Dictionary of Literary Biography

1. *The American Renaissance in New England,* edited by Joel Myerson (1978)
2. *American Novelists Since World War II,* edited by Jeffrey Helterman and Richard Layman (1978)
3. *Antebellum Writers in New York and the South,* edited by Joel Myerson (1979)
4. *American Writers in Paris, 1920–1939,* edited by Karen Lane Rood (1980)
5. *American Poets Since World War II,* 2 parts, edited by Donald J. Greiner (1980)
6. *American Novelists Since World War II, Second Series,* edited by James E. Kibler Jr. (1980)
7. *Twentieth-Century American Dramatists,* 2 parts, edited by John MacNicholas (1981)
8. *Twentieth-Century American Science-Fiction Writers,* 2 parts, edited by David Cowart and Thomas L. Wymer (1981)
9. *American Novelists, 1910–1945,* 3 parts, edited by James J. Martine (1981)
10. *Modern British Dramatists, 1900–1945,* 2 parts, edited by Stanley Weintraub (1982)
11. *American Humorists, 1800–1950,* 2 parts, edited by Stanley Trachtenberg (1982)
12. *American Realists and Naturalists,* edited by Donald Pizer and Earl N. Harbert (1982)
13. *British Dramatists Since World War II,* 2 parts, edited by Stanley Weintraub (1982)
14. *British Novelists Since 1960,* 2 parts, edited by Jay L. Halio (1983)
15. *British Novelists, 1930–1959,* 2 parts, edited by Bernard Oldsey (1983)
16. *The Beats: Literary Bohemians in Postwar America,* 2 parts, edited by Ann Charters (1983)
17. *Twentieth-Century American Historians,* edited by Clyde N. Wilson (1983)
18. *Victorian Novelists After 1885,* edited by Ira B. Nadel and William E. Fredeman (1983)
19. *British Poets, 1880–1914,* edited by Donald E. Stanford (1983)
20. *British Poets, 1914–1945,* edited by Donald E. Stanford (1983)
21. *Victorian Novelists Before 1885,* edited by Ira B. Nadel and William E. Fredeman (1983)
22. *American Writers for Children, 1900–1960,* edited by John Cech (1983)
23. *American Newspaper Journalists, 1873–1900,* edited by Perry J. Ashley (1983)
24. *American Colonial Writers, 1606–1734,* edited by Emory Elliott (1984)
25. *American Newspaper Journalists, 1901–1925,* edited by Perry J. Ashley (1984)
26. *American Screenwriters,* edited by Robert E. Morsberger, Stephen O. Lesser, and Randall Clark (1984)
27. *Poets of Great Britain and Ireland, 1945–1960,* edited by Vincent B. Sherry Jr. (1984)
28. *Twentieth-Century American-Jewish Fiction Writers,* edited by Daniel Walden (1984)
29. *American Newspaper Journalists, 1926–1950,* edited by Perry J. Ashley (1984)
30. *American Historians, 1607–1865,* edited by Clyde N. Wilson (1984)
31. *American Colonial Writers, 1735–1781,* edited by Emory Elliott (1984)
32. *Victorian Poets Before 1850,* edited by William E. Fredeman and Ira B. Nadel (1984)
33. *Afro-American Fiction Writers After 1955,* edited by Thadious M. Davis and Trudier Harris (1984)
34. *British Novelists, 1890–1929: Traditionalists,* edited by Thomas F. Staley (1985)
35. *Victorian Poets After 1850,* edited by William E. Fredeman and Ira B. Nadel (1985)
36. *British Novelists, 1890–1929: Modernists,* edited by Thomas F. Staley (1985)
37. *American Writers of the Early Republic,* edited by Emory Elliott (1985)
38. *Afro-American Writers After 1955: Dramatists and Prose Writers,* edited by Thadious M. Davis and Trudier Harris (1985)
39. *British Novelists, 1660–1800,* 2 parts, edited by Martin C. Battestin (1985)
40. *Poets of Great Britain and Ireland Since 1960,* 2 parts, edited by Vincent B. Sherry Jr. (1985)
41. *Afro-American Poets Since 1955,* edited by Trudier Harris and Thadious M. Davis (1985)
42. *American Writers for Children Before 1900,* edited by Glenn E. Estes (1985)
43. *American Newspaper Journalists, 1690–1872,* edited by Perry J. Ashley (1986)
44. *American Screenwriters, Second Series,* edited by Randall Clark, Robert E. Morsberger, and Stephen O. Lesser (1986)
45. *American Poets, 1880–1945, First Series,* edited by Peter Quartermain (1986)
46. *American Literary Publishing Houses, 1900–1980: Trade and Paperback,* edited by Peter Dzwonkoski (1986)
47. *American Historians, 1866–1912,* edited by Clyde N. Wilson (1986)
48. *American Poets, 1880–1945, Second Series,* edited by Peter Quartermain (1986)
49. *American Literary Publishing Houses, 1638–1899,* 2 parts, edited by Peter Dzwonkoski (1986)
50. *Afro-American Writers Before the Harlem Renaissance,* edited by Trudier Harris (1986)
51. *Afro-American Writers from the Harlem Renaissance to 1940,* edited by Trudier Harris (1987)
52. *American Writers for Children Since 1960: Fiction,* edited by Glenn E. Estes (1986)
53. *Canadian Writers Since 1960, First Series,* edited by W. H. New (1986)
54. *American Poets, 1880–1945, Third Series,* 2 parts, edited by Peter Quartermain (1987)
55. *Victorian Prose Writers Before 1867,* edited by William B. Thesing (1987)
56. *German Fiction Writers, 1914–1945,* edited by James Hardin (1987)
57. *Victorian Prose Writers After 1867,* edited by William B. Thesing (1987)
58. *Jacobean and Caroline Dramatists,* edited by Fredson Bowers (1987)
59. *American Literary Critics and Scholars, 1800–1850,* edited by John W. Rathbun and Monica M. Grecu (1987)
60. *Canadian Writers Since 1960, Second Series,* edited by W. H. New (1987)
61. *American Writers for Children Since 1960: Poets, Illustrators, and Nonfiction Authors,* edited by Glenn E. Estes (1987)
62. *Elizabethan Dramatists,* edited by Fredson Bowers (1987)
63. *Modern American Critics, 1920–1955,* edited by Gregory S. Jay (1988)
64. *American Literary Critics and Scholars, 1850–1880,* edited by John W. Rathbun and Monica M. Grecu (1988)
65. *French Novelists, 1900–1930,* edited by Catharine Savage Brosman (1988)
66. *German Fiction Writers, 1885–1913,* 2 parts, edited by James Hardin (1988)
67. *Modern American Critics Since 1955,* edited by Gregory S. Jay (1988)
68. *Canadian Writers, 1920–1959, First Series,* edited by W. H. New (1988)
69. *Contemporary German Fiction Writers, First Series,* edited by Wolfgang D. Elfe and James Hardin (1988)
70. *British Mystery Writers, 1860–1919,* edited by Bernard Benstock and Thomas F. Staley (1988)

71 *American Literary Critics and Scholars, 1880–1900,* edited by John W. Rathbun and Monica M. Grecu (1988)

72 *French Novelists, 1930–1960,* edited by Catharine Savage Brosman (1988)

73 *American Magazine Journalists, 1741–1850,* edited by Sam G. Riley (1988)

74 *American Short-Story Writers Before 1880,* edited by Bobby Ellen Kimbel, with the assistance of William E. Grant (1988)

75 *Contemporary German Fiction Writers, Second Series,* edited by Wolfgang D. Elfe and James Hardin (1988)

76 *Afro-American Writers, 1940–1955,* edited by Trudier Harris (1988)

77 *British Mystery Writers, 1920–1939,* edited by Bernard Benstock and Thomas F. Staley (1988)

78 *American Short-Story Writers, 1880–1910,* edited by Bobby Ellen Kimbel, with the assistance of William E. Grant (1988)

79 *American Magazine Journalists, 1850–1900,* edited by Sam G. Riley (1988)

80 *Restoration and Eighteenth-Century Dramatists, First Series,* edited by Paula R. Backscheider (1989)

81 *Austrian Fiction Writers, 1875–1913,* edited by James Hardin and Donald G. Daviau (1989)

82 *Chicano Writers, First Series,* edited by Francisco A. Lomelí and Carl R. Shirley (1989)

83 *French Novelists Since 1960,* edited by Catharine Savage Brosman (1989)

84 *Restoration and Eighteenth-Century Dramatists, Second Series,* edited by Paula R. Backscheider (1989)

85 *Austrian Fiction Writers After 1914,* edited by James Hardin and Donald G. Daviau (1989)

86 *American Short-Story Writers, 1910–1945, First Series,* edited by Bobby Ellen Kimbel (1989)

87 *British Mystery and Thriller Writers Since 1940, First Series,* edited by Bernard Benstock and Thomas F. Staley (1989)

88 *Canadian Writers, 1920–1959, Second Series,* edited by W. H. New (1989)

89 *Restoration and Eighteenth-Century Dramatists, Third Series,* edited by Paula R. Backscheider (1989)

90 *German Writers in the Age of Goethe, 1789–1832,* edited by James Hardin and Christoph E. Schweitzer (1989)

91 *American Magazine Journalists, 1900–1960, First Series,* edited by Sam G. Riley (1990)

92 *Canadian Writers, 1890–1920,* edited by W. H. New (1990)

93 *British Romantic Poets, 1789–1832, First Series,* edited by John R. Greenfield (1990)

94 *German Writers in the Age of Goethe: Sturm und Drang to Classicism,* edited by James Hardin and Christoph E. Schweitzer (1990)

95 *Eighteenth-Century British Poets, First Series,* edited by John Sitter (1990)

96 *British Romantic Poets, 1789–1832, Second Series,* edited by John R. Greenfield (1990)

97 *German Writers from the Enlightenment to Sturm und Drang, 1720–1764,* edited by James Hardin and Christoph E. Schweitzer (1990)

98 *Modern British Essayists, First Series,* edited by Robert Beum (1990)

99 *Canadian Writers Before 1890,* edited by W. H. New (1990)

100 *Modern British Essayists, Second Series,* edited by Robert Beum (1990)

101 *British Prose Writers, 1660–1800, First Series,* edited by Donald T. Siebert (1991)

102 *American Short-Story Writers, 1910–1945, Second Series,* edited by Bobby Ellen Kimbel (1991)

103 *American Literary Biographers, First Series,* edited by Steven Serafin (1991)

104 *British Prose Writers, 1660–1800, Second Series,* edited by Donald T. Siebert (1991)

105 *American Poets Since World War II, Second Series,* edited by R. S. Gwynn (1991)

106 *British Literary Publishing Houses, 1820–1880,* edited by Patricia J. Anderson and Jonathan Rose (1991)

107 *British Romantic Prose Writers, 1789–1832, First Series,* edited by John R. Greenfield (1991)

108 *Twentieth-Century Spanish Poets, First Series,* edited by Michael L. Perna (1991)

109 *Eighteenth-Century British Poets, Second Series,* edited by John Sitter (1991)

110 *British Romantic Prose Writers, 1789–1832, Second Series,* edited by John R. Greenfield (1991)

111 *American Literary Biographers, Second Series,* edited by Steven Serafin (1991)

112 *British Literary Publishing Houses, 1881–1965,* edited by Jonathan Rose and Patricia J. Anderson (1991)

113 *Modern Latin-American Fiction Writers, First Series,* edited by William Luis (1992)

114 *Twentieth-Century Italian Poets, First Series,* edited by Giovanna Wedel De Stasio, Glauco Cambon, and Antonio Illiano (1992)

115 *Medieval Philosophers,* edited by Jeremiah Hackett (1992)

116 *British Romantic Novelists, 1789–1832,* edited by Bradford K. Mudge (1992)

117 *Twentieth-Century Caribbean and Black African Writers, First Series,* edited by Bernth Lindfors and Reinhard Sander (1992)

118 *Twentieth-Century German Dramatists, 1889–1918,* edited by Wolfgang D. Elfe and James Hardin (1992)

119 *Nineteenth-Century French Fiction Writers: Romanticism and Realism, 1800–1860,* edited by Catharine Savage Brosman (1992)

120 *American Poets Since World War II, Third Series,* edited by R. S. Gwynn (1992)

121 *Seventeenth-Century British Nondramatic Poets, First Series,* edited by M. Thomas Hester (1992)

122 *Chicano Writers, Second Series,* edited by Francisco A. Lomelí and Carl R. Shirley (1992)

123 *Nineteenth-Century French Fiction Writers: Naturalism and Beyond, 1860–1900,* edited by Catharine Savage Brosman (1992)

124 *Twentieth-Century German Dramatists, 1919–1992,* edited by Wolfgang D. Elfe and James Hardin (1992)

125 *Twentieth-Century Caribbean and Black African Writers, Second Series,* edited by Bernth Lindfors and Reinhard Sander (1993)

126 *Seventeenth-Century British Nondramatic Poets, Second Series,* edited by M. Thomas Hester (1993)

127 *American Newspaper Publishers, 1950–1990,* edited by Perry J. Ashley (1993)

128 *Twentieth-Century Italian Poets, Second Series,* edited by Giovanna Wedel De Stasio, Glauco Cambon, and Antonio Illiano (1993)

129 *Nineteenth-Century German Writers, 1841–1900,* edited by James Hardin and Siegfried Mews (1993)

130 *American Short-Story Writers Since World War II,* edited by Patrick Meanor (1993)

131 *Seventeenth-Century British Nondramatic Poets, Third Series,* edited by M. Thomas Hester (1993)

132 *Sixteenth-Century British Nondramatic Writers, First Series,* edited by David A. Richardson (1993)

133 *Nineteenth-Century German Writers to 1840,* edited by James Hardin and Siegfried Mews (1993)

134 *Twentieth-Century Spanish Poets, Second Series,* edited by Jerry Phillips Winfield (1994)

135 *British Short-Fiction Writers, 1880–1914: The Realist Tradition,* edited by William B. Thesing (1994)

136 *Sixteenth-Century British Nondramatic Writers, Second Series,* edited by David A. Richardson (1994)

137 *American Magazine Journalists, 1900–1960, Second Series,* edited by Sam G. Riley (1994)

138 *German Writers and Works of the High Middle Ages: 1170–1280,* edited by James Hardin and Will Hasty (1994)

139 *British Short-Fiction Writers, 1945–1980,* edited by Dean Baldwin (1994)

140 *American Book-Collectors and Bibliographers, First Series,* edited by Joseph Rosenblum (1994)

141 *British Children's Writers, 1880–1914,* edited by Laura M. Zaidman (1994)

142 *Eighteenth-Century British Literary Biographers,* edited by Steven Serafin (1994)

143 *American Novelists Since World War II, Third Series,* edited by James R. Giles and Wanda H. Giles (1994)

144 *Nineteenth-Century British Literary Biographers,* edited by Steven Serafin (1994)

145 *Modern Latin-American Fiction Writers, Second Series,* edited by William Luis and Ann González (1994)

146 *Old and Middle English Literature,* edited by Jeffrey Helterman and Jerome Mitchell (1994)

147 *South Slavic Writers Before World War II,* edited by Vasa D. Mihailovich (1994)

148 *German Writers and Works of the Early Middle Ages: 800–1170,* edited by Will Hasty and James Hardin (1994)

149 *Late Nineteenth- and Early Twentieth-Century British Literary Biographers,* edited by Steven Serafin (1995)

150 *Early Modern Russian Writers, Late Seventeenth and Eighteenth Centuries,* edited by Marcus C. Levitt (1995)

151 *British Prose Writers of the Early Seventeenth Century,* edited by Clayton D. Lein (1995)

152 *American Novelists Since World War II, Fourth Series,* edited by James R. Giles and Wanda H. Giles (1995)

153 *Late-Victorian and Edwardian British Novelists, First Series,* edited by George M. Johnson (1995)

154 *The British Literary Book Trade, 1700–1820,* edited by James K. Bracken and Joel Silver (1995)

155 *Twentieth-Century British Literary Biographers,* edited by Steven Serafin (1995)

156 *British Short-Fiction Writers, 1880–1914: The Romantic Tradition,* edited by William F. Naufftus (1995)

157 *Twentieth-Century Caribbean and Black African Writers, Third Series,* edited by Bernth Lindfors and Reinhard Sander (1995)

158 *British Reform Writers, 1789–1832,* edited by Gary Kelly and Edd Applegate (1995)

159 *British Short-Fiction Writers, 1800–1880,* edited by John R. Greenfield (1996)

160 *British Children's Writers, 1914–1960,* edited by Donald R. Hettinga and Gary D. Schmidt (1996)

161 *British Children's Writers Since 1960, First Series,* edited by Caroline Hunt (1996)

162 *British Short-Fiction Writers, 1915–1945,* edited by John H. Rogers (1996)

163 *British Children's Writers, 1800–1880,* edited by Meena Khorana (1996)

164 *German Baroque Writers, 1580–1660,* edited by James Hardin (1996)

165 *American Poets Since World War II, Fourth Series,* edited by Joseph Conte (1996)

166 *British Travel Writers, 1837–1875,* edited by Barbara Brothers and Julia Gergits (1996)

167 *Sixteenth-Century British Nondramatic Writers, Third Series,* edited by David A. Richardson (1996)

168 *German Baroque Writers, 1661–1730,* edited by James Hardin (1996)

169 *American Poets Since World War II, Fifth Series,* edited by Joseph Conte (1996)

170 *The British Literary Book Trade, 1475–1700,* edited by James K. Bracken and Joel Silver (1996)

171 *Twentieth-Century American Sportswriters,* edited by Richard Orodenker (1996)

172 *Sixteenth-Century British Nondramatic Writers, Fourth Series,* edited by David A. Richardson (1996)

173 *American Novelists Since World War II, Fifth Series,* edited by James R. Giles and Wanda H. Giles (1996)

174 *British Travel Writers, 1876–1909,* edited by Barbara Brothers and Julia Gergits (1997)

175 *Native American Writers of the United States,* edited by Kenneth M. Roemer (1997)

176 *Ancient Greek Authors,* edited by Ward W. Briggs (1997)

177 *Italian Novelists Since World War II, 1945–1965,* edited by Augustus Pallotta (1997)

178 *British Fantasy and Science-Fiction Writers Before World War I,* edited by Darren Harris-Fain (1997)

179 *German Writers of the Renaissance and Reformation, 1280–1580,* edited by James Hardin and Max Reinhart (1997)

180 *Japanese Fiction Writers, 1868–1945,* edited by Van C. Gessel (1997)

181 *South Slavic Writers Since World War II,* edited by Vasa D. Mihailovich (1997)

182 *Japanese Fiction Writers Since World War II,* edited by Van C. Gessel (1997)

183 *American Travel Writers, 1776–1864,* edited by James J. Schramer and Donald Ross (1997)

184 *Nineteenth-Century British Book-Collectors and Bibliographers,* edited by William Baker and Kenneth Womack (1997)

185 *American Literary Journalists, 1945–1995, First Series,* edited by Arthur J. Kaul (1998)

186 *Nineteenth-Century American Western Writers,* edited by Robert L. Gale (1998)

187 *American Book Collectors and Bibliographers, Second Series,* edited by Joseph Rosenblum (1998)

188 *American Book and Magazine Illustrators to 1920,* edited by Steven E. Smith, Catherine A. Hastedt, and Donald H. Dyal (1998)

189 *American Travel Writers, 1850–1915,* edited by Donald Ross and James J. Schramer (1998)

190 *British Reform Writers, 1832–1914,* edited by Gary Kelly and Edd Applegate (1998)

191 *British Novelists Between the Wars,* edited by George M. Johnson (1998)

192 *French Dramatists, 1789–1914,* edited by Barbara T. Cooper (1998)

193 *American Poets Since World War II, Sixth Series,* edited by Joseph Conte (1998)

194 *British Novelists Since 1960, Second Series,* edited by Merritt Moseley (1998)

195 *British Travel Writers, 1910–1939,* edited by Barbara Brothers and Julia Gergits (1998)

196 *Italian Novelists Since World War II, 1965–1995,* edited by Augustus Pallotta (1999)

197 *Late-Victorian and Edwardian British Novelists, Second Series,* edited by George M. Johnson (1999)

198 *Russian Literature in the Age of Pushkin and Gogol: Prose,* edited by Christine A. Rydel (1999)

199 *Victorian Women Poets,* edited by William B. Thesing (1999)

200 *American Women Prose Writers to 1820,* edited by Carla J. Mulford, with Angela Vietto and Amy E. Winans (1999)

201 *Twentieth-Century British Book Collectors and Bibliographers,* edited by William Baker and Kenneth Womack (1999)

202 *Nineteenth-Century American Fiction Writers,* edited by Kent P. Ljungquist (1999)

203 *Medieval Japanese Writers,* edited by Steven D. Carter (1999)

204 *British Travel Writers, 1940–1997,* edited by Barbara Brothers and Julia M. Gergits (1999)

205 *Russian Literature in the Age of Pushkin and Gogol: Poetry and Drama,* edited by Christine A. Rydel (1999)

206 *Twentieth-Century American Western Writers, First Series,* edited by Richard H. Cracroft (1999)

207 *British Novelists Since 1960, Third Series,* edited by Merritt Moseley (1999)

208 *Literature of the French and Occitan Middle Ages: Eleventh to Fifteenth Centuries,* edited by Deborah Sinnreich-Levi and Ian S. Laurie (1999)

209 *Chicano Writers, Third Series,* edited by Francisco A. Lomelí and Carl R. Shirley (1999)

210 *Ernest Hemingway: A Documentary Volume,* edited by Robert W. Trogdon (1999)

211 *Ancient Roman Writers,* edited by Ward W. Briggs (1999)

212 *Twentieth-Century American Western Writers, Second Series*, edited by Richard H. Cracroft (1999)

213 *Pre-Nineteenth-Century British Book Collectors and Bibliographers*, edited by William Baker and Kenneth Womack (1999)

214 *Twentieth-Century Danish Writers*, edited by Marianne Stecher-Hansen (1999)

215 *Twentieth-Century Eastern European Writers, First Series*, edited by Steven Serafin (1999)

216 *British Poets of the Great War: Brooke, Rosenberg, Thomas. A Documentary Volume*, edited by Patrick Quinn (2000)

217 *Nineteenth-Century French Poets*, edited by Robert Beum (2000)

218 *American Short-Story Writers Since World War II, Second Series*, edited by Patrick Meanor and Gwen Crane (2000)

219 *F. Scott Fitzgerald's* The Great Gatsby: *A Documentary Volume*, edited by Matthew J. Bruccoli (2000)

220 *Twentieth-Century Eastern European Writers, Second Series*, edited by Steven Serafin (2000)

221 *American Women Prose Writers, 1870–1920*, edited by Sharon M. Harris, with the assistance of Heidi L. M. Jacobs and Jennifer Putzi (2000)

222 *H. L. Mencken: A Documentary Volume*, edited by Richard J. Schrader (2000)

223 *The American Renaissance in New England, Second Series*, edited by Wesley T. Mott (2000)

224 *Walt Whitman: A Documentary Volume*, edited by Joel Myerson (2000)

225 *South African Writers*, edited by Paul A. Scanlon (2000)

226 *American Hard-Boiled Crime Writers*, edited by George Parker Anderson and Julie B. Anderson (2000)

227 *American Novelists Since World War II, Sixth Series*, edited by James R. Giles and Wanda H. Giles (2000)

228 *Twentieth-Century American Dramatists, Second Series*, edited by Christopher J. Wheatley (2000)

229 *Thomas Wolfe: A Documentary Volume*, edited by Ted Mitchell (2001)

230 *Australian Literature, 1788–1914*, edited by Selina Samuels (2001)

231 *British Novelists Since 1960, Fourth Series*, edited by Merritt Moseley (2001)

232 *Twentieth-Century Eastern European Writers, Third Series*, edited by Steven Serafin (2001)

233 *British and Irish Dramatists Since World War II, Second Series*, edited by John Bull (2001)

234 *American Short-Story Writers Since World War II, Third Series*, edited by Patrick Meanor and Richard E. Lee (2001)

235 *The American Renaissance in New England, Third Series*, edited by Wesley T. Mott (2001)

236 *British Rhetoricians and Logicians, 1500–1660*, edited by Edward A. Malone (2001)

237 *The Beats: A Documentary Volume*, edited by Matt Theado (2001)

238 *Russian Novelists in the Age of Tolstoy and Dostoevsky*, edited by J. Alexander Ogden and Judith E. Kalb (2001)

239 *American Women Prose Writers: 1820–1870*, edited by Amy E. Hudock and Katharine Rodier (2001)

240 *Late Nineteenth- and Early Twentieth-Century British Women Poets*, edited by William B. Thesing (2001)

241 *American Sportswriters and Writers on Sport*, edited by Richard Orodenker (2001)

242 *Twentieth-Century European Cultural Theorists, First Series*, edited by Paul Hansom (2001)

243 *The American Renaissance in New England, Fourth Series*, edited by Wesley T. Mott (2001)

244 *American Short-Story Writers Since World War II, Fourth Series*, edited by Patrick Meanor and Joseph McNicholas (2001)

245 *British and Irish Dramatists Since World War II, Third Series*, edited by John Bull (2001)

246 *Twentieth-Century American Cultural Theorists*, edited by Paul Hansom (2001)

247 *James Joyce: A Documentary Volume*, edited by A. Nicholas Fargnoli (2001)

248 *Antebellum Writers in the South, Second Series*, edited by Kent Ljungquist (2001)

249 *Twentieth-Century American Dramatists, Third Series*, edited by Christopher Wheatley (2002)

250 *Antebellum Writers in New York, Second Series*, edited by Kent Ljungquist (2002)

251 *Canadian Fantasy and Science-Fiction Writers*, edited by Douglas Ivison (2002)

252 *British Philosophers, 1500–1799*, edited by Philip B. Dematteis and Peter S. Fosl (2002)

253 *Raymond Chandler: A Documentary Volume*, edited by Robert Moss (2002)

254 *The House of Putnam, 1837–1872: A Documentary Volume*, edited by Ezra Greenspan (2002)

255 *British Fantasy and Science-Fiction Writers, 1918–1960*, edited by Darren Harris-Fain (2002)

256 *Twentieth-Century American Western Writers, Third Series*, edited by Richard H. Cracroft (2002)

257 *Twentieth-Century Swedish Writers After World War II*, edited by Ann-Charlotte Gavel Adams (2002)

258 *Modern French Poets*, edited by Jean-François Leroux (2002)

259 *Twentieth-Century Swedish Writers Before World War II*, edited by Ann-Charlotte Gavel Adams (2002)

260 *Australian Writers, 1915–1950*, edited by Selina Samuels (2002)

261 *British Fantasy and Science-Fiction Writers Since 1960*, edited by Darren Harris-Fain (2002)

262 *British Philosophers, 1800–2000*, edited by Peter S. Fosl and Leemon B. McHenry (2002)

263 *William Shakespeare: A Documentary Volume*, edited by Catherine Loomis (2002)

264 *Italian Prose Writers, 1900–1945*, edited by Luca Somigli and Rocco Capozzi (2002)

265 *American Song Lyricists, 1920–1960*, edited by Philip Furia (2002)

266 *Twentieth-Century American Dramatists, Fourth Series*, edited by Christopher J. Wheatley (2002)

267 *Twenty-First-Century British and Irish Novelists*, edited by Michael R. Molino (2002)

268 *Seventeenth-Century French Writers*, edited by Françoise Jaouën (2002)

269 *Nathaniel Hawthorne: A Documentary Volume*, edited by Benjamin Franklin V (2002)

270 *American Philosophers Before 1950*, edited by Philip B. Dematteis and Leemon B. McHenry (2002)

271 *British and Irish Novelists Since 1960*, edited by Merritt Moseley (2002)

272 *Russian Prose Writers Between the World Wars*, edited by Christine Rydel (2003)

273 *F. Scott Fitzgerald's* Tender Is the Night: *A Documentary Volume*, edited by Matthew J. Bruccoli and George Parker Anderson (2003)

274 *John Dos Passos's* U.S.A.: *A Documentary Volume*, edited by Donald Pizer (2003)

275 *Twentieth-Century American Nature Writers: Prose*, edited by Roger Thompson and J. Scott Bryson (2003)

276 *British Mystery and Thriller Writers Since 1960*, edited by Gina Macdonald (2003)

277 *Russian Literature in the Age of Realism*, edited by Alyssa Dinega Gillespie (2003)

278 *American Novelists Since World War II, Seventh Series*, edited by James R. Giles and Wanda H. Giles (2003)

279 *American Philosophers, 1950–2000*, edited by Philip B. Dematteis and Leemon B. McHenry (2003)

280 *Dashiell Hammett's* The Maltese Falcon: *A Documentary Volume*, edited by Richard Layman (2003)

281 *British Rhetoricians and Logicians, 1500–1660, Second Series*, edited by Edward A. Malone (2003)

282 *New Formalist Poets*, edited by Jonathan N. Barron and Bruce Meyer (2003)

283 *Modern Spanish American Poets, First Series*, edited by María A. Salgado (2003)

284 *The House of Holt, 1866–1946: A Documentary Volume*, edited by Ellen D. Gilbert (2003)

285 *Russian Writers Since 1980*, edited by Marina Balina and Mark Lipoyvetsky (2004)

286 *Castilian Writers, 1400–1500*, edited by Frank A. Domínguez and George D. Greenia (2004)

287 *Portuguese Writers*, edited by Monica Rector and Fred M. Clark (2004)

288 *The House of Boni & Liveright, 1917–1933: A Documentary Volume*, edited by Charles Egleston (2004)

289 *Australian Writers, 1950–1975*, edited by Selina Samuels (2004)

290 *Modern Spanish American Poets, Second Series*, edited by María A. Salgado (2004)

291 *The Hoosier House: Bobbs-Merrill and Its Predecessors, 1850–1985: A Documentary Volume*, edited by Richard J. Schrader (2004)

292 *Twenty-First-Century American Novelists*, edited by Lisa Abney and Suzanne Disheroon-Green (2004)

293 *Icelandic Writers*, edited by Patrick J. Stevens (2004)

294 *James Gould Cozzens: A Documentary Volume*, edited by Matthew J. Bruccoli (2004)

295 *Russian Writers of the Silver Age, 1890–1925*, edited by Judith E. Kalb and J. Alexander Ogden with the collaboration of I. G. Vishnevetsky (2004)

296 *Twentieth-Century European Cultural Theorists, Second Series*, edited by Paul Hansom (2004)

297 *Twentieth-Century Norwegian Writers*, edited by Tanya Thresher (2004)

298 *Henry David Thoreau: A Documentary Volume*, edited by Richard J. Schneider (2004)

299 *Holocaust Novelists*, edited by Efraim Sicher (2004)

300 *Danish Writers from the Reformation to Decadence, 1550–1900*, edited by Marianne Stecher-Hansen (2004)

301 *Gustave Flaubert: A Documentary Volume*, edited by Éric Le Calvez (2004)

302 *Russian Prose Writers After World War II*, edited by Christine Rydel (2004)

303 *American Radical and Reform Writers, First Series*, edited by Steven Rosendale (2005)

304 *Bram Stoker's* Dracula: *A Documentary Volume*, edited by Elizabeth Miller (2005)

305 *Latin American Dramatists, First Series*, edited by Adam Versényi (2005)

306 *American Mystery and Detective Writers*, edited by George Parker Anderson (2005)

307 *Brazilian Writers*, edited by Monica Rector and Fred M. Clark (2005)

308 *Ernest Hemingway's* A Farewell to Arms: *A Documentary Volume*, edited by Charles Oliver (2005)

309 *John Steinbeck: A Documentary Volume*, edited by Luchen Li (2005)

310 *British and Irish Dramatists Since World War II, Fourth Series*, edited by John Bull (2005)

311 *Arabic Literary Culture, 500–925*, edited by Michael Cooperson and Shawkat M. Toorawa (2005)

312 *Asian American Writers*, edited by Deborah L. Madsen (2005)

313 *Writers of the French Enlightenment, I*, edited by Samia I. Spencer (2005)

314 *Writers of the French Enlightenment, II*, edited by Samia I. Spencer (2005)

315 *Langston Hughes: A Documentary Volume*, edited by Christopher C. De Santis (2005)

316 *American Prose Writers of World War I: A Documentary Volume*, edited by Steven Trout (2005)

317 *Twentieth-Century Russian Émigré Writers*, edited by Maria Rubins (2005)

318 *Sixteenth-Century Spanish Writers*, edited by Gregory B. Kaplan (2006)

319 *British and Irish Short-Fiction Writers 1945–2000*, edited by Cheryl Alexander Malcolm and David Malcolm (2006)

320 *Robert Penn Warren: A Documentary Volume*, edited by James A. Grimshaw Jr. (2006)

321 *Twentieth-Century French Dramatists*, edited by Mary Anne O'Neil (2006)

322 *Twentieth-Century Spanish Fiction Writers*, edited by Marta E. Altisent and Cristina Martínez-Carazo (2006)

323 *South Asian Writers in English*, edited by Fakrul Alam (2006)

324 *John O'Hara: A Documentary Volume*, edited by Matthew J. Bruccoli (2006)

325 *Australian Writers, 1975–2000*, edited by Selina Samuels (2006)

326 *Booker Prize Novels, 1969–2005*, edited by Merritt Moseley (2006)

327 *Sixteenth-Century French Writers*, edited by Megan Conway (2006)

328 *Chinese Fiction Writers, 1900–1949*, edited by Thomas Moran (2007)

Dictionary of Literary Biography Documentary Series

1 *Sherwood Anderson, Willa Cather, John Dos Passos, Theodore Dreiser, F. Scott Fitzgerald, Ernest Hemingway, Sinclair Lewis*, edited by Margaret A. Van Antwerp (1982)

2 *James Gould Cozzens, James T. Farrell, William Faulkner, John O'Hara, John Steinbeck, Thomas Wolfe, Richard Wright*, edited by Margaret A. Van Antwerp (1982)

3 *Saul Bellow, Jack Kerouac, Norman Mailer, Vladimir Nabokov, John Updike, Kurt Vonnegut*, edited by Mary Bruccoli (1983)

4 *Tennessee Williams*, edited by Margaret A. Van Antwerp and Sally Johns (1984)

5 *American Transcendentalists*, edited by Joel Myerson (1988)

6 *Hardboiled Mystery Writers: Raymond Chandler, Dashiell Hammett, Ross Macdonald*, edited by Matthew J. Bruccoli and Richard Layman (1989)

7 *Modern American Poets: James Dickey, Robert Frost, Marianne Moore*, edited by Karen L. Rood (1989)

8 *The Black Aesthetic Movement*, edited by Jeffrey Louis Decker (1991)

9 *American Writers of the Vietnam War: W. D. Ehrhart, Larry Heinemann, Tim O'Brien, Walter McDonald, John M. Del Vecchio*, edited by Ronald Baughman (1991)

10 *The Bloomsbury Group*, edited by Edward L. Bishop (1992)

11 *American Proletarian Culture: The Twenties and The Thirties*, edited by Jon Christian Suggs (1993)

12 *Southern Women Writers: Flannery O'Connor, Katherine Anne Porter, Eudora Welty*, edited by Mary Ann Wimsatt and Karen L. Rood (1994)

13 *The House of Scribner, 1846–1904*, edited by John Delaney (1996)

14 *Four Women Writers for Children, 1868–1918*, edited by Caroline C. Hunt (1996)

15 *American Expatriate Writers: Paris in the Twenties*, edited by Matthew J. Bruccoli and Robert W. Trogdon (1997)

16 *The House of Scribner, 1905–1930*, edited by John Delaney (1997)

17 *The House of Scribner, 1931–1984*, edited by John Delaney (1998)

18 *British Poets of The Great War: Sassoon, Graves, Owen*, edited by Patrick Quinn (1999)

19 *James Dickey*, edited by Judith S. Baughman (1999)

See also DLB 210, 216, 219, 222, 224, 229, 237, 247, 253, 254, 263, 269, 273, 274, 280, 284, 288, 291, 294, 298, 301, 304, 308, 309, 315, 316, 320, 324

Dictionary of Literary Biography Yearbooks

1980 edited by Karen L. Rood, Jean W. Ross, and Richard Ziegfeld (1981)

1981 edited by Karen L. Rood, Jean W. Ross, and Richard Ziegfeld (1982)

1982 edited by Richard Ziegfeld; associate editors: Jean W. Ross and Lynne C. Zeigler (1983)

1983 edited by Mary Bruccoli and Jean W. Ross; associate editor Richard Ziegfeld (1984)

1984 edited by Jean W. Ross (1985)

1985 edited by Jean W. Ross (1986)

1986 edited by J. M. Brook (1987)

1987 edited by J. M. Brook (1988)

1988 edited by J. M. Brook (1989)

1989 edited by J. M. Brook (1990)

1990 edited by James W. Hipp (1991)

1991 edited by James W. Hipp (1992)

1992 edited by James W. Hipp (1993)

1993 edited by James W. Hipp, contributing editor George Garrett (1994)

1994 edited by James W. Hipp, contributing editor George Garrett (1995)

1995 edited by James W. Hipp, contributing editor George Garrett (1996)

1996 edited by Samuel W. Bruce and L. Kay Webster, contributing editor George Garrett (1997)

1997 edited by Matthew J. Bruccoli and George Garrett, with the assistance of L. Kay Webster (1998)

1998 edited by Matthew J. Bruccoli, contributing editor George Garrett, with the assistance of D. W. Thomas (1999)

1999 edited by Matthew J. Bruccoli, contributing editor George Garrett, with the assistance of D. W. Thomas (2000)

2000 edited by Matthew J. Bruccoli, contributing editor George Garrett, with the assistance of George Parker Anderson (2001)

2001 edited by Matthew J. Bruccoli, contributing editor George Garrett, with the assistance of George Parker Anderson (2002)

2002 edited by Matthew J. Bruccoli and George Garrett; George Parker Anderson, Assistant Editor (2003)

Concise Series

Concise Dictionary of American Literary Biography, 7 volumes (1988–1999): *The New Consciousness, 1941–1968; Colonization to the American Renaissance, 1640–1865; Realism, Naturalism, and Local Color, 1865–1917; The Twenties, 1917–1929; The Age of Maturity, 1929–1941; Broadening Views, 1968–1988; Supplement: Modern Writers, 1900–1998.*

Concise Dictionary of British Literary Biography, 8 volumes (1991–1992): *Writers of the Middle Ages and Renaissance Before 1660; Writers of the Restoration and Eighteenth Century, 1660–1789; Writers of the Romantic Period, 1789–1832; Victorian Writers, 1832–1890; Late-Victorian and Edwardian Writers, 1890–1914; Modern Writers, 1914–1945; Writers After World War II, 1945–1960; Contemporary Writers, 1960 to Present.*

Concise Dictionary of World Literary Biography, 4 volumes (1999–2000): *Ancient Greek and Roman Writers; German Writers; African, Caribbean, and Latin American Writers; South Slavic and Eastern European Writers.*

Dictionary of Literary Biography® • Volume Three Hundred Twenty-Eight

Chinese Fiction Writers, 1900–1949

Dictionary of Literary Biography® • Volume Three Hundred Twenty-Eight

Chinese Fiction Writers, 1900–1949

Edited by
Thomas Moran
Middlebury College

A Bruccoli Clark Layman Book

Detroit • New York • San Francisco • New Haven, Conn. • Waterville, Maine • London • Munich

ST. PHILIP'S COLLEGE LIBRARY

PL
2652
.C475
2007

Dictionary of Literary Biography
Volume 328: Chinese Fiction Writers, 1900–1949
Thomas Moran

Advisory Board
John Baker
William Cagle
Patrick O'Connor
George Garrett
Trudier Harris
Alvin Kernan

Editorial Directors
Matthew J. Bruccoli and Richard Layman

© 2007 Thomson Gale, a part of The Thomson Corporation.

Thomson and Star Logo are trademarks and Gale is a registered trademark used herein under license.

For more information, contact
Thomson Gale
27500 Drake Rd.
Farmington Hills, MI 48331-3535
Or you can visit our Internet site at
http://www.gale.com

ALL RIGHTS RESERVED
No part of this work covered by the copyright hereon may be reproduced or used in any form or by any means—graphic, electronic, or mechanical, including photocopying, recording, taping, Web distribution, or information storage retrieval systems—without the written permission of the publisher.

For permission to use material from this product, submit your request via Web at http://www.gale-edit.com/permissions, or you may download our Permissions Request form and submit your request by fax or mail to:

Permissions Department
Thomson Gale
27500 Drake Rd.
Farmington Hills, MI 48331-3535
Permissions Hotline:
248-699-8006 or 800-877-4253, ext. 8006
Fax: 248-699-8074 or 800-762-4058

While every effort has been made to ensure the reliability of the information presented in this publication, Thomson Gale does not guarantee the accuracy of the data contained herein. Thomson Gale accepts no payment for listing; and inclusion in the publication of any organization, agency, institution, publication, service, or individual does not imply endorsement of the editors or publisher. Errors brought to the attention of the publisher and verified to the satisfaction of the publisher will be corrected in future editions.

LIBRARY OF CONGRESS CATALOGING-IN-PUBLICATION DATA

Chinese fiction writers, 1900-1949 / edited by Thomas Moran.
   p. cm. — (Dictionary of literary biography ; v. 328)
"A Bruccoli Clark Layman book."
Includes bibliographical references and index.
ISBN-13: 978–0–7876–8146–3
ISBN-10: 0–7876–8146–6 (hbk. : alk. paper)
  1. Chinese fiction—20th century—Bio-bibliography—Dictionaries.
  2. Novelists, Chinese—20th century—Biography—Dictionaries.
  3. Chinese fiction—20th century—Dictionaries. I. Moran, Thomas.
II. Series.
PL2652.C4175 2006
895.1'35109—dc22
                                     2006015676

Printed in the United States of America
10 9 8 7 6 5 4 3 2 1

Contents

Plan of the Series xiii
Introduction xv

Ai Wu (1904–1992) 3
  Alexandra R. Wagner

Ba Jin (1904–2005) 10
  Nicholas A. Kaldis

Bao Tianxiao (1876–1973) 26
  Feng-ying Ming

Bing Xin (1900–1999) 33
  Lingzhen Wang

Cheng Xiaoqing (1893–1976) 43
  Timothy C. Wong

Ding Ling (1904–1986) 53
  Thomas Moran

Jiang Guangci (1901–1931) 66
  John A. Crespi

Lai He (1894–1943) 73
  Rosemary M. Haddon

Lao She (1899–1966) 79
  William A. Lyell

Ling Shuhua (1900–1990) 95
  Amy D. Dooling

Liu E (1857–1909) 104
  Christopher Lupke

Lu Ling (1923–1994) 116
  Kirk A. Denton

Lu Xun (1881–1936) 129
  Jon Eugene von Kowallis

Lu Yin (1898?–1934) 151
  Kristina M. Torgeson

Mao Dun (1896–1981) 164
  Charles A. Laughlin

Mu Shiying (1912–1940) 178
  Yingjin Zhang

Qian Zhongshu (1910–1998) 183
  Xiaobin Yang

Shen Congwen (1902–1988) 192
  Jeffrey C. Kinkley

Shi Tuo (Lu Fen) (1910–1988) 206
  Steven P. Day

Wu Jianren (Wo Foshanren)
  (1866–1910) 212
  Theodore Huters

Wu Zuxiang (1908–1994) 220
  Philip F. Williams

Wumingshi (Bu Baonan)
  (1917–2002) 228
  Carlos Rojas

Xiang Kairan (Pingjiang Buxiaosheng;
  Buxiaosheng) (1890–1957) 235
  Roland Altenburger

Xiao Hong (1911–1942) 241
  Nicole Huang

Xu Dishan (Luo Huasheng)
  (1893–1941) 250
  Steven Riep

Xu Zhenya (1889–1937) 257
  Jianhua Chen

Yang Kui (1905–1985) 264
  Angelina C. Yee

Ye Shaojun (Ye Shengtao)
  (1894–1988) 272
  Xinmin Liu

Yu Dafu (1896–1945) 282
  Ann Huss

Zeng Pu (1872–1935) 290
   Hu Ying

Zhang Ailing (Eileen Chang)
   (1920–1995) 296
   Zhang Jingyuan

Zhang Henshui (1895–1967) 311
   T. M. McClellan

Zhang Tianyi (1906–1985) 320
   Thomas Moran

Zhao Shuli (1906–1970) 333
   T. M. McClellan

Books for Further Reading 341
Contributors 345
Cumulative Index 349

Plan of the Series

> ... Almost the most prodigious asset of a country, and perhaps its most precious possession, is its native literary product—when that product is fine and noble and enduring.
>
> Mark Twain*

The advisory board, the editors, and the publisher of the *Dictionary of Literary Biography* are joined in endorsing Mark Twain's declaration. The literature of a nation provides an inexhaustible resource of permanent worth. Our purpose is to make literature and its creators better understood and more accessible to students and the reading public, while satisfying the needs of teachers and researchers.

To meet these requirements, *literary biography* has been construed in terms of the author's achievement. The most important thing about a writer is his writing. Accordingly, the entries in *DLB* are career biographies, tracing the development of the author's canon and the evolution of his reputation.

The purpose of *DLB* is not only to provide reliable information in a usable format but also to place the figures in the larger perspective of literary history and to offer appraisals of their accomplishments by qualified scholars.

The publication plan for *DLB* resulted from two years of preparation. The project was proposed to Bruccoli Clark by Frederick G. Ruffner, president of the Gale Research Company, in November 1975. After specimen entries were prepared and typeset, an advisory board was formed to refine the entry format and develop the series rationale. In meetings held during 1976, the publisher, series editors, and advisory board approved the scheme for a comprehensive biographical dictionary of persons who contributed to literature. Editorial work on the first volume began in January 1977, and it was published in 1978. In order to make *DLB* more than a dictionary and to compile volumes that individually have claim to status as literary history, it was decided to organize volumes by topic, period, or genre. Each of these freestanding volumes provides a biographical-bibliographical guide and overview for a particular area of literature. We are convinced that this organization—as opposed to a single alphabet method—constitutes a valuable innovation in the presentation of reference material. The volume plan necessarily requires many decisions for the placement and treatment of authors. Certain figures will be included in separate volumes, but with different entries emphasizing the aspect of his career appropriate to each volume. Ernest Hemingway, for example, is represented in *American Writers in Paris, 1920-1939* by an entry focusing on his expatriate apprenticeship; he is also in *American Novelists, 1910-1945* with an entry surveying his entire career, as well as in *American Short-Story Writers, 1910-1945, Second Series* with an entry concentrating on his short fiction. Each volume includes a cumulative index of the subject authors and articles.

Between 1981 and 2002 the series was augmented and updated by the *DLB Yearbooks*. There have also been nineteen *DLB Documentary Series* volumes, which provide illustrations, facsimiles, and biographical and critical source materials for figures, works, or groups judged to have particular interest for students. In 1999 the *Documentary Series* was incorporated into the *DLB* volume numbering system beginning with *DLB 210: Ernest Hemingway*.

We define literature as the *intellectual commerce of a nation:* not merely as belles lettres but as that ample and complex process by which ideas are generated, shaped, and transmitted. *DLB* entries are not limited to "creative writers" but extend to other figures who in their time and in their way influenced the mind of a people. Thus the series encompasses historians, journalists, publishers, book collectors, and screenwriters. By this means readers of *DLB* may be aided to perceive literature not as cult scripture in the keeping of intellectual high priests but firmly positioned at the center of a nation's life.

DLB includes the major writers appropriate to each volume and those standing in the ranks behind them. Scholarly and critical counsel has been sought in deciding which minor figures to include and how full their entries should be. Wherever possible, useful refer-

---

*From an unpublished section of Mark Twain's autobiography, copyright by the Mark Twain Company ences are made to figures who do not warrant separate entries.

Each *DLB* volume has an expert volume editor responsible for planning the volume, selecting the figures for inclusion, and assigning the entries. Volume editors are also responsible for preparing, where appropriate, appendices surveying the major periodicals and literary and intellectual movements for their volumes, as well as lists of further readings. Work on the series as a whole is coordinated at the Bruccoli Clark Layman editorial center in Columbia, South Carolina, where the editorial staff is responsible for accuracy and utility of the published volumes.

One feature that distinguishes *DLB* is the illustration policy—its concern with the iconography of literature. Just as an author is influenced by his surroundings, so is the reader's understanding of the author enhanced by a knowledge of his environment. Therefore *DLB* volumes include not only drawings, paintings, and photographs of authors, often depicting them at various stages in their careers, but also illustrations of their families and places where they lived. Title pages are regularly reproduced in facsimile along with dust jackets for modern authors. The dust jackets are a special feature of *DLB* because they often document better than anything else the way in which an author's work was perceived in its own time. Specimens of the writers' manuscripts and letters are included when feasible.

Samuel Johnson rightly decreed that "The chief glory of every people arises from its authors." The purpose of the *Dictionary of Literary Biography* is to compile literary history in the surest way available to us—by accurate and comprehensive treatment of the lives and work of those who contributed to it.

The DLB Advisory Board

Introduction

The periodization used in China since 1949 in scholarship on literature from after the mid-nineteenth century is as follows: early modern *(jindai)*, 1844 to 1917; modern *(xiandai)*, 1917 to 1949; and contemporary *(dangdai)*, post-1949. This tripartite scheme still has influence, but scholars have offered alternatives that make finer distinctions, and while any periodization is at least partially arbitrary, the history of modern Chinese literature up to 1949 may be divided into five periods, with some overlap across divisions. Late-Qing literature extends from 1895 to 1911, the Mandarin Ducks and Butterflies School of fiction from 1912 to 1918, early May Fourth literature from 1919 to 1927, late May Fourth literature from 1928 to 1936, and the literature of the war with Japan and the Chinese civil war from 1937 to 1949.

During the last decades of the Qing dynasty, which began in 1644 and ended in 1911, much foreign fiction was translated—often quite freely—into Chinese; the classics of Chinese vernacular fiction, regarded as common cultural property, were rewritten or added to; and several thousand new works of fiction were published. In *Zhongguo xiaoshuo shilüe* (1923–1924; translated as *A Brief History of Chinese Fiction*, 1959) Lu Xun, modern China's foremost writer, sorts late-Qing fiction into novels about prostitutes *(xiaxie xiaoshuo)*, novels of adventure and detection *(gongan xiayi xiaoshuo)*, and novels of exposure *(qianze xiaoshuo)*. Lu Xun praises only the last, which "expose social abuses and lash out at contemporary politics, sometimes at social conventions as well."

By 1900 there was much for writers to expose and criticize. In the seventeenth and eighteenth centuries the Qing emperors ruled a sophisticated, powerful civilization, but in the nineteenth century China faced problems. Since the mid eighteenth century the British had been importing opium into China, and in the 1820s and 1830s they and other foreign nationals did so in exponentially increasing quantities because opium, which sold well and created permanent customers, was the only product that could offset the large imbalance of trade between foreign nations, which paid in silver for Chinese exports, and China, where there was only a small market for imports. According to Jonathan D. Spence in *The Search for Modern China* (1990), by the 1820s "enough opium was coming into China to sustain the habits of around 1 million addicts." The Qing dynasty government's first efforts to ban the opium trade were not successful, but starting in 1838 it used arrests and confiscations to slow the traffic of opium inside China; and in the spring of 1839, in the southern port city of Guangzhou, Imperial Commissioner Lin Zexu forced the British to surrender the opium stored in their warehouses. Lin oversaw the destruction of several million pounds of British opium. The British military response began in the fall of 1839 and was quickly effective. The treaty that ended the war on 29 August 1842 punished the Chinese, who agreed to cede Hong Kong to Great Britain; pay for the opium destroyed in Guangzhou, as well as an additional amount as recompense to the British for costs incurred in the fighting; and open five cities to foreign trade and permanent foreign residence. The Chinese suffered a succession of military and diplomatic defeats in the ensuing decades in which a series of *bu pingdeng tiaoyue* (unequal treaties) gave foreign nations rights and privileges in China, and Britain, France, Germany, and other nations took and held parts of China as semicolonial enclaves. Between 1851 and 1864 the Taiping Rebellion killed millions in the south. The Taiping Rebellion was led by Hong Xiuquan, who was from a rural area in what is now Guangxi province and was a member of the Hakka minority. After personal setbacks and an illness, Hong came to believe that he was the brother of Jesus Christ and began to preach his millenarian interpretation of Christianity. Between 1851 and 1853 Hong recruited an estimated sixty thousand people to his cause. His army crossed southern China to the city of Nanjing, which fell to the Taiping rebels in March 1853. The Taiping ruled much of southern China from Nanjing until 1864, when Qing troops finally defeated them. Scholars estimate that the direct and indirect effects of the Taiping Rebellion, including the massacre of the population of Nanjing in 1853, killed twenty million people. In the late 1870s the first Chinese students went abroad to study, ending assumptions that China was the center of all knowledge. The nascent modern Chinese navy was destroyed in wars with France in 1885 and with Japan in 1894–1895; after the latter war, Japan took Taiwan as its possession. In 1898 the young Guangxu emperor attempted to implement a slate of reforms crafted by his advisers; but his aunt, the empress dowager Cixi, had six reformers executed and the emperor placed under house arrest. In 1900 the presence in China of foreign traders, troops, and missionaries sparked a violent backlash known in Chinese as the Yihetuan (Society United in Righteousness) movement and in English as the Boxer Rebellion, after Yihequan (The United Righteous Fists), the name of one of the movement's founding groups. The Boxers attacked Chinese Christians and foreign missionaries, killed a German diplomat, and laid siege to the foreign quarter in Beijing. An allied force of eight nations drove out the Boxers, occupied Beijing, and punished the Qing, enforcing a settlement that further eroded Chinese sovereignty and impoverished the government. The Qing attempted belated reforms, abolishing the traditional civil service examination system in 1905. The Guangxu emperor died in 1908 and the empress dowager a year later. On 10 October 1911 a revolution got off to an accidental start when a munitions dump exploded. Insurrection followed. In some places the Qing military fought, in others it did not; the Qing collapsed, and Sun Yat-sen was inaugurated as the president of the Republic of China on 1 January 1912. The *Xinhai geming* (Revolution of the Year *Xinhai*) was, however, followed by twenty-five years of political instability and disunion.

In this context Liang Qichao published "Yi yin zhengzhi xiaoshuo xu" (1898; translated as "Foreword to the Publication of Political Novels in Translation") and "Lun xiaoshuo yu qunzhi zhi guanxi" (1902; translated as "On the Relationship Between Fiction and the Government of the People"), both of which are translated in *Modern Chinese Literary Thought: Writings on Literature, 1893–1945* (1996), edited by Kirk A. Denton. In the former, Liang wrote that fiction appealed to the masses and influenced society, but "taken as a whole, Chinese novels invariably teach us either robbery or lust," in the latter that "If one intends to renovate the people of a nation, one must first renovate its fiction." Liang was not the only intellectual to suggest that fiction could change China, but he gave the idea its most forceful articulation. His conviction that literature had didactic utility and his distrust of fiction were traditional notions. In China the category of "literature"—writing deserving of appreciation and study—consisted of poetry, belletristic prose, history, and philosophy, which were held to be true to the feelings of the poet or prose writer, the historical record, and the correct moral order. In *A Guide to Chinese Literature* (1997), Wilt Idema and Lloyd Haft argue that while the literary merit of some stories and novels was recognized, fiction, by definition untrue, was in general regarded as trivial and "at best tolerated as muddled history."

The authors of late-Qing novels of exposure shared Liang's ideas about the utility of fiction but not his distrust of it. The men identified by Lu Xun as exemplifying the genre—Liu E, Li Boyuan (Li Baojia), Wu Jianren (Wu Woyao), and Zeng Pu—are still regarded as the most important authors of their time. Their novels observe many of the conventions of traditional Chinese fiction but are credited by scholars with thematic and formal innovations. For example, in *C. T. Hsia on Chinese Literature* (2004) Hsia argues that Liu E's *Lao Can youji* (1903–1907; translated as *The Travels of Lao Ts'an,* 1952) subordinates storytelling conventions to individual vision, includes descriptive passages unexcelled in the Chinese tradition, and in one passage explores the consciousness of the protagonist with a mode of writing that approximates stream of consciousness.

Liu E and the others published their fiction after the turn of the century, and for this and other reasons the year 1900 can be taken as a convenient marker of the horizon of Chinese literary modernity. The turn of the twentieth century in China has been called a transitional age, and nothing was more indicative of a transition in the pattern of the lives of China's educated elite than the abolition of the examination system in 1905. This step was only one of several taken by the Qing government in a belated attempt to reform education, government, and commerce, but it was, according to R. Keith Schoppa, "the most revolutionary act of the twentieth century." For eight hundred years the three-tiered examination system buttressed the Confucian orthodoxy and produced the degree-holding scholar-gentry class that dominated China's political and intellectual life. By 1905 Liu E, Li Boyuan, Wu Jianren, and Zeng Pu had all either entered and left the civil service or opted out of it. Because of bad luck, personal choice, and changing times, all four men pursued careers outside the civil service before it was abolished. Wu Jianren did not take the examinations, and Liu E failed at the provincial level. Li Boyuan passed the local but failed the provincial examination in 1897. Zeng Pu passed both but, famously, stormed out of the metropolitan examination without finishing it.

Liu E, Li, Wu, and Zeng Pu came from scholar-gentry families, were trained in the classics, and were the inheritors of a literati culture going back two thousand years, but they were modern men. Liu E, for example, was a consultant on flood control, developed railways and mines, and participated in several commercial ventures. The novelists of the late Qing have been called journalist-littérateurs. Li owned newspapers and was also a journalist, editor, and publisher; Wu edited and managed newspapers; and Zeng Pu, who read French, was a publisher and translator and founded two book companies.

Between 1872 and 1908 automatic inking, lithographic printing, photolithography, the rotary press, and metal type were introduced to China. Between 1895 and 1911 more than two hundred progressive journals and newspapers were established, reaching a readership of between two and four million. Leo Ou-fan Lee and Andrew J. Nathan, who provide this estimate in an essay included in *Popular Culture in Late Imperial China* (1985), edited by Nathan, David G. Johnson, Evelyn Sakakida Rawski, and Judith A. Berling, write that in about a decade beginning at the turn of the twentieth century "the modern press had created the largest, most far-flung audience in Chinese history." Many periodicals of the late-Qing period and after included literary supplements; some of these supplements became literary journals that published fiction, which facilitated the development of modern Chinese literature.

From the 1910s through the 1920s the most popular fiction was that of the Mandarin Ducks and Butterflies School. Technically, this label refers to sentimental love stories; but in usage dating to the 1920s it encompasses all entertainment fiction. It was also called the Saturday School after the magazine *Libailiu* (Saturday), a venue for popular fiction. According to Timothy C. Wong's afterword to his anthology *Stories for Saturday: Twentieth-Century Chinese Popular Fiction* (2003), Mandarin Ducks and Butterflies fiction included stories of love *(aiqing)*, social satire *(shehui fengci)*, crime detection *(zhentan)*, scandal *(heimu)*, and martial gallantry *(wuxia)*. Mandarin Ducks and Butterflies fiction inherited the long tradition of stories about love, adventure, heroism, good and evil, mystery, and miracles, and, David Der-wei Wang argues in *Fin-de-Siècle Splendor: Repressed Modernities of Late Qing Fiction, 1849–1911* (1997), also inherited the late-Qing tradition of sentimental novels, chivalric and court-case novels, sensationalized exposé novels, and science fiction and fantasy novels.

Mandarin Ducks and Butterflies fiction developed during a time of change and disorder. The revolution of 1911 ended the Qing dynasty, and the Republic of China was founded on 1 January 1912 with Sun Yat-sen as provisional president. On 12 February, Yuan Shikai replaced Sun, in 1914 Yuan dissolved Parliament and in January 1916 declared himself emperor. In March he restored the republic; but by then three southern provinces had declared their independence, and more seceded in April and May. Yuan died in June, and power devolved to *junfa* (warlords). The major division was between the south, where the Nationalist Party was active, and the north, where warlords kept a national government in place to give their activities legitimacy. China remained divided until 1928.

E. Perry Link Jr. argues in his *Mandarin Ducks and Butterflies: Popular Fiction in Early Twentieth-Century Chinese Cities* (1981) that the appeal of Mandarin Ducks and Butterflies fiction was more than its entertainment value; it had stylistic links to traditional fiction and endorsed traditional values, which was comforting to urban middle-class readers unsettled by revolution and modernization. Exemplary authors of Mandarin Ducks and Butterflies fiction include Xu Zhenya, whose *Yuli hun* (1912, Jade Pear Spirit) is regarded by literary historians as having begun the flourishing of the genre; Bao Tianxiao, a writer, translator, publisher, editor, and patron of younger writers; Cheng Xiaoqing, who created Huo Sang and Bao Lang, the Chinese Sherlock Holmes and Dr. Watson; Xiang Kairan, who, as Roland Altenburger writes in his entry on Xiang in this volume, "virtually invented the modern genre of the martial arts novel based on popular lore"; and Zhang Henshui, whose best-selling *Tixiao yinyuan* (1930, Fate in Tears and Laughter), combines romance, social commentary, and a bit of martial arts.

The term "Mandarin Ducks and Butterflies School" was first used disparagingly by leaders of the iconoclastic New Culture Movement. They believed that literature should be progressive and were hostile to popular fiction. Their movement began in 1915 with the founding of the magazine *Xin qingnian* (New Youth) by Chen Duxiu, a veteran revolutionary and propagandist who held an imperial degree and had studied in Japan and France. In the first article of the first issue Chen attacked tradition and, alluding to social Darwinism, argued that unless Chinese culture and society changed radically, the Chinese were in danger of disappearing because they were "unfit for survival." In 1919 Chen summarized the editorial stance taken by his magazine in its first three years. *Xin qingnian*, he wrote, supported science and democracy and opposed Confucianism, traditional ethics, old-fashioned politics, and traditional arts, religion, and literature. Excerpts from the essay are translated in Chow Tse-tsung's *The May 4th Movement: Intellectual Revolution in Modern China* (1960).

Articles in *Xin qingnian* in January and February 1917 by Chen and by Hu Shi, who had studied in the United States, began a literary revolution *(wenxue geming)* that led to the creation of a new literature *(xin wenxue)*. Key to the transformation of the theory and practice of fiction in China were assertions by Hu Shi and others that fiction should be written in a "plain speech" *(baihua)* vernacular and that this fiction could become a new national literature.

There are two forms of written Chinese. Classical Chinese *(wanyan)* was modeled on the language of the Confucian classics, was developed from the Han dynasty (206 B.C. to A.D. 220) onward, and was the written language of government and elite culture until the early twentieth century. It is a written language only and is difficult to understand when read aloud, even for native speakers of Chinese. Written vernacular Chinese, which had developed by the time of the Song dynasty (960 to 1279), was based on the spoken Chinese of northern China and was the language of written popular culture, including fiction. Classical Chinese and the vernacular influenced each other but remained different in grammar and lexicon. Texts in Classical Chinese were held in high regard as literature, but texts in the vernacular, including fiction, were not. In a 1918 essay in *Xin qingnian,* "Jianshe de wenxue geming lun" (On Constructive Literary Revolution), Hu Shi denounced Classical Chinese as a dead language, argued for the use of vernacular Chinese as the "gongju" (tool) for the creation of a "Guoyu de wenxue" (Chinese literature of national speech), and encouraged his readers to study the language of traditional vernacular fiction. Hu Shi's recognition of the value of vernacular fiction as literature was revolutionary.

Because of the influence of late-Qing fiction and journalism, much of which was in the vernacular, and broad support for social and political reform, the movement to replace Literary with vernacular Chinese succeeded quickly: experiments with vernacular poetry began in 1918; in the early 1920s the Ministry of Education adopted the vernacular as the standard language for textbooks; authors of Mandarin Ducks and Butterflies fiction abandoned their semi-Literary style and began to write in the vernacular; and journals were founded to publish new literature in the vernacular.

In May 1918 Lu Xun published the story "Kuangren riji" (translated as "A Madman's Diary," 1981) in *Xin qingnian*. Lu Xun had studied in Japan, was well read in foreign literature, and took the title for his story from Nikolai Gogol. "Kuangren riji" is often identified as the first work of modern Chinese literature because of its use of vernacular fiction for a serious purpose, manipulation of formal elements such as narrative perspective and symbolism, foreign influences, and condemnation of tradition—it calls Confucianism cannibalistic, an epithet popular among reformers. According to Lee's *Voices from the Iron House: A Study of Lu Xun* (1987), in stories such as "Kuangren riji" Lu Xun created "something new in both form and content by transforming and thereby transcending traditional Chinese influences, while consciously borrowing from Western literary models."

At the beginning of World War I in 1914 Japan declared war on Germany, seized German-controlled territory in China's Shandong province, and forced the Chinese government to grant it economic privileges and the right to station police in the northeastern part of the country. At the Paris Peace Conference after the war the Chinese delegation could not block a provision that granted Japan continued control of Shandong. The news reached China in late April 1919, and on 4 May more than three thousand students gathered at the northern end of Tiananmen Square in Beijing to protest the government's failure to resist Japanese encroachment. They distributed a manifesto written, according to Chow, "in vivid and clean-cut vernacular Chinese, which reflected the effect of the literary revolution," and left letters of protest at foreign legations. Students beat one government official, burned the home of another, and fought with police. After the Beijing demonstration, student unions were formed across China, strikes took place in Shanghai and elsewhere, and the publication and distribution of progressive periodicals expanded.

Named for the date of the Tiananmen demonstration, the patriotic May Fourth Movement *(Wu si yundong)* promoted cultural, social, economic, and political reform. It is generally regarded as having ended by the mid 1920s, by which time cultural and political activity in China was beginning to organize itself along the lines of the split between the Nationalist Party and the Chinese Communist Party, founded in 1921. The term "May Fourth Literature," however, is used to refer to fiction, drama, and poetry written from 1918 until 1937 that reflected and promoted the liberalism of the early 1920s and the left-leaning ideology of the late 1920s and 1930s. During the 1920s and 1930s both May Fourth fiction, which was the literature of the intellectual elite, and Mandarin Ducks and Butterflies popular fiction were produced and read.

Beijing was the center of intellectual activity until the late 1920s, when its place was taken by Shanghai. In these cities May Fourth writers and critics discussed and debated literary techniques, the purpose of literature, the role of the writer in society, and the history of literature in the West. They founded journals, translated, wrote, and organized themselves into groups, among which the Wenxue yanjiu hui (Literary Research Association) and the Chuangzao she (Creation Society), both founded in 1921, were the most influential. Chow writes that the "former emphasized the revelation of human and social realities; the latter emphasized unrestricted expression of human feelings."

The Literary Research Association and its periodicals promoted literary realism and opposed theories that emphasized fiction's utility for conveying a moral message or that argued that fiction was for entertainment and aesthetic contemplation. Mao Dun, one of the founders of the Literary Research Association, became the editor of *Xiaoshuo yuebao* (Short Story Monthly) beginning with the first issue of 1921 and changed the magazine's content from popular to May Fourth fiction. *Xiaoshuo yuebao* carried the first published fiction by Xu Dishan, Lao She, Ba Jin, Ding Ling, and Mao Dun himself and helped establish the careers of other important writers, including Lu Yin, Bing Xin, and Ling Shuhua.

Before 1925 the Creation Society promoted Romanticism. In *The Romantic Generation of Modern Chinese Writers* (1973) Lee argues that in the early 1920s much new literature, including writing by authors who were not members of the Chuangzao she, was subjective and expressive. Other literary groups were the Xinyue she (Crescent Moon Society), founded in 1923, which included Hu Shi and Shen Congwen and was influenced by Anglo-American humanism; the Spinners of Words Society, a liberal group founded in 1924 by Lu Xun and his brother that believed that serious writers should pursue their individual interests; and the Sun Society, established in 1927 by Jiang Guangci, Qian Xingcun, and others, with the support of the Chinese Communist Party, to promote Marxist theories of literature. After 1925 the Creation Society also advocated communism and revolutionary literature.

Some advocates of the new literature were pioneers in the study of traditional Chinese fiction. In the early 1920s Lu Xun wrote the first comprehensive history of Chinese fiction, *Zhongguo xiaoshuo shilüe*; in 1928 Hu Shi published one volume of a planned longer history of vernacular literature, *Baihua wenxue shi, shang juan* (A History of Vernacular Literature, volume 1)—the rest never appeared; and in 1937 Qian published a history of late-Qing fiction, *Wan Qing xiaoshuo shi* (A History of Late-Qing Fiction), that remains a standard source. May Fourth writers were familiar with and fond of traditional fiction, some were expert in aspects of traditional culture, and several wrote fiction inspired by traditional works; Lu Xun, for example, reworked several Chinese legends in his *Gushi xinbian* (1936; translated as *Old Tales Retold*, 1961). While May Fourth writers were influenced by tradition, they consciously and conspicuously embraced new foreign models.

The introduction of foreign literature and literary theory to China in the 1920s was neither systematic nor thorough, but it was enthusiastic and extensive. Anton Chekhov, Maksim Gorky, Ivan Turgenev, Rabindranath Tagore, Gustave Flaubert, Charles Dickens, Emile Zola, Guy de Maupassant, and Natsume Sōseki are among the many foreign writers who were favorites of the authors discussed in this volume. Ling Shuhua majored in English and French in college and minored in Japanese; Bing Xin earned an M.A. from Wellesley College; Qian Zhongshu studied English literature at the University of Oxford; Lao She lived in England for five years; Ba Jin studied in France; and Lu Xun, Yu Dafu, Lu Yin, Mao Dun, and Yang Kui spent time in Japan. In her essay on the impact of Western literary trends on May Fourth literature, included in Merle Goldman's *Modern Chinese Literature in the May Fourth Era* (1977), Bonnie S. McDougall writes that "The impact of Western literature in China in the twenties and thirties above all fostered a sense of internationalism among Chinese writers."

The always ongoing evolution of Chinese prose style accelerated in the 1920s because of an increase in the number of works translated from foreign languages, a change in translation practice to increased fidelity to the original work, and efforts by writers to borrow features of foreign languages. In *Rewriting Chinese: Style and Innovation in Twentieth-Century Chinese Prose* (1991) Edward Gunn argues that the "innovations derived from foreign languages beginning in 1918 reached almost every category of linguistic analysis in terms of grammar, rhetorical invention, and sentence cohesion." According to Gunn, however, stylistic innovations based on European languages did not displace but rather added to existing Chinese linguistic structures and were "employed for conventional stylistic purposes, such as cohesion, emphasis, elegant variation, emotiveness, and irony." The "Europeanized" (*Ouhua*) style used by May Fourth writers marked them as different both from traditional Chinese fiction writers and from modern popular writers; but, Gunn concludes, Chinese readers were comfortable with both the conservative style of commercial writers and the experimental style of May Fourth writers: "whether one eschewed innovations in the manner of Zhang Henshui or employed them lavishly in the manner of Ba Jin made little difference to the market for fiction."

In the 1920s the dominant fictional form was the short story; novels did not rival or surpass short stories in popularity or critical success until the 1930s. Scholars speculate that May Fourth writers in the early period preferred the short story because it was easier to write an original work that borrowed techniques of foreign short fiction—and so seemed modern—than it was to imitate carefully structured nineteenth-century European novels without falling back on the quite different conventions of the traditional Chinese novel. Also, the new magazines found short fiction convenient to publish. Lu Xun, the most important writer of the decade, wrote no novels; he wrote all of his short stories between 1918 and 1926.

In his *Zhongguo xiandai xiaoshuo liupai shi* (1989, A History of the Schools of Modern Chinese Fiction) Yan Jiayan sums up the thematic concerns of Chinese fiction from 1918 to 1937 by identifying ten "liupai" (schools). In the 1920s writers of "Xiangtu wenxue" (Native-Soil Fiction), including Ye Shaojun, turned attention to life in the countryside and experimented with the use of realism to capture regional characteristics. The Romantic fiction advocated by the Creation Society in its early period included "Ziwo xiaoshuo" ("I" Fiction), which was influenced by expressionist theories of literature; Yu Dafu is a representative Romantic writer. The Sun Society and, after 1925, the Creation Society promoted "Geming xiaoshuo" (Revolutionary Fiction), a jejune form of proletarian literature; Jiang Guangci is a well-known writer of this school of propagandistic literature.

In a 1967 essay reprinted in the third edition of his *A History of Modern Chinese Fiction* (1999) Hsia writes that Chinese literature of the 1920s and 1930s was distinguished by "its obsessive concern with China as a nation afflicted with a spiritual disease and therefore unable to strengthen itself or change its set ways of inhumanity." Another prominent feature of fiction of the 1920s is subjectivism: many stories are autobiographical or semi-autobiographical, and many use first-person narration. Some writers experimented with unreliable narrators, the depiction of unusual psychological states, and rural settings and characters.

Many wrote about love, and many wrote about the lives of women who were either oppressed by tradition or liberated and challenged by modernity.

Beginning in the 1890s reformers, including women, wrote and argued for new educational opportunities for women and the abolition of foot binding. The emancipation of women was a central goal of the May Fourth Movement. Schools for women were founded, and in 1920 the first female students were admitted to Beijing University. The identity and experience of the "xin nüxing" (new woman) became a preoccupation of much fiction and commentary. China had always had some women writers, but in the May Fourth period they were prominent in unprecedented numbers. Scholars speculate that because women were excluded from traditional literati culture, they may have found it relatively easy to depart from that culture and adapt to new literary conventions. Some of the first successful May Fourth writers were women, including Bing Xin, Lu Yin, Ling Shuhua, and Ding Ling. Significant women fiction writers who could not be treated in this volume for space or other reasons include Chen Hengzhe, who went to a girls' school in Shanghai, graduated Phi Beta Kappa from Vassar College in 1915, was the first woman professor at Beijing University, and published only one book of short stories but, according to Amy D. Dooling and Kristina M. Torgeson in their *Writing Women in Modern China: An Anthology of Women's Literature from the Early Twentieth Century* (1998), has the distinction of writing what may have been the first modern short story composed in vernacular Chinese: "Yi ri" (1917; translated as "One Day," 1998); Bai Wei, who was primarily a playwright and a poet; Lin Huiyin, who was an architect, historian, artist, poet, and novelist; Xie Bingying, whose most important works are autobiographical accounts of her time in the military; Su Qing, whose novel *Jiehun shinian* (1944, Ten Years of Marriage) was highly popular; and Shi Pingmei. Male writers who are not treated include Li Boyuan, Duanmu Hongliang, Sha Ting, Wang Tongzhao, Xiao Jun, and Shi Zhecun.

In 1925 the division between the political right and left deepened, and the truce between the Nationalist Party and the Communist Party weakened. In 1926 the Beifa (Northern Expedition), a military campaign led by Chiang Kai-shek, defeated or made alliances with warlords and began to unite the country. In late 1926 and early 1927 Communists had success in organizing labor unions in major cities. In March 1927 Communists in Shanghai organized a general strike and an armed rebellion, allowing Northern Expedition troops to take the city; but in April Chiang broke the truce and ordered the arrest and killing of Communists and union members. By the end of 1928 the Communists withdrew to beleaguered base areas in the southeastern countryside, and Chiang and the Nationalists controlled China from the new capital of Nanjing.

Political change caused a change in literature. In a February 1928 article in a Creation Society magazine Cheng Fangwu, a writer and one of the founders of the Creation Society, contended that the new fiction was petit bourgeois in ideology and of interest only to a segment of the intellectual class and proposed a move from literary revolution to revolutionary literature. Some writers defended the independence of art and the artist and argued against the Marxist notion that all literature was class based, but much of the debate over revolutionary literature from 1928 to 1930 was between rival groups of leftists who were divided by personal animosity. Young radicals attacked older writers for failing to produce literature that would mobilize the masses in revolution. Lu Xun and Mao Dun, who were among those attacked, considered the radicals naive and arrogant.

Shanghai was the center of left-wing literary activity. The publishing industry was based there; and parts of the city were governed and policed by foreign nations and so were beyond the control of the Chinese government, affording writers some relief from government censorship. The Zhongguo zuoyi zuojia lianming (League of Left-Wing Writers) was founded in Shanghai in March 1930 at the instigation of the Chinese Communist Party, bringing together most of those who had been divided in the debate of the previous two years. At its largest, the organization had branches in various cities, including Beiping (as Beijing was known from 1928 to 1949), and more than four hundred members divided into groups and committees that operated independently of one another but under the direction of the leadership. The league was banned by the Nationalist Party, which arrested and executed some members, but continued to operate. It organized demonstrations, pamphleteered, published journals, promoted the popularization of literature, and moderated disputes among its members. It debated and criticized anyone who argued in support of literature that did not promote the revolutionary cause. League theorist Qu Qiubai argued that the written vernacular had become Westernized and called for proletarian mass literature written in a language closer to that used by the masses and in forms familiar and appealing to them. Qu's ideas had no immediate effect; fiction in the conventional vernacular remained the dominant genre.

In the periodization used by Sima Changfeng in *Zhongguo xin wenxue shi* (1975–1978, A History of the New Chinese Literature), the years 1929 to 1937 were the "shouhuo qi" (period of results; literally, "harvest season") when the new literature movement flourished. Mao Dun, Zhang Tianyi, Ding Ling, and Ai Wu were leading fiction authors who were members of the League of Left-Wing Writers. Mao Dun's long novel *Ziye* (1933; translated as

Midnight, 1979), a portrayal of the social, economic, and political conditions in Shanghai in the early 1930s, exemplifies what Yan terms the school of "Shehui pouxi xiaoshuo" (Fiction of Social Analysis). Ding Ling's fiction of the early 1930s typifies efforts by left-wing writers to find a politically and aesthetically satisfying resolution to the thematic formula of "geming jia lian'ai" (revolution plus love), popular since the 1920s. Liu Jianmei writes in *Revolution plus Love: Literary History, Women's Bodies, and Thematic Repetition in Twentieth-Century Chinese Fiction* (2003) that Ding Ling's 1930 novel *Wei Hu* shows that "Ding Ling was caught in a dilemma between her original identity as a modern, urbanized, and liberated woman and her new, vague Communist identity." The "Dongbei zuojia qun" (Northeastern Writers)—Duanmu Hongliang, Xiao Jun, and Xiao Hong, all of whom started their careers in the 1930s—wrote about their home provinces and the Japanese occupation of the northeast, which began in 1931.

In the 1930s the audience for May Fourth fiction finally matched that for popular fiction. Link writes that by 1935 "most urban readers no doubt read both kinds of literature, though in somewhat different moods." According to Link, Zhang Henshui's *Tixiao yinyuan* (1930, Fate in Tears and Laughter) "was probably the most widely read Chinese novel in the first half of the twentieth century." *Tixiao yinyuan* is a work of Mandarin Ducks and Butterflies fiction that owes its success, T. M. McClellan writes in his entry on Zhang Henshui in this volume, to its "exuberant mix of traditional and modern style, technique, content, and themes." Ba Jin's *Jia* (1933; translated as *Family,* 1958) is a canonical work of May Fourth fiction but shares the sentimentality and melodrama of entertainment fiction and was almost as popular as *Tixiao yinyuan.*

Ba Jin, Shen Congwen, Wu Zuxiang, Shi Zhecun, Mu Shiying, and Lao She were leading authors of the 1930s who were independent of the League of Left-Wing Writers. Shen is one of Yan's examples of authors of "Jing pai xiaoshuo" (Fiction of the Beijing School): writers who lived in Beijing for some or all of their careers and were united by opposition to the commercialization and politicization of literature. Shi, Mu, and Liu Na'ou were leaders of the Shanghai-based "Xin ganjue" (New Perceptionist) school of modernist fiction; it was modeled on a similarly named Japanese type of fiction, which, in turn, had been influenced by expressionism, Surrealism, futurism, and American and English stream-of-consciousness literature. Shi, who experimented with the incorporation of Freudian theories in his short stories, was first the editor and then the co-editor of the nonpartisan magazine *Xiandai/Les Contemporains* (The Moderns) from 1932 to 1935. *Xiandai/Les contemporains* published almost all leading left-wing and independent writers. It was, Shu-mei Shih writes in *The Lure of the Modern: Writing Modernism in Semicolonial China, 1917–1937* (2001), "arguably the most important literary forum in all of China."

In Taiwan, occupied by Japan since 1895, the New Culture Movement shared the social and political agenda of the mainland's May Fourth Movement. May Fourth fiction was reprinted in journals in Taiwan, and writers published realist fiction in vernacular Chinese. The first author to use the vernacular instead of Classical Chinese in Taiwan was Lai He, who published his first story in 1926. Lai He was well trained in Classical Chinese and identified culturally with China. Many of his stories, Rosemary Haddon writes in her entry on Lai He in this volume, "portray the brutality and hardship of Japanese colonial rule and the adverse effects of assimilationist policies."

The majority of people in Taiwan spoke Southern Min (Taiwanese), and in 1931–1932 some intellectuals advocated the creation of a written language based on it. This idea was, however, impractical, because Chinese characters do not exist for many words in Taiwanese and because the Japanese discouraged the Taiwanese-language movement. After 1931 the influence of May Fourth literature on Taiwan lessened, and, because of a generational change and government policy, the use of Japanese by Taiwanese fiction writers increased. Yang Kui, one of the writers to whom Lai He served as mentor, was educated in Japanese-language schools in Taiwan and studied in Japan; he wrote his fiction in Japanese, publishing his first story in 1936. Sung-sheng Yvonne Chang argues in her essay on Taiwanese literature during the Japanese occupation in *Taiwan: A New History* (1999), edited by Murray A. Rubinstein, that Yang Kui and his contemporaries "consciously shifted to more detailed depictions of local customs, rural life, and folk traditions of Chinese/Taiwanese origin in order to register their resentment of the Japanization program."

On the Chinese mainland the Communist Party was driven out of its base in Jiangxi province by Nationalist forces in late 1934 and reached Yan'an in the north central province of Shaanxi after a year-long journey of six thousand miles. War between China and Japan began in July 1937. The Japanese captured the eastern cities; the Nationalist government moved inland, reaching its wartime capital of Chongqing in Sichuan province in October 1938. The extent of Japanese control was at its greatest in 1941–1942, reaching up the Yangtze River to Changsha in Hunan province and threatening the Communist base at Yan'an.

After 1937 most writers relocated to the Nationalist-controlled interior. Many—including, most prominently, Lao She, Wu Zuxiang, and Zhang Tianyi—joined the Zhonghua quanguo wenyijie kangdi xiehui (All-China Association of Literary Resistance), which was sponsored by both the Nationalists and the Communist Party during the Second United Front, an unstable truce between the two while they fought the Japanese. Lao She and others contributed works in various genres, including fiction, that celebrated heroic Chinese soldiers, called for sacrifice and dedication in the war effort, and condemned the Japanese invaders. Authors who published significant works of fiction in Nationalist areas during or just after the war include Xiao Hong, Wu Zuxiang, Ba Jin, Lu Ling, and Wumingshi ("Anonymous"; pseudonym of Bu Baonan); the latter two published their first books during the war. Wumingshi's eccentric mix of Romantic and modernist elements typifies what Yan calls the "Houqi langman pai xiaoshuo" (Later Romantic School of Fiction).

The major fiction writers in occupied Shanghai were Shi Tuo, Zhang Ailing, and Qian Zhongshu. Under the pseudonym Lu Fen, Shi Tuo wrote stories and a novella and in 1941 published *Shanghai shouzha* (Shanghai Correspondence); "this literary montage," Steven P. Day writes in his entry on Shi Tuo in this volume, "reads as part essay and part novel, as commentary is blended harmoniously with eighteen fictional vignettes that juxtapose everyday life against wartime in Shanghai." Yan terms Zhang Ailing's work, which refers only indirectly to the war, "Xinli fenxi xiaoshuo" (Psychological Fiction) and groups it with the New Perceptionist fiction of the 1930s. Beginning in 1938 Qian taught at Southwest Associated University in Kunming and then at a college in rural Hunan but was in Shanghai in 1941 and could not leave after the Japanese took control of the city. In Shanghai, Qian taught and wrote essays, criticism, and short stories. He also began a novel, *Weicheng* (1947; translated as *Fortress Besieged,* 1979). In *A History of Modern Chinese Fiction* Hsia calls *Weicheng* "the most delightful and carefully wrought novel in modern Chinese literature" and "perhaps also its greatest."

Several writers spent some or all of the war years in and around Yan'an, the Communist capital. In *War and Popular Culture: Resistance in Modern China, 1937–1945* (1994) Chang-tai Hung writes that "Communist leaders were superb craftsmen in utilizing a rich array of popular culture forms to wage war against Japan, to win public support, and, most important, to spread revolutionary ideas and socialist reforms." Ding Ling went to Shaanxi after escaping from Nationalist custody in 1936. She wrote an essay that was critical of the treatment of women in Yan'an and became a target of the rectification campaign of 1942. She recanted and wrote works of reportage and fiction that observed the guidelines laid out by Mao Zedong in May 1942 at the Yan'an Forum on Literature and Art. These guidelines specified that writers should reform themselves so that they could better empathize with the masses; that they should write for workers, peasants, and soldiers; and that their work should be evaluated by its efficacy in promoting revolutionary change.

The "Qiyue pai xiaoshuo" (July School of Fiction) is named after a journal founded in 1937 by Hu Feng; its writers, including Lu Ling, were Communists but followed Hu Feng in his insistence that authors maintain their independence and refuse to submit to the control of the party. Zhao Shuli's *Xiao Erhei jiehun* (Young Blacky Gets Married; translated as "Little Erhei's Marriage," 1979) and *Li Youcai banhua* (The Rhymes of Li Youcai; translated as "The Rhymes of Li Yu-ts'ai," 1950), both published in 1943, were among the first works written in accordance with Mao's guidelines and are praised by critics for their wit and combination of popular fictional forms and communist themes. Zhao is the exemplar of what Yan and others call the "Shanyaodan pai" (Potato School).

After the founding of the People's Republic of China in 1949, the political control of fiction became absolute; but politics and literature intersect throughout the history of modern Chinese fiction, which is evident in the fates of writers. In 1908 Liu E was falsely accused of crimes against the Qing government and banished to the far northwest, where he died in 1909. In 1931 Jiang Guangci was criticized and expelled from the Communist Party; he died of a heart ailment a month later. In Taiwan the Japanese arrested Lai He twice, releasing him the second time because he was ill with the heart disease that killed him in 1943. Yu Dafu was executed by the Japanese in Sumatra in 1945. Mu Shiying, who had gone to work for the pro-Japanese government of Wang Jingwei, was assassinated, probably by Nationalist agents, in 1940. Taiwan's Yang Kui was imprisoned more than a dozen times by the Japanese before 1945, and in 1949 the Nationalist government put him in prison for twelve years. By the early 1950s Ling Shuhua, Zhang Ailing, and Bao Tianxiao had left China; only Ling ever went back. Wumingshi moved to Hong Kong in 1982 and to Taiwan a year later.

Most writers who stayed in China after 1949 stopped writing altogether or kept to politically safe genres such as reportage, essays, memoirs, and children's literature. Several became cultural bureaucrats in the socialist literary system. Some writers suffered. The persecution was egalitarian, targeting authors of both popular and May Fourth fiction and both independents and Communists. Shen Congwen was in Beiping when the Communists took the city in December 1948 and became the target of what Jeffrey C. Kinkley, in *The Odyssey of Shen Congwen* (1987), calls "a war of psychological terror." Lu Ling was arrested in 1955 and spent twenty-five years in prisons, psychiatric wards, and labor camps. Ding Ling was expelled from the Communist Party in 1957, sent into internal exile, and then imprisoned. Xiang Kairan's death in 1957 may have resulted from a stroke brought on by physical abuse during the Anti-Rightist Campaign. In a 1979 speech the playwright Yang Hansheng read a list of more than one hundred writers and artists who had been driven to their deaths or wrongly vilified during the Cultural Revolution of 1966 to 1976. In 1966 Cheng Xiaoqing was abused before a crowd at a Suzhou theater; Ba Jin was forced to kneel on broken glass as he was humiliated and criticized on the field at a Beijing sports stadium; Lao She was beaten by Red Guards and a day later was found dead in a Beijing lake (indications are that he drowned himself); Qian Zhongshu and his wife, playwright Yang Jiang, survived the Cultural Revolution, but their son-in-law, who was also the target of criticism, killed himself in 1970; Zhao Shuli, whose stories had been held up for twenty years as exemplars of the use of popular forms to create literature that was entertaining to the masses and ideologically healthy, died in 1970 of an injury sustained at the hands of the Red Guards during the Cultural Revolution.

From 1949 through the 1970s literary historians in and outside of China emphasized the newness of Chinese fiction in the first half of the twentieth century and the thoroughness of its break with the past. Standard histories taught that China's traditional literature had reached its end by the late nineteenth century and identified 1917 to 1919 as the years in which Chinese literature suddenly, and under the influence of the West, became modern. These histories also took the year 1949 as marking the end of modern literature and the beginning of a different era of contemporary literature. Starting in the 1970s, however, contributions from many scholars corrected the misleading assertion that there was an absolute separation between a monolithic modern literature that arose after 1917 and a discarded premodern literature. These scholars documented the process whereby literature in China in the first fifty years of the twentieth century emerged in its complexity and diversity from late-Qing dynasty literature in specific and from the richness of the Chinese literary tradition in general. Scholars also expanded the canon by turning their attention to popular writers and modernists who had been ignored in standard histories, which concentrated on the critical realists of the May Fourth movement. Some scholars have questioned the validity of dividing twentieth-century Chinese literature by political chronology, which separates pre-1949 modern literature from post-1949 contemporary literature, or geography, which separates the literature of Taiwan and Hong Kong from that of the rest of China. In China and Taiwan for many years scholars have edited volumes of research materials and compiled detailed life chronologies and exhaustive bibliographies for each of many modern Chinese writers and have also edited and annotated collections of these writers' complete or selected works. These Chinese-language sources, along with important English-language biographies of individual authors, are indispensable to research into modern Chinese literature and are credited individually by title and author in the lists of references that follow the entries in this volume.

With few exceptions, this volume uses Hanyu pinyin (Chinese Phonetic Spelling) to romanize Chinese personal and place names, book titles, and terms. The pinyin system was adopted in the People's Republic of China in 1958, replacing other schemes used to represent the sounds of Mandarin Chinese with the Roman alphabet. In English-language writing about China since the 1980s, pinyin has become the standard, replacing the Wade-Giles system, which dates to 1912, although Wade-Giles spellings remain familiar to China scholars and general readers; "modern literature" is "hsien-tai wen-hsueh" in Wade-Giles and "xiandai wenxue" in pinyin. In Taiwan, which has been governed independently as the Republic of China since 1949, a different system was used until 2002, when Taiwan, too, adopted pinyin—albeit inconsistently, with some modifications, and at the cost of controversy. Before pinyin came into use, the English spelling of Chinese personal names was unpredictable, and spellings of Chinese toponyms conformed to the usage in an atlas published in 1903 by the Directorate General of Posts. This atlas used a system based on Cantonese pronunciation, which is why, for example, the southern city called Xianggang in Mandarin is known in English as Hong Kong, which approximates the Cantonese pronunciation. In this volume "Hong Kong" is used, and old spellings are also used for some personal names, including that of Chiang Kai-shek, whose name in pinyin is Jiang Jieshi. Most English-language books about China published before the introduction of pinyin used Wade-Giles in their titles, and in this volume such titles are cited as they originally appeared.

Speakers of English who do not know Chinese can approximate Mandarin pronunciation when reading pinyin by mastering a few conventions. In many contexts, including the names Ding Ling and Bing Xin, the vowel *i* is pronounced like the *i* in *machine* or *chlorine*; but when following *c, r, s,* or *z*, as in the titles of Lao She's books *Zhao Ziyue* (1928), *Niu Tianci zhuan* (1936, The Biography of Niu Tianci; translated as *Heavensent*, 1951), and *Si shi tong tang* (1946, Four Generations under One Roof), the *i* sound is "a weakly buzzing syllabic *z*," as S. Robert Ramsey explains in *The Languages of China* (1987). When following *r, ch, sh,* or *zh, i* is pronounced like the *ir* in *sir* or *bird;* the surname of the writer Shi Tuo is thus pronounced something like *sure*.

E, as in the names Lai He, Lao She, and Liu E, sounds similar to the *u* in *bud. U,* as in the surnames Lu and Wu, is similar to the vowel sound in *shrew;* but written with an umlaut, as in *lü* (green), it sounds like the vowel in the French *une* or the *ü* in the German *lügen.* By convention the umlaut is not written when *u* follows *j, q, x,* or *y,* as in the surnames Xu and Yu; but in these cases the vowel sounds like that in *lü* and not like that in the surname Lu. The initial consonants *j, q, x, ch, sh, zh, c,* and *z* are especially puzzling to the uninitiated. *J,* as in Ba Jin's given name, sounds like the *j* in *jeep. Q,* as in the name of the Marxist theorist Qu Qiubai, sounds like the *ch* in *cheap. X,* as in the surnames of the writers Xiang Kairan, Xiao Hong, and Xu Dishan, sounds like the *sh* in *sheep. Ch,* as in the name Cheng Xiaoqing, is similar to the *ch* in *church. Zh,* as in the surnames Zhang and Zhao, sounds like the *j* in *Joe* and *joust. Sh,* as in the names Ling Shuhua, Mu Shiying, and Ye Shaojun, sounds like the *sh* in *shirt. C,* as in the names Shen Congwen and Jiang Guangci, is like the *ts* in *nuts* or *cheats. Z,* as in the name Zeng Pu, stands for a sound similar to the final sound in *adze* or *bids.* These rules are approximations only; they do not take pitch or tone into account and do not attempt to represent important features of Mandarin pronunciation—for example, *ch, sh,* and *zh* are retroflex sounds made with the tip of the tongue curled up and placed behind the alveolar ridge.

In the bibliographies that begin the entries in this volume, English courtesy translations are given for the titles of books for the convenience of researchers; the Chinese language has many homophones and near-homophones, and the pinyin romanization used in this volume deletes diacritics over vowels, which are required in proper pinyin and convey the "tone" or pitch contour of a word. Diacritics distinguish, for example, *mā* (mom) from *má* (hemp), *mǎ* (horse), and *mà* (to scold). Courtesy translations prevent confusion where the meaning of a title in pinyin is not immediately apparent; for example, without Chinese characters to refer to, one cannot tell if the title of Ai Wu's fifth book means "Night Scenes" or "Wild Scenery," because both Chinese words are romanized *Yejing.* Diacritic marks make it obvious that the title is *Yèjǐng* (Night Scenes), not *Yějǐng* (Wild Scenery); in this volume the distinction is accomplished with courtesy translations.

In the bibliographies of primary materials and in the entries, all Chinese personal names are given in the Chinese order of surname first, then given name; the same is true for the names of authors of Chinese-language reference works. With few exceptions, Chinese surnames are one syllable, and given names are one or two syllables. In both spoken and written Chinese, people are rarely if ever referred to by surname alone; when the surname is used, it is preceded by a familiar term of address such as *lao* (old) or *xiao* (young) or followed by the given name or a title, nickname, or other designation such as *shifu* (master). Most English-language writing about Chinese people observes this convention at least in part, favoring the use of the full name—surname and given name—on every mention; this practice avoids both the typographical inelegance of repeated mentions of a short surname such as Ai or Mu and the semantic confusion caused by the surname He. In the entries in this volume, surnames are used alone on the second and subsequent mentions of people who have two-syllable given names; for example, after the first mention, Qian Zhongshu is referred to as Qian. People whose given names are of one syllable, such as Ai Wu, however, are always referred to by the full name in this volume, which observes Chinese convention and respects the logic of names such as Ba Jin, Bing Xin, Lao She, and Mao Dun, which are pen names that cannot be shortened without a loss of meaning.

The typical Chinese writer in the first half of the twentieth century had a *yuanming* (original given name), a *zi* (style name), perhaps a *hao* (literary name), and several *biming* (pen names). The use of different names at different stages of life and the liberal use of literary sobriquets are conventions rooted in Chinese culture and history, but the term *biming* is apparently a late-nineteenth- or early-twentieth-century coinage. In the modern period pen names were useful to writers who wanted to avoid political persecution and to editors who wanted to publish more than one work by an author in a single issue of a journal. Pen names, like traditional alternative names, can be meaningful; for example, Yang Kui, who wrote in the language of the Japanese colonial occupiers of Taiwan, changed his given name from Gui to Kui after Li Kui, a character from a traditional Chinese novel who is an "impetuous daredevil," as Angelina Yee puts it in her essay on Yang Kui in this volume; Shen Yanbing's pen name, Mao Dun, is a play on the word *maodun* (contradiction), perhaps in reference to Marxism, perhaps in reference to personal, political, and philosophical tensions in general, perhaps both; and Xu Dishan used Huashang (peanuts) in his pen name to allude to the importance of hard work and humility. Only a few of the authors included in this book published fiction under their original names, a practice that did not become prevalent until the 1980s. Ye Shaojun did so, but he is just as well known by his style name, Shengtao, and he used at least seventeen pen names in his career. Authors tended to use only one or two pen names for books, but it was not uncommon for a modern Chinese fiction writer to publish in journals under many pen names. Ding Ling used a dozen; Shen Congwen used forty. Modern China's most famous writer, Lu Xun, had four style names and seven literary names and used 141 pen names. The name given to him at birth, Zhou Zhangshou, is probably unfamiliar to even well-read Chinese.

–Thomas Moran

Acknowledgments

This book was produced by Bruccoli Clark Layman, Inc. Philip B. Dematteis was the in-house editor.

Production manager is Philip B. Dematteis.

Administrative support was provided by Carol A. Cheschi.

Accountant is Ann-Marie Holland.

Copyediting supervisor is Sally R. Evans. The copyediting staff includes Phyllis A. Avant, Caryl Brown, Melissa D. Hinton, and Rebecca Mayo. Freelance copyeditors are Brenda Cabra, Jennifer Cooper, and Dave King.

Pipeline manager is James F. Tidd Jr.

Editorial associates are Elizabeth Leverton, Dickson Monk, and Timothy C. Simmons.

In-house vetter is Catherine M. Polit.

Permissions editor is Amber L. Coker.

Layout and graphics supervisor is Janet E. Hill. The graphics staff includes Zoe R. Cook.

Office manager is Kathy Lawler Merlette.

Photography editor is Crystal A. Leidy.

Digital photographic copy work was performed by Zoe R. Cook.

Systems managers are James Sellers and Donald Kevin Starling.

Typesetting supervisor is Kathleen M. Flanagan. The typesetting staff includes Patricia M. Flanagan.

Library research was facilitated by the following librarians at the Thomas Cooper Library of the University of South Carolina: Elizabeth Suddeth and the rare-book department; Jo Cottingham, interlibrary loan department; circulation department head Tucker Taylor; reference department head Virginia W. Weathers; reference department staff Laurel Baker, Marilee Birchfield, Kate Boyd, Paul Cammarata, Joshua Garris, Gary Geer, Tom Marcil, Rose Marshall, and Sharon Verba; interlibrary loan department head Marna Hostetler; and interlibrary loan staff Bill Fetty and Nelson Rivera.

The volume editor was assisted by Middlebury College librarians in the interlibrary loan, acquisitions, and circulation departments, including Rachael Manning, Joy Pile, and Elin Waagen; by Cornell University librarians Thomas Hahn, Curator of the Wason Collection on East Asia-China in the Kroch Asia Library, and David Louis Jones, digitization specialist; and by Middlebury College students James Meader '02, Olatokunbo "Tixo" Augustus '06, and Anastasia Aurol '07, who did research and copyediting and were supported by the Middlebury College Collaborative Research Fund.

Dictionary of Literary Biography® • Volume Three Hundred Twenty-Eight

Chinese Fiction Writers, 1900–1949

Dictionary of Literary Biography

Ai Wu

(2 June 1904 – 5 December 1992)

Alexandra R. Wagner

BOOKS: *Shanzhong muge* [Shepherd's Mountain Song] (Shanghai: Tianma shudian, 1934);

Piaobo zaji [Random Notes from a Wandering Life] (Shanghai: Shenghuo shudian, 1935);

Nanguo zhi ye [Nights in the South] (Shanghai: Liangyou tushu gongsi, 1935)—includes "Paoxiao de xujia tun," translated by Wendy Locks as "Rumbling in Xu Family Village," in *Furrows, Peasants, Intellectuals, and the State: Stories and Histories from Modern China,* edited by Helen F. Siu (Stanford, Cal.: Stanford University Press, 1990), pp. 75–94;

Nanxing ji [Notes from Travels South] (Shanghai: Wenhua shenghuo chubanshe, 1935; revised edition, Beijing: Zuojia chubanshe, 1963; revised again, Beijing: Renmin wenxue chubanshe, 1980)—includes "Shanxia zhong," translated by Chen Haiyan as "In the Gorge," *Chinese Literature,* 2 (Summer 1992): 26–39;

Yejing [Night Scenes] (Shanghai: Wenhua shenghuo chubanshe, 1936);

Haidao shang [On an Island] (Shanghai: Wenhua shenghuo chubanshe, 1936)—includes title story, translated by W. J. F. Jenner as "On the Island," in *Modern Chinese Stories,* translated by Jenner and Gladys Yang, edited by Jenner (London & New York: Oxford University Press, 1970), pp. 107–119;

Chuntian [Spring] (Shanghai: Liangyou tushu gongsi, 1937);

Bajiao gu [Banana Vale] (Shanghai: Shangwu yinshuguan, 1937)—title story translated by Shi Junbao as "Banana Vale," *Chinese Literature,* 2 (Summer 1992): 3–25;

Taohuang [Flight from Famine] (Shanghai: Wenhua shenghuo chubanshe, 1939);

Ai Wu (from Hu Depei, ed., Ai Wu, *1984; Collection of Thomas Moran)*

Mengya [Sprouts] (Chongqing: Fenghuoshe, 1939);

Yaoyuan de houfang [The Distant Rear] (Guilin: Dashidai chubanshe, 1939);

Zacao ji [Weeds] (Yong'an: Gaijin chubanshe, 1940);

Wenxue shouce [Handbook of Literature] (Guilin: Wenhua gongyingshe, 1941; revised and enlarged, 1942; revised edition, Shanghai: Wenhua gongyingshe, 1949);

Huangdi [Wasteland] (Guilin: Wenhua gongyingshe, 1942);

Huanghun [Twilight] (Guilin: Wenxian chubanshe, 1942);

Qiushou [Autumn Harvest] (Chongqing: Dushu chubanshe, 1942);

Women de laba [Sound Our Horns] (Chongqing: Fenghuoshe, 1942);

Ai [Love] (Guilin: Dadi tushu gongsi, 1943);

Dongye [Winter Night] (Guilin: Sanhu tushushe, 1943); republished as *Ai Wu chuangzuo ji* [A Collection of Ai Wu's Works] (Shanghai: Xin xin chubanshe, 1947);

Miandian xiaojing [Burmese Vignettes] (Guilin: Wenxue shudian, 1943);

Jiangshang xing [On the River] (Chongqing: Xinqun chubanshe, 1945);

Tongnian de gushi [Childhood Stories] (Chongqing: Jianguo shudian, 1945);

Duanlian [Tempering] (Chongqing: Huamei shuwu, 1945);

Fengrao de yuanye [Fertile Plains] (Chongqing: Ziqiang chubanshe, 1946);

Wo de lüban [My Traveling Companion] (Shanghai: Huaxia shudian, 1946);

Xiangchou [Homesickness] (Shanghai: Wenhua gongzuoshe, 1946);

Guxiang [Hometown], 2 volumes (N.p.: Dushu chubanshe, 1946);

Wo de qingnian shidai [My Youth] (Shanghai: Kaiming shudian, 1948);

Shanye [Mountain Wilderness] (Shanghai: Wenhua shenghuo chubanshe, 1948; revised edition, Beijing: Zuojia chubanshe, 1954);

Yanwu [Smoke and Mist] (Shanghai: Zhongyuan chubanshe, 1948)—includes "Shiqing saozi," translated by Wen Xue as "Mrs. Shih Ching," *Chinese Literature*, 3 (1954): 84–97; translation republished as "Mrs. Shi Qing," in *Stories from the Thirties*, volume 2 (Beijing: Chinese Literature, 1982), pp. 209–231;

Yige nüren de beiju [A Woman's Tragedy] (Hong Kong: Xin zhongguo shuju, 1949);

Xin de jia [A New Home] (Beijing: Renmin wenxue chubanshe, 1955)— title story translated by Yeh Yung as "A New Home," *People's China*, 2 (1954): 31–37; also includes "Yu," translated by Vivian Ling Hsu and Katherine Holmquist as "Rain," in *Born of the Same Roots: Stories of Modern Chinese Women*, edited by Hsu (Bloomington: Indiana University Press, 1981), pp. 140–146; and "Yegui," translated by Yuan Ko-chia as "Homeward Journey," in *Homeward Journey and Other Stories by Contemporary Chinese Writers* (Beijing: Foreign Languages Press, 1957), pp. 53–64;

Xingfu de kuanggongmen [The Happy Miners] (Shenyang: Liaoning renmin chubanshe, 1955);

Bai lian cheng gang (Beijing: Zuojia chubanshe, 1958); translated as *Steeled and Tempered* (Beijing: Foreign Languages Press, 1961);

Yegui [Homeward Journey] (Beijing: Zuojia chubanshe, 1958; Washington, D.C.: Center for Chinese Research Materials, Association of Research Libraries, 1973; revised edition, Chengdu: Sichuan renmin chubanshe, 1978);

Chuchun shijie [In Early Spring] (Tianjin: Baihua wenyi chubanshe, 1958);

Ouxing ji [Notes from Travels in Europe] (Tianjin: Baihua wenyi chubanshe, 1959);

Wenxue rumen [An Introduction to Literature] (Hong Kong: Zhongliu chubanshe, 1959);

Langhua ji [Surf] (Beijing: Beijing chubanshe, 1959);

Nanxing ji xu pian [Notes from Travels South: A Sequel] (Beijing: Zuojia chubanshe, 1964)–includes "Yeniu zhai," translated by Su Chin as "Wild Bull Village," *Chinese Literature*, 9 (1962); and "Jieha zhai," translated as "Under the Bo Tree," *China Reconstructs*, 12 (June 1963): 32–35;

Wo de younian shidai [My Childhood] (Tianjin: Xinlei chubanshe, 1981);

Nanxing ji xin pian [Notes from Travels South: A New Sequel] (Kunming: Yunnan renmin chubanshe, 1983);

Tan xiaoshuo chuangzuo [On Writing Fiction] (Changsha: Hunan renmin chubanshe, 1984);

Chuntian de wu [Spring Mist] (Beijing: Renmin wenxue chubanshe, 1985);

Fengbo [Wave] (Shanghai: Shanghai wenyi chubanshe, 1987).

Editions and Collections: *Guxiang* [Hometown], 2 volumes (Shanghai: Ziqiang chubanshe, 1947);

Ai Wu duanpian xiaoshuo ji [Short Stories by Ai Wu] (Beijing: Renmin wenxue chubanshe, 1953);

Ai Wu xuanji [Selected Works by Ai Wu] (Hong Kong: Wenxue chubanshe, 1957);

Ai Wu zhongpian xiaoshuo ji [Novellas by Ai Wu] (Tianjin: Tianjin renmin chubanshe, 1958);

Dushi de youyu [City Melancholy] (Hong Kong: Xinyue chubanshe, 1959);

Ai Wu xuanji [Selected Works by Ai Wu] (Beijing: Renmin wenxue chubanshe, 1959);

Ai Wu xiaoshuo xuan [Selected Fiction by Ai Wu] (Changsha: Hunan renmin chubanshe, 1981);

Ai Wu jin zuo [Recent Works by Ai Wu] (Chengdu: Sichuan renmin chubanshe, 1981);

Ai Wu wenji [Ai Wu's Works], 10 volumes (Chengdu: Sichuan renmin chubanshe/Sichuan wenyi chubanshe, 1981–1989);

Ai Wu ertong wenxue zuopin xuan [A Selection of Children's Literature by Ai Wu], edited by Tang Jixiang and Wang Sha (Chengdu: Sichuan shaonian ertong chubanshe, 1983);

Ai Wu, edited by Hu Depei (Hong Kong: Sanlian shudian xianggang fendian / Beijing: Renmin wenxue chubanshe, 1984);

Bingzhong suixiang lu [Thoughts in Illness] (Shanghai: Shanghai shudian, 1996);

Ai Wu, edited by Tang Wenyi (Beijing: Huaxia chubanshe, 1997);

Wangshi suixiang [Thoughts on the Past], edited by Tang Wenyi and Liu Ping (Chengdu: Sichuan renmin chubanshe, 2000).

Editions in English: "A New Home" ("Xin de jia"), translated by Yeh Yung, in *A New Home and Other Stories by Contemporary Chinese Writers* (Beijing: Foreign Languages Press, 1955), pp. 85–102;

"Wild Bull Village" ("Yeniu zhai"), translated by Su Chin, in *Wild Bull Village: Chinese Short Stories* (Beijing: Foreign Languages Press, 1965), pp. 1–22;

"Return by Night," translated by Raymond Hsu, *Renditions,* no. 7 (1977): 39–44;

"One Night in Hong Kong" ("Xianggang zhi yiye"), translated by Zhiyu Zhu, *Renditions,* nos. 29–30 (Spring–Fall 1988): 59–62,

Banana Vale (Beijing: Chinese Literature Press, 1993)—comprises "Banana Vale" ("Bajiaogu"), translated by Shi Junbao; "Going Home" ("Hui jia"), translated by Wang Chiying; "In the Gorge" ("Shanxia zhong"), translated by Chen Haiyan; "Seeing off Guests in the Mountains," translated by Chen; "Song of the Crows," translated by William Bishop; "Mrs. Shi Qing" ("Shiqing saozi"), translated by Wen Xue; and "The Night Xujia Village Roared" ("Paoxiao de xujia tun"), translated by Jeff Book.

OTHER: "The Freedom of the Writer," *China Reconstructs,* nos. 8–10 (October 1959): 58–60;

"One Night in Hong Kong" ("Xianggang zhi yiye"), in *Hong Kong: Somewhere between Heaven and Earth. An Anthology,* edited by Barbara-Sue White (Hong Kong & New York: Oxford University Press, 1996), pp. 189–192.

With short stories, novellas, essays, and several full-length novels filling the ten volumes of his collected works (1981–1989), Ai Wu was one of China's most prolific modern writers. His career has earned him a place among the major literary figures of Republican China, as well as among those of the People's Republic of China. The title of his autobiographical essay "Moshuiping gua zai jingzi shang xiezuo de" (Writing with the Ink Bottle around My Neck) first published in July 1934 in *Wo yu wenxue,* a special issue commemorating the first anniversary of the journal *Wenxue* (Literature), suggests that travel drove and distinguishes much of Ai Wu's life and work; it indicates his readiness to write despite being frequently on the move and provides a clue both to his personality and to the productivity that characterized his career.

Ai Wu is best known for the travel writings and short stories he published in the 1930s and 1940s. The travel writings describe his journey as an itinerant worker through southern China and Burma (today Myanmar) between 1925 and 1931 and provide insights into the little-known lives and customs of minority groups in the region. Many of the protagonists in Ai Wu's short stories are poor villagers and peasants who suffer from an oppressive social order and an unjust political system; others are bandits, thieves, and petty criminals. Lyrical descriptions of natural beauty contrast with and heighten the harsh lives of the protagonists. Some of his early stories, however, include Gothic elements, portraying nature as hostile in order to strengthen their eerie atmosphere. Critics typically categorize Ai Wu as a leftist author whose most significant works are written in a critical-realist mode and portray the suffering of common people and the poor during the Sino-Japanese War of 1937 to 1945 and the Chinese civil war of 1945 to 1949. Ai Wu is, however, devoted above all to uncovering his characters' humanity in all of its facets.

Ai Wu was born Tang Daogeng on 2 June 1904 into a literate but poor family in Sichuan's Xinfan district. His father, Tang Kunyong, was a village elementary-school teacher. Tang Daogeng had four younger brothers and a younger sister. In 1925 he ended his formal education at Chengdu First Normal School to embark on a journey through southern China. Inspired by the innovative publications that had sprung up in the wake of the May Fourth movement, which had begun in 1919, he wanted to learn through personal experience. He also wanted to escape an impending marriage that his parents had arranged for him in 1917. His travels took him through Sichuan and Yunnan and, in 1927, into Burma. He supported himself with menial work, including odd jobs for the Kunming Red Cross, sweeping horse manure for a Burmese innkeeper and teaching the innkeeper's children, and proofreading for a Burmese daily newspaper. In 1927 a fellow Sichuan native who was studying Sanskrit and Buddhism in Rangoon provided the destitute and ailing Tang with room and board

Cover for Ai Wu's novella Jiangshang xing *(1945, On the River),*
about the Yangtze River journey of four students
fleeing the Japanese occupation of Shanghai
(Cornell University Library)

and encouraged him to publish his short stories and essays in the supplement to the Overseas Chinese newspaper *Yangguan ribao* (Rangoon Daily); he began to use the pseudonym Ai Wu at this time.

Except for a short trip to Singapore in 1930, Ai Wu remained in Burma until he was expelled by the British colonial government in early 1931 for supporting the peasant rebellion and the Communist movement. In "Xianggang zhi yiye" (translated as "One Night in Hong Kong," 1988), first published in June 1931 in *Dushu yuekan* (Reading Monthly), he gives an account of the night he spent in a Hong Kong prison during his extradition back to China; he sarcastically describes the inhumane conditions and appalling treatment of the prisoners and vents his contempt for the British oppression of the Chinese people in the colony. "Wo de airen" (1933, My Lover), describes a female fellow inmate in the Rangoon prison where Ai Wu and two of his friends were awaiting their extradition trial. Many of Ai Wu's first-person narratives, including "Wo de airen," reveal a subtle distance between the narrator and the other characters; in some of the stories this distance manifests itself as suspicion, annoyance, or mistrust. The stories suggest, however, that these sentiments result from the narrator's incomplete understanding of the circumstances the other characters are facing.

After Ai Wu returned to China, he decided to become a professional writer and moved in with his friend Sha Ting, another aspiring writer, in Shanghai. They wrote to the eminent author Lu Xun, asking for instruction in the proper material for fiction writing. Lu Xun replied with encouragement and with advice not only on material but also on the proper position for the writer to take toward his or her subject.

In 1932 Ai Wu joined the Zhongguo zuoyi zuojia lianmeng (Chinese League of Left-Wing Writers). His article "Sanshi niandai de yifu jianying: Wo canjia zuolian qianqian houhou de qingxing" (1979, A Sketch of the Thirties: The Story of My Membership in the League) describes his economic hardships and the problems an unknown writer faced in the Shanghai publishing market. The article also furnishes insight into the frustrations of league members who were assigned to transform illiterate workers into "Wenyi tongxunyuan" (literature and arts correspondents).

In 1932 Ai Wu's autobiographical short story "Rensheng zhexue de yike" (A Lesson in Life's Philosophy) was published in the League journal *Wenxue yuekan* (Literature Monthly) and earned him his first recognition by left-leaning writers and critics. Reaching Kunming on his journey south, the narrator is hungry and out of money; although he is willing to try his hand at virtually any occupation, getting a job is much harder than he anticipated. "Rensheng zhexue de yike" is written in a humorous tone that highlights the narrator's indefatigable spirit in the face of adversity. The story also reflects his growing sympathy for the poor, whose lot he is beginning to understand because of his own hardships.

In March 1933 Ai Wu was arrested by the Nationalist government and imprisoned for six months; Lu Xun was among those who provided financial help to obtain his release. In 1933 more of Ai Wu's short stories were published in literary journals and received acclaim in leftist circles. In "Paoxiao de xujia tun" (translated as "Rumbling in Xu Family Village," 1990), collected in his *Nanguo zhi ye* (1935, Nights in the South), villagers take spontaneous action against their oppressors, furiously killing all the Japanese soldiers stationed in their community. The story derives its forcefulness from a swiftly developing plot composed of brief scenes and written in concise language. Ai Wu demonstrates his ability to capture a situation and its full range of ramifications by combining simple images:

> Half a dozen Japanese soldiers . . . came to a halt at the entrance to a small alley. They peered down the narrow passage, looked at each other and laughed, then sauntered down the alley.
>
> A pink shirt, white blouse, and a pair of blue striped trousers hung out to dry, swaying slightly in the cool spring breeze. Against the old grey wall of the alley grew a peach tree, its bright pink blossoms smiling to anyone who visited this dusty, narrow lane. . . .
>
> Soldiers, who just the night before had talked about the blossoms of their homeland, were now intoxicated in the spring of another country.
>
> As they walked towards a house, they spotted ahead of them a girl of sixteen or so who, with a distraught look on her face, was darting around like a cornered mouse as she frantically pulled the few garments off the line. The soldiers stopped and stared at the girl for a moment, and laughed lustily (translation by Jeff Book).

On 2 August 1934 Ai Wu married Wang Leijia. They had two sons and three daughters.

Between 1935 and 1940 various Shanghai publishing houses brought out collections of Ai Wu's short stories that had originally appeared in literary journals. "Paoxiao de Xujiatun" was included in his first collection, *Nanguo zhi ye*. His second collection, *Nanxing ji* (Notes from Travels South), was published that same year. Besides "Rensheng zhexue de yike" and other stories about life in Yunnan and Burma, *Nanxing ji* includes "Shanxia zhong" (1934; translated as "In the Gorge," 1992), perhaps Ai Wu's best-known and most often republished short story. Traveling through the mountainous south, the narrator temporarily joins up with a band of outlaws. One of them is a young man who was badly beaten after a botched theft attempt; with his severe injuries he has become a liability to his comrades. The group spends the night in a deserted temple. During the night the other bandits throw the injured man from a bridge outside the temple into the roaring river below. Unbeknownst to them, the narrator witnesses the gruesome act from a distance. The next morning, he and the outlaws go their separate ways. The scene in the desolate temple before the murder and the dramatic backdrop of the river gorge where the killing takes place give the story a haunting beauty, despite its gloomy plot. As in many of Ai Wu's works, the narrator here is ultimately sympathetic to the criminals: living under an unjust social system, morality is a privilege they cannot afford.

Piaobo zaji (1935, Random Notes from a Wandering Life) consists of forty-one succinctly written essays chronicling Ai Wu's experiences on his journey to the south. Some of them are quite similar to his first-person fictional narratives in form and content.

"Bajiao gu" (translated as "Banana Vale," 1992), the well-known title story of Ai Wu's 1937 collection, is representative of many of his third-person narratives of the period. At an inn along a trade route through a forested region of Yunnan near the Burmese border the capable and courageous innkeeper, aided by her young son, fatally beats and stabs her fourth husband to keep him from raping her daughter. The murder is discovered by Burmese and British authorities patrolling the area, and the woman will probably receive the death penalty for her deed. Her fate exemplifies the cruel situation of women in a male-dominated society. Later stories such as "Shiqing saozi" (1948, Mrs. Shi Qing; translated as "Mrs. Shih Ching," 1954), collected in *Yanwu* (1948, Smoke and Mist) and "Yige nüren de beiju" (1949, A Woman's Tragedy) also focus on women. While "Yige nüren de beiju" ends with the protagonist jumping off a cliff with her children, "Shiqing saozi" concludes with the desperate heroine determined to survive.

Ai Wu's first novella, *Chuntian* (1937, Spring), about the struggle of a group of peasants against a corrupt landlord in a Sichuan village, was the first part of a planned four-part novel. In October 1937 Ai Wu and his family fled Shanghai after the Japanese occupation of the city. In early 1939 they settled in Guilin. Ai Wu's short-story collections *Taohuang* (Flight from Famine) and *Mengya* (Sprouts) were published that year. Ai Wu was active in various political groups and committees in Guilin; in October 1939, for example, he was one of the organizers of the Guilin branch of the Zhonghua quanguo wenyijie kangdi xiehui (All-China Association of Literary Resistance), of which he was elected managing director. In 1940 he published the collection *Zacao ji* (Weeds), comprising thirty-three essays written since his departure from Shanghai. He devoted some of his time to the instruction of young writers, an effort that resulted in the publication of his *Wenxue shouce* (1941, Handbook of Literature).

In 1944 the approach of the Japanese army forced Ai Wu and his family to relocate to Chongqing, the Chinese wartime capital. There Ai Wu helped to establish political-literary organizations such as the Chongqing branch of the All-China Association of Literary Resistance and became editor of the branch publication *Banyue wenyi* (Literature and Arts Semimonthly).

Ai Wu's novella *Jiangshang xing* (1945, On the River) recounts the Yangtze River journey of four students trying to reach home after fleeing the Japanese occupation of Shanghai as each tries to determine his role and identity in a time of war. *Jiangshang xing* demonstrates Ai Wu's inclination to explore complex human factors rather than make political statements. One of the

Cover for Ai Wu's novel Bai lian cheng gang *(1958; translated as* Steeled and Tempered, *1961), which correlates the love of two factory workers for each other with their devotion to building their country (Collection of John Berninghausen)*

students, for example, comments that not all Japanese soldiers are equally bad and reminds his friends that some secretly distributed antiwar leaflets. He also denounces revenge as a feudal and unjust notion.

In 1946 Ai Wu published *Fengrao de yuanye* (Fertile Plains), which comprises *Chuntian* and "Luohua de shijie" (Season of Falling Flowers), the second part of his planned tetralogy. That same year he published the collection *Wo de lüban* (My Traveling Companion). It includes the story "Hui jia" (translated as "Going Home," 1993), which depicts the inner conflicts of a man who is trying to decide whether to send his wife away after she becomes pregnant by another man. As the tale progresses, the husband's sympathy for his wife, who in reality was raped by a fellow villager, increases. Ultimately, however, he yields to social pressure to drive her out of the village, dashing the reader's hope that he will defy the cruel customs of the community.

Ai Wu had worked on the long novel *Guxiang* (Hometown) from 1941 to 1945, but the chaos of war prevented it from being published in book form until 1946. It is an ambitious work that paints on a broad canvas the complex social, political, and economic conditions in the remote countryside during the Sino-Japanese War. By contrast, *Shanye* (1948, Mountain Wilderness), the other novel Ai Wu wrote during the 1940s, portrays the confrontation of a group of villagers with the Japanese advancing on their area. The much more compressed time frame in which the plot unfolds makes *Shanye* a tighter, more dynamic, and, therefore, ultimately more successful literary endeavor than *Guxiang*.

Ai Wu also completed two memoirs. *Wo de younian shidai* (My Childhood), serialized in 1948 but not published in book form until 1981, and *Wo de qingnian shidai* (1948, My Youth) provide a detailed account of his life up to 1927. Both are marked by candid and unaffected language.

Ai Wu assumed leading positions in various political and government organizations that structured literary life after the establishment of the People's Republic of China in 1949; for example, he was made vice chairman of the Sichuan branch of the Zhongguo zuojia xiehui (Chinese Writers' Association). In his official functions or as a member of government-sponsored groups he continued his travels across China, visiting steel mills and oil fields in the north to learn about the lives of workers under the Communist regime. His first short story about industrial workers, "Xin de jia" (1953; translated as "A New Home," 1954), was followed in 1954 by the well-received "Yegui" (translated as "Homeward Journey," 1957), about the late-night trip home of a young man and woman who live in the countryside and work in a village. Both aspire to become productive contributors to the building of a new country, and their commitment and enthusiasm are revealed as they talk about their hopes and plans during their journey. Their budding friendship and suggested romantic feelings for each other become a metaphor for their love of their country.

In 1954 Ai Wu made an extended tour of Eastern European countries and the Soviet Union as a delegate to the first National People's Congress. Those travels are documented in his essay collection *Ouxing ji* (1959, Notes from Travels in Europe).

Ai Wu's best-known novel, *Bai lian cheng gang* (1958; translated as *Steeled and Tempered*, 1961), correlates the characters' romantic love with their devotion to building the country. Three factory workers are in a competition to produce high-quality steel in record time; one of the workers, the capable and heroic young Qin Degui, is in love with Sun Yufen, a girl who works in a nearby electrical plant. The novel has all the ingredients of a suspenseful story: budding love, heroism, intrigue, jealousy, and crisis. In addition, by paralleling the workers' competition and the love story, Ai Wu skillfully "romanticizes" the work at the steel furnace. He creates convincing personalities and psychologies for the main characters, who are players in an intricate and engaging plot. Ai Wu's in-depth knowledge of the machinery, production procedures, and administrative system of a steel factory add to the appeal and realism of the work. Finally, rather than portraying an idealized harmonious relationship between the factory management and the Communist Party, the novel presents a convincing picture of the conflicting interests of these two forces. *Bai lian cheng gang* has been acclaimed as one of the best Chinese industrial novels.

After an official journey to the south in 1961–1962, Ai Wu wrote *Nanxing ji xu pian* (1964, Notes from Travels South: A Sequel). Like the original *Nanxing ji*, it offers tragic stories set in the old society; it also includes tales that portray life in small borderland villages after the foundation of the People's Republic.

While Ai Wu's most creative period came between 1935 and 1949, he continued writing until he was forced to stop during the Cultural Revolution of 1966 to 1976; he was imprisoned from 1968 to 1972. He was, however, luckier than many of his peers: he emerged fairly unscathed from that period and soon resumed his place in the literary establishment. He began writing fiction and articles again in 1977 but increasingly focused on editing and revising his collected works. In 1980 he visited Japan with a Chinese writers' delegation, and in 1981 he led a similar delegation to North Korea. In 1983 he published *Nanxing ji xin pian* (Notes from Travels South: A New Sequel), based on a journey to southern China in 1981; the stories in the collection present an idyllic picture of life in the area after 1949. The novels *Chuntian de wu* (1985, Spring Mist), about the "Siqing yundong" (Four Clean-ups Movement) in the countryside during the mid 1960s, and *Fengbo* (1987, Wave), about the "Chuguo re" (Going-Abroad Craze) in the 1980s, were the last major works he wrote before his death on 5 December 1992.

Ai Wu's fiction displays a wide variety of styles, forms, and tones. Compared to his third-person narratives, his semi-autobiographical first-person tales are more intimate, reflective, and often humorous. On the other hand, stories such as "Ye yingtao" (1963, Wild Cherries) and "Qunshan zhong" (1964, In the Mountains), both of which are collected in *Nanxing ji xu pian*, although loosely embedded in a first-person narrative, are essentially told as legends or folktales. His longer stories, novellas, and novels make ample use of dialogue. Ai Wu's fiction is distinctive for presenting in unaffected yet poignant language a nuanced picture of human virtues, flaws, and motivations. Spanning an extremely eventful and volatile period, his work bears literary testimony to the Chinese twentieth century.

Bibliography:
"Ai Wu de chuangzuo ji pingjia ziliao mulu suoyin," in *Ai Wu zhuan ji,* edited by the Sichuan University Chinese Department (Chengdu: Gai xi, 1979), pp. 295–355.

Biographies:
Sichuan University Chinese Department, ed., *Ai Wu zhuan ji* (Chengdu: Gai xi, 1979);

Lian Zhengxiang, *Ai Wu zhuan: Liulang wen hao* (Taiyuan: Beiyue wenyi chubanshe, 1992);

Ge Mai, "A Profile of Ai Wu," translated by Lei Ming, *Chinese Literature,* no. 2 (Summer 1992): 40–43.

References:
Feng Yongqi, ed., *Nanxing dage–Ai Wu yu Yunnan* (Kunming Shi: Yunnan jiaoyu, 2001);

Mao Wen and Huang Liru, eds., *Ai Wu yanjiu zhuanji* (Chengdu: Sichuan wenyi chubanshe, 1986);

Nanxing ji: Cong xiaoshuo dao pingmu (Beijing: Zhongguo dianying chubanshe, 1994);

Shi Chuan, *Sha Ting Ai Wu zuopin xinshang* (Nanning: Guangxi jiaoyu chubanshe, 1994);

Tan Xingguo, *Ai Wu de shengping he chuangzuo* (Chongqing: Chongqing chubanshe, 1985);

Tan, *Ai Wu ping zhuan* (Chongqing: Chongqing chubanshe, 1995);

Wang Xiaoming, *Sha Ting Ai Wu de xiaoshuo shijie* (Shanghai: Shanghai wenyi chubanshe, 1987);

Zhang Xiaomin, *Ai Wu ping zhuan* (Chengdu: Xinan caijing daxue chubanshe, 1988);

Zhang, *Ai Wu zhuan: Liulang wen hao zhi mi* (Chengdu: Sichuan minzu chubanshe, 1997);

Zuojia chubanshe Editorial Department, ed., *"Bailian chenggang" pingjie* (Beijing: Zuojia chubanshe, 1958).

Papers:
In 2005 Ai Wu's son Tang Jixiang donated his father's manuscripts, letters, diaries, photographs, and book collection, as well as the furniture and utensils from Ai Wu's study, to the Zhongguo xiandai wenxue guan (Museum of Modern Chinese Literature) in Beijing.

Ba Jin

(25 November 1904 – 17 October 2005)

Nicholas A. Kaldis
Binghamton University

BOOKS: *Miewang* [Destruction] (Shanghai: Kaiming shudian chubanshe, 1929);

Fuchou [Revenge] (Shanghai: Xin Zhongguo shuju, 1931);

Siqu de taiyang [The Dead Sun] (Shanghai: Kaiming shudian chubanshe, 1931);

Wu [Fog] (Shanghai: Xin Zhongguo shuju, 1931);

Hai di meng [Dream on the Sea] (Shanghai: Xin Zhongguo shuju, 1932);

Chuntian li de qiutian (Autumn in Spring] (Shanghai: Kaiming shudian chubanshe, 1932);

Guangming [Light] (Shanghai: Xin Zhongguo shuju, 1932)–includes "Gou," translated as "Dog," in *Living China: Modern Chinese Short Stories,* edited by Edgar Snow (London: Harrap, 1936; New York: Reynal & Hitchcock, 1936), pp. 174–180; Chinese version republished as *Ai de shizijia* [The Crucifixion of Love] (Shanghai: Wenhua shenghuo chubanshe, 1941);

Haixing [Sea Voyage] (Shanghai: Xin Zhongguo shuju, 1932); republished as *Haixing zaji* [Sea Voyage Notebook] (Shanghai: Kaiming shudian chubanshe, 1935);

Yu [Rain] (Shanghai: Liangyou tushu yinshua gongsi, 1932);

Shading [The Antimony Miners] (Shanghai: Kaiming shudian chubanshe, 1933);

Xinsheng [New Life] (Shanghai: Kaiming shudian chubanshe, 1933);

Dianyi [Electric Chair] (Shanghai: Xin Zhongguo shuju, 1933);

Jia (Shanghai: Kaiming shudian chubanshe, 1933); chapter 34 translated by Wang Chi-chen as "The Puppet Dead," in *Contemporary Chinese Stories,* edited by Wang (New York: Columbia University Press, 1944), pp. 80–94; complete novel translated by Sidney Shapiro as *The Family* (Beijing: Foreign Languages Press, 1958; San Francisco: China Books and Periodicals, 1969);

Ba Jin (from Zhongguo dabaike quanshu zongbianji weiyuanhui, ed., Zhongguo dabaike quanshu: Zhongguo wenxue, volume 2, 1986; Collection of Thomas Moran)

Lei (Shanghai: Liangyou gongsi, 1933); edited and translated by Larry Kent Browning as "Thunder," M.A. thesis, Stanford University, 1961;

Mengya [Sprouts] (Shanghai: Xiandai shuju, 1933); republished as *Xue* [Snow] (San Francisco: Pingshe, 1935; Shanghai: Wenhua shenghuo chubanshe, 1936); republished as *Zhaoyang* [Morning Sun] (Shanghai: Xin shenghuo chubanshe, 1939);

Mobu [Dustcloth] (Beiping: Beiping xingyuntang shudian, 1933);

Ba Jin zizhuan [Ba Jin's Autobiography] (Shanghai: Diyi chubanshe, 1934);

Jiangjun [The General], as Yu Yi (Shanghai: Shenghuo shudian, 1934); as Ba Jin (Shanghai: Shenghuo shudian, 1937)–includes "Yijian xiaoshi," translated by Stanley R. Munro as "A Tiny Incident," in *Genesis of a Revolution: An Anthology of Modern Chinese Short Stories,* edited and translated by Munro (Singapore: Heinemann Educational [Asia], 1979), pp. 5–12; and "Yueye," translated by Shapiro as "A Moonlit Night," in *Masterpieces of Modern Chinese Fiction 1919–1949* (Beijing: Foreign Language Press, 1983), pp. 354–363;

Chenmo [Deep Silence], 2 volumes (Shanghai: Shenghuo shudian, 1934);

Lütu suibi [Random Notes of a Voyage] (Shanghai: Shenghuo shudian, 1934);

Dian [Lightning] (Shanghai: Liangyou tushu yinshua gongsi, 1935);

Diandi [Drops] (Shanghai: Kaiming shudian chubanshe, 1935);

Shen gui ren [God, Ghost, Man] (Shanghai: Wenhua Shenghuo chubanshe, 1935);

Chenluo [Sinking Low] (Shanghai: Shangwu yinshuguan, 1936)–includes "Huaxue de rizi," translated by Tang Sheng (Dang Sheng) as "When the Snow Melted," *Modern Chinese Literature,* 5 (1962): 50–63;

Fa de gushi [The Story of Hair] (Shanghai: Wenhua shenghuo chubanshe, 1936);

Sheng zhi chanhui [Confessions of a Life] (Shanghai: Shangwu yinshuguan, 1936);

Yi [Memoirs] (Shanghai: Wenhua shenghuo chubanshe, 1936);

Changsheng ta [Pagoda of Long Life] (Shanghai: Wenhua Shenghuo chubanshe, 1937);

Duanjian [Short Notes] (Shanghai: Liangyou tushu yinshua gongsi, 1937);

Kongsu [I Accuse] (Shanghai: Fenghuo she, 1937);

Chun [Spring] (Shanghai: Kaiming shudian chubanshe, 1938);

Meng yu zui [Dream and Drunkenness] (Shanghai: Kaiming shudian chubanshe, 1938);

Ganxiang [Impressions] (Chongqing: Fenghuo chubanshe, 1939);

Heitu [Black Earth] (Shanghai: Wenhua shenghuo chubanshe, 1939);

Lütu tongxun [Letters from the Road] (Shanghai: Wenhua shenghuo chubanshe, 1939);

Huo: Di yi bu [Fire: Part One] (Chongqing: Kaiming shudian chubanshe, 1940);

Li'na [Leena] (Shanghai: Wenhua Shenghuo chubanshe, 1940);

Qiu [Autumn] (Shanghai: Kaiming shudian chubanshe, 1940);

Wuti [Untitled] (Guilin: Wenhua shenghuo chubanshe, 1941);

Long hu gou [Dragon, Tiger, Dog] (Shanghai: Wenhua shenghuo chubanshe, 1942);

Feiyuan wai [Behind a Desolate Garden] (Chongqing: Fenghuoshe, 1942);

Huanhun cao [The Grass of Resurrection] (Shanghai: Wenhua Shenghuo chubanshe, 1942);

Huo: Di er bu [Fire: Part Two] (Shanghai: Kaiming shudian chubanshe, 1942);

Xiaoren xiaoshi [Little People, Little Affairs] (Shanghai: Wenhua shenghuo chubanshe, 1943; revised, 1945);

Qiyuan [Garden of Repose] (Chongqing: Wenhua Shenghuo chubanshe, 1944; revised edition, Shanghai: Chenguang chuban gongsi, 1953);

Huo: Di san bu [Fire: Part Three] (Shanghai: Kaiming shudian chubanshe, 1945);

Di si bingshi (Shanghai: Liangyou fuxing tushu gongsi, 1946); translated by Howard Goldblatt as *Ward Four: A Novel of Wartime China* (San Francisco: China Books and Periodicals, 1999);

Lütu zaji [Travel Notebook] (Shanghai: Wanye shudian, 1946);

Hanye (Shanghai: Chenguang chuban gongsi, 1947); translated by Nathan K. Mao and Liu Ts'un-yan as *Cold Nights: A Novel* (Hong Kong: Chinese University Press / Seattle: University of Washington Press, 1978);

Huainian [Reminiscences] (Shanghai: Kaiming shudian chubanshe, 1947);

Jingye de beiju [Tragedy on a Quiet Night] (Shanghai: Wenhua shenghuo chubanshe, 1948);

Huashacheng de jieri–Bolan zaji [Warsaw Holiday–Notes from Poland] (Shanghai: Pingmin chubanshe, 1951);

Weiwen xin ji qita [Letter of Sympathy and Other Pieces] (Shanghai: Pingming chubanshe, 1951);

Shenghuo zai yingxiongmen de zhongjian (Beijing: Renmin wenxue chubanshe, 1953); translated as *Living amongst Heroes* (Beijing: Foreign Languages Press, 1954);

Women huijianle Peng Dehuai Silingyuan [Our Meeting with Commander Peng Dehuai] (Beijing: Renmin wenxue chubanshe, 1953);

Wu yu dian [Fog, Rain, Lightning] (Shanghai: Pingming chubanshe, 1953);

Yingxiong de gushi [Stories of Heroes] (Shanghai: Pingming chubanshe, 1953);

Baowei heping de renmen [People Guarding Peace] (Beijing: Zhongguo qingnian chubanshe, 1954);

Ba Jin duanpian xiaoshuo xuanji [Selected Short Stories of Ba Jin] (Beijing: Renmin wenxue chubanshe, 1955);

Ba Jin sanwenxuan [Ba Jin: Selected Prose] (Beijing: Renmin Wenxue chubanshe, 1955);

Tan Jiehefu [On Chekhov] (Shanghai: Pingming chubanshe, 1955);

Da huanle de rizi [Joyful Times] (Beijing: Zuojia chubanshe, 1957);

Jianqiang zhanshi [Stalwart Warriors] (Beijing: Zhongguo shaonian ertong chubanshe, 1957); translated by Zhang Dang as "Perseverance," *Chinese Literature*, 6 (1963): 47–62;

Mingzhu he Yuji [Mingzhu and Yuji] (Beijing: Zhongguo shaonian ertong chubanshe, 1957);

Ba Jin duanpian xiaoshuo ji [Short Stories by Ba Jin], 4 volumes (Hong Kong: Jindai tushu gongsi, 1958);

Yichang wanjiu shengming de zhandou (Beijing: Zhongguo qingnian chubanshe, 1958); translated by Zheng Zhiyi and Shen Zigao as *A Battle for Life: A Full Record of How the Life of Steel-Worker Chiu Tsai-kang Was Saved in the Shanghai Kwangtze Hospital* (Beijing: Foreign Languages Press, 1959);

Luoche shang [On the Mule Cart] (Hong Kong: Xinyue, 1959);

Xinsheng ji [New Voices] (Beijing: Renmin wenxue chubanshe, 1959);

Youyi ji [Friendship] (Beijing: Zuojia chubanshe, 1959);

Zhu yu ji [Piglet and Chickens] (Beijing: Zuojia chubanshe, 1959);

Zan'ge ji [Song of Praise] (Shanghai: Wenyi chubanshe, 1960);

Li Dahai [Li Dahai] (Beijing: Zuojia chubanshe, 1961);

Qingtu bujin de ganqing [Inexhaustible Feelings] (Tianjin: Baihua wenyi chubanshe, 1963);

Xianliang qiaopan [At the Xianliang Bridge] (Beijing: Zuojia chubanshe, 1964);

Dazhai xing [A Trip to Dazhai] (Xi'an: Shanxi renmin chubanshe, 1965);

Juehuo ji [Torch Fire] (Beijing: Renmin wenxue chubanshe, 1979);

Suixiang lu [Random Thoughts] (Beijing: Renmin wenxue chubanshe, 1980);

Ba Jin zhongpian xiaoshuo xuan [Selected Novellas by Ba Jin], 2 volumes (Sichuan: Renmin chubanshe, 1980);

Tansuo ji: Suixiang lu [Explorations: Random Thoughts] (Beijing: Renmin wenxue chubanshe, 1981);

Chuangzuo huiyi lu [Memoirs of a Writing Life] (Beijing: Renmin wenxue chubanshe, 1982);

Huainian ji [Recollections] (Yinchuan shi: Ningxia renmin chubanshe, 1982);

Xuba ji [Prefaces and Postscripts] (Guangzhou: Huacheng chubanshe, 1982);

Zhenhua ji: Suixiang lu [The Truth: Random Thoughts] (Hong Kong: Sanlian shudian chubanshe, 1982).

Editions and Collections: *Aiqing de sanbu qu* [Love: A Trilogy] (Shanghai: Liangyou tushu yinshua gongsi, 1936)–comprises *Wu* [Fog], *Yu* [Rain], and *Dian* [Lightning];

Ba Jin duanpian xiaoshuo ji [Short Stories by Ba Jin], 3 volumes (Shanghai: Kaiming shudian chubanshe, 1936-1942);

Ba Jin wenji [Ba Jin's Works] (Shanghai: Kaiming shudian chubanshe, 1948);

Miewang [Destruction] (Shanghai: Kaiming shudian chubanshe, 1948);

Ba Jin wenji [Ba Jin's Works], 14 volumes (Beijing: Renmin wenxue, 1958-1962);

Ba Jin wenji [Ba Jin's Works], 14 volumes (Hong Kong: Nan'guo chubanshe, 1970);

Ba Jin sanwen xuan [Selected Essays by Ba Jin], 2 volumes (Hangzhou: Zhejiang renmin chubanshe, 1982);

Ba Jin quanji [Ba Jin's Complete Works], 15 volumes (Beijing: Renmin wenxue chubanshe, 1982-1990);

Ba Jin quanji [Ba Jin's Complete Works], 25 volumes published to date (Beijing: Renmin wenxue chubanshe, 1986–);

Ba Jin xiaoshuo quanji [Ba Jin's Complete Fiction] (Taipei: Yuanliu, 1993);

Ba Jin yiwen quanji [Ba Jin's Complete Translations], 10 volumes (Beijing: Renmin wenxue chubanshe, 1997).

Editions in English: *Han-Ying dui zhao Ba Jin duanpian xiaoshuo xuan = Short Stories by Pa Chin, with English Translations*, translated by Mo Jinyi (Hong Kong: Huitong shudian, 1940);

"Nanny Yang" ("Yang sao"), translated by E. Perry Link Jr.; "The General" ("Jiangjun"), translated by Nathan K. Mao; "Sinking Low" (*Chenluo*), translated by Link; and "Piglet and Chickens" ("Zhu yu ji"), translated by Anita M. Brown and Jane Parish Yang, in *Modern Chinese Stories and Novellas, 1919-1949,* edited by Joseph S. M. Lau, Leo Ou-Fan Lee, and C. T. Hsia (New York: Columbia University Press, 1981), pp. 293-321;

Autumn in Spring and Other Stories (Beijing: Chinese Literature, 1981)–comprises "Autumn in Spring" ("Chuntian li de qiutian"), translated by Wang Mingjie; "The Heart of a Slave" ("Nuli di xin"), translated by Gladys Yang; "A Moonlit Night" ("Yueye"), translated by Sidney Shapiro; "When the Snow Melted" ("Huaxue de rizi"), translated by Tang Sheng (Dang Sheng); and "An Interview with Ba Jin," by Yang Yi;

Random Thoughts, translated by Geremie Barmé (Hong Kong: Joint Publishing Company, 1984);

Selected Works of Ba Jin, translated by Shapiro and Wang Mingjie (Beijing: Foreign Languages Press, 1988)—comprises "The Family" *(Jia),* "Autumn in Spring" ("Chuntian li de qiutian"), "Garden of Repose" *(Qiyuan),* and "Bitter Cold Nights" *(Hanye);*

"Dog" ("Gou"), translated by Lance Halvorsen, in *The Columbia Anthology of Modern Chinese Literature,* edited by Lau and Howard Goldblatt (New York: Columbia University Press, 1995), pp. 121-125;

"Paradise for Birds" ("Niao de tiantang"), "In Memoriam of Mr. Lu Xun" ("Yi Lu Xun xiansheng"), and "Independent Thoughts" ("Duli sikao"), as Yu Yi, translated by Martin Woesler; "A Writer's Courage and Sense of Duty" ("Zuojia de yongqi he zerenxin"), translated by Du Xianju; "The Small Dog Baodi" ("Xiaogou Baodi"), translated by Woesler; and "In Memoriam of Xiao Shan II" ("Zaiyi Xiao Shan"), translated by Jin Li, in *20th Century Chinese Essays in Translation,* edited by Woesler (Bochum, Germany: University Press of Bochum, 2000), pp. 102-104, 112-132.

SELECTED PERIODICAL PUBLICATIONS–UNCOLLECTED: "Zenyang jianshe zhenzheng pingdeng ziyou de shehui" [How to Establish a Truly Equal and Free Society], as Li Feigan, *Banyue,* no. 17 (1921);

"'Wen'ge bowuguan" [Cultural Revolution Museum], *Xinmin wanbao,* 8 August 1986; translated by Geremie Barmé as "Ba Jin: A Cultrev Museum," in *Seeds of Fire: Chinese Voices of Conscience,* edited by Barmé and John Minford (Hong Kong: Far Eastern Economic Review, 1986; New York: Hill & Wang, 1988; Newcastle upon Tyne, U.K.: Bloodaxe, 1989), pp. 381-384.

Ba Jin is one of the best-loved Chinese writers of the twentieth century; in Chinese readers' polls of the 1930s and 1940s he was ranked second in popularity only to Lu Xun. From the late 1920s to the late 1940s he wrote sometimes melodramatic but consistently humanistic novels and short stories that criticize poverty, war, greed, and other social injustices. His works from the early decades of the People's Republic of China, on the other hand, are seen by many as little more than political exercises. Although he complied with the demands placed on writers by the Communist authorities, because of his pre-1949 anarchist political activities and writings he suffered persecution from the late 1950s—and especially during the Cultural Revolution of 1966 to 1976—until he was rehabilitated in 1977.

Despite Ba Jin's popularity, some scholars have found his stories and novels lacking in quality. C. T. Hsia, for example, writes in his influential *A History of Modern Chinese Fiction* (1971) that while Ba Jin is one of the most popular and prolific authors from the late 1920s through the mid 1930s, "he is not one of the most important," his work shows no "striving for excellence," and he "never outgrew his own adolescence." W. J. F. Jenner puts his criticism in the context of cultural differences: "we could easily find modern Chinese works highly thought of by Chinese readers that tend to leave Anglophone readers cold (most of Ba Jin, for example)." Ba Jin's worldwide following and his nomination for the 1975 Nobel Prize in literature stem from his confronting his characters with difficult ethical situations that demand the sacrifice of personal interests for a greater good, rather than from the overall literary merit or stylistic virtuosity of his works. Some of his novels, however, have received consistent scholarly praise, and his popularity has never diminished among Chinese readers.

Ba Jin was born Li Yaotang on 25 November 1904 into a large, wealthy landowning family in Chengdu, the capital of Sichuan province; his *zi* (style name) was Li Feigan. The household was ruled over by Li Yaotang's grandfather, a retired magistrate whose father had served as a government official. Li's mother, the preeminent influence in the first decade of his life, was a practicing Buddhist who taught her son compassion for all living things. She also recited favorite poems to her sons.

Li's father held an official position but encountered legal difficulties during his son's infancy. In 1907 his name was cleared, and he was promoted to magistrate of the city of Guangyuan in northern Sichuan. The author's earliest memories were of a happy and peaceful existence during their two years in Guangyuan.

Li Yaotang was tutored in the Chinese classics, required learning for a future government official. He shared a room with his brother Yaolin, who was a year older, and a maidservant, Yang sao ("Sister" Yang), whom he remembers fondly in "Yang sao" (translated as "Nanny Yang," 1981) in the 1933 collection *Mobu* (Dustcloth). Her death when Li Yaotang was around six ended an idyllic era for him. It coincided with the beginning of his struggle to understand the unequal treatment of women in Chinese society, which was precipitated by the deaths and disfigurements of "exemplary" women that he saw illustrated in Liu Xiang's classical text *Lienü zhuan* (79-78 B.C., Biographies of Distinguished Women).

In early 1911, with Sichuan experiencing violent demonstrations against the Qing dynasty's policies, Li's father resigned from his government post and moved

Cover for a 1948 edition of Ba Jin's first novel, Miewang (Destruction), first published in 1929, about a union organizer whose martyrdom inspires his girlfriend to lead a successful weavers' strike (Wason Collection on East Asia–China, Kroch Asia Library, Cornell University)

the family back to Chengdu. The revolution reached its peak in October, and the emperor abdicated in February 1912. Ba Jin later remembered this period as an exciting phase of his childhood, even though the Li family had tried to keep him and his young siblings and cousins insulated from the revolutionary chaos. During these years spent in isolation in the family's luxurious compound, the foundations for a life in letters were being laid: several of the well-educated family elders had some literary talent; the children's tutor focused almost exclusively on Chinese literary classics; and the children's games and family social gatherings often involved literature and literary lore.

Despite the sumptuousness of his surroundings, Li became sensitive to the unequal and often cruel treatment of the household servants. He counted many of them among his companions, and in a 1937 essay, "Wode jige xiansheng" (A Few of My Teachers), he refers to some of them as his early "xiansheng" (teachers). Most biographers and scholars of Ba Jin's works agree on the importance of his childhood experiences with members of the working class. Nathan K. Mao, for example, writes that Ba Jin defended the poor in his work because he had learned as a child to appreciate their virtues.

Li Yaotang's mother died after a three-week illness when he was nine. Mao notes the impact of the loss on Ba Jin's writings: "In novel after novel, his fictional characters seem unable to shake off the memories of their mothers." Four months after his mother's death, his eldest sister died. In the years after his mother's death, Li read many of the Chinese literary classics in the family's private library; there, according to his biographer Olga Lang, he found "friends in books" who understood him when no one else seemed to. His father died in 1917. Li turned to Buddhism briefly but found little solace in faith. During this period of loneliness and sorrow he began to see the cruelty, corruption, greed, hypocrisy, and misogyny that underlay the congeniality and propriety of members of his family. Some of the most pernicious acts he witnessed were visited upon servants and the poor. Such revelations coincided with his exposure to critical political and literary writings that eventually motivated him, as Michael S. Duke says, to "bring hope, courage, and strength to life" through fiction writing.

According to Lang, Li's grandfather kept him inside the family compound after the father's death to protect him from the "pernicious influence of modern schools and modern ideas." But as early as 1918 Li began to read Western works of fiction in translation, and in 1919, the year his grandfather died, news of the May Fourth movement reached the compound in journals and pamphlets. Through their reading of such journals as Xin qingnian (New Youth) Li and his brothers and cousins absorbed radical ideas about world affairs, Chinese nationalism, culture, and society. Li's intellectual, political, and literary development was heavily influenced by the Western ideas and literary styles promoted in these journals. Lang observes that "in the formation of his ideals three Western ideological complexes were of primary importance: international anarchism, Russian populism, and, to a lesser extent, the Great French Revolution." Anarchism had by far the greatest impact. In Lang's account, Li understood anarchism as the belief in "a new social order based on liberty unrestricted by man-made law; the theory that all forms of government rest on violence, and are therefore wrong and harmful as well as unnecessary."

By the winter of 1920 Li was referring to himself as an "anarchist." He made his first real friends outside the family compound in youthful anarchist clubs, and his first act of social protest was to join in a student boycott to express grievances against a warlord. In 1921 his first published essay, "Zenyang jianshe zhenzheng ziyou pingdeng de shehui" (How to Establish a Truly Equal and Free Society), appeared under the name Li Feigan. Impressed by Russian, German, and French writers such as Ivan Turgenev, Leopold Kampf, Emile Zola, Guy de Maupassant, and Romain Rolland, Li emulated the style and content of their work, most notably in his emotional, realistic, sympathetic portrayals of the poor and dispossessed. In his study of modern Chinese prose styles Edward Gunn identifies Ba Jin's as "prolix, Europeanized writing" and refers to the "overall density of his Euro-Japanese usage in the pre-1950s texts." Lang points out that "to whatever degree Ba Jin used foreign forms and ideas, he did so because they helped him represent the new realities of Chinese life."

An important rite of passage for members of the iconoclastic generation of Chinese intellectuals who came of age in the early years of the twentieth century was to study abroad. After studying in Shanghai from 1923 to 1926, Li boarded a French mail boat, the *Angers,* for Marseilles on 14 January 1927. He spent most of the next two years in Paris and Château-Thierry, a small town outside Paris, where, according to Lang, he was either alone or in the company of "anarchists from various countries, his Chinese friends, and Frenchmen of the lower middle classes." He studied French at the French Cultural Association Auxiliary Night School. His years in France were marked by news of his family's bankruptcy and by boredom, loneliness, depression, and consternation over the 23 August 1927 executions in Boston of the anarchists Nicola Sacco and Bartolomeo Vanzetti. In Lang's account, the executions were the "deepest emotional experience" of Li Yaotang's time abroad. Mao suggests that he became a fiction writer at this time "as a form of self-therapy."

Between March 1927 and August 1928 Li completed the novel *Miewang* (1929, Destruction). He published it under the pen name Ba Jin, which he had first used for a 1928 translation; he went on to achieve fame as Ba Jin, although he published under at least thirty-seven pen names during his career. According to a well-known account, he created the name from the Chinese transliterations of the surnames of the anarchist thinkers he most admired, the Russians Mikhail Bakunin and Petr Kropotkin. Lang notes, however, that Ba Jin claimed in his 1958 essay "Tan *Miewang*" (Discussion of *Destruction*) that the "Ba" came from the name of a Chinese student he met in France who later committed suicide; the "Jin" did stand for the last syllable of Kropotkin and had been "half-jokingly" suggested by a friend. Considering the political persecution he experienced because of his anarchist sympathies, his denial may have been made under duress. He sent the manuscript for *Miewang* to a friend in Shanghai, who was supposed to have a few copies printed at Ba Jin's expense and distribute them only to the author's brothers and close friends. Instead, the friend submitted it to the leading literary journal *Xiaoshuo yuebao* (Short Story Monthly). The novel was serialized from January to April 1929; enthusiastic reader response led to publication in book form that same year.

In *Miewang* the young, sensitive, tubercular intellectual Du Daxin, angered and frustrated by the social injustices he sees, and ineffective in his work for a Shanghai labor union, commits suicide after a botched assassination attempt on a murderous antiunion garrison commander. Du's passionate conviction and martyrdom incite his girlfriend to lead a successful weavers' strike. The novel depicts a world of cruelty and injustice to which the only possible response is hatred of the system and commitment to its destruction. The plot was inspired by contemporary events in China, the executions of Sacco and Vanzetti, and, Lang argues, Ba Jin's "intensive preoccupation with Russian literature and with the history of the Russian revolutionary movement." Chen Sihe reports in his article "Ba Jin chuangzuo fengge de yanbian" (The Evolution of Ba Jin's Creative Style), included in *Ba Jin zuopin pinglun ji* (1985, Collected Commentaries on the Works of Ba Jin), edited by Chen, Jia Zhifang, Tang Jinhai, and Zhang Xiaoyun, that Ba Jin followed the dictates of his emotions in writing the novel, which resulted in a collection of unrelated sections that he then rearranged and edited. Written in a straightforward style, it is easy to read; but, as Mao notes, it is predictable, relying on hackneyed plot devices and one-dimensional characters.

Ba Jin's next novel, *Siqu de taiyang* (1931, The Dead Sun), deals with bourgeois intellectuals during the May Thirtieth Movement. In Shanghai a college student, Wu Yangqing, witnesses the 30 May 1925 massacre, ordered by a British police officer, of unarmed students and workers protesting the murder of a Chinese union leader by a Japanese factory guard. Inspired by the martyred protesters and by hatred of China's foreign oppressors, Wu commits himself to the workers' movement. The novel attacks imperialism and idealizes the working class; the latter is personified by Wang Xueli, the leader of a group of striking workers. Demonstrating greater resolve and fortitude than do cowardly, wavering intellectuals such as Wu, Wang is executed for an act of sabotage. As in most of Ba Jin's

Ba Jin in 1934 (from Zhongguo dabaike quanshu zongbianji weiyuanhui, ed., Zhongguo dabaike quanshu: Zhongguo wenxue, *volume 2, 1986; Collection of Thomas Moran)*

fiction, the struggle between good and evil in *Siqu de taiyang* is absolute. Characters are guided by powerful emotions and judged by the author for their commitment to fighting oppression. The novel demonizes foreigners, shames uncommitted intellectuals, and points to the need for unity and courage in the face of aggression. The book resonated with the sentiments of many readers in the early 1930s but has not been highly regarded by critics. According to Lang, Ba Jin considered it a failure.

In August 1931 Ba Jin published *Fuchou* (Revenge), a collection of short stories based on his experiences in France. In October his novel *Wu* (Fog) began to appear in serial form in *Dongfang zazhi* (The Eastern Miscellany); it was published as a book that same year. The protagonist, Zhou Rushui, is a weak, indecisive intellectual who acquiesces in the status quo. The married Zhou falls in love with a student, Zhang Roulan. By the end of the novel he has missed his chance to be with Zhang, experienced unrequited love for another woman, lost his wife to illness, and drowned himself in the Huangpu River.

In 1931 Ba Jin had completed *Xinsheng* (New Life), the sequel to *Miewang*. In January 1932, while the book was in press, the original manuscript and many copies were destroyed in the Japanese bombing of the Zhabei district of Shanghai. Ba Jin rewrote the novel in less than two weeks in July, adding ten thousand Chinese characters, and it was published in 1933. The protagonist of *Xinsheng* is the martyred Du Daxin's friend Li Leng, a Shanghai poet. Du's death has left him in deep mourning. A self-obsessed, nihilistic intellectual, Li Leng denies the efficacy of action. He prefers to revel in shame, self-pity, and alienation, while struggling to ignore Du's example and to reject his sister's argument that life must have a cause to be meaningful. His girlfriend, Wenru, a union organizer, is also unable to move him from his existential lethargy. Finally, after prolonged agonizing, Li Leng joins a labor union, is arrested for the attempted murder of a police official, and is sentenced to be executed. Facing death, he loses his cynicism, and he finds peace in the knowledge that he is giving his life in a noble cause.

In their chronology of Ba Jin's life (1989) Zhang Xiaoyun and Tang Jinhai report that on 2 March 1932, as the Japanese bombed Shanghai, he witnessed the night sky "half lit up with firelight, accompanied by the cries of despair coming from several middle-aged people wandering about." He vowed to turn the short story he was then writing into a scathing novella that would "drown the invaders in a roaring sea of blood." *Hai di meng* (1932, Dream on the Sea) is, as Zhang and Tang note, an allegory "in the guise of a children's tale." The native people of an island nation have been invaded by foreigners. Some of the locals collaborate and others resist. Li'na, from a well-to-do family of collaborators, marries an intellectual who has become the leader of the "slave" resistance to the invaders. Though her husband is executed, she is undaunted by the clear threat to her own life and would rather die than yield to her oppressors. Li'na tells her story to the autobiographical narrator, her fellow passenger on a boat in the Mediterranean. The following day she has disappeared.

After finishing *Hai di meng*, Ba Jin took less than a week to write the novella *Chuntian li de qiutian* (1932, Autumn in Spring). It takes the form of a diary kept by the teacher Lin, in which he quotes from his brother's diary and letters. Lin learns that his older brother has killed himself because his girlfriend's parents forced her to marry a man of their choosing. Lin faces a similar problem when the parents of his student and lover, Rong, force her to sever her relationship with him and marry someone else. She becomes ill, avoids taking her medicine, and dies. Mao finds literary "artistry" in the juxtaposing in the novel of the "intoxicating bliss of courtship" with "feelings of doom."

Ba Jin's second collection of short stories, *Guangming* (Light), was published in the spring of 1932. It includes "Nuli di xin" (translated as "The Heart of a Slave," 1981), which allegorically addresses the social inequalities in China in terms of slaves and slave owners. The narrator, Zheng, a selfish man from a slave-holding family, recalls a heated discussion he had many years ago with his friend Peng, a college classmate from China's slave class. Peng passionately related the story of his family's destruction at the hands of their master and his profligate son; he also lamented his inheritance: a slave's heart. While listening to Peng's tragic tale, Zheng was overwhelmed with shame, guilt, and fear. He fainted; when he awakened, Peng was gone. Zheng lost touch with Peng after this incident. Now, relaxing in his garden with his wife while being attended to by five slaves, Zheng reads in the newspaper that a revolutionary with the same name as Peng has been executed. He sighs and decides to forget about Peng. "Gou" (translated as "Dog," 1995), also included in *Guangming*, is one of Ba Jin's best-known stories. It is a simple anecdote about a young beggar who feels less than human, especially in comparison to foreigners. He prays to be turned into a dog so that he might have access to the love and luxury enjoyed by white people's pets. Deluding himself that his prayers have been answered, he winds up in prison after getting into a fight with the dog of a white woman whose pet he longs to be.

In 1932 Ba Jin also published *Yu* (Rain), a sequel to *Wu*. Zhou Rushui's friend, the recently widowed Wu Renmin, struggles in a more heroic fashion than Zhou to reconcile his need for romantic love with his devotion to revolutionary work. Interior monologues allow readers to follow his progress and share his anguish. The women in Wu's life suffer and die for him. His former love, Zheng Yuwen, is trapped in an unhappy marriage; realizing that she can never have Wu, she kills herself. Wu and his former student, Zhijun, fall in love; but Zheng's death precipitates a series of events that separates them, and Zhijun, too, dies. With help from staunch revolutionary companions and more inner struggle, Wu sheds the burden of love and emerges at the end of the novel with renewed dedication to the revolution.

In the allegorical novella *Lei* (1933; translated as "Thunder," 1961) a romantic triangle creates tensions among a group of revolutionary youths: Mr. De (Virtue) and Mr. Min (Sensitivity) are both in love with Miss Hui (Intelligence). Resolution comes when De sacrifices his life to save Min, who then commits himself to revenge in the name of revolution. Hui's advocacy of total sexual liberation is radical for the time, but the story exalts male bonding and revolutionary passion over women's liberation or sensual hedonism.

In January 1933 Ba Jin published *Shading* (The Antimony Miners). Poor laborers are promised high wages for working in an antimony mine but instead are enslaved, starved, and tortured. After a deadly cave-in, the wealthy mine owners simply hire new workers. Also in January 1933 Ba Jin began serializing a longer novel about miners, *Mengya* (Sprouts), in a weekly newspaper; it was published in book form seven months later. The title is taken from the novel it imitates, Zola's *Germinal* (1885, Germination Month; translated as *Germinal*, 1885). Like Zola, Ba Jin did research for the work by spending a week at a mine. The two mining novels stand out from his previous work in their focus on nonurban laborers and their transparent attack on the capitalist class associated with the Guomindang (Nationalist) regime. Owing to its obvious targets, *Mengya* was banned. In response, Ba Jin changed characters' names and changed the title to "Mei" (Coal); but the revised version was also banned and was never published. In late 1936 the novel was republished under the title by which it is generally known, *Xue* (Snow).

While revising *Mengya*, Ba Jin published two more collections of short stories, *Dianyi* (1933, Electric Chair) and *Mobu*. The seven stories in *Dianyi* cover a broad range of topics and are notable for their degree of psychological depth. *Mobu* comprises only two stories, "Yang sao," about Ba Jin's beloved childhood nanny, and "Di'er de muqin" (Second Mother).

In April 1931 Ba Jin's novel "Jiliu" (Torrent) had begun to appear in serial form in the Shanghai newspaper *Shi bao* (The Eastern Times) and had created a sensation. Published in book form in 1933 as *Jia* (Family), it became his best-known work and established him as one of the most admired and successful Chinese writers of the 1930s and 1940s. *Jia* chronicles the breakdown of the Gaos, a large and wealthy extended family of the scholar-gentry class. The main characters are the brothers Gao Juexin, Juemin, and Juehui, who struggle to gain control over their lives in defiance of the rules that demand the subjugation of the individual to a predetermined role in the family and in society. Ba Jin portrays the traditional Chinese family structure as designed to crush the aspirations and dreams of young people, and he uses the brothers' grandfather, the patriarch Master Gao, to show that this structure is not an impersonal system but is embodied in the conservative tyrants who uphold it. Master Gao tolerates no debate or dissension; he dictates every aspect of his grandsons' lives, and most of his decisions run counter to their desires. The main dramatic movement of the novel is generated by the brothers' acquiescence in, resistance to, or rebellion against their grandfather's dictums. Other plotlines depict the suffering of women under the traditional Chinese family and social systems.

Cover for Xue *(1936, Snow), Ba Jin's novel about coal miners that was originally serialized under the title* Mengya (Sprouts) *in 1933 (from Yu Runqi, ed.,* Tang Tao cang shu, *2004; Bruccoli Clark Layman Archives)*

Jia takes place between 1919 and 1923, China's warlord era and the period of the student-led May Fourth movement. The relationships among literature, enlightenment, and the transformation of Chinese society can be discerned both in the content of the story and in the popular reception of the novel: the characters are inspired by May Fourth ideas as found in the journals of the 1920s; likewise, readers in the 1930s and 1940s were inspired by the indictment in the novel of the traditional family system. The work treats the characters as victims but also suggests that some of them are at least partly to blame for their own fates. Juexin, the eldest son, for example, is faulted by the narrator for habitually bending to his grandfather's will. In the essay "He duzhe tan *Jia*" (A Discussion of *Family* with Readers), included in volume four of *Ba Jin wenji* (1958–1962, Ba Jin's Works), Ba Jin writes that Juexin "is my own eldest brother" (Lang's translation). Ba Jin's brother killed himself rather than have his dreams crushed by the Li family patriarchs; news of the suicide reached Ba Jin while he was writing chapter 6 of *Jia*. Acutely aware of his brother's complicity in his own misfortune, Ba Jin is careful to demonstrate that much of Juexin's suffering results from cowardice. Any judgment of Juexin and the other male characters must take into account this critical stance toward willful ignorance and passivity, which is revealed in the most common literary device in the novel: the didactic depiction of characters' responses to decisive events. For example, after Juehui—the youngest and most rebellious brother and an alter ego of Ba Jin—gives money to a beggar, "a voice seemed to shout at him in the silence: 'Do you think deeds like that are going to change the world? Do you think you've saved that beggar child from cold and hunger for the rest of his life? You—you hypocritical "humanitarian"; what a fool you are!'" Juehui is the "courageous rebel" of the story, but his commitment to changing China through intellectual means rather than through action is his tragic flaw. Juehui's servant and secret love, Mingfeng, pleads for Juehui to save her from becoming a concubine to a "lecherous old man." Juehui, absorbed in editorial duties for a journal "introducing new ideas and attacking all that was unreasonable of the old," is oblivious to Mingfeng's crisis, and, with no one else to turn to, she commits suicide.

While the young male characters in *Jia* are partially responsible for the evils of the patriarchy, the same cannot be said of the young women. Mingfeng's plight is typical of the women and girls in the novel: they are helpless without a man's intervention. Rey Chow notes that Mingfeng becomes just another victim of tradition, while readers are encouraged to sympathize and commiserate with Juehui, the man who could have saved her. As Chow points out, the female characters are ancillary to the main concern in the novel: the rebellious young Juehui's heroic fight against the male-dominated family system.

Along with publishing translations, writing essays on his recent travels in southern China, and cofounding a literary magazine, Ba Jin found time to publish two more collections of stories. *Jiangjun* (The General) and *Chenmo* (Deep Silence) appeared in August and October 1934, respectively. *Jiangjun* comprises eleven stories. The title work (translated as "The General," 1981) is about a former Russian lieutenant in exile in China who gets drunk nightly in an attempt to drown memories of his brief, happy youth in Russia—a stark contrast to the poverty in which he now lives. He pays for his wine with money his young wife earns as a prostitute. He is a pitiful and despicable drunk who often hurls insulting nationalistic epithets at the waiters who serve him, but Ba Jin finds pathos in his situation. In "Yueye" (translated as "A Moonlit Night," 1981), peasants are terrorized by landlords and gentry. Other stories in

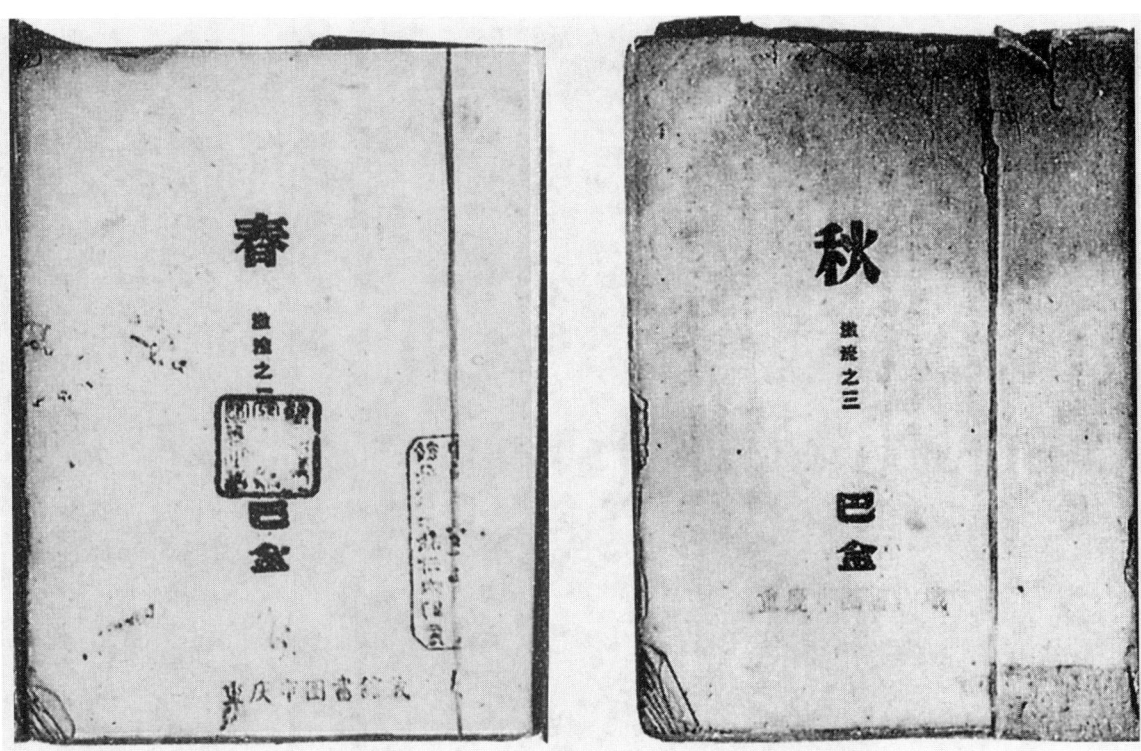

Covers for Chun (1938, Spring) and Qiu (1940, Autumn), the second and third novels in Ba Jin's "Jiliu" (Torrent) trilogy about the Gao family (from Lin Mohan, Fang Jing, and Shen Shiming, eds., Zhongguo kang Ri zhanzheng shiqi dahoufang wenxue shuxi, di san pian: Xiaoshuo, volume 4, 1989; Collection of Thomas Moran)

Jiangjun, such as "Wushi duoge" (More Than Fifty), address the suffering of peasants and portray the military in a negative light. *Chenmo* consists of seven stories and an essay. Three of the stories deal with key figures of the French Revolution: Jean-Paul Marat, Georges-Jacques Danton, and Maximilien Robespierre. "Zhishi jieji" (The Intellectuals) is a castigating portrayal of self-serving, dishonest intellectuals. "Chunyu" (Spring Rain) is also about intellectuals but is less stridently moralizing. The stories in *Jiangjun* and *Chenmo* are didactic but display some mastery in their use of a variety of characters and contexts to lend emotional appeal to political arguments.

Since China had become a dangerous place for a known anarchist and an author of banned materials, Ba Jin went to Japan in November 1934 under an assumed name. Just before a visit to Tokyo by Henry Puyi, the Japanese puppet emperor of Manchuria, he and others were arrested by plainclothes police in a predawn raid and imprisoned for half a day. Ba Jin returned to Shanghai in August 1935. By mid November he had published two translations and his next collection of short stories, *Shen gui ren* (God, Ghost, Man). The stories had been written in Japan, and each has a Japanese protagonist. "Shen" and "Gui" are mild indictments of the ways in which religion and superstition provide illusory alternatives to action and rigorous critical thinking, while "Ren" is a sympathetic portrayal of an atheist who is arrested for stealing books by André Gide, Friedrich Nietzsche, and Leo Tolstoy.

In 1935 Ba Jin published *Dian* (Lightning), a sequel to *Yu*. More than two years have passed since the events of that novel. Wu Renmin, now a committed revolutionary, comes to the city of E, the setting of *Yu*, with a mission for a group of young revolutionaries. Their struggles are used to illustrate the conflicts between peaceful, organized revolutionary activity and solitary acts of terrorism, and between romantic love and revolution. Wu Renmin resolves these conflicts by finding success as a leader of peaceful revolutionary agitation and happiness with a pretty fellow revolutionary, Li Peizhu.

Wu, *Yu*, and *Dian* were republished together in 1936 as *Aiqing de sanbu qu* (Love: A Trilogy). The fictional world of these works is an unforgiving but simple place in which characters are usually presented with a choice between yielding to the forces of evil or pursuing the path of uncompromising commitment and martyr-

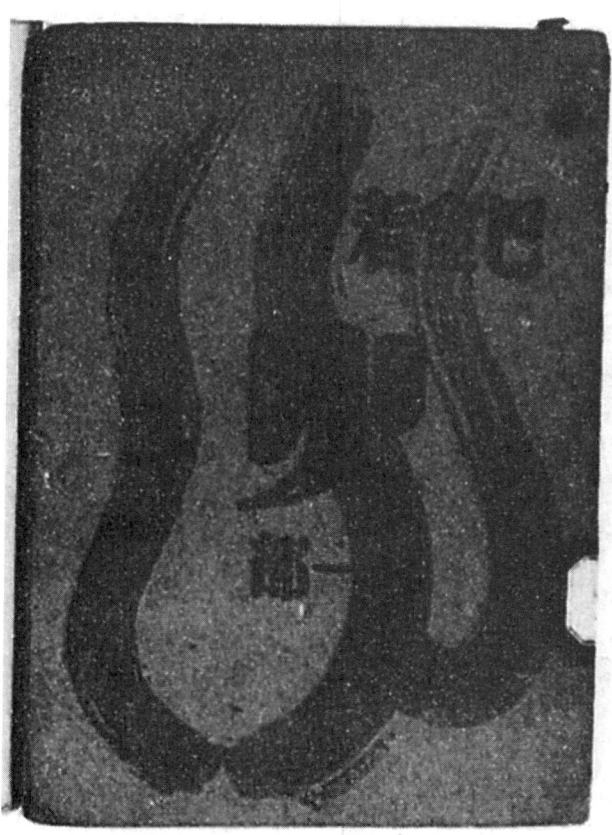

Cover for Huo: Di yi bu *(Fire: Part One, 1940)*, Ba Jin's novel about a group of young people in Shanghai during the Japanese siege of 1937 *(from Lin Mohan, Fang Jing, and Shen Shiming, eds.,* Zhongguo kang Ri zhanzheng shiqi dahoufang wenxue shuxi, di san pian: Xiaoshuo, *volume 4, 1989; Collection of Thomas Moran)*

dom. Evil is found throughout the system, which is a mixture of Confucianism, capitalism, bourgeois mores, individualism, and reactionary politics—because of censorship, Ba Jin could not directly name one of his targets, the Guomindang. Some characters fall into gray areas, but they, too, are judged by how short they fall of fighting the system. Chen notes in his 1985 article that many characters in *Aiqing de sanbu qu* are mere "continuations and derivations" of Du Daxin from *Miewang*. In *Aiqing de sanbu qu,* however, romantic love is no longer equated with selfish individualism, as some revolutionaries fall in love with each other. As Jianmei Liu explains, the formula of *geming jia lian'ai* (revolution plus love) was popular in the late 1920s and 1930s. In Liu's determination, "Ba Jin adopts revolution plus love as the main theme" in five of his novels, including all three parts of *Aiqing de sanbu qu* (the other two are *Miewang* and *Xinsheng*).

In early 1936 Ba Jin published the short-story collections *Chenluo* (Sinking Low) and *Fa de gushi* (The Story of Hair). The title story of the former (translated as "Sinking Low," 1981) is about an aging, self-important literature professor's realization that he has wasted his life. Confronted by the narrator, who is one of his students, he breaks into sobs, confessing that he has been blind to the world, merely aping the words of the books in which he immerses himself. He likens the feeling to "sinking" and believes that it is too late for him to change. The collection also includes the two-part epistolary novella *Li'na* (Leena). In letters written from prison the title character, a young Russian aristocrat who has become a revolutionary, tells of her passionate romance with her nihilist boyfriend, Boris, her rejection of her class background, and her resistance to the tsarist autocracy, for which she has been incarcerated. (The novella was published separately in 1940.) Overall, the five stories in *Chenluo* do not stray far from themes already well explored in Ba Jin's works, such as the conflict between personal romantic desire and commitment to the revolutionary cause. *Fa de gushi* comprises four stories and a postscript. The title story is another of Ba Jin's idealized portrayals of revolutionary characters, in this case Korean rebels who resist the Japanese.

According to Lang, Ba Jin once stated that "'pure literature' does not help humanity in its struggles"; Hsia quotes Ba Jin's desire as a writer to "bring some light to the masses and strike a blow at darkness." Lang notes that Ba Jin's specific intent was to expose the inequality and oppression of Chinese social structures so that "those who built their happiness on the suffering of others must perish." In an essay collected in *Sheng zhi chanhui* (1936, Confessions of a Life) Ba Jin writes, "Many, many people are taking hold of my pen to express their sorrow.... Do you think I can still pay attention to form, plot, perspective, and other such trivial matters?" Lang comments that Ba Jin "suffered with" his characters, but his negative characters lack depth and complexity and are frequently little more than allegorical representations of a perceived evil. Didactic, undisguised political content and unambiguous, emotionally charged characterizations are the hallmarks of Ba Jin's fiction and the sources of his popularity.

In October 1936 Ba Jin signed a manifesto calling for solidarity among writers in resisting Japan and for freedom of expression in literature. In March 1937 he published *Changsheng ta* (Pagoda of Long Life), a somber collection of children's fables; the title story had already appeared in *Chenluo*. After Japan's full-scale invasion of China a few months later, he wrote fewer short stories. He had never belonged to any of China's many literary societies before the invasion, but in March 1938 he joined the Zhonghua quanguo wenyijie kangdi xiehui (All-China Association of Literary Resistance). The content of his work began to reflect his enthusiastic participation in the war effort.

During the early war years Ba Jin published several volumes of essays and translations and a sequel to *Jia* titled *Chun* (1938, Spring); a third novel, *Qiu* (Autumn), was added in 1940, forming a trilogy that Ba Jin called "Jiliu"–the original title of *Jia*. *Chun* and *Qiu* follow the breakdown of the Gao family after Master Gao's death. The tyrannical Zhou Botao, who is related to the Gaos through marriage, takes over as head of the household. Zhou's daughter and son, cousins of the Gao brothers, die as the result of their father's stubborn conservatism and suspicion of Western medicine. A third cousin, inspired by a Russian play, flees the Gao household to freedom in Shanghai. Juemin and his sister, Shuhua, aided by Juexin, must contend with family infighting. The climax in *Qiu* is a series of impassioned quarrels between the siblings and their aunts and uncles. Tempered by their previous failures and armed with knowledge of the imperfection–even degeneracy– of their older relatives, the young people stand their ground until they pass into adulthood and independence. The Gao family disbands into smaller and smaller units; the compound is sold; and the members of the younger generation appear to be free to determine their own futures. Hsia argues that *Qiu* offers a more authentic emotional exploration than do the first two parts of the trilogy, as Ba Jin eschews the "didacticism of the shallow philosopher and revolutionary." Nevertheless, while the trilogy received critical acclaim, only *Jia* has been canonized as a masterpiece of modern Chinese literature. Some scholars even compare it favorably with the eighteenth-century classic, *Honglou meng* (Dream of the Red Chamber).

In late 1940 and early 1942 Ba Jin published the first and second installments of the trilogy *Huo* (Fire). Part 1 concerns a group of patriotic, educated young people in Shanghai during the Japanese siege of 1937, which Ba Jin had experienced. Working in dangerous circumstances, they promote the war effort, enlighten their fellow citizens, help the wounded, and fight the Japanese; assassination, portrayed negatively in Ba Jin's earlier novels, becomes a heroic act in *Huo*. In part 2 educated youth working in a propaganda unit in a mountainous war zone (possibly in Anhui province) unite with peasant masses in patriotic solidarity against a common enemy during the late 1930s.

After completing parts 1 and 2 of *Huo,* Ba Jin published the short-story collection *Huanhun cao* (1942, The Grass of Resurrection). The four stories describe grief, loss, and patriotic unity during war.

According to Hsia, Ba Jin expressed disappointment with the first two parts of *Huo*, admitting their literary deficiencies even as propaganda pieces. Part 3, completed in 1943 and published in 1945, portrays the events that befall the Tians, a Christian family of five befriended by two leftist activists. Parts of the story cover ground familiar from other Ba Jin novels, but Tian Huishi is unlike his previous male characters. A fifty-two-year-old devout Christian and social activist who publishes a Christian patriotic resistance magazine, he stands out in Ba Jin's repertoire because, Lang writes, he is "neither a young man nor an atheistic revolutionary." Conversely, many of the negative characters in part 3 are young; in Ba Jin's earlier novels the negative characters are usually older, traditional, and conservative. Tian's faith is positively portrayed; Ba Jin added a postscript to assure readers that he was not religious himself. Several commentators note that the war and Ba Jin's marriage in 1944 to the writer Chen Yunshen, who used the pen name Xiao Shan, had a maturing effect on his powers of characterization as displayed in part 3 of *Huo*.

In December 1945 Ba Jin published a revision of *Xiaoren xiaoshi* (Little People, Little Affairs), his last collection of stories before 1949. He had first used this title in 1943 for a collection of essays and short stories; the 1945 book eliminates the essays and adds two stories.

Cover for a 1945 edition of Ba Jin's 1944 novel Qiyuan (translated as "Garden of Repose," 1988), about the decline of the wealthy Yang family (from Yu Runqi, ed., Tang Tao cang shu, 2004; Bruccoli Clark Layman Archives)

Unlike most of his previous wartime stories, those in *Xiaoren xiaoshi* bring to light the devastation of domestic social relations in a country at war. For example, "Zhu yu ji" (translated as "Piglet and Chickens," 1981) makes only passing reference to the Japanese; instead, it focuses on arguments and hilarious exchanges of obscenities among urban dwellers trying to make do in rented quarters. The contentious, ill-behaved tenants are portrayed more sympathetically than their landlady, the villainess of the story. Other stories in *Xiaoren xiaoshi* show the petty behavior of average people in time of war. In comparison to the heroic and romantic hyperbole of much of his earlier work, Ba Jin displays a subtle touch in this collection.

The 1944 novel *Qiyuan* (translated as "Garden of Repose," 1988), originally planned as a sequel to *Qiu*, revisits the theme of the decline of a Chinese family. In *Qiyuan* the characters are more developed, and the representation of family life is more nuanced than in the "Jiliu" trilogy. The narrator, a writer, is invited to stay in a house called the Leisure Garden that once belonged to the wealthy Yang family, whose decline at the hands of the improvident Yang Laosan is mainly told by Yang's young son. The boy sneaks into his former garden to pick flowers for his father and is befriended by the writer and Mrs. Yao, the second wife of the estate's current owner. The kind and sensitive Mrs. Yao is struggling to discipline her unruly teenage stepson; he is spoiled by his grandmother, who delights in making things difficult for her dead daughter's replacement. The disobedient teenager's drowning is the result of the grandmother's coddling and Mr. Yao's failure to take charge and defend his second wife against his former mother-in-law. Yang Laosan is a more complex adult version of the Yao boy. A wastrel and a womanizer who has ruined his family, he repents, resorts to petty theft, and dies in prison. Unlike patriarchs of wealthy gentry families in Ba Jin's previous fiction, Yang is a tragic figure. No dedicated revolutionaries are to be found among the young people and women in the story.

In 1946 Ba Jin published *Di si bingshi* (translated as *Ward Four: A Novel of Wartime China*, 1999), based on his stay in 1944 in a hospital in Guiyang and partially modeled after Anton Chekhov's "Palata No. 6" (1892, Ward No. Six). The narrator's diary entries provide information about his fellow patients and the hospital staff. His bed is one of twelve in an unsanitary, poorly staffed ward where most of the patients receive inadequate care. The heroine, Dr. Yang, a conscientious, compassionate woman and an admirer of Mohandas Gandhi, shows that it is not neglect or incompetence that plagues the hospital but financial problems. Despite her efforts, all but the richest of the patients suffer, frequently to extremes. *Di si bingshi* is didactic but shows Ba Jin's increasing maturity, combining a kind of literary naturalism with sympathy for the sufferings of the poor. Unlike many of his previous works, this novel portrays suffering as a result of poverty, not a symptom of a corrupt tradition or system that must be overthrown through collective revolutionary action. Likewise, compassion and cruelty are present; but there is no stark division of characters and social groups along these lines, only the reduction of all human circumstances to harsh economic realities.

Many critics consider *Hanye* (1947; translated as *Cold Nights: A Novel*, 1978), Ba Jin's last work of fiction prior to 1949, his best novel. Set in 1945, the bleak final year of the war, the work conveys a sense of the time through a dual focus on the siege atmosphere and constant threat of air raids, on the one hand, and the economic deprivation and gloom of city life in Chongqing, on the other hand. Night scenes and sunless days predominate. The characters suffer under desperate social conditions and are tormented by private problems. The protagonist, Wang Wenxuan, is educated but weak; he

Cover for Ba Jin's Hanye (1947; translated as Cold Nights: A Novel, 1978), about the tribulations of a married couple in Chongqing amid the hardships of the final year of the 1937–1945 war with Japan (Wason Collection on East Asia–China, Kroch Asia Library, Cornell University)

cannot find a higher-paying job to help his family deal with the rapid inflation. He contracts tuberculosis; his wife, Zeng Shusheng, and his widowed mother despise and torment one another; a friend, Tang Baiqing, steps in front of a truck and is killed; and another friend, the avuncular Zhong, dies of cholera in an overcrowded wartime hospital. Wang and his wife are in their thirties; they are mature, disillusioned versions of the heroic young revolutionaries in Ba Jin's works of the 1930s. When they were younger they shared a dream of promoting education in rural areas, but now their marriage is falling apart. Zeng still loves Wang but cannot tolerate the combination of a bad relationship with her son, criticism and suspicion from her mother-in-law, boredom, and poverty. She leaves Wang, following her supervisor at the bank in which she works to a city farther removed from the Japanese threat. Despairing over his wife's abandonment and the loss of his job, Wang dies just as victory over the Japanese is being celebrated in the streets. Zeng returns home to find her husband dead and her son and mother-in-law gone. Lang reports that Ba Jin summarized *Hanye* as an indictment of the corrupt Guomindang regime. For example, on her return to Chongqing during the victory celebration Zeng hears someone in the street say, "Victory is for them, not for us. We have not made profits out of the country's misfortune." Nevertheless, much that goes on in the characters' lives is not blamed on the Guomindang. Rather, the unrelenting problems of the public and private worlds overlap and influence one another. This notion is conveyed through one of Wang's nightmares: the Japanese have attacked Chongqing; with crowds of refugees fleeing the city, Zeng urges him to abandon his disoriented and apparently wounded mother; when Wang decides that he cannot do so, Zeng takes their son and leaves without him. National and domestic crises coalesce in this dream, and no simple solution to either problem presents itself. Complexity and ambiguity are also evident in the personalities of Zeng and Wang's mother, neither of whom is a one-

Cover for a 1948 collection of Ba Jin's works
(Middlebury College Library)

dimensional or purely negative character; they are both flawed, but they love Wang and wish the best for him. Hsia regards the focus on the psychological reality of "ordinary Chinese family life" in *Hanye* as Ba Jin's greatest achievement. He calls the novel a "parable of China" and a "morality play."

During the early decades of the People's Republic of China, Ba Jin published less than at any prior time in his life. Such a falling off in productivity was common among writers who had been active before 1949. Like many such writers, too, Ba Jin experienced political persecution from the late 1950s through the mid 1970s, even though he complied with the political demands placed on writers in the early decades of the People's Republic. Duke includes Ba Jin's work of these decades as part of a trend toward "decidedly inferior work in an attempt to adapt to the new literary regime." Despite his conciliatory literary efforts, Ba Jin was officially labeled "a great poisonous weed" and "the Big Literary Tyrant" in 1968. During the Cultural Revolution he was forced to kneel on broken glass while being harangued at a rally in People's Stadium in Shanghai, he was tormented at other *pidouhui* (struggle sessions),

and his art collection and library were destroyed; according to Mao, the library contained an "impressive collection of anarchist literature." Ba Jin recounts many of these experiences in his "Suixiang lu" essays of the 1980s (collected and translated as *Random Thoughts*, 1984).

Ba Jin was nominated for the Nobel Prize in literature in 1975, losing out to the Italian poet Eugenio Montale. He was officially rehabilitated by the Communist Party in 1977. In 2002 the *China Daily* called him "the only survivor of the 'six contemporary literature giants of China.'" He remained influential in the literary world, playing an instrumental role in establishing the Zhongguo xiandai wenxue guan (Museum of Modern Chinese Literature), which opened in 2000. A lifelong heavy smoker, Ba Jin suffered from chronic bronchitis and Parkinson's disease. He was reportedly confined to the Shanghai Huadong Hospital starting in 1999. On 3 July 2002 the *China Daily* quoted him as saying that "longevity is a punishment for me." He died on 17 October 2005.

Bibliographies:

Nathan K. Mao, "Selected Bibliography," in his *Pa Chin* (Boston: Twayne, 1978), pp. 161–166;

"Ba Jin zhuzuo yizuo bianmu" and "Wenxue chuangzuo bufen," in *Ba Jin yanjiu ziliao*, edited by Li Cun'guang (Fuzhou: Haixia wenyi chubanshe, 1985), pp. 143–374;

"Ba Jin zhuyao zuopin mulu," in *Ba Jin daibiaozuo*, edited by Liu Huizhen (Zhengzhou: Henan renmin chubanshe, 1989), pp. 539–548.

Biographies:

Olga Lang, *Ba Chin and His Writings: Chinese Youth between the Two Revolutions* (Cambridge, Mass.: Harvard University Press, 1967);

Chen Sihe, *Ren'ge de fazhan: Ba Jin zhuan* (Taipei: Yeqiang chubanshe, 1991);

Li Cun'guang, *Ba Jin zhuan* (Beijing: Beijing shiyue wenyi chubanshe, 1994).

References:

Rey Chow, "Ba Jin's *Jia* (The Family) (1930)," in her *Woman and Chinese Modernity: The Politics of Reading between West and East* (Minneapolis: University of Minnesota Press, 1989), pp. 96–102;

Michael S. Duke, "The Problematic Nature of Modern and Contemporary Chinese Fiction in English Translation," in *Worlds Apart: Recent Chinese Writing and Its Audiences,* edited by Howard Goldblatt (Armonk, N.Y.: Sharpe, 1990), pp. 198–227;

Edward Gunn, *Rewriting Chinese: Style and Innovation in Twentieth-Century Chinese Prose* (Stanford, Cal.: Stanford University Press, 1991), pp. 43, 73, 88–89, 108;

C. T. Hsia, "Pa Chin (1904–)," in his *A History of Modern Chinese Fiction* (New Haven: Yale University Press, 1971), pp. 237–256;

W. J. F. Jenner, "Insuperable Barriers? Some Thoughts on the Reception of Chinese Writing in English Translation," in *Worlds Apart: Recent Chinese Writing and Its Audiences*, pp. 177–197;

Jia Zhifang, Tang Jinhai, Zhang Xiaoyun, and Chen Sihe, eds., *Ba Jin zuopin pinglun ji* (Beijing: Zhongguo wenlian chubanshe gongsi, 1985);

Wendy Larson, "Shen Congwen and Ba Jin: Literary Authority against the 'World,'" in her *Literary Authority and the Modern Chinese Writer: Ambivalence and Autobiography* (Durham, N.C.: Duke University Press, 1991), pp. 61–85;

Joseph S. M. Lau, "Pa Chin (1904–)," in *Modern Chinese Stories and Novellas, 1919–1949*, edited by Lau, Leo Ou-fan Lee, and Hsia (New York: Columbia University Press, 1981), p. 292;

Lin Mohan, Fang Jing, and Shen Shiming, eds., *Zhongguo kang Ri zhangheng shiqi dahoufang wenxue shuxi, di san pian: Xiaoshuo*, volume 4 (Chongqing: Chongqing chubanshe, 1989);

Jianmei Liu, *Revolution plus Love: Literary History, Women's Bodies, and Thematic Repetition in Twentieth-Century Chinese Fiction* (Honolulu: University of Hawai'i Press, 2003), pp. 54, 62, 176, 236;

Nathan K. Mao, *Pa Chin* (Boston: Twayne, 1978);

Ming Xingli (Father Jean Monsterleet), *Ba Jin de shenghuo he zhuzuo* (Shanghai: Wenfeng chubanshe, 1950);

Stanley R. Munro, "Ba Jin," in *Genesis of a Revolution: An Anthology of Modern Chinese Short Stories*, edited and translated by Munro (Singapore: Heinemann Educational Books [Asia], 1979);

Craig Sadler Shaw, "Ba Jin's Dream: Sentiment and Social Criticism in *Jia* (Family)," dissertation, Princeton University, 1993;

Tang Xiaobing, "The Last Tubercular in Modern Chinese Literature: On Ba Jin's *Cold Nights*," in his *Chinese Modern: The Heroic and the Quotidian* (Durham, N.C.: Duke University Press, 2000), pp. 131–160;

Xu Shanshu, ed., *Ba Jin yu Shijieyu* (Beijing: Zhongguo shijieyu chubanshe, 1995);

Yu Runqi, ed., *Tang Tao cang shu* (Beijing chubanshe, 2004), pp. 131, 178, 198;

Zhang Xiaoyun and Tang Jinhai, eds., *Ba Jin nianpu (1950–1986 nian)*, 2 volumes (Sichuan: Wenyi chubanshe, 1989);

Zhongguo dabaike quanshu zongbianji weiyuanhui, ed., *Zhongguo dabaike quanshu: Zhongguo wenxue*, volume 2 (Beijing & Shanghai: Zhongguo dabaike quanshu chubanshe, 1986).

Bao Tianxiao

(26 February 1876 – 24 November 1973)

Feng-ying Ming
California State University, Long Beach

BOOKS: *Yi nian hong* [A Pinch of Red] (Shanghai: Xiaoshuolin she, 1906);

Duanpian xiaoshuo congkan [A Serial Collection of Short Stories], by Bao and Leng Xue [Chen Jinghan] (Shanghai: Guanwen shukan she, 1906–1907);

Guchu ganyuji [A Record of the Experience of a Lonely Fledgling] (Shanghai: Shangwu shuju, 1915);

Kaocha Riben xinwen lüeshu [A Brief Record of My Observation on Japanese Newspapers] (Shanghai: Shangwu shuju, 1918);

Tongzi zhentan dui [The Children's Detective Brigade] (Shanghai: Shangwu shuju, 1920);

Liufangji [The Lingering Fragrance] (Shanghai: Zhonghua shuju, 1922);

Shanghai chunqiu [Annals of Shanghai] (Shanghai: Zhonghua shuju, 1926);

Jiazi sutan [An Account of Events and Incidents from the Year of 1924] (Shanghai: Dadong shuju, 1926);

Furen zhi nü [Rich Man's Daughter] (Shanghai: Shanghai ziyou zazhi she, 1926);

Renjian diyu ji [Living Hell Collection] (Shanghai: Shanghai ziyou zazhi she, 1927);

Maishi qishi ji [Stones Buried, Stones Tossed Away] (Shanghai: Shangwu shuju, 1931);

Dashidai fufu [Couples of a Great Era] (Guilin: Zhongguo lüxingshe, 1943);

Xin Baishezhuan [New Story of the White Snake] (Shanghai, 1958);

Chuanyinglou huiyi lu [Memoirs from the Pavilion of the Bracelet Shadow] (Hong Kong: Dahua chubanshe, 1971; Shanxi: Shanxi guji chubanshe, 1999);

Chuanyinglou huiyi lu xupian [A Sequel to *Memoirs from the Pavilion of the Bracelet Shadow*] (Hong Kong: Dahua chubanshe, 1973; Shanxi: Shanxi guji chubanshe, and Shanxi jiaoyu chubanshe, 1999);

Shi yi zhu xing de bainian bianqian [Food, Clothes, Living, and Transportation in the Past One Hundred Years] (Hong Kong: Dahua chubanshe, 1974).

Bao Tianxiao (from Tang Wenyi, Mu Dingsheng, and Ji Lei, eds., *20 shiji Zhongguo wenxue tudian*, 2001; Collection of Thomas Moran)

Editions and Collections: *Tianxiao duanpian xiaoshuo* [Tianxiao's Short Stories], 2 volumes (Shanghai: Zhonghua shudian, 1920);

Bao Tianxiao xiaoshuoji [A Collection of Stories by Bao Tianxiao] (Shanghai: Dadong shuju, 1926);

Chuanyinglou huiyi lu xupian [A Sequel to *Memoirs from the Pavilion of the Bracelet Shadow*] (Shanxi: Shanxi guji chubanshe & shanxi jiaoyu chubanshe, 1999).

Edition in English: "So Near, So Far," in *Stories for Saturday: Twentieth-Century Chinese Popular Fiction*, translated by Timothy C. Wong (Honolulu: University of Hawai'i Press, 2003).

PRODUCED SCRIPTS: *Keliande Nülin,* motion picture, Mingxing yingpian gufen youxian gongsi, 1926;

Konggulan, motion picture, Mingxing yingpian gufen youxian gongsi, 1926.

TRANSLATIONS: H. Rider Haggard, *Jiayin xiaozhuan* [A Little Biography of Jiayin], translated by Bao and Yang Zilin (Shanghai: Wenming shuju, 1901);

"Sanqianli xunqin ji" [Looking for Mother], by an unknown Italian author, and "Tie shijie" [Iron World], by an unknown French author, in *Lixue yibian* [Translations of the Learning Endeavor Society] (Suzhou: Lixue yibian she, 1901);

Xiner jiuxue ji [Xiner Went to School], by an unknown French author (Shanghai: Shangwu chubanshe, 1909).

SELECTED PERIODICAL PUBLICATIONS—UNCOLLECTED: "Yilüma: Qiuxingge biji zhi san" [A Twist of Hemp: The Third Piece of Work from the Autumn Inspiration Studio], *Xiaoshuo shibao,* 2 (13 November 1909);

"Minghong" [Letters to the Other World], *Xiaoshuo daguan* (1915);

"Yuxiao zhuxiang," *Ziluolan banyuekan* (1926);

"Huiyi," *Shanhu banyuekan* (1932);

"Zhao jiugui," *Meigui banyuekan* (1937);

"Huanchao luanfeng," *Xiaoshuo yuebao* (1940);

"Buru guiqu," *Da Shanghai zhoukan* (1941);

"Xiaoshuojia de shenpan" [Judgment on a Novelist], *Xiaoshuo yuebao* (1941);

"Qiuxinge biji," *Dazhong yuekan* (1943);

"Wo yu xinwenjie," *Wanxiang yuekan* (1944);

"Wo yu zazhishe," *Wanxiang yuekan* (1944);

"Daxiaxie shikao," *Xinwanbao* (Hong Kong), 7 November 1973.

With a seventy-year writing career, Bao Tianxiao was one of the most productive and long-lived authors in modern Chinese literary history. The key figure in the Mandarin Ducks and Butterflies school of writers, he was also one of the representative literatus-writers born in the transitional period between the traditional and modern phases of Chinese literature. Raised to participate in the traditional civil examination system to become a government official, he instead became a prolific writer of popular novels and an influential editor of fiction journals. Throughout much of his career Bao alternated among writing, editing, journalism, and teaching, sometimes pursuing all four occupations at the same time. His participation in literary activities in the late-Qing and early-Republican eras made him an eyewitness to the early modern phase of Chinese literary production. He recorded his memories of this period in his *Chuanyinglou huiyi lu* (1971, Memoirs from the Pavilion of the Bracelet Shadow).

Bao was born Bao Qingzhu on 26 February 1876 in Suzhou, a city in southeastern China known for its scenery, literati culture, folk arts, outdoor entertainment, and pleasure quarters (high-class brothels). His father was Bao Yingxun; his mother's name is unknown. According to Bao's account, his father was an employee of a *qianzhuang* (traditional Chinese bank) who disapproved of the treachery and dishonesty involved in his work. As the only son in a family that was not wealthy, Bao was expected to become a government official by passing the traditional civil examination. He started school at four and studied the Chinese classics but soon discovered that these standard texts were not as interesting as traditional novels and the newly ascendant newspapers and magazines. He read the Shanghai newspaper *Shen bao* (Shanghai Journal) from the age of eight. Later he read the Shanghai newspaper *Xinwen bao* (The News) and the monthly news magazine *Zhongwai yuebao* (Monthly News of China and the West) regularly.

Bao's father died in 1892. To support himself and his mother, Bao became a private tutor. In 1894 he passed the preliminary level of the civil service examination and was awarded the title *xiucai* (cultivated talent). He continued to teach while preparing for more-advanced levels of the examination. He and his friends exchanged ideas on current affairs and intellectual issues in a group they called the Lixuehui (Learning Endeavor Society).

Modern newspapers had only recently been introduced in China, and they played an important part in Bao's development. Liang Qichao's pioneering *Shiwu bao* (The China Progress) influenced a generation of Chinese and was one of the major inspirations for Bao. From it and other newspapers he learned about notions of internal reform, new-style schools, *xin xue* (the New Learning, mostly referring to the new knowledge from the West), women's education, the prohibition of foot-binding, and Western science. He became curious, he says in his memoir, about "sound, light, transformation, and electricity" (that is, acoustics, optics, chemistry, and electrical engineering). He also studied mathematics, Japanese, and English.

By 1900 many Chinese students had begun to go abroad to study. Bao could not afford to do so, but friends who had gone to Japan sent him books and student journals. Excited about the new knowledge, Bao and his friends in the Learning Endeavor Society came up with the idea of using a bookstore as a medium for sharing their interests and learning with others. They called the shop they founded in 1900 Donglai Shuzhuang (Books from the East). It mainly sold imported books and magazines in Japanese, such as the Japanese version of T. H. Huxley's *Evolution and Ethics* (1893), which were popular at the time.

Also in 1900 the Learning Endeavor Society founded a journal, *Lixue yibian* (Translations of the Learning Endeavor Society). Published for a year in a total of twelve issues, it was directed at literati and intellectual readers and included translations of Japanese articles about politics, law, nation building, and other social issues. Bao and Yang Zilin published in the journal their translation of the second part—the only part available to them at the time—of the English writer H. Rider Haggard's *Joan Haste* (1895) as *Jiayin xiaozhuan* (A Little Biography of Jiayin). Like many of the first generation of Chinese translators of fiction, Bao and Yang freely adapted and expanded the original story. The newly founded Commercial Press in Shanghai published the translation as a book in 1901. A short time later the eminent translator Lin Shu produced a translation of Haggard's entire novel. Commenting on the two books, the author Lu Xun wrote: "The first translator attacked the second translator for affecting his sales. Only [by reading the later translation], however, do we realize that the first translation left out an important episode about the heroine's giving birth to a son out of wedlock. It would seem that the first translator found an excuse for not translating this morally ambivalent episode." Bao explains in *Chuanlingyou huiyi lu* that he considered Lin Shu's translation superior to his own and was never jealous of it. (He also said that his translation was based on the second part of Haggard's work, not on the first, as Lu Xun had said.)

Immediately after *Lixue yibian* was discontinued, Bao Tianxiao started one of the earliest newspapers in vernacular rather than Classical Chinese, the *Suzhou baihua bao* (Suzhou Vernacular News); he served as the sole editor, translator, publisher, and distributor. Based primarily on Japanese articles, the newspaper published pieces on politics, women's education, opium addiction, foot-binding, and popular superstitions. It was aimed at semiliterate townspeople, women, and peddlers. In pursuit of this audience, Bao adapted folk songs and ballads. The enterprise lasted for about two years.

At age twenty-five Bao married Chen Zhensu, to whom he had become engaged when he was eighteen, in his hometown. In 1901 he went to Nanjing to serve as a special consultant to the high-ranking official Kuai Guangdian. In 1902 Kuai sent Bao to Shanghai to direct the Jinsuzhai yishu chu (Jinsuzhai Translation Center). In that capacity Bao edited and published Yan Fu's translations of Adam Smith's *The Wealth of Nations* (1776), John Stuart Mill's *A System of Logic* (1843), and Herbert Spencer's *The Study of Sociology* (1873). He also organized a public talk by Yan Fu in Shanghai. And he published *Renxue* (On Humanity), a controversial work advocating reform in China and attacking Chinese tradition. The manuscript had been left behind by Tan Sitong, who had been executed after the failure of the Hundred Days' Reform in 1898, and had first been published in Japan by Chinese exiles. Bao published the book in China in cooperation with the Commercial Press in Shanghai, and the 1,500 copies sold out quickly.

After the Jinsuzhai Translation Center was forced to close for financial reasons in 1904, Bao was invited by a Qing government official to be the *jiandu* (principal) of a new-style school in Qingzhou in Shandong province. During his two years in this position, for which he was paid the handsome salary of 60 yuan a month, he initiated a series of new policies, redesigned the class schedule, and promoted student self-government.

During the early years of the twentieth century Bao began the lifelong habit of visiting brothels that earned him the nickname "Tianxiao haopiao" (the licentious Tianxiao). Bao records his experiences candidly in his memoir:

> I visited brothels wherever I traveled, purely out of curiosity. Though I never went to brothels in my native town, I did so in both Shanghai and Nanjing. In Qingzhou, since I was serving as the school principal, I was concerned about my reputation and didn't take the risk. . . . After resigning from the principal's position, however, I took the chance of paying a visit to a brothel before I left Qingzhou. The girl was tall and energetic. She wore a red cotton jacket, and a pair of green pants. She had medium size feet, long braided hair with bangs on her forehead, a powdered face with rouge on her cheeks. It was a rather earthy country look. She was innocent, genuine, hospitable, outgoing, and neither coy nor pretentious. I found her quite pleasant. . . . I thought that she could make a popular courtesan in a big city, if only she could learn to dress better, wear more fashionable clothes, and learn to sing and dance.

Soon after he returned to Shanghai with a wife and daughter, Bao accepted positions at the two most significant Shanghai publications, the newspaper *Shi bao* (The Eastern Times) and the magazine *Xiaoshuo lin* (Forest of Fiction), as editor and contributing author

Cover for a post-1949 edition–probably from the 1980s–of Bao's novel Shanghai chunqiu (Annals of Shanghai), originally published in 1926 (from Tang Wenyi, Mu Dingsheng, and Ji Lei, eds., 20 shiji Zhongguo wenxue tudian, 2001; Collection of Thomas Moran)

under contract. He also taught half-time at two girls' schools and served as an assistant manager of the Jiangsu Province Educational Association. By this time he had become a celebrity in Shanghai literary circles. He was well connected with various groups of Shanghainese, such as old-style scholars (those who had passed the civil examinations), students returned from overseas, publisher-merchants, and political progressives. His experience as a new-style school principal made him a suitable candidate to write the "educational novels" that were deemed necessary at the time.

In 1909 Di Chuqing, the founder of *Shi bao*, started a magazine, *Shi bao xiaoshuo* (Novels of *The Eastern Times*), and appointed Bao and Chen Jinghan editors. Though Chen was officially the editor in chief, Bao claims in his memoir that he did most of the work because Chen was away much of the time. He initiated several editorial policies that were significant in the development of the novel in China: instead of serializing works, he published them in full in each issue; instead of publishing only novels by a small group of contracted writers, he called for contributions from the public; and to attract the readers' attention he printed pictures of famous courtesans at the beginning of each issue. The last approach seems to have been successful in increasing sales, but it invited criticism from more-serious readers and critics, especially those responsible for launching the Xin wenhua yundong (New Culture Movement) after 1915. These young radicals considered the pictures an example of the frivolity that characterized what they labeled the Mandarin Ducks and Butterflies school of writing. (Mandarin ducks and butterflies were traditional symbols of happily paired lovers.)

Meanwhile, Bao kept publishing his creative works and translations, including science-fiction novels, romance novels, philosophical novels, social novels, detective novels, comic stories, commentaries, and personal notes. They appeared mostly in literary journals such as *Xiaoshuo lin*, *Xinxin xiaoshuo* (The New New Novel), *Yueyue xiaoshuo* (Monthly Fiction), and *Nübao* (Women's News). While these works were written for leisure reading and entertainment, they are marked by pronounced patriotic sentiments, stress the need to react against foreign threats, and express concern for China's future. Bao also wrote educational novels such as the well-received *Xiner jiuxue Ji* (1909, Xiner Went to School).

A representative work of Bao's early period is his short story "Yilüma: Qiuxingge biji zhi san" (A Twist of Hemp), which was published in *Xiaoshuo shibao* (The Fiction Times) in 1909. A beautiful and talented girl is forced by her family to separate from the man she loves and marry a retarded man from a rich family. She refuses to sleep in the same bed with her husband. Soon, however, she contracts a serious illness. Her servants will not go near her for fear of catching it, but her husband cares for her attentively despite her rude treatment of him. She recovers; but by then her husband has been infected, and he dies. The woman is touched by his patient devotion and chooses to observe a widow's chastity for her dead spouse, refusing a renewed proposal from her former lover. To many critics the story reflects Bao's wavering between traditional and modern values: it begins as an attack on arranged marriage but ends up honoring the custom of widow's chastity. Bao himself regarded it as emblematic of an attempt to maintain a society built on "new institutions as well as old moral standards." Mei Lanfang adapted "Yilüma" as an opera, and it was also made into a 1927 movie, *Guaming de fuqi* (The Nominal Husband and Wife), starring the popular actress Ruan Lingyu.

Through his editorial work Bao became acquainted with several young writers who later became famous, including prominent representatives of the Mandarin Ducks and Butterflies school such as Zhou Shoujuan and Zhang Yihan. In 1910 he joined the poetry group Nan she (Southern Society), through which he met the writers Zhe Zhenchang, Yu Youren, Wang Jingwei, Chen Duxiu, Li Shutong, Hu Jichen, and Deng Qiumei.

In 1911 *Shi bao* founder Di started another magazine, *Funü shibao* (Women's Times), and appointed Bao and Chen as co-editors. Although *Funü shibao* was aimed at a female audience, male writers were the primary contributors, because the limited number of women writers at the time mainly produced poetry in the *shi* (short and lyrical) and *ci* (originally sung) forms or short essays on details of daily life. Like *Shi bao xiaoshuo, Funü shibao* carried pictures of famous beauties on its opening pages. It lasted for six years and twenty-one issues. As editor of *Funü shibao* Bao discovered two young talents, Shao Piaoping and Bi Yihong, who went on to become well-known writers.

In 1912 Bao edited *Zhonghua Minguo dashi ji* (Important Events in the Republic of China), an annotated monthly chronicle of the major events that transpired since the founding of the republic in January. That same year he compiled for the Commercial Press a four-volume extracurricular reader, *Xin shehui* (The New Society), for advanced primary-school students. The reader was supposed to provide "new knowledge" and "new thinking" to the citizens of the newly established Republic of China. In spite of Bao's experience as a teacher and principal in new-style schools, the volumes did not sell well.

In 1915, while still serving as editor of *Shi bao xiaoshuo* and *Funü shibao,* Bao started another fiction quarterly, *Xiaoshuo daguan* (Fiction Spectacle), under the sponsorship of the Shanghai Wenming Bookstore. Of a substantial size—three million Chinese *zi* (characters) in each issue—the magazine published novels with "decent," "moral," and "entertaining" themes by well-known authors such as Zhou, Zhang, Bi, Ye Chuchang, Yao Wanzhou, Chen Diexian, and Fan Yanqiao. Bao also published his own novels and translations in the magazine, including "Minghong" (1915, Letters to the Other World), which is considered a predecessor of the modern Chinese epistolary novel. The work comprises a dozen letters written in beautiful Classical Chinese by a woman to her husband, who died during the 1911 revolution that ended the Qing dynasty. Before he left home to join the revolution, he asked his wife to write to him every week. She has kept her promise even after his death, writing to him on a weekly basis about household details, their son's schoolwork, sociopolitical changes in China, and her loneliness without him, and then burning the letters.

Bao's story "Buguo" (Repentance) was published in *Xiaoshuo daguan* in 1916. Like "Yilüma," it is a sad story about love and marriage—a timely subject for young Chinese men and women caught between new and traditional values in a period of drastic changes. A student falls in love with the girl who lives next door in his poverty-stricken neighborhood but leaves her behind to pursue social and academic advancement. He becomes engaged to the brilliant and kindly daughter of his mentor, a well-known doctor. But when the young man learns that his former lover has led a miserable life and has suffered because of the pregnancy that resulted from their relationship, he is tortured by guilt. He breaks his engagement and marries his former lover, only to find that his new wife is awkward, dependent, and inadequate in every way. But there is nothing he can do. He has lost his chance at a happy marriage and a career as director of his mentor's hospital and is tormented by disappointment and guilt, especially after discovering that his erstwhile fiancée has remained unmarried after their breakup.

Xiaoshuo daguan ran for twelve issues. In 1919 Bao left *Shi bao* and *Shi bao xiaoshuo* and traveled to Beijing hoping to find either a job or a subject for a novel. He did not find a job but decided to adapt Beijing Opera star Mei Lanfang's life story as the main thread of a novel that could be read as a microcosm of contemporary China. In 1921 he finished a seven-chapter novel titled, with a pun on the last syllable of Mei's given name, *Liufangji* (1922, The Lingering Fragrance). Written in graceful style and language, *Liufangji* is considered by critics one of Bao's best works in spite of flaws such as weak characterization and a fragmented structure. The main character, Mei Lanfang, disappears from the story after the first third of the novel. In addition, the book includes factual mistakes, unwarranted generalizations, and far-fetched episodes set abroad. Finally, while Bao claimed that the novel was a comprehensive treatment of contemporary history, it is ill focused and reads like a fragmented journalistic report. Much as "Yilüma" vacillates between opposing social values, *Liufangji* seems to be caught between an ambition to produce a significant historical novel, in accord with the demands of May Fourth critics, and Bao's background as a fashioner of popular tales of ordinary life.

After the May Fourth Movement began in 1919, the novels and magazines that had been popular in the mid and late 1910s gradually lost readers. In February 1923 the leading popular literary magazine *Libailiu* (Saturday) closed because of decreasing sales. No longer able to make a living writing in the Mandarin Ducks and Butterflies style, Bao took a job in 1924 writing scripts for the Mingxing Film Company. He worked there for about four years; of the movies based on his scripts, *Kelian de guinü* (1925, The Pitiful Girl) and *Konggulan* (1925, Orchid in the Quiet Valley) are the best known. He also wrote the novel *Shanghai chunqiu* (1926, Annals of Shanghai), as well as short stories that were published in magazines such as *Banyue* (The Fortnightly); *Jiating zazhi* (Family Magazine); the *Shen bao* literary supplement, *Xiaoxian yuekan* (Entertainment Monthly); *Xiaoshuo shijie* (The World of Fiction); and *Xiaohua* (Laughter Pictorial). In addition, he founded two small literary magazines, *Xingqi* (The Week) and *Changqing* (Evergreen).

Bao's responsibilities as the breadwinner for his family gradually lightened as his children grew up. Trying to break away from his earlier role as someone who "maiwen" (sold words) for a living and concentrate on the art rather than the business of literature, he stopped writing for money and contributed to magazines only to help the editors who were his friends. He occasionally filled in as an editor by invitation; in 1935, for example, he was asked to serve as substitute editor for the literary supplement of the newspaper *Libao* while the regular editor, Zhang Henshui, was on leave.

In 1936 Bao joined his Shanghai colleagues in issuing two pronouncements: "Shanghai xinwen jizhe wei zhengqu yanlun ziyou xuanyan" (A Freedom of Speech Declaration by Shanghai Journalists) called on all journalists in Shanghai to unite in condemning Japanese imperialism in China, and "Wenyijie tongren wei tuanjie yuwu yu ziyou xuanyan" (A Declaration of Unification and Freedom of Speech by Writers and Artists) urged writers and artists of different political perspectives to join in resisting Japanese incursions. After the outbreak of the war with Japan in 1937 he wrote several stories promoting anti-Japanese sentiments; they are not considered successful as literature, because their anti-Japanese themes are presented too blatantly. In his short novel "Xiaoshuojia de shenpan" (Judgment on a Novelist), published in *Xiaoshuo yuebao* (Short Story Monthly) in 1941, an idealistic and patriotic novelist risks his life by using his writings to arouse anti-Japanese feelings in his readers and to promote left-wing political ideas. In 1946 Bao moved to Taiwan to live with his eldest son; in 1950 he moved to Hong Kong to live with his second son, remaining there until his death.

In the last twenty-five years of his life he continued to work as a freelance writer. In 1971 he published *Chuanyinglou huiyi lu*, which he had begun in 1949. It is a detailed memoir of a life spent witnessing the rise of modern print culture in Shanghai. The book was extremely well received, which inspired Bao to write the posthumously published *Chuanyinglou huiyi xubian* (1973, A Sequel to Memoirs from the Pavilion of the Bracelet Shadow). While also considered a valuable reference book, the sequel lacks the focus of the first book. The serialization of Bao's last book-length work, *Shi yi zhu xing de bainian bianqian* (Food, Clothes, Living, and Transportation in the Past One Hundred Years), was completed in *Xin wanbao* (The New Evening News) in October 1973. On 7 November *Xin wanbao* published his final article, "Dazhaxie shikao" (On the History of the *Dazha* Crab). Bao died on 24 November. *Shi yi zhu xing de bainian bianqian* was published in book form the following year.

Bao Tianxiao was one of the most important professional writers in China at the turn of the twentieth century, a time when a new world of magazines and newspapers was arising in Shanghai. During his long life he edited eight major periodicals devoted to popular fiction, as well as the literary supplements of three newspapers. Because he discovered several young talents on the Shanghai literary scene, he has long been considered one of the most important contributors to Mandarin Ducks and Butterflies literature. He has also been called the "leader of low-brow literature"; because popular literature has been accorded little regard by scholars, Bao has been largely excluded from Chinese literary history. His position in modern Chinese literature and intellectual life is marked by paradox. Bao considered himself to be inspired by the "new knowledge," but he was neither a late-Qing reform-minded "new novelist" nor "new" by the standards of the May Fourth literary agenda. His early contemporaries might have viewed him as a new-style writer because of his connoisseur's interest in everything new and foreign; later generations, however, saw him as an old-style literatus who dabbled in fashionable new knowledge but was essentially "old." To the May Fourth generation he was merely a decadent Mandarin Ducks and Butterflies writer who indulged himself with everything retrograde from traditional China, including publishing photographs of prostitutes in his fiction magazines. In actuality, Bao combines all of these aspects. While he manifestly published what was popular to make a living, he also produced historical and detective novels, the genres promoted by the "new novelists" in the late-Qing period. While leading a "decadent" lifestyle that included keeping two wives in the same household, he also joined his colleagues in issuing politically progressive statements. And while motivated mainly by the income generated by his writing, after 1937 he produced several stories that aimed to inspire patriotism during the war with Japan. Because of—rather than in spite of—these and many other contradictions in his life and work, Bao Tianxiao remains an important figure in modern Chinese literary history and deserves continued attention.

Biography:

Luan Meijian, *Tongsu wenxue zhi wang: Bao Tianxiao* (Shanghai: Shanghai shudian chuban she, 1999).

References:

A Ying, *Wanqing xiaoshuo shi* (Beijing: Renmin chubanshe, 1980);

Fan Boqun, *Libailiu de hudiemeng* (Shanghai: Renmin wenxue chubanshe, 1989);

Fan, *Zhongguo jinxiandai tongsu wenxue shi* (Jiangsu: Jiangsu jiaoyu chubanshe, 2000);

Fan, ed., *Tongsu mengzhu: Bao Tianxiao* (Taiwan: Yeqiang chubanshe, 1993);

E. Perry Link Jr., *Mandarin Ducks and Butterflies: Popular Fiction in Early Twentieth-Century Chinese Cities* (Berkeley: University of California Press, 1981);

Lu Xun, "Shanghai wenyi zhi yibi," in *Erxinji* (Shanghai: Hezhong shudian, 1932);

Tang Wenyi, Mu Dingsheng, and Ji Lei, eds., *20 shiji Zhongguo wenxue tudian* (Chengdu: Sichuan renmin chubanshe, 2001);

Wei Shaochang, *Huaqian xinji* (Shanghai: Wenyi chubanshe, 1984);

Wei, ed., *Yuanyang hudiepai yanjiu ziliao* (Shanghai: Wenyi chubanshe, 1984);

Zhang Jinglu, ed., *Zai chubanjie ershinian* (Shanghai: Shanghai zazhi gongsi, 1938);

Zhang, ed., *Zhongguo jindai chuban shiliao* (Shanghai: Zhonghua shuju, 1957).

Bing Xin

(5 October 1900 – 28 February 1999)

Lingzhen Wang
Brown University

BOOKS: *Fanxing* [Myriad Stars] (Shanghai: Shangwu yinshuguan, 1923]–includes twenty-eight poems translated by John Cayley as "Selections from *A Maze of Stars*," *Renditions*, no. 32 (1989): 108–117;

Chunshui [Spring Water] (Shanghai: Beixin shuju, 1923)–includes thirty-three poems translated by Grace M. Boynton as "Selections from *Spring Water*," *Renditions*, no. 32 (1989): 98–107;

Chaoren [Superman] (Shanghai: Shangwu yinshuguan, 1923)–title story translated by Gong Shifen as "Superman," *Renditions*, no. 32 (1989): 124–129; also includes "Jimo," translated by R. A. Roberts as "Loneliness," in *One Half of the Sky: Selections from Contemporary Women Writers of China*, edited by Roberts and Angela Knox (London: Heinemann, 1987), pp. 1–14;

Ji xiao duzhe [Letters to Young Readers] (Shanghai: Beixin shuju, 1926; enlarged, 1927);

Wang shi [Reminiscences] (Shanghai: Kaiming shudian, 1930)–includes "Meng," translated by Janet Ng as "A Dream," *Renditions*, no. 46 (1996): 103–105;

Nan gui [Return South] (Shanghai: Beixin shuju, 1931);

Gugu [The Paternal Aunt] (Shanghai: Beixin shuju, 1932)–includes "Fen," translated as "Separation," in *Genesis of a Revolution: An Anthology of Modern Chinese Short Stories*, edited and translated by Stanley R. Munro (Singapore: Heinemann Educational Books [Asia], 1979), pp. 13–30;

Xian qing [Leisurely Mood] (Shanghai: Beixin shuju, 1932; revised and enlarged edition, Guangzhou: Huacheng chubanshe, 1988);

Qu guo [Leaving My Country] (Shanghai: Beixin shuju, 1933);

Pingsui yanxian lüxing ji [A Record of a Journey along the Railway Line from Beiping to Suiyuan] (Beiping: Pingsui tielu guanliju, 1935); republished as *Bing Xin youji* [Bing Xin's Travel Sketches] (Shanghai: Beixin shuju, 1935);

Donger guniang [Miss Donger] (Shanghai: Beixin shuju, 1935)–title story translated by Jennifer Anderson and Theresa Munford as "Miss Winter," in *Chinese Women Writers: A Collection of Short Stories by Chinese Women Writers of the 1920s and 30s*, edited by Anderson and Munford (Hong Kong: China Books and Periodicals, 1985), pp. 32–39;

Guanyu nüren [About Women], as Nan Shi (Chongqing: Tiandi chubanshe, 1943; republished, with a new preface, as Bing Xin, Shanghai: Kaiming shudian, 1945; republished, with a new preface, Ningxia: Renmin chubanshe, 1980)–includes "Zhang sao," translated by Samuel Ling as "Chang Sao," in *Born of the Same Roots: Stories of Modern Chinese Women*, edited by Vivian Ling Hsu (Bloomington: Indiana University Press, 1981), pp. 56–61;

Ruhe jianshang Zhongguo wenxue [How to Appreciate Chinese Literature] (Tokyo: Tokyo da riben xiongbianhui jiangtanshe, 1949);

Xi feng [West Wind] (Kowloon: Nanhua shudian, 1950)–title story translated by Ling as "West Wind," in *Born of the Same Roots: Stories of Modern Chinese Women*, pp. 44–56;

Tao Qi de shuqi riji [Tao Qi's Summer Diary] (Shanghai: Shaonian chubanshe, 1956);

Huanxiang zaji [Notes on a Trip Home] (Shanghai: Shaonian chubanshe, 1957);

Guilai yihou [After Returning] (Beijing: Zuojia chubanshe, 1958);

Women ba chuntian chaoxingle [We Have Woken the Spring] (Tianjin: Baihua wenyi chubanshe, 1960)–includes "Wo shi zenyang xie *Fanxin* he *Chunshui* de," translated by Cayley as "How I Wrote *A Maze of Stars* and *Spring Water*," *Renditions*, no. 32 (1989): 88–91;

Xiao ju deng [The Little Orange Lamp] (Beijing: Zuojia chubanshe, 1960; revised edition, Beijing: Renmin chubanshe, 1978)–title story translated by Gong Shifen as "The Little Orange Lamp," *Renditions*, no. 32 (1989): 130–132;

Yinghua zan [Ode to Cherry Blossoms] (Tianjin: Baihua wenyi chubanshe, 1962);

Shisui xiaozha [Gleanings] (Beijing: Zuojia chubanshe, 1964);

Bing Xin (from Zhongguo dabaike quanshu zongbianji weiyuanhui, ed., Zhongguo dabaike quanshu: Zhongguo wenxue, *volume 2, 1986; Collection of Thomas Moran)*

Wanqing ji [The Golden Years Collection] (Tianjin: Baihua wenyi chubanshe, 1980);

San ji xiao duzhe [Third Batch of Letters to My Young Readers] (Beijing: Shaonian ertong chubanshe, 1981);

Ji shi zhu [Pearls from a Record of Events] (Beijing: Renmin wenxue chubanshe, 1982);

Wo de guxiang [My Hometown] (Fuzhou: Fujian renmin chubanshe, 1983);

Guanyu nanren [About Men] (Beijing: Renmin chubanshe, 1988);

Bing Xin jinzuo xuan [A Selection of Bing Xin's Recent Works] (Beijing: Zuojia chubanshe, 1991);

Bing Xin jiuxun wenxuan [Selected Works of Bing Xin in Her Nineties] (Hong Kong: Qinshiyuan chubanshe, 1992);

Bing Xin sanwen jinzuo [Recent Essays by Bing Xin] (Taiwan: Yeqiang chubanshe, 1992);

Guanyu nüren he nanren [About Women and Men] (Beijing: Renmin chubanshe, 1993).

Collections: *Bing Xin quanji* [Bing Xin's Complete Works], 3 volumes (Shanghai: Beixin shuju, 1932–1933);

Bing Xin zhuzuoji [Bing Xin's Works], 3 volumes (Shanghai: Kaiming shudian, 1943);

Bing Xin xiaoshuo sanwen xuanji [A Selection of Fiction and Essays by Bing Xin] (Beijing: Renmin chubanshe, 1954);

Ertong wenxue ji [Children's Literature] (Beijing: Renmin chubanshe, 1963);

Bing Xin zuopin xuan [A Selection of Bing Xin's Works] (Beijing: Shaonian ertong chubanshe, 1982);

Bing Xin lun chuangzuo [Bing Xin on Writing] (Shanghai: Wenyi chubanshe, 1982)—includes "Bing Xin zhuanlüe," translated by John Cayley as "Autobiographical Notes," *Renditions*, no. 32 (1989): 84–87;

Bing Xin wenji [A Collection of Bing Xin's Literature], 6 volumes (Shanghai: Wenyi chubanshe, 1982–1993);

Bing Xin sanwen xuan [A Selection of Bing Xin's Essays] (Beijing: Renmin wenxue chubanshe, 1983);

Bing Xin, edited by Zhuo Ru (Hong Kong: Sanlian shudian youxian gongsi, Renmin wenxue chuibanshe, lianhe bianji chuban, 1983);

Bing Xin xuanji [Selected Works by Bing Xin], 3 volumes (Chengdu: Sichuan renmin chubanshe, 1983–1984);

Bing Xin (Beijing: Renmin chubanshe / Hong Kong: Sanlian shudian, 1985);

Bing Xin daibiaozuo [Representative Works by Bing Xin] (Zhengzhou: Huanghe wenyi chubanshe, 1986);

Bing Xin he ertong wenxue [Bing Xin and Children's Literature] (Beijing: Shaonian ertong chubanshe, 1990);

Bing Xin sanwen xuanji [A Selection of Bing Xin's Essays] (Tianjin: Baihua chubanshe, 1992);

Qingche rensheng [A Life That Is Clear and Enlightened] (Guangzhou: Huacheng chubanshe, 1992);

Lü de ge [Song of Green] (Huhehaote: Neimenggu renmin chubanshe, 1992);

Bing Xin meiwen jingcui [The Best of Bing Xin's Elegant Prose] (Beijing: Zuojia chubanshe, 1992);

Bing Xin sanwen suibi xuanji [A Selection of Essays and Jottings by Bing Xin] (Shenyang: Shenyang chubanshe, 1993);

Bing Xin shi quanbian [The Complete Poems of Bing Xin] (Hangzhou: Zhejiang chubanshe, 1994);

Bing Xin quanji [The Complete Works of Bing Xin], 9 volumes, edited by Zhuo Ru (Fuzhou: Haixia wenyi chubanshe, 1994; revised, 1999).

Edition in English: *The Photograph,* translated by Jeff Book (Beijing: Chinese Literature Press, 1992)—includes "Year away from Home" ("Lijia de yinian"), "The Painting and the Poem" ("Hua–Shi"), "Notes from the Mountain" ("Shan zhong zaji"), "Return South" ("Nan gui"), "My Childhood" ("Wo de tongnian"), "Treasures Imperishable" ("Diubudiao de zhenbao"), "Sissy Liuyi" ("Liuyi zi"), "The First Dinner Party" ("Diyici yanhui"), "The Photograph" ("Xiangpian"), "Our Madam's Parlor" ("Women taitai de keting"), "My Landlady" ("Wo de fangdong"), "My Most Unforgettable Experience" ("Ji yijian zui nanwang de shiqing"), and "An Empty Nest" ("Kong chao").

TRANSLATIONS: *Yindu tonghua ji* [Collection of Indian Fairy Tales] (Beijing: Zhongguo qingnian chubanshe, 1955);

Rabindranath Tagore, *Jitanjiali* [Gitanjili] (Beijing: Renmin wenxue chubanshe, 1955);

Tagore, *Taige'er shixuan* [Selected Poems by Tagore], translated by Bing Xin and Shi Zhen (Beijing: Renmin chubanshe, 1958);

Tagore, *Taige'er juzuoji* [Selected plays by Tagore] (Beijing: Zhongguo xiju chubanshe, 1959).

Cover for a 1923 Beijing edition of Chunshui *(Spring Water), a collection of poems by Bing Xin published that same year in Shanghai (from Yu Runqi, ed.,* Tang Tao cang shu, *2004; Bruccoli Clark Layman Archives)*

Bing Xin was one of the best-known woman writers of twentieth-century China. She first rose to prominence between 1919 and 1922 on the strength of her *wenti xiaoshuo* (problem fiction), which describes the struggles of young intellectuals at the intersection of traditional and modern societies. The only woman poet of the May Fourth cultural movement of 1919 to 1925, Bing Xin fashioned short free-verse poems after the style of the Bengali poet Rabindranath Tagore's *Stray Birds* (1916). She was also an author of short stories and, most important, an acclaimed writer of essays. Her *Ji xiao duzhe* (1926, Letters to Young Readers) is still one of the best-loved Chinese literary works for children. In the 1920s Bing Xin's simple language and poetic diction created the *Bing Xin ti* (Bing Xin style), which attracted many imitators. After the establishment of the People's Republic of China in 1949, she devoted herself mainly to children's literature and the translation of Tagore's works; except during the period of the Cultural Revolution of 1966 to 1976, however, she continued to publish essays, memoirs, and autobiographies until the mid 1990s, leaving behind a corpus of work of great historical importance and inestimable literary value.

The significance of Bing Xin's writing lies in its insistence on the value of motherly love, the innocence and purity of childhood, and the beauty of nature. Her early representative works evince a confluence of influences from her childhood: the Christian idea of love, disseminated by the missionary school she attended; Tagore's "philosophy of love" as expressed in his poetry; and modern Western humanism, introduced to China at the turn of the twentieth century. As one of the better-known contributors to the iconoclastic May Fourth cultural movement, Bing Xin provided her readers with an idealistic solution to the social problems that were arising in a changing China: the universal power of love. Her focus on the role of the good mother and on the power of maternal love reflected the influence of a tradition, which had developed among the Chinese elite in the late imperial period, that situated the mother at the emotional center of the family. Her claims that maternal love is a universal good and that the mother-child bond is the most ideal relationship conformed, however, to the modern Western concept of love and human nature. Although the idealization of the mother had emerged in the modern nationalist writings of Liang Qichao and other Chinese male intellectuals during the late nineteenth century, Bing Xin's view of motherhood and maternal love contained personal, emotional, and religious aspects that resisted the ideological repudiation of the mother in modern Chinese literature after its turn to the Left in the late 1920s. Praised by many critics as the most talented and influential woman writer of the May Fourth Movement, Bing Xin was criticized in the late 1920s and 1930s by powerful left-wing male critics such as Mao Dun, A Ying, and He Yubo, who called her writing sentimentalist, elitist, pessimistic, and lacking in social and class consciousness. In response, Bing Xin published several stories focusing on people of the working class, but none were as influential as her earlier works.

Bing Xin was born Xie Wanying on 5 October 1900 in Fuzhou, Fujian province. Her father, Xie Baozhang, a naval officer who had fought in the Sino-Japanese War of 1894–1895, was a follower of nationalist and reformist ideas promoted by intellectuals such as Yan Fu. He raised his daughter as a son, dressing her in boy's clothing and indulging her interest in outdoor activities until she was eleven; the courage, self-confidence, and appreciation of nature this upbringing cultivated in her contributed to her success as a writer in the early 1920s. Her mother, Yang Fuci, was from a gentry family, well educated, and an avid reader of literature. She subscribed to *Xiaoshuo yuebao* (Short Story Monthly) and *Funü zazhi* (Women's Journal); the latter promoted the ideal of *liangmu xianqi* (the good mother and virtuous wife), which had arisen in late-imperial China and was revitalized in nationalist ideology in the early modern period to redefine women's domestic roles in relation to nation building: the "good mother" was held to be crucial for nurturing and raising good citizens for the new nation. Her mother taught Xie to read when she was four and later became the first reader of the drafts of her early literary works. Xie's maternal uncles Yang Zijing and Wang Xiangfeng introduced her to Chinese vernacular fiction and taught her to read classical Chinese and compose classical-style poems. A voracious reader of classical as well as popular Chinese fiction, Xie wrote her first story when she was ten.

Xie spent her childhood in Yantai on the Shandong Peninsula, where the sea made such a deep impression on her that it became one of the most important images in her writing. The family moved to Beijing in 1913, and in 1914 Xie entered the Bridgman Academy for Girls, a missionary school where she was influenced by the Christian doctrine of universal love. In 1918 she entered Peking Union College for Women, also a missionary school (it was later incorporated into Yenching [Yanjing] University). In 1919 she changed her major from medicine to literature, became absorbed in the nationalist May Fourth Movement, and, using the pen name Bing Xin, began publishing short stories and essays.

Bing Xin published five short stories in *Chen bao* (Morning Post) in 1919. The first two, "Liangge jiating" (Two Families) and "Siren du qiaocui" (Personal Grief), deal with the central issues of the May Fourth Movement: nationalism, family, the role of women, and the conflict between father and son. The first story, by comparing the different fates of two families, emphasizes the role of "good mothers and virtuous wives" in sustaining a healthy domestic space at a moment of national and social crisis; the latter, set during the nationwide antigovernment demonstrations on and after 4 May 1919, concerns the frustrations felt by college students whose political and cultural iconoclasm is undermined by their economic and emotional dependence on their authoritarian fathers.

By 1919, as a result of the introduction of Western individualism and feminism, the model of the good mother and virtuous wife was being criticized by Chinese reformers as conservative and constraining. Bing Xin was, therefore, exceptional in adhering to her personal experience and affirming the value of the "old" model. She did not believe that the only appropriate social role for a woman was that of a wife and mother, but she did think that the notion of the good mother and virtuous wife captured something of fundamental importance to emotional and spiritual life and the maintenance of human relationships.

Bing Xin discovered Tagore's poems and biography in 1919. In her essay "Yao ji Yindu zheren Taige'er" (To Indian Philosopher Tagore), published in *Yanda jikan* (Yenching [Yanjing] University Quarterly) in 1920, she describes how Tagore's belief in the harmony of the universe and the individual spirit, together with his writings on natural beauty, helped her to articulate her own philosophy of love and her views on the natural world. She felt a similar resonance when she read the Bible. In 1921 she composed some short poems in Tagore's style as a response to her Bible reading and published fourteen of them in the magazine *Shengming* (Life). The poems express her ideas about God, love, life, children, and nature. In "Wenyi congtan" (Reflections on Art and Literature), an essay published in *Xiaoshuo yuebao* in 1921, Bing Xin argues that the essence of literature is the expression of a personal truth that is formed by one's upbringing, environment, experience, and attitude toward the world. Such truth does not follow social trends nor imitate others.

Most of the protagonists of Bing Xin's early stories are young intellectuals caught up in the discrepancy between the reality of traditional Chinese society and the ideals and values of their modern Westernized education. By focusing on her characters' psychological and emotional struggles and political uncertainties, she illustrates the dilemmas that young people encountered during a period of unprecedented historical transition and implicitly questions the possibility of any political solution to those problems. According to Bing Xin, political interests can, despite good intentions, separate people and damage human relationships. In her story "Guo qi" (The National Flag), published in the literary supplement of *Chen bao* in 1921, an innocent friendship between a Chinese boy and a Japanese boy is endangered by the political hostility between their nations. Bing Xin believed that modern nationalism, represented by the flag in the story, should be discarded if it undermines and destroys the fundamental human values manifested in friendship and love.

Bing Xin's best-known short story, "Chaoren" (translated as "Superman," 1989), was published in *Xiaoshuo yuebao* in 1921 and is set during the post–May Fourth period. He Bing, a young man who has been influenced by Friedrich Nietzsche's philosophy, is determined to become a self-sufficient "superman," independent of human emotions and relationships. But when Lu'er, a twelve-year-old from a poor family who is a helper in He Bing's landlady's kitchen, moans during the night because of his injured leg, He Bing cannot help thinking of his happy childhood and his bond with his loving mother, a relationship he has tried to deny. A few days later he pays for the treatment of the boy's leg in an attempt to silence the moaning, which brings back the memory of his mother. But the boy has sparked an irreversible process that drives He Bing to exclaim, "Oh, Mother! I want sit in your arms; hold me and let me sit in your arms. Oh, Mother! We are purely tied to each other and never separated from each other." Moved by a letter in which Lu'er says that all mothers are good friends and, thus, all sons are also good friends, He Bing becomes aware of the cost of his denial of his mother; he also becomes aware of the grandeur of the universe, the value of human life, and the importance of love and sympathy. Lu'er has taught him that people are bound to one another through their mothers and should never reject one another. The change in He Bing's attitude illustrates Bing Xin's belief that the answer to problems modern young intellectuals face is to be found neither in political ideologies nor in modern Western philosophies but in universal love, which is manifested first and foremost in a mother's love.

In Bing Xin's philosophy love is a given, but it can be realized only through conscious effort and interaction. In "Ai de shixian" (Realization of Love), a poetic short story published in *Xiaoshuo yuebao* in 1921 and collected in *Chaoren* in 1923, the young poet Jingbo goes to a seaside resort to complete a long, ambitious essay with the same title as the story. In these beautiful natural surroundings, he has no difficulty in beginning his work. Before long, however, he finds that he cannot continue writing without hearing the footsteps and laughter of two children, a sister and brother, who walk past his house every day in the morning and return at dusk. When he comes to the conclusion of his essay, it is a stormy day; he is unable to write because the children, who passed by that morning, have not returned. As the weather turns worse, he goes out into the storm and searches for them in vain. When he struggles back to his house, however, he finds them sleeping in his rocking chair with beautiful smiles on their faces. He is instantly inspired, and his thoughts flow onto the paper. The story shows that love is the origin of literature and stresses the poet's role in sensing, seeking, and realizing love in his or her daily life.

Although Bing Xin's short stories center on the major social issues of the new culture movement, her style is not realistic in the sense of an objective representation of reality but tends toward the poetic and the idealistic; her stories, which use innovative language and invoke lyrical moods, were frequently described by critics as *shi xiaoshuo* (poetic fiction), and she was often referred to as the most talented young poet of the 1920s. Her training in classical Chinese poetry and the influence of Tagore and the Bible helped her produce a unique style that is manifested in all her works, regardless of genre. This fresh, delicate, and simple style, first called the "Bing Xin style" by A Ying in 1934, made

Bing Xin in 1923 (from Bing Xin, *edited by Zhuo Ru, 1983; East Asian Collection, Hillman Library, University of Pittsburgh)*

Bing Xin's writing, in Shen Congwen's words, "fly into the hearts of young people."

Bing Xin began writing about children in 1921 with "Lijia de yinian" (translated as "Year away from Home," 1992), which describes the emotions of a thirteen-year-old who has to leave his parents and older sister to go to school in another city. In "Jimo" (translated as "Loneliness," 1987) Bing Xin again demonstrates unusual sensitivity and skill in describing children's inner lives and subtle feelings: seven-year-old Xiaoxiao experiences an indescribable, wistful sadness after the unexpected departure of his younger cousin, who had visited his family with her mother and played with him. The cousin's father arrived earlier than scheduled to pick up his wife and daughter on a morning when Xiaoxiao was attending a ceremony at school, and Xiaoxiao rushed home only to find that she was gone. Bing Xin strove to stay close to the sensibility of children and write from their perspective and to them. The stories were published in *Xiaoshuo yuebao* in 1921 and 1922, respectively, and collected in *Chaoren*.

In 1922 Bing Xin began publishing short vernacular free-verse poems in *Chen bao*, initiating a fad for the genre in China. Modeled after Tagore's *Stray Birds*, the poems, collected in 1923 in her *Fanxing* (Myriad Stars) and *Chunshui* (Spring Water), express her thoughts and feelings about motherly love, childhood, youth, nature, family, poetry, and life and death. In the imagery-laden 105th poem in *Chunshui* Bing Xin unifies the mother, the self, and nature in describing her ideal state of being: "I am in my mother's arms, / Mother in the small boat, / and the small boat is in the moonlit sea." She elaborates on the childhood experiences that produced this ideal in the essay "Wang shi" (Reminiscences), which appeared in *Xiaoshuo yuebao* in late 1922.

Bing Xin graduated from Peking Union College for Women in 1923 and went to the United States to study literature at Wellesley College. Bing Xin published a series of twenty-nine essays under the heading "Ji xiao duzhe" (Letters to Young Readers) in *Chen bao* from 1923 to 1926. She received her M.A. in 1926 and was appointed professor of literature at Yenching (Yanjing) University when she returned to China in the summer. The *Chen bao* essays were collected that year as *Ji xiao duzhe;* the book was reprinted forty times in ten years and established Bing Xin as a leading writer of children's literature. In her preface to the fourth edition (1927) she states that the subject of the book is her mother, "the first and last person I love." Among the essays, most of which were written in the United States, are four long ones in which she details her longing for her mother while she is abroad. In the tenth letter she recounts that as a child she asked one day why her mother loved her; her mother replied, "No reason, just because you are my daughter!" Bing Xin says that the unconditional love expressed by her mother was such a powerful statement about the value of being a daughter that it formed the core of her sense of self, a sense that could never be detached from her mother and her mother's love.

In June 1929 Bing Xin married Wu Wenzao, a sociologist. Six months later, her mother died. "Diyici yanhui" (translated as "The First Dinner Party," 1992), a semi-autobiographical short story published in *Xin yue* (Crescent Moon) in 1929 and collected in her *Gugu* (The Paternal Aunt) in 1932, marks a change of perspective in Bing Xin's writing by touching on the tension between a daughter's devotion to her mother and a wife's commitment to her husband. A bride, Ying, is caring for her sick mother in the south of China but yields to the mother's entreaties to go to her newly built home in Beiping (as Beijing was known from 1928 to 1949) to prepare a dinner party for one of her husband's American friends before the friend leaves China. Ying panics when she finds that the interior of the house is not finished. After five days of intensive work, the house is in order but looks empty and is in need of further decoration. On the day of the party Ying goes to tidy the bedroom and is surprised to discover a packet of silver flower holders that her mother tried to give her as a wedding gift and slipped into her suitcase when she refused to accept them. The memory of her mother in the sickbed, urging her to leave for her new home and to take the flower holders, generates guilt feelings in Ying, and she condemns herself for getting married and not being able to serve her mother all her life. When one of the housekeepers comes in and suggests that there should be flowers on the dinner table, Ying realizes that the flower holders match the silverware perfectly. The mother's gift adds grace to the daughter's first dinner party and helps to make it a success. Though contented with the evening and with her new married life, Ying cannot help crying when she thinks of her loving, sick mother, who has put her daughter's happiness ahead of her own. When her husband is surprised to see her in tears, Ying conceals her conflicting feelings by telling him that she is crying for joy. Unconditional maternal love is represented in "Diyici yanhui" as a kind of self-sacrifice, in that the mother purposely removes herself as the main object of her daughter's love; the daughter's guilt is a reaction to her awareness of the mother's self-sacrifice and to the realization that leaving one's mother is unavoidable.

In the 1930s Bing Xin experimented with narrative forms and techniques and explored topics such as mother-daughter relationships, romantic love, marriage, family, and class, paying particular attention to the psychology of her characters. "San nian" (Three Years), published in *Xiaoshuo yuebao* in 1930 and collected in *Gugu*, probes the psyches of a modern young couple when the wife extends a dinner invitation to a former admirer who was also once a close friend of her husband's. "San nian" is reminiscent of "Jiu hou" (1925; translated as "Intoxicated," 1998), a story by another woman author, Ling Shuhua; Ling's work also depicts the tension between a modern married couple and a male friend of both and explores sexual desire, love, friendship, family, and morality in the new historical circumstances of the 1920s. Although sexual desire is less emphasized in Bing Xin's story, "San nian" departs from her previous work in its attention to the psychological complexity of the married couple, who are tempted to commit transgressions and restrained by social convention.

Bing Xin and Wu Wenzao had a son in 1931. After becoming a mother, Bing Xin wrote less, and the style and subject matter of her stories changed significantly. In the long essay (translated as "Return South," 1992) that forms the title piece of her collection *Nan gui* (1931) and is dedicated to her mother's soul in heaven, she details the last three weeks of her mother's life with emotional intensity. She quotes from a letter she wrote to her husband shortly after her mother's death: "the essence of life is pain, and the origin of the pain is too much love. Even so, we still drink the poison to quench our thirst, and we still search for comfort from love that generates pain. How silly and unreasonable, and how contradictory!" The death of her mother made Bing Xin realize how much pain love can produce, but it also brought an end to the guilt she felt for her happy marriage. More significantly, it changed Bing Xin's relationship to her mother from a purely loving one to a form of identification. At the end of "Nan gui" she writes, "I have received all the love [from my mother], and now it is time for me to love others. . . . Help me, remind me, and let me become a person just like my mother!" Bing Xin continued to write about her mother for the rest of her life both in fiction and nonfiction.

"Fen" (translated as "Separation," 1979), which first appeared in *Xin yue* in 1931 and was collected in *Gugu* in 1932, stands out because of its subject matter and narrative invention. "Fen" is narrated by the newborn son of rich parents. Conversing with a working-class infant in the maternity ward, he feels sorrow for the inequality in the society into which he has just been born and inadequate in comparison to his robust companion, who is proud of his class origin and anxious to go out and change society. The story won praise from the left-wing literary critic Mao Dun for its emphasis on class and social reality.

Bing Xin's pursuit of a variety of styles and themes is apparent in "Women taitai de keting" (1933; translated as "Our Madam's Parlor," 1992), first serialized in the newspaper *Dagong bao/L'Impartial* and collected in *Donger guniang* (Miss Donger) in 1935. It is a sarcastic story about a cosmopolitan woman whose "salon" in Beiping becomes a stage for the performance of various soap opera-style romantic entanglements in the 1930s. The story is narrated by an invisible, omnipresent servant who addresses the heroine as "our mistress," producing the illusion that the reader is telling stories about his or her own mistress.

"Donger guniang" (1934; translated as "Miss Winter," 1985), originally published in *Wenxue jikan* (Literature Quarterly) and collected as the title story of Bing Xin's 1935 volume, focuses on a lower-class girl whose difficult life has made her strong, boyish, and fearless. Despite her rebelliousness, she is devoted to her mother. "Donger guniang" is told in colloquial language by the mother, a servant, to her mistress, who serves as a silent interlocutor. This narrative strategy not only enhances the vividness of the Bing Xin's representation of the lives of working-class people but also avoids the class gap between narrator and characters, a problem common in writing about the masses at the time. Mao Dun grouped "Donger guniang" with "Fen," praising both for their critical realism. Both stories show admiration for the strength and courage of working-class people, indicating an effort on Bing Xin's part to incorporate contemporary left-wing ideology. At the same time, the narrative forms of the two stories reveal the interest in stylistic experiment that characterizes her fiction of the early 1930s.

Bing Xin explores the feeling of loss experienced by single career women after they reach a certain age in "Xiangpian" (translated as "The Photograph," 1992), first published in *Wenxue jikan* in 1934 and collected in *Donger guniang*. The beautiful American missionary teacher, Miss Shi, devoted her youth to teaching in China, ignoring her need for love and family. She adopts a Chinese girl, Shuzhen, and takes her to the United States, where Shuzhen falls in love with a young Chinese man. One day Shuzhen shows her mother some photographs taken at a picnic. Miss Shi, by then in her fifties, is struck by Shuzhen's youth and charm in one of the pictures, and she bursts into tears as she also sees in the photograph the China she remembers and the faces of two men she met there: an American who loved her and a Chinese man she liked. "Xi feng" (translated as "West Wind," 1981), also published in *Wenxue jikan* in 1936 and collected as the title story of a 1950 volume, is a sentimental account of a middle-aged woman who, having chosen career over marriage more than ten years previously, unexpectedly encounters her former boyfriend, now happily married, during a trip to Shanghai and finds herself regretting her choice.

Bing Xin and Wu Wenzao had a second son in 1935. In 1936 Bing Xin traveled to Japan, the United States, the Soviet Union, and western Europe; during the trip she visited Virginia Woolf in England. She returned to Beiping in June 1937 and in November gave birth to her last child, a daughter. War with Japan broke out in 1937. Bing Xin and her family moved to Kunming in Yunnan province in 1938 and to Chongqing in Sichuan province, the Chinese capital during the war, in 1940.

Bing Xin had written about her childhood as early as 1922, in "Wang shi"; she did not write another autobiographical work until 1942, when she published in *Funü xinyun* (Women's New Movement) "Wo de tongnian" (translated as "My Childhood," 1992). It is collected in her *Wanqing ji* (1980, The Golden Years Collection). Also in 1942 she published in Wentan (Literary World) the essay "Guanyu zizhuan" (About Autobiography), in which she claims that she never felt qualified to write an autobiography—despite the fact that she always wrote autobiographical fiction and essays. She says that Woolf had urged her to write an autobiography when the two women met in 1936; later, she says, she was further encouraged by friends who viewed autobiography as an important means of illustrating the relationships between heredity and environment and between individual ideal and achievement. She also reasoned, she writes, that autobiography can provide later generations with a more vivid and detailed historical record. She emphasizes that the self in an autobiography does not occupy the center but functions only as the thread that connects historical events. This modesty reflects a cultural convention that mostly excluded women from writing autobiographies. Bing Xin did not write any further autobiographical works until the early post–Mao Zedong era.

During the war Bing Xin did not write much, but her *Guanyu nüren* (About Women), a collection of fourteen short stories first serialized in *Xingqi pinglun* (Weekly Criticism), became a best-seller when it was published in Chongqing in 1943. Writing under the pen name Nan Shi (Mr. Man), Bing Xin uses a male narrator to tell the stories of various women he knows: his mother, nanny, sisters-in-law, teacher, classmates, student, neighbor, friends' mothers and wives, landlady, and servant. By quoting a long paragraph from Cao Xueqin's *Honglou meng* (1791; translated as *Hung Lou Meng; or, The Dream of the Red Chamber*, 1892–1893) as a preface to her stories Bing Xin indicates that her narrator's perspective is similar to that of the male narrator of that classic late-imperial novel, who is not only sympathetic to women's fate in history but also highly praises their virtues and talents. Most of the stories are about women Bing Xin knew personally, the most obvious example being "Wo de muqin" (My Mother). She creates a vivid gallery of portraits of women of various classes, regions, and ages.

Bing Xin, Wu Wenzao, and their children returned to Beiping in July 1946. In November they went to Kyoto, Japan, where Bing Xin taught Chinese literature and published essays in Japanese journals and newspapers. In 1952 they returned to Beijing, where Bing Xin held a variety of official positions in the People's Republic of China. Between 1949, when the People's Republic was established, and 1965 she published a few reprints of her earlier works, but her major literary activities were writing children's literature, translating, and composing essays. Her "Xiao ju deng" (translated as "The Little Orange Lamp," 1989), which was published in *Zhungguo shaonianbao* (Chinese Juvenile Newspaper) in 1957 and became the title piece of a 1960 collection, is regarded as one of the best children's stories of the time. In a pre-1949 Chongqing suburb an eight- or nine-year-old girl cares for her sick mother while waiting for the return of her father, a carpenter, who has been arrested on suspicion of Communist activity. The narrator meets the girl at a public telephone and later visits her home, bringing some oranges as a gift. When the narrator leaves in the evening, the girl skillfully makes a lamp for the narrator (whose sex is never specified in the story) to carry in the dark by putting a candle in an orange peel tied to a bamboo stick. The story places Bing Xin's interest in children and love in a political context: hope for the new China and its people is expressed through the character of the girl, who is not only caring, loving, and considerate but also strong, courageous, and optimistic; the last quality is symbolized by the little orange lamp illuminating the darkness. Bing Xin also wrote another twenty-one letters to young readers from 1958 to 1960 that were published in *Renmin ribao* (People's Daily) and *Ertong shidai* (Children's Times). She translated many works of South Asian literature from English into Chinese, especially Tagore's poems, stories, plays, and memoirs. Her essays follow the demands of the dominant political ideology, praising socialist society, working-class people, and the new nation. They are collected in *Guilai yihou* (1958, After Returning), *Yinghua zan* (1962, Ode to Cherry Blossoms), and *Shisui xiaozha* (1964, Gleanings).

In January 1970, during the Cultural Revolution, Bing Xin was sent to a Wu qi ganbu xuexiao (cadre school) in Hubei Province to "be reformed"; in June she was moved to another school in the same province, where she remained with her husband until August 1971. Meanwhile, her children were scattered across China. Bing Xin and her husband returned to Beijing in August 1971; she resumed writing in 1978 and enjoyed the second-most-productive period of her career, publishing children's literature, fiction, memoirs, poetry, and literary criticism through the mid 1990s. From 1978 to 1980 she published another series of letters to young readers in *Ertong shidai;* they were collected in 1981 as *San ji xiao duzhe* (Third Batch of Letters to My Young Readers). She also wrote many essays on Chinese children's literature and on her experience in writing children's works. In 1984 she published "Mingzi he Mizi" (Mingzi and Mizi), a short story about a cat, a boy, and his grandmother, in *Renmin ribao*. From 1979 to 1987 she wrote seven autobiographical pieces covering the period from her childhood to the first three years after she returned from the United States in 1926; they were published in *Fujian wenyi* (Fujian Literature and Art), *Shouhuo* (Harvest), *Renmin ribao,* and *Shaonia zhi you* (Friend of Youth). Written in a succinct and documentary-like style, they include many references to significant historical events.

Most of Bing Xin's short stories of the late 1970s and 1980s center on intellectuals in their sixties or seventies who have survived the turbulent periods in twentieth-century China but are facing various new problems in their lives. In "Kong chao" (translated as "Empty Nest," 1992), published in *Beifang wenxue* (Northern Literature) and collected in *Wanqing ji*, a professor who left China when the Communist Party took power returns in the early post-Mao period to visit one of his former college classmates. The story creates a sentimental retrospective mood similar to that of "Xi feng" as the professor

Cover for a 1939 edition of Fanxing *(Myriad Stars), a collection of poems first published in 1923, modeled after the Bengali poet Rabindranath Tagore's 1916 volume* Stray Birds *(Wason Collection on East Asia–China, Kroch Asia Library, Cornell University)*

reviews his years of struggle to survive financially in the United States and finds his life quite meaningless: his wife is dead; his son has married and left home; and his research has deviated from his true interests. In contrast, the former classmate's "nest is full" with three generations of his family living together and a career that is developing quickly after the Cultural Revolution.

"Ganshe" (Interference), the last short story written by Bing Xin, was published in *Renmin wenxue* (People's Literature) in 1988. It addresses one of the most contested issues of the 1980s in China: the remarriage of senior citizens. Beijing professor Yang Qian, who has lived a lonely life since the death of his wife, meets another widowed professor, Liu Qing, at a conference in Shanghai. They fall in love and decide to marry. Yang Qian's daughter, who has moved into his spacious apartment to take care of him, is concerned about what their friends and neighbors will think about her father's remarriage and also about where she will live afterward. She invokes the memory of her late mother to dissuade him from remarrying. The story ends with a dialogue between the two professors in which Yang Qian says, "I am afraid we will be like two railway tracks, never coming together."

From 1985 to 1992 Bing Xin published in *Zhongguo zuojia* (Chinese Writers) a series of twelve pieces under the general title "Guanyu nanren" (About Men); the first six were collected in a volume of that title in 1988. Unlike those in the similarly titled *Guanyu nüren*, these works are not fiction but memoirs of men Bing Xin had known, including other writers and her grandfather, father, three brothers, cousins, uncle, husband, teachers, and friends. Despite their difference in genre, the series of works about women and men were published together as *Guanyu nüren he nanren* (About Women and Men) in 1993. Bing Xin died on 28 February 1999.

As indicated by the title of one of her essays, "Shengming cong bashisui kaishi" (Life Begins at Eighty), published in *Ertong shidai* in 1980 and included as the preface to *San ji xiao duzhe*, the final period of Bing Xin's life was filled with activity. A woman writer who had lived through the twentieth century and produced literary works in almost every decade of it, Bing Xin is more than a representative of May Fourth literature. Her works raise important questions regarding the relationship between tradition and modernity, personal experience and public literary production, foreign culture and native heritage, gender and cultural politics, and individual sentiment and political ideology in twentieth-century China.

Bibliographies:

"Bing Xin zhuyi nianbiao," "Bing Xin zhuyi mulu," and "Bing Xin yanjiu ziliao mulu suoyin," in *Bing Xin yanjiu ziliao*, edited by Fan Boqun (Beijing: Beijing chubanshe, 1984), pp. 419–494;

"Bing Xin shengping, zhuzuo nianbiao jianbian," in *Bing Xin quanji*, revised edition, 9 volumes, edited by Zhuo Ru (Fuzhou: Haixia wenyi chubanshe, 1999), IX: 3–32.

Biographies:

Fan Boqun and Zeng Huapeng, *Bing Xin pingzhuan* (Beijing: Renmin chubanshe, 1983);

Xiao Feng, *Bing Xin zhuan* (Beijing: Shiyue chubanshe, 1987);

Zhou Ming, *Jing Bing Xin* (Changsha: Hunan renmin chubanshe, 1987);

Zhuo Ru, *Bing Xin zhuan* (Shanghai: Wenyi chubanshe, 1990).

References:

Colena M. Anderson, "A Study of Two Modern Chinese Women: Ping Hsin and Ting Ling," dissertation, Claremont Graduate School and University Center of Pomona, 1954;

Gloria Bien, "Images of Women in Ping Hsin's Fiction," in *Women Writers of Twentieth-Century China*, edited by Angela Jung Palandri (Eugene: Asian Studies Publications, University of Oregon, 1982), pp. 19–40;

Marcela Bouskova, "On the Origin of Modern Chinese Prosody: An Analysis of the Prosodic Components in the Works of Ping Hsin," *Archiv Orientalni*, 32, no. 5 (1946): 619–643;

Bouskova, "The Stories of Ping Hsin," in *Studies in Modern Chinese Literature*, edited by Jaroslav Prusek (Berlin: Akademie-Verlag, 1964), pp. 114–129;

Rey Chow, "Loving Women: Masochism, Fantasy, and the Idealization of the Mother," in her *Women and Chinese Modernity: The Politics of Reading between West and East* (Minneapolis & Oxford: University of Minnesota Press, 1991), pp. 121–170;

Fan Boqun, ed., *Bing Xin yanjiu ziliao* (Beijing: Beijing chubanshe, 1984);

C. T. Hsia, "The Literary Association (Yeh Shao-chün, Ping Hsin and Ling Shu-hua, Lo Hua-sheng)," in his *A History of Modern Chinese Fiction*, second edition (New Haven: Yale University Press, 1971), pp. 55–92;

Wendy Larson, "Female Subjectivity and Gender Relations: The Early Stories of Lu Yin and Bing Xin," in *Politics, Ideology, and Literary Discourse in Modern China: Theoretical Interventions and Cultural Critique*, edited by Tang Xiaobing and Liu Kang (Durham, N.C.: Duke University Press, 1993), pp. 278–299;

Li Xitong, ed., *Bing Xin lun* (Shanghai: Beixin shuju, 1932);

Sally Taylor Lieberman, "The Idealized Mother and the Politics of Personhood," in her *The Mother and Narrative Politics in Modern China* (Charlottesville & London: University Press of Virginia, 1998), pp. 19–50;

Lu Wencai and Zhang Jie, *Zhongguo xiandai nü zuojia lun* (Jinan: Shandong wenyi chubanshe, 1988);

Mao Dun, "Bing Xin lun," in his *Mao Dun lun chuangzuo*, edited by Ye Ziming (Shanghai: Shanghai wenyi chubanshe, 1980), pp. 184–204;

Yu Runqi, ed., *Tang Tao cang shu* (Beijing: Beijing chubanshe, 2004), p. 40;

Zhongguo dabaike quanshu, ed., *Zhongguo wenxue*, volume 2 (Beijing & Shanghai: Zhongguo dabaike quanshu chubanshe, 1986).

Cheng Xiaoqing

(2 August 1893 – 12 October 1976)

Timothy C. Wong
Arizona State University

SELECTED BOOKS: *Wodao ji* [The Dagger] (Shanghai: Shangwu yinshuguan, 1920);

Jiangnan Yan [South-China Swallow] (Shanghai: Huating shuju, 1921);

Chuangwai ren [The Man outside the Window] (Shanghai: Dadong shuju, 1923);

Tiegui shang [On the Tracks] (Shanghai: Dadong shuju, 1923);

Wu fu chuan [The Five Blessings Boat] (Shanghai: Dadong shuju, 1923);

Dongfang Fu'ermosi tan'an [The Cases of the Holmes of the East] (Shanghai: Dadong shuju, 1926);

Yulan hua [Magnolia Blossoms] (Shanghai: Shehui xinwen she, 1928);

Huo Sang tan'an waiji [The Other Cases of Huo Sang], 6 volumes, (Shanghai: Dazhong shuju, 1932);

Huo Sang tan'an huikan [The Collected Cases of Huo Sang], 2 volumes (Shanghai: Wenhua meishu tushu gongsi, 1933);

Zhu xiangquan [The Pearl Necklace], Huo Sang tan'an xiuzhen congkan [The Cases of Huo Sang: Pocket Edition Series], no. 1 (Shanghai: Shijie shuju, 1942?);

Huangpu Jiang zhong [On the Huangpu River], Huo Sang tan'an xiuzhen congkan, no. 2 (Shanghai: Shijie shuju, 1942);

Bashisi [Eighty-four], Huo Sang tan'an xiuzhen congkan, no. 3 (Shanghai: Shijie shuju, 1942?–1944?);

Lun xia xue [The Blood on the Tracks], Huo Sang tan'an xiuzhen congkan, no. 4 (Shanghai: Shijie shuju, 1942?–1944?);

Guomian dao [The Cotton-Wrapped Sword], Huo Sang tan'an xiuzhen congkan, no. 5 (Shanghai: Shijie shuju, 1942?–1944?);

Kongbu de huo ju [The Scary Play], Huo Sang tan'an xiuzhen congkan, no. 6 (Shanghai: Shijie shuju, 1942?–1944?);

Wuhou de guisu [After the Ball], Huo Sang tan'an xiuzhen congkan, no. 7 (Shanghai: Shijie shuju, 1942?–1944?); republished as *Yu ye qiang sheng* [Gunfire on a Rainy Night];

Cheng Xiaoqing (from Tang Wenyi, Mu Dingsheng, and Ji Lei, eds., 20 shiji Zhongguo wenxue tudian, 2001; Collection of Thomas Moran)

Baiyi guai [The Ghost in White], Huo Sang tan'an xiuzhen congkan, no. 8 (Shanghai: Shijie shuju, 1942?–1944?);

Cuiming fu [The Deadly Spell], Huo Sang tan'an xiuzhen congkan, no. 9 (Shanghai: Shijie shuju, 1942?–1944?);

Maodun quan [The Circle of Contradiction], Huo Sang tan'an xiuzhen congkan, no. 10 (Shanghai: Shijie shuju, 1942?–1944?);

Zi xinjian [The Note in Purple], Huo Sang tan'an xiuzhen congkan, no. 11 (Shanghai: Shijie shuju, 1944);

Moku shuang hua [Twin Beauties in the Devil's Den], Huo Sang tan'an xiuzhen congkan, no. 12 (Shanghai: Shijie shuju, 1944);

Liangli zhu [Two Pearls], Huo Sang tan'an xiuzhen congkan, no. 13 (Shanghai: Shijie shuju, 1944);

Huiyi ren [The Man in Gray], Huo Sang tan'an xiuzhen congkan, no. 14 (Shanghai: Shijie shuju, 1944);

Yeban husheng [The Cry at Midnight], Huo Sang tan'an xiuzhen congkan, no. 15 (Shanghai: Shijie shuju, 1944);

Shuang ren bi xue [Frosty Blade, Martyr's Blood], Huo Sang tan'an xiuzhen congkan, no. 16 (Shanghai: Shijie shuju, 1944);

Xinhun jie [The Postnuptial Disaster], Huo Sang tan'an xiuzhen congkan, no. 17 (Shanghai: Shijie shuju, 1944);

Nan xiong nan di [Refugee Brothers], Huo Sang tan'an xiuzhen congkan, no. 18 (Shanghai: Shijie shuju, 1944);

Jiangnan Yan [South-China Swallow], Huo Sang tan'an xiuzhen congkan, no. 19 (Shanghai: Shijie shuju, 1944);

Huo shi [Living Corpse], Huo Sang tan'an xiuzhen congkan, no. 20 (Shanghai: Shijie shuju, 1944?-1946?);

Anzhong an [The Case within a Case], Huo Sang tan'an xiuzhen congkan, no. 21 (Shanghai: Shijie shuju, 1944?-1946?);

Qingchun zhi huo [The Fire of Youth], Huo Sang tan'an xiuzhen congkan, no. 22 (Shanghai: Shijie shuju, 1944?-1946?);

Wufu dang [The Five Blessings Gang], Huo Sang tan'an xiuzhen congkan, no. 23 (Shanghai: Shijie shuju, 1944?-1946?);

Wu gong mo ying [Ghostly Shadows in the Dance Palace], Huo Sang tan'an xiuzhen congkan, no. 24 (Shanghai: Shijie shuju, 1944?-1946?);

Huqiu nü [The Woman in Fox Furs], Huo Sang tan'an xiuzhen congkan, no. 25 (Shanghai: Shijie shuju, 1944?-1946?);

Duanzhi tuan [The Finger Choppers], Huo Sang tan'an xiuzhen congkan, no. 26 (Shanghai: Shijie shuju, 1944?-1946?);

Zhanni hua [The Mud-Splattered Flower], Huo Sang tan'an xiuzhen congkan, no. 27 (Shanghai: Shijie shuju, 1944?-1946?);

Tao fan [Escaped Convict], Huo Sang tan'an xiuzhen congkan, no. 28 (Shanghai: Shijie shuju, 1944?-1946?);

Xue shouyin [The Bloody Handprint], Huo Sang tan'an xiuzhen congkan, no. 29 (Shanghai: Shijie shuju, 1944?-1946?);

Hei dilao [Dark Dungeon], Huo Sang tan'an xiuzhen congkan, no. 30 (Shanghai: Shijie shuju, 1944?-1946?);

Ta weishenme bei sha [Why Was She Murdered?] (Shanghai: Shanghai wenhua chubanshe, 1956);

Dashucun xuean [A Bloody Case in Big Tree Village] (Shanghai: Shanghai wenhua chubanshe, 1956);

Sheng si guantou [A Matter of Life and Death] (Nanjing: Jiangsu renmin chubanshe, 1957);

Cheng Xiaoqing wenji: Huo Sang tan'an xuan [The Collected Writings of Cheng Xiaoqing: Selected Cases of Huo Sang], 4 volumes, edited by Zhongguo zuojia xiehui Jiangsu fenhui [the Jiangsu branch of the Chinese Writers' Association] (Nanjing: Zhongguo wenlian chuban gongsi, 1986)—includes in volume 4, "Bieshu zhi guai," translated as "The Ghost in the Villa," in *Stories for Saturday: Twentieth-Century Chinese Popular Fiction*, translated by Timothy C. Wong (Honolulu: University of Hawai'i Press, 2003), pp. 175-189;

Zhongguo zhentan xiaoshuo zongjiang–Cheng Xiaoqing [The Grand Master of Chinese Detective Fiction–Cheng Xiaoqing], edited by Fan (Nanjing: Nanjing chubanshe, 1994).

Collections: *Jianlu shici yigao* [Poetry from the Cocoon Cottage] (New York: Lianhe yinshu gongsi, 1982);

Huo Sang tan'an ji [Collected Cases of Huo Sang], 13 volumes (Beijing: Qunzhong chubanshe, 1986-1988);

Huqiu nu: Huo Sang tan'an ji [The Woman in Fox Furs: Collected Cases of Huo Sang] (Beijing: Qunzhong chubanshe, 1997).

Edition in English: *Sherlock in Shanghai: Stories of Crime and Detection by Cheng Xiaoqing*, edited and translated by Timothy C. Wong (Honolulu: University of Hawai'i Press, 2006).

TRANSLATIONS: S. S. Van Dine (Willard Huntington Wright), ed., *Shijie mingjia zhentan xiaoshuo ji* [A Collection of Stories by the World's Great Writers of Detective Fiction] (Shanghai: Dadong shuju, 1931);

Van Dine, *Shenmi zhi quan* [Kennel Murder Case] (Shanghai: Shijie shuju, 1934);

E. Bramah and others, *Gu zhentan* [The Blind Detective] (Shanghai: Dadong shuju, 1948);

Edgar Allan Poe and others, *Maige Lu de xiong an* [The Murders in the Rue Morgue] (Shanghai: Dadong shuju, 1948).

OTHER: "Tan zhentan xiaoshuo" [Discussing Detective Fiction], in *Yuanyang hudie pai wenxue ziliao* [Materials on Mandarin Ducks and Butterflies Literature], volume 1, edited by Rui Heshi and others (Fuzhou: Fujian renmin chubanshe, 1984), pp. 61–67;

"Zhuanshi xiangchuan" [The Diamond Necklace], in *Yuanyuan hudie–libailiu pai zuopin xuan* [Selected Works from the Mandarin Ducks and Butterfly–*Saturday* School], edited by Fan Boqun (Beijing: Renmin wenxue chubanshe, 1991), pp. 282–325;

"Ji Yun Tieqiao xiansheng" [In Memory of Mr. Yun Tieqiao], in *Yuanyang hudie pai sanwen daxi, 1909–1949: Huozai weixiaozhong* [Compendium of Writings on the Mandarin Ducks and Butterflies School, 1909–1999: Living among Smiles], edited by Yuan Jin (Shanghai: Dongfang chuban zhongxin, 1997), pp. 140–141;

"Huahou qu" [The Floral Melody], "Siji ren" [The Chauffeur], and "Shishang ming" [The Name Carved in Stone], in *Zhentan juan* [Volume on Detective Fiction] of *Qingmo-minchu xiaoshuo shuxi* [Collection of Late Qing and Early Republican Fiction], edited by Yu Runqi (Beijing: Zhongguo wenlian chubanshe, 1997), pp. 346–363, 368–376, 471–486;

"Zhentan xiaoshuo yu '?'" [Detective Fiction and "?"], in *Yuanyang hudie pai sanwen daxi, 1909–1949: Yihai tan you* [Compendium of Writings on the Mandarin Ducks and Butterflies School, 1909–1949: Exploring the Depths of the Sea of Art], edited by Yuan Jin (Shanghai: Dongfang chuban zhongxin, 1997), pp. 221–223.

SELECTED PERIODICAL PUBLICATIONS–UNCOLLECTED: "Xiaye de Canju" [One Summer Night], *Hong meigui*, 3, no. 7 (1927): 1–13;

"Wuchang zhong," [At the Ball], *Hong meigui*, 6, no. 1 (1930): 1–16.

Among twentieth-century writers of Chinese fiction Cheng Xiaoqing equals or surpasses many of his better-known contemporaries in talent, seriousness of effort and purpose, self-awareness, and popularity. Cheng, however, wrote mostly during the first half of the century, a time of upheaval in Chinese history, politics, and culture. Consequently, he has not been given the critical attention he might have received had he plied his craft in a different time and place. From the start he was classified as a writer of the "Mandarin Ducks and Butterflies School," an appellation first applied to maudlin and politically pointless love stories, or the "Saturday School," a name for the type of entertainment fiction made popular by the magazine *Liubailiu* (Saturday). According to traditionalists, Cheng's stories were suitable reading only "chayu jiuhou" (after tea and wine), not for "deng daya zhi tang" (entering the halls of grand elegance). If Cheng's novellas and stories evince any didactic concern, it is to demonstrate the "scientific" validity of the rigorous intellectual examination of particulars, not to point out and condemn China's social ills in the manner of mainstream realist fiction of the May Fourth period.

Study of Cheng's writings yields, partly by contrasting it with canonical May Fourth literature, a better understanding of the Chinese literary scene during the 1920s and 1930s–the period when he was most productive–than can be gained by consideration of May Fourth literature alone. Like his revered contemporary Lu Xun, Cheng wanted to use his fiction to better his society; but whereas Lu Xun's stories point out what is wrong with the nation, Cheng wrote his works at least partly to show his readers how to improve themselves individually. Like all writers of his generation, he was influenced by Liang Qichao, the most intellectually prominent of the leaders of the Hundred Days' Reform of 1898. In "Lun xiaoshuo yu qunzhi zhi guanxi" (1902; translated as "On the Relationship between Fiction and the Government of the People," 1996) Liang urged writers to "renovate" their fiction so as to renovate the Chinese people by making progressive use of the ability of fiction "to surprise, to startle, to make us feel sad, and to move us." Liang was not concerned that the use of fiction for social reform might threaten its traditional appeal, and Cheng also rejected the notion that didacticism can detract from the ability of fiction to captivate the reader. In "Tan zhentan xiaoshuo" (Discussing Detective Fiction), first published in the magazine *Hong meigui* (Red Roses) on 11 and 21 May 1929, Cheng maintains that detective fiction is a means of stimulating the reader's curiosity and convincing him or her of the superiority of modern science; in "Zhentan xiaoshuode duo fangmian" (The Many Aspects of Detective Fiction), included in *Huo Sang tan'an huikan* (1933, The Collected Cases of Huo Sang), he calls his own popular tales of crime detection "textbooks in disguise," written to educate readers to the advantages of careful observation and rigorous reasoning. But because he held that fiction could entertain in order to be effective, Cheng remained a "Butterfly-Saturday" writer: that is, one who was read avidly but not taken seriously. At a time when writers such as Lu Xun were seeking to wake readers up to harsh national realities, Cheng was seen as wanting no more than to follow the traditional practice of providing them with respite from their daily cares. Moreover, he adapted his best-known central characters and plot devices from the Sherlock Holmes stories of Sir Arthur Conan Doyle. As a consequence,

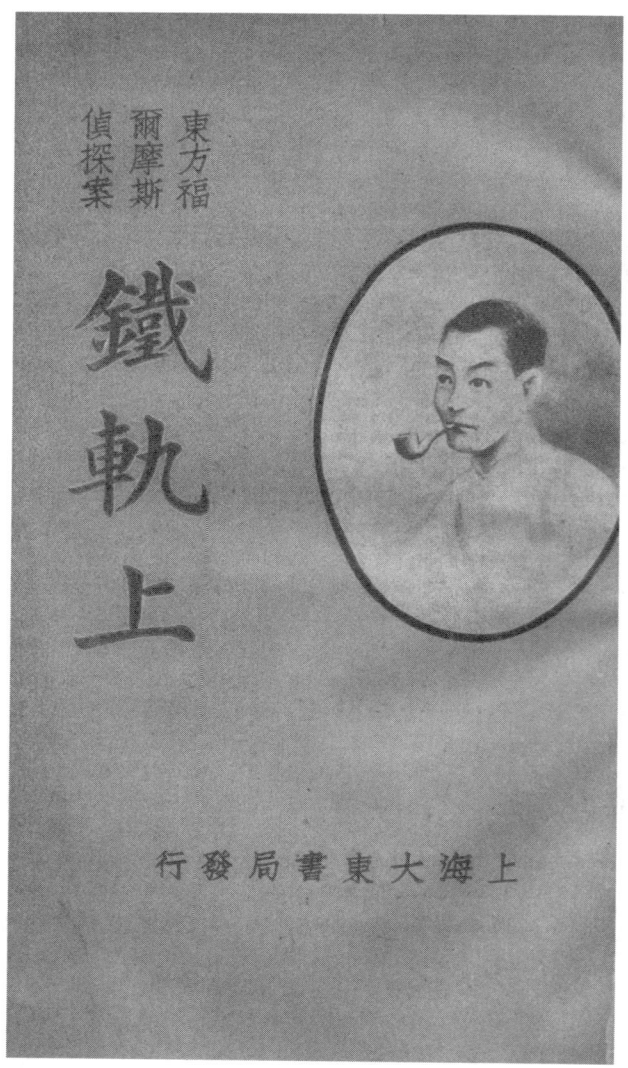 

Cover for and illustrated opening page of Cheng Xiaoqing's novella Tiegui shang (1923, On the Tracks), featuring his detective character Huo Sang (Wason Collection on East Asia–China, Kroch Asia Library, Cornell University)

his place in the history of Chinese literature has been undermined both by the long-standing Chinese disrespect for fiction and, in the modern era, by the premium placed on originality.

A series of events that shaped China's modern transformation occurred during the early years of Cheng's life: the Sino-Japanese War of 1894–1895, when he was two; the Hundred Days' Reform of 1898, when he was five; the fall of the Dynasty in 1911, when he was eighteen; and the May Fourth Movement of 1919, which set off sweeping cultural changes throughout the country, when he was twenty-five. These events spawned a new wave of socially engaged fiction in the vernacular language. The hybrid character of Cheng's fiction—its seamless blending of Chi-

nese and Western and of traditional and modern—was a product of the hybrid urban culture Leo Ou-fan Lee has called "Shanghai Modern." As the country's leading center of publication, Shanghai was the major venue for the production and consumption of both the new vernacular fiction and the more traditional Butterfly-Saturday fiction, which, as E. Perry Link Jr. points out, continued to provide comfort to an increasingly literate urban populace caught in the throes of swift economic and social change.

Cheng was born Cheng Qingxin on 2 August 1893 in the old Nanshi (Southern City) district of Shanghai. His father, Cheng Wenzhi, worked in a fabric store and sold newspapers; his mother's surname was Chen. The parents could not afford to raise Cheng's brother, Jinghai, who was born in 1897; they gave him to their neighbors to bring up as their own. A sister, Yinbao, was born in 1901. The father died in 1903, leaving the family in straitened circumstances, but Cheng managed to remain in school for another five years.

The first translation of a Sherlock Holmes story had been published in Liang's Shanghai newspaper *Shiwu bao* (The China Progress) in 1896, and subsequent translations of other Western detective stories appeared in such popular Shanghai publications as *Xiaoshuo lin* (The Forest of Fiction). Cheng's biographer Wei Shouzhong reports that Cheng read his first Sherlock Holmes story when was twelve. His first job after leaving school was playing clarinet in a Western-style band; the band soon broke up, and he became an apprentice in a shop that sold and repaired clocks and watches. A fellow employee owned many books; Cheng regularly borrowed them, taking notes on everything that piqued his interest. Between 1902 and 1910 he wrote short stories but had limited success in getting them published; these early stories, written in Classical Chinese, are no longer available, but he revised and rewrote some of them in the vernacular years later. Around 1910 he began taking English-language classes at the Shanghai YMCA.

Cheng began using the pen name Cheng Xiaoqing in 1911. That year he submitted a love story to *Xiaoshuo yuebao* (Short Story Monthly), a Butterfly-Saturday publication founded the year before. It was rejected, but the editor, Yun Tieqiao, advised Cheng to develop his talent by reading and reflecting on classical texts. Cheng's first success as a writer came when he won a competition held in 1914 by the fiction supplement *Kuaihuo lin* (Forest of Happiness) of *Xinwen bao* (The News), one of Shanghai's two leading commercial newspapers. His story, "Dengguang renying" (The Shadow in the Lamplight), which is no longer extant, featured a Holmes-like detective named Huo Sen; the name was changed to Huo Sang when the story was published, probably because of a typesetter's error. Cheng was not bothered by the mistake and continued to use the new name. He claims in "Zhentan xiaoshuode duo fangmian" that he merely wanted his protagonist's name to be of two syllables, rather than the more common three, because he was concerned about meeting the word limit for submissions to the contest; he also thought, he writes, that a two-syllable name better suited "a new kind of Chinese detective, one worth looking up to, who possesses scientific thinking and attitude, who values reason and truth."

In 1915 Cheng married Huang Hanzhang, the older sister of Huang Shanmin, who edited the Butterfly-Saturday magazine *Xiaoshuo hai* (The Ocean of Fiction), and took a job teaching Shanghainese to foreigners at the high school attached to Dongwu University (later Suzhou University) in Suzhou, a cultural mecca near Shanghai. He improved his English by exchanging lessons with an American teacher. In 1916 he joined Zhou Shoujuan and others in rendering Doyle's Sherlock Holmes stories into Classical Chinese; the collection, *Fuermosi tan'an quanji* (The Complete Cases of Sherlock Holmes), was reprinted more than twenty times. The translations stimulated imitations from native writers, including Cheng himself; three of his early detective stories, written in Classical Chinese and not featuring Huo Sang, can be found in *Zhentan juan* (1997, Volume on Detective Fiction), edited by Yu Runqi as part of a collection of late-Qing and early Republican fiction. In 1917 a friend took him to a Methodist church near the high school, and he converted. Cheng and his wife had a son, Yude, in 1918.

In 1919 Cheng published the highly successful "Jiangnan Yan" (South-China Swallow), which features the Sherlock Holmes–like detective Huo Sang and is narrated by Huo Sang's friend, the Dr. John H. Watson–like Bao Lang. Written in Classical Chinese, it established Cheng as the Chinese Doyle and Huo Sang as the Sherlock Holmes of the East. Cheng and his wife had a daughter, Yuzhen, in 1921.

By the time "Jiangnan Yan" was published, modern Western-style detective fiction was highly popular in China. Cheng writes in "Zhentan xiaoshuode duo fangmian" that many talented Chinese writers were producing stories in the genre during the late 1910s, but "regrettably, so many authors proved to be following a transient trend, soon directing their energies in a different direction." Aside from Cheng, the most notable of such writers was Sun Liaohong, who published a series of stories in the 1920s and 1930s about the "antidetective" Lu Ping, a master thief adapted from the French author Maurice Leblanc's popular Arsène Lupin. In 1923 Sun staged a duel between Huo Sang and Lu Ping—as Jeffrey C. Kinkley calls it, "'the Oriental Holmes' versus 'the Oriental Lupin'"—in the story "Kueileiju" (Puppet Show).

The popularity of Cheng's new kind of detective stimulated speculation that the character's name was taken from a Chinese transliteration of the last name of the American writer Nathaniel Hawthorne and that Huo Sang's initials were intended to be the reverse of Sherlock Holmes's. Cheng left the questions unanswered. Such speculations are indicative of the popularity of Western-style detective fiction in China in the 1920s, a time when the country's urban centers were struggling with sweeping cultural changes accelerated by the May Fourth Movement of 1919 to 1925. Begun by the political protests of university students in Beijing over the decision of the Versailles Conference after World War I to turn defeated Germany's "interests" in Shandong province over to Japan, the movement attributed China's persistent political ineptitude to its inability to put aside its cultural traditions and come to terms with modern realities. The difficult classical language in which China's respectable literature had been written since the first millennium B.C. was exchanged for the vernacular, previously found only in the fictional narratives of the last two dynasties, the Ming (1368 to 1644) and the Qing (1644 to 1911), a principal reason why fiction was considered unfit for elite attention. Like his fellow Butterfly-Saturday writers, Cheng was affected. He used the classical language in the stories he published up to the early 1920s and the vernacular afterward.

Cheng and his wife had a son, Yugang, in 1926. In March 1930 Cheng became chief editor of the Shijie shuju (World Book Company) of Shanghai retranslation of the 1916 Sherlock Holmes collection from Classical into vernacular Chinese; it remains the official Chinese version.

In his 1933 article "Zhentan xiaoshuo yu '?'" (Detective Fiction and "?") Cheng explains that his crime stories are meant to lead his readers to go beyond emotional prejudice, to question all preconceptions and appearances. He uses "the hidden power of detective stories" to place a question mark inside the brains of his readers and set them free to confront reality. In making fiction a tool to open minds, Cheng is unique in trying to solve China's problems by changing his countrymen's thinking processes rather than by persuading them to adopt certain political positions.

In 1937, as the Japanese threatened the area around Shanghai, Cheng and his family fled to Anhui province. There Cheng and his colleagues from Suzhou started the first high school in the village where they were staying. In 1938 Cheng and his family moved to Shanghai. During the war Cheng wrote stories and screenplays, employing other pen names for work that appeared in pro-Japanese publications.

In 1917 Cheng had published the story "Juezhi ji" (Battle of Wits) in Classical Chinese. More than a quarter of a century later, with the help of his daughter, Yuzhen, he revised the story and translated it into the vernacular as "Zhuanshi xiangquan" (The Diamond Necklace). He paired it with another story, "Qianting tu" (Submarine Blueprints), and serialized them under the general title "Longhu dou" (The Battle of Dragon and Tiger) in eleven issues of the fiction magazine *Zi luolan* (Violets) in 1943. In these stories all traces of China are removed: the settings are London and Paris, and the protagonists retain their original names in transliteration based on Shanghainese—Xieloke Fuermosi (Sherlock Holmes), Yuehan Huasheng (John Watson), and Asen Luoping (Arsène Lupin). "Zhuanshi xiangchuan" has been collected in *Yuanyuang hudie–libailiu pai zuopin xuan* (1991, Selected Works from the Mandarin Ducks and Butterfly–*Saturday* School) and "Qianting tu" in *Zhongguo zhentan xiaoshuo zongjiang–Cheng Xiaoqing* (1994, The Grand Master of Chinese Detective Fiction–Cheng Xiaoqing), both edited by Fan Boqun. In August 1945 Cheng and his family returned to Suzhou.

From the 1920s to the 1940s Cheng produced a series of Huo Sang stories that, along with his translations of detective stories from English into Chinese, secured his place as what Fan calls "The Grand Master of Chinese Detective Fiction." Liu Ts'un-yan points out that aside from his translations of the works of Doyle, Leblanc, Earl Derr Biggers, Leslie Charteris, and S. S. Van Dine (pseudonym of Willard Huntington Wright), Cheng wrote "a hundred-odd cases involving the great detective Huo Sang . . . and his exploits in Shanghai," earning "tremendous fame." Liu does not mention the many screenplays and the lyrics to at least one successful popular song that Cheng also wrote; his participation in the Qing she (Green Society) and Xing she (Star Society) literary associations, both founded in 1922 by writers of popular fiction; his occasional essays; or his editing of various Butterfly-Saturday periodicals. Indisputably, however, the thirty Huo Sang stories he wrote from the late 1910s through the early 1930s and republished in the 1940s are the works that will secure his reputation.

Like other Butterfly-Saturday writers, Cheng serialized his stories in popular fiction periodicals; with the exception of the most prominent, such as *Liubailiu* and *Hong meigui*, these periodicals had short life spans and were not regularly collected by libraries. Some of the Huo Sang stories, which were mostly of novella length, were reedited and republished as separate volumes, with no indication of the dates or venues of their initial serializations. Identifying the first dates of publication for much of his fiction ranges, therefore, from difficult to impossible. The most important of the republications were the thirty books in Huo Sang tan'an xiuzhen congkan (The Cases of Huo Sang: Pocket Editions Series), put out by the World Book Company in the 1940s. These thirty undated editions are regarded as the core of Cheng's oeuvre.

Jiangnan Yan (1944) was number 19 in the pocket editions. Sometime in the quarter century between its initial appearance and its republication in the series, Cheng rewrote the story in the vernacular, which is the version that is available today. In both form and content it serves as a paradigm for all of the Huo Sang stories. Like *A Study in Scarlet* (1887), Doyle's initial Sherlock Holmes story, *Jiangnan Yan* begins with Bao Lang, Watson's counterpart as the first-person narrator, introducing himself and the detective hero. Bao Lang explains that he and his friend and housemate Huo Sang were fellow students in high school and at the university. He describes Huo Sang as solidly built and strong, with an angular face and a high-bridged nose, and as determined and alert, with a highly retentive memory and superhuman deductive abilities. The setting is Suzhou, where Bao Lang (like Cheng) teaches at the high school attached to Dongwu University. One of his students, the son of a retired government official, comes to ask for help after his home is robbed of a fortune in jewelry by someone who signed the crime by writing the name of the notorious jewel thief South-China Swallow on the wall. The student has heard about Huo Sang from his teacher and wants the detective to help with the investigation. Bao Lang visits the crime scene with Huo Sang and presents the reader with each of the clues and the list of suspects, which includes the owner's concubine and the household servants. The reader is thus invited to match wits with Huo Sang, who solves the case through careful reasoning and then explains everything in detail to Bao Lang and hence to the reader. He knew from the start—as the reader should have—that the real South-China Swallow could not have been involved.

Though the two characters eventually relocate to Shanghai, the main site of their adventures, the general narrative pattern of *Jiangnan Yan* is followed in all of the Huo Sang stories, including those not included in the pocket series. In "Yizhi xie" (1923, The Shoe), for example, a police detective comes to Huo Sang and Bao Lang's residence on Aiwen Road in Shanghai to ask for help in solving the murder of a stockbroker's young wife; Huo Sang arrives at the solution by reasoning that a pretty shoe left at the scene is not a clue.

The shadowy character of the South-China Swallow, who is referred to but never appears in the story that bears his name, emerges not as Huo Sang's nemesis but as his silent partner in *Huangpu Jiang zhong* (1942; translated as "On the Huangpu," 2006), number 2 in the pocket series. The Swallow operates outside the law but, in Robin Hood fashion, seeks social justice as fervently as Huo Sang does. (In "Wuchang zhong" [1930, At the Ball], in which Huo Sang and Bao Lang do not appear, the Swallow steals an emerald necklace at an elaborate dance party put on by a corrupt official to show off his wealth and his beautiful daughter.) His appearance in the Huo Sang stories usually changes their nature from cerebral to more sensational: the climax of *Huangpu Jiang zhong* features "a bloody battle" aboard a gangsters' ship, where Huo Sang has gone to rescue a businessman's kidnapped son; he succeeds not through his reasoning powers but through his own courage and the Swallow's help.

Cover for the first volume of the thirteen-volume Huo Sang tan'an ji *(1986–1988, Collected Cases of Huo Sang), the adventures of Cheng's "Sherlock Holmes of the East" (East Asian Library, Princeton University)*

In effect, in his Huo Sang stories Cheng transports Sherlock Holmes to Shanghai, even though the city did not then have private investigators engaging in official police business. Holmes, in London, lives in an apartment with a servant, plays the violin for relaxation, and smokes as he contemplates a case, and Huo Sang can be portrayed as doing similar things in cosmopolitan Shanghai without straining the reader's credulity. Cheng increases the naturalness of the transfer by minor adaptations and by direct reference to Shanghai's realities. In *Zi xinjian* (1944, The Note in Purple), number 11 in the pocket series, Huo Sang notices that tracks left in the mud are from Denglupu (Dunlop) tires and that the automobile concerned has rear-wheel drive. In "Bai shajin" (The White Handkerchief), the date of which is uncertain but which is included in volume one of *Huo Sang tan'an ji* (1986–1988, Collected Cases of Huo Sang), Huo Sang smokes Baijinlong (Golden Dragon) cigarettes, a popular brand manufactured in Shanghai; catches the electric tram in an area known as Shiliu Pu by the docks on the Huangpu River; and takes

Illustrated opening page of Cheng's novella Wu fu chuan *(1923, The Five Blessings Boat). Like all of his early Huo Sang stories, it is written in Classical Chinese. Cheng later rewrote many of them in the vernacular (Wason Collection on East Asia–China, Kroch Asia Library, Cornell University).*

the Ningbo Ferry. He concludes that the traces of hair pomade left on a straw hat is of the Xi Shi brand, named after a famous ancient beauty. Although the plots may be, as Cheng insists in "Zhentan xiaoshuode duo fangmian," inspired by actual events, they are essentially "kongzhong louge" (castles in the air), made up in the imagination. The frequent references to Shanghai reality, however, make the imaginary seem actual. They are both the result and the cause of Cheng's success in turning the foreign and bizarre into the domestic and familiar. Huo Sang fits as naturally into the Shanghai of his time as Holmes fits into the London of his. So believable were the stories that in the summer of 1932 readers had demanded that Cheng solve the mystery of who stole his own bicycle from in front of the Gongyuan dianyingyuan (Park Cinema),

and he had done so. As King-fai Tam writes, Cheng exploited "to his . . . advantage the ambiguous relationship between fact and fiction," and his reader was in turn "encouraged . . . to take as literal truth whatever is recorded." Tam does not mention that traditional Chinese storytellers had habitually exploited this relationship. Well before the 1920s, what the world called "fiction" the Chinese called—and continue to call—*xiaoshuo* ("minor narratives"), because such writings were not expected to deal with important matters. The Chinese term gives no indication as to whether what is written about is factual or invented. Traditional respect for the literal truth of anything that is written down had encouraged Chinese readers to take *xiaoshuo* not as "castles in the air" but as fact, albeit not of moral or intellectual significance. When Cheng made Shanghai an equivalent of London, therefore, he was following China's native traditions even as he was "renovating" them to fit in with imported attitudes and ideas.

The *xiaoshuo* tradition also played a role in Cheng's casual transfer of Sherlock Holmes, the major figure of modern detective fiction, from England to China. Whereas readers in the modern West assume fictional texts to be the created products of an individual author who retains—legally, through copyright—sole proprietorship of what he writes, traditional authors of *xiaoshuo* narratives were little more than transient participants in a potentially endless evolutionary process. Every well-known premodern *xiaoshuo* comes in a variety of versions that differ significantly one from another; in old China *xiaoshuo* writers did not so much own what they wrote as share it. Readers in China accepted Huo Sang from Doyle's admitted imitator because Cheng was writing *xiaoshuo*, something insignificant or made up and hence not more or less valid as the product of one author or another. This attitude made it easy for Cheng and his readers not just to cross the borders between what was Chinese and what was British, or between the traditional and the modern, but to obliterate them.

The dissolution of cultural "self" and "other" is clearer in the case of Bao Lang, the sinicized Watson who relates Huo Sang's exploits to the reader. Before the modern era, the first-person narrator did not exist in *xiaoshuo*. The vernacular fiction of the Ming and Qing dynasties invariably features an intrusive and omniscient narrator-cum-commentator who directly addresses the reader, and narrator and reader both regard the plot and the characters from a detached distance. Like Watson, Bao Lang is neither omniscient nor detached; he is limited by his own observations as he participates in and describes Huo Sang's cases. Yet, in a way that is not so different from a narrator in traditional *xiaoshuo*, he does not hesitate to comment on or to dramatize the action. *Zi xinjian* begins with an extended quotation detailing the speaker's discovery of the murder victim "well after the clock had struck twelve" on a blustery, rainy night in autumn. The doorbell rings twice. The speaker's servant answers the front door and yells for him. With the stinging wind shooting raindrops through the open door, and the servant trembling off to one side, the speaker, relying on the light from a low-wattage electric bulb in the corridor, looks out and reports that "all the hairs on my body involuntarily stood on end." Not until three pages later does Bao Lang finally introduce him as Xu Zhigong; he explains that Xu's testimony was "very dramatic" and that he therefore decided "to change the usual order of my reports, to begin with what he related."

In this work, as in many of Cheng's stories, Chinese tradition and Western modernity are thoroughly amalgamated. Playing with chronological order in a narrative to increase dramatic effect was rare in old vernacular *xiaoshuo* but not altogether absent. Involving the reader by increasing mystery and surprise is as common in old Chinese stories as it is in their modern Western counterparts. It is, therefore, impossible to say whether the opening of *Zi xinjian* borrows from tradition or is inspired by Western fiction. Likewise, the description of the murder victim Xu sees—a man "lying across the doorsill, half inside the door, and half still remaining on the flagstones outside"—could be considered traditional, since descriptions of characters in traditional fiction often begin with their clothing: "What he was wearing was a lined robe of a light color, along with a dark vest. The black felt hat he was wearing had already tumbled onto the floorboards inside." In this case, however, the reader is expected to deduce that the victim is a well-heeled dandy, just as Watson's tanned and haggard face, injured left arm, and military bearing reveal to Holmes, when they first meet in *A Study in Scarlet,* that he is an army doctor "just come from the tropics." Cheng's Huo Sang stories affirm Lee's contention that modern Shanghai authors "never imagined themselves, nor were they so regarded, as so 'foreignized' *(yanghua)* as to become slaves to foreigners *(yangnu).*" In short, Cheng Xiaoqing's appropriation of the Sherlock Holmes detective story does not make him or his fiction any less Chinese or any more Western.

In 1948 Cheng's daughter Yuzhen graduated from Dongwu University and went to the United States to study; she did not return to China. With the establishment of the People's Republic in 1949, Cheng's writing largely ceased. Kinkley reports that for the nearly three remaining decades of Cheng's life "Modern Chinese and most foreign crime fiction, traditional Chinese 'court case fiction,' and chivalric or martial-arts fiction were all banned, with minor exceptions during the Hundred Flowers and other thaws." Cheng thus spent the last third of his life watching the "?" of his 1933 essay disappear from his countrymen's consciousness, to be replaced by a quasi-religious faith in political ideology. In the 1950s Cheng continued to teach and, during one of the thaws mentioned by Kinkley, published the *jingyan xiaoshuo* (thrillers) *Ta weishenme bei sha* (1956, Why Was She Murdered?), *Dashucun xuean* (1956, A Bloody Case in Big Tree Village), and *Sheng si guantou* (1957, A Matter of Life and Death). In 1958 he joined the Jiangsu provincial branch of the Zhongguo zuojia xiehui (Chinese Writers' Association). In August 1966, at the beginning of the Cultural Revolution, he was publicly castigated in front of the Kaiming Theater in Suzhou, and his home was ransacked by Red Guards. His friend and colleague Zhou, who was subjected to abuse alongside Cheng, killed himself in 1968. Cheng was placed under house arrest in 1970 and released in 1971. His wife died in September 1975; Cheng died on 12 October of the following year.

When Liang Qichao urged his countrymen in 1902 to renovate Chinese fiction, he was writing from a Japan that also looked out to the modernized West. By the time the May Fourth Movement began seventeen years later, however, serious writers were no longer as interested in renovation as they were in transformation—in using fiction to engage with China's immediate problems. In the much-quoted preface to his *Nahan* (1923, Outcry; translated as *Call to Arms,* 1981) Lu Xun declared that he was writing fiction "to change the spirit" of his countrymen, whom he saw as unable to free themselves from their attachment to the past. In 1902 Liang had called for the renovation of tradition; a little more than two decades later Lu Xun called for tradition to be replaced. Because of his innate cosmopolitanism, Cheng Xiaoqing can be seen as one of the few to follow Liang's true directive—that tradition be made new, rather than abandoned. Even though he never lived abroad, throughout his life Cheng had what Lee calls "an abiding curiosity in 'looking out'—locating oneself as a cultural mediator at the intersection between China and other parts of the world." Cheng's natural tendency to look beyond China, evident in his writings, ties him culturally to Shanghai, which Lee calls "the cosmopolitan city par excellence" in the 1930s. Since 1986 the publication in Beijing and Nanjing of major collections of Cheng's detective fiction is an indication that his literary legacy—and the cosmopolitanism it embodies—have revived.

Biographies:

Fan Boqun, "Zhongguo zhentan xiaoshuo zhi zongjiang–Cheng Xiaoqing pingzhuan," in *Zhongguo zhentan xiaoshuo zongjiang–Cheng Xiaoqing,*

Zhongguo jinxiandai tongsu zuojia pingzhuan congshu, no. 3, edited by Fan (Nanjing: Nanjing chubanshe, 1994), pp. 11–25;

Wei Shouzhong, "Cheng Xiaoqing shengping yu zhuyi nianbiao," in *Shenmide zhentan shijie: Cheng Xiaoqing, Sun Liaohong xiaoshuo yishu tan,* edited by Lu Runxiang (Shanghai: Xuelin chubanshe, 1996), pp. 131–155.

References:

Fan Boqun, "Cheng Xiaoqingde 'Huo Sang tan'an,'" in his *Yuanyang hudie pai* (Beijing: Renmin wenxue chubanshe, 1989), pp. 201–215;

Eva Hung, "Giving Texts a Context: Chinese Translations of Classical English Detective Stories 1890–1916," in *Translation and Creation: Readings of Western Literature in Early Modern China, 1840–1918,* edited by David Pollard (Amsterdam & Philadelphia: Benjamin, 1998), pp. 151–176;

Jeffrey C. Kinkley, *Chinese Justice, the Fiction: Law and Literature in Modern China* (Stanford, Cal.: Stanford University Press, 2000), pp. 170–240;

Leo Ou-fan Lee, *Shanghai Modern: The Flowering of a New Urban Culture in China, 1930-1945* (Cambridge, Mass.: Harvard University Press, 1999), pp. 307–323;

Joseph R. Levenson, *Liang Ch'i-chao and the Mind of Modern China* (Berkeley: University of California Press, 1967);

Liang Qichao, "On the Relationship between Fiction and the Government of the People," translated by Gek Nai Cheng, in *Modern Chinese Literary Thought: Writings on Literature, 1893–1945,* edited by Kirk A. Denton (Stanford, Cal.: Stanford University Press, 1996), pp. 74–81;

E. Perry Link Jr., *Mandarin Ducks and Butterflies: Popular Fiction in Early Twentieth-Century Chinese Cities* (Berkeley: University of California Press, 1981), pp. 22, 147, 168–169;

Liu Ts'un-yan, "Introduction: 'Middlebrow' in Perspective," *Renditions,* nos. 17–18 (Spring–Autumn 1982): 1–40;

Lu Xun, "*Nahan* zixu," translated by Yang Hsien-yi and Gladys Yang as "Preface to *Call to Arms,*" in *Modern Chinese Literary Thought,* pp. 238–242;

King-fai Tam, "Cultural Ambiguities of Modern Chinese Fiction," in *The Post-Colonial Detective,* edited by Ed Christian (Basingstoke, U.K.: Macmillan/Palgrave, 2001), pp. 112–139;

Tam, "The Detective Fiction of Ch'eng Hsiao-ch'ing," *Asia Major,* third series, 5 (1992): 113–132;

Tang Wenyi, Mu Dingsheng, and Ji Lei, eds., *20 shiji Zhongguo wenxue tudian* (Chengdu: Sichuan renmin chubanshe, 2001);

Timothy C. Wong, "Commentary and *Xiaoshuo* Fiction," *Journal of the American Oriental Society,* 120, no. 3 (2000): 400–409.

Ding Ling
(12 October 1904 – 4 March 1986)

Thomas Moran
Middlebury College

BOOKS: *Zai hei'an zhong* [In Darkness] (Shanghai: Kaiming shudian, 1928)—includes "Shafei nüshi de riji," translated by A. L. Chin as "The Diary of Miss Sophia," in *Straw Sandals: Chinese Short Stories, 1918-1933,* edited by Harold Robert Isaacs (Cambridge, Mass.: MIT Press, 1974), pp. 129-169;

Zisha riji [A Suicide's Diary] (Shanghai: Guanghua shuju, 1929)—includes "Qingyunli zhong de yijian xiao fangjian," translated by Stanley R. Munro as "On Qing Yun Lane," in *Genesis of a Revolution: An Anthology of Modern Chinese Short Stories,* edited and translated by Munro (Singapore: Heinemann Educational, 1979), pp. 35-48; and "Guonian," translated as "New Year," in *Chinese Women Writers: A Collection of Short Stories by Chinese Women Writers of the 1920s and 30s,* translated by Jennifer Anderson and Theresa Munford (Hong Kong: Joint Publishing Company, 1985), pp. 13-29;

Wei Hu (Shanghai: Dajiang shupu, 1930);

Yige nüren [A Woman], by Ding Ling and Hu Yepin (Shanghai: Zhonghua shuju, 1930)—includes Ding Ling's "Ri," translated by Amy D. Dooling and Kristina M. Torgeson as "Day," in *Writing Women in Modern China: An Anthology of Women's Literature from the Early Twentieth Century,* edited by Dooling and Torgeson (New York: Columbia University Press, 1998), pp. 267-273;

Yige ren de dansheng [The Birth of a Person], by Ding Ling and Hu (Shanghai: Xinyue shudian, 1931);

Fawang [Net of Law] (Shanghai: Liangyou tushu yinshua gongsi, 1931);

Shui [Water] (Shanghai: Hufeng shuju, 1931)—chapter 1 of title story translated by Edgar Snow as "The Flood," in *Living China: Modern Chinese Short Stories,* edited by Snow (London: Harrap, 1936; New York: Reynal & Hitchcock, 1937), pp. 154-164; also includes "Yi tian," translated by Gary Bjorge as "A Day," in *Revolutionary Literature in China: An Anthology,* edited by John Berninghausen and Ted Huters (New York: Sharpe, 1976), pp. 53-55;

Ding Ling (from Yi-tsi Mei Feuerwerker, Ding Ling's Fiction: Ideology and Narrative in Modern Chinese Literature, *1982; Middlebury College Library)*

Muqin [Mother] (Shanghai: Liangyou tushu yinshua gongsi, 1933; enlarged edition, Beijing: Renmin wenxue chubanshe, 1980);

Yehui [Night Meeting] (Shanghai: Xiandai shuju, 1933)—includes "Mouye," translated by George A. Kennedy as "One Certain Night," *China Forum* (Shanghai), 1 (July 1932): 9, republished in *Straw Sandals,* pp. 254-260; and "Xiaoxi," translated as

"News," in *Living China: Modern Chinese Short Stories,* pp. 165–173;

Ding Ling xuanji [Selected Works of Ding Ling], edited by Peng Zi (Shanghai: Tianma shudian, 1933)—includes "Wo de chuangzuo shenghuo," translated by Zha Jianying as "Foolish Dreams: Like a Blind Person Going Fishing," in *Modern Chinese Writers: Self-Portrayals,* edited by Helmut Martin and Jeffrey Kinkley (Armonk, N.Y.: Sharpe, 1992), pp. 302–306;

Yiwai ji [Unforeseen] (Shanghai: Liangyou tushu yinshua gongsi, 1936);

Yi ke weichutang de qiangdan (Chongqing: Shenghuo shudian, 1938); title story revised as *Yige xiaohongjun de gushi* [The Story of a Little Red Soldier] (Shanghai: Shaonian ertong chubanshe, 1956); original version of title story translated by Tommy McClellan as "A Bullet Never Fired," *Renditions,* 58 (November 2002): 117–126;

Suqu de wenyi [Literature and Arts in Soviet District] (Shanghai: Nanhua chubanshe, 1938);

Henei Yilang [Kawachi Ichiro] (Xi'an: Shenghuo shudian, 1938);

Yi nian [One Year] (Xi'an: Shenghuo shudian, 1939);

Yi tian [One Day] (Shanghai: Qingnian wenhua chubanshe, 1939);

Tuanju [Reunion] (Shanghai: Yiliu shudian, 1941);

Wo zai Xia cun de shihou, edited by Hu Feng (Guilin: Yuanfang shudian, 1944)—includes title story, translated by Gary Bjorge as "When I Was in Hsia Village," in *Modern Chinese Stories and Novellas 1919–1949,* edited by Joseph S. M. Lau, Leo Ou-Fan Lee, and C. T. Hsia (New York: Columbia University Press, 1981), pp. 268–278;

Taiyang zhao zai Sangganhe shang (Harbin: Guanghua shudian, 1948); translated by Yang Hsien-yi and Gladys Yang as *The Sun Shines over the Sangkan River* (Beijing: Foreign Languages Press, 1954); translation republished as *The Sun Shines over the Sanggan River* (Beijing: Foreign Languages Press, 1984);

Shanbei fengguang [The Scenery of Northern Shaanxi] (Jiamusi: Xinhua shudian Dongbei zhongfendian, 1948);

Yi er jiu shi yu Jin Ji Lu Yu bianqu: Dihou kang Ri genjudi jieshao [The 129th Infantry and the Shanxi, Hubei, Shandong and Henan Frontiers: A Portrayal of the Base Areas for Resistance against Japan behind Enemy Lines] (Shanghai: Xinhua shudian chubanshe, 1950);

Ouxing sanji [European Travelogue] (Beijing: Renmin wenxue chubanshe, 1951);

Kuadao xinde shidai lai [Step over into the New Era] (Beijing: Renmin wenxue chubanshe, 1951);

Dao qunzhong qu luohu [Going to Live among the Masses] (Beijing: Zuojia chubanshe, 1954);

Ding Ling jinzuo [Ding Ling's Recent Works] (Chengdu: Sichuan renmin chubanshe, 1980)—includes "'Niu peng' xiaopin (san zhang)," excerpts translated by R. A. Roberts as "Sketches from the 'Cattle Shed,'" in *One Half of the Sky: Stories from Contemporary Women Writers of China,* translated by Roberts and Angela Knox (London: Heinemann, 1987; New York: Dodd, Mead, 1988), pp. 38–50;

Shenghuo, chuangzuo, xiuyang [Life, Writing, Self-Cultivation] (Beijing: Renmin wenxue chubanshe, 1981);

Shenghuo, chuangzuo, shidai linghun [Life, Writing, and the Spirit of the Times] (Changsha: Hunan renmin chubanshe, 1981);

Wo de shengping yu chuangzuo [My Life and My Works] (Chengdu: Sichuan renmin chubanshe, 1982);

Ding Ling xiju ji [A Collection of Ding Ling's Plays] (Beijing: Zhongguo xiju chubanshe, 1983);

Fang Mei sanji [American Travelogue] (Changsha: Hunan renmin chubanshe, 1984);

Ding Ling xiezuo shengya [Ding Ling's Writing Life] (Tianjin: Baihua wenyi chubanshe, 1984);

Ding Ling lun chuangzuo [Ding Ling Discusses Writing] (Shanghai: Shanghai wenyi chubanshe, 1985);

Ding Ling quanji (Ding Ling's Complete Works), 12 volumes, edited by Zhang Jiong (Shijiazhuang: Hebei renmin chubanshe, 2001)— includes in volume 4, "Zai yiyuan zhong," translated by Gary J. Bjorge as "In the Hospital," in *Modern Chinese Stories and Novellas 1919–1949,* pp. 279–291; in volume 8, "Wode shengping yu chuangzuo," translated by Kathy Yeh and others as "Daughter of the Chinese People," in *China for Women: Travel and Culture* (New York: Feminist Press, 1995), pp. 71–78.

Collections: *Ding Ling xuanji* [Selected Works of Ding Ling], edited by Xu Chensi and Ye Wangyou (Shanghai: Wanxiang shuwu, 1940);

Ding Ling daibiaozuo [Representative Works of Ding Ling] (Shanghai: Quanqiu shudian, 1947);

Ding Ling wenji [Ding Ling's Writings], edited by Feng Xuefeng (Shanghai: Kaiming shudian, 1947);

Ding Ling wenji [Ding Ling's Writings], 8 volumes (Changsha: Hunan renmin chubanshe, 1983–1991);

Wangliang shijie [A World of Demons and Monsters] (Changsha: Hunan renmin chubanshe, 1987);

Fengxue renjian [Stormy Life] (Xiamen: Xiamen daxue chubanshe, 1987);

Zai yanhan de rizi li [In the Coldest Days] (Beijing: Renmin wenxue chubanshe, 1990);

Ding Ling quanji [A Complete Collection of Ding Ling's Works], 12 volumes, edited by Zhang Jiong

(Shijiazhuang shi: Hebei renmin chubanshe, 2001).

Editions in English: *When I Was in Sha Chuan and Other Stories,* translated by Kung Pusheng (Pune, India: Kutub, 1945);

Miss Sophie's Diary and Other Stories, translated by W. J. F. Jenner (Beijing: Chinese Literature Press, 1985)—includes "From Dusk to Dawn" ("Cong yewan dao tianliang"), "The Hamlet" ("Tianjia chong"), "Rushing" ("Ben"), "The Reunion" ("Tuanju"), and "Night" ("Ye");

I Myself Am a Woman: Selected Writings of Ding Ling, edited by Tani E. Barlow and Gary J. Bjorge (Boston: Beacon, 1989)—includes "A Woman and a Man" ("Yige nüren he yige nanren"), translated by Ruth Keen and Hal Pollard; "Yecao," translated by Charlotte Calhoun; "Shanghai, Spring 1930" ("Yijiusanling nian chun Shanghai"), translated by Shu-ying Ts'ao and Donald Holoch; "Net of Law" *(Fawang),* translated by Bjorge; "Mother" (excerpt from *Muqin*), translated by Barlow, Bjorge, and Catherine Lo; "Affair in East Village" ("Dongcun shijian"), translated by Jean James; "New Faith" ("Xinde xinnian"), translated by James and Barlow; "Du Wanxiang" ("Du Wanxiang") translated by Barlow; "Thoughts on March 8" ("San ba jie you gan"), translated by Gregor Benton; and "People Who Will Live Forever in My Heart: Remembering Chen Man" ("Yongyuan huozai wo xinzhong de renmin"), translated by James;

Ding Ling xiao shuo xuan = Selected Stories by Ding Ling, bilingual edition (Beijing: Chinese Literature Press, 1999).

OTHER: Hu Yepin, *Yepin shixuan* [Selected Poems of Hu Yepin], edited by Ding Ling (Shanghai: Honghei chubanchu, 1929).

Ding Ling and her common-law husband, the poet Hu Yepin, in 1927 (from Ding Ling quanji, *edited by Zhang Jiong, 2001; Collection of Thomas Moran)*

A canonical May Fourth fiction writer, Ding Ling may well be the best-known woman writer of twentieth-century China. She became famous in the late 1920s for her stories about young women. In the early 1930s she was among the writers who shifted attention in their fiction from love to revolution. She joined the Communist Party and was arrested, but she escaped to the Communist capital, Yan'an. She was at first critical of life there but soon yielded to party discipline. In the late 1950s she was expelled from the party, sent to the countryside for twelve years, and imprisoned for five years before being rehabilitated. Ding Ling's life is well documented, and her fiction is much discussed; but some biographical facts are disputed, and disagreement remains as to the quality and significance of her fiction.

Ding Ling was born on 12 October 1904; her *ruming* (infant name) was Bingzi. She was the first of two children of Jiang Baoqian (also called Jiang Yulan) and Jiang Manzhen, who at the time of her marriage was named Yu Manzhen but, in a departure from Chinese custom, took her husband's surname. When Jiang Bingzi was born, her father was in Japan, and her mother was staying with her family in Wuling, Changde prefecture, Hunan province. After Jiang Baoqian came back from Japan, the family lived in his hometown, Woshaxi, in Aufu (today Linli) county, about thirty-five miles north of Wuling.

In 1937 Ding Ling told the story of her childhood to Helen Foster Snow, who recorded it in *Women in Modern China* (1967). According to Ding Ling, the men in the Jiang clan were landlords, government officials, and merchants; but her father "did no work," was "weak and passive, with no ambition for the future," and was incapable of managing the small estate granted him by his older brothers when his father died. Jiang Baoqian "liked his own freedom and was willing to give freedom to others." Ding Ling's mother, who had been educated by her liberal father, was strong, energetic, and disciplined, and because "of her knowledge of western novels, she had imagination to envision a new future."

Jiang Manzhen was thirty and pregnant with a son when Jiang Baoqian died in 1908, leaving his wife and daughter "nearly bankrupt" because of his casualness with money and his refusal to allow Manzhen to help manage their finances. She took her daughter and baby son to her hometown, where they lived with her brothers and their families, and changed her given name to Shengmei; according to Ding Ling's biographer Wang Zhousheng, the name expressed her desire to "shengguo xumei" (be better than "beards and eyebrows"—that is, better than men). She changed her daughter's name to Jiang Wei and her son's name to Jiang Zongda; the combination of the daughter's name and the last syllable of the son's name, Wang says, expressed her wish that her children achieve something *weida* (great).

In 1911 Jiang Shengmei enrolled in a new women's school in Wuling; Jiang Wei attended the kindergarten at the school. The school closed in 1912; Jiang Shengmei attended school in the provincial capital, Changsha, for a year, then taught in Taoyuan, near Wuling. In 1915 Jiang Shengmei took a job as *shejian* (dormitory warden) at the girls' primary school her daughter was attending in Wuling. That spring and summer Jiang Wei read the books stored in her uncle's attic, including classic Chinese novels and translations of Daniel Defoe's *Robinson Crusoe* (1719), Jonathan Swift's *Gulliver's Travels* (1726), and Charles Dickens's *David Copperfield* (1849–1850).

Jiang Wei's brother died of pneumonia in the spring of 1918. She finished primary school in the early summer and enrolled in the Di er nüzi shifan xuexiao (Second Women's Normal School) in Taoyuan. She was an excellent student, but, as she recalls in "Wode zhongxue shenghuo de pianduan: Gei sunnü de xin" (Episodes from My Middle School Years: A Letter to My Granddaughter), written in September 1978 and collected in volume eleven of her complete works (2001), she began to be dissatisfied with the social status quo. She and her classmates cut their hair in the modern style and organized night classes for the poor. Ding Ling told her biographers that she was an "activist," but Charles J. Alber writes in his *Enduring the Revolution: Ding Ling and the Politics of Literature in Guomindang China* (2002) that "Jiang Wei was more a follower than a leader."

In the summer of 1919 Jiang Wei transferred to the Zhounan nüxiao (Zhounan Women's School) in Changsha, where she continued to study foreign literature and began to learn about China's new literature. In the fall of 1921 she transferred to Changsha's Yueyun zhongxue (Yueyun Middle School), a boys' school with a progressive curriculum, because the girls' school had become more conservative. One of her classmates at the boys' school was Yang Kaihui, who married the future Communist leader Mao Zedong the same year. In late 1921 Wang Jianhong, who had been a classmate of Jiang Wei's at the Second Women's Normal School, urged Jiang Wei to go with her to enroll in the Pingmin nüxiao (Common People's Girls School) in Shanghai, which had been established by the newly founded Communist Party to promote Marxism among students and workers.

Jiang Shengmei supported Jiang Wei's decision to go to Shanghai and her refusal to accept an arranged marriage to a cousin, and in February 1922 Jiang Wei and Wang enrolled in the school. According to Wang Zhousheng, Jiang Wei stopped using her surname and began using the single name Bingzhi, which was similar to her original given name, Bingzi, but simpler to write. She did propaganda work and collected money to support a strike by women textile workers. Ding Ling told Snow that she learned about anarchism from Wang Jianhong, met and was influenced by anarchists from Beijing, and joined the Anarchist Party but soon lost interest in it because it did little.

The Common People's Girls' School closed in August 1922. According to Tani E. Barlow's introduction to *I Myself Am a Woman: Selected Writings of Ding Ling* (1989), the Chinese women's movement split in 1922 into a "bourgeois feminist wing" and a "socialist-feminist wing." Bingzhi and Wang Jianhong belonged to the former and, Barlow writes, were "Unwilling to submit to the seemingly arbitrary authority of the Communists." For the next year Bingzhi moved between her mother's home and Nanjing, often in the company of Wang, whom Ding Ling later described as her closest friend.

In the early summer of 1923 Bingzhi and Wang met Qu Qiubai, who had returned six months earlier from a trip to the Soviet Union. Qu encouraged them to enroll at Shanghai daxue (Shanghai University), where he had been teaching since April. Ding Ling told Snow that she decided to attend the school "because it was then a revolutionary school and had been organized by the communists." In "Wo suo renshi de Qu Qiubai tongzhi" (Comrade Qu Qiubai as I Knew Him), published in *Wenhui zengkan* (*Wenhui* Supplement) on 20 February 1980 and collected in volume six of her complete works, however, she writes that at first she suspected that Shanghai University was "another Common People's Girls' School," a center for Communist propaganda rather than a serious academic institution, but that Qu and others assured her that while it did train young Communists, it was a "zhengshi xuexiao" (proper school). Bingzhi and Wang enrolled at the university in late July 1923. At this time Bingzhi selected the easily written two-stroke character *Ding* as her new surname.

At Shanghai University Ding Bingzhi studied foreign and Chinese literature, history, and geography. In "Wo suo renshi de Qu Qiubai tongzhi" Ding Ling writes that the faculty included many prominent intellectuals, but "the best teacher was Qu Qiubai." Qu and Wang became lovers and married. In 1923 Ding Bingzhi encountered Xiang Jingyu, a former classmate of her mother's at the women's school in Wuling and an early member of the Chinese Communist Party, and the two women discussed communism. In her essay "Xiang Jingyu tongzhi liugei wo de yingxiang" (The Influence that Comrade Xiang Jingyu had on Me), published in *Shouhuo* (Harvest) on 25 January 1980 and collected in volume six of her complete works, Ding Ling writes that she was not interested in joining the Communist Party in 1923 because she wanted to retain the freedom to find her own way in life.

Wang Jianhong died of tuberculosis in July 1924; Ding was disconsolate and also angry at Qu for seeming to treat Jianhong's death lightly. Bingzhi went to Beijing in the fall to enroll in Beijing University but either missed or failed the entrance examination. In the spring of 1925 she moved into the dormitory of a *buxiban* (privately run tutorial center) on the west side of the city. She audited Lu Xun's lectures at Beijing University and briefly took private art lessons. In "Lu Xun xiansheng yu wo" (Mr. Lu Xun and I), published in *Xin wenxue shiliao* (Historical Materials on the New Literature) on 22 August 1981 and collected in volume six of her complete works, Ding Ling says that her life would have been easier had she been an artist instead of a writer. She made and dropped plans to go to France with her French teacher and to work as a secretary for a Hong Kong businessman. In May she met Hu Yepin, the editor of a newspaper literary supplement, and Hu's friend Shen Congwen, who later wrote the memoir *Ji Ding Ling* (1934, Remembering Ding Ling). She began using the name Ding Ling at this time.

In the spring of 1925 Ding Ling went home to Hunan. In the essay "Hu Yepin," written in October 1980, published in *Wenhui zengkan* on 10 January 1981, and collected in volume six of her complete works, she wrote that she felt "like a soldier defeated in battle. . . . I was ashamed to face my mother, I felt I hadn't lived up to her hopes and faith in me." Hu Yepin, who had fallen in love with her, arrived in Changde uninvited. In the fall he and Ding Ling moved into a small house near the Temple of Azure Clouds, west of Beijing. There Ding Ling read French and Russian literature in Chinese or English translation, the latter of which she read imperfectly. According to Wang Zhousheng, she was particularly fond of Alexandre Dumas *fils*'s *La Dame aux Camélias* (1852; translated as *The Lady of the Camellias*, 1852), Gustave Flaubert's *Madame Bovary* (1857; trans-

Cover for a 1939 edition of Ding Ling's first book, Zai hei'an zhong *(1928,* In the Darkness*), a collection of some of her early short stories (Wason Collection on East Asia–China, Kroch Asia Library, Cornell University)*

lated, 1881), and Ivan Turgenev's *Ottsy i deti* (1862; translated as *Fathers and Sons*, 1867). In *Ji Ding Ling*, Shen claims that she read *Madame Bovary* at least ten times; according to Shen, from the women in *Madame Bovary* and in Guy de Maupassant's *Notre cour* (1890, Our Heart; translated as *The Human Heart,* 1890) Ding Ling "learned how to analyze herself, and from the men who wrote the books she learned how to write about women." In 1926 Ding Ling made a brief attempt to become an actress but found the movie business unsavory. She told Snow, "I tried out twice and they said, 'She is pretty enough,' and appreciated me like a commodity, which infuriated me."

In April 1927 the tense truce between the Nationalist Party and the Communist Party ended when Nationalist agents arrested and killed Communists and labor union members. The Communist Party had no effective response and by late 1927 was in retreat. Ding Ling told Snow that because she could not go south to join the revolution, she began writing short stories. Her first, "Mengke," was published in December in *Xiaoshuo yuebao* (Short Story Monthly). The title character's name is a transliteration of the French *mon coeur* (my heart), a term of endearment Qu used for Wang Jianhong. Mengke comes to Shanghai from the countryside to attend art school but leaves the school after confronting a teacher for taking advantage of a model. She falls in love with her cousin, but he is unfaithful. Disillusioned and in need of money, Mengke sacrifices her principles and becomes an actress. In makeup, she sees in the mirror that she looks like a prostitute.

"Shafei nüshi de riji" (translated as "The Diary of Miss Sophia," 1974), published in *Xiaoshuo yuebao* in February 1928, comprises entries from a young woman's diary over three winter months. Shafei has tuberculosis and is in psychological distress because of the conflict between her desires and her socialization. She lives apart from her family, the traditional source of identity, and struggles to create herself as a modern woman. A young man is pursuing her, but she finds him weak; she feels guilty about her sexual attraction to the handsome but shallow Singaporean Ling Jishi; and she is similarly conflicted by the sexual feelings she has for women. Ding Ling's frank exploration of the psychology of a young urban woman, including her sexual desires, was appealing to many readers. With "Shafei nüshi de riji," Yi-tsi Mei Feuerwerker writes, "Ding Ling was well on her way to becoming one of China's most celebrated—and in the eyes of some, notorious—women writers."

In December 1927 Ding Ling fell in love with Feng Xuefeng, a Communist Party member and translator of Marxist works from Japanese and Russian. She followed him to Shanghai, Hu followed her, and the three went on to Hangzhou together. Fearing that Hu would kill himself if she left him, Ding Ling told Feng that their relationship would have to remain platonic. Feng returned to Shanghai; Ding Ling and Hu remained in Hangzhou until July 1928, when they, too, moved to Shanghai. In October, Ding Ling published her first book, *Zai hei'an zhong* (In Darkness), a collection of most of her published short stories. In addition to "Mengke" and "Shafei nüshi de riji," it includes "Shujia zhong" (Summer Vacation), about the same-sex love affairs, jealousies, and frustrations of young female teachers at a girls' school. Tze-lan D. Sang writes that "Ding Ling unflinchingly discloses the sexual nature of certain relationships between women teachers, but the plot degrades lesbian eroticism to the level of a second-rate sexual outlet and a form of self-deception."

Ding Ling's second short-story collection, *Zisha riji* (A Suicide's Diary), was published in May 1929. In the title piece a young woman, Isa, finds life meaningless and tries to talk herself into committing suicide in her diary entries. "Qingyunli zhong de yijian xiao fangjian" (A Small Room on Qingyun Lane; translated as "On Qing Yun Lane," 1979) relates a day in the life of Aying, a prostitute, as she jokes with friends and daydreams about marrying her lover back home. She realizes, however, that she does not want to live the life of an "anfen de funü" (well-behaved woman). "Guonian" (translated as "New Year," 1985) is based on an incident in 1913, when Jiang Shengmei had left her daughter behind in Changsha when she went to Taoyuan with her son. In Feuerwerker's estimation it "captures and counterpoints the many moods of childhood, ranging from almost magical happiness to desolate loneliness." In "Suimu" (The End of the Year), set on Chinese New Year's Eve, the college student Peifang is jealous and resentful because her roommate, Yunying, has a boyfriend.

In 1929 Ding Ling, Hu, and Shen started the literary journals *Hong hei yuekan* (Red and Black Monthly) and *Renjian yuekan* (The World Monthly). Both went out of business after eight issues. Ding Ling's first long work of fiction, *Wei Hu,* was serialized in *Xiaoshuo yuebao* beginning in January 1930 and published in book form later that year. It is based on the romance of Wang and Qu. Wang Zhousheng presents the orthodox reading of the novella: "The work describes the conflict between revolution and love in the relationship of the revolutionary Wei Hu and the petit bourgeois woman Lijia; in the end, revolution wins out over love." Feuerwerker, however, argues that *Wei Hu* weights "its descriptive interest on the side of love" and "is a nostalgic lingering on what has already been or will soon be lost and past, rather than a positive affirmation of the revolutionary future." Liu Jianmei maintains that *Wei Hu* is evidence that "Ding Ling was caught in a dilemma between her original identity as a modern, urbanized, and liberated woman and her new, vague Communist identity."

In early 1930 Ding Ling and Hu went to Jinan, Shandong, where Hu took a teaching job. Wang Zhousheng writes, "All day long Hu preached Marxism, historical materialism, . . . and proletarian literature." In April, Ding Ling and Hu published *Yige nüren* (A Woman), a collection of six stories. Ding Ling's four stories—"Ta zou hou" (After He Left), "Yige nüren he yige nanren" (translated as "A Woman and a Man," 1989), "Ri" (translated as "Day," 1998), and "Yecao" (translated, 1989)—explore the consciousnesses of young women in various everyday situations.

In May 1930 the Shandong government issued an order for Hu's arrest, and he and Ding Ling, who was pregnant, fled to Shanghai. In the same month Hu joined the Zhongguo zuoyi zuojia lianmeng (Chinese League of Left-Wing Writers), recently organized by the Communist Party. In June, Ding Ling published in *Xiaoshuo yuebao* "Nianqian de yitian" (The Day before New Year's), a story about two writers struggling to make enough money to live.

From September through December 1930 *Xiaoshuo yuebao* serialized "Yijiusanling nian chun Shanghai" (translated as "Shanghai, Spring 1930," 1989), which is widely regarded as marking Ding Ling's transition from the romantic exploration of female consciousness to a socially engaged realism. Each of the two parts of the work is a story of lovers who are drifting apart because one is committed to revolution and the other to individual desires. In the first story Meilin grows dissatisfied with her egotistical lover and their bourgeois life. When her friend Ruoquan, a disciplined, confident Communist, praises her ideological awakening, Meilin is so happy that she blushes. In the second story Wang Wei is distracted from his revolutionary work when his lover, Mali, arrives from Beijing. Mali, a hedonist, makes a brief attempt to enter Wang Wei's world; Wang Wei hopes that she will change but knows that she will not. They separate, and at the end of the story Wang Wei is arrested for agitating for communism in a street demonstration while Mali is shopping.

On 8 November 1930 Ding Ling gave birth to a son, Jiang Zulin. In December, Hu joined the Communist Party. On 17 January 1931 British police raided a secret meeting, arresting Hu and twenty-four other Communists and handing them over to Nationalist authorities. They were executed on 7 February; five of those killed, including Hu, who was twenty-four, were writers. Tsi-an Hsia cites Harold Robert Isaacs's 1938 suggestion that Hu and the others were betrayed by their Communist Party comrades in an intraparty struggle. Ding Ling told Snow:

> After my husband was killed, I sent my baby to my mother in Hunan and began a new life alone. I read a great deal, wrote stories and worked in the Left Writers' League. My writing changed both in style and in content. . . . my viewpoint had been changing gradually for some time, so this was not a sudden break in thought. I changed my literary style from writing in a personal autobiographical manner and concentrating on individuals, to describing social background. . . . I felt that merely to write stories was not enough. I wanted to get down to real revolutionary work.

Ding Ling's story *Fawang* (translated as "Net of Law," 1989), published as a book in April 1931, is about people in a working-class neighborhood whose lives are ruined when their disappointment over social injustice and natural disaster leads to rage, and they turn on one another. In May, Ding Ling met the American journalist Agnes Smedley and her secretary and translator, Feng Da, who was a member of the Communist Party. She attended her first meeting of the League of Left-Wing Writers and gave a speech at Guanghua (Aurora) University, published as "Wode zibai" (Vindicating Myself) in *Dushu yuekan* (Reading Monthly) on 10 August 1931 and collected in volume seven of her complete works, in which she said that while she intended to stop writing about love, she would not write about workers or peasants because she had no understanding of their lives. In June, Feng Xuefeng asked her to become the editor of the League of Left-Wing Writers journal *Beidou* (Big Dipper), and she accepted. In her memoir *Wangliang shijie* (1987, A World of Demons and Monsters) she writes about the distress and loneliness she felt in 1931. In November she moved in with Feng Da.

In the title story of Ding Ling's collection *Shui* (Water), published in late 1931, poor rural villagers become refugees after their homes are destroyed by a flood but discover that their anger can be turned into power if they work together. Marston Anderson notes that several critics, including Feng Xuefeng, "credited Ding Ling with having invented a new form that overcame the individualism of May Fourth literature and took 'the unfolding of collective action' as its theme." Other stories in *Shui* include "Tianjia chong" (Tian Family Village; translated as "The Hamlet," 1985), which, in Feuerwerker's words, depicts peasants as "reservoirs of revolutionary virtue and energy," and "Cong yewan dao tianliang" (translated as "From Dusk to Dawn," 1985), which describes the emotions of a young writer over the course of one night as she thinks about her brother, who died years earlier; her baby son, whom she has sent home to her mother; and her dead husband, who has been "flung into some dark hole." She tries to overcome despair with reason and the determination to keep working.

In 1931–1932 the ruling Nationalists grew more authoritarian, urban left-wing intellectuals put increased energy into cultural work and propaganda, the Communist Party's military resisted Nationalist efforts to surround and destroy its mountain bases, and patriotic feeling grew stronger as Japanese aggression intensified. In February 1932 Ding Ling joined the Communist Party. In July *Beidou* ceased publication on orders of the government. In the fall Ding Ling took over from Qian Xingcun (also known as A Ying) as secretary of the Communist group in the League of Left-Wing Writers.

On 14 May 1933 Ding Ling and Feng Da were arrested by Nationalist agents and taken to Nanjing; Ding Ling later blamed Feng Da for revealing their address. Ding Ling's arrest was protested by left-wing intellectuals and by moderates such as Song Qingling, the widow of the statesman and revolutionary leader Sun Yat-sen, and Cai Yuanpei, a former president of Beijing University. The

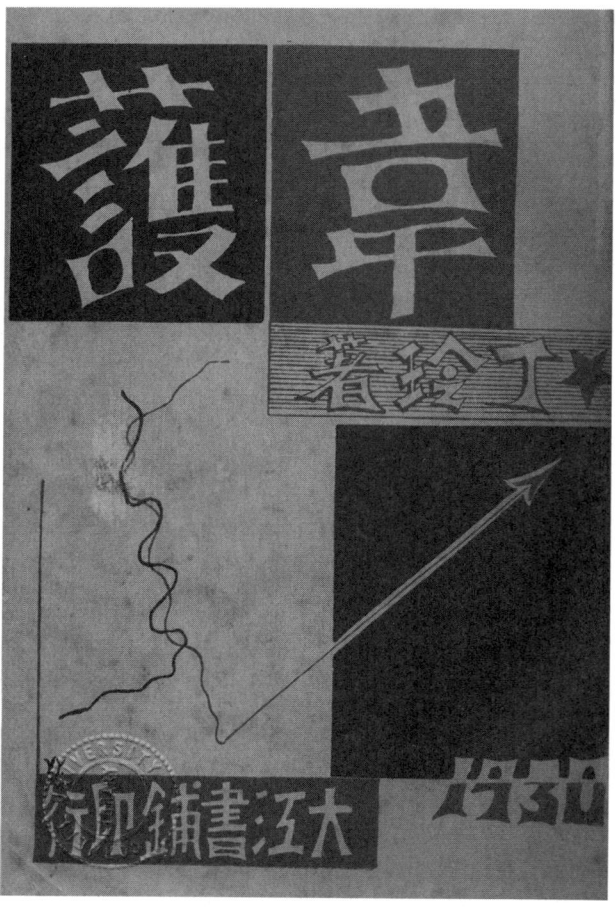

Cover for a 1933 edition of Ding Ling's first long work of fiction, Wei Hu (1930), about the conflict between revolution and love in the relationship of the title character and a woman of the petite bourgeoisie (Wason Collection on East Asia–China, Kroch Asia Library, Cornell University)

government denied knowledge of Ding Ling's whereabouts, and a rumor circulated that she was dead.

On 1 June *Fawang* and six other stories were published as *Yehui* (Night Meeting). The collection includes "Mouye" (translated as "One Certain Night," 1932), which imagines the last moments of a young poet who is shot to death along with twenty-four comrades. The executioners are brutal and profane; the poet finds comfort in thinking of his lover's eyes and dies singing the *Internationale*.

Also in June 1933 Ding Ling's unfinished novel *Muqin* (excerpt translated as "Mother," 1989) was published in Shanghai. After the death of her husband, Manzhen returns home to Wuling with her children, goes to school, unbinds her feet, and becomes an advocate of women's rights and social reform. In "Gender and Identity in Ding Ling's *Mother*" (1989) Barlow writes that the novel "shifted Ding Ling's discursive focus from the individual female personality to the shared identity of the revolutionary sisterhood." Qian Xingcun argues that *Muqin* succeeds in depicting the many small changes in society that occurred in the years leading up to the 1911 revolution and in showing the disintegration of the traditional social system under the pressure of new economic and ideological realities. But the work "is not necessarily a success," according to Qian, because it is simplistic in depicting the motivation for changes in Manzhen's thinking, vague about the revolutionary events that took place in Wuling, and tediously long in its description of life at Manzhen's school. Qian forgives the faults of the book, because Ding Ling was unable to devote sustained attention to it; as published, *Muqin* is only part of what was planned as a much longer work.

In the summer of 1933 Shen Congwen began to serialize parts of *Ji Ding Ling;* it was published as a book in 1934 and republished in 1939, both times with portions deleted by government censors. Jeffrey C. Kinkley writes that the book is a sympathetic account but "certainly does not show Ding Ling as she would have depicted herself" and reports that Ding Ling later rejected Shen's book as "bad fiction." Kinkley describes the falling-out between Ding Ling and Shen and offers possible reasons why Ding Ling hated *Ji Ding Ling,* but he concludes that these reasons do not fully explain Ding Ling's "vindictive attitude" toward Shen.

In September 1933 a letter from Ding Ling to Feng Xuefeng was published in the magazine *Wenxue* (Literature) under the title "Bu suan qingshu" (Not a Love Letter). Dated August 1931 to January 1932, it is signed with a pseudonym and replaces Feng's name with "XX" but mentions Ding Ling and Hu Yepin by name. Ding Ling writes of wanting to lie in the arms of "XX" and spend time with him at home, reading and writing. She repeatedly professes her love for him but acknowledges that they will never be together.

In November, Ding Ling's unfinished "Shafei nüshi ri ji di er bu" (The Diary of Miss Sophia, Part 2), written two years earlier, was published in *Wenxue*. It comprises two diary entries. In the first, Shafei says that she sent her baby home to her mother in Hunan after her lover was shot to death by the government and expresses her determination to improve herself and put worry aside. In the second entry, dated 5 May, she writes that she wanted to buy a peony to commemorate the flower she and her lover saw the night they met on the same date six years ago, but peonies are hard to find in Shanghai.

In February 1934 Ding Ling's books were banned by the government censors. In April, Jiang Shengmei arrived in Nanjing with Ding Ling's son. That same month Feng Da agreed to go to work for the Nationalist as a translator. On 3 October, Ding Ling gave birth to her and Feng Da's daughter, Zuhui. In 1935 she and Feng Da moved to a village outside Nanjing; Feng Da had tuberculosis, and Ding Ling told Snow that she herself "almost died of typhoid fever." In April 1936 Jiang Shengmei returned to Hunan with both of Ding Ling's children. Ding Ling asked the Communist Party to help her get away from Nanjing. The Nationalists had greatly relaxed their supervision of Ding Ling, and on 18 September 1936 she walked away from her Nanjing home without a word to Feng Da or anyone else. According to Alber's *Enduring the Revolution,* Feng Xuefeng sent a party member to meet Ding Ling and accompany her to Shanghai. In mid October she traveled in disguise to Xi'an, the capital of Shaanxi province, and arrived in Bao'an, a Communist Party base, in mid November. Among those who welcomed her were Mao and the future premier of the People's Republic of China, Zhou Enlai.

In that same month Ding Ling's *Yiwai ji* (Unforeseen) was published in Shanghai. It comprises a preface and eight stories, one identified as an "experiment in reportage" and all previously published in magazines, including "Bu suan qingshu" and "Shafei nüshi ri ji di er bu." The stories are about a boy whose family has been displaced and impoverished by flooding and drought, the economic polarization of Chinese society, a prison guard, a print-shop apprentice, a gentry family in decline, and a woman from the countryside who works as a maid in the city. "Slim as it is," Feuerwerker writes, the book "reveals an unusual range of subject matter and formal diversity."

In Bao'an, Ding Ling helped to establish the Zhongguo wenyi xiehui (Chinese Literary and Artistic Association). In January 1937 she accompanied Smedley to Yan'an, the Communist Party headquarters. War with Japan began in July, and in September Ding Ling left Yan'an to lead the Xibei zhandi fuwutuan (Northwest Battlefield Service Corps). In *China Fights Back: An American Woman with the Eighth Route Army* (1938), Smedley writes that the corps was "a kind of flying squadron of propaganda" that went "far into the territory near the enemy lines to arouse the people to struggle, to give plays, to speak, collect material, make reports." The corps traveled and performed in several places in Shaanxi and Shanxi through early 1938. In March, Ding Ling returned briefly to Yan'an, then took the Northwest Battlefield Service Corps to Xi'an. In July, Ding Ling and the corps returned to Yan'an, and in August, Ding Ling's children joined her in Yan'an.

The backgrounds and worldviews of the many intellectuals who came to Yan'an in the late 1930s separated them from Communist cadres and peasants, but the party welcomed them because of their usefulness for agitprop work. In November 1938 Ding Ling was assigned to study at the Yan'an Institute for Marxism and Leninism in Lanjiaping. According to Alber, by this time she was living with Chen Ming, a member of the Northwest Battlefield Service Corps who was twelve years younger than she.

In 1938 Ding Ling published *Yi ke weichutang de qiangdan* (A Bullet Not Yet Fired), a collection of essays about soldiers and scenes at the front and two stories that are, in Chang Jun-mei's opinion, "crude propaganda without literary value." *Yi nian* (1939, One Year) comprises stories and essays about Ding Ling's experiences with the Northwest Battlefield Service Corps.

In May 1939 Ding Ling took part in the formation of the Yan'an branch of the Zhonghua quanguo wenyijie kangdi xiehui (All-China Association of Literary Resistance), and in November she became assistant director of the Shan Gan Ning bianqu wenhua xiehui (Shaanxi-Gansu-Ningxia Border Region Cultural Association). Because of persistent rumors that she had betrayed the Communist cause while under arrest, she asked the party to take a position on her case. The Central Organizational Department issued a report rejecting all accusations against Ding Ling as unfounded and declaring her to have been always loyal to the party (the report is included in volume ten of her complete works). Her story "Ruwu" (Entering the Ranks), which satirizes a left-wing writer who is useless in real revolutionary situations, was published in *Zhongguo wenhua* (Chinese Culture) on 25 May 1940.

By 1941 a division existed between those who wanted writers to be free to criticize aspects of life in Yan'an and those who did not. Zhou Yang was the principal spokesman for the latter group. Biographers agree that Ding Ling was a moderate, but her writing was perceived as liberal at the time. In June 1941 she published the story "Wo zai Xiacun de shihou" (translated as "When I Was in Hsia Village," 1981), in which she criticizes the persistence of discriminatory attitudes toward women in the areas "liberated" by the Communists. The narrator, a Communist Party cadre, visits Xia Village. There she meets Zhenzhen, a young woman who was raped by the Japanese, taken from the village, and forced to be a concubine to a Japanese officer. She escaped but was sent back to the Japanese to work as a spy. The villagers regard Zhenzhen as tainted and scorn her. She decides to leave for Yan'an, where she can get treatment for venereal disease and start a new life. Critics agree that the story attacks the continued presence in the "liberated areas" of discriminatory attitudes toward women.

In "Women xuyao zawen" (We Need Topical Essays), published in *Jiefang ribao wenyi fukan* (Liberation Daily Literary Supplement) on 23 October 1941 and collected in volume seven of her complete works, Ding

Cover for a 1940 edition of Ding Ling's unfinished novel Muqin *(1933, Mother), in which the title character, based on the author's mother, goes to school, unbinds her feet, and becomes an advocate of women's rights and social reform after her husband's death (Collection of John Berninghausen)*

Ling writes that because Yan'an culture does not encourage free debate, people refrain from expressing their opinions and only mutter complaints in private, which is unproductive. She concedes that advances have been made in Yan'an but insists that problems remain and that complacency must be avoided. To call attention to problems and promote change, she argues for the use of the *zawen* (topical essay) of the type written by Lu Xun; Lu Xun's *zawen* were famed for the economy and ferocity of their satire.

In "Zai yiyuan zhong" (translated as "In the Hospital," 1981), published in *Guyu* (Grain Rain) on 15 November 1941, Lu Ping comes to Yan'an and is assigned to work in a hospital. The facility is poorly equipped, and the directors, who are veteran members of the Communist Party, have no medical knowledge. Lu Ping becomes the subject of gossip when she falls in love with a surgeon, who is not a Communist, and is criticized for ideological shortcomings. She is troubled by the dogmatism of the hospital administrators and begins to doubt her loyalty to the party and her usefulness to the revolution. Her request to transfer away from the hospital is granted. Before she leaves, she meets a patient who has lost both feet because of his doctors' incompetence. He tells her that he is no longer resentful, because he has come to understand that the hospital staff is doing the best it can under difficult circumstances, and he encourages Lu Ping to be patient and remain confident. The story ends with a claim that a new life had begun for Lu Ping and that all people must endure trials to mature, but this optimism is muted.

"San ba jie you gan" (translated as "Thoughts on March 8," 1989), written in March 1942 and published on 9 March in *Jiefang ribao wenyi fukan,* describes the predicament women face in Yan'an: if they are unmarried, they are the subject of gossip and rumors; if they are married, they must sacrifice their ambitions to the demands of their families; if they are unschooled, their educated husbands may divorce them; if they are educated, they are regarded with suspicion by men; if they wish to remain unfettered by children, they must undergo risky abortions; and if they have children, they are praised but must withdraw from work and are left behind. The essay concludes with an appeal to women to take charge of and improve their lives.

The April 1942 Zhengfeng yundong (Rectification Campaign) imposed discipline and the authority of Mao on the Chinese Communist Party and specifically targeted cultural workers for ideological retraining. In May a meeting, the Yan'an Forum on Literature and Art, was held to criticize Ding Ling's "San ba jie you gan" and a *zawen* titled "Ye baihehua" (Wild Lilies), by Wang Shiwei, that faulted the party leadership for ruling as a privileged class. Ding Ling attended the meeting; in "Yan'an wenyi zuotanhui de qianqian houhou" (The Whole Story of the Yan'an Forum on Literature and Art), published in *Xin wenxue shiliao* (Historical Materials on the New Literature) on 22 May 1982 and collected in volume eleven of her complete works, she writes that Mao identified Wang as an enemy of the party but said, "Ding Ling is not like Wang Shiwei. Ding Ling is a comrade." Mao outlined the party's literary policy, making it clear that writers were to follow orders from the party and specifically refuting the claim that the topical essay was still needed. Wang Shiwei was put on trial; on the last day of the trial Ding Ling renounced her essay "San ba jie you gan" and denounced Wang. She said that all involved should show Wang the way to reform but called him "despicable, petty, capricious, and scheming" for having gone against the party in thought and deed. Ding Ling's remarks were published in *Jiefang ribao* (Liberation Daily) on 16 June 1942 as "Wenyijie dui Wang Shiwei yingyou de taidu ji fanxing" (How Literary and Art Should Regard Wang Shiwei, and Self-reflections), which is collected in volume seven of her complete works. Wang was imprisoned until he was executed in 1947.

Ding Ling and Chen Ming were married in 1942. After a period of self-criticism during the Shencha ganbu yundong (Cadre Inspection Movement) in 1942, and with increasing frequency in 1944 and 1945, Ding Ling wrote reportage about workers, peasants, and soldiers; nine of these works are collected in *Shanbei fengguang* (1948, The Scenery of Northern Shaanxi). In late 1945 Ding Ling, Chen, and her children went to Zhangjiakou, one hundred miles northwest of Beiping (as Beijing was known from 28 June 1928 to 27 September 1949). In Communist-controlled areas, land was being confiscated and redistributed to peasants; the former landlords were humiliated and beaten in public, and some were killed. Ding Ling observed land reform in several areas and wrote a socialist-realist novel about it. *Taiyang zhao zai Sangganhe shang* (1948; translated as *The Sun Shines over the Sangkan River*, 1954) is set in the fictional village of Nuanshui on the Sanggan River; the locale is based on an area where Ding Ling spent two months in the summer of 1946. A Communist Party land-reform team helps the Nuanshui peasants take action against their landlords, dismantles the traditional social structure of the village, replaces it with collective organizations, and teaches the people to value class solidarity instead of kinship ties and personal loyalties. The public denunciation of landlord Qian Wengui in chapter 50 is, critics agree, the high point of the work. Qian has sought to protect himself by sending his son to join the Communist army and marrying his daughter to a cadre. He is overthrown when Cheng Ren, chairman of the peasants' association, puts aside his love for the landlord's niece and mobilizes the people. Wang Yao writes that the novel "demonstrates that local tyrants despised by the masses must first be overthrown; only then will the masses believe in their own strength, eliminate ideas that stand in the way of revolutionary change, and enthusiastically join the struggle of land reform." Chang Jun-mei argues, on the other hand, that the denunciation of Qian makes it "utterly clear how the ignorance of these simple people is used in a well-calculated plan for political purposes." Even commentators who fault the novel for sacrificing art to propaganda agree that Ding Ling portrays her characters and their times as complex and multifaceted. The novel won the Stalin Prize.

In early 1949 Ding Ling contributed articles to the campaign to criticize Xiao Jun, a colleague from Yan'an who was outspoken in his criticism of Communist Party's policies; Xiao Jun was sent to work in a coal mine, remaining there until 1951. In June 1949 Ding Ling moved to Beiping, which the Communists had taken in January. She became a member of the standing committee of the Zhongguo quanguo wenxue yishujie lianhehui (All-China Federation of Literature and Art Circles), vice chairperson of the All-China Association of Literary Workers, a member of the standing committee of the National Women's Federation, and a member of the National Committee of the Chinese People's Political Consultative Conference. In 1950 she helped organize the Zhongyang wenxue yanjiusuo (Central Literary Research Institute) and became its director. In the early 1950s she was the editor of *Wenyi bao* (Literary Gazette) and then deputy editor in chief of *Renmin wenxue* (People's Literature). Her mother died in Beijing in May 1953 at seventy-five.

In the early 1950s Zhou Yang, who had been an opponent of moderate and liberal members of the literary left wing since the mid 1930s, expanded his power, and in 1952–1953 Ding Ling quit or was forced out of her positions. In the fall of 1955 the Communist Party committee of the All-China Association of Literary Workers sent a report to the propaganda department of the party Central Committee denouncing Ding Ling as part of a "fan dang xiao jituan" (antiparty clique). In early 1956 the party's policy toward intellectuals was liberalized, and Ding Ling asked the Central Committee to reopen her case. In May the director of the propaganda department, Lu Dingyi, gave a speech in which, quoting a phrase used by Mao, he said, "To artists and writers, we say, 'Let a hundred flowers bloom.'" Writers, especially young ones, responded with stories that placed art above politics or criticized aspects of New China. On 6 June 1957 the party committee of the All-China Association of Literary Workers agreed that the 1955 verdict on Ding Ling should be rescinded. Two days later, however, the party announced the beginning of the Fanyou yundong (Anti-Rightist Campaign). According to R. David Arkush, the writers who were attacked during the Fanyou yundong were mostly older ones—including, "above all," Ding Ling—despite the fact that "most had been rather cautious in 1956–1957." In August a front-page editorial in *Renmin ribao* (People's Daily) attacked Ding Ling by name. Throughout the spring of 1958 "Shafei nüshi ri ji di er bu," "Wo zai Xiacun de shihou," "San ba jie you gan," and "Zai yiyuan zhong" were criticized in the press. By mid 1958 an estimated three hundred thousand people had been labeled "rightists" and removed from their jobs; thousands were imprisoned or sent into internal exile. In the summer Ding Ling and Chen Ming were condemned as rightists and sent to the collective Tangyuan Farm near Jiamusi Heilongjiang province. Ding Ling was initially assigned to look after the poultry, but after 1959 she spent most of her time as a cultural-affairs worker, help-

Cover for a 1957 edition of Ding Ling's 1948 novel, Taiyang zhao zai Sangganhe shang (translated as The Sun Shines over the Sangkan River, 1954), about a Communist Party land-reform team helping peasants take action against their landlord (Wason Collection on East Asia–China, Kroch Asia Library, Cornell University)

ing to promote literacy, organizing cultural activities, and writing. In December 1964 Ding Ling and Chen Ming were transferred to Baoquanling Farm.

Early in the Cultural Revolution of 1966 to 1976 Ding Ling was subjected to public abuse and beatings. In the summer of 1968 she was confined to a *niu peng* (cattle shed), a term for any room in which prisoners of the Red Guards were kept. In May 1969 she was sent to the Twenty-First Production Brigade in Baoquanling, where she cleaned buildings, emptied latrines, spread fertilizer, fed pigs, cut the grass, planted vegetables, and performed any other tasks assigned by the Red Guards. In April 1970 she and Chen Ming were taken to Qincheng prison in Beijing; they were kept in solitary confinement until May 1975, when they were sent to a village in Shaanxi province. By this time Ding Ling had diabetes and back trouble. She writes about her experiences during the Cultural Revolution in "'Niu peng' xiaopin" (excerpts translated as "Sketches from the 'Cattle Shed,'" 1987), the second part of her memoir *Fengxue renjian* (1987, Stormy Life).

Ding Ling's "rightist" label was removed in July 1978. In January 1979 the Central Committee allowed her and Chen Ming to return to Beijing. According to Wang Zhousheng, on 25 January 1980 the Central Committee of the Communist Party approved the recommendation from the Zhongguo zuojia xiehui (Chinese Writers' Association) that Ding Ling's "Rightist" label be removed and that she be restored to her position in the party. Her earlier works were republished, and she published memoirs and essays; met with foreign writers, journalists, scholars, and students; attended conferences; traveled; and underwent treatment for breast cancer. From August to December 1981 she visited the United States at the invitation of the International Writing Center in Iowa. In 1983, to the surprise and disappointment of many of her admirers, she spoke out in support of the campaign against "jingshen wuran" (spiritual pollution). Alber writes that Ding Ling "wholeheartedly supported" the campaign "not because she believed Western influence was harmful or that alienation was impossible under socialism, but simply to get political revenge" on Zhou Yang, who was by this time on the side of moderates and liberals and was under attack by the party. Jingyuan Zhang argues that Ding Ling's behavior in 1983 was consistent with her life-long "nonconformist attitudes and strong convictions."

Ding Ling's health worsened in 1984. She was hospitalized in late 1985 and died on 4 March 1986. Interest in Ding Ling and her work has continued undiminished since her death. Some scholars emphasize Ding Ling's feminism, others her conversion to communism, others her consistent interest in progressive causes. Her fame as a writer is inseparable from her reputation as a person who lived a remarkable and often difficult life. All commentators recognize that Ding Ling was one of the most popular and influential writers of the late 1920s and early 1930s, when she published innovative short stories that were provocative in their exploration of female identity and sexuality during a time of great social change. Her career as a writer for the Communist Party has captured lasting interest because she was an outspoken critic of the party's policies toward women but also a successful author of propaganda. In general, Ding Ling's best-known works of fiction are respected as much for their personal candor and political daring as for their art, but her permanent place among the leading writers of twentieth-century China is assured. The most thorough English-language discussion of Ding Ling's fiction is Feuerwerker's *Ding Ling's Fiction: Ideology and Narrative in Modern Chinese Liter-*

ature (1982). Yuan Liangjun's *Ding Ling yanjiu ziliao* (1982, Research Materials on Ding Ling), *Ding Ling yanjiu wushinian* (1990, Fifty Years of Ding Ling Studies), edited by Yuan, and *Ding Ling yanjiu* (1992, Ding Ling Studies) collect important critical articles in Chinese.

Bibliographies:

"Chronological List of Ding Ling's Fiction," in *Ding Ling's Fiction: Ideology and Narrative in Modern Chinese Literature,* by Yi-tsi Mei Feuerwerker (Cambridge, Mass.: Harvard University Press, 1982), pp. 185–189;

"Ding Ling zhuzuo nianbiao" and "Ding Ling zhuzuo mulu," in *Ding Ling yanjiu ziliao,* edited by Yuan Liangjun (Tianjin: Tianjin renmin chubanshe, 1982), pp. 613–702;

"Ding Ling wannian zhuzuo mulu (1979–1987)," in *Ding Ling yanjiu wushinian,* edited by Yuang (Tianjin: Tianjin jiaoyu chubanshe, 1990), pp. 286–341;

"Ding Ling zhuzuo biannian (1927–1998), in *Ding Ling quanji,* 12 volumes, edited by Zhang Jiong (Shijiazhuang: Hebei renmin chubanshe, 2001), XII: 309–363.

Biographies:

Shen Congwen, *Ji Ding Ling* (Shanghai: Liangyou tushu yinshua gongsi, 1934);

Shen, *Ji Ding Ling xuji* (Sequel to Remembering Ding Ling) (Shanghai: Liangyou fuxing tushu yingshua gongsi, 1934);

Chang Jun-mei, *Ting Ling: Her Life and Her Work* (Taibei: Institute of International Relations, National Chengchi University, 1978);

Zhou Liangpei, *Ding Ling zhuan* (Beijing: Beijing shiyue wenyi chubanshe, 1993);

Wang Zhousheng, *Ding Ling nianpu* (Shanghai: Shanghai shehui kexueyuan chubanshe, 1997);

Chen Ming, "Yijiuwuwu nian zhi yijiuqijiu nian you guan Ding Ling de zhongyao jishi," in *Ding Ling quanji,* 12 volumes, edited by Zhang Jiong (Shijiazhuang: Hebei renmin chubanshe, 2001), X: 191–199;

Charles J. Alber, *Enduring the Revolution: Ding Ling and the Politics of Literature in Guomindang China* (Westport, Conn.: Praeger, 2002);

Alber, *Embracing the Lie: Ding Ling and the Politics of Literature in the People's Republic of China* (Westport, Conn.: Praeger, 2004).

References:

Marston Anderson, *The Limits of Realism: Chinese Fiction in the Revolutionary Period* (Berkeley: University of California Press, 1990), pp. 69, 73, 184–187;

R. David Arkush, introduction to *Literature of the Hundred Flowers,* 2 volumes, edited by Hualing Nieh (New York: Columbia University Press, 1981), I: xiii–xlv;

Tani E. Barlow, "Gender and Identity in Ding Ling's *Mother,*" in *Modern Chinese Women Writers: Critical Appraisals,* edited by Michael S. Duke (New York: Sharpe, 1989), pp. 1–24;

Ding Ling yanjiu (Changsha: Hunan shifan daxue chubanshe, 1992);

Yi-tsi Mei Feuerwerker, *Ding Ling's Fiction: Ideology and Narrative in Modern Chinese Literature* (Cambridge, Mass.: Harvard University Press, 1982);

David Holm, *Art and Ideology in Revolutionary China* (Oxford: Clarendon Press, 1991);

Tsi-an Hsia, "Enigma of the Five Martyrs," in his *The Gate of Darkness: Studies on the Leftist Literary Movement in China,* by Hsia (Seattle: University of Washington Press, 1968), pp. 163–233;

Ellen R. Judd, "Prelude to the 'Yan'an Talks': Problems in Transforming a Literary Intelligentsia," *Modern China,* 11 (July 1985): 377–408;

Jeffrey C. Kinkley, *The Odyssey of Shen Congwen* (Stanford, Cal.: Stanford University Press, 1987);

Liu Jianmei, *Revolution plus Love: Literary History, Women's Bodies, and Thematic Repetition in Twentieth-Century Chinese Fiction* (Honolulu: University of Hawai'i Press, 2003), pp. 13, 19–21, 54, 100, 105, 126–134, 165, 168–169, 191;

Qian Xingcun, "Guanyu *Muqin,*" *Xiandai,* 4 (November 1933): 58–66;

Tze-lan D. Sang, *The Emerging Lesbian: Female Same-Sex Desire in Modern China* (Chicago: University of Chicago Press, 2003), pp. 6, 150–153, 270;

Agnes Smedley, *China Fights Back: An American Woman with the Eighth Route Army* (New York: Vanguard, 1938), pp. 6–7, 140–144;

Helen Foster Snow, *Women in Modern China* (Paris: Mouton, 1967), pp. 190–211;

Wang Yao, *Zhongguo xin wenxue shigao,* volume 2 (Shanghai: Shanghai wenyi chubanshe, 1982), pp. 663–664;

Yuan Liangjun, *Ding Ling yanjiu ziliao* (Tianjin: Tianjin renmin chubanshe, 1982);

Yuan, ed., *Ding Ling yanjiu wushinian* (Tianjin: Tianjin jiaoyu chubanshe, 1990);

Jingyuan Zhang, "Feminism and Revolution: The Work and Life of Ding Ling," in *The Columbia Companion to Modern East Asian Literature,* edited by Joshua S. Mostow (New York: Columbia University Press, 2003), pp. 395–400.

Jiang Guangci

(11 September 1901 – 31 October 1931)

John A. Crespi
Colgate University

BOOKS: *Xin meng* [New Dreams] (Shanghai: Shanghai shudian, 1925);

Shaonian piaobozhe [The Youthful Tramp] (Shanghai: Yadong tushuguan, 1926);

Ai Zhongguo [A Lament for China] (Hankou: Changjiang shudian, 1927);

Yalujiang shang [On the Yalu River] (Shanghai: Yadong tushuguan, 1927);

Yeji [Sacrifice in the Wilderness] (Shanghai: Chuangzaoshe chubanbu, 1927);

Duankudang [The Sansculottes] (Shanghai: Taidong shuju, 1927);

Jinianbei [Monument], by Jiang and Song Ruoyu (Shanghai: Yadong tushuguan, 1927);

Kusu [Complaint] (Shanghai: Chunye shudian, 1928);

Jufen (Shanghai: Xiandai shuju, 1928);

Zuihoude weixiao [The Final Smile] (Shanghai: Xiandai shuju, 1928); republished as *Shenglide weixiao* [The Victorious Smile] (Shanghai: Guanghua shuju, 1930);

Zhangu [War Drums] (Shanghai: Beixin shuju, 1929);

Lishade aiyuan [The Sorrows of Lisa] (Shanghai: Xiandai shuju, 1929);

Chongchu yunweide yueliang [The Moon Bursts through the Clouds] (Shanghai: Beixin shuju, 1930);

Yibang yu guguo [Foreign Land and Native Country] (Shanghai: Xiandai shuju, 1930);

Xiangqing ji [Love of Home] (Shanghai: Beixin shuju, 1930);

Suilede xin yu xun ai [Broken Heart and Seeking Love] (Shanghai: Aili shudian, 1930);

Lishaji [Sorrows of Lisa and Other Stories] (Shanghai: Beixin shuju, 1931);

Tianyede feng [The Wind over the Fields] (Shanghai: Hufeng shuju, 1932).

Collections: *Jiang Guangci xuanji* [The Selected Works of Jiang Guangci] (Beijing: Kaiming shudian, 1951);

Jiang Guangci shiwen xuanji [The Selected Poetry and Prose of Jiang Guangci] (Beijing: Renmin wenxue chubanshe, 1955);

Jiang Guangci (from Tang Wenyi, Mu Dingsheng, and Ji Lei, eds., *20 shiji Zhongguo wenxue tudian,* 2001; Collection of Thomas Moran)

Jiang Guangci wenji [The Works of Jiang Guangci], 4 volumes (Shanghai: Wenyi chubanshe, 1982–1988).

TRANSLATIONS: Ilya Ehrenburg and others, *Dongtiande chunxiao* [Spring Smile in the Wintertime] (Shanghai: Taidong shuju, 1929);

Iurii Libedinsky, *Weiyuan* [Commissars] (Shanghai: Beixin shuju, 1930);

Libedinsky, *Yi zhou zian* [A Week] (Shanghai: Beixin shuju, 1931).

SELECTED PERIODICAL PUBLICATION—UNCOLLECTED: "Laotaipo yu A San" *Tuohuangzhe*, no. 1 (January 1930)–"A San," translated by Harold R. Isaacs as "Hassan," in *Straw Sandals: Chinese Short Stories 1918–1933*, edited by Isaacs (Cambridge, Mass. & London: MIT Press, 1974), pp. 170–173.

Jiang Guangci's prolific though unpolished efforts at combining revolution and romance won him a significant readership among China's educated youth during the late 1920s and early 1930s; by the time he died at age thirty, he was penniless and had alienated himself from his colleagues in China's nascent leftist literary movement. Though he is remembered primarily as a novelist and a poet, Jiang's literary endeavors range from short stories to critical essays, journal editing, and translations from Russian, as well as the publication of his diary and romantic correspondence. The brief span of his popularity was inseparable from the embryonic milieu of modern Chinese leftist writing during the late 1920s, when inchoate literary conventions and turbulent political passions often resulted in works notable less as successful art than as indicators of the era's unsettled mood.

Jiang was born Jiang Ruheng on 11 September 1901 in the village of Baitapan in the Dabie Mountains of western Anhui province. His father Jiang Congfu, was a self-educated shopkeeper; his mother's surname was Chen. Jiang's education began in 1907 at the local village school, where he displayed a facility with reading and writing that distinguished him among his siblings—two older brothers and a younger sister—and raised his parents' hopes that he would pursue a career in officialdom. Political events, along with exposure to the new-style education that was then taking hold in China, soon deflected Jiang from a traditional vocation, however. In 1914, three years after the revolution that ended the Qing dynasty, he enrolled at a boarding school in neighboring Henan province that taught mathematics, English, history, geography, and hygiene along with the Confucian Five Classics and Four Books. Jiang's keen awareness of social injustice developed and found direction during the next several years through the tutelage of progressive-minded mentors who introduced him to foreign political thought entering China at the time but also through his affinity for traditional Chinese tales of knight-errantry.

In 1917 Jiang began studying at the Number 5 Provincial Middle School in the Yangtze River treaty-port town of Wuhu. Like many young educated Chinese of the time he was inspired by Russia's October (New Style, November) Revolution; but he was attracted most powerfully by the anarchist thought of Prince Petr Kropotkin and the rebellious exploits of Sophia Perovskaya. The pen names he adopted as a youth, Jiang Guangchi (*chi* means "red") and Xiaseng (knight-errant monk), reflect his early efforts at political and literary self-fashioning. His socially progressive aspirations found their first outlet in the local chapter of the student-run Anarchist Society, where he gained editing experience working on the society's mimeographed flyer, "Ziyou zhi hua" (Flower of Freedom). During the 1919 May Fourth Movement he played an active role in Wuhu's student-led protests and boycotts and soon drew the attention of leftist intellectuals such as Chen Duxiu who were preparing to form the Chinese Communist Party. In 1920 Jiang accepted a secret invitation to enroll in the Communist Youth League's foreign-language school in Shanghai to study Russian under the tutelage of Communist International (Comintern) agent Yang Mingzhai.

In the summer of 1921 Jiang was a member of a group that traveled across war-torn Siberia to Moscow to study at the new University of the Toilers of the East, a political training school for ethnic minorities from the Soviet Union as well as students from countries such as China, Korea, Japan, India, and Turkey. During his three years in a land recovering from devastating civil strife Jiang and the other Chinese students, among whom were the future political leader Liu Shaoqi and Marxist theorist Qu Qiubai, endured hunger, a chronic shortage of clothing, and a formidable language barrier. Yet, the new-style poetry Jiang wrote during this span, collected in his first book, *Xin meng* (1925, New Dreams), expresses little of the physical hardship or homesickness he must have suffered but projects the extravagant self-image of a revolutionary-romantic poet. The portrait falls short of success, however, because in his exuberance Jiang ignores telling detail and linguistic nuance in favor of spontaneity and political sloganeering. Only in a series of untitled epigrammatic poems does he seem fleetingly, and quite uncharacteristically, to hint at a darker and more reflective side of his inner experience: "I fear nothing more than the dim shadow before me, / It is a fugitive thing, / Yet at times stabs my soul."

Jiang joined the Chinese Communist Party in Moscow in 1922. Returning to China in 1924, he taught Marxist sociology and Russian at the leftist Shanghai University and began to establish connections with the local literary scene. The following year he was recruited into Guo Moruo and Yu Dafu's Chuangzao she (Creation Society), formed his own short-lived Chunlei she (Spring Thunder Society), wrote several theoretical pieces on revolutionary literature, and published *Xin meng*. That same year, wearying of the routine of lecturing, he accepted an assignment as translator for the Soviet advisers of the warlord general Feng Yuxiang in Zhangjiakou, Hebei province. The demanding work at Feng's headquarters, however, conflicted with Jiang's self-image as a romantic wanderer and revolutionary poet. Also, throughout his stay in Shanghai and Zhangjiakou he had been carrying on a passionate correspondence with Song Ruoyu, a teacher at a middle school in Kaifeng to whom he had first written during their student days in 1920. They met face to face for the first time in August 1925 in Beijing. Song then went to Nanjing to study, and Jiang, flouting party orders by deserting his post after six months, went back to Shanghai so that he could visit her more easily.

Jiang's first major work of fiction, the short novel *Shaonian piaobozhe* (1926, The Youthful Tramp), is a slackly structured refraction of the author's romantic vision of himself as a drifter, lover, and champion of social justice. Jiang frames the story as a long confessional letter written by the young protagonist, Wang Zhong, to an established writer and mentor figure. It begins with the death of Wang's parents under a tyrannical landlord and develops into a record of his suffering when he is cast adrift in an unjust society. The ill-starred but defiant Wang encounters a pederastic itinerant scholar, unscrupulous merchants, a corrupt innkeeper, a despotic British silk-mill owner, the evil minions of the union-crushing warlord Wu Peifu, and callous foreign residents of Shanghai; he also engages in a tragically doomed love affair. An addendum informs the reader that after attending the Whampoa Military Academy in Guangzhou, Wang met a heroic end in a hail of bullets crying, "Down with the warlords! Down with imperialism!" Although *Shaonian piaobozhe* was criticized for its crudity and immaturity, the novel found a readership among educated, romantically minded Chinese youth. For Jiang, who invested much of his own sketchy but firmly held personal vision into his writing, the disappointing critical reception that met both this first novel and *Xin meng*–which had, nevertheless, gone into three printings by mid 1926–was assuaged in part by a growing measure of literary celebrity.

Jiang's next effort at fiction was a collection of eight short stories written in 1926 and published in 1927 as *Yalujiang shang* (On the Yalu River). Most of the stories weave autobiographical elements into the dual fixation on love and revolution that became the hallmark of his writing. Perhaps the best known of these stories is the title piece, in which Jiang appeals to the contemporary Chinese reader by selecting the exotic locales of Moscow and Japanese-occupied Korea for his setting. Several students at the University of the Toilers of the East sit around a stove on a winter evening exchanging stories of their experiences in love. After some prodding from the narrator and a Persian classmate, the taciturn Korean Lee Maeng-han tells how his idyllic childhood on the verdant banks of the Yalu River was shattered when his aristocratic parents were killed by the barbaric Japanese police and he was forced to leave Korea and his betrothed, Kim Yun-ku. Kim died in a Japanese prison after being arrested for labor agitation with the Korea Socialist Youth Alliance, leaving Lee heartbroken yet passionately devoted to liberating his homeland from its imperialist oppressors.

Cover for a 1949 edition of Jiang's Yalujiang shang *(1927, On the Yalu River), a collection of stories with autobiographical elements (Wason Collection on East Asia–China, Kroch Asia Library, Cornell University)*

The final story in the volume, "Xun ai" (Seeking Love), delivers a failed effort at parody through the misadventures of Liu Yisheng, a down-at-the-heels art student in Shanghai whose poetic talent is said to rival those of Li Bai, Heinrich Heine, and William Butler Yeats. Liu—and, the reader suspects from certain autobiographical details, Jiang—believes that a sensitive "poet of genius" like himself should naturally attract female admirers. When none are forthcoming, he seeks the affections of a beautiful classmate, an entertainer, and waitresses at the upscale Sun Company coffee shop and the teahouse theaters of the Fairy World Department Store. Liu's amorous fantasies are deflated when the women snub him for smartly dressed swells or berate him for leaving a niggardly tip. The frustrated and resentful Liu concludes that "today's world is a world of money where poets of genius, love, purity and the like are no more than dog farts!" He burns his poetry, severs all ties with the literary arena, and plunges into the workers' movement so that he may "expunge the insults he has suffered and change the world." The story is notable on one level for its depiction of libidinal drives split between literature, love, and social justice and on another as an early portrayal of a literary man whose masculinity is threatened by the urban modern girl, a schema developed with much greater complexity by the Shanghai modernists in the early to mid 1930s. Jiang's inept treatment of these themes leaves the reader unsure whether to view Liu Yisheng as an object of pity, satire, or heroic revolutionary resolve.

Song moved in with Jiang in Shanghai in the fall of 1926. In November she died of tuberculosis in the Jiangxi province resort town of Guling. A year after her death, Jiang published a portion of their correspondence as *Jinianbei* (Monument).

Jiang's second novel, *Duankudang* (1927, The Sansculottes), is an ambitious attempt to dramatize the series of massive strikes organized by Communist labor leaders in Shanghai in the months preceding the April 1927 arrival of Chiang Kai-shek's Beifa (Northern Expedition), a two-year military campaign that united China under Nationalist Party rule. Jiang wrote the novel in the midst of the uprisings and based several of the main characters on his close acquaintances among the movement's organizers, including Qu. Nevertheless, critics pointed out that *Duankudang* falls far short of its grand aspirations. The narrative lurches clumsily to and fro among an array of shallow, unconvincing heroes and villains as it follows several pairs of revolutionary lovers through a series of secret meetings, blood-spattered clashes with police, and melodramatic declarations of passion for revolution and for one another. After the actual insurrection ended in a violent counterrevolutionary coup on 12 April, Jiang fled up the Yangtze River to Wuhan. In the interest of self-preservation during the ensuing White Terror, he changed his pen name from Guangchi to Guangci (*ci* means "kind").

After Jiang returned to Shanghai in September 1927, he and some colleagues established the Taiyang she (Sun Society) literary association and a small publishing company, the Chunye Bookstore, where they produced a sectarian journal, *Taiyang yuekan* (Sun Monthly). The Sun Society launched a bid for leadership of the latest vogue in Shanghai literary circles: revolutionary literature. The ferment of interest in a literature of revolution during the late 1920s arose in part from the wave of urban uprisings that had swept China's coastal cities during 1927 but also resonated with similar leftist literary movements in Japan, the United States, and various European countries. At this initial stage in 1927–1928 the burning issue was not so much the practical problem of how to write such a literature but the more vainglorious question of which literary group—the Sun Society or the rival Creation Society, from which Jiang had split—could claim credit for originating it on the Chinese scene. Soon, however, the two groups formed a loose alliance and shifted their strategy to denouncing the revolutionary credentials of the new literature movement's most authoritative figure, Lu Xun. For his efforts Jiang earned from Lu Xun the derisive epithets "Guang-X," "Guang-Y," and "Guang-Z." The spate of high-profile polemics, however, helped create an expanded readership for this self-styled revolutionary—or, as it was also called, proletarian—literature. Jiang in particular profited from sympathetic, though not wholly uncritical, reviews of his work by his colleague and fellow Anhui native A Ying.

Jiang continued to exploit the links between love and revolution in his next several novels. In *Yeji* (Sacrifice in the Wilderness), written in Wuhan and published at the end of 1927, he sets up a romantic triangle among Chen Jixia, a "semi-proletarian" writer who lives under an assumed name on the fringes of the Shanghai labor movement; Zhang Shujun, his landlord's daughter; and Zheng Yuxuan, a schoolteacher. Soon after Chen moves into the Zhang household, Shujun detects his true identity as a Communist Party member-cum-revolutionary writer, falls secretly in love with him, and is inspired to enter the Shanghai labor movement. The misguided Chen, however, initiates an affair with the bland and apolitical Yuxuan, even as his conscience tugs at him for ignoring the unspoken love of the increasingly activist Shujun. Fearing association with the political Left, Yuxuan rebuffs Chen after the April 1927 counterrevolutionary coup. The bold, pure-

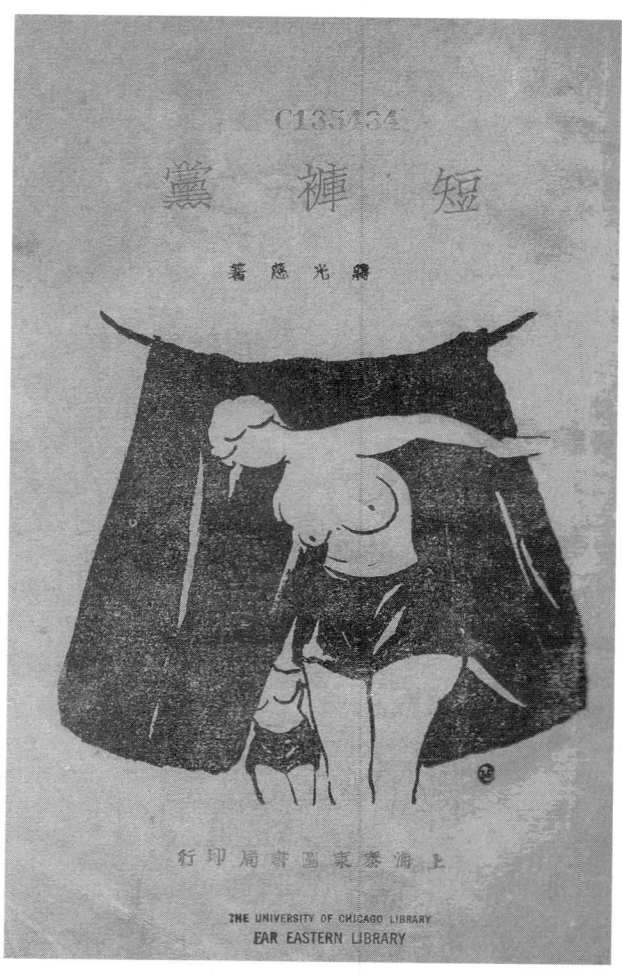

Cover for Jiang's novel Duankudang (1927, The Sansculottes), about a series of strikes organized by Communist labor leaders in Shanghai in April 1927 (Joseph Regenstein Library, University of Chicago)

hearted revolutionary Shujun is arrested during the White Terror and executed in secret, leaving Chen consumed with remorse for having spurned her and, by implication, the revolutionary project. To relieve his guilt and recommit himself to the path of righteous rebellion, he carries a bottle of wine and a bouquet of flowers to the desolate seaside at Wusongkou, where he tearfully performs a ritual sacrifice and composes a poem that concludes: "Let this bottle of wine be my blood and tears; / Let this bouquet be my oath; / You were sacrificed in the pursuit of the light, / And I shall forever take the darkness as my sworn foe. / Alas! My girl! / May your soul bring me succor."

A similar guiding female figure appears in Jiang's next novel, *Zuihoude weixiao* (1928, The Final Smile), the first four chapters of which were published serially in *Taiyang yuekan* in 1928 under the title "Zuiren" (The Guilty). The hero, nineteen-year-old Wang Agui, represents Jiang's skewed conception of a typical urban proletarian's coming to revolutionary consciousness. Wang is drawn into the Shanghai labor movement while attending classes taught by a young woman revolutionary, Shen Yufang, at a commoners' night school. Shen and one of Wang's comrades are arrested and executed at the instigation of Agui's overseer at the silk filature, Zhang Jinkui, who later fires Agui from his job. The remainder of the novel follows the semidelirious Wang on a murderous, anarchic vendetta against the overseer and his coconspirators. Spurring him along on his killing spree are hallucinations of mocking yellow ants and visions of Yufang. At one point Yufang appears to him in Revolutionaries' Heaven, a sylvan paradise where pure-willed martyrs to the anticapitalist, anti-imperialist struggle relax in lawn chairs and rowboats. As the dream fades, Yufang reminds Wang of his sacred revolutionary mission: "Have you forgotten your responsibility? Zhang Jinkui is still out there harming others! Can it be you've forgotten that your parents are suffering and your worker comrades are oppressed? Go! Go and avenge us. Go and avenge the oppressed, avenge yourself. Make haste!" After killing Zhang, Wang consummates his bloody mission of revolutionary vengeance by bursting in on two union-busting toughs as they lie, naked, smoking opium in a hotel room. He shoots them dead and then, surrounded by police and with a "smile of victory" on his face, turns the pistol on himself.

The excesses of Jiang's style began to attract damaging criticism from leftist literary circles after the release of *Lishade aiyuan* (1929, The Sorrows of Lisa). In this novel, which Jiang described as an "experiment," he attempts a psychological portrait in the confessional mode of a beautiful young Russian aristocrat who flees to Shanghai with her husband after the October Revolution. Dire economic straits compel Lisa to become an exotic dancer and then a prostitute catering to foreign men. After ten years, her body ridden by syphilis, her homeland lost to the Bolsheviks, and her husband benumbed with depression, Lisa decides to commit suicide by throwing herself into the ocean.

The harshest attacks on *Lishade aiyuan* were directed not at its stylistic flaws, the most notable of which is Jiang's clumsy and tedious use of first-person narration, but at its ambiguous political message. At a moment when brutal repression threatened to extinguish the Chinese leftist movement, Jiang's largely sympathetic portrayal of a character who both hates the Bolsheviks—whom she calls "black worms"—and idealizes her former aristocratic life could hardly be condoned as properly revolutionary writing. In the eyes of leftist critics, Jiang's "experiment" was worse than a failure; they pointed out the ideological inconsistencies of the novel, and at least one recommended that Jiang be formally punished by the party for his transgression.

Jiang wrote his next novel, *Chongchu yunweide yueliang* (1930, The Moon Bursts through the Clouds), in three months in late 1929 while convalescing in Tokyo from tuberculosis of the lungs; he was also suffering from the as-yet-undiagnosed intestinal tuberculosis that eventually took his life. Despite his deteriorating physical condition he also translated Iurii Libedinsky's novel *Nedelya* (1922) as *Yi zhou zian* (1931, A Week) from the Russian, kept a diary that he published under the title *Yibang yu guguo* (Foreign Land and Native Country) in 1930, and read books of Russian and Soviet literary theory that he borrowed on visits to the home of the Japanese Marxist critic Kurahara Korehito.

After its publication in January 1930, *Chongchu yunweide yueliang* went through eight reprints in as many months. The popular appeal of the novel can be attributed to Jiang's integration of sexual escapades into a revolutionary bildungsroman. Wang Manying, an attractive young woman of high patriotic and progressive ideals, studies at the Whampoa Military Academy and endures the hardships of the Northern Expedition. When the expedition's hoped-for liberation of Shanghai ends in the Nationalists' bloody suppression of the Communists, the disillusioned but still rebellious Manying launches herself on a personal mission of vengeance against society by seducing and sexually humiliating a series of men—including a comprador's son, a corrupt politician, and the seventeen-year-old son of a banker—whom she perceives as enemies of the revolution. But she reencounters and falls in love with a former classmate, Li Shangzhi, who is now an underground Communist Party activist pursuing the more orthodox revolutionary path of union organizing. Humbled by Li's high-minded commitment to the cause, Manying descends into tortured self-recriminations that climax when she discovers that Li, who is unaware of her sexual adventuring, harbors a secret love for her. At the hastily expedient conclusion of the novel Manying suddenly emerges from her despair while viewing the sunrise from the train to Wusongkou, where she had planned to drown herself in the ocean. Two months later, she and Li are reunited when he finds the reborn Manying, now a laborer in a filature, lecturing to a crowd of other workers.

In January 1930 Jiang met and married the art student, actress, and self-styled bohemian Wu Sihong. Living in Shanghai under an assumed name, he attended meetings of the newly formed Zhongguo zuoyi zuojia lianmeng (League of Left-Wing Writers) and worked on his final novel, *Tianyede feng* (1932, The Wind over the Fields); the first thirteen chapters appeared in 1930 in the league journal that Jiang helped to edit, *Tuohuangzhe* (Cultivator on Barren Land), under the title "Paoxiaolede tudi" (The Roaring Earth). The novel, which is modeled loosely on Ivan Turgenev's *Ottsy i deti* (1862; translated as *Fathers and Sons*, 1867), represents something of a departure for Jiang in its depiction of rural rather than urban revolutionary activism. An educated young revolutionary, Li Jie, returns to his home village and leads the struggle to organize a farmers association and overturn the reactionary local gentry, of which his own father is a member. In terms of technique, however, *Tianyede feng*, like much of Jiang's previous work, suffers greatly from the author's stilted imagination combined with what his acquaintances describe as a habitual disinclination to revise or edit his manuscripts. Jiang clumsily shepherds his prop-like characters through one contrived plot device after another, neutralizing any dramatic tension that might have emerged from Li Jie's relations with his father, among the rogues' gallery of peasants he seeks to win over, or between Li and his several love interests. The novel was banned by the Nationalist authorities before publication; when it appeared in print posthumously in 1932, it was promptly banned again.

Terminally ill with intestinal tuberculosis, chafing under the demands of party membership, and his marriage collapsing under the dual strain of constant police harassment and the economic hardship caused by the banning of his books, Jiang ceased producing during his last year of life. His isolation was compounded when he applied in October 1930 to resign from the party to devote his diminishing stamina more fully to writing. The party responded with an announcement of his expulsion in the *Hongqi ribao* (Red Flag Daily News) that called his application "the most dastardly act of a petit-bourgeois" and labeled him an opportunist and a coward. Jiang died in Shanghai's Tongren Hospital on 31 October 1931.

Since the early 1950s, critics and literary historians in the People's Republic of China have largely excused Jiang's political and literary shortcomings in order to add him to the canon of modern patriotic leftist writers. Outside of China, Jiang Guangci is regarded as a flawed, headstrong, and misguided writer but one whose short, troubled career reflects vividly the passions, distortions, and contradictions of a tumultuous era. For the reader willing to tolerate the idiosyncrasies of his style, Jiang Guangci's fiction remains a testament to the fecund and undisciplined nature of China's earliest modern revolutionary literature.

Bibliography:

"Jiang Guangci zhuyi shumu" and "Jiang Guangci yanjiu ziliao mulu suoyin," in *Jiang Guangci yanjiu ziliao,* edited by Fang Ming (Yinchuan: Ningxia renmin chubanshe, 1983), pp. 62–68, 541–552.

Biography:

Wu Tenghuang, *Jiang Guangci zhuan* (Hefei: Anhui renmin chubanshe, 1982).

References:

Fang Ming, ed., *Jiang Guangci yanjiu ziliao* (Yinchuan: Ningxia renmin chubanshe, 1983);

Marian Galik, "Studies in Modern Chinese Literary Criticism: VI. Chiang Kuang-tz'u's Concept of Revolutionary Literature," *Asian and African Studies* (Bratislava), 8 (1972): 43–69;

C. T. Hsia, "Communist Fiction, I," in his *A History of Modern Chinese Fiction* (New Haven: Yale University Press, 1961), pp. 257–280;

Tsi-an Hsia, "The Phenomenon of Chiang Kuang-t'zu," in his *The Gate of Darkness: Studies on the Leftist Literary Movement in China* (Seattle & London: University of Washington Press, 1968), pp. 55–100;

Leo Ou-fan Lee, "Chiang Kuang-tz'u," in his *The Romantic Generation of Modern Chinese Writers* (Cambridge, Mass.: Harvard University Press, 1973, pp. 201–221;

Tang Wenyi, Mu Dingsheng, and Ji Lei, eds., *20 shiji Zhongguo wenxue tudian* (Chengdu: Sichuan renmin chubanshe, 2001);

Philip F. Williams, "Pierrot Figures in the Modern Chinese Novella," *Asian Review,* 9, no. 1 (1989): 21–24.

Lai He

(25 April 1894 – 31 January 1943)

Rosemary M. Haddon
Massey University

BOOKS: *Yi gan chengzi*, edited by Zhong Zhaozheng and Ye Shitao, Guangfuqian Taiwan wenxue quanji 1, Yuanjing congkan, no. 126 (Taibei: Yuanjing chubanshe, 1979)–title story translated by Jane Parish Yang as "The Steelyard," in *The Unbroken Chain: An Anthology of Taiwan Fiction since 1926*, edited by Joseph S. M. Lau (Bloomington: Indiana University Press, 1983), pp. 3–11; also includes "Shansong de ren de gushi," translated as "The Advocate," in *Oxcart: Nativist Stories from Taiwan, 1934–1977*, translated by Rosemary M. Haddon, Edition Cathay, volume 18 (Dortmund: Project, 1996), pp. 59–71;

Lai He xiansheng quanji [The Complete Works of Lai He], edited by Li Nanheng, Rijuxia Taiwan xinwenxue: Mingji, volume 1 (Taibei: Mingtan chubanshe, 1979).

Collections: *Lai He xiaoshuo ji* [Collected Stories by Lai He] (Taibei: Hongfan shudian, 1994);

Lai He shougao ji: Xin wenxue juan [Lai He's Manuscripts: New Literature Volume], edited by Lin Ruiming (Taiwan: Lai He wenjiao jijinhui/Taiwan Sheng wenxian weiyuanhui, 2000).

Lai He (from the back cover for Lai He shougao ji: Xin wenxue juan *(2000, Lai He's Manuscripts: New Literature Volume), edited by Lin Ruiming (Davis Library, University of North Carolina at Chapel Hill)*

Known as "Taiwan xinwen xue zhi fu" (the father of Taiwan's new literature), Lai He lived during the Japanese colonial period (1895 to 1945) and played a key role in Taiwan's New Literature Movement of 1920 to 1937. The movement promoted the use of *baihua* (the Chinese vernacular), and Lai was the first Taiwanese writer to use the vernacular rather than *wenyanwen* (Classical Chinese) in his works. Lai He's reputation is based on his vernacular writings, which comprise poems, stories, and essays in the subgenres *sanwen* (prose essay), *suibi* (informal essay), *zawen* (topical essay), and *tongxun* (dispatch). As the first writer to use the vernacular as a literary language, Lai paved the way for Taiwan's modern literary development. He was also a mentor to important writers such as Yang Kui; the first half of Yang Kui's debut short story, "Shinbun hai-tatsufu" (Paperboy), was published in the journal *Taiwan xinmin bao* (Taiwan New People's Press) in 1932 owing to Lai's recommendation. A nationalist, Lai resisted Japanese colonial rule and its policies of assimilation and grew a queue–a Manchu, Qing dynasty-style braid–to symbolize his anti-Japanese sentiments.

Lai He was born in Zhanghua in central Taiwan on 25 April 1894, a few months prior to the outbreak of the first Sino-Japanese War. Japan's victory in 1895 began fifty years of colonial rule, which shaped Lai He's attitude toward the Japanese. His name is a homophone of his best-known pen name; the only difference is the character used for "He." (His other pen names included Lan Yun, Fu San, An Dusheng, Zou Jiesheng, Hui, and Xuan.) Lai He's family belonged to the "lesser tradition" of the Chinese social order—that is, the folk tradition as opposed to the Confucian tradition of elite culture. His father, Lai Tiansong, was a Daoist priest; his mother's name was Dai Yun. As a boy Lai He was greatly influenced by his grandfather, Lai Zhi, a practitioner of an occult Daoist healing art involving cymbals.

Lai He was required to attend public school, where the language of instruction was Japanese. But before and after school, he studied Chinese at a private academy in which his family enrolled him when he was nine. In 1907 he began private lessons with a tutor, Huang Zhaoqi, under whose instruction he developed a deep understanding of the Chinese classical tradition.

Lai He gained access to the best educational route open to the Taiwanese when he entered the colonial government's medical school in Taibei at fifteen. In 1914 he received his medical degree; the following year he obtained a position at Jiayi Hospital. His salary, however, was less than half that of the hospital's Japanese doctors. In November 1915 he married Wang Cao in Zhanghua. When he returned to the hospital, he was not reinstated as a doctor. For the next year he was assigned the menial duty of recording patients' illnesses.

In 1917 Lai He resigned from the hospital and returned to Zhanghua, where he opened a private clinic. His career as a writer commenced that year when he began writing poetry in Classical Chinese. The poems appeared in *Taiwan,* a journal published by Taiwanese living in Tokyo. The themes of the poems include Liu Mingchuan, a well-known Taiwanese entrepreneur of the Qing period; bereavement; opium addiction; and issues of equality and justice. A 1997 study of Lai He edited by the Donghai University Chinese Department compares his 102 poems in Classical Chinese to the poetry of the sixteenth-century Ming scholar-official Gui Youguang.

Lai He and his wife had a son in 1918. In 1919 Lai He began working at the Bo'ai Hospital in Xiamen, Fujian province, in mainland China, where he was exposed to the Xin wenhua yundong (New Culture Movement) that began in 1915. He returned to Taiwan in 1920 for the birth of his second son and remained there. He and his wife had four more sons and three daughters. The first, second, and sixth sons died in infancy or as toddlers; their first daughter died at age three. During the following two decades he devoted himself to writing and to his clinic, where, according to hearsay, he occasionally treated the poor of Zhanghua free of charge.

The Taiwan wenhua xiehui (Taiwan Cultural Association) was formed in July 1921 and provided the major impetus for social and political reform. Lai He joined in October and was elected executive officer. In 1923 the association began sponsoring lecture tours to promote modernization.

Lai He began to write in the vernacular in 1925. This enterprise was fraught with difficulty for two reasons: first, the vernacular was not yet fully formed as a literary language; second, Lai He's formal education in the colonial school system had been conducted in Japanese. Nontheless, he refused to write in Japanese because he associated the language with colonial occupation. Writing in the vernacular was an arduous three-stage process: first, he wrote a draft in Classical Chinese; then he translated the draft into the vernacular; finally, he revised the translation to bring the language closer to the Taiwanese dialect, a version of the Min dialect spoken in Fujian province. The Taiwanese dialect is quite different from the vernacular Mandarin in which most modern Chinese literature is written, and many Taiwanese words do not have matching Chinese characters. In his essays Lai He discusses views about Classical Chinese, the need for a vernacular literature that would be accessible to the people, and the difficulty of using Chinese characters to write the Taiwanese dialect.

Lai He's first vernacular work was an experimental prose piece, "Wu ti" (Untitled); it was published in the August 1925 issue of *Taiwan minbao* (Taiwan People's Press), a journal linked to the New Literature Movement. The narrator's former girlfriend has rejected him in favor of a man from a wealthy family; he watches her wedding procession as it takes her to her new home and offers himself to the reader as a "model to the foolish" who fall in love. The romanticism of "Wu ti" is an anomaly in Lai He's corpus, most of which is realist or social realist. During the period of China's May Fourth Movement, 1919 to 1925, social realism, which is concerned with social and political injustice, superseded Romanticism as the preferred mode of literary expression; Taiwan's New Literature movement, which was influenced by the May Fourth Movement, was generally realist. May Fourth ideas about democracy, socialism, and Westernization reached Taiwan through Zhang Wojun, a Taiwanese intellectual who traveled to Beijing, and through journals such as *Taiwan minbao,* which published nineteenth-century European literary works and selections from May Fourth writers, including stories by Lu Xun. May Fourth fiction stimulated the development of Taiwan's new literature.

"Juewuxia de xisheng" (Calculated Sacrifice), Lai He's first vernacular poem, was published in the

December 1925 issue of *Taiwan minbao*. It commemorates the 23 October Erlin Incident in Zhanghua in which Taiwanese sugar-cane farmers organized a cooperative to negotiate with the Japanese Sugar Association, the cartel that had controlled the sugar industry in Taiwan since 1909, for better prices. The negotiations failed, a confrontation occurred, and thirty-nine members of the cooperative were jailed. "Juewuxia de xisheng" expresses sympathy for the farmers, to whom the poet refers as "ruozhe" (the weak).

The fiction reprinted in *Taiwan minbao* was a source of inspiration for Lai He. Many of his stories portray the brutality of Japanese colonial rule and the hardships it inflicts on Taiwan's weak and disempowered, including peasants, vendors, students, women, and the indigenous Austronesians. Other stories critique the attitudes, lifestyles, and social ills that were the legacy of the old Chinese society. His themes include opium smoking and intellectuals who have not made the transition to the new thinking. He published his first short story, "Dou nao're" (Much Ado), in *Taiwan minbao* in January 1926. Realist in orientation, it opens with an idyllic portrait of a quiet, moonlit town that contrasts with a subsequent description of street life in one of the town's neighborhoods. The neighborhood is the scene of nightly pitched battles between gangs fighting for face and prestige. The neighborhood people are educated and of an elevated class status, but they lack unity and purpose. In their folly they give money to the gangs as payment for the entertainment provided by the battles. "Dou nao're" offers a stark portrayal of the foibles of Taiwan's traditional society.

Lai He's next work, the social realist short story "Yi gan chengzi" (translated as "The Steelyard," 1983), was published in the February 1926 issue of *Taiwan minbao* and is one of his best-known and most-loved works. The farmer Qin Deshen goes into town to sell some vegetables to earn a few extra dollars for the approaching New Year. A Japanese policeman accuses him of using a scale—the "steelyard" of the title—that does not conform to the colonial government's standards of weights and measures. It does not occur to the guileless Qin to bribe the policeman by giving him a few vegetables, and the officer breaks the steelyard in two and records Qin's name and address. In court Qin refuses to pay his fine and is sent to jail. His wife pawns a piece of jewelry and pays the fine to free her husband in time for the New Year. Qin is released but has no money to buy presents for their children. He recalls his mother at the moment of her death and the peace that accompanied her release from a lifetime of suffering. "Yi gan chengzi" concludes with the children's cries of disappointment and a rumor that a Japanese policeman has been murdered in the early hours of New Year's Day. In a postscript Lai He refers to the story as a "tragedy" and states that it was inspired by Anatole France's story "Crainquebille" (1901; translated, 1915), about a gendarme who victimizes a vegetable vendor. He then says that an incident such as that recounted in "Yi gan chengzi" can occur in any place that is subject to authoritarian rule. From the remarks the reader may conclude that Qin killed the policeman, then possibly committed suicide. Such a reading would account for Lai He's calling the story a tragedy.

Cover for *Lai He xiaoshuo ji* (Collected Stories by Lai He), published in 1994 (Wason Collection on East Asia–China, Kroch Asia Library, Cornell University)

In 1926 Lai He was appointed editor of the literature and arts section of *Taiwan minbao*. In 1927 ideological disagreements among the members split the Taiwan Cultural Association into a left-wing faction, which advocated class struggle, and a right-wing faction, which favored national unity. Lai He's works reflect the debates within the association.

The recruitment of Taiwanese into the Japanese police force is reflected in Lai He's story "Bu Tai-lin" (Officer Bu), published in the Tokyo journal *Xin sheng* (New Life) in 1927. Officer Bu is an irascible Taiwanese patrolman who, because of assimilation, becomes a running dog of the Japanese. "Bu ruyi de guonian" (Unhappy New Year's), which was published in the January 1928 issue of *Taiwan minbao,* is also concerned with the police. A policeman named Tai-lin acts out his resentment over an unexpected decrease in his year-end bonus by knocking street hawkers down, fining people he deems slow in sweeping the footpaths in front of their houses, and breaking the weighing scales of shops in a crude attempt to enforce the colonial weights and measures law. At the conclusion of the story Tai-lin is incensed yet again by the indifference of the local people to Japanese social customs.

The essay "Qianjin" (Advance) is significant for the insight it offers into Lai He's political thought. It appeared in the May 1928 inaugural issue of *Taiwan dazhong shibao* (Taiwan Masses Times), a journal associated with the leftist faction in the 1927 split within the Taiwan Cultural Association. The essay features two children who symbolize Taiwan's abandonment by China and who are driven to seek solace in a "meng zhi guo" (world of dreams). An allegory of the post-1927 political factions and their unrealized potential to cooperate in the creation of a utopia, "Qianjin" describes Taiwan as a "land covered in darkness." Critics acclaimed it as a masterpiece.

Lai He's next story, "She xiansheng" (Mr. Snake), is a tongue-in-cheek anecdote that was serialized in the 1, 11, and 18 January 1930 issues of *Taiwan minbao.* It opens with the hero in a snake-infested marshland at midnight, stalking frogs to sell in the local market. The frogs fall over each other to leap into Mr. Snake's basket, grateful to be rescued from the snakes even though they will soon fall victim to the butcher's knife. After some years, Mr. Snake becomes an expert in treating people for snakebite but is detained for questioning because his treatments are not recognized by the law. Later, a doctor trained in Western medicine pressures Mr. Snake to share his snakebite remedies; in exasperation, Mr. Snake picks a handful of grass and hands it to the doctor. The doctor has the grass analyzed; but when the results emerge from the laboratory two years later, they show an ingredient that has long been known in local medical circles. In a metaphorical reading of the story, Mr. Snake symbolizes traditional values that fend off the mores that have seeped into Taiwan with modernization.

Lai He's story "Qipanbian" (Beside the Chessboard) appeared in *Xiandai shenghuo* (Modern Life) in October 1930. The protagonist is a member of the traditional Chinese intellectual elite; his life revolves around the opium he smokes with like-minded companions. His "Ru!?" (Insult!?) was published in the January 1931 issue of *Taiwan xinmin bao,* the successor to *Taiwan minbao.* The birthday celebration of Zhusheng niangma (the Goddess of Birth), a local deity in Chinese popular religion, includes opera performances that present a story within the story and provide an ironic commentary on colonialism by depicting a fantasy world that is at odds with the events that unfold in the "real" world of the narrative. Prior to the evening performance, street vendors set up their stalls and angrily discuss the police, who have been called in to watch over the meetings of the Taiwan Cultural Association; the duty entails an extra expense for the police, which they make up for by fining the street vendors. The more meetings the police are called in to watch over, the more the street vendors are fined. The opera presents a story that is similar to that of the street vendors, involving inequality, suffering, and injustice; in the opera, however, a knight-errant obtains revenge on behalf of the people. The vendors are mesmerized by the opera; but as they watch, the police descend on them again, depriving them of even a vicarious vengeance. The reader is reminded of the hopelessness that dominates day-to-day life in the real world of colonialism.

In April and May 1931 Lai He serialized the long poem "Nan'guo aige" (Lament of the South) in three issues of *Taiwan xinmin bao.* It commemorates the Wushe Incident of 1930, which commenced on 27 October when a group of the Taiya people of the village of Wushe in southern Taiwan disrupted a Japanese athletic competition. In the conflict that followed, the Taiya killed more than one hundred Japanese. The colonial government ordered the uprising quelled, and Japanese troops moved in with tanks, airplanes, and poison gas. During the following two months the troops killed more than nine hundred villagers. In a contrast with the mournful tone of traditional elegies, "Nan'guo aige" celebrates the bravery of the Taiya Austronesians. The poem was originally published in censored form: the first stanza was cut because it includes references to the Japanese troops' use of poison gas, a violation of international law.

"Kelian ta sile" (Death of a Woman), published in censored form in *Taiwan xinmin bao* in May and June 1931, is similar to May Fourth stories about women who are oppressed because of their sex. A-jin is sold as a child bride by her impoverished parents to raise money for the *hushui* (residency tax). She moves in with a family that includes a son who will become her husband; but the son and the father are killed by the police during a labor dispute, and A-jin's widowed mother-in-law is forced to sell her as a concubine. A-jin's new husband, A-li Ge (Brother A-li), has an uncontrollable appetite for sex. When he tires of her, he sends her back to her former mother-in-law and moves on to seek a new conquest. Discovering that she is pregnant, A-jin decides to bear the child and raise it on her own. One day she goes to a nearby river to do the laundry, is caught up in the swift current, and drowns. "Kelian ta sile" concludes with A-li Ge submitting a request for a new wife to the go-between, who asks, horrified, whether A-li Ge knows that A-jin has drowned.

"Fengzuo" (Harvest), published in January 1932 in the *Taiwan xinmin bao,* deals with the exploitation of the sugarcane farmers by the Japanese Sugar Association. The cartel confiscated or bought up large tracts of land, leaving the farmers with no alternative but to work for it. Tianfu plants cane on land he leases from the cartel. His heart is set on exceeding the production quota, which will win him a prize that will enable him to afford the dowry to buy a wife for his son. But the cartel announces new regulations, which have the potential of wiping out Tianfu's profit. Tianfu labors hard, determined to win the award. At harvesttime, however, the Japanese fix the scales, and Tianfu's harvest weighs in at four thousand kilos less than he actually turned in. After deducting the costs of the lease, fertilizer, seedlings, and interest, Tianfu is left with nothing.

"Reshi" (Provocation), serialized in the magazine *Nanyin* (Voices of the South) in January, April, and July 1932, is another story about police oppression. A policeman's chicken wanders into the house of an elderly woman and gets trapped under a basket. The policeman discovers the chicken and accuses the woman of stealing it. A young man defends the woman and tries to muster support for her among the villagers, but his attempts are met with indifference. He denounces the policeman, then departs for Taibei, ostensibly for work but more likely because he is afraid that the policeman will retaliate. The Mukden Incident of 18 September 1931, which launched Japanese military aggression in northeastern China, and the resulting tightening of Japanese control in Taiwan explain why in "Reshi" Lai He turns from the resistance he depicted in earlier works to a portrayal of apathetic indifference on the part of the people.

In 1934 Lai He participated in the formation of the Taiwan wenyi lianmeng (Alliance of Taiwan's Literary Artists), the high point in the effort to bring about cultural renaissance and social and political reform. His story "Shansong de ren de gushi" (translated as "The Advocate," 1996), which was published in *Taiwan wenyi* (Taiwan Literary Arts) in December of that year, continues the low irony of "Reshi." The story was written as a *chuanqi* (legend) with elements of myth and divine intervention, which masked a blunt political message. This form enabled it to evade the tightened censorship in an increasingly militarized Taiwan. The story includes elements of divine intervention. Mr. Lin, an Austronesian, goes to the Fujian provincial court in

Cover for the collection Lai He shougao ji: Xin wenxue juan *(2000, Lai He's Manuscripts: New Literature Volume), edited by Lin Ruiming (Davis Library, University of North Carolina at Chapel Hill)*

Fouzhou to try to restore land stolen by a landlord to the local people, who want to use it for cattle grazing and as a cemetery. In a teahouse he meets a beggar-like individual who, mysteriously, knows why he has come to Fuzhou and gives him some pointers that help him succeed in the lawsuit. The land is declared public property, and harmony and order are restored. The theft symbolizes the confiscation of land under enclosure policies and practices and the loss of native sovereignty.

In the mid 1930s militarism led to the adoption by the colonial government of *Kôminka undô* (Imperialization program), which compelled the Taiwanese to speak Japanese and take Japanese surnames. The difficulties of this period are reflected in the mood of Lai He's final works, which include "Yige tongzhi de pixin" (Letter from a Comrade) and "Fule chunyan huilai" (Return from a Banquet). "Yighe tongzhi de pixin" was published in December 1935 in *Taiwan xin wenxue* (Taiwan's New Literature) and includes many phrases from the Taiwanese dialect, which make it difficult to read. Both stories possess a low-key, dispirited tone that is similar to that in Lai He's "Di qiya de shanding–Bagua shan" (1931, Low-Pressure Summit—Bagua Mountain), a poem that expresses despair over the deepening shadow of colonialism. The narrator of the ostensibly autobiographical "Fule chunyan huilai," published in the first issue of *Dongya xinbao* (East Asia New Press), possibly in January 1936 (there is some uncertainty about the year), has sunk into bar life and womanizing. In "Yige tongzhi de pixin" the former political activist Shi Hui receives a letter from an old comrade in jail asking for a loan, but before he can respond, he is compelled to donate funds to the Japanese and is left with nothing to lend to his friend.

In 1937 full-scale war broke out between China and Japan. With the declaration of war, the Chinese-language sections of Taiwan's journals and newspapers were banned, leaving writers with nowhere to publish their works, and the New Literature Movement came to an end.

Lai He was arrested on 8 December 1941 for violating Japanese colonial law. His "Yuzhong riji" (Prison Dairy) is an account of thirty-nine of the fifty days he spent in prison—after the thirty-ninth day, he became ill and was no longer able to write—and his refusal to succumb to Japanese intimidation. He was released because of heart disease. He died on 31 January 1943. His prison diary was edited by the writer Yang Shouyu and published in the November 1945 issue of *Zhengjing bao* (Political and Economic Press).

Since the 1980s Lai He has received increased recognition for his contribution to Taiwanese literature. His work provides insight into the period of Japanese occupation of Taiwan and has become a focus of critical attention in Taiwan studies. He was one of a few writers during the colonial period who used literature to subvert imperialism. His social realism exposes the worst abuses of colonial rule, which include political and economic oppression and the arbitrary use of the law. Besides colonialism, Lai He critiqued what he perceived to be the benighted, backward, and feudal aspects of traditional Chinese society. Lai He's work is subversive in that it takes the position of the weak, the poor, and the disadvantaged and exposes a society in need of reform. His humanism and his recognition of the need for equality and justice have gained him the appellation "the Lu Xun of Taiwan."

References:

Chen Fangming, *Zuoyi Taiwan—zhimindi wenxue yundong shilun* (Taibei: Maitian chuban gufen youxian gongsi, 1998), pp. 5–73;

Donghai daxue Zhongguo wenxuexi (Donghai University Chinese Department), ed., *Taiwan wenxuezhong de lishi jingyan* (Taibei: Wenjin chubanshe youxian gongsi, 1997), pp. 19–46;

Huang Zhongtian and others, *Taiwan xinwenxue gaiguan* (Taibei: Daohe chubanshe, 1992), pp. 29–39;

Lin Ruiming, *Taiwan wenxue yu shidai jingshen: Lai He yanjiu lunji* (Taibei: Yunchen wenhua chuban, 1993);

Wang Jinjiang, "Lai Lanyun lun," in *Lai He xiansheng quanji*, Rijuxia Taiwan xinwenxue: Mingji, volume 1, edited by Li Nanheng (Taibei: Mingtan chubanshe, 1979), pp. 399–406;

Xu Junya, *Riju shiqi Taiwan xiaoshuo yanjiu*, Renwen shehui kexue congshu 1 (Taibei: Wenshizhe chubanshe, 1995), pp. 203–208;

Jane Parish Yang, "The Evolution of the Taiwanese New Literature Movement from 1920 to 1937," dissertation, University of Wisconsin–Madison, 1981.

Papers:

Lai He's papers are in the National Museum of Taiwanese Literature, Tainan City.

Lao She

(3 February 1899 – 25 August 1966)

William A. Lyell
Stanford University

BOOKS: *Lao Zhang de zhexue* [Old Zhang's Philosophy] (Shanghai: Shangwu yinshuguan, 1928);

Zhao Ziyue (Shanghai: Shangwu yinshuguan, 1928);

Er Ma [The Two Mas] (Shanghai: Shangwu yinshuguan, 1931); translated by Jean M. James as *Ma and Son: A Novel by Lao She* (San Francisco: Chinese Materials Center, 1980);

Wenxue gailun jiangyi [Introductory Talks on Literature], as Shu Sheyu (Jinan: Privately printed by Qila daxue wenxue yuan, circa 1931–1934; Beijing: Beijing chubanshe, 1984);

Mao cheng ji [The Chronicle of the City of Cats] (Shanghai: Xiandai shuju, 1933); translated by William A. Lyell as *Cat Country: A Satirical Novel of China in the 1930's* (Columbus: Ohio State University Press, 1970);

Lihun (Shanghai: Liangyou tushu yinshua gongsi, 1933; revised edition, Shanghai: Chenguang chuban gongsi, 1947); translated by Evan King as *Divorce* (St. Petersburg, Fla.: King, 1948); Chinese version revised (Beijing: Renmin wenxue chubanshe, 1963);

Lao She youmo shi wen ji [A Collection of Lao She's Humorous Poems and Essays] (Shanghai: Shidai tushu gongsi, 1934)–includes "Yousheng dianying," translated by Lin Yutang as "Talking Pictures," in *A Nun of Taishan and Other Translations* (Shanghai: Commercial Press, 1936), pp. 115–122;

Gan ji [Deadliners] (Shanghai: Liangyou tushu yinshua gongsi, 1934)–includes "Weishen," translated by Gladys Yang as "A Vision," *Chinese Literature*, 6 (1962): 77–88; and "Kaishi daji," translated by Lyell as "The Grand Opening," *East-West Review*, 3, no. 2 (1967): 170–182;

Xiao Po de shengri [Little Pore's Birthday] (Shanghai: Shenghuo shudian, 1934);

Ying hai ji [Red Cherries and Green Sea] (Shanghai: Renjian shuwu, 1935)–includes "Shangren," translated by Sidney Shapiro as "Brother Yu Takes Office," *Chinese Literature*, 6 (1962): 58–76;

Lao She (frontispiece to Dragon Beard Ditch, *translated by Liao Hung-ying, 1956; Middlebury College Library)*

"Xisheng," excerpt translated by George Kao as "Dr. Mao," in *Chinese Wit and Humor*, edited by Kao (New York: Coward-McCann, 1946), pp. 309–327; "Liu tun de," translated by Stanley R. Munro as "The Woman from Liu Tun," in *Genesis of a Revolution: An Anthology of Modern Chinese Short Stories*, edited and translated by Munro (Singapore: Heinemann Education Books [Asia], 1979), pp. 52–89; "Laonian de langman," translated by Lyell as "Old Liu," in *Two Writers and the*

Cultural Revolution: Lao She and Chen Jo-hsi, edited by Kao (Hong Kong: Chinese University Press, 1980), pp. 57–65; "Maomaochong," translated by Michael S. Duke as "Caterpillar," in *Born of the Same Roots: Stories of Modern Chinese Women,* edited by Vivian Ling Hsu (Bloomington: Indiana University Press, 1981), pp. 2–7; "Shanren," translated by Roberta Raine as "Kind People," *Chinese Literature,* no. 1 (Spring 1997): 127–134; "Linjumen," translated by Lyell as "Neighbors," in *K'uei Hsing: A Repository of Asian Literature in Translation,* edited by Liu Wu-chi (Bloomington: Indiana University Press, 1974), pp. 81–95; and "Yueya'r," translated by Shapiro as "Crescent Moon," *Chinese Literature,* no. 4 (1957): 66–88;

Niu Tianci zhuan [The Biography of Niu Tianci] (Shanghai: Renjian shuwu, 1936)–translated by Xiong Deni as *Heavensent* (London: Dent, 1951; Hong Kong: Joint Publishing Company, 1986);

Ge zao ji [Clams and Seaweed] (Shanghai: Kaiming shudian, 1936)–includes "Lao zihao," translated by Lyell as "An Old and Established Name," *Renditions,* no. 10 (1978): 62–67; "Xin shidai de beiju," translated by Duke as "An Old Tragedy in a New Age," in *Modern Chinese Stories and Novellas, 1919–1949,* edited by Joseph S. M. Lau, Leo Ou-fan Lee, and C. T. Hsia (New York: Columbia University Press, 1981), pp. 159–194; and "Qie shuo wuli," translated by K. C. Yeh as "Portrait of a Traitor," *T'ien Hsia Monthly,* 12 (August–September 1941): 75–93;

Lao niu po che [An Old Ox and a Broken-down Cart] (Shanghai: Renjian shuwu, 1937); revised as *Lao niu po che xinbian* [An Ox and a Broken-down Cart: New Edition] (Hong Kong: Sanlian shudian, 1986)–includes "Wo zenyang xie *Niu Tianci zhuan,*" translated by Xiong Deni as "How I Wrote *Heavensent,*" in *Heavensent,* pp. 253–255;

San si yi [Three, Four, and One] (Chongqing: Duli chubanshe, 1938);

Luotuo Xiangzi [Camel Xiangzi] (Shanghai: Renjian shuwu, 1939); unauthorized and bowdlerized translation by King as *Rickshaw Boy* (New York: Reynal & Hitchcock, 1945); Chinese version republished with new preface (Shanghai: Chenguang chuban gongsi, 1950; abridged edition with new postscript, Beijing: Renmin wenxue chubanshe, 1955); translated by James as *Rickshaw: The Novel Lo-t'o Hsiang Tzu* (Honolulu: University of Hawaii Press, 1979); 1955 edition translated by Shi Xiaoqing as *Camel Xiangzi* (Beijing: Foreign Languages Press, 1981);

Huoche ji [Train on Fire] (Shanghai: Zazhi gongsi, 1939)–includes "'Huo' che," translated as "The Last Train," in *Contemporary Chinese Short Stories,* edited and translated by Yuan Chia-hua and Robert Payne (London: Noel Carrington, 1946), pp. 48–66; "Ren tong ci xin," translated by Richard L. Jen as "They Gather Heart Again," *T'ien Hsia Monthly,* 7 (November 1938): 406–417; enlarged as *Donghai bashan ji* [From the Shandong Seacoast to the Sichuan Mountains] (Shanghai: Xinfeng chubanshe, 1946);

Canwu [Lingering Fog] (Changsha: Shangwu yinshuguan, 1940);

Wen boshi [Dr. Wen, Ph.D.] (Hong Kong: Zuozhe shushe, 1940; Chengdu: Zuojia shuwu, 1940);

Mianzi wenti [The Problem of Face] (Chongqing: Zhengzhong shuju, 1941);

Zhang Zichong (Hankou: Huazhong tushu gongsi, 1941);

Da di long she [Dragons and Snakes across the Land] (Shanghai: Guomin tushu chubanshe, 1941);

Jian bei pian [North of the Jianmen Pass: Odes] (N.p.: Dalu tushu gongsi, 1942);

Gui qu lai xi [The Return] (Chongqing: Zuojia shuwu, 1943);

Guojia zhi shang [The Country above All], by Lao She and Song Zhidi (N.p.: Nanfang yinshuguan, 1943);

Shei xian daole Chongqing [Whoever Arrives in Chongqing First] (Chongqing: Lianyou chubanshe, 1943);

Tao li chun feng [Peaches and Plums in the Spring Breeze: Students in Their Youth], by Lao She and Zhao Qingge (Chengdu?: Zhongxi shuju, 1943);

Huozang [Cremation] (Chongqing: Chenguang chuban gongsi, 1944);

Pinxue ji [The Anemic Collection] (Chongqing?: Wenyu chubanshe, 1944);

Huanghuo: Si shi tong tang, di yi bu [Apprehension: Four Generations under One Roof, Part 1] (Chongqing: Liangyou fuxing tushu yinshua gongsi, 1946);

Tousheng: Si shi tong tang, di er bu [Just Living: Four Generations under One Roof, Part 2], 2 volumes (Shanghai: Chenguang chuban gongsi, 1946);

Fang Zhenzhu [Pearl Fang] (Shanghai: Chenguang chubanshe, 1950);

The Yellow Storm, translated by Ida Pruitt (New York: Harcourt, Brace, 1951)–comprises abridged translations of *Huanghuo, Tousheng,* and "Jihuang" [Destitution];

Longxu gou (Beijing: Dazhong chubanshe, 1951); translated by Liao Hung-ying as *Dragon Beard Ditch* (Beijing: Foreign Languages Press, 1956);

Guo xinnian [Celebrating the New Year] (Shanghai: Chenguang chubanshe, 1951);

The Drum Singers, translated by Helena Kuo (New York: Harcourt, Brace, 1952); translated into Chinese by Ma Xiaomi as *Gushu yiren* (Beijing: Renmin wenxue chubanshe, 1980);

Liushu jing [Willow Well] (Beijing: Baowen tang shudian, 1952);

Chunhua qiushi [Spring Flowers and Fall Fruit] (Beijing: Renmin wenxue chubanshe, 1953);

Dajia pingli [Everybody Take a Stand] (Beijing: Dazhong chubanshe, 1953);

He gongren tongzhimen tan xiezuo [Talking with Comrade Workers about Writing] (Beijing: Gongren chubanshe, 1954);

Qingnian tujidui [The Young Shock Brigade] (Beijing: Dazhong chubanshe, 1955);

Wuming gaodi you le ming [That Nameless Stretch of High Ground Is Famous Now] (Beijing: Renmin wenxue chubanshe, 1955);

Xiwang Chang'an [Gazing West toward Chang'an] (Beijing: Zuojia chubanshe, 1956);

Shiwu guan [Fifteen Strings of Cash] (Beijing: Renmin chubanshe, 1956);

Fuxing ji [Lucky Stars] (Beijing: Beijing chubanshe, 1958);

Chaguan (Beijing: Zhongguo xiju chubanshe, 1958); translated by John Howard-Gibbon as *Teahouse: A Play in Three Acts* (Beijing: Foreign Languages Press, 1984);

Hong dayuan [Red Courtyard] (Beijing: Zuojia chubanshe, 1959);

Nü dianyuan [The Salesgirl] (Tianjin: Baihua wenyi chubanshe, 1959);

Qingxia Danxue [Qingxia and Danxue] (Beijing: Beijing chubanshe, 1959);

Quanjia fu [Family Portrait] (Beijing: Zuojia chubanshe, 1959);

Baochuan [The Magic Boat] (Beijing: Zhongguo shaonian ertong chubanshe, 1961);

He Zhu pei [A Match for He Zhu] (Beijing: Zhongguo xiju chubanshe, 1962);

Xiao huaduo ji [Small Flowers] (Tianjin: Baihua wenyi chubanshe, 1963);

Shenquan [Miraculous Fists] (Beijing: Zhongguo xiju chubanshe, 1963);

Chu kou cheng zhang [Spoken So Well That It Is Fit to Print] (Beijing: Zuojia chubanshe, 1964);

Wo re ai xin Beijing [I Adore the New Beijing] (Beijing: Beijing chubanshe, 1979?);

Lao She lun chuangzuo [Lao She on Writing] (Shanghai: Shanghai wenyi chubanshe, 1980);

Lao She shenghuo yu chuangzuo zishu [Lao She's Autobiographical Essays on His Life and Work] (Hong Kong: Sanlian chubanshe, 1980)—includes "Tule yi kou qi: *Shenquan* houji," translated by Beata Grant as "Suppressed Furor against Foreign Troops: An Unwritten Novel and a Play about the Boxer Uprising," in *Modern Chinese Writers: Self-Portrayals,* edited by Helmut Martin (Armonk, N.Y.: Sharpe, 1992), pp. 268–271;

Zheng hongqi xia (Beijing: Renmin wenxue chubanshe, 1980); translated by Don J. Cohn as *Beneath the Red Banner* (Beijing: Chinese Literature Press, 1982);

Lao She xiaoshuo jiwai ji [Lao She's Uncollected Stories] (Beijing: Beijing chubanshe, 1982);

Si shi tong tang bubian [Four Generations under One Roof] (Tianjin: Baihua wenyi chubanshe, 1983)—comprises *Huanghuo, Tousheng,* and "Jihuang," chapters 88–100 of "Jihuang" translated into Chinese by Ma Xiaomi from Pruitt's English translation;

Wenniu [Literary Beast of Burden] (Hong Kong: Sanlian shudian, 1986)—includes "Wode muqin," translated by Carmen Li and D. E. Pollard as "My Mother," *Renditions,* no. 38 (Autumn 1992): 60–61, 63;

Lao She jiutishi jizhu [An Annotated Compilation of Lao She's Old-style Poetry], edited and annotated by Zhang Guixing (Xuzhou: Zhongguo Kuangye daxue chubanshe, 1994; revised and enlarged edition, Beijing: Zhongguo guoji guangbo chubanshe, 2000);

Lao She quanji [The Complete Works of Lao She], 19 volumes (Beijing: Renmin chubanshe, 1999);

Lao She, edited by Shu Ji (Taibei: Shulin chuban youxian gongsi, 1992).

Editions and Collections: *Weishen ji* [Vision] (Shanghai: Chenguang chubanshe, 1947);

Yueya'r ji [Crescent Moon] (Shanghai: Chenguang chubanshe, 1948);

Lao She xuanji [Selected Works by Lao She] (Beijing?: Kaiming chubanshe, 1951);

Lao She duanpian xiaoshuo xuan [Selected Short Stories of Lao She] (Beijing: Renmin wenxue chubanshe, 1956);

Shangren (Beijing: Zuojia chubanshe, 1958);

Yueya'r [Crescent Moon] (Beijing: Zuojia chubanshe, 1959);

Lao niu po che: Essai autocritique sur le roman et l'humour, translated and annotated by Paul Bady (Paris: Presses universitaires de France, 1974);

Lao She, edited by Shu Ji (Taibei: Shulin chuban youxian gongsi, 1992).

Editions in English: "Black Li and White Li" ("Hei Bai Li" [abridged]), "The Glasses" ("Yanjing"), "Grandma Takes Charge" ("Bao sun"), "The Philanthropist" ("Shanren"), and "Liu's Court" ("Liu jia dayuan"), translated by Chi-chen Wang, in

Contemporary Chinese Stories, edited by Wang (New York: Columbia University Press, 1944), pp. 25–79;

"Talking Pictures" ("Yousheng dianying"), translated by Lin Yutang, in *Chinese Wit and Humor,* edited by George Kao (New York: Coward-McCann, 1946), pp. 305–309;

"They Take Heart Again" ("Ren tong ci xin"), translated by Richard L. Jen; "Portrait of a Traitor" ("Qie shuo wuli"), translated by K. C. Yeh; and "The Letter from Home" ("Yi feng jiaxin"), translated by Wang Chi-chen, in *Stories of China at War,* edited by Wang (New York: Columbia University Press, 1947), pp. 96–132;

The Quest for Love of Lao Lee (Lihun), translated by Helena Kuo (New York: Reynal & Hitchcock, 1948);

"Black and White Li" ("Hei Bai Li"), translated by Gene Hanrahan, in *50 Great Oriental Stories,* edited by Hanrahan (New York: Bantam, 1965), pp. 81–94;

"An Old and Established Name" ("Lao zihao"), translated by William A. Lyell, in *Two Writers and the Cultural Revolution: Lao She and Chen Jo-hsi,* edited by Kao (Hong Kong: Chinese University Press, 1980), pp. 51–56;

Crescent Moon and Other Stories (Beijing: Chinese Literature Press, 1985)—comprises "A Day in the Life" ("Yi tian"), translated by Don J. Cohn; "Filling a Prescription" ("Zhua yao"), translated by Cohn; "By the Temple of Great Compassion" ("Dabei si wai"), translated by Cohn; "Mr. Jodhpurs" ("Maku xiansheng"), translated by Cohn; "A Vision" ("Weishen"), translated by Gladys Yang; "Black Li and White Li" ("Hei Bai Li"), translated by Cohn; "Brother You Takes Office" ("Shangren"), translated by Sidney Shapiro; "The Soul-Slaying Spear" ("Duanhun qiang"), translated by Cohn; "'The Fire Chariot'" ("'Huo' che"), translated by Cohn; "Crescent Moon" ("Yueya'r"), translated by Shapiro; and "This Life of Mine" ("Wo zhe yi beizi"), translated by W. J. F. Jenner;

Blades of Grass: The Stories of Lao She, translated by William A. Lyell and Sarah Wei-ming Chen (Honolulu: University of Hawaii Press, 1999)—comprises "The Grand Opening" ("Kaishi daji"), "An Old and Established Name" ("Lao zihao"), "No Distance Too Far, No Sacrifice Too Great" ("Buyuan qianli er lai"), "Also a Triangle" ("Ye shi sanjiao"), "An Old Man's Romance" ("Laonian de langman"), "Hot Dumplings" ("Re baozi"), "Life Choices" ("Shengmie"), "Neighbors" ("Linjumen"), "Crooktails" ("Wai mao'r"), "Ding" ("Ding"), "Rabbit" ("Tu"), "Attachment" ("Lian"), "Autobiography of a Minor Character" ("Xiao renwu zishu"), and "How I Wrote My Stories" ("Wo zenyang xie duanpian xiaoshuo").

Lao She has always been associated with Beijing—with the Beijing dialect, with the city's streets and alleys, with the typical Beijinger's character, and with the Beijinger sense of humor. As a writer he falls somewhere between the popular Mandarin Ducks and Butterflies School *(Yuanyang hudie pai)* and the more-intellectual authors of the May Fourth period: he was close to the former in his somewhat conservative view of the world and to the latter in that he eschewed the Mandarin Ducks and Butterflies School's use of the traditional storyteller's diction (whether vernacular or classical) and created a new vernacular based on the Beijing dialect. Lao She's vast array of characters are taken from almost every walk and rank of Chinese society. He had the Beijinger's love of words and ability to coin phrases that were fresh, memorable, and witty, as well as revealing. He wrote in many genres, all of which involved playing with words and crafting sentences. In textbooks of the 1930s the Ministry of Education often used examples from Lao She's works; it is, therefore, difficult to overestimate his influence on the language itself.

Lao She shared with the May Fourth intellectuals a deep concern with social issues, as well as with telling a good story, but above all he was a humorist—the first real humorist of the New Literature movement. In contrast to Lu Xun, whose style of humor was typically the intellectual's satire, Lao She's humor could be understood by minimally educated readers. Humor was suspect in traditional China—at least among the Confucian upper class that ruled the country and equated humor with frivolity. Humor was also mistrusted by most members of the new intellectual elite of the May Fourth period—Lao She's peers. Most of them were as serious about politics and ideologies as their forebears had been about the classics.

A Manchu, Lao She was born Shu Qingchun in Beijing on 3 February 1899. His father, Shu Yongshou, was an imperial guard who died in what is known in the West as the Boxer Rebellion the year after Shu was born. His mother then supported Shu and his siblings by working as a cleaning lady in primary schools. Shu received an education only because a philanthropic relative took an interest in him and helped out financially. In June 1919 he graduated from the Beijing shifan xuexiao (Beijing Normal School), where he learned to read Classical Chinese and to write essays and poetry; the following month he was appointed principal of a primary school in Beijing. While many of his peers were out demonstrating, he worked to help support his mother and siblings. By custom, around this time he would have taken his *zi* (style name), Shu Sheyu. His rise within the new system of education was rapid, and over the next few years he served in an impressive number of positions as a teacher and as an administrator.

In 1921 Shu's first short story, "Tade shibai" (Her Failure), appeared in *Haiwai xinsheng* (New Voices from Overseas), a magazine published in Japan. It is a seven-hundred-word vignette describing the mixed emotions of a modern young woman on receiving a letter from her boyfriend. At some point between January and July 1922 he converted to Christianity and was baptized at the London Missionary Society's Gangwashi Church. In July he helped draft a document in Chinese outlining the church's activities and organization. In September he accepted a teaching position at the Nankai Middle School in Tianjin, where, according to Gan Hailan, he gave talks on Christianity and took part in performances put on by a Christian organization. In December he published in *Shengming* (Life) his first translation, rendering of Bao Guanglin's "The Ideal Society in Christianity" into Chinese as "Jidujiao de datong zhuyi." Bao had studied theology at London University and was active in a Christian youth organization in Beijing, where he was often in contact with Shu.

On 28 January 1923 Shu published his first fully developed story, "Xiaoling'r" (Little Bell), in the Nankai Middle School journal, *Nankai jikan* (Nankai Quarterly). The title character is a Beijing elementary-school student who is known, even to his teachers, by that nickname because he is "xiang ge xiao tong ling'r, yi peng jiu xiang de" (as lively as a little bronze bell, bound to ring out at a touch). Xiaoling'r's father died fighting the Japanese, and the boy vows to avenge his death. He organizes a quasi-military group at school; having built themselves up physically through calisthenics and inured themselves to fighting by giving and taking hard blows, they beat up the "little [foreign] devil" who bicycles past their school from a nearby church every day. Identified as the perpetrators the next day, the group is expelled from school.

In February 1923 Shu returned to Beijing, where he taught at the Beijing shi di yi zhongxue (Beijing City No. 1 Middle School) and taught Sunday School at the Gangwashi Church. Bao introduced him to Yenching (Yanjing) University professor Robert Kenneth Evans, who allowed Shu to audit classes in English at the university. The London Missionary Society was looking for someone from China as a candidate for a lectureship at London University's School of Oriental Studies; Evans recommended Shu for the position, and in the summer of 1924 Shu left Shanghai by boat for England. By early September he was teaching the Chinese classics and colloquial Mandarin at the School of Oriental Studies. He advised Clement Egerton, who was translating the seventeenth-century erotic novel of manners, *Jin ping mei;* Egerton's translation, published in four volumes as *The Golden Lotus* in 1939, is dedicated to "C. C. Shu" (for Shu Ch'ing-ch'un, as Shu Qingchun was romanized in the Wade-Giles system used before 1949).

Cover for a 1949 edition of Lao She's first book, the novel Lao Zhang de zhexue *(1928, Old Zhang's Philosophy), about an unscrupulous miser's efforts to rise in the world and procure a concubine (Collection of John Berninghausen)*

Shu wrote his first three novels in London. *Lao Zhang de zhexue* (1928, Old Zhang's Philosophy) was serialized in the Shanghai magazine *Xiaoshuo yuebao* (Short Story Monthly) from July to December 1926; the first installment was published under the name Shu Qingchun, but the rest carried the name by which he is universally known: Lao She. It was published as a book by the Shangwu yinshuguan (Commercial Press) in in Shanghai in 1928. The novel is set in Beijing in the early 1920s and concerns the efforts of the unscrupulous, miserly Old Zhang to rise in the world and acquire a concubine. The first few chapters present a form of humor that is easily appreciated by ordinary readers and with which Lao She was identified during much of his career; Old Zhang and his nefarious band of cohorts are the objects of most of the jokes. These chapters reveal another characteristic of much of Lao

She's fiction: because they are presented with an overlay of humor, his villains are not entirely despicable. In the literary ambience of the late 1920s and the 1930s this approach was virtually unheard of. One does find arrant villains in Lao She's writings, but there are many Old Zhangs, as well. The second half of the novel centers around a favorite May Fourth issue—freedom from arranged marriages and the right to choose one's own mate. In pace and tone this part of the novel differs greatly from the fast-moving burlesque humor of the early chapters. Many readers thought that the social criticism in the work was diluted by the humor.

Lao She was virtually alone among May Fourth intellectuals in his negative view of students, a group many other writers idealized. His disdain for and mistrust of students shows up in much of his fiction, including his second novel. *Zhao Ziyue* was published in installments in *Xiaoshuo yuebao* from March to November 1927 and in book form in 1928. The title is the name of the protagonist and contains a satirical echo of the phrase *Zi yue* (the Master [Confucius] says). Whereas in *Lao Zhang de zhexue* Lao She was content to describe and criticize Chinese society, in his second novel he offers a positive program to make China wealthy and powerful. In addition to addressing the reader directly, a style he uses liberally in both novels, he promotes his program through the voice of the character Li Jingchun. Unlike his fellow students, Li will have nothing to do with demonstrations or strikes; instead, he advocates hard work and diligent study. The passages that present Li's beliefs imply that the phrase "let the student study" should be added to the Confucian admonition that the ruler, minister, father, and son should each perform the role proper to his place. Despite this seeming endorsement of the Confucian notions of *zhengming* (rectification of terms) and *ming shi* (name and reality)—that is, the reality should match the name, and the name should match the reality—one should not mistake Lao She for a narrow-minded disciple of Confucianism. He was, on the contrary, a critic of traditional Chinese systems of thought. Li Jingchun tells his schoolmate Zhao that three roads are open to him: he can pick a subject and put in years learning it; he can buy books on modern agriculture and go home and work the family's land; or he can take whatever job he can find, even though he may lack the learning to do it properly. This last path, Li comments, is the most unworthy, because doing nothing but filling one's rice bowl is tantamount to theft. Later, Li mentions the assassination of warlords as another possible direction for Zhao to take. In the first part of chapter 11 Lao She addresses the reader directly on the futility of resisting foreign domination with sloganeering: "Unfortunately, imperialism's cannons and imperialism's citizens, trained as they all are in the firing of guns, can't be chased away by shouting slogans at them."

These themes are further explored in *Er Ma* (The Two Mas; translated as *Ma and Son: A Novel by Lao She*, 1980), the last novel Lao She wrote in London. It was serialized in *Xiaoshuo yuebao* from May to December 1929 and published as a book in 1931. The basic plot is simple and symmetrical: Ma Zeren leaves China to take over a London curio shop he has inherited from his younger brother. He is accompanied by his grown son, Ma Wei. The Mas take rooms with Mrs. Winter and her daughter, Mary. Romance blossoms between Ma Zeren and Mrs. Winter and between Ma Wei and Mary, but the relationships are terminated by racial prejudice: mother and daughter worry about what others would think if they married Chinese men. The framework allows Lao She to explore generational conflict between the two Mas and cultural conflict between the Mas and English society. It also gives him an opportunity to castigate foreign businessmen for their superficial knowledge of China and to criticize well-meaning missionaries who claim to "love the Chinese people." A theme of the novel is that "the ordinary Englishman despised Chinese," and "wealthy Englishmen and women regarded them as mere objects of amusement." The novel is preoccupied with comparisons, comments, and programs of action, becoming in part an essay on Anglo-Chinese relations. As in his first two works, Lao She is often didactic:

> Is there a foreigner in China who, possessed of artillery and airplanes, science and technology, and financial power as well, doesn't laugh at the antics of students—spending their time banner-waving, crying for justice, and jockeying for positions of leadership instead of studying? . . . Put down your banners and take up your books, or go to work. Stop wailing about lost loves and concentrate on your goals, your responsibilities, your career. These two prescriptions are essential for the youth of China, a battered but still lovable China.

Li Zirong, an overseas Chinese student who has long worked in the curio shop, serves as an alter ego of Lao She as he articulates what he sees as wrong with China and sets forth the only way that Chinese of the younger generation can hope to set things right. Li becomes close to Ma Wei, and the two discuss relationships, marriage, business practices, culture, and politics. As representatives of China's activist younger generation, they are opposed to the passive, acquiescent attitude of the lazy Ma Zeren, who, in turn, looks down on Li as someone who belongs to a lower stratum in the class hierarchy.

Lao She repeatedly addresses the reader directly on the issue of how to make China rich and strong; he also speaks in the thinly veiled voices of his characters, so that even the weaker are mouthpieces for his favorite ideas. In his later novels and short stories Lao She moved away from the didacticism of the early novels to more objective narration. The first three novels are, nevertheless, eminently readable, and *Er Ma* provides a portrayal of culture clash and racial prejudice unprecedented in modern Chinese literature.

Lao She left England in the summer of 1929 and spent three months touring Europe. After failing to find a job in Paris, he booked passage in the fall to Singapore. There he planned to write a novel about Southeast Asia on the rough model of works by Joseph Conrad, a writer he greatly admired. But unlike Conrad's European characters, who are overcome by Southeast Asia, the Chinese settlers in his novel would prosper as they overcame every difficulty. When he arrived in Singapore, Lao She found a branch of the Commercial Press, asked for the latest two issues of *Xiaoshuo yuebao*, and told the clerk and then the manager that he was the author of *Er Ma*, which was then being serialized in the journal. Through the manager he gained an introduction to the administrators of a middle school run by overseas Chinese; he was given a job at the school, where he taught for almost half a year to earn funds for his return to China. He had saved relatively little in England because he had been sending money to his mother.

Lao She gave up his plans for a Conradesque novel because to understand the area he wanted to write about he would have had to learn Malayan, Fukienese, and Cantonese. Instead, he wrote a story in his native Mandarin about the children with whom he had daily contact. In *Xiao Po de shengri* (Little Pore's Birthday), which was serialized in *Xiaoshuo yuebao* from January to April 1931 and published as a book in 1934, he captures both the simplicities and the complexities of childhood. The first eleven chapters deal with events in the life of Little Pore (Pore [Po] is a play on the Chinese for Singapore [Xinjiapo]): a day at school; a trip to the park; an episode of playing hooky, during which he carries a heavy basket home for an old woman; an excursion to the wharf to look at the ships and boats; his birthday celebration; and trips to the beach, the botanical gardens, and the movies. In chapter 12, after he and his sister have been put to bed by their mother, Little Pore begins to dream. Lao She presents the boy's dreamworld as offering freedom from the restrictions and rules that hem in a child during waking hours: "Your teacher can tell you not to do this or not to do that, but can your teacher tell you not to *dream* when you sleep? Your dad can tell you to eat your food slowly and not to make any loud slurping sounds as you drink your tea, but can he tell you how you ought

Cover for a 1964 edition of Lao She's second book, the novel *Zhao Ziyue* (1928), in which the title character receives advice from a diligent fellow student about how to work for the improvement of Chinese society (Collection of John Berninghausen)

to dream?" Little Pore dreams that he is in a movie theater. Invited into the movie world, he crawls under the curtain into "Shadowland," a world of movie magic where the rain does not get one wet, where faucets dispense tea or milk, where things are never what they seem. Shadowland's shortcomings are catalogued along with its wonders. In his essay "Wo zenyang xie 'Xiao Po de shengri'" (How I Wrote "Little Pore's Birthday"), which was published in *Yuzhou feng* (Cosmic Wind) on 1 November 1935 and collected in *Lao niu po che* (1937, An Old Ox and a Broken-Down Cart), Lao She expresses particular satisfaction in noting that he was able to say everything he wanted to say using only the simple language of children.

When Lao She arrived in Shanghai in March 1930, he was already a novelist of some note. In August he secured a position as a professor of literature at Qilu University in Jinan, Shandong province. Ranbir Vohra speculates that Lao She's conversion to Christianity may have made him all the more attractive to the school, which was a missionary institution. On winter vacation in Beiping (as Beijing was known from 1928 to 1949) early in 1931, he was introduced to Hu Jieqing, a student at Beiping Normal University; they were married in Beiping in the summer.

While teaching at Qilu University, Lao She heard firsthand accounts of the "May Third Incident" of 1928 in which Japanese forces had attacked Jinan, causing widespread destruction and loss of life. In 1931 he wrote a novel based on the incident titled "Daming hu" (Daming Lake) after the body of water that covers approximately a quarter of the area of the Jinan municipality; dotted with teahouses and temples, it is still a tourist attraction. The only copy of the manuscript was lost in 1932, when some of the Commercial Press buildings were destroyed in a Japanese military assault that quickly became infamous as the "January 28th Incident." Lao She rewrote one episode from it as a long short story, "Yueya'r" (translated as "Crescent Moon," 1957), which was serialized in *Guowen zhoubao* (National News Weekly) in April 1935; it was collected in his *Ying hai ji* (1935, Red Cherries and Green Sea).

In 1932, depressed by increasing Japanese aggression and China's apparent helplessness to resist it, Lao She wrote *Mao cheng ji* (The Chronicle of the City of Cats; translated as *Cat Country: A Satirical Novel of China in the 1930's*, 1970); it was serialized in *Xiandai/ Les Contemporains* (The Moderns) from August 1932 to April 1933 and published as a book in 1933. The novel is narrated by a Chinese astronaut who crash-lands in Cat Country on Mars. There he is shown around by a Martian of approximately his own age called Xiao Xie (Young Scorpion). In analyzing the various social systems of Cat Country, which is an allegorical representation of China, Young Scorpion is describing the shortcomings of Chinese society in the 1930s. Like Li Jingchun in *Zhao Ziyue* and Li Zirong in *Er Ma*, Xiao Xie is, in part, an alter ego of Lao She. But whereas Li Jingchun and Li Zirong hold out hope for the future, Xiao Xie sees none, and his dialogue is marked by a strong note of cynicism. *Mao cheng ji* lampoons nationalistic pride in Chinese antiquity and mocks the shallow affectations of intellectuals who make a big show of the little knowledge they possess of the West. Chapter 23 introduces a military hero, Daying (Hawk), the sort of unsophisticated man of direct action whom the narrator and the author admire. Daying, however, has given up all hope of restoring integrity and good sense among the people of Cat Country and commits suicide by eating "reverie leaves," the narcotic to which the cat people are addicted. As the novel ends, Cat Country collapses into utter helplessness before the onslaught of an enemy that contemporary readers would understand to represent Japan, and nobody of any political persuasion is able to save it. Lao She found this novel profoundly dissatisfying. In the essay "Wo zenyang xie *Mao cheng ji*" (How I Wrote *Cat Country*, 1937), published in *Yuzhou feng* on 1 December 1935 and collected in *Lao niu po che*, he wrote: "As I see it, *Cat Country* is a failure.... Some people think it is really worthy of praise simply because it is not my usual humorous self—much the same way that any performance by Mei Lanfang [a Beijing opera singer famous for ingenue roles] in a male role would be worthy of praise." He admits that while he might be at home in writing humor, he is not capable of good satire.

Lao She and his wife had a daughter, Shu Ji, in 1933. Lao She turned to his hometown, Beiping, for the setting of his next novel, *Lihun* (1933; translated as *Divorce*, 1948). He wrote the novel quickly; the plot is tight and fast-moving. The two chief protagonists, surnamed Zhang and Li and known as Lao Zhang (Old Zhang) and Lao Li (Old Li), are bureaucrats in the Beiping city finance bureau. They are diametrically different characters. The realistic, comfortable Lao Zhang accepts life as it comes and is content to play out the role he has been allotted. Lao Li is a middle-aged, sentimental man; though married, he is on the prowl for a bit of the romance that he thinks will give meaning to his life. Despite his romantic bent, Lao Li is at times envious of Lao Zhang's easy acceptance of the banality of everyday life. In chapter 1 Lao Li visits Lao Zhang and begins to consider the differences between them:

> What did Big Brother Zhang have that he did not, Lao Li wondered to himself unhappily. What made Big Brother Zhang so happy? How did he always manage to appear so busy, doing nothing? Just carrying packages into the kitchen was a far cry from lofty words like "life" and "truth." The packages Big Brother Zhang had taken into the kitchen were obviously ordinary ones. They could be nothing more than just toilet paper, bed linens, and things like that.
>
> But if he went to the kitchen, he might find something significant there—something with deep meaning applicable to life—that he had hitherto missed. There were certain attractions about the kitchen, with the fire, the smell of the meat and the cooking, and the meowing of the cat. Perhaps these things were *truth*, perhaps they were *life*. Who could tell?

While granting the logic behind Zhang's rejection of romance, however, Lao Li wonders:

> And yet . . . and yet, if you looked at it from a slightly different point of view, in putting an end to romance didn't common sense *also* destroy idealism and any thought of revolution? Once again Lao Li had thought himself into a dead end where there was no moving forward and where backing out left a bad taste in the mouth, too [translations by Helena Kuo, with spelling of names changed to pinyin romanization].

Lao Li falls in love with his neighbor, Mrs. Ma—or, more accurately, he falls in love with the image he has of her, for they never become intimate. Mrs. Ma had married her high-school teacher, a superficial Marxist revolutionary who promptly left her for another woman. She now lives alone, an ideal situation for Lao Li's romantic fantasies; but her husband returns, and, much to Lao Li's surprise and consternation, she takes him back. Eventually reconciling himself to his traditional, unromantic wife, Lao Li decides to make a life for them in countryside, far removed from the sophistication of the city.

In July 1934 Lao She resigned from Qilu University. In August he went to Shanghai to see whether he could make a living as a writer. In the early fall he gave up and took a post as a professor in the Department of Chinese Literature at Shandong University in Qingdao.

In the novel *Niu Tianci zhuan* (The Biography of Niu Tianci; translated as *Heavensent*, 1951), which was serialized in *Lunyu* (The Analects) from 16 September 1934 to 16 October 1935 and published as a book in 1936, Lao She examines the influence of the Chinese class structure and the new ways of thinking brought in by the May Fourth Movement on an orphan boy. Around 1905 a peanut vendor finds a baby in front of the residence of the childless Mr. and Mrs. Niu in the northern town of Yuncheng. He presents the child to the couple, who are doubly delighted since they are both in their fifties. They call him "Tianci" ("Heaven's Gift" or "Bestowed by Heaven"). The couple is well off and has a woman servant, Mrs. Liu, and a handyman, Fourth Tiger. Now they must hire a wet nurse, and Ji Ma (Mother Ji) is brought in from the countryside to fulfill this duty. She has mixed feelings about the situation, for she is poor and must sell her milk to strangers while her own child goes hungry at home. Mr. Niu hopes that the baby will grow up and follow in his footsteps as a merchant; Mrs. Niu, on the other hand, comes from an official family, disdains merchants—including her henpecked husband—and dreams that the boy will become a high official. When the novel ends in 1925, Tianci's adoptive parents have died, and he is able to go to Beijing to pursue his higher education only through the generosity of a man beholden to Mr. Niu.

In "Wo zenyang xie *Niu Tianci*" (How I Wrote *Heavensent*), published in *Yuzhou feng* on 1 August 1936 and collected in *Lao niu po che*, Lao She says that *Niu Tianci* might have been better had he written it under different circumstances. He had begun it in late March 1934 and completed it in early August; as he worked, a heat wave in Jinan sent the temperature in his room to ninety degrees Fahrenheit: "Foggy brained and half asleep, I'd use my left hand to hold my fan and swat flies while holding my pen in my right. With sweat rolling down the backs of my fingers and dripping on to the paper, I'd write as fast as I could" (translation by Xiong Deni).

Cover for a 1947 edition of Lao She's Mao cheng ji *(1933, The Chronicle of the City of Cats; translated as* Cat Country: A Satirical Novel of China in the 1930's, *1970), an allegory in which a Martian society represents China (Wason Collection on East Asia–China, Kroch Asia Library, Cornell University)*

Lao She and his wife had a son, Shu Yi, in 1935. In 1936 Lao She resigned from Shandong University and once again tried to devote himself to writing; he still could not earn enough to support his family, so he rejoined the faculty of Qilu University. (In 2000 the Lao She scholar Zhang Guixing compiled a book about Lao She's Shandong years titled *Lao She yu di er guxiang* [Lao She and His Second Homeland]; Beijing, of course, was his first.)

Since his return to China in 1930, Lao She had written short stories as well as novels. Most of his stories from this period are collected in *Gan ji* (1934, Deadliners), *Ying hai ji*, and *Ge zao ji* (1936, Clams and Seaweed). The stories depict a broad range of characters, occupations, and themes. *Gan ji*, for example, includes "Kaishi daji" (translated as "The Grand Opening," 1967), about an incompetent crew that opens a hospital; "Liu jia dayuan" (The Liu Family Courtyard; translated as "Liu's Court," 1944), an autobiographical celebration of growing up poor in a Beijing *siheyuan* (four-sided courtyard); and "Dabei si wai" (translated as "By the Temple of Great Compassion," 1985), about the Christ-like dedication of a supervisor of students. Among the stories in *Ge zao ji* is "Lao zihao" (translated as "An Old and Established Name," 1980), about the quixotic loyalty to tradition shown by an apprentice in the silk trade. During this same period Lao She wrote lectures, poetry, plays, and essays on wide-ranging topics and translated articles on literary criticism. In 1935 he began to write a series of essays on the art of fiction writing and his own experiences as a novelist; they were collected in 1937 as *Lao niu po che*. (A 1974 French translation by Paul Bady includes copious, useful notes.)

From 16 September 1936 to 1 October 1937 *Yuzhou feng* serialized *Luotuo Xiangzi* (Camel Xiangzi), by critical and popular consensus the most successful of Lao She's novels; it was published as a book in 1939. In the late 1920s Xiangzi (his surname is never given), an honest, ambitious eighteen-year-old orphan, comes to Beiping from the countryside. He tries to earn a living as a laborer, then settles on ricksha pulling; he believes that he can become successful in the profession through diligence and hard work. Lao She skips everything that happens to Xiangzi before he comes to Beijing and quickly covers in a flashback his first few years in the city and the misadventure that leaves him with the nickname "Camel": Xiangzi is press-ganged by soldiers and taken into the hills west of Beijing but escapes, taking three camels with him; he sells the camels before reentering the city. At first he avoids the bad habits of the other pullers, such as smoking, drinking, gambling, and whoring, but he is gradually beaten down by the capitalist society until he acquires all of these habits and worse. His fortunes rise and fall three times before he meets with final disappointment and failure and ends up cynical, syphilitic, and penniless. To blame for Xiangzi's decline are Detective Sun, Old Liu, the Yangs, and Old Lady Chen, each of whom represents a real or perceived problem of Chinese society in the early twentieth century: respectively, warlordism and political oppression, feudal despotism, class oppression, and superstition. The narrator says that Xiangzi is a victim of unhappy circumstance: "Had his environment been a little better, had he had a little education, he certainly would not have ended up in the 'rubber tire corps.'" But the narrator also makes the case that Xiangzi is complicit in his own exploitation because of his "individualism." In C. T. Hsia's opinion, at the time it was published *Luotuo Xiangzi* was the "finest modern Chinese novel" yet written.

In 1945 *Luotuo Xiangzi* became a best-selling American Book-of-the-Month Club selection in an unauthorized translation by Evan King titled *Rickshaw Boy*. King invented characters, deleted all references to communism, and gave the novel a conclusion that is hopeful if not happy. Xiangzi has just emerged from a brothel to which he has gone to rescue the woman he loves:

> With quick movements he lifted the frail body up, folding the sheet about it, and, crouching to get through the door, he sped as fast as he could through the clearing into the woods.
>
> In the mild coolness of a summer evening the burden in his arms stirred slightly, nestling closer to his body as he ran. She was alive. He was alive.

In the original, when Xiangzi goes to the brothel to seek out his love he is told that the woman hanged herself long ago. In Jean M. James's authoritative translation of the original version, *Rickshaw: The Novel Lo-t'o Hsiang Tzu* (1979), the novel ends:

> Handsome, ambitious, dreamer of fine dreams, selfish, individualistic, sturdy, great Hsiang Tzu. No one knows how many funerals he marched in, and no one knows when or where he was able to get himself buried, that degenerate, selfish, unlucky offspring of society's diseased womb, a ghost caught in Individualism's blind alley.

A third translation, *Camel Xiangzi* (1981), by Shi Xiaoqing, is based either on the version of the novel included in *Lao She xuanji* (1951, Selected Works by Lao She) or from the 1955 edition, which Lao She altered to fit the requirements of the Communist society. The 1955 edition and Shi's translation delete all references to sex and all criticism of the hypocritical revolutionary character Ruan Ming.

Xuanmin (The Electorate) was serialzed in *Lunyu* from October 1936 to July 1937; it was published in book form in 1940 as *Wen boshi* (Dr. Wen, Ph.D.). It is the last novel Lao She wrote with Jinan as the setting. After returning to China with an American doctorate, the self-important Wen blames his failure to find a suitable job on the short-sightedness of Chinese employers and marries Lillian Yang for her money and social status. Like the works of many other authors at the time, *Wen boshi* directs its satire at amoral social climbers whose petty selfishness renders them ignorant of, or indifferent to, China's crisis.

Lao She and his wife had a second daughter, Shu Yu, in 1937. Further evidence of Lao She's strength as a writer of short stories is provided by "Tu" (translated as "Rabbit," 1999), published in *Wenyi yuekan* (Literary Arts Monthly) on 1 July 1937, and "Wo zhe yi beizi" (translated as "This Life of Mine," 1985), published on the same day in *Wenxue* (Literature); both are included in the 1939 collection *Huoche ji* (Train on Fire). "Tu" is the sad tale of a young government clerk and amateur opera singer who, against the advice of his friend, the narrator, turns professional and ends up in an opium-clouded abyss of moral degradation. "Wo zhe yi beizi" is the autobiography of a policeman in the capital who joined the force as a young man, shortly before the end of the Qing dynasty in 1915. Policemen were poorly paid and held in contempt, and the narrator's life becomes even more difficult when he is fired from his job just before he turns fifty. He takes what work he can find, but at the end of the story he is alone and penniless.

When Jinan was about to fall to the Japanese in November 1937, Lao She fled to Wuhan; his wife and their three children stayed in Jinan until the fall of 1938, when they moved to Beiping—most likely to be with Lao She's mother but perhaps also because the city, though occupied by the Japanese, was relatively safe. In Wuhan, Lao She served in administrative positions in many organizations formed to further the war effort; he was elected president of the Zhonghua quanguo wenyijie kangdi xiehui (All-China Association of Literary Resistance). He engaged enthusiastically and indefatigably in writing wartime propaganda; to reach the largest possible audience he turned to writing popular poetry and various types of *quyi* (folk art forms), including ballads, stories for storytellers, comic dialogues, *kuaiban* (clapper talks, in which a story is told in rhyme to the quick beat of bamboo clappers), and *guci* (drum songs). He became particularly skilled not only in writing but also in drum songs in which the storyteller accompanies the tale with drum and clackers. Many of the drum songs he wrote were designed to celebrate the fighting spirit of the Chinese while condemning Japanese cruelties. "Zhang Zhong ding ji" (Zhang Zhong Hits on a Plan), for example, is about a Hebei peasant who, on hearing of the atrocities committed by the invading forces, bids farewell to wife and family and organizes a guerrilla group to ambush the Japanese outside the village. It was published in *Da shidai* (Great Age) on 28 December 1937 and collected in *San si yi* (1938, Three, Four, and One).

Lao She's novel *Tui* (Transformation) began its serialization in *Kang dao di* (Resist to the End) on 16 February 1938; he stopped writing it when the magazine ceased publication with the 16 March 1939 issue. The unfinished work is collected in *Lao She xiaoshuo jiwai ji* (1982, Lao She's Uncollected Stories). When the Japa-

Cover for a 1951 edition of Lao She's novel Luotuo Xiangzi *(1939, Camel Xiangzi), about the rise and fall of a Beiping ricksha puller in the late 1920s (Collection of Thomas Moran)*

nese occupy Beiping, five students flee the city and engage in anti-Japanese acts. The heroine is determined to toughen herself physically and spiritually in preparation for a long struggle against a powerful enemy. She and the other students seek to achieve a "transformation" like that of a cicada shedding its skin. Propaganda in service of the struggle against Japan, the novel is typical of everything Lao She wrote during the war.

On 30 July 1938 Lao She, representing the All-China Association of Literary Resistance, left Wuhan for Chongqing in Sichuan province, the wartime capital. In June 1930 he left Chonqing with a group that traveled a reported 18,500 *li* (about 6,000 miles) to boost the morale of civilians and soldiers. In the course of this trip Lao She met Mao Zedong in Yan'an, the Communist capital in Shaanxi Province. The following year he wrote a series of new-style poems celebrating the places he had seen and the people he had met; this poetic travel diary sings the praises of cultural and historical sites while deploring the brutality of the Japanese invaders. The poems were published in seven different magazines from February 1940 to December 1940; it is not clear if all were published in periodicals before being gathered together as *Jian bei pian* (North of the Jianmen Pass: Odes) in 1942. While on the 1939 trip Lao She also wrote traditional-style poetry, including "Paomao zhi hou" (After Breakdown), which captures the difficulty of his travels: "One stretch of two or three *li* / We'd break down four or five times / We'd get off the truck six or seven times / And eight, nine or ten of us would push." "Paomao zhi hou" was written in 1939 and first published in volume thirteen of *Lao She quanji* (1999, The Complete Works of Lao She). Lao She continued to write traditional poetry for the rest of his life.

Canwu (Lingering Fog), Lao She's first wartime play, was performed in 1939–1940, serialized in *Wenyi yuekan: Zhanshi tekan* (Literary Arts Monthly: Wartime Edition) from 20 August 1939 to 16 January 1940, and published as a book in 1940. The four-act piece is propaganda, though well written. Set in Chongqing, it pits patriots against collaborators and mahjong-playing members of the upper classes who seem oblivious to the war effort. In 1941 Lao She wrote the play *Mianzi wenti* (The Problem of Face) to show how concern with "face" stood in the way of unified resistance to the invaders. The success of *Canwu* inspired the Huijiao jiuguo xiehui (Muslim Association for the Protection of the Country) to ask Lao She to write a play for them. The result was *Guojia zhi shang* (1943, The Country above All), written in collaboration with Song Zhidi, who, like, like Lao, was a non-Muslim. The play is about the conversion of an older Muslim man from a parochial and narrow-minded worldview to a more liberal one and a new willingness to cooperate with his non-Muslim countrymen in the war against the Japanese invaders. *Guojia zhi shang* is perhaps Lao She's most successful wartime play. *Gui qu lai xi* (1943, The Return), set in 1941 Chongqing, is a five-act play that includes many subplots but in the main is a patriotic call for all Chinese to pull together in the war against Japan.

Lao She's mother died in August 1942, freeing Hu Jieqing to leave Beiping. The next year she and the children made an arduous fifty-three-day trip to Chongqing, reuniting the family. Lao She's story "Lian" (translated as "Attachment," 1999) was published in the premiere issue of *Shi yu chao wenyi* (Time and Tide Literature and Art) on 15 March 1943; it was republished in *Pinxue ji* (1944, The Anemic Collection), so named because it is a thin volume and because Lao She was suffering from anemia when he put it together. "Lian" is a sympathetic story about a man who agrees to serve in the Japanese puppet government to save his collection of paintings by minor Shandong artists, the only thing that lends his life a touch of color.

The arrival of his wife and children prompted Lao She to try a novel set in Japanese-occupied China. The result was *Huozang* (1944, Cremation), a patriotic story about collaborators and traitors, all of whom are punished in the end. The novel is set in the fictional Japanese-occupied city of Wencheng. Wang Menglian, the heroine, is the daughter of a *juren* (holder of the second-level degree in the civil examination system); throughout the novel the father is referred to as "Juren gong" (His Honor, the *Juren*). Filial piety and loyalty to country are set at odds when Menglian's father decides to serve in the Japanese puppet government. Menglian "tui" (sheds) her old identity and metamorphoses into a new person: "Had there been no war, no spilling of blood, no massacres, no destruction, no starvation, no torturing of people, Menglian would, no doubt, simply have remained Menglian." Her fiancé, Ding Yishan, is as patriotic as she is and joins the Nationalist army to fight the Japanese. Menglian has a second suitor, more to her father's liking, who is as traitorous as Ding is loyal: Liu Ergou (Second Dog Liu), whom Menglian scorns. Ding returns to Wencheng surreptitiously to reconnoiter prior to a planned attack on the Japanese-held city and is discovered by Liu Ergou, who has him killed. Nonetheless, the guerrilla force proceeds with the attack and, with the aid of the townspeople, kills 150 Japanese, as well as Menglian's father and Liu Ergou. At the end of the novel Menglian leaves the city to join the Nationalist forces. In the preface Lao She admits that *Huozang* is flawed, in part because he had not lived in occupied China and was not writing from experience. Lao She and his wife had a third daughter, Shu Li, in 1945.

Lao She's lack of firsthand experience in occupied China also posed a problem in his writing of *Si shi tong tang* (1946–1950, Four Generations under One Roof); but in this work he was writing about Beiping, which he knew well. *Si shi tong tang* is a trilogy of one hundred chapters with a complicated publishing history. *Huanghuo* (Apprehension), comprising chapters 1 to 34, was written in 1944, serialized in the Chongqing magazine *Saodang bao* (The Mopping-Up Post) from 10 November 1944 to 2 September 1945, and published as a book in 1946. *Tousheng* (Just Living), comprising chapters 35 to 67, was written in 1945, serialized in *Shijie ribao* (The World News) from 1 May 1945 to 15 December 1945, and published in two volumes in 1946. "Jihuang" (Destitution), comprising chapters 68 to 100, was written in New York City in 1947–1948; chapters 68 to 87 were published in the first six issues of *Xiaoshuo* (Fiction) for 1950. An abridged English translation of the trilogy by Ida Pruitt was published in 1951 as *The Yellow Storm*; Pruitt translated the final thirteen chapters (88 to 100) that are missing from the published Chinese version from Lao She's manuscript, which was subsequently lost. Those chapters were translated into Chinese from

Pruitt's English by Ma Xiaomi and published as "*Si shi tong tang* shi pian" (*Four Generations under One Roof*: Lost Chapters) in *Shiyue* (1982, October). The entire novel, including the chapters translated by Ma, was published in 1983.

Si shi tong tang focuses on the ways in which the Qi and Guan families, who live in Xiao yangquan hutong (Sheepfold Alley) in Beiping, react to the Japanese occupation of the city. Each of the various members of the Qi family acquits himself in a different way, while the Guans are all traitors and are shunned by their neighbors. Lao She's knowledge of conditions in occupied Beijing was based on what Hu Jieqing and other refugees from the city told him. The first novel of the trilogy, *Huanghuo*, deals with the four generations of the Qi family, from the patriarch of the clan to his great-grandson, but the story revolves around the three grandsons. The eldest briefly considers joining the resistance but decides to remain in Beijing to tend to the family's affairs; the middle grandson is a collaborator; and the youngest, Qi Ruiquan, heroically drops out of college to join the army and fight the Japanese. The second novel, *Tousheng*, places the Guans at the center of the action. Mr. Guan has a wife and a concubine; the latter proves to be a patriot, while Guan and his wife are willing to sell anyone out to the Japanese for their own profit or advancement. Qi Ruiquan falls in love with one of the Guan daughters, Zhaodi, but she defects to the Japanese. Toward the end of the third novel, "Jihuang," Qi Ruiquan strangles Guan Zhaodi in retribution for the suffering and death she has caused through her betrayal. The trilogy ends with the patriarch of the Qi clan, supported by his grandson Qi Ruiquan, inviting all the neighbors to his home to celebrate the victory over Japan. Writing in 1975, Prudence Chou says that "*Four Generations Under One Roof* is the best of Lao She's wartime literary products. Nonetheless . . . it offers no strong literary merit. Possibly because of its rarity as a study of occupied Beijing, the novel still attracts a great number of readers, Chinese as well as English."

In 1946 Lao She and the playwright Cao Yu arrived in Seattle at the invitation of the United States Department of State. Lao She spent three and a half years in the United States, touring, giving lectures, taking part in writing groups, and helping Pruitt translate *Si shi tong tang* into English. In 1948–1949 he wrote his only novel set in Chongqing. The story, about drum singers driven out of Beiping during the war, their subsequent lives in Chongqing, and their return to Beiping after Japan's defeat, is based on Fu Shaofang and his foster daughter, Fu Guihu, a drum-singing team Lao She knew in China. Helena Kuo translated the novel from Lao She's manuscript as he wrote it, and he proof-

Cover for a 1949 edition of Lao She's novel Huozang (1944, Cremation), about Chinese collaborators and traitors in a fictitious Japanese-occupied city (Collection of John Berninghausen)

read her work as it progressed. The Chinese manuscript was lost after Lao She returned to China, before the novel could be published in Chinese; Kuo's translation was published as *The Drum Singers* in 1952. In 1980 Ma Xiaomi translated Kuo's work into Chinese as *Gushu yiren*. Both Kuo's English version and Ma's Chinese version are included in volume six of *Lao She quanji* (1999, Complete Works of Lao She).

Lao She returned to China aboard the *President Wilson*; he left San Francisco on 13 October 1949, twelve days after Mao Zedong announced the establishment of the People's Republic of China. Because the manuscript for the Chinese version of *The Drum Singers* had been lost, he wrote a four-act play on a similar theme, comparing the lives of folk performers before and after *jiefang* (liberation). On the advice of friends, he added a fifth act to emphasize the positive changes that liberation had brought. The play was published in 1950 as *Fang Zhenzhu* (Pearl Fang). In "*Fang Zhenzhu* de ruodian" (The Weaknesses of *Fang Zhenzhu*), published in the Beijing newspaper *Xinmin bao* (New People's Post) on 11 January 1951 and collected in *Lao She lun chuang-*

zuo (1980, Lao She on Writing), he says that adding the fifth act was like adding hot water to tea without putting in more tea leaves: the result is weaker tea. He confesses that one of his own weaknesses is listening too readily to the advice of friends, thus relinquishing his responsibility as a creative writer and turning himself into a "yijian xiang" (suggestion box).

After 1949 Lao She wrote in favor of a variety of Communist Party programs and policies. In the play *Longxu gou* (1951; translated as *Dragon Beard Ditch*, 1956), for example, the new government repairs an unhealthful, foul-smelling sewage canal and gives poor people an opportunity to stand up for themselves. The mayor of Beijing liked *Longxu gou* so much that he conferred on Lao She the title "Renmin yishujia" (Artist of the People).

By all accounts, Lao She was optimistic about the new society and did all that he could to help in its building. At the end of October 1953 he was part of a delegation that went to North Korea to show the homeland's care for and appreciation of the Chinese *zhiyuanjun* ("volunteers") who had fought there in the Korean War and had yet to return to China (the armistice had been signed on 27 July). Lao She was so impressed by the experience that he remained in Korea for five months after the rest of the group returned to China. He interviewed veterans of the series of battles, from the summer of 1952 to the spring of 1953, that ended with the Chinese in control of a hill called "Lao tu shan" (Old Baldy), known to American soldiers officially as Hill 266 and unofficially as "Old Baldy" and "Suicide Hill." He decided that five months was not enough time for him to get to know the soldiers and their experiences intimately enough to turn the material into effective fiction; instead, he wrote the nonfiction *Wuming gaodi you le ming* (1955, That Nameless Stretch of High Ground Is Famous Now).

Two of Lao She's works of the late 1950s show some dissatisfaction, however faint, with the Communist order. His 1956 play *Xiwang Chang'an* (Gazing Westward toward Chang'an) hints that corruption persists in the new society, even among the Communist cadres. Lao She intended the work as friendly criticism. Most critics agree that *Chaguan* (1958; translated as *Teahouse: A Play in Three Acts*, 1984) is the best of Lao She's forty-four plays. Written in 1956 in the midst of the brief period of liberalization known as the Hundred Flowers Movement and published in the premiere (July 1957) issue of *Shouhuo* (Harvest) and as a book in 1958, *Chaguan* presents seventy characters against the background of three periods of Chinese history. Act 1 is set in 1898, during the declining days of the Manchu Dynasty; the rise of warlordism after the founding of the Chinese Republic in 1912 is the background to act 2; and act 3 takes place in 1945, after the end of the war with Japan, when "Nationalist agents and American soldiers are running amuck." All three acts are set in a Beijing teahouse; Lao She thought that such a locale could serve as a microcosm of society, and he was familiar with the habits and language of teahouse patrons. The use of the same setting and the appearance of the same main characters in all three acts give the history covered in the play a sense of continuity. The work is explicitly critical of the Nationalists but is open to a reading that suggests that the suffering of the Chinese people continues regardless of changes in regime. To that extent, *Chaguan*, like *Xiwang Chang'an*, can be taken as mild criticism of the Communist government.

In 1961–1962 Lao She worked on the only full-length novel he attempted after 1949; he never completed it. The autobiographical *Zhenghong qi xia* (translated as *Beneath the Red Banner*, 1982) was not published until 1980. It was his last major work. A collection of essays on writing appeared under the title *Chu kou cheng zhang* (Spoken So Well It's Fit to Print) in 1964. Many of these essays, like those in *Lao niu po che* of 1937, deal with dialogue, description of scenery, and use of metaphor, while others are related to the new subject of playwriting.

The Cultural Revolution began in 1966. On 23 August of that year Lao She and other writers and artists were humiliated and beaten during a *pidouhui* (struggle session) at Beijing's Kong miao (Confucius Temple). According to Zheng Zhi and Fu Guangming's *Taiping hu de jiyi: Lao She zhi si* (2001, Taiping Lake Memory: The Death of Lao She), among the Red Guards who beat Lao She and his colleagues with the buckles of their belts were students from a Beijing girls' middle school. At two o'clock in the morning of 24 August, Lao She's wife, Hu Jieqing, took Lao She home; he was ordered to report to the offices of the Beijing shi wenyijie lianhehui (Beijing Federation of Literary and Artistic Circles) later in the day. He left home later in the morning and disappeared. The next day his body was found in the water close to the shore of Taiping Lake on the western edge of Beijing. According to his son's *Lao She zhi si* (1987, The Death of Lao She), in 1966 Taiping Lake, which no longer exists, was quiet and suburban, lined with poplar trees and benches by the water. The lake was north and west of Desheng Gate, the spot where Xiangzi wanders alone as a crowd follows a man to his execution at the end of *Luotuo Xiangzi*. Lao She knew the neighborhood well: from 1920 to 1922 he had worked as a educational administrator in an office near Desheng Gate, and his first novel is set in the area. Taiping Lake was north of a place called Huokou (Breach), which was named for a gap in the Beijing city wall.

*Lao She (center) with the writer and critic Mao Dun (left) and the poet Yu Liqun in Chongqing, 1945
(from* Lao She, *edited by Shu Ji, 1992; Collection of Thomas Moran)*

The wall had been torn down in the 1950s as part of the dismantling of old Beijing; in his "Death and the Novel: On Lao She's 'Suicide,'" collected in *Two Writers and the Cultural Revolution: Lao She and Chen Jo-hsi* (1980), edited by George Kao, Bady wonders if Lao She's suicide was motivated by more than political attacks: "How could he survive if there were no more tea-houses and story-tellers in Tianqiao, if the city-gates and walls and the marble bridges were being destroyed forever?" Shu Yi notes that after the wall was demolished, Taiping Lake, which had been outside the wall, became an easy walk from the alley where Lao She's mother had lived until her death in 1942; he speculates that Lao She's last act was to pay his respects to his mother's memory. According to the Taiping Lake gatekeeper, Lao She sat on a bench and stared into the waters of the lake for hours on 24 August. Early on the morning of 25 August his body was found in the lake near the shore; he had drowned. Although the time and circumstances of Lao She's death have never been completely established, the consensus is that he committed suicide.

On 3 June 1978–almost twelve years after Lao She's death and two years after the end of the Cultural Revolution–his ashes were interred in a ceremony at the Babaoshan cemetery. In 1999, the one hundredth anniversary of Lao She's birth, the home where Lao She lived from 1950 until his death was opened as the Lao She jinianguan (Lao She Memorial and Museum), with Lao She's daughter Shu Ji as curator. That same year the nineteen-volume *Lao She quanji* was published. Lao She's son, Shu Yi, is the curator of the Zhongguo xiandai wenxue guan (Museum of Modern Chinese Literature), which opened in Beijing in 2000. At the Lao She chaguan (Lao She Teahouse) in Beijing, tourists can enjoy a gentrified facsimile of the teahouse depicted in the play *Chaguan*.

Letters:

Lao She Yingwen shuxin ji: Zhong Ying duizhaoben [Lao She's English Correspondence: Chinese-English Edition] (Hong Kong: Qin + yuan chubanshe, 1993).

Bibliographies:

Zbigniew Slupski, "List of Lao She's Short Stories" and "Bibliography of the Works of Lao She," in his *The Evolution of a Modern Chinese Writer: An Analysis of Lao She's Fiction with Biographical and Bibliographi-*

cal *Appendices* (Prague: Oriental Institute in Academia, 1966), pp. 101–120;

"Lao She zhuyi nianbiao he zhuzuo mulu," in *Lao She yanjiu ziliao,* 2 volumes, edited by Wu Huaibin and Zeng Guangcan (Beijing: Shiyue wenyi chubanshe, 1985), II: 1031–1263;

Zhang Guixing, ed., *Lao She zhuyi pianmu* (Beijing: Zhongguo guoji guangbo chubanshe, 2000).

Biographies:

"Lao She zhuanlüe" and "Lao She nianpu," in *Lao She yanjiu ziliao,* 2 volumes, edited by Wu Huaibin and Zeng Guangcan (Beijing: Shiyue wenyi chubanshe, 1985), I: 3–107;

Hao Changhai and Wu Huaibin, *Lao She nianpu* (Hefei: Huangshan shushe, 1988);

Gan Hailan, *Lao She nianpu* (Beijing: Shumu wenxian chubanshe, 1989);

Zhang Guixing, *Lao She nianpu,* 2 volumes (Shanghai: Shanghai wenyi chubanshe, 1997);

Shu Ji, Hao Changhai, and Wu Huaibin, "Lao She nianpu," in *Lao She quanji,* 19 volumes (Beijing: Renmin chubanshe, 1999), XIX: 487–663;

Shu Yi, *Lao She* (Beijing: Zhongguo huaqiao chubanshe, 1999);

Zhang Guixing, *Lao She yu di er guxiang* (Qingdao: Haiyang daxue chubanshe, 2000).

References:

Robert A. Bickers, "New Light on Lao She, London, and the London Missionary Society, 1921–1929," *Modern Chinese Literature,* 8 (Spring/Fall 1994): 21–40;

Cyril Birch, "Lao She: The Humorist in His Humor," *China Quarterly,* 8 (October–December 1961): 45–62;

Wei-ming Chen, "Pen or Sword: The Wen-Wu Conflict in the Short Stories of Lao She (1899–1966)," dissertation, Stanford University, 1985;

Prudence Chou, "Lao She: An Intellectual's Role and Dilemma in Modern China," dissertation, University of California, Berkeley, 1975;

C. T. Hsia, "Lao She" and "The Veteran Writers: Lao She," in his *A History of Modern Chinese Fiction* (New Haven: Yale University Press, 1961), pp. 165–188, 366–374;

George Kao, ed., *Two Writers and the Cultural Revolution: Lao She and Chen Jo-hsi* (Hong Kong: The Chinese University Press, 1980), pp. 5–128;

Peter Li, "Lao She and Chinese Folk Literature," *CHINOPERL Papers,* no. 18 (1996): 1–19;

Meng Guanglai and others, eds., *Lao She yanjiu lunwen ji* (Jinan: Shandong renmin chubanshe, 1983);

Thomas Moran, "The Reluctant Nihilism of Lao She's *Camel Xiangzi,*" in *The Columbia Companion to Modern East Asian Literature,* edited by Joshua Mostow, Kirk A. Denton, Bruce Fulton, and Sharalyn Orbaugh (New York: Columbia University Press, 2003), pp. 452–457;

David Pollard, "Lao She, *Luotuo Xiangzi* (Camel Xiangzi), 1936–37," in *A Selective Guide to Chinese Literature 1900–1949,* volume 1: *The Novel,* edited by Milena Dolezelová-Velingerová (Leiden: Brill, 1988), pp. 106–108;

Shu Ji, ed., *Lao She wenxue cidian* (Beijing: Beijing shiyue wenyi chubanshe, 2000);

Shu Yi, *Lao She zhi si* (Beijing: Guoji wenhua chuban, 1987);

Zbigniew Slupski, *The Evolution of a Modern Chinese Writer: An Analysis of Lao She's Fiction with Biographical and Bibliographical Appendices* (Prague: Oriental Institute in Academia, 1966);

Britt Towery, *Lao She, China's Master Storyteller* (Waco, Tex.: Tao Foundation, 1999);

Ranbir Vohra, *Lao She and the Chinese Revolution* (Cambridge, Mass.: Harvard University Press, 1974);

Wu Huaibin and Zeng Guangcan, eds., *Lao She yanjiu ziliao,* 2 volumes (Beijing: Shiyue wenyi chubanshe, 1985);

Zeng Guangcan, *Lao She yanjiu zonglan, 1929–1986* (Tianjin: Tianjin jiaoyu chubanshe, 1987);

Zhang Guixing, *Lao She ziliao kaoshi (xiudingben)* (Beijing: Zhongguo guoji guangbo chubanshe, 2000);

Zheng Zhi and Fu Guangming, *Taiping hu de jiyi: Lao She zhi si* (Shenzhen: Haitian chubanshe, 2001).

Ling Shuhua
(25 March 1900 – 22 May 1990)

Amy D. Dooling
Connecticut College

BOOKS: *Hua zhi si* [The Temple of Flowers] (Shanghai: Xinyue shudian, 1928)–includes "Jiu hou," translated by Amy D. Dooling as "Intoxicated," in *Writing Women in Modern China: An Anthology of Women's Literature from the Early Twentieth Century,* edited by Dooling and Kristina M. Torgeson (New York: Columbia University Press, 1998), pp. 179–184; "Xiu zhen," translated by Jane Parish Yang as "Embroidered Pillows," in *Modern Chinese Stories and Novellas, 1919–1949,* edited by Joseph S. M. Lau, C. T. Hsia, and Leo Ou-fan Lee (New York: Columbia University Press, 1981), pp. 197–199; "Zhongqiu wan," translated by Nathan K. Mao as "The Night of the Mid-Autumn Festival," in *The Columbia Anthology of Modern Chinese Literature,* edited by Lau and Howard Goldblatt (New York: Columbia University Press, 1995), pp. 110–119; "Shuo you zheme yihui shi," translated by Dooling as "Once upon a Time," in *Writing Women in Modern China,* pp. 185–195; "You fuqi de ren," translated by Jennifer Anderson as "The Lucky One," in *Chinese Women Writers: A Collection of Short Stories by Chinese Women Writers of the 1920s and 30s,* edited by Anderson and Theresa Munford (San Francisco: China Books and Periodicals, 1985), pp. 62–74;

Nüren [Women] (Shanghai: Shangwu yinshuguan, 1930)–includes "Xiao Liu," translated by Vivian Ling Hsu as "Little Liu," in *Born of the Same Roots: Stories of Modern Chinese Women,* edited by Hsu (Bloomington: Indiana University Press, 1981), pp. 62–80; "Fengle de shiren," translated by Ling and Julian Bell as "A Poet Goes Mad," *T'ien Hsia Monthly,* 4, no. 4 (1937): 401–420; "Song che," translated by Donald Holoch as "The Send Off," in *The Longman Anthology of World Literature by Women, 1875–1975,* edited by Marian Arkin and Barbara Shollar (New York: Longman, 1989), pp. 413–419;

Xiaohai [Children] (Shanghai: Shangwu yinshuguan, 1930); enlarged as *Xiao ge'er lia* [Two Brothers] (Shanghai: Liangyou chubanshe, 1935);

Ancient Melodies, introduction by Vita Sackville-West (London: Hogarth Press, 1953; New York: Universe, 1988); translated into Chinese by Fu Guangming as *Gu yun* (Taibei: Yejiang chubanshe, 1991);

Aishanlu mengying [Dreams from a Mountain Lover's Studio] (Singapore: Xingzhou shijie chubanshe, 1960).

Collections: *Ling Shuhua zixuan duanpian xiaoshuo ji* [A Collection of Short Stories by Ling Shuhua] (Singapore: Xingzhou shijie shuju, 1960);

Ling Shuhua xuanji [Selected Works of Ling Shuhua] (Hong Kong: Wenxue yanjiushe, 1979);

Ling Shuhua xiaoshuo ji [The Collected Fiction of Ling Shuhua], 2 volumes (Taibei: Hongfan chubanshe, 1984).

While neither prolific nor particularly representative of her generation of early-twentieth-century women writers, Ling Shuhua has earned a lasting place in the modern Chinese literary canon. Written at a time when authors were often more concerned about sociopolitical content than formal technique, her fiction has been appreciated for its subtle, unsentimental descriptive style and adept use of symbolism. Her short stories from the mid 1920s to the early 1930s capture the subtle nuances of human psychology, and her most acclaimed works offer skillful portraits of middle- and upper-class women. Despite the promise of her early stories, Ling had ceased writing fiction by the late 1930s, although she went on to publish a poignant memoir of her childhood and a volume of short essays on topics ranging from traditional and modern Chinese art to the natural landscape. In addition to her writing, Ling was an accomplished painter in the classical literati style.

Ling Shuhua was born Ling Ruitang on 25 March 1900 in Beijing. Her father, Ling Fupeng, had earned the highest-level academic degree after passing

Cover for Ling's first book, Hua zhi si (1928, The Temple of Flowers), a collection of twelve short stories. The title piece is about a clever woman who pretends to be her husband's secret admirer (Sterling Memorial Library, Yale University).

the imperial civil service examination and held several important bureaucratic posts, including serving as a top-ranking official in Beijing and Tianjin during the final years of the Qing dynasty. After the founding of the Republic in 1912, he was handpicked by President Yuan Shikai for the lucrative job of overseeing the restoration of the Qing imperial tombs southwest of Beijing. Ling's mother, Pan Zhulan, the adopted daughter of an affluent family of Cantonese merchants, was the fourth of her father's six wives. She bore four daughters, of whom Ling was the youngest; but owing to the traditional value accorded to male heirs, her failure to produce a son caused her great disappointment. In *Ancient Melodies* (1953) Ling writes candidly of her mother's unhappiness and of the tensions and bitter rivalries among her father's wives as they competed for his favor.

Nevertheless, Ling seems to have enjoyed a relatively carefree, if extremely sheltered, childhood in the sprawling mansion where her family resided. She developed a taste for traditional popular culture from her mother, who often sang old Cantonese ballads and romantic tales to entertain the large household. Her father was a connoisseur of classical Chinese painting and calligraphy and cultivated an atmosphere of aesthetic refinement in the home. Her father doted on her, and she, unlike her sisters, was permitted to study alongside her brothers with their private tutor. When she was still quite young, her artistic potential caught the attention of the painter Wang Zhuling, a friend of her father's, who took her as his pupil and later introduced her to the former imperial court artist Miao Sujun. The foreign-educated scholar Gu Hongming, another of her father's close associates and a frequent guest at the Ling residence, gave her English lessons.

At seven Ling, together with several siblings and a cousin, was sent to school in Kyoto, Japan; her studies came to an end when two of her older sisters drowned in a swimming accident. She returned home not to Beijing but to Tianjin, where the family had moved into a residence in the foreign concession. She was sent to a private girls' school, where she was elected secretary of the student union formed amid the May Fourth Movement and participated in various student movement activities. An essay she wrote about the local demonstrations and boycotts was published in the *Tianjin ribao* (Tianjin Daily). Her budding interest in classical Chinese philosophy, particularly in the Daoist classic *Zhuangzi*, along with her father's opposition to the May Fourth Movement, however, kept her from being drawn into the more radical activism of many of her peers.

In 1922 Ling matriculated in the foreign languages department of the newly reorganized Yenching (Yanjing) University in Beijing, joining one of the first cohorts of female students to attend the prestigious institution. Her classmates included Xie Wangying, soon to be known as the female poet and writer Bing Xin, with whom she would remain lifelong friends. She majored in English and French and minored in Japanese. In 1924 several of her short stories—beginning with "Nü'er shenshi tai qiliang" (Tragic Is a Girl's Fate), which she published under the pen name Rui Tang—and essays appeared in the literary supplement of the Beijing *Chen bao* (Morning Post), although none received much attention. Knowing how much he disapproved of the new vernacular writing, Ling never showed any of her literary work to her father.

In the spring of 1924 Ling met her future husband, Chen Yuan, an English professor at Beijing University and an influential literary critic who wrote under the pen name Chen Xiying. Chen Yuan gained fame the following year in a public dispute with the writer Lu Xun over an incident at the Beijing Women's Higher Normal School. Ling and Chen Yuan initially kept their relationship secret from their families. Through Chen Yuan, Ling came into frequent contact with many notable young writers, including Xu Zhimo and Shen Congwen.

Ling's fiction first began to draw critical notice with her story "Jiu hou" (1925; translated as "Intoxicated," 1998), which was published while was still in college. She began to use the pen name Ling Shuhua at this time. "Jiu hou" appeared in *Xiandai pinglun* (Contemporary Review), a liberal weekly journal edited by Chen Yuan, which served as a forum for a group of mostly Anglo-American-educated scholars affiliated with universities in Beijing. The opening passages of the tightly written story set up what appears at first to be a scene of conjugal harmony as Caitiao and her husband relax after a dinner party they have hosted: the room is bathed in the warm glow of the fire, and a sweet aroma emanates from a bowl of fruit. Caitiao, however, is not listening to the drunken revery of her amorous spouse; her attention is riveted on the handsome writer who has passed out in an armchair across the room. Unable to suppress her feelings any longer, she impulsively asks her husband's permission to kiss the man; he grants the request, albeit reluctantly. But before she goes through with the deed, her desire cools, and she returns to sit next to her husband. Ling provides few clues as to why she changes her mind, leaving the ending open to interpretation.

The success of this story, which was adapted as a one-act domestic comedy by the playwright Ding Xilin in 1925, was followed by several equally impressive publications over the next few months. Among them was "Xiu zhen" (1925; translated as "Embroidered Pillows," 1981), one of her best-known works. Eldest Young Miss is a well-bred lady who dedicates herself to fine needlework in hopes of attracting a husband, even though such "feminine" practices seem to belong to a bygone age. The story is neatly divided into two contrasting parts: the first describes the heroine's painstaking efforts one sweltering summer afternoon to complete a pair of intricately embroidered pillow cushions that are to be presented to Cabinet Secretary Bai, who is considering a match for his second son. With characteristic subtle narrative technique, Ling conveys the emotional state of the protagonist through minutely observed details rather than through a direct representation of her feelings. The faint blush that creeps over Eldest Young Miss's face when the maidservant Zhang Ma indiscreetly remarks on her marital prospects, for instance, indicates to the reader both the nervousness and the wishful anticipation that underlie the heroine's labors. Despite the buildup, little appears to have changed in the second part, set two years later: Eldest Young Miss is still living at home, still dutifully embroidering, and still unmarried. No explicit comment is made about the character's predicament; instead, the fate of the exquisite pillows, a symbol for the young woman, is related: on the night the gifts were presented, "a drunk guest vomited all over a large part of one of them; the other one was pushed off onto the floor by someone playing mahjong. Someone used it as a footstool, and the beautiful black satin backing was covered with muddy footprints." Like the unappreciated ornamental objects, the story suggests, women such as Eldest Young Miss retain little value in the emerging modern social order. The story exemplifies Ling's mastery of two formal techniques for which her writing became known: rich symbolism and powerful use of narrative irony. According to C. T. Hsia, who ranks Ling as the most accomplished woman writer of her generation, the story represented a formal breakthrough as "the first modern Chinese short to be sustained on the dramatic irony of a pervading symbolism."

Ling's fascination with old-fashioned ladies whose lifestyles and mentalities remain steeped in the established ways, yet whose lives are inexorably being altered by the rise of modern values and conventions, can be seen in several other works from this period. The tradition-bound protagonist of "Zhongqiu wan" (1925; translated as "The Night of the Mid-Autumn Festival," 1995) clings so stubbornly to outmoded rituals and superstitious beliefs that she alienates her new husband. She fails to achieve even a modicum of awareness of what is happening and fatalistically attributes the destruction of her marriage to a bad omen portended during the festival described at the beginning of the story.

In "Chicha" (1925, The Tea Party), "Chahui yihou" (1925, After the Tea Party), and "Shuo you zheme yihui shi" (1926, It Is Said This Once Happened; translated as "Once upon a Time," 1998) Ling places her female protagonists in more-modern social settings. The first story is a light-hearted comedy that presents the awkwardness and misunderstanding that arise when the young, naive, and self-absorbed Fangying meets the urbane foreign-educated older brother of a friend and misreads his politeness as an indication of romantic interest. After days of pining, in a scene that parodies the classical motif of the boudoir lament, the love-stricken Fangying receives a much-anticipated letter—only to open an invitation to the man's wedding. Yet, if the author laughs at her foolish heroine, in acknowledging the confusion borne of rapidly changing social mores she also renders Fangying's plight with

Cover for Ling's short-story collection Nüren (Women), published in 1930 (East Asia Collection, University of California, Berkeley Library)

sympathy. Fangying is a victim of her own naiveté; but in a culture that traditionally restricted women of elite households to the inner quarters, she is hardly to blame for her lack of worldliness. The sisters A Ying and A Zhu in "Chahui yihou" are not sequestered at home, like Eldest Young Miss, or as easily deluded as Fangying, but they are nevertheless bewildered by the fashionable tea party they have attended. Their seemingly trivial commentary on the stylish young ladies at the party, who interacted freely with male guests and sported the latest hairdos and shoes, betrays apprehension toward the unfamiliar social terrain that they must now navigate. "Shuo you zheme yihui shi" depicts a brief lesbian romance between two college students, Yingman and Yunluo, who fall in love while rehearsing their respective roles as Romeo and Juliet in a school play. The Shakespearean reference foreshadows the doomed nature of the relationship, but it is also key to the story's irony: Yunluo's family arranges for her to meet a man during the summer break; instead of committing suicide like Shakespeare's protagonists, Yunluo yields to social pressure and marries the man, and Yingman faints on hearing the news. Homosexuality was not an uncommon theme in fiction at the time, and for writers such as Lu Yin and Chen Xuezhao love between women embodied an ideal alternative to conventional husband-wife roles. In "Shuo you zheme yihui shi" Ling uses the theme to make a statement about conformity: even when afforded the benefits of modern education and greater social freedoms, women such as Yunlou remain imprisoned by their adherence to social norms. The idea for the story was not Ling's: according to the preface that accompanied the story when it first appeared in Chen bao in 1926, the writer Yang Zhensheng was so dissatisfied with his "Ta weishenme fafeng le" (Why She Went Mad), which was also published in Chen bao in 1926, that he asked Ling to rewrite it.

Ling and Chen Yuan were married on Ling's graduation from college in 1927. They spent the following year in Japan, where Ling studied the works of modern Japanese writers such as Natsume Soseki, Tanizaki Jun'ichiro, and Kawabata Yasunari.

Ling's first short-story collection, Hua zhi si (The Temple of Flowers), came out not long after she and her husband returned from Japan in 1928. It was one of the initial publications of the Crescent Moon Bookstore, which had been founded in Shanghai by Xu Zhimo following the exodus of scholars and writers from Beijing during the political turmoil of 1926–1927. In addition to books, the Crescent Moon Bookstore published the literary journal Xin yue yuekan (Crescent Moon Monthly), modeled after the British Yellow Book, from 1928 to 1933. The writers whose works appeared in Xin yue yuekan, including Ling, were distinguished for their Western cultural sensibilities and their promotion of the aesthetic value of literature over its potential to reflect sociopolitical concerns.

Hua zhi si comprises twelve stories, primarily works Ling had published in 1925 and 1926 in Xiandai pinglun, including "Jiu hou," "Xiu zhen," "Zhongqiu wan," "Chicha," "Chahui yihou," and "Shuo you zheme yihui shi." The title piece, "Hua zhi si" (1925, The Temple of Flowers), is a mildly satirical tale of a shrewd middle-class woman who tries to put a romantic spark back into her marriage while at the same time teaching her husband a lesson about fidelity. As the story opens, Youquan, a poet, is restless and bored with the daily routine at home. That evening he receives a letter from a secret admirer who proposes a rendevous the next day at the Temple of Flowers. While the locale fails to live up to its poetic-sounding name, he waits with great anticipation—only to be mortified when the mystery woman turns out to be his wife. The cleverly structured plot keeps the reader, as well as the husband, in suspense as to the identity of the letter writer. The greatest virtue of the work, however, is the precision with which Ling captures the shifting moods of the male character, from his ennui at the beginning of the story to his guilty eagerness and, finally, to the mixture of embarrassment and delight he experiences when the truth is revealed.

The brief "Zaijian" (1925, See You Again/Farewell) also depicts with great nuance the elusive emotional dynamics of human relationships. A pair of former lovers accidentally encounter each other at West Lake in Hangzhou. At first the reader detects the flicker of renewed romantic attraction as each makes discreet inquiries as to the other's marital status. As their conversation progresses, however, Yaoqiao, who, like so many of Ling's female characters, is endowed with keen powers of observation, begins to notice details about Ju Ren—his rudeness toward the waiter and his new interest in playing cards, for instance—that reveal how much he has changed since becoming a petty government bureaucrat. The imperceptive Ju Ren, on the other hand, fails to pick up the signals and grows ever more animated as he fondly recalls the past and angles for a future date. But as they part ways, the pun in the title is revealed: while he uses the expression *zaijian* in the sense of "see you again," for her it conveys a firm "farewell."

In 1929 Chen Yuan took the directorship of the prestigious School of Letters of National Wuhan University. Ling developed close friendships with two prominent women literary scholars and writers at the university, Yuan Changying and Su Xuelin. In a reminiscence of those years, "Ling Shuhua qiren qiwen" (1980, Ling Shuhua—Her Life and Her Writing) Su notes that the trio spent so much time together that they became known as the "Three heroes of Luojia Hill," after the ancient site near which they all lived. During her years in Wuhan, Ling's work appeared in such leading literary journals as *Xin yue yuekan*, *Xiaoshuo yuebao* (Short Story Monthly), *Beidou* (Big Dipper), and *Wenxue zazhi* (Literature Magazine). In 1930 many of the stories were collected by the Shanghai Commercial Press in the volumes *Nüren* (Women) and *Xiaohai* (Children).

In *Nüren* the reader finds echoes of many themes from Ling Shuhua's earlier work. Reminiscent of "Hua zhi si," the title piece is a short play about a resourceful wife who devises a clever plan to deal with an unfaithful husband. The plot is efficient and well executed, but, without the descriptive detail Ling uses in her narrative fiction, it falls somewhat flat and is among the weaker selections in the volume. Several of the seven short stories in *Nüren* feature middle-class wives. "Xiao Liu" (translated as "Little Liu," 1981) is one of the few stories in which Ling uses a first-person narrator. The narrator's fond memories of the title character as a feisty, if somewhat cruel, modern female student are juxtaposed with a disappointing reunion with her in the present. Barely recognizable, Little Liu has turned into a harried housewife bogged down in the drudgery of everyday routine and child rearing. The passages capturing the chaos and drab domesticity that the narrator witnesses attest to Ling's descriptive abilities: the shabby living room, remnants of peanut shells littering the carpet, a wailing baby, and a demanding boy whose grotesque antics include relieving himself in the spittoon and wiping his nose on his mother's dress are rendered in painfully realistic detail. Whereas the disillusioned "new women" characters popularized by writers such as Lu Yin openly resent or defy their domestic predicaments, Ling's characters are not rebels and evince little awareness that other life choices may be available. The narrative details themselves, however, unmistakably impart the author's distaste for the oppressive dreariness of bourgeois family life.

The realist narrative "Song che" (translated as "The Send Off," 1989) presents a humdrum afternoon at the Bai household. The story opens in midconversation as Mrs. Bai, a pretentious middle-aged housewife, complains about the weight of a chicken recently purchased by the cook and the price he claims to have paid for bean sprouts. The stream of superficial chatter and gossip continues with the arrival of Mrs. Zhou and her daughter, who have made plans with Mrs. Bai to see their friend Mrs. Xu off at the train station that afternoon. Eventually, Mr. Bai, who has been reading the newspaper all the while, impatiently reminds his wife of the time; but the women continue to dillydally until it is too late to get to the station. So they prattle on, turning their focus to the modern Mrs. Xu and her newfangled, free-love marriage, of which they all greatly disapprove. This mildly satirical narrative in which nothing of any consequence happens depicts the empty nature of middle-class domesticity. At the same time, Ling uses the banal exchange among the housewives to provide clues to their psychology: Mrs. Bai's preoccupation with the honesty of her cook—a tedious topic to which she returns at the end of the story, much to her husband's exasperation—reveals the narrow scope of her monotonous life, while the scorn she and her friends heap upon Mrs. Xu smacks not only of jealousy but also of the insecurities they feel in their own marriages at a moment of changing social values and roles.

Other stories in *Nüren* deal with women of other social classes. The title character in "Li xiansheng"

(1930, Schoolmistress Li), for example, is a lonely attendant at a girl's school who is past her prime. While she enjoys a friendly rapport with the energetic students, the vivacious, fashionably dressed schoolgirls make her conscious of her age; love letters in the incoming mail she sorts recall missed opportunities for marriage; and the plain, uncomfortable furniture of the school's reception room evokes a longing for warmth of a home of her own. Critics thought that *Nüren* lacked the thematic unity of Ling's first volume of stories.

Xiaohai, which was enlarged to include several new stories and republished as *Xiao ge'er lia* (Two Brothers) in 1935, has been somewhat misleadingly categorized as children's literature. Most of the stories do feature children, but, like most of Ling's fiction, they are experiments in narrative perspective rather than children's stories as such. "Didi" (1927, Little Brother), for instance, captures a boy's perspective on his sister's engagement and the unwitting role he plays early on in the courtship: forgetting that he is to stay out of his sister's bedroom, he goes there in search of a copy of the ancient epic *Shuihu zhuan* (The Story of the Water Margin; translated as *All Men Are Brothers*, 1933) and innocently exposes her romantic desires by showing the young man the photograph that she has stashed in a drawer. "Xiao Ying" (1935, Little Ying) examines marriage from the viewpoint of a naive girl. Little Ying can hardly contain her excitement about her Third Aunt's impending wedding. She imagines how lovely the bride will look in her gown and admires the growing assortment of objects and clothing that have been purchased for the trousseau. At night after the wedding, however, as she replays the scenes of the day in her mind, she is haunted by the image of the ferocious old woman she met at the ceremony: Third Aunt's new mother-in-law. Her fairy-tale vision of marriage is further shattered when she visits her aunt and sees that the latter is treated like a household servant. The story includes none of the strident protest against arranged marriage or the traditional family structure common in fiction of the era; instead, Ling unfolds her critique through the eyes of an innocent child and allows readers to draw their own conclusions.

Other stories in *Xiao ge'er lia* indirectly take up the dynamics of nation and class, both of which were major concerns of Chinese writers at the time. The title character of "Kaiselin" (1935, Katherine) is a neglected rich girl with a somewhat pretentious Westernized name who accidently breaks her mother's expensive watch while playing with the daughter of the maid at her family's summer villa. The girls bury the incriminating evidence in the garden. The next day, when Katherine's mother interrogates her about the missing watch, she lies her way out of trouble, unaware that the blame is bound to fall on someone else: the maid is accused of stealing and summarily fired. While the story lacks the satiric undertone that drives many of Ling's best stories, it illustrates her characteristic style of showing rather than overtly protesting the moral and emotional vacuum beneath the aesthetic refinement and polite manner of the Chinese elite. Another story in the collection explores how personal relationships are altered by national affairs: in "Yiguo" (1935, A Foreign Country) a Chinese student receives kind treatment at a Japanese hospital, but the attitude of her nurses abruptly changes when news breaks that several Japanese soldiers have been killed in northern China. Two other stories, "Qiandaizi" (1931, Chiyoko) and "Shengri" (1935, Birthday), are also set in Japan and center on Japanese children. The most successful work in the volume, though also the most disturbing, is "Fenghuang" (1930, Phoenix), in which an imaginative girl named Zhi'er wanders away from home, drawn by the sights and sounds of the busy street. Of particular appeal to Zhi'er are the colorful toys made from soft dough sold by a street peddler, including a magnificent phoenix that she desperately wants to buy. As she begins to despair because she has no money, a man buys the toy for her and lures her even farther from her home with the promise of a real phoenix. Zhi'er is located before anything serious transpires, but Ling develops a powerful narrative tension between the innocent, almost magical world inhabited by her gullible young heroine and the dangers lurking in the adult world.

By the mid 1930s Ling had a solid reputation as a modern short-story writer. The critical reception of her fiction, however, varied greatly. Many of her contemporaries regarded Ling as a breed apart from the so-called New Woman writers, such as Lu Yin, Feng Yuanjun, and Ding Ling, who were highly popular at the time. Whereas the latter were known for their innovative use of an intensely confessional narrative voice and for their explicit treatment of current sociopolitical problems, Ling was often labeled a practitioner of "guixiu wenxue" ("literature by and for ladies," in Clara Yu Cuadrado's translation). The genre, as it was understood by critics, embodied a quintessentially "feminine" literary style consisting of a delicate lyricism and an attention to trifling domestic concerns. Other women writers to whom this label was sometimes applied included Ling's friends Su and Bing Xin. Even critics such as Yi Zhen, who recognized the detached sarcasm that lends Ling's fictional narratives their critical edge, referred to her as a "new *guixiu*" writer whose primary interest was in women in love. Lu Xun avoided the somewhat derogatory label when he included "Xiu zhen" in the fiction volume he edited in 1935 for *Zhongguo xin wenxue daxi* (A Comprehensive Anthology of

China's New Literature), but he also emphasized the contrast he saw between Ling's muted literary style and the "dadan" (bold), "ganyan" (outspoken) approach of Feng, the only other female author represented in the volume.

In the politically charged, class-conscious climate of 1930s literary culture, other critics objected more specifically to what they considered the elitist orientation of Ling's work. In his 1936 book on modern Chinese women's writing, the leftist critic He Yubo characterized Ling's fiction as mere entertainment for readers of the leisure class. Ling was not the only writer He and other like-minded contemporary critics targeted for attack. Feminist literary historians have noted that with the narrowing definition of the "political" at the time, many female authors who focused on personal life and the domestic realm were charged with writing fiction that was at best insignificant and at worst politically reactionary.

Other critics, however, were impressed by Ling's mastery of modernist formal techniques; above all, they praised the narrative finesse she brought to her psychological portraits. In a 1931 review of *Hua zhi si* and *Nüren*, Shen Congwen observed that Ling's approach is descriptive rather than analytical and compared her style to that of the New Zealand–born British author Katherine Mansfield, whose work was widely translated and read in China in the 1920s. (Xu Zhimo had published a collection of translations of Mansfield's fiction in 1927.) Su further consolidated Ling's reputation as the "Mansfield of China" in her 1936 essay "Ling Shuhua de *Hua zhi si* yu *Nüren*" (Ling Shuhua's *Temple of Flowers* and *Women*), in which she analyzes the similarities between Ling's "You fuqi de ren" (1926; translated as "The Lucky One," 1985) and Mansfield's "An Ideal Family" (1922). Both stories portray elderly heads of affluent households who come to realize how greedy and materialistic their children are.

After the mid 1930s, Ling's fiction writing dropped off considerably. In 1935 she assumed the editorship of *Xiandai wenyi* (Contemporary Literature and Art), a supplement of the *Wuhan ribao* (Wuhan Daily), and much of her time was devoted to carrying out the responsibilities of the position. She also formed a relationship with the nephew of the British writer Virginia Woolf, Julian Bell, who was teaching English literature at National Wuhan University. In collaboration with Bell she translated several of her short stories, including "Fengle de shiren" (1928; translated as "A Poet Goes Mad," 1937), into English for *T'ien Hsia Monthly*, the leading journal of translation in China at the time. Her most significant literary project during these years, however, was her evocative memoir of her childhood, *Ancient Melodies*. War with Japan broke out in 1937; in

Title page for Ling's Xiao ge'er lia *(1935, Two Brothers), a collection of stories written from the perspective of children (from Yao Zhimin, Wang Zhongming, Zhang Zhenhua, and Bian Qiansheng, eds.,* Shuying, *volume 2, 2003; Bruccoli Clark Layman Archives)*

the winter of 1938 Wuhan University was evacuated to Luoshan in Sichuan Province. Around this time Ling began corresponding with Woolf. Like most Chinese intellectuals, she was familiar with Woolf's work—including *A Room of One's Own* (1929), which had been translated into Chinese in the 1930s—although the correspondence may have been prompted by news of Bell's death in the Spanish Civil War in 1937. Whether or not the idea of writing a memoir was triggered by Woolf's suggestion in a letter of 15 April 1938 is not certain; Ling had previously published several autobiographical vignettes in magazines: "Banjia" (1929; translated as "Moving House," 1953), "Bayue jie" (1937; translated as "Sakura Festival," 1953), and "Yijian xishi" (1938; translated as "A Happy Occasion," 1953). All were included, with minor revisions, in *Ancient Melodies*. What is certain is that Ling decided to start writing in English, which bespeaks a new orientation toward a foreign readership. Woolf supplied her with literary texts such as Elizabeth Cleghorn Gaskell's *The Life of Charlotte Brontë, Author of "Jane Eyre," "Shirley," "Villette," etc.*

(1857) and Charles Lamb's essays and offered advice on the drafts of the manuscript Ling sent her. Woolf wrote on 15 October 1938 that she was charmed by the work and urged Ling to preserve the "Chinese flavor" in her English prose.

In 1946 Chen Yuan was appointed the Chinese representative to the United Nations Educational, Scientific and Cultural Organization (UNESCO), and he and Ling relocated briefly to Paris and then settled in London. Woolf had committed suicide in 1941, so Ling never met her in person. *Ancient Melodies* was published in 1953 by the Hogarth Press, which Woolf had founded with her husband, Leonard; it included an introduction by Woolf's friend, the writer Vita Sackville-West, with whom Ling became acquainted after moving to England, and hand-drawn illustrations by the author.

Ancient Melodies comprises eighteen autobiographical vignettes; all but "Moving House," "Sakura Festival," and "A Happy Occasion" were originally composed in English. The title, an allusion to a poem by the Tang Dynasty master Bo Juyi, reflects Ling's view that the way of life she knew growing up has long since vanished. A translation of the poem by Arthur Waley (pseudonym of Arthur David Schloss), whom Ling met in England, is included in the introduction:

Of cord and cassia-wood is the lute compounded;
Within it lie ancient—melodies.
Ancient melodies-weak and savorless;
Not appealing to present men's taste.
Light and color are faded from the jade stops;
Dust has covered the rose-red strings,
Decay and ruin came to it long ago,
But the sound that is left is still cold and clear.
I do not refuse to play it, if you want me to;
But even if I play, people will not listen.

Ancient Melodies constitutes one of the most valuable sources of biographical information about Ling's life from early childhood to the May Fourth era, when she was a young teenager. It is a self-consciously literary work that draws on many novelistic techniques, although some scholars have thought that it lacks the subtlety that distinguishes her earlier fiction and occasionally caters to the foreign reader in its exotic details. Reminiscent of several stories in *Xiao ge'er lia*, the work unfolds through the perspective of a first-person child narrator, which Ling captures in a simple, yet elegant, lyrical prose. On the surface the vignettes paint a picture of an almost idyllic childhood. Grim and often tragic details punctuate the narrative, however, creating a disturbing disjunction between the narrator's childish vision and the world she inhabits. In the first chapter, for instance, Ling and her favorite servant, Ma Tao, are on an afternoon outing and join a throng of onlookers watching a public execution. Despite the servant's explanation, the uncomprehending child sees the scene as a lively theatrical performance. Not until the prisoner lies decapitated in a pool of blood does a vague sense of horror begin to take hold—though even then she remains innocently curious about what is in store next for the poor fellow. Readers versed in modern Chinese literature will have little difficulty in spotting the reference here to Lu Xun, who represented China's modern national condition through a similar scene of execution and depraved spectatorship. In general, however, the memoir avoids the well-worn historical paradigms found in other accounts of the period, and the complex historical setting of Ling's youth comes into view only indirectly as it is reflected in everyday details woven into the story. The chapter contrasting the noisy Confucian rituals at her older brother's marriage with her sister's Western-style wedding ceremony, complete with morose orchestral music and a groom in a clownish top hat, for instance, is a refreshing look at the themes of modernization versus tradition and native versus foreign practices.

The reception of the book in Great Britain was enormously positive, with a glowing review in *The Times Literary Supplement*. The essayist J. B. Priestley called it the "book of the year," and it received further publicity when it was read over the BBC. *Ancient Melodies* was translated into several European languages, but readers in China had to wait until 1991 for the work to become available in Chinese translation.

Ling took teaching positions at Nanyang University in Singapore from 1956 to 1960 and at the University of Toronto in 1967–1968; she also delivered occasional lectures on Chinese literature and art at the University of Oxford, the University of London, and the University of Edinburgh. Her paintings were shown in Paris in 1955, and works from her private collection were displayed at the Arts Council of Great Britain in 1967. After Chen Yuan's death in 1970 at seventy-four, she made several trips back to China.

Ling wrote virtually no fiction during the latter half of her life, when she lived abroad, despite the abiding interest in her work among Chinese readers. On occasion she wrote brief articles on classical and modern Chinese art and culture for newspapers and magazines in Hong Kong and Singapore. In 1960 the Singapore Xinzhou World Press published a compilation of her essays, *Aishanlu mengying* (Dreams from a Mountain Lover's Studio), mostly written during her sojourn in Singapore. The collection includes both *suibi* (informal essays) on art and lyrical prose pieces. Many of the latter are inspired by her travels and are characterized by a classical-style evocation of nature and the landscape. Full of references to places and people she knew in her past, they also express a nostalgia for China. Collections of her early short stories have been published in Hong Kong, Taiwan, and Singapore since the early 1960s.

At the end of 1989 Ling Shuhua realized a long-held dream of moving back to Beijing, where her old friend Bing Xin helped her find permanent housing. She died on 22 May 1990.

References:

A Chinese Painter's Choice: Some Paintings from the 14th to the 20th Century from the Collection of Ling Su-hua (London: Arts Council of Great Britain, 1967);

Rey Chow, "Virtuous Transactions: A Reading of Three Stories by Ling Shuhua," *Modern Chinese Literature,* 4 (1988): 71–86;

Clara Yu Cuadrado, "Portraits of a Lady: The Fictional World of Ling Shuhua," in *Women Writers of 20th Century China,* edited by Angela Jung Palandri (Eugene: Asian Studies Publications, University of Oregon, 1982), pp. 41–62;

He Yubo, *Zhongguo xiandai nüzuojia* (Shanghai: Fuxing Shuju, 1936), pp. 49–88;

Don Holoch, "Everyday Feudalism: The Subversive Stories of Ling Shuhua," in *Women and Literature in China,* edited by Anna Gerstlacher and others (Bochum, Germany: Studienverlag Brockmeyer, 1985), pp. 379–393;

C. T. Hsia, *A History of Modern Chinese Fiction,* second edition (New Haven: Yale University Press, 1971), pp. 77–84;

Huang Renying, *Dangdai Zhongguo nüzuojia lun* (Shanghai: Guanghua shuju, 1933), pp. 1–36, 259–264;

Wendy Larson, *Women and Writing in Modern China* (Stanford, Cal.: Stanford University Press, 1998), pp. 118–122, 194–195;

Patricia Laurence, "The China Letters: Julian Bell, Vanessa Bell, and Ling Shu Hua," *South Carolina Review,* 29 (1996): 122–131;

Leo Ou-fan Lee, *The Romantic Generation of Modern Chinese Writers* (Cambridge, Mass.: Harvard University Press, 1973), pp. 17–18;

Sally Taylor Lieberman, *The Mother and Narrative Politics in Modern China* (Charlottesville: University Press of Virginia, 1998), pp. 141–145;

Lu Qiyuan and Xu Zhichao, eds., *Fan fengjian de chunlei xiyu: Su Xuelin, Lu Yin, Ling Shuhua, Feng Yuanjun, Zhongguo xinwenxue dashi mingzuo shangxi,* volume 26 (Taibei: Haifeng chubanshe, 1992);

Bonnie McDougall, "Dominance and Disappearance: A Post-Feminist Review of Fiction by Mao Dun and Ling Shuhua," in *Autumn Floods: Essays in Honour of Marián Gálik,* edited by Raoul Findeisen and Robert Gassmann (Bern: Peter Lang, 1997), pp. 283–306;

Meng Yue and Dai Jinhua, *Fuchu lishi dibiao* (Taibei: Shibao wenhua chubanshe, 1993), pp. 135–155;

Janet Ng, "Writing in Her Father's World: The Feminine Autobiographical Strategies of Ling Shuhua," *Prose Studies,* 16, no. 3 (1993): 235–250;

Qiao Yigang, *Zhongguo nüxing de wenxue shijie* (Wuhan: Hubei jiaoyu chubanshe, 1993), pp. 278–287;

Shu-mei Shih, "Gendered Negotiations with the Local: Lin Huiyin and Ling Shuhua," in her *The Lure of the Modern: Writing Modernism in Semicolonial China, 1917–1937* (Berkeley: University of California Press, 2001), pp. 204–230;

Su Xuelin, "Ling Shuhua de *Hua zhi si* yu *Nüren,*" in her *Su Xuelin wenji,* volume 3 (Hefei: Anhui wenyi chubanshe, 1996), pp. 223–234;

Su, "Ling Shuhua nüshi de hua," in her *Su Xuelin wenji,* volume 2 (Hefei: Anhui wenyi chubanshe, 1996), pp. 398–399;

Su, "Ling Shuhua qiren qiwen," in *Zhongguo jindai zuojia yu zuopin,* edited by Lin Haiyin (Taibei: Chunwenxue chubanshe, 1980), pp. 71–76;

Yao Zhimin, Wang Zhongming, Zhang Zhenhua, and Bian Qiansheng, eds. *Shuying,* volume 2 (Shanghai: Yuandong chubanshe, 2003);

Yi Zhen, "Ji wei dangdai Zhongguo nü xiao shuojia," in *Dangdai Zhongguo nüzuojia lun,* edited by Huang Renying (Beiping: Guanghua shuju, 1933), pp. 1–36;

Zhang Ruogu, "Zhongguo xiandai de nüzuojia," *Zhen Mei Shan: Nüzuojia hao* (1928): 1–73;

Zhao Qingge, *Changxiang yi* (Shanghai: Xuelin chubanshe, 1999), pp. 68–70.

Liu E
(29 September 1857 – 3 August 1909)

Christopher Lupke
Washington State University

Liu E (from the cover for Meipi xiangzhu Lao Can youji, *1979; Collection of Thomas Moran)*

BOOKS: *Yu Zhi Lu san sheng Huanghe tu* [A Chart of the Course of the Yellow River through the Provinces of Henan, Zhili, and Shandong], by Liu E and others (N.p., 1890);

Zhi He qi shuo [Seven Methods for Yellow River Flood Control] (N.p., 1890–1892?);

Lidai Huanghe bianqian tukao [Maps and Studies of Changes to the Yellow River through History] (N.p.: Xiuhai shanfeng, 1893);

Tieyun cang gui [Tortoise Shells in the Collection of Tieyun], 6 volumes (N.p., 1903);

Tieyun cang tao [Pottery in the Collection of Tieyun], as Liu Tieyun, 2 volumes (N.p., 1904);

Lao Can youji [The Travels of Lao Can], 2 volumes (Shanghai: Shenzhou ribaoguan, 1907); translated by Harold E. Shadick as *The Travels of Lao Ts'an* (Ithaca, N.Y.: Cornell University Press, 1952);

Lao Can youji erji [The Sequel to the Travels of Lao Can] (Shanghai: Liangyou tushu gongsi, 1935)—comprises chapters 21–26; translated as "A Nun of Taishan," in *A Nun of Taishan (a Novelette) and Other Translations,* edited and translated by Lin Yutang (Shanghai: Commercial Press, 1936), pp. 1–112; translation revised in *Widow, Nun and Courtesan: Three Novelettes from the Chinese,* edited and translated by Lin (New York: John Day, 1951), pp. 113–180;

Lao Can youji quanbian [The Complete Travels of Lao Can] (Taibei: Yiwen chubanguan, 1972)—comprises chapters 1–29 and the *waipian* fragment;

Tieyun shicun [The Extant Poetry of Tieyun], as Liu Tieyun, edited by Liu Huisun (Ji'nan: Qi Lu shushe, 1980);

Tieyun cang huo [Coins in the Collection of Tieyun], as Liu Tieyun (Beijing: Zhonghua shuju, 1986).

Editions: *Lao Can youji* [The Travels of Lao Can], annotated by Chen Xianghe and Dai Hongsen (Beijing: Renmin wenxue chubanshe, 1957—comprises chapters 1–26; enlarged, 1982—comprises chapters 1–29);

Lao Can youji [The Travels of Lao Can] (Hong Kong: Taiping shuju, 1969)—comprises chapters 1–26;

Lidai Huanghe bianqian tukao [Maps and Studies of Changes to the Yellow River through History] (Taibei: Wenhai chubanshe, 1971);

Meipi xiangzhu Lao Can youji [The Travels of Lao Can with Full Annotation at the Top of the Page], edited by Lü Ziyang, annotated by Yu Guoji (Gaoxiong: Heban chubanshe, 1979);

Lao Can youji, annotated by Yan Weiqing (Ji'nan: Qi Lu shushe, 1981);

Lao Can youji, annotated by Yan (Taibei: Jian'an, 1997);

Lidai Huanghe bianqian tukao [Maps and Studies of Changes to the Yellow River through History] (Beijing: Beijing chubanshe, 1997);

Tieyun cang tao [Pottery in the Collection of Tieyun], 2 volumes (Yangzhou: Jiangsu guangling guji keyinshe, 1998);

Tieyun cang gui [Tortoise Shells in the Collection of Tieyun], 6 volumes (Beijing: Beijing tushuguan chubanshe, 2000);

Xinshi Lao Can youji [The Newly Annotated Travels of Lao Can], annotated by Wu Shaozhi and Wu Yiling (Tainan: Xiangyi chubanshe, 2000).

Editions in English: *Tramp Doctor's Travelogue,* translated by Lin Yi-chin and Ko Te-shun (Shanghai: Commercial Press, 1939);

Mr. Decadent, translated by H. Y. Yang and G. M. Tayler (Nanjing: Duli shudian, 1947); republished as *Mr. Derelict* (London: Allen & Unwin, 1948); revised as *Lao Can youji* (Beijing: Chinese Literature Press, 1983).

Liu E wrote only one novel, *Lao Can youji* (1907, The Travels of Lao Can; translated as *The Travels of Lao Ts'an,* 1952); but it is recognized by scholars as one of the four great novels of the late Qing Dynasty period (1844 to 1911). Shuen-fu Lin argues that Liu E's book is "the last classic Chinese novel" in that it reflects, even in its structure, the retreat of the traditional Chinese worldview in the face of modernity and the West. *Lao Can youji* also marks the beginning of modern Chinese literature: its influence on Chinese writing in the twentieth century was as great as, if not greater than, that of any other late-Qing novel. Liu E's work combines features of the traditional *zhanghui* (linked) novel with innovations such as shifts in narrative point of view; sustained descriptions of people, places, and landscape; and the exploration of the protagonist's psychology. Liu E was also a connoisseur of traditional Chinese culture and interested in science and technology. He collected antique coins and published the first collection of rubbings made from inscriptions of "oracle bones" (inscribed tortoise shells and animal bones dating to before 1000 B.C.). And he engaged in many business ventures, including planning railroads and opening a printing press. His straightforward manner and frustration with vested interests, combined with his unflagging opposition to corruption, led to his downfall: he accrued enemies and rivals throughout his life; some of them rose to positions of power, which was fateful for Liu E.

Liu E was born into a literati family in Liuhe on the lower Yangtze River in Jiangsu province on 29 September 1857. His *yuanming* (original given name) was Mengpeng; his name as recorded in the Liu family genealogy is␣Zhenyuan. He is well known by both his *zi* (style name), Liu Tieyun, and his *ming* (personal name), Liu E. He came from a long line of government servants, officials, and military men; while politically prominent and well educated, the Liu clan accumulated only modest wealth. Liu E's father, Liu Chengzhong, who had earned the *jinshi* (highest-level) degree in 1852, served as an examination official, censor, and prefect. According to Fang Chao-ying's entry on Liu E in Arthur W. Hummel's *Eminent Chinese of the Ch'ing Period (1644–1912)* (1943), Liu Chengzhong "collected many books on mathematics, on world geography, and on other studies recently introduced from the West." Liu E's mother, who was from a prominent Liuhe family, was surnamed Zhu. According to *Tieyun xiansheng nianpu changbian* (1982, A Complete Chronology of the Life of Mr. Tieyun), by Liu E's grandson Liu Huisun, Liu E's mother "was intelligent and widely read, well informed about current affairs, skilled in music and knowledgeable about medicine." Liu E had one older brother, Mengxiong, and three older sisters. His second eldest sister taught him to read when he was four *sui* (in traditional Chinese reckoning, a person is one *sui* at birth).

Liu E lived with his parents until the age of nineteen *sui*. He read broadly under the tutelage of his father and other family members. As a youth he had a reputation for brashness and for having little patience for deception, incompetence, dogma, or superciliousness and was known for his fairness in argument and loyalty to friends. He detested the procrustean nature of the *baguwen* (eight-legged essay), the mastery of which was necessary to pass the various levels of the civil service examinations.

In 1873 Liu E married a woman surnamed Wang, who was sixteen. In 1875 Liu E and Wang *Shi* (the Chinese equivalent of "Mme Wang") were still childless; to fulfill his filial obligation to carry on the family line, Liu E formally adopted his brother's third son, Dazhang. In the spring of 1875 Liu E moved to Huai'an in Jiangsu province, where his family had property and where, according to Harold E. Shadick's introduction to *The Travels of Lao Ts'an,* he had spent his early years. In the fall of 1876 Liu E failed the provincial civil service examination. He and his wife had a daughter, Ruzhen, in the fall of the following year. Liu E took his first concubine, a woman surnamed Heng, in 1878. In 1881 his wife gave birth to a son, Dafu; in 1883 his concubine gave birth to a daughter, Fobao.

In 1884 Liu E opened a tobacco store in Huai'an, but the venture soon failed. In early 1885 his concubine gave birth to a son, Dajin. Around this time Liu E went to Yangzhou to study with Li Longchuan, a teacher of the sect known as the Taigu xuepai (Taigu School) that combined elements of Confucianism, Daoism, and Buddhism. He studied with Li, whom he had first met in 1876, for several years and found in Taigu an inclusive philosophy that did not reject tradition but could still meet the unprecedented challenges facing modern China. Shadick writes that under Li's influence Liu E, "who had been so headstrong and undisciplined apparently experienced what might very well be called a religious conversion" and "developed a sense of social responsibility." The Taigu School figures prominently in Liu E's novel.

According to "Guanyu *Lao Can youji*" (1940, On *The Travels of Lao Can*), by Liu E's son Dashen, in 1885 Liu E tried to make money by practicing traditional Chinese medicine but failed to attract patients. In 1886 Liu undertook the imperial examinations for the second time but quit before completing them. On the way home from Nanjing, he stopped in Jinjiang and took a woman surnamed Mao as his second concubine; she gave birth to his son Dashen in 1887. That same year, in Shanghai, Liu opened one of China's first Chinese-owned lithographic printing presses. The press went out of business in 1888, and Liu E returned to Huai'an.

In 1887 the Yellow River had broken through its dikes in several places, including Zhengzhou in Henan province, and massive flooding had resulted. In 1888 Wu Dacheng, the governor of Guangdong province and a friend of Liu E's father, was put in charge of the Yellow River conservancy in Zhengzhou. Liu E went to Zhengzhou and offered his services to Wu. According to Liu Huisun, Liu E proposed to "zhu di shu shui, shu shui gong sha" (build dikes so as to manage the flow of water, and manage the flow of water so as to control sedimentation). Wu implemented the plan, and Liu E shed his long gown, donned boots, and got into the trenches with the workers. The dikes were strengthened and protected, and the persistent problem of flooding in the area was solved by the winter of 1888–1889. Wu offered Liu E an official post, but Liu E gave it to his brother and remained in Henan to contribute to a work published in 1890 as *Yu Zhi Lu san sheng Huanghe tu* (A Chart of the Course of the Yellow River through the Provinces of Henan, Zhili, and Shandong).

In 1890 Liu E's concubine Heng gave birth to a daughter, Mabao. That same year Zhang Yao, the governor of Shandong, brought Liu E to the province as an adviser on flood control. Shadick writes that Zhang Yao appointed Liu E to "the rank of subprefect, later raised to prefect"; Fang claims that Liu E purchased the rank of "expectant sub-prefect," an accepted practice, before going to Henan. Zhang Yao died in 1891 and was replaced as governor by Furun (a Chinese transliteration of a Manchu name), whom Liu E continued to serve as an adviser on flood control until 1893. While in Shandong, Liu E wrote books on mathematics and river conservancy, including *Lidai Huanghe bianqian tukao* (1893, Maps and Studies of Changes to the Yellow River through History) and *Zhi He qi shuo* (1890–1892? Seven Methods for Yellow River Flood Control); according to some sources, the title is *Zhi He wu shuo* (Five Methods for Yellow River Flood Control). Also, some sources claim Liu E wrote one or two appendixes to the book; according to Jiang Yixue's *Liu E nianpu* (1980, A Chronology of Liu E's Life), Liu E wrote and published a work titled *Zhi He xushuo* (Additional Methods for Yellow River Flood Control). In the latter, according to Liu Huisun, Liu E refutes the theory, ascribed to Jia Rang of the Han Dynasty (206 B.C. to A.D. 220), that one should not "fight the river" and that floods were best controlled by widening the space between dikes to accommodate floods. Liu E advocated a contrasting method ascribed to Wang Jing, who lived around A.D. 100 and taught, Shadick writes, that one should "narrow and deepen the river bed so that the current would be swift and prevent the silt from forming a deposit."

In the introduction to his translation of Liu E's novel Shadick, drawing on information provided to him by Liu Dashen that was later published as "Guanyu *Lao Can youji*," writes that Yuan Shikai (who became president of the Republic of China in 1912 and then made himself emperor) and the Manchu officials Gangyi and Yuxian were working in Shandong and that all of them regarded Liu E with enmity. Shadick, following Liu Dashen, contends that Yuan Shikai "turned against Liu because the latter could not or would not persuade Governor Zhang to give him a position of responsibility." According to the biography of Yuan Shikai in Howard L. Boorman and Richard C. Howard's *Biographical Dictionary of Republican China* (1967–1979), however, Yuan Shikai was in Korea as China's top-ranking representative there during Liu E's years in Shandong. Shadick, following Liu Dashen, claims that Gangyi and Yuxian disagreed with Liu E on flood control and were displeased when the governor sided with Liu E. In "*The Travels of Lao Ts'an*: An Exploration of Its Art and Meaning" (1969), however, C. T. Hsia contends that Gangyi did not serve in Shandong when Liu E was there. All scholars, including Hsia, agree that the two main villains in *Lao Can youji*, the officials Gang Bi and Yu Xian, are based on Gangyi and Yuxian.

Liu E's wife died at thirty-six in August 1893. In the same month his concubine Mao Shi gave birth to a daughter, Longbao. Liu E's mother died in September, and he returned to Huai'an for the mourning period. In 1895 Shandong governor Furun recommended that Liu E be brought to the capital to work for the Zongli yamen (Foreign Office); Liu E was offered the position and accepted it. In the summer and fall of 1896 Liu E went to Hubei on an assignment for Zhang Zhidong, governor-general of Hubei and Hunan, to implement Zhang's plan to build a railway from Beijing to Hankou. The industrialist Sheng Xuanhuai, an associate of Zhang's, disagreed with Liu E on details of the plan, and Liu E quit and returned to Beijing. Liu E next proposed a railway between Tianjin and Jinjiang, the city in Jiangsu on the Yangtze River where Liu E's paternal grandfather had settled. (Shadick says that Jinjiang was Liu E's "native place," but other sources name Dantu, a town near Jinjiang, and still others claim that Dantu and Jinjiang are two names for the same town.) Jinjiang officials who were in Beijing opposed the railway, and it was not built.

In 1896 Liu E took his third concubine, a seventeen-year-old surnamed Wang. Mao Shi gave birth to his son Dajing in 1897. That same year Liu E made three trips to Shanxi province as the Chinese manager for an English company that planned to open mines there (coal mines, according to Shadick; iron mines or coal and iron mines, according to other sources). According to Liu Huisun, the enterprise was Liu E's idea. The contract stipulated that after thirty years, the mines and the railroads built to service them would revert to Chinese control. Liu E either quit or was fired when he argued with his English partners over contractual details that he found not to be in China's interests. According to Luke S. K. Kwong, in 1898 officials from Shanxi asked the emperor to criticize the governor of Shanxi "for granting privileges to foreigners in exchange for a loan for railway construction." Kwong says that "Liu E, a go-between in the negotiations, was identified as a culprit," and the government in Beijing demanded that the governor explain his actions, claimed Liu E was of "exceedingly ill repute," and banned him from participation in projects in Shanxi. In 1899 Liu E began participating in the planning and construction of a railway in Henan; it was a segment of a line he had planned from Shanxi to Jiangsu to bring the products of the mines in Shanxi to the east coast.

Liu E's daughter Mabao died in 1899. In late spring of the next year his concubine Wang Shi gave birth to his last son (his sixth, counting the adopted Dazhang), Dalun. Shortly afterward, Liu married Zheng Anxiang as his *jishi* (new wife of a widower).

Cover for a 1907 edition, the earliest that can be confirmed, of Liu E's novel Lao Can youji (translated as The Travels of Lao Ts'an, 1952) (from Yu Runqi, ed., Tang Tao cang shu, 2004; Bruccoli Clark Layman Archives)

Either before or after this marriage, he took a fourth concubine, Guo Shi.

According to Liu Huisun, in 1900 the powerful Manchu official Gangyi filed a petition with the government asking that Liu E be disciplined because of the Shanxi railroad and mining venture. In "*The Travels of Lao Ts'an:* An Exploration of Its Art and Meaning" Hsia claims that Gangyi "accused Liu E of treason"; Hsia, however, suggests that this event happened in 1897. Hsia questions Shadick's claim in the introduction to *The Travels of Lao Ts'an* that Gangyi was settling a personal score with Liu E; he argues that as an "antiforeign conservative" Gangyi would naturally have been troubled by Liu E's involvement with an English company intending to build railroads and mines in the Chinese interior"—especially at the time of the antiforeign Boxer Rebellion, which Gangyi supported. Liu E was in Shanghai, where he was involved in a failed plan to build a five-story department store, and escaped trouble.

In August 1900 twenty thousand troops from eight foreign nations entered Beijing to complete the suppression of the Boxer Rebellion. Sometime shortly thereafter, Liu E returned to the city and engaged in relief work for the populace. According to Liu Huisun, when the supply of relief rice ran out in April or May 1901, a businessman from Ningbo named Zhang put Liu E in touch with the Russian troops who had taken control of the imperial granary and wanted to get rid of the rice in the storehouses so that they could use the buildings. Liu E bought the rice and resumed the distribution of food aid. According to Liu Dashen, Liu E had friends in the British, Italian, and Japanese embassies and in the Chinese government and was asked to participate on the periphery of the discussions of details of the Boxer Protocol, the document that ended the rebellion and imposed severe penalties on the Chinese.

In 1901 Liu E resumed efforts to promote railway construction and mining in Henan, started a mint in Baoding, purchased government offices for himself and four of his sons, and discussed starting a company to install running water in Beijing. His concubine Guo Shi died that year. Liu E's 1902 business ventures included a plan to start a company to refine salt in the northeast for export to Korea. He also continued to work on mining and railway schemes and bought land in Pukou in Jiangsu, intending to develop the area as a commercial port. The land became valuable with the completion of a railway line from Tianjin to Pukou.

By this time Liu E was quite well off. His primary domicile was in Huai'an, but he also owned homes in Beijing, Shanghai, and in Henan and Shandong provinces. He had become an important collector of antiques and in 1902 bought a large collection of oracle bones that had belonged to Wang Yirong, the chancellor of the Imperial Academy, who had committed suicide after foreign troops entered Beijing in 1900. Liu E had known Wang, and he bought the bones from Wang's son.

In 1903 Liu E again took up his plan of refining salt in the northeast for export to Korea. That same year he moved his whole family to Shanghai and began to write *Lao Can youji*. This complex novel is reputed to have been unplanned and to have been composed in his spare time. According to both Liu Dashen and Liu Houze's "Liu E yu *Laocan youji*" (Liu E and *The Travels of Lao Can*), included in a 1985 volume edited by Liu Delong, Zhu Xi, and Liu Deping, a friend of Liu E's named Lian Mengqing was wanted by the Qing government on charges of conspiring to reveal information about the government's support for the Boxer Rebellion and had fled the capital for Shanghai, where he made his living as a writer. Liu E knew that Lian was too proud to take gifts of money, so he used his spare time to write something that Lian could publish. He allowed Lian to submit the manuscript and collect the royalties. Hsia repeats the story in "*The Travels of Lao Ts'an:* An Exploration of Its Art and Meaning" but expresses doubt about it in a footnote, pointing out that according to Liu Dashen's own account, the fee paid to authors by *Xiuxiang xiaoshuo* (Fiction Illustrated), the Shanghai journal that initially serialized the novel, was negligible. Hsia suggests that Liu E could have found easier ways to provide larger sums of money to his friend.

The novel was published in *Xiuxiang xiaoshuo* from September (some sources say March) 1903 through January 1904. The author was named as "Hongdu Bailiansheng" (The Scholar of One Hundred Temperings from Hongdu); the public was not aware that Liu E wrote the work until Hu Shi established his authorship in 1925. After *Xiuxiang xiaoshuo* expurgated the last part of chapter 10, all of chapter 11, and the first part of chapter 12 without consulting him, Liu E broke off his relationship with the journal and had the novel republished, starting from the first chapter, in the Tianjin newspaper *Riri xinwen bao* (The Daily News), which was under the editorial direction of his friend Fang Yaoyu. Liu E resumed writing with chapter 14, and the serialization in *Riri xinwen bao* continued through chapter 20. The first twenty chapters are customarily referred to as the *chuji* or *chupian* (text proper). Hsia's "*The Travels of Lao Ts'an:* An Exploration of Its Art and Meaning," Timothy C. Wong's "Notes on the Textual History of the *Lao Ts'an Yu-chi*" (1983), and Liu Delong, Zhu Xi, and Liu Deping's *Liu E xiao zhuan* (1987, A Concise Biography of Liu E) discuss the publishing history of the text proper. All three sources mention A Ying's claim in his "*Lao Can youji* banben kao" (1936, A Study of the Editions of *The Travels of Lao Can*) that he owned a one-volume edition of the first ten chapters published by *Riri xinwenbao* in 1904; all three mention the claim by Liu Houze, Liu E's grandson, that sometime after 1904—probably in 1906—*Riri xinwenbao* published all twenty chapters in two volumes. According to Liu, Zhu, and Liu, the first volume of Liu Houze's copy of the book—the only surviving copy—was destroyed during the Cultural Revolution. A two-volume edition of the text proper was published in Shanghai by the Riri xinwenguan (Office of the Daily News) in 1907, and copies of this book survive.

The second set of authentic chapters, referred to variously as the *erji, erpian,* or *xuji* (sequel), of which nine are extant, was probably written in 1907 after one of Liu E's business failures afforded him time to write. These chapters were rediscovered in the offices of *Riri xinwen bao* in 1929, and four of them were published in Lin Yutang's periodical *Renjian shi* (The World Age) in 1934. These chapters and two more were published the following year as *Lao Can youji erji* (1935, The Sequel to the Travels of Lao Can) and translated by Lin Yutang in 1936 as "A Nun of Taishan." The remaining three chapters of the sequel were suppressed by the Liu family because of their phantasmagorical quality and were first published in 1972. A *waipian* (fragment) of approximately a chapter in length was discovered in the Liu home in 1929 and is likely to have been written by Liu E. Other chapters have been rumored to exist, but none has surfaced.

The earliest English translation of part of *Lao Can youji* is Lin Yutang's rendition of the sequel in *A Nun of Taishan (A Novelette) and Other Translations*, published by the Commercial Press in Shanghai in 1936. In 1939 the Commercial Press brought out an abridged translation of chapters 1 through 20 by Lin Yi-chin and Ko Te-shun under the title *Tramp Doctor's Travelogue*. A translation by H. Y. Yang (Yang Xianyi) and G. M. Tayler (later known as Gladys Yang) was published in Nanjing in a bilingual edition as *Mr. Decadent* in 1947 by the Duli shudian (Independent Bookstore) and as *Mr. Derelict* in London in 1948 by George Allen and Unwin. *Tramp*, *Decadent*, and *Derelict* are efforts to convey the meaning of the name Lao Can, which is sometimes glossed as "Old Decrepit." In "The Name 'Lao Ts'an' in Liu E's Fiction" (1989) Wong cites scholars such as Qian Zhongshu in arguing that *Decrepit* and its variants do not convey the meaning of the Chinese; he offers "Old Remnant" as the accurate translation. The hero's real name is Tie Ying; his *hao* (literary name or sobriquet) is Bucan, in which *can* (remnants) is an allusion to a carefree Tang Dynasty Buddhist priest; Lao Can is the affectionate nickname by which his friends know him. In a footnote to chapter 1 of his translation of the novel Shadick glosses the name "Bucan" as "he who mends broken things or leftovers" and says that it "probably refers to the profession of medicine," since Lao Can is a healer. The Yang-Tayler 1947 translation, which deletes chapters 9 through 11, 16, 18, 19, and part of chapter 20, was republished in 1983, with minor changes in wording and punctuation, by the Chinese Literature Press in Beijing as *Lao Can youji*. The first, and still only complete, translation of the "text proper" is Shadick's *The Travels of Lao Ts'an* of 1952; it is exemplary, annotated, and the standard one.

Lao Can youji features lyrical passages, idyllic renderings of the natural landscape, political and philosophical repartee, digressions, and apocalyptic imagery. It is a "linked" or episodic work, not an integrated one in the fashion of a modern novel. It is, however, unified in its overall tone, stylistic continuity, and sustained attention to the picaresque adventures of the protagonist, Lao Can. The travels of the peripatetic Lao Can are also a spiritual and moral quest. Treating the work as a "series of ascending lyrical tableaux," Leo Ou-fan Lee in "The Solitary Traveler: Images of the Self in Modern Chinese Literature" (1985) identifies the concern of the novel as an exploration of nature, politics, and spirituality. By using several styles of expression that were in favor in China in the early twentieth century, Liu E also explores the culture of the emergent modern Chinese nation-state and the values and modes of thought that underpin it. Donald Holoch calls the novel "one author's excursion into the various genres of his day" and argues that the "characters and events function as illustrations of moral positions and of typical actions."

In the manner of traditional Chinese fiction, *Lao Can youji* begins with a preface. The preface is a meditation on "strong" and "weak" *kuqi* (weeping): weak weeping is the crying of spoiled children, while strong weeping is the profound expression of emotion found in great literature. "The quality of a man," the narrator says, "is measured by his much or little weeping, for weeping is the expression of a spiritual nature." Shuen-fu Lin suggests that the theme of the prologue—a man's worth is demonstrated by his affective response to injustice and crisis—is exemplified by the various stories of social realism told in the novel.

The preface is followed by the allegorical prologue of chapter 1. It begins with a reference to the "Penglai Pavilion," named after a legendary abode of immortals, and presents the national allegory of the novel. From a spot near the Penglai Pavilion on Penglai Hill on the Shandong coast Lao Can and his friends spy a boat in peril. The sailors are fighting with the passengers and, Lao Can notices, have no compass and cannot find their way to safe waters. The compass, invented by the Chinese, was used by Western mariners to navigate the globe and colonize territories. The allegory suggests that China should use any methods necessary to right its ship of state. Lao Can's vision of a ship in distress turns out to be a dream. This chapter and the others in the book end in the traditional manner, with variations on the phrase "to learn what happened, hear the next chapter tell."

In chapter 2 Lao Can visits a famous lake in Ji'nan and listens to the singing of Hei Niu (the Dark Maid) and Bai Niu (the Fair Maid). Qian Zhongshu (Ch'ien Chungshu) argues that this passage represents an attempt by the author to apply the principles of traditional poetry to modern Chinese prose. Milena Doleželová-Velingerová and Tao Tao Liu Sanders include these parts of chapter 2 as examples of passages in *Lao Can youji* that allow readers to envisage the events and places described "with a clarity seldom experienced in any literature."

In chapters 3 through 7 Lao Can hears about Yu Xian, a draconian magistrate who emerges as the chief

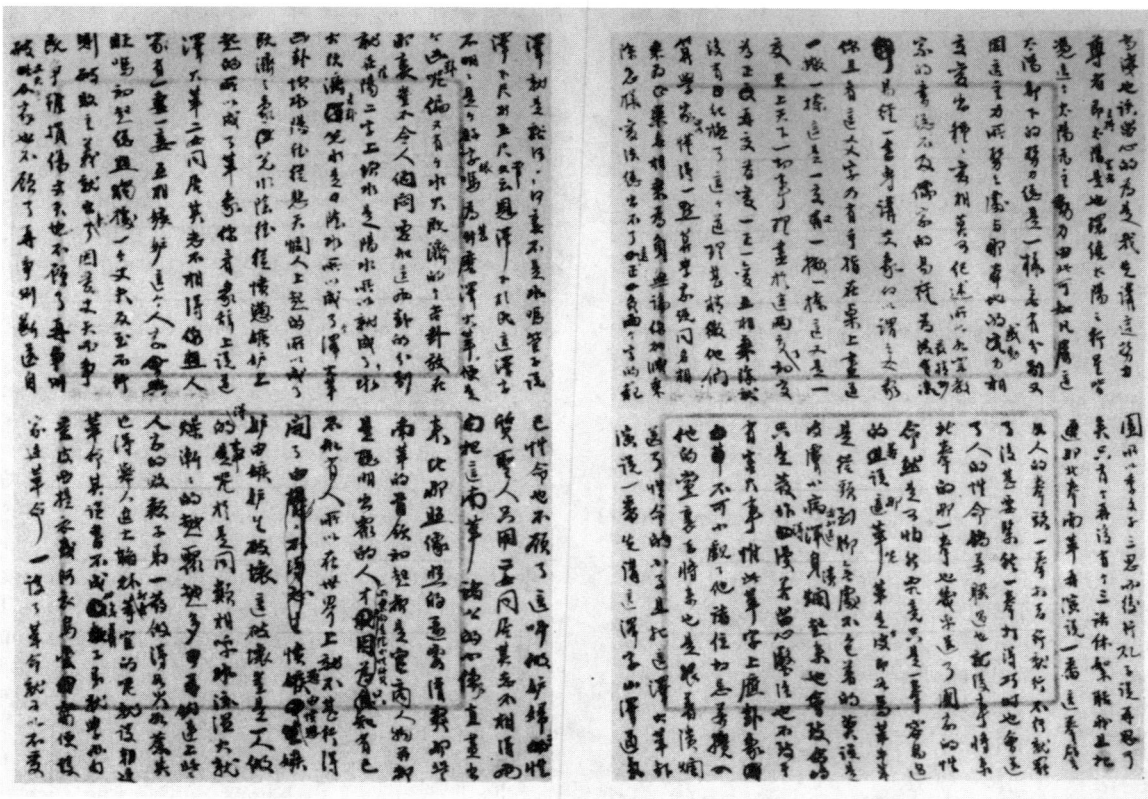

Pages from the manuscript for the end of chapter 11 of Lao Can youji (from Liu Delong, Zhu Xi, and Liu Deping, eds., Liu E ji Lao Can youji ziliao, 1985; Charles E. Shain Library, Connecticut College)

villain of the first half of the work. He is proud of his incorruptibility and overly confident in his powers of judgment; his hubris has led him to torture an innocent father and son to death, driving the son's wife to suicide. The abuse of power by sanctimonious officials convinced of their infallibility deters Lao Can from serving in the government. In this respect he is like a Daoist sage who has talent but also the wisdom to know that his small contribution to the state will be ineffectual. Also in line with the Daoist tradition, Lao Can can heal illness and does so several times in the novel. Lao Can writes a letter to Provincial Governor Zhuang (who is based on Zhang Yao, for whom Liu E worked) informing on Yu Xian and recommending the *xia* (knight-errant) Liu Renfu to bring order to the county. Shen Ziping, the cousin of a friend of the governor, is sent to find Liu Renfu.

Shen's quest takes him to Taohua shan (Peach Blossom Mountain). By Chinese literary convention, the name "Peach Blossom" suggests a utopia; this notion is reinforced by the natural imagery of this section of the novel and the enlightened attitudes of the people Shen meets: a young woman called Yu Gu (Miss Jade) and an older man who calls himself Huang Longzi (Yellow Dragon). Liu E often uses the voices of women to convey crucial information; here Yu Gu explains to Shen that Huang Longzi's poems articulate a synthesis of Confucianism, Daoism, and Buddhism (an allusion to Taigu). She laments that the true understanding of Confucianism has been lost and tells Shen that one should not shun emotions and feelings, as puritanical Neo-Confucians do. Yu Gu says that Neo-Confucianism (the Song Dynasty reworking of Confucian philosophy into a new orthodoxy) has made "the Confucianism of Confucius and Mencius more and more narrow until it was quite destroyed."

In chapter 11 Huang Longzi predicts China's future, which he says holds "bei quan nan ge" (Boxers in the north, revolution in the south). He says that a "political force in the north" will create a great clash and much upheaval, which will invite the wrath of a massive Western incursion in the year *Gengzi* (1900 by the Western calendar). The Boxer Rebellion and its suppression by a military alliance of eight imperialist nations had, of course, already occurred by the time the novel was written. Huang Lonzi's second prediction is that the "political force in the south" will incite revolution in 1910. Liu E may have had in mind anti-Qing revolutionary groups that took their inspiration from two southern revolutionaries, Sun Yat-sen (Sun Zhongshan) and Zou Rong. Huang Longzi says that the movements in the north and south will bring disaster to China but will open up a new era. He predicts that "the introduction of new culture from Europe will revivify our ancient culture . . . and very rapidly we shall achieve a universal culture. But these things are still far off, not less than thirty or fifty years." In an apocalyptic vision rare in Chinese literature he goes on to postulate a supreme force known as "zun zhe" (the August One) or "shi li zun zhe" (Force Supreme).

Shen's sojourn to Peach Blossom Mountain has been the subject of much discussion by scholars. Some suggest that chapters 8 through 11 are a digression that betrays the disjunct quality of the narrative. In *"The Travels of Lao Ts'an:* An Exploration of Its Art and Meaning" Hsia offers the most ambitious account of this portion of the work, arguing that it is indicative of a split in the author: Lao Can represents the practical, active side of his nature, while Huang and Yu Gu represent his philosophical side.

In chapters 12 through 16 Lao Can is unable to cross the Yellow River because unusually cold weather has left the ferryboats frozen in ice. As he contemplates the natural surroundings, the stark sky brings to his mind a poem from the *Shijing* (circa 600 B.C., The Classic of Poetry) that describes the Big Dipper. The poem, a veiled criticism of the gentry class, causes Lao Can to reflect on idle and corrupt officials; and in this reverie, which Hsia and others have called stream of consciousness, he is overcome by emotion and by thoughts of the passage of time and the urgency of China's crisis: "When he reached this point in his thinking, unconsciously the tears began to trickle down his face." Lao Can realizes that he is crying only when he feels ice—his frozen tears—sliding down his cheeks. Many scholars have remarked on the elegant prose of this passage.

Waiting to cross the river, Lao Can lodges at an inn. There he encounters an old acquaintance, Huang Renrui. The worldly Huang Renrui is a counterpoint to the philosophical Huang Longzi; their identical surnames are an example of the preoccupation of the novel with the synthesis of opposites. Huang Renrui invites Lao Can to his room to share his dinner and a cup of wine. Two courtesans Huang Renrui has retained for the night, Cuihua and Cuihuan, arrive and recount how the teenage Cuihuan, who came from a wealthy household, ended up poor and with no recourse but to become a prostitute when she lost her family two years previously in an ill-conceived flood-abatement scheme authorized by Governor Zhuang. Zhuang, who is not a villain but tolerates wrongdoing that it would be impolitic to address, sanctioned a scholar-official's plan to flood land along the Yellow River inhabited mainly by peasants in order to avert a flood downstream. Several hundred thousand people, including Cuihuan's family, were drowned. The account of Cuihuan's travails justifies Lu Xun's description in *Zhongguo xiaoshuo shilüe* (1935; translated as *A Brief History of Chinese Fiction*, 1959) of *Lao Can youji* as a *qianze xiaoshuo* (novel of exposure).

When Lao Can learns that Cuihuan is to be sold to a man with a reputation for cruelty, he is filled with pity, anger, and grief, and a "slight moistness" comes to his eyes. He and Huang Renrui agree that the best way to save Cuihuan is for Lao Can to take her as his concubine. Lao Can is uncomfortable with the plan, however, and in chapter 17 he is surprised and "rather disgruntled" when Huang Renrui arranges a ceremony to formalize Cuihuan's sale to him as concubine.

Lao Can, Huang Renrui, and the two women talk from chapter 12 through chapter 16. The telling of Cuihuan's story is interrupted by and intermingled with banter between Lao Can and Huang, Huang's periodic opium smoking, and a fire that breaks out in Lao Can's room. Liu E introduces the final episode of the novel by having Huang Renrui mention at the end of chapter 12 "a most amazing law case," on which he does not begin to elaborate until chapter 15. Praising Liu E's craftsmanship, Hsia says in *"The Travels of Lao Ts'an:* An Exploration of Its Art and Meaning" that "this continuous scene records undoubtedly the longest night in traditional Chinese literature and, in terms of fictional art, the most triumphant."

The final episode of the first twenty chapters is a *gongan* (criminal case) story that returns to the theme of the rigidly incorruptible magistrate whose belief in his grasp of the truth leads to the suffering of innocents. Several members of the Jia family and their attendants have been murdered, and the Jias' daughter-in-law, Jia Wei, and her father, the elderly Mr. Wei, have been arrested for the crime. Magistrate Gang Bi orders Jia Wei and Mr. Wei tortured until they confess. This tale of *qi yuan* (strange injustice), as the heading of chapter 18 puts it, plays out in chapters 15 through 20.

Having secured a letter from the governor, Lao Can marches into Gang Bi's court and forces him to suspend sentencing of Jia Wei and Mr. Wei. In chapter 18, Prefect Bai, a benevolent and astute high-ranking politician, arrives and acquits the accused. In the next chapter Lao Can treats Jia Wei's injuries from her torture and carries out his own inquiries. Mr. Wei tells Lao Can that Wu Er Langzi (Wastrel Wu) held a grudge against Mr. Wei for refusing him Jia Wei's hand in marriage. On Lao Can's instructions Xu Liang, a *yamen chairen* (assistant at the local government headquarters), tracks Wu down and tricks him into revealing his guilt: he used a poison called *qian ri zui* (Thousand Days'

Sleep) on the Jias. Lao Can discovers an antidote that revives all thirteen of the characters who had been presumed dead.

The quest for the truth in chapters 15 through 20 increases the suspense by mixing several modes of perception and transmission: hearing (the tale Huang tells Lao Can about the law case), writing (the letter that Lao Can writes to Governor Zhuang), seeing (the imagery of the story itself), retelling (the story Mr. Wei tells Lao Can that confirms Wei's innocence and reveals the true malefactor), and whispering (the plan that Lao Can tells Xu Liang to enact). Stuart H. Sargent suggests that Gang Bi's refusal to give speculation their due and his insistence on an unrealistic standard for truth lead to his draconian behavior. Sargent further argues that Gang Bi's behavior is implicitly contested and rejected by the fictitiousness of the novel itself; in other words, the explicit and implicit celebration in the novel of imagination, sentiment, and fiction refutes Gang Bi's approach to the world. In a *meipi* (marginal or "eyebrow" annotation) to the 1979 edition of *Lao Can youji*, Yu Guoji argues that Prefect Bai's reasoning by inference and close questioning of witnesses are unusual in traditional Chinese crime fiction, in which prosecutors usually arrive at the truth abruptly through flashes of insight.

Hsia writes in "*The Travels of Lao Ts'an*: An Exploration of Its Art and Meaning" that in modeling Yu Xian and Gang Bi on the real Manchu officials Yuxian and Gangyi, Liu E intended a critique of more than self-righteous zealotry. Yuxian and Gangyi supported the antiforeign activities of the Boxers in 1899–1900, and Yuxian supervised the murder of Chinese Christians and foreign missionaries. Liu E, Hsia writes, made Yuxian and Gangyi his targets in his novel to denounce their "crime of inciting and supporting a fanatic movement of grave national consequence."

Chapters 21 through 26 are reminiscent of the storytelling modes employed in the traditional *huaben* genre (short or medium-length stories in vernacular Chinese from the late imperial period). Though these chapters are referred to as "the sequel," there is no indication that they are not simply a continuation of Liu E's serial novel. In these chapters the narrative voice is fully assumed by women, and the issue of sexuality, which is referred to obliquely in the "text proper," is brought to the fore.

Lao Can and Cuihuan happen upon Lao Can's old friend De Huisheng, who appeared in his dream of the ship of state in the first chapter, and De's wife, and the two couples make an excursion to Tai shan (Mt. Tai). There they meet the Buddhist nuns Qingyun, Yiyun, and Jingyun, who is in hiding from the son of a corrupt magistrate who wishes to subject her to his will. The nuns reside in a temple that is an hour's hike up the mountain. Their convent is, as Lin Yutang writes in the prefatory note to his translation, "irregular": by a tradition dating back to the Ming Dynasty, Yiyun explains, the younger nuns dress attractively and entertain guests. "Sometimes a few young men like to flirt with us, which we don't mind," she says. Jingyun's reputation is such that Lao Can has heard of her. (In late-Qing China, courtesans were celebrities known for their beauty and their talent for poetry and music.) Mrs. De asks Yiyun if "all of you remain virgins until the end of your days." Yiyun answers, "ye bu jinran" (not exactly). Some of the nuns occasionally spend a night with a guest, she says, but not often: "After all, this is a temple and not a brothel." At the age of thirty the nuns cut off their hair and enter religious life.

Yiyun accompanies the party on the climb to the peak of Mt. Tai. On the way she relates the story of her life and her first love, Ren Sanye (Third Master Ren). Yiyun's account of her infatuation gives Mrs. De vicarious pleasure and alludes to the female romantic imagination as it is presented in traditional Chinese literature, which is filled with sons, scholars, and fantasies of political careers and fancy clothing, as well as conflicts with mothers-in-law. Yiyun explains how she was courted by Ren, fell in love with him, dreamed of having sons who would become scholars—one successful at the traditional examinations, the other a distinguished student abroad—and how it all came to naught because of the restrictions on autonomous love in late imperial China.

In chapter 5 of the sequel (chapter 25 of the novel) the group spends the night on the mountain. In conversation with Mrs. De, Yiyun explains the outlines of her spiritual progress and quotes from the *Diamond Sutra* and the *Vimalakirti Sutra,* works in which she finds the distillation of the teaching that has enlightened her and freed her from "mortal desires." The next day the group goes down the mountain and returns to the temple, where Jingyun greets them. They talk about Buddhism, and Lao Can is impressed by Yiyun's intimate understanding of the subtleties of the philosophy. Yiyun's comments expound the Buddhist doctrine of "nonduality" and, as Lin Yutang writes in a footnote, suggest "that there is no absolute truth, and that if one sincerely desires a truth, 'wants' it," then this is the truth of salvation.

Chapters 27 through 29 center on Lao Can's dream visit to Yama, the King of Hell, who exacts reparation throughout eternity for the conduct of people such as Yu Xian and Gang Bi. In his "Crime or Punishment? On the Forensic Discourse of Modern Chinese Literature" (2000) Wang Dewei suggests that while Lao Can's foray into hell is a "belated" form of "poetic justice" because it shows that those who escaped punishment in the living world are punished in the afterlife, readers finish the book thinking "that justice on earthly

China is only an expensive fantasy." According to Wang, even in the world "beyond life" Liu E does not offer the reader an alternative to draconian magistrates.

During and after the writing of *Lao Can youji*, Liu E distinguished himself as a prolific and respected arbiter on subjects such as oracle bones, inscriptions on ancient pottery, music, poetry, and seals. His *Tieyun cang gui* (1903, Tortoise Shells in the Collection of Tieyun) and *Tieyun cang tao* (1904, Pottery in the Collection of Tieyun) catalogue antiques in his collection. The former is an important early contribution to the study of *jiaguwen*, the oldest Chinese script. A bibliography in *Liu E ji Lao Can youji ziliao* (1985, Research Materials on Liu E and *The Travels of Lao Can*), edited by Liu Delong, Zhu Xi, and Liu Deping, lists similar works written or compiled by Liu E: fourteen are lost; twenty-three are extant; and three of the extant titles survive only in part. The bibliography gives no information as to which have been published and which have not. *Tieyun cang huo* (Coins in the Collection of Tieyun), published in 1986 from Liu E's manuscript, is a survey of his collection of antique coins. Like any member of the traditional literati, Liu E wrote poetry; it is collected in *Tieyun shicun* (1980, The Extant Poems of Tieyun), annotated by his grandson Liu Huisun.

From 1905 to 1907 Liu E undertook new business ventures, including textile mills and a steel refinery and, in Beijing, a waterworks (resuming an effort he had first made in 1901), a streetcar line, and an electric-light company; none came to full fruition. He made at least two trips to Japan and in 1906 took a Japanese woman as his fifth and last concubine; Liu E brought her to China in the winter of 1906–1907, but she returned permanently to Japan not long afterward.

Most sources chronicle the same series of events that led to Liu E's death, although the accounts differ on details. In 1907 Chen Liu, a member of the Pukou gentry whom Liu E had not allowed to participate in his 1902 land deal, charged that Liu E had bought the land for foreigners. All sources refute Chen Liu's claim and record that Liu bought the land with a group of friends and relatives with the intent of developing it as a commercial port. According to Shadick's introduction to his translation of *Lao Can youji* and according to Liu Huisun, in 1907 Yuan Shikai and a man named Shi Xu, both of whom were in the Junjichu (Grand Council of State) in Beijing, charged Liu E "with being a traitor to the country and buying land at Pukow for certain foreign interests." According to Liu Huisun, Shi Xu held a grudge because of a perceived slight from Liu E's father. According to Shadick, Liu E had alienated Yuan in Shandong in 1890, but there is reason to doubt that this claim is true. It is certain that the government ordered Liu E's arrest in 1907. According to Shadick,

Cover for the bilingual edition (1947) of Lao Can youji, with translation by H. Y. Yang (Yang Xianyi) and G. M. Tayler (Wason Collection on East Asia–China, Kroch Asia Library, Cornell University)

Liu E's brother-in-law, Ding Baoquan, the governor of Shanxi, intervened, and Liu E was not detained. In June 1908 Yuan Shikai revived Chen Liu's allegation, added to it a charge that Liu E had misappropriated imperial grain in 1901, and ordered Liu's arrest. The official ordered to carry out the arrest warrant, Duanfang, knew Liu E and tried to warn him, but to no avail. (Fang Chao-ying writes that Duanfang had an old score to settle with Liu E and benefited from Liu's arrest by confiscating many of his antiques, but Liu Huisun dismisses this version of events). Liu E was exiled to Xinjiang province in the far northwest, where he died of a stroke on 3 August 1909. His body was retrieved and prepared for interment by the governor of Gansu province and was met at stops along the trip home to Huai'an by each of his sons in succession. He was buried in Huai'an, Jiangsu province.

The half century of Liu E's life fits between the Opium Wars of the mid eighteenth century and the revolution that toppled the Qing Dynasty. During this time the challenges of domestic rebellion and foreign imperialism compelled China to alter its political and cultural structures. Liu E's life and work exemplify this transformation. Hsia writes in "*The Travels of Lao Ts'an*: An Exploration of Its Art and Meaning" that Liu E cannot be understood apart from the political turmoil of the late Qing dynasty, and Shuen-fu Lin argues that the challenge to moral values brought on by the Western incursion into China created a "split" in Liu E's value system and in his novel. Lin writes that in its form *Lao Can youji* combines "narrative devices from the native tradition with experimental innovations from the West," and in its meaning it highlights the tension between Liu E's "unswerving commitment to the heritage of China's humanistic culture and his sensitive (and in many ways farsighted) response to Western civilization." Liu E's lone novel has remained a favorite of readers and critics since it was published as a book in 1925.

Bibliographies:

Li Tien-yi, "Lao Ts'an yu-chi," in his *Chinese Fiction: A Bibliography of Books and Articles in Chinese and English* (New Haven: Yale University Press, 1968), pp. 219–223;

Shimmatsu shōsetsu kenkyūkai, "Ryū Tetsuun kenkyū shiryō mokuroku," *Shinmatsu Shōsetsu kenkyū*, 1 (October 1977): 87–111;

Winston L. Y. Yang, Peter Li, and Nathan K. Mao, "The Travels of Lao Ts'an (Lao Ts'an yu-chi)," in their *Classical Chinese Fiction: A Guide to Its Study and Appreciation. Essays and Bibliographies* (Boston: G. K. Hall, 1978), p. 262;

"Liu E zhuzuo cunmu" and "*Lao Can youji* banben mulu," in *Liu E ji Lao Can youji ziliao*, edited by Liu Delong, Zhu Xi, and Liu Deping (Chengdu: Sichuan renmin chubanshe, 1985), pp. 532–545;

Ma Youyuan (Y. W. Ma), Robert E. Hegel, and William H. Nienhauser, "Liu E," in *The Indiana Companion to Traditional Chinese Literature*, volume 2, edited by Nienhauser Jr. (Bloomington: Indiana University Press, 1998), pp. 368–369.

Biographies:

Jiang Yixue, *Liu E nianpu* (Ji'nan: Qi Lu shushe, 1980);

Liu Huisun, *Tieyun xiansheng nianpu changbian* (Ji'nan: Qi Lu shushe, 1982);

Liu Delong, Zhu Xi, and Liu Deping, *Liu E xiao zhuan* (Tianjin: Tianjin renmin chubanshe, 1987).

References:

A Ying, "*Lao Can youji* banben kao," in his *A Ying wenji* (Hong Kong: Sanlian shudian, 1979), pp. 279–280;

A Ying, *Wan Qing xiaoshuoshi* (Beijing: Dongfang chubanshe, 1996), pp. 29–33;

Howard L. Boorman and Richard C. Howard, eds., *Biographical Dictionary of Republican China*, volume 4 (New York & London: Columbia University Press, 1971), pp. 78–89;

Cao Naimu and Huang Zongbao, eds., *Lao Can youji ciyu, renwu suoyin* (Beijing: Shangwu yinshuguan, 1998);

Chen Liao, "Lao Can Youji," in *Mingqing xiaoshuo jianshang cidian*, edited by He Manzi and Li Shiren (Hangzhou: Zhejiang guji chubanshe, 1992), pp. 933–942;

Chen, *Liu E yu Lao Can youji* (Zhengzhou: Zhongzhou guji chubanshe, 1989);

Ch'ien Chungshu (Qian Zhongshu), "A Note to the Second Chapter of Mr. Decadent," *Philobiblon* (Nanjing), 2 (September 1948): 8–14;

Milena Doleželová-Velingerová, "Typology of Plot Structures in Late Qing Novels" and "Narrative Modes in Late Qing Novels," in *The Chinese Novel at the Turn of the Century*, edited by Doleželová-Velingerová (Toronto: University of Toronto Press, 1980), pp. 38–75;

Doleželová-Velingerová and Tao Tao Liu Sanders, "Liu E, *Lao Can youji*," in *A Selective Guide to Chinese Literature 1900–1949: Volume 1, The Novel*, edited by Doleželová-Velingerová (Leiden: Brill, 1988), pp. 122–123;

Fang Chao-ying, "Liu E," in *Eminent Chinese of the Ch'ing Period (1644–1912)*, edited by Arthur W. Hummel (Washington, D.C.: U.S. Government Printing Office, 1943), pp. 516–518;

Gao Zheng, "Liu E shouji kaoshi," *Daojia wenjua yanjiu*, 5 (1994): 477–491;

Donald Holoch, "*The Travels of Lao Can*: Allegorical Narrative," in *The Chinese Novel at the Turn of the Century*, pp. 139–149;

C. T. Hsia, "Liu E's *Travels of Lao Can*," in *Masterworks of Asian Literature in Comparative Perspective*, edited by Barbara Stoler Miller (Armonk, N.Y.: Sharpe, 1994), pp. 299–308;

Hsia, "*The Travels of Lao Ts'an*: An Exploration of Its Art and Meaning," *Tsing Hua Journal of Chinese Studies*, new series 7, no. 2 (1969): 40–68;

Frederic Jameson, "Third-World Literature in the Era of Multinational Capitalism," *Social Text*, 15 (1986): 65–88;

Luke S. K. Kwong, "Self and Society in Modern China: Liu E (1857–1909) and *Laocan Youji*," *T'oung Pao*, 87 (2001): 360–392;

Leo Ou-fan Lee, "Literary Trends I: The Quest for Modernity, 1895–1927," in *The Cambridge History of China Vol. 12: Republican China 1912–1949*, edited by John K. Fairbank (Cambridge: Cambridge University Press, 1983), pp. 452–504;

Lee, "The Solitary Traveler: Images of the Self in Modern Chinese Literature," in *Expressions of Self in Chinese Literature,* edited by Robert E. Hegel and Richard C. Hessney (New York: Columbia University Press, 1985), pp. 282–423;

Lee and Andrew J. Nathan, "The Beginnings of Mass Culture: Journalism and Fiction in the Late Ch'ing and Beyond," in *Popular Culture in Late Imperial China,* edited by David Johnson, Andrew J. Nathan, and Evelyn S. Rawski (Berkeley, Los Angeles & London: University of California Press, 1985), pp. 360–395;

Li Ruiteng, *Lao Can meng yu ai: Lao Can youji de yixiang yanjiu* (Taibei: Jiuge, 2001);

Shuen-fu Lin, "The Last Classic Chinese Novel: Vision and Design in *The Travels of Laocan,*" *Journal of the American Oriental Society,* 121, no. 4 (2001): 549–564;

Liu Dashen, "Guanyu *Lao Can youji,*" *Yuzhoufeng yikan,* 20 (January 1940): 18–21; 21 (February 1940): 103–106; 22 (March 1940): 198–200; 23 (April 1940): 262–266; 24 (May 1940): 340–343; revised, with notes by Liu Houze, in *Lao Can youji ziliao,* edited by Wei Shaochang (Beijing: Zhonghua Shuju, 1962), pp. 54–104;

Liu Delong, *Liu E san lun* (Kunming: Yunnan renmin chubanshe, 1998);

Liu Delong, Zhu Xi, and Liu Deping, eds., *Liu E ji Lao Can youji ziliao* (Chengdu: Sichuan renmin chubanshe, 1985);

Lu Xun, *Zhongguo xiaoshuo shilüe,* revised edition (1935), in his *Lu Xun quanji,* volume 9 (Beijing: Renmin wenxue chubanshe, 1991), pp. 288–290; translated by Yang Hsien-yi and Gladys Yang as *A Brief History of Chinese Fiction* (Beijing: Foreign Languages Press, 1959), pp. 361–363;

Ma Youyuan (Y. W. Ma), "Du Liuzhu Lao Can youji erpian cunyi," *Zhongyang ribao,* 20–22 June 1981;

Ma, "Liu E," in *The Indiana Companion to Traditional Chinese Literature,* edited by William H. Nienhauser (Bloomington: Indiana University Press, 1984), pp. 580–583;

Jaroslav Průšek, "Liu O et son roman, le *Pèlerinage du Lao Ts'an,*" in his *Chinese History and Literature: Collection of Studies* (Dordrecht, Netherlands: Reidel, 1970), pp. 139–169;

Stuart H. Sargent, "Lao-Ts'an and Fictive Thinking," *Journal of the Chinese Language Teachers Association,* 12 (October 1977): 215–220;

Harold E. Shadick, "*The Travels of Lao Ts'an*: A Social Novel," *Yenching Journal of Social Studies,* 2 (1939): 36–69;

Shi Meng, *Wan Qing xiaoshuo* (Shanghai: Shanghai guji chubanshe, 1989), pp. 81–84;

Tarumoto Teruo, "Rôzan Yûki Gaihen Wa Gisaji Ka?" *Ia,* 5 (December 1975): 1–13;

Tarumoto, "Rôzan Yûki jimmei sakuhin," *Ôsaka Keidai ronshû,* 193 (1990): 101–170;

Tarumoto, "Shunen no Hito–Rôzan Yûki no Sakusha Ryu Aju ni Tsuite," *Yasô,* 3 (January 1971): 13–31;

Wang Dewei (David Der-wei Wang), "Crime or Punishment? On the Forensic Discourse of Modern Chinese Literature," in *Becoming Chinese: Passages to Modernity and Beyond,* edited by Wen-hsin Yeh (Berkeley, Los Angeles & London: University of California Press, 2000), pp. 260–297;

Wang, *Fin-de-siècle Splendor: Repressed Modernities of Late Qing Fiction, 1849–1911* (Stanford, Cal.: Stanford University Press, 1997), pp. 34–39, 145–155, 174–182;

Wang, "Lao Can youji yu gong'an xiaoshuo," in his *Cong Liu E dao Wang Zhenhe: Zhongguo xiandai xieshi xiaoshuo sanlun* (Taibei: Shibao wenhua chuban gongsi, 1985), pp. 55–64;

Wang Xuejun, *Liu E yu Lao Can youji* (Shenyang: Liaoning jiaoyu chubanshe, 1992);

Wei Shaochang, ed., *Lao Can youji ziliao* (Beijing: Zhonghua shuju, 1962);

Kam-ming Wong and Chung-min Tu, "The Road Less Traveled By: Rectifying Liu E's *Laocan youji* in the Name of Post/Modernity," in *The Great Book of Aesthetics: Proceedings of the 15th International Congress of Aesthetics,* edited by Ken-ichi Saski and Tanehisa Otabe, CD-ROM (Tokyo, 2003);

Timothy C. Wong, "The Facts of Fiction: Liu E's Commentary to the Travels of Lao Can," in *Excursions in Chinese Culture: Festschrift in Honor of William R. Schultz,* edited by Marie Chan, Chia-lin Pao Tao, and Jing-shen Tao (Hong Kong: The Chinese University Press, 2002), pp. 159–171;

Wong, "Liu E in the Fang-shih Tradition," *Journal of the American Oriental Society,* 112, no. 2 (1992): 302–306;

Wong, "The Name 'Lao Ts'an' in Liu E's Fiction," *Journal of the American Oriental Society,* 109, no. 1 (1989): 103–106;

Wong, "Notes on the Textual History of the *Lao Ts'an Yu-chi,*" *T'oung Pao,* 69, nos. 1–3 (1983): 23–32;

Zhang Bilai, "Lao Can youji de fandongxing he Hu Shi zai *Lao Can youji* pingjiazhong suo biaoxiande fandong zhengzhi lichang," *Renmin wenxue,* 2 (February 1955): 122–133.

Lu Ling
(23 January 1923 – 12 February 1994)

Kirk A. Denton
Ohio State University

BOOKS: *Ji'e de Guo Su'e* [Hungry Guo Su'e] (Shanghai: Xiwang she, 1943; Beijing: Renmin wenxue, 1988);

Qingchun de zhufu [Blessings of Youth] (Chongqing: Nantian, 1945; Shanghai: Xiwang she, 1947)—includes "Guancai," translated by Jane Parish Yang as "Coffins," in *Modern Chinese Stories and Novellas, 1919-1949,* edited by Joseph S. M. Lau, Leo Ou-fan Lee, and C. T. Hsia (New York: Columbia University Press, 1981), pp. 510-527;

Caizhu di ernümen [Children of the Rich] (Shanghai: Nanwu, 1945; revised and enlarged edition, 2 volumes, Shanghai: Xiwang she, 1948);

Qiu'ai he qita [In Search of Love and Other Stories] (Shanghai: Haiyan, 1946);

Woniu zai jingji shang [Snails on Brambles] (Shanghai: Xinxin, 1946);

Yunque [Skylark] (Shanghai: Xiwang she, 1948);

Zai tielian zhong [In Chains] (Shanghai: Haiyan, 1949);

Ranshao de huangdi [The Burning Wasteland] (Shanghai: Zuojia shuwu, 1951);

Yingxiong de muqin [The Heroic Mother] (Shanghai: Nitu she, 1951);

Yingzhe tian ming [Greeting Daybreak] (Shanghai: Tianxia, 1951); republished as *Renmin wansui* [Long Live the People], in *Lu Ling juzuo xuan* (Beijing: Zhongguo xiju, 1986), pp. 99-102;

Pingyuan [The Plain] (Shanghai: Lianying shudian, 1952);

Zhu Guihua de gushi [The Story of Zhu Guihua] (Tianjin: Zhishi, 1952);

Zuguo zai qianjin [The Fatherland Marches Forward] (Shanghai: Nitu she, 1952);

Banmendian qianxian sanji [Accounts from the Panmunjom Front] (Shanghai: Zuojia, 1954);

Chu xue (Ningxia: Ningxia renming, 1981)—title story translated as "First Snow," *Chinese Literature,* 3 (1954): 109-128;

Zhanzheng, weile heping [War, for Peace] (Beijing: Zhongguo wenlian, 1985);

Lu Ling (from Lu Ling, *edited by Zhu Yanqing, 1994; Baker-Berry Library, Dartmouth College)*

Lu Ling xiaoshuo xuan [Collected Fiction of Lu Ling], edited by Zhu Hengqing (Beijing: Zuojia, 1992);

Lu Ling daibiao zuo [Representative Works of Lu Ling], edited by Zhu Hengqing (Beijing: Huaxia, 1998).

Collections: *Lu Ling xiaoshuo xuan* [Collected Fiction of Lu Ling] (Chengdu: Sichuan wenyi, 1986);

Lu Ling juzuo xuan [Selected Dramatic Writings of Lu Ling] (Beijing: Zhongguo xiju, 1986);

Lu Ling, edited by Zhu Yanqing (Hong Kong: Sanlian shudian, 1994);

Lu Ling wenji [Collected Writings of Lu Ling], 4 volumes (Hefei: Anhui wenyi, 1995);

Lu Ling piping wenji [Lu Ling's Literary Criticism] (Guangzhou: Zhuhai, 1998);

Lu Ling wannian zuopin ji [The Collected Later Works of Lu Ling], edited by Zhang Yesong and Xu Lang (Shanghai: Dongfang, 1998).

PLAY PRODUCTION: *Yunque* [Skylark], Nanjing, fall 1947.

SELECTED PERIODICAL PUBLICATION—UNCOLLECTED: "Menglong de qidai" [Waiting in Obscurity], *Dasheng ribao,* 17 November 1938).

Lu Ling's reputation as a writer is inseparable from the politics and the political construction of a modern Chinese literature in the early years of the People's Republic of China. In June 1955, six years after the founding of the People's Republic, Lu Ling and at least one hundred other writers and intellectuals were arrested as members of the *Hu Feng jituan* (Hu Feng Clique) in the largest-scale cultural purge yet undertaken by the leadership of the Chinese Communist Party. Hu Feng was an important leftist literary critic who, like the Hungarian theorist György Lukács in a different socialist context, fought literary tendentiousness and the bureaucratic control of creative writers by political authorities. Lu Ling, it was claimed, was the preeminent member of Hu Feng's literary coterie, and his work embodied Hu Feng's view that literature should be infused with the subjectivity of the writer and should focus as much on matters of the spirit as on social issues, class oppression, and political objectives—a view that did not mesh well with Marxist materialism and the official party cultural policy that promoted a literature for "workers, peasants, and soldiers." Lu Ling's fiction, which perhaps more than that of any other modern Chinese writer depicted the psychology of its characters, was reviled as "bourgeois" and "individualist." From 1955 until his rehabilitation in 1980 Lu Ling was persona non grata on the Chinese literary scene, removed from his official positions and incarcerated in detention centers, prisons, psychiatric wards, and labor camps. Only in the 1980s, with the post–Mao Zedong liberalization, did scholars rediscover Lu Ling's writing, which was generally praised as representing a humanist alternative to the mainstream leftist literary tradition. It is difficult to gauge Lu Ling's place in literary history, because his reputation is so intertwined with his political fate; but at the height of his career in the 1940s he enjoyed national fame as a "genius" writer with a unique psychological style.

Lu Ling belonged to the post–May Fourth generation of modern Chinese writers who came of age during the war with Japan of 1937 to 1945. By forcing them to leave their homes and encounter alien cultures and social classes in the Chinese hinterland, the war had a strong influence on their development. It is clear from the abundance of refugees, drifters, and displaced indigents in Lu Ling's stories that this period of his life deeply affected and inspired him. The war gave a strong social dimension to his writing, which exhibits a consistent interest in the psychological effects of social oppression. But in giving rise to rigid Marxist theories of materialist determinism and collectivist action, the war also caused writers such as Lu Ling to seek to resurrect the "discredited" values of the May Fourth New Culture Movement of 1915 to 1925, particularly its individualism. Although Lu Ling's ties to Hu Feng placed him solidly in the leftist camp, his psychological fiction developed in part as a reaction to forces that conspired against the individual.

Lu Ling was born Xu Sixing on 23 January 1923 in Suzhou. His father, Zhao Zhenhuan, who enjoyed singing Beijing opera and telling stories, had been trained as a Western-style doctor. He had opened a clinic when he married Xu Juying; the Xu family, whose only male heir had recently died, had given him money in return for his agreeing to allow any sons born of the marriage to take the Xu name. Zhao died when Xu Sixing was two; although Xu was later told that he had died of an illness, he apparently committed suicide because his medical practice was failing. The family then moved to Nanjing to "avoid his ghost." Not long after her husband's death, Xu Juying married Zhang Jidong, who worked in the General Accounting Office of the Ministry of Economics. Typical of the petit-bourgeois clerks who filled the Nationalist bureaucracy in Nanjing, Zhang's fortunes fluctuated from difficult periods to times of relative prosperity. Xu's mother taught him to read and write; according to Hu Feng, he inherited his good looks and fiery temperament entirely from her. In a 27 February 1941 letter to Hu Feng, Lu Ling described his stepfather as "a functionary, spiritually impoverished, petty; angry, bad-tempered, and complaining."

In 1927 Xu entered the Lianhua Bridge Elementary School. He was a diligent, if sometimes outspoken, student; according to the recollections of the aging writer, who was no doubt motivated by a desire to restore his tarnished political reputation, he was "politically conscious" even in his childhood, aware of and willing to act against social and political injustices. The Mukden Incident of 18 September 1931, in which the Japanese garrison in Mukden (today Shenyang) used the pretext of an explosion along the Japanese-owned

Cover for a 1947 edition of Lu Ling's first and most celebrated novel, Ji'e de Guo Su'e *(1943, Hungry Guo Su'e)*, about a woman whose desire for a better life leads to her being beaten, burned, raped, and murdered (Wason Collection on East Asia–China, Kroch Asia Library, Cornell University)

South Manchurian Railway to occupy the city and then the rest of Manchuria, stirred his first feelings of patriotism; he wanted to join the resistance forces after the Japanese bombing of Shanghai in January 1932, but his teachers persuaded him that he was too young. Lu Ling's reading in his grade-school years was typical of young urban Chinese; as he matured it became more sophisticated, progressing from children's editions of Johann Wolfgang von Goethe's *Faust* (1808, 1832) and Miguel de Cervantes's *Don Quixote* (1605–1615) to Lu Xun's *Nahan* (1923, Outcry; translated as *Call to Arms*, 1981), traditional novels such as Cao Xueqin's *Honglou meng* (1791, Dream of the Red Chamber; translated as *The Story of the Stone*, 1973–1986) and Luo Guanzhong's fourteenth-century *Sanguo yanyi* (translated as *San Kuo, or, Romance of the Three Kingdoms*, 1925); fiction by Bing Xin, Mao Dun, and Ba Jin; Greek tragedies; Leo Tolstoy's *Voina i mir* (1868–1869; translated as *War and Peace*, 1800); and Fyodor Dostoevsky's first novel, *Bednye liudi* (1846; translated as *Poor Folk*, 1887). He earned praise and high marks for his school essays.

Xu entered Jiangsu Provincial Jiangning Middle School in the fall of 1935. Education beyond elementary school was not common in China in the 1930s, in part because of the cost, but Xu was a talented and enthusiastic student, and his family could afford the tuition. He continued to receive praise and encouragement for essays in middle school. He also continued to read the works of foreign authors–Ivan Turgenev and Aleksandr Pushkin, in particular–but also kept up with the latest publications in Chinese literature by such important writers as Lao She and Cao Yu.

Xu's schooling was disrupted by the outbreak of the war with Japan in July 1937. In August the family fled to Zhang Jidong's ancestral home in Hanchuan in central Hubei. During the two months they stayed there Xu wrote anti-Japanese essays under pen names that included Feng Song, Xu Feng, and Liu Feng; some were later published in small literary journals and literary supplements. When Wuhan was about to fall to the Japanese during the winter of 1937–1938, Lu Ling and several of his classmates went by boat up the Yangtze River to Chongqing in Sichuan province; his parents seem to have reached Chongqing separately. In the spring of 1938 Xu entered the Second National Sichuan Middle School in Wenxingchang, north of Chongqing; it was a makeshift school, and classes were given only sporadically. The Nationalist government relocated its wartime capital to Chongqing in October 1938, and Xu's stepfather continued to work for the Ministry of Economics as an accountant in the Mines and Metallurgy Research Institute.

Xu read voraciously during this time, especially political theory and Russian fiction by Turgenev, Dostoevsky, and Nikolai Gogol. The school soon moved to Hechuan, a county seat about one hundred miles north of Chongqing. With a friend from Nanjing, Liu Guoguang, Xu organized a literary society, Shaobing (Sentinel), and began a literary supplement of the same name for the Hechuan newspaper, *Dasheng ribao* (The Alarm Daily). In addition to editing the supplement, he contributed short articles promoting resistance to the Japanese and criticizing government corruption, as well as his first published short story, "Menglong de qidai" (Waiting in Obscurity), which won a five-yuan prize as the best story received from the society's call for submissions; it was never reprinted in any of Lu Ling's many short-story collections. "Menglong de qidai" narrates the thoughts of a Japanese military pilot who longs to return home to his family; it reveals a nascent concern with the depiction of the mind and a rejection of wartime literary stereotypes. Xu also contributed essays to *Qingguang* (Light of Youth), the literary supplement of the newspaper *Shishi xinbao* (New Current Affairs Times).

Ostensibly as punishment for engaging in extracurricular activities when he should have been studying, but perhaps really to get rid of an increasingly radical youth, the school expelled Xu in the spring of 1939. (Liu Guoguang says that he was expelled not for political reasons but because he was not interested in schoolwork and wanted to "throw himself into society.") He then joined a propaganda troupe of the Three Principles of the People Youth Corps, a Nationalist Party organization, in which he performed in anti-Japanese plays and fell in love with Li Luling, an actress. The theatrical world of Chongqing is the object of much satire in Lu Ling's novel *Caizhu di ernümen* (1945, 1948, Children of the Rich). Xu quit the troupe after his trunk was searched; his diary was read; and he was informed by a colleague that his thought was too far to the left for the organization.

By September 1939 Xu was devoting all of his spare time to writing. The publication of "Yaosai tuichu yihou" (After the Fort Retreated), a short story that describes the thoughts of a student caught in a military retreat, marks his entry into the Sichuan literary world; it was also his first work to be published under the pen name Lu Ling and his first to appear in *Qiyue* (July), a journal edited by Hu Feng, whom he had long admired. A poet, Hu Feng had been the administrative secretary of the Zhongguo zuoyi zuojia lianmeng (League of Left-Wing Writers) in 1933–1934 and had gained a reputation as a literary critic during a series of vehement debates within the progressive literary world in the mid 1930s. He had also been close to Lu Xun, the titular head of the Zhongguo zuoyi zuojia lianmeng. In his theoretical writings and in founding journals such as *Qiyue* Hu Feng established himself as a leftist literary critic, but his views diverged in important ways from the official Communist Party position. He mentored many young writers; but Lu Ling was one of the protégés who was most important to him, and he harbored strong fatherly feelings for the promising youth. Lu Ling came to share many of Hu Feng's ideas, including his respect for Lu Xun, his defense of subjectivity in the creative process, and his distaste for formulaic literature.

Near the end of 1939, under Hu Feng's sponsorship, Lu Ling attended the Yucai xuexiao (School for the Development of Talent) in Beibei, about fifty miles north of Chongqing. As a "study friend"—not officially registered as a student and not employed as a teacher—he had the opportunity to read more extensively and systematically in classical Chinese texts and Western leftist literature and to lecture occasionally to younger students. During this period Li Luling left him for their friend Yao Lunda. The breakup devastated him, and to commemorate the loss of his lover and his friend he adopted the pen name Lu Ling—homophonous with her given name and using one of the characters Yao had used in a pen name of his own. Li Luling appears in various guises in several of his works, including *Caizhu di ernümen;* "Gu" (Valley), collected in his *Qingchun de zhufu* (1945, Blessings of Youth); and the play *Yunque* (Skylark; produced 1947, published 1948).

Financial exigencies forced Lu Ling to leave the school after just a few months, bringing an end to his sporadic formal education. (It was not uncommon for writers in the Republican era to lack advanced levels of education.) In the late summer of 1940, through his stepfather's connections, he became a clerk in an accounting office of the Mines and Metallurgy Research Institute in the village of Houfengyan. Some sources assert that he was a miner; he was not, but he drew heavily from his observations of the lives of the workers in and around the mines for fictional material. With Hu Feng and the wartime campus of Fudan University in the vicinity, Lu Ling was able to find a small community of like-minded intellectuals with whom he could discuss literature and politics.

In April 1942 Lu Ling completed his first and most celebrated novel, *Ji'e de Guo Su'e* (1943, Hungry Guo Su'e), a horrific tale of a sexually and spiritually hungry woman whose passionate desire for a better life leads to her being beaten, branded with hot irons, and finally raped to death. The animalistic sexuality and the mine setting have led critics to compare the novel to the work of D. H. Lawrence. *Ji'e de Guo Su'e* is no mere formulaic tale of class oppression; it is a well-wrought tragedy that makes use of a complex array of symbolic and mythic imagery to paint a bleak, yet not entirely hopeless, fictional world. The novel ends with the demise of the corrupt village power structure.

In the spring of 1942 Lu Ling quit his job in Houfengyan after a fight with a fellow clerk. He then obtained a position as a library manager at the Nationalist Party Central Political Academy on the recommendation of a philosophy teacher at the school, Fang Guan, who wrote under the pen name Shu Wu. The two lived in the same dormitory and often discussed politics, philosophy, and literature, and Lu Ling incorporated material from his friend's oral narratives into his fiction. Lu Ling enjoyed the "university" environment but was upset at only watching others study when he was forced to work in the library. In his spare time he read Romain Rolland's bildungsroman *Jean-Christophe* (1905–1912); it exerted some influence on his *Caizhu di ernümen,* which Yang Yi sees as a

Cover for the first volume of Lu Ling's novel Caizhu di ernümen *(1945, Children of the Rich), about the disintegration of a wealthy family (from Lin Mohan, Fang Jing, and Shen Shiming, eds.,* Zhongguo kang Ri zhanzheng shiqi dahoufang wenxue shuxi, di san pian: Xiaoshuo, *volume 4, 1989; Collection of Thomas Moran)*

mélange of Tolstoy's long and convoluted sentences and Rolland's art of dissection of the spirit. During his tenure at the library Lu Ling rewrote *Caizhu di ernümen* from memory: Hu Feng had lost his draft of the novel in 1941 in the chaos following a Japanese air raid on Hong Kong.

Lu Ling's experiences during the early 1940s are reflected in the short stories and novellas in his 1945 collection *Qingchun de zhufu*. They are set for the most part in fictional mining villages of Sichuan, and the characters include miners and factory workers. Though it was increasingly common for leftist writers to write about the proletariat, Lu Ling's workers are not the formulaic heroes armed with Marxist ideology seen in some literature produced in Yan'an, the wartime Communist capital, in the 1940s; instead, they are psychologically complex figures who struggle with a primitive defiance against their oppressors. In this first collection of his fiction Lu Ling's concern is less with the politicized representation of class struggle than with the psychological exploration of the unconscious and irrational mind. The volume is dominated by characters who are drifters—loners, without families or homes and the stable moral system associated with them; they defy authority, though they lack the will or consciousness for sustained struggle. Xia Jinqian argues that Lu Ling's disparate fictional work is united by the theme of "liulang" (wandering), of physical and spiritual displacement. "Heise zisun zhi yi" (A Descendant of Black), first published in 1941 in *Qiyue*, treats the tensions among mine workers who have migrated to Sichuan from various cultural regions of China. This emphasis on a lack of national unity is strikingly at odds with the discourse of patriotic collectivism that dominated the war period. "Guancai" (translated as "Coffins," 1981), probably written in 1942, describes the conflict between two brothers—one miserly, the other dissolute—over coffins made from trees in the family compound. Both brothers are corrupt, and the families who work for them suffer greatly. Lu Ling's fiction offers few characters who are positive models.

An exception to the stories about workers in the collection is "Gu," which deals with alienation and the impossibility of love between two young teachers in a rural Sichuan high school. Di Siliu recalls that "Gu" was exceptional in Chinese wartime literature in general, which was dominated by politically zealous novels of battlefield heroics and anti-Japanese propaganda. Lu Ling's concern with the minds of his characters is so intense in this story that Hu Feng, his most ardent supporter, advised him in a 16 October 1941 letter to temper it: "I worry that the criticism directed at 'Valley' will stir misunderstandings and explanations that are harmful to your work. The technique of reflecting society through the minds and personalities of your characters is essentially correct, but 'Valley' uses too much long dialogue (actually, the male protagonist's monologues) to express it." The absence of "the enemy" in the stories in *Qingchun de zhufu* is striking; it suggests that for Lu Ling the true foe of social regeneration was not Japan but something far less tangible that resided in the core of the national psyche. Exposing these "spiritual" enemies was a role for literature that Lu Ling inherited from Lu Xun through Hu Feng.

In both *Qingchun de zhufu* and *Ji'e de Guo Su'e* Lu Ling depicts characters who exude a primitive, bestial strength that Hu Feng termed "the primitive power of the people." This primitivism may be seen as part of a literary trend of the late 1930s and 1940s that glorified the unconscious and primal power of the people, a power related to but different from the power of the masses as the motive force of history that was being promoted in Yan'an. In these and other stories by Lu Ling the *kuangye* (wilderness) is the spatial embodiment of a powerful primitive desire that will well up and destroy traditional morality, social convention, and political oppression.

In late 1943 Lu Ling returned to the mining region north of Chongqing to work as a clerk in a fuel-management office in the village of Huangjueshu, the wartime location of Fudan University. He befriended several students and helped organize student *bibao* (wall newspapers), to which he contributed short essays. He also briefly taught Chinese at the Wenchang Middle School. In April 1944 he completed *Caizhu di ernümen*. The first volume was published in 1945; a revised version of that volume, and the second volume, appeared in 1948.

Caizhu di ernümen is a massive novel. The first volume portrays the disintegration of the wealthy gentry/bourgeois Jiang family of Nanjing and Suzhou; Yang Yi suggests that the family is modeled on that of one of Lu Ling's maternal uncles. Of the many characters, this volume focuses on the two elder sons, Jiang Weizu and Jiang Shaozu; according to Daiyun Yue, the former represents a generation of intellectuals still tied to tradition, while the latter represents the liberal May Fourth generation of intellectuals. Volume two centers on the youngest son, Jiang Chunzu, and his struggles to understand himself and his place in the world. Whereas volume one is panoramic and multilayered, volume two is a bildungsroman. The most remarkable feature of the novel as a whole is its relentless attention to the characters' thoughts. There is a plot, but Lu Ling's main concern is the psychological conflicts within the three main characters as they struggle with society's demands and try to discover themselves. The mental processes of the protagonists are depicted in a Europeanized prose style that is characteristic of Lu Ling: he rigorously avoided the parallelism, four-character phrases, reduplicatives, and simple syntax of the more traditional fictional language to which many writers returned during the war and experimented with a complex syntax that he thought could better capture the intricacies of thought and emotion. The novel garnered some positive critical attention before 1949 but was the object of critical scorn during the anti–Hu Feng campaign of 1955, when its characters, particularly Jiang Chunzu, were attacked as solipsistic and megalomaniacal, exulting in their heroic individualism, their alienation from society, and their disdain for politics. Post-Mao scholarship, by contrast, has hailed *Caizhu di ernümen* as a psychological novel—a genre that is rare in Chinese literary history.

Soon after completing *Caizhu di ernümen*, Lu Ling married Yu Mingying, a native of Hubei with a middle-school education who had been a friend of Li Luling's. After a month's honeymoon, Yu returned to her job as a telegraph operator for the Central Communications Bureau in Chongqing; the couple visited each other as often as possible during this time of separation. The first of their three daughters was born in 1945.

Writing made the tedium of Lu Ling's clerk's position bearable: during this period he wrote short fiction that was collected in *Qiu'ai he qita* (1946, In Search of Love and Other Stories) and *Zai tielian zhong* (1949, In Chains). The stories in the former volume, written between 1944 and 1946, are atypically short; some are almost vignettes in their brevity and lack of plot. Most are satires that depict the relationship between personal ambition and oppression; a few take on an ironic tone in the disparity between the matter-of-factness of the narration and the absurdity and cruelty of what is being narrated. Like most of Lu Ling's fiction, these stories are antiheroic: their concern is not the glorification of the soldier or worker but the depiction of a dark world in a tragic age. In "Xinqi de yule" (A Novel Amusement) a group of bored people waiting for a bus amuse themselves by sadistically directing a blind man to bump into various objects. In many of the stories a minor incident sparks a rage that is the product of repressed unconscious feelings. In "Yingxiong de wudao" (Heroes' Dance) an aging storyteller who loses his clientele to some newcomers goes mad and begins performing a wild spirit dance, imagining himself a great hero of old. His dance becomes so frenetic that he attracts the attention of the newcomers' audience across the street; but he soon collapses of exhaustion and dies. Through a depiction of an idealist intellectual's failure to stop an unjust beating "Renquan" (Human Rights) attacks the intelligentsia as morally impotent and intellectually bankrupt. In "Qiu ye" (Fall Night) a petty clerk studying accounting late into the night indulges in delusions of heroic grandeur. As he envisions his glorious future, a rat appears. He traps and tortures it. Suddenly, he becomes frightened, haunted by images of rats' eyes and the plague that rats will bring to the world to avenge his cruel act. Yang Yi says that *Qiu'ai he qita* marks Lu Ling's maturation as a writer of fiction, revealing a refinement and lyricism lacking in his earlier works.

Around the time he was composing the stories in *Qiu'ai he qita*, Lu Ling wrote *Woniu zai jingji shang* (1946, Snails on Brambles). In this novella, which was first published in a journal in 1944, Huang Shutai, a former soldier who both harbors delusions of heroic machismo and suffers from feelings of impotence and inadequacy, vents his frustrations by beating his wife. Lu Ling also wrote "Jialing jiang pan de chuanqi" (Legend on the Shores of the Jialing River), a long novella about the conflict between good and evil in a middle-aged failure of a man that was serialized in the 8 September to 10 October 1946 issues of *Lianhe wanbao* (United Evening

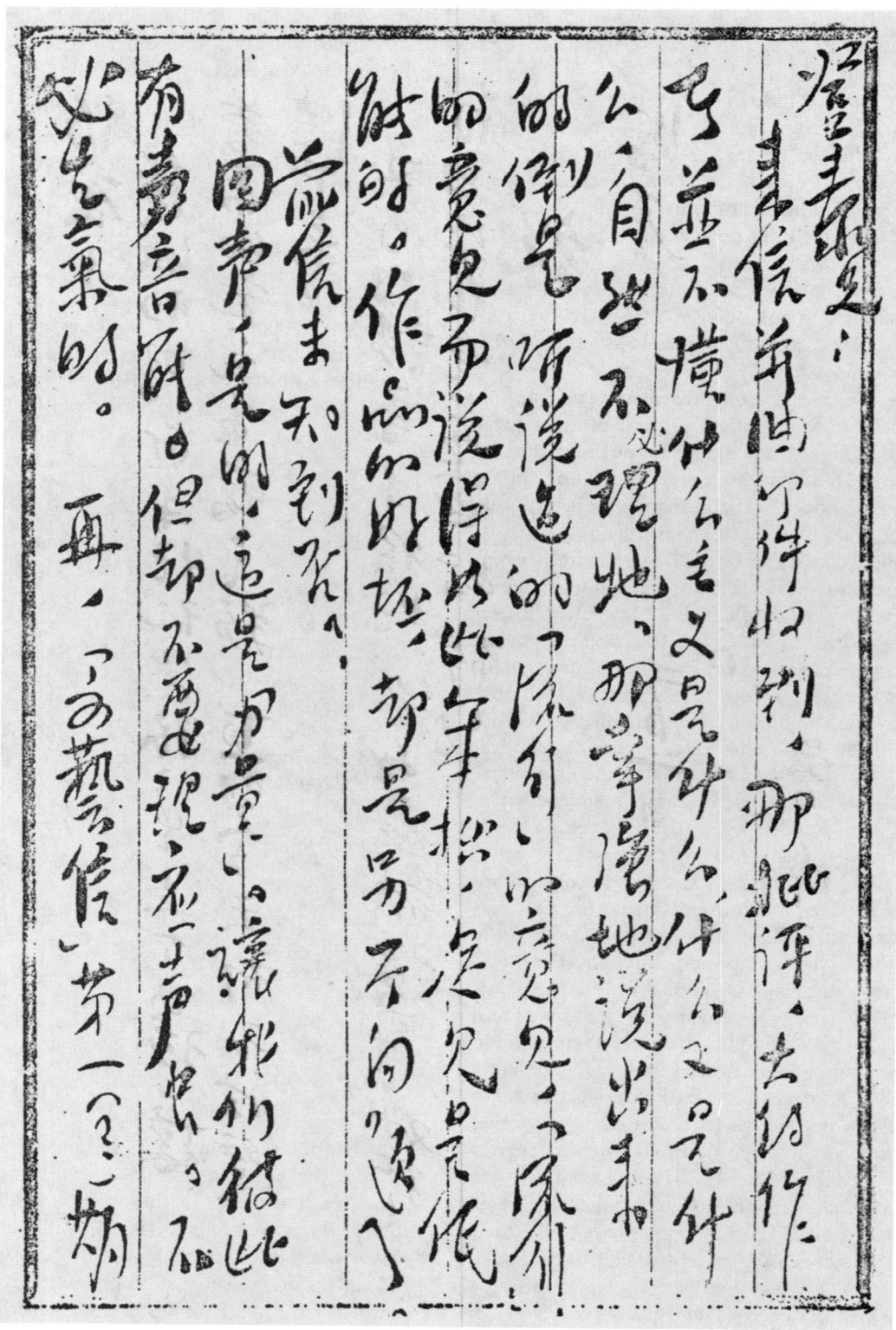

First page of a 29 January 1946 letter in which Lu Ling advises Lu Dengtai, a student at Fudan University in Shanghai, not to pay attention to the critical comments of an unnamed person about something Lu Dengtai had written (from Lu Ling shuxin ji, edited by Zhang Yiying, 1989; Harvard-Yenching Library, Harvard-Yenching Institute, Harvard University)

News) and first collected in *Lu Ling daibiao zuo* (1998, Representative Works of Lu Ling).

The stories in *Zai tielian zhong*, written between 1944 and 1946, are much longer and more concerned with the representation of characters' thoughts than those in *Qiu'ai he qita*. In "Wang Bingquan de daolu" (The Way of Wang Bingquan) the title character returns to his village after years of drifting to find that his wife, thinking him dead, has remarried. The story portrays Wang's thoughts and feelings about his past life with his wife and his present loneliness. His encounter with his wife near the end of the story is mostly presented through Wang's thoughts, which are a complex interplay of feelings of guilt, anger, jealousy, loyalty, and desire for freedom. In "Luo Dadou de yisheng" (A Life of Luo Dadou) the title character has been reduced by a series of failures and disappointments to begging in the streets, while his mother fends off the squalor of her real existence by surrounding herself with old perfume bottles and imagining a beautiful life of bourgeois ease. Seeking solace in his despair, Luo becomes a passionate believer in local divinities and spirits. Critics have compared the story to Lu Xun's "A Q zheng zhuan" (1921; translated as "The True Story of Ah Q," 1981).

Lu Ling's fiction was first attacked by Communist Party–sponsored critics during the Rectification Campaign, initiated in Yan'an in 1942 to eliminate expressions of discontent with the party and later extended to areas under Nationalist Party control. The main object of the Chongqing Rectification was Hu Feng, whose theories on realism and subjectivism were at odds with those espoused by Mao in his 1942 "Talks at the Yan'an Forum on Literature and Art." To show his displeasure with the Rectification Campaign, Hu Feng founded the literary periodical *Xiwang* (Hope). Lu Ling's "Luo Dadou de yisheng" was the first piece in the January 1945 inaugural issue of the journal, which also included a polemic by Hu Feng reiterating his view that subjectivity was needed to portray objective reality in literature, and the essay "Lun zhuguan" (On Subjectivism), by Shu Wu (Lu Ling's friend Fang Guan). In April 1945 "Lun zhuguan," which provided a philosophical foundation for Hu Feng's theories, became the focus of an attack by Communist Party officials, who sought to obstruct publication of *Xiwang*. During the campaign against subjectivism Lu Ling's work was criticized by Communist critics for being too obscure and complex for the masses. Critics not affiliated with the party, on the other hand, generally praised it as vital, imaginative, passionate, and psychologically probing. Hu Feng was an ardent promoter of Lu Ling's work; he viewed Lu Ling as continuing the "spirit of Lu Xun" and predicted in an often-quoted sentence in his preface to *Caizhu di ernümen* that "time will prove that the publication of *Children of the Rich* is a great event in the history of modern Chinese literature."

In June 1946 Lu Ling returned to Nanjing. He was unemployed for several months, and the family subsisted on his wife's meager salary. Though their lives were difficult, unemployment at least afforded Lu Ling time to revise the stories that were collected in *Qiu'ai he qita* and to work on other stories; twenty-eight of the latter were collected in 1952 as *Pingyuan* (The Plain). Like those in *Qiu'ai he qita*, the stories in *Pingyuan* are relatively short and are concerned with the psychological effects of oppression on the victims rather than with attacking the oppressors. The characters are psychologically unstable, unheroic, and too weak to fight their oppressors; instead, they fly into irrational fits of rage that they take out on animals, their wives, their children, or themselves. In "Yi Xuefu he ta de niu" (Yi Xuefu and His Ox) Yi Xuefu, burdened by the death of his wife and debts incurred to pay for her burial, vents his anger on his ox by smashing its eye with a rock; he then commits suicide. The protagonist of "Quru" (Humiliation) strangles his newborn baby in a paroxysm of anger provoked by the loss of his job; by his meddling father, who caused him to be fired; and by his clinging wife. Lu Ling was criticized in 1955 for the bestiality and cruelty of his characters and for having them direct their rage at the innocent rather than at their oppressors; he was said to have imposed his own bourgeois desperation on his working-class characters, thereby sullying their purity. Some of the characters in the collection express a longing for a world of light and weightlessness through dreams and flights of imagination. In "Ge chang" (A Song to Be Sung) Lin Futian, to the accompaniment of his fiddle, imagines a wild horse that destroys his oppressive surroundings and then soars to a mountain wilderness where it drinks madly the pure water of a stream.

Only after the birth of their second daughter in 1947 were Lu Ling and his wife able to find a permanent residence and set up a stable home. Around this time Huang Ruohai, an associate of Hu Feng, asked Lu Ling to write a script for the local drama company he directed. Written from April to July 1947, *Yunque* was produced by Huang's troupe that fall. Huang considered the play a challenge to what he called the "superficial, clamoring" theater that was the rule in postwar China. *Yunque* is a complex psychological chamber drama in four acts about a couple who teach at a middle school. The husband has estranged the wife emotionally through his neglect of her and his unbending adherence to lofty ideals; she feels that he has not lived up to his progressive ideals in their relationship, where he expects her to play the traditional role of the submissive wife. She succumbs to the renewed advances of a cynical former lover who abandoned her years earlier; although dissolute and immoral, the former lover spurs her to rebel against her husband and to see her own hypocrisy: she sought out the ease and comfort of married life, even though it meant the suffocation of her passions. In the end she returns to her husband, begs his forgiveness, then takes her own life. During the anti–Hu Feng campaign *Yunque* was criticized as a decadent bourgeois drama about a defiant intellectual hero struggling alone for truth and justice. After its production, Lu Ling received many letters from young spectators praising the play for its emotional energy and for featuring characters who spoke for the times. Several of these admirers, including Hua Tie and Ouyang Zhuang, became friends with whom Lu Ling founded in 1947 an irregularly published literary journal, *Mayi xiaoji* (Ants). Lu Ling assisted in editing the journal and contributed essays, book reviews, and short fiction.

In 1948 Hua Tie and Ouyang Zhuang took over the editorship of *Mayi xiaoji* and moved its headquarters to Shanghai; Lu Ling remained in Nanjing. Early the following year Ouyang Zhuang was arrested by the Nationalists; the copy of *Mayi xiaoji* found on his person was used as evidence of seditious intentions against the government. Arrested as an associate of Ouyang Zhuang, Hua Tie informed on Lu Ling. Regretting his betrayal, Hua Tie smuggled out a note to Lu Ling's parents, who were living in Shanghai, warning them of the danger in which he had put their son and asking them to alert Lu Ling in Nanjing. Lu Ling received the warning in time and fled to Shanghai. According to a 1955 account by Li Zhihua, Lu Ling contacted Hu Feng's wife and A Long, a friend from Chongqing and a member of Hu Feng's Qiyue poetry group; with the collusion of some politically powerful acquaintances, they helped him secure the release of his two imprisoned colleagues. When Lu Ling returned to Nanjing, he found that his house had apparently not been searched. During the anti–Hu Feng campaign this incident was taken as evidence of Lu Ling's intimate association with the Nationalist Party and as sufficient grounds for his being labeled a counterrevolutionary. The accusation, however, overlooked the fact that the original arrest of Ouyang Zhuang was made by Nationalist military police for what they viewed as the anti-Nationalist nature of the journal with which Lu Ling was involved.

According to several accounts, Lu Ling was outspoken, passionate, defiant of authority, and wary of political movements and empty ideologies. Invited to speak at a student literary meeting to celebrate the anniversary of the May Fourth Movement in 1948, he declined in an article for *Mayi xiaoji* in which he reviled the students for chanting leftist slogans against reactionary art; true revolutionary struggle, he said, would not emerge from this kind of thoughtless recitation of hollow political incantations.

Lu Ling completed his novel *Ranshao de huangdi* (The Burning Wasteland) in 1948; it was published in 1951 by the Hu Feng–controlled publishing house (Writers' Bookstore). Guo Zilong, the son of a landlord, returns to his hometown after years of wandering and soldiering. His youthful idealism for a new China has faded, and he is looking for a quiet place to live out his middle age in ease and comfort. Much of the novel is taken up by the thoughts of Guo, a "chedi de wangmingzhe" (character in total exile). He is alienated from society, from his own class, and from the peasantry, to which he can never belong. Wu Shunguang, a landlord and an enemy from Guo's youth, now rules the village. Guo befriends Zhang Lao'er, a peasant whose land Wu has confiscated, and promises to take revenge on his behalf. But Guo, torn psychologically by his allegiance to his class background, his personal hatred of Wu, and his disappointment at failing to live up to his youthful revolutionary ideals, is unable to act; all he can do is to brood on his failures and unrealized hopes. Guo is a despicable character; yet, his anguish provokes sympathy in the reader. At the end of the novel Zhang compulsively—almost unconsciously—kills the landlord with an ax blow to the head. The novel made a deep impression on Lu Ling's friend Lu Dian, who compared it in a 9 October 1949 letter to Lu Ling to Lu Xun's "A Q zheng zhuan" in its "grasp of history and in the psychological world of its characters." Zhang's murder of Wu was the source of much criticism in 1955 because it is not politically or ideologically motivated but is an act of personal hatred.

In the spring of 1949, shortly after the Communist takeover of Nanjing, Lu Ling became an instructor of creative writing at Nanjing University with a concurrent appointment as a teacher at the Nanjing First Girls' Middle School. He was also made a member of the creative-writing division of the Nanjing Literature and Arts Union. The union encouraged its members to "study from the masses"; Lu Ling did so with great zeal, visiting factories and eating and living with the workers. In 1950, through Hu Feng's connections, he became the head of a creative-writing group at the China Youth Arts Theater in Beijing and immediately set to work reworking scripts he had begun before 1949. He wrote *Yingxiong de muqin* (1951, The Heroic Mother), *Yingzhe tian ming* (1951, Greeting Daybreak), and *Zuguo zai qianjin* (1952, The Fatherland Marches Forward); none of them was ever produced because of alleged flaws in their political content, although all were published by Hu Feng–controlled houses.

Lu Ling spent the summer of 1951 in Dalian with a group of writers led by the playwright Tian Han to learn about the conditions of "volunteer" soldiers taking part in the Korean War. Early in 1953 he was sent to the war front to learn from the soldiers and peasants. He spent several months with various companies of the Thirty-ninth Army, two weeks at command headquarters interviewing officers, and several days with a Korean family in Kaicheng. Out of these experiences came another play, which was eventually lost by the China Youth Arts Theater and never produced or published; some short stories and essays; and an unfinished novel, *Zhanzheng, weile heping* (War, for Peace), which was not published until the 1980s—first in serialized form and in 1985 as a book.

The attack on members of the Hu Feng group had begun in July 1949 when Mao Dun, in his speech to the first meeting of the Zhongguo quanguo wenxue yishujie lianhehui (All-China Federation of Literary and Art Circles [ACFLAC]), presented an overview of "behind-the-lines" literature in which he criticized the theory of "subjectivism" without mentioning Hu Feng. In 1950 Communist Party cultural figures had attacked the poet Ah Long, a member of Hu Feng's group, for articles in which he expressed opposition to literary tendentiousness and stereotypical characters. Lu Ling's dramas had been the object of published criticism in 1951, but the criticism intensified during the 1952 Three-Antis and Five-Antis Campaigns, mass movements that targeted capitalists and corrupt bureaucrats. Lu Ling's fiction was attacked for "distorting" the proletariat; Merle Goldman records that one critic wrote: "The proletariat under his pen are petty, wild, barbarous, cruel, disorganized, undisciplined and irrational. Almost all of his working people have such a backward ideology . . . that they stand in opposition to their own class." On 8 June, Shu Wu, one of Hu Feng's closest colleagues and Lu Ling's friend from his days in Sichuan, wrote a self-criticism renouncing his connection to Hu Feng and urging writers such as Lu Ling to follow him in accepting Mao's Yan'an talks as literary doctrine. In September a published letter by Shu Wu pleaded with Lu Ling to repent his literary sins. ACFLAC organized a meeting in December 1952 to discuss Hu Feng's literary theories. Articles by two of the most powerful critics in China, Lin Mohan and He Qifang, in early 1953 summed up the case against Lu Ling and hinted that Hu Feng would be the next target.

The campaign against Lu Ling had died down by the spring of 1953, a year of relaxation and liberalization in Communist Party literary policy during which Hu Feng was appointed a representative to the National People's Congress, placed on the editorial board of the prestigious journal *Renmin wenxue* (People's Literature), made a member of the executive board of the Zhonghua quanguo wenxue gongzuozhe xiehui (National

Cover for Lu Ling's Qiu'ai he qita (1946, In Search of Love and Other Stories), a collection of extremely brief, mostly satirical pieces that depict a dark world in a tragic age (Wason Collection on East Asia–China, Kroch Asia Library, Cornell University)

Assembly of Literary and Art Workers [the name of this organization was changed to the Chinese Writers' Association in September 1953]), and expanded several of the publishing houses he controlled. Meanwhile, Lu Ling published a series of essays on his experiences in Korea; seven were collected in 1954 as *Banmendian qianxian sanji* (Accounts from the Panmunjom Front). He also published short stories that drew on his experience on the Korean front in *Renmin wenxue*.

Believing that his opportunity to confront cultural-policy makers had arrived, in July 1954 Hu Feng submitted a long report expounding his views on literature to the Central Committee. Perhaps the most forthright and outspoken attack on the Communist Party literary bureaucracy in the history of Maoist China, it summed up ideas Hu Feng had been propounding since the mid 1930s: an empirical approach to literary creation is superior to one dictated by doctrinaire ideology or inflexible party policy; the writer's individual subjective spirit is the necessary means of capturing objective reality; literary creation should not be controlled by a party bureaucracy; and popular (that is, traditional and folk) forms mark a retreat from literary progressiveness and the spirit of internationalism introduced during the May Fourth Movement. Lu Ling helped Hu Feng prepare the report.

For several months there was no reaction to Hu Feng's report from the Central Committee or the Zhongguo zuojia xiehui (Chinese Writers' Association). Hu Feng interpreted the lack of a response as a positive sign, and at a combined meeting of the Chinese Writers' Association and ACFLAC on 11 November he gave a speech in which he criticized the Communist Party cultural official Zhou Yang by name and lambasted the literary bureaucracy for the fear they had instilled in young writers, for their "religious zealotry," and for being "warlords of the literary world." The publication of Hu Feng's speech in the 10 December issue of the official *Wenyi bao* (Literary Gazette) signaled the beginning of the campaign against him. In January 1955 journals and newspapers throughout China were mobilized in the attack on Hu Feng. On 11 January his perfunctory self-criticism was published as evidence of his recalcitrance, and at a meeting of the Chinese Writers' Association and ACFLAC in February a resolution was passed calling for an all-out criticism of Hu Feng and the members of his "clique." Lu Ling was generally recognized as the most significant member of the Hu Feng group and the one whose writing most clearly embodied Hu Feng's literary ideals. From January to July dozens of articles criticizing Lu Ling's Korean War stories, his pre-1949 fiction, and his dramas appeared in all of the major literary periodicals and newspapers. The first three issues of the 1955 volume of *Wenyi bao* featured his long and defiant retort to the criticism of his Korean War stories. On 22 February, at a meeting of the China Dramatists Union convened to criticize Hu Feng, Lu Ling—likely with the blessing of Hu Feng, who was by this time well aware of the desperateness of their situation—laid the blame for the error of his ways on his mentor. Hu Feng was expelled from the Chinese Writers' Association in May and officially labeled a counterrevolutionary in June. Lu Ling lost his membership in the Dramatists Union on 16 May, when he was "geli fanxing" (separated for self-reflection). Two weeks later he was arrested, given a perfunctory trial, and found guilty of counterrevolution. Recent research has corroborated what many had long suspected: the political charges against members of the "Hu Feng Clique" were fabricated, and the clique itself was largely a fiction manufactured by the party.

From his arrest in 1955 until the spring of 1959, except for a brief stay in a Beijing hospital for treatment of meningitis, Lu Ling was in the custody of the Public Security Bureau. He was forced to go through "self-reflection," which Denton describes as a "psychologically grueling process of responding to the verbal and physical abuse of hard-nosed political cadres by endlessly writing and rewriting self-criticisms." That his self-reflection lasted for four years suggests what later memoirs have confirmed: Lu Ling refused to confess to the crimes of which he was accused. (By contrast, Hu Feng's self-reflection lasted only three months.) In June 1959 he was sent to Qincheng, an elite prison north of Beijing where important political prisoners continue to be locked up. There he joined at least a dozen other members of the Hu Feng group; most of the minor members had been released. In July 1961 he was taken to a Beijing hospital and treated for schizophrenia with insulin injections. He remained in the hospital until early 1964, when he was released on bail and allowed to return home to recuperate. In 1965 he wrote a series of more than thirty "memorials"—letters to the Central Committee—to protest his mistreatment and seek judicial redress. He had written memorials that had caused him much trouble during his imprisonment, and it is hard to believe that the writing of these letters was not the irrational act of an insane man. He was returned to the hospital, where he remained until the outbreak of the Cultural Revolution. In October 1966 he was discovered by Red Guards; interrogated, humiliated, and abused; and sent back to Qincheng prison. The "revolutionary" courts took up his case anew in 1973 and sentenced him to twenty years in prison, retroactive to 1955. He joined several prison work teams, making shoes in a factory and doing a variety of jobs on the Yanqing prison farm northwest of Beijing. He was released on 19 June 1975 and permitted to return to his family; by then two of his daughters had married and left home. During his long absence his wife had supported the family by taking jobs such as working in a hemp-sack factory. Unlike the relatives of many individuals condemned during the Cultural Revolution, she had never given in to pressure to renounce her ties with him.

After his release from prison, Lu Ling was forced to sweep the streets and clean out the public toilets of his Beijing neighborhood; the labor was supposed to bring about his spiritual and political cleansing. According to Du Gao, Lu Ling heard the news of his official rehabilitation in 1980 "without an outburst of happiness or painful tears. . . . Silent, without uttering a word, he continued sweeping the street with lowered head." After his rehabilitation, he was given a nominal post as an editor of the periodical *Juben* (Script). Gradually, he was recognized by the cultural world that had

Lu Ling with his wife, Yu Mingying, in 1948 (from Lu Ling, edited by Zhu Yanqing, 1994; Baker-Berry Library, Dartmouth College)

excluded him for more than twenty years. He was seen, silent and pensive, at the Di si ci Zhongguo wenxue yishu gongzuozhe daibiao dahui (Fourth Congress of Writers and Artists) in 1979 and at Hu Feng's funeral in 1985. He slowly began to write again, producing poetry, essays, and fiction–including an unfinished novel about the campaigns against intellectuals in the 1950s–but his work garnered little critical attention apart from a few literary historians and biographers who were interested in restoring his reputation.

A reappraisal of Lu Ling's fiction in the People's Republic began in 1980. Since then, most of his works have been republished, dozens of articles and a handful of books have been written about him, and research materials, including letters exchanged between members of the Hu Feng group and reminiscences, have appeared. Scholarly interest in the writers of the Hu Feng group was particularly strong in the late 1980s; it was promoted by state journals and cultural bureaucrats, perhaps as a calculated response to a growing interest in avant-garde literature and postmodernist theory. Lu Ling died of a cerebral hemorrhage on 12 February 1994.

Letters:
Lu Ling shuxin ji, edited by Zhang Yiying (Guilin: Lijiang chabanshe, 1989).

Bibliographies:
"Lu Ling de biming," *Wenjiao ziliao*, 4 (1985): 46;
Shen Yongbao and others, "Lu Ling zuopin xinian mulu," *Wenjiao ziliao*, 4 (1985): 51–60;
Yang Yi, Zhang Huan, Wei Lin, and Li Zhiyuan, eds., *Lu Ling yanjiu ziliao* (Beijing: Shiyue wenyi, 1993);
"Lu Ling zhuzuo nianbiao," in *Lu Ling wenji*, volume 4 (Hefei: Anhui wenyi, 1995), pp. 379–390;
Xu Lang, "Lu Ling wannian chuangzao nianbiao," *Xin wenxue shiliao*, 4 (1997): 22–25.

Biographies:
Di Siliu, "Lu Ling de zaoyu," *Jingbao yuekan*, 31 (February 1980): 31–35;
Hua Tie, "Wo suo zhidao de Lu Ling," *Xin wenxue shiliao*, 2 (1985): 172–175;
Shen Yongbao and others, "Lu Ling shengping jiqi chuangzuo de ruogan kaoding," *Wenjiao ziliao*, 4 (1985): 47–50;
Du Gao, "Yige shounanzhe de linghun," *Juben*, 2 (1986): 73–76;
Yang Yi, "Lu Ling zhuanlüe," *Xin wenxue shiliao*, 1 (1987): 193–204;
Zhang Yiying, "Lu Ling de nianpu jianbian," in *Lu Ling shuxin ji*, edited by Zhang (Guilin: Lijiang, 1989), pp. 174–259;

Ji Pang, "Ai Lu Ling," *Xin wenxue shiliao*, 1 (1995): 137–154;

Yu Mingying, "Lu Ling yu wo," *Xin wenxue shiliao*, 4 (1997): 9–11;

Zhang Yesong, ed., *Lu Ling yinxiang* (Shanghai: Xuelin, 1997);

Zhu Hengqing, *Lu Ling: Wei wancheng de tiancai* (Jinan: Shandong wenyi, 1997);

Liu Tingsheng, *Sisuozhe xiongda lixiang de lüxingzhe: Lu Ling zhuan* (Shanghai: Huadong shifan daxue, 1999).

References:

Kirk A. Denton, *The Problematic of Self in Modern Chinese Literature: Hu Feng and Lu Ling* (Stanford, Cal.: Stanford University Press, 1998);

Fan Jun, "Cong *Qiu ai*, *Zai tielian zhong*, he *Pinyuan* kan Lu Ling zenyang tongguo zuopin jinxing fan'geming goudang," *Wenxue yanjiu jikan*, 2 (1957): 26–27;

Fan Ning, "Jin yi nian lai Lu Ling jinmi peihe Hu Feng jingong he tuique de jidian shishi," *Wenyi bao*, 12 (1955): 26–27;

Merle Goldman, *Literary Dissent in Communist China* (New York: Atheneum, 1971);

Hao Yimin, "Hu Feng de zhuguan zhandou jingshen he Lu Ling de xiaoshuo chuangzuo," *Zhongguo xiandai wenxue yanjiu congkan*, 3 (1988): 54–72;

Theresa Kuskowski-Pieroni, "The Writings of a Poet-Warrior: Hu Feng's Vision of Realism in China (1928–1948)," dissertation, University of Wisconsin–Madison, 1987;

Li Hui, *Lishi beige: Zhongguo zuida de wentan yuan'an* (Taibei: Fengyun shidai, 1989); republished as *Hu Feng jituan yuan'an* (Beijing: Renmin ribao, 1989);

Li Ming, "Jielu Hu Feng fenzi zai Nanjing wenyijie de zuixing," *Wenyi yuebao* (July 1955): 25–27;

Li Zhihua, "Fangeming de Lu Ling," *Xin Hunan bao* (19 August 1955): 14–17;

Lin Mohan, "Hu Feng shijian qianqian houhou," *Xin wenxue shiliao*, 3 (1989): 4–28;

Lin, Fang Jing, and Shen Shiming, eds., *Zhongguo kang Ri zhangzheng shiqi dahoufang*, volume 4 (Chongqing: Chongqing chabanshe, 1989);

Kang Liu, "Individualism and Realism: Lu Ling and Modern European Literature," dissertation, University of Wisconsin–Madison, 1989;

Liu, "The Language of Desire, Class, and Subjectivity in Lu Ling's Fiction," in *Gender and Sexuality in Twentieth-Century Chinese Literature and Society*, edited by Lu Tonglin (Albany: State University of New York Press, 1993), pp. 67–83;

Liu, "Mixed Style in Lu Ling's Novel *Children of the Rich*: Family Chronicle and Bildungsroman," *Modern Chinese Literature*, 7, no. 1 (1993): 61–87;

Liu, "Revolution and Desire in Lu Ling's Fiction: Modern Chinese Literature in the 1940s," *Chinese Culture*, 34, no. 3 (1993): 39–57;

Liu Tingsheng, *Yige shenmi de wenxue tiancai: Lu Ling* (Shanghai: Huadong shifan daxue, 1997);

William A. Lyell Jr., "Lu Ling's Wartime Novel: *Hungry Guo Su'e*," in *La littérature au temps de la guerre de résistance contre le Japon (de 1937 à 1945)* (Paris: Editions de la fondation Singer-Poulignac, 1982), pp. 267–280;

Qian Liqun, "Tansuozhe de de yu shi," *Zhongguo xiandai wenxue yanjiu congkan*, 3 (1981): 265–279;

Qian, "Zhanshi zhishifenzi xinling licheng de shishi–Lu Ling de *Caizhu di ernümen* jianlun," *Kangzhan wenyi yanjiu*, 4 (1983): 44–50;

Shu Wu (Fang Guan), "Cong tou xuexi 'Zai Yan'an wenyi zuotanhui de jianghua,'" *Renmin ribao*, 8 June 1952, p. 4;

Shu Wu, "Zhi Lu Ling de gongkai xin," *Wenyi bao*, no. 18 (26 September 1952);

Yunzhong Shu, *Buglers on the Home Front: The Wartime Practice of the Qiyue School* (Albany: State University of New York Press, 2000), pp. 107–151;

Suqing Hu Feng heibang fenzi–Lu Ling (Hong Kong: Zhongguo xin wenxue ziliao shi, 1975);

Tang Shi, "Lu Ling yu tade *Qiu Ai*," *Wenyi fuxing*, 4, no. 2 (November 1947): 189–192;

Wu Qian, "Ping Lu Ling de duanpian xiaoshuo ji *Pingyuan*," *Renmin wenxue* (September 1952): 61–65;

Xia Jinqian, "*Caizhu di ernümen* yu xiandai zhishizhe de jingsheng liulang," *Kangzhan wenyi yanjiu*, 3 (1988): 1–19;

Xiao Feng, ed., *Hu Feng, Lu Ling wenxue shujian* (Hefei: Anhui wenyi, 1994);

Yang Yi, "Lu Ling–linghun aomi de tansuozhe," *Wenxue zhenglun*, 5 (1983): 114–127;

Daiyun Yue, *Intellectuals in Chinese Fiction* (Berkeley: Center for Chinese Studies, University of California, 1988), pp. 83–107;

Zhang Yiying, ed., *Lu Ling shuxin ji* (Guilin: Lijiang, 1989);

Zhao Yuan, *Jiannan de xuanze* (Shanghai: Shanghai wenyi, 1986), pp. 321–342;

Zhao, "Lu Ling xiaoshuo de xingxiang yu meigan," *Kangzhan wenyi yanjiu*, 4 (1985): 3–11.

Lu Xun

(25 September 1881 – 19 October 1936)

Jon Eugene von Kowallis
University of New South Wales, Sydney

BOOKS: *Zhongguo kuangchan zhi* [A Survey of Mineral Resources in China], as Zhou Zhangshou (Shanghai: Shanghai puji shuwu/Nanjing: Nanjing qixin shuju/Tokyo: Riben Dongjing liuxuesheng huiguan, 1906);

Nahan [Outcry] (Beijing: Beijing daxue di yi yuan xinchao she, 1923); translated by Yang Xianyi and Gladys Yang as *Call to Arms* (Beijing: Foreign Languages Press, 1981);

Zhongguo xiaoshuo shilüe, 2 volumes (Beijing: Beijing daxue di yi yuan xinchao she, 1923, 1924; revised edition, 1 volume, Beiping: Beixin shuju, 1931; revised again, 1935); translated by Yang Xianyi and Gladys Yang as *A Brief History of Chinese Fiction* (Beijing: Foreign Languages Press, 1959);

Re feng [Hot Wind] (Beijing: Beixin shuju, 1925)—includes "Suiganlu sanshiba," translated by Kirk A. Denton as "Impromptu Reflection No. 38: On Conceitedness and Inheritance," *Republican China*, 16 (November 1990): 90–97;

Huagai ji [Bad Luck] (Beijing: Beixin shuju, 1926);

Panghuang [Hesitation] (Beijing: Beixin shuju, 1926); translated by Yang Xianyi and Gladys Yang as *Wandering* (Beijing: Foreign Languages Press, 1981);

Fen [The Grave] (Beijing: Weiming she, 1927)—includes "Moluo shi li shuo," abridged and translated by Donald Holoch and Shu-ying Tsau as "On the Power of Māra Poetry," and "Lun zhaoxiang zhi lei," translated by Denton as "On Photography," in *Modern Chinese Literary Thought: Writings on Literature, 1893–1945*, edited by Denton (Stanford, Cal.: Stanford University Press, 1996), pp. 96–203;

Huagai ji xubian [Bad Luck II] (Beijing: Beixin shuju, 1927);

Yecao (Beijing: Beixin shuju, 1927)—translated by Yang Xianyi and Gladys Yang as *Wild Grass* (Beijing: Foreign Languages Press, 1974);

Lu Xun (from Lu Xun Selected Works, *volume 1, 1985; Collection of Thomas Moran)*

Zhao hua xi shi (Beiping: Weiming she, 1928); translated by Yang Xianyi and Gladys Yang as *Dawn Blossoms Plucked at Dusk* (Beijing: Foreign Languages Press, 1976);

Eryi ji [And That's That] (Shanghai: Beixin shuju, 1928)—includes "Lüe tan Xianggang," translated by Zhu Zhiyu as "On Hong Kong," *Renditions*, nos. 29–30 (Spring-Autumn 1988): 47–53;

San xian ji [Three Leisures] (Shanghai: Beixin shuju, 1932);

Er xin ji [Two Hearts] (Shanghai: Hezhong shudian, 1932); preface and twenty-two essays removed on order of government censors from the fourth edition (Shanghai: Hezhong shudian, 1933), republished as *Shiling ji* [Tidbits] (Shanghai: Hezhong shudian, 1934);

Chuangzuo de jingyan [The Experience of Creation] (Shanghai: Tianma shudian, 1933);

Wei ziyou shu [False Liberty] (Shanghai: Qingguang shuju, an imprint of Beixin shuju, 1933);

Nanqiang beidiao ji [Southern Accent, Northern Inflection] (Shanghai: Tongwen shudian, 1934);

Zhun feng yue tan [Semi-Frivolous Talk] (Shanghai: Xingzhong shuju, 1934)–includes "Nanren de jinhua," translated as "The Evolution of the Male Sex," in *The Chinese Essay*, translated and edited by David E. Pollard (Hong Kong: Research Centre for Translation, The Chinese University of Hong Kong, 1999; New York: Columbia University Press, 2000; London: Hurst, 2000), pp. 113–116;

Jiwai ji [Collection of the Uncollected] (Shanghai: Qunzhong tushu gongsi, 1935)–includes "Wenyi yu zhengzhi de qitu," translated by Holoch and Tsau as "The Divergence of Art and Politics," in *Modern Chinese Literary Thought*, pp. 328–334; and "Zichao," translated by Jon Eugene von Kowallis as "Laughing at My Own Predicament," in his *The Lyrical Lu Xun: A Study of His Classical-Style Verse* (Honolulu: University of Hawai'i Press, 1996), pp. 202–208;

Menwai wentan [A Layman's Remarks on Writing] (Shanghai: Tianma shudian, 1935);

Gushi xinbian [Old Tales Retold] (Shanghai: Wenhua shenghuo chubanshe, 1936)–translated by Yang Xianyi and Gladys Yang as *Old Tales Retold* (Beijing: Foreign Languages Press, 1961);

Huabian wenxue [Fringed Literature] (Shanghai: Lianhua shuju, 1936);

Qiejieting zawen [Essays From Demi-Concession Studio] (Shanghai: Sanxian shuwu, 1937);

Qiejieting zawen er ji [Essays From Demi-Concession Studio II] (Shanghai: Sanxian shuwu, 1937);

Qiejieting zawen mobian [Essays from Demi-Concession Studio III] (Shanghai: Sanxian shuwu, 1937);

Ye ji [Night Jottings], edited by Xu Guangping (Shanghai: Wenhua shenghuo chubanshe, 1937);

Jiwai ji shiyi [Addendum to the Collection of the Uncollected] (Shanghai: Lu Xun xiansheng jinian weiyuanhui/Lu Xun quanji chubanshe, 1938);

Lu Xun riji [Lu Xun's Diaries] (24 volumes, Shanghai: Shanghai chuban gongsi, 1951; enlarged edition, 2 volumes, Beijing: Renmin wenxue chubanshe, 1976);

Lu Xun shiji [Collected Poems of Lu Xun] (Beijing: Wenwu chubanshe, 1963);

Lu Xun quanji [The Complete Works of Lu Xun], (16 volumes, Beijing: Renmin wenxue chubanshe, 1981; revised, 1991; enlarged, 18 volumes, 2005)–includes in volume 8, "Po e'sheng lun," translated by Kowallis as "Toward a Refutation of the Voices of Evil," *Renditions*, 26 (Autumn 1986): 108–119.

Editions and Collections: *Lu Xun zagan xuanji* [Selected Essays of Lu Xun], edited by Qu Qiubai as He Ning (Shanghai: Qingguang shuju, 1933);

Lu Xun zixuan ji [Lu Xun's Selection of His Own Works] (Shanghai: Tianma shudian, 1933);

Lu Xun quanji [The Complete Works of Lu Xun], 20 volumes, edited by Lu Xun xiansheng jinian weiyuanhui (Shanghai: Lu Xun quanji chubanshe, 1938);

Lu Xun sanshi nian ji [Lu Xun's Works over Thirty Years], 30 volumes (Shanghai: Lu Xun quanji chubanshe, 1941);

Lu Xun zizhuan ji qi zuopin [Lu Xun's Autobiography and His Works], edited by Meng Jindie (Shanghai: Yingwen xuehui, 1941);

Lu Xun quanji buyi [Addendum to the Complete Works of Lu Xun], edited by Tang Tao (Shanghai: Shanghai chuban gongsi, 1946);

Manhua "A Q zhengzhuan" [The Illustrated "True Story of Ah Q"], illustrated by Feng Zikai (Shanghai: Jiliu shudian, 1949);

Lu Xun quanji buyi xubian [Continuation of the Addendum to the Complete Works of Lu Xun], edited by Tang Tao (Shanghai: Shanghai chuban gongsi, 1952);

Lu Xun xiaoshuo ji [Collected Short Stories of Lu Xun] (Beijing: Renmin wenxue chubanshe, 1952);

Lu Xun quanji [The Complete Works of Lu Xun], 10 volumes (Beijing: Renmin wenxue chubanshe, 1956–1958);

Lu Xun, *A Lu Hsun Reader*, edited by William A. Lyell (New Haven: Far Eastern Publications, Yale University, 1967);

Lu Xun quanji [The Complete Works of Lu Xun], 20 volumes (Beijing: Renmin wenxue chubanshe, 1973);

Lu Xun lun wenxue yu yishu [Lu Xun on Literature and Art], 2 volumes, edited by Wu Zimin and others (Beijing: Renmin wenxue chubanshe, 1980);

Lu Xun shougao quanji: Riji [Complete Works of Lu Xun Reproduced in Handwritten Manuscript Form: Diaries], 8 volumes (Beijing: Wenwu chubanshe, 1983);

Lu Xun zawen quanbian [Complete Miscellaneous Essays of Lu Xun], 2 volumes, edited by Wang Dehou and Qian Liqun (N.p.: Zhejiang wenyi chubanshe, 1993);

Lu Xun shougao quanji: Zhuzuo [Complete Works of Lu Xun Reproduced in Handwritten Manuscript Form: Stories and Essays], 12 volumes (Fuzhou: Fujian jiaoyu chubanshe, 2000).

Editions in English: *Ah Q and Others: Selected Stories of Lusin,* translated by Chi-chen Wang (New York: Columbia University Press, 1941);

Selected Stories of Lu Hsun, translated by Yang Hsien-yi and Gladys Yang (Peking: Foreign Languages Press, 1954; San Francisco: China Books and Periodicals, 1990);

Selected Works of Lu Xun, 4 volumes, translated by Yang Xianyi and Gladys Yang (Beijing: Foreign Languages Press, 1956–1960)—includes in volume 2 (1957), "My Views on Chastity" ("Wo zhi jielie guan"); "What Happens after Nora Leaves Home?" ("Nuola zou hou zenyang"); "More Roses without Blooms [excerpts]" ("Wuhua de qiangwei zhi er"); and "In Memory of Miss Liu Hezhen" ("Jinian Liu Hezhen jun") and "Literature of a Revolutionary Period" ("Geming shidai de wenxue"); in volume 3 (1959), "How I Came to Write Stories" ("Wo zenme zuoqi xiaoshuo lai"); in volume 4 (1960), "The Case of Mrs. Qin Lizhai" ("Lun Qin Lizhai furen zhuan"); and "Death" ("Si"); republished as *Lu Xun, Selected Works,* 4 volumes (Beijing: Foreign Languages Press, 1980);

The True Story of Ah Q, translated by Yang Xianyi and Gladys Yang (Beijing: Foreign Languages Press, 1972; Boston: Cheng & Tsui, 1990);

Silent China: Selected Writings of Lu Xun, edited and translated by Gladys Yang (Oxford: Oxford University Press, 1973);

Lu Xun: Writing for the Revolution: Essays by Lu Xun and Essays on Lu Xun from Chinese Literature Magazine (San Francisco: Red Sun, 1976);

Poems of Lu Hsun, translated by Huang Hsin-chyu (Hong Kong: Joint Publishing Company, 1979);

The Complete Stories of Lu Xun: Call to Arms, Wandering, translated by Yang Xianyi and Gladys Yang (Bloomington: Indiana University Press in association with Foreign Languages Press, Beijing, 1981);

Selected Poems, translated by W. J. F. Jenner (Beijing: Foreign Languages Press, 1982);

Lu Hsun Complete Poems: A Translation with Introduction and Annotation, edited and translated by David Y. Ch'en (Tempe: Center for Asian Studies, Arizona State University, 1988);

Diary of a Madman and Other Stories, translated by William A. Lyell (Honolulu: University of Hawai'i Press, 1990);

Warriors of the Spirit: The Early Wenyan Essays of Lu Xun, edited and translated by Jon Eugene von Kowallis (Berkeley: University of California, East Asian Institute Monographs, 2006)—includes "On Imbalanced Cultural Development" ("Wenhua pianzhi lun") and "On the Power of Māra Poetry" ("Moluo shi li shuo" [complete translation]).

OTHER: *Zhongguo xiaoshuo de lishi bianqian* [Historical Changes in Chinese Fiction], edited by Lu Xun (Xi'an: Xibei daxue chubanbu, 1925);

Xiaoshuo jiu wen chao [Old Anecdotes on Chinese Fiction], edited by Lu Xun (Beijing: Beixin shuju, 1926);

Tang Song chuanqi ji [Selected Tang and Song Stories], 2 volumes, edited by Lu Xun (Shanghai: Beixin shuju, 1927, 1928);

Beiping jianpu [Beiping Stationery], 6 volumes, edited by Lu Xun and Xidi [Zheng Zhenduo] (Beiping: Rongbaozhai, 1933);

Yin yu ji [Collection to Attract Jade], edited by Lu Xun (Shanghai: Sanxian shuwu, 1934);

Muke jicheng [A Milestone in Woodcuts], edited by Lu Xun (Shanghai: Tiemu yishu she, 1934);

Zhongguo xinwenxue daxi: Xiaoshuo er ji [China's New Literature Series: Fiction Volumes], edited by Lu Xun (Shanghai: Liangyou tushu yinshua gongsi, 1935);

Hai shang shu lin [Account of a Forest on the Sea], 2 volumes, translated by Qu Qiubai, edited by Lu Xun (Shanghai: Zhu Xia huai shuang she, 1936).

TRANSLATIONS: Jules Verne, *Yuejie lüxing* [A Trip to the Moon] (Tokyo: Jinhua she, 1903);

Verne, *Didi lüxing* [Journey to the Center of the Earth] (Nanjing: Qixin shuju, 1906);

Yuwai xiaoshuo [Tales from Abroad], 2 volumes, translated by Lu Xun, as Zhou Zhangshou, and Zhou Zuoren (Tokyo & Shanghai: Privately printed, 1909);

Friedrich Nietzsche, *Chalatusitela de xuyan* [Prologue to *Thus Spake Zarathustra*], *Xinchao* [New Tide], 2 (September 1920);

Vasilii Eroshenko, *Ailuoxianke tonghua ji* [Eroshenko's Tales for Children], translated by Lu Xun, Hu Yuzhi, Wang Fuquan, and others (Shanghai: Shangwu yinshuguan, 1922);

Mikhail Artzybashev, *Gongren Suihuilüefu* [Worker Shevyryov] (Shanghai: Shangwu yinshu guan, 1922);

Xiandai xiaoshuo yicong [Renditions of Modern Fiction], translated by Lu Xun, Zhou Zuoren, and Zhou Jianren (Shanghai: Shangwu yinshuguan, 1922);

Xiandai Riben xiaoshuo ji [A Collection of Modern Japanese Short Stories], translated by Lu Xun and Zhou Zuoren (Shanghai: Shangwu yinshuguan, 1923);

Kuriyagawa Hakuson, *Kumen de xiangzheng* [Symbols of Anxiety] (Beijing: Xinchao she, 1924);

Kuriyagawa, *Chu liao xiangya zhi ta* [Out of the Ivory Tower] (Beijing: Weiming she, 1925);

Katakami Shin, "Xin shidai de yugan" [Harbingers of a New Age], *Chun chao* [Spring Tide], 1 (May 1929);

Anatoli Lunacharsky, *Yishu lun* [On Art] (Shanghai: Dajiang shupu, 1929);

Lunacharsky, *Wenyi yu piping* [Literature and Criticism] (Shanghai: Shuimo shudian, 1929);

Georgii Plekhanov, *Yishulun* [On Art] (Shanghai: Guanghua shuju, 1930);

Iwasaki Akira, "Xiandai dianying yu youchan jieji" [Modern Film and the Bourgeoisie], *Mengya yuekan* [Sprouts Monthly], 1 (1 March 1930);

Aleksandr Fadeev, *Hui mie* [The Rout] (Shanghai: Dajiang shupu, 1931);

Aleksandr Yakolev, *Shi yue* [October] (Shanghai: Shenzhou guoguang she, 1933);

Maksim Gorky, *E'luosi de tonghua* [Russian Folktales] (Shanghai: Wenhua shenghuo chubanshe, 1935);

Nikolai Gogol, *Si hunling* [Dead Souls] (Shanghai: Shenghuo shudian, 1935);

Anton Chekhov, *Huai haizi he biede qiwen* [The Bad Child and Other Strange Tales] (Shanghai: Lianhua shuju, 1936);

Lu Xun yiwen ji [Lu Xun's Collected Translations], 10 volumes (Beijing: Renmin wenxue chubanshe, 1958).

Zhou Shuren, better known since the early 1920s by his pen name Lu Xun, is generally considered the father of modern Chinese literature and was regarded by many in his own day as the foremost representative of the nation's conscience. In 1995 he was hailed by Japanese Nobel laureate Ōe Kenzaburō as "the greatest writer Asia has produced in the twentieth century." His initial fame rested on a series of sometimes bleak, sometimes humorous, often satirical short stories written in the modern Chinese vernacular. But he also wrote poetry, prose, literary history, cultural criticism, and polemical essays. He gained renewed fame and influence as a master of the feuilleton, which he wielded as a rhetorical dagger first against the warlord government in Beijing in the late 1920s and then in the 1930s against the Nationalist Party, which took over the government of the republic from the warlords in 1927 but continued dictatorial rule.

The eldest of three surviving children, all boys (a sister died in infancy and a brother around age two), Zhou was born into a gentry family on 25 September 1881 in the town of Shaoxing (known in ancient times as Kuaiji in the former kingdom of Yue) on China's southeastern seaboard; today it is in the province of Zhejiang. His name at birth was Zhou Zhangshou; he was also known as Zhou Yucai. Under the pen name Zhou Zuoren the middle brother, Zhou Kuishan, also achieved prominence as a writer. The Zhou clan were absentee landlords, and Zhou Zhangshou's grandfather had risen to the upper echelons of the imperial civil service through the examination system. His mother was literate and eventually unbound her feet in response to an anti-foot-binding campaign. With her independent spirit she obviously made a stronger impression on Zhou than did his alcoholic, opium-smoking father, Zhou Boyi, for he adopted her surname, Lu, as part of his best-known pen name.

From the age of six Zhou was tutored in the Confucian classics—first at home by an uncle, then in a clan-run, one-room schoolhouse. There his teacher encouraged his extracurricular reading in texts such as an illustrated edition of the *Shanhaijing* (Classic of Mountains and Oceans), an ancient book about fantastic creatures and imaginary foreign countries; it became his favorite book as a child. These works, along with ghost stories; tales of the Taiping Rebellion of 1851 to 1864, which had a major impact on Shaoxing; and regional opera and local legends nurtured his interest in literature. In an unfinished biography Tang Tao stresses the importance of his growing up in the Shaoxing region for the formation of his unique personality and interests.

In 1893 Zhou's grandfather Zhou Fuqing was denounced by a personal enemy and arrested for abetting cheating on the imperial civil-service examinations. Although the offense was relatively common in those days, the law called for harsh punishment. Zhou Fuqing was initially sentenced to death, and because of fear of further reprisals against his family, Zhou Zhangshou and Zhou Kuishan were sent into hiding at the homes of maternal relatives in the countryside; the third brother, Zhou Jianren, was too young to be sent away. The experience became a traumatic memory for him: "I was sometimes even called a beggar," he recounts in "Lu Xun zizhuan" (Lu Xun's Autobiography), written in 1930 and published in volume eight of *Lu Xun quanji* (1981, The Complete Works of Lu Xun). In the preface to the short-story collection *Nahan* (1923, Outcry; translated as *Call to Arms*, 1981) he writes that "those who come down in the world will probably learn in the process what society is really like."

The one-room school in Shaoxing that Lu Xun attended as a child (from Jon Eugene von Kowallis, The Lyrical Lu Xun: A Study of His Classical-Style Verse, *1996; Thomas Cooper Library, University of South Carolina)*

Returning home six months later, after the danger had passed, Zhou watched as the family's resources were drained in appeals for clemency for his grandfather. The death sentence was eventually commuted, but the grandfather was imprisoned for almost seven years. Meanwhile, Zhou's father became ill. As the eldest son, Zhou was sent to a pawnshop with family heirlooms that he offered to a broker who handed the money down contemptuously. He then proceeded to an herbalist to procure the exotic medicines that had been prescribed for his father by a traditional physician of high repute in the locale. By the time his father died in 1896, these experiences had turned Zhou against traditional Chinese medicine for the rest of his life.

Because of the family's economic straits, in the spring of 1898 Zhou was withdrawn from the traditional studies that prepared young men for the old civil-service examinations and sent to the government-funded Jiangnan shuishi xuetang (Jiangnan Naval Academy) in Nanjing, where he could study on a scholarship. At this time he took the name Zhou Shuren. Within a year he transferred to the Kuangwu tielu xuetang (School of Mines and Railroads), run by the Jiangnan lushi xuetang (Jiangnan Army Academy). There he was impressed by the notion that Western science had served to prompt the enthusiasm for the reforms of the Meiji era (1867 to 1912) in Japan. He also gained a critical exposure to the nineteenth-century European doctrine of "social Darwinism" through Yan Fu's 1896 translation—more precisely, adaptation—of T. H. Huxley's *Evolution and Ethics* (1893). Reading about the "survival of the fittest" in the wake of China's defeat by Japan in 1895 and by the army of the Eight Allied Nations that suppressed the Boxer Rebellion in 1900 contributed to his vision of China as a weak nation pressed upon by dynamic competitors while being ruled by an effete dynasty bent on preserving its own privileges.

Zhou graduated from the School of Mines and Railroads in January 1902. The following month he received a scholarship, administered through the office of the Qing Dynasty viceroy for the Jiangnan region, to study in Japan. For the first two years he studied Japanese at the Kōbun Institute in Tokyo. His fellow provincial Xu Shoushang, who attended the school in 1902 and remained a friend for the rest of his life, recalled that Zhou's desk was covered with books, including the poetry of Qu Yuan; a work on George Gordon, Lord Byron; a biography of Friedrich Nietzsche (probably by Tobari Chikufû); and works on Greek and Roman mythology. From this testimony it seems that Zhou's attraction to the writers he later called the "Māra poets" was already forming. *Māra* was Zhou's more neutral, Sanskrit-based translation of "satanic," the English Poet Laureate Robert Southey's pejorative epithet for Byron and his school of poetry. Aside from Byron, whom Zhou placed at the head of his list, the group included Byron's friend and fellow Englishman Percy Bysshe Shelley, the Russians Aleksandr Pushkin and Mikhail Lermontov, the Poles Adam Mickiewicz and Juliusz Słowacki, and the Hungarian Sándor Pettöfi, who wrote revolutionary verse around 1848. What Zhou appreciated most about this group of romantic poets, as he expresses it in his nine-part 1908 treatise "Moluo shi li shuo" (translated as "On the Power of Māra Poetry," 1996)—published in *Henan*, a Japanese journal published by Chinese students and collected in his *Fen* (1927, The Grave)—was their passionate commitment to justice for the "captive nations," the oppressed peoples of Greece, Eastern Europe, and the Baltic held down by the Ottoman Turks, Tsarist Russia, and the Austro-Hungarian Empire. He drew a connection between the fates of these countries and the condition of China under the rule of the alien Manchu Qing Dynasty; the legacy of Mongol, Manchu, Western, and Japanese invasion; and the shame of subjugation. He suggests that China needs to produce figures like Byron—"jingshenjie zhi zhanshi" (warriors in the spiritual realm)—with the courage to awaken the nation to its plight and shake its people out of their lethargy and self-deception. In mid 1903 he published in two issues of *Zhejiang chao* (Zhejiang Tide), a monthly magazine edited by Chinese students in Japan, the article "Sibada zhi hun" (The Soul of Sparta), in which he calls on the youth of China to learn from the self-sacrificing spirit of the ancient Spartan resistance against the invading Persians at Thermopylae; it is included in his *Jiwai ji* (1935, Collection of the Uncollected). But he remained disposed toward writing and study rather than direct engagement with political causes.

Reformers such as Yan Fu and Liang Qichao had written about the potential for popularizing new knowledge through fiction, and in 1903 Zhou began a project aimed at the popularization of science. He first made abridged translations of two Jules Verne novels (1903, 1906) in the hope that reading science fiction would inspire an enthusiasm for scientific invention among Chinese youth. Also, thinking back on his father's illness and death, he decided that he could persuade people in China of the validity of reform by curing their illnesses with Western medicine. Thus, in the autumn of 1904 he entered Sendai Provincial Medical Academy in northern Honshû. But his dream was shattered in his second year of medical studies. In biology classes lantern slides were used to show magnified photographs of microbes; if time remained at the end of the period, the instructor might show slides of news events. The 1904–1905 Russo-Japanese War was then being fought in Manchuria (known in Chinese as Dongbei [the Northeast]); Lu Xun writes in the preface to *Nahan* that one day the students were shown a slide of a Chinese man about to be beheaded by the Japanese for spying for the Russians. He was dismayed at the crowd of Chinese onlookers, "those people milling around who had just come to enjoy the spectacle of seeing someone's head lopped off":

> I dropped out of school before the semester was over and went back to Tokyo, because this one slide had convinced me that the study of medicine was no longer important. For it matters little how physically strong the bodies of a citizenry racked by its own ignorance may be. As they are in their present state, they are good for nothing more than to serve as victims or provide the audiences at such spectacles. So it is not necessarily lamentable even if large numbers of them perish from illness. The most important task that lay ahead, then, was to change them in spirit; and since I thought that literature might serve this purpose, I decided to promote a literary movement.

In June 1906 Zhou made a brief trip back to China in response to a letter from his mother, who had feigned illness to get him to return for an arranged marriage to Zhu An, the daughter of a local gentry family. Unhappy but feeling unable to refuse, he went through with the ceremony. A few days later, he returned to Japan, taking his brother Kuishan with him but leaving his bride behind.

In the summer of 1908 the Zhou brothers attended lectures by the exiled scholar and former newspaper editor Zhang Taiyan (pseudonym of Zhang Binglin) on the ancient etymological dictionary *Shuowen jiezi*. Zhang, who had served time in prison for publishing Zou Rong's subversive *Geming jun* (1903; translated as *The Revolutionary Army*, 1968), peppered his lectures with anti-Manchu remarks, deriding the ruling house as descendants of primitive tribesmen from the periphery of the civilized world who had usurped the Chinese throne and whose cruelty, ineptitude, and misrule had brought the nation to the verge of collapse in the face of pressure from the imperialist powers of the West and Japan. But Zhang's racial orientation held little appeal for Zhou, who was more interested in developing a critique of what had gone wrong with China internally. Zhang's influence can be most directly seen in the laconic style of prose that Zhou had begun developing from reading Zhang's works.

The major essays of Zhou's early period were published in 1908 in *Henan*. In "Wenhua pianzhi lun" (translated as "On Imbalanced Cultural Development," 2005) he analyzes the rise and problems of the West, drawing conclusions relevant to China's modernization process. "Moluo shi li shuo" deals with the role literature can play in a nation's cultural, political, and social transformation and may be viewed as a literary manifesto written at the outset of his career. In "Po e'sheng lun" (translated as "Toward a Refutation of the Voices of Evil," 1986) he criticizes China's gentry for blaming the country's backwardness on the "ignorance and superstition" of the peasants, rather than admitting their own responsibility. He also critiques social Darwinism as a pseudoscientific theory used by the industrialized nations to justify their subjugation of weaker countries. *Henan* was banned by the Japanese government at the request of the Qing authorities before Zhou could publish a sequel to "Moluo shi li shuo."

In 1909 the Zhou brothers published their first short-story translations in two volumes under the title *Yuwai xiaoshuo* (Tales from Abroad); the works are rendered in an erudite style of Classical Chinese. The work presents an informed selection of stories by Oscar Wilde from England; Edgar Allan Poe from the United States; Guy de Maupassant and Marcel Schwob from France; Hans Christian Andersen from Denmark; Sergei Stepniak (pseudonym of Sergei Kravchinski), Vsevolod Garshin, Anton Chekhov, Fyodor Sologub, and Leonid Andreev from Russia; Henryk Sienkiewicz from Poland; Milena Mrazovic from Bosnia; Argyris Ephtaliotis from Greece; and Juhani Aho from Finland. Zhou Shuren conceived of the collection and chose the stories but translated only two by Andreev and one by Garshin; the rest were translated by Zhou Zuoren, then edited for style by Zhou Shuren.

During this period Zhou Shuren was most influenced by Sienkiewicz and Nikolai Gogol. From Sienkiewicz and Gogol, according to Zhou Zuoren's "Guanyu Xu Xun zhi er" (1937, On Lu Xun II), he learned the technique of maintaining a distance in the treatment of cruelty and oppression. He was also impressed by Andreev, Garshin, and the Japanese authors Natsume Sōseki and Mori Ogai. From Natsume, Zuoren observed in 1936 in "Guanyu Lu Xun zhi er" Zhou Shuren obtained a model for "the poignant wit and subtle beauty" of his satire.

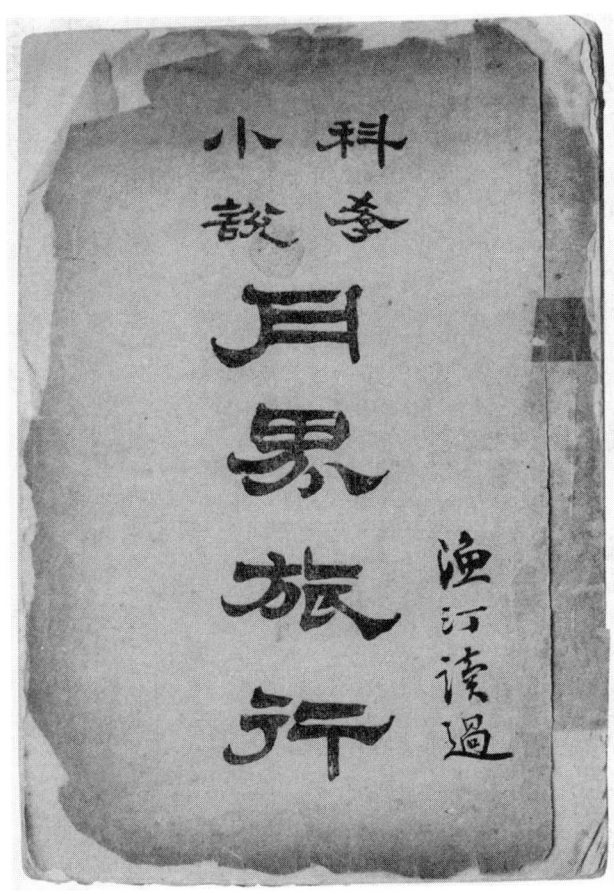

Cover for Yuejie lüxing *(A Trip to the Moon)*, Lu Xun's 1903 translation of Jules Verne's novel De la Terre à la lune *(1865; translated as* From the Earth to the Moon, *1869), (from Yu Runqi, ed.,* Tang Tao cang shu, *2004; Bruccoli Clark Layman Archives)*

Although Zhou Shuren had placed high hopes on these translations to inspire his compatriots, the sales figures in Tokyo were only twenty copies for volume one and no more than that for volume two. The book fared no better in Shanghai. Zhou later noted that the foreign fiction for which Chinese readers had acquired a taste mostly comprised the works of H. Rider Haggard and Sir Arthur Conan Doyle, which turned on suspense, adventure, and sensation. Part of the problem, however, was that the abstruse language used by the Zhou brothers under the influence of Zhang Taiyan's archaistic style proved a challenge even to highly educated readers; another part lay in their penchant for literalness, which made their translations somewhat choppy; and yet another part was their lack of a distributor in China, where the books were sold through a silk-goods shop.

Because he believed that China had much to learn from abroad, Lu Xun's translations over a period of four decades were vast and wide-ranging; in terms of volume they dwarfed his creative output. He worked mostly from Japanese but also from German versions, producing ten substantial volumes of translations of Eastern European, Russian, Japanese, and Western European texts. In addition to Verne's science fiction, they include Vasilii Eroshenko's tales for children (1922); Kuriyagawa Hakuson's *Kumon no shôchô* (1924, Symbols of Anxiety), a Freudian-influenced work on the psychological aspects of literary creation; the critical works of Anatoly Lunacharsky (1929), Georgii Plekhanov, and Katakami Shin (1929); Maksim Gor'ky's Russian fables (1935); Gogol's *Pokhozhdeniia Chichikova, ili Mertvye dushi* (1842, The Adventures of Chichikov, or Dead Souls [1935]); and Chekhov's stories (1936).

In 1909 Zhou Shuren returned to China and took a job teaching science at the Zhejiang liangji shifan xuetang (Zhejiang Normal School) in Hangzhou, partly to finance Zuoren's university studies in literature. Zuoren had married Nobuko, their Japanese former servant, and had decided to remain in Japan.

When the 1911 revolution began, Zhou was teaching in a middle school in Shaoxing. He was among the first to realize that though the Qing Dynasty had been overthrown, little else had changed. In fact, the nightmare scenario he had foreseen in his essay "Wenhua pianzhi lun" seemed to be materializing in the form of a republic. Warlords, old-style gentry, and opportunists of every sort took over the government at the national and local levels, and the weak, far from being liberated, became victims. He addresses the failure of the revolution in several of his short stories and particularly with the black humor of his novella "A Q zheng zhuan" (1923, The True Biography of A Q; translated as "Our Story of Ah Q," 1941).

Zhou's classmate from Japan, Xu Shoushang, obtained a position for Zhou at the new Ministry of Education through Cai Yuanpei, who was also a native of Shaoxing. The ministry was initially located in Nanjing but moved to Beijing in 1912. The move came at a particularly fortunate juncture for Zhou, because tension had arisen between him and Wang Jinfa, a petty warlord who had taken power in Shaoxing. Zhou left his wife behind and lived at the Shaoxing huiguan (Hostel), where many of his fellow townsmen boarded and congregated when in Beijing. In response to a program initiated by Cai, he wrote an article on the necessity of promoting aesthetic education, "Ni bobu meishu yijian shu" (1913, A Proposal for the Dissemination of the Arts), and lectured on aesthetics. The liberal Cai was forced to resign from the ministry under pressure from Yuan Shikai, the dictatorial president and former Qing general who had betrayed the dynasty (and later betrayed the republic by attempting to proclaim himself emperor). As the political situation grew increasingly discouraging, Zhou retreated into the study of antiquity. He researched Buddhist writings, copied ancient bronze and stone inscriptions, and collated historical materials about his native region.

Yuan Shikai's death marked the beginning of the Warlord Era of 1916 to 1927, a period of political chaos in which military men seized territory and fought for control of Beijing and national power. In 1919 the warlord government in Beijing agreed to terms dictated by Japan at the Versailles peace conference after World War I, and protests by college students in Beijing spread nationwide. The date of the Beijing demonstration, 4 May 1919, was adopted to name the broad cultural and political reform movement of the 1910s and 1920s. Two years before 1919, the "May Fourth Era" in literature began with demands for "literary reform" and "literary revolution" by Hu Shi and Chen Duxiu, both of whom gave early encouragement to Zhou's literary career. Hu and Chen argued that Chinese literature should abandon Classical Chinese and ancient models in favor of vernacular language and innovation. Chiefly at the urging of Chen and of Qian Xuantong, a former classmate from the course taught by Zhang Taiyan, Zhou began in April 1918 to contribute stories to *Xin qingnian* (New Youth), a liberal magazine with a nationwide circulation; it was a principal mouthpiece of the New Culture Movement, which was closely allied with the May Fourth Movement. He first used the pen name Lu Xun for the story "Kuangren riji" (translated as "A Madman's Diary," 1981) in the May 1918 issue of *Xin qingnian*.

The readers of *Xin qingnian* were mostly young intellectuals eager to resolve the contradiction between the dictates of tradition and the imperative to change. Lu Xun had grappled with this problem for years, and this experience, more than anything else, gave him the ability to strike a responsive chord with his readers. In a short time he became nationally famous. Aside from his personal experiences, the material for his stories was drawn, he explains in "Wo zenme zuoqi xiaoshuo lai" (translated as "How I Came to Write Stories," 1959), first published in his *Chuangzuo de jingyan* (1933, The Experience of Creation), "from the plight of unfortunates in a sick society. It was my intention to expose this sickness and suffering so as to draw attention to it, in the hope that a cure might thereby be sought." His goal was not to castigate tradition but to criticize its misappropriation.

From 1918 to 1926 Lu Xun wrote stories in which the Shaoxing of his childhood—variously referred to as "S Cheng" (S-town), "Luzhen" (Luville), and "Weizhuang" (Nowheresville)—is reworked into a fictional microcosm for all of China, and its inhabitants

Covers for the first (right) and third editions of Lu Xun's first story collection, Nahan (1923, Outcry; translated as Call to Arms, 1981). The third edition, published in 1924, reproduces Xun's calligraphy for the title; the first edition uses a standard typeface (from Yu Runqi, ed., Tang Tao cang shu, 2004; Bruccoli Clark Layman Archives).

are transformed into representational types. The stories are in many ways thematically related to his essays of this period, examining the cruelty of conventional attitudes and beliefs. V. I. Semanov points to what makes Lu Xun's social critique so thoroughgoing: his stories "not only show disgust for those who prevent 'the little guy' from struggling or even crawling up the social ladder, he brands the slaves themselves for naively believing that they will secure freedom from the hands of their masters."

Lu Xun was a conscious stylist: he went over his stories again and again, working hard on wording and striving to eliminate inconsequential detail. The stories are often stark and have been compared to a traditional woodblock print in which the characters are delineated with a minimum of lines and an economical use of shading. His first story to appear in *Xin qingnian*, "Kuangren Riji," was collected as the first story in *Nahan*. Although it borrows elements from Gogol's "Zapiski sumasshedshego" (1835, The Diary of a Madman), it differs significantly from its Russian predecessor both in form and in content. The story established the theme with which Lu Xun became identified by most of his Chinese readers: the denunciation of traditional ethical codes as hypocritical cant formulated by the oppressors to justify an inhumane order that permits the strong to prey on the weak. A scholar treated as a paranoiac by his family and the community notices that the work of Chinese history he is reading "contains no dates or periods, only the words 'benevolence,' 'righteousness,' and 'morality' [*ren, yi,* and *daode*] scrawled throughout its pages." Continuing his reading far into the night, he makes out in the spaces between the lines of printed characters that the whole of history "is filled with two words: 'Eat people!'" The reader of the story suspects that the madman sees more clearly than those who try to ignore the brutal aspects of society. Lu Xun later wrote that he had used cannibalism in this story as a metaphor for exploitation and inhumanity. "Kuangren Riji" was structurally innovative, taking the form of a

Illustration by Feng Zikai for a 1949 edition of Lu Xun's novella A Q zheng zhuan *(translated as "Our Story of Ah Q," 1941), which was first published in 1921 and collected in* Nahan *two years later (Wason Collection on East Asia–China, Kroch Asia Library, Cornell University)*

quirky, random diary, and it quickly engendered discussion among Chinese intellectuals concerning the "cannibalistic" nature of their society's traditional social mores and the old family system. Largely owing to its Western-influenced technique, as well as the fact that it was written primarily in the colloquial language, "Kuangren Riji" is considered China's first "modern" short story.

"Kong Yiji" (translated as "Kong Yiji," 1981), written in March 1919, was published in *Xin qingnian* in April 1919 and is included in *Nahan*. The title of the story is the rather singular name of the protagonist: *yi* and *ji* are the first characters in a child's calligraphy primer, and Kong is the surname of the sage known in English as Confucius; hence, the name means something like "Confucius ABC." A scholar who has failed the official examinations and ekes out a meager living copying books for wealthy families, Kong Yiji is accepted neither by the gentry nor by the peasants, with whom he is forced to stand to drink his wine in the Xianheng (Prosperity for All) Wineshop. The narrator, a boy employed by the shop as a wine warmer, initially joins the crowd in laughing at Kong but gradually develops a guarded sympathy for him. In the end Kong is beaten so severely for stealing the books he was entrusted to copy that he is crippled; he eventually disappears from the town altogether. The narrator is left to wonder if he really is dead, as rumor has it. Lu Xun called this story his favorite, which underscores the value he placed on the qualities of brevity, subtle suggestion, and irony, as well as the importance he gave to its theme of man's inhumanity to man.

"Yao" (translated as "Medicine," 1981), written in April 1919, was published in *Xin qingnian* in May 1919 and collected in *Nahan*. "Yao" begins in the late Qing era and involves the beheading of a revolutionist, an intellectual concerned for the welfare of his people. The execution is depicted only indirectly, through the description of the reaction of the crowd as seen from a distance by an old man. The old man then warily approaches the executioner, "whose entire body was [clad in] black," to buy a *mantou* (steamed bun) dipped in fresh blood—a traditional cure for the tuberculosis from which his young son suffers. After the boy dies, exposing the belief in the cure as a superstition, his mother meets the revolutionist's mother in the graveyard where their sons are buried. Mistaking a Western-style wreath left there in secret, perhaps by his comrades, for a sign from the spirit world, the revolutionist's mother prays to her son to make a crow perched on a branch fly down to his grave as a sign that his death will be avenged. At first nothing happens; but after the mothers decide to leave and walk twenty or thirty paces away together, the silence is pierced by a loud caw from the crow. As they turn to look, startled, it "spread its wings, stood up, then flew off straight as an arrow into the distant sky."

In his *History of Modern Chinese Fiction* (1971) C. T. Hsia points to this scene as an important turning point for China. Milena Dolezelová-Velingerova concludes her structuralist analysis of the story by speculating that the crow represents "a frightening but cathartic symbol of revolution." One might also interpret its flight away from the grave as a sign that the path ahead will be determined not by the spirit world but by human initiative.

In 1920 Lu Xun was invited to teach Chinese literature at Beijing University. Other institutions in the capital followed suit—most notably, Beijing nüzi gaodeng shifan xuexiao (Beijing Women's Higher Normal School), where he began teaching in October 1923.

"Guxiang" (My Old Hometown; translated as "My Old Home," 1981), written in January 1921, was published in *Xin qingnian* in May 1921 and collected in *Nahan*. It was, in part, inspired by Lu Xun's trip south in December 1919 to help his mother sell off the family home and join him in Beijing; his wife also joined him at this time. It is an artistic re-creation of his feelings on his last trip home. The opening paragraph reads:

> I braved the bitter cold, to return over two thousand *li* to the old home I had left over twenty years ago. Though it was late winter, as we gradually neared my hometown, the weather became wet and overcast, and a cold wind blew through the cabin of our boat, howling, while all one could see through the cracks in the boat's covering were a few desolate villages, scattered far and near, under the pallid yellow sky. My heart was unable to hold back the feeling of sadness that came over it.

Attempting to reconnect with the poverty-stricken Runtu, a childhood friend who can now only meekly address him as "Lao Ye!" (Master!), the narrator learns that there is no going back. But his nephew, Hong'er, makes friends with Runtu's youngest son, Shuisheng, causing the narrator to muse:

> although there is such a barrier between Runtu and myself, our children still have much in common, for wasn't Hong'er thinking of Shuisheng just now? I hope they will not be like us, that they will not allow a barrier to grow up between them. But again I would not like them, because they want to be one, to have a treadmill existence like mine, nor to suffer like Runtu until they become stupefied, nor yet, like others, to devote all their energies to dissipation. They should have a new life, a life we never experienced. . . .
>
> As I dozed, a stretch of jade-green seashore spread itself before my eyes, and above a round golden moon hung from a deep blue sky. I thought: hope cannot be said to exist, nor can it be said not to exist. It is just like roads across the earth. For actually the earth had no roads to begin with, but when many men pass one way, a road is made.

The Communists shortened the last sentence to an axiom that they then ascribed to Lu Xun: "Lu shi ren zou chulai de!" (A road is formed by people walking it!).

The best known of Lu Xun's fictional creations is the nine-part novella "A Q zheng zhuan," serialized in the weekly literary supplement of the Beijing newspaper *Chen bao* (Morning Post) in 1921 under the pseudonym Ba Ren (A Simple Man) and collected in *Nahan*. It is a tragicomic tale of a homeless coolie whose given name is written with the Latin letter Q, suggesting pictographically (and perhaps also as a pun on the English word *queue*) the head of a typical Chinese man during the last years of the Qing era with his queue, or pigtail, hanging down. In that sense A Q is "John Chinaman," a representative both of the victimization of his nation and of its own benighted thinking: A Q is victim and oppressor at different points in the story. But in another sense he is a new Everyman, an international symbol of human folly whose penchant for self-delusion is crystallized in his "jingshen shengli fa" (method of attaining psychological victories): whenever he is humiliated by a rival, he quickly turns the experience around in his mind and imagines himself to have come out on top. The novella ends with A Q's ignoble execution, by firing squad instead of beheading, under the newly proclaimed republic. The disappointed crowd of onlookers in Weizhuang conclude that they have followed the cart to his execution for nothing.

"A Q zheng zhuan" is often read as a national allegory, but when it was published, several individuals thought themselves to be the butt of the satire; some wrote letters to the newspaper in protest. Lu Xun was clearly influenced by the "national character" discourse in vogue when he studied in Japan at the turn of the century, as discussed by Lydia He Liu, and also by Eastern European models, such as Sienkiewicz's "Bartek Zwyciezca" (1882, Bartek the Victor), as Patrick D. Hanan explains; but A Q is Lu Xun's own unforgettable creation. The novella was made into a motion picture in 1981 with a screenplay by the playwright Chen Baichen that preserves much of the humor of the original.

In July 1923 Lu Xun and Shou Zuoren, once his closest companion, had a permanent falling-out. Although a charge of sexual harassment against Lu Xun brought by Zuoren's wife, Nobuko, precipitated the break, both Bonnie S. McDougall and Zhou Haiying, Lu Xun's son, argue that there is no real evidence for such an incident having occurred. Perhaps Zuoren simply used the accusation as a excuse to throw off his older brother's smothering influence; as David E. Pollard observes, Zuoren was an academician in his own right and wanted to develop as a writer in different directions from Lu Xun.

In 1923–1924 Lu Xun published *Zhongguo xiaoshuo shilüe* (translated as *A Brief History of Chinese Fiction*, 1959); the pioneering work of its type, it remains largely unsurpassed today. In 1924 he and Lin Yutang founded the literary journal *Yusi* (Threads of Talk).

In "Zhufu" (Benediction; translated as "The New-Year Sacrifice," 1981), written in 1924 and included in Lu Xun's second story collection, *Panghuang* (1926, Hesitation; translated as *Wandering*, 1981), the narrator is an intellectual who has come home for a visit after a long absence studying abroad and working the hereafter. Cast out of the uncle's home, she wanders the streets. The story ends with a passage describing the narrator's reaction to the Lunar New Year celebration immediately after her death: "the doubt which had preyed on my mind from dawn till night was swept clean away by the festive atmosphere, and I felt only that the saints of heaven and earth had accepted the sacrifice and incense and were reeling with intoxication in the sky, preparing to give Luzhen's people boundless good fortune." If this ending is read ironically, the "benediction" of the title becomes a curse: the weak are trampled by the powerful, and heaven is indifferent.

Much of "Zhufu" has to do with the narrator's inability to communicate meaningfully with the townspeople; thus, it encapsulates the tragedy not only of Xianglin Sao but also of China's modern intelligentsia and their inability to change, or even influence, conditions in the country. This aspect of the story is lost in the 1956 movie adaptation; the screenplay by Xia Yan eliminates the narrator's character, concentrating on Xianglin Sao's tragedy and emphasizing an antisuperstition theme. The movie also creates positive characters among the workers and peasants; such characters are largely absent from the original story.

Lu Xun's only story set in Beijing, "Feizao" (translated as "Soap," 1981), was serialized in the 27 and 28 March 1924 issues of the supplement to the Beijing newspaper *Cherbao* (Morning News) and collected in *Panghuang*. It satirizes hypocrisy and sexist attitudes among conservative urbanites. Mr. Siming–his name means "Four Stone Tablets," signifying a moral exemplar–is an absentee landlord who spends his days bullying his wife and browbeating his son, whom he suspects of harboring liberal sympathies. One day he sees a young woman begging in the street, accompanied by an old lady. Moved by his mistaken idea that the young woman gives the money to the older one–her grandmother, Mr. Siming assumes–he and his associates in the Moral Rearmament League place an advertisement in a newspaper for a contest calling for the best essay in praise of filial piety. The uncontrollable laughter of a middle-aged friend at a reported remark about how much a good scrubbing with a cake of soap would do for the girl's sex appeal throws Siming's household into an uproar.

In "Zai jiulou shang" (In the Wineshop; translated as "In the Tavern," 1981), written in 1924, published that same year in *Xiaoshuo yuebao* (Short Story Monthly), and collected in *Panghuang*, the narrator returns to his hometown and goes to a wineshop; there he encounters an old friend from school, Lü Weifu. The character for *Lü*, two pictograms meaning "mouth" joined together, hints that he is an alter ego of the narrator. Lü has come back to town at the urging of his

Cover for a 1947 edition of Lu Xun's second short-story collection, Panghuang (Hesitation; translated as Wandering, 1981), first published in 1926 (Wason Collection on East Asia–China, Kroch Asia Library, Cornell University)

in the capital. He is profoundly disturbed by his encounters with his conservative uncle and the unfolding story of one of the uncle's servants, Xianglin Sao (Sister-in-Law Auspicious Grove). The peasant woman is a widow whose son by her second husband was carried off by a wolf. As Xianglin Sao repeats her tragic tale over and over, the villagers tire of hearing it and begin to mock her; the uncle wants to rid himself of her because, as a widow, she is inauspicious. She presses the narrator with the question, "When people die, do their souls live on?" Not knowing the context of her question and hoping to comfort her, he suggests that there may, indeed, be life after death. The answer only increases her anxiety: Liu Ma, a rival servant in the household, has told her that because she was married twice, she will be sawed in two by King Yama of the Netherworld so that she can be divided between her two husbands in mother to move the grave of his younger brother, which is being threatened by a rising river. He hires a team of men to dig up the grave and discovers that nothing remains of his brother. Yü-sheng Lin is among the commentators who have speculated that the absence of any trace of the body, even hair, suggests allegorically that the substance of tradition is gone. Lü is also searching for a pure-hearted peasant girl from his past, Ah Shun, to whom he wants to give some velvet flowers. When he learns that she has died, he tries to leave the flowers for her younger sister, a superficial girl who rebuffs the stranger. Lü has compromised his ideals to make a living: his goal was to teach mathematics and modern subjects to the nation's youth, but he teaches the Confucian classics and the *Nüer jing* (Canon for Girls), because his students' parents do not want the subjects he learned abroad taught to their children. He concludes, "Just think: is there even one thing that turned out as we hoped of all we planned in those days?" At the end the narrator pays the bill and walks off in an opposite direction from Lü, refreshed by the cold wind and the snow beating against his face. One reading of this ending is that the narrator intends to struggle on, despite the disillusionment of his interlocutor.

"Guduzhe" (The Loner; translated as "The Misanthrope," 1981) was written in 1925 and first published in *Panghuang*. Wei Lianshi, who majored in zoology abroad, ends up teaching history in a middle school in S-town. A bachelor, he spends his evenings at home talking with a group of intellectuals. The narrator says:

> I wanted very much to ask why he had remained single for so long, but I did not know him well enough. Once you got to know him, he was a good talker and full of ideas, many of them quite remarkable. But what exasperated me were some of his guests. As a result, probably, of reading [Yu Dafu's story] "Sinking," they went around referring to themselves as "young unfortunates" or "superfluous men"; and, sprawling on the big chairs like lazy and arrogant crabs, they would sigh, smoke, and frown all at the same time.

An overly sensitive idealist, Wei offends people and loses his job. He appeals to the narrator, who has gone back to Beijing and is powerless to help. Eventually, Wei becomes a private secretary to a warlord, whereupon he gains tremendous prestige in the community that once spurned him; the warlord-controlled press celebrates him in its society pages. Wei dies; when the narrator returns for the funeral, he is surprised to see Wei dressed in a uniform: "khaki military trousers with broad red stripes, and a tunic with glittering epaulettes. . . . In his awkward costume he lay placidly, with closed mouth and eyes. There seemed to be an ironical smile on his lips, mocking the ridiculous corpse." Wei's transformation from *wen* (literary) to *wu* (military) symbolizes the compromises made by a would-be reformer.

Female protagonists are featured in "Shangshi" (translated as "Regret for the Past," 1981) and "Lihun" (translated as "The Divorce," 1981). In "Shangshi," written in 1925 and first published in *Panghuang*, the young couple Juansheng and Zijun thwart convention in the early years of the republic by living together, but they are ground down by economic pressures after Juansheng loses his job because of the scandal their cohabitation creates. Zijun, the stronger of the two, urges him to work as a self-employed literary translator; but he loses heart and sends her home, where she is received with scorn. After she dies, Juansheng regrets having given up. He visits their old home on Jizhao hutong (Lucky Lane) and is startled by the unexpected return of their abandoned and half-starved dog. His closing reflection is an ironic play on Xianglin Sao's question to the narrator of "Zhufu" about life after death:

> If only there really were ghosts, really were a hell! Then, no matter how the infernal wind roared, I would seek out Zijun and tell her to her face of my remorse and grief, to beg her for forgiveness. Failing this, the poisonous flames of hell would simply engulf me and fiercely consume all my remorse and grief.
>
> In the whirlwind and flames I would put my arms round Zijun and ask her pardon, or let her take her revenge. . . .

In "Lihun," also published in 1925 in *Yusi* and included in *Panghuang*, the assertive Ai Gu (Loving Girl) is denied justice in her divorce "hearing" by the town patriarchs. The gentry adjudicators, headed by a man referred to as "Seventh Master," pretend to consult a person with a "Western education" to justify their decision, while Seventh Master, a self-styled antiquarian, rubs his nose with a jade anus-stopper recently excavated from a Han-era tomb.

Lu Xun's position on women in Chinese society is even clearer in his essays than in his stories. He stresses the importance of economic and legal rights for women in "Nuola zou hou zenyang" (translated as "What Happens after Nora Leaves Home?" 1957), a lecture he delivered at the Beijing Women's Higher Normal School on 26 December 1923 and collected in *Fen*, and he attacks the hypocritical attitudes toward women in both traditional and contemporary society in "Wo zhi jielie guan," published in *Xin qingnian* (New Youth) in 1918 (translated as "My Views on Chastity," 1957) and "Lun Qin Lizhai furen zhuan" (translated as "The Case of Mrs. Qin Lizhai," 1961), included in *Fen*

Lu Xun with his long-time lover, Xu Guangping, and their son, Haiying, in 1933 (from Zhongguo dabaike quanshu, ed., Zhongguo wenxue, volume 2, 1986; Collection of Thomas Moran)

and *Huabian wenxue* (1936, Fringed Literature), respectively. These essays are but three of many examples.

In a 1925 political dispute Lu Xun sided with student activists against Yang Yinyu, the conservative American-educated woman chancellor of Beijing Women's Higher Normal School, which resulted in his being fired by the Ministry of Education. He was reinstated after a lawsuit, but the controversy continued in his *bizhan* (pen war) against Chen Yuan (Chen Xiying), a British-educated professor and prominent literary critic who supported Yang, and others, including Liang Shiqiu, who were associated with the conservative minister of education Zhang Shizhao. The debate spilled over into larger questions of philosophy and the role of the intellectual in society.

Sometime between July and October 1925 Lu Xun entered into a relationship with a former student, Xu Guangping, while remaining married to Zhu An. The product of this intense period is the volume of prose poetry *Yecao* (1927; translated as *Wild Grass*, 1974), a somberly lyrical work compared by Jaroslav Průšek

and Leo Ou-fan Lee with Charles Baudelaire's *Les Fleurs du mal* (1857; translated as *The Flowers of Evil*, 1909). The twenty-three pieces in *Yecao* were written primarily between 1 December 1924 and 19 April 1926 and first published serially in *Yusi*; prototypes of several pieces, published in *Guomin gongbao* (National Gazette) in August and September 1919, are gathered as "Ziyan ziyu" (Talking to Myself) in the 1991 edition of *Lu Xun quanji*. Lu Xun's "tici" (inscription or foreword) speaks in veiled terms of lives having been "trampled upon and mown down," perhaps during the Nationalist purge of the Communists on 12 April 1927 in Shanghai and on 15 April in Guangzhou, and of a "subterranean fire" that "is spreading, raging, underground," perhaps referring to the forces of the revolution, which had been driven underground. The foreword was banned by Nationalist censors in 1931 and not restored to the collection until the compendium *Lu Xun sanshi nian ji* (Lu Xun's Works over Thirty Years) came out in Shanghai in 1941 during the Gudao shiqi (Orphan Island period), when the International Settlement and French concession remained under the control of European powers and were encircled by the invading Japanese army.

The pieces in this short collection are often called "prose poems"; but perhaps it is more accurate to think of them as "poetic prose," because only one—a spoof—is in verse form, and several resemble short stories and autobiographical fiction. Since the 1920s they have been singled out by Chinese critics for the highest praise accorded to any examples of the new *baihua wen* (writings in vernacular Chinese) since the literary revolution began around 1917. The critic Tsi-an Hsia writes of "the strange beauty of 'frozen flames,'" an image in *Yecao*, and expresses the opinion that Lu Xun "let *paihua* [baihua] do things that it had never done before—things not even the best classical writers had ever thought of doing in *wen-yan* [Classical Chinese]." He suggests that the lyrical imagery of *Yecao* is imbued with "a kind of terror and anxiety, an experience which we might call modern." In *Voices from the Iron House: A Study of Lu Xun* (1987) Lee comments that the most successful of the pieces present a linguistic texturing that takes on metaphorical layers of meaning and constitute the essential core of Lu Xun's modernist project. Interpretations of the pieces have been many and diverse. Susanne Weigelin-Schwierdrzik and Katrin Sievers propose in their unpublished paper "The Hidden Message of *Yecao*" (1995) that some of the pieces were written in response to philosophical points in the works of Nietzsche. (Lu Xun had studied Nietzsche during his first years in Japan and had subsequently embarked on a translation of *Also sprach Zarathustra: Ein Buch für Alle und Keinen* [1883–1885; translated as *Thus Spake*

Zarathustra: A Book for All and None, 1896]. His translation of the prologue into vernacular Chinese was published in *Xinchao* [New Tide] in September 1920; he had already translated the prologue and the first three sections of the book into Classical Chinese in 1918, but this translation was not published during his lifetime.)

Lu Xun's protégé Feng Xuefeng published a somewhat forced Marxist reading of *Yecao* titled *Lun "Yecao"* (On *Wild Grass*) three years after the founding of the People's Republic of China in 1949, shortly before he was purged as a rightist. In *"Yecao" yanjiu* (1982, Research on *Wild Grass*) Sun Yushi cautions that "*Yecao*, like Lu Xun, is a product of an era and its history" and that only by acquiring a familiarity with the historical background of the works can one understand their meaning. *Yecao* is a product of the Warlord Era, when Beijing was under the repressive control of "Chief Executive" Duan Qirui; the warlords Zhang Zuolin, Wu Peifu, Cao Kun, and Feng Yuxiang vied for power; and Japan sought to increase its control over Manchuria and the whole of northern China. It was a bleak period in Lu Xun's life, as two of his former students at Beijing Women's Higher Normal School, Liu Hezhen and Yang Dequn, were among the more than forty people gunned down by troops of the Duan Qirui government on 18 March 1926 during a demonstration in front of Government House in Beijing to protest government compliance with Japanese interference in China. In *"Yecao Yingwen yiben xu"* (Preface to the English Translation Edition of *Wild Grass*), which is included in his essay collection *Er xin ji* (1932, Two Hearts), Lu Xun muses:

> For the most part these are merely short reflections written on the spur of the moment. Because at that time it was difficult to speak out directly, occasionally their language became quite ambiguous.
> To cite a few examples now, I wrote "Wo de shilian" (My Lost Love) as a satire on the fact that poems about lost loves were so prevalent then. Because I was repulsed by the number of people in society who just stood by and watched, I wrote "Fuchou" (Revenge) #1. Out of astonishment at the passivity of our youth, I wrote "Xiwang" (Hope). "Zhe yang de zhanshi" (A Fighter Such as This) was written as a reaction to those men of letters and scholars who abetted the warlords. "La ye" (The Dried Leaf) was written for those who loved me and wanted to preserve me. After the Duan Qirui government fired on unarmed demonstrators, I wrote "Dandan de xue hen zhong" (Amid Pale Bloodstains) while I was living in hiding. When the Fengtian and Zhili warlord cliques were fighting, I wrote "Yi jue" (The Awakening), after which I could no longer live in Beijing.
> So it may also be said that these were mostly small pale flowers on the edges of a neglected hell, which of course cannot be beautiful. But this hell was bound to be lost. This became clear to me through the expressions and tones of a handful of eloquent and ruthless "heroes" who had not at that time realized their ambitions. At that point I wrote "Shidiao de hao diyu" (The Good Hell That Was Lost).
> Afterwards I could no longer compose these sorts of things. In an age when things were changing daily, such writing, and even such reflections, were no longer allowed to exist. I think this is probably a good thing.

Cover for *Liang di shu* (translated as Letters between Two: Correspondence between Lu Xun and Xu Guangping, 2000), published in 1933 (from Yu Runqi, ed., *Tang Tao cang shu*, 2004; Bruccoli Clark Layman Archives)

Although his statement ends on an ambiguous note, its import is to place these pieces within an historical context of political and artistic repression that grew worse after the Northern Expedition defeated the warlords and reunified China for the "Nanjing decade" of 1927 to 1937 under the centralized rule of Chiang Kai-shek's Nationalist Party. Xu Shoushang, who knew Lu Xun best, quotes him as saying that the prose poems in *Yecao* comprise nothing less than his personal philosophy. *Yecao* has a pivotal place in the development of modern Chinese literature, and its poems have been read as metaphors for the political and intellectual struggles of the time, philosophical musings, symptoms of despair, psychological nightmares, reflections of the zeitgeist of the mid 1920s, seminal works of modernism, and literary manifestations of Nietzschean ideas.

Lu Xun commemorated his former students killed in the 18 March 1926 demonstration in two of his most moving essays, "Jinian Liu Hezhen jun" (translated as "In Memory of Ms Liu Hezhen," 1957) and "Wuhua de qiangwei zhi er" (excerpts translated as "More Roses without Blooms," 1957), calling the date of the shooting the "darkest day since the founding of the Republic." The essays were published in *Yusi* in 1926 and included in his *Huagai ji xubian* (1927, Bad Luck II). A warrant went out for his arrest as a ringleader of the disturbances and forced him to go into hiding for several months. Chen Yuan, the educator and critic with whom he had clashed earlier, implied that he had manipulated the students into getting themselves killed for someone else's cause—that is, the cause of the Communists.

In August 1926 Lu Xun and Xu Guangping left Beijing. Largely at the initiative of Lin Yutang, Lu Xun had been invited to teach Chinese literature at Xiamen (Amoy) University in Fujian province, newly founded with donations from overseas Chinese in Southeast Asia. Lin and the school's chancellor, Lin Wenqing, were sympathetic to his plight in Beijing and wanted to help him with the position. But Lu Xun grew restless in Xiamen; he was bored by his colleagues, felt that his academic duties were pointless, and resented the Western-colonial-educated Singaporean chancellor's veneration of Confucius and deference to wealthy donors. Also, he was separated from Xu Guangping, who had returned to her native Guangzhou to teach. "I was living alone in a stone house in Xiamen," he writes in the preface to *Gushi xinbian* (1936; translated as *Old Tales Retold*, 1961), "looking out over the ocean. I leafed through old books, no breath of life around me, a void in my heart." Though he continued to work on his fictionalized reminiscences for the collection *Zhao hua xi shi* (1928; translated as *Dawn Blossoms Plucked at Dusk*, 1976), at this time he largely abandoned the short-story genre—a decision lamented in the field of Chinese letters ever since. He claimed to have despaired of the misinterpretations to which his fiction had been subjected.

Lu Xun had considered joining Xu Guangping in Guangzhou sooner than planned—their initial understanding was that they would spend two years apart—so when he received a formal invitation to serve as professor of Chinese literature and dean at Guangzhou's Zhongshan (Sun Yat-sen) University in late 1926, he accepted it with little hesitation. For some time Guangzhou had served as the base for a "second revolution"—the first being the revolution of 1911, which many progressive intellectuals considered to have failed. Under the leadership of the Nationalist Party and with the participation of the Chinese Communists and Russian advisers, a "Northern Expedition" to destroy the warlords and reunite the country was on the move.

In January 1927 Lu Xun, accompanied by several of his students from Beijing, arrived at Guangzhou amid much fanfare from the Nationalist authorities. Nevertheless, his enthusiasm for the self-proclaimed revolutionary government was guarded, and appropriately so, for by 15 April of that same year, Chiang Kai-shek's purge of the Communists had spread from Shanghai to Canton, and Lu Xun suddenly became witness to more carnage. When his attempts at gaining the release of imprisoned students failed, he resigned his positions at Zhongshan University in protest. He never returned to teaching, devoting himself to polemical essays, translations, and other projects including editing (Lu Xun edited many journals during his career—fourteen, by one count) and promoting the works of young writers. In Beijing he had encouraged newcomers such as Tai Jingnong and Wei Suyuan, and he acquired more protégés in the last decade of his life, including Rou Shi, Xiao Hong, Xiao Jun, the translator Huang Yuan, and Communist activists Feng Xuefeng and Hu Feng). Lu Xun helped with their translating, edited their manuscripts, introduced them to publishers, and in some instances financed their publications or even gave them money for living expenses. A third project of Lu Xun's was the encouragement of a woodblock engraving movement in the arts. It is not without good reason that Lu Xun later became known as the father of the woodcut movement. He advocated this art form for its accessibility and ease of reproduction, organizing classes for artists and himself serving as a translator when lectures were given in Japanese. He published and popularized woodblock prints by leading artists in Europe such as Kaethe Kollwitz, as well as premodern examples of this nearly forgotten traditional art form in order to provide references for young artists.

In early autumn 1927 Lu Xun and Xu Guangping moved to Shanghai. Lu Xun thought that he could combine his efforts with those of leftist literary groups flourishing there, such as the Chuangzao she (Creation Society) and the Taiyang she (Sun Society). But the leadership of these groups, which were controlled by Guo Moruo and Cheng Fangwu, respectively, proved unwilling to halt the barrage of abuse they had been leveling at Lu Xun since the mid 1920s and continued to characterize him as a "feudal element" and an "outsider to the proletariat." Their motivation stemmed partly from jealously of an older, more successful writer who had become an independent leader of the Left (Lu Xun had made sarcastic jabs at the new, propagandistic "revolutionary" literature being turned out by younger writers who were members of these "editorial collectives") and partly out of a conviction that they, as members of the Communist Party, represented a discipline and an orthodoxy to which Lu Xun did not conform. According to Zhou Haiying's *Lu Xun yu wo qishi nian* (2001, Lu Xun and I through Seventy Years), in 1959 Cheng Fangwu told the Soviet scholar Nikolai Petrov that he and his colleagues had been incensed by Lu Xun's decision to go to Guangdong University in the wake of the defeat of the 1927 revolution, where he would be used for propaganda purposes by the Nationalists; but Cheng named the wrong university, and his dating was off by some months, as well: Lu Xun had gone to Zhongshan University, a more progressive institution than Guangdong University, several months prior to Chiang Kai-shek's putsch against the Communists.

The criticism from the Left led Lu Xun to undertake a systematic study of Marxist literary criticism so that he could expose his detractors' lack of theoretical sophistication, and he translated theoretical works by Lunacharsky, Plekhanov, and Katakami. As Jon Eugene von Kowallis writes in *The Lyrical Lu Xun: A Study of His Classical-Style Verse* (1996), to "provide examples by which Chinese writers and critics could better gauge their work, he translated representative pieces from both the proletarian and 'fellow traveler' schools in Russian fiction." But he rejected arguments that "geming wenxue" (revolutionary literature) and "shehui zhuyi xianshi zhuyi" (socialist realism) were valid literary forms for the China of his day. In "Geming shidai de wenxue" (translated as "Literature of a Revolutionary Period," 1957), a talk he gave at the Huangpu Military Academy on 18 April 1927 and collected in his *Eryi ji* (1928, And That's That), he commented that "the people had not yet opened their mouths" and that such works were merely the creations of "onlookers who put words in the people's mouths."

In 1928 the Nationalist regime began enacting laws to control the press, but literary journals remained relatively unaffected until the early 1930s. Having friends copy manuscripts for him so that his handwriting would not be recognized and using scores of pen names, Lu Xun managed to continue publishing critical essays that satirized the government and mocked its apologists. In 1929 Xu Guangping gave birth to a son, Lu Xun's only child; they named him Haiying ("Shanghai Baby").

The Nationalist regime embarked in the late 1920s on a systematic program of intimidation, harassment, assassination, arrest, torture, and execution to rid China of the threat of Communist subversion. The campaign, which affected not only the Communist Party but its liberal sympathizers and "fellow travelers," as well, came to be known as *Baise kongbu* (the White

Lu Xun (left) with George Bernard Shaw and Cai Yuanpei in Shanghai in 1933 (from Beijing Lu Xun bowuguan, Lu Xun 1881–1936, 1976; Collection of Jon Eugene von Kowallis)

Terror). Lu Xun and many among his coterie were potential targets of this campaign. Throughout the 1930s Lu Xun had to move about Shanghai in secret because of the constant threat of arrest or assassination. Zhou Haiying writes of being told by former Nationalist assassin Shen Zui at a 1992 meeting of the Zhongguo renmin zhengzhi xieshang huiyi quanguo weiyuan hui (National Committee of the Chinese People's Political Consultative Conference), to which they were both delegates, that "at some point in the 1930s" he had been sent to watch Lu Xun's residence in preparation for killing the writer; but the plan was never carried out, because the Nationalists realized that Lu Xun was too prominent a figure to assassinate without repercussion.

Lu Xun's relations with the Communist Party's underground leadership in Shanghai were not smooth in his last years. Although the Communists needed him as an ally and wanted to use his name in their propaganda struggle against the Nationalists, they resented his deviationist positions—most notably during the "Battle of the Slogans" in 1936, when he refused to take the official Communist Party line on "Guofang wenxue"

Lu Xun (left) with a Japanese bookseller in Shanghai in 1933
(from Jon Eugene von Kowallis, The Lyrical Lu Xun: A
Study of His Classical-Style Verse, 1996; Thomas
Cooper Library, University of South Carolina)

(Literature for National Defense) and proposed his own slogan, "Minzu geming zhanzheng de dazhong wenxue" (Mass Literature for the National Revolutionary War), instead.

In January 1936 Lu Xun returned to the short-story genre with *Gushi xinbian,* a collection of eight parodies written between 1922 and 1935 that deconstruct traditional attitudes and approaches to the sages and ancient legends of his culture, while making veiled comments on the present and speculating on the future of China. He died of tuberculosis on 19 October 1936.

After Lu Xun's death, the Communists spared no effort to claim him as their own. The campaign started with his lavish funeral: an organized march by students, workers, and dissidents turned into a tumultuous demonstration at which he was hailed as "the soul of the nation." In 1938 Mao Zedong praised him as "a sage for a new China." Mao further eulogized him in "Xin minzhu zhuyi lun" (1940, The Culture of New Democracy):

> The chief commander of China's cultural revolution, he was not only a great man of letters but a great thinker and revolutionary. Lu Xun was a man of unyielding integrity, free from all sycophancy or obsequiousness; this quality is invaluable among colonial and semicolonial peoples. Representing the great majority of the nation, Lu Xun breached and stormed the enemy citadel; on the cultural front he was the bravest and most correct, the firmest, the most loyal and the most ardent national hero, a hero without parallel in our history. The road he took was the very road of China's new culture.

Mao was convinced that Lu Xun's contributions to the struggle for a revolution had been enormous; but the Communist government did not tolerate his brand of dissent in its own press, as became clear after Mao's 1942 "Zai Yan'an wenyi zuotanhui shang de jianghua" (Talks at the Yan'an Forum on Literature and Art). Several of Lu Xun's protégés–including Hu Feng and Feng Xuefeng, both Communists–were persecuted in the early 1950s.

As Harriet C. Mills sums him up, Lu Xun

> had but one subject–China. The main concern of his life was that China should become great and strong. For him greatness lay not in military power but in the creative energy of a healthy, educated and responsible citizenry. The cannibalism of the traditional society had sacrificed the many to the few. A new and more rational order had to take its place. But the new could not succeed until the old had been destroyed. The real urgency was to secure for the new the chance to be born. The defeat of the old was of more practical moment than the blueprinting of the new. His work is therefore in a sense negative. He was not concerned with the good in China, nor with the details of the future, but with what was wrong. It was the evil that threatened the future. His work is essentially a commentary on the attitudes and practices he felt most endangered China.

On 20 October 1980, during the political thaw after the Cultural Revolution of 1966 to 1976, a young writer, Zhang Yu'an, published the poem "Jiaru Lu Xun xiansheng hai huozhe" (translated as "If Lu Xun Were Still Alive," 1989) in the newspaper *Renmin ribao* (People's Daily). The poem asks whether Lu Xun would be honored or imprisoned if he were still alive and suggests that even if he ascended to a position of importance, he would not cut himself off from the people. It concludes, "He might be rather happier and more cheerful, / But he might too have felt new unease and wrath." The poem addresses–with the understatement characteristic of Lu Xun's style–a question frequently asked since the 1950s: what would have happened to Lu Xun had he lived to see the Communist victory? The seventh line, "In high office he would not forget to be an ox to a child," refers to Lu Xun's old-style poem "Zichao" (translated as "Laughing at My Own Predicament," 1996) in his *Jiwai ji,* in which the line "But bowing my head, I gladly agree, / an ox for the children to be" can be interpreted as expressing his desire to serve the oppressed and down-

Lu Xun (left) talking with young artists at the Second National Woodcut Exhibition on 8 October 1936, eleven days before his death (from Jon Eugene von Kowallis, The Lyrical Lu Xun: A Study of His Classical-Style Verse, *1996; Thomas Cooper Library, University of South Carolina)*

trodden; this imagery is discussed in Kowallis's *The Lyrical Lu Xun*. Playing on the titles of Lu Xun's two short-story anthologies, Zhang Yu'an goes on to say that in contemporary China, Lu Xun would feel new "Outcries" and new "Hesitations." The next line, "In jail he'd have written new 'Permitted Conversations' and 'Pseudo-Free Letters,'" refers to the titles of Lu Xun's essay collections *Zhun feng yue tan* (1934, Semi-Frivolous Talk) and *Wei ziyou shu* (1933, False Liberty), which protest the lack of press freedom under the Nationalist regime, and suggests that the Communists would have censored Lu Xun, too.

In an essay he wrote in the last weeks of his life, "Si" (translated as "Death," 1961), which is included in his *Qiejieting zawen mobian* (1937, Essays from Demi-Concession Studio III), Lu Xun says:

> I remember also how during a fever I recalled that when a European is dying there is usually some sort of ceremony in which he asks pardon of others and pardons them. Now I have a great many enemies, and what should my answer be if some modernized person asked me my views on this? After some thought I decided: Let them go on hating me. I shall not forgive a single one of them either.

Letters:

Liang di shu [Letters between Two Places], edited by Lu Xun (Shanghai: Qingguang shuju, 1933); translated by Bonnie S. McDougall as *Letters between Two: Correspondence between Lu Xun and Xu Guangping* (Beijing: Foreign Languages Press, 2000);

Lu Xun shujian [The Correspondence of Lu Xun], edited by Xu Guangping (Shanghai: Sanxian shuwu, 1937); enlarged as *Lu Xun shuxin ji* [Collected Letters of Lu Xun], 2 volumes (Beijing: Renmin wenxue chubanshe, 1976);

A Selection of Lo Shun's Letters Translated, translated by Wei Yin (Singapore: Shijie shuju youxian gongsi, 1973);

Lu Xun shougao quanji: Shuxin [Complete Works of Lu Xun Reproduced in Handwritten Manuscript Form: Correspondence], 8 volumes (Beijing: Wenwu chubanshe, 1978–1980);

Liang di shu zhenji: Yuan xin shou gao [The Authentic Letters between Two Places: The Original Letters in Handwritten Format and a Hand-copied Version by Lu Xun], edited by Zhou Haiying (Shanghai: Shanghai guji chubanshe, 1996).

Bibliographies:

Donald A. Gibbs, *A Bibliography of Studies and Translations of Modern Chinese Literature, 1918–1942* (Cambridge, Mass.: East Asian Research Center, Harvard University, 1975), pp. 98–135;

Lu Xun yanjiu ziliao suoyin, 2 volumes (Beijing: Renmin wenxue chubanshe, 1980, 1982);

Zhongguo shehuikexue, yuan wenxue yanjusuo ziliaoshi, ed., "Lu Xun zhu yi nianbiao," in *Lu Xun quanji,* volume 16 (Beijing: Renmin wenxue chubanshe, 1981), pp. 1–40;

Zhou Guowei, ed., *Lu Xun zhuyi banben yanjiu bianmu* (Shanghai: Shanghai wenyi chubanshe, 1996).

Biographies:

Zheng Xuejia, *Lu Xun zhengzhuan* (Jiangxi: Shengli chubanshe, 1942);

Xiaotian Yuefu (Oda Takeo), *Lu Xun zhuan,* translated from the Japanese by Fan Quan (Shanghai: Kaiming shudian, 1946);

Wang Shijing, *Lu Xun zhuan* (Shanghai: Xinzhi shudian, 1948; revised edition, Beijing: Zhongguo qingnian chubanshe, 1981; revised again, 1991);

Zhu Zheng, *Lu Xun zhuanlüe* (Beijing: Zuojia chubanshe, 1956; revised edition, Beijing: Renmin wenxue chubanshe, 1982);

Cao Juren, *Lu Xun pingzhuan* (Hong Kong: Xin wenhua chubanshe, 1957);

Cao, *Lu Xun nianpu* (Hong Kong: San yu tushu wenju gongsi, 1967);

Lin Fei and Liu Zaifu, *Lu Xun zhuan* (Beijing: Zhongguo shehui kexue chubanshe, 1981);

Lin Zhihao, *Lu Xun zhuan* (Beijing: Beijing chubanshe, 1981);

Wu Zhongjie, *Lu Xun zhuanlüe* (Shanghai wenyi chubanshe, 1981);

Zeng Qingrui, *Lu Xun pingzhuan* (N.p.: Sichuan renmin chubanshe, 1981);

Peng Dingan, *Lu Xun pingzhuan* (Changsha: Hunan renmin chubanshe, 1982);

Xue Suizhi, ed., *Lu Xun shengping shiliao huibian,* 5 volumes (Tianjin: Tianjin renmin chubanshe, 1983);

Wang Shiqing, *Lu Xun a Biography,* translated by Zhang Peiji (Beijing: Foreign Languages Press, 1984);

Tang Tao, "Lu Xun zhuan," *Lu Xun yanjiu yuekan,* nos. 5–10 (1992);

Wu Jun, *Lu Xun pingzhuan* (Nanchang: Baihuazhou wenyi chubanshe, 1992);

Wang Xiaoming, *Wufa zhimian de rensheng: Lu Xun zhuan* (Shanghai: Shanghai wenyi chubanshe, 1993);

Chen Shuyu, *Lu Xun* (Beijing: Zhongguo huaqiao chubanshe, 1997);

Niu Daifeng, *Lu Xun zhuan* (Beijing: Zhongguo wenlian chubanshe, 1999);

David E. Pollard, *The True Story of Lu Xun* (Hong Kong: Chinese University Press, 2002).

References:

Charles J. Alber, "Soviet Criticism of Lu Hsün (1881–1936)," dissertation, Indiana University, 1971;

Alber, "Symmetry and Parallelism in Lu Hsün's *Prose Poems,*" in *Critical Essays on Chinese Literature,* edited by William H. Nienhauser Jr. (Hong Kong: Chinese University of Hong Kong, 1976), pp. 1–29;

Beijing Lu Xun bowuguan, *Lu Xun 1881–1936* (Beijing: Wenwu chubanshe, 1976);

Pingleung Chan and Tak-wai Wong, eds., *An Index to Personal Names in Lu Hsün's Diaries* (Hong Kong: University of Hong Kong, Centre of Asian Studies, 1981);

Chiu-yee Cheung, *Lu Xun: The Chinese "Gentle" Nietzsche* (Frankfurt am Main: Peter Lang, 2001);

Milena Dolezelová-Velingerova, "Lu Xun's *Medicine,*" in *Modern Chinese Literature in the May Fourth Era,* edited by Merle Goldman (Cambridge, Mass.: Harvard University Press, 1977), pp. 221–231;

Fang Xiangdong, *Lu Xun yu ta ma guo de ren* (Shanghai: Shanghai shudian, 1996);

Feng Xuefeng, *Huiyi Lu Xun* (Beijing: Renmin wenxue chubanshe, 1981);

Gao Yuanbao, *Lu Xun liu jiang* (Shanghai: Shanghai sanlian shudian, 2000);

Patrick D. Hanan, "The Technique of Lu Hsün's Fiction," *Harvard Journal of Asiatic Studies,* 34 (1974): 53–96;

C. T. Hsia, *A History of Modern Chinese Fiction,* second edition (New Haven: Yale University Press, 1971), pp. 28–54, 257–258, 541–544;

Tsi-an Hsia, "Lu Hsün and the Dissolution of the League of Leftist Writers" and "Aspects of the Power of Darkness in Lu Hsün," in his *The Gate of Darkness: Studies on the Leftist Literary Movement in China* (Seattle: University of Washington Press, 1968), pp. 101–162;

Raymond S. W. Hsü, *The Style of Lu Hsün: Vocabulary and Usage* (Hong Kong: University of Hong Kong, Centre of Asian Studies, 1979);

Sung-k'ang Huang, *Lu Hsün and the New Culture Movement of Modern China* (Amsterdam: Djambatan, 1957);

W. J. F. Jenner, "Lu Xun's Disturbing Greatness," *East Asian History,* 16 (June 2000): 1–26;

Nicholas Andrew Kaldis, "The Prose Poem and Aesthetic Insight: Lu Xun's 'Yecao,'" dissertation, Ohio State University, 1998;

Jon Eugene von Kowallis, "Interpreting Lu Xun," *Chinese Literature: Essays, Articles, Reviews,* 18 (1996): 153–164;

Kowallis, "Lu Xun and Gogol," *Soviet and Post-Soviet Review,* 28, nos. 1–2 (2002): 101–112;

Kowallis, "Lu Xun and Terrorism: A Study of Revenge and Violence in *Māra* and Beyond," in *Creating Chinese Modernity: Knowledge and Everyday Life, 1900–1940,* edited by Peter Zarrow (New York: Peter Lang, 2006), pp. 83–97;

Kowallis, "Lu Xun's Classical Poetry," *Chinese Literature: Essays, Articles, Reviews,* 13 (1991): 101–118;

Kowallis, "Lu Xun's *wenyan* Essay Moluo Shi Li Shuo (On the Power of Māra Poetry) and the Concerns of the May Fourth Movement," in *Proceedings of the International Symposium on Interliterary and Intraliterary Aspects of the May Fourth Movement of 1919 in China,* edited by Marian Galik (Bratislava: Slovak Academy of Sciences, 1990), pp. 45–58;

Kowallis, "Lu Xun: The Sexier Story," *Chinese Literature: Essays, Articles, Reviews,* 27 (2005): 151–166;

Kowallis, *The Lyrical Lu Xun: A Study of His Classical-Style Verse* (Honolulu: University of Hawai'i Press, 1996);

Berta Krebsova, "Lu Hsün and His Collection *Old Tales Retold,*" *Archiv Orientalni,* 28 (1960): 640–656; 29 (1961): 268–310;

D. C. Lau, *Lu Xun xiaoshuo ji: Vocabulary–Selected Stories of Lu Xun* (Hong Kong: Chinese University Press, 1979);

Leo Ou-fan Lee, *Voices from the Iron House: A Study of Lu Xun* (Bloomington: Indiana University Press, 1987);

Lee, ed., *Lu Xun and His Legacy* (Berkeley: University of California Press, 1985);

Simon Leys, "Fire under the Ice: Lu Xun," in his *The Burning Forest: Essays on Chinese Culture and Politics* (New York: Holt, Rinehart & Winston, 1986), pp. 100–107;

Tianming Li, "A Thematic Study of Lu Xun's Prose Poetry Collection *Wild Grass,*" dissertation, University of British Columbia, 1998;

Lim Buan Chay, *Lun Lu Xun xiuci: Cong jiqiao dao guilü* (Singapore: Wan Li, 1986);

Yü-sheng Lin, *The Crisis of Chinese Consciousness: Radical Anti-traditionalism in the May Fourth Era* (Madison: University of Wisconsin Press, 1979), pp. 7–9, 105–115, 125–136, 143–150;

Liu Fuqin, *Lu Xun qingshu jianshang* (Guilin: Guangxi shifan daxue chubanshe, 1993);

Lydia He Liu, *Translingual Practice: Literature, National Culture, and Translated Modernity–China 1900–1937* (Stanford, Cal.: Stanford University Press, 1995), pp. 67–74, 223–227;

Liu Xinhuang, *Lu Xun zheige ren* (Taibei: Dongda tushu gongsi, 1986);

Lu Xun zuopin cidian (Anyang: Henan jiaoyu chubanshe, 1990);

Lu Xun da cidian editorial group, ed., *Lu Xun zhuzuo suoyin wuzhong* (Chengdu: Sichuan renmin chubanshe, 1980);

Lennart Lundberg, *Lu Xun as a Translator: Lu Xun's Translation and Introduction of Literature and Literary Theory, 1903–1936,* Skrifter utgivna av Föreningen för Orientaliska Studier, no. 23 (Stockholm: Orientaliska Studier, Stockholm University, 1989);

William A. Lyell, *Lu Hsün's Vision of Reality* (Berkeley: University of California Press, 1976);

Maruo Tsuneki and others, eds., *Rojin Bungen Goi Sakuin,* Tooyoogaku Bungen Sentaa Sokan, no. 36 (Tokyo: Tokyo Daigaku Tooyoo Bunka Kenkyuu Jo Fuzoku Tooyoo Bengen Sentaa, 1981);

Bonnie S. McDougall, *Love Letters and Privacy in Modern China: The Intimate Lives of Lu Xun and Xu Guangping* (Oxford & New York: Oxford University Press, 2002);

McDougall, "Lu Xun Hates China, Lu Xun Hates Lu Xun," in *Symbols of Anguish: In Search of Melancholy in China–in Memoriam Helmut Martin (1940–1999),* edited by Wolfgang Kubin (Bern: Peter Lang, 2001), pp. 385–440;

Harriet C. Mills, "Lu Hsün, 1927–1936, the Years on the Left," dissertation, Columbia University, 1963;

Mao Zedong, "Xin minzhu zhuyi lun," in his *Mao Zedong xuanji* (Beijing: Renmin chubanshe, 1968);

Ni Moyan, *Lu Xun jiushi qianshuo* (Shanghai: Renmin chubanshe, 1977);

Ni, *Lu Xun jiushi tanjie* (Shanghai: Shanghai shudian chubanshe, 2002);

Ōe Kenzaburō, "Interview with Ōe Kenzaburō," *Mingbao yuekan* (Hong Kong), 3 March 1995, p. 13;

Ouyang Fanhai, *Lu Xun de shu* (Guangzhou: Hua-Mei tushu gongsi, 1949);

Jaroslav Průšek and Leo Ou-fan Lee, *The Lyrical and the Epic: Studies of Modern Chinese Literature* (Bloomington: Indiana University Press, 1980);

James Reeve Pusey, *Lu Xun and Evolution* (Albany: State University of New York Press, 1998);

William R. Schultz, "Lu Hsün: The Creative Years," dissertation, University of Washington, 1955;

V. I. Semanov, *Lu Hsün and His Predecessors,* translated by Charles Alber (White Plains, N.Y.: Sharpe, 1980);

Su Xuelin, *Wo lun Lu Xun* (Taibei: Wenxing shudian, 1967);

Sun Yushi, *Xianshide yu zhexuede Lu Xun "Yecao" chongshi* (Shanghai: Shanghai shudian chubanshe, 2001);

Sun, *"Yecao" yanjiu* (Beijing: Zhongguo shehui kexue chubanshe, 1982);

Tsau Shu-ying, "Lu Xun and Kuriyagawa Hakuson's *Symbols of Anguish*" in *Symbols of Anguish,* pp. 441–469;

Wang Hui, *Fankang juewang: Lu Xun de jingshen jiegou yu "Nahan" "Panghuang" yanjiu* (Shanghai: Shanghai renmin chubanshe, 1991);

Wang Yeqiu, *Minyuan qian de Lu Xun* (Chongqing: Emei chubanshe, 1943);

Xu Shoushang, *Wang you Lu Xun yinxiang ji* (Shanghai: Emei chubanshe, 1947);

Xu, *Wo suo renshi de Lu Xun* (Beijing: Renmin chubanshe, 1952);

Xue Suizhi and others, eds., *Lu Xun zawen cidian* (Jinan: Shandong jiaoyu chubanshe, 1986);

Yu Runqi, ed., *Tang Tao cang shu* (Beijing: Beijing chubanshe, 2004), pp. 10, 41, 157;

Zhang Enhe, *Lu Xun jiushi jijie* (Tianjin: Tianjin renmin chubanshe, 1981);

Zhang Xiangtian, *Lu Xun jiushi jian zhu* (Guangzhou: Guangdong renmin chubanshe, 1959; revised and enlarged edition, 2 volumes, Hong Kong: Yadian meishu yinzhi gongsi, 1972, 1973);

Zhang Yu'an, "If Lu Xun Were Still Alive," translated by Geremie Barmé and John Minford in *Seeds of Fire: Chinese Voices of Conscience,* edited by Barmé and Minford (New York: Hill & Wang, 1988), p. 314;

Zhongguo dabaike quanshu, ed., *Zhongguo wenxue,* volume 2 (Beijing & Shanghai: Zhongguo dabaike quanshu chubanshe, 1986);

Zhou Haiying, *Lu Xun yu wo qishi nian* (Haikou: Nanhai chuban gongsi, 2001);

Zhou Jianren and Zhou Ye, *An Age Gone By: Lu Xun's Clan in Decline* (Beijing: New World Press, 1988);

Zhou Zhenfu, *Lu Xun shi ge zhu* (Hangzhou: Zhejiang renmin chubanshe, 1962);

Zhou Zuoren, "Guanyu Lu Xun zhi er," in his *Gua dou ji* (Shanghai: Yuzhou feng she, 1937), p. 239;

Zhou, as Zhou Qiming, *Lu Xun de qingnian shidai* (Beijing: Zhongguo qingnian chubanshe, 1957);

Zhou, as Zhou Xiashou, *Lu Xun xiaoshuo li de renwu* (Shanghai: Shanghai chuban gongsi, 1953);

Zhou, *Zhitang huixiang lu,* 2 volumes (Hong Kong: San yu tushu wenju gongsi, 1971).

Papers:

Lu Xun's papers and private library are at the Lu Xun Museum in Beijing.

Lu Yin

(4 May 1898? – 13 May 1934)

Kristina M. Torgeson

BOOKS: *Haibin guren* [Seaside Friends] (Shanghai: Shangwu yinshuguan, 1925)–includes "Linghun keyi mai ma?" [Can a Soul Be Sold?], translated by Jennifer Anderson and Theresa Munford as "Factory Girl," in *Chinese Women Writers: A Collection of Short Stories by Chinese Women Writers of the 1920s and 30s,* edited and translated by Anderson and Munford (San Francisco: China Books and Periodicals, 1985), pp. 85–95;

Manli (Beijing: Beijing gucheng shushe, 1928);

Guiyan [Returning Goose] (Shanghai: Shenzhou guoguang she, 1930);

Linghai chaoxi [The Tides of the Ocean of the Spirit] (Shanghai: Kaiming shudian, 1931)–includes "Shengli yihou," translated by Amy D. Dooling and Kristina M. Torgeson as "After Victory," in *Writing Women in Modern China: An Anthology of Women's Literature from the Early Twentieth Century,* edited by Dooling and Torgeson (New York: Columbia University Press, 1998), pp. 143–156;

Yun Ou qingshu ji [Collected Love Letters of Yun and Ou], by Lu Yin and Li Weijian (Shanghai: Shenzhou guoguang she, 1931);

Meigui de ci [Rose Thorns] (Shanghai: Zhonghua shuju, 1933);

Nüren de xin [A Woman's Heart] (Shanghai: Shanghai sishe chubanbu, 1933);

Xiangya jiezhi [Ivory Rings] (Shanghai: Shanghai shuju, 1934);

Lu Yin zizhuan [The Autobiography of Lu Yin] (Shanghai: Di yi chubanshe, 1934); excerpts translated by Torgeson as "Autobiography (Excerpts)," in *May Fourth Women Writers: Memoirs,* edited by Janet Ng and Janice Wickeri (Hong Kong: Research Centre for Translation, Chinese University of Hong Kong, 1996), pp. 94–119;

Dongjing xiaopin [Tokyo Sketches] (Shanghai: Beixin shuju, 1935);

Huoyan [Flame] (Shanghai: Beixin shuju, 1936);

Lu Yin xuanji [The Selected Works of Lu Yin], 2 volumes, edited by Qian Hong (Fuzhou: Fujian

Lu Yin (from Lu Yin, *edited by Xiao Feng, 1983; Sawyer Library, Williams College)*

renmin chubanshe, 1985)–volume 1 includes "Chuangzuo de wo jian," translated by Paul Foster and Sherry Mou as "My Opinions on Creativity," in *Modern Chinese Literary Thought: Writings on Literature, 1893–1945,* edited by Kirk A. Denton (Stanford, Cal.: Stanford University Press, 1996), pp. 235–236;

Lu Yin jiwai ji [The Previously Uncollected Works of Lu Yin], edited by Qian Hong (Beijing: Shumu wenxian chubanshe, 1989)–includes "Haibin xiaoxi–ji Bowei," translated by Dooling and Torgeson as "News from the Seashore–A Letter to Shi Pingmei," in *Writing Women in Modern China*, pp. 139–141.

Collections: *Lu Yin duanpian xiaoshuo xuan* [Selected Short Stories by Lu Yin] (Shanghai: Nüzi wenku, nüzi shudian, 1935);

Lu Yin xuanji [The Selected Works of Lu Yin] (Shanghai: Wanxiang shudian, 1936);

Lu Yin jiazuo xuan [A Selection of Lu Yin's Best Works] (Shanghai: Xinxiang shudian, 1947);

Lu Yin, edited by Xiao Feng (Hong Kong: Sanlian shudian, 1983);

Haibin guren, Guiyan [Seaside Friends, Returning Goose] (Beijing: Renmin wenxue chubanshe, 1985);

Lu Yin xiaoshuo quanji [The Complete Fiction of Lu Yin], 2 volumes, edited by Guo Junfeng and Wang Jinting (Changchun: Shidai wenyi chubanshe, 1997).

SELECTED PERIODICAL PUBLICATION–UNCOLLECTED: "Liji zhuyi yu lita zhuyi [Self-Reliance and Reliance on Others], as Huang Ying, *Beijing nüzi gaodeng shifan wenyi huikan*, no. 2 (April 1920).

Some of the facts of Lu Yin's life, including the year of her birth and the years of publication of several of her books, remain in some question. She was born in Fujian province, probably on 4 May 1898; most sources give her name at birth as Huang Ying, though some give it as Huang Shuyi. During her career she published under several pseudonyms besides Lu Yin, including Huang nüshi (Miss Huang), Lusha, Huang Ying, and Huang Luyin. Her father, Huang Zhixian, was an official in the bureaucracy of the Qing dynasty. Her mother, whose name is unknown, was an illiterate, superstitious woman and the source of much pain in Lu Yin's life. After giving birth to three sons, the mother was hoping for a daughter when she became pregnant. Although her prayers were answered, her feelings toward the newborn changed drastically when, on the day of the birth, her own mother died. She interpreted this event as an omen that the girl harbored an evil spirit. In *Lu Yin zizhuan* (1934, The Autobiography of Lu Yin; excerpts translated as "Autobiography [Excerpts]," 1997) Lu Yin recalls that she "never experienced motherly love or affection"; her mother was unable to bring herself to look at the baby, let alone breast-feed her. Pitying the neglected and often sick baby, a wet nurse offered to care for the child at her own home in the countryside.

In 1902 Huang Zhixian was appointed county magistrate of Changsha, Hunan province, and Huang Ying was called home to move with the family. She missed the warmth and friendship she had found at the wet nurse's farm, and her dissatisfaction irritated her parents. In her autobiography she describes her father as impatient with her constant crying and as menacing her on at least one occasion. Three years after taking his new position in Changsha, Huang Zhixian died of a heart attack; he left a thirty-six-year-old widow and four children, the oldest of whom was fifteen. Lu Yin writes in her autobiography, "My mother was a dedicated and strong woman, but faced with this unexpected and difficult situation, there was simply no way she could cope." With the help of two maids and her husband's associates, the mother converted the family assets to cash. In 1907, while one of the sons accompanied their father's corpse to Fujian for burial, the rest of the family went to Beijing and moved in with Huang Ying's uncle.

Although the uncle had a large family with many young children, Lu Yin describes her stay there as lonely. A tutor was hired for her brothers, while her aunt, who "had never once set foot inside a school" but had been taught by her husband to read the moral tracts for Confucian wives, *Nü si shu* (The Four Books for Women), was considered adequate to keep Huang Ying busy learning to read a few Chinese characters. Her mother once became so angry at her disobedience and inattention to her studies that she beat Huang Ying fiercely with a duster. Gradually, the child became immune to such treatment: "this kind of serious punishment could no longer control my youthful temper." She dealt with her mother's rejection by keeping to herself as much as possible.

As Huang Ying grew older, her relationship with her mother deteriorated even further. When guests came for a special family event, her siblings were dressed up "like little angels" for the occasion, but Huang Ying was told that her "sad appearance would make them lose face" and locked up in a separate courtyard. Lu Yin's fiction reveals that she attributed much of the unhappiness of her later life to her distressing childhood. In her best-known work, the novella "Haibin guren" (Seaside Friends), which was serialized in *Xiaoshuo yuebao* (Short Story Monthly) on 10 October and 10 December 1923 and republished as the title story in a 1925 collection, the autobiographical main character, Luo Sha, is described as "The first unlucky one . . . who, influenced by the old atmosphere of her childhood, had developed an eccentric and stubborn temperament, and yet her nature was extremely full of emotion. And so she ended up being a person whose intelligence and emotion were often in conflict." Lu Yin frequently characterizes herself as "eccentric," "stubborn," and "emotional" and writes of the pain she felt from her mother's neglect and the feelings of inadequacy that resulted from it.

In 1908 Huang Ying was sent to a missionary boarding school in Beijing, purportedly to tame her mischievous nature; but because the school had a low tuition and waived the costs of room and board for girls who converted to Christianity, Lu Yin concluded in retrospect that her mother merely took advantage of an economical way to get rid of her. To get the nine-year-old admitted, her aunt told the school administrators that she was eleven. Her young age and small size led the other girls to tease her, and she was forced to do work beyond her abilities.

Huang Ying used the writing skills she acquired at the school to send a letter to her mother complaining about the conditions there. The mother was so surprised and impressed that her "stupid" daughter was able to write a letter that she visited the following Saturday and agreed to spend a little more money so that Huang Ying could eat a bit better. This occasion was Lu Yin's first indication of the power of the written word, but, she says in her autobiography, "I was too used to following a path of adversity to think that my luck had changed for the better."

The foreign headmistress of the school came to Huang Ying during a prayer meeting, asked her to believe in God, and began praying aloud for God to convert this "lost little lamb." Lu Yin writes in her autobiography, "My little heart at that time was so weak. My mother did not love me, my siblings had abandoned me, and my illnesses weakened me, so I too was moved to tears. My empty heart took in God. With tears in my eyes I said to Mrs. Jewell, 'I believe, I really believe!'" In "Miaohui" (Temple Festival), which was first published in *Funü zazhi* (Women's Journal) in December 1930 and collected posthumously in her *Dongjing xiaopin* (Tokyo Sketches) in 1935, she claims that "the influence of God on my mind passed away along with the innocence of my childhood. In the end I became an atheist." In her autobiography, however, she admits that "Although I did not stay with the church, religion helped to comfort me during many difficult times in my life."

The missionary school provided Huang Ying with self-confidence, affection, and two things rare for girls in China: a high level of literacy and a degree of independence. Since the late nineteenth century, male reformers had—with varying degrees of enthusiasm—been agitating for the emancipation of women as part of their program to make China wealthy and strong. Women supported one other in unbinding their feet, cutting their long braids into *modeng* (modern) bobs, and resisting arranged marriages. The flood of translations of Western writings in the early 1900s gave Chinese women a set of "distinguished women" as role models who were thoroughly different from those in

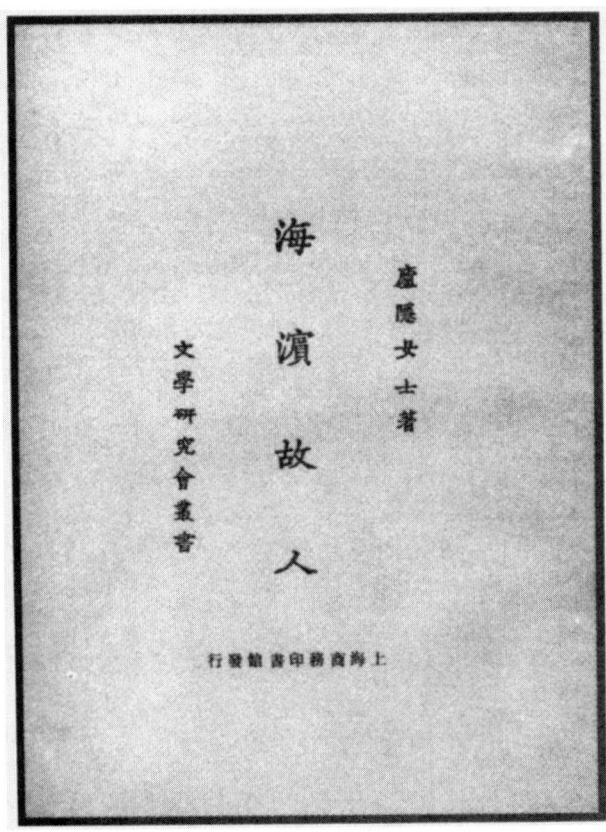

Cover for Lu Yin's first book, Haibin guren (1925, Seaside Friends), a collection of short stories (from Tang Wenyi, Mu Dingsheng, and Ji Lei, eds., 20 shiji Zhongguo wenxue tudian, 2001; Collection of Thomas Moran)

Liu Xiang's *Lienü zhuan* (79–78 B.C., Biographies of Distinguished Women), including the French Revolutionary figure Mme. Roland (Viscountess Jeanne Marie Roland de la Platière), Florence Nightingale, Joan of Arc, and the Russian assassin Sophia Perofskaya. A homebred feminist radical, Qiu Jin, who was executed in 1907 for organizing a revolutionary uprising against the Qing, provided a symbol of bravery and determination. And, perhaps most important, young, idealistic women were brought together in new schools for girls. In Huang Ying's case, while her education began as a way for her mother to get rid of her, it became the means by which she freed herself from the restrictions of family and tradition.

In 1911 Huang Ying's family briefly fled to Tianjin to escape the violence of the Republican Revolution. When they returned to Beijing, Huang Ying was to be sent back to the mission school; but with the help and encouragement of one of her brothers she took the entrance examination for a newly established government middle school, the Beijing nüzi shifan xuexiao

(Beijing Women's Normal School). The rest of her family was shocked to learn that their "stupid little duckling" had been admitted to the institution. She enrolled in 1912.

The school was so strict and the curriculum so difficult that for the first time Huang Ying looked forward to visiting her family on the weekends, especially since her mother was treating her somewhat better. Nevertheless, although she was the smallest and youngest student at the school, she flourished academically and socially. Spirited and mischievous, she soon formed an alliance with five other students who enjoyed finding ways of getting around the school rules. Dubbing themselves the "Liu junzi" (Six Gentlemen) after a group of scholars from the Ming dynasty (1368 to 1644), the girls played pranks on their more-severe classmates and teachers. Lu Yin writes about her middle-school days in her autobiography and in "Zhongxue shidai shenghuo de huiyi" (Memories of Middle School Life), which was first published in *Nüsheng* (Women's Voice) in September 1933 and collected in *Lu Yin jiwai ji* (1989; The Previously Uncollected Works of Lu Yin).

The advent of education for women in China was revolutionary not only because it led to the abolition of female illiteracy and foot binding but also because it gave the students the opportunity to form bonds with women outside of their immediate families. An aspect of school life that Lu Yin recalls in "Zhongxue shidai shenghuo de huiyi" was the students' frequent experiments with "tongxing ai" (homosexual love). Huang Ying's classmates teased any girl who said something nice about another by referring to the two as a couple. Subjected to such teasing, Lu Yin writes, many girls unwittingly "fashengle tongxing ai" (fell in homosexual love), and "pair after pair of 'fake husbands and wives' filled the school's yard and dormitories." The one time she was the target of such teasing, she kept her composure and, without the slightest embarrassment, continued talking about novels with the girl with whom she was supposedly infatuated. Their classmates were left befuddled: "all they could do was walk away in disappointment." This atmosphere of adventure and friendship during her first few years of the five-year teacher's course, Lu Yin writes, salvaged something of the "huangjin shidai" (golden age) that her childhood should have been.

After Huang Ying turned seventeen, her relationship with the other five "gentlemen" cooled because she made friends with a student the others felt to be unworthy. She found comfort in books: "At about this time I first discovered the fun of reading novels. Every day, after doing the little homework I had, I spent all my time reading." Since school rules forbade the reading of novels, Huang Ying had to hide her habit. Once, she claims, she played sick for several days to read the entire three-hundred-volume series of translations by Lin Shu, including works by Charles Dickens and H. Rider Haggard and Alexandre Dumas *fils*'s wildly popular *La Dame aux Camélias* (1852; translated as *The Lady of the Camellias,* 1852). (The leading translator of foreign fiction in China in the early twentieth century, Lin Shu produced elegantly written Chinese-language versions of nearly two hundred works. He could not read any foreign language but took dictation as others translated orally for him.) She also enjoyed reading *tanci* ballads, a classical genre popular in the late nineteenth century for their romantic tales of talented men and beautiful women.

In 1916 her love of books led Huang Ying to her first painful encounter with a man. Lin Hongjun, a relative of Huang Ying's aunt, was studying in Japan when he was called home to his father's deathbed. After the father died, Lin did not have enough money to resume his studies and came to Beijing looking for work. On his frequent visits with Huang Ying's family, he noticed that Huang Ying liked to read and lent her a copy of Xu Zhenya's *Yuli hun* (1912, Jade Pear Spirit). This melodramatic story of unrequited love so moved Huang Ying that she left tearstains on the pages and cover. Lin found an intermediary to plead his case as a suitor to her mother. The mother refused to consider his proposal, because he had only a middle-school education, and Lu Yin's brother was already looking for a suitable match for her.

Despite Huang Ying's lack of enthusiasm for marriage in general, her mother's rejection of Lin stimulated her to defiance. She wrote a letter to her mother requesting permission to marry Lin. Knowing how stubborn her daughter could be, the mother yielded but laid down the condition that Lin finish college before the marriage. It is not known whether Huang Ying actually loved Lin, or how much time they spent together, but their engagement stopped her mother from making any other marriage arrangements for her.

Lu Yin writes in her autobiography that in 1917 "I graduated from high school and was only eighteen years old—at that time there were no women's colleges and other colleges were not yet open to women, so I didn't have many routes to take." Her mother thought that Huang Ying could earn some money for the family by taking a teaching job, the conventional choice for an unmarried educated woman. Huang Ying taught in elementary schools in Beijing, Anhui province, and Henan province, her displeasure with teaching leading her to change schools three times in a year and a half: "Ah, tired, tired everything made me tired. Even more tiresome was the life of a teacher. Around this time I thought again of getting married in order to avoid so much trouble but he had not yet graduated from college, so I had to put that idea aside again." One of her early stories, "Panghuang" (Hesitation), first published in *Xiaoshuo yuebao* on 10 January 1923 and included in *Haibin guren,* describes the tribulations of a young teacher on his first job.

When Huang Ying learned that her former middle school in Beijing was planning to open one of the first institutions of higher education for women in 1919, she immediately decided to attend. Her mother, however, opposed the idea and refused to support her financially. Huang Ying taught for another semester, saved money for the tuition, and borrowed the rest from a friend. When she returned to Beijing in 1919, the date for the entrance examination for the Beijing nüzi gaodeng shifan xuexiao (Beijing Women's Higher Normal School) had passed; but she was allowed to audit the fall semester, with formal admission depending on her performance. The only other auditor that year was Su Xuelin, who, like Huang Ying, went on to become one of China's foremost women writers. Six women writers whose works began to appear in literary journals during the 1920s attended the school; and three—Lu Yin, Su, and Feng Yuanjun—were in the first class admitted to the institution.

As an auditor, and faced with competition from talented students from all over the country, Huang Ying felt intimidated. Her characteristic response was to work doubly hard. In her autobiography she describes writing her first essay in the terse, elliptical language of Classical Chinese. The topic was the moral values expressed in the *Liji* (Book of Rites), which dates to the *Zhan guo* (Warring States) period of 403 to 221 B.C., when various states fought for control of what is now China: "I had no idea about how to write on this topic. I thought to ask some other students but was afraid they would laugh at me, so in the end I hurried off to the library and found a copy of the *Book of Rites,* read it, and carefully studied the notes before I began to understand even a little. I spent an entire day on the essay, industriously writing one thousand words." She was astounded when her composition was picked for inclusion in a booklet of student essays: "From then on my confidence began to rise, and I wouldn't allow the others to make fun of me, and even the older students began to value me as well." After their first semester as auditors, Huang Ying and Su were admitted as regular students.

Attending college in Beijing from 1919 to 1922, the period of the *Xin wenhua yundong* (New Culture Movement) and the *Wu si yundong* (May Fourth Movement), Huang Ying could not be oblivious to the political and intellectual ferment around her. (The New Culture Movement, which began in 1915, was an intel-

Cover for Lu Yin's story collection Linghai chaoxi *(The Tides of the Ocean of the Spirit), published in 1931 (from Yu Runqi, ed.,* Tang Tao cang shu, *2004; Bruccoli Clark Layman Archives)*

lectual renaissance in which reformers acted in myriad ways to revitalize Chinese culture by liberating it from the inhibiting influence of tradition; the May Fourth Movement, named for antigovernment demonstrations that took place in Beijing on 4 May 1919, encompassed reform in all aspects of society. Most historians regard the two movements as having ended by 1927 at the latest.) Huang Ying was caught up in the excitement and, unlike the majority of her conservative classmates, read the new magazines and embraced the opinions expressed in them.

In the fall of 1919 the Fujian Students' Association was formed in Beijing in response to the killing of a student and the wounding of others in Huang Ying's native province, when students demonstrating in support of the boycott of Japanese goods clashed with police. Huang Ying was chosen as the representative from the Beijing Women's Higher Normal School, vice chairperson of the organization, and editor of its magazine. The association broke up before long, but several of the former members, including Huang Ying, formed a study society they called "SR"–the initial letters of the English words "social research." Lu Yin describes the society in her "Guo Mengliang xingzhuang" (Obituary for Guo Mengliang), which was first published in *Shishi xinbao: Xue deng* (New Current Affairs Times: The Study Lamp) on 7 December 1925 and is collected in *Lu Yin jiwai ji*.

In the midst of these events Huang Ying received a letter from her family asking her to come home: Lin had graduated from college and wanted to get married. Lu Yin writes in her autobiography:

> How could I think about marriage at such a time? I told him that I wanted to wait until I graduated from college before I got married. At the time he did not oppose me, but he pressed me with a lot of talk about how all my running around outside all day was really laughable and asked why should a girl be worrying about such things! From this one conversation I discovered the commonness of his thoughts and I was very unhappy and returned to the school that evening as usual.

The next day she received a letter of apology from Lin. She "sent him a letter immediately in which I set forth to him my thoughts on life and society and how the common attitude to life he was advocating was exactly what I was opposed to." Although Lin "always remained an upright and honest person, and from beginning to end he was very warm and cordial," Huang Ying broke off the engagement; he married a rich woman soon afterward.

During her first year in college Lu Yin attended Hu Shi's lectures on the history of Chinese philosophy. (Hu Shi was among the most prominent intellectuals of the May Fourth Movement and, later, the leading anti-Communist intellectual. During the 1937 to 1945 war with Japan he was Chinese ambassador to the United States; he was chancellor of Beijing University from 1946 to 1948 and president of the Academia Sinica in Taiwan from 1958 until his death in 1962.) In her autobiography she recalls that during this course her "thinking progressed the most quickly" but that

> At this time I was also the most depressed, I often felt that there was something stuck inside my heart that I would have to spit out before I could be happy. Only later when I took classes in introductory literature and literary history and read about artistic impulses did I feel that I too had such impulses and begin to think about writing. But what to write? . . . I simply could not think of anything until finally I decided to go ahead and write about my own life.

Seeking refuge in a corner of the library, she wrote for several days; but when she reread the piece, "Yin niang xiao zhuan" (A Little Biography of Miss Yin), she discovered that it was a "plotless mess" and hid it away in a trunk. In her autobiography she writes that she recently came across the manuscript and, unable to do anything with it, burned it.

Huang Ying studied the composition of several novels before coming to the conclusion that it would be better for her to start out with short stories. She wrote one and showed it to her literature instructor, Professor Chen. He glanced over it and advised her to give up writing. When she realized that Chen knew only about the Confucian classics and nothing of the new literature, she regained her self-confidence. In an essay written after Lu Yin's death, "Guanyu Lu Yin de huiyi" (Memories of Lu Yin), published in the magazine *Wenxue* (Literature) in 1934 and republished in Xiao Feng's *Lu Yin zhuan* (1982, A Biography of Lu Yin) and *Lu Yin* (1983), Su recalls:

> When she talked or laughed, the sound of her high-pitched voice could be heard several rooms away. Whenever she came or went she would be surrounded by a crowd of Fujianese classmates, chattering away in Fujianese, which I could not understand. She liked cracking jokes and making fun of other students. She was not so willing to get close to us pedants who had read quite a bit of classical literature. . . . Whenever she spoke, she would always stick in a few curses, she was always saying "bullshit" *[pi]*. When this impolite word came from her, it sounded quite funny.

Descriptions of Lu Yin never fail to refer to her sharp tongue and abrasive personality. Su also recalls that

> She sat right in front of me, and every time we had to write compositions and the teacher announced the topic, we would all chatter and moan about it, and perhaps not write a word the whole day. Lu Yin, however, sitting straight in her chair, with her head bent, her hand holding down the paper, and her pen not stopping, would be writing on and on, and in a flash her manuscript would be complete. She never copied her notes over a second time, but they were still more complete than ours. She wrote in big characters, which although they did not take any time, came out adorable.

Another former classmate, Feng Yuanjun, writes in "Yi Lu Yin" (Remembering Lu Yin), published in *Renjian shi* (The World Age) on 20 September 1934 and included in *Lu Yin zhuan*: "In the group of students at school she was the most capable of accepting the new ideas, and while others were still hesitating over the new poetry and fiction, she was already publishing it in newspapers."

The first known use of the name Lu Yin in print was in the byline of her first published piece, "'Nüzi chengmeihui' xiwang yu funü" ("The Association for Women's Advancement": The Hope Lies with Women), published in *Chen bao fukan* (Supplement to the [Beijing] *Morning Post*) on 19 February 1920. It was a letter criticizing an article by Guo Mengliang, a philosophy student at Beijing University, that had called for women to be liberated by men rather than liberating themselves. In April, under the name Huang Ying, she published two pieces in the second issue of *Beijing nüzi gaodeng shifan wenyi huikan* (The Journal of the Literature and Arts Association of Beijing Women's Higher Normal School): "Jinling" (Nanjing), a short poem in the classical style, and an essay, "Liji zhuyi yu lita zhuyi" (Self-Reliance and Reliance on Others). During the remainder of 1920 she wrote poems and essays on women's liberation for student publications.

Through the Fujian Students Association Lu Yin made the acquaintance of the literary critic and writer Zheng Zhenduo, who was also a native of Fujian. In January 1921, probably at Zheng's invitation, she was the only woman among the twenty-one people who met in a Beijing park to found the Wenxue yanjiu hui (Literary Research Association). Through Zheng she met Mao Dun, who had assumed the editorship of *Xiaoshuo yuebao* at the end of 1920 and was intent on turning it into a vehicle of the literary revolution. On 25 and 26 January 1921 the prominent Shanghai newspaper *Shishi xinbao* (New Current Affairs Times) serialized Lu Yin's first published short story, "Haiyang li di yi chu canju" (Tragedy at the Bottom of the Sea); it is collected in *Lu Yin jiwai ji*. But the work that established her as one of the foremost writers—and one of the few female authors—of the new literary movement was the melodramatic "Yige zhuzuojia" (A Writer), which was published on 10 February in Mao Dun's *Xiaoshuo yuebao* and is collected in *Haibin guren*. A brilliant but poor young mathematics scholar is visited by his old flame; her parents had not allowed them to marry because of his poverty, and she is now married to someone else. At their encounter she faints, spits blood, and dies; the mathematician goes insane and also dies. This romantic treatise on "free love" and the evils of arranged marriage is no masterpiece, but its theme of young intellectuals of a new age battling against tradition became a common one in fiction during the May Fourth period.

"Yige zhuzuojia" was Lu Yin's first contribution to the genre of *wenti xiaoshuo* (problem fiction), which was especially popular in the late 1910s and early 1920s and is distinguished by its attention to social and psychological problems arising from conflicts between tra-

Cover for Yun Ou qingshu ji *(1931, Collected Love Letters of Yun and Ou), by Lu Yin and Li Weijian (from Yu Runqi, ed.,* Tang Tao cang shu, *2004; Bruccoli Clark Layman Archives)*

ditional society and new ideas. In rapid succession she wrote several other stories in the genre, but she was never comfortable within its bounds. Typically in these early works she employs a first-person narrator—usually a young, educated woman like herself—to frame a story about an unfortunate maidservant or a working-class girl, but she never explores her characters' thoughts or motives. Her narrator rarely goes beyond exclamations such as one in "Yifeng xin" (A Letter), published in *Xiaoshuo yuebao* on 10 June 1921 and collected in *Haibin guren*: "Friends, poor people certainly are pitiful! . . . What is this world but a sad and bitter jail!" After her stories of "problem fiction," Lu Yin turned to—and for most of her career continued—writing about relationships and experiences from her own life.

At this time reformers were advocating the use in literature of *baihua* (vernacular Mandarin). The written vernacular had existed for centuries, but works composed in it, instead of in Classical Chinese, had been regarded as frivolous and not deserving of respect as literature. The written vernacular underwent change in the 1920s under the influence of foreign literatures and conscious attempts by writers to make their language reflect modern spoken Mandarin. The new generation of writers, both male and female, were thus faced with the challenge of writing about new experiences in a "new" language. The men, however, had the benefit of a tradition of thousands of years of male literary voices, while the women had the task of finding a voice and a mode of expression to convey the female experience. The search led them in a variety of directions. Lu Yin's classmate Su, for example, turned to the past in many of her stories, writing in a flowery, descriptive style that drew heavily on the techniques of classical *ci* poetry—a genre that had always been considered feminine and that often took on a female voice even when written by men. Another writer, Ling Shuhua, turned to Western models, fashioning her carefully constructed vignettes of love and family life on the style of Katherine Mansfield.

Through the Fujian Students Association Lu Yin met Guo Mengliang, whose ideas she had attacked in "'Nüzi chengmeihui' xiwang yu funü." They began exchanging letters daily and strolling through parks together on weekends and eventually became lovers. Guo, however, had a wife by an arranged marriage who had remained in Fujian while he was away at college. Despite Guo's insistence that he never loved his wife and planned to divorce her, Lu Yin was pressured by her family, friends, and moral principles to break off the relationship.

Lu Yin graduated from the Beijing Women's Higher Normal School in the summer of 1922 and took a teaching job in a progressive rural middle school. She quit after one semester because of the pressure and abuse she received as a woman teacher in a rural area. She returned to Beijing early in 1923 and, ignoring the protests of her friends and family, married Guo, who had divorced his first wife.

After her experiments with "problem fiction," Lu Yin turned to the highly subjective style represented by "Haibin guren." In college she and three of her classmates had called themselves the "Si gongzi" (Four Princes), a reference to the Warring States period. A long, loosely constructed story about four friends and the troubles they encounter after graduating from college, "Haibin guren" is based on the group. The four friends are "closer than any of their classmates, because all of them are very ambitious, different from those lost in drunken lives and dreams. Therefore, in the midst of all the other classmates, they built up a fortress and cut themselves off." After graduation, the women's supportive friendship and lofty ambitions are pulled apart by the responsibilities of marriage. In a technique that became typical of her new style, Lu Yin tells much of the story through a confusing assortment of letters and conversations among the friends. The theme of the educated, idealistic female disappointed by life and love became Lu Yin's trademark.

"Haibin guren" is melodramatic, but it focuses on an issue that was pressing to Lu Yin's young female readers: what were young, educated, ambitious women to do in a society that offered them few opportunities other than marriage? Luo Sha, the autobiographical main character, says that when she was a girl,

> I did not leave the house all day long. I had no idea what the world was. Outside of relying on my parents and living without any cares, I had no thoughts at all.... After I entered school my outlook on life changed. I could not tolerate my relatives or parents and gradually I began to feel lonely, depressed and bored.... Wasn't it knowledge that harmed me?"

Education showed women the inequalities of Chinese society, but that society offered them no opportunity to change the situation. Luo Sha responds to this frustration by imagining a refuge: a house in a village by the ocean that she can share with her friends. Life in a quiet place by the seashore, alone with her friends, writing, taking walks, and talking remained a fantasy of Lu Yin's. Like her creator, Luo Sha also faces the dilemma of a married boyfriend and worries about the disaster that will befall his wife if they divorce. That the modern idea of "freedom in love" was not as beneficial to women as to men became a prominent theme in Lu Yin's fiction and essays.

In her autobiography Lu Yin writes that after her marriage and the publication of "Haibin guren," her life was not what she had imagined it would be. She did not write for nearly half a year. Her mother died in the summer of 1924. When she began writing again, she produced several short stories and essays dealing with the question of happiness and the meaning of love. The idyllic dreams of her "Haibin guren" days were over. Most of her friends were married and, like her, dissatisfied with their situations. Characters similar to those in "Haibin guren" appear in these works. They were able to marry for love rather than through family arrangement but have found that little has changed in the traditional role of women in the family. In "Shengli yihou" (After the Victory), published in *Xiaoshuo yuebao* on 10 June 1925 and collected in *Linghai chaoxi* (1931, The Tides of the Ocean of the Spirit), Lu Yin describes the frustrations encountered by the friends after they achieve the "victory" of marrying for love; they conclude that "women's education in China is really a great failure" because after educated women marry, they are too occupied by the trivial matters of the household, in which they have little interest, to take up work in society. In "Hechu shi guicheng" (Where to Return?), published in *Xiaoshuo yuebao* on 10 February 1927 and collected in *Linghai chaoxi*, the protagonist looks at her aging face in the mirror and laments that child rearing, housework, and waiting on her husband have worn her down and put any thought of a career out of the question.

The characters in Lu Yin's short stories often display a defeatist attitude, but her essays reveal that she was looking for a way to improve her own situation. In "Zhongguo de funü yundong wenti" (Problems of the Chinese Women's Movement), published in *Min feng* (The People's Vanguard) on 1 March 1924 and collected in volume one of *Lu Yin xuanji* (1985, The Selected Works of Lu Yin), an angry Lu Yin addresses her audience: "as I have a pessimistic view of the women's movement so far, you probably are saying I should note how many schools have opened to women." But, she continues, allowing more women to be educated is only a "superficial" measure for which men get a great deal of credit while doing little. To make any real changes in the position of women in Chinese society, she argues, women must have economic equality, beginning with equal wages for equal work. Lu Yin was one of the first women to question the motives and efficacy of male champions of women's causes.

In July 1925 the Shanghai firm Shangwu yinshuguan (The Commercial Press) published the collection *Haibin guren* to enormous success. Lu Yin's popularity is explained in great part by the fact that her characters gave a voice to the emotions and frustrations of young women readers of the time. In October, however, just as her career was taking off and she had apparently adjusted to married life, Guo died of lung disease at twenty-seven. Lu Yin found herself a widow with an infant daughter. She moved in with her in-laws and taught in a girls' school in Fujian for six months, then left her daughter with her mother-in-law and taught in a girls' school in Shanghai. In the spring of 1927 she returned to Beijing, where she taught in a variety of schools and edited a literary journal. Between the spring of 1927 and the end of 1931 she published thirteen short stories in magazines and two short-story collections; the works are based mainly on her own experiences and sorrows. She describes her life in Beijing, which was known as Beiping from 1928 until 1949, in diary form in the novella *Guiyan* (Returning Goose), which was serialized in the first eight issues of *Huayan yuekan* (China's Dignity Monthly) in 1929 and published as a book in 1931. Her autobiographical protagonist is in a state of deep depression, drinking and smoking with abandon; she wants to cut herself off from society but, at the same time, feels lonely. Her unsettled state of mind becomes only more complicated when she has an affair with a friend of her late husband's brother.

Unlike many of her contemporaries, Lu Yin never addresses politics directly in her writing, but her subtle references in *Guiyan* to the tense and dangerous political situation in China reveal another source of her disillusionment. In 1925 a military expedition defeated warlords and began to bring the country under the control of the Nationalist government. In 1927 the government broke a truce with the Communist Party and arrested or killed many Communists and their allies. In *Guiyan* the protagonist goes to a lecture by a member of a political party and is inspired to try to rouse her students to action. The next day the students only parrot what she says, showing little excitement or initiative. She loses her own enthusiasm, saying, "I am a machine, they are machines too."

The collection *Manli* (1928) includes stories and essays that Lu Yin wrote after Guo's death. The title story is written as the diary of Manli, an educated girl who wants to do political work to save the country. She joins "some party"—Lu Yin carefully refrains from specifying which party—only to find that its members talk but do not act and are pursuing personal profit in ways that are little different from those of the bureaucracy they are ostensibly trying to overturn. Manli dies, as do many characters in the fiction of the 1920s, of exhaustion and heartbreak. In the essay "Zui hou" (After Getting Drunk) Lu Yin writes that in the past she saw herself as a brave martyr, "standing alone on a high peak of the Himalayas, proudly looking down at the human world as if to say: I will sacrifice myself for all inequalities; I will shake my twin swords at all that is evil." At present, however, she feels weak and alone. According to "Zui hou," there was only one person during this period to whom Lu Yin "opened the door to my heart which had been tightly shut for so long": the poet Shi Pingmei. Four years younger than Lu Yin, Shi had also attended the Beijing Women's Higher Normal School and was teaching physical education in the middle school attached to it when Lu Yin returned to Beijing in 1927. Their similar romantic experiences and current sorrows drew the two women together. In college Shi had fallen in love with Gao Junyu, a student and member of the Communist Party. Gao, like Guo at the time Lu Yin met him, was already married. Over Shi's objection that she did not want to ruin another woman's life, Gao divorced his wife and asked Shi to marry him; Shi refused. Gao died suddenly in 1925.

In 1927 Shi was not as accomplished a writer as Lu Yin but was gaining fame as a member of a movement of new-style poetry in Beijing. It was common at the time for writers to engage in literary battles in print; Lu Yin and Shi, in contrast, carried out a "friendship in print" in stories, essays, and poems. Shi died of meningitis on 30 September 1928 with Lu Yin at her bedside. Going against conventional morality and the advice of her friends, Lu Yin had Shi buried beside Gao with matching

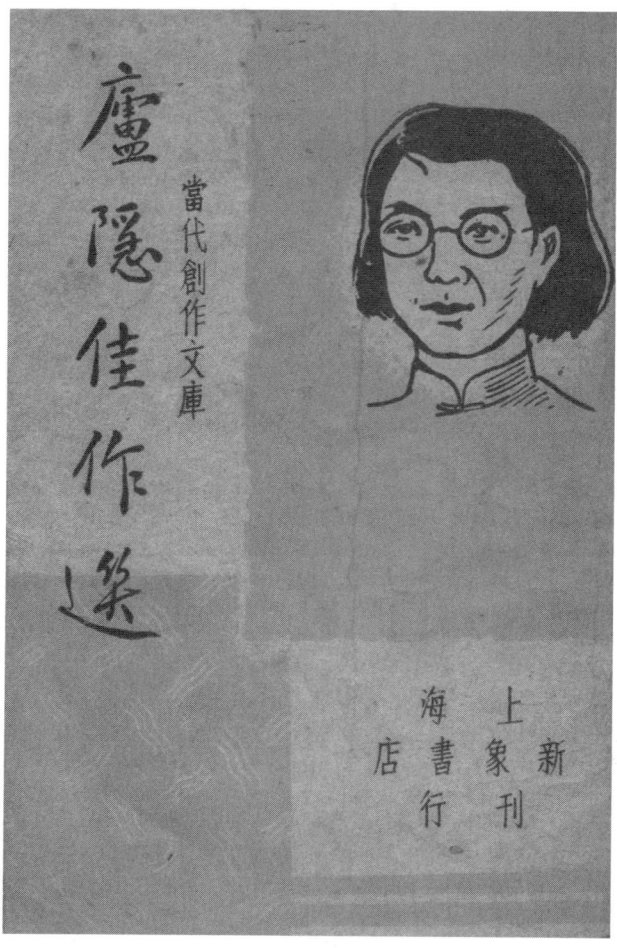

Cover for Lu Yin jiazuo xuan *(A Selection of Lu Yin's Best Works),* posthumously published in 1947 *(Wason Collection on East Asia–China, Kroch Asia Library, Cornell University)*

couplets carved into their headstones. The grave was a pilgrimage spot for young lovers until it was destroyed during the Cultural Revolution of 1966 to 1976.

Shi's death was followed two or three months later by that of Lu Yin's eldest brother. Lu Yin fell back into a state of depression. Soon, however, she was again meeting with friends and writing and even started a literary journal, *Huayan yuekan,* with a poet friend. Hoping to publish some of his poems in the journal, Li Weijian, a student at Qinghua University, asked a mutual acquaintance to introduce him to Lu Yin. Li arrived more than an hour late to the meeting with Lu Yin at the acquaintance's house. In the essay "Wo he Lu Yin de chuci jianmian" (The First Time Lu Yin and I Met), published in *Shidai huabao* (Times Pictorial) in 1935 and republished in *Lu Yin jiwai ji,* Li says that he asked what she was currently working on; her answer was curt and cold. He went on to ask why she was so sad and told her that he, too, had been depressed recently but was trying to be more optimistic. She answered that although she had been optimistic in her younger days, she now felt that optimism was "nothing but a dream." Before leaving, Li asked Lu Yin if she would look over his poems, and she gave him her address.

Lu Yin recalls her initial impression of Li in her autobiography: "He was the first person I had ever met in my life who was this sharp, and . . . my whole spirit filled with darkness was completely swept clear by his brightness." Li began visiting Lu Yin every Sunday for an outing in a park or a walk in the suburbs. In an essay titled "Huang Luyin" that is included in Xiao Feng's *Lu Yin,* Xie Bingying writes that the love affair of Lu Yin and the much younger Li "caused a sensation in the journalistic circles of Beiping, and an even greater sensation in the literary world."

Lu Yin's story "Yunmeng guniang" (Miss Yunmeng), published in *Xiaoshuo yuebao* on 10 January 1929 and included in *Linghai chaoxi,* is a fictionalized account of Li's courtship of the initially reluctant and cautious author. The most important documents of the affair are the sixty-eight love letters that were published as "Yunmeng de tongxin" (Yunmeng's Correspondence) in the supplement to the Tianjin newspaper *Yishi* from 14 February to 8 April 1930 and in book form as *Yun Ou qingshu ji* (The Collected Love Letters of Yun and Ou) in 1931. It was not uncommon at the time for writers to publish their love letters; what made the letters between Lu Yin and Li so interesting to their readers was that Lu Yin was a famous woman writer, a widow with a young child, and nine years older than her dashing poet-lover. Covering the period of exactly a year from their first meeting in 1928, the letters, written in highly sentimental language, demonstrate Li's persistent and finally successful attempt to break through Lu Yin's depression and win her love.

In August 1930, to escape social pressure, she and Li eloped to Tokyo, where they planned a quiet life of study and writing. Tokyo was undergoing rebuilding and industrialization in the wake of an earthquake that had destroyed the city in 1923, and the couple enjoyed exploring it together.

For economic reasons, Lu Yin and Li returned to China at the end of 1930; they settled first in Hangzhou and then, in August 1931, in the British concession area of Shanghai. There they lived with the publisher Shu Xincheng, who gave Li an editorial job; Lu Yin found a teaching position at the Gongbuju nüzi zhongxue (Department of Works Women's Middle School). Soon after their arrival in Shanghai, Lu Yin gave birth to a daughter.

The time in Hangzhou and Shanghai was particularly productive for Lu Yin. In Hangzhou she wrote a novel based on the life of Shi Pingmei. *Xiangya jiezhi*

(Ivory Rings) was serialized in *Xiaoshuo yuebao* from June to December 1931; it was still incomplete when Japanese bombs destroyed the Commercial Press buildings in January 1932, putting the magazine out of business. The complete novel was published as a book in 1934. Lu Yin tells the poignant story of Shi's stormy love affair with Gao Junyu with obvious sympathy for her friend's difficult position. This dramatic and sad work is reminiscent of Lu Yin's early writing and so is an exception to the change in her style after 1930. In her autobiography Lu Yin notes that she had promised Shi that she would write the work.

Lu Yin recalls her and Li's wanderings around Tokyo in a series of nine short essays or "sketches"; four were published in *Funü zazhi* in December 1930 and four more from May through August 1931. They were posthumously collected, along with a previously unpublished sketch, in *Dongjing xiaopin* in 1935; the volume also includes other essays and some short stories. In the first of the Tokyo sketches, "Kafei guan" (The Coffee Shop), she describes the opening of a new business that employs young female hostesses. Watching the girls put on their makeup and smile, sing, and dance for their male customers, Lu Yin comments sarcastically that "all Oriental women have a remarkable ability for hosting guests!" Other sketches describe a helpful neighbor, the refreshing naturalness of Japanese women at the public baths, and the superstitions displayed at a temple festival. Lu Yin emphasizes to her no doubt skeptical Chinese audience the kindness of most Japanese and the value of many of their customs and attitudes; but in the third sketch, "Linju" (Neighbors), she criticizes Japanese women for being the "slaves and puppets" of their men. In the seventh sketch, "Liudao zhi yi pie" (A Glance at Yanagishima), she recounts a trip with Li and a male friend to a geisha district in Tokyo. Lu Yin had suggested the excursion because she had always been curious about the lives of prostitutes. She dressed for the trip in Western clothing like a Japanese "modern girl" in order to be less conspicuously foreign. The geishas' heavily made-up faces and soft calls to men, which she heard as cries of "humiliation and sorrow," disgusted and scared her. She observes that her male companions were much less "sensitive" to the scene than she was. In one of the other essays in the book, "Jinhou funü de chulu" (The Way Out for the Women of the Future), first published in *Nüsheng* on 16 March 1933, she states that not all women have to walk out of their homes like Nora in Henrik Ibsen's play *Et Dukkehjem* (1879; translated as *Nora*, 1880, and as *A Doll's House*, 1889) but that family responsibilities—including financial ones—should be shared equally by husband and wife. (The character of Nora was well known to Chinese readers and writers of the time: the play had been published in Chinese translation in 1918 and was widely performed and discussed.) Lu Yin's "slogan," she says, is that women should "not only be women but should also be persons." In "Huaping shidai" (The Vase Age), first published in *Qingguang* (The Light of Youth), a supplement to *Shishi xinbao*, on 11 August 1933, she sarcastically thanks men for liberating women in order to make them "good looking flower vases" on bank counters and office desks so that when a male worker is tired, he has only to glance at a "vase" to be revitalized. She warns the "vases" that although poets may write verses to them, one never knows when "these men who once admired and inspired you" might "break you into pieces." She ends the essay by warning, "don't expect men to help you," and encouraging women to break out of the degrading "flower vase age."

In the amusing short story "Hao zhangfu" (Good Husbands), first published in the periodical *Nüsheng* on 15 January 1933 and collected in *Lu Yin jiwai ji*, a group of women teachers turn the tables on men who constantly discuss "what makes a good wife" by describing the qualities that would make a man a good husband. All agree that such a husband has to respect his wife and share in the burdens of running the household and raising children.

Lu Yin records her and Li's stay in Hangzhou in essays collected in *Meigui de ci* (1933, Rose Thorns), which also includes some short stories; three of the ten pieces that comprise the book had previously been published in magazines. She describes their various homes as "salons" where the doorbells never stopped ringing during the afternoon as all sorts of people came to visit. She and Li wrote all morning and strolled along the shores of West Lake in the evening.

In the final two years of her life Lu Yin wrote two short novels that are far more carefully constructed and thought out than her earlier writings. In *Nüren de xin* (The Heart of a Woman), which was serialized in *Shishi xinbao* from 14 February to 5 May 1933 and published as a book the same year, Supu has been in an arranged marriage for four years. Her husband, Heshi, has gone to study in Germany; she is studying in Beiping, having left her daughter in the care of her mother in Suzhou. Lonely, and knowing that her husband is free to do whatever he pleases overseas, Supu falls in love with another student, Chunshi, and accompanies him to California when he goes there for graduate school. But having the "tangled heart of a woman," she feels guilty about her daughter and husband and decides to resolve the situation by visiting Heshi in Germany. There she discovers that he is involved with a German woman, and they agree to divorce. Supu returns to the United States and marries Chunshi, but guilt over the divorce haunts her. A friend explains her predicament to her new husband: "she wants to be at the forefront of women in this society, but her courage is still not quite enough, so her actions bother people all the more. This is the illness of the age!" The clear prose, complicated plot, and effective character portrayal in *Nüren de xin* contrast with Lu Yin's early rambling, first-person narratives based on her own experiences.

The clearest evidence of Lu Yin's literary transformation is the other novel, *Huoyan* (1936, Flame), which she was still revising when she died. It describes the events of 28 January 1932, when the boycott of Japanese goods in Shanghai to protest the Japanese invasion of Manchuria set off a skirmish between Chinese and Japanese troops that ended in the Japanese bombing of a Chinese working-class neighborhood. Lu Yin focuses on a group of young worker-revolutionaries and their strong feelings against the Japanese. Criticism of Chiang Kai-shek's corrupt Nationalists is delivered in the voices of the workers. The merit of the work lies in the characterization of the soldiers and their ambiguous political and social positions rather than in a realistic portrayal of historical incidents.

Lu Yin's resolve to change her attitude and her writing style was, in part, an effort to regain control over her life after a long period of depression, but it may largely have been a response to increasing political pressures on writers during the early 1930s. The sort of subjective style that she used in her early writing was popular in the 1920s, but it was increasingly criticized as the sympathies of a new generation of intellectuals moved leftward and as literature turned to social, political, and national crises.

Li gives an account of his wife's death in his preface to *Dongjing xiaopin*. One evening in the spring of 1934 Lu Yin went to bed ill; Li continued to write in his office before falling asleep on the couch. During the night he was repeatedly awakened by Lu Yin's cries. He went to her side, waited until the pain subsided, and then returned to the couch. After "many days," Lu Yin agreed to call a doctor. She was taken to a hospital; after examining her, the doctor reported that she was hemorrhaging from a torn womb and that there was nothing he could do. Li had her moved to another hospital, where doctors agreed to operate. Lu Yin survived the operation but died several days later, on 13 May. Shortly before her death, she called her husband and daughters to her side. She told her daughter with Guo Mengliang to call Li "father" from then on, and told the younger daughter to respect her father. Turning to Li, she said, "I will take an impression of you with me." It is unclear what her exact medical condition was or what procedures were taken, but sources consistently record that Lu Yin died from complications of pregnancy or labor.

In the essay "Huang Luyin," published in *Renjian shi* on 5 June 1934 and included in *Lu Yin zhuan*, Lu Yin's friend and mentor, the critic Liu Dajie, describes her speaking before large groups of men. If a man made a sarcastic comment about women, Liu writes, "with her face and ears burning, she would argue with him until he admitted he had lost." Liu also points out, however, that "On the surface, she was an optimist, but on the inside, she was a pessimistic person." This dichotomy may be the reason why, despite her firm stance on women's issues and her willingness to change her ideas and writing style, she never threw herself completely into the political debates that were raging during her time. The theme of alienation that runs throughout her works certainly stems in part from her experiences as a neglected child, but being a female in the largely male first generation of modern writers in China contributed greatly to her estrangement. Literature, political involvement, and moral responsibility had never been the domain of women in traditional China. That Lu Yin, along with almost the entire first generation of modern Chinese women writers, remained uninvolved in the political activities and literary debates of the period suggests that they did not feel welcome in the many political and literary cliques and groups of the time. Lu Yin, for example, was a founding member of the Association for Literary Studies, and her work appeared regularly in the group's journal, *Xiaoshuo yuebao*, but these distinctions did not gain her recognition as a member of the almost entirely male literary elite—and in many literary histories they still have not. While the position of women was a focus of Lu Yin's writing throughout her career, her dream life was always to be away from the pressures of society, either with women friends in a secluded hut on a beach or in a country village home with an intimate companion. She came close to this ideal in her marriage to Li Weijian, which was cut short by her untimely death.

In "Lu Yin lun" (On Lu Yin), which was published in *Wenxue* in July 1934 and is included in *Lu Yin zhuan*, Mao Dun writes: "Reading her complete works today is like breathing the air of the May Fourth era again." He goes on to use what he calls the "stagnation of Lu Yin" as a symbol of the general stagnation that overcame the bourgeois May Fourth Movement. Mao Dun's opinions carry so much weight that criticism of Lu Yin's work seldom questions his appraisal. The reception of Lu Yin's work, both during her lifetime and after her death, was also influenced by Hu Shi's admonition in his 1917 essay, "Wenxue gailiang chuyi" (A Preliminary Discussion of Literary Reform), that modern Chinese writers should "reject melancholy" that was characteristic of mournful writers of the Chinese past. This notion set the tone for criticism of writers such as Lu Yin who expressed personal depression and discontent in their work. Finally, nearly all of the first generation of May Fourth women authors turned from writing to careers in literary research and teaching because of the predominance of the idea that writing "personal," "domestic," or "individualistic" fiction was not helping to change China and that they would be able to contribute more in some other pursuit. The persistent assertion that a "broadness of vision" in literature equates solely with socially engaged critical realism perpetuated a canon of Chinese modern writers that excluded many women, as well as men, whose literary styles and forms fall outside this mainstream. Since the late 1980s, however, the canon has been widened to include a variety of literary styles and approaches and to accept deserving writers such as Lu Yin.

Bibliographies:

Xiao Feng, "Lu Yin nianbiao," in *Lu Yin*, edited by Xiao Feng (Hong Kong: Sanlian shudian, 1983);

"Lu Yin zhuzuo xinian mulu," in *Lu Yin jiwai ji*, edited by Qian Hong (Beijing: Shumu wenxian chubanshe, 1989), pp. 569–584.

Biographies:

Xiao Feng, *Lu Yin zhuan* (Beijing: Beijing shifan daxue chubanshe, 1982);

Xiao Feng, ed., *Lu Yin* (Hong Kong: Sanlian shudian, 1983).

References:

Paul A. Cohen, "Christian Missions and their Impact to 1900," in *The Cambridge History of China*, volume 10: *Late Ch'ing, 1800–1911, Part 1*, edited by John K. Fairbank (Cambridge: Cambridge University Press, 1978), pp. 543–590;

Yi-tsi Feuerwerker, "Women as Writers in the 1920's and 1930's," in *Women in Chinese Society*, edited by Margery Wolf and Roxanne Witke (Stanford, Cal.: Stanford University Press, 1975), pp. 143–168;

Wendy Larson, "Female Subjectivity and Gender Relations: The Early Stories of Lu Yin and Bing Xin," in *Politics, Ideology, and Literary Discourse in Modern China: Theoretical Interventions and Cultural Critique*, edited by Xiaobing Tang and Kang Liu (Durham, N.C.: Duke University Press, 1993), pp. 124–146;

Leo Ou-fan Lee, *The Romantic Generation of Modern Chinese Writers* (Cambridge, Mass.: Harvard University Press, 1973), pp. 20, 23, 262, 270;

Jianmei Liu, "Feminizing Politics: Reading Bai Wei and Lu Yin," *Journal of Modern Literature in Chinese*, 5, no. 2 (2002): 55–80;

Peng Ming, *Wu si yundong shi* (Beijing: Renmin chubanshe, 1984), pp. 629–636;

Tang Wenyi, Mu Dingsheng, and Ji Lei, eds., *20 shiji Zhongguo wenxue tudian* (Chengdu: Sichuan renmin chubanshe, 2001), p. 83;

Yu Runqi, ed., *Tang Tao cang shu* (Beijing: Beijing chubanshe, 2004), p. 128.

Mao Dun
(4 July 1896 – 27 March 1981)

Charles A. Laughlin
Yale University

SELECTED BOOKS: *Huanmie* [Disillusionment] (Shanghai: Shangwu yinshuguan, 1928);

Dongyao [Vacillation] (Shanghai: Shangwu yinshuguan, 1928);

Zhuiqiu [Pursuit] (Shanghai: Shangwu yinshuguan, 1928);

Xiaoshuo yanjiu ABC [The ABC's of Studying Fiction] (Shanghai: Shijie shuju, 1928);

Ouzhou dazhan yu wenxue [The European Great War and Literature] (Shanghai: Kaiming shudian, 1928);

Zhongguo shenhua yanjiu ABC [The ABC's of Studying Chinese Mythology], as Xuan Zhu, 2 volumes (Shanghai: Shijie shuju, 1929);

Xiandai wenyi zalun [Assorted Essays on Modern Literary Art] (Shanghai: Shijie shuju, 1929);

Qishi wenxue ABC [The ABC's of Chivalric Literature] (Shanghai: Shijie shuju, 1929);

Shenhua zalun [Assorted Essays on Mythology] (Shanghai: Shijie shuju, 1929);

Liuge Ouzhou wenxuejia [Six European Authors] (Shanghai: Shijie shuju, 1929);

Ye qiangwei [Wild Roses] (Shanghai: Dajiang shupu, 1929)—includes "Zisha," translated by Edgar Snow and Hsiao Ch'ien [Xiao Qian] as "Suicide," in *Living China: Modern Chinese Short Stories*, edited by Snow (London: Harrap, 1936), pp. 128–141;

Xiyang wenxue [Western Literature] (Shanghai: Shijie shuju, 1930);

Xila wenxue ABC [The ABC's of Greek Literature] (Shanghai: Shijie shuju, 1930);

Bei Ou shenhua ABC [The ABC's of Northern European Mythology] (Shanghai: Shijie shuju, 1930);

Hong [Rainbow] (Shanghai: Kaiming shudian, 1930); translated by Madeline Zelin as *Rainbow* (Berkeley: University of California Press, 1992);

San ren xing [When Three Walk Together] (Shanghai: Kaiming shudian, 1931);

Su mang [Sleeping in the Wild], as MD (Shanghai: Dajiang shupu, 1931)—includes "Nining," translated by Snow and Hsiao Ch'ien (Xiao Qian) as "Mud," in *Living China*, pp. 142–151; translation

Mao Dun (photograph by Pan Derun; from Mao Dun, *edited by Zhuang Zhongqing, 1986; Collection of Thomas Moran)*

republished as "War and Peace Come to the Village," in *A Treasury of Modern Asian Stories*, edited by Daniel L. Milton and William Clifford (New York: New American Library, 1961), pp. 206–213;

Lu [The Road] (Shanghai: Guanghua shuju, 1932);

Ziye (Shanghai: Kaiming shudian, 1933); translated by Hsü Meng-hsiung as *Midnight* (Beijing: Foreign

Languages Press, 1957; Washington, D.C.: Center for Chinese Research Materials, Association of Research Libraries, 1970);

Chun can [Spring Silkworms] (Shanghai: Kaiming shudian, 1933);

Mao Dun sanwen ji [An Anthology of Essays by Mao Dun] (Shanghai: Tianma shudian, 1933);

Hua xiazi [Chatterbox] (Shanghai: Liangyou tushu yinshua gongsi, 1934);

Suxie yu suibi [Literary Sketches and Informal Essays] (Shanghai: Kaiming shudian, 1935);

Shijie wenxue mingzhu jianghua [Talks on Famous Works of World Literature] (Shanghai: Kaiming shudian, 1936);

Chuangzuo de zhunbei [Preparation for Literary Creation] (Shanghai: Shenghuo shudian, 1936);

Paomo [Froth] (Shanghai: Shenghuo shudian, 1936)–includes "Dangpu qian," translated by John Berninghausen as "In Front of the Pawnshop," in *Revolutionary Literature in China: An Anthology,* edited by Berninghausen and Theodore Huters (White Plains, N.Y.: Sharpe, 1976), pp. 56–61;

Yinxiang, ganxiang, huiyi [Impressions, Thoughts, and Memories] (Shanghai: Wenhua shenghuo chubanshe, 1936);

Duojiao guanxi [Multifaceted Relations] (Shanghai: Shenghuo shudian, 1936);

Xiaocheng chunqiu [The Annals of a Small Town] (Shanghai: Wenhua shenghuo chubanshe, 1937);

Shaonü de xin [The Heart of a Young Girl] (Shanghai: Wenhua shenghuo chubanshe, 1937);

Guling zhi qiu [Autumn in Guling] (Shanghai: Wenhua shenghuo chubanshe, 1937);

Can dong [Winter's End] (Shanghai: Wenhua shenghuo chubanshe, 1937);

Yanyun ji [Mists and Clouds Anthology] (Shanghai: Liangyou tushu yinshua gongsi, 1937)–includes "'Yige zhenzhengde Zhongguo ren,'" translated by Wang Chi-chen as "'A True Chinese,'" in *Contemporary Chinese Stories* (New York: Columbia University Press, 1944), pp. 159–164;

Paohuo de xili [Baptism by Cannon Fire] (Chongqing: Fenghuo she, 1939);

Fushi [Putrefaction] (Shanghai: Huaxia shudian, 1941);

Jiehou shiyi [Gathering Remnants after Disaster] (Guilin: Xueyi chubanshe, 1942);

Wenyi lunwen ji [Treatises on Literary Art] (Chongqing: Qunyi chubanshe, 1942);

Shuangye hong si eryue hua [Frosted Leaves as Red as February Flowers] (Guilin: Huahua shudian, 1943);

Jianwen zaji [Jottings on the Seen and Heard] (Guilin: Wenguang shudian, 1943);

Yesu zhi si [The Death of Jesus] (Shanghai: Zuojia shuwu, 1943);

Mao Dun suibi [Informal Essays by Mao Dun] (Guilin: Wenren chubanshe, 1943);

Baiyang lizan [In Praise of the White Poplar] (Guilin: Roucao she, 1943);

Zenyang lianxi xiezuo [How to Practice Writing] (Chongqing: Wenfeng shuju, 1944);

Shijian de jilu [The Recording of Time] (Chongqing: Liangyou fuxing tushu yinshua gongsi, 1945);

Weiqu [Grievances] (Chongqing: Jianguo shudian, 1945)–includes "Bao shi," translated by Wang Chi-chen as "Heaven Has Eyes," *Mademoiselle* (March 1945): 134–135, 222–227; translation republished in *Stories of China at War,* edited by Wang (New York: Columbia University Press, 1947), pp. 27–38; and "Chuanshang," translated by W. J. F. Jenner as "On the Boat," in *Modern Chinese Stories,* edited by Jenner (London & New York: Oxford University Press, 1970), pp. 75–84;

Di yi jieduan de gushi [Story of the First Stage] (Chongqing: Yazhou tushu chubanshe, 1945);

Tieshu hua [Flowers of the Iron Tree] (Shanghai: Wenhua shenghuo chubanshe, 1945);

Qingming qianhou [Before and after the Qingming Festival] (Chongqing: Kaiming shudian, 1945);

Fang sheng wei si zhi jian [Between Living and Dying] (Nanjing: Xiaoya shudian, 1947);

Shenghuo zhi yi ye [One Page from Life] (N.p.: Xinqun chubanshe, 1947);

Sulian jianwen lu [Seen and Heard in the Soviet Union] (Shanghai: Zhiyong shudian, 1948);

Zatan Sulian [Miscellaneous Remarks on the Soviet Union] (N.p.: Zhiyong shudian, 1949);

Mao Dun duanpian xiaoshuo xuanji [A Selection of Short Stories by Mao Dun] (Beijing: Renmin wenxue chubanshe, 1955);

Yedu ouji [Occasional Notes on Night Reading] (Tianjin: Baihua wenyi chubanshe, 1958);

Mao Dun wenji [Mao Dun's Collected Works], 10 volumes (Beijing: Renmin wenxue chubanshe, 1958–1961)–includes in volume 9, "Dazhonghua yu liyong jiu xingshi," translated by Yu-shih Chen as "Literature and Art for the Masses and the Use of Traditional Forms," in *Modern Chinese Literary Thought: Writings on Literature, 1893–1945,* edited by Kirk A. Denton (Stanford, Cal.: Stanford University Press, 1996), pp. 433–435;

Guchui ji [In Advocation Anthology] (Beijing: Zuojia chubanshe, 1959);

Guchui xuji [The Second Advocation Anthology] (Beijing: Zuojia chubanshe, 1962);

Guanyu lishi he lishi ju [On History and Historical Drama] (Beijing: Zuojia chubanshe, 1962);

Dushu zaji [Miscellaneous Notes on Reading] (Beijing: Zuojia chubanshe, 1963);

Mao Dun pinglun wenji [Mao Dun's Collected Critical Articles], 2 volumes (Beijing: Renmin wenxue chubanshe, 1978);

Mao Dun shici [Mao Dun's Poetry] (Shijiazhuang: Hebei renmin chubanshe, 1979);

Mao Dun lun chuangzuo [Mao Dun on Literary Creation], edited by Ye Ziming (Shanghai: Shanghai wenyi chubanshe, 1980)–includes "Cong Guling dao Dongjing," translated by Yu-shih Chen as "From Kuling to Tokyo," in *Revolutionary Literature in China: An Anthology,* pp. 37–43; and "*Ziye* shi zenyang xiecheng de" [How *Midnight* Was Written], translated by Theodore Huters as "Shanghai's Silk Industry: World Economic Crisis, Workers, and Civil War," in *Modern Chinese Writers: Self-Portrayals,* edited by Helmut Martin and Jeffrey Kinkley (Armonk, N.Y.: Sharpe, 1992), pp. 285–288;

Mao Dun lun Zhongguo xiandai zuojia zuopin [Mao Dun on Works by Modern Chinese Authors] (Beijing: Beijing University Press, 1980)–includes "Du *Ni Huanzhi*," translated by Yu-Shih Chen as "On Reading *Ni Huanzhi*," in *Modern Chinese Literary Thought,* pp. 289–306;

Mao Dun sanwen suxie ji [An Anthology of Essays and Literary Sketches by Mao Dun] (Beijing: Renmin wenxue chubanshe, 1980);

Mao Dun jinzuo [Recent Articles by Mao Dun] (Chengdu: Sichuan renmin chubanshe, 1980);

Duanlian [Discipline] (Beijing: Wenhua yishu chubanshe, 1981);

Wo zouguo de daolu [The Road I Have Walked], 3 volumes (Beijing: Renmin wenxue chubanshe, 1981–1988);

Mao Dun quanji [The Complete Works of Mao Dun], 40 volumes (Beijing: Renmin wenxue chubanshe, 1984–2001)–includes in volume 14, "Zenyang fang neng shi funü yundong you shili," translated as "How Do We Make the Women's Movement Truly Powerful?" *Chinese Studies of History,* 31 (Winter 1997–1998): 84–87; in volume 18, "Wenxue yu rensheng," translated by Berninghausen as "Literature and Life," in *Modern Chinese Literary Thought,* pp. 190–195;

Mao Dun riji [Mao Dun's Diaries], edited by Zha Guohua (Taiyuan: Shanxi jiaoyu chubanshe, 1988).

Editions and Collections: *Shi* [Eclipse] (Shanghai: Kaiming shudian, 1930)–comprises *Huanmie* [Disillusionment], *Dongyao* [Vacillation], and *Zhuiqiu* [Pursuit];

Mao Dun zixuan ji [Works by Mao Dun Selected by the Author] (Shanghai: Tianma shudian, 1933);

Mao Dun duanpian xiaoshuo ji [An Anthology of Short Stories by Mao Dun] (Shanghai: Kaiming shudian, 1934);

Chun can (Shanghai: Chenguang chuban gongsi, 1935?);

Mao Dun xuanji [Selected Works by Mao Dun] (Shanghai: Wanxiang shuwu, 1935);

Mao Dun chuangzao xuan [A Selection of Creative Works by Mao Dun] (Shanghai: Wenhua shenghuo chubanshe, 1936);

Mao Dun daibiao zuo [Representative Works by Mao Dun] (Shanghai: Chunqiu shudian, 1937);

Mao Dun duanpian xiaoshuo ji, di er ji [An Anthology of Short Stories by Mao Dun, Part 2] (Shanghai: Kaiming shudian, 1939);

Mao Dun wenxuan [A Selection of Works by Mao Dun] (Shanghai: Qingchun chubanshe, 1946);

Ziye (Beijing: Kaiming shudian, 1947);

Mao Dun wenji [A Collection of Mao Dun's Works] (Shanghai: Chunming shudian, 1948);

Mao Dun xuanji [Selected Works by Mao Dun] (Beijing: Kaiming shudian, 1952);

Mao Dun zixuan sanwen ji [Essays by Mao Dun Selected by the Author] (Hong Kong: Xiandai wenjiao she, 1954);

Mao Dun xuanji [Selected Works by Mao Dun] (Beijing: Renmin wenxue chubanshe, 1959);

Mao Dun zixuan ji [Works by Mao Dun Selected by the Author] (Hong Kong: Xinyue chubanshe, 1962);

Shijie wenxue mingzhu zatan [Miscellaneous Remarks on World Literature] (Tianjin: Baihua wenyi chubanshe, 1980);

Mao Dun duanpian xiaoshuo ji [The Collected Short Stories of Mao Dun], 2 volumes (Beijing: Renmin wenxue chubanshe, 1980);

Mao Dun wenyi pinglun ji [An Anthology of Mao Dun's Literary Criticism], 2 volumes (Beijing: Wenhua yishu chubanshe, 1981);

Mao Dun, edited by Zhuang Zhongqing (Hong Kong: Sanlian shudian Xianggang fendian, 1986);

Mao Dun quan ji: Fu ji [The Complete Works of Mao Dun: Appendix] (Beijing: Renmin wenxue chubanshe, 2001).

Editions in English: *Spring Silkworms and Other Stories,* translated and edited by Sidney Shapiro (Beijing: Foreign Languages Press, 1956)–comprises "Spring Silkworms" ("Chun can"), "Autumn Harvest" ("Qiu shou"), "Winter Ruin" ("Can dong"), "Epitome" ("Xiao wu"), "The Shop of the Lin Family" ("Lin jia puzi"), "Wartime" ("You di'er zhang"), "Big Nose" ("Da bizi de gushi"), "Second Generation" ("Erzi kaihui qule"), "The Bewilderment of Mr. Chao" ("Zhao xiansheng xiangbutong"), "A True Chinese Patriot" ("Yige zhenzhengde Zhongguo ren'"), "Frustration"

("Weiqu"), "First Morning at the Office" ("Diyi ge bantian de gongzuo"), and "Great Marsh District" ("Da ze xiang");

"Spring Silkworms" ("Chun can"), "Comedy" ("Xiju"), Isaacs "Autumn Harvest" ("Qiu shou"), and "Notes on Chinese Left-Wing Periodicals" ("Zhongguo zuoyi wenyi dingqi qikan jieshao"), in *Straw Sandals: Chinese Short Stories, 1918–1933,* edited by Isaacs (Cambridge, Mass.: MIT Press, 1974), pp. 274–336, 242–253, 438–444;

"In Front of the Pawn Shop" ("Dangpu qian"), in *Genesis of a Revolution: An Anthology of Modern Chinese Short Stories,* edited and translated by Stanley R. Munro (Singapore: Heinemann Educational Books [Asia], 1979), pp. 94–108;

The Vixen (Beijing: Chinese Literature, 1987)—comprises "Creation" ("Chuangzao"), translated by Gladys Yang; "The Vixen" ("Xiao wu"), "The Shop of the Lin Family" ("Lin jia puzi"), and "Spring Silkworms" ("Chun can"), translated by Shapiro; "A Ballad of Algae" ("Shuizao xing"), translated by Simon Johnstone; "Second Generation" ("Erzi kaihui qule"), translated by Shapiro; "Liena and Jidi" ("Liena he Jidi"), translated by Johnstone; "Frustration" ("Weiqu"), translated by Shapiro; "The Beancurd Pedlar's Whistle" ("Mai doufu de xiaozi"), "Mist" ("Wu"), "Rainbow" ("Hong"), "An Old Country Gentleman" ("Lao xiangshen"), "The Incense Fair" ("Xiang shi"), "Before the Storm" ("Leiyu qian"), "Evening" ("Huanghun"), "Footprints on the Sand" ("Shatan shang de jiaoji"), "On Landscapes" ("Fengjing tan"), "In Praise of the White Poplar" ("Baiyang lizan"), "Mountains and Rivers of Our Great Land" ("Dadi shanhe"), "Night on Mount Qinling" ("Qinling zhi ye"), and "Recollections of Hainan" ("Hainan zayi"), translated by Yang; and "Mao Dun, Master Craftsmen of Modern Chinese Literature," by Fan Jun, translated by Niu Jin;

"Mud" ("Nining"), translated by Theodore Huters, in *Furrows, Peasants, Intellectuals and the State: Stories and Histories from Modern China,* edited by Helen F. Siu (Stanford, Cal.: Stanford University Press, 1990), pp. 33–39;

"Algae" ("Shuizao xing"), translated by Yi-tsi Mei Feuerwerker, in *Reading the Modern Chinese Short Story,* edited by Huters (Armonk, N.Y.: Sharpe, 1990), pp. 137–152.

OTHER: *Zhongguo yuyan chubian* [A Preliminary Collection of Chinese Fables], edited by Mao, as Shen Dehong (Shanghai: Shangwu yinshuguan, 1917);

Chuci xuanzhu [An Annotated Selection from the *Songs of Chu*], edited by Mao, as Shen Dehong (Shanghai: Shangwu yinshuguan, 1928);

Jindai wenxue mianmian guan [Aspects of Modern Literature], edited by Mao (Shanghai: Shijie shuju, 1929);

Hanyi xiyang wenxue mingzhu [On Famous Works of Western Literature in Chinese Translation], edited by Mao (Shanghai: Zhongguo wenhua fuwushe, 1935);

Zhongguo de yiri [One Day in China], edited by Mao (Shanghai: Shenghuo shudian, 1936); excerpts translated by Sherman Cochran, Andrew C. K. Hsieh, and Janis Cochran as *One Day in China: May 21, 1936* (New Haven: Yale University Press, 1983).

TRANSLATIONS: *Mao Dun yiwen xuanji* [Selected Translations by Mao Dun], 2 volumes (Shanghai: Shanghai yiwen chubanshe, 1981).

Mao Dun was, perhaps, the most influential leftist writer and critic in twentieth-century China. While many give that distinction to Lu Xun, the latter's fictional output was not nearly as large as that of Mao Dun; and, perhaps more important, Lu Xun did not leave behind a substantial and influential corpus of criticism and literary theory. Mao Dun did leave such a corpus, and he played the central role in defining the poetics of realistic fiction in China throughout most of the century. His many essays on works by major and minor modern Chinese authors are collected in *Mao Dun lun Zhongguo xiandai zuojia zuopin* (1980, Mao Dun on Works by Modern Chinese Authors) and *Mao Dun lun chuangzuo* (1980, Mao Dun on Literary Creation). A founding member of the Wenxue yanjiu hui (Literary Research Association), one of the principal goals of which was the study and introduction into China of Western literature, Mao Dun contributed articles describing literary trends in other countries and translated works of fiction and essays by Spanish, northern and Eastern European, and Russian and Soviet authors. In these ways he exerted an enormous influence on readers' and writers' understanding of modern naturalist and realist literature and on the technical development and artistic standards of modern Chinese fiction. He also published adaptations of Chinese myths and classics.

The best source of information on Mao Dun's childhood and youth is his own three-volume *Wo zouguo de daolu* (1981–1988, The Road I Have Walked), which narrates his life up to the point at which he began his creative writing. He was born Shen Dehong in Wuzhen, Zhejiang province, on 4 July 1896; his *zi* (style

Mao Dun in 1929 (from Mao Dun, edited by Zhuang Zhongqing, 1986; Collection of Thomas Moran)

name) was Shen Yanbing. His ancestors had worked their way up from the peasantry to become merchants and public officials, and the Shen home commanded prime waterfront space overlooking the river in the center of town. His father, Shen Yongxi, attained the degree of *xiucai* (the first of the three levels of the traditional civil service examination system) and was an accomplished practitioner of traditional Chinese herbal medicine. He aligned himself with the reformers at the end of the Qing dynasty who desired modernization on a Western model. Shen Yanbing's mother, Chen Aizhu, was relatively well educated and played an important role in his early education. He had a brother, Zemin, who was born in 1900. Their father died in 1905.

As the child of progressive-minded parents, Shen was able to attend the newest, most Westernized schools in his area; but by the time he was in middle school he was chafing at the persistence of old-fashioned thinking among the teachers and administrators. He enrolled in the preparatory school for Beijing University in 1913, but his family could not afford to send him to the university. Therefore, in 1916 he took a position at the Shangwu yinshuguan (Commercial Press) in Shanghai, correcting English papers for correspondence courses and participating in translation projects. He married Kong Dezhi in his hometown in March 1918.

After serving as an editor for the magazine *Xuesheng zazhi* (The Student Magazine), Shen began writing the column "Xiaoshuo xinchao lan" (New Tides in Fiction) for the prominent journal *Xiaoshuo yuebao* (Short Story Monthly) in 1920. In this role, and in step with the current Xin wenhua yundong (New Culture Movement), he published several polemical and prescriptive articles regarding the role of fiction in society. According to Marián Gálik in *The Genesis of Modern Chinese Literary Criticism (1917–1930)* (1980), at the beginning of his literary career Mao Dun believed in a "uniform process of the development of literature, applying to the entire world" and proposed a plan for translating important works of foreign literature into Chinese as models for Chinese writers. He also spoke out against art for art's sake and in support of works of fiction that were, in his view, aesthetically accomplished or, more important, presented truths about contemporary society. At the end of the year he joined Zhou Zuoren, Ye Shaojun, Zheng Zhenduo, and Wang Tongzhao in establishing the Literary Research Association and was given full editorial responsibility for *Xiaoshuo yuebao*, which in 1921 became the de facto organ of the association. He was one of the founders of the Chinese Communist Party, which was established in Shanghai in 1921. His daughter, Shen Xia, was born that same year, and his son, Shen Shuang, was born in December 1923.

Shen Yanbing participated in Communist Party organizational work throughout the early 1920s under the cover of his editorial and literary activities. In 1925 he served as one of the two Shanghai representatives of the "Left faction of the Nationalist Party"—as the Communist Party was called pursuant to the first United Front policy, a truce between the Communists and Nationalists while they combated warlords and imperialists. He and Zheng set up a radical newspaper, *Gongli bao* (The Truth), to report on the repression of demonstrations; the publication quickly went out of business: the government either shut it down officially or hired thugs to terrorize it until it shut itself down. Near the end of 1925 Shen served under Mao Zedong as director of the Central Propaganda Department of the Nationalist Party in Guangzhou.

At the end of 1926 the Beifa (Northern Expedition)—a military campaign to unify China under Nationalist rule—reached Wuhan in Hubei province. A "people's government" was established, and in January 1927 Shen assumed an administrative post at the

Wuhan campus of the Zhongyang junshi zhengzhi xuexiao (Central Military and Political Academy). In March the Communist Party assigned him to be the editor of the *Hankou Minguo ribao* (Hankou Republic Daily), but in July he quit and went into hiding when the local Nationalist leader, Wang Jingwei, initiated a purge of Communists in the city. In his article "Cong Guling dao Dongjing" (translated as "From Kuling to Tokyo," 1976), published in *Xiaoshuo yuebao* in 1928, Shen writes that he went to the mountain town of Guling to recuperate from an illness and then went to Shanghai in August. In fact, however, he left Wuhan in late July, on orders from the party, to take a bank draft to a contact in Jiujiang, Jiangxi province. In Jiujiang he was told to deliver the money to the party organization in Nanchang, about fifty-six miles south of Jiujiang. Unable to get a train ticket to Nanchang, he took a detour over Mt. Lu and through the town of Guling. In Guling he learned that the road to Nanchang was blocked. On 26 July he was preparing to leave for Shanghai but fell ill with dysentery. Communists took over Nanchang on 1 August, but troops allied with Jiang Jieshi forced them to withdraw four days later. Shen, in Guling, learned that the Communist uprising in Nanchang had failed. In mid August he went to Shanghai, where, according to Marston Anderson, he lived "in hiding and great despair over the outcome of the revolution."

Blacklisted by the Nationalists, Shen began his creative-writing career with the novella *Huanmie* (Disillusionment), which he published in *Xiaoshuo yuebao* in 1927 under the pen name Mao Dun. According to John Berninghausen in "The Central Contradiction in Mao Dun's Earliest Fiction" (1977), he took the name from the Chinese word *maodun* (contradiction); the writer Ye Shaojun changed the name "by adding the grass element to the character 'mao,' thus making it an actual surname and giving it a twist something like 'Kontradiction' in English." *Huanmie* was the first novella in a trilogy that Mao Dun completed with *Dongyao* (Vacillation) and *Zhuiqiu* (Pursuit), which were published serially in *Xiaoshuo yuebao* beginning in January and June 1928, respectively. In July 1928 Mao Dun went to Japan. The Shangwu yinshuguan (Commercial Press) in Shanghai published *Huanmie* and *Dongyao* as books in August and *Zhuiqiu* as a book in December. Over the next two years he wrote in Tokyo and Kyoto his first full-length novel, *Hong* (1930; translated as *Rainbow*, 1992); several short stories, essays, poems, and works of literary criticism; and his influential "ABC" guidebooks to Western literature and Chinese and Western mythology.

Western critics have been most interested in Mao Dun's early fiction, because it is less obviously tendentious than other works in the leftist canon. His early fiction is characterized by a focus on modern young intellectuals struggling with the conflicting values of their time, as well as with the tension between sociopolitical ideals and human nature. Many of these early short stories, novellas, and novels have female protagonists, and Mao Dun stands apart from virtually all progressive male writers of his time in consistently writing from a woman's perspective. According to C. T. Hsia, in his early works Mao Dun "records the passive feminine response to the chaotic events of contemporary Chinese history" in a "feminine . . . , romantic, sensuous, melancholic" idiom. His female protagonists' thoughts and desires are probed deeply and, by most accounts, convincingly. Much has been said about the allegorical and symbolic uses of women in modern Chinese literature to represent both tradition and modernity and to embody China's passivity and weakness in relation to the West; while maintaining these levels of meaning, Mao Dun portrays his female characters with a substantial degree of psychological realism.

This combination is demonstrated in his debut trilogy of novellas, *Huanmie, Dongyao,* and *Zhuiqiu,* which were collected in 1930 under the title *Shi* (Eclipse). *Huanmie* is the story of two women struggling with love and political engagement in 1920s Shanghai. Jing is an idealist of provincial origins, attracted to the big city by the stimulating possibility of living an unfamiliar but meaningful life. Hui was originally naive and idealistic like Jing but has experienced enough bitterness to have become cynical and hedonistic; yet, she is haunted by her conscience. The two women are plagued by unscrupulous suitors and a progression of political developments that extinguish any simple faith they may have had in historical progress. Jing believes that she has found true love with Qiang Meng, but at the end of the novella he is discharged from the hospital and recalled to the front lines of the Northern Expedition.

Dongyao narrates the deterioration of a political reform in Hubei province into a mindless riot. The hapless Nationalist official Fang Luolan is sent to administer the town; an idealist, he is unable to cope with the political factions and opportunists he finds there. In addition to his public dilemma, Fang has to deal with his ambivalent feelings about his meek, relatively traditional wife Meili and his attraction to his dynamic coworker Sun Wuyang. The price of his vacillation is a bloodbath in the political realm and the collapse of his family. Feng, his wife, and Sun hide in a dilapidated convent from the factional violence. Sun describes the killings and rapes that have taken place in town, and Meili imagines the gory details of these events in a hallucinatory vision.

Cover for Mao Dun's novel Ziye (1933; translated as Midnight, 1957), about the struggle between an industrialist committed to Chinese economic development and a financier working on behalf of foreign investors (from Yu Runqi, ed., Tang Tao cang shu, 2004; Bruccoli Clark Layman Archives)

In the final novella of the trilogy, *Zhuiqiu*, some of the characters from *Huanmie* and *Dongyao* return to Shanghai in the wake of the violent purge of Communists by the Northern Expedition. They still hope to accomplish something meaningful, but the choices they make—settling down with a family, teaching, journalism, and so forth—bring them misery, disfigurement, and disease. Those choices were reasonable, but, the novel makes it clear, they can lead to no good in a stagnated society in which progressive change has been aborted. The trilogy drew harsh criticism from leftist critics who believed that revolutionary literature should be uplifting and should reflect the struggles and nobility of the lower classes, rather than the despair of petite bourgeois intellectuals.

Mao Dun's early "feminine" period also includes *Ye qiangwei* (1929, Wild Roses), a collection of five stories that explore moral dilemmas from the points of view of young educated women. While less explicitly engaged with historical transformation than his longer works, the stories more clearly demonstrate the mechanics of gender in Mao Dun's fiction.

By critical consensus, Mao Dun's crowning achievement in the depiction of history through a feminine subjectivity is his novel *Hong*. While Ye Shengtao's *Ni Huanzhi* (1928; translated as *Schoolmaster Ni Huan-chih*, 1958) was modern China's first revolutionary bildungsroman, *Hong* was its first artistically successful one. Mao Dun's essay "Du *Ni Huanzhi*" (1929; translated as "On Reading *Ni Huanzhi*," 1996), published in *Wenxue zhoubao* (Literature Weekly) in July 1929, while he was in the midst of writing *Hong* or had just completed it, suggests that with his novel Mao Dun intended not only to vindicate himself as a revolutionary novelist but also to achieve what he believed Ye had tried to accomplish in *Ni Huanzhi*: to depict a young intellectual's struggle to contribute to a rapidly changing society and illustrate those changes without losing the character's individuality or psychological verisimilitude.

According to Mao Dun's "*Hong* ba" (Afterword to *Rainbow*)," *Hong* was supposed to be an epic narrative of the previous ten years; but he was unable to finish it during his sojourn in Japan and decided to publish it as it was. *Hong*, which was serialized in three issues of

Xiaoshuo yuebao starting in June 1929 and published in book form in 1930, relates the vagaries faced by Mei, a young woman from Sichuan, between 1919 and 1925. Running away from an arranged marriage, Mei becomes a schoolteacher; but, as would have been the case with many independent women at the time, she is ostracized amid rumors of sexual scandal. Like the schoolmaster Ni Huanzhi in Ye Shengtao's novel, and roughly at the same historical juncture, Mei travels to Shanghai to participate in revolutionary activity. While she experiences fulfillment in doing so, she also finds herself in the midst of a paradigmatic dilemma of revolutionary fiction: conflict between her "bourgeois" romantic feelings for her colleague Liang Gangfu and the purity of revolutionary consciousness, embodied by the cool-headed Liang, to which such feelings are an obstacle. *Hong* does not resolve the "love versus revolution" conflict: it ends with Mei setting out to participate in the fateful demonstration of 30 May 1925, in which twelve demonstrators were shot to death by British police in Shanghai's International Settlement. Mao Dun's later fiction turns away from an emphasis on private feelings and, for the most part, from the depiction of female protagonists; but traces of "femininity" can be found in his work throughout his career.

When Mao Dun returned to Shanghai in April 1930, the Zhongguo zuoyi zuojia lianmeng (Chinese League of Left-Wing Writers) had just been established. The group, in which he served for a time as acting secretary, attempted to consolidate the literary Left after years of divisiveness and government persecution. The league flourished from 1930 to 1933, waned after 1934, and dissolved in the spring of 1936. It was the most successful attempt since the Literary Research Association in the early 1920s to unify the modern Chinese literary scene.

Mao Dun is best known in China for the unambiguously revolutionary stories and novels he wrote after 1930, the most prominent of which are "Chun can" (1932; translated as "Spring Silkworms," 1956), "Lin jia puzi" (1932; translated as "The Shop of the Lin Family," 1956), and *Ziye* (1933; translated as *Midnight*, 1957). Hsia argues that these works bend to external pressures in the increasingly leftist literary scene of the 1930s yet still demonstrate Mao Dun's craftsmanship and sophistication as a writer.

"Chun can" was published in the journal *Xiandai/Les Contemporains* (The Moderns) in 1932 and is the title piece of a 1933 collection of Mao Dun's stories. Praised by Hsia as his "best story and the outstanding achievement in Chinese proletarian fiction," it is Mao Dun's first attempt to dramatize larger historical forces within the confines of a short story. One of his earliest uses of a rural setting, "Chun can" depicts a silk-producing village threatened by industrialization and economic imperialism; it is a portrait of immemorial, idyllic rural harmony slowly disintegrating under the pressure of an impersonal global capitalism. The peasants overcome great obstacles to bring their crop to market, but alien economic forces render their hard work meaningless. The fluctuations in cocoon prices caused by Japanese automated processing and man-made silk substitutes are unintelligible to the peasants, who never conceived of a world in which a bumper crop could be a burden. Responses to the crisis range from millenarian religious fanaticism to youthful calls for rebellion, but none are informed by an awareness of the nature of the economic and historical situation. The story is continued and takes a much more politically tendentious direction in "Qiu shou" (1933; translated as "Autumn Harvest," 1956) and "Can dong" (1937, Winter's End; translated as "Winter Ruin," 1956), but "Chun can" poses the issue in the most vivid human terms.

"Lin jia puzi," published in 1932 in *Zhongxuesheng* (The Middle-School Student) and collected in *Chun can*, is also about the collapse of an economic system and the consequences for individuals who are caught up in a process outside their control. Mr. Lin owns a general store in a small town and functions as a banker for many of his customers. But the availability of cheaper Japanese alternatives to his traditional merchandise and price fluctuations on the wholesale market so damage Lin's retail business that he cannot return his banking customers' savings, and the former pillar of the community is forced to flee ignominiously from the town. "Lin jia puzi" was made into a motion picture in 1959; it was criticized for being overly sympathetic to the bourgeois Mr. Lin.

Ziye portrays a titanic struggle for economic power between the forces of national industry, embodied by Wu Sunfu, and international market capital—and by extension, economic imperialism—represented by his nemesis, Zhao Botao. It is a grand narrative of social disintegration involving upper-class decadence, student and worker activism, rural and urban development, and financial intrigues. *Ziye* was intended to be the first installment in a multivolume epic about the historical and economic landscape of China in the early 1930s, but Mao Dun completed only one of the projected volumes.

The industrialist Wu is depicted in mythic proportions: he is physically large, charismatic, cunning, and ruthless but passionately committed to the success of Chinese industry in the face of foreign competition. He views the world economic crisis of 1930 as an opportunity to create a textile-manufacturing empire out of the ruins of dozens of small domestic factories, but to do so he must deal with the comprador financier

Cover for a 1935 edition of Chun can (1933, Spring Silkworms), a collection of Mao Dun's stories about economic hardships faced by peasants and small merchants in the 1930s (Wason Collection on East Asia–China, Kroch Asia Library, Cornell University)

Zhao and the latter's foreign investors and network of connections in the banking sector. Wu attempts to overwhelm Zhao by purchasing failing factories and engaging in a war of stock speculation; his failure is precipitated not by his own inadequacy but by his betrayal by relatives and friends whose support he needs to wage the battle.

Wu's grand Western-style mansion in Shanghai is the setting for many of the climactic scenes in the novel; the contrast between the metropolis and Wu's hometown in Zhejiang province, which he is attempting to industrialize, is depicted through the encounters with Shanghai of other members of his family. Wu's aged father dies within hours of his arrival, overwhelmed by the sensual overload of the city and his son's lifestyle, and Wu's younger sister, Huifang, never succeeds in fitting in with her urban peers. The rural-urban connection is also examined in satirical caricatures of rural gentry such as Feng Yunqing, who comes to Shanghai to make a fortune, prostitutes his daughter to get inside information about stocks, and loses his family's fortune. The novel also includes a younger generation of educated poets, revolutionaries, and scholars who resemble the main characters in Mao Dun's earlier fiction, as well as opportunists among the wealthy Shanghai elite such as the gold digger Xu Manli. Finally, Mao Dun meticulously presents the complex interactions of the workers and management of Wu's factories with each other and with Wu. In *Lun Mao Dun de shenghuo yu chuangzuo* (1980, On Mao Dun's Life and Work) Sun Zhongtian notes that the Communist writer and political leader Qu Qiubai called *Ziye* China's "first successful realistic novel."

These transitional works display two important characteristics that are absent from Mao Dun's earlier fiction: first, the depiction of the historical and economic forces preying on Chinese peasants in their everyday lives and work that is evident in "Chun can," "Qiu shou," and "Can dong," as well as in "Shuizao xing" (translated as "A Ballad of Algae," 1990), in Mao Dun's 1937 collection *Yanyun ji* (Mists and Clouds Anthology); second, the representation of Chinese society in a broad perspective, including all classes and social groups, that is found in *Ziye*. Yu-shih Chen argues in her *Realism and Allegory in the Early Fiction of Mao Dun* (1986) that works such as *Shi* and *Hong* allegorize the personalities and behaviors of characters, representing various facets of the complicated revolutionary movement during the Northern Expedition. In this way Mao Dun was able to dramatize the complex forces at work within the revolutionary ranks, as well as to express his disappointment at the failure of the first United Front. By not using a strictly realist aesthetic but employing the multi-edged tool of allegory, however, Mao Dun was not clearly expressing a political position, as leftist writers were expected to do; and he was setting himself up as a target for doctrinaire Marxist critics, because each allegorical detail could have many political meanings.

David Der-wei Wang argues in *Twentieth Century Chinese Fictional Realism: Mao Dun, Lao She, Shen Congwen* (1992) that the relationship of time and money becomes increasingly prominent from the rural setting of "Chun can" through the Lin family's town to the Shanghai metropolis in *Ziye*. That is, while the villagers manage their economy on a rigid yearly cycle, Mr. Lin, as a merchant, is accustomed to maximizing profit by responding to the unpredictable, changing circumstances of the market; the fluidity of the relationship of time and money is brought to the extreme in *Ziye*.

In 1934 Mao Dun and Lu Xun established the influential journal *Yiwen* (Translation). The two men also assisted Harold R. Isaacs in putting together his collection *Straw Sandals: Chinese Short Stories, 1918–1933* (1974), and they collaborated in drafting proclamations of the Chinese League of Left-Wing Writers that decried the violent suppression of revolutionary activity and congratulated the Communist Party on its arrival in the northeast after the Long March of 1934 to 1935.

The leftist literary community emphasized investigation of the living conditions of the working class and the integration of political activity with creative life. Mao Dun was interested enough in the new *baogao wenxue* (reportage literature) promoted by the League of Left-Wing Writers to write critical articles on it, and one of his most ambitious and successful experiments was the collective-writing project *Zhongguo de yiri* (1936; excerpts translated as *One Day in China: May 21, 1936*, 1983). Inspired by Maksim Gorky's idea of compiling newspaper clippings from all over the world on a single date into a book to be called "Den Mira" (One Day in the World), *Zhongguo de yiri* was limited to China but included a much broader variety of entries. The project began with a call for contributions in which people from all walks of life were to write about their activities on a certain day, 21 May 1936, in whatever form or genre they wished. About four hundred pieces were chosen for publication from the three thousand submissions; the preface attributes the smallness of the selection to financial limitations, particularly the consideration that many intended readers would not be able to afford a large book. *Zhongguo de yiri* has a decidedly raw and miscellaneous look; therefore, the reader is given the impression that the leftist political slant of the book is an accidental feature of a random sample of contributions, when, in fact, it is the outcome of a conscious selection of a small fraction of them.

During the 1937 to 1945 war with Japan, Mao Dun edited the journal *Nahan* (Outcry), later retitled *Fenghuo* (Beacon Fire), that combined several peacetime journals that closed at the outbreak of the war. In early 1938 he went to the provisional capital, Wuhan, where he participated in establishing the Zhonghua quanguo wenyijie kangdi xiehui (All-China Association of Literary Resistance) and served as one of its forty-five *lishi* (elected directors). The next year he started one of the most important wartime literary magazines, *Wenyi zhendi* (Literary Battlefront), in Guangzhou; edited *Yan lin* (Forest of Words), the literary supplement to the Hong Kong newspaper *Li bao*; and completed a novel, "Ni wang nali pao" (Where Will You Run?), which was serialized in *Li bao* in 1938 and republished in 1945 as *Di yi jieduan de gushi* (Story of the First Stage). The work dramatizes the choices faced by young, ambitious people during and after the Japanese invasion in the summer of 1937: to follow the Communists into their remote, mountainous base areas; to retreat into the cities of the interior, as the Nationalist government did; or to remain in the occupied cities and resist or cooperate with the invaders. Citing the character Pan Xueli, a stock speculator's daughter, as an example, Hsia says that Mao Dun "achieves his best effects in scenes depicting the weakness of bourgeois youth after a brief flirtation with patriotism."

In December 1938 Mao Dun went to Dihua (now Urumqi) in Xinjiang province, where he taught and served as chairman of the Xinjiang Cultural Association under the apparently leftist-sympathizing warlord Sheng Shicai. In 1940 Sheng betrayed the Communist cultural figures who had been attracted to his territory, and Mao Dun escaped to the Communist base at Yan'an. He taught for a few months at the Lu Xun Academy of Arts and brought his daughter and son to Yan'an to complete their studies. He then went to the wartime capital, Chongqing, and worked under Guo Moruo, minister of culture in the Nationalist government's Political Department. On the collapse of the Second United Front in 1941 he fled to Hong Kong, where he serialized his novel *Fushi* (Putrefaction) in Zou Taofen's magazine *Dazhong shenghuo* (Mass Life) from May to September 1941; it was published as a book in Shanghai in October. *Fushi* is the diary of Huiming, a young Nationalist secret-police agent. In the preface Mao Dun claims that the diary was found in an abandoned air-raid shelter in Chongqing. Huiming's work for the Nationalist regime troubles her conscience, and although she attempts to hide her guilt feelings by adopting a nihilistic attitude, her hostility toward the corruption and decadence that surrounds her shows that her moral sense has survived. She resolves to help a college girl escape employment with the secret police, at which point her diary ends. The preface raises the possibility that she has been killed.

The Japanese occupied Hong Kong in December 1941; with the help of Communist guerrillas, Mao Dun escaped to Guilin. There he wrote *Shuangye hong si eryue hua* (1943, Frosted Leaves as Red as February Flowers) in nine months. The title is an alteration of a line from a poem by the Tang dynasty poet Du Mu: "The frosted leaves are redder than February flowers." *Shuangye hong si eryue hua* was intended as the first volume of a trilogy that was to contrast the opportunistic, false appearance of revolutionary zeal, symbolized by "frosted red leaves," on the part of many activists during the period of the Northern Expedition in 1926–1927 with the less ostentatious but genuine commitment to the revolutionary cause that survived the 1927 Communist purge, symbolized by the "February flowers." The novel dramatizes the clash between traditional agriculture and landownership and modern industrial capitalism, which

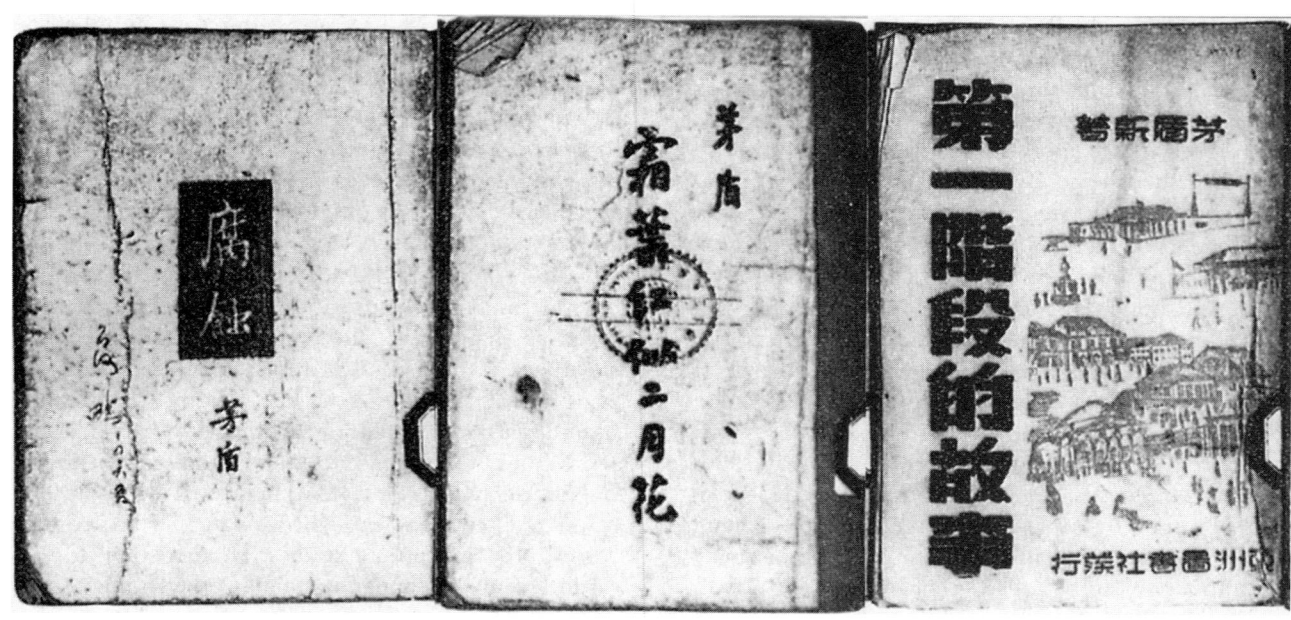

Covers for three novels by Mao Dun published during the war with Japan: Fushi *(1941, Putrefaction)*, Shuangye hong si eryue hua *(1943, Frosted Leaves as Red as February Flowers)*, and Di yi jieduan de gushi *(1945, Story of the First Stage) (from Lin Mohan, Fang Jing, and Shen Shiming, eds.*, Zhongguo kang Ri zhanzheng shiqi dahoufang wenxue shuxi: Di san pian. Xiaoshuo, *volume 4, 1989; Collection of Thomas Moran)*

are represented by the Zhao and Wang families, respectively. The focus is on the Zhang family, who are of scholarly civil-servant stock, with Zhang Xunru's marriage and its challenges at the center. Zhang's relative Qian Liangcai is an ineffectual and conflicted activist who tries to resist the exploitation of the local people by Wang Boshen's steamship company. Mao Dun interweaves domestic problems with social frictions and evenhandedly and realistically depicts both the recalcitrant and sympathetic sides of his peasant characters.

Mao Dun returned to Chongqing in 1942. In June 1945 the All-China Association of Literary Resistance held a banquet in honor of his twenty-five years of literary creation and established a literary prize in his name. It seems likely that he never saw his daughter again after leaving her in Yan'an five years earlier, as she died of an illness there in the late summer of 1945.

After the Japanese surrender in 1945, an armed conflict broke out between the Communists and the Nationalists that is often referred to as the Chinese civil war. To resist the Nationalists' efforts to regain control over China, Mao Dun drafted proclamations that were published in Chinese newspapers or sent to international organizations in which he decried human-rights abuses, such as the 1946 assassination of the poet and scholar Wen Yiduo by Nationalist agents, and called for international support for peace and democracy in China. He also endeavored to promote a better understanding of contemporary life in the Soviet Union, publishing translations of Soviet works and traveling to the country with his wife in late 1946 at the invitation of the Soviet cultural relations association. He wrote extensively about his tour of the Soviet Union, and his *Sulian jianwen lu* (1948, Seen and Heard in the Soviet Union) served the next generation as an influential account of the leading Communist nation. His daughter-in-law, Xiao Yi, a war correspondent, was killed during the battle for Taiyuan on 15 April 1949.

As a member of the Chinese Communist Party's cultural bureaucracy during the civil war and after the founding of the People's Republic in 1949, Mao Dun was forced to conform to the principles laid down by Mao Zedong in his 1942 "Zai Yan'an wenyi zuotanhui shang de jianghua" (Talks at the Yan'an Forum on Literature and Art). Hsia argues that some of Mao Dun's wartime fiction, such as *Shuangye hong si eryue hua*, written outside the jurisdiction of the party in Hong Kong or in China's interior, is still of literary significance; but during the civil war and after 1949 the European standards he had promoted in the 1930s had to be discarded in favor of Stalinist socialist realism.

Mao Dun was the editor of *Xiaoshuo yuebao* from 1946 to 1949. After 1949, because he was occupied with political and administrative work and because of the increased repression of artistic expression, he published only essays, articles, and travelogues. In 1949 he became minister of culture, president of the Zhonghua quanguo wenxue gongzuozhe xiehue (National Assembly of Literary and Art Workers)—renamed the Zhongguo zuojia xiehui (Chinese Writers' Association) in 1953—and vice president of the Zhongguo quanguo wenxue yishujie lianhehui (All-China Federation of Literary and Art Workers). He was also the first editor in chief of two of the flagships of Chinese Communist literature: *Renmin wenxue* (People's Literature), founded in 1949, and the English-language *Chinese Literature*, founded in 1951.

Between 1949 and the beginning of the Cultural Revolution in 1966 Mao Dun, like many other writers, had to distance himself from his pre-1949 work because it was ideologically suspect when judged from a Maoist point of view. Unlike some authors, he was at least partly sincere in rejecting his early works, particularly his novels that express sympathy for the travails of young bourgeois intellectuals at the expense of the masses. The only works of Mao Dun's that were made part of the Maoist canon were "Chun can," "Lin jia puzi," and *Ziye*.

According to Zhuang Zhongqing's "Mao Dun zhuyi jianbiao" (1986, A Concise Bibliography of Mao Dun's Publications), Mao Dun stepped down as minister of culture in January 1965. According to the *Biographical Dictionary of Republican China* (1967–1979), edited by Howard L. Boorman, Mao Dun was forced to leave office "on charges of ideological heresy in connection" with the 1959 movie version of his story "Lin jia puzi." Though he still held official positions during the Cultural Revolution, he rarely left his residence on the east side of Beijing; he enjoyed the protection of key political figures, but according to the 1998 memoir by his son, Shen Shuang (writing under the pen name Wei Tao), and Chen Xiaoman, he privately expressed dismay at the worsening situation. After the Cultural Revolution ended in 1976, he attended and spoke at conferences, published essays and occasional poetry, and oversaw the publication of collections of his work. His health worsened in February 1981, and he died on 27 March.

Western scholarly reception of Mao Dun's work divides into two camps. One is exemplified by Hsia, who proceeds from the conviction that standards of literary quality are universal—a position with which Mao Dun himself and most of his colleagues on the literary Left would have disagreed. Hsia praises the sophistication of Mao Dun's early writing but finds that his later work shows a "steady deterioration of a powerful imagination in the service of propaganda." Two articles in *Modern Chinese Literature in the May Fourth Era* (1977), edited by Merle Goldman, represent the other camp. John Berninghausen argues that Mao Dun's fiction is artistically compelling not despite his political convictions but because of them: Mao Dun's work, Berninghausen contends, is consistent with Marxist aesthetic theory. Yu-shih Chen theorizes that Mao Dun's early fiction is not only a realistic depiction of the frustration of bourgeois intellectual youths in the crucible of revolution but also an allegory of the inner and outer conflicts of the Chinese Communist Party, particularly in its relationship with the Nationalist Party. Chen elaborates on this reading in his *Realism and Allegory in the Early Fiction of Mao Dun* (1986). For Chen, Mao Dun was a passionately devoted Communist, and his early fiction was a sincere effort to create a truly revolutionary literature; this literature did not adhere to later Marxist recipes calling for stock character types and tendentious themes but was meant to be read as an allegory of the struggles of the Communist Party in the early years of its existence. These struggles are embodied in the romantic and political entanglements of the female protagonists of his novellas *Huanmie*, *Dongyao*, and *Zhuiqiu* and of his first long novel, *Hong*. Critics in both groups agree that Mao Dun was engaged throughout his career in a struggle between what he wished to accomplish in the form of politically engaged creative expression and what he was able to achieve. The consensus is that he is a compelling literary artist who was prevented from realizing his artistic vision but nevertheless made a significant contribution to the culture of modern China.

Bibliographies:

"Mao Dun zhu yi nianbiao," in *Mao Dun yanjiu ziliao*, 3 volumes, edited by Sun Zhongtian and Zha Guohua (Beijing: Zhongguo shehui kexue chubanshe, 1983), III: 2–269;

Zhuang Zhongqing, "Mao Dun zhuyi jianbiao," in *Mao Dun*, edited by Zhuang (Hong Kong: Sanlian shudian Xianggang fendian, 1986), pp. 259–273;

"Mao Dun shengping zhu yi nianbiao" and "Mao Dun zhuyi shumu," in *Mao Dun quanji: Fu ji* (Beijing: Renmin wenxue chubanshe, 2001), pp. 1–409.

Biographies:

Zha Guohua, *Mao Dun nianpu* (Wuhan: Changjiang wenyi chubanshe, 1985);

Wan Shuyu, *Mao Dun nianpu* (Suzhou: Zhejiang wenyi chubanshe, 1986);

Li Biaojing, *Mao Dun zhuan* (Beijing: Tuanjie chubanshe, 1990);

Zhong Guisong, *Mao Dun zhuan* (Beijing: Dongfang chubanshe, 1996).

References:

Marston Anderson, "Mao Dun, Zhang Tianyi, and the Social Impediments to Realism," in his *The Limits of Realism: Chinese Fiction in the Revolutionary Period*

(Berkeley: University of California Press, 1990), pp. 119–179;

Dorothee Balthus, *Die moderne Frau im Fruhwerk des Schriftstellers Mao Dun* (Bochum, Germany: Brockmeyer, 1989);

John Berninghausen, "The Central Contradiction in Mao Dun's Earliest Fiction," in *Modern Chinese Literature in the May Fourth Era,* edited by Merle Goldman (Cambridge, Mass.: Harvard University Press, 1977), pp. 233–259;

Berninghausen, "Mao Dun's Fiction, 1927–1936: The Standpoint and Style of His Realism," dissertation, Stanford University, 1979;

Lorenz Bichler, "Conjectures on Mao Dun's Silence as a Novelist after 1949," in *Autumn Floods: Essays in Honour of Marián Gálik,* edited by Raoul Findeison and Robert Gassmann (Bern: Peter Lang, 1997), pp. 195–206;

Chingkiu Stephen Chan, "Eros as Revolution: The Libidinal Dimension of Despair in Mao Dun's *Rainbow*," *Journal of Oriental Studies,* 24, no. 1 (1986): 37–53;

Susan W. Chen, "Mao Tun the Translator," *Harvard Journal of Asiatic Studies,* 48 (1988): 71–84;

Chen, "The Personal Element in Mao Tun's Early Fiction," *Harvard Journal of Asiatic Studies,* 43 (1983): 187–213;

Yu-shih Chen, "False Harmony: Mao Dun on Women and Family," *Modern Chinese Literature,* 7, no. 1 (1993): 131–152;

Chen, "Mao Dun and the Use of Political Allegory in Fiction: A Case Study of His 'Autumn in Kuling,'" in *Modern Chinese Literature in the May Fourth Era,* pp. 261–280;

Chen, *Realism and Allegory in the Early Fiction of Mao Dun* (Bloomington: Indiana University Press, 1986);

Hilary Chung, "Questing the Goddess: Mao Dun and the New Woman," in *Autumn Floods: Essays in Honour of Marián Gálik,* pp. 165–183;

Yi-tsi Mei Feuerwerker, "The Dialectics of Struggle: Ideology and Realism in Mao Dun's 'Algae,'" in *Reading the Modern Chinese Short Story,* edited by Theodore Huters (Armonk, N.Y.: Sharpe, 1990), pp. 51–73;

Marián Gálik, "From Chuang-tzu to Lenin: Mao Tun's Intellectual Development," *Asian and African Studies* (Bratislava), 3 (1967): 98–110;

Gálik, *Mao Tun and Modern Chinese Literary Criticism* (Wiesbaden: Steiner, 1969);

Gálik, "Mao Tun's Midnight: Creative Confrontation with Zola, Tolstoy, Wertherism and Nordic Mythology," in *Milestones in Sino-Western Literary Confrontation (1898–1979),* edited by Gálik (Wiesbaden: Harrassowitz, 1986), pp. 73–100;

Gálik, "Mao Tun's Struggle for a Realistic and Marxist Theory of Literature," in his *The Genesis of Modern Chinese Literary Criticism, 1917–1930* (London: Curzon Press, 1980), pp. 191–213;

Gálik, "The Names and Pseudonyms Used by Mao Tun," *Archiv Orientalni,* 31 (1968): 80–108;

Gálik, "Studies in Modern Chinese Literary Criticism: I. Mao Tun, 1919–1920," *Asian and African Studies* (Bratislava), 3 (1967): 113–140;

Gálik, "Studies in Modern Chinese Literary Criticism: II. Mao Tun on Men of Letters, Character and Functions of Literature (1921–1922)," *Asian and African Studies* (Bratislava), 4 (1968): 30–43;

Fritz Gruner, "Der Roman Tzu-yeh von Mao Tun—ein bedeutendes realistisches Werk der neuen chinesischen Literatur," *Asian and African Studies* (Bratislava), 11 (1975): 57–72;

Michel Hockx, *Questions of Style: Literary Societies and Literary Journals in Modern China, 1911–1937* (Leiden: Brill, 2003), pp. 31, 47, 54, 57, 59–60, 64, 69, 70, 72, 194, 204, 209, 212–214, 217, 220, 251;

C. T. Hsia, *A History of Modern Chinese Fiction* (New Haven: Yale University Press, 1961), pp. 155–160, 350–359;

Theodore Huters, "Mao Dun's *Fushi*: The Politics of the Self," *Modern Chinese Literature,* 5, no. 2 (1989): 242–268;

Wilt Idema, "Mao Dun and Speenhoff, or How a Fallen Woman from Rotterdam Started a New Life in Shanghai," in *Words from the West: Western Texts in Chinese Literary Context. Essays to Honor Erich Zürcher on His Sixty-Fifth Birthday,* edited by Lloyd Haft (Leiden: Centre of Non-Western Studies, 1993), pp. 35–47;

Oldrich Kral, "Researches into Mao Dun's Aesthetics," *Acta Universitatis Carolinae-Philologica,* 2 (1965): 75–90;

Joseph S. M. Lau, "Naturalism in Modern Chinese Fiction," *Literature East and West,* 12 (1968): 149–158;

Li Biaojing, *Mao Dun wenti lun chugao* (Xiamen: Xiamen daxue chubanshe, 1991);

Li and Wang Jialiang, eds., *Jianming Mao Dun cidian* (Lanzhou: Gansu jiaoyu chubanshe, 1993);

Li Xiu, *Mao Dun bijiao yanjiu lun gao* (Taiyuan: Beiyue wenyi chubanshe, 1988);

Li Xiu, ed., *Mao Dun yanjiu zai guowai* (Changsha: Hunan renmin chubanshe, 1984);

Lin Mohan, Fang Jing, and Shen Shiming, eds., *Zhongguo kang Ri zhangzheng shiqi dahoufang wenxue shuxi, di san pian: Xiaoshuo,* volume 4 (Chongqing: Chongqing chubanshe, 1989);

Sylvia Li-chun Lin, "Unwelcome Heroines: Mao Dun and Yu Dafu's Creations of a New Chinese

Woman," *Journal of Modern Literature in Chinese,* 1 (January 1998): 71–94;

Hiromi Matsui, ed., *Mao Dun pinglun ji,* 5 volumes (Tokyo: Tōkyō Toritsu Daigaku Jinbun Gakubu Chūgoku Bungaku Kenkyūjo, 1957–1966);

Bonnie S. McDougall, "Dominance and Disappearance in May Fourth: A Post-Feminist Review of Fiction by Mao Dun and Ling Shuhua," in *Autumn Floods: Essays in Honour of Marián Gálik,* pp. 283–306;

McDougall, "The Search for Synthesis: T'ien Han and Mao Tun in 1920," in *Search for Identity: Modern Literature and the Creative Arts in Asia,* edited by A. R. Davis (Sydney: Angus & Robertson, 1974), pp. 225–254;

Jaroslav Průšek, "Mao Tun," in his *The Lyrical and the Epic: Studies of Modern Chinese Literature* (Bloomington: Indiana University Press, 1980), pp. 121–142;

"Shen Yen-ping," in *Biographical Dictionary of Republican China,* 5 volumes, edited by Howard L. Boorman (New York: Columbia University Press, 1967–1979), III: pp. 110–115;

Shi Yao, Wang Jialiang, Qian Chengyi, and Luo Hanchao, *Mao Dun wenyi meixue sixiang lungao* (Hangzhou: Hangzhou daxue chubanshe, 1991);

Vincent Y. C. Shih, "Mao Tun: The Critic," *China Quarterly,* no. 19 (1964): 84–98; no. 20 (1964): 128–162;

Sun Zhongtian, *Lun Mao Dun de shenghuo yu chuangzuo* (Tianjin: Baihua wenyi chubanshe, 1980);

Sun, *Zi ye de yishu shijie* (Shanghai: Shanghai wenyi chubanshe, 1990);

Wan Shuyu and Li Xiu, eds., *Mao Dun he wo* (Zhongguo guangbo dianshi chubanshe, 1996);

David Der-wei Wang, "Mao Tun and Naturalism: A Case of 'Misreading' in Modern Chinese Literary Criticism," *Monumenta Serica,* 37 (1986–1987): 169–195;

Wang, *Twentieth Century Chinese Fictional Realism: Mao Dun, Lao She, Shen Congwen* (New York: Columbia University Press, 1992);

Wang Jialiang, *Mao Dun xiaoshuo lun* (Shanghai: Shanghai wenyi chubanshe, 1989);

Wei Tao (Shen Shuang) and Chen Xiaoman, *Fuqin Mao Dun de wannian* (Shanghai: Shanghai shudian chubanshe, 1998);

Tak-wai Wong and M. A. Abbas, "Mao Tun's 'Spring Silkworms': Rhetoric and Ideology," in *The Chinese Text: Studies in Comparative Literature,* edited by Ying-hsiung Chou (Hong Kong: Chinese University Press, 1986), pp. 191–207;

Richard H. Yang, "*Midnight:* Mao Tun's Political Novel," in *China's Literary Image,* edited by Paul K. T. Sih (Jamaica, N.Y.: St. John's University Press, 1975);

Ye Ziming, *Lun Mao Dun sishi nian de wenxue daolu* (Shanghai: Shanghai wenyi chubanshe, 1959);

Ye, *Mao Dun man ping* (Tianjin: Baihua wenyi chubanshe, 1983);

Ye, *Meng hui xing yi–Mao Dun wannian de shenghuo jianwen* (Nanjing: Nanjing daxue chubanshe, 1991);

Yu Runqi, ed., *Tang Tao cang shu* (Beijing: Beijing chubanshe, 2004), p. 148;

Zhongguo kang Ri zhangzheng shiqi dahoufang wenxue shuxi: Di san pian. Xiaoshuo, volume 4 (Chongqing: Chongqing chubanshe, 1989);

Zhongguo Mao Dun yanjiu hui, ed., *Mao Dun yu ershi shiji* (Beijing: Huaxia chubanshe, 1997);

Zhuang Zhongqing, *Mao Dun de chuangzuo licheng* (Beijing: Renmin wenxue chubanshe, 1982);

Zhuang, *Mao Dun de wenlun licheng* (Shanghai: Shanghai wenyi chubanshe, 1996);

Zhuang, *Mao Dun shi shi fa wei* (Changsha: Hunan renmin chubanshe, 1985);

Zhuang, ed., *Mao Dun ji shi* (Chengdu: Sichuan wenyi chubanshe, 1986);

Zhuang, ed., *Mao Dun yanjiu lun ji* (Tianjin: Tianjin renmin chubanshe, 1984).

Mu Shiying

(1912 – June 1940)

Yingjin Zhang
University of California, San Diego

SELECTED BOOKS: *Jiaoliu* [Interflow] (Shanghai: Fangcao shudian, 1930);

Nanbeiji [North-and-South-Poles] (Shanghai: Hufeng shuju, 1932; enlarged edition, Shanghai: Xiandai shuju, 1933)–includes "Hei xuanfeng," translated by Wiu-kit Wong as "Black Whirlwind," *Renditions,* no. 37 (Spring 1992): 23–34;

Gongmu [The Public Cemetery] (Shanghai: Xiandai shuju, 1933)–includes "Yezonghui li de wuge ren," translated by Randolph Trumbull as "Five in a Nightclub," *Renditions,* no. 37 (Spring 1992): 5–22;

Baijin de nüti suxiang [The Platinum Nude] (Shanghai: Fuxing shuju, 1934; Shanghai: Xiandai shuju, 1934);

Sheng chunü de ganqing [The Love of St. Virgin] (Shanghai: Liangyou tushu yinshua gongsi, 1935).

Collections: *Zhongguo xin ganjue pai shengshou: Mu Shiying xiaoshuo quanji* (Masters of New Perceptionism: The Complete Stories of Mu Shiying), edited by Yue Qi (Beijing: Zhongguo wenlian chuban gongsi, 1996);

Mu Shiying xiaoshuo quanji [The Complete Stories of Mu Shiying] (Shanghai: Xuelin chubanshe, 1997);

Mu Shiying xiaoshuo quanji, 2 volumes (Changchun: Shidai wenye chubanshe, 2001).

Mu Shiying (from Mu Shiying xiaoshuo quanji, *2001; Collection of Thomas Moran)*

Mu Shiying was a precocious talent in the ideologically divided, polemical literary scene of early 1930s China. His two distinct styles–proletarian vernacular and modernist *xin ganjue* (variously translated as "New Perceptionist" and "New Sensationalist," though the former more closely reflects these writers' intention of experimenting with the literary representation of new urban perceptions)–made him a literary sensation and won him a following among young urban readers, many of whom were would-be writers. Mu's writing career was short: he published little after 1935 and was forgotten until scholarly interest in New Perceptionism was renewed in the 1980s.

Mu was born in 1912–the exact date is unknown–in the coastal province of Zhejiang. His father ran a small bank. Mu majored in Chinese literature at Guanghua (Aurora) University in Shanghai, which by the early 1930s had replaced Beiping (as Beijing was known from 1928 to 1949) as the cultural center of China and was also the country's economic and financial center. At the university Mu became acquainted with a group of upcoming writers that included Dai Wangshu, Du Heng (pseudonym of Su Wen), Liu Na'ou, Shi Zhecun, and Ye Lingfeng. He and Ye, who had just made the transition from writing in the May Fourth realist style to a more popular type of urban fiction, rented rooms in a house owned by Liu. Born in Taiwan and educated in Japan, Liu single-handedly launched a literary fashion by introducing Japanese *Shin kangaku kai* (New Perceptionism) into China in 1928. Mu was quick to learn this new mode of writing, and in a few years he surpassed Liu to become the leading figure of Chinese New Perceptionism.

The stories that marked Mu's entry into the literary arena lack ostentatious modernist trimmings. On the contrary, his *Nanbeiji* (1932, North-and-South Poles), which stunned the literary establishment with its distinctive voice, is a collection of eccentric stories about poverty-stricken lower-class people struggling to survive in a ruthless world. The title piece was first published in *Xiaoshuo yuebao* (Short Story Monthly), a stronghold of May Fourth and leftist writers. A few of his other stories appeared in *Xin wenyi* (New Literature and Art), a monthly edited by Shi. In 1932 Shi became the editor of *Xiandai/Les Contemporains* (The Moderns), an influential journal that helped cultivate literary modernism in China, and several of Mu's stories were published there.

Immediately after Mu began to publish, the literary historian Wang Zhefu called him a new literary star. For Wang, Mu was a promising writer not so much because of the subject matter of his stories but because of his distinctive use of a proletarian vernacular characterized by street-smart humor, natural liveliness, sensational primitivism, and deliberate vulgarism. The eminent literary scholar Zhu Ziqing also gave high praise to Mu's first collection (quoted by Liu Xinhuang. For Zhu, Mu's proletarian vernacular achieved a naturalness unsurpassed by the writers of so-called *puluo wenxue* (proletarian literature), which was more ideological than artistic and, therefore, earned the appellation "slogan literature."

The first story in *Nanbeiji*, "Hei xuanfeng" (translated as "Black Whirlwind," 1992), which bears the completion date of 24 September 1929, retells the traditional *Shuihu zhuan* (Outlaws of the Marsh or The Story of the Water Margin; translated as *All Men Are Brothers*, 1933), attributed to Shi Nai'an; a silk factory, a college campus, and a small town, all in the suburbs of contemporary Shanghai, provide the locations for Mu's investigation of social issues and sexual tensions as a preindustrial community enters the modern age. "Shouzhi" (Fingers), dated 6 October 1930, depicts the death of a female silk-factory worker. In the title story, dated 1 August 1930, Yu Shangyi, nicknamed Little Lion, leaves his hometown after his sweetheart is corrupted by urban commercialism and takes a train to Shanghai. At first homeless, he becomes a ricksha puller, a customer of rundown brothels, and, finally, a bodyguard for the wealthy Liu family. In this job he serves as the reader's witness to the decadent bourgeois lifestyle. Old Master Liu is so rich that he is willing to pay a ransom of 80,000 yuan for his kidnapped Fifth Mistress. While one of Liu's concubines is having an affair with Liu's son, Liu is involved with a movie star, Miss Duan, who also takes both Little Lion and another young man as lovers. "Nanbeiji" ends with an act of rebellion: Little Lion pushes Master Liu out of the way as he walks off the job. Class conflict runs throughout the stories in *Nanbeiji*. The homeless protagonist of "Zamen de shijie" (Our World), dated 1930, vents the author's anger at the capitalist system, declaring that he hates "money and all moneyed people." At the end of the story he becomes a pirate and plunders commercial ships. Mu gives the same rebellious spirit to a group of striking fishermen in "Shenghuo zai haishang de renmen" (People Living on the Sea), dated 2 January 1931.

Three features of Mu's first—and often neglected—collection of stories deserve attention. First, he adopts the tone of a traditional marketplace storyteller, writing as if he himself were poor, angry, and rebellious. This imaginary identification with the working class is a narrative strategy rather than a political statement. Second, Mu's writing evinces a kind of raw masculinity in its graphic description of violence: eyeballs are poked out; heads are chopped off; and corpses are burned. Mu shared his preoccupation with fictional violence with Shi, and both men foreshadow a fascination with brutality in the work of avant-garde writers of the late 1980s such as Su Tong and Yu Hua. Third, the figure of the femme fatale, a favorite of Mu's in his later work, makes her initial appearance in *Nanbei ji*; here she is either an unfilial daughter corrupted by commercialism or an urban seductress exuding depraved sexuality.

With the publication of *Gongmu* (The Public Cemetery) in 1933 Mu made the transition from the proletarian vernacular to New Perceptionism. In the preface he declares that he will be "faithful to himself and thus to others." Unlike certain hypocritical—presumably leftist—writers who use "phony slogans" to increase their visibility with the public, he prefers to record his own observations of reality, note occurrences of chance or accident, and transcribe his subconscious as it appears to him in dreams. He says that he uses the name Pierrot, from the clown figure in French pantomime, to refer to people who are squeezed or crushed by life and cannot fight back against their oppressors. According to Mu, all except the utterly insensitive bury deep in their hearts a feeling of inescapable loneliness; everyone is

Cover for Mu's Nanbeiji (1932, North-and-South-Poles), a collection of stories about poor people struggling to survive (from Yu Runqi, ed., Tang Tao cang shu, 2004; Bruccoli Clark Layman Archives)

spiritually isolated; and everyone is either partially or completely misunderstood by others.

In *Gongmu*, Mu explores human psychology; the setting for this exploration is, for the most part, the city. "Shanghai de hubuwu" (Shanghai Fox-Trot) was first published in *Xiandai/Les Contemporains* in 1932; it was intended as part of a novel to be called "Zhongguo 1931" (China 1931), which Mu never completed. The story demonstrates Mu's skill in presenting slices of urban life and fragments of human perception in a fashion reminiscent of a motion-picture montage. Quick shots of random street scenes of murder and prostitution are interspersed with longer descriptions of the urban mise-en-scène such as a foreign-style mansion in which mistresses demand money from their men, a dance hall where music intensifies the melancholy mood of pleasure seekers, and a hotel in which trafficking in sex and drugs takes place. "Yezonghui li de wuge ren" (translated as "Five in a Nightclub," 1992) is a longer story in which five characters get drunk in a nightclub to forget their losses, at least temporarily: Hu Junyi, a stockbroker, has lost all of his assets, 800,000 yuan, in a single day; Zheng Ping, a college student, has lost his sweetheart, and his hair has turned white overnight; Daisy Huang, a twenty-eight-year-old socialite, has lost her youth and her charm; Ji Jie, a scholar of Shakespearean theater, has lost himself in the daily interaction of fact and fiction; and Miao Zongdan, a dutiful clerk, has lost his job as first secretary to the mayor. The story ends with loss of life: first, the wife and newborn baby of Johnny, the club's saxophone player, die at the hospital after Johnny's boss refuses to let him leave work early to be with them; then, Hu Junyi commits suicide outside the nightclub.

In contrast to these two stories about urban disillusionment, "Bei dangzuo xiaoqianpin de nanzi" (Men Kept as Playthings), about fashionable college students' dating and nightlife, shows Mu's fascination with what the city can offer. A character named Rongzi expresses her admiration for Mu and for Mu's kindred spirits: the writers Paul Morand, Yokomitsu Riichi, Horiguchi Daigaku, Sinclair Lewis, and Liu Na'ou and the graphic artist Guo Jianying. In return, the narrator expresses his admiration for her as the quintessential urban woman: "Rongzi, what a modern girl thriving on stimulation and speed! You are a mixture of Jazz, machinery, speed, urban culture, American flavor, and modern beauty." The story begins with the male narrator's judgmental look at a female student: her mouth that tells lies, her eyes that deceive, her cat-like head, her red silk *qipao* that shows off her snake-like curves, and her red satin high-heeled shoes. In short, he sees her as a creature that embodies both tenderness and danger and consumes male passions like chocolates. As these passages demonstrate, narcissism and voyeurism are fully at work in Mu's New Perceptionist fiction.

From voyeurism Mu ventures into eroticism, which sometimes verges on pornography. In "Craven 'A,'" named after a brand of cigarette, Mu takes the reader on a tour of a grand imaginary land, beginning with its dark forests, winding through its twin lakes and twin peaks, and finally entering its bustling commercial port. With a little reflection, the reader realizes that this description is an allegorical map of the female body as an imaginary vacationland for male adventurers to explore.

In other stories Mu envisions the suburbs as a fantastic place where battered and dazed urbanites can indulge themselves and find temporary escape from the pressures of city life. "Hei mudan" (Black Peony) follows a dance-hall hostess who pretends to be a peony—a spirit flower from a classic Chinese story of the marvelous—and seeks refuge in a suburban mansion owned by a recluse. The title story, first published in *Xiandai/Les Contemporains* in May 1932, is sentimental in tone. Distant from disorienting urban street life, the public cemetery nurtures a doomed love affair between the narrator and a fairy-like terminally ill girl. The cemetery gardens provide the metaphor of life as a cycle and add to the lament for passing youth and withering love.

The story collection *Baijin de nüti suxiang* (1934, The Platinum Nude) continues Mu's obsession with urban psychology and precarious human emotions. In the preface Mu likens himself to someone who has been thrown out of a fast-moving train and realizes in his dying moments that "all concepts and all beliefs are gone; all standards, laws, and values are obscured; . . . all human joys, sorrows, anxieties, dreams, and hopes . . . are gathered and then dispersed again, reshaped in a turning kaleidoscope." Another passage in the preface continues the train metaphor and gives further testimony to Mu's pessimistic view of urban life:

> Life is an express train. Yet we are not vacationers sitting comfortably in the train viewing beautiful scenery. Rather, we are professional travelers forced to run as quickly as we can in pursuit of the ever-rolling train. In such a fierce competition with an inorganic steam-engine train, an organic man is surely to exhaust himself some day and abruptly fall dead on the road!

Despite Mu's grim philosophizing in the preface, the title story is almost playful in its probing of the sudden sexual awakening of a doctor as he stands before a naked female patient. The theme of sexual awakening is also addressed in "Luotuo, Nicai zhuyi zhe yu nüren" (Camel, the Nietzschean Scholar, and Women). More lighthearted than many of Mu's stories, these two pieces explore the prominent place that "looking" has in the fantasy life of modern urbanites—particularly men looking at women. "PIERROT," on the other hand, dramatizes the alienation of a writer who is misunderstood by his lovers, critics, and readers. Pan participates in social activism, is imprisoned, and ends up abandoned by almost everyone with whom he has associated. When he is released from prison, he walks alone in the street. Returning to the interest in social issues evident in Mu's first short-story collection, "Benbu xinwenlan bianjishi li yizha feigao shang de gushi" (Story from a Batch of Manuscripts Discarded by the Editorial Staff of the Local News Section) takes the form of an investigative report on an abused and imprisoned dance-hall hostess.

Critics in the 1980s and 1990s tended to overlook Mu's attention to social issues and concentrated on his contribution to a brief phase of modernism in 1930s China. One of his modernist techniques is fragmented perceptions: rather than give the reader panoramic descriptions, Mu prefers to "zoom in" on specific objects—most often parts of the female body,

Cover for the enlarged edition (1933) of Nanbeiji
(Wason Collection on East Asia–China, Kroch
Asia Library, Cornell University)

such as eyes, lips, and legs, but also parts of objects, such as the leg of a table. A second modernist technique is inventive orthography: Mu uses unusual arrangements of characters, numbers, and punctuation to convey the intensity of the experiences he records in his fiction. In "Gongmu," for example, a series of 3s represents crawling ants: "Life is as trivial as ants. . . . There are 3 3 3 3 3 3 3 3 3 3 3 3 . . . crawling toward me in all directions and in endless processions . . . Crushed! I am really crushed!" A third technique is repetition: Mu often describes the same action over and over again, changing only the performer or the recipient of the action; in this way he intimates urbanites' loss of individuality as they go about their similar daily routines.

In the mid 1930s Mu became interested in cinema. He edited the movie sections of the newspaper

Chen bao (Morning Post) and the magazine *Wenyi huabao* (Literature and Art Pictorial), on the latter as coeditor with Ye Lingfeng in 1934–1935. He began writing movie criticism and participated in a heated debate with leftist writers over the issue of *ruanxing dianying* (soft cinema), a type of motion picture that Liu Na'ou and Huang Jiamo, coeditors of *Xiandai dianying* (Modern Cinema), proposed in opposition to the heavily ideological leftist movies that had become popular. Liu and Huang argued that movies should provide the audience with "soft" images and "soft" feelings: they should be "ice cream for the eyes" and "a comfortable sofa for the heart." Soft cinema was widely regarded as irrelevant—or, indeed, detrimental—to the *Guofang wenxue* (Literature for National Defense) and *guofang dianying* (cinema of national defense) against the Japanese invasion of China that was being produced by leftist and progressive writers and moviemakers. Thus, Mu, like Liu, came onto the literary scene as a leftist, only to end his career as an opponent of the Left.

After the Japanese occupied Shanghai in 1937, Mu fled to Hong Kong. There he worked for the *Xingdao ribao* (Hong Kong Daily), served as a screenwriter for the Hua'nan Film Company, and is reported to have directed *Ye mingzhu* (1937, Night Pearl), a tragic story about a dance hostess, for the Dapeng Film Company. For unknown reasons he returned to Shanghai in 1939 and went to work in the media and moviemaking agencies of the pro-Japanese government of Wang Jingwei. Some of Mu's friends speculated that his wife, Qiu Feifei, who had been a well-known dance hostess in Shanghai, might have pressured him to come back. In Shanghai, Mu was responsible for the literary supplements of the newspapers *Zhonghua ribao* (China Daily) and *Guomin xinwen* (National News). After Liu Na'ou was assassinated in 1939, Mu succeeded him in helping to coordinate activities in the Shanghai movie industry. In 1939 and 1940 he made two visits to Japan under the sponsorship of the Japanese military government. There he was paraded as an accomplished Chinese writer and friend of Japan, and he met with some of his Japanese New Perceptionist counterparts. He was shot to death on his way to work in June 1940, presumably by underground Nationalist agents; one source gives the date of his assassination as 8 June, another as 28 June, and some sources erroneously give the year of his death as 1939. After his death, some of the writers he had met in Japan published articles commemorating him.

Mu Shiying's creative career lasted only about five years; nevertheless, it demonstrates the vitality of modernist aesthetics and urban sensibility in China. The change in Mu's literary style and political affiliation points to the volatile climate of the 1930s, as well as the relative freedom enjoyed by Chinese writers of all ideological persuasions during the period. Since the 1980s, fascination with modernism in China has focused renewed attention on Mu Shiying and his fellow New Perceptionists in Asia, Europe, and North America. These studies highlight the similarities between the 1930s and the 1980s and 1990s, two periods when Chinese cultural life reacted to changing political circumstances and a vibrant commercial economy.

References:

Huang Jundong, "Mu Shiying he ta de zuopin," *Siji* (Hong Kong) 1 (1972): 38–42;

Leo Ou-fan Lee, *Shanghai Modern: The Flowering of a New Urban Culture in China, 1930–1945* (Cambridge, Mass.: Harvard University Press, 1999), pp. 211–231;

Liu Xinhuang, *Kangzhan shigi lunxiangu wenxue shi* (Tabei: Chengwen chubanshe, 1980), p. 81;

Liu Yichang, "Shuangchong renge: Maodun de laiyuan," *Siji* (Hong Kong), 1 (1972): 31–37;

Shu-mei Shih, *The Lure of the Modern: Writing Modernism in Semicolonial China, 1917–1937* (Berkeley: University of California Press, 2001), pp. 302–338;

Su Xuelin, *Er san shi niandai zuojia yu zuopin* (Taibei: Guangdong chubanshe, 1979), pp. 420–427;

Randolph Trumbull, "The Shanghai Modernists," dissertation, Stanford University, 1989, pp. 152–191;

Wang Zhefu, *Zhongguo xin wenxue yundong shi* (Beiping: Jiecheng yinshuju, 1933), pp. 235–236;

Yan Jiayan, *Zhongguo xiandai xiaoshuo liupai shi* (Beijing: Renmin wenxue chubanshe, 1989), pp. 137–140;

Yang Yi, *Zhongguo xiandai xiaoshuoshi*, 3 volumes (Beijing: Renmin wenxue chubanshe, 1986–1991), II: 685–698;

Ye Lingfeng, "Tan Mu Shiying," *Siji* (Hong Kong), 1 (1972): 27–30;

Yu Runqi, ed., *Tang Tao cang shu* (Beijing: Beijing chubanshe, 2004), p. 138;

Yingjin Zhang, *The City in Modern Chinese Literature and Film: Configurations of Space, Time, and Gender* (Stanford, Cal.: Stanford University Press, 1996), pp. 160–168.

Qian Zhongshu
(21 November 1910 – 19 December 1998)

Xiaobin Yang
Academia Sinica

BOOKS: *Xie zai rensheng bianshang* [Written at the Margin of Human Life] (Shanghai: Kaiming shudian, 1941)–includes "Lun wenren," translated by Phillip F. Williams as "On Writers," in *Modern Chinese Literary Thought: Writings on Literature, 1893–1945*, edited by Kirk A. Denton (Stanford, Cal.: Stanford University Press, 1996), pp. 443–449;

Ren shou gui [Humans, Beasts, and Ghosts] (Shanghai: Kaiming shudian, 1946)–includes "Linggan," translated by Dennis T. Hu as "The Inspiration," and "Jinian," translated by Nathan K. Mao as "The Souvenir," in *Modern Chinese Stories and Novellas, 1919–1949*, edited by Joseph S. M. Lau, C. T. Hsia, and Leo Ou-fan Lee (New York: Columbia University Press, 1981), pp. 416–453;

Weicheng (Shanghai: Chenguang chuban gongsi, 1947); translated by Mao and Jeanne Kelly as *Fortress Besieged* (Bloomington: Indiana University Press, 1979; London: Allen Lane, 2005);

Tan yi lu [Notes on Poetics] (Shanghai: Kaiming shudian, 1948; revised edition, Beijing: Zhonghua shuju, 1984);

Zhongguo shi yu Zhongguo hua [Chinese Poetry and Chinese Painting] (Hong Kong: Longmen shudian, 1969);

Jiuwen sipian [Four Old Essays] (Shanghai: Shanghai guji chubanshe, 1979)–includes "Tonggan," translated by Mark Bender and Xie Jianzhen as "Synaethesia," *Cowrie: A Chinese Journal of Comparative Literature*, 1 (1983): 1–20;

Guanzhui bian [Pipe and Awl Collection], 5 volumes (Beijing: Zhonghua shuju, 1979–1982); excerpts translated by Ronald Egan as *Limited Views: Essays on Ideas and Letters* (Cambridge, Mass.: Harvard University Asia Center, 1998);

Yeshi ji [Also So Collection] (Hong Kong: Guangjiaojing chubanshe, 1984)–includes "Shi ke yi yuan," translated by Siu-kit Wong as "Poetry as a Vehicle for Grief," *Renditions*, nos. 21–22 (Spring/Autumn 1984): 21–40;

Qi zhui ji [Collection of Seven Patchings] (Shanghai: Shanghai guji chubanshe, 1985);

Shi yu [Words of Stone] (Beijing: Zhongguo shehui kexue chubanshe, 1986);

Qian Zhongshu lunxue wenxuan [Collection of Scholarly Essays by Qian Zhongshu] (Guangzhou: Huacheng chubanshe, 1989);

Huaiju shicun [Extant Poems of Huaiju] (Beijing: Sanlian shudian, 1995);

Qian Zhongshu ji [Collected Works of Qian Zhongshu], 13 volumes (Beijing: Sanlian shudian, 2001).

OTHER: *Songshi xuanzhu* [An Annotated Selection of Song Dynasty Poetry], edited by Qian (Beijing: Renmin wenxue chubanshe, 1958);

Yang Jiang, *Ganxiao liuji*, preface by Qian (Beijing: Sanlian shudian, 1981); translated as "Preface," in *Six Chapters from My Life "Downunder,"* by Yang Jiang, translated by Howard Goldblatt (Seattle: University of Washington Press / Hong Kong: Chinese University Press, 1984), pp. 1–3.

SELECTED PERIODICAL PUBLICATION–UNCOLLECTED: "Wushiliao duanshu" [A Brief Account of a Leisurely Chat], *Qinghua zhoukan*, 33 (28 February 1930).

Qian Zhongshu was not only an erudite scholar and polyglot whose works on comparative literature touch on a wide range of Chinese and Western texts but also a novelist, short-story writer, and essayist whose distinctive narrative style had a profound impact on modern Chinese literature. Although most of his masterpieces were written in the 1940s, Qian's literary achievements were not recognized until the 1980s, and his reputation culminated in the 1990s.

Qian was born on 21 November 1910 in Wuxi, the birthplace of many distinguished literati, in Jiangsu province. His father, Qian Jibo, was a distinguished literary historian; his mother, whose given name is not known, was the sister of Wang Yunzhang, a popular writer of the time. According to custom, at the age of one Qian Zhongshu was made to play the game of *zhuazhou*, in which the child grabs an object from a group of

Qian Zhongshu (Museum of Modern Chinese Literature, Beijing)

randomly arranged items; the object picked is supposed to predict the child's future. Qian gripped a book; his given name, which means "cherishing books," was selected as a result of the game. (This story is contested in some accounts of his life.)

Qian Jibo's family and those of two of his brothers shared a family compound. Because Qian Zhongshu was the first-born male child, his grandfather decided that he would be adopted by his uncle Qian Jicheng, who was fourteen years older than Qian Jibo and had no male heir.

Qian Zhongshu began learning to read at four. When he was six, he was sent to an elementary school but had to withdraw after a few months because of his health. He started attending a private school at seven and began to learn Chinese classics such as the *Shijing* (circa 600 B.C., The Classic of Poetry). After a year, his uncle decided to teach him at home. There Qian read bulky classic novels of the sixteenth and seventeenth centuries such as Wu Cheng'en's *Xiyou ji* (circa 1592; translated as *Journey to the West*, 1977–1983), Shi Nai'an's *Shuihu zhuan* (The Story of the Water Margin; translated as *All Men Are Brothers*, 1933), and Luo Guanzhong's *Sanguo yanyi* (translated as *San kuo, or, Romance of the Three Kingdoms*, 1925). He also avidly read popular traditional novels such as Wang Mengji's *Jigong zhuan* (Biography of Jigong), Shi Yukun's *Qixia wuyi* (1889, Seven Heroes and Five Gallants), and Luo Guanzhong's *Shuo Tang* (Stories from the Tang Dynasty), which he obtained from a book-rental concern. In 1919 he entered Donglin Elementary School. His uncle died shortly thereafter, and his father resumed the responsibility for his upbringing and education.

Qian's earliest encounter with Western literature occurred at the age of eleven when he began reading Lin Shu's translations (actually, rewritings) of English novels by such authors as Jonathan Swift, Charles Dickens, and Sir Walter Scott. At thirteen he entered Taowu Middle School in Suzhou, a missionary school affiliated with the American Episcopal Church, where he learned English as quickly as he could so that he could read novels by authors such as H. Rider Haggard in the original. Later he transferred to Furen Middle School in Wuxi, founded by Chinese Christians, where he received solid training in English language and literature.

Qian's first substantial education in the Chinese classics was received during summer vacation from the middle school when he was sixteen. Under the guidance of his father, who was on vacation from his teaching post at Qinghua University in Beijing, he read anthologies of Classical Chinese prose and poetry. He also began to compose classical-style prose and poetry, often ignoring the techniques his father had taught him yet winning his father's approval because of the splendor of his style. Qian's *wenyanwen* (Classical Chinese) was so superb that he was occasionally asked to write in his father's name. For example, Qian Jibo's introduction to a book by the historian Qian Mu was actually written by the teenage Qian Zhongshu and published without the slightest revision by Qian Jibo.

Qian graduated as the top student at Furen Middle School and entered the Department of Foreign Languages and Literatures at Qinghua University; the story goes that he failed the mathematics portion of the entrance examination but was admitted as an exceptional case by the university's president because of his superior performance in Chinese and English. When Qian matriculated at the university in 1933, it boasted not only eminent professors such as the philosopher of language and literary theory I. A. Richards and Wu Mi, who had studied under Irving Babbitt at Harvard University and taught Western literature at Qinghua, but also outstanding students such as Li Jianwu, who became a playwright, translator, and critic, and Ji Xianlin, who later earned recognition as a linguist, historian, and translator. On the Qinghua campus Qian and his classmates Wan Jiabao (later known as the playwright Cao Yu) and Yan Yuheng were called the *san jie* (three talents).

Because Qian was fascinated with writing traditional-style Chinese poetry or *lüshi* (regulated verse), his father arranged for him to study with the renowned poet Chen Yan; he visited Chan Yan occasionally during the early 1930s. Chen Yan encouraged Qian to learn the poetry of the Song dynasty (960–1279) instead of that of the Tang dynasty (618–907), even though the latter was conventionally thought to be superior. This advice resulted much later in his acclaimed anthology, *Songshi xuanzhu* (1958, An Annotated Selection of Song Dynasty Poetry).

Qian published his first piece, a poem titled "Wushiliao duanshu" (A Brief Account of a Leisurely Chat), in the 28 February 1930 issue of *Qinghua zhoukan* (Qinghua Weekly); he published another poem in the 26 March 1932 issue in response to a poem Chen Yan wrote to him. His literary interaction with a well-known poet was admired and envied by his fellow students. He also contributed essays and book reviews to magazines, primarily the leading literary journal *Xinyue* (Crescent Moon). His reviews not only praised but also candidly exposed flaws in the works of both senior and young writers, such as the master essayist Zhou Zuoren and the novice poet Cao Baohua. In the March and June 1933 issues of *Xinyue* he applauded the mysticism and sensual correspondence of a collection of the latter's poems and said that the trite metaphors and gaudy ornamentation reveal the immaturity of Cao's "readable" but not "rereadable" poetry. Qian's focus on aesthetics and poetics is reflected in everything he wrote while at Qinghua. In "Zuozhe wuren" (1933, Five Authors), for example, he assesses some Western philosophers not for the content of their ideas but for their poetic spirit and stylistic characteristics.

Qian received his bachelor's degree in the summer of 1933. Confident of his ability to study literature on his own, he did not accept the suggestion of the university president and many of his professors that he enroll in the graduate program at Qinghua but took a teaching position in the Department of Foreign Languages at Guanghua (Aurora) University in Shanghai, where his father was chairman of the Chinese Department. During the following two years he focused on writing classical-style poetry under the pen name Huaiju; the poems are collected in *Huaiju shicun* (1995, Extant Poems of Huaiju). He was also a frequent contributor to the English-language journals *China Critic Weekly* and *T'ien Hsia Monthly* and the Chinese-language semi-monthly *Guofeng* (Airs of the States).

During his years at Guanghua, Qian engaged in debates on the problem of moral law with his departmental colleagues and on the issue of vernacular versus Classical Chinese with an historian. He also published essays on controversial topics, including "Lun suqi" (1933, On Bad Taste), "Lun buge" (1934, On "No Estrangement"), and "Lun fugu" (1934, On Restoring the Old Ways). In these works Qian expresses his dialectical insights into the self-reversing nature of the concepts at issue and shows how ideas deviate in unexpected directions—a theme that is developed in his later fiction. For example, in "Lun suqi" he maintains that because excessiveness is the essence of vulgarity, vulgarity can include excessive elegance; in "Lun fugu" he argues that the effort to restore the old ways may well result in a reformation or even a revolution, which will not succeed if tradition is completely abandoned. Qian's early literary and cultural ideas were quite different from the May Fourth paradigm that endorsed only absolute truth, as opposed to Qian's belief in relative truths, and absolute novelty.

In March 1933 Qian submitted his manuscript "Zhongguo wenxue xiaoshi" (A Short History of Chinese Literature) to the Shangwu yinshuguan (Commercial Press) in Shanghai; the book was never published, and the manuscript was lost. His article "Zhongguo wenxue xiaoshi xulun" (1933, Prolegomena to "A Short History of Chinese Literature"), however, discloses some of his early literary theories, including his opposi-

Qian's diploma from Qinghua University, dated 22 June 1933, with his photograph at bottom left (from Yang Yan, Yi dai caizi: Qian Zhongshu, *2005; Collection of Thomas Moran)*

tion to the May Fourth promotion of *pingmin wenxue* (commoners' literature) and the equating of Western and Chinese literary concepts without detailed analysis.

In the summer of 1935 Qian married Yang Jiang, who shared his interest in Chinese and Western literature; like his, her father was an eminent literatus from Wuxi. They had met for the first time in the spring of 1932, even though their families had long been acquainted. Yang Jiang later became a playwright, translator, and essayist.

In 1935 Qian and Yang Jiang went to England, where Qian had a Boxer Indemnity Scholarship to study English literature at Exeter College of the University of Oxford. His thesis on the image of China in seventeenth- and eighteenth-century English literature is a pioneering work on the cultural interaction of China and the West. He also wrote several essays, including "Lun jiaoyou" (1937, On Friendship), in which he criticizes the Confucian notion of friendship based on practical considerations and embraces the traditional Chinese value placed on unaffected, pure friendship. In 1937 he received the B.Litt. degree with First Class Honors, which was rarely awarded to a Chinese student at that time. He declined the offer of a readership at the college and moved to Paris with Yang Jiang to study at the Sorbonne. Their daughter, Qian Yuan, was born that year.

The Sino-Japanese War broke out in 1937; the news from his homeland increasingly concerned Qian, and he and Yang Jiang decided to discontinue their study in Europe and return to China. They arrived in Hong Kong by ship in 1938. Qian joined the faculty of Xi'nan lianhe daxue (Southwest Associated University) in Kunming, which gathered outstanding scholars from Beijing, Qinghua, and Nankai Universities and was the most prestigious institution of higher education in the areas of China not occupied by the Japanese.

Between January and May 1939 Qian published in *Jinri pinglun* (Criticism Today) a series of four essays—"Lun wenren" (translated as "On Writers," 1996), "Shi wenmang" (Explaining Illiteracy), "Yige pianjian" (A Prejudice), and "Shuo xiao" (Talking about Laughter)—to which he gave the collective title "Lengwu suibi" (Jottings from the Cold House); they are his earliest major literary works. In these essays he draws on his own observations and on his wide reading in Chinese and Western literary classics to make sarcastic remarks about human follies.

In the summer of 1939 Qian took a position at the Lantian Normal College in rustic Baoqing county in Hunan province, where he helped establish the Department of Foreign Languages; his father had accepted an invitation from the president of the college to chair the Chinese Department. Qian's arduous trip to the hinterland of Hunan and his isolated life there are depicted, with fictional adaptations, in his novel *Weicheng* (1947; translated as *Fortress Besieged,* 1979).

Qian returned to Shanghai in the summer of 1941. He was trapped there in December, when the Japanese occupied areas of Shanghai that had been held by European powers and sealed off the city. That month he published *Xie zai rensheng bianshang* (Written at the Margin of Human Life); it comprises ten of his essays, including the "Lengwu suibi" series. Dealing with topics such as eating, laughter, happiness, and the literati, the book is full of humorous, illuminating, and sophisticated observations that undermine cultural conventions. If human life is a big book, Qian says in his preface, then his essays are fragmented marginalia, written for entertainment—rather than the enlightenment that most writers were seeking to impart at the time—and are offered without systematic structure and without avoiding contradictions or exaggerations. This self-marginalizing stance was rare among Chinese writers of the 1930s and 1940s.

"Mogui yefang Qian Zhongshu xiansheng" (A Demon Visits Mr. Qian Zhongshu at Night), the first essay in *Xie zai rensheng bianshang,* epitomizes the spirit of the book. A conversation between a demon and the author reveals the knowledge and wisdom of the demon and encourages the reader to consider the possibility that humans are as demonic as—or even more demonic than—demons. In other essays Qian reveals the contradictory elements in seemingly simple aspects of life. Laughter, he observes in "Shuo xiao," may well be appropriated to conceal emotional poverty, as in professional *youmo wenxue* (humor literature). "Chifan" (Eating) probes the ramifications of the act of eating in Chinese society: politics, art, love, and hypocrisy all come into play in the social arena of the meal and are at odds with or complicate the original purpose of eating. In "Lun kuaile" (On Happiness) he points out that happiness is always overshadowed by unhappiness.

In 1942 Qian became a professor at Aurora Women's College in Shanghai; he remained there until the end of the war. His loneliness and bitterness during this period are recorded in his poetry. In the mid 1940s he wrote some short stories that were collected in 1946 as *Ren shou gui* (Humans, Beasts, and Ghosts). Like his essays, the stories are either witty sarcasm directed at vanity, greed, and hypocrisy or tragicomic dramas of family life. The first story in the volume, "Shangdi de meng" (God's Dream), is an allegorical and satirical piece that portrays God as having human emotions such as loneliness, anger, joy, ennui, and chagrin. Vanity is the motive for his creation of humanity, which leads to consequences that are contrary to those he expected: God makes humans because he wants creatures who will praise him; but he comes to realize that humans have become the masters who demand more and more from him, so he creates beasts to subdue them and insects to sicken them. God's plan ends catastrophically before he awakens to find that it was all a dream. In "Linggan" (translated as "The Inspiration," 1981) a dead writer is harassed in hell by his characters, who accuse him of disposing of their lives irresponsibly or arbitrarily in his works. The writer is sentenced to serve as a character for another writer, but he escapes from the latter's brain and transmigrates into a fetus in the womb of the second writer's sweetheart. The story is a satire of the worst of the cheap, shoddy literature of the time and the prevailing self-important intellectual style. "Mao" (The Cat) is about an intellectual husband and wife, a topic that Qian later developed further in *Weicheng.* Li Jianhou and his wife, Aimo, host a literary salon in Beiping (as Beijing was called from 1928 to 1949) where cultural celebrities are eager to show off their highbrow pedantry. Aimo falls in love with Qi Yigu, a young male secretary hired by Jianhou to help him write the memoir that he believes will bring him fame. When Jianhou leaves Aimo for his mistress, she turns to Qi Yigu but finds her love unrequited. Their pet cat creates incidents—tearing up manuscripts, scratching people, and so on—that disrupt the normal relationships among the characters and the logical development of the plot. In the last story in *Ren shou gui,* "Jinian" (translated as "The Souvenir," 1981), Xu Manqian marries the childish and simple-minded Caishu but soon becomes bored with her. When she meets his cousin, the handsome air force pilot Zhou Tianjian, she is attracted to him but is determined to keep the relationship a chaste, spiritual one so that she can enjoy romance and maintain an intact family at the same time. But he rapes her while they are on an outing, and she becomes pregnant. Shortly thereafter, Tianjian dies in an accident. Unaware of his wife's liaison and assuming that the child she carries is his, Caishu suggests that the baby be named Tianjian in memory of his cousin. In "Jinian," as in the other stories in the collection, Qian highlights the lack of connection between intention and result.

While writing the stories in *Ren shou gui,* Qian also wrote some of his most important critical works. Among them is "Zhongguo shi yu Zhongguo hua" (Chinese Poetry and Chinese Painting), published in February 1940, which examines the differences between the aesthetic standards of poetry and the visual arts in China. The essay reveals Qian's profound understanding of the fissures and irregularities in the Chinese aesthetic tradition, which was assumed by many to be a monolithic whole.

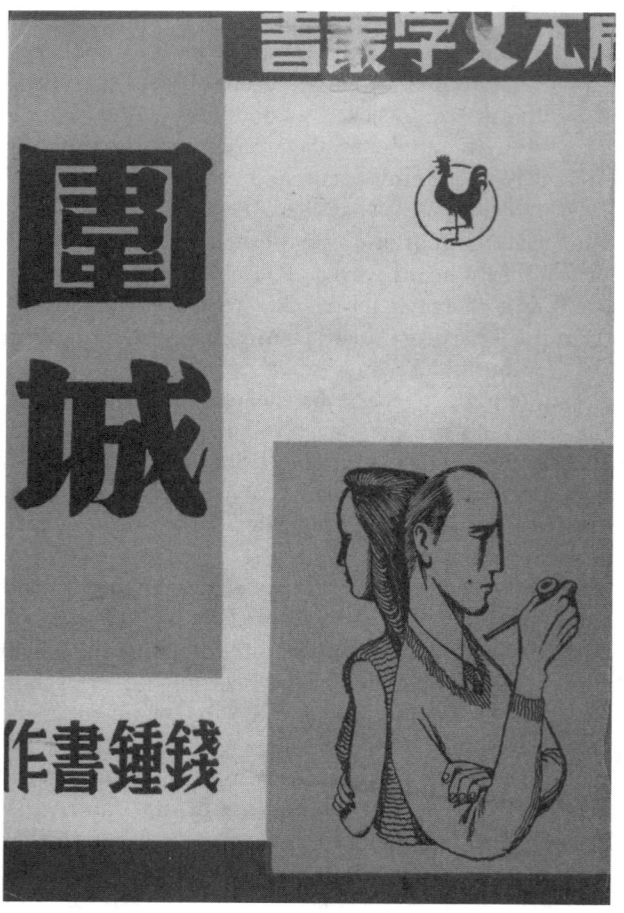

Cover for Qian's novel Weicheng (1947; translated as Fortress Besieged, 1979), in which the protagonist escapes the plotting and backbiting of academic life but finds himself trapped in an unhappy marriage (Wason Collection on East Asia–China, Kroch Asia Library, Cornell University)

In 1944 Qian watched a performance of Yang Jiang's play, *Chenxin ruyi* (Satisfied), and was inspired to write his only novel. It took him two years to complete *Weicheng,* which was serialized in the magazine *Wenyi fuxing* (Literary Renaissance) from February to December 1946 and published as a book in 1947 by the Shanghai Chenguang chuban gongsi (Chenguang Publishing Company). Following the tradition of social satire in vernacular Chinese novels such as Wu Jingzi's *Rulin waishi* (circa 1750, Unofficial History of the Literati; translated as *The Scholars,* 1957), Qian portrays educated people who are inept, vulgar, and faithless and exemplify the shallow "intellectual" lifestyle of modern times. Fang Hongjian comes back to China with a Ph.D. that he bought, rather than earned, abroad. He has apparently learned little beyond how to flirt with a woman he meets on the ship. Invited to give a lecture at a school, all he can manage are rambling comments about opium and syphilis. His courtship of the attractive Tang Xiaofu arouses the jealousy of his admirer, Su Wenwan; she tells Tang about Fang's misconduct, ruining his chance for romance with Tang. Fang takes a job at a college in the interior, far from the Japanese army occupying the eastern seaboard. The faculty of the college includes Su Wenwan's former suitor, who considered Fang a rival; a professor of Chinese literature, who has brought rare medicine with him to sell at an inflated price; the chairman of the foreign-languages department, who has the same counterfeit credentials as Fang; and the chairman of the Chinese department, who has secured his position through his connection with a high official. Flattering and plotting against one another, Fang and the others experience frustration and misfortune. After he is fired, Fang marries Sun Roujia, a lecturer in English who has used various ruses to lure him. Their marriage ends in misery when they become caught up in their families' squabbles and are overcome by their own selfish natures. Fang discovers that the family unit is just as ensnaring as the academic environment that he was determined to escape. The title of the novel is explained by a character who refers to a French saying that marriage is like a besieged fortress: people outside are trying to get in, and people inside are trying to get out. The work suggests that the simile applies not just to marriage but to all of the situations in which one finds oneself: love affairs, friendship, work, travel, and so on. The novel distances itself from mainstream May Fourth and war-era literature by presenting dilemmas and paradoxes rather than a straightforward, one-dimensional message about saving the nation or redeeming society.

Weicheng won applause from many critics for its wit and imagination, but the reception was not universally favorable. The harshest censure came from leftist critics who either categorized the novel as an encyclopedia of lewd desires or accused the author of being the avatar of the cultures of Eastern feudalism and Western capitalism. But even leftist revolutionaries had a use for *Weicheng:* in the late 1940s a clandestine Communist group studied the book, looking for a deeper understanding and a thoroughgoing critique of "reactionary individualism."

The Japanese surrendered in 1945. In early 1946 Qian took a position at the National Central Library in Nanjing as editor in chief of its English-language journal, *Philobiblon*. In the summer he accepted an invitation to join the faculty of Jinan University in Shanghai as a professor of Western literature and literary criticism.

Since his days at Lantian Normal College in Hunan, Qian had written down his thoughts about traditional Chinese poetry and poetics. These jottings went into his *Tan yi lu* (1948, Notes on Poetics). In the preface Qian says that the book was written in a time of chaos and represents his concern for China and its culture, which were under threat both from Japanese occupation and from global modernity. *Tan yi lu* deals with issues of poetic form, such as language, style, structure, and rhythm, as well as the relationship between poetry and nature. The copious quotations from more than a thousand Chinese and Western sources allow the book to be viewed as an innovative, though unintentional, contribution to the field of comparative literature.

Qian taught at Jinan University until the takeover of Shanghai by the Communists in 1949. Reluctant to leave his homeland, he declined offers from Oxford and from Hong Kong University and in September took a position at Qinghua University in Beijing. The manuscript for a novel titled "Baihe xin" (The Heart of Artichoke), which he had begun after the publication of *Weicheng,* was lost when he moved from Shanghai to Beijing. The title was derived from Charles Baudelaire's phrase "le coeur d'artichaut," indicating the empty center of the bulb within layers and layers of leaves. Qian later joked that because it had never been completed, people could imagine that "Baihe xin" would have been even better than his first novel.

In 1950 Qian was appointed chairman of the Committee on English Translation of the *Selected Works of Mao Tse-Tung* (1961–1977), a position that saved him from serious persecution during political upheavals such as the Anti-Rightist Campaign of 1957. In 1952 he became one of the few senior fellows at the Institute of Literature at Beijing University; a year later the institute was placed within the Division of Philosophy and Social Science of the Chinese Academy of Sciences. (The Division of Philosophy and Social Science has been renamed the Chinese Academy of Social Sciences and is now separate from the Chinese Academy of Sciences.) He held the position for the rest of his life.

In the mid 1950s Qian was involved in collective work on such books as *Zhongguo wenxue shi* (1962, History of Chinese Literature) and *Tangshi xuan* (1978, Selected Tang Dynasty Poetry). His major work during the decade was his groundbreaking 1958 anthology *Songshi xuanzhu,* which is accessible to a popular audience but still conveys Qian's profound understanding of Chinese poetics and literary and cultural history. His introduction to the book is not only a scholarly presentation of the subject matter but also an elegantly written, pleasant essay that brings Song dynasty poets to life as vivid characters.

At the beginning of the 1960s Qian participated in the team in charge of finalizing the English translation of Mao Zedong's poetry. Even this position did not protect him during the Cultural Revolution of 1966 to 1976, however, and he was "uncovered" as a "zichan jieji xueshu quanwei" (bourgeois academic authority) in August 1966. Qian and his family underwent extreme hardship, including the persecution and suicide of Qian's son-in-law. At the end of the 1960s Qian and Yang Jiang were sent to the Wu qi ganbu xuexiao (cadre school) in Luoshan, Henan province, to receive "reeducation" through physical labor. Their experiences there are recorded in Yang Jiang's memoir *Ganxiao liuji* (1981; translated as *A Cadre School Life: Six Chapters,* 1984).

Qian and Yang Jiang were released from the cadre school and returned to Beijing in March 1972. The following year Qian engaged in a fistfight with a young couple who were assigned to occupy half of their apartment. Qian and Yang Jiang moved out and lived illegally in an office at the Institute of Literature for three years. During this period Qian became seriously ill and was hospitalized; the rumor that he was dead traveled beyond China, and several articles memorializing him were published overseas. In 1979 *Renmin ribao* (The People's Daily) published a brief, easily overlooked announcement listing those, including Qian, from whom the Chinese Academy of Social Sciences had removed the label "intellectuals whose bourgeois worldview has not been reformed."

Qian's latest major work was *Guanzhui bian* (1979–1982, Pipe and Awl Collection; excerpts translated as *Limited Views: Essays on Ideas and Letters,* 1998), a five-volume study of ten Chinese classics that he began in 1972 and completed in 1975. It was a daring act to study Chinese classics during the Cultural Revolution, when almost all old books were condemned as poisonous. The first four volumes of *Guanzhui bian* were published in 1979, the year when scholars began using the term *Qianxue* (Qian Studies)—recognition that Qian was a writer whose work was rich enough to support its own academic field. *Guanzhui bian* addresses a wide range of themes extending beyond the boundaries of literature and includes quotations from four thousand publications in Classical Chinese, Latin, English, French, German, Spanish, and Italian.

The erudition that Qian displays in *Guanzhui bian* is a quality for which he had been known since his student days at Qinghua University, if not before. In the late 1970s he gave lectures in Italy, the United States, and Japan. His audiences were amazed at his ability to recite, impromptu and in the original language, any poems that were mentioned and to comment accurately on any detail of any book about which a question was asked. Qian's performance on this lecture tour has passed into legend.

Qian's international reputation rose in the late 1970s and the 1980s with the publication of translations of *Weicheng* into many languages, including English, French, German, Russian, and Japanese. The signifi-

Qian and his wife, Yang Jiang, in 1961 (from Modern Chinese Stories and Novellas, 1919–1949, *edited by Joseph S. M. Lau, C. T. Hsia, and Leo Ou-fan Lee, 1981; Chinese Collection, Middlebury College Main Library)*

cance of *Weicheng*, as well as Qian's status as a writer, were ignored by almost all official histories of modern Chinese literature in mainland China from 1949 until the 1980s, when C. T. Hsia's *A History of Modern Chinese Literature* (1961), which celebrates *Weicheng* as one of the greatest works of modern China, was translated into Chinese. From 1982 until his death he served as vice president of the Chinese Academy of Social Sciences and published essays, poems, and revisions of and appendices to his previous books. The first issue of the journal *Qian Zhongshu yanjiu* (Qian Zhongshu Studies) was published in 1988. Qian's literary style, previously considered frivolous and erotic, was in tune with the carnivalesque and sardonic cultural imagination of "postmodern" China, exemplified by such popular writers as Wang Shuo. His popularity in China reached its zenith when a television miniseries adaptation of *Weicheng* was broadcast in December 1990.

Qian was, however, adamantly opposed to "Qian studies" and all other efforts to apotheosize him. He declined to take part in a 1991 series, *Zhongguo dangdai wenhua mingren* (Cultural Celebrities of Contemporary China), produced by eighteen television stations. His last publications were *Shi yu* (1986, Words of Stone), a dialogue on traditional poetics with Chen Yan from the 1930s, and the 1995 *Huaiju shicun*, a collection of his old-style poems written from 1934 to 1991.

Qian Zhongshu died on 19 December 1998. In early 2001 the Beijing branch of Sanlian shudian (Joint Publishing Company) published the *Qian Zhongshu ji* (Collected Works of Qian Zhongshu) in thirteen volumes. It is a nearly complete collection of his works, including previously unpublished material.

Bibliographies:

Yi Fu, "Qian Zhongshu zhuzuo mulu," *Qian Zhongshu yanjiu* (1989): 305–310;

Yi Fu, "Qian Zhongshu zhuzuo mulu (xubian)," *Qian Zhongshu yanjiu* (1990): 347–350;

Yi Fu, "Qian Zhongshu zhuzuo mulu (xubian, han dingzheng)," *Qian Zhongshu yanjiu, di san ji* (1992): 326–331;

"Qian Zhongshu nianbiao" and "Qian Zhongshu zhu yi mulu," in *Qian Zhongshu Yang Jiang yanjiu ziliao ji*, edited by Tian Huilan, Ma Guangyu, and Chen Keyu (Wuhan: Huazhong shifan daxue chubanshe, 1997), pp. 6–35.

Biographies:

Ai Mo, *Qian Zhongshu zhuan gao* (Tianjin: Baihua wenyi chubanshe, 1992);

Kong Qingmao, *Qian Zhongshu zhuan* (Nanjing: Jiangsu wenyi chubanshe, 1992).

References:

Jana Benická, "Some Remarks on the Satirical in Qian Zhongshu's Novel *Fortress Besieged*," in *Autumn Floods: Essays in Honour of Marián Gálik*, edited by Raoul D. Findeisen and Robert H. Gassmann (Bern: Peter Lang, 1998), pp. 351–361;

Shen Tai Chang, "Reading Qian Zhongshu's 'God's Dream' as a Postmodern Text," *Chinese Literature, Essays, Articles, Reviews / Chung-kuo wen hsüeh*, 16 (1994): 93–110;

Chen Bing, ed., *Buyiyang de jiyi: Yu Qian Zhongshu zai yiqi* (Beijing: Dangdai shijie chubanshe, 1999);

He Hui and Fang Tianxing, eds., *Yi cun qian si: Yi Qian Zhongshu* (Shenyang: Liaohai chubanshe, 1999);

C. T. Hsia, "Ch'ien Chung-shu," in his *A History of Modern Chinese Fiction*, second edition (New Haven: Yale University Press, 1971), pp. 432–460;

Dennis T. Hu, "A Linguistic-Literary Approach to Ch'ien Chung-shu's Novel *Wei-ch'eng*," *Journal of Asian Studies*, 37 (1978): 427–443;

Hu, "A Linguistic-Literary Study of Ch'ien Chung-shu's Three Creative Works," dissertation, University of Wisconsin, 1977;

Theodore Huters, "Illumination of Chinese Fictional Conventions in Qian Zhongshu's *Weicheng*," *Selected Papers in Asian Studies*, 1 (1976): 50–60;

Huters, "In Search of Qian Zhongshu," *Modern Chinese Literature and Culture*, 11 (Spring 1999): 193–199;

Huters, *Qian Zhongshu* (Boston: Twayne, 1982);

Huters, "Traditional Innovation: Qian Zhong-shu (Ch'ien Chung-shu) and Modern Chinese Letters," dissertation, Stanford University, 1977;

Li Hongyan and Fan Xulun, *Wei Qian Zhongshu shengbian* (Tianjin: Baihua wenyi chubanshe, 2000);

Liu Zhongguo, *Qian Zhongshu: 20 shiji de renwen beige* (Guangzhou: Huacheng chubanshe, 1999);

Lu Wenhu, *"Weicheng" neiwai: Qian Zhongshu de wenxue shijie* (Beijing: Jiefangjun wenyi chubanshe, 1992);

Mou Xiaoming and Fan Xulun, eds., *Ji Qian Zhongshu xiansheng* (Dalian: Dalian chubanshe, 1995);

Qian Zhongshu yanjiu bianji weiyuanhui, ed., *Qian Zhongshu yanjiu* (Beijing: Wenhua yishu chubanshe, 1989);

Tian Huilan, Ma Guangyu, and Chen Keyu, eds., *Qian Zhongshu, Yang Jiang yanjiu ziliao ji* (Wuhan: Huazhong Shifan daxue, 1990);

Wang Weiping, *Dongfang ruizhi xueren: Qian Zhongshu de dute gexing yu meili* (Shijiazhuang: Hebei jiaoyu chubanshe, 1997);

Wang Yinfeng, *Zouchu mojing de Qian Zhongshu* (Beijing: Jincheng chubanshe, 1999);

Xin Guangwei and Li Hongyan, eds., *Liaodong Miusi zhi hun: Qian Zhongshu de wenxue shijie* (Shijiazhuang: Hebei jiaoyu chubanshe, 1995);

Yang Jiang, *Ganxiao liuji* (Beijing: Sanlian shudian, 1981); translated by Geremie Barmé and Bennett Lee as *A Cadre School Life, Six Chapters* (Hong Kong: Joint Publishing Company / New York: Readers International, 1984); translated by Howard Goldblatt as *Six Chapters from My Life "Downunder"* (Seattle: University of Washington Press / Hong Kong: Chinese University Press, 1984);

Yang Jiang, *Women sa* (Beijing: Sanlian shudian, 2003);

Yang Yan, *Yi dai caizi: Qian Zhongshu* (Shanghai: Shanghai renmin chubanshe, 2005);

Zhang Mingliang, *Huaiyin xia de huanjing: Lun "Weicheng" de xushi yu xugou* (Shijiazhuang shi: Hebei jiaoyu chubanshe, 1997);

Zhang Wenjiang, *Yingzao Babita de zhizhe: Qian Zhongshu zhuan* (Shanghai wenyi chubanshe, 1993);

Zhou Jin, *"Weicheng" yanjiu* (Taibei: Chengwen chubanshe, 1980).

Shen Congwen

(28 December 1902 – 10 May 1988)

Jeffrey C. Kinkley
St. John's University, New York

BOOKS: *Yazi* [Duck] (Beijing: Beixin, 1926);

Di'er ge Feifei [The Second Feifei] (Beijing: Chenbaoshe, 1926?);

Shiji [At Market] (Beijing: Chenbaoshe, 1926?);

Migan [Sweet Mandarins] (Shanghai: Xinyue, 1927);

Yazhai furen [Captive Mistress of the Stockade] (Shanghai: Shangwu, 1927);

Dao shijie shang [Into the World] (Shanghai? 1927?);

Ruwu hou [After Entering the Ranks] (Shanghai: Beixin, 1928);

Laoshi ren [The Simpleton] (Shanghai: Xiandai shuju, 1928);

Alisi Zhongguo youji [Alice's Adventures in China], 2 volumes (Shanghai: Xinyue, 1928);

Haoguan xianshi de ren [The Busybody] (Shanghai: Xinyue, 1928);

Huang jun riji [The Diary of Master Huang] (Beiping: Beiping wenhua xueshe, 1928);

Yu hou ji qita [After Rain, and Other Stories] (Shanghai: Chunchao shuju, 1928)–includes "Baizi," translated anonymously as "Pai Tzu" in *Living China: Modern Chinese Short Stories,* edited by Edgar Snow (New York: Reynal & Hitchcock, 1936; London: Harrap, 1936), pp. 182–187;

Chang xia [Long Summer] (Shanghai: Guanghua, 1928);

Guizishou [The Executioner] (Shanghai: Guanghua, 1928);

Shangui [Mountain Spirit] (Shanghai: Guanghua, 1928);

Bu si riji [A Pre-posthumous Diary] (Shanghai: Renjian shudian, 1928);

Yi ge wunü de tongxin [Correspondence from a Danseuse] (Shanghai, 1928?)–Shen's authorship is disputed by some scholars;

Dai guan riji [Diary of a Dumb Bureaucrat] (Shanghai: Yuandong, 1929);

Nanzi xuzhi [What a Man Must Know] (Shanghai: Honghei, 1929);

Shisi ye jian [Night of the Fourteenth] (Shanghai: Guanghua, 1929);

Shenwu zhi ai [The Shaman's Love] (Shanghai: Guanghua, 1929);

Diyici lian'ai [The First Love] (Shanghai: Honghei, 1929?);

Gemingzhe [The Revolutionary] (Shanghai: Honghei, 1929?);

Yi ge tiancai de tongxin [Correspondence from a Born Talent] (Shanghai: Daguang, 1930);

Lüdian ji qita [The Inn, and Other Stories] (Shanghai: Zhonghua, 1930)–includes "Qi ge yeren yu zui hou yi ge yingchun jie," translated as "Seven Barbarians and the Last Spring Festival," in *Genesis of a Revolution,* edited and translated by Stanley R. Munro (Singapore: Heinemann Educational, 1979), pp. 109–129;

Shen Congwen jia ji [Shen Congwen's "A" Collection] (Shanghai: Shenzhou guoguang she, 1930);

Jiu meng [Past Dreams] (Shanghai: Shangwu, 1930);

Zhongguo xiaoshuo shi jiangyi [Lectures on the History of Chinese Fiction] (Shanghai: Ji'nan Daxue chubanshe, 1930);

Chen [Sinking] (Shanghai? 1930);

Shizi chuan [The Marble-Carrying Boat] (Shanghai: Zhonghua, 1931);

Congwen xinzhu [New Works by Congwen] (Shanghai: Dadong, 1931);

Shen Congwen zi ji [Shen Congwen's "AA" Collection] (Shanghai: Xinyue, 1931)–includes "Zhangfu," first five pages translated by Shih Ming as "Husband," *Asia,* 37 (July 1937): 524–525;

Long Zhu (Shanghai: Xiaoxing, 1931);

Yi ge nü juyuan de shenghuo [The Life of an Actress] (Shanghai: Dadong, 1931);

Xin wenxue jiangyi [Lectures on the New Literature] (Wuhan: Wuhan Daxue, 1931?);

Huchu [Tiger Cub] (Shanghai: Xin Zhongguo shuju, 1932);

Ji Hu Yepin [Remembering Hu Yepin] (Shanghai: Guanghua, 1932);

Nitu [Mud] (Beiping: Xingyuntang shudian, 1932);

Dushi yi furen [A Lady of the City] (Shanghai: Xin Zhongguo shuju, 1932);

Yilin ji [Fragments] (Hangzhou: Cangshan, 1932?);

Shen Congwen (from Shen Congwen xuan ji, *volume 4, 1983; Collection of Thomas Moran)*

Ahei xiao shi [The Story of Ahei] (Shanghai: Xin shidai, 1933);

Kangkai de wangzi [The Generous Prince] (Shanghai: Liangyou, 1933);

Fengzi [Fengzi] (Beiping: Lidai, 1933);

Yi ge muqin [A Mother] (Shanghai: Hecheng shuju, 1933);

Yuexia xiaojing [Under Moonlight] (Shanghai: Xiandai shuju, 1933);

Nuofu [The Coward] (Shanghai: Xin shidai shuju, 1933?);

Shenshi de taitai [The Gentry Wife] (Shanghai: Santong shuju, 1933?);

Momo ji [Froth] (Shanghai: Dadong, 1934);

Youmu ji [The Roving Eye] (Shanghai: Dadong, 1934);

Rurui ji [Rurui Collection] (Shanghai: Shenghuo, 1934);

Congwen zizhuan [Congwen's Autobiography] (Shanghai: Diyi, 1934);

Ji Ding Ling [Remembering Ding Ling] (Shanghai: Liangyou, 1934);

Bian cheng [The Frontier City] (Shanghai: Shenghuo shudian, 1934); translated by Emily Hahn and Shing Mo-lei as "Green Jade and Green Jade," *T'ien Hsia Monthly,* 2 (January 1936): 87–107; (February 1936): 174–196; (March 1936): 271–299; (April 1936): 360–390;

Baoban [Leopard Spots] (Beiping: Lida, 1934);

Ba jun tu [Portrait of Eight Steeds] (Shanghai: Wenhua shenghuo, 1935);

Xiang xing san ji [Discursive Notes on a Trip through Hunan] (Shanghai: Shangwu, 1936);

Congwen xiaoshuo xizuo xuan [Selective Exercises from Congwen's Fiction Writing] (Shanghai: Liangyou, 1936);

Xin yu jiu [The New and the Old] (Shanghai: Liangyou, 1936)—includes "Xiaoxiao," translated by Lee Yi-hsieh as "Hsiao-hsiao," *T'ien Hsia Monthly,* 7 (October 1938): 295–309;

Feiyou cundi [Letters Never Mailed], by Shen and Xiao Qian (Shanghai: Wenhua shenghuo, 1937);

Xiangxi [West Hunan] (Changsha: Shangwu, 1939);

Ji Ding Ling xuji [Sequel to *Remembering Ding Ling*] (Shanghai: Liangyou, 1939);

Kunming dongjing [Winter Scenes in Kunming] (Shanghai: Wenhua shenghuo, 1939);

Zhufu ji [Housewife] (Shanghai: Shangwu, 1939);

Guolingzhe [The One Who Crossed over the Mountains] (Shanghai: Xinguang, 1940?);

Zhu xu [The Candle Extinguished] (Shanghai: Wenhua shenghuo, 1941);

Yunnan kan yun ji [Gazing at Clouds in Yunnan] (Chongqing: Guomin tushu, 1943);

Ajin [Ajin] (Guilin: Kaiming, 1943);

Heifeng ji [Black Phoenix] (Guilin: Kaiming, 1943);

Chang he [Long River] (Guilin: Kaiming, 1943); chapters 1, 3, and 5 translated by Lillian Chen Ming Chu as "*The Long River* by Shen Ts'ung-wen," M.A. thesis, Columbia University, 1966;

Chun Deng ji ["Spring" and "Lamp" Collection] (Guilin: Kaiming, 1943);

Hei ye [Dark Night] (Guilin: Kaiming, 1943);

Chun [Spring] (Guiling: Kaiming, 1943);

Zhanguo qiqi [Lacquerware of the Warring States Period] (Beijing, 1954);

Shen Congwen xiaoshuo xuan ji [A Collection of Shen Congwen's Selected Fiction] (Beijing: Renmin wenxue chubanshe, 1957);

Zhongguo sichou tu'an [Patterns on Chinese Fabrics], by Shen and Wang Jiashu (Beijing: Zhongguo gudian yishu chubanshe, 1957);

Tang Song tong jing [Bronze Mirrors of the Tang and Song Dynasties] (Beijing: Zhongguo gudian yishu chubanshe, 1958);

Ming jin [Ming Dynasty Brocades] (Beijing: Wenwu chubanshe, 1959);

Longfeng yishu [The Art of Dragons and Phoenixes] (Beijing: Zuojia chubanshe, 1960);

Zhongguo gudai fushi yanjiu [Researches into Ancient Chinese Costume] (Hong Kong: Shangwu, 1981);

Shen Congwen wen ji [The Works of Shen Congwen], 12 volumes, edited by Shao Huaqiang and Ling Yu (Hong Kong: Sanlian/Guangzhou: Huacheng, 1982–1985)—includes, in volume 8, "Shuiyun" [Water and Clouds]; translated into French by Isabelle Rabut as *L'Eau et les nuages* (Paris: Bleu de Chine, 1996);

Shen Congwen xuan ji [Selected Works by Shen Congwen], 5 volumes, edited by Ling Yu (Chengdu: Sichuan renmin chubanshe, 1983);

Shen Congwen bie ji [Other Works by Shen Congwen], 20 volumes, edited by Liu Yiyou, Xiang Chengguo, and Shen Huchu (Changsha: Yuelu shushe, 1992);

Shen Congwen quanji [The Complete Works of Shen Congwen], 32 volumes, edited by Zhang Zhaohe and others (Taiyuan: Beiyue wenyi chubanshe, 2002).

Editions in English: *The Chinese Earth: Stories*, translated by Ching Ti and Robert Payne (London: Allen & Unwin, 1947)—comprises "Pai Tzu" ("Baizi"); "The Husband" ("Zhangfu"); "San-San" ("Sansan"); "Under Moonlight" ("Yuexia xiaojing"); "Three Men and a Girl" ("San ge nanzi he yi ge nüren"); "Lung Chu" ("Long Zhu"); "Fufu" ("The Lovers"); "Tang Wang" [*Congwen zizhuan* (Congwen's Autobiography), chapter 16]; "The Rainbow" ("Kan hong lu"); and "The Frontier City" *(Bian cheng)*;

"Little Flute" ("Xiaoxiao"), translated by Li Ru-mien, *Life and Letters*, 60, no. 137 (1949): 20–29;

"Long Zhu," translated by Ch'u Chai and Winberg Chai as "Lung Chu," in *A Treasury of Chinese Literature: A New Prose Anthology, Including Fiction and Drama*, edited by Ch'u Chai and Winberg Chai (New York: Appleton-Century-Crofts, 1965), pp. 320–341;

"A Bandit Chief" (*Congwen zizhuan* [Congwen's Autobiography], chapter 16), translated by William L. MacDonald, in *Anthology of Chinese Literature*, volume 2: *From the Fourteenth Century to the Present Day*, edited by Cyril Birch and Donald Keene (New York: Grove, 1972), pp. 276–285;

The Border Town and Other Stories, translated by Gladys Yang (Beijing: Chinese Literature, 1981)—comprises "The Border Town" *(Bian cheng)*, "Xiaoxiao" ("Xiaoxiao"), "The Husband" ("Zhangfu"), "Guisheng" ("Guisheng"), and "My Uncle Shen Congwen," by Huang Yongyu;

"The Orange Grower and the Old Sailor" (*Chang he* [Long River], chapter 3), translated by Nancy Gibbs, in *Chinese Civilization and Society: A Sourcebook*, edited by Patricia Buckley Ebrey (New York: Free Press, 1981), pp. 321–331;

"Hsiao-hsiao" ("Xiaoxiao"), translated by Eugene Eoyang, and "Pai-tzu" ("Baizi") and "Three Men and One Woman" ("San ge nanzi he yi ge nüren"), translated by Kai-yu Hsu, in *Modern Chinese Stories and Novellas, 1919–1949*, edited by Joseph S. M. Lau, C. T. Hsia, and Leo Ou-Fan Lee (New York: Columbia University Press, 1981), pp. 22–36, 222–226, 253–265;

Recollections of West Hunan, translated by Yang (Beijing: Chinese Literature, 1982)—comprises "I Study a Small Book and at the Same Time a Big Book" and "While Continuing My Schooling I Stick to That Big Book" (*Congwen zizhuan* [Congwen's Autobiography], chapters 3 and 5); "A Night at Mallard-Nest Village," "An Amorous Boatman and an Amorous Woman," "Chest Precipice," and "Five Army Officers and a Miner" (*Xiang xing san ji* [Discursive Notes on a Trip through Hunan], chapters 3, 5, 7, and 8); "The People of Yuanling" and "Fenghuang" (*Xiangxi* [West Hunan], chapters 4 and 9); "After Snow" ("Xue qing"); "Qiaoxiu and Dongsheng" ("Qiaoxiu he Dongsheng"); and "Truth Is Stranger than Fiction" ("Chuanqi bu qi");

Imperfect Paradise, edited by Jeffrey Kinkley (Honolulu: University of Hawai'i Press, 1995)—comprises "The New and the Old" ("Xin yu jiu"), translated by Kinkley; "The Husband" ("Zhangfu"), translated by Kinkley; "The Lovers" ("Fufu"), translated by Kinkley; "Ah Jin" ("Ajin"), translated by William MacDonald; "My Education" ("Wo de jiaoyu"), translated by Kinkley; "Ox" ("Niu"), translated by Caroline Mason; "Sansan" ("Sansan"), translated by Kinkley; "Life" ("Sheng"), translated by Peter Li; "Guisheng" ("Guisheng"), translated by Kinkley; "The Vegetable Garden" ("Caiyuan"), translated by Li; "Eight Steeds" ("Ba jun tu"), translated by MacDonald; "Winter Scenes in Kunming" ("Kunming dongjing"), translated by Kinkley and Wong Kam-ming; "Amah Wang" ("Wang sao"), translated by Li; "Qiaoxiu and Dongsheng" ("Qiaoxiu he Dongsheng"), translated by Kinkley; "The Housewife" ("Zhufu"), translated by MacDonald; "Suicide" ("Zisha"), translated by Kinkley; "Gazing at Rainbows" ("Kan hong lu"), translated by Kinkley; "Songs of the Zhen'gan Folk" ("Ganren yaoqu"), translated by Kinkley; and *The Celestial God* (*Xiaoshen*), translated by Kinkley.

OTHER: Liu Yu, *Liu Yu shi xuan* [Poetry by Liu Yu], edited by Shen (Shanghai: Beixin, 1932);

Xiandai shi jiezuo xuan [Masterpieces of Modern Poetry], edited by Shen (Shanghai: Qingnian shudian, 1932);

Fushi ji ["Floating World" Collection], edited by Yao Pengzi, Shen, and others (Shanghai: Liangyou, 1935);

Xiandai riji wenxuan [A Selection of Modern Diary Literature], edited by Shen (Shanghai: Dongfang shuju, 1936?);

Ershi ren suoxuan duanpian jiazuo ji [A Book of Outstanding Short Stories as Recommended by Twenty Guest Editors], edited by Zhao Jiabi, Shen, and others (Shanghai: Liangyou, 1937);

Meili de Beijing [Beautiful Beijing], edited by Cao Yu and Shen (Hong Kong: Sanlian, 1956).

Shen Congwen, recognized as one of the great writers of the first half of the twentieth century and one of the finest Chinese prose stylists of all time, played a major role in shaping China's new vernacular literature after the May Fourth Movement of 1919. Prolific, versatile, and a partisan of literary revolution, he shunned politically revolutionary literature and writers' organizations. After two decades of popularity among students, other young people, and intellectuals, Shen went on in the late 1930s and the 1940s to experiments in modernism that even many of his friends thought too Westernized, difficult, and erotic for China. After the Communist revolution in 1949, he ceased writing, attempted suicide, and ultimately found a new career in art history. Mainland China and Taiwan banned his works in the 1950s and nearly erased the memory of his literary contributions until both sides liberalized in the 1980s. "Shen Congwen manias" ensued, with critics lauding him as an iconic independent writer of the revolutionary era. From 1982 until his death Shen was one of the few Chinese writers in serious contention for a Nobel Prize in literature.

Shen was best known for writing about country folk and rural places. His rendering of the scenery, customs, and moods of his native region, West Hunan, endowed it with the breadth and development of a literary character. Many of his other masterpieces are about modern Chinese urbanites and their discontents. For all his experimentalism, he was respected by his peers for his steadfast devotion to the classic short-story writer's craft—for creating exquisite language, archetypal characters, and intriguing plot twists.

Shen was born Shen Yuehuan into a military-gentry family with minor landholdings in Fenghuang, West Hunan, on 28 December 1902; he styled himself "Congwen" in late adolescence. His father was Shen Zongsi; his mother was Huang Ying. Many May Fourth writers were of similar background, but Shen's ancestry had exotic regional, ethnic, and military colorations that figure in his prolific early fiction and earned him the reputation of the "Dumas of China." His native region was the upriver, mountainous portion of West Hunan, an area so isolated from the rest of Hunan province that it gained autonomy under homegrown warlords and invaded neighboring provinces. Some of the ethnic minorities, such as the Miao (Méo, Hmong) and Tujia, who had settled there centuries earlier, remained unassimilated in the twentieth century, even as their mores colored the regional culture of the lowland Chinese. That Shen's mother was a Tujia and his paternal grandmother a Miao were hidden from him until he came of age. The Han elite saw those ethnic groups as low-status tribespeople, useful only as bodyguards, servants, and concubines.

Shen's male relatives were entrenched in the local system of Han and Miao farmer-soldier colonies that originated in eighteenth-century military campaigns to suppress the Miao. They also figured in the Gelaohui secret society, which rose up to overthrow the Manchus in the 1911 revolution. Shen entered the armies of local warlords as a teenager and rose, by dint of his fine calligraphy, to the position of personal clerk to Chen Quzhen, who became the warlord of West Hunan in 1921.

Shen left for Beijing in 1923 intending to join the May Fourth literary revolution and become a new-style intellectual dedicated to social change and the new

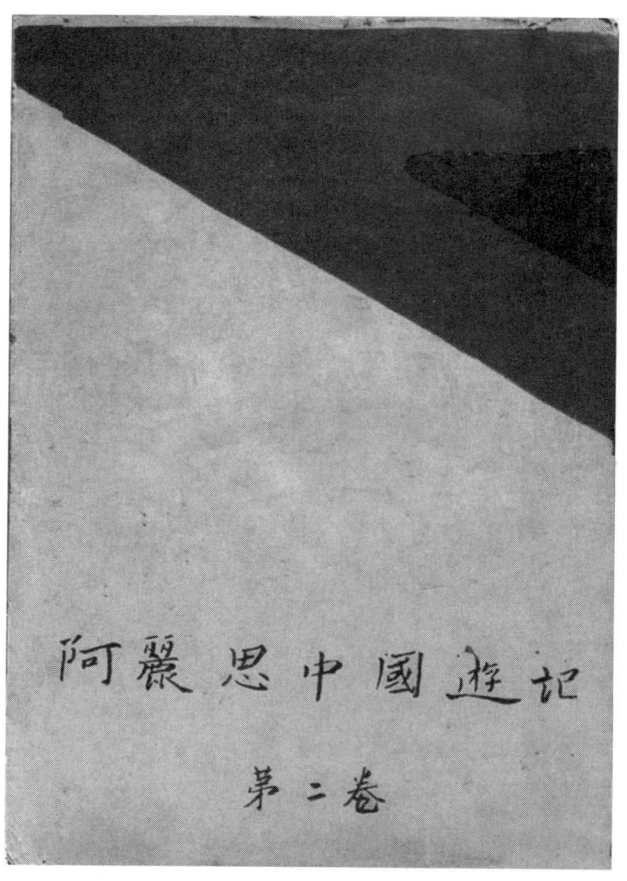

Cover for volume two of a 1931 edition of Shen's Alisi Zhongguo youji *(1928, Alice's Adventures in China), a satirical contrast of bourgeois urban Chinese with poor and downtrodden rural members of the Miao ethnic minority in West Hunan (from Yao Zhimin, Wang Zhongming, Zhang Zhenhua, and Bian Qiansheng, eds.,* Shuying, *2003; Bruccoli Clark Layman Archives)*

thought from Japan and the West. He did not plan to be a professional writer—few Beijing intellectuals were able to live off their royalties; Shen later claimed that he was among the first to do so. But as an autodidact without even a primary-school degree who found it impossible to learn a foreign language, he could not pass the entrance examinations for any of the universities, nor could he afford tuition at a private school. He was, however, able to audit the classes of professors at Beijing University free of charge.

Living in genteel poverty in the 1920s at the margins of Beijing's student-poet subculture, then moving to Shanghai at the end of the decade to be close to his publishers, Shen wrote short fiction, essays, character sketches, diaries, letters, poems, and plays to earn a meager living and attack the status quo. In the 1920s China's elite intellectuals of the Xin wenhua yundong (New Culture Movement) advocated a new Chinese vernacular literature enriched with local customs, dialect, and folklore. Readers were particularly curious about Shen's "barbarous" homeland and its mores. He satisfied that interest by sketching regional characters in works such as "Daigou" (1925, Miao for "Young Fella"), which was included in his first book, *Yazi* (1926, Duck), and by depicting local curses and Sino-Miao creole expressions in "Xiang jian de xia" (1925, Summer in the Countryside), collected in volume fifteen of *Shen Congwen quanji* (2002, The Complete Works of Shen Congwen). Shen's stories, sketches, and plays depict regionally distinctive but comfortably preindustrial aspects of ordinary Han people's culture, including rural markets, festivals, childhood pastimes, and rustic crafts and manufacturing processes. The play *Xiaoshen* (1925? translated as *The Celestial God,* 1995), collected in *Yazi,* may be based on extemporized masked folk dramas performed to requite the Nuo gods that had survived in West Hunan from ancient times. (Shen's other short plays were mostly one-act situation comedies about young urban people in the manner of Ding Xilin.) In "Ganren yaoqu" (1926; translated as "Songs of the Zhen'gan Folk," 1995), collected in volume fifteen of *Shen Congwen quanji,* Shen transcribes his region's Chinese-language Sino-Miao "mountain songs" and explains how to use them to attract a sexual partner or ridicule a rival.

Proud of having been a soldier, Shen wrote tales of life in the warlord armies to shock and titillate urban readers unaware of the harsh realities of life in the provinces. "Zai bie yi ge guodu li" (In a Separate Realm), serialized in *Xiandai pinglun* (Contemporary Review) in April and May 1926 and republished as the title story of the collection *Nanzi xuzhi* (1929, What a Man Must Know), features letters between bandits and victims negotiating a ransom after a kidnapping. "Ruwu hou" (1927, After Entering the Ranks), the title story of a 1928 collection, depicts the aspirations of the young soldiers who filled out West Hunan's rough-hewn armies. The satirical *Alisi Zhongguo youji* (1928, Alice's Adventures in China) contrasts bourgeois urban Chinese with destitute and downtrodden rural assimilated Miao; the novel combines and parodies many genres. "Wo de jiaoyu" (1929; translated as "My Education," 1995), collected in *Shen Congwen jia ji* (1930, Shen Congwen's "A" Collection), is a fictional diary depicting a surfeit of executions in a primitive rural world without morality; the diarist relates the needless deaths with deadpan humor, joking about officers who jostle to see the "action."

In an era given to ideological nostrums of nation, race, and strength in unity, the feel of "home" and the celebration of regional cultural diversity in Shen's works won him a reputation as a strong writer on rural and local themes. Most of China's modern literature was weak in local color and devoted to urban life and problems; peasants made many intellectuals think not of rural life or of rustic themes in the ancient poetic tradition but of their own exalted social status and mission. Shen was an exception; feeling inadequate as an urban intellectual, he called himself a "country boy" and identified with his region and its people. During his writing career he was not called a *xiangtu* (native-soil, local, nativist, or rural-local) author, one who celebrates a region's scenery, customs, dialect, and lore and represents its rural folk's interests against the encroachment of outlanders; but during his 1980s revival on both sides of the Taiwan Strait his rural writing was seen in retrospect as the epitome of *xiangtu* literature.

In his fiction Shen upholds even the "unspoiled" honor and "country" integrity of déclassé figures such as small-town prostitutes and the rough boatmen who brave the rapids of inland rivers to remain true to such women. "Baizi" (translated as "Pai Tzu," 1936), included in his collection *Yu hou ji qita* (1928, After Rain, and Other Stories), depicts a joyous reunion of two such characters. "Zhangfu" (1930; translated as "The Husband," 1937), collected in *Congwen xinzhu* (1931, New Works by Congwen), evokes the distress of a peasant husband who, having sent his wife out as a prostitute, brings her back home out of shame and, perhaps, love.

On the other hand, Shen also presents critical views of common people's stubbornness, conservatism, and materialism. In "Fufu" (1929; translated as "The Lovers," 1947), collected in *Congwen xiaoshuo xixuo xuan* (1936, Selective Exercises from Congwen's Fiction Writing), ignorant peasants persecute an "enlightened" young married couple whom they catch enjoying sex out of doors. "Niu" (1929; translated as "Ox," 1995), included in *Shen Congwen jia ji*, is on first reading a realistic tale about a rough peasant who mistreats his ox and comes to regret it when the animal loses its strength. Read in conjunction with stories about confrontations between workers and managers, such as "Da cheng zhong de xiao shiqing" (1929, A Small Matter in a Big City), collected in volume eight of *Shen Congwen wen ji* (1982–1985, The Works of Shen Congwen), and the title story of *Shizi chuan* (1931, The Marble-Carrying Boat), however, one can see an allegory of the Hegelian master-slave dialectic. The endings of these stories are not only surprising but also nonideological. Though always showing sympathy for the underdog, Shen attempts to transcend class ideological analysis with modern psychological explanations of dominance and the discontents it causes.

There was another side to Shen in the 1920s—a decade when he was so prolific that he resembled Alexandre Dumas *père* not only as a "creole" but also as a "fiction factory." With sensibilities molded by classical Chinese belles-lettres and the better-educated writers who preceded him in the May Fourth literary revolution, such as Zhou Zuoren and Yu Dafu, Shen wrote vernacular poems, essays, and stories about his experiences in Beijing. Many of these works are in the voice of a poor, hypersensitive, young intellectual writer angry at social injustice. Even in these self-commiserating or satirical pieces, such as "Mian xie" (1925, Cotton Shoes), collected in volume eight of *Shen Congwen wen ji*, and "Yi ge tiancai de tongxin" (1929, Correspondence from a Born Talent), the title story of a 1930 collection, Shen evokes the familiar comforts of hometown values, particularly of kith and kin. His social criticism and his late-1920s romantic potboilers about young urban or tribal lovers, often written in flamboyantly long sentences and using unconventional grammar, gave him a large following among students. Many of these works were written hurriedly and are no longer well regarded except as vivid documentation of the author's life and times. Among them are the comedies of manners "Shenshi de taitai" (The Gentry Wife), in *Shen Congwen zi ji* (1931, Shen Congwen's "AA" Collection), and the title story of *Dushi yi furen* (1932, A Lady of the City).

By the end of the 1920s Shen was developing new skills in plotting. He was inspired by the works of Western writers available in Chinese translation, particularly French and Russian short-fiction masters of the nineteenth and early twentieth centuries: Anton Chekhov, Alphonse Daudet, Anatole France, Maksim Gor'ky, Guy de Maupassant, and Ivan Turgenev. He took plots from ghost stories he had heard as a soldier and from great Ming and Qing novels. "Ajin" (1928; translated as "Ah Jin," 1995), included in *Lüdian ji qita* (1930, The Inn, and Other Stories), is a transitional piece, built on broadly sketched comic characters reminiscent of Shen's earlier local-color stories but with a brisk plot. The title character is a young assimilated Miao who goes to market to pay the bride price for an attractive young widow, but a "friend," the busybody village headman, repeatedly blocks his way. An ironic narrator's patter affirms that the headman cannot be called bad just because he "loves to talk," even though he wants the widow for himself and Ajin as a match for his niece. Distressed and distracted, Ajin enters a gambling booth and loses the bride price. Hearing that the wedding is off, the headman congratulates Ajin for his unexpected resolve and himself for having helped a friend. The plot is from a Miao folktale, but the surprise ending is reminiscent of O. Henry.

Cover for the first edition of Shen's Huang jun riji (The Diary of Master Huang), published in 1928 (from Yu Runqi, ed., Tang Tao cang shu, 2004; Bruccoli Clark Layman Archives)

Shen's best-known "Miao legend" is "Long Zhu" (1929; translated as "Lung Chu," 1947), the title story of a 1931 collection, about a tribal prince who is superlative in looks, intelligence, and singing voice; his very perfection hinders him from finding a mate until he encounters a beautiful maiden whose sung repartee is as witty as his own. The story is flavored with vernacular Chinese poems composed by Shen to represent real Miao songs with their extravagant metaphors (the mountain songs he inserted into his earlier stories were composed originally in Chinese and are pithier and more linguistically ingenious). A dwarf companion is a foil for the hero; a similar foil accompanies the mute hero of *Shenwu zhi ai* (1929, The Shaman's Love), the ethnographic highlight of which is a description of an archaic Miao Nuo exorcism.

Su Xuelin suggests that Shen's readers loved the raw vigor and spontaneity of his exotic tribal characters. One can see in his "Miao stories" the attitude of the historian and folklorist Gu Jiegang, who theorized that China's diverse regional cultures took their distinctiveness and vitality from the border peoples whom Han Chinese had for centuries despised as barbarians. Shen's tribal folk bear a vital and unspoiled primal culture that, he claimed, the Han had once possessed but had lost through Confucian bureaucratism, puritanism, and urban worldliness. His characters reminded some critics of noble savages, but Shen's concern was Social Darwinist and not specific to the Miao: he worried that China, owing more to cultural than to racial-national enervation, had lost the strength to survive in the modern world. The Chinese, he believed, needed to reject thousands of years of Han cultural decadence produced by Confucianism, Daoism, and Buddhism—Shen decried them all—by simultaneously adopting the modern merits of the West and returning to the "root" Chinese mores that had been retained only by ethnic minorities.

The clash between commercial-official and tribal cultures is clearest in the parable "Qi ge yeren yu zui hou yi ge yingchun jie" (1929; translated as "Seven Barbarians and the Last Spring Festival," 1979), included in *Lüdian ji qita*. Miao braves hide from the Han so as to continue freely making love, hunting, and drinking their corn liquor, but technologically advanced and hypocritically Confucian urban people conquer them in the end. Because Shen more often blurred the racial and ethnic identities of his rural and southwestern characters, much of his fiction about plain village folk took on the coloration of his Miao stories. Han obscurantism and ruthless modernization, though seemingly opposed, are on the same morally decadent side in his fiction—although, as a May Fourth intellectual, Shen in practice embraced the most modern and modernistic aspects of Western culture and was fascinated by town life and its crafts.

Despite his lack of formal education, in 1929 introductions from his friends Xu Zhimo, Hu Shi, and Wen Yiduo enabled Shen to support himself by teaching creative writing and the history of modern Chinese literature at the China Institute in Shanghai. There he fell in love with a student, Zhang Zhaohe. He worked his way up to positions at Wuhan University in 1930–1931 and Qingdao University from 1931 to 1933. The steady income gave him time to refine the prose style of the works that are now known as his classics. He continued to follow the "revolution" of using modern colloquial syntax, but, like writers in the classical language, he lyrically exploited the unique lexical resources of written Chinese, whose building blocks are not words but the far larger universe of morphemes represented by Chinese characters.

In the late 1920s and the 1930s Shen was known for well-made short stories about the city people who constituted his new social milieu. An early example is "Caiyuan" (1929; translated as "The Vegetable Garden," 1995), collected in *Xin yu jiu* (1936, The New and the Old), which begins as a nostalgic tale about old Beijing and the long-Sinicized Manchu families who remained its backbone. The main family in the story grows cabbages like no other, and it keeps up old traditions such as poetry, art, and lifelong marriage. When the son becomes a revolutionary "new poet," his widowed old mother adapts to the situation with love and understanding. In the meantime the cabbages, a staff of life for the Beijing folk, are joined in the family garden by beautiful chrysanthemums. The government, by contrast, resolves political manifestations of the generation gap through bloodshed: the Nationalists, who have harbored a prejudice against the Manchus since overthrowing them in 1911, shoot the son and his bride as supposed Communists, and the new ruling class appropriates the garden for its own use. The old widow decides that she has lived long enough and hangs herself. The story had a second round of popularity in Taiwan in the 1980s: the 1911 revolution was the founding myth of the Nationalist regime that still ruled on the island, and there was much nostalgia for the old, unhurried way of life on the mainland. Taiwan itself seemed like a garden, walled off from the vicissitudes of the world but in danger from the outside, and Shen's jaundiced view of revolution, violence, and cultural know-nothingism seemed, in retrospect, prophetic of the 1949 revolution.

"San ge nanzi he yi ge nüren" (1930; translated as "Three Men and a Girl," 1947), collected in *Youmu ji* (1934, The Roving Eye), is a complicated tale with a hint of mystery in which West Hunanese soldiers puzzle over a rural beancurd-shop owner who disinters and sleeps beside the corpse of his lost love—perhaps from love, perhaps from superstition. Hua-ling Nieh considers the story an existentialist work and the shopowner not only one of Shen's quintessential "country folk" but also a human being confronting the same kind of absurdity as that represented in Albert Camus's *L'Etranger* (1942; translated as *The Stranger*, 1946).

Shen's sagas of young love among the hill people, such as the story cycle *Ahei xiao shi* (The Story of Ahei), published in periodicals between 1928 and 1933 and collected in book form in the latter year, fascinated Chinese urbanites in the throes of their own Western-influenced sexual revolution. His later works, however, evoke a mythic atmosphere that is outside of time. Love between the sexes and courtship by alternating boy-girl songs trilled across long distances and deep valleys are still the subject matter, but the premarital sexual unions known to Ahei are sublimated in these pieces into heroic romances; Shen claimed that he wrote the later works to nourish young people's imaginations. "Yuexia xiaojing" (1933, translated as "Under Moonlight," 1947) is ostensibly the legend of a double love-suicide by star-crossed young lovers—a folkloric theme familiar from southwestern China to Japan. The lovers want to pledge eternal love and fidelity, but their loss of virginity with each other has made each of them the mate that the other is forbidden to marry under tribal law. "Yuexia xiaojing" is the title piece in a 1933 volume of nine stories; the others are adaptations of the Jataka tales, stories about the lives of the Buddha before he was born as Siddhartha Gautama around 563 B.C. that were transcribed from Sanskrit into Chinese centuries later.

In the 1930s Shen wrote the lyric "pastoral" works that brought his reputation to its pinnacle. His maddening ambiguity, refusal to depict society in Marxist class terms, and avoidance of anti-imperialist themes led the leftists who dominated literary politics to see him as an apologist for China's "old society," while his social criticism and Westernized ideas caused the government to regard him as a malcontent undermining the status quo, tradition, and respect for authority. Like Lu Xun, Shen eschewed the common urban nationalism of his day. His painterly technique, detachment from topical social concerns, and depiction of the beauty of human nature were appreciated by many critics, but others thought that he created archetypes instead of characters and painted tableaux instead of delving deeply into reality. David Der-wei Wang points to Shen's "imaginary nostalgia," defining it as a longing for something he never experienced. Most who scorned Shen's work attacked his "idealism"—his beautiful subject matter and his nonadherence to any conventional doctrine of realism. Perhaps in response, Shen set his naturalistic stories "Fulan" (1929, Rot), collected in *Youmu ji*, and "Nitu" (Mud), the title piece of a 1932 collection, in slums—but, characteristically, made chaos, garbage, and putrefaction into eerily beautiful scenery.

"Xiaoxiao" (1930; translated as "Hsiao-hsiao," 1938) exemplifies Shen's ambiguity even when he is setting innocent country folk against inimical forces. The eponymous adolescent heroine is a child bride premarried to an infant husband. An adult hired hand deflowers her; the punishment for the ensuing pregnancy could be death, but she is "forgiven" when the child is a boy. Xiaoxiao survives, and society goes on without change. Critics could not agree as to whether society is depicted as paying a price for its lack of change, but a subtle theme of feminism is sounded through Xiaoxiao's socially "inappropriate" envy of modern schoolgirls she sees in town.

In urban stories such as "Bohan" (1930, Chill), included in *Xin yu jiu*, and "Chun" (1932, Spring), in *Dushi yi furen*, as in his tales of Miao romance, Shen opposes sexual inhibition. He was attracted to and supportive of strong and intellectual females but without going so far as to call for a revolution in gender roles.

Shen and his wife, Zhang Zhaohe, in Beijing in 1934, the year after their marriage (from Shen Congwen xuan ji, *volume 4, 1983; Collection of Thomas Moran)*

At the same time, he argued for a more confident and assertive masculinity that he felt was lacking in himself.

Shen's interest in psychology and the ideas of Sigmund Freud, manifested even in his rural works such as *Bian cheng* (1934, The Frontier City; translated as "Green Jade and Green Jade," 1936), found most forceful expression in his treatment of urban intellectuals. He often put himself, his family, and colleagues into such pieces. "Disi" (1930, Number Four), included in *Shen Congwen jia ji,* is the story of a "garrulous" friend of Shen's who overcomes a psychological problem by talking about it. The incident offers consolation for the narrator, a professional writer: perhaps there is a "writing cure," as well as a "talking cure." Shen speaks in his own voice as the left-wing foil and amateur psychoanalyst of a repressed and conservative Nationalist friend, Ruomo yisheng (Dr. Ruomo), the title character of a 1931 story included in *Dushi yi furen.*

The title character of "Sansan" (1931; translated as "Sansan," 1947), collected in *Huchu* (1932, Tiger Cub), is an innocent girl just beginning to discover her sexuality in the confines of a patriarchal society. She feels drawn to a rich older man with tuberculosis who comes to the countryside to convalesce and is dependent on a nubile nurse he brings from the city. The outsiders are images of modernity, spelling danger and even corruption, and yet they have their own attractions. The man dies before Sansan can be betrothed to him, saving her from an unsuitable match.

Shen was not always apolitical. He criticized both the "white terror" of the Nationalists and the ignorant naiveté of youthful Communist idealists in emotional biographies of two of his leftist writer friends, *Ji Hu Yepin* (1932, Remembering Hu Yepin) and *Ji Ding Ling* (1934, Remembering Ding Ling), followed by *Ji Ding Ling xuji* (1939, Sequel to *Remembering Ding Ling*); he depicts Ding Ling as a young Madame Bovary.

Shen also wrote of common city folk, showing special interest as always in those with colorful professions. He imagined for them tragic pasts and stoic ways of coping with everyday life and the rigors of modernity. In "Sheng" (1933; translated as "Life," 1995), included in Shen's *Rurui ji* (1934, Rurui Collection), a pathetic old puppeteer performs simple skits in a losing competition with jugglers and street actors in the old Beijing Drum Tower district. He is revealed at the end to be trying symbolically to reverse, through dramatic reenactments, the death of his son several years before.

"San ge nüxing" (1933, Three Women), included in *Rurui ji,* presents in thinly disguised form the personalities and philosophies of Shen's fiancée, Zhang Zhaohe; his younger sister; and his old friend Ding Ling as they argue with each other about the meaning of life, love, art, and revolution. Shen and Zhang were married in 1933.

Shen explores the meaning of his past and his mission as a writer in the complex first-person allegorical novel *Fengzi* (1933, Phoenix). He reshapes his life in a more conventionally factual, chronological—and, given the sordidness of warlordism, almost incongruously elegant—literary form in *Congwen zizhuan* (1934, Congwen's Autobiography). Like Daudet's *Le petit chose: Histoire d'un enfant* (1868; translated as *The Little Good-for-Nothing,* 1878), from which it drew inspiration, it is the autobiography of a mere twenty-year-old; but it is colorful, sophisticated, and socially aware. The book reveals the author's own experiences to have been as fantastic as anything he depicted in his military and tribal fiction and the incidence of executions in rural "pacifications" in his earlier fiction to have been understatements.

"Sansan" seems, in retrospect, to have been a study for one of Shen's masterpieces: the novella *Bian cheng.* Cuicui ("Green Jade"), the pubescent orphan granddaughter of a ferryman, discovers her sexuality in a lush rural setting. She does not dwell on her poverty; like Shen's other country folk, she has her own life of the mind. Cuicui's dreams and the local customs, including courtship by mountain song, arouse subliminal fantasies, fears, and awareness of death. She dreams in Freudian symbols; her growing ambivalence toward her grandfather and other males lend the novella a rare psychological depth. The idyllic natural setting, lapidary prose, and lack of political referents epitomize Shen's lyric creativity; yet, there are presentiments of the tragedy that arrives in the end.

Shen wrote essays attacking the revival of classical Chinese and castigated Nationalist neotraditionalism, dictatorship, and reliance on military force to change China. His treatment of such problems in fiction was often symbolic. "Xin yu jiu" (1935; translated as "The New and the Old," 1995), the title piece of his 1936 collection, allows moral, social, and political readings. Its hero, an old-style headsman (decapitator) in the Miao Defense Army in the Qing dynasty, is superannuated in the new republic, but not because morality has progressed; on the contrary, his killing method has become too slow, and his ritual means of atoning for killing has become superfluous. Yet, a new regime revives the headsman's old mode of killing—without the atonement—as a "new" way of terrorizing young people suspected of Communism. Shen's immediate target in the story was Chiang Kai-shek's New Life Movement of 1934–1935, which, he believed, hypocritically revived the old Confucian morality to speed up modernization. The greatest insights in the story lie in its dissection of modernization itself.

In the roman à clef "Ba jun tu" (translated as "Eight Steeds," 1995), the title story of a 1935 collection, the narrator and eight professor friends are summering at a seaside resort in Qingdao. All but one are middle-aged men paying a psychological price for repressing their emotions. The narrator-"therapist," Shen's alter ego, tries to cure them by encouraging spontaneity, only to discover that his fidelity to his fiancée may be stifling him. In "Zisha" (1935; translated as "Suicide," 1995), collected in *Xin yu jiu,* and "Zhufu" (1936; translated as "The Housewife," 1995), collected in *Zhufu ji,* Shen delves into the difficult psychologies of suicide and marriage.

Shen's lyrical yet exciting prose and his eye for detail and social contradictions in rural China appear in his episodic travelogue *Xiang xing san ji* (1936, Discursive Notes on a Trip through Hunan; excerpts translated in *Recollections of West Hunan,* 1982), which was inspired by a rare visit home in 1933–1934 during which he had to leave Fenghuang in a hurry when the locals began to accuse him of Communist sympathies. In the book he returns to scenes of his adolescent memories, wistfully noting tragedies of both change and lack of change among his countrymen and imagining tribulations that they will soon face.

Even in his "pastoral" mode Shen sometimes created rustic scenes as a foil for the dark side of humanity, in the manner of Thomas Hardy. The eponymous hero of "Guisheng" (1937; translated as "Guisheng," 1980), collected in *Zhufu ji* (1939, Housewife), is a hired worker—below poor-peasant status in Mao Zedong's later categorization of rural social classes. He does not feel oppressed, however, but enjoys his life and freedom in the luxuriant countryside. He grows to love a shopkeeper's daughter but seeks to marry her only after overcoming fears that her horoscope dooms those around her. By then she has been sold off as a concubine to a rich and profligate landlord—not to procreate but so that her virginity, according to local belief, may bring the landlord luck at gambling. At the end of the story the shopkeeper's home is in flames, and so is Guisheng's. Guisheng may have lit the fires to kill his tormentors and himself.

On a conventional May Fourth intellectual and social reading, "Guisheng" is an attack on the feudal superstitions that made Guisheng more attentive to a horoscope than to his heart's desire and motivated the landlord to deflower yet another virgin. Concubinage and the excessive power and prerogatives of the rich appear in a bad light—although the oppressed girl is of the shopkeeper class, Guisheng does not resent landlords as a class, and he is not portrayed as economically oppressed and pitiable. An alternative *xiangtu* reading would emphasize that the natural vigor and morality of the native region have succumbed to vapid, upper-class, "urban" corruption from the landlords. On yet another reading, the gentry do not control their destiny but are also victims; decadence comes from the rural culture's own contradictions as symbolized by Guisheng, a man whose human nature bears the seeds of his own decline.

Shen edited major journals and literary feuilletons, including the *Wenyi* (Literature and Arts) page of the Tianjin newspaper *Dagong bao/L'Impartial* beginning in 1933. He passed on most of the work to his protégé Xiao Qian in 1935. In the paper Shen published a body of nonideological literary criticism; some of it was collected in *Feiyou cundi* (1937, Letters Never Mailed), co-authored with Xiao Qian. He continually asserted the importance of craft over "genius," aesthetic values, and seriousness of purpose as opposed to the values of "merely popular" literature and agitprop. His polemics against the commercialism, trendiness, frivolity (allegedly found in Lin Yutang's "humor"), and political correctness of "Shanghai Types" led critics in the 1930s and again in the 1980s to speak of an academic "Beijing School," led by Shen and including his protégés Bian Zhilin, He Qifang, Li Guangtian, and a host of young poets, that upheld literary professionalism against a more popular and changeable "Shanghai School."

Cover for a 1946 edition of Shen's novella Bian cheng *(1934, The Frontier City; translated as "Green Jade and Green Jade," 1936), about a country girl's discovery of her sexuality (Wason Collection on East Asia–China, Kroch Asia Library, Cornell University)*

Shen made a harrowing escape from Beiping (as Beijing was known from 1928 to 1949) two weeks after it fell to the Japanese on 29 July 1937. He helped compile textbooks in Wuhan for a few months and taught at temporary institutions retreating in front of the Japanese. By then, autonomous West Hunan belonged to the past. Positioned between warring Nationalist and Communist armies, it had fallen in 1935 to the pro-Nationalist warlord He Jian. Sending in his own Peace Preservation Corps from Changsha, He Jian transferred Shen's old employer Chen Quzhen's fierce Miao soldiers east to defend Chiang Kai-shek's hometown of Fenghua and nearby Ningbo in Zhejiang province. Shen's younger brother and one of their cousins went with them as commanders. A "Miao rebellion" in 1937 cost He Jian his governorship and earned West Hunan a reputation as a region of bandits and barbarians.

Late in 1937 Shen took up residence in his elder brother's home in Yuanling, West Hunan. There he hosted Wen Yiduo and Wen's students, who were collecting folklore while trekking to their southwestern refuge from the Japanese. From 1939 until the end of the war Shen taught at the Xi'nan lianhe daxue (Southwest Associated University) in Kunming, a union of the Beijing, Qinghua, and Nankai universities in exile.

In 1938 Shen helped persuade the rebel "Miao King," Long Yunfei, to surrender his troops for the greater cause of resisting Japan. For his part Shen preferred, as always, to stay aloof. He declined an appointment to the Hunan provincial assembly and refused to join even the broadest of patriotic writers' associations, though they gave him honorary directorships in absentia. That great numbers of Nationalists and Communists were already enrolled made him more, rather than less, leery of such front groups. When Wen Yiduo tried to engage Shen in his third-party movement in Kunming, Shen demurred, fearing that Wen's group served the interests of the Kunming warlord Long Yun; he sardonically called for a fourth-party movement.

Shen was moved by his region's and nation's recent tragedies to resume his role as regional chronicler, with West Hunan representing both its own "unique" original purity and the troubles besetting China as a whole. The darker mood foreshadowed in *Xiang xing san ji* takes definite shape in "Xiaozhai" (1937, Little Stockade), collected in volume seven of *Shen Congwen wen ji*, which begins by depicting the subhuman existence of cave-dwelling country folk outside a West Hunanese riverport after the 1935 takeover by the corrupt militarists from Changsha. The main characters include a diseased prostitute, her madam, and a boy with dropsy who is just learning how to cheat people at the market. The war stopped publication of the magazine in which the story was being serialized, and Shen did not resume this negative mirror image of the pastoralism of *Bian cheng*.

Shen's first major regional work after the war broke out and he visited his home province was *Xiangxi* (1939, West Hunan). It is less a travelogue in the manner of *Xiang xing san ji* than an impressionistic gazetteer, meditating on the strengths and weaknesses of all the West Hunanese—boatmen, literati, shamans, prostitutes, marketplace magicians, and tribal girls convinced that a god has taken them in marriage. His purpose in writing *Xiangxi* was not to continue the story of his region's degradation but to rehabilitate West Hunan from its reputation as a place of outlawry and to preserve memories of its ancient cultural roots before they were swept away by the tide of refugees from the east.

From his sanctuary in Kunming, which was controlled neither by the Nationalists nor the Communists, Shen wrote several other paeans to the country folk, including "Kunming dongjing" (translated as "Winter

Scenes in Kunming," 1995), the title story of a 1939 collection, and "Wang sao" (1940; translated as "Amah Wang," 1995), collected in volume seven of *Shen Congwen wen ji*. "Xiang cheng" (1940, A Country Town; translated as "Old Mrs. Wang's Chickens," 1940–1941), also collected in volume seven of *Shen Congwen wen ji*, tells of the resilience of country folk in the face of war mobilizers and propagandists.

In his literary criticism Shen defended those who wrote about subjects other than the war. He accused China's many mediocre wartime writers of a herd mentality—of writing "all about the same." He, on the contrary, was absorbed in rapturous philosophical-religious meditations in the essay collection *Zhu xu* (1941, The Candle Extinguished). Shen ponders the massive wartime corruption from the point of view of a pacifist and pantheist, worshipping noumenal Beauty and a vitalistic Life Spirit. Despite the war and poverty, Shen and his university colleagues found Kunming's spirit of freedom, intellectualism, and genuine self-sacrifice relatively uplifting.

Shen's prose in *Zhu xu* was experimental—"difficult" in both concepts and syntax. Kunming was far more upset by his new experiments in fiction, which were erotic, modernist, and unrelated to the wartime sacrifice. In "Kan hong lu" (1943; translated as "The Rainbow," 1947), collected in volume ten of *Shen Congwen quanji*, Shen splits himself and an imaginary female companion into conscious and subconscious personalities to explore desire, memory, and the illusiveness of reality. The erotic symbolism and the bilevel discourse between lovers communicating simultaneously in speech and in mutually understood streams of consciousness are a modern version of the old alternating boy-girl mountain songs. Chinese audiences in the wartime atmosphere found the work offensive, and it was not reprinted in Shen's lifetime. Still more conceptually difficult is "Shuiyun" (1943, Water and Clouds), a psychological autobiography about how libido shaped Shen's romances and works, in which he cleaves his soul into the mutually questioning voices of ego, alter ego, and superego. It is collected in volume ten of *Shen Congwen wen ji*. There is no English translation of this monumental and difficult work, but it was translated into French in 1996 as *L'Eau et les nuages*.

In 1943 Shen published *Chang he* (Long River), an epic work that he had begun in 1938 about the decline of his beloved region. The scene is a village near a riverport in the late 1930s: the heroes are a tangerine grower, the boatmen who deliver his goods to market, and the orchard owner's prenubile daughter, Yaoyao, who is more pert than Xiaoxiao, Sansan, or Cuicui but just as vulnerable. Shen's finely chiseled prose conveys natural color and local customs as in *Bian cheng*—although this setting is wholly Han—without neglecting the vital energies of wharfside folk, but evil intrudes in the person of the new Peace Preservation officer from Changsha whose job is to extract booty from the region instead of nourish its native riches. A full panorama of local manners, *Chang he* provides an exceptional view of the subtlety of corruption and sexual harassment beneath a veil of conservative etiquette. The suave but rapacious Changsha man hardly has to hint that he wants a boatload of tangerines free of charge—or little Yaoyao; the irony is that rural hospitality offers the passing traveler as many free tangerines as he needs to quench his thirst. Like Yaoyao, the pristine countryside is not used to defending itself against this old and yet new urban rapacity. It is ripe for the picking.

Volumes two and three were to follow the course of local history with a tale of resistance and rebellion, but censorship delayed and nearly prevented the publication even of volume one. Several stories about rural China and two other books by Shen were banned by the government. The republication of his works in thirty-odd individually titled volumes was delayed for four years, and some of the textbooks he compiled were rejected for insufficient patriotism. The bowdlerization of *Chang he* was unsurprising, however, for that work pursues revenge not only against He Jian but also Chiang Kai-shek, who proclaims, astride his white horse, a "New Life." "New Life" is not just a stand-in for Nationalist neotraditionalism, hypocritical use of armed force on innocent country folk (as in "Xin yu jiu"), and the Chiang personality cult; it is also a symbol of the costs of modern life, from bureaucratic capitalism and other sins conventionally attributed to the Nationalists to the faster and more calculating way of life inherent in modernization itself.

The remnants of the West Hunan armies were nearly annihilated; they were cannon fodder in a battle for eastern China that was fought after the Nationalist generals had already decided to abandon the area to the enemy. Shen contemplated the sacrifice of his old army in the elegiac "Dongjing" (1943, Stirrings), collected in volume ten of *Shen Congwen quanji*, about a wounded West Hunanese colonel, based on his younger brother, who remains idealistic after the great slaughter but is resented by the local Nationalist Party branch as a worthless "petit bourgeois." Less modernist in style than "Kan hong lu" and "Shuiyun" but more pantheistic and mystical, with hints of Buddhist color symbolism, are Shen's meditations about the meaning of life in his "nightmare" cycle, beginning with "Lü yan" (1944, Green Nightmare), collected in volume ten of *Shen Congwen wen ji*.

The return to rural residence when he joined the evacuation of Kunming to avoid air raids gave Shen much comfort. His prose style grew complex and classi-

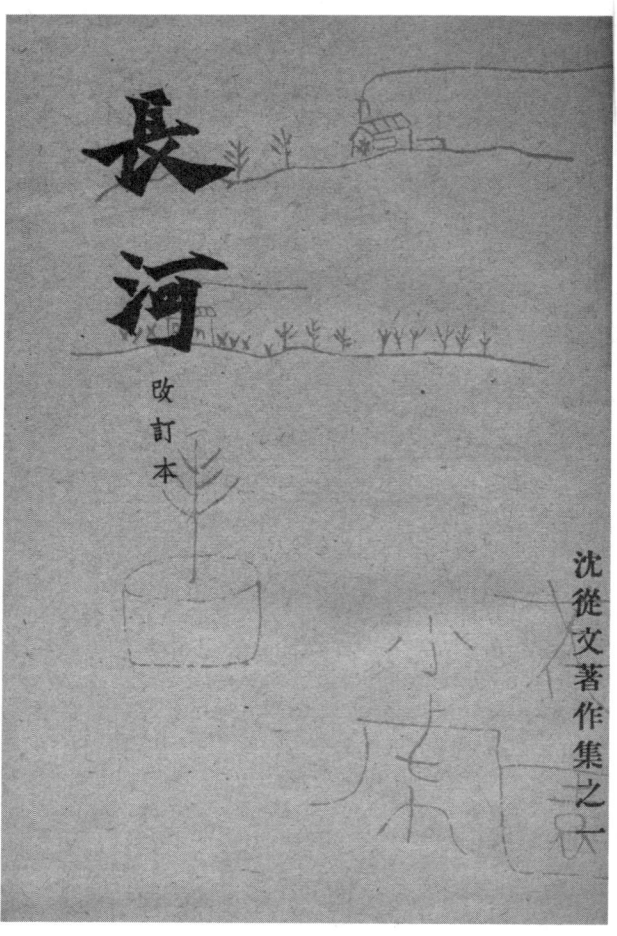

Cover for a 1946 edition of Chang he (1943, Long River), an epic work about the decline of Shen's native West Hunan province (Wason Collection on East Asia–China, Kroch Asia Library, Cornell University)

cal in syntax—some called it flowery—but the quantity of his output declined. His many unfinished projects, works never collected after their original publication in periodicals, and pieces delayed by censorship indicate that he was thwarted by the chaos in the publishing industry brought on by the war.

Returning to Beiping after the war, Shen taught at Beijing University from 1946 to 1949. He resumed the editorship of *Dagong bao*/*L'Impartial* and also edited the literary supplement of the Tianjian *Yishibao* (Social Welfare News). He published pieces of his regional saga that were originally intended as later chapters of *Chang he*. His last great story cycle was collected in volume seven of *Shen Congwen wen ji* as "Xue qing," the title of a constituent story (1946; translated as "After Snow," 1982). Like "Xiaozhai" and *Chang he*, the story "Xue qing" sets a scene of solid West Hunanese country folk whose social comity is starting to be poisoned by violence and mutual ruination; "Qiaoxiu he Dongsheng" (1947; translated as "Qiaoxiu and Dongsheng," 1982) and "Chuanqi bu qi" (1947; translated as "Truth Is Stranger than Fiction," 1982) turn the saga into a Proustian tale of the author/narrator's search for his roots and selfhood in the exotic Chinese southwest. The work resumes the first-person allegorical ventures into the meaning of his past that Shen first attempted in *Fengzi*.

Shen tells the story of incompetence and betrayal by those on top in the slaughter of the West Hunan armies fighting Japanese to the east, in Zhejiang, in "Yi ge chuanqi de benshi" (1947, Material for a Fairy Tale), collected in volume ten of *Shen Congwen wen ji*. Like his younger brother, who witnessed the debacle in east China, Shen's older brother in West Hunan got into trouble with the Nationalists; Shen began serializing a novel about him titled "Yunlu jishi" (1947, Yunlu Chronicles), but it remained unfinished. It is collected in volume ten of *Shen Congwen quanji*.

Vilified by articles and in wall posters prior to the Communist siege of Beiping in 1948, Shen attempted suicide early in 1949 by slashing his wrists; he was found before he bled to death. After recovering, writing many confessions at a revolutionary university (including confessing to having been influenced by James Joyce), taking a turn in 1950 as a docent in the Palace Museum, and handing over his collection of antiques to the state, he became a professional researcher in the history of ancient artifacts, crafts, and costumes. At times he seemed to try to find an accommodation with the new regime, and in 1962 he went on a retreat to write a novel about a Communist martyr in his wife's family. But he could not produce what the times required. His only output was poems in classical Chinese, some of which appear to mock Mao. Shen never wrote another major creative work; yet, being mostly forgotten meant that he was at least never labeled a rightist, as were several of his leftist friends (including Ding Ling, from whom he had become estranged). During the Cultural Revolution of 1966 to 1976 his house was raided several times, and he and his wife, like most intellectuals, were sent to the countryside for ideological rehabilitation; but the main hardship he suffered was lack of medical care. His *Zhongguo gudai fushi yanjiu* (Researches into Ancient Chinese Costume) received official encouragement in post-Mao times, though it was not published until 1981. Specialists found it a contribution to knowledge but not a work requiring the genius of a Shen Congwen.

Shen's literary reputation was revived by interest in him in America, Europe, and Japan, and his works were republished in China after 1981 and in Taiwan after 1986. His rural and regional themes led both mainland and Taiwanese critics to see him as a great *xiangtu* writer equal to—some said better than—Lu Xun.

He reminded both sides of how much of China's modernity they had lost. In the People's Republic, Shen seemed to be the antithesis of the country's revolutionary writers: he was China's non-Lu Xun, nonrealist and nonsocialist, treading his own anti-Confucian, pro-Western, yet nonurban and apolitical path. Taiwan recast him as a great "native" writer–rustic, non-Communist, and not as Westernized as he appeared to be to mainland critics. Shen died on 10 May 1988.

As a documenter of his native West Hunan, Shen developed the craft of the traditional literati poet, gazetteerist, and travel writer. His style and rural themes influenced many Hunanese writers, including Gu Hua, Sun Jianzhong, He Liwei, Xiao Jianguo, and Cai Cehai; Bai Xianyong, who published in Taiwan; Han Shaogong, Acheng, and Jia Ping'ao, who in the mid 1980s went to China's hinterlands (Han to West Hunan) to "search for roots" of Chinese literature; and Shen's old "Beijing School" protégés Xiao Qian and Wang Zengqi, whose own revivals in the 1980s helped spur a new literature of urban local color and lifestyles.

Shen's work is also a milestone in a less "earthbound" tradition–that of southwestern exoticism, primalism, and quests of the soul. The tradition is as ancient as the *Chu ci* (translated as *Ch'u T'z'u: The Songs of the South*, 1957), attributed to Qu Yuan (circa 338–278 B.C.), in which that wronged Chu poet communes with shamans and female goddesses on a vision quest in the wondrous southwest of his day (West Hunan, Shen believed); and as recent as Gao Xingjian's *Ling shan* (1990; translated as *Soul Mountain*, 2000), in which Gao, persecuted by the Communist Party, searches for his identity in the southwest (the book won Gao the 2000 Nobel Prize in literature). In *Yuanfang you ge nüer guo* (1988; translated as *The Remote Country of Women*, 1994), Bai Hua uses southwestern tribal society as a foil for Han civilization, as did Shen; and many post-Mao authors, of whom Zhang Xianliang and Gao Xingjian are the best known, wrote autobiographical novels splitting their souls into mutually disputatious parts. As a standard-bearer for the independence of art from politics, Shen Congwen's influence was widest of all.

Letters:

Congwen jiashu: Congwen Zhaohe shuxin xuan [Congwen's Letters Home: Selected Correspondence of Congwen and Zhaohe] (Shanghai: Yuandong chubanshe, 1996).

Bibliography:

Jeffrey C. Kinkley, *The Odyssey of Shen Congwen* (Stanford, Cal.: Stanford University Press, 1987), pp. 387–438.

Biographies:

Jeffrey C. Kinkley, "Shen Ts'ung-wen's Vision of Republican China," dissertation, Harvard University, 1977;

Kinkley, *The Odyssey of Shen Congwen* (Stanford, Cal.: Stanford University Press, 1987);

Ling Yu, *Shen Congwen zhuan* (Beijing: Shiyue wenyi chubanshe, 1988);

Wu Lichang, *Renxing de zhiliaozhe: Shen Congwen zhuan* (Taibei: Yeqiang chubanshe, 1992).

References:

Ba Jin, Huang Yongyu, and others, *Chang he bu jin liu: Huainian Shen Congwen xiansheng* (Changsha: Hunan wenyi chubanshe, 1989);

C. T. Hsia, *A History of Modern Chinese Fiction*, revised edition (New Haven: Yale University Press, 1971), pp. 189–211, 359–366;

Huang Xianwen, *Shen Congwen chuangzuo xinlun* (Wuhan: Huazhong Ligong Daxue chubanshe, 1996);

Liu Hongtao, *Hunan xiangtu wenxue yu Xiang Chu wenhua* (Changsha: Hunan jiaoyu chubanshe, 1997);

William L. MacDonald, "Characters and Themes in Shen Ts'ung-wen's Fiction," dissertation, University of Washington, 1970;

Hua-ling Nieh, *Shen Ts'ung-wen* (New York: Twayne, 1972);

Peng Hsiao-yen, *Antithesis Overcome: Shen Congwen's Avant-Gardism and Primitivism* (Taibei: Institute of Chinese Literature and Philosophy, Academia Sinica, 1994);

Shen Congwen yanjiu, edited by Jishou Daxue Shen Congwen yanjiushi (Changsha: Hunan Daxue chubanshe, 1988);

Su Xuelin, "Shen Congwen lun," *Wenxue*, 3 (September 1934): 712–720;

David Der-wei Wang, *Fictional Realism in Twentieth-Century China: Mao Dun, Lao She, Shen Congwen* (New York: Columbia University Press, 1992);

Wong Yoon Wah (Wang Runhua), *Shen Congwen xiaoshuo xinlun* (Shanghai: Xuelin chubanshe, 1998);

Xiang Chengguo, *Huigui ziran yu zhuixun lishi: Shen Congwen yu Xiangxi* (Changsha: Hunan Shifan Daxue chubanshe, 1997);

Yao Zhimin, Wang Zhongming, Zhang Zhenhua, and Bian Quiansheng, eds., *Shuying*, volume 2 (Shanghai: Yuandong chubanshe, 2003), p. 53;

Yu Runqi, ed., *Tang Tao cang shu* (Beijing: Beijing chubanshe, 2004), p. 100.

Shi Tuo
(Lu Fen)
(10 March 1910 – 7 October 1988)

Steven P. Day
Swarthmore College

BOOKS: *Gu* [The Valley], as Lu Fen (Shanghai: Wenhua shenghuo chubanshe, 1936); as Shi Tuo (Beijing: Renmin wenxue chubanshe, 2001);

Limen shiji [Sketches Gathered at My Native Place], as Lu Fen (Shanghai: Wenhua shenghuo chubanshe, 1937); as Shi Tuo (Hong Kong: Xinyue chubanshe, 1962);

Huanghua tai [Day Lily Moss], as Lu Fen (Shanghai: Liangyou tushu gongsi, 1937);

Luori guang [Light of Dusk], as Lu Fen (Shanghai: Kaiming shudian, 1937; as Shi Tuo (Shanghai: Kaiming shudian, 1949);

Yeniao ji [Wild Birds], as Lu Fen (Shanghai: Wenhua shenghuo chubanshe, 1938);

Jianghu ji [Itinerant], as Lu Fen (Shanghai: Kaiming shudian, 1938); as Shi Tuo (Beijing: Zhongguo qingnian chubanshe, 1995);

Wuming shi [Anonymous], as Lu Fen (Shanghai: Wenhua shenghuo chubanshe, 1939);

Kan ren ji [Observing Humanity], as Lu Fen (Shanghai: Kaiming shudian, 1939); as Shi Tuo (Beijing: Zhongguo qingnian chubanshe, 1995);

Wuwangcun de guanzhu [Master of Wuwang Village], as Ji Meng (Shanghai: Kaiming shudian, 1941); as Shi Tuo (Fuzhou: Fujian renmin chubanshe, 1983);

Shanghai shouzha [Shanghai Correspondence], as Lu Fen (Shanghai: Wenhua shenghuo chubanshe, 1941);

Guoyuan cheng ji [An Account of Orchard Town], as Lu Fen (Shanghai: Shanghai chuban gongsi, 1946; revised edition, Shanghai: Xinwenyi chubanshe, 1958)—includes "Yi wen," translated by Theodore D. Huters as "A Kiss," in *Reading the Modern Chinese Short Story,* edited by Huters (Armonk, N.Y.: Sharpe, 1990), pp. 153–161;

Jiehun [Marriage] (Shanghai: Shanghai chenguang chuban gongsi, 1947; Chengdu: Sichuan renmin chubanshe, 1982);

Shi Tuo (Museum of Modern Chinese Literature, Beijing)

Ma Lan (Shanghai: Wenhua shenghuo chubanshe, 1948; revised edition, Guangzhou: Huacheng chubanshe, 1982);

Da maxituan [The Big Circus] (Shanghai: Wenhua shenghuo chubanshe, 1948);

Ye dian [Night Inn], by Shi Tuo and Ke Ling (Shanghai: Shanghai chuban gongsi, 1948);

Lishi wu qing [History Is Merciless] (Shanghai: Shanghai chuban gongsi, 1951);

Chun meng [Spring Dream] (Hong Kong: Xianggang Yimeishu gongsi, 1956);

Shi jiang [The Mason] (Beijing: Zuojia chubanshe, 1959);

Baojialiya xing ji [Travelogue of Bulgaria] (Shanghai: Shanghai wenyi chubanshe, 1960);

Shanchuan–lishi–renwu [Nature–History–Personage] (Shanghai: Shanghai wenyi chubanshe, 1979);

Lu Fen duanpian xiaoshuo xuanji [Selected Short Stories by Lu Fen] (Nanchang: Jiangxi renmin chubanshe, 1983).

Collections: *Emeng ji* [Nightmare] (Hong Kong: Xianggang wenxue yanjiushe, 1981);

Lu Fen sanwen xuanji [Selected Essays by Lu Fen] (Nanjing: Jiangsu renmin chubanshe, 1981);

Shanghai san zha [Three Shanghai Missives] (Yinchuan: Ningxia renmin chubanshe, 1984);

Shi Tuo sanwen xuanji [Selected Essays of Shi Tuo] (Tianjin: Baihua wenyi chubanshe, 1992);

Guoyuan cheng [Orchard Town], edited by Luo Gang (Zhuhai: Zhuhai chubanshe, 1997);

Shi Tuo daibiao zuo [Shi Tuo's Representative Works], edited by Ren Haideng (Beijing: Huaxia chubanshe, 1998);

Shi Tuo quanji [Complete Works of Shi Tuo], 8 volumes (Kaifeng: Henan daxue chubanshe, 2004).

PLAY PRODUCTIONS: *Da maxituan* [The Big Circus], adapted by Shi Tuo, as Lu Fen, from Leonid Andreyev's play *Tot, kto poluchaet poshchechiny* (1915; translated as *He, the One Who Gets Slapped*, 1921), Shanghai, Carlton Theatre, 5 October 1942;

Ye dian [Night Inn], adapted by Shi Tuo, as Lu Fen, and Ke Ling from Maksim Gor'ky's play *Na dne* (performed 1902, published 1903; translated as *The Lower Depths*, 1906), Shanghai, Carlton Theatre, December 1945.

PRODUCED SCRIPT: *Ye dian* [Night Inn], motion picture, screenplay by Shi Tuo and Ke Ling, adapted from Maksim Gor'ky's play *Na dne* (performed 1902, published 1903; translated as *The Lower Depths*, 1906), Wenhua, 1947.

SELECTED PERIODICAL PUBLICATIONS–UNCOLLECTED: "Qingyuan zheng pian" [Petition: The Official Version], *Beidou*, 2 (20 January 1932): 115–128;

"Qingyuan wai pian" [Petition: The Unofficial Version], *Wenxue yuebao*, 1 (10 June 1932), 145–151.

Shi Tuo is a major "minor" writer in modern Chinese literature: though never officially canonized, he achieved critical acclaim at various points in his five-decade career. His choice of rural subject matter and the lyrical quality of his writing earned him the labels of a *xiangtu* (native-soil) and Jing pai (Beijing School) writer. His views on the virtues of country life and the human condition are, however, less sanguine than those of writers usually associated with these groups. Though he was sympathetic with the Left, throughout much of his life Shi Tuo maintained a relatively independent position in both politics and literature and expressed doubts about ideologies and even about the role of literature itself as solutions to society's problems. This critical attitude is articulated in his fiction through satire and irony, and his work has formal and thematic affinities with Lu Xun's. Though writing almost exclusively in a realist mode, Shi Tuo was willing to experiment formally in his fiction and at times pushed the boundaries of both narrative point of view and genre to their limits. Predominantly a fiction writer, Shi Tuo also produced poems, essays, travelogues, screenplays, and historical fiction and dramas and adapted extant plays.

Early critical commentary on Shi Tuo's fiction frequently remarks on his use of language, as well as the somber tone and worldview expressed in his works. Although he was widely acknowledged to be adept at creating vivid lyrical depictions of rural scenery and at adding local color through the inclusion of regional patois, he was faulted for his often flowery and overwrought diction. "Excess" is a common criticism of his writing, whether of his ornate language, his indignant tone and pessimistic outlook, his lengthy descriptions and sometimes intrusive commentaries, or his early pastoralism. Otherwise, Shi Tuo was, generally speaking, regarded favorably by his contemporaries. One prominent critic remarked on his ability, uncommon at a time when realism and romanticism were competing modes of writing fiction, to combine detailed observations with vivid imagination.

Shi Tuo was born into a fallen landlord family in Qi county, Henan province, on 10 March 1910; his birth name was Wang Changjian. After receiving basic instruction in the Chinese classics at a small private school, he went to middle school in Qi County; there he developed an interest in literature through his exposure to local storytellers and Li He's poetry. Wang attended high school in Kaifeng until the Beifa (Northern Expedition of 1926–1927) forced him to return home; many schools closed at this time. He resumed his studies in 1927 and started a small magazine with some classmates.

After graduating in 1931, Wang went to Beiping (as Beijing was known from 1928 to 1949) on the pre-

Cover for Shanghai shouzha (1941, Shanghai Correspondence), Shi Tuo's part-essay, part-novel about life in the Japanese-surrounded foreign zone of Shanghai, published under his pen name, Lu Fen (Memorial Library East Asian Collection, University of Wisconsin–Madison)

text of sitting for college entrance examinations, but he never took them and never attended college. Caught up in the fervor of the Mukden Incident of 18 September 1931, when the Japanese military stationed in Manchuria sabotaged a South Manchurian railway line near Mukden (today Shenyang) and used the incident as a pretext to seize Manchuria, he took part in the Anti-Imperialist Alliance in Beiping. In 1932 he began his writing career in earnest under the pen name Lu Fen, a transliteration of the English word "ruffian." After establishing a journal, Jianrui (Sharp), he published his first short stories, "Qingyuan zheng pian" (Petition: The Official Version) and "Qingyuan wai pian" (Petition: The Unofficial Version), in two other journals.

Between 1932 and 1936 Lu Fen produced forty-three short stories; the majority were written in a pastoral mode during the last three years of this period. The title character of "Jinzi," which was published in December 1934 in Wenxue jikan (Literature Quarterly) and collected in Lu Fen's Luori guang (1937, Light of Dusk), is a young man who drops out of school and goes to work after his father dies. After initial misfortunes Jinzi is given opportunities to enjoy both familial affection and an education. But he falls ill, and at the end he lies delirious in his "coffin-like room." The narration alternates deftly between showing Jinzi and seeing the world through his eyes. Lu Fen merges the objective and subjective viewpoints at the end of the story as Jinzi, in his delirium, transcends bodily restraints by envisioning those closest to him suffering equally tragic fates. Stories such as "Lao Baozi" (1934, Old Baozi), collected in Lu Fen duanpian xiaoshuo xuanji (1983, Selected Short Stories by Lu Fen), and "Jianghu ke" (1937, The Itinerant) and "Niao" (1937, Bird), collected in Luori guang, anticipate a trend in late-1930s Chinese fiction that favored depiction of character over plot.

In Lu Fen's pastoral works majestic landscapes stand in stark contrast to the cruelty that permeates rural society. The cruelty takes both individual and collective forms and stems from entrenched customs and mores. In "Duzhou" (A Malicious Curse), collected in Limen shiji (1937, Sketches Gathered at My Native Place), individual cruelty arises from inability to produce a male heir. Master Bi decides to "switch land," even though his wife argues that his "seed," not her "soil," is at the root of the problem. When the new "land"—Master Bi's young new concubine—becomes pregnant, the wife poisons her rival in an attempt to induce a miscarriage. The girl dies, leaving Master Bi distraught and his wife cursing the land as "poisoned"—a double entendre referring both to the concubine and to their homestead. Cruelty takes the form of collective violence invoked to maintain an unjust social order in "Tou" (1935, The Head), collected in Lu Fen's first book, Gu (1936, The Valley). After the affable but wayward Sun San is executed for a petty crime, his head is nailed to a tree as a warning to others. The disembodied head both frightens and enlivens the dull village, creating a macabre, yet morbidly fascinating spectacle for the residents. After his name and bar tab are wiped from the tavern slate at the end of the story, the memory of Sun San will presumably pass into oblivion. Yet, no sooner has this action been taken than another character enters the bar, ordering "half a catty" of wine in the same manner as Sun San. The uncanny sense of repetition implied in this final scene disrupts the closure initially held out by the erasure of Sun San's name, leaving the reader with the unsettled feeling that similar events will transpire again. Other stories that depict collective cruelty include "Ren xia ren" (1936, The Downtrodden), collected in Gu, and "Juantan ji" (1936, Collection of Laggard Talks), "Baishun jie" (Baishun Street, 1936), and "Qiu yuan" (1937, Autumn Plain), all collected in Limen shiji.

Although in the preface to *Luori guang* Lu Fen writes that nature provides a source of personal solace for him, he seldom holds out this consolation to his characters. Rather, a notion akin to "cosmic irony" appears in his fiction as nature frustrates or even mocks characters' ambitions, as is illustrated by the inclement weather and difficult terrain in the title story of *Gu*. The indifference of nature creates an underlying sense of alienation as characters appear to be estranged both from each other and from their environment. In "Guo ling ji" (1935, Crossing the Ridge), collected in *Gu*, sublime scenery and recollections of accounts of mishaps in the mountains in traditional fiction inspire awe and dread in the three main characters and bind them closer during their journey. Yet, after crossing the ridge safely, they part with a quick farewell and continue on their separate ways. The narrator suggests that even their destinations—their homes—offer little hope of refuge.

In August 1936 social and political upheaval in Beiping impelled Lu Fen to move to Shanghai. *Gu*, his collection of seven short stories, won the *Dagong bao wenyi fukan (L'Impartial Literary Supplement)* prize for fiction in 1937, establishing him as an important figure on the Chinese literary scene. His works from the outbreak of war with Japan in 1937 to the end of 1941 generally concern war themes, as in the collection *Wuming shi* (1939, Anonymous), or themes of returning home. Inspired by his layover in the provinces en route to Shanghai, "Guoyuan cheng" (1938, Orchard Town), collected in *Guoyuan cheng ji* (1946, An Account of Orchard Town), describes the narrator Ma Shu'ao's impressions when he returns home after a seven-year absence. Pleasant recollections of the past stand out against the grim reality of a stagnating rural town left behind by modernization. Visiting with his relatives, Ma realizes that "time has not really spared us"; yet, despite the changes that the passage of time has wrought, the story ends with tea being served to each guest in a covered cup, just as Ma remembers. This constancy amid change offers little peace of mind, however, but leaves the reader with an unsettled feeling that lingers after the story concludes.

The war story "Wuyan zhe" (1939, Silent One), collected in *Wuming shi*, exemplifies Lu Fen's willingness to undertake formal innovations as he extends the bounds of narrative perspective by employing the modernist technique of *fenshen fa* (disembodied consciousness) to relate the thoughts and visions of a soldier dying on the battlefield. The soldier's consciousness drifts back home, where he witnesses injustices suffered by members of his family at the hands of a corrupt military regime. He can utter no protest; his silence symbolizes the Chinese peasantry's unheard voices. At the end of the story the narrator declares that the soldier

Cover for Shi Tuo's short-story collection Guoyuan cheng ji *(1946, An Account of Orchard Town), published under his pen name, Lu Fen (Wason Collection on East Asia–China, Kroch Asia Library, Cornell University)*

has the right to speak but cannot do so, because he is dead; this enforced silence authorizes the narrator to speak on the soldier's behalf.

Although the novella *Wuwangcun de guanzhu* (1941, Master of Wuwang Village), published under the pseudonym Ji Meng, nominally has only one narrator, it shifts between first- and third-person narrative voices to create an effect that combines the omniscience and cordial tone of the traditional storyteller's voice with the modern interiority of a self-conscious, dramatized narrator. Near the end of the work the narrator reveals that his narrative authority, which allows him to relate the most private details of the master's life, has for the most part been gained from his wife, Lily, the master's former spouse, whom the narrator "saved" by marrying and reeducating her. But this authority is undercut by the various voices and points of view that he surreptitiously appropriates without acknowledgment. Themat-

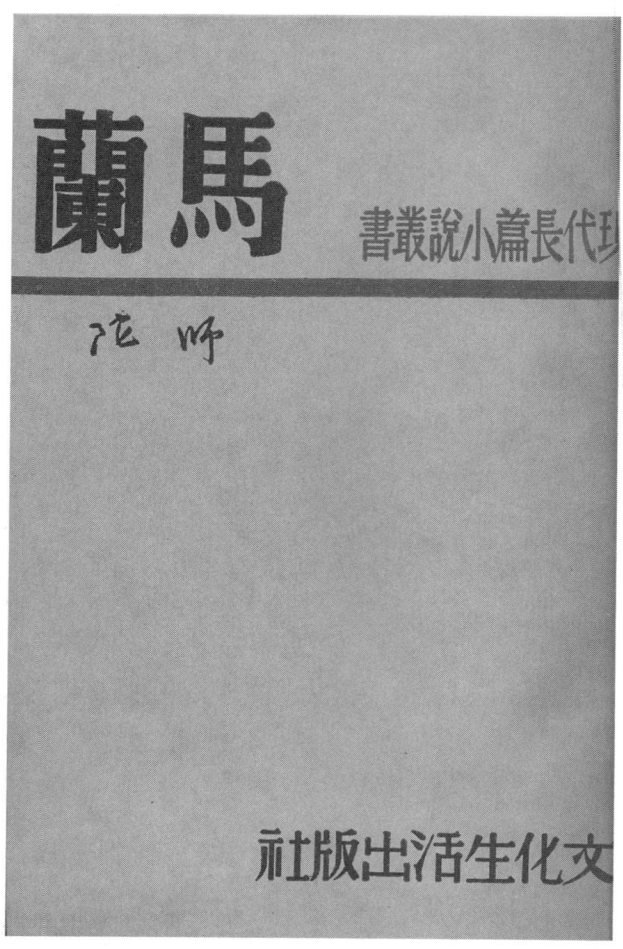

Cover for Shi Tuo's novel Ma Lan (1948), in which the title character suffers through a series of unfulfilling relationships with men before breaking the cycle by escaping to the mountains (Wason Collection on East Asia–China, Kroch Asia Library, Cornell University)

ically and formally the novella calls into question the relationship between morality and writing that dominated discussions of Chinese literature at the time: should writers follow the dictates of realism and depict the world as it is, or try to ameliorate social conditions by portraying the world as it should be?

Lu Fen's *Shanghai shouzha* (1941, Shanghai Correspondence) is a literary montage that reads as part essay and part novel; commentary is blended harmoniously with eighteen fictional vignettes of everyday life in the Japanese-surrounded foreign zone of Shanghai, which was known as the "Gudao" (Orphan Island) from 12 November 1937 until the entire city fell to the Japanese on 8 December 1941. In one vignette a couple goes through their belongings before fleeing to Hong Kong; various objects evoke fond memories for them, but they can cherish such moments only briefly as they are interrupted by telephone calls from prospective subletters of their apartment. In another scene three sisters sit on a park bench dreaming of the things they will purchase with the next remittance from their father, who left Shanghai after the war broke out. *Shanghai shouzha* is part of a trend in 1940s Chinese fiction of resisting tight structuring and purity of form or genre in a manner akin to the composition of traditional Chinese prose essays.

Lu Fen supported himself throughout the occupation by working as an editor at the Soviet Broadcasting Center. He also made successful forays into new genres, writing a screenplay and adapting plays from the Russian stage; his adaptations of *Da maxituan* (performed 1942, published 1948, The Big Circus) and Maksim Gor'ky's *Na dne* (performed 1902, published 1903; translated as *The Lower Depths*, 1906) as *Ye dian* (produced 1945, published 1948, Night Inn) had long runs. The war brought greater economic hardship to Shanghai and forced Lu Fen to leave the city for nearby Jiaxing until 1949.

The Sino-Japanese War ended in 1945 and was succeeded by the civil war between the Nationalist Party and the Communists. As the Nationalists' search for "traitors" intensified, Lu Fen decided to change his pseudonym to differentiate himself from another Lu Fen who had published in "treasonous" magazines. He began to use Shi Tuo regularly in 1946, and he published his first novel, *Jiehun* (Marriage), under that name in 1947. The first part of the work consists of the letters of the young teacher Hu Qu'e (Barbarian Eliminating Evil) to his fiancée, who is waiting for him in the relative security of the countryside while he remains in wartime Shanghai to earn money to support them. The letters reveal Hu's transformation from an upright educator dedicated to ensuring his family's financial future to the kind of money-hungry Shanghainese he initially despised. After Hu breaks off the engagement and further correspondence with his former fiancée, the narration shifts to the third person. The second part of the novel relates Hu's downfall, which is brought about by his desire to get ahead; though he is duped by others, he bears the ultimate responsibility for his fate. Hu's undoing stems not from the evils of society but from his blindness about himself, which makes him something of a tragic figure. Blindness is a major trope of the novel: the third-person narrator's account reveals blind spots in Hu's earlier epistolary version of events, and the actually blind Mr. Huang possesses greater insight into the ways of the world than the self-deluded intellectual Hu. Huang, not Hu, marries in the end, making a mockery of the institution as he weds "Old Maid" Zhang, with whom he has been cohabiting until his divorce came through.

In his next novel, *Ma Lan* (1948), Shi Tuo creates a *Rashomon* effect by relating the same events through various narrative perspectives. The eponymous heroine's tale is told partly in her own voice through her journal entries but is related primarily from the point of view of her unrequited lover, Li Botang. As in *Jiehun*, this technique is effective in suggesting how easily people can delude themselves—in this case, in matters involving love. Ma Lan suffers through a series of unfulfilling relationships, each of which ends up serving the immediate interests of her male partner. She finally breaks the cycle by escaping to the mountains. Her perseverance, like the resilience of the aster plant that is her namesake, offers a more optimistic view of human fate and agency than is usually found in Shi Tuo's fiction, although at times the work reads too much like a didactic novel.

In early 1949 Shi Tuo returned to Shanghai, where he worked as an editor and screenwriter while continuing his literary output of fiction, essays, and historical dramas and novels. Like other writers in the 1950s, he took part in the Land Reform Movement. After spending time in Henan, Shandong, and the northeast provinces, he visited Bulgaria in 1957; his impressions of his travels there were published as *Baojialiya xing ji* (1960, Travelogue of Bulgaria). In the 1960s he wrote several historical plays and novels, which were lost during the Cultural Revolution of 1966 to 1976 when his home was ransacked and his writings confiscated by Red Guards. He published sparingly after 1976; most of these works were either revisions of, or reflections on, earlier pieces. He stopped publishing in 1982. He died on 7 October 1988 and is survived by his wife, Chen Wanfang, and a son who lives in New York.

Following political and economic liberalization in the People's Republic of China in the 1980s and 1990s, Shi Tuo again attracted attention from critics and literary scholars. Though he was labeled a realist and a regional writer, his fiction exhibits clear affinities with modernist concerns and sensibilities. His exploration of alienation and of the corrosive effects of time and memory for the possibility of reliable narrative, as well as his formal innovations in narrative voice and point of view, do not, however, belong to either a strict Western or Chinese modernism—or, for that matter, to any other school. Moreover, though his fiction is marred by certain excesses and inconsistencies, the fact that he pursued his own intellectual aims and aesthetic designs and produced high-quality work under wartime conditions, which brought great political and economic pressures to bear on writers—especially in Beiping and occupied Shanghai—makes him a significant figure in modern Chinese literature.

Bibliography:
"Shi Tuo zhuzuo nianbiao," "Shi Tuo zhuzuo mulu," and "Shi Tuo yanjiu ziliao mulu suoyin," in *Shi Tuo yanjiu ziliao*, edited by Liu Zengjie (Beijing: Beijing chubanshe, 1984), pp. 347–419.

Biography:
"Shi Tuo zhuan lüe," "Shi Tuo shengping nianbiao," and "Shi Tuo zi shu," in *Shi Tuo yanjiu ziliao*, edited by Liu Zengjie (Beijing: Beijing chubanshe, 1984), pp. 3–36.

References:
Edward M. Gunn, "Shih T'o," in his *Unwelcome Muse: Chinese Literature in Shanghai and Peking, 1937–1945* (New York: Columbia University Press, 1980), pp. 77–102;

C. T. Hsia, "Shih T'o," in his *History of Modern Chinese Fiction*, second edition (New Haven: Yale University Press, 1971), pp. 461–468;

Theodore D. Huters, "The Telling of Shi Tuo's 'A Kiss': Few Words and Several Voices," in *Reading the Modern Chinese Short Story*, edited by Huters (Armonk, N.Y.: Sharpe, 1990), pp. 74–91;

Liu Zengjie, ed., *Shi Tuo yanjiu ziliao* (Beijing: Beijing chubanshe, 1984);

Qian Liqun, "Lu Fen: Zhishizhe de piaobo zhi lü," in his *Jingshen de lianyu: Zhongguo xiandai wenxue cong "Wusi" dao kangzhan de licheng* (Nanning: Guangxi jiaoyu chubanshe, 1996), pp. 241–253;

Zbigniew Slupski, "The World of Shih T'o," *Asian and African Studies*, 9 (1973): 11–28;

Tang Diwen, "*Guoyuan cheng ji*," in *Ershi shiji zhongguo xiaoshuo lilun ziliao*, edited by Qian, volume 4 (Beijing: Beijing daxue chubanshe, 1997), pp. 367–368;

Tang Shi, "Shi Tuo de *Jiehun*," in *Ershi shiji zhongguo xiaoshuo lilun ziliao*, volume 4, pp. 517–522;

Wang Peiyuan, "Shi Tuo de xiangtu xiaoshuo: fushi hui–yongtan diao," *Zhongguo xiandai wenxue yanjiu congkan*, 3 (1991): 145–159;

Xie Weimin, "You gexing de xushuzhe: Du Shi Tuo de *Wuwangcun de guanzhu*," *Zhongguo xiandai wenxue yanjiu congkan*, 2 (1991): 95–105;

Yang Yi, "Shi Tuo: Paihuai yu xiangtu shuqing he dushi xinli xiezhao zhi jian," in his *Zhongguo xiandai xiaoshuo shi*, volume 3 (Beijing: Renmin wenxue chubanshe, 1998), pp. 413–435;

Yin Xueman, "Shi Tuo yu ta de *Guoyuan cheng ji*," in his *Kangzhan shiqi de xiandai xiaoshuo* (Taibei: Chengwen chubanshe, 1980), pp. 135–154;

Zhang Yingjin, "The Orchard Town" and "Speculation as Prostitution: Shi Tuo's Marriage," in his *The City in Modern Chinese Literature and Film: Configurations of Space, Time, and Gender* (Stanford, Cal.: Stanford University Press, 1996), pp. 40–58, 148–153.

Wu Jianren
(Wo Foshanren)
(29 May 1866 – 21 October 1910)

Theodore Huters
University of California, Los Angeles

BOOKS: *Haishang mingji sida jin'gang qishu* [Strange Tales of the Four Guardian Spirit Shanghai Courtesans], attributed to Wu (Shanghai: Shanghai shuju, 1898);

Zhengzhi weixin yaoyan [Crucial Words on Political Reform], 2 volumes (Shanghai: Shanghai shuju, 1902);

Wu Jianren ku [Wu Jianren Laments] (Shanghai, 1902);

Dianshu qitan [The Marvels of Electricity] (Shanghai: Guangzhi shuju, 1905);

Jiuming qiyuan [Strange Injustice to Nine Lives], 3 volumes (Shanghai: Guangzhi shuju, 1906);

Henhai: Xieqing xiaoshuo [The Sea of Regret: Novel of Feeling] (Shanghai: Guangzhi shuju, 1906); translated as "The Sea of Regret," in *The Sea of Regret: Two Turn-of-the-Century Chinese Romantic Novels*, translated by Patrick Hanan (Honolulu: University of Hawai'i Press, 1995), pp. 101–205;

Hutu shijie [A World of Muddle] (Shanghai: Shijie fanhua bao, 1906);

Hu Baoyu [Hu Baoyu] (Shanghai: Lequn chuban she, 1906);

Zhongguo zhentan an [The Chinese Detective Files] (Shanghai: Guangzhi shuju, 1906);

Ershi nian mudu zhi guai xianzhuang [Strange Events Eyewitnessed in the Past Twenty Years], 8 volumes (Shanghai: Guangzhi shuju, 1906–1911); abridged and translated by Liu Shih Shun as *Vignettes from the Late Ch'ing: Bizarre Happenings Eyewitnessed over Two Decades* (Shatin, Hong Kong: Chinese University of Hong Kong, 1975);

Huitu xin shitou ji [The Illustrated New Story of the Stone] (Shanghai: Gailiang xiaoshuo she, 1908);

Xiapian qiwen [Strange Tales of Random Deceptions] (Shanghai: Shangwu yinshuguan, 1908);

Shanghai youcan ji [A Sojourn in Shanghai] (Shanghai: Qunxue she, 1908);

Facai mijue [The Secret of Striking It Rich] (Shanghai: Qunxue she, 1908);

Wu Jianren (from Liu Ts'un-yan, ed., Chinese Middlebrow Fiction from the Ch'ing and Early Republican Eras, *1984; Collection of Thomas Moran)*

Jieyu hui [Ashes of the Holocaust] (Shanghai: Guangzhi shuju, 1909);

Qiaopi hua [Witticisms] (Shanghai: Qunxue she, 1909);

Huitu zuijin shehui wochuo shi [The Illustrated Recent History of a Vile Society] (Shanghai: Shiwu shuguan, 1910);

Liangjin yanyi [Romance of the Two Jin Dynasties] (Shanghai: Qunxue she, 1910);

Tongshi [A Painful History] (Shanghai: Guangzhi shuju, 1911);

Jianchan biji [Jottings from Jianren's Place] (Shanghai: Guangzhi shuju, 1911);

Huaji tan [Humorous Tales], 2 volumes (Shanghai: Saoye shanfang, 1915);

Wo Foshan ren zhaji xiaoshuo [I Am a Man of Foshan's Book of Tales], 3 volumes (Shanghai: Saoye shanfang, 1922).

Collections: *Wo Foshan ren wenji* [Collected Writings of I Am a Man of Foshan], 8 volumes (Guangzhou: Huacheng chubanshe, 1988–1989);

Wu Jianren quanji [Complete Works of Wu Jianren], 10 volumes (Harbin: Beifang wenyi chubanshe, 1998).

Wu Jianren was among the most prolific of the many novelists who began writing and publishing their fiction during the last decade of the Qing dynasty–roughly between 1902 and 1910. Relatively well educated in the traditional style, Wu composed–in addition to novels–poetry, anecdotes, fiction criticism, and joke collections. While he wrote in several novelistic genres, the bulk of his fiction deals with the cultural and political crises facing modern China. In devoting himself primarily to what he calls in the preface to *Huitu zuijin shehui wochuo shi* (1910, The Illustrated Recent History of a Vile Society) the "shehui xiaoshuo" (social novel), Wu was in the mainstream of his time, following the reformist trend sparked by Liang Qichao's calls for the "New Novel" in the period between 1898 and 1902. Wu is distinguished from his cohort, however, by his narrative innovations and the complexity of his characters and situations. In his oeuvre the paradoxes and contradictions of the transitional period in which he lived and worked are set out in agonizing and compelling detail.

Born in Beijing on 29 May 1866, Wu was a member of a highly educated family that had had government affiliations for several generations. His original given name, Baozhen, was soon changed to Woyao. Wu Jianren, his first literary name, is the one by which he is now best known; another of his literary names was Wo Foshanren (I Am a Man of Foshan), a reference to his family's hometown in Nanhai county of Guangdong province. The family was living in Beijing at the time of Wu's birth because Wu's father, Wu Yunji, had been assisting his own father, Wu Xinshe, a government official; with the death of Wu Xinshe in 1863 the family's fortunes had gone into decline. In 1867 Wu Yunji went to Ningbo, near Shanghai, in search of work; the rest of the family returned to Foshan. Wu Woyao began school in 1874 at the age of eight *sui* (a child was considered one *sui* old at birth and aged one *sui* at each lunar New Year). He enrolled in the Foshan shuyuan (Foshan Academy) in 1878.

After Wu Yunji died in Ningbo in 1882, Wu Woyao sought employment in Shanghai. Probably arriving there in the fall of 1883, he went to work at the Jiangnan zhizao ju (Jiangnan Arsenal) south of the old city. A mammoth military enterprise that dated from the Tongzhi restoration in the 1860s, the arsenal was the main site for the importation of Western scientific and industrial technology into China in the late nineteenth century; it comprised a shipyard, a weapons factory, various metallurgical facilities, and a technical translation bureau. Wu began as a copyist and worked his way up to draftsman. It is reported that in 1888 he built by himself a scale-model steamboat that he sailed on the Huangpu River. He went to Beijing in 1891 to attend to the remains of a recently deceased uncle and brought his two orphaned cousins back to Shanghai; in 1896 he went to Yichang to arrange the funeral of his other uncle. Both events appear in thinly fictionalized form in his 108-chapter novel *Ershi nian mudu zhi guai xianzhuang* (1906–1911, Strange Events Eyewitnessed in the Past Twenty Years; translated in abridged form as *Vignettes from the Late Ch'ing: Bizarre Happenings Eyewitnessed over Two Decades,* 1975).

Wu appears to have left his job at the arsenal in 1897; he reports in the preface to *Zhengzhi weixin yaoyan* (1902, Crucial Words on Political Reform) that "in the *Dingyou* [1897] and *Wuxu* [1898] years, I closed myself up at home to nurse an illness." He spent the next several years writing for and managing a succession of Shanghai newspapers, including *Xiaoxian bao* (Entertainment News), *Caifeng bao* (Folksong-collector News), *Qixin bao* (Astounding News), and *Yuyan bao* (Fabulous News). Most were small papers oriented toward the city's burgeoning entertainment industry. In 1902 he noted in *Wu Jianren ku* (Wu Jianren Laments) that "looking back over the past five or six years," he could see that "being in editorial charge of various small newspapers has been, in fact, a great impediment to my progress. I threw away five or six years of my time in this way." While he may have regretted the time spent as a journalist, it aided his development as a writer, if only because of the vast number of stories it put him in a position to hear and later use in his novels.

In March 1901 Wu spoke at a demonstration at the Zhang yuan (Zhang Garden)–the preeminent public space in Shanghai–against the liberal concessions China had granted in its most recent treaty with Russia. From his departure from the arsenal through the first two years of the new century he wrote a series of essays on current affairs that he collected as "Jianyi waibian" (Jianren's Somniloquy: The Outer Chapters); he added a preface in January 1902. When the collection was published in two small volumes in April 1902, the title was changed to *Zhengzhi weixin yaoyan*, a more precise description of the contents. In the essays Wu follows a political line characteristic of Shanghai scholars of the time: he is aware of the corruption and decline of the Chinese government and supportive of needed reforms but also mindful of the need to guard national sovereignty against the incursions of the imperialist powers. He advocates a middle course between radical reform based on Western law, on the one hand, and adherence to indigenous ways and values, with Confucianism at the core, on the other hand. He revisits most of the themes he raises in the essays in the novels that began to appear shortly thereafter. The compromises he advocates, however, never seem to work out as well in his fiction as they do in the essays.

In March 1902 Wu resigned as editor of *Yuyan bao;* he traveled to Hankou a month later to take up the editorship of the *Hankou ribao* (Hankou Daily). In July he published in an entertainment monthly a collection of fifty-seven satirical comments on Shanghai life titled "Wu Jianren ku" (Wu Jianren Laments). Each entry consists of an ironic observation on modern life in the big city, followed by the remark "Wu Jianren laments." The cynical tone of the collection can be seen in the entry: "I often thought to myself that the reason that China is not progressive and open and able to reform is because of a shortage of educated people. Suddenly, however, a different thought came to me: It is precisely because it contains too many educated people that China has been unable to be progressive and open and able to reform. Wu Jianren laments." He does not hold himself exempt from censure and often turns a cynical eye on his own shortcomings: "Wu Jianren of course has not made any progress, but I can clearly see that neither has anyone else. Wu Jianren laments."

According to the preface to *Huitu zuijin shehui wochuo shi,* Wu took up the writing of fiction during his stay in Hankou in 1903. Motivated by discontent with forms of writing that did not allow him to use an "imposing, masculine" style that could "shout up the winds, move mountains, seize the soul and lament the spirits," he says, he took advantage of his capacity to describe minutiae and linked up such descriptive passages to form *zhanghui xiaoshuo* (episodic novels). Liang Qichao's journal *Xin xiaoshuo* (New Fiction) had commenced publication in Yokohama, Japan, in November 1902 and moved to Shanghai the next year; the eighth issue, published on 5 October 1903, included initial chapters of three novels on which Wu was working: *Ershi nian mudu zhi guai xianzhuang, Dianshu qitan* (1905, The Marvels of Electricity), and *Tongshi* (1911, A Painful History). *Dianshu qitan* is based on a Japanese translation of an English novel and includes exotic foreign characters and settings, while *Tongshi* is Wu's version of the tragic patriotism of the Southern Song dynasty. Each subsequent issue of *Xin xiaoshuo* featured chapters of these and other of Wu's novels.

In the autumn of 1904 Wu was diagnosed with *xuqie zheng* (nervous exhaustion) and left Hankou. He was married to a woman surnamed Feng; their daughter, Jingjing, was born in March 1905. Their only other child, a boy, died in infancy. Around the time his daughter was born, Wu accepted the position of editor of *Chubao,* the newly founded Chinese edition of the English-language *Central China Post,* an American-owned newspaper published in Hankou. He had not been on the job long when the question of the renewal of the discriminatory Chinese exclusion acts came up in the U. S. Congress, and Chinese patriotic organizations organized a boycott of American goods and interests in China to put pressure on the American government to revise the treaties. Wu responded to the call in July by resigning from the American-owned newspaper and returning to Shanghai, where he spoke at patriotic rallies held throughout the summer.

In late September 1905 Wu began serializing his novel "Xin shitou ji" (The New Story of the Stone) in the newly founded Shanghai daily *Nanfang bao* (The Southern News). Wu uses a familiar text–Cao Xueqin's *Honglou meng* (1791, Dream of the Red Chamber; translated as *The Story of the Stone,* 1973–1986)–to convey the transformation China was undergoing. Sequels to the eighteenth-century novel had been common in the nineteenth century, much to the dismay of those who considered themselves connoisseurs of the original. Wu opens his work in a defensive mode, noting the many sequels to well-known novels and fearing that his effort will only "add feet to [the portrait] of a snake" (a Chinese expression for ruining something with a superfluous addition). Though he depended on the market for his fiction for his living, Wu nonetheless concludes his introduction by asserting that writers must write to please themselves: "If the readers say it is good, that is fine; if they think it is absurd *[chou],* that is fine, too. I won't be able to hear [the comments] in any case."

Most of the previous sequels to *Honglou meng* retold Cao's love story, maintaining the original setting and characters and trying to ingratiate themselves with the audience by making the ending happier. Wu omits the female characters who occupy the greater part of Cao's novel and uses only three of the male characters from the original: Jia Baoyu; his page, Beiming; and Jia's ne'er-do-well brother-in-law, Xue Pan. "Xin shitou ji" is constructed of two roughly equal but antithetical parts. The first twenty-one chapters bring the characters to early-twentieth-century Shanghai and Beijing and points beyond, where Jia bears repeated witness to the chaos of the modern world and the varieties of foolishness that have prevented the implementation of sound policy. The nineteen chapters of the second half resolve this chaos into order by the creation of a science-fiction realm.

The shock of the modern embodied by Shanghai is registered by the responses of Jia and Xue Pan to the city after their 150-year hibernation. In Cao's novel Jia is a young man determined not to follow the path of a career in officialdom; in Wu's novel he is determined to gain an understanding of economics so as to find the reasons for the inferior position to which the Chinese are relegated in their own country and to publicize what he learns. Xue Pan adapts smoothly to the changed circumstances and shows no sign of surprise at them. He makes money in trade in Shanghai and spends it liberally in pursuit of the same mindlessly dissolute life he leads in the original novel. The Shanghai in which every human relationship is commodified is a congenial place for Xue Pan and his licentious style of life.

The "wenming jingjie" (civilized realm) that Jia visits in the second half of "Xin shitou ji" is a utopia in which technology and morality come together in perfect accord. After a thorough introduction to this realm, he returns to actual places in China and finds them transformed beyond recognition. Of all the things that he observes, urbanization impresses him the most: a Shanghai projected into the future has reached out to colonize the rest of China. As in a dream, he suddenly finds himself aboard a steamer, then on a train, and then in the capital, Beijing, where he hears the emperor deliver a speech announcing a new era of world peace. As Jia begins to applaud and stamp his feet in appreciation, he breaks through the floor and falls into an abyss. His terror wakes him up; he finds himself still in the civilized realm, but the transformation of the actual places in China that he has just visited turns out to have, indeed, been a dream. The sequence serves as a reminder of the remoteness and inaccessibility of the utopian vision of a perfect Chinese order that Wu sets out in the second half of the novel. The work was published in book form in 1908 as *Huitu xin shitou ji* (The Illustrated New Story of the Stone).

The final issue of *Xin xiaoshuo* appeared in January 1906. Only the novel *Jiuming qiyuan* (1906, Strange Injustice to Nine Lives) ran in its entirety in the journal; the other works by Wu that had been appearing in serialization in *Xin xiaoshuo* were eventually completed in book form. *Jiuming qiyuan* is set in the Yongzheng period (1723 to 1736) of the Qing dynasty but treats the issues of official corruption and popular superstition that Wu saw as major contemporary problems; Wu called it a "social novel" rather than a *lishi xiaoshuo* (historical novel). In form the work bears a close resemblance to the popular *gongan* (criminal case) genre, in which a complicated case involving serious injustice has remained unsolved through several investigations and is finally solved by a wise magistrate. *Jiuming qiyuan* is based on a murder that occurred in Guangdong province in 1738 and was rendered into a short novel, *Liang Tianlai jingfu qishu* (1809, Liang Tianlai: The Strange Story of a Warning to the Rich), by An He. The basic plot was used in popular texts and ballads throughout the nineteenth century, and in *Jiuming qiyuan* Wu admits to having "chongbian" (reedited) the work. His augmentation of the original material is so extensive, however, that the novel should be considered an original work.

The major innovative feature of *Jiuming qiyuan* is found in the first chapter: an assault led by Master Ling on an otherwise unidentified stone edifice of the Liang family is described in detail, primarily through the dialogue of the attackers. Other than a desire to kill the people inside, no motive or background for the attack is provided. While the inversion of time sequence had a long history in the Chinese novel, to begin a tale in medias res was unprecedented. The device of using dialogue to represent a significant action was almost certainly influenced by translated European novels: a friend of Wu's, Zhou Guisheng, had published a translation of a French novel that begins with dialogue a few months before the initial appearance of *Jiuming qiyuan* and had written a short apologia for this way of opening a work of fiction; Zhou felt the explanation necessary because of its novelty for the Chinese reader.

After the account of the assault on the stone house, Wu reverts to standard Chinese narrative practice with a direct address to his audience:

> Ai, readers! Look at the way I recklessly narrate this swift assault by a gang of robbers. For what reason did the instigator, one Master Ling, rich as Croesus himself, wish only to murder the dwellers in the stone house without regard to any money they might have? I am sure you readers were most perplexed upon reading this, and were I to continue telling the story in such a heedless fashion, you still wouldn't understand even when you finished with the book.

After alerting his readers to his innovation, Wu proceeds to fill in the background and aftermath of the attack. Master Ling ordered the attack on the Liangs' stone house because it was impeding his *fengshui* (geomantic fortune) and thus preventing him from passing the provincial-level examinations. Ling continually intercedes into the official investigation into the murders and uses bribery to ensure that he is not charged. In due course, however, although not without multiple complications, an honest, competent official uncovers the truth, and justice is meted out.

Ershi nian mudu zhi guai xianzhuang, Wu's longest novel, is considered one of the most important works published during the boom in fiction during the late Qing dynasty. Among its distinctions, according to Theodore Huters, is that it is the "earliest sustained first-person narrative in Chinese vernacular literature." The initial chapters appeared in the eighth number of *Xin xiaoshuo* in October 1903; when the journal ceased publication in January 1906, the first forty-five chapters had been serialized in its pages. The novel was published as a book in eight volumes, beginning in February 1906; the final volume, comprising chapters 95 to 108, appeared posthumously in January 1911. The work has been republished many times and remains one of the most popular late-Qing texts.

The "twenty years" in *Ershi nian mudu zhi guai xianzhuang* are, roughly, 1883 to 1903. In 1884 a brief war between China and France for influence in Annam (today Vietnam) ended when the French navy destroyed the Chinese fleet in the harbor at Fuzhou. In 1894–1895 China fought a war with Japan; China lost and ceded Taiwan to Japan as part of the settlement. In 1897–1898 the Japanese, French, British, Germans, and Russians pushed for concessions and influence in China. In 1898 the Guangxu emperor's Hundred Days' Reform ended with a coup by the empress dowager; some reformers were executed, others went into exile, and the emperor lost control of the government. In 1900 an anti-Christian, antiforeigner millenarian movement known in English as the Boxer Rebellion ended with the Boxers defeated, the Qing government in disarray, and foreign troops occupying Beijing. The Boxer Protocol signed in 1901 imposed severe penalties on China. From the perspective of 1903 the twenty years since 1883 were disastrous for China, which at the start of the twentieth century found itself weakened and impoverished.

Ershi nian mudu zhi guai xianzhuang is presented as the diary of a young man whose name, Jiusi Yisheng, means "Nine Deaths, One Life"—in other words, "still alive despite multiple perils." A third-person prologue creates a provenance for the diary, recounting that a Sili Taosheng (Escapee from the Jaws of Death) bought it on the street in Shanghai from a person who claimed that it was more instructive than a *shanshu* (book of morality). Huters suggests that given the popularity of translated European novels in China in the early twentieth century (in 1904 Wu's friend Zhou wrote that he had read several hundred English and French novels), the motif of a discovered diary might be a borrowing from Western fiction; he adds that the discovery of the diary might also "represent a kind of secularization of the mystical process of discovering the narrative-covered stone at the beginning of" *Honglou meng.*

Ershi nian mudu zhi guai xianzhuang presents a dismal picture of contemporary life among the upper classes, with a focus on the higher rungs of the nonmetropolitan bureaucracy. The diary takes events and experiences from Wu's life: for example, it begins when Jiusi is fifteen and his father dies unexpectedly. Many of the characters and incidents depicted are thinly disguised versions of actual people, including members of Wu's family, and the gossip that surrounded them.

Jiusi's diary reveals his immaturity and his inability to make the correct decision when confronted with a range of plausible alternatives. His inexperience is established at the beginning of the work when he arrives in Hangzhou to find that his father has died. Jiusi must choose an executor of his father's estate from among three men, each of whom explains why the others cannot be trusted. Jiusi decides to honor Confucian principle in making his choice on the basis of familial connection and selects his uncle, against whom his father's trusted shop assistant had warned him. The uncle embezzles all of Jiusi's inheritance. Jiusi then takes a job as assistant to a friend who is an official, which allows him to observe, Huters writes, "a world gripped by a virtually universal corruption, in which everything turns up for sale sooner or later" and behind which lies "a terrible breakdown of Confucian values, particularly those having to do with the family." Jiusi says that he meets only "pests, beasts, and demons"; he cannot comprehend the corruption, incompetence, ignorance, and immorality he sees.

Gradually, however, Jiusi learns to understand and deal with the world. A turning point occurs when he returns from Nanjing, where he has been working as an assistant to the official who befriended him, to his home in the south in response to an urgent telegram reporting that his mother is seriously ill. He finds that his mother has not been sick and knows nothing of the telegram. She does, however, hint at plots by relatives to swindle their branch of the family. This information, combined with Jiusi's own observations of the sinister environment at home, leads him to dispose of the family property and take his mother and the proceeds from the sale back to Nanjing, in the process thwarting the machinations of various conniving family members and acquaintances.

As Jiusi gains maturity, his function in the novel is reduced to that of witness and collector of tales. He goes to work for a private company founded by the official for whom he had been working and travels to many places on business, which allows him to observe many more "strange affairs." Huters argues that "from the standpoint of narrative possibility," modern means of transportation and communication are "perhaps the most important material legacy of the coming of the

Cover for the first volume of a 2006 ediiton of Wu's 108-chapter novel Ershi nian mudu zhi guai xianzhuang *(Strange Events Eyewitnessed in the Past Twenty Years; translated in abridged form as* Vignettes from the Late Ch'ing: Bizarre Happenings Eyewitnessed over Two Decades, *1975), first published in eight volumes between 1906 and 1911 (Collection of Thomas Moran)*

West." The dramatic quality of the episodes in the later chapters is more powerful than in the earlier ones as the level of depravity represented increases markedly. Each episode provides further evidence of the truth of the theme announced by Sili Taosheng at the outset: "I had known that Shanghai was no good, but according to [this] book, although the world is wide, it is just no place for human beings." Jiusi's newfound sense of intellectual control ultimately proves inadequate to allow him to impose a sense of order to the chaotic events that he observes.

One of the paradoxes in *Ershi nian mudu zhi guai xianzhuang* is the contrast between Jiusi's—and, presumably, the author's—commitment to Confucian values and the conspicuous failure of these values to work out in practice. While the values are admired by all of the positive characters, the episodes almost invariably show a failure by society at large to observe them—or any other values.

In October 1906 Wu published the tragic romance *Henhai* (translated as "The Sea of Regret," 1995), subtitled *Xieqing xiaoshuo* (Novel of Feeling). Unlike most late-Qing fiction, *Henhai* was not first serialized in a magazine or newspaper. The ten-chapter work was written almost in one sitting and features a unity of event and character not found in Wu's other novels. Moreover, Wu departs significantly from the norm followed in most other writings devoted to fictionalizing contemporary events by withholding authorial judgment on the principal characters. *Henhai* is regarded as the novel that inspired the sentimental love stories that dominated the Chinese literary scene after 1910 and have become known as the *Yuanyang hudie* (Mandarin Ducks and Butterflies) genre.

The Chen and Wang families, all of whom are southerners, live together in a Beijing compound. The heads of the two families are cousins and degree holders on probationary appointments in the capital. They invite the merchant Zhang family, who are, like the Chens, Cantonese, to share their spacious house. The Chens have two children, Bohe and his younger brother Zhongai; the other families each have a daughter, Zhang Dihua and Wang Juanjuan. Because the children are about the same ages, go to school together, get along well, and come from comparable backgrounds, Zhang Dihua is affianced to Chen Bohe and Wang Juanjuan to Chen Zhongai. As the narrative proceeds, Chen Bohe is presented from an almost purely external perspective, while long, detailed accounts are given of Zhang Dihua's thoughts and feelings. Historians have pointed out that the depiction of female subjectivity is associated with the rise of the novel in more than one literary tradition.

At first, Zhang Dihua is portrayed as being so fussy about propriety as to seem a negative character, and her prissiness causes many problems. Chen Bohe, on the other hand, seems to be a paragon of the practical morality lacking in Zhang Dihua's fastidiousness. Soon, however, the reader finds out how unsatisfactory Chen Bohe's combination of impulsive action and lack of introspection can be. With the coming of the Boxer disturbances to Beijing in 1900, Wang Letian takes a leave of absence from his official post and goes home to Suzhou with his family; Zhang Heting departs for Shanghai at about the same time, leaving his family in the care of Chen Jilin. The government forbids any more leaves of absence, obliging Chen Jilin to stay in the capital, despite his awareness that his life is in danger should the rebels take control of Beijing. As the situation deteriorates, he orders his sons to escort Zhang Dihua and her mother to safety in Shanghai. Chen Zhongai refuses to abandon his parents, so Chen Bohe becomes the leader of a party that includes Zhang Dihua and her mother.

During the journey south Chen Bohe becomes separated from the others. Zhang Dihua becomes responsible for the small party and leads it southward through terrible trials, including the death of her mother. They finally reach Shanghai. Chen Bohe arrived long ago, after having made a small fortune along the way. In the metropolis he has lost himself in a life of dissipation, squandered his ill-gotten wealth, and become addicted to opium. Zhang Dihua and her father attempt to rehabilitate him, but he dies. Zhang Dihua declares that she will remain chaste in memory of her "husband" and becomes a nun. Meanwhile, Chen Zhongai finds that Wang Juanjuan has become a prostitute, and he becomes a hermit.

For all the care with which they are expressed, Zhang Dihua's moral scruples are never presented as practical or realistic. Even her rigidly moralistic father is bewildered by her devotion to her wastrel fiancé. Zhang Dihua takes upon herself the responsibility for all that has transpired, giving expression to her self-blame in neo-Confucian terms as she thinks:

> There is no one in the world insensible to the earnestness of others. [So] how can he be like this, just so indifferent and apathetic whenever he sees me? Perhaps my heart still isn't free of insincerity *[bucheng]*, and that's the reason? Or perhaps I can't express myself well enough, and that's why I'm unable to persuade him? Oh! How can I lay bare my heart so that he can see into it?

Her moral perspective, while admirable, seems quaint in the context of the circumstances with which she is faced. Once again, Wu has created a novel in which ideals fall short when they collide with reality.

In November 1906 the first issue of *Yueyue xiaoshuo* (Monthly Fiction) appeared, with Wu and Zhou listed as editors. Wu was primarily responsible for producing original fiction for the periodical; Zhou was in charge of translating foreign novels, which were at the height of their popularity in China. In his introduction to the first issue Wu says that the purpose of the magazine is to publish fiction that will provide moral uplift in trying times. The journal ceased publication temporarily after the eighth issue, for May 1907. When it resumed in October 1907, Wu and Zhou no longer had the main responsibility for producing texts for it, although they did continue to publish in the magazine before it closed for good in 1909. Most of Wu's commentaries about the nature and goals of fiction and most of his many short stories appeared in *Yueyue xiaoshuo*.

In 1908 Wu published the novelette *Facai mijue* (The Secret of Striking It Rich), in which he focuses, as he does throughout his fiction, on lapses in moral propriety. He confesses in the afterword that "when it came to writing this story, I became enraged by what I was attempting to write." As a result, he claims, he was unable to gain control of the book, and *Facai mijue* ended up as "the worst novel I have written." The conflict of morality and immorality is also the theme of *Jieyu hui* (1909, Ashes of the Holocaust), which centers around a gruesome episode of perfidy within a family.

During the last years of his life Wu completed novels he had begun earlier and wrote short stories and novelettes; many of the latter remained unfinished. Other than his participation in the founding and administration of a school for the Cantonese community in Shanghai, few records exist of his activities between 1907 and 1910. On 21 October 1910 he completed moving his family into a new residence and celebrated the occasion with some friends. That night he died in bed of an asthma attack. For all the success his writing had enjoyed, Wu is said to have had only 40¢ to his name at his death, and it was left to his many friends to pay for his funeral.

Although Wu Jianren's writings continued to be published throughout the 1920s, his concern with social critique fell out of fashion shortly after his death and was replaced by the lurid romances and exposés that have since been grouped in the Mandarin Ducks and Butterflies category. With the coming of the Xin wenhua yundong (New Culture Movement) in the late 1910s, the reputation of Wu and the late-Qing "New Novel" in general suffered. Lu Xun, in his Beijing University lectures that were later collected as the celebrated *Zhongguo xiaoshuo shilüe* (1923, 1924; translated as *A Brief History of Chinese Fiction*, 1959), labeled the late-Qing fiction of Wu and his colleagues "qianze xiaoshuo" (fiction of censure or novels of exposure): "Although they were intent upon reforming the age and thus seem to be in the same category as novels of satire, their expression is superficial and their biting style is without any subtlety. More than that, however, they are full of exaggeration in order to accord with the predilections of the time." Wu's standing in scholarship has suffered ever since because of Lu Xun's exalted image in Chinese letters. His name and work were, however, kept alive between 1920 and 1980 by such scholars as A Ying (Qian Xingcun) and Wei Shaochang. Since the 1980s Wu has received renewed attention from scholars both in and outside China, and his best-known novels have been widely republished.

Bibliography:
Pei Xiaowei, "Wu Jianren zhuzuo xinian," in *Wu Jianren quanji*, volume 10, edited by Hai Feng (Harbin: Beifang wenyi chubanshe, 1998), pp. 337–401.

References:
A Ying (Qian Xingcun), *Wan Qing xiaoshuo shi*, revised edition (Shanghai: Shangwu yinshuguan, 1954);
Chen Pingyuan, *Ershi shiji Zhongguo xiaoshuo shi, 1897–1916* (Beijing: Beijing daxue chubanshe, 1989);
Chen, *Zhongguo xiaoshuo xushi moshi de zhuanbian* (Taibei: Jiuda wenhua gongsi, 1990);
Chen Xinghui, *"Ershi nian mudu zhi guai xianzhuang" yanjiu* (Taibei: National Taiwan University, 1983);
Milena Dolezelová-Velingerová, ed., *The Chinese Novel at the Turn of the Century* (Toronto: University of Toronto Press, 1980);
Theodore Huters, "The Shattered Mirror: Wu Jianren and the Reflection of Strange Events," in *Culture and State in Chinese History: Conventions, Accommodations, and Critiques,* edited by Huters, R. Bin Wong, and Pauline Yu (Stanford, Cal.: Stanford University Press, 1997), pp. 277–299;
Lin Mingde, ed., *Wan Qing xiaoshuo yanjiu* (Taibei: Lianjing chuban gongsi, 1988);
Liu Ts'un-yan, ed., *Chinese Middlebrow Fiction from the Ch'ing and Early Republican Eras* (Hong Kong: Chinese University Press, 1984), p. 341;
Lu Xun, *A Brief History of Chinese Fiction,* translated by Yang Xianyi and Gladys Yang, second edition (Beijing: Foreign Languages Press, 1964), pp. 372, 377–381;
Mei Qingji, *Zhongguo gudian xiaoshuo lungao* (Harbin: Heilongjiang jiaoyu chubanshe, 1995);
Ouyang Jian, *Wanqing xiaoshuo shi* (Hangzhou: Zhejiang guji chubanshe, 1997), pp. 125–155;
Tang Xiaobing, "Trauma and Passion in *The Sea of Regret:* The Ambiguous Beginnings of Modern Chinese," in his *Chinese Modern: The Heroic and the Quotidian* (Durham, N.C.: Duke University Press, 2000), pp. 11–48;
David Wang, *Fin-de-Siècle Splendor: Repressed Modernities of Late Qing Fiction, 1849–1911* (Stanford, Cal.: Stanford University Press, 1997);
Wei Shaochang, *Wan Qing si da xiaoshuo jia* (Taibei: Shangwu yinshuguan, 1993);
Wei, ed., *Wu Jianren yanjiu ziliao* (Shanghai: Guji chubanshe, 1980);
Yuan Jin, *Zhongguo xiaoshuode jindai biange* (Beijing: Zhongguo shehui kexue chubanshe, 1992).

Wu Zuxiang

(5 April 1908 – 11 January 1994)

Philip F. Williams
Massey University

BOOKS: *Xi liu ji* [West Willow Collection] (Shanghai: Shenghuo shudian, 1934)—includes "Li jia de qianye," translated by Stanley R. Munro as "The Night before Leaving Home," in *Genesis of a Revolution: An Anthology of Modern Chinese Short Stories,* edited by Munro (Singapore: Heinemann Educational Books [Asia], 1979), pp. 133–143;

Fan yu ji [An After-Hours Anthology] (Shanghai: Wenhua shenghuo chubanshe, 1935)—includes "Nüren," translated by Paul Crescenzo and Vivian Ling Hsu as "Two Women," in *Born of the Same Roots: Stories of Modern Chinese Women,* edited by Hsu (Bloomington: Indiana University Press, 1981), pp. 8–11;

Yazui lao [Duckbill Falls] (Chongqing: Shi yu chao yinshua suo, 1943); republished as *Shan hong* [Mountain Torrent] (Shanghai: Xingqun chubanshe, 1946);

Wu Zuxiang xiaoshuo sanwen ji [An Anthology of Wu Zuxiang's Fiction and Prose] (Beijing: Renmin wenxue chubanshe, 1954).

Editions and Collections: *Wu Zuxiang xuanji* [An Anthology of Wu Zuxiang] (Hong Kong: Xianggang wenxue yanjiu she, 1978);

Shan hong [Mountain Torrent] (Beijing: Renmin wenxue chubanshe, 1982);

Xi liu ji [West Willow Collection] (Shanghai: Shanghai shudian, 1987);

Shuo bai ji: Gudian Xiaoshuo lunping juan [Informal Discussions: Collected Essays on Classics of Chinese Fiction] (Beijing: Beijing daxue chubanshe, 1987);

Su cao ji: Xiaoshuo juan [Grass of Yore: Collected Fiction] (Beijing: Beijing daxue chubanshe, 1988);

Shi huang ji: Sanwen juan [Foraging for Gleanings: Collected Prose] (Beijing: Beijing daxue chubanshe, 1988);

Yuan wai ji: Wenyi pinglun juan [Outside the Garden of Letters: Collected Literary Criticism] (Beijing: Beijing daxue chubanshe, 1988).

Editions in English: "Young Master Gets His Tonic" ("Guanguan de bupin"), translated by Cyril Birch; "Let There Be Peace" ("Tianxia taiping"), translated by James C. T. Shu; and "Fan Village" ("Fan jia pu"), translated by Russell McLeod and C. T. Hsia, in *Modern Chinese Stories and Novellas, 1919-1949,* edited by Hsia, Joseph S. M. Lau, and Leo Ou-fan Lee (New York: Columbia University Press, 1981), pp. 372–415;

Green Bamboo Hermitage (Beijing: Chinese Literature Press, 1989)—includes "Green Bamboo Hermitage" ("Lu zhu shanfang"), translated by Yu Fanqin; "Buddhist *Wan*-Character-Shaped Honeysuckle" ("Wanzi jinyinhua"), translated by Yu; "Eighteen Hundred Piculs" ("Yiqianbabai dan"), translated by Gladys Yang; "The Boxcar" ("Tie menzi"), translated by Jeff Book; "Twilight" ("Huanghun"), translated by Susan Dewar; "The Sights of Mount Taishan" ("Taishan fengguang"), translated by Geremie Barmé; and "Firewood" ("Chai"), translated by Denis Mair;

"Young Master Gets His Tonic" ("Guanguan de bupin"), translated by Birch, in *The Columbia Anthology of Modern Chinese Literature,* edited by Lau and Howard Goldblatt (New York: Columbia University Press, 1995), pp. 159–173.

OTHER: "Mouri," in *Shinian* (A Decade), edited by Xia Mianzun (Shanghai: Kaiming shudian, 1936), pp. 197–217; translated by Marston Anderson as "A Certain Day," in *Furrows: Peasants, Intellectuals, and the State—Stories and Histories from Modern China,* edited by Helen F. Siu (Stanford, Cal.: Stanford University Press, 1990), pp. 40–54.

In spite of the acceleration of urbanization in China during the twentieth and early-twenty-first centuries, a plurality of the nation's citizenry continues to live in the countryside. Until the third and fourth decades of the twentieth century, however, the setting of Chinese fiction was overwhelmingly urban and thereby highly unrepresentative of Chinese society. Considered by prominent Chinese literary historians the most dis-

Wu Zuxiang (Museum of Modern Chinese Literature, Beijing)

tinguished specialist in rural or "peasant" fiction of the 1930s and early 1940s, Wu Zuxiang played a significant role in rectifying this imbalance. With more than 90 percent of his fiction set in his rural homeland of southern Anhui province, Wu helped to overcome widespread urban stereotypes about the supposed simple-mindedness of villagers and the presumed "idiocy" of their rural folkways.

Wu did not, however, champion rural traditions or prettify his portrayals of his home area. He viewed himself as a progressive, urban-trained intellectual whose criticisms of problems and shortcomings in the southern Anhui countryside might hasten the arrival of reforms there. Global economic turmoil and local political instability exacerbated the problems and added a sense of urgency and immediacy to Wu's fiction. An independent leftist intellectual who did not join the Chinese Communist Party until the mid 1950s, well after he had abandoned creative writing near the beginning of that decade, Wu avoided the sort of preordained conclusions and pat answers in which his more ideologically rigid confreres tended to indulge. His nonconformist approach cost him support among some leading figures in the Zhongguo zuoyi zuojia lianmeng (League of Left-Wing Writers) during the 1930s but has helped his fiction retain its fascination for subsequent generations of readers at home and abroad.

One of eleven children, Wu was born on 5 April 1908 in the hill-ringed southern Anhui village of Maolin; a relatively prosperous town of a few thousand residents, it was nearly as populous as the county seat, Jingxian, the largest municipality in the county. Wu's pen name, which he first used in 1923, is homonymous with his original name, differing only in the two characters used to write his given name, Zuxiang; he wanted to delete the old-fashioned respectful reference to zu (ancestors) in favor of the value-neutral term zu (organize). The Wu clan was Maolin's dominant lineage and had built one of the most architecturally impressive ancestral temples in the region. For centuries Wu's ancestors had been prominent merchants or government officials; among them was Wu Fangpei, who had been inducted into the prestigious Hanlin Academy in Beijing during the latter half of the Qing dynasty (1644 to 1911). Wu Zuxiang's father, Wu Qingyu, was a scholar and calligrapher who engaged in teaching, small-scale landholding, and entrepreneurship. His mother, Feng Suzhu, was the illiterate daughter of a Feng clan landlord from Fengcun, a village near Maolin.

Wu benefited from growing up in a highly cultured household of the local elite, and his early education was a combination of private and public schooling. In 1921 he left his village to board at prominent middle schools in the Anhui paper-manufacturing town of Xuancheng and the major Yangtzee River ports of Wuhu and Nanjing. In 1925 he moved to China's preeminent metropolis, Shanghai, where he completed college preparatory work; he enrolled in a private liberal arts college the following year. In 1927 he married Shen Shuyuan and went back to Maolin for a one-year stint as a schoolteacher. Thenceforth he regularly returned to his village not in the capacity of a resident but as a visitor from urban China. During his many years of periodic observation of changes affecting the village society he combined the inside knowledge and contents of a native with the relative dispassion and informed perspective of an urban-educated outsider.

Unlike many of his generation who felt a strong attraction to the cosmopolitan and free-wheeling atmosphere of Shanghai, Wu detested what he saw as the city's overcommercialized decadence and its subservience to the foreigners who controlled treaty-port foreign concessions in the city; under the treaty-port system, which was finally abrogated in 1943, the Chinese endured a humiliating compromise of their national sovereignty at the hands of powers such as Britain, France, and Japan. Wu thus sought to use his educational opportunities in Shanghai as a stepping-stone to a truly first-class university education in the ancient city of Beiping (as Beijing was known from 1928 to 1949), still the cultural capital of China and a foil to the Westernized brashness of Shanghai.

In the summer of 1929 Wu passed the difficult entrance examinations for the top-notch Qinghua University in Beiping; he began studying there in the autumn. Qinghua's Department of Chinese had a rigorous yet creatively designed curriculum, as well as some of the country's most distinguished professors and most talented students. Wu's teachers included the versatile scholar and essayist Zhu Ziqing and the vernacular-literature scholar Zheng Zhenduo; among his classmates was Qian Zhongshu, who became the century's most brilliant all-around Chinese scholar and writer. The contribution of this intellectual atmosphere to Wu's development as a writer can be gauged by comparing the sophomoric stories he published in the 1920s with the discipline and restraint evident in his fiction of the early 1930s. The difference is so striking that Wu did not admit publicly until the 1980s that he had even published any fiction during the 1920s. Even at eighty he insisted that his raw and often maudlin stories of the 1920s be relegated to an appendix in his anthology *Su cao ji: Xiaoshuo juan* (1988, Grass of Yore: Collected Fiction) because they were unworthy of being placed side by side with his well-wrought fiction of the 1930s and 1940s.

In 1931 Wu published the semi-autobiographical stories "Li jia de qianye" (translated as "The Night before Leaving Home," 1979) in *Fenü zazhi* (The Women's Magazine) and "Liangzhi xiao maque" (Two Young Sparrows) in *Wenxue yuekan* (The Literary Monthly), which accentuate the cultural gulf between city and countryside. Each story features a young urban couple vacationing in the husband's old village home, where a nursemaid helps the husband's widowed mother care for their child. Both were included in Wu's first book, *Xi liu ji* (1934, West Willow Collection).

The main conflict in "Li jia de qianye" is between the wife's desire to return to full-time university study in the city and her yearning to stay with their toddler in the genteel village household headed by her mother-in-law. Wu's characteristic mastery of highly individualized dialogue appears in the conversations about whether she should go; the aural emphasis in his descriptive language manifests itself in the onomatopoetic rendering of the child's cries and coos. The urban-rural dichotomy and the generational divide largely determine how each character reacts to the idea of the wife's departure: her twenty-two-year-old husband and their young nursemaid are supportive, the mother-in-law is opposed, and the wife herself is ambivalent. She finally decides to delay her academic aspirations and remain in the village with her child, as Wu's wife, Shen, did on one of the two occasions when she faced this dilemma in her own life; in the other instance she left their child in the care of her mother-in-law to pursue her urban collegiate studies in elementary education.

In "Liangzhi xiao maque" the wife, who is the narrator of the storty, feels indirectly responsible for the death of her son's nursemaid, a farmer's wife. The narrator's spoiled child had been clamoring for new birds to replace his two pet sparrows that had recently died; on her own initiative, the nursemaid went to a nearby river to catch some waterfowl for the boy and drowned in a flood. Earlier in the story the nursemaid's husband had asked the narrator's husband about the doubtful stability of the Nationalist government's mandate; the narrator's husband had been unable to offer the worried farmer anything more than a flippant response peppered with stale urban political clichés. Exasperated, the farmer had turned away to have a few words with the narrator's mother-in-law before departing, illustrating

The elementary school that Wu attended in the village of Maolin (photograph by Philip F. Williams; from his Village Echoes: The Fiction of Wu Zuxiang, *1993; Collection of Philip F. Williams)*

the dearth of meaningful communication between the urban and rural realms.

Wu's first-person narrators invariably come from the educated elite; he switches to third-person narration when focusing on a humbler social stratum in his first story of 1932, "Xiao Hua de shengri" (Young Hua's Birthday), which was published in *Zhongguo shehui* (Chinese Society), reprinted in *Quinghua zhoukan* (The Qinghua Weekly) in 1933, and also collected in *Xi liu ji*. Unemployed because his shop went bankrupt in the Great Depression, a former clerk has to depend on the money his wife earns by sewing and by hosting mahjongg parties in their village home. At one party, held on the day of their younger child's birthday, he sees his wife warding off a player's unwanted sexual advances and jumps to the conclusion that she has been unfaithful to him. As he rains blows on the hapless woman, he shouts insults at her guests; the latter flee, vowing to have nothing more to do with such a family. Escaping from her husband's brutality, the wife scoops up their two sobbing children and runs down the road that leads out of the village. In an ironic twist, moments before the violent rupture of the marriage, one of the wife's well-heeled clients had been praising the husband's patience in the face of economic adversity.

In "Zhizi hua" (1932, The Flowering Gardenia) the unemployed rural shopkeeper Xiangfa persuades his uncle, who works at a university in Beiping, to help him find a job as a petty clerk in a government bureau in the capital. Though Xiangfa works hard, after a few months budget cuts result in his being laid off. On his way back to his village he consoles himself with the thought that he will, at least, be reunited with his beloved wife and will be able to enjoy his gardenia bush by the courtyard wall. When he arrives, he is stunned to find that the courtyard wall has caved in on the gardenia bush; and there is no trace of his wife except for some funeral paraphernalia strewn about. As in many of Wu's stories, no explanation is given: the work breaks off with Xiangfa fainting in the wake of his discovery of his wife's death.

Wu was far less interested in amatory motifs than most Chinese writers of his generation, but later in 1932 he published in *Qinghua zhoukan* a story featuring a narrator enmeshed in an urban love triangle. In "Jin Xiaojie yu Xue Guniang" (Miss Jin and the Xue Girl) Miss Jin, who embodies rural virtues, breaks up with the passive college-boy narrator after discovering that he has been dating the city girl Xue on the side. Having been morally corrupted by unscrupulous associates in

Shanghai, Xue decides to abort the illegitimate child she is carrying by another man to improve her prospects of marrying the narrator. The back-alley abortionist botches the operation, and the narrator's search for Xue leads him to her bloody corpse. The story breaks off at that point, leaving readers to form their own conclusions about the moral. This story was also collected in *Xi liu ji*.

The final story Wu published in 1932, "Guanguan de bupin" (Guanguan's Tonic; translated as "Young Master Gets His Tonic," 1981), also appeared in *Qinghua zhouken*. It represents his most successful use of an unreliable narrator—a challenging technique of ironic presentation that is almost never encountered in premodern Chinese fiction and was seldom used even by Wu's contemporaries. The narrator, Guanguan, the skirt-chasing son of a wealthy rural landlord, is taken to a Shanghai hospital after an automobile accident. His family pays a modest amount for life-saving blood transfusions from the very tenant, Baldy, whom his uncle had evicted from the farm for late payment of rent. When Guanguan returns to his home village to recuperate, his mother hires Baldy's buxom wife to provide a cup or two of breast milk a day for him to drink as a tonic. Guanguan's parasitical relationship with the farm family turns poisonous when he agrees with his uncle's decision to behead Baldy as an alleged bandit courier and with the family's head maid's rebuke of Baldy's wife for crying out against her husband's unjust execution. A work with a narrator as unreliable as Guanguan calls for a careful reader. Such as reader would likely react with mirth to Guanguan's sentimental description of how he swore that he would have liked to die in his pretty companion's arms just before their car flipped over, killing her and badly injuring him. The alert reader would find his later comparison of Baldy's wife to a cow, which Guanguan deems hilarious, pathetic if not disgusting. "Guanguan de bupin" was Wu's first story to be reviewed in a major journal—the same issue of *Qinghua zhoukau* in which it was published—where it was praised. Unfortunately, some of the rich texture of irony in "Guanguan de bupin" is lost in the English and French translations, which are based on the heavily bowdlerized version of the story in *Wu Zuxiang xiaoshuo sanwen ji* (1954, An Anthology of Wu Zuxiang's Fiction and Prose). For example, the scene in which Baldy's fellow tenant farmers stone their "class comrade" to death after the executioner's sword misses its mark is excised, leaving the ending of the story dangling in a way that is not the case in either its original journal publication or in *Xi liu ji*.

The contrast between city and countryside that dominates Wu's fiction in 1931–1932 gives way to an almost exclusive focus on the countryside in "Lu zhu shanfang" (1933; translated as "Green Bamboo Hermitage," 1989), also included in *Xi liu ji*. The narrator describes his widowed Second Aunt's eccentric ways in her secluded abode in a hillside bamboo grove. His wife grows increasingly frightened by the aunt's nonchalant references to the supernatural, and an almost Gothic mood of being trapped in a haunted house takes hold. But—in a manner reminiscent of Jane Austen's parody of the Gothic novel, *Northanger Abbey* (1817)—Wu dissolves the suspense at the end of the story with a clever and thoroughly naturalistic plot twist.

An urban-based narrator and his wife are on vacation in the countryside in Wu's other stories of 1933, "Huanghun" (translated as "Twilight," 1989), published in *Wenxue* (Literature), and "Wanzi jinyinhua" (Splay-petaled Honeysuckle; translated as "Buddhist Wan-Character-Shaped Honeysuckle," 1989), published in *Qinghua zhoukan;* both are included in *Xi liu ji*. "Huanghun" consists mostly of conversations the narrator and his wife overhear from neighboring compounds while they enjoy cool twilight breezes in their courtyard. Because the neighbors' worsened economic circumstances have increased tensions in other aspects of their lives, the tone of the somewhat musical "Huanghun" is definitely in a minor key. On the other hand, Wu avoids the kind of tendentious commentary in which less reflective leftist writers were apt to indulge when dealing with similar topics. The influential critic and novelist Mao Dun had stories such as "Huanghun" in mind when he lambasted Wu in *Wenxue* 1934 as an "out-and-out objectivist"—Mao Dun had secretly joined the Chinese Communist Party, which at that time often condemned art that refrained from taking a clear and "correct" ideological standpoint as "objectivist." Wu rejected the label.

In "Wanzi jinyinhua" the narrator discovers a woman in the throes of childbirth in a ramshackle forest hut. She recognizes him as a childhood friend, but he cannot recall her until she mentions splay-petaled honeysuckle, the unusual hybrid vine he had shown her when they had met more than a decade previously. The thought of the plant unlocks a stream of dormant memories, much as a madeleine cookie and an uneven flagstone do in Marcel Proust's *A la recherche du temps perdu* (1913–1925, In Search of Lost Time; translated as *The Remembrance of Things Past,* 1922–1929). Shaken to see the girl, on whom her well-to-do family once doted, placed in such life-threatening circumstances by unforgiving clan elders, the narrator hurries home to get help for her; but she and the baby are dead when he returns. The narrator's vivid descriptions of his clouded awareness and concluding bout of Dostoevskian brain fever are probably based on Wu's memories of suffering from malaria during his childhood and adolescence.

Wu received his B.A. in 1933 and began graduate work at Qinghua University, but worsening economic circumstances and a disagreement with a professor led him to abandon his studies in the middle of 1934. The three works for which he is best known were published that year: "Yiqianbabai dan" (translated as "Eighteen Hundred Piculs," 1989), published in *Wenxue jikan* (Literature Quarterly), and "Tianxia taiping" (The World at Peace; translated as "Let There Be Peace," 1981), published in *Wenxue*, are included in *Xi liu ji*; "Fan jia pu" (translated as "Fan Village," 1981), published in *Wenxue jikan*, was collected in *Fan yu ji* (1935, An After-Hours Anthology).

The dominant role of dialogue in "Yiqianbabai dan," Wu's best-known and most influential work within China, makes this novella the closest thing to a play that he ever wrote. The main plot consists of several Song clan discussions about what to do with the 1,800 bushels of rice stored in their ancestral temple. A dozen personages in the clan, from Manager Botang and Militia Head Shaoxuan to a pettifogger and a lowly beancurd seller, achieve distinct characterizations through their individualized speech patterns. The secondary plot traces the rumblings of discontent among the Songs' impoverished tenant farmers. The plots come together in the finale, when the tenants storm the temple and pillage the rice. Although a food riot during a drought year does not really amount to a politically revolutionary act, the incident has often been interpreted as such by Communist critics.

In sharp contrast to "Yiqianbabai dan," "Tianxia taiping" consists almost entirely of narration. In part, Wu wanted to prove that his writing skills were not limited to dialogue-based "sketches," as some of his stories had been categorized by hostile critics. After the village shop in which he worked as a clerk goes bankrupt during the Depression, Wang Xiaofu is forced to fall back on peddling, day labor, and, finally, thievery to feed his family. At the end he falls to his death from a temple rooftop while trying to steal a sacred ornament.

In "Fan jia pu" poverty drives the husband of the tea-stand proprietor Xianzi to rob a nunnery. After he is arrested, one of the jailers solicits Xianzi for a bribe to ensure better treatment for him. Xianzi's mother is the only family member with money to spare, but she refuses to lend any of it to Xianzi. Xianzi seethes with anger at her mother and has nightmares of her husband lying in a pool of blood in his cell. One night, when her mother is sleeping in Xianzi's cottage, Xianzi tries to steal the money hidden inside her mother's headband. The mother wakes up, and during the ensuing struggle Xianzi stabs her to death. She sets fire to the murder scene—her own home—and is about to run to the jail with the money when she learns that her husband has

Cover for Shan hong *(1946, Mountain Torrent), originally published in 1943 as* Yazui lao *(Duckbill Falls), Wu's novel about changing attitudes among southern Anhui villagers toward the war against the Japanese (Wason Collection on East Asia–China, Kroch Asia Library, Cornell University)*

been freed by a bandit gang that has driven the local government officials from their offices. The fragrant osmanthus tree that goes up in smoke next to Xianzi's burning cottage symbolizes the destruction of her family's harmony and continuity in the face of economic disaster and political chaos.

After withdrawing from graduate school, Wu worked for several months in a minor administrative post in Nanjing. In 1935 he became a private tutor and personal secretary to General Feng Yuxiang. Known as "the Christian General," Feng was a former warlord who had accepted a sinecure under Chiang Kai-shek, his long-time political rival. Feng's position permitted him to choose his place of residence; he settled with his entourage in the foothills of Mt. Tai, a sacred landmark in Shandong province that has attracted pilgrims and sightseers for more than 2,500 years.

"Taishan fengguang" (translated as "Sights at Mount Tai," 1989), first published in *Wenxue* and collected in *Fan yu ji*, is Wu's most anthologized work of 1935. It is a satirical, semi-autobiographical account of his observations of the pilgrims to the holy mountain and those who profit from their presence. The latter

Wu at his home, probably in the late 1980s (Museum of Modern Chinese Literature, Beijing)

include not only the usual peddlers and preachers but also a family of "official" beggars who ply their trade in rags and then change back into fine clothing on returning to their huge, well-furnished house. The narrator's friends erupt in laughter when one of the beggars mistakes him for a pilgrim, grasping him firmly by his clothing in an aggressive demand for alms. After the narrator escapes from the beggar's clutches, he vows to observe such activities henceforth only from a safe distance.

In 1936 Wu's "Mouri" (translated as "A Certain Day," 1990), his last major short story set in his southern Anhui homeland, was published in an anthology. In contrast with his stories of the early 1930s that feature victims of economic and social crises, this work portrays a self-sufficient farmer who fends off a blackmail attempt by a member of the gentry. The farmer's long history of treating his neighbors and laborers fairly results in their solidarity with him in the face of the interloper's scheme, in spite of the latter's high status in the clan hierarchy. Although the farmer remains modest after his victory, the concluding image of a rooster crowing on a dunghill symbolizes resistance to any attempt to wrest away the fruits of one's labors, regardless of a mismatch in social status.

Japanese aggression in northern China led to war between the two countries in 1937. Wu played a major role in organizing a patriotic Chinese writers' organization in the temporary capital, Wuhan, in 1938; he subsequently moved to the long-term wartime capital, Chongqing, in Sichuan province. He used his writing talent on behalf of the Chinese war effort, but he also satirized corruption in the ranks and directed attention to other problems that interfered with the prosecution of the war. His 1938 story "Chai chuan" (The Requisitioned Boat), published in *Qixue* (July) and collected in *Wu Zuxiang xiaoshuo sanwen ji*, exposes the plight of wounded soldiers suffering delays in medical treatment because of irresponsible officers' indulgence in river-port wining and dining. In "Tie menzi" (1942; translated as "The Boxcar," 1989), published in *Zhongguo qingnian* (Chinese Youth), a shackled soldier is being taken in a boxcar to be punished for rape. Though the other men in the car find his crime deplorable, they loosen his bindings; after all, they have to admit, his behavior was not much worse than that of his commanding officers, who had frequently demanded that local leaders supply them with young women to serve as their concubines. The train is attacked by Japanese bombers, and the soldier disappears during the confusion; but instead of running away, he lays down his life to save one of the boxcars by decoupling it from the rest of the train, which is on fire. The suggestion seems to be that irresponsible behavior by officers has prevented the potential for heroic national struggle by the rank and file from being realized.

Wu's lone novel was published in 1943 as *Yazui lao* (Duckbill Falls); it was retitled *Shan hong* (Mountain Torrent) when it was republished in 1946. Set in the southern Anhui countryside, it explores changing local attitudes toward the war effort. At first the villagers hide in the hills when Chinese troops march through the region, because they have been imbued with a traditional fear of soldiers as plunderers—"bandits in uniform"—and the young men are afraid of being dragooned into the army. But they gradually discover that improved discipline in the military has made these traditional fears obsolete, and reports of Japanese atrocities against Chinese civilians embolden them to support the troops as porters carrying ammunition and other military supplies.

The war ended with Japan's surrender in 1945 and was succeeded by the civil war between the Nationalists and the Communists. Like most of the major May Fourth Era writers who remained in China after the Communist victory in 1949, Wu abandoned the writing of fiction rather than grapple with the Mao Zedong government's controls on literature. He spent the last half of his life as a professor of Chinese literature at Beijing University, where he specialized in premodern fiction and served as a mentor to younger faculty members and graduate students.

Mao died in 1976, and Deng Xiaoping's reforms in 1978 set the stage for a relaxation of political restrictions on literature. Literary historians and scholars produced considerably higher evaluations of Wu Zuxiang's fiction than had been the case during the Mao era, and more of his work was republished in the 1980s than in any previous decade. Full-length studies of his fiction were published in Chinese and in English in the late 1980s and early 1990s, and by the time of his death on 11 January 1994 no one doubted his stature as a leading twentieth-century Chinese writer of rural fiction.

Bibliographies:

Philip F. Williams, "Wu's Creative Works" and "Other Writings by Wu," in his *Village Echoes: The Fiction of Wu Zuxiang* (Boulder, Colo.: Westview Press, 1993), pp. 259–270;

Fang Xide, "Wu Zuxiang zhuzuo nianbiao," in *Wu Zuxiang Xiansheng jinian ji*, edited by the Beijing University Department of Chinese (Beijing: Beijing daxue chubanshe, 1995), pp. 395–415.

References:

Catherine Pease Campbell, "Political Transformation in Wu Zuxiang's Wartime Novel *Shan hong*," *Modern Chinese Literature*, 5, no. 2 (1989): 293–324;

C. T. Hsia, "Wu Tsu-hsiang," in his *A History of Modern Chinese Fiction, 1917–1957*, second edition (New Haven: Yale University Press, 1971), pp. 281–287;

Bonnie S. McDougall and Kam Louie, "Wu Zuxiang, 1908–94," in their *The Literature of China in the Twentieth Century* (New York: Columbia University Press, 1997), pp. 144–146;

Su Hsüeh-lin, "Present-Day Fiction and Drama in China," in *1500 Modern Chinese Novels and Plays*, edited by Joseph Schyns (Hong Kong: Lung Men Bookstore, 1966), pp. iii–lviii;

Tang Yuan, *Wu Zuxiang zuopin xinshang* (Nanning: Guangxi renmin chubanshe, 1986);

Philip F. Williams, "The Problem of Bowdlerization in the Translation of 20th-Century Chinese Literature," *Tamkang Review: A Quarterly of Comparative Studies between Chinese and Foreign Literature*, 27, no. 4 (1998–1999): 103–115;

Williams, as Wei Lun, "Shishi qiu shi yu huanxiang chuangzuo: Tan Wu Zuxiang de xiandai xiaoshuo," *Jiuzhou xuekan*, 1, no. 3 (1987): 127–130;

Williams, "20th-Century Iconoclasm in a Classical Tragedy: Wu Zuxiang's 'Fan Hamlet,'" *Republican China*, 18, no. 1 (1993): 1–22;

Williams, *Village Echoes: The Fiction of Wu Zuxiang* (Boulder, Colo.: Westview Press, 1993);

Williams, as Wei Lun, "Wu Zuxiang bixia de san'ge 'nü qiangren,'" in *Zhongguo funü yu wenxue lunji, di'erji*, edited by Williams and Yenna Wu (Taibei: Daw shiang Publishing, 2001), pp. 171–199;

Yan Jiayan, "Shehui pouxi pai xiaoshuo," in his *Zhongguo xiandai xiaoshuo liupai shi* (Beijing: Renmin wenxue chubanshe, 1989), pp. 175–204.

Wumingshi
(Bu Baonan)
(1 January 1917 – 11 October 2002)

Carlos Rojas
University of Florida

Wumingshi (from Tang Wenyi, Mu Dingsheng, and Ji Lei, eds., 20 shiji Zhongguo wenxue tudian, 2001; Collection of Thomas Moran)

BOOKS: *Hanguo de fennu* [Korean Fury], as Li Fanshi (N.p., 1942);

Zhong Han waijiao shihua [An Historical Narrative of the Foreign Relations between China and Korea], as Min Shilin (N.p.: Dongfang chuban gongsi, 1942);

Luxiya zhi lian [Luxiya's Love] (Chongqing: Zhongguo bianyi chubanshe, 1942);

Beiji fengqing hua [A Picture of an Arctic Romance] (Shanghai: Wuming shuwu, 1943);

Yibaiwan nian yiqian [A Million Years in the Past] (Hong Kong: Huanghe chubanshe, 1943);

Tali de nüren [Woman in the Pagoda] (Shanghai: Shidai shenghuo chubanshe, 1944);

Yeshou, yeshou, yeshou [Beast, Beast, Beast] (Shanghai: Shidai shenghuo chubanshe, 1946); republished as *Yin Di* (Hong Kong: Xinwen tiandi she, 1977); revised as *Yeshou, yeshou, yeshou* (Taibei: Yuanjing chuban shiye gongsi, 1984);

Huoshao de dumen [City Gates in Conflagration] (Shanghai: Zhenshanmei tushu chuban gongsi, 1947); republished as *Xielu* [Sprouting Bulb] (Hong Kong: Xinwen tiandishe, 1977);

Hai yan [Siren of the Sea] (Shanghai: Zhenshanmei tushu chuban gongsi, 1947; revised edition, Taibei: Hanguang wenhua shiye gufen youxian gongsi, 1986);

Longku [Dragon Cave] (Shanghai: Zhenshanmei tushu chuban gongsi, 1947);

Chensi shiyan [Experimental Reflections] (Shanghai: Zhenshanmei tushu chuban gongsi, 1948); republished as *Mingxiang oushi* [A Random Collection of Profound Thoughts] (Hong Kong: Xinwen tiandishe, 1977); revised as *Hudie chensi* [Butterfly Reflections] (Taibei: Liming wenhua gongsi, 1992);

Jinse de she ye [Golden Night of the Serpent] (Shanghai: Zhenshanmei tushu chuban gongsi, 1949);

Si de yanceng [The Stone Strata of Death] (Hong Kong: Xinwen tiandi she, 1981);

Jinse de she ye, xuji [Golden Night of the Serpent, Part 2] (Hong Kong: Xinwen tiandi she, 1982);

Wumingshi shipian [A Collection of Wumingshi's Poetry] (Hong Kong: Xinwen tiandi she, 1982);

Shengdan hong [Christmas Red] (Hong Kong: Shanhe chubanshe, 1982);

Kaihua zai xingyun yiwai [Blooming Flowers beyond Stars and Clouds] (Hong Kong: Xinwen tiandi she, 1983);

Chuang shiji da puti [Great Enlightenment of the Creation of a New Era] (Hong Kong: Xinwen tiandi she, 1983; revised edition, Taibei: Yuanjing chuban shiye gongsi, 1984);

Haixia liang an qi da qi ji: Wumingshi yanjiangji [Seven Miracles on the Two Sides of the Taiwan Straits: A Collection of Talks by Wumingshi] (Taibei: Liming wenhua shiye gongsi, 1983);

Lüse de huisheng: Qingchun aiqing zizhuan [Green Echoes: Autobiographical Reflections on Youthful Love] (Taibei: Zhanwang zazhishe, 1983);

Wumingshi shici moji [Ink Stains of Wumingshi's Poetry and Lyric Poetry] (Taibei: Liming wenhua shiye gongsi, 1984);

Yuzhong shichao: Xie zai naozhi shang de 125 shou shi [Poem Drafts from Prison: 125 Poems Written on the Paper of My Mind] (Taibei: Liming wenhua shiye gongsi, 1984);

Hai de chengfa: Xiasha xiang jizhongying shilu [Punishment of the Sea: A True Record of My Experiences at the Xiasha Concentration Camp] (Taibei: Xinwen tiandi she, 1985); translated by "Mr. Anonymous" as *The Scourge of the Sea: A True Account of My Experiences in the Hsia-sa Village Concentration Camp* (Taibei: Compilation Department, Kuang Lu Publication Service, 1985);

Wo zhanzai jinmen wang dalu [I Stand at Jinmen and Gaze toward the Mainland] (Taibei: Liming wenhua shiye gongsi, 1985);

Wumingshi zixuanji [Wumingshi's Self-Selected Collection] (Taibei: Liming wenhua shiye gongsi, 1985);

Wumingshi xun hui Mei, Jia, Ri yanjiang jiyao [Summaries of Wumingshi's Lectures from his Tour of the United States, Canada, and Japan] (Taibei: Guanglu chubanshe, 1985);

Dushu, shidai, shenghuo [Reading, Historical Period, and Life] (Taibei: Liming wenhua shiye gongsi, 1986);

Wumingshi yanjiang [Wumingshi's Lectures], 2 volumes (Taibei: Liming wenhua shiye gongsi, 1986);

Zouxiang gegeta [Walking toward the Cavalry] (Taibei: Xinwen tiandi she, 1986);

Hua de kongbu [Flower Terror] (Taibei: Liming wenhua shiye gongsi, 1988); republished as *Hua yu hua shi* [Flowers and Fossils] (Taibei: Zhongtian chubanshe, 1999); translated by Richard Ferris and Andrew Morton as *Flower Terror: Suffocating Stories of China* (Dumont, N.J.: Homa & Sekey, 1999);

Zhongguo da beiju shidai duihua [A Discussion about China's Tragic Historical Period] (Taibei: Liming wenhua shiye youxian gongsi, 1988);

Hong sha [Red Shark] (Taibei: Liming wenhua shiye gufen youxian gongsi, 1989); translated by Tung Chung-hsuan as *Red in Tooth and Claw: Twenty-Six Years in Communist Chinese Prisons* (New York: Grove, 1994);

Tawai de nüren [Woman outside the Pagoda] (Taibei: Fengyun shidai chuban gongsi, 1990);

Guweng [Poison Urn] (Taibei: Liming wenhua chubanshe, 1991);

Konglong shiji [Era of Dinosaurs] (Taibei: Liming wenhua gongsi, 1992);

Danshui yu mingsi [Profound Thoughts on a Freshwater Fish] (Guangzhou: Huacheng chubanshe, 1995);

Yuzhou touying: Rensheng shi meng de fangshe [Projections of the Universe: Human Life Is an Oneiric Radiance] (Taibei: Zhongtian chubanshe, 1997);

Zai shengming de guanghuan shang tiaowu [Dancing on the Halo of Life] (Taibei: Zhongtian chubanshe, 1997);

Shuqing yanyun [Expressing Emotions of Clouds and Mist], 2 volumes (Taibei: Wenshizhe chubanshe, 1998);

Yi gen qian si huo gou [A Fiery Hook Made from a Filament of Lead] (Taibei: Zhongtian chubanshe, 1999).

Wumingshi (Anonymous), the pen name used by Bu Baonan throughout most of his long career, came to assume an irony that he did not anticipate when he selected it: although he published more than thirty books, he remains relatively unknown, particularly by scholars in the English-speaking world. While his writings span a wide range of genres, including poetry, essays, reportage, lectures, correspondence, and memoirs, his most influential publications are his novels and short stories. His works can be divided into three main categories: romantic fiction, particularly the extremely popular novels *Beiji fengqing hua* (1943, A Picture of an Arctic Romance) and *Tali de nüren* (1944, Woman in the Pagoda); philosophical fiction, the most important of which is the six-novel series "Wuming shu" (1946–1983, Anonymous Book), also known as "Wuming shugao" (Anonymous Manuscript); and political works, particularly his critiques of Communism. The political dimension is most prominent in his short stories and reportage of the 1980s and 1990s but is present throughout his career.

Bu Baonan was born in Nanjing on 1 January 1917; he was also known as Bu Ning and Bu Naifu. His father, Bu Shanfu, whose original name was Bu Shiliang, had moved to Nanjing from his hometown, Yangzhou, and had become a successful practitioner of Chinese medicine; his mother, Lu Shuzhen, had a minimal education. Bu was the fourth of six children, all boys, three of whom died young. His second eldest brother, Bu Baoyuan, became a successful reporter in China and later in Hong Kong under the name Bu Shaofu.

Bu Baonan studied the Confucian classics from the age of five. His father died when he was six, and he was sent to live with his widowed maternal grandmother in Yangzhou, east of Nanjing. He attended elementary school there until 1927, when he returned home and enrolled in the fourth grade at the Nanjing guoli Dongnan daxue shiyan xiaoxue (Experimental Elementary School of the Southeast State College of Nanjing); he was quickly moved up to the sixth grade. According to his biographers Wang Yingguo and Zhao Jiangbin, the school was run in accordance with the progressive theories of the American philosopher and educator John Dewey. Bu impressed his teachers with his writing skills, and some of his essays were published in the magazine *Xiao pengyou* (Young Friends). He graduated in a year and a half. During the summer after graduation he did not study for the placement examinations and failed to gain acceptance to a good public middle school. In 1929–1930 he studied at private middle schools. Unable to afford tuition, he did not attend school in the 1930–1931 academic year but spent his time reading his brother Bu Baoyuan's collection of Chinese and foreign fiction.

In the fall of 1931 Bu enrolled at a private school in Nanjing, the Leyu zhongxue (Leyu High School); he played on the basketball team, published essays in a magazine edited by his brother, acted in performances of plays by the left-wing playwright Tian Han, and was stirred to political activity by the Japanese incursions into China's northwest. He forged documents to facilitate his transfer in the early spring of 1933 to a better school, the Nanjing sanmin zhongxue (Three Principles of the People Middle School), from which he was expelled for writing stories and essays critical of the faculty and administration; he was readmitted after his brother intervened. He dropped out in April 1934, two months before graduation, and refused to take the national placement examination for college, which he considered biased in favor of students in schools supported by the Nationalist government.

In April 1934 Bu went to Beiping (as Beijing was known from 1928 to 1949), where he spent his days reading in the city library and sitting in on lectures at Beijing University. In 1935 he briefly studied Russian at a junior college but returned to Nanjing when the school was closed because of government suspicion that it had ties to the Soviet Union and Communists.

The work considered by scholars to mark the beginning of Wumingshi's career as a writer is "Beng tui" (1937, Decline and Fall) an essay inspired by the ideas of the philosopher Friedrich Nietzsche; it was written in 1937 and first published in his 1947 collection, *Huoshao de dumen* (City Gates in Conflagration). Wuminghsi returned, in a more nuanced way, to his early Nietzschean concerns in his later writings, including "Wuming shu."

War with Japan began in the summer of 1937. In November, Japanese troops threatened to move into the area of Yangzhou, where Bu and his family had been living since August, and he left for the interior. In 1938 he arrived in Chongqing, the wartime capital, where he was active in the Japanese resistance effort as a journalist and interpreter. In 1941 he fell in love with a woman named Li Yanwen, but she left Chongqing. Some of his essays and prose poems from this period are included in *Huoshao de dumen*.

Bu's first two books were ghostwritten for others. *Hanguo de fennu* (1942, Korean Fury), is a collection of memoirs published under the name of the Korean Restoration Army's chief of staff, General Li Fanshi. In the same year he wrote *Zhong Han waijiao shihua* (An Historical Narrative of the Foreign Relations between China and Korea) under the name of his acquaintance Min Shilin. According to Wang and Zhao, Bu fell in love with Min's daughter, but that romance, like the one with Li Yanwen, failed.

In 1942 Bu moved to Xi'an. That year he published his first book under the pen name Wumingshi, the short-story collection *Luxiya zhi lian* (Luxiya's Love). The title piece, a romance set in Nazi Germany, was part of a larger project that he subsequently abandoned. His first novel, *Beiji fengqing hua,* was serialized starting in November 1943 in the periodical *Huabei xinwen* (North China News), published in Xi'an, and appeared in book form the same year. Based on the experiences of the Korean general Li, *Beiji fengqing hua* opens with the unnamed narrator coming to Mt. Hua in Shaanxi province, hoping to be cured of meningitis. One of the five Taoist sacred mountains of China, Mt. Hua is known as "the Sacred Mountain of the West"; Wumingshi had visited it in the early 1940s. The narrator meets a Korean soldier, who recounts his love affair in Siberia with a Polish woman who initially mistook him for her boyfriend. Their romance ended in tragedy: the soldier was sent back to Korea, and the lovesick woman committed suicide. The success of the novel can be attributed in part to the ways in which it builds on the romantic conventions of popular "Mandarin Ducks and Butterflies" fiction; the portrayal of two young people seeking love under the shadow of Japanese imperialism also appealed to readers' political sympathies.

In 1943 Wumingshi became involved with a woman of mixed Chinese and Russian heritage; her Chinese name was Liu Yage, and her Russian name was Tamara. They were engaged, but the relationship ended in June 1944. Toward the end of the year Wumingshi returned to Chongqing.

Wumingshi's second romantic novel, *Tali de nüren*, opens with a direct reference to the earlier one: the narrator says, "In early summer of 1944, about three months after I finished writing *Arctic Romance*, I felt extraordinarily depressed. Often, for days at a time, I found myself unable to read a line of text or to write a single word. I couldn't even bring myself to read the letters from my friends but rather simply burned them unopened." At Mt. Hua a doctor tells the narrator that when he was younger he had been a musician and had fallen in love with a woman, but his parents had arranged a marriage for him to someone else. The woman he loved married unhappily, and he still grieves over her fate. *Tali de nüren* is loosely based on the story of Wumingshi's acquaintances Zhou Shantong and Qu Nong. Because Wumingshi was unhappy with the way his publisher had handled the release of *Beiji fengqing hua*, he published *Tali de nüren* at his own expense. Both books quickly went through multiple editions, and they are still popular in Taiwan.

After the war with Japan ended in 1945, Wumingshi went to Shanghai. In 1946 he moved to Hangzhou, where he rented rooms in a Buddhist convent, and embarked on the writing of "Wuming shu." The seven-volume, five-thousand-page narrative, which he did not complete until 1960, is one of the most ambitious literary projects of twentieth-century China. Owing, perhaps, to the difficulty and political untimeliness of the work, compounded by the fact that the second half was written underground and not published until more than thirty years after the first half, it has received relatively little critical attention. Although several Chinese-language overviews of modern Chinese literary history, such as those by Sima Changfeng, Yang Yi, and Yan Jiayan, include discussions of the work, it has received virtually no mention in English-language studies. Wumingshi's conflicted relationship with Chinese literature's canonical orthodoxy, particularly in English-language scholarship, is illustrated by the fact that while he is not mentioned in C. T. Hsia's influential *A History of Modern Chinese Fiction 1917–1957* (1961), Hsia wrote the preface to *Red in Tooth and Claw: Twenty-Six Years in Communist Chinese Prisons* (1994), the translation of Wumingshi's *Hong sha* (1989, Red Shark). There Hsia says that "Wuming shu"—which he calls *Book without a Title*—is "a work of unprecedented ambition and scope in modern Chinese literature, far superior to the famous trilogies of the acknowledged leading writers, such as [Lao She's] *Four Generations under One Roof* and Ba Jin's *Turbulent Stream*.... Whatever its ultimate position in modern Chinese literature, *Book without a Title* was certainly the most magnificent undertaking by an individual writer to be completed on the mainland during the Maoist era."

The six novels—one of which is split into two volumes published thirty-three years apart—that comprise "Wuming shu" follow the quest of the protagonist, Yin Di, for the meaning of existence amid the social and political maelstrom of 1930s and 1940s China. Each novel, however, treats this theme from a distinct perspective. The first, *Yeshou, yeshou, yeshou* (1946, Beast, Beast, Beast) emphasizes revolutionary engagement. *Yeshou, yeshou, yeshou* opens in the early summer of 1920, when Yin Di abruptly leaves the college from which he is about to graduate and embarks on his quest. In 1927 he becomes involved in the Communist resistance to the Nationalist Party's White Terror and in the Autumn Harvest Uprisings. The revolution fails, and he is arrested and tortured. On emerging from prison he is disturbed by the coldness and suspicion with which he is greeted by his former comrades and becomes disillusioned with Communism. In *Hai yan* (1947, Siren of the Sea) the focus shifts to romance. Yin Di attempts to retire from political activity amid accusations that he is a Communist. On a ship he encounters a beautiful woman dressed in white. He is entranced, but later he discovers that she is his cousin, Qu Ying. The remainder of the novel concerns Yin Di's struggle to reconcile his attraction to Qu Ying with his realization that the time is not right for them to be together. The idealized romance in *Hai yan* contrasts with Yin Di's decadent infatuation with a high-class prostitute in *Jinse de she ye* (1949, Golden Night of the Serpent). Yin Di is initially drawn to Sha Kaluo when he glimpses her portrait by his friend Ma Erti. The theme of decadence and desire is counterbalanced by a series of reflections on the relationship between contemporary modernist Western art and traditional Chinese art that Yin Di shares with his artist friends Ma and Lin Suzi. These reflections likely developed out of Wumingshi's friendship with the influential painter Lin Fengmian. An essay on Lin is included in his *Chensi shiyan* (1948, Experimental Reflections), and some commemorative pieces he wrote following Lin's death in 1991 are in the collection *Shuqing yanyun* (1998, Expressing Emotions of Clouds and Mist).

Jinse de she ye was published in August 1949. The People's Republic of China was founded the following October. Because of the unflattering discussions of Communism in "Wuming shu," Bu Baonan was careful

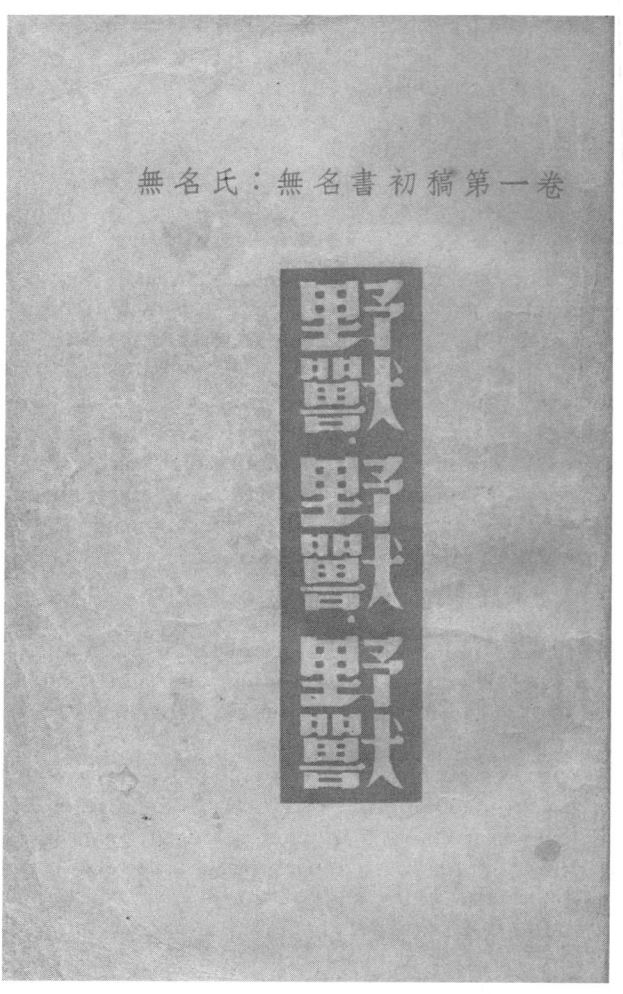

Cover for a 1948 edition of Wumingshi's Yeshou, yeshou, yeshou (1946, Beast, Beast, Beast), the first work in his six-novel cycle about a man's search for the meaning of existence (Wason Collection on East Asia–China, Kroch Asia Library, Cornell University)

not to let himself be identified with the writer known as Wumingshi.

In 1949 Wumingshi brought his mother and her adopted daughter, Liu Baozhu, to Hangzhou to live with him; later, they moved to Hangzhou. Liu Baozhu was Wumingshi's cousin and had lived with Lu Shuzhen since she was ten; her name before the adoption had been Liu Jing. Wumingshi fell in love with a woman named Zhao Wuhua, but she died in 1950. In 1954 he married his adopted sister, Liu Baozhu. Shortly after the wedding, she took a job in Shanghai; thereafter, she and Wumingshi saw each other only a few times a year and never spent more than a month together at a time. They had no children. At some point Liu Baozhu became Bu Baozhu.

Wumingshi continued to work on "Wuming shu" in secret. He completed a second volume of *Jinse de she ye* in 1950, *Si de yanceng* (1981, The Stone Strata of Death) in 1957, and *Kaihua zai xingyun yiwai* (1983, Blooming Flowers beyond Stars and Clouds) in 1958. He was imprisoned for a little more than a month in a *laodong gaizao* (reeducation through labor) camp during the Anti-Rightist Campaign in 1957 and again, for fourteen months, in 1960–1961. In 1968, at the height of the Cultural Revolution, he was imprisoned for more than a year. He and his wife separated that year. He finished the final volume of "Wuming shu," *Chuang shiji da puti* (1983, Great Enlightenment of the Creation of a New Era), in 1969. He and Bu Baozhu were divorced in 1972. His mother died in 1977.

In 1979 Wumingshi began mailing the manuscripts for the remaining parts of "Wuming shu" page by page to his brother Bu Shaofu in Hong Kong. To ensure against loss, he reportedly sent eight copies of each page; and to avoid arousing the suspicion of the postal authorities, he arranged for friends to mail the letters from various cities throughout China. This process continued until 1981, and the remaining four volumes of "Wuming shu" were published between 1981 and 1983.

When *Si de yanceng* opens, Yin Di has converted to Catholicism; in a letter he describes how he came to turn to Christianity. He relates his attempts to escape the inner demons that plagued him throughout *Jinse de she ye* by dedicating himself to rescue work with a military medical unit. His legs were injured in an explosion, and during his long convalescence in the hospital he met several Western priests and turned to religion for answers to the questions with which he had been wrestling. Although Wumingshi was an agnostic, *Si de yanceng* is one of the most systematic engagements with religion to be found in modern Chinese literature.

In *Kaihua zai xingyun yiwai* Yin Di retreats from society to the relative isolation of Mt. Hua, where he reflects on various philosophical and spiritual issues. With the exception of events such as the death of Yin Di's mother, *Kaihua zai xingyun yiwai* lacks conventional plot movement. One of the philosophical musings in the work begins with a reflection on the Buddhist expression "jinghua shuiyue" (flowers in the mirror and the reflection of the moon in water), which refers to the ephemerality of material existence:

"Flowers in the mirror and the reflection of the moon in water" is not a reference to life's true flower and true moon, but it is nevertheless still an apparent flower and an apparent moon. An apparent object is not an original object, "resemblance" is not the same as "truth"; nevertheless, it is only not the "truly true," and still remains "apparently true." In the eye's cornea and conjunctiva, flowers in the mirror still retain the form and appearance of flowers, and the reflection of the moon in water still retains the form of the moon—the former has color, while the latter has illumination. And even if it is the case that this color and illumination are not true color and illumination, are not original color and illumination, then we must still ask to what extent actual moon and flowers themselves can be said to possess true light and color?

Wumingshi's synthesis in this passage of modern Western medical and traditional Buddhist terminology is emblematic of his attempts throughout the novel to get beyond simplistic dichotomies of Western and Eastern culture.

The concluding volume of "Wuming shu," *Chuang shiji da puti,* opens with the end of the Sino-Japanese War in 1945 and Yin Di's decision to descend from Mt. Hua and return to society. His marriage to his cousin Qu Ying completes his romantic quest, if not his philosophical one. The account of their connubial bliss is layered with complex discussions of the process of realizing one's own subjectivity through a dialogic interaction with another autonomous individual. The tone of the volume is utopian; Wumingshi once remarked that in *Chuang shiji da puti* he sought to present a model for a new human existence and more-perfect interpersonal relations. Like *Kaihua zai xingyun yiwai,* the second half of *Chuang shiji da puti* departs almost entirely from a conventional plot and becomes a long philosophical rumination. One of the main themes of the work, the relationship between Western and Eastern cultural and philosophical traditions, can be discerned in the title, which combines explicit allusions to Buddhism and Christianity: *puti* (great enlightenment) is a Buddhist concept, while *chuang shijie* means "creation of a new area" but is also the conventional Chinese term for Genesis.

Wumingshi's writing style in "Wuming shu" is a pastiche of modernist and traditional influences. His fascination with the plasticity of language evokes comparisons with the Shanghai Xin ganjue pai (New Perceptionist School) of the 1930s and 1940s such as Mu Shiying, Liu Na'ou, and Shi Zhecun: like the New Perceptionists, Wumingshi relies heavily on repetition, onomatopoeia, and florid description. The work is also reminiscent of late-imperial "literati novels" in its tendency to abandon narrative continuity in favor of abstract philosophical discussions of politics, aesthetics, religion, art, and literature. But "Wuming shu" repeatedly returns to a set of core issues: the meaning of human life, the relationship between perception and existence, similarities and differences of the Eastern and Western cultural traditions, and the nature of interpersonal relations. Large portions of "Wuming shu" are highly abstract and impersonal philosophical reflections, but the work is also a personal creation with individualized characters; many of the latter are based on prominent acquaintances of Wumingshi's. The painter Lin Fengmian and the Korean general Li Fanshi, for example, provide the models for Lin Suzi and Han Muhan, respectively, and Tang Jingqing is based on Zhou Shantong.

In December 1982 Wumingshi went to Hong Kong to join Bu Shaofu, who was editor in chief of the periodical *Xinwen tiandi/Newsdom.* In 1983 he moved to Taiwan. On 19 May 1985 he married twenty-seven-year-old Ma Fumei.

Wumingshi's later works of fiction are significantly less aesthetically ambitious than "Wuming shu" and tend to take the form of stridently anti-Communist tracts. *Hai de chengfa: Xiasha xiang jizhongying shilu* (1985, Punishment of the Sea: A True Record of My Experiences at the Xiasha Concentration Camp; translated as *The Scourge of the Sea: A True Account of My Experiences in the Hsia-sa Village Concentration Camp,* 1985) describes Wumingshi's 1958 incarceration. His short-story collection *Hua de kongbu* (1988, The Terror of Flowers; translated as *Flower Terror: Suffocating Stories of China,* 1999) includes several semi-autobiographical pieces that express indignation at the way people were treated during the early decades of the People's Republic of China. The 1989 *Hong sha* is based on the experiences of Han Weitian, who was arrested by the Communists in 1967 and imprisoned in a dry well for more than two years; when he emerged, he had gone blind and was near death. He endured even more horrors as he spent the next two decades in various prisons. Wumingshi had experienced imprisonment, and his exposé of the penitentiary system is heartfelt. The work, however, remains at the level of straightforward description and fails to reflect on the events described. The romantic tradition in which Wumingshi began his literary career influenced many of his subsequent works; in *Hong sha* it can be seen in the narrator's account of having sex with his illicit lover:

If 'Lusa was indeed a volcano, she never ceased to erupt, and I never ceased to burn with her love. . . . There were times when I could not help but make love to her. In the height of pleasure, however, I would become suddenly panic-stricken; not because of her strong embraces at the peak of passion or her gentle murmurs afterward, but because I was doing something forbidden by the Communists, something for which I could die.

Revised editions of some of the novels in "Wuming shu" were published in Taiwan in the late 1980s, and more-thoroughly revised versions of several of the volumes appeared through the late 1990s. Wumingshi continued to revise his earlier works until his death on 11 October 2002. His most enduring legacy is "Wuming shu." Like Wumingshi's corpus as a whole, it is an eclectic blend of narrative genres, including memoir, reportage, philosophical reflection, and sentimental romance. Begun during a period of social upheaval and foreign aggression and completed in defiance of the orthodoxies of social realism imposed during the first three decades of the People's Republic of China, "Wuming shu" challenges conventional periodizations of mid-twentieth-century Chinese literary history. It also represents an intriguing combination of historical pertinence and universalizing abstraction: it is set during the period of the formation of the Chinese Communist Party and the Sino-Japanese War, and its main plot is grounded in the political and cultural struggles of that era; but as it progresses it becomes increasingly disconnected from this historical backdrop and moves into timeless philosophical meditations. The main theme of the work as a whole is the impact of the political, social, and cultural upheaval of mid-twentieth-century China on the human spirit.

Letters:

Yujian (Beijing: Yuanjing chuban shiye gongsi, 1983).

Bibliographies:

Sima Changfeng, "Zuopin pianming," in his *Zhongguo xinwenxue shi*, volume 3 (Hong Kong: Zhaoming chubanshe youxian gongsi, 1978), pp. 101–103;

Geng Zhuanming, "Wumingshi wenxue chuangzuo nianbiao," in his *Duxing renzong: Wumingshi zhuan* (Jiangsu: Jiangsu wenyi chubanshe, 2001), pp. 241–244;

Peng Zhengxiong, "Zuopin nianpu," in *Wumingshi de wenxue zuopin tansuo yu jihuai*, edited by the Wenshizhe chubanshe bianweihui (Taibei: Wenshizhe chubanshe, 2004), pp. 350–362.

Biographies:

Wang Yingguo and Zhao Jiangbin, *Wumingshi chuanqi* (Shanghai: Shanghai wenyi chubanshe, 1998);

Geng Zhuanming, *Duxing renzong Wumingshi zhuan* (Jiangsu: Jiangsu wenyi chubanshe, 2001).

References:

Bu Shaofu, ed., *Wumingshi yanjiu* (Hong Kong: Xinwen tiandi she, 1981);

Bu and Qu Zhancai, eds., *Xiandai xinling de tansuo: Wumingshi zuopin yanjiu* (Taibei: Liming wenhua gongsi, 1989);

Chen Sihe, "Shilun *Wumingshu*," in his *Tan hu tan tu* (Guilin: Guangxi shifan daxue chubanshe, 2001), pp. 81–107;

Qu Zhancai, ed., *Wumingshi juan* (Taibei: Yuanjing chuban shiye gongsi, 1983);

Sima Changfeng, *Zhongguo xinwenxue shi*, volume 3 (Hong Kong: Zhaoming chubanshe youxian gongsi, 1978), pp. 100–108;

Tang Wenyi, Mu Dingsheng, and Ji Lei, eds., *20 shiji Zhongguo wenxue tudian* (Chengdu: Sichuan renmin chubanshe, 2001), p. 286;

Wenshizhe chubanshe bianweihui, ed., *Wumingshi de wenxue zuopin tansuo yu jihuai* (Taibei: Wenshizhe chubanshe, 2004);

Yan Jiayan, *Zhongguo xiandao xiaoshuo liupai shi* (Beijing: Renmin wenxue chuanshe, 1989), pp. 302–309;

Yang Yi, *Zhongguo xiandai xiaoshuo shi*, volume 3 (Beijing: Beijing wenxue chubanshe, 1993), pp. 500–512.

Xiang Kairan
(Pingjiang Buxiaosheng; Buxiaosheng)
(26 February 1890 – December 1957)

Roland Altenburger
Universität Zürich

BOOKS: *Liu dong waishi* [Unofficial History of Sojourners in the East], 10 volumes, as Buxiaosheng (Shanghai: Minquan chubanbu, 1916–1922)–includes commentary by Bozi (Zhang Mingfei);

Quanshu jianwen lu [Records Seen and Heard on the Technique of Boxing], as Xiang Kui (Shanghai: Taidong shuju, 1919);

Long hu chunqiu [Chronicle of Dragon and Tiger], 2 volumes, as Xiang Kui (Shanghai: Jiaotong tushuguan, 1919);

Jianghu guaiyi zhuan [Stories of the Strange in the World of Adventure], as Buxiaosheng (Shanghai: Shijie shuju, 1923);

Jianghu qi xia zhuan [Stories of Amazing Knights-Errant in the World of Adventure], 12 volumes, by Xiang as Buxiaosheng and Zhao Tiaokuang as Zouxiaosheng (Shanghai: Shijie shuju, 1924–1930)–includes commentary by Shi Jiqun (Zhao Tiaokuang);

Jianghu yiren zhuan [Stories of Otherworldly People in the World of Adventure] (Shanghai: Shijie shuju, 1924);

Jianghu xiao xia zhuan [Stories of Minor Knights-Errant in the World of Adventure] (Shanghai: Shijie shuju, 1925);

Jindai xiayi yingxiong zhuan [Stories of Chivalric Heroes from the Recent Era], 8 volumes (Shanghai: Shijie shuju, 1926–1929); republished as *Xiayi yingxiong zhuan* [Stories of Chivalric Heroes], 12 volumes, edited by Zhao Tiaokuang and Lu Dan'an (Shanghai: Shijie shuju, 1929–1933);

Yu jue jin huan lu [Record of the Jade Bangle and the Golden Ring], 2 volumes, edited by Fan Yanqiao (Shanghai: Zhongyang shudian, 1927); republished as *Jianghu da xia zhuan* [Stories of Great Knights-Errant in the World of Adventure], edited by Chen Zijing (Shanghai: Zhongyang shudian, 1938);

Xiang Kairan (photograph in Dagong bao *[Hong Kong], 17 February 1957; from E. Perry Link Jr.,* Mandarin Ducks and Butterflies: Popular Fiction in Early Twentieth-Century Chinese Cities, *1981; Collection of Thomas Moran)*

Xiandai qi ren zhuan [Stories of Amazing Men from the Present Era] (Shanghai: Shijie shuju, 1928);

Liu dong waishi bu [Supplement to the Unofficial History of Sojourners in the East], 2 volumes (Shanghai: Dadong shuju, 1929)–includes critical commentary by Bao Tianxiao;

Nan bei qi xia [Amazing Knights-Errant from North and South], 2 volumes (Shanghai: Huanqiu shuju, 1930);

Liu dong xin shi [New History of Sojourners in the East], 3 volumes (Shanghai: Shijie shuju, 1931);

Banye fei tou ji [Tale of the Head Flying in the Middle of the Night], 2 volumes (Shanghai: Shihuan shuju, 1936).

Collections: *Minguo wuxia xiaoshuo dianji ren: Pingjiang Buxiaosheng* [The Founder of the Republican Martial Arts Novel: Pingjiang Buxiaosheng], edited by Fan Boqun (Nanjing: Nanjing chubanshe, 1994);

Wuxia bizu Xiang Kairan daibiaozuo [Representative Works by Xiang Kairan, Originator of Martial Arts Fiction], edited by Fan Boqun and Fan Zijiang (Nanjing: Jiangsu wenyi chubanshe, 1996);

Pingjiang Buxiaosheng daibiaozuo [Representative Works by Pingjiang Buxiaosheng], edited by Fan Boqun (Beijing: Huaxia chubanshe, 1999);

Pingjiang Buxiaosheng wenji [Collected writings by Pingjiang Buxiaosheng], edited by Fan Boqun (Beijing: Huaxia chubanshe, 2000).

Xiang Kairan, better known by his pseudonyms Pingjiang Buxiaosheng or just Buxiaosheng, was among the most successful authors of popular fiction in Republican China. In the 1920s he virtually invented the modern genre of the martial-arts novel based on popular lore. The enormous popularity his serialized works enjoyed among the urban population quickly made *wuxia xiaoshuo* (martial-arts fiction) the best-selling genre of commercial writing and stimulated the first major wave of Chinese martial-arts fiction in the twentieth century; the second wave occurred in the 1950s and 1960s in Hong Kong and the third in the 1980s. While Xiang's aesthetic achievements have commonly been undervalued by scholars, his influence is evident in the works of the *wuxia xiaoshuo* masters of the 1930s and 1940s. His greatest success, the serially published novel *Jianghu qi xia zhuan* (1924–1930, Stories of Amazing Knights-Errant in the World of Adventure), is considered one of the two representative major works of Republican martial-arts fiction (the other is the monumental *Shushan jianxia zhuan* [circa 1932, Stories of Sword Fighters in the Sichuanese Mountains], by Huanzhu Louzhu [Li Shoumin]). Some leftist critics, however, grouped Xiang with Zhang Henshui as epitomes of the purely commercial escapist mass entertainment to which they were fiercely opposed. Therefore, the name Buxiaosheng assumed a notorious ring to leftists, and after the establishment of the People's Republic of China in 1949, Xiang's writings were labeled *ducao* (poisonous weeds). As a consequence of his infamous place in post-1949 orthodox literary history, only superficial biographical and critical research into Xiang's life and career has been undertaken. Although he wrote a brief autobiographical essay in 1951, knowledge about his life is fragmentary and often anecdotal.

Xiang was born on 26 February 1890 into a fairly wealthy family that was native to the Pingjiang district of Hunan province and lived in the province's Xiangtan district. His grandfather had made a fortune manufacturing umbrellas, and his father, Xiang Biquan, held the degree of *shengyuan* (government student) and won local renown for his erudition. Xiang Kairan's original name was Xiang Kui; he later took Kairan as his *zi* (style name). His full pen name, Pingjiang Buxiaosheng, means "the unworthy student from Pingjiang." From early on he was fascinated by the martial arts, and he received training in various fighting techniques. He was educated at home in the traditional fashion from the age of five, and at eleven he began to learn to write in the style required to pass the civil service examination. In 1905 the examination system was abolished and new-style schools were established, and Xiang entered the *gaodeng shiye xuetang* (practical high school) in Changsha, Hunan province.

In 1906 a public funeral was held in Changsha for Hunan native Chen Tianhua; Chen had been a member of the Revolutionary Alliance, an anti–Qing dynasty organization founded in Tokyo by exiles from China, and had committed suicide in Japan in protest against the Qing government. The funeral turned into a prorevolutionary demonstration, and Xiang was expelled from school for taking part in it. After this incident it would have been difficult for him to gain admission to any other school. Therefore, in 1907 his family sent him to Tokyo to study at the Kōbun Institute, established to teach Chinese students enough Japanese to enable them to enter institutions of higher learning in Japan. During his stay in Japan he began serious study of the martial arts under the guidance of a Chinese master. After graduating from the Kōbun Institute, he may have attended another school before returning to Changsha in February 1911. There he became active in the Guojihui (National Fighting Association) and serialized his first work, *Quanshu jiangyi* (Instructions in Chinese Boxing), in the newspaper *Changsha ribao* (Changsha Daily). The work includes an appendix of anecdotes about Chinese boxing (*quanshu* is not "boxing" in the Western sense but fighting with the fists, as opposed to fighting with any of the weapons of the Chinese martial arts). The appendix, which in 1919 was published separately as *Quanshu jianwen lu* (Records Seen and Heard on the Technique of Boxing), represents Xiang's earliest attempt to write stories on the subject of martial arts.

The revolution of 1911 ended the Qing dynasty but led to the autocratic government of President Yuan Shikai. Xiang participated in the movement against Yuan, and in 1913, after efforts to remove Yuan from power failed, he used the royalties from his first book to go back to Japan and enroll in the School of Politics and Economics at Tokyo's Central University. He did not earn a degree. In late 1914 he began writing a novel about Chinese expatriates in Tokyo. He returned to China in 1915 and settled in Shanghai, where he hoped to make a living as a writer. He also joined the Revolutionary Party, which had been established by Sun Yat-sen in Tokyo in 1914.

Xiang had difficulty finding a publisher for the novel he had begun in Tokyo and finally sold it for less than he had hoped to a minor publishing house. The 106 chapters of *Liu dong waishi* (Unofficial History of Sojourners in the East) were published serially in installments of around 15 chapters, beginning in 1916 and ending in 1922. The work was a great commercial success.

Liu dong waishi purports to be a "confession"; if it is, then Xiang did not study in Tokyo but idled away his time in socializing, gambling, drinking, and frequenting brothels. For *Liu dong waishi* Xiang adopted the pseudonym Buxiaosheng (Unworthy Student), which is how the narrator presents himself in his introduction. Various characters are thinly veiled portraits of real people; their depiction is satirical, in some cases abusive. The main protagonist, Zhou Zhuan, generally taken to be Xiang's negative "self-portrayal," is highly unsympathetic: he tries to cheat girls into marrying him, and, worse, he spies on other students on behalf of the Yuan government. Although the picture of Chinese expatriates in Japan drawn by the novel is overwhelmingly negative, there are a few good characters, particularly those exiles who are genuinely involved in revolutionary activities. Nevertheless, the main ingredients of the work are social scandal and gossip. According to Fan Boqun in *Libailiu de hudie meng* (1999, The Butterfly Dreams of *Saturday*), the lengthy descriptions of life in Tokyo's brothels, which are reminiscent of late-Qing dynasty courtesan novels, met all the criteria for cynical readers to call the novel a "piaoxue jiaokeshu" (textbook for the science of frequenting brothels).

The first novel ever published about the lives of Chinese students abroad, *Liu dong waishi* became a model for fictional representations of Chinese students' experiences in Europe. The early 1920s were, however, a difficult time for Xiang. He temporarily stopped writing, and his friend Zhang Mingfei, a fellow Hunan native who wrote a commentary for *Liu dong waishi*, described him as constantly depressed.

Xiang's home in Shanghai reportedly served as a gathering place for martial artists, adventurers, eccentrics, and members of the city's underworld. From conversation with his guests, Xiang is said to have picked up many anecdotes that served as material for his fiction. An obscure 1919 novel, *Long hu chunqiu* (Chronicle of Dragon and Tiger), which long went unnoticed by scholars, indicates that he began to write martial-arts fiction as early as the late 1910s. Moreover, *Liu dong waishi* includes fighting scenes and frequently refers to the values of chivalry. Thus, though several sources refer to Xiang's "shift" to

Cover for a 1960 edition of Xiang's Jindai xiayi yingxiong zhuan *(1926–1929, Stories of Chivalric Heroes from the Recent Era), an historical novel (Wason Collection on East Asia–China, Kroch Asia Library, Cornell University)*

wuxia xiaoshuo in the early 1920s, it appears that he was working within, or near, that genre from the beginning.

Bao Tianxiao, an accomplished writer of entertainment fiction, claims in his memoirs a pivotal role in Xiang's career. In 1922 Bao asked Xiang to contribute to his small-format weekly magazine *Xingqi* (The Week). Xiang's work for *Xingqi* came to the notice of Shen Zhifang, the founder of the publishing house Shijie shuju (World Book Company), who hired Xiang to write for his weekly, *Hong zazhi* (Red Magazine). For years afterward, Shen tied Xiang to Shijie shuju and prevented him from writing for any other publisher or magazine.

At a time when knight-errantry fiction written in vernacular Chinese was not yet popular, Shen encouraged Xiang to write his first novel set in a fantasy world of adventure and including extensive descriptions of martial-arts performances and fighting scenes. *Jianghu qi xia zhuan* was serialized in *Hong zazhi* in installments of half a chapter, beginning with the first issue of 1923. In July 1924 the title of the magazine was changed to *Hong meigui* (Red Roses); it continued to serialize *Jianghu qi xia zhuan,* which had quickly caught readers' attention. Xiang was still writing the novel as it was simultaneously serialized in the magazine and published in books of about a dozen chapters each. By 1927 social unrest and political fighting had made Shanghai unsettled and dangerous, and Xiang suspended the novel abruptly after 106 chapters and moved back to his home province of Hunan. Reluctant to discontinue his most popular serial novel, the editor asked another editor, Zhao Tiaokuang, to write chapters 107 through 160. These chapters were published under the pseudonym Zouxiaosheng (The Unworthy Student Has Gone), a reference to the original author's departure from Shanghai. Xiang was unhappy about the unauthorized continuation of his work but declined the editor's invitation to write a sequel of his own.

Jianghu qi xia zhuan was remarkably successful in the 1920s and early 1930s. The novel introduced a new subgenre to the field of popular fiction, which hitherto had been dominated by tragic romance. In terms of the evolution of the *wuxia xiaoshuo* genre, Xiang's work was groundbreaking for its departure from the type of adventure novel prevalent in the nineteenth century: *Jianghu qi xia zhuan* placed new emphasis on fantasy and magic and the description of martial-arts performance. Xiang based his novel largely on popular tales and legends, relying on oral accounts and written sources; some of the latter can be identified. But he embellished and expanded his source material and increased the element of exaggeration inherent in the folk tradition of marital-arts tales. In terms of narrative aesthetics, however, *Jianghu qi xia zhuan* is not considered a significant achievement: its structure is loose, episodic, and open-ended, with extensive digressions. These shortcomings are related to the manner in which the novel was produced—Xiang wrote it chapter by chapter in unplanned fashion. Thematically, the most lasting contribution of the novel to martial-arts fiction was the introduction of the motif of factional strife among rival schools of martial arts, which became one of the favorite ingredients of the genre. The main story line is provided by the conflict between the competing Kunlun and the Kongtong martial-arts schools. When the Kunlun and Kongtong groups are challenged by a third faction, which they consider "heterodox" because of its reliance on sorcery, they unite against the common enemy and gradually bring harmony to their relationship.

Jianghu qi xia zhuan gained wider renown through the motion-picture adaptation, *Huo shao Honglian si* (1928, Burning Down of the Red Lotus Monastery), produced by the Mingxing Film Company in early 1928 with Zhang Shichuan as the director and major stars in the cast. The movie was based on chapters 65 to 86 of the novel, in which a group of Kunlun sword fighters tries to subdue the wicked monk Zhiyuan, whose gang of bandits has committed every possible crime, and destroy his monastery near Changsha; but with help from the Kongtong faction, Zhiyuan always escapes at the last minute. The success of the movie led to the production of seventeen subsequent serial parts through 1931 in which the leading actress Hu Die took over the role of the female knight-errant Honggu. Owing to the popularity of the movie, the title *Huo shao Honglian si* was used for some print versions of Xiang's novel. The success of the series launched a wave of Chinese martial-arts movies, and the genre quickly came to dominate the Chinese motion-picture industry.

While *Jianghu qi xia zhuan* is remembered for the enormous impact it made on the popular culture of the early Republican period, the lesser-known novel *Jindai xiayi yingxiong zhuan* (1926–1929, Stories of Chivalric Heroes from the Recent Era) may be Xiang's more important legacy to *wuxia xiaoshuo*. Serialized beginning in June 1923 in *Zhentan shijie* (Detective World), a semimonthly magazine that had recently been launched by Shijie shuju, the eighty-four-chapter work is quite different from *Jianghu qi xia zhuan,* even though Xiang wrote the two novels simultaneously. In sharp contrast to the fantastic *Jianghu qi xia zhuan*, *Jindai xiayi yingxiong zhuan* is set in the real world, and its mode of representation is realistic. Based largely on historical sources and anecdotes, *Jindai xiayi yingxiong zhuan* presents a linked series of biographies of martial-arts masters who lived during the late Qing period around the turn of the twentieth century and is almost an unofficial history of Chinese martial arts in the early modern era. The two principal characters are "Big Knife" Wang Zhengyi (Wang Five) and Huo Yuanjia, martial-arts champions who, motivated by patriotic fervor and a chivalric spirit of righteousness, engage the urgent national questions of their time. Xiang regarded China's age-old martial-arts tradition as a remedy for the nation's weakness, and in the novel Huo sets up a school of physical culture in this same patriotic spirit: he intends to cure "the sick man of Asia," as China was called by both Chinese and foreigners in the early twentieth century.

Another historical character in *Jindai xiayi yingxiong zhuan* is Tan Sitong, an influential thinker and charismatic politician; the novel opens with a famous poem by Tan. When the 1898 reform movement is crushed by its conservative enemies at court, Wang offers to take Tan to safety; but Tan refuses to be saved, preferring to die a martyr.

Jindai xiayi yingxiong zhuan advocates resistance to foreign aggression; at the same time, however, it favors the introduction of Western scientific knowledge and physical culture. Thus, while nationalistic, it is free of antiforeign sentiment. Although Huo's victories over three foreign "strong men" who claim to be "world champions" inevitably appear to exemplify cultural chauvinism, the two heroes are appalled by the atrocities committed against foreigners and Chinese Christians during the fiercely xenophobic *Yihetuan* (Society United in Righteousness) movement—known in English as the Boxer Rebellion—that raged through Beijing and Tianjin in 1900. Obligated by their chivalric credo to support the weak and help those whose lives are in danger, Wang and Huo publicly offer protection to the victims of the uprising and turn a private residence into a fortress that they defend against the Boxers. (This episode, comprising chapters 15 to 19, was excised in a 1984 edition of the novel published in the People's Republic of China: in Communist historiography the Boxer Rebellion is considered a progressive revolutionary event.) Wang later dies fighting against the foreign military forces that moved in to suppress the rebellion.

Aesthetically, *Jindai xiayi yingxiong zhuan* is superior to *Jianghu qi xia zhuan*. Following the "billiard ball" technique of shifting the narrative focus from anecdote to anecdote, which has a long tradition in Chinese storytelling, it is made up of a series of loosely interconnected short narratives. Although Xiang's fame rests on his novels, his strength as a fiction writer was not in that form; he was, instead, a master of the short story. He wrote many short narratives about martial-arts matters—at first in Classical Chinese and then, beginning in the early 1920s and following the general trend, in the vernacular. All of these stories were published in *Hong zazhi* and its successor, *Hong meigui*, the magazines that carried *Jianghu qi xia zhuan*. Unlike many other authors, Xiang never cared to collect his stories in book form; for him they were less independent narratives than sources of material on which he could draw as he composed his novels, and protoversions of some episodes in the novels are found in the short stories. In essence, then, Xiang's basic aesthetic unit was the short narrative; his novels merely combine many such stories. *Jianghu yiren zhuan* (1924, Stories of Otherworldly People in the World of Adventure), for example, is a collection of individual tales unified by only a minimal novelistic framework. Xiang's outstanding skill as a storyteller is best appreciated in his shorter tales.

The novel *Yu jue jin huan lu* (Record of the Jade Bangle and the Golden Ring) was Xiang's third major work of *wuxia xiaoshuo*. It was serialized in 1925–1926 in *Xinwen bao* (The News), Shanghai's third-largest newspaper, and published in book form in 1927. The father of the hero, Zeng Fuchou, is accused of banditry and executed by a local tyrant. After his mother commits suicide, Zeng is brought up first by a loyal servant and later by a troupe of martial-arts performers, who teach him swordsmanship. Finally, he is adopted by a prefect and changes his name. Returning to his native village, he gains entry, by claiming to be a martial-arts performer, to a party being held for the tyrant who had his father killed. He avenges his father's death by killing the tyrant. The jade bangle and golden ring in the

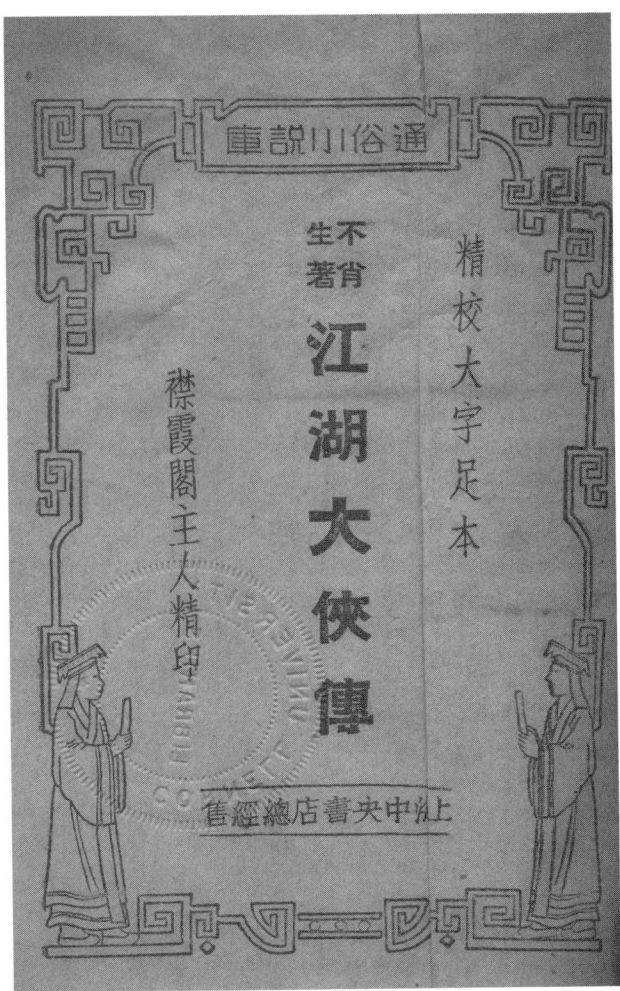

Title page for a 1938 edition of Xiang's Jianghu qi xia zhuan *(Stories of Amazing Knights-Errant in the World of Adventure), originally published in 1930 (Wason Collection on East Asia–China, Kroch Asia Library, Cornell University)*

title are tokens that were handed down to him by his parents. This classic revenge story has been widely acclaimed.

The 1920s were successful for Xiang in the sense that his writing paid handsomely. His publisher is said to have given him eight thousand *yuan* for *Jianghu qi xia zhuan*, an unprecedented sum. He wrote only between midnight and dawn, filling each sheet of paper with an enormous amount of text in tiny but clear handwriting, and had a reputation for being fast and prolific. But providing chapters for several serial novels running at the same time and meeting tight deadlines put him under enormous pressure and appears to account, at least in part, for his addiction to opium during these years—a condition that was endemic among popular writers at the time.

Xiang returned from Hunan to Shanghai in 1930. From 1927 to 1932 he wrote martial-arts instruction manuals rather than fiction. Unlike most other major authors of *wuxia xiaoshuo*, he was a practitioner of the martial arts. His wife, Cheng Yize, specialized in *neigong* (inner technique), which is described as the supreme martial art in *Jianghu qi xia zhuan*.

The total number of major works written by Xiang is estimated by scholars at between twelve and fourteen. This count, however, is unreliable, because most of his works from the 1930s and after have never been published in book form. He began an historical novel about the Wuchang uprising of 1907, "Tiexue yingxiong zhuan" (Stories about Heroes of Iron and Blood), involving revolutionary martyrs such as Qiu Jin. It was serialized in the early 1930s in the newspaper *Mingxing ribao* (Bright Star News) but remained unfinished, and no book edition is known to exist.

After the Japanese assault on Shanghai in January 1932, Xiang left the city and became a private secretary to He Jian, the governor of Hunan province. Around this time Xiang was also actively involved with two regional martial-arts training centers. In the mid 1930s Xiang described himself as exhausted by the fiction business and relieved to have withdrawn from professional writing. The Sino-Japanese War began in 1937; in 1938 Xiang resigned from He Jian's staff and accepted a position with the Nationalist army's Twenty-first Military Corps, which sent him to Lihuang in Anhui province as an adviser to the provincial government. For a short time he also taught in the literature department of Anhui University.

The Communist army took Anhui in the spring of 1947, and Xiang was taken prisoner, questioned, and released. He then returned to Changsha. After the Communists took power in Hunan in 1949, Xiang served as a representative at the Hunan sheng zhengzhi xieshang huiyi (Provincial Consultative Conference) and was a member of the Zhongyang wenshiguan (Central Institute for the Research of Literature and History). Information about the last years of his life is vague and contradictory. Several sources claim that he became a Buddhist monk on a hill near Changsha; on the other hand, there is evidence that he wrote two middle-length stories for local magazines. In 1956 he was a member of the jury for the first national martial-arts contest, held as part of the Hundred Flowers Movement. This service established him as a leading authority in the field, and he began to draft his last book project: a general history of Chinese martial arts. It was left unfinished at his death in Changsha in December 1957. At least one biographical sketch claims that he died of a stroke brought on by being physically mistreated during an Anti-Rightist Campaign "struggle session."

Xiang Kairan began to make his name as a writer of popular fiction in the late 1910s, and in the 1920s he became the leading author of martial-arts novels. His most active period was limited to about a decade, during which he wrote his two most important serial novels. The more famous of the two, *Jianghu qi xia zhuan*, established the genre of the modern martial-arts novel, which flourished as a form of popular literature throughout the twentieth century.

Biographies:

Guan Zhichang, "Xiang Kairan (1889–1957)," *Zhuanji wenxue*, 42, no. 3 (1983): 146–147;

Zhang Gansheng, *Minguo tongsu xiaoshuo lungao* (Chongqing: Chongqing chubanshe, 1991), pp. 111–124;

Fan Boqun, "Minguo wuxia xiaoshuo dianjiren: Pingjiang Buxiaosheng pingzhuan," in his *Minguo wuxia xiaoshuo dianjiren: Pingjiang Buxiaosheng* (Nanjing: Nanjing chubanshe, 1994), pp. 11–30;

Fan, ed., *Zhongguo jinxiandai tongsu wenxue shi*, 2 volumes (Nanjing: Jiangsu jiaoyu chubanshe, 1999), I: 513–532.

References:

Bao Tianxiao, *Chuanyinglou huiyi lu* (Hong Kong: Dahua chubanshe, 1971);

Cheng Yize, "Yi Kairan xiansheng," in *Jianghu qi xia zhuan*, by Pingjiang Buxiaosheng (Xiang Kairan), volume 2 (Changsha: Yuelu shushe, 1986), pp. 558–586;

Fan Boqun, "Cong Buxiaosheng de heimu yu wuxia daibiaozuo tanqi," in his *Libailiu de hudie meng* (Beijing: Renmin wenxue chubanshe, 1999), pp. 180–210;

Fan, *Minguo wuxia xiaoshuo dianjiren: Pingjiang Buxiaosheng* (Nanjing: Nanjing chubanshe, 1994);

E. Perry Link Jr., *Mandarin Ducks and Butterflies: Popular Fiction in Early Twentieth-Century Chinese Cities* (Berkeley: University of California Press, 1981);

James J. Y. Liu, *The Chinese Knight-Errant* (London: Routledge & Kegan Paul, 1967), pp. 135–137;

Qin Heming, ed., *Minguo zhanghui xiaoshuo daguan* (Beijing: Zhongguo wenlian chuban gongsi, 1995), pp. 6–9, 49–65;

Rui Heshi and others, eds., *Yuanyang hudie pai wenxue ziliao*, 2 volumes (Fuzhou: Fujian renmin chubanshe, 1984);

Wei Shaochang, *Wo kan Yuanyang hudie pai* (Taibei: Taiwan shangwu yinshuguan, 1992), pp. 132–138;

Ye Hongsheng, *Lun jian: Wuxia xiaoshuo tan yi lu* (Shanghai: Xuelin chubanshe, 1997), pp. 90–120;

Zheng Yimei, "Xiang Kairan shuxi wushu," in his *Qing mo Min chu wentan yishi* (Shanghai: Xuelin chubanshe, 1987), pp. 283–287.

Xiao Hong
(1 June 1911 – 22 January 1942)

Nicole Huang
University of Wisconsin–Madison

BOOKS: *Bashe* [Trudging], by Xiao Hong as Qiao Yin, and Xiao Jun as San Lang (Harbin: Privately printed by Harbin wu ri huabao she, 1933);

Sheng si chang [The Field of Life and Death] (Shanghai: Nulishe, 1935);

Shangshi jie [Market Street] (Shanghai: Wenhua shenghuo chubanshe, 1936)–translated by Howard Goldblatt as *Market Street: A Chinese Woman in Harbin* (Seattle: University of Washington Press, 1986);

Qiao [Bridge], as Qiao Yin (Shanghai: Wenhua shenghuo chubanshe, 1936)–includes "Shou," translated by Goldblatt as "Hands," in *Modern Chinese Stories and Novellas, 1919–1949,* edited by Joseph S. M. Lau, Leo Ou-fan Lee, and C. T. Hsia (New York: Columbia University Press, 1981), pp. 456–464;

Niuche shang [On the Oxcart] (Shanghai: Wenhua shenghuo chubanshe, 1937)–includes "Niuche shang," translated by Goldblatt as "On the Oxcart," in *Born of the Same Roots: Stories of Modern Chinese Women,* edited by Vivian Ling Hsu (Bloomington: Indiana University Press, 1981), pp. 13–22; and "Jiazu yiwai de ren," translated by Goldblatt as "The Family Outsider," in *Modern Chinese Stories and Novellas, 1919–1949,* pp. 465–483;

Kuangye de huhan [Cries in the Wilderness] (Chongqing: Da shidai shuju, 1939; revised edition, Shanghai: Shanghai zazhi gongsi, 1946);

Xiao Hong sanwen [Essays by Xiao Hong] (Chongqing: Da shidai shuju, 1940);

Huiyi Lu Xun xiansheng [A Remembrance of Mr. Lu Xun] (Chongqing: Funü shenghuo chubanshe, 1940);

Ma Bole (Chongqing: Da shidai shuju, 1941; enlarged edition, Harbin: Heilongjiang renmin chubanshe, 1981);

Hulan he zhuan [A Biography of Hulan River] (Guilin: Heshan chubanshe, 1942);

Xiaocheng sanyue [March in a Small Town] (Hong Kong: Haiyang shuwu, 1948)–title story translated by

Xiao Hong (from Xiao Hong, *edited by Wang Shu, 1987; Clapp Library, Wellesley College)*

Sidney Shapiro as "Spring in a Small Town," *Chinese Literature,* 8 (1961): 59–82;

Xiao Hong xuanji [Selected Works by Xiao Hong] (Beijing: Renmin wenxue chubanshe, 1958; enlarged, 1981)–enlarged edition includes "Shimian zhi ye," translated by Amy D. Dooling and Kristina M. Torgeson as "A Sleepless Night," in *Writing Women in Modern China: An Anthology of*

Women's Literature from the Early Twentieth Century, edited by Dooling and Torgeson (New York: Columbia University Press, 1998), pp. 363–366; and "Yongjiu de chongjing yu zhuiqiu," translated by Goldblatt as "Perpetual Longing and Pursuit," in his introduction to "The Field of Life and Death" in *The Field of Life and Death and Tales of Hulan River: Two Novels,* translated by Goldblatt and Ellen Yeung, edited by Goldblatt (Bloomington: Indiana University Press, 1979), pp. xv–xvi;

Xiao Hong quanji [The Complete Works of Xiao Hong], 3 volumes (Harbin: Harbin chubanshe, 1998)—volume 3 includes "Qi er," translated by Dooling and Torgeson as "Abandoned Child," in *Writing Women in Modern China,* pp. 347–361.

Collections: *Xiao Hong duanpian xiaoshuo ji* [Short Stories by Xiao Hong] (Harbin: Heilongjiang renmin chubanshe, 1982);

Xiao Hong: "Zhongguo xiandai zuojia xuanji" congshu [Xiao Hong: "Selected Works of Modern Chinese Authors" Series], edited by Wang Shu (Hong Kong: Shudian Xianggang fendian, 1982);

Xiao Hong sanwen xuanji [Selected Essays by Xiao Hong] (Tianjin: Baihua wenyi chubanshe, 1982);

Xiao Hong daibiao zuo [Representative Works by Xiao Hong] (Zhengzhou: Henan renmin chubanshe, 1987);

Xiao Hong, edited by Wang Shu (Hong Kong: Shudian Xianggang fendian, 1987);

Xiao Hong quanji [The Complete Works of Xiao Hong], 2 volumes (Harbin: Harbin chubanshe, 1991);

Hou huayuan [Rear Garden] (Beijing: Yanshan chubanshe, 1998).

Editions in English: "Harelip Feng" (Chapter 7 of *Hulan he zhuan* [A Biography of Hulan River]), translated by Gladys Yang, *Chinese Literature,* 2 (1963): 3–24;

The Field of Life and Death and Tales of Hulan River: Two Novels, translated by Howard Goldblatt and Ellen Yeung, edited by Goldblatt (Bloomington: Indiana University Press, 1979);

Selected Stories of Xiao Hong, translated and edited by Goldblatt (Beijing: Chinese Literature Press, 1982; San Francisco: China Books and Periodicals, 1982)—comprises "The Death of Wang Asao" ("Wang asao de si"), "The Bridge" ("Qiao"), "Hands" ("Shou"), "On the Oxcart" ("Niuche shang"), "The Family Outsider" ("Jiazu yiwai de ren"), "Flight from Danger" ("Taonan"), "Vague Expectations" ("Menglong de qidai"), "North China" ("Bei Zhongguo"), and "Spring in a Small Town" ("Xiaocheng sanyue");

Tales of Hulan River, translated by Goldblatt (Hong Kong: Joint Publishing Company, 1988).

Xiao Hong is remembered as the author of the fiction masterpieces *Sheng si chang* (1935; translated as "The Field of Life and Death," 1979) and *Hulan he zhuan* (1942, A Biography of Hulan River; translated as "Tales of Hulan River," 1979) and as a talented woman who lived a tumultuous life and died at a tragically young age. By the mid 1940s her life had become part of the mythology of the romantic strain of modern Chinese literature. Many critics and literary historians regard her as the most important disciple of the literary giant Lu Xun; they consider her nostalgic accounts of an imagined homecoming in her fiction and essays an effort to carry on the tradition of Xiangtu wenxue (Native-Soil Literature) exemplified by Lu Xun's early writing. Xiao Hong's association with Lu Xun and other leftist writers situates her in the left-wing literary movement of the 1930s. Critics and historians also consider her one of the most significant realist writers of that decade. This characterization of her as an orthodox May Fourth critical-realist chronicler of Chinese rural life has long dominated Xiao Hong scholarship. But while Xiao Hong's intellectual lineage thus seems to place her firmly in the modern Chinese literary mainstream, Howard Goldblatt's analyses and translations of Xiao Hong's works paint a picture of a unique modern Chinese author. Other scholars, including Lydia Liu, Meng Yue, and Dai Jinhua, argue that Xiao Hong's highly personalized writing about war, women, the homeland, and nostalgia was often at odds with the mainstream narratives of her time. All agree that Xiao Hong occupies an important and yet peculiar place in the literary imagination of twentieth-century China.

Xiao Hong was born into a wealthy landlord family on 1 June 1911 in Hulan in the northernmost region of Manchuria in what is now Heilongjiang province. Published accounts of her birth name differ, but the information in the chronology of her life in the third volume of *Xiao Hong quanji* (1998, The Complete Works of Xiao Hong) is definitive: her *ruming* (infant name) was Zhang Ronghua; her *xueming* (formal name used at school) was Zhang Xiuhuan, but her grandfather later changed it to Zhang Naiying. Located in the southern Heilong (Amur) River valley and on the north shore of the Songhua (Sungari) River, Hulan was a prosperous county seat.

In 1936 the American leftist journalist Edgar Snow asked Xiao Hong to submit a short autobiographical sketch for a collection of translations of modern Chinese fiction he was compiling. Which of her stories he was considering for the collection is not known, because the published volume, *Living China:*

Modern Chinese Short Stories (1936), includes none. But Xiao Hong's sketch, "Yongjiu de chongjing yu zhuiqiu" (translated as "Perpetual Longing and Pursuit," 1979), was published in the inaugural issue of *Baogao* (The Report) in January 1937. In this rare autobiographical account, which is indicative of her candid and yet complex prose style, Xiao Hong writes of the two "fangmian" (aspects) of her complicated childhood experience; the notion of "two aspects" has been adopted as a model of interpretation by both critics and admirers of her work. One aspect was represented by her cold and distant father, the other by her loving and sensitive grandfather. Xiao Hong depicts her father, Zhang Tingju (courtesy name Xuansan), as a cruel and inhumane man who was the root cause of the troubles in her life: "My father often gave up his humanity over his own covetousness. His relationships with servants, or with his own children, as well as with Granddad were all characterized by his stinginess, aloofness, and even hard-heartedness" (translation by Howard Goldblatt). Her mother died when she was nine, and her father became even more threatening; his eyes "underwent a change, and each time I passed by him I felt as though there were thorns stuck all over my body." Her grandfather was the only person in the family who understood her, shared her passion for poetry and nature, and encouraged her to cultivate her artistic sensibilities: "Whenever my father beat me, I would go to Granddad's room and stare out the window from dusk to late into the night—the white snow beyond the window floated there like white fleece, while the lid of the water jug on the radiator vibrated, sounding like the accompaniment of a musical instrument. . . . I learned from Granddad that besides coldness and hatred, life also includes warmth and love." Xiao Hong's biographers contend that her childhood set the pattern for her relationships with her friends and lovers in later life: she saw herself either as cherished and protected or as abandoned and tormented.

Archival documents and memoirs by family members, however, contradict Xiao Hong's characterization of her father. These accounts portray Zhang Tingju as an open-minded member of the local gentry, an educated man of vision, and a champion of modern education in Hulan county. Records show that he joined the Nationalist Party soon after the founding of the Republic in 1911 and began to advocate equal access to public education for girls.

When Zhang Naiying graduated from primary school, her father and other members of the family wanted her to switch to home schooling. Dissatisfied with life in the quiet town, she refused. In 1927 she went to Harbin, a major metropolis twenty miles away, to attend the Dongsheng tebiequli nüzi di yi zhong

Xiao Hong (left) and her lover, the novelist Xiao Jun (Liu Honglin), in Harbin in 1934 (from Xiao Hong, *edited by Wang Shu, 1987; Clapp Library, Wellesley College)*

xuexiao (Eastern Provincial Special District First Women's Middle School). At this time she became an avid reader of the New Literature; she appears to have been particularly fond of Lu Xun's fiction and essays and of works by major Russian authors.

In 1929 Zhang's grandfather died. Soon afterward her father informed her that she was to leave school for an arranged marriage to Wang Enjia, the son of a local warlord. To escape from her father's control she became romantically involved with a cousin who took her to Beiping (as Beijing was known from 1928 to 1949), where she continued her education at a middle school. Their families cut off all financial support, leaving them penniless, and they returned to Harbin in January 1931. Zhang's family brought her home and put her under the supervision of an uncle. After ten months of confinement, she escaped and made her way back to Harbin, where she lived on the streets.

In Harbin, according to some sources, Zhang formed a relationship with Wang, the intended groom she had initially loathed. They lived together at a small hotel from late 1931 until Wang abandoned her in the summer of 1932. Unable to pay the rent, she moved into a dark, damp storage room. Sick, hungry, and eight months pregnant, she began to compose poetry—her earliest known writing. These first poems are written in simple, straightforward language and filled with sorrow, anguish, and despair.

On the verge of a nervous breakdown, Zhang wrote to the local newspaper *Guoji xiebao* (International Gazette) pleading for help. The editor was taken aback by the wretched state she described in the letter and sent a young reporter, Liu Honglin, who wrote for the paper under the pen name Xiao Jun, to the hotel to confirm its truthfulness. Xiao Jun was an aspiring writer who published his literary work under the pseudonym San Lang; at their first meeting he discovered that Zhang was also an aspiring writer. Struck by the contrast between the frailty of the sick young woman and the strength of her poetic talent, he determined to rescue her. Zhang's encounter with Xiao Jun gave her renewed hope, and her poetry became increasingly optimistic. She titled her short verses "Chun qu" (Songs of Spring) and published them under the pen name Qiao Yin ("gentle chanting") in the literary supplement of *Guoji xiebao*.

In August, Zhang gave her child up for adoption, and she and Xiao Jun began living together. Over the next year and a half she contributed poetry, essays, and short stories to local newspapers under the pen name Qiao Yin. Her first published story, "Qi er" (translated as "Abandoned Child," 1988), about a young unmarried woman who gives her baby up for adoption but meets a man who looks after her, was serialized in the literary supplement of the newspaper *Dagong bao/L'Impartial* in May 1933. In August, using the pen names Qiao Yin and San Lang, Zhang and Xiao Jun privately published a joint collection of stories and essays titled *Bashe* (Trudging). Zhang contributed the "Chun qu" poems, an essay, and four short stories, three of which had already been published; among them was "Wang asao de si" (translated as "The Death of Wang Asao," 1982), which had appeared in the *Dagongbao/L'Impartial* literary supplement the same month as "Qi er." "Wang asao de si" is a story of the brutal mistreatment of the poor by the wealthy; the main characters are the widow Wang Asao, whose husband's death was caused by the landlord for whom she works, and Little Huan, whose mother died after being raped by the landlord's son.

In the spring of 1934 Zhang and Xiao Jun fled the Japanese occupation of Manchuria by traveling to Qingdao in Shandong province. During their six-month stay in Qingdao they began working on their first full-length novels: Xiao Jun on a narrative of anti-Japanese resistance by a group of guerrilla patriots, *Bayue de xiangcun* (1935; translated as *Village in August*, 1942), and Zhang on *Sheng si chang*. They sent their manuscripts to Lu Xun in Shanghai prior to their departure for the city; by the time they arrived, Lu Xun had read their works and readily accepted the couple into his growing entourage of young leftist authors. Lu Xun published both novels in his "Nuli congshu" (Slave Series). With the publication of her first major work, Zhang began using Xiao Hong as her pseudonym.

Though canonized in the same leftist context, *Sheng si chang* is different from *Bayue de xiangcun* and other anti-Japanese resistance literature of the time: it is not dominated by anti-Japanese sentiments, and the awakening and revolt of a rural population against foreign invasion, a central theme in most such works, takes up only the last third of Xiao Hong's novel. Instead, she paints a dark and powerful picture of rural life in China's northeast, with stark depictions of the animal-like existence of the residents of a village stricken by poverty and sickness. Most of the narration follows a cyclical rhythm: daily life flows from summer into autumn, which is succeeded by a long winter and a spring that arrives gingerly. Difficult births, sadness in old age, catastrophic disease, and death in various forms are ever present. Xiao Hong's narration changes from cyclical to linear in the last third of the book as the sudden invasion of Japanese forces renders life even more unbearable and death even more grotesque and cruel.

As soon as they were published, Xiao Hong's *Sheng si chang* and Xiao Jun's *Bayue de xiangcun* were praised as models of patriotic and anti-imperialist literature. But while the case for Xiao Jun's admittance to the ranks of left-wing writers was clear-cut, Xiao Hong's advocates met a critical impasse when trying to integrate her work into the social-realist mainstream. Some of the most authoritative figures in the leftist camp insisted that her female voice, though fresh and distinctive, needed to be guided and corrected to serve the calling of the time. Hu Feng, a literary critic widely regarded as the spiritual leader of the leftist writers of the 1930s and 1940s, wrote an epilogue for the first edition of *Sheng si chang* titled "Duhou ji" (After Reading; translated as "Appendix II: Epilogue to *The Field of Life and Death*," 1979). Praising the novel's "masculine" style, he says that Xiao Hong's direct and daring revelations are rarely found among female authors. But he criticizes what he considers an immature work by a promising young author: the organization of the material is weak; there is no central development for readers to follow; focused descriptions of the main figures are lacking; and the characters are not representative of China's rural population. By branding Xiao Hong's fiction a national allegory in the making, Hu Feng's remarks have prevented readers from understanding the uniqueness and complexity of her vision of history and her original prose style. The final criticism Hu offers in his frequently quoted epilogue is that Xiao Hong's grammar and syntax are too idiosyncratic, a fault he attributes to her lack of formal training in literary writing. By contrast, readers of later generations often marvel at Xiao Hong's testing of the capacity of the modern Chinese vernacular to represent local color and regional history. Hu Feng's comments are an indication of the uneasiness Xiao Hong's writing generated even among male writers and critics who were her primary supporters in the 1930s.

Following the success of *Sheng si chang*, Xiao Hong published *Shangshi jie* (1936, Market Street; translated as *Market Street: A Chinese Woman in Harbin,* 1986), a series of sketches of daily occurrences based on her first two years with Xiao Jun in Harbin. The translator, Goldblatt, characterizes the text as an autobiography "thinly disguised as fiction." Seemingly linear, the narrative is actually a modernist subversion of the conventions of autobiographical fiction: if Xiao Hong's critics had trouble comprehending the language and style of *Sheng si chang,* they found the episodic structure and the narrator's pronounced inward turn in *Shangshi jie* even harder to grasp. In contrast to *Sheng si chang, Shangshi jie* is not concerned with the social and historical context; it focuses on the spiritual journey of a young woman who nurtures her literary sensibilities in the midst of hunger, poverty, love, loneliness, sickness, and exile. Though largely ignored by critics at the time, *Shangshi jie* remains one of Xiao Hong's most daring attempts to distance herself from the "master narrative" of the period, in which the concerns of the individual were sacrificed to the interests of the group, and the quotidian and the sentimental were overwhelmed by the grand drama of revolution, and to undermine conventional boundaries between fiction and nonfiction.

Shangshi jie consists of forty-one episodes set in Harbin. Though the first-person narrator is omnipresent, the true protagonist in the early episodes is the hunger she endures during her prolonged seclusion in the rundown Hotel Europa:

> I opened the little window by standing on the table. That little window was our sole link with the outside world. Through it we maintained contact with the skyline—roofs and chimneys—the falling snow, the dark, floating, moisture-laden clouds—street lamps, policemen, hawkers, beggars.... The streets were noisy and bustling. Small though the room was, I had the sensation of being in the middle of a vast deserted public square. The walls enclosing me seemed farther away than the heavens themselves; I was all alone, com-

Cover for Xiao Hong's novel Sheng si chang *(1935; translated as "The Field of Life and Death," 1979), about the grim lives of villagers in northeast China before and during the Japanese invasion (from Yu Runqi, ed.,* Tang Tao cang shu, *2004; Bruccoli Clark Layman Archives)*

pletely cut off from the outside world. It all boiled down to this: I had an empty stomach (translation by Howard Goldblatt).

The narrator's hunger is depicted realistically, but as in other modernist writing of the time, hunger is also a trope of alienation and longing.

The narrator and her lover, Langhua, are introduced to a literary circle of people their age who are equally poor and hungry. Although the others share her rootlessness, the narrator feels excluded from the close-knit group. Her sense of loneliness and helplessness is increased in the eighth episode, when she and her lover move to a small apartment on Market Street. This "home" brings no joy to the narrator; it reduces her to the role of a "little housewife": "I stayed home and waited for him. I began to pace the floor around the stove. Every day it was the same: eat, sleep, worry about firewood, fret over rice." In this loathed state of prolonged loneliness, writing becomes a necessity and a path of salvation for the narrator. She begins to write, as does Langhua. The narrative ends with the publication of a joint collection of fiction and essays by the lovers, mirroring Xiao Hong and Xiao Jun's publication of *Bashe* in 1933.

In 1936 Xiao Hong also published *Qiao* (Bridge), a collection of short stories and essays. Most notable in this book is the story "Shou" (translated as "Hands," 1981), in which Wang Yaming, a girl from a poor family, goes through a series of ordeals to fulfill her dream of getting a proper education. She is rejected at school because her frail body carries a reminder of her humble origin: her hands, "blue, black, and even showing a touch of purple," are signs of hard labor in her family's dyeing business. They are a source of shame from which Wang cannot escape even by wearing thick gloves.

In 1935–1936 Xiao Hong developed a close relationship with Lu Xun and his wife, Xu Guangping. Xiao Hong's biographers, following the "two worlds" theory, suggest that she saw in Lu Xun the image of her deceased grandfather. But in 1936 Lu Xun was beset by a series of physical ailments, and he and Xu could afford less and less time and energy to comfort Xiao Hong, whose relationship with Xiao Jun was deteriorating. In July, Xiao Hong traveled alone to Tokyo. During her six-month stay she wrote "Jiazu yiwai de ren" (translated as "The Family Outsider," 1981), a short story based on her childhood memories of a household servant; it was published in the Shanghai journal *Zuojia* (The Writer) in 1936. In Tokyo she experienced loneliness and homesickness. Adding to her depression was the news of Lu Xun's death on 19 October; she felt that she had lost the only person in her life other than her grandfather who treated her with unreserved kindness, understanding, and love. Xiao Hong returned to Shanghai and Xiao Jun soon after Lu Xun's death.

When the Sino-Japanese War broke out in July 1937, Shanghai entered into the so-called *gudao* (Orphan Island) era. The International Settlement and French concession remained under the control of European powers, but this territory was encircled by the Japanese army that was overrunning much of eastern China. Those who resided in the besieged city had to decide whether to stay within the confines of the concessions or to leave Shanghai for the interior. Xiao Hong and Xiao Jun joined a massive migration to the inland city of Wuhan, where Xiao Hong met and became romantically involved with another young Manchurian writer, Duanmu Hongliang. In 1938 Xiao Hong, Xiao Jun, and Duanmu made a one-month journey together to northern China. Afterward, Xiao Hong and Xiao Jun ended their six-year relationship. Xiao Hong returned to Wuhan with Duanmu, while Xiao Jun went on to the Communist-controlled region in the north.

Xiao Hong's decision to return south instead of going north to the Communist capital, Yan'an in Shaanxi province, with Xiao Jun surprised and disappointed many of her leftist friends. Even her fellow female writers put class struggle ahead of gender solidarity and failed to understand her choice. An essay Xiao Hong published in October 1937 in the Wuhan journal *Qiyue* (July) reveals when and how she decided that she was different from Xiao Jun and other literary leftists. "Shimian zhi ye" (translated as "A Sleepless Night," 1998) captures the last moments of Xiao Hong's life with Xiao Jun and shows that their separation was an indication of the divergent political paths they had chosen; it demonstrates her ambivalence about the cause of nationalism and conveys her sense of being an outsider to collective movements. She recalls listening to her lover and her friends sharing happy memories of their hometowns in the northeast and longing for the day when the Chinese win the war and they are able to return there. She wondered whether the notion of a homecoming meant as much to her as it did to the others. Her lover talked about taking her home as his bride: "'And what about me?' I was thinking to myself. 'How would your family treat a "daughter-in-law" brought home from somewhere else?' I then spoke my thoughts to him aloud" (translation by Amy D. Dooling and Kristina M. Torgeson). She discovered that she felt neither sadness at the loss of home nor joy at the prospect of returning there; long before the Japanese took over her homeland, she was already homeless.

In Wuhan, Xiao Hong found out that she was pregnant again. Left alone for months while Duanmu traveled to Chongqing, the wartime Nationalist capital in Sichuan province, she once again experienced poverty, sickness, and depression. Shortly after joining Duanmu in Chongqing, she gave birth to her second child. What happened to the child remains in question: one theory is that the baby was stillborn; another is that, as in the case of her first child, she gave it away.

After two years of being unable to write, Xiao Hong began the autobiographical novel that some critics consider her finest work: *Hulan he zhuan*. Its genesis was the short story she had written in Japan, "Jiazu yiwai de ren"; as more of her childhood memories surfaced, they inspired her to write an expansive history of a time and place that were closest to her heart. She wrote most of *Hulan he zhuan* in Chongqing amid air raids, scarcity, hunger, and sickness. In the spring of 1940 she and Duanmu moved to Hong Kong, where she finished the novel. Published serially in the *Xingzuo fukan* (Constellation Supplement) of the Hong Kong newspaper *Xingzuo ribao* (Constellation Daily) from September to December 1940, it first appeared in book form in 1942, after her death. In this novel, as in *Shangshi jie*, Xiao Hong resists the call of ideology and separates herself from the master narrative of her time. Conceived during her voluntary exile in Japan, written in the wartime capital of Chongqing, and completed in Hong Kong amid poverty and failing health, the novel imagines a world untouched by the violent times; many of the episodes are permeated by beauty and innocence. The literal meaning of the title is "a biography of Hulan River," indicating that the protagonist is a place and the memories associated with it.

The novel is divided into seven episodes, including a montage-style survey of various sites and personalities of the small town of Hulan, a lyrical essay depicting the seasonal rituals that punctuate local life, a melancholy reminiscence of the days the narrator and her grandfather shared in the rear garden of the family compound, and a haunting account of the death of a child bride told from the point of view of the young, innocent narrator. Each episode has its own structure and constructs a unique picture. The narrator's position shifts throughout the work: in some episodes she hides behind the narrative and observes daily life like a local historian; at other moments she emerges as the first-person "I," bringing a sense of immediacy to the flow of memories. These changes and shifts give the novel a musical rhythm. The persona of the narrator, however, is consistent: she is characterized by nostalgia, melancholy, a meticulous sense of time and place, a pervading loneliness and sadness, and a sense of history as it is experienced on a daily basis. The narrator's voice emerges in full force in the short epilogue: "The little town of Hulan River, in earlier days it was where my Granddad lived, and now it is where he is buried. When I was born Granddad was already in his sixties, and by the time I was four or five he was nearly seventy. As I approached the age of twenty Granddad was almost eighty; soon after he reached the age of eighty Granddad was dead." Now, far removed from the time and the place of which she has written, the narrator engages in a final intimate dialogue with her memories: "Do drops of morning dews still gather on the flower-vase stands? Does the noonday sun still send its rays down on the large sunflowers? Do the red clouds at sunset still form into the shape of a horse, only to shift a moment later into the shape of a dog?" (translation by Howard Goldblatt). Xiao Hong ends her novel, as is the Chinese custom, by noting the time and place of the completion of her writing: "December 20, 1940, Hong Kong."

An unprecedented attempt to weave personal history together with the history of a region, *Hulan he zhuan* has presented a dilemma for literary historians of mod-

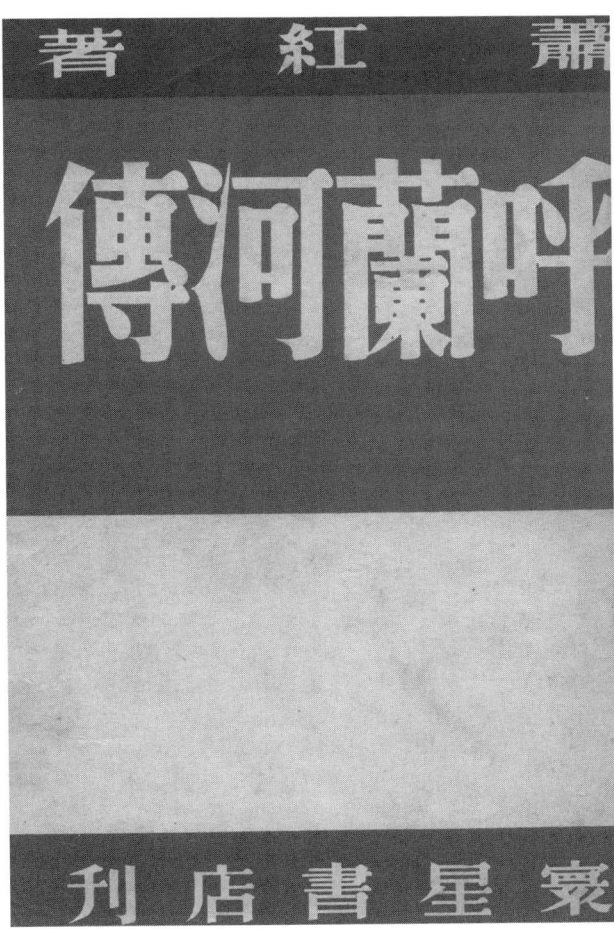

Cover for a 1947 edition of Xiao Hong's posthumously published novel Hulan he zhuan *(1942, A Biography of Hulan River; translated as "Tales of Hulan River," 1979), an evocation of her childhood that some critics consider her finest work (Wason Collection on East Asia–China, Kroch Asia Library, Cornell University)*

ern China. Xiao Hong searched for a voice that was true to the time and yet uniquely hers. She was a rebel but concealed her rebellious spirit beneath a frail sensibility, which caused many critics to characterize her as a quintessentially female writer: in Republican China male critics assumed that women were best suited to and most interested in writing about their domestic and emotional lives. In the latter half of the twentieth century literary historians made Xiao Hong a canonical modern Chinese writer and identified her as among the most important two or three women writers since 1900. Until the mid 1980s scholars in China and abroad favored left-leaning critical realism when writing histories of modern Chinese literature, and Xiao Hong was understood in these terms. Since then some critics have labeled her writing feminist and antipatriarchal. None of these characterizations takes into account Xiao Hong's lifelong struggle to move away from collective causes.

Xiao Hong wrote another narrative set in the imagined homeland she created in *Hulan he zhuan*. The short story "Xiaocheng sanyue" (March in a Small Town; translated as "Spring in a Small Town," 1961), about a young woman's doomed attempt to seek a life outside of her isolated chambers, was published in the Hong Kong literary magazine *Shidai wenxue* (Literature of the Times) in 1941. In 1941 Xiao Hong was also working on *Ma Bole*, a satirical novel set in Qingdao and Shanghai; it was published that year and in an enlarged edition in 1981 that includes the nine chapters of the incomplete "Ma Bole, di er bu" (Ma Bole, Part Two), previously unpublished in book form. In December she was hospitalized for a respiratory condition. She died on 22 January 1942. Her doctors were unable to provide a clear diagnosis of the cause of Xiao Hong's death; various accounts cite the respiratory condition, a stomach ailment, tuberculosis, complications from childbearing, and prolonged depression. Her ashes were buried in the area of Hong Kong known as Repulse Bay.

Ding Ling, a leading leftist and feminist author whom Xiao Hong had met on her travels with Xiao Jun and Duanmu in 1938, wrote "Fengyu zhong yi Xiao Hong" (Remembering Xiao Hong in Wind and Rain) in 1942 after hearing of Xiao Hong's death. In this emotionally charged essay Ding Ling laments the loss of a great talent but blames Xiao Hong for making the wrong choice at a critical moment in Chinese history. Ding Ling did not realize that Xiao Hong had begun to distance herself from the nationalist cause and its advocates long before she separated from Xiao Jun and returned south.

A poem by the modernist poet Dai Wangshu, "Xiao Hong mupan kouzhan" (1944, By Xiao Hong's Grave, a Quatrain), idealizes Xiao Hong's image and illustrates the meaning of her life and career in the literary culture of wartime China. The poem was written after a visit to Xiao Hong's makeshift grave at Repulse Bay at a time when Dai was at a personal and political impasse. Relating his own fate of perpetual exile to that of the young woman author whose resting place was far from her hometown, Dai expresses the faint hope that in death Xiao Hong has found release from the difficulties that everyone in their generation experienced:

Six hours of lonely walk, I arrived
at your grave, to dedicate a bouquet of red camellias
I await the endless darkness of the night
while you lie listening to the gentle flutters of ocean waves.

In her final days Xiao Hong had never expressed a wish to be taken back to her hometown in the northeast. She had, however, indicated to Duanmu that she would like to have her ashes shipped back to Shanghai and buried next to the grave of Lu Xun. This wish was never fulfilled. In August 1957 Xiao Hong's ashes were transferred to Guangzhou (Canton) for permanent burial in Yinhe Public Graveyard.

Letters:

Xiao Hong shujian jicun zhushi lu, edited by Xiao Jun (Harbin: Heilongjiang renmin chubanshe, 1980);

Lu Xun gei Xiao Jun Xiao Hong xinjian zhushi lu, edited by Xiao Jun (Harbin: Heilongjiang renmin chubanshe, 1981).

Bibliographies:

"Xiao Hong zhuzuo bianmu," in *Xiao Hong: "Zhongguo xiandai zuojia xuanji" congshu*, edited by Wang Shu (Hong Kong: Sanlian shudian Xianggang fendian, 1982), pp. 223–240;

"Xiao Hong shengping shiyi kao," in *Xiao Hong quanji*, volume 3 (Harbin: Harbin chubanshe, 1998), pp. 1389–1531.

Biographies:

Luo Binji, *Xiao Hong xiao zhuan* (Shanghai: Jianwen shudian, 1947);

Xiao Feng, *Xiao Hong zhuan* (Tianjin: Baihua wenyi chubanshe, 1980);

Ge Haowen (Howard Goldblatt), *Xiao Hong ping zhuan* (Taibei: Shibao wenhua chuban shiye youxian gongsi, 1980);

Xiao Jun, *Cong Linfen dao Yan'an* (Taiyuan: Shanxi renmin chubanshe, 1983);

Wang Guanquan, ed., *Huainian Xiao Hong* (Harbin: Heilongjiang renmin chubanshe, 1984);

Lu Xiang, *Xiao Hong Xiao Jun wai zhuan* (Harbin: Beifang funü ertong chubanshe, 1986);

Xiao Si, "Loneliness among the Mountain Flowers: Xiao Hong in Hong Kong," translated by Janice Wickeri, *Renditions*, no. 29–30 (1988): 177–181;

Ge Haowen (Howard Goldblatt), *Xiao Hong xin zhuan* (Hong Kong: Joint Publishing Company, 1989);

Li Chonghua, ed., *Hulan xueren shuo Xiao Hong* (Harbin: Harbin chubanshe, 1991);

Zhong Yaoqun, *Duanmu yu Xiao Hong* (Beijing: Zhongguo wenlian chuban gongsi, 1998);

Ji Hongzhen, *Xiao Hong zhuan* (Beijing: Beijing shiyue wenyi chubanshe, 2000);

Ji, ed., *Xiaoxiao luohong* (Beijing: Renmin wenxue chubanshe, 2001).

References:

Marston Anderson, *The Limits of Realism: Chinese Fiction in the Revolutionary Period* (Berkeley: University of California Press, 1990);

Tani Barlow, "Theorizing Women: Funu, Guojia, Jiating (Chinese Women, Chinese State, Chinese Family)," *Genders,* 10 (1991): 132–160;

Barlow, ed., *Gender Politics in Modern China: Writing and Feminism* (Durham, N.C.: Duke University Press, 1993);

Rey Chow, *Woman and Chinese Modernity: The Politics of Reading between West and East* (Minneapolis: University of Minnesota Press, 1991), pp. 128–133;

Ding Ling, "Fengyu zhong yi Xiao Hong," in *Xiaoxiao luohong,* edited by Ji Hongzhen (Beijing: Renmin wenxue chubanshe, 2001), pp. 179–183;

Howard Goldblatt, *Hsiao Hung* (Boston: Twayne, 1976);

Goldblatt, "Life as Art: Xiao Hong and Autobiography," in *Woman and Literature in China,* edited by Anna Gerstlacher and others (Bochum, Germany: Brockmeyer, 1985), pp. 345–363;

Goldblatt, "Lu Xun and Patterns of Literary Sponsorship," in *Lu Xun and His Legacy,* edited by Leo Ou-fan Lee (Berkeley: University of California Press, 1985), pp. 199–215;

Huang Renying, *Dangdai Zhongguo nü zuojia lun* (Shanghai: Guanghua shuju, 1933);

Wendy Larson, *Women and Writing in Modern China* (Stanford, Cal.: Stanford University Press, 1998);

Leo Ou-fan Lee, *The Romantic Generation of Modern Chinese Writers* (Cambridge, Mass.: Harvard University Press, 1973);

Lydia Liu, "The Female Body and Nationalist Discourse: Manchuria in Xiao Hong's *Field of Life and Death,*" in *Body, Subject and Power in China,* edited by Angela Zito and Tani Barlow (Chicago: University of Chicago Press, 1994), pp. 157–177;

Liu, "Invention and Intervention: The Making of a Female Tradition in Modern Chinese Literature," in *From May Fourth to June Fourth: Fiction and Film in Twentieth-Century China,* edited by Ellen Widmer and David Der-wei Wang (Cambridge, Mass.: Harvard University Press, 1993), pp. 194–220;

Liu, *Translingual Practice: Literature, National Culture, and Translated Modernity—China, 1900–1937* (Stanford, Cal.: Stanford University Press, 1995), pp. 199–213;

Meng Yue and Dai Jinhua, *Fuchu lishi dibiao* (Zhengzhou: Henan renmin chubanshe, 1989);

Xiao Hong yanjiu (Harbin: Beifang luncong, 1983);

Yue Gang, "Embodied Spaces of Home: Xiao Hong, Wang Anyi, and Li Ang," in his *The Mouth That Begs: Hunger, Cannibalism, and the Politics of Eating in Modern China* (Durham, N.C.: Duke University Press, 1999), pp. 293–330;

Yu Runqi, ed., *Tang Tao cang shu* (Beijing: Beijing chubanshe, 2004), p. 168;

Zhao Yuan, *Jiannan de xuanze* (Shanghai: Shanghai wenyi chubanshe, 1986).

Xu Dishan
(Luo Huasheng)
(14 February 1893 – 4 August 1941)

Steven Riep
Brigham Young University

BOOKS: *Yuti wenfa dagang* [Outline of Prose Grammar] (Shanghai: Shenghuo shudian, 1921);

Zhuiwang laozhu [The Vain Labors of a Spider], as Luo Huasheng (Shanghai: Shangwu yinshuguan, 1925)—includes "Huanghun hou," translated by J. B. Kyn Yn Yu and E. H. F. Mills as "After Dusk," in *The Tragedy of Ah Qui and Other Modern Chinese Stories* (London: Routledge, 1930), pp. 13–26; "Kuyang shenghua," translated by Sidney Shapiro as "Blooms on a Dried Poplar," *Chinese Literature*, 1 (1957): 63–78; "Shangren fu," translated by William H. Nienhauser as "The Merchant's Wife," in *Modern Chinese Stories and Novellas, 1919–1949*, edited by Joseph S. M. Lau, C. T. Hsia, and Leo Ou-fan Lee (New York: Columbia University Press, 1981), pp. 41–50; "Zhuiwang laozhu," translated by Douglas McComber as "The Web-Mending Toiling Spider," in his "Hsu Ti-shan and the Search for Identity: Individuals and Families in the Short Stories of Luo Hua Sheng (1894–1941)," dissertation, University of California, Berkeley, 1980, pp. 150–177;

Kongshan lingyu [Timely Rain on an Empty Mountain], as Luo (Shanghai: Shangwu yinshuguan, 1925);

Wufa toudi zhi youjian [Letters That Could Not Be Sent Anywhere], as Luo (Beijing: Beijing wenhua shushe, 1927);

Yindu wenxue [Indian Literature] (Shanghai: Shangwu yinshuguan, 1930);

Da zhong ji: Yapian zhanzheng qian Zhong Ying jiaoshe shiliao [Meeting Halfway: Historical Materials on Negotiations between China and England before the Opium War] (Shanghai: Shangwu yinshuguan, 1931);

Fozang zimu yinde: Combined Indices to the Authors and Titles of Books and Chapters in Four Collections of Buddhistic Literature, 3 volumes, Harvard-Yenching Institute Sinological Index Series, no. 11 (Beiping: Gaichu, 1933);

Xu Dishan (from Xu Dishan, *edited by Zhou Junsong and Xiang Yunxiu, 1984; Neilson Library–East Asian Collection, Smith College)*

Jiefangzhe [The Liberator], as Luo (Beiping: Xingyuntang shuju, 1933)—includes "Zai Fei zongli de ketingli," translated by Gladys Yang as "Director Fei's Reception Room," *Chinese Literature*, 9 (1964): 64–73;

Daojiao shi [A History of Daoism] (Shanghai: Shangwu yinshuguan, 1934);

Chuntao [Spring Peach] (Shanghai: Shenghuo shudian, 1935)–title story translated by Shapiro as "Big Sister Liu," *Chinese Literature*, 1 (1957): 79-96;

Fuji mixin de yanjiu [Research on the Superstitious Belief of the Planchette] (Shanghai: Shangwu yinshuguan, 1941);

Guocui yu guoxue [Chinese National Essence and National Culture] (Shanghai: Shangwu yinshuguan, 1946);

Zagan ji [Miscellaneous Thoughts], as Luo, edited by Zhou Sisong (Shanghai: Shangwu yinshuguan, 1946);

Weichao zhuijian [Letters from an Endangered Nest], edited by Zheng Zhenduo (Shanghai: Shangwu yinshuguan, 1947)–includes "Tieyu de sai," translated by Yang as "The Iron Fish with Gills," *Chinese Literature*, 9 (1964): 73-84; and "Yuguan," translated by Cecile Chu-chin Sun as "Yü-kuan" in *Modern Chinese Stories and Novellas, 1919-1949*, pp. 51-87;

Luo Huasheng wenji [The Collected Works of Luo Huasheng], 5 volumes (Taibei: Qiming shuju, 1957).

Collections: *Luo Huasheng chuangzuo xuan* [A Selection of Luo Huasheng's Work] (Shanghai: Shanghai fanggu shudian, 1936);

Xu Dishan yuwen lunwen ji [Xu Dishan's Treatises on the Chinese Language] (Xianggang: Xinwenzi xuehui, 1941);

Xu Dishan xuanji [Selected Works by Xu Dishan] (Beijing: Kaiming shudian, 1951);

Xu Dishan xuanji [The Selected Works of Xu Dishan], 2 volumes (Beijing: Renmin wenxue chubanshe, 1958);

Xu Dishan xiaoshuo xuan [The Selected Fiction of Xu Dishan], edited by Yang Mu (Taibei: Hongfan shudian, 1984);

Xu Dishan, edited by Zhou Junsong and Xiang Yunxiu (Hong Kong: Sanlian shudian, 1984);

Xu Dishan sanwen quanbian [The Complete Essays of Xu Dishan], edited by Chen Pingyuan (Hangzhou: Zhejiang wenyi chubanshe, 1992);

Xu Dishan wenji [The Collected Works of Xu Dishan], 2 volumes, edited by Gao Wei (Beijing: Xinhua chubanshe, 1998).

PLAY PRODUCTION: *Nü guoshi* [The Woman Patriot], as Luo Huasheng, Hong Kong, Hong Kong University, 1938.

TRANSLATIONS: *Mengjiala minjian gushi* [Popular Bengali Stories] (Shanghai: Shangwu yinshuguan, 1929);

Ershi ye wen [Questions Asked over Twenty Nights] (Beijing: Zuojia chubanshe, 1955);

Taiyang de xiajiang [The Setting Sun] (Beijing: Zuojia chubanshe, 1956).

An accomplished fiction writer, poet, and essayist and a founding member of the Wenxue yanjiu hui (Literary Research Association), Xu Dishan was a pioneer in the development of new literature in China. He was also a scholar of Asian religions and compiled a history of Daoism and an index to Buddhist texts. He lived and studied in Burma (today Myanmar) and India, which serve as settings for his early works; translated several collections of Indian literature; and wrote articles on the influence of Indian culture on China, particularly on Chinese drama. He distinguished himself by arguing for the continued relevance of religious principles and values such as redemption, compassion, and charity in an age when most authors dismissed religion as superstition. His fiction explores the nexus of the traditional and the modern in the May Fourth period and the two decades that followed it.

Born on 14 February 1893 in Tainan, Taiwan, Xu was named Xu Zankun at birth. He was the fourth of eight children (six boys and two girls) of Xu Nanying, a scholar and government official, and Wu Shen. In 1895 China lost the first Sino-Japanese War and ceded Taiwan to Japan, and Xu Nanying moved his family to Fujian province; two years later they relocated to Guangdong province. Xu Zankun studied in private academies and with tutors. In 1911 he took a position at a teachers' school in Qiangzhou Zhangzhou, Fujian province. Two years later he moved to Rangoon, Burma, to teach in a Chinese school. By convention he would have taken his *zi* (style name) at age twenty; he chose Dishan. In 1915 he returned to China, where he taught at the Huaying Middle School and at the Second Fujian Provincial Teacher's College in Qiangzhou. He joined a Christian sect, the Fujian London Church, in 1916.

In 1917 Xu began studying literature at Yenching (Yanjing) University in Beijing. He returned to Fujian in early 1918 to marry Lin Yuesen from Taizhong, Taiwan; they had a daughter later that year. Lin lived with Xu's family while her husband continued his studies at Yenching University. With the rise of the May Fourth Movement in 1919, Xu participated in and organized student associations and meetings. He received his bachelor's degree in 1920 and enrolled in Yenching University's seminary to study comparative religion. In October he went back to Fujian to bring his wife and daughter to Beijing; his wife died of an illness en route.

Xu's unusual style of dress and grooming–he favored a long gown of his own design, wore his hair long, and grew a goatee–earned him a reputation as an eccentric. He edited the journal *Xin shehui xunkan* (New

Xu (back row, fourth from right) and other founding members of the Wenxue yanjiu hui (Literary Research Association) on 4 January 1921. Huang Ying, who later adopted the pen name Lu Yin, is in the front row, third from left; Guo Mengliang, whom Lu Yin married in 1923, is at the right end of the front row (from Zhongguo dabaike quanshu zongbianji weiyuanhui, ed., Zhongguo wenxue, volume 2, 1986; Collection of Thomas Moran).

Society Thrice Monthly) with Zheng Zhenduo and Qu Qiubai; the first issue appeared on 1 November 1919 and the last–the nineteenth–on 1 May 1920. In 1921 he, Zheng, Mao Dun (Shen Yanbing), and Ye Shaojun were among the founders of the Wenxue yanjiu hui, a pioneering literary society of the May Fourth period. The association assumed editorial responsibility for the magazine *Xiaoshuo yuebao* (Short Story Monthly), in which Xu published his first stories later that year under the pen name Luo Huasheng.

Xu's autobiographical essay "Luohuasheng," published in *Xiaoshuo yuebao* in 1922 and collected in his *Kongshan lingyu* (Timely Rain on an Empty Mountain) in 1925, is perhaps his most frequently anthologized and widely read work in China, Taiwan, and Hong Kong. The title can be read either as "Peanuts" or as the pen name under which he published virtually all of his creative writing. In the essay he recalls an incident in his youth when his family gathered to eat the peanuts they had grown in their yard. Xu's father asked the children to tell him the good qualities peanuts possess; the children replied that they smell good, can be made into oil, and–Xu's own answer–are affordable and taste good. The father offered another attribute: unlike showier fruits, such as apples and peaches, the peanut grows underground; only after harvest can one judge the quality of the peanuts a plant produces. He reminded the children that he expected them, like a peanut plant, to be productive without being showy. Xu and his siblings assented to their father's call for hard work and humility, the central theme of the essay.

Critics hold diverse opinions as to the quality of Xu's fiction, but they agree that his stories have a style that is distinct from that of any of his contemporaries. His early works share exotic South and Southeast Asian settings, religious themes and imagery, and strong female protagonists and comparatively weak male supporting characters. His first story, "Mingming niao" (Birds Fated for Each Other), published in 1921 in *Xiaoshuo yuebao* and collected in *Zhuiwang laozhu* (1925, The Vain Labors of a Spider), is set in Burma under British colonial rule. The teenagers Jialing and Minming, classmates at a Buddhist school, want to marry, but Jialing's aristocratic father insists that he become a Buddhist monk, while Minming's father wants her to perform in the troupe he manages. Minming's father hires a sorcerer to cast a spell to break up the relationship. Minming discovers the plan, flees to her room in tears, then confronts her father and drives the sorcerer away. The next morning she is entranced by a light emanating from the Shwedegon Pagoda, one of the most sacred Buddhist sites in Burma. Transported in a vision to Nirvana, she becomes enlightened as to the uncertainty and impermanence of romantic love. On the night of the Nirvana Festival she tells Jialing about her experience. Believing that they will enter Nirvana if they commit suicide, they drown themselves in a nearby lake.

Of the two lovers, Minming is the focus of the story. She takes the initiative in expressing her love for Jialing in song; she uncovers her father's attempt to break up their relationship, confronts him, and drives the sorcerer away; and she dreams of Nirvana and shares her experiences with Jialing, who agrees to follow her without argument. She ponders, prays, and acts, while he simply follows her lead.

"Mingming niao" touches on many of the conflicts common in May Fourth–era literature. The contrast between traditional ways and modern practices is seen in Jialing's father's attempt to dissuade his son from entering a Western school; he relents only when Jialing agrees to attend one that respects Burmese culture. The two youths forge a relationship based on mutual affection rather than on family arrangements, which leads to conflicts with their parents. Xu also offers a critique of superstition in his references to the sorcerer and to the incompatibility of the lovers' horoscopes, which, according to both Burmese and Chinese custom, would preclude any possibility of marriage. But whereas May Fourth writers tended to view romantic love as superior to custom and familial obligations, Xu has Minming discover that enlightenment surpasses even love, which is transitory. Where most authors would have dismissed Buddhism along with tradition and superstition, Xu respects religion and the desire for transcendence. At the end of the story he reconciles the romantic and religious themes by noting that Minming and Jialing are "birds fated for each other" and comparing their entry into the lake to a newly married couple "entering the bridal chamber hand in hand."

By setting "Mingming niao" in Burma, a non-Chinese yet still Asian cultural milieu, Xu gives his readers a new perspective on contemporary social issues. He also resists simple conclusions about the superiority of the modern over the traditional or the foreign over the native: while Western education has its place, it must respect traditional Burmese culture. Westerners threaten to destroy the traditional cultural fabric not only by establishing new schools but also by removing sacred relics from Mandalay and posting troops at the Shwedegon Pagoda. Xu tries to find a middle ground that acknowledges the benefits and costs of both the new and the old ways of life. He also distinguishes religion from superstition so that he can explore the principles and values of the former, while critiquing the latter. Much of Xu's fiction considers the role of religion in the individual's search for meaning and contentment.

Xu's second story, "Shangren fu" (translated as "The Merchant's Wife," 1981), also appeared in *Xiaoshuo yuebao* in 1921. When her husband gambles away his store in Fujian, Xiguan gives him some of her jewelry so that he can start a new business in Singapore. After waiting ten years for him to return for her, she goes to Singapore and discovers that he has made a fortune and taken a Malaysian wife. After a week, Xiguan is sold to Ahuja, a Muslim Indian cloth merchant, as his sixth wife. Ahuja takes her to his home in Madras, where she develops a friendship with his third wife. The third wife not only teaches her to read Bengali and Arabic and to survive in a Muslim household but also assists her in giving birth to a son. After Ahuja's death, Xiguan flees the household with her child, sells the diamond nose ring she had to wear as Ahuja's wife, purchases a home with the money, gets an education, and becomes a schoolteacher. The narrator, a Chinese fellow ship passenger in whom Xiguan confides, treats her with smug condescension at first but comes to respect her when he hears her story. When the narrator characterizes Xiguan's life as one of tragedy and suffering, she tells him to save his pity. Life, she believes, is inevitably filled with pain; that pain can become meaningful and even beneficial in retrospect, when one can see one's accomplishments. She rejects the fatalism of Islam and Hinduism and embraces the compassion and charity found in Buddhism and Christianity; a mixture of the principles of the latter two religions defines her view of life as suffering leading to knowledge, patience, and courage, which give one hope for the future. Significantly, Xiguan's liberation takes place outside of China: she learns to read, buys a home, goes to school, and takes a job in India. She cannot read Chinese and considers herself Indian. For her, independence can only exist outside the Chinese cultural setting—a commentary on the lack of freedom available to women in China in the May Fourth period.

In 1922 Xu received his bachelor's degree in religious studies from Yenching University. The following year he entered Columbia University in New York City, where he earned his master's degree in comparative religion and the history of religion in 1924. He then studied Indian philosophy, Sanskrit, religious history, and folklore at the University of Oxford. He earned a bachelor's degree in 1926, and, after spending almost a year in India studying Sanskrit, Buddhism, and Indian literature, he returned to China and joined the faculty at his alma mater, Yenching University. During this period he continued to publish stories, poems, and

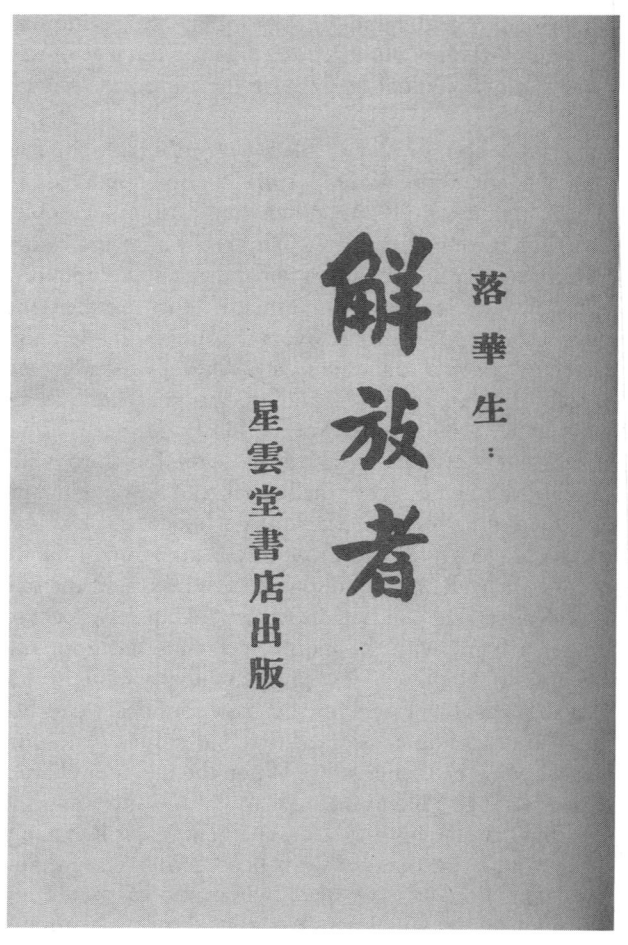

Cover for Xu's short-story collection Jiefangzhe (The Liberator), published in 1933 (Wason Collection on East Asia–China, Kroch Asia Library, Cornell University)

essays in *Xiaoshuo yuebao;* his stories were collected in *Zhuiwang laozhu* and his essays in *Kongshan lingyu*. He also wrote articles on Indian and Iranian influences on Chinese literature, prepared an anthology of Indian fiction in Chinese translation (1929), published a monograph on Indian literature (1930), compiled a collection of English-language materials on the Opium Wars (1931), and prepared an index to Buddhist sacred texts (1933). In 1929 he married Zhou Sisong; they had a son and a daughter.

In the late 1920s and the early 1930s Xu wrote satires and critiques of Republican China's urban society, its manners, and the corruption that was rampant during the period. "Zai Fei zongli de ketingli" (1928; translated as "Director Fei's Reception Room," 1964) describes at length the room in which the corrupt businessman Director Fei greets his guests. The carefully displayed copies of Confucian classical texts, calligraphy by eminent intellectuals, and scrolls bearing politically correct maxims are intended to convince visitors that Fei is a gentleman of the highest scholarly attainment and noblest propriety. In fact, the tongue-in-cheek narrative reveals, he is an opium addict, has several concubines, and makes a tidy profit from a factory that purportedly exists to provide employment and charity to women in need. Carefully placed bribes to Nationalist government officials and police keep his corrupt commercial empire in operation. In "San boshi" (1931, The Three Ph.D.s) Xu exposes the deception practiced by some members of the educated elite to impress women and potential employers: Chinese students go to America to earn bogus doctorates with dissertations on such topics as the origin of mah-jongg tiles and the ingredients in various Chinese foods. Xu collected these stories in *Jiefangzhe* (1933, The Liberator).

Xu rose to the rank of professor at Yenching University and also taught at Beijing and Qinghua universities. His scholarly projects included translations of Indian literature (1929, 1955, and 1956), two volumes of which appeared posthumously; the first volume of a never-completed comprehensive history of Daoism in China (1934); and a series of articles on the history of Chinese women's clothing. In 1935 he accepted an offer to become the first professor of Chinese at the University of Hong Kong. His responsibilities included teaching Confucian texts and the literature of the Tang and Song dynasties. After the outbreak of the second Sino-Japanese War in 1937, he engaged in patriotic and resistance activities. These activities included writing a one-act historical spoken drama, *Nü guoshi* (1938, Woman of the Nation), for performance by the University of Hong Kong's Women Student Association. During this period he wrote several other plays in modern standard Chinese (Mandarin) and in Cantonese. He also promoted Chinese language reform, calling for the adoption of romanization as a means to achieve universal literacy. He also produced a story that combines the religious and satirical strains of his earlier writing and has been widely praised as his masterpiece.

Published in 1939 in the magazine *Dafeng* (The Wind), "Yüguan" (translated as "Yü-kuan," 1981) is Xu's longest work of fiction and includes his most fully developed protagonist. His maturity as a writer emerges in his balanced critique of Christianity in China and in his depiction of a woman's struggles to live a meaningful life in an era of political and social upheaval. The title character's husband, a sailor, is killed in combat at the beginning of the first Sino-Japanese War in 1894, leaving her to bring up their son alone. To provide for the two of them and help her son get an education, she accepts a job with a foreign Christian minister; later she agrees to join and proselytize for his church. At heart, however, she remains devoted to her traditional culture: while she struggles to accept the finer points of Christian doctrine, she maintains her belief in ghosts, in the power of classical Chinese philosophical and religious texts to exorcize them, and in ancestor worship. She devotes much of her energy to seeing that her son becomes successful so that he can take care of her in her old age and build a memorial to her as a model Confucian woman and mother after she dies. She spends her savings to pay for his wedding but fails to receive the respect she thinks she deserves from her new daughter-in-law. After the son's wife dies, he goes abroad to study; Yuguan anxiously awaits for him to return and care for her. In the meantime she continues her missionary work, even though she lacks a solid knowledge of and belief in the religious principles she teaches. Yet, in spite of her doubts, Yuguan has a positive impact on the villagers she teaches and on the village women she protects from the Nationalist soldiers who want to rape them during the second war with Japan. She preaches to the women and the soldiers, recites verses from the Bible, appeals to their Confucian and Christian senses of decency, and persuades the Chinese soldiers that they should treat the women as their sisters. As a result, the soldiers treat the women with respect and decency and protect them from the predations of the enemy. Ultimately, she realizes that her missionary work, like her desire for her son's support, is motivated by a selfish hunger for reward. As the story concludes, Yuguan finds fulfillment by dedicating herself to serving the villagers she has come to love and respect and by aiding the friends who have supported her through the years.

"Yuguan" brings together Xu's interest in religion and the individual's quest for spiritual enlightenment, hallmarks of his early stories, with the satiric style found in his later works. While he pokes fun at the difficulty Yuguan has in understanding and accepting her "foreign" faith, he also criticizes the foreign clergymen and their families who do not fully understand their own doctrine and fail at times to practice the principles they preach. He never reduces the protagonist's religious quest to a struggle in which Western religion simply displaces traditional Chinese beliefs. Yuguan develops her own religious views, which combine ancestor worship and Chinese folk practices with Christian values. By this time Xu's theological interest had shifted away from the major organized religions toward a personal synthesis of beliefs that drew on a variety of native and nonnative sources.

Xu's last story, "Tieyu de sai" (The Gills of the Iron Fish; translated as "The Iron Fish with Gills," 1964), which originally appeared in the February 1941 issue of *Dafeng*, is a social satire much like his works of the late 1920s and early 1930s. Despite having studied

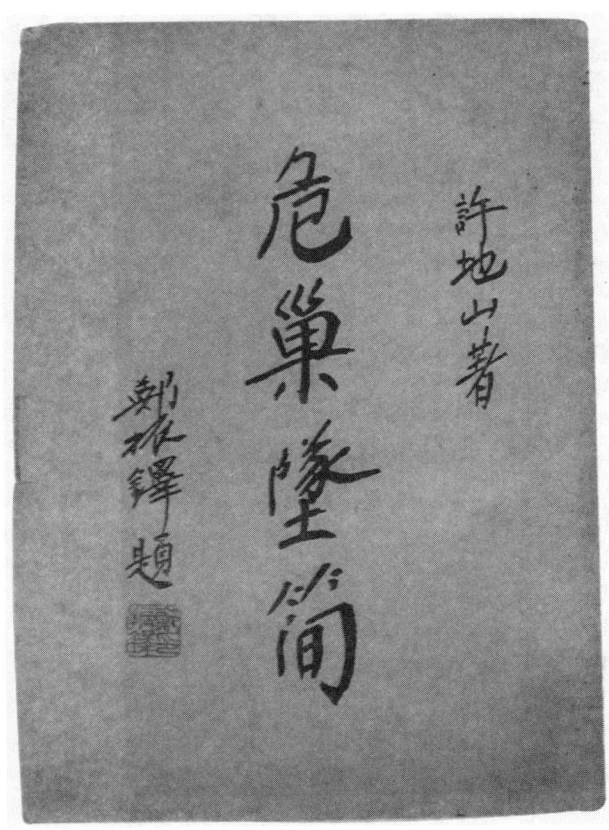

Cover for Weichao zhuijian *(1947, Letters from an Endangered Nest), a collection of Xu's final stories posthumously published by his friend Zheng Zhenduo (from Yu Runqi, ed.,* Tang Tao cang shu, *2004; Bruccoli Clark Layman Archives)*

abroad, the protagonist is never given a chance to put his talents to use but works as a factory manager or as a weapons repairman. That he has invented a revolutionary submarine and an underwater breathing device that could help the Chinese win the war against Japan remains known only to him and a friend. When the Japanese attack southern China, he flees inland by ship to Guangxi. As he disembarks, he drops the prototype of his iron gill into the ocean; he jumps into the water to save it and drowns. "Tieyu de sai" exposes the Nationalists' blindness to valuable ideas and lack of respect for those who discover and develop them.

Xu Dishan died in Hong Kong of a heart attack on 4 August 1941. His final stories were collected by his friend Zheng as *Weichao zhuijian* (1947, Letters from an Endangered Nest). He also left behind poetry and extensive writings on religion, language reform, and South Asian literature and culture. While not a prolific author, Xu distinguished himself from other May Fourth–era writers with his focus on non-Chinese settings as backgrounds for analyzing social problems, his balanced treatment of the significance of religion in a modernizing China, and his strong women protagonists. His blending of social satire with meditations on the importance of compassion, mercy, and the individual's search for enlightenment and redemption make his works worth reading today.

Bibliography:

Wang Sheng, "Xu Dishan zhuyi mulu jianbian," in *Xu Dishan pingzhuan,* edited by Wang Sheng (Nanjing: Nanjing chubanshe, 1989), pp. 93–98.

Biography:

Wang Sheng, ed., *Xu Dishan pingzhuan* (Nanjing: Nanjing chubanshe, 1989).

References:

C. T. Hsia, "Lo Hua-sheng (1893–1941)," in his *A History of Modern Chinese Fiction,* third edition (Bloomington & Indianapolis: Indiana University Press, 1999), pp. 84–92;

Douglas Adrian McComber, "Hsu Ti-shan and the Search for Identity: Individuals and Families in the Short Stories of Luo Hua Sheng (1894–1941)," dissertation, University of California, Berkeley, 1980;

Steven L. Riep, "Religion Reconsidered: Redemption and Women's Emancipation in Xu Dishan's 'The Merchant's Wife' and 'Yuguan,'" *Literature and Belief,* 24, nos. 1–2 (2004): 101–115;

Lewis Stewart Robinson, *Double-Edged Sword: Christianity and 20th Century Chinese Fiction* (Hong Kong: Tao Fong Shan Ecumenical Centre, 1986), pp. 35–60, 183–201;

Robinson, "The Stories of Hsu Ti-shan: Literature for Life," M.A. thesis, University of California, Berkeley, 1977;

Robinson, "'Yü-kuan': The Spiritual Testament of Hsü Ti-shan," *Tamkang Review,* 8 (October 1977): 147–167;

Yu Runqi, ed., *Tang Tao cang shu* (Beijing: Beijing chubanshe, 2004), p. 203;

Zhongguo dabaike quanshu zongbianji weiyuanhui, ed., *Zhongguo wenxue,* volume 2 (Beijing & Shanghai: Zhongguo dabaike quanshu chubanshe, (1986);

Zhou Sisong and Xiang Yunxiu, *Xu Dishan* (Taibei: Shulin chuban youxian gongsi, 1992);

Zhu Chuanyu, *Xu Dishan yanjiu ziliao* (Taibei: Tianyi chubanshe, 1981).

Xu Zhenya

(5 August 1889 – July? 1937)

Jianhua Chen
Hong Kong University of Science and Technology

BOOKS: *Yuli hun* [Jade Pear Spirit] (Shanghai: Minquan chubanbu, 1913); revised as *Xuehong leishi* [A Sad History of the Snow and the Swan] (Shanghai: Zhenxiage, 1916);

Zhenya langmo [The Wasted Ink of Zhenya] (Shanghai: Xiaoshuo congbao she, 1915);

Shuanghuan ji [Two Maids] (Shanghai: Xiaoshuo congbao she, 1916);

Huayue chidu [Model Correspondence of Flower and Moon], annotated by Dong Na (Shanghai: Xiaoshuo congbao she, 1917; revised, Shanghai: Xiaoshuo congbao she, 1920);

Qinghai zhinan [A Guide on the Sea of Love] (Shanghai: Xiaoshuo congbao she, 1917);

Yu zhi qi [My Wife] (Shanghai: Xiaoshuo congbao she, 1917);

Langui hen [Regrets of the Boudoir] (Shanghai: Xiaoshuo congbao she, 1918);

Chunyan bishi [A Secret History of the Fatal Women] (Shanghai: Xinxin shushe, 1921);

Yan yan lihun ji [The Swallow and the Wild Goose: The Record of a Tragic Death] (Shanghai: Shijie shuju, 1924);

Yu zhi fu [My Husband], 2 volumes (Shanghai: Xiaoshuo shijieshe, 1927);

Kegu xiangsi ji [Eternal Longing for Love] (Shanghai: Qinghua shuju, 1927);

Rangxu ji [The Given-Away Son-in-Law] (Shanghai: Qinghua shuju, 1929);

Guang xie duo [Enlarged Collection of Comic Anecdotes] (Shanghai: Dazhong shuju, 1934);

Yi zi yi lei [One Word, One Tear] (Hong Kong: Wuguitang, 1936);

Zhenya Langmo xuji [The Wasted Ink of Zhenya, Continued] (Shanghai: Zhenxiage, n.d.);

Zhenya Langmo sanji [The Wasted Ink of Zhenya, Volume 3] (Shanghai: Dazhong shuju, n.d.);

Zhenya Langmo siji [The Wasted Ink of Zhenya, Volume 4] (Shanghai: Dazhong shuju, n.d.).

Xu Zhenya (photograph from Hsing-kuang *[Hong Kong], no. 2, 1923; in E. Perry Link Jr.,* Mandarin Ducks and Butterflies: Popular Fiction in Early Twentieth-Century Chinese Cities, *1981; Collection of Thomas Moran)*

SELECTED PERIODICAL PUBLICATION–UNCOLLECTED: "Baiyang shuaicao qui fan hun" [The Grieving Ghosts among the White Poplar and Withered Grass], *Xiaoshuo congbao* (1915).

Ducks and butterflies are symbols of romantic fidelity and gave their name to a genre of popular fiction, Yuanyang hudie pai xiaoshuo (Mandarin Ducks and Butterflies School of Fiction), that originated in a wave of sentimental romances published in Shanghai in the 1910s. The boom in Mandarin Ducks and Butterflies fiction was set off by Xu Zhenya's novel *Yuli hun* (1913, Jade Pear Spirit). Xu influenced many other writers not only with *Yuli hun* and his other novels of tragic love but also as an editor and publisher. He edited a series of periodicals and from 1918 to 1934 owned a publishing house. The main contributors to the journals, such as Wu Shuangre, Yu Tianfen, and Yao Min'ai, came, like Xu, from Changshu county, a prosperous "land of fish and rice" in southern Jiangsu province. They made important contributions to the development of popular genres of the 1910s and early 1920s, including tragic romance, comic romance, the historical novel, and detective fiction. Their writing was culturally and morally conservative, particularly from the perspective of the iconoclastic May Fourth generation that came of age in the late 1910s. They—especially Xu—did innovate, but they wrote in classical Chinese (albeit the "new style" classical Chinese that developed in the late nineteenth century), favoring four-six parallel prose (alternating clauses of four and six Chinese characters), a style that was nostalgic for the literary elegance born in the Six Dynasties period (222–589).

Xu was born Xu Jue on 5 August 1889 in Changshu; he was the third of three children of Xu Maosheng, a Confucian scholar who was also talented in poetry and music. Unsuccessful in the imperial examinations, the usual path to a career as a government official, Xu Maosheng devoted himself to educating his two sons, Xu Jue and Xu Jue's elder brother, Xu Xiaoyao. A child prodigy, Xu Jue started studying the classics at age five and devoted most of his time to reading literature; he was able to compose respectable poetry when he was ten. In 1903 he was sent to a normal school; the following year he began teaching in a school near his home. In 1909 he took a teaching job at a primary school in Wuxi, the administrative seat of Changshu county. Around this time he adopted the *zi* (style name) Zhenya, which can be read to mean "pillowing" *(zhen)* one's head on "Asia" *(Ya* [from *Yazhou]*). He explains in the essay "Zhenya shiming" (The Implications of Zhenya), a short, playful essay that is highly allusive and infused with black humor, that when he rests his head on the imaginary "pillow" of Asia, he is dreaming; and yet, as if awake, he can see people going about their daily lives; likewise, after he wakes up, he can see what people are dreaming. His "pillow of Asia" looks normal, with space only for his head, but it is also limitless and can accommodate hundreds of thousands of heads. It brings magic to, and affects the nature of, his dreams: a pillow of lotus flowers brings dreams of romantic love; a pillow of stone, a dream of a beautiful landscape; and a dragon pillow, dreams of hurricanes and thunderstorms. "On my pillow," says Xu, "I dream of demons and evils who appear and transform before me until I am awakened by the chimes of freedom." The essay is included in his collection *Zhenya langmo* (1915, The Wasted Ink of Zhenya).

According to published remarks by Xu, *Yuli hun* is based on events in his life that took place while he was teaching in Wuxi. He was hired by a man named Cai Yinting to tutor Cai's grandson, moved in with the Cai family, and fell in love with Chen Peifen, his pupil's widowed mother. Since widows were forbidden by custom to remarry, the conventional wisdom has been that Chen introduced Xu to her sister-in-law, Cai Ruizhu, to free herself from Xu's courtship. Xu married Cai Ruizhu at the end of 1910. Xu, however, hints that his relationship with Chen was not as pure as that between He Mengxia and Li Niang in his novel. Moreover, in the 1990s the scholar Shi Meng discovered love letters from Chen to Xu in which Chen expresses herself boldly and makes it clear that she and Xu met frequently in 1909 and 1910.

By 1912 Xu and his brother Xu Xiaoyao, who had taken the style name Xu Tianxiao, were living in Shanghai and editing *Minquan bao* (People's Rights Journal), a political newspaper devoted to attacking Yuan Shikai, the authoritarian first president of the Republic of China. *Yuli hun* was serialized in *Minquan bao* from June 1912 to June 1913. *Minquan bao* was banned in 1913, and Xu became the chief editor of *Xiaoshuo congbao* (Fiction Miscellany).

In *Yuli hun* He Mengxia, a young teacher, is hired as a live-in tutor to an eight-year-old boy, Penglang. Penglang's mother, Bai Liying, called Li Niang (Lady Pear Blossom), is a young, beautiful widow; she and her son live in her father-in-law's household. He Mengxia and Li Niang fall in love. Restricted by traditional norms, they must communicate secretly by exchanging letters via Penglang. As their passion—which remains entirely chaste—grows, they suffer acutely. No widow in the moral universe in which Li Niang lives could even begin to consider remarrying, and she knows that He Mengxia is wasting his talents and squandering his future on a love that cannot be. To extricate herself from this dilemma she proposes that Mengxia marry her sixteen-year-old sister-in-law, Yunqian, but he rejects the idea. After additional complications and great emotional drama, Li Niang commits suicide by refusing to eat or, when she falls ill with tuberculosis, to take medicine. Yunqian, who has emotional and intellectual conflicts of her own, dies soon afterward. The grief-stricken He Mengxia travels to Japan to study, as Li Niang had wanted him to do. In

1911 he joins the revolution against the Qing dynasty and dies in battle.

Yuli hun brought Xu immediate fame. Republished in book form in 1913, it sold twenty thousand copies within two years; counting the many unauthorized editions, hundreds of thousands of copies were sold. The novel touched a nerve with youth at a time when Western ideas of free love and choice in marriage were beginning to spread in China, because it questioned patriarchal authority and the custom of arranged marriage and spoke up for the legitimacy of the romantic leanings of the individual heart. The popularity of the novel also rested on its sophisticated style and artistry. *Yuli hun* inherits the long sentimental-erotic tradition of Chinese literature, from lyrical love ballads in classical poetry to romances in vernacular drama and fiction, and is firmly within the conventions of *yanqing xiaoshuo* (romantic novels) and *aiqing xiaoshuo* (novels of tragic love), which celebrated the nobility of ill-fated love. Its classical language toys with the rhetorical devices of parallelism and poetic allusion. It appealed to the conservative aesthetic tastes of readers of popular fiction, while also including references to, and narrative techniques from, Western literary works such as William Shakespeare's *Romeo and Juliet* (circa 1595–1596) and Alexandre Dumas *fils*'s *La Dame aux camélias* (1852; translated as *The Lady with the Camellias,* 1887), both of which had been introduced to Chinese readers in translations by Lin Shu. For all its seeming traditionalism, *Yuli hun* is recognizably modern in the way that it reveals the inner world of its protagonists and builds to a climax of considerable psychological intensity. It was republished many times in Shanghai over the next two decades and also published in Hong Kong and Singapore. A 1933 vernacular Chinese translation of the novel widened its impact still further. It was also adapted for the stage and made into a movie.

In the mid to late 1910s the Chinese intellectual class was disillusioned by the failure of the new republic to bring the order and prosperity to the country that the 1911 revolution had promised. In contrast to the sentimental bent of his fiction, Xu's many essays for newspapers and periodicals are tough-minded, target political and social evils, and display his talents for keen observation, trenchant criticism, and wicked satire and humor. "Shuizu geming ji" (A Record of the Revolution in the World of Aquatic Animals), for example, is a political animal allegory—George Orwell's *Animal Farm* (1945) on a much smaller scale. Xu poignantly mocks the 1911 revolution for changing only the form rather than the fact of authoritarian rule: after the revolution, the "aquatic world" is as dark and farcical as ever. The essay concludes, "Ha ha, even in such a world of cold-blooded animals a revolution was called for, and the kind of revolution called for succeeded. The greedy whale became the Great President and all the officials he hired were his old cronies. While happily escaping from the dictator Dragon King, how could you have expected to fall into the mouth of the tyrannical whale?" In "Feiren hui canguan ji" (A Visit to a Meeting of Disabled Men) Xu depicts a gathering of blind, mute, lame, and hunchbacked men who feel that they are superior to everyone else. Each makes a speech that is both outrageously funny and poignantly critical of social and political absurdities. For example, a crippled man ridicules women who are obsessed with footbinding and also the president, who says that he wants to walk like a dragon—a bold reference to Yuan, who tried to make himself emperor. The essay ends by praising the disabled as wiser and purer in heart than the powerful men who govern them. Both essays are included in *Zhenya langmo*.

In Xu's short story "Baiyang shuaicao gui fan hun" (The Grieving Ghosts among the White Poplar and Withered Grass), published in *Xiaoshuo congbao* in 1915, two brothers filled with Chinese nationalistic pride join the 1911 revolution against the Manchu Qing dynasty; one dies in a battle, and the other loses an arm and a leg. The latter comes home to find only his mother there; his father has gone to look for his sons. Soon they learn that the father has died. Son and mother live in poverty until the son is hired by a rich man to operate a machine. Happy to have the job, he is unaware that he is, in fact, working for an antigovernment party and is making bombs. Soon he is arrested, sentenced to death, and executed. The story ends with his mother refusing to eat because she wants to die. The unremitting succession of horror and death is manipulative of the reader's emotions, but the story is notable as a rare example of fiction of the time that reveals what the revolution of 1911 meant to ordinary people.

To mollify conservative critics who decried the "indecent" depiction of a widow's love affair in *Yuli hun,* Xu revised the work as "He Mengxia riji" (The Diary of He Mengxia) and serialized it in eighteen issues of *Xiaoshuo congbao* from May 1914 through January 1916. Perry Link argues that another reason Xu rewrote *Yuli hun* was that all of the profit from the sale of his first book went to the publisher; Xu made no money beyond his initial fee for the serialization of the work. Xu owned and published his second novel himself. This radical revision of *Yuli hun,* retitled *Xuehong leishi* (A Sad History of the Snow and the Swan) when it was published as a book in 1916, changes the third-person narration of the original into a first-person diary kept by He Mengxia. The commentary Xu attached to it

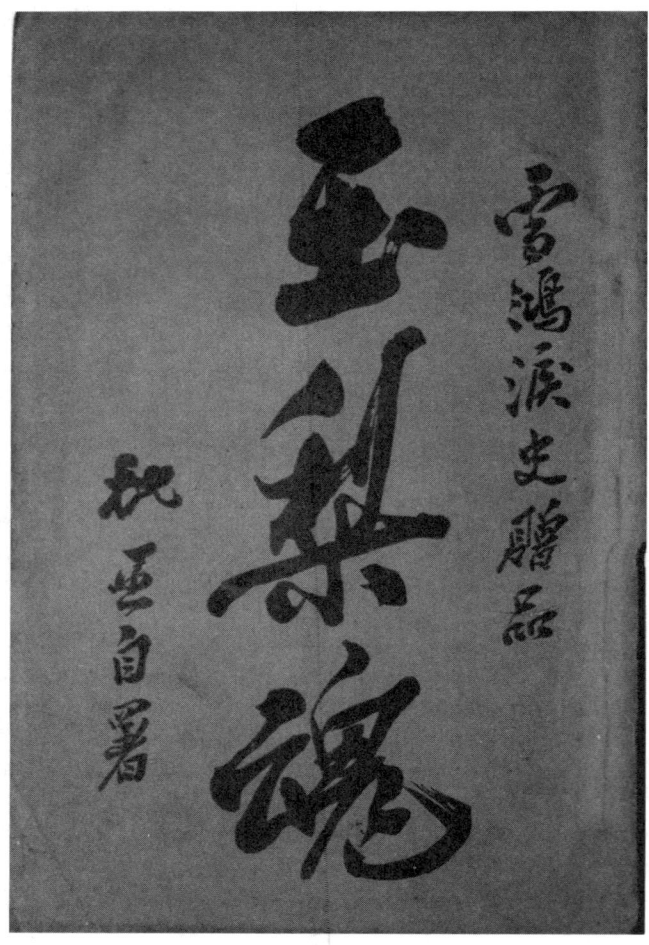

Cover for Xu's first book, Yuli hun (1913, Jade Pear Spirit), the novel that set off the boom in Mandarin Ducks and Butterflies fiction (from Yu Runqi, ed., Tang Tao cang shu, 2004; Bruccoli Clark Layman Archives)

begins with the claim that "My life is very similar to Mengxia's"; he says that the revised work is the authentic version of He Mengxia's love story and, therefore, more valuable than *Yuli hun,* in which, he maintains, he made many mistakes. Although the novel sold well both in serialized and book form, critics considered it an artistic regression from the heights of *Yuli hun* and deplored its moral didacticism—Li Niang, for example, is depicted as a defender of traditional Confucian values. The same critics, however, acknowledged that as the first Chinese novel in the form of a diary, *Xuehong leishi* made a significant contribution to modern Chinese literature.

Each month Xu and his brother took turns going home to check on their families in Changshu. In January 1915 Xu Tianxiao received an urgent letter informing him that his daughter was ill. He rushed back to Changshu to find not only that his daughter had died but that his wife was dead, too. Xu Zhenya fictionalized the incident in "Yu gui ye wan" (My Late Return Home), which was first published in his collection *Zhenya langmo*. In the story he laments that "Family matters are bitter and yet cannot be spoken of." What Xu could not say was that his mother had a suspicious, hysterical temperament, was tyrannical at home, and made her daughters-in-law suffer. According to some sources, Xu Tianxiao's wife hanged herself because she could no longer endure the criticism and ill treatment from her mother-in-law. Xu Zhenya's wife, Cai Ruizhu, returned to her parents' home as often as she could and stayed there as long as possible.

Xu sympathized with his wife, but as a dutiful son he could express his anger at his mother only in his fiction, where he turns it into criticism of the repressive traditional family and of arranged marriages. But he is pessimistic about the possibility for any resolution to the problem and skeptical of the value of individualism, a new concept in early-twentieth-century China. His story "Qifu duanchang shi" (A History of an Abandoned Wife), also published in *Zhenya langmo,* is a woman's account of how her life was ruined by the older women who have authority over her. The narrator is an orphan who is maltreated by the aunt who is raising her. Sent away to school, she receives a modern education that instills in her a belief in the value of individual freedom. She chooses her own husband, rather than have one chosen for her by her aunt, and is married in a Western-style ceremony. But her new mother-in-law turns out to be even more ferocious than her aunt, and her modern "free marriage" has left her trapped in the yoke of feudal tyranny. After she gives birth to a girl, her mother-in-law demands that her husband divorce her because she has failed to produce a son; he has no choice but to obey. She takes a refuge in a monastery and writes her "history" on her deathbed as a plaint against the old society and a warning to young women who aspire to modern love. In "Du" (Poison), published in the magazine *Zhonghua xiaoshuo jie* (Chinese Fiction World) in 1914 and collected in *Zhenya langmo,* a young couple caught up in the contradiction between new and old is led by the force of love to a catastrophic end. Studying in the United States, Yu Renjun meets another Chinese student, Chen Binghua. They fall in love and are engaged to be married. But when Yu returns to China, his father forces him to break off the engagement and accept an arranged marriage. On the wedding night, Yu's bride is mysteriously poisoned and dies. Chen reappears at this point, and, after an interval, they are married. On their wedding night Chen reveals that she murdered Yu's first wife, and to complete her revenge on Yu for leaving her, she kills herself by drinking poison. "Love is the most deadly poison," Yu concludes, and drinks the poison that remains. In these stories tradition and patriarchy are condemned, but free love and individualism are shown to be self-destructive.

The metaphysical connection between romantic love and death is a common theme in traditional Chinese fiction; it is treated, for example, in such masterpieces as Cao Xueqin's *Honglou meng* (1791, Dream of the Red Chamber; translated as *The Story of the Stone,* 1973–1986) and Wei Xiuren's *Hua yue hen* (1858, Traces of Flower and Moon), both of which were highly popular in early-twentieth-century China and were favorites of Xu's. In late-imperial China these romances, which are imbued with the doctrine of "wei qing er si" (dying for the sake of love), shaped popular beliefs by endorsing the value of individual romantic passion and free choice in the exercise of that passion; death was represented as the absolute force that could shield love from, or allow it to transcend, orthodox morality. Literary sentimentalism revived in the early Republican era, resonating with popular despair over the dismal social reality of the time, and was lent new charm by Lin Shu's translations of Western romances, such as *La Dame aux camélias* and H. Rider Haggard's *Joan Haste* (1894), each of which created a sensation among Chinese readers.

The theme of an excess of passion leading to illness and death is presented with unusual intensity in Xu's fiction. In part, this preoccupation is evidence of his indebtedness to the foreign and Chinese literature that he favored. A more significant source, however, was his contradictory feelings about the worth of liberating romantic passion, on the one hand, and the importance of moral values, on the other hand. In his preface to the novel *Lanniang aishi* (1913, The Sad Story of Madam Lan), by his friend Wu Shuangre, Xu asserts that both morality and passion are inbred in human nature (the preface is included in *Zhenya langmo*). Whereas traditional morality is tied to and serves the old familial authority and is, therefore, to be rejected, unfettered passion is no less reprehensible. Traditional morality, Xu writes, is a cold-blooded killer, and passion should be cursed and destroyed. In Xu's fiction the conflict between romantic love and morality is drawn out and dramatized, and in the end the opposing forces smother each other in the confined space of domestic melodrama.

Xu's novel "Bangda yuanyang lu" (Punishment of the Mandarin Ducks) was published in serial form in *Xiaoshuo congbao* from August 1915 to July 1916; it appeared in book form in 1916 under the title *Shuanghuan ji* (Two Maids). Shielded by the patriarch of a large family, the shrewd maids Tang Er and Qiu Hong vie for power by manipulating the love affairs and marriage plans of their young masters. At the maids' instigation the parents tear their children from their lovers and arrange unhappy marriages for them. As the maids' conspiracies spin out of control, the family unravels in a sequence of absurd and brutal events that result in the deaths of one family member after another. In the end the maids take their own lives. Critics were disappointed in *Shuanghuan ji* because it shows less concern for the social and emotional costs of arranged marriage and traditional morality than does *Yuli hun:* they expected him to attribute the deaths explicitly to the old marriage system, rather than to the maids. In writing *Shuanghuan ji* Xu was apparently more interested in formal experimentation than in social commentary. The narrative structure and the cast of characters are reminiscent of *Honglou meng,* but in traditional novels maids never manipulate their masters like puppets.

Yu zhi qi (1917, My Wife) deals with the connection between love and money, a new topic for Xu. The novel opens with a theatrical, heart-rending scene in which Qin Yuxian meets her long-time fiancé, Shi Qiuxing, in a forlorn garden and tells him that her father has ordered her to break off their engagement because Qiuxing has been left in poverty after the recent death of his father. Her father has already arranged for her to marry another man. Qiuxing travels to a northern city, makes his fortune, and returns home three years later. Although he is rich, and Yuxian's husband has died, they still cannot be together because conventional morality prohibits a widow from remarrying. Yuxian introduces Qiuxing to her sister Mingxia and removes herself as an obstacle to his happiness by committing suicide. At the beginning of the fifth chapter Xu says that "a truly sad romance should make readers cry from the beginning to the end." In most of his fiction, passion frustrated by morality inevitably leads to the lover's death. *Yu zhi qi,* however, shows that when money is added to the equation—China was becoming increasingly commercialized at the time the story was written—the outcome is changed: on the night of Yuxian's marriage Qiuxing is in extreme despair; yet, he overcomes his initial impulse to kill himself because of his desire to make money. Becoming rich is a form of revenge; it is also his way of proving his love and the value of his life.

The critical consensus is that Xu's creative energy was exhausted after 1917. The more his fiction conformed to traditional morality, the less it appealed to the younger generation of readers, who aspired to be modern in all things. Xu continued to practice a degree of formal experimentation, but the worldview implicit in his writing was out of touch with contemporary life. He wanted to use his fiction to manifest his identity as a member of the traditional Chinese literati, a group that was increasingly under attack from progressives in the late 1910s. His novel *Yu zhi fu* (My Husband), which he began in 1917 but did not complete and publish until 1927, is the self-portrait of a melancholy antihero, an iconoclastic artist who becomes a homeless wanderer. Xu's fictional autobiography is narcissistic and fantastic and includes imitations and parodies of traditional poetry and essays and popular ballads. Despite its genuine innovation, which was rarely matched by Xu's contemporaries, such self-indulgent use of literary tradition proved to be even more at odds with the "progressive" literary current and decreased the commercial appeal of the work.

Xu missed his home and was nostalgic for the way of life enjoyed by literati in the past. In an essay about Shanghai collected in *Zhenya langmo* he criticizes the metropolis as a "hell" where, despite superficial splendor and spectacle, crime and fraud prevail. He points to prostitutes as the most miserable victims of the city; Shanghai in the 1910s had a huge sex industry, and men of Xu's convictions would have deplored the fact that the sophisticated courtesan culture was being replaced by the vulgar business of sex for hire. Depressed by social ills and personal problems, he sought comfort in opium and alcohol. In 1918 his editorship of *Xiaoshuo congbao* came to an end, largely because his colleagues were more interested in profit than in literary quality, and he founded a publishing house, Qinghua shuju.

The fate of the "abandoned wife" depicted in Xu's early fiction befell his own wife, Cai Ruizhu, who had remained in Changshu with her mother-in-law when Xu moved to Shanghai. Xu's mother mistreated Cai and wanted him to send her away. To appease his mother, Xu said that he intended to divorce Cai; instead, he brought her to Shanghai to live with him in 1915. Soon, however, his mother discovered the deception and went to Shanghai to force Xu and Cai to separate; they pretended to do so. In 1923 Cai Ruizhu died shortly after giving birth to a son.

Liu Ruanying—the only daughter of Liu Chunlin, famous for placing first in the final imperial examination given before the system was abolished in 1905—was an admirer fan of Xu's fiction and was moved by his poems of mourning for his wife, which were published in a Shanghai newspaper. She wrote to Xu, expressing as much affection as sympathy. They exchanged photographs by mail, and Xu went to Beijing to meet her. Liu Chunlin despised Xu as a Shanghai popular novelist and was outraged that his daughter had taken the initiative in a modern "free love" affair. He eventually relented, in part yielding to the persuasion of his friend the poet Fan Zengxiang. Xu and Liu Ruanying were married in 1924. The celebrity match was a popular sensation. Zhang Henshui, just beginning to make a name as a writer of popular fiction, produced a thinly disguised version of the story of Xu and Liu Ruanying in his novel *Chunming waishi* (An Unofficial History of Beijing), which was serialized in the literary supplement of the Beijing newspaper *Shijie wanbao* (The World Evening News) from April 1924 until January 1929 and published in book form in 1930.

Also in 1924 *Yuli hun* was adapted for the screen; the silent movie was produced by the Mingxing Film Company and directed by Zhang Shichuan and Xu Hu. Two years later the novel was staged as a *huaju* (spoken drama) in Shanghai. In response to this revival of popular interest, Xu confirmed that *Yuli hun* was autobiographical. In the public eye he became something of a legendary romantic figure whose biography seemed to combine fiction and reality and tradition and modernity.

Xu's success, however, did nothing to improve his economic fortunes or his personal life. Before long, Liu Ruanying lost patience with her mother-in-law, who was as insufferable as ever, and she lost hope in her husband, who could not overcome his addiction to opium. They lived separately in Shanghai until Liu moved back to Beijing in 1927; she died shortly thereafter. In 1934 Xu sold his publishing house and went back to Changshu, where he opened an antique shop. Details are sketchy, but Xu seems to have become seriously ill in 1937; he died of his illness in the middle of a Japanese air raid sometime after war broke out in July of that year.

Biographies:

Wei Shaochang, "Xu Zhenya," in his *Yuanyang hudie pai yanjiu ziliao* (Shanghai: Wenyi chubanshe, 1962), pp. 461–462;

Chen Jingzhi, "Yuanyang hudie pai dashi Xu Zhenya," *Zhanggu yuekan* (October 1971): 65–70;

Zheng Yimei, "Xu Zhenya," in his *Nanshe congtan* (Shanghai: Renmin chubanshe, 1981), pp. 234–235;

He Zhenqiu, "Yuanyang hudie pai dianji zuojia Xu Zhenya," in his *Changshuo wenshi lungao* (Nanjing: Nanjing University Press, 1989), pp. 185–204;

Wei, *Wo kan Yuanyang hudie pai* (Taibei: Taiwan shangwu yinshuguan, 1992), pp. 50–58;

Chen Ziping, "Aiqing juzi: Yuanyang hudie pai kaishanzu–Xu Zhenya pingzhuan," in *Zhongguo jin xiandai tongsu zuojia pingzhuan congshu*, volume 4, edited by Fan Boqun (Nanjing: Nanjing chubanshe, 1994), pp. 250–269;

Zhou Wenxiao, "Xu Jue," in *Nanshe renwu zhuan*, edited by Liu Wuji and Yin Anru (Beijing: Shehui kexue wenxian chubanshe, 2002), pp. 543–547.

References:

Fan Boqun, "Zaoqi Yuanyang hudie pai daibiao zuo–*Yuli hun*," in his *Minguo tongsu xiaoshuo Yuanyang hudie pai* (Taibei: Guowen tiande zazhishe, 1990), pp. 101–116;

Fan and others, "Lun Yuan die pai zushi Xu Zhenya de *Yuli hun*," in Fan's *Zhongguo jin xiandai tongsu wenxueshi* (Nanjing: Jiangsu jiaoyu chubanshe, 2000), pp. 269–278;

Fan Yanqiao, "Xu Zhenya zhi *Yuli hun* yu *Xuehong leishi*," in his *Zhongguo xiaoshuo shi* (Jiulong: Huaxia chubanshe, 1967), pp. 267–270;

C. T. Hsia, "Hsu Chen-ya's *Yu-li hun*: An Essay in Literary History and Criticism," in *Chinese Middlebrow Fiction from the Ch'ing and Early Republican Era*, edited by Liu Ts'un-yan and John Minford (Hong Kong: Chinese University Press, 1984), pp. 199–240;

Hsia, "*Yuli hun* xin lun," *Mingbao*, no. 9 (1985): 59–64; no. 10 (1985): 93–97; no. 11 (1985): 94–98;

E. Perry Link Jr., *Mandarin Ducks and Butterflies: Popular Fiction in Early Twentieth-Century Chinese Cities* (Berkeley: University of California Press, 1981), pp. 40–78;

Liu Yangti, "Xu Zhenya he *Yuli hun*," in his *Liubian zhong de liupai–Yuanyang hudie pai xinlun* (Beijing: Zhongguo wenlian chuban gongsi, 1997), pp. 86–102;

Shi Meng, "*Yuli hun* zhenxiang dabai," *Suzhou zazhi*, no. 1 (1997): 55–57;

Yu Runqi, ed., *Tang Tao cang shu* (Beijing: Beijing chubanshe, 2004), p. 26;

Yuan Jin, *Yuanyang hudie pai* (Shanghai: Shanghai shudian chubanshe, 1994), pp. 41–51.

Yang Kui
(18 October 1905 – 12 March 1985)

Angelina C. Yee
Hong Kong University of Science and Technology

BOOKS: *Sangokusi butsugo* [Tales of the Three Kingdoms], 4 volumes (Taibei: Shengxing chubanbu, volume 1, 1941?–1944);

Me moyuru [Sprouts] (Taibei: Shengxing chubanbu, 1944);

Udori no yome iri [Mother Goose Gets Married] (Taibei: Sanxing tang, 1946); translated from Japanese into Chinese as *E mama chujia* [Mother Goose Gets Married] (Tainan: Dahang chubanshe, 1975; revised edition, Taibei: Qianwei chubanshe, 1985); title story translated by Jane Parish Yang as "Mother Goose Gets Married," in *The Unbroken Chain: An Anthology of Taiwan Fiction since 1926*, edited by Joseph S. M. Lau (Bloomington: Indiana University Press, 1983), pp. 33–54;

Songbaofu/Shinbun haitatsufu (Taibei: Taiwan pinglun she, 1946); translated by Rosemary M. Haddon as "Paperboy," *Renditions*, no. 43 (1995): 25–58;

Yangtou ji [Ram's Head Essays] (Taibei: Huihuang chubanshe, 1976);

Yabubian de meigui [The Uncrushable Rose] (Taibei: Huihuang chubanshe, 1976); title story translated by Daniel Tom as "The Indomitable Rose," *Chinese Pen* (Autumn 1978): 86–94; enlarged edition (Taibei: Qianwei chubanshe, 1985)—includes "Ni wawa," translated as "Mud Dolls," in *Oxcart: Nativist Stories from Taiwan, 1934–1977*, edited and translated by Haddon (Dortmund, Germany: Projekt, 1996), pp. 73–84;

Songbaofu [Newspaper Boy], edited by Zhong Zhaozheng and Ye Shitao, Guangfu qian Taiwan wenxue quanji [Complete Works of Taiwan Literature before Reunification], volume 6 (Taibei: Yuanjing chuban shiye gongsi, 1979);

Yang Kui de wenxue shengya [The Literary Life of Yang Kui], edited by Chen Fangming (Irvine, Cal.: Taiwan chubanshe, 1986; Taibei: Qianwei chubanshe, 1988);

Lüdao jiashu [Letters Home from Green Island] (Taizhong: Chenxing chubanshe, 1987);

Yang Kui (from Yang Kui quanji, *edited by Peng Xiaoyan, 1998–2001; Van Pelt Library–East Asia, University of Pennsylvania)*

Letian pai [The Optimist] (Taibei: Hesen wenhua shiye youxian gongsi, 1990);

Zheng yan de xiazi [Blind Man Eyes Open] (Taibei: Hesen wenhua shiye youxian gongsi, 1990);

Yang Kui quanji [Complete Works of Yang Kui], 14 volumes, edited by Peng Xiaoyan (Taibei & Tainan: Guoli wenhua zichan baocun yanjiu zhongxin choubeichu, 1998–2001).

Collections: *Yang Kui zuopin xuanji* [Selected Works by Yang Kui] (Beijing: Renmin wenxue chubanshe, 1985);

Yang Kui xuanji [Selected Works of Yang Kui], edited by Cong Su (Hong Kong: Wenyi feng chubanshe, 1986);

Yang Kui ji [Collected Works of Yang Kui], edited by Zhang Henghao, Taiwan zuojia quanji–duanpian xiaoshuo juan, Riju shidai: 7 [Complete Works of Taiwan Authors: Short Stories of the Period of Japanese Occupation, Volume 7] (Taibei: Qianwei chubanshe, 1991);

Yō Ki [Yang Kui], edited by Kawahara Isao, Nihon tōchiki Taiwan bungaku Taiwanjin sakka sakuhinshū [Collected Works of Taiwan Writers under Japanese Occupation], volume 1 (Tokyo: Ryokuin Shobō, 1999).

PLAY PRODUCTION: Sergiel Tret'iakov, *Hoero Shina* [Roar! China], adapted by Yang Kui, Taizhong, 1944.

TRANSLATIONS: Lu Xun, *A Q Seiden* [The True Story of Ah Q], translated into Japanese by Yang Kui (Taibei: Donghua shuju, 1947);

Mao Dun, *Da bizi de gushi* [The Story of Big Nose], translated into Japanese by Yang Kui (Taibei: Donghua shuju, 1947);

Yu Dafu, *Weixue de zaochen* [A Morning of Light Snow], translated into Japanese by Yang Kui (Taibei: Donghua shuju, 1947?).

Yang Kui is recognized by scholars as one of the most important Taiwanese writers of the period of the Japanese occupation of the island (1895 to 1945). He wrote fiction and plays; worked as an editor, publisher, and translator; and was involved in social, cultural, and political activities. He has been hailed as Taiwan's conscience, a forerunner of a native Taiwanese literature, and an anticolonialist fighter.

The 1920s Xin wenhua yundong (New Culture Movement) on the Chinese mainland included the use of vernacular instead of classical Chinese in literature; a corresponding movement was spawned on Taiwan, but it developed with difficulty. The majority of Taiwan's populace spoke Southern Min (Taiwanese) and found Mandarin unintelligible, while the educated were schooled only in classical Chinese. For the Taiwanese the Mandarin vernacular was an acquired language and was subjected to colonial censorship, and a written Taiwanese vernacular did not exist. During the Japanese occupation the literature of Taiwan was written in classical Chinese through the first decades of the twentieth century and, after Japanization took effect, mostly in Japanese. This literature was submerged after the Nationalist government assumed control of Taiwan at the end of World War II and banned the use of Japanese. In the 1970s, when the search for a native Taiwanese consciousness reached back to the island's colonial roots, publishers recovered writings from the period that included those of Yang Kui.

Yang Kui was born in Xinhua township in Tainan county on 18 October 1905 to Yang Bi and Su Zu. His name at birth was Yang Gui. His father owned a small tin shop. He had three older brothers and four older sisters, but only three of his sisters and one of his brothers lived to adulthood. He grew up hearing stories of Japanese atrocities, and decades later he recalled in his essays childhood images of colonial trauma: Japanese tanks crushing a peasant revolt, executions after anticolonialist uprisings, his brother being conscripted into the Japanese army, and a family friend being beaten to death by the colonial police.

Yang Gui was a sickly child and did not attend grade school until he was nine. He was educated in colonial public schools, where Japanese was used exclusively. He studied mathematics and English, as well as Japanese and Western literature. He was particularly fond of the novels of Victor Hugo, Leo Tolstoy, Nikolai Gogol, and Fyodor Dostoevsky. He also read widely in philosophy and social science texts and, in an interview by Wang Shixun published in 1988, singled out the flamboyant, eccentric anarchist Ōsugi Sakae as having made the deepest impression on him in his youth.

In 1924 Yang Gui spurned an arranged marriage and went to Japan, where he took courses in modern literature, movies, and playwriting in the literary arts evening extension program at Japan University. To support himself he took jobs as a factory worker, a newspaper boy, and a construction worker, all of which provided material for his earliest stories. Unlike most other Taiwanese students in Japan, who came from the landed gentry and were inclined toward nationalism, Yang Gui was attracted to Marxism. He embraced the cause of Japanese workers, joined student organizations, and, as a member of a worker study group, investigated the slum areas near Asakusa, where he saw people die from the cold. He worked with Japanese students to alert workers to capitalist exploitation and participated in Korean students' demonstrations against the Japanese occupation of Korea: he was arrested, held for two days, and released after a hearing. The latter activity brought about his first brush with the law. He also took part in student demonstrations against the Giichi Tanaka government's invasion of Manchuria. He frequented playwright Sasaki Takamaru's avant-garde theater group and mingled with Japanese leftist writers. It is unclear whether he joined the Japanese Communist Party, which was established in 1923, but he had close ties with party members and sym-

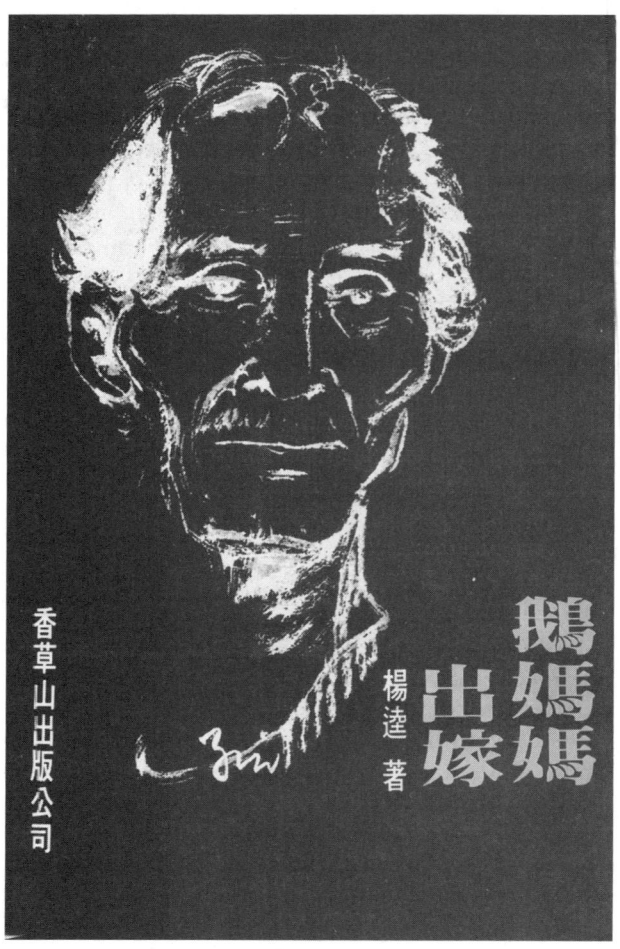

Cover for a 1976 edition of Yang Kui's short-story collection E mama chujia (Mother Goose Gets Married), originally published in 1975 (Wason Collection on East Asia–China, Kroch Asia Library, Cornell University)

pathizers. He joined the Taiwan qingnian xiehui (Taiwan Youth Association) but took no part in Chinese organizations; he professed ignorance of the political situation on the mainland because he could not read Chinese, and because of the gap between spoken Mandarin and spoken Taiwanese he would have had difficulty talking to mainlanders. In Japan, Yang Gui learned of mainland China's 1911 revolution and read Sun Yat-sen's *Sanmin zhuyi* (Three Principles of the People) in Japanese translation. When news of the 1927 Nationalist liquidation of the Communist Party reached Japan, he watched Chinese students of opposing camps come to blows and lamented the internecine feuding. He spoke admiringly of two Taiwanese brothers he knew who decided to join the Communist revolution in China.

In the 1920s Japan's tenant farmers unionized and fought to win better terms from their landlords. Eager to emulate the Japanese peasant movement, Yang Gui returned to Taiwan in 1927. He took charge of the political, organizational, and educational wings of the Taiwan nongmin zuhe (Taiwan Peasant Collective) and worked as a reporter for the official publication of the Taiwan wenhua xiehui (Taiwan Cultural Association). He was imprisoned eight times in two years. By 1929 the movement was riven by internal conflicts within and was on the verge of collapse in the face of a crackdown by the colonial authorities.

Angelina Yee writes that Yang Gui "remained undaunted in the face of adversity and found solace in humor in the worst of times." An example is his arrest the night before he was to be married. On 11 February 1927 Yang Gui and his fiancée, Ye Tao, gave speeches at a meeting of the Tainan zonggonghui (Tainan Federation of Labor Unions). They were to go to Xinhua, Yang Gui's hometown, the next day for their wedding, but they were arrested before dawn, put in handcuffs and shackles, taken to the prison in Tainan, and then transferred to a prison in Taizhong. Yee reports that Yang Gui joked that anyone who saw him and Ye Tao in chains and handcuffs in the street would have thought that they had been caught trying to elope, that their stay in prison in Taizhong was "an all expenses paid honeymoon courtesy of the government," and that the Japanese police who trailed him after his release from prison "gave him free protection for his reclusive life as a woodcutter." Yang Gui and Ye Tao were two of the four hundred thousand people arrested on the island in 1927.

Yang Gui and Ye Tao were married after their release from prison. Yang Gui retreated to the slopes of Mt. Shou, near the city of Gaoxiong, where he chopped wood for a living. During the following years he took other odd jobs. Encouraged by the writer Lai He, soon to become a venerated figure in Taiwan literary circles, he started to write. At Lai He's suggestion he changed his given name, Gui (High Office), to Kui (Reaching All Paths), a name that recalls the impetuous daredevil Li Kui in the popular Chinese novel *Shuihu zhuan* (The Story of the Water Margin; translated as *All Men Are Brothers*, 1933), by Shi Nai'an.

In 1930 Yang Kui and Ye Tao had a daughter, Sujuan. That same year Yang Kui's second eldest brother, Yang Chen, killed himself. In 1920 Yang Chen had given up his plan to go to medical school because of financial problems and, at the urging of his family, moved in with his wife's family. In 1932 Yang Kui and Ye Tao had a son, Zibeng (Collapse of Capitalism); later, they had another son, Jian.

Yang Kui's first short story, "Shinbun haitatsufu" (translated as "Paperboy," 1995), appeared in the *Taiwan xinmin bao* (Taiwan New People's Press) in 1932 with help from Lai He; the censors, however, permitted the publication of only the first half of the story. In 1934 the complete story was carried in the leftist Tokyo journal *Bungaku Hyoron* (Literary Review) and won a "second prize"–no first prize was awarded–in the journal's writing competition for the year. A member of the first generation in Taiwan to become fully literate in Japanese, Yang Kui was also the first writer from the colony of Taiwan to win a literary prize in Japan. "Shinbun haitatsufu" was translated into Chinese as "Songbaofu" by Hu Feng and included in the anthologies he published in Shanghai in 1936: *Shanling: Chaoxian Taiwan xiaoshuo xuan* (Mountain Spirits: Selected Stories from Korea and Taiwan) and *Ruoxiao minzu xiaoshuo xuan* (Stories of Small, Weak Nations).

"Shinbun haitatsufu" is narrated by a poor Taiwanese student in Japan who delivers newspapers for a dishonest distributor who cheats him out of his pay. Yang Kui infuses scenes of pathos with humor, as when the narrator gets up to use the toilet at night in dire fear of treading on the men crowded together on the dormitory floor. The use of interior monologue and flashback marks the stylistic modernism of the story.

In contrast to mainland and Taiwanese writers of the period who were obsessed with national humiliation, Yang Kui emphasizes the generosity of Tanaka, a Japanese fellow worker, when the narrator comes under financial duress. In fact, no hint is given that the narrator himself is not Japanese until the second half of the story, when a family calamity brings back memories of his fellow villagers' misery under occupation, including his father's death after being imprisoned for refusing to yield his land to a Japanese sugar monopoly. Debating with himself whether he should stay in Japan or leave, the narrator contrasts his Japanese friend's loyalty with the treachery of his own brother in Taiwan, who became a Japanese colonialist bailiff, as he ruminates on his discovery that Japan, as a nation, is not his enemy:

> At home, I had thought that all Japanese were evil, and I hated them one and all. But since I've arrived here, I have found that not all Japanese are bad. I have warm feelings for the innkeeper; as for Tanaka, there is more affection between us than between brothers. . . . No, when I think of my own brother, who is now a policeman, what a brother! To mention the two in the same breath would be an insult to Tanaka.

Tanaka, the benefactor who represents his ideal of manhood, is the main reason for the narrator's affection for Japan. The thoughts with which the narrator consoles himself in his darkest hour are Japanese: "The Japanese have always said, 'though there are ghosts in the world, there are Buddhas too.'"

"Shinbun haitatsufu" ends with a Japanese labor unionist helping the newspaper boys expose their boss's wrongdoing, an experience the narrator decides to replicate back home. The moral is that workers everywhere suffer from exploitation. The heroes are not people such as the narrator's parents, whose resistance to colonialist encroachment and economic deprivation can only be passive, but those who fight: the trade unionist, the newspaper boys who unite against capitalist exploitation, and people such as Tanaka.

From 1935 to 1937, while struggling to make ends meet with odd jobs as a tutor, secretary, janitor, and bricklayer, Yang Kui edited and published the bilingual literary journal *Taiwan xin wenxue* (Taiwan New Literature). He continued his adulatory portrayal of the Japanese spirit in "Ori seibatsu" (1936, How the Naughty Boys Vanquished the Demon), which was published in *Taiwan xin wenxue* and is included in *Yang Kui quanji* (1998–2001, Complete Works of Yang Kui). Written at the height of his creative power, "Ori seibatsu" is his most modernist story and one of the most experimental works by any Chinese author of the period. The narrator is a Japanese artist visiting Taiwan. Besotted with official propaganda about Taiwan's beauty and plenty, which testify to Japan's colonial success, the artist is stunned by the squalor he sees. In the midst of decrepit dwellings a group of children of various nationalities play together, oblivious to the rubble surrounding them, until a capitalist appropriates the playground to build a mansion guarded by dogs. Deciding that the meaning of art lies in its power to change people's lives, the artist gives the children a painting of themselves piling on top of one another, clutching primitive weapons aimed at the watchdogs. The picture inspires the children to fight the capitalist, and they reclaim their playground. While Yang appears to pander to the colonizers by giving the Japanese hero a god-like role, the moral of transnational unity against capitalism is only thinly disguised.

In the only story he wrote in the third person, "Denen shokei" (1936, Pastoral Scenes), republished in *Yang Kui quanji* as "Mohan mura" (Model Village), Yang Kui satirizes a Japanese overlord and a Chinese collaborator for rushing to beautify a village for a visiting prefect. Farm implements and haystacks are hidden, while ancestral pictures and Buddhist icons are replaced by images of Japanese gods. The two main characters—Chen Wenzhi, a traditional Chinese scholar idled by the colonial government's suppression of the Chinese language, and Ruan Xinmin, a landlord-collaborator's Japanese-educated son appalled by the misery of his fellow villagers—undergo a crisis of conscience and find inspiration in the united strength of the local farmers, who emulate Japanese peasants' struggle to reclaim land appropriated by the government.

When Yang Kui fell ill with tuberculosis and was taken to court for failing to pay his rice bill at a local grain store, a Japanese policeman, Irita Haruhiko, who was an admirer of "Shinbun haitatsufu," gave him money that enabled him to pay off his debts and start a farm in 1937. Though an overseas colonial assignment was considered a lucrative position, Irita quit his job soon afterward and started writing articles exposing Japanese police corruption. When his leftist leanings became apparent, Irita was recalled to Japan; he committed suicide days before his scheduled departure by taking an overdose of sleeping pills. Yang Kui was at his bedside to hear him call out the name of Yang Kui's oldest son, Zibeng, with his last breath. Irita willed that his ashes be used to fertilize Yang Kui's flowerbeds and bequeathed to Yang Kui his books, among which were Lu Xun's collected works. In this way Yang discovered Lu Xun, whose works were banned in Japan and Taiwan.

Yang Kui called the garden at his farm Shouyang; the name was an allusion to the legendary brothers Bo Yi and Shu Qi, who chose to remain loyal to the Shang dynasty and starve to death in the Shouyang Mountains rather than accept high offices in the new government. In "Syuyoen zakki" (1938, Miscellaneous Notes of Shouyang) Yang Kui confesses that he is "not reconciled to following Bo Yi and Shu Qi all the way"; instead, he finds existential meaning in his daily chores: "When the vegetables and flowers are invaded by bugs, we kill the bugs one by one; when weeds overgrow, we pull them out one by one: this is our call of duty." He saw the garden as a metaphor for self-cultivation and for combat against external forces of oppression.

During the Sino-Japanese War of 1937 to 1945 strict censorship was enforced, and the Kominka (Japanization or Imperialization) campaign was rigorously waged. The works Yang Kui wrote during the war are lyrical and allegorical. In the lyrical essay "Ni wawa" (translated as "Mud Dolls," 1996), written in 1942 but first published in *Yangtou ji* (1976, Ram's Head Essays), the narrator's son clamors to join the Japanese army, as all Taiwanese boys were taught to do. The narrator's lament that "there is nothing crueler than to have the children of a fallen nation subjugate other nations" reflects Yang Kui's anxiety about human malleability and moral decline. The remedy, he suggests, is self-transformation and self-creation through physical labor and engagement with the natural world. In other essays and in letters and stories he celebrates the joy of productive labor and compares the aesthetic satisfaction of gardening to the pleasure of writing. His wartime Japanese-language collections *Me moyuru* (1944, Sprouts) and *Udori no yome iri* (1946, Mother Goose Gets Married) include lyrical, meditative essays and writings that fuse fiction and autobiography. In the title story of *Me moyuru*, he depicts an ideal world in which a child is raised with love amid beauty. In the title story of *Udori no yome iri* the narrator draws a moral parallel between his taking a goose from its flock to give as a gift to a Japanese hospital administrator to secure a favor, on the one hand, and a friend's father's betrayal of his daughter to appease his Japanese creditor, on the other hand. The analogy recognizes that subjugated peoples, like their oppressors, are prone to corruption.

Colonial repression intensified during Japan's Pacific War from 1942 to 1945, and death and regeneration are recurrent themes in Yang Kui's works of the period. "Mu i son" (1942, The Doctorless Village) describes a young country doctor's awakening to the futility of medical knowledge when villagers cannot afford to pay for health care. Shaken by his helplessness in the face of death, he retreats into writing poetry; but this capitulation only deepens his sense of guilt.

In "Zosan no kage ni—nonki na josan no hanashi" (1944, Behind Increased Production—The Story of the Old Buffoon) Yang Kui goes further in expounding an idealized version of Sino-Japanese relations than he had in "Ori seibatsu." Published at the height of the war, when Taiwan intellectuals were pressured to declare their support of the Japanese war effort, the story was written on commission from the colonial government's Information Office and is ostensibly a government investigator's report on the lives of miners. Impressed by the miners' fortitude, the investigator likens them to Japanese soldiers. The driving force behind the group, he soon discovers, is an old Japanese man who animates the community with his optimism and altruism. The old man teaches his adopted Taiwanese daughter, Jinlan, to speak perfect Japanese and display exquisite traditional Japanese manners. The reporter departs, lauding those "who have the progressive idea of following the Japanese.... Such an ingenuous attitude of following beauty, of not hesitating to leap into danger, signals the sprouting of a beautiful Japanese spirit." The story is included in *Yang Kui quanji*.

As censorship became more severe, Yang Kui wrote veiled criticisms of Japan's invasion of China. In 1944 he and some friends founded the Taizhong yineng fenggonghui (Taizhong Arts Society); they secretly named it the Jiaotuhui (Scorched Earth Society), an allusion to the mainland slogan of "scorching the earth to resist the Japanese invaders." In a concealed attack on Japanese aggression he adapted *Hoero Shina* (Roar! China), a Russian play by Sergiel Tret'iakov that denounced British imperialism in China. The play was staged in Taizhong, Zhanghua, and Taibei, presumably in Japanese, in 1944. Plans for its performance in the Southern Min language were abandoned when Japan surrendered in 1945.

The day of Japanese surrender was, according to Yang Kui, the happiest day of his life; for the first time he felt "the dignity and happiness of being Chinese." Exulting in Taiwan's retrocession to China, he led volunteer groups, named Xin shenghuo cujindui (New Life Brigades) after Chiang Kai-shek's New Life Movement, to clean up the streets; and to fill the vacuum left by the collapse of the colonial government he organized the Minshenghui (People's Livelihood Society) to maintain order in Taizhong. He started learning Mandarin from his daughter, who belonged to the first postwar Taiwanese generation to receive a Chinese-language education. Although most journals and newspapers continued to print some pages in Japanese in the initial postwar period, Yang Kui renounced writing in Japanese and relinquished a post as editor of a Japanese section of a newspaper. He also painstakingly translated his Japanese stories into unsophisticated Chinese. In 1946 he revised Hu Feng's Chinese version of "Shinbun Haitatsufu" and published it as *Songbaofu* in a crudely printed booklet; it was the first complete edition of the work to appear in Taiwan. He also renamed his garden Yi Yang (One Sun) in celebration of the victory over Japan. Declining offers of government positions, he took the editorship of the *Heping ribao* (Peace Daily) literary supplement. In 1947 he translated works by Lu Xun, Yu Dafu, and Mao Dun into Japanese and published them in bilingual editions. A collection of his translations of stories by Zheng Zhenduo was advertised in 1948 but never published. In a 1982 interview with He Xu included in *Yang Kui de wenxue shengya* (1988, The Literary Life of Yang Kui), edited by Chen Fangming, he said that he also published bilingual versions of works by Shen Congwen and Lao She, but the translations have not been republished.

On 28 February 1947 the Nationalist government, which was composed largely of Mandarin-speaking mainlanders who had arrived on Taiwan in 1945, began a repression of dissent that led to the arrests and executions of thousands of people. Yang had published some poems satirizing government corruption, and he and his wife were jailed for more than three months. On his release, Yang Kui assumed the editorship of the *Lixing bao* (Endeavor News) literary supplement and founded the *Taiwan wenyi congkan* (Taiwan Arts and Literature Journal). He helped to organize a cultural association to bridge the differences between mainlanders and Taiwanese and drafted a "Heping xuanyan" (Peace Declaration) that called for reconciliation between the two groups, freedom of expression, release of political prisoners, legalization of opposition political parties, return of government to the people, economic equality, and local autonomy. Published in Shanghai's *Dagong bao/L'Impartial* on 21 January 1949, the "Heping xuanyan" deeply offended Chen Cheng, the governor of Taiwan. Yang was brought before a military tribunal and, after intensive questioning, convicted of insurrection and sentenced to twelve years in prison. Yang Kui greeted his most lengthy prison term with his most trenchant humor,

Cover for the collection Yang Kui de wenxue shengya *(1986, The Literary Life of Yang Kui), edited by Chen Fangming (East Asian Library, Princeton University)*

observing that drafting the brief "Heping xuanyan" earned him his highest pay ever as a writer: a twelve-year meal ticket.

While serving his sentence on Lüdao (Green Island), Yang Kui continued to solicit contributions to the journals he edited, the *Xin shenghuo bibao* (New Life Bulletin) and the *Xinsheng yuebao* (New Life Monthly); worked on his Mandarin; and wrote many stories and essays. Among the essays was "Yuanding riji" (A Gardener's Diary), written in 1956 and published in *Yangtou ji*, in which, as in "Udori no yome iri," he describes his battle with the ants infesting his garden; but here he satirizes his own "imperialism" from the ants' point of view. In 1957 he wrote "Chunguang guanbuzhu" (Spring Light Cannot Be Shut Out), which was included in his collection *E mama chujia* (1975, Mother Goose Gets Married); renamed "Yabubian de meigui" (The Uncrushable Rose; translated as "The Indomitable Rose," 1978), it was the title story of a 1976 collection of his works. The story is set in the war years 1941 to 1945, when Taiwanese students were conscripted into Japanese construction units.

As the conscripts toil, the sight of a small fishing boat—the first sign of life outside the labor camp that the students have seen since being confined—causes an excited stir, and a rose growing under a rock symbolizes inextinguishable yearning for freedom and striving for life. Though the story is situated in the colonial era, the parallel between the predicament of Taiwan under the Japanese and under the Nationalist regime is clear. In "Yabubian de meigui," as in Yang Kui's other postwar works, anti-Japanese rhetoric is minimal, even though he was free to indulge in it: his interest had turned to uprooting the enemy within. In "Cai bashiwu sui de nüren" (The Woman Who Is Only Eighty-Five), written in 1957 and collected in the 1985 enlarged edition of *Yabubian de meigui*, an eighty-five-year-old woman hikes up a mountain, scorning bystanders who think that she needs help.

While imprisoned on Lüdao, Yang Kui wrote a series of letters to his wife and children; the letters never reached his family, who did not see them until they were published posthumously as *Lüdao jiashu* (1987, Letters Home from Green Island). One letter thanks Zibeng for sacrificing his education to take care of the family during his father's imprisonment and encourages him to carry on despite setbacks. A 1956 letter, "Wo de xiao xiansheng" (My Little Teacher), portrays his Mandarin sessions with his seven-year-old daughter, a picture of domestic bliss signifying his happiness about Taiwan's return to the motherland. "Taitai dailaile hao xiaoxi" (My Wife Brings Good News), also written in 1956, is an intimate celebration of Yang's family; family, he says, is the surest basis for a "commonwealth of nations."

In 1959 Yang Kui expressed his discontent with the strife between the Communists and the Nationalists in a play, *Niu li fenjia* (The Cow and the Plough Split Up), a thinly veiled political allegory in which both sides of a feuding family are denounced. It was performed as a street play in the Lüdao penal colony in 1959 and collected posthumously in his *Zheng yan de xiazi* (1990, Blind Man Eyes Open). Also in 1959 he was asked to serve as a spy in Japan for the Nationalist government; he agreed to do so, on the condition that his son accompany him, but the mission never took place.

Yang Kui was released from prison in 1961. In the years that followed he bought a small plot of land in Taizhong and started building his Donghai (Eastern Sea) Garden, which became a mecca for young writers as his literary fame spread. His wife died in 1965. In the 1970s his works were republished and anthologized as part of a movement in Taiwan to promote native literature. In his seventies Yang Kui became an avid long-distance runner and delighted in challenging young people to race him. His short memoir, "Bingshan dixia guohuo qishinian" (Seventy Years under an Iceberg), was published in *Yangtou ji*. By 1976 "Yabubian de meigui" was included in the national high-school literature curriculum—the first piece of writing by a native Taiwanese author to be so recognized. Yang Kui was invited to the International Writers' Workshop at the University of Iowa in 1982 and awarded Taiwan's Wu Sanlian Literary Prize in 1983. He died on 12 March 1985 and was eulogized both as a Chinese nationalist and a native son of Taiwan. Many of his works were rediscovered, translated, and anthologized posthumously.

In Taiwan, Yang Kui is respected for putting his ideals into practice and for the complexity of his ideology. Although he kept a cautious distance from the mainland and mainlanders, particularly in the wake of the imposition of martial law on 28 February 1947, Yang was not a Taiwan nationalist. While expressing understanding of the Taiwan Independence Movement, he called for a gradual process of unification between Taiwan and the mainland based on the wishes of the people. In his "'Caogen wenhua' de zai chufa" (Relaunching a Grassroots Culture), published in *Yabubian de meigui*, and in an interview in *Yang Kui de wenxue shengya* Yang Kui declared that Taiwanese tradition "by and large constitutes a minor tradition of mainland tradition, with, however, a new content" and called for a "grassroots culture" and a "realist, radical and exalted literature of social change." Yang Kui was anticapitalist and anti-imperialist, but because of his mistrust of governments he does not easily fit the description of a socialist. In a 1981 interview with Lin Jinkun he called himself a "humane socialist." He refrained from joining political parties, renounced the use of violence to effect social change, and never held out a vision of an ideal system of government. In the years immediately preceding and following the war he increasingly gave priority to the strength of the individual. This notion is a key component of his literary legacy.

Interviews:

Lin Jinkun, "Yang Kui fangwenji," *Jinbu zazhi* (April 1981);

Dai Guohui and Uchimura Gousuke, "Yang Kui de qishiqi nian suiyue—1982 nian Yang Kui xiansheng fangwen Riben de tanhua jilu," translated into Chinese by Chen Zhongyuan, *Wenji*, 1 (November 1983): 8–30;

Dai and Wakabayashi Masahiro, "Taiwan lao shehui yundongjia de huiyi yu zhanwang—Yang Kui guanyu Riben, Taiwan, Zhongguo dalu de tanhua jilu," *Taiwan yu shijie*, 21 (May 1985): 37–44; republished, *Wenji*, 2 (June 1985): 26–42;

Wang Shixun, "Yang Kui huiyi lu," and He Xu, "Ererba shijian qianhou," in *Yang Kui de wenxue shengya*, edited by Chen Fangming (Taibei: Qianwei chubanshe, 1988), pp. 143–174.

Bibliographies:

Lin Fan, "Yang Kui duizhao nianpu," in *Yang Kui huaxiang*, by Lin Fan (Taibei: Bijiashan chubanshe, 1978), pp. 245-294;

Zhang Henghao, "Yang Kui shengping xiezuo nianbiao," in *Yang Kui ji*, edited by Zhang, Taiwan zuojia quanji–duanpian xiaoshuo juan, Riju shidai, no. 7 (Taibei: Qianwei chubanshe, 1991), pp. 363-375;

Huang Huizhen, "Yang Kui shengping xiezuo nianbiao," "Heyuan Gong [Kawahara Isao] bian: Yang Kui shi 'zhuzuo mulu,'" and "Xubu Heyuan Gong [Kawahara Isao] bian: Yang Kui shi 'zhuzuo mulu,'" in his *Yang Kui ji qi zuopin yanjiu* (Taibei: Maitian chuban youxian gongsi, 1994), pp. 192-231.

Biographies:

Lin Fan, *Yang Kui huaxiang* (Taibei: Bijiashan chubanshe, 1978);

Yang Sujuan, ed., *Yang Kui de ren yu zuopin* (Taibei: Minzhong ribao chubanshe, 1979);

Chen Fangming, ed., *Yang Kui de wenxue shengya* (Taibei: Qianwei chubanshe, 1988);

Huang Huizhen, *Yang Kui ji qi zuopin yanjiu* (Taibei: Maitian chuban youxian gongsi, 1994).

References:

Bai Suying, "Cong wenxue zuopin kan Riju shidai de minzu xinli–Yang Kui, Wu Zhuoliu zuopin tantao," *Shiyuan*, 33 (May 1980): 26-34;

Chen Chunmei, "Zhuiqiu yige meiyou yapo, meiyou boxue de shehui–fang rendao de shehui zhuyi zhe Yang Kui," *Qianjin guangchang*, 15 (19 November 1983): 4-7;

Chen Ruoxi, "Yang Kui jingshen bu xiu," *Zhongguo shibao* (Taibei), 29 March 1985;

Chen Yingzhen, "Lishi de jimo–Yang Kui xiansheng yongchui buxiu," *Zhonghua zazhi*, no. 261 (April 1985): 51-52;

Dai Guohui, "Zuihou de jianzheng," *Zhongguo shibao* (Taibei), 13 March 1985;

Hu Qiuyuan, "Lun Yang Kui xiansheng ji qi zuopin," *Zhonghua zazhi*, 14, no. 160 (1976): 42-44;

Jiang Fan, "Yuanding lao qu cun weixiao–Yang Kui xiansheng de wenxue jingshen," *Zili wanbao* (Taibei), 13 March 1985;

Kawahara Isao, "Taiwan xin wenxue yundong de zhankai (shang)–Riben tongzhi xia zai Taiwan de shehui yundong," translated into Chinese by Ye Shitao, *Wenxue Taiwan*, 1 (December 1990): 217-245;

Kawahara, "Yang Kui de wenxue huodong," translated into Chinese by Yang Jingding, *Taiwan wenyi*, no. 94 (May 1985): 182-199; no. 95 (July 1985): 194-213;

Lin Yingwen, "Lao bing jingshen bu si–zhuiyi Yang Kui," *Wenxue jie*, 14 (April 1985): 138-140;

Liu Jingjuan, "Na chutou zai dishang xiezuo–fang yongyuan bu lao de Yang Kui xiansheng," *Zhongyang yuekan*, 14 (May 1982): 65-67;

Qiu Xiuzhi and others, "Bu xiu de lao bing: Yang Kui yinxiang," *Wenxun yuekan*, 17 (April 1985): 245-264;

Song Dongyang, "Fang dan wenzhang pinmin jiu–lun Yang Kui zuopin zhong de fan zhimin jingshen," *Taiwan wenyi*, no. 94 (May 1985): 144-164;

Song, "Xianren zhi xue, tudi zhi hua–Riju shidai Taiwan zuoyi wenxue yundong de fazhan beijing," *Taiwan wenyi*, no. 88 (May 1984): 6-22;

Tsukamoto Terukazu, "Yang Kui zuopin 'Shinbun Haitatsufu' (Songbaofu) de banben zhi mi," translated into Chinese by Xiang Yang, *Taiwan wenyi*, no. 94 (May 1985): 165-180;

Yang Jian, "Nitu de huigui–huainian xianfu Yang Kui xiansheng," *Lianhe wenxue*, 8 (June 1985): 22-25;

Yang Sujuan, "Xinjin shang de baihua–fuqin yu wo, jian ji muqin Ye Tao nüshi," *Lianhe wenxue*, no. 8 (June 1985): 26-32;

Ye Shitao, "Liulei sa zhong de, bi huanhu shouge–guangfu chuqi de Taiwan Riwen wenxue," *Wenxue jie*, 9 (February 1984): 2-9;

Ye, "Riju shidai de kangyi wenxue," *Lianhe wenxue*, no. 56 (June 1989): 162-169;

Ye, "Riju shidai de Yang Kui–ta de Riben jingyan yu yingxiang," *Lianhe wenxue*, no. 8 (June 1985): 21;

Ye Yunyun, "Shi lun zhanhou chuqi de Taiwan zhishi fenzi ji qi wenxue huodong (1945-1949)," *Wenji*, 2 (June 1985): 1-18;

Angelina Yee, "Writing the Colonial Self: Yang Kui's Texts of Resistance and National Identity," *Chinese Literature: Essays, Articles, Reviews*, 17 (1995): 111-132;

Zhang Henghao, "Guanyu 'Heping xuanyan' ji qita," in *Yang Kui de wenxue shengya*, edited by Chen Fangming (Taibei: Qianwei chubanshe, 1988), pp. 309-322;

Zhang Liangze, "Buqu de wenxue hun–lun Yang Kui jian tan Riju shidai de Taiwan wenyi," *Qianjin guangchang*, 15 (19 November 1983);

Zhong Zhaoqing, "Xuelei de wenxue, zhengzha de wenxue–qishi nian Taiwan wenxue fazhan zongheng tan (zongxu)," in *Taiwan zuojia quanji: Lai He ji* (Taibei: Qianwei chubanshe, 1991), pp. 1-38.

Ye Shaojun
(Ye Shengtao)
(28 October 1894 – 16 February 1988)

Xinmin Liu
University of Pittsburgh

SELECTED BOOKS: *Gemo* [Barriers] (Shanghai: Shangwu yinshuguan, 1922)–includes "Yi sheng," translated as "A Lifetime," in *Genesis of a Revolution: An Anthology of Modern Chinese Short Stories,* edited and translated by Stanley R. Munro (Singapore: Heinemann Educational [Asia], 1979), pp. 147–154;

Xuezhao [Snowy Morning], by Ye, Zhou Zuoren, Zhu Ziqing, Yu Pingbo, Liu Yanling, Zheng Zhenduo, Guo Shaoyu, and Xu Yunuo (Shanghai: Shangwu yinshuguan, 1922);

Daocaoren [The Scarecrow] (Shanghai: Shangwu yinshuguan, 1923)–includes "Yi li zhongzi," translated as "The Seed," *Chinese Literature,* no. 7 (1961): 115–119; title story translated as "The Scarecrow," *Chinese Literature,* no. 7 (1961): 107–114;

Huozai [Conflagration] (Shanghai: Shangwu yinshuguan, 1923);

Jianqiao [The Scabbard], by Ye and Yu (Shanghai: Pushe, 1924);

Zuowen lun [On Composition] (Shanghai: Shangwu yinshuguan, 1924);

Xianxia [Under the Line] (Shanghai: Shangwu yinshuguan, 1925)–includes "Qiaoshang," translated by Donald Holoch as "On the Bridge," in *Revolutionary Literature in China: An Anthology,* edited by John Berninghausen and Theodore Huters (White Plains, N.Y.: Sharpe, 1976), pp. 21–26; "Pan xiansheng zai nan zhong," translated by Tang Sheng as "How Mr. Pan Weathered the Storm," *Chinese Literature,* 5 (1963): 3–22;

Chengzhong [In the City] (Shanghai: Kaiming shudian, 1926);

Fenglang [The Storm] (Shanghai: Shangwu yinshuguan, 1928);

Weiyan ji [Without Satiety] (Shanghai: Shangwu yinshuguan, 1928)–includes "Yifuzi," translated by Richard J. Jen as "A Man Must Have a Son," *T'ien*

Ye Shaojun (from Ye Shengtao, *edited by Ye Zhishan, 1989; Collection of Thomas Moran)*

Hsia Monthly, 6 (April 1938): 377–387; "Kangzheng," translated by George A. Kennedy as "Resistance," *China Forum,* 1 (April 1932): 7–8; and "Ye," translated by Zhang Su as "Night," *Chinese Literature,* no. 5 (1963): 23–32;

Ni Huanzhi (Shanghai: Kaiming shudian, 1929); translated by A. C. Barnes as *Schoolmaster Ni Huan-chih* (Peking: Foreign Languages Press, 1958);

Gudai yingxiong de shixiang [The Statue of the Ancient Hero] (Shanghai: Shangwu yinshuguan, 1931)—includes "Gudai yingxiong de shixiang," translated as "The Statue of the Ancient Hero," *Chinese Literature*, no. 3 (1954): 129–133; and "Huangdi de xinyi," translated as "The Emperor's New Clothes," *Chinese Literature*, no. 3 (1954): 133–138;

Jiaobu ji [Footsteps Collection] (Shanghai: Xin Zhongguo shuju, 1931);

Mifeng [Honeybees], by Ye and He Mingzhai (Shanghai: Shangwu yinshuguan, 1932);

Weiyan ju xizuo [Practice Compositions from the Without Satiety Residence] (Shanghai: Kaiming shudian, 1935);

Sisan ji [Forty-Three] (Shanghai: Liangyou fuxing tushu yinshua gongsi, 1936)—includes "Yipian xuanyan," translated by Yu Fanqin as "A Declaration," *Chinese Literature*, no. 5 (1963): 32–38; and "Duo shou le san wu dou," translated by Gladys Yang as "A Year of Good Harvest," *Chinese Literature*, no. 4 (1960): 37–45;

Shengtao duanpian xiaoshuo ji [A Collection of Shengtao's Short Stories] (Shanghai: Shangwu yinshuguan, 1936);

Shengtao suibi [Shengtao's Jottings] (Shanghai: Santong shuju, 1940);

Xi Chuan ji [West Sichuan Collection] (Chongqing: Wenguang shudian, 1945);

Hanjia de yi tian [One Day during Winter Vacation] (Beijing: Renmin wenxue chubanshe, 1953);

Yige lianxisheng [A Trainee] (N.p.: Tongsu duwu chubanshe, 1955);

Ye Shengtao xuanji [Selected Works by Ye Shengtao] (Beijing: Renmin wenxue chubanshe, 1956);

Kangzheng [Fighting Back] (Beijing: Renmin wenxue chubanshe, 1958);

Xiaoji shi pian [Ten Notes] (Tianjin: Baihua wenyi chubanshe, 1958);

Qiecun ji [From a Valise] (Beijing: Zuojia chubanshe, 1960);

Pinggai liang pian zuowen [Revisions and Commentary on Two Articles] (Beijing: Renmin chubanshe, 1964);

Pinggai liang pian baodao [Revisions and Commentary on Two Reports] (Beijing: Renmin chubanshe, 1964);

Riji san chao [Three Transcripts from a Diary] (Guangzhou: Huacheng chubanshe, 1982);

Ye Shengtao lun chuangzuo [Ye Shengtao on Literary Creation] (Shanghai: Wenyi chubanshe, 1982)—includes "Wenyi tan," excerpts translated by Kirk A. Denton as "On the Literary Arts (Excerpts)," in *Modern Chinese Literary Thought: Writings on Literature, 1893–1945,* edited by Denton (Stanford, Cal.: Stanford University Press, 1996), pp. 162–168;

Wo yu Sichuan [Sichuan and I] (Chengdu: Sichuan renmin chubanshe, 1984).

Collections: *Ye Shaojun daibiao zuo* [Representative Works by Ye Shaojun] (Shanghai: Santong shuju, 1941);

Ye Shengtao wenji [Ye Shengtao's Collected Works] (Shanghai: Chunfeng shudian, 1948);

Ye Shengtao xuanji [Selected Works by Ye Shengtao] (Shanghai: Kaiming shudian, 1951);

Ye Shengtao duanpian xiaoshuo ji (Beijing: Renmin wenxue chubanshe, 1954);

Ye Shengtao tonghua ji [Stories for Children by Ye Shengtao] (Beijing: Zhongguo shaonian ertong chubanshe, 1956);

Ye Shengtao wenji [Ye Shengtao's Collected Works], 3 volumes (Beijing: Renmin wenxue chubanshe, 1958);

Ye Shengtao xuanji [Selected Works by Ye Shengtao] (Beijing: Renmin wenxue chubanshe, 1959);

"Daocaoren" he qita tonghua ["The Scarecrow" and Other Stories for Children] (Beijing: Zhongguo shaonian ertong chubanshe, 1979);

Ye Shengtao yuwen jiaoyu lunwen ji [Ye Shengtao's Treatises on Chinese Language Arts Education], 2 volumes (Beijing: Jiaoyu kexue chubanshe, 1980);

Ye Shengtao, edited by Ye Zhishan, "Zhongguo xiandai zuojia xuanji" congshu ["Selected Works of Modern Chinese Authors" Series] (Hong Kong: Sanlian shudian [Xianggang] youxian gongsi; Renmin wenxue chubanshe, 1983);

Ye Shengtao sanwen jiaji [The First Collection of Ye Shengtao's Essays] (Chengdu: Sichuan renmin chubanshe, 1983);

Ye Shengtao xu ba ji [Ye Shengtao's Prefaces and Postscripts] (Beijing: Sanlian shudian, 1983);

Ye Shengtao sanwen yiji [The Second Collection of Ye Shengtao's Essays] (Beijing: Sanlian shudian, 1984);

Ye Shengtao lun yuwen jiaoyu [Ye Shengtao on Chinese Language Arts Education] (Zhengzhou: Henan jiaoyu chubanshe, 1986);

Ye Shengtao ji [The Collected Works of Ye Shengtao], 5 volumes (Nanjing: Jiangsu jiaoyu chubanshe, 1987–1988);

Ye Shengtao, edited by Ye Zhishan (Hong Kong: Sanlian shudian [Xianggang] youxian gongsi; Renmin wenxue chubanshe, 1989);

Ye Shengtao sanwen xuanji [The Selected Essays of Ye Shengtao] (Tianjin: Baihua wenji chubanshe, 1992).

Editions in English: "Mrs. Li's Hair" ("Li taitai de toufa") and "Neighbors" ("Linju"), in *Contemporary Chinese Stories,* translated by Wang Chi-chen (New York: Columbia University Press, 1944), pp. 165–180;

"The Torrential Rain of May 31" ("Wu yue sayi ri jiyu zhong"), translated by Thomas Goo, *Journal of Oriental Literature,* 2 (June 1948): 8–11;

The Scarecrow: A Collection of Stories for Children (Peking: Foreign Languages Press, 1961)—comprises "The Seed" ("Yi li zhongzi"), "The Thrush" ("Huamei niao"), "The Scarecrow" ("Daocaoren"), "The Statue of the Ancient Hero" ("Gudai yingxiong de shixiang"), "The Emperor's New Clothes" ("Huangdi de xinyi"), "The Sensitive Plant" ("Hanxiu cao"), "The Silkworm and the Ant" ("Can he mayi"), "The Experience of a Locomotive" ("Huochetou de jingli"), and "The Language of Birds and Animals" ("Niao yu shou yan");

"Mr. Pan in Stress" ("Pan xiansheng zai nan zhong") and "Three to Five Bushels More" ("Duo shou le san wu dou"), translated by Harold R. Isaacs, in *Straw Sandals: Chinese Short Stories, 1918–1933,* edited by Isaacs (Cambridge, Mass.: MIT Press, 1974), pp. 84–106, 337–347;

"Rice" ("Fan") and "Solitude" ("Gudu"), translated by Frank Kelly; "Horse-Bell Melons" ("Maling gua"), translated by Jason C. S. Wang; and "Autumn" ("Qiu"), translated by Kelly, in *Modern Chinese Stories and Novellas 1919–1949,* edited by Joseph S. M. Lau, C. T. Hsia, and Leo Ou-Fan Lee (New York: Columbia University Press, 1981), pp. 90–122;

How Mr. Pan Weathered the Storm, edited by Wei Shang (Beijing: Chinese Literature, 1987)—includes "Bitter Greens" ("Ku cai"), translated by Simon Johnstone; "A Stroll at Dawn" ("Xiao xing"), translated by Wenxue; "The Package" ("Yi bao dongxi"), translated by Wenxue; "A Trainee" ("Yige lianxisheng"), translated by Johnstone; "A Minor Flutter" ("Yige xiao langhua"), translated by Wenxue; "Lotus Root and Water Shield" ("Ou yu chuncai"), translated by Alison Bailey; "Before Leaving" ("Jiang li"), translated by Bailey; "Traveller's Words" ("Keyu"), translated by Bailey; "Late-Night Food" ("Shenye de shipin"), translated by Johnstone; "Three Kinds of Boat" ("Sanzhong chuan"), translated by Bailey; and "To Goose Sands by Sheepskin Raft" ("Zuo yangpifa dao yantan"), translated by Johnstone;

"Yifuzi," translated by Bonnie S. McDougall as "The Posthumous Son," in *The Columbia Anthology of Modern Chinese Literature,* edited by Lau and Howard Goldblatt (New York: Columbia University Press, 1995), pp. 35–43;

"Three Kinds of Boat" ("Sanzhong chuan"), "My Own Patch of Green" ("Tianjing li de zhongzhi"), and "Intellectuals" ("Zhishi fenzi"), in *The Chinese Essay,* edited and translated by David E. Pollard (New York: Columbia University Press, 2000), pp. 167–187.

OTHER: *Jie ben Xunzi* [Primer of Xunzi], compiled by Ye as Ye Shengtao (Shanghai: Shangwu yinshu guan, 1937);

Wen yiduo quanji [Complete Works of Wen Yiduo], edited by Ye and Zhu Ziqing (Shanghai: Kaiming shudian, 1948),

Wen xin [The Soul of Literary Writings], edited by Ye and Xia Mianzun (Hong Kong: Tatong shujü, 1959);

Zhu ziqing wenji [Selected Works of Zhu Ziqing], edited by Ye and others (Hong Kong: Wenxue yanjiu she, 1972);

Wen zhang ping gai [Editorial Comments on Literary Writings], edited by Ye and others (Shanghai: Shanghai jian yü chubanshe, 1979);

Wen yan du ben [A Reader of Classical Chinese], edited by Ye and Lü Shuxiang (Shanghai: Jiaoyü chubanshe, 1980);

Wen zhang jiang hua [Commentary on Creative Writing], edited by Ye and others (Beijing: Yü wen chubanshe, 1992).

Ye Shaojun was one of the most versatile and renowned Chinese intellectuals of the twentieth century. During his life of more than nine decades he wrote literary works and children's fiction, edited books and journals, and was an educator, linguist, and government official. He took Ye Shengtao as his *zi* (style name) in 1911 and published his first work under that name in the same year. He used at least seventeen pen names during his career, but he published the majority of his work as either Ye Shaojun—his birth name—or Ye Shengtao. When he died in 1988, he was mourned as one of the most important authors of modern Chinese literature.

Ye was born on 23 October 1894 on the outskirts of Suzhou in Jiangsu province. His father, Ye Renbo, was a bookkeeper; his mother's surname was Zhu. He attended *sishu* (traditional private schools) from 1900 to 1905. In 1905, in keeping with his father's wishes, he took the imperial examination but did not pass; the examinations were abolished that year. From 1906 to 1911 he studied in Suzhou's first modern public primary and middle schools. One of his primary-school classmates was Gu Jiegang, who became famous as an

Ye Shaojun (center) with the authors Gu Xiegang (left) and Wang Boxiang in 1911 (from Ye Shengtao, *edited by Ye Zhishan, 1989; Collection of Thomas Moran)*

historian in the 1920s; the two formed a lifelong friendship. Ye was forced to discontinue his schooling after he graduated from middle school, because his family could not afford the tuition for high school.

Ye taught elementary school in Suzhou from 1912 until he lost the job in 1914. His elderly father was unemployed, and to continue to support his family Ye began to sell his writing. In the summer of 1914 he published two short stories written in Classical Chinese, one in *Xiaoshuo congbao* (Fiction Miscellany) and the other in the popular Shanghai magazine *Libailiu* (Saturday). In 1915 he moved to Shanghai, where he edited primary-school Chinese-language textbooks for the Shangwu yinshuguan (Commercial Press) and taught Chinese language arts at a primary school operated by the firm for its employees' children. In the summer of 1916 he married Hu Molin from Hangzhou, who had graduated from the Beijing nüzi shifan xuexiao (Beijing Women's Normal School) and taught at the Nantong Women's Normal Academy.

In 1917 Ye began teaching at a *gaodeng xiaoxue* (higher primary school)—grades five and six—in Luzhi, near Suzhou. He and his reform-minded colleague Wu Binruo proposed to revise the standard curriculum by replacing some traditional classics with modern texts that treated subjects more relevant to students' lives and that were written in, or translated into, *baihua* (the vernacular). Inspired by the American educator John Dewey's notion of "learning by doing," Ye and Wu believed that effective schooling must place students in an environment that is like the larger society in miniature and where they can achieve growth by way of "controlled social development." Accordingly, they set up an experimental school farm where students could apply book knowledge to change "social" conditions. One of the goals of the farm experiment was to knock down the social barrier between the children of landowners and those of ordinary peasants; that goal was not reached because the barrier persisted even on the farm. Also, the farm was built on an abandoned graveyard, which angered the townsfolk. Ye and Wu also held that teachers must act as ethical role models in times of social change. Ye published commentaries on how traditional pedagogy impeded young learners and made it difficult for them to learn to read, think, and write well. He advocated adopting new teaching methodologies and promoted the use of the vernacular in schools in place of Classical Chinese.

In 1918 Ye and Hu had a son, Ye Zhishan. In the same year Ye published his first short story written in the vernacular, "Chun yan suotan" (Table Talk on a Spring Evening), in *Funü zazhi* (Women's Journal). In 1919, inspired by the May Fourth Movement, he joined the circle of student activists, mostly from Beijing, who founded the Xinchao she (New Tide Society), and he contributed short stories to the society's journal, *Xinchao/The Renaissance*.

In the 1920s Ye edited and annotated editions of classical texts and poetry and co-authored books of literary criticism and essays on language with his friends Xia Mianzun and Zhu Ziqing. According to C. T. Hsia, the introductory Chinese literature and rhetoric textbooks Ye wrote with Xia and Zhu were "quite popular with high school students." Ye's writings on pedagogy are collected in *Ye Shengtao yuwen jiaoyu lunwen ji* (1980, Ye Shengtao's Treatises on Chinese Language Arts Education), and much of his literary criticism is collected in *Ye Shengtao lun chuangzuo* (1982, Ye Shengtao on Literary Creation).

In 1921 Gu assisted Ye in establishing connections with the leftist writers Mao Dun and Zheng Zhenduo, who invited Ye to be a fellow founding member of the Wenxue yanjiu hui (Literary Research Association) that year. When these writers called for a new "wenxue wei rensheng" (literature as the expression of human life), they reaffirmed what Ye believed and implemented in his writing. Ye wrote in "Wenyi tan" (excerpts translated as "On the Literary Arts," 1996), a series of forty essays that appeared in the supplement of the Shanghai newspaper *Chen bao* (Morning Post) from March to June 1921, that the purpose of "true literary works" is to "draw the reader in without his being aware of it. The reader feels the profound feeling seep into his spirit, and from this he can increase his own understanding, compassion, and delight. This is something that humankind needs and expects and something to which writers should devote themselves." He contends that "literature is the expression and the critique of life" and that "the humanist tendency to empathize with the plight of the weak" is an example of the "profound feeling" expressed in all writing worthy of being called "literature," and he offers "sincerity" as "the essential condition necessary" for the profession of writer (translations by Kirk A. Denton). Ye's essays on literature combine traditional beliefs, such as the assumption that the purpose of writing is the cultivation and expression of the self in order to move others emotionally, with modern notions, such as the conviction that fiction should serve the downtrodden and instigate social reform. In Marston Anderson's summation, "Wenyi tan" blends "self-expression and moral earnestness." Leaning heavily on the subjective and the emotive, Ye's views on literature are cogent, composed, and unassuming. In Hsia's words, throughout his career Ye "evinced a civilized sensibility which, while nourished upon the prevailing attitudes of the time, remains nearly always invulnerable to cant and pretentiousness." Also in 1921 Ye contributed to *Libailiu* an essay attacking the frivolity of the literature published in the magazine and objecting to the cynical, decadent tone of the magazine's advertising slogan: "You can take away my concubine, just don't take away my *Saturday*."

Ye's opinions on literature were faulted by his more militant leftist colleagues for being prosaic and individualistic. Leftists such as Qian Xingcun took Ye's self-assurance as an indulging of personal sentiments and an escape from social engagement. Anderson notes that in the 1920s, Qian's Taiyang she (Sun Society) attacked Ye, Mao Dun, and Lu Xun "in part for their continued focus on the problems of intellectuals and the middle class, in part for failing to offer a positive message of hope to the workers and peasants." Receptive to criticism but not swayed by it, Ye never countered his critics directly but wove his responses and defense of his opinions into his essays. He seems not to have deviated from this approach decades later: Hsia finds that Ye's preface to *Ye Shengtao xuanji* (1956, Selected Works by Ye Shengtao) "actually reads like a sly rebuke" to the Communist requirement that all fiction be about workers and peasants, a policy with which Ye could not disagree openly.

In June 1921 Ye went to Shanghai to teach in a middle school but left three months later after a disagreement between conservative members of the faculty and the progressive faction to which he belonged. He followed his friend Zhu to Hangzhou and got a teaching position there. In January 1922 he began teaching composition at Beijing University at the invitation of the university's president and the chairman of the Chinese department, but he resigned a month later to return to Suzhou and be with his wife during her difficult pregnancy. Hu gave birth to a daughter, Ye Zhimei, in April.

Ye's first collection of short stories, *Gemo* (Barriers), was published by the Commercial Press in March 1922. The stories exude empathy for representative poor, illiterate, and downtrodden working-class figures such as the abused wife, the child bride, the gardener, and the rice farmer. Posing as the incarnated spirit of the May Fourth Movement, the educated narrator bluntly exposes the abusive and voracious bullies among the citizens of a typical small town. He describes the landowner, the school official, and the patriarch in brief but compelling passages that are reminiscent of the highlights of Chekhovian drama, and his expression of passionate amity for the victimized among the townsfolk reaches a lyrical epiphany. In the meantime, however, the plot stagnates. In "Yi ke" (One Class), while the teacher lectures on the orbits of the planets, one pupil lets his mind play truant as he ponders where to pick tender mulberry leaves for the pet silkworm he secretly keeps in his desk drawer. Interior monologue reveals that the boy is mistreated by the school officials because of his family's inability to pay for textbooks. In other stories women are treated as chattel to be bought and sold. The title character of "A Feng" is a child bride for whom a day never passes without a scolding or beating from her mother-in-law. When she has a rare moment to rest, A Feng sings lullabies and plays with a kitten. Ye's early stories are melodramatic and didactic, and the narrators are often thinly disguised versions of the author.

In the spring of 1923 Ye took a job as an editor in the language arts division of the Commercial Press. He and Gu wrote a middle-school Chinese composition and literary studies textbook that sold well through the 1940s. Ye also taught at Fudan University and other schools in Shanghai. In November 1923 he published a book for children, *Daocaoren* (The Scarecrow), in which he reworks stories and legends from Chinese folklore. According to Hsia, Ye's best-known stories for children, including the title piece in this volume (translated as "The Scarecrow," 1961), are all written in imitation of Hans Christian Andersen, but this claim does not diminish his status as one of the most important and successful writers of children's fiction in modern China.

Ye's second collection of fiction for adults, *Huozai* (Conflagration), was also published in November 1923. It shows a critical shift in narrative approach that continues in his next two collections, *Xianxia* (1925, Under the Line) and *Chengzhong* (1926, In the City). "Ku cai" (translated as "Bitter Greens," 1987) is typical of the stories in *Gemo* in that the working-class world remains impenetrable to the narrator: the narrator is perplexed that the gardener he hires to grow vegetables for him loathes gardening and toiling in the soil; he had assumed that all gardeners savor and nurture life and

Cover for a 1949 edition of Ye's children's book Daocaoren *(1923, The Scarecrow), a collection of reworked stories and legends from Chinese folklore (Wason Collection on East Asia–China, Kroch Asia Library, Cornell University)*

are at one with nature. In the stories in *Huozai*, in contrast, the narrators are more self-conscious about the elite status that alienates them from the wretched commoners they encounter. "Xiao tongjiang" (The Little Coppersmith) identifies the barrier between the narrator, who is a self-absorbed teacher, and a student from a poor family as having been formed by class differences; the narrator calls the class barrier "a wall both tall and thick blocking each from the other." When the student, whose poverty has forced him to withdraw from school, returns to help fix broken classroom equipment and displays considerable skill in doing so, the teacher realizes that the educated classes do not know what life is like for workers.

In May 1925 striking Chinese textile workers in Shanghai vandalized a Japanese-owned mill; the Japanese guards fired on the workers and killed one of them. On 30 May about two thousand students and workers demonstrated on Shanghai's Nanjing Road in the center of the city; when the demonstration threatened to grow violent, Chinese and Sikh police opened fire on the command of a British officer, killing at least ten and wounding dozens. The following day, street demonstrators defied armed patrols in the city's foreign concessions. Ye's "Wu yue sayi ri jiyu zhong" (1925; translated as "The Torrential Rain of May 31," 1948) provides an eyewitness account of the events. His observations are conveyed powerfully and lyrically, and his indictment of the repressive violence of the foreign imperialist powers comes through clearly.

The stories in *Xianxia* and *Chengzhong* show an increase in realism, with a corresponding decrease in lyricism. Critics classified many of the stories in the two collections as belonging to the literature of *huise shenghuo* (lives in gray), in which characters live out their humdrum existences and fall short in their attempts to get ahead and to bring meaning to their lives. The narrators are able to view the characters and events from a distance and engage in a sober appraisal of the gap between moral ideals and the exigencies of reality. In tales such as "Jin erhuan" (The Golden Earrings) and "Waiguo qi" (Foreign Flags) in *Xianxia* and "Qiantu" (The Future) in *Chengzhong*, Ye unmasks the genteel guises of vain urbanites who are proud of what the reader knows to be petty and self-serving acts. In the end, each of these urban sophisticates is dealt a shattering blow by reality.

The motif of the educator struggling to cope with social change dominates Ye's writing during much of the 1920s. He reveals the naive intentions, psychological failings, and narrow social vision of his schoolteacher and administrator characters, many of whom are modeled on his colleagues from his teaching days. In "Xiaozhang" (The Headmaster), which is included in *Xianxia*, Headmaster Shuya carries out a curriculum reform that includes having his pupils grow corn, potatoes, and vegetables in some reclaimed wasteland behind the school. Just as "the young shoots of an ideal school"—both the literal shoots of the students' crops and the students as metaphorical shoots beginning to grow—are sprouting, three teachers are discovered gambling before and after school, and one is accused of having extramarital sex. Such scandalous deeds could ruin the school's reputation. Shuya tries to persuade his teachers to mend their ways, to no avail. In the end he yields to their pleas and agrees to renew their contracts. Ye's message is that the headmaster should direct to himself the same moral scrutiny he applies to others when he is confronted with the hardest part of his reform: firing those who are unfit to teach.

In the title story of *Xianxia* the young teacher Ding Yusheng returns to his hometown to open a progressive middle school but meets resistance from the local bureaucrats. Ding and his colleagues seize every opportunity to publicize their agenda of a socially responsible educational system, coeducation, and low tuition, despite the danger of being arrested as political radicals. Ye brings the story to an abrupt end with Ding standing firm against the politicians, leaving unanswered the question of whether his new school will survive.

Also included in *Xianxia* is "Pan xiansheng zai nan zhong" (translated as "How Mr. Pan Weathered the Storm," 1963), perhaps Ye's best-known short story. Pan has brought his family to Shanghai because their town is about to be attacked by a warlord's army, but he is summoned home to resume teaching. There he joins the local Red Cross and offers his school as a shelter for women refugees should the need arise. He is given a Red Cross badge to wear and a Red Cross banner to display at the school. Knowing that the warlord will respect these emblems, Pan finds excuses to ask for more badges, which he intends to give to his family when they return from Shanghai, and a second banner, which he hangs in front of their house. At the end of the story officials from the Bureau of Education ask Pan to provide the calligraphy for inscriptions welcoming the arrival of the triumphant warlord, General Du, and his troops. Pan writes the inscriptions praising Du's virtue and benevolence, even though he knows that the fighting has brought only destruction, suffering, and death. Pan's use of the charitable organization for his own self-interest and his surrender to that which he formerly despised reveal his moral decline. For Ye, Pan's personal failure is symbolic of the failure of realist fiction, which merely describes social problems, to effect real change.

Ye and Hu's last child, their son Ye Zhicheng, was born in August 1926. In 1927 Ye became editor in chief of *Xiaoshuo yuebao* (Short Story Monthly). In the position, which he held through late 1930, he compiled special issues in memory of the revolutionary youths who had been arrested or killed in the Nationalist crackdown on the Left. He published Mao Dun's "Lu Xun lun" (1927, On Lu Xun), a pioneering critical study of a modern Chinese author. He also put together special issues devoted to emerging fiction writers such as Ding Ling, Shi Zhecun, and Zhang Tianyi; Ding Ling's "Shafei nüshi de riji" (1928; translated as "The Diary of Miss Sophia," 1974) is one of several stories he selected for these issues that have important places in the history of modern Chinese literature. And he helped to energize the new genre of free-verse vernacular poetry by facilitating the debut of Dai Wangshu. Ye's editorial notes and columns appealed to nonliterary youths and other common readers by offering encouragement, advice, and social commentary, in addition to literary criticism.

Ye's fourth book of stories, *Weiyan ji* (1928, Without Satiety), includes "Kangzheng" (Fighting Back; translated as "Resistance," 1932). The protagonist, Guo, is a member of the executive committee of his town's *jiaozhiyuan lianhehui* (teachers and administrators union). When the press reports that the town authorities have decided to hold back the payment of teachers' salaries and plan a salary reduction for the following year, Guo is enraged and calls a meeting of the teachers to launch a protest. Despite his wife's words of caution, he confronts the authorities with a list of demands and leads the teachers in a strike. Weeks later, with no response from the authorities, the other teachers call off the strike. Guo loses his job, and his family is faced with destitution.

Ye's only novel, *Ni Huanzhi* (translated as *Schoolmaster Ni Huanzhi*, 1958), was serialized in *Jiaoyu zazhi* (Journal of Education) from January through December 1928 and published as a book in August 1929. The title character is an educator who, as Anderson observes, goes through three rites of passage—pedagogical, romantic, and political. Though each stage ends in dissatisfaction for Ni, his journey in search of a fulfilling life lays out the course of personal development one must follow to serve society. At the invitation of the reform-minded headmaster Jiang Bingru, Ni arrives at a new school to teach and put his ideals of *cheng* (sincerity) and *tongqing* (compassion) into practice. (Anderson traces Ye's preoccupation with *cheng* and *tongqing* in his work in general.) Instead of scolding the son of a town notable for bullying a carpenter's son during a ballgame, Ni appeals to the youngster's empathy and self-respect and persuades him to admit his wrongdoing. Ni believes that students should be trained in life skills and prepared to meet the needs of society, and he proposes to establish a farm where the pupils can grow produce. His progressive ideas, however, arouse the hostility of his fellow teachers and the townspeople, who prefer the status quo. Scandalous rumors are circulated about the school, and a powerful local figure, Tiger Jiang, threatens a lawsuit. To save the farm project Ni and the headmaster are forced to make deals with the local elite. Ni learns bitter lessons about the political obstacles standing in the way of school reform and about the social pressure that makes it difficult for him to be the person he wants to be.

Ni's romance with Miss Jin, a cultured young woman with liberal ideals who recently graduated from a normal college and is helping out at the school as an instructor, also leads to disappointment and compromise. Ni and Miss Jin express their feelings for each other by talking about teaching; as Anderson notes,

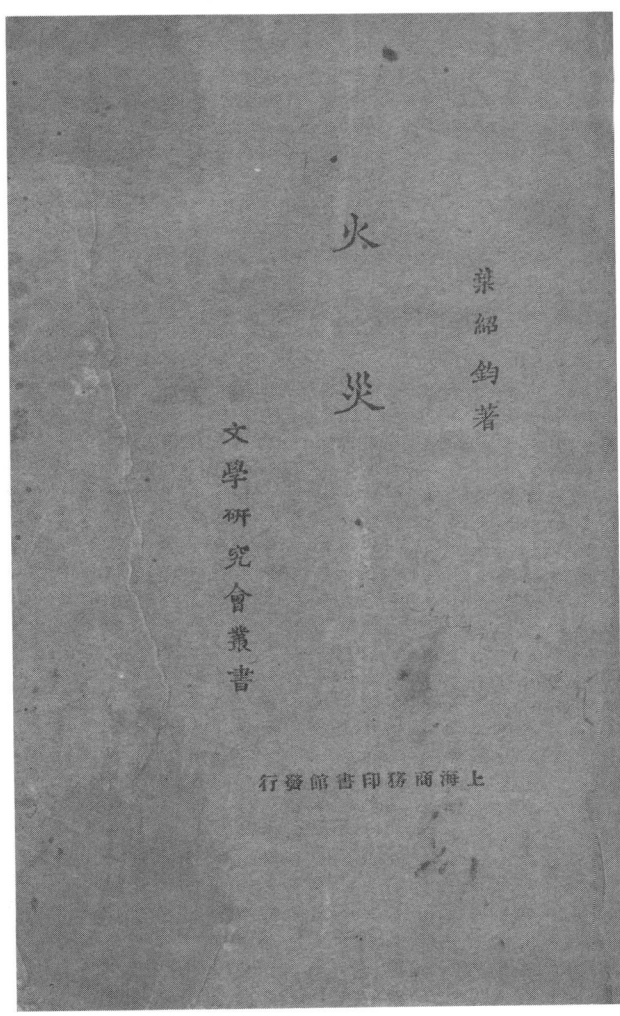

Cover for a 1928 edition of *Huozai* (1923, Conflagration), Ye's second collection of fiction for adults (Wason Collection on East Asia–China, Kroch Asia Library, Cornell University)

"Though the couple's early conversations are limited to a discussion of pedagogical matters, they are colored by an awkward adolescent eroticism." The couple soon turn to love letters, which spare them the embarrassment of speaking face to face. Ni writes to Jin in the vernacular; Anderson points out that "during the May Fourth period . . . the sexual encoding of the colloquial language . . . made it the expressive ground for the potency of both a new politics and a new sexuality." But she writes back in the classical language, thus remaining within the bounds of traditional etiquette and propriety for women. Their marriage is a harsh letdown for Ni; he becomes bored by household chores and is disappointed by his wife's wilting interest in social and pedagogical reform in favor of caring for

Cover for a 1949 edition of Ye's only novel, Ni Huanzhi (1929; translated as Schoolmaster Ni Huanzhi, 1958), about a teacher who goes through three rites of passage—pedagogical, romantic, and political—all of which end badly (Collection of John Berninghausen)

their baby son. Like his educational ideals, Ni's hopes for love and happiness fail to match dreary reality.

The last part of *Ni Huanzhi* deals with the "May Thirtieth Movement" of 1925 and the "White Terror"—the violent purge of leftists—of 1927–1928. Ni is visited by Wang Leshan, a former classmate who has been a labor activist in Beijing. Wang's radical left-wing ideology is appealing to Ni, who comes to Shanghai to teach in a girls' middle school and soon joins Wang and other activists in the labor movement. On 30 May 1925 the activists lead a general strike in Shanghai; Ni participates in street protests, makes speeches, and is caught up in clashes with the police. But some of the Nationalist troops suddenly mutiny and massacre workers, students, and city residents who have gathered in support of the protests. The labor movement is routed, and Wang is executed along with hundreds of other revolutionaries. Disillusioned, Ni suffers from hallucinations, falls into a coma, and dies. Though his wife carries on his cause after his death, Ye makes it clear that Ni was an idealist who pursued a fantasy and was unable to accept reality or to continue to embrace revolution when it met defeat. Anderson and other scholars have observed that Ni Huanzhi is Ye's alter ego: Ye was a staunch left-wing nationalist and collaborated with the Chinese Communist Party, but he remained on the margins of partisan politics. According to *Ye Shengtao yanjiu ziliao* (1988, Research Materials on Ye Shengtao), edited by Liu Zengren and Feng Guanglian, he did not join the Zhongguo zuoyi zuojia lianmeng (Chinese League of Left-Wing Writers) when it was founded in 1930 because Feng Xuefeng, an undercover Communist who was also one of the leading figures among the left-wing writers, artists, and moviemakers in Shanghai, believed it would be better for Ye to preserve the facade of neutrality so that he could serve the Communist cause without attracting notice. Anderson, however, cites a memoir in which Mao Dun expresses his unhappiness that Ye was not invited to join the league; if Ye's exclusion was a Communist undercover operation, it is puzzling that Mao Dun was not aware of the fact.

In 1930 Ye left the Commercial Press and became an editor for the Shanghai publishing firm Kaiming shudian (Kaiming Bookstore). His second collection of fiction for children, *Gudai yingxiong de shixiang* (The Statue of the Ancient Hero), appeared in 1931 with illustrations by the renowned cartoonist Feng Zikai. The collection includes the stories "Hanxiu cao" (translated as "The Sensitive Plant," 1978) and "Can he mayi" (translated as "The Silkworm and the Ant," 1978), allegories that expose the injustices and abuses of China's class-based society of the 1930s. Also in 1931 Ye published *Jiaobu ji* (1931, Footsteps Collection), a volume of essays. In his essays on political topics Ye tends to address his readers—especially young people—as a public-minded pedagogue who offers counsel on the purposes of education and its role in personal fulfillment. In "Jiaru wo you yige didi" (If I Had a Younger Brother), for example, he discusses schooling, careers, and options for living a meaningful life with an imagined youthful reader, addressed as "you," as though the two were engaged in an intimate conversation.

In 1935 Ye moved back to Suzhou but remained active in the increasingly politicized literary life of Shanghai, which was fifty miles away by rail. His circle of friends and associates in Shanghai included most of the leading men and women of letters of his generation. In 1936 he helped found the Wenyijia xiehui (Association of Writers and Artists). In March of that year he published *Shengtao duanpian xiaoshuo ji* (A Collection of Shengtao's Short Stories), his own selection of the best of his earlier fiction along with two new stories. The following month he published in the Shanghai newspaper *Dagong bao/L'Impartial* the story "Yipian xuanyan" (translated as "A Declaration," 1963), in which a principal receives a telegram from the Bureau of Education ordering him to find out who on his faculty wrote a letter objecting to Japanese encroachments on Chinese territory; the bureau regards protests against Japan as interference with state policy and suspects protesters of having Communist sympathies. When the principal identifies Wang Yongyi as the author of the letter, which merely reported the consensus opinion of the faculty, a second telegram orders that Wang's students' composition books be sent to the bureau. Nothing suspicious is found in the books, but the principal and Wang have been reminded of the environment of political repression and paranoia in which they live.

In September 1937, two months after war with Japan began, Ye, his wife and children, his mother, and his younger sister left Suzhou, which was increasingly threatened by the Japanese advance, and went to Hankou. In December, Ye left his family in Hankou and traveled to Yichang and then to Chongqing in Sichuan province, where he taught, wrote, edited, and participated in literary organizations. His family joined him in January 1938. In October they moved to Leshan, also in Sichuan; there Ye took a teaching job at Wuhan University, which had relocated to the city. In the fall of 1940 they moved to Chengdu, where Ye participated in the Zhonghua quanguo wenyijie kangdi xiehui (All-China Association of Literary Resistance), edited journals and books, taught, worked for the Sichuan sheng jiaoyu kexue guan (Sichuan Provincial Educational Science Office), and published literary criticism, poetry, and essays on education and on patriotic themes. He also published a few short stories, but, like many of his contemporaries, he wrote little fiction in the late 1930s and 1940s. He returned to Shanghai in 1946, where he directed the daily affairs of the Association of Writers and Artists and resumed his position as an editor for the Kaiming Bookstore.

In January 1949 Ye left Shanghai, stayed briefly in Hong Kong, and then traveled on to Beiping (as Beijing was known from 1928 to September 1949), where he attended the ceremony celebrating the founding of the People's Republic of China on 1 October. In the 1950s he was a delegate to the National People's Congress, deputy director of the Publications Bureau, director of the People's Education Publishing House, and vice minister of education. His wife died in 1957. According to the chronology in *Ye Shengtao yanjiu ziliao*, Ye escaped persecution during the Cultural Revolution of 1966 to 1976 because he spent August and September 1966 in the hospital and then made a decision to "kao bian" (stand to one side), removing himself from public life. A directive by Premier Zhou Enlai protected Ye through the early 1970s, stating that he was to be left alone because he was old. In the late 1970s and early 1980s he occasionally published poetry and commentaries and made appearances at public events and conferences.

Ye Shaojun died in Beijing on 16 February 1988. The Ye Shengtao jinian guan (Ye Shengtao Memorial Museum), in Luzhi commemorates his contributions as an educator and writer.

Bibliographies:

Li Jingbing, *Ye Shengtao daibiao zuo* (Zhengzhou: Huanghe wenyi chubanshe, 1987), pp. 361-364;

Liu Zengren and Feng Guanglian, "Ye Shengtao zhuyi nianbiao he zhuzuo mulu," in *Ye Shengtao yanjiu ziliao*, edited by Liu and Feng (Beijing: Shiyue wenyi chubanshe, 1988), pp. 823-1092;

Shang Jinlin, "Ye Shengtao nianbiao," in *Ye Shengtao*, edited by Ye Zhishan, "Zhongguo xiandai zuojia xuanji" congshu (Hong Kong: Sanlian shudian [Xianggang] youxian gongsi; Renmin wenxue chubanshe, 1989), pp. 263-282.

Biographies:

Liu Zengren, *Shan gao shui chang: Ye Shengtao zhuan* (Taibei: Ye jiang chubanshe, 1994);

Shang Jinlin, *Ye Shengtao zhuan lun* (Hefei: Anhui jiaoyu chubanshe, 1995).

References:

Marston Anderson, *The Limits of Realism: Chinese Fiction in the Revolutionary Period* (Berkeley: University of California Press, 1990), pp. 93-118;

Chen Liao, *Ye Shengtao ping zhuan* (Tianjin: Baihua wenyi chubanshe, 1981);

C. T. Hsia, *A History of Modern Chinese Fiction, 1917-1957* (New Haven: Yale University Press, 1961), pp. 57-70;

Jin Mei, *Lun Ye Shengtao de wenxue chuangzuo* (Shanghai: Shanghai wenyi chubanshe, 1985);

Leo Ou-fan Lee, *The Romantic Generation of Modern Chinese Writers* (Cambridge, Mass.: Harvard University Press, 1973), pp. 177-178;

Liu Zengren and Feng Guanglian, eds., *Ye Shengtao yanjiu ziliao*, (Beijing: Shiyue wenyi chubanshe, 1988);

Ren Tianshi, *Ye Shengtao xiaoshuo lun* (Nanjing: Jiangsu jiaoyu chubanshe, 1988);

Wang Song, *Ye Shengtao xinlun* (Lanzhou: Lanzhou daxue chubanshe, 1991).

Yu Dafu

(7 December 1896 – September 1945)

Ann Huss
Wellesley College

BOOKS: *Chenlun* [Sinking] (Shanghai: Taidong tushuju, 1921)–title story translated by Joseph S. M. Lau and C. T. Hsia as "Sinking," in *Twentieth-Century Chinese Stories,* edited by Hsia with the assistance of Joseph S. M. Lau (New York: Columbia University Press, 1971), pp. 1–33;

Yingluo ji [Convolvulus] (Shanghai: Taidong tushuju, 1923)–includes "Xue lei," translated as "Blood and Tears," in *Genesis of a Revolution: An Anthology of Modern Chinese Short Stories,* edited and translated by Stanley R. Munro (Singapore: Heinemann Educational Books [Asia], 1979), pp. 158–175; and "Yingluo xing," translated as "Wistaria and Dodder," in *Living China,* edited by Edgar Snow (New York: Reynal & Hitchcock, 1936), pp. 247–266;

Xiaoshuo lun [On Fiction] (Shanghai: Guanghua shuju, 1926);

Wenyi lunji [On Literature and Art] (Shanghai: Guanghua shuju, 1926)–includes "Wenxue shang de jieji douzheng," translated by Haili Kong and Howard Goldblatt as "Class Struggle in Literature," in *Modern Chinese Literary Thought: Writings on Literature, 1893–1945,* edited by Kirk A. Denton (Stanford, Cal.: Stanford University Press, 1996), pp. 263–268;

Xiju lun [On Drama] (Shanghai: Shangwu yinshuguan, 1926);

Hanhui ji: Dafu quanji, di yi juan [Cold Ashes: Dafu's Complete Works, Volume One] (Shanghai: Chuangzao she chubanbu, 1927)–includes "Chunfeng chenzui de wanshang," translated by George A. Kennedy as "One Spring Night," *China Forum,* 1 (March 1932): 7–8;

Wenxue gaishuo [An Introduction to Literature] (Shanghai: Shangwu yinshuguan, 1927);

Riji jiuzhong [Nine Diaries] (Shanghai: Beixin shuju, 1927);

Jilei ji: Dafu quanji, di er juan [Chicken Ribs: Dafu's Complete Works, Volume Two] (Shanghai: Chuangzao she, 1927);

Yu Dafu (1934 photograph inscribed to Lin Yutang; from Jon Eugene von Kowallis, The Lyrical Lu Xun: A Study of His Classical-Style Verse, *1996; Thomas Cooper Library, University of South Carolina)*

Guoqu ji: Dafu quanji, di san juan [The Past: Dafu's Complete Works, Volume Three] (Shanghai: Kaiming shudian, 1927);

Miyang [The Stray Sheep] (Shanghai: Beixin shuju, 1928);

Jiling ji: Dafu quanji, di si juan [Odd Lots: Dafu's Complete Works, Volume Four] (Shanghai: Kaiming shudian, 1928);

Dafu daibiao zuo [Representative Works by Dafu] (Shanghai: Chunye shudian, 1928);

Bizhou ji: Dafu quanji, di wu juan [Battered Brooms: Dafu's Complete Works, Volume Five] (Shanghai: Beixin shuju, 1928);

Zai hanfeng li [In a Cold Wind] (Xiamen: Shijie wenyi shushe, 1929);

Weijue ji: Dafu quanji, di liu juan [Ferns: Dafu's Complete Works, Volume Six] (Shanghai: Beixin shuju, 1930);

Ta shi yige ruo nüzi [She Is a Weak Woman] (Shanghai: Hufeng shuju, 1932); republished as *Raole ta* [Forgive Her] (Shanghai: Xiandai shuju, 1933);

Chanyu ji [Regret] (Shanghai: Tianma shudian, 1933);

Dafu zixuan ji [Stories by Dafu, Selected by the Author] (Shanghai: Tianma shudian, 1933);

Duancan ji: Dafu quanji, di qi juan [Fragments: Dafu's Complete Works, Volume Seven] (Shanghai: Beixin shuju, 1933);

Zhedong jingwu jilüe [Sketches of Eastern Zhejiang] (N.p.: Hang Jiang tieluju, 1933);

Jihen chuchu: Sanwen youji ji [Footprints Here and There: Essays and Travel Writing] (Shanghai: Xiandai shuju, 1934);

Dafu riji ji [A Collection of Dafu's Diaries] (Shanghai: Beixin shuju, 1935);

Dafu duanpian xiaoshuoji, shang xia [A Collection of Short Stories by Dafu in Two Volumes], 2 volumes (Shanghai: Beixin shuju, 1935);

Dafu youji [Dafu's Travel Writing] (Shanghai: Wenxue chuangzao she, 1936);

Dafu sanwenji [Dafu's Essays] (Shanghai: Beixin shuju, 1936);

Xian shu [Book for Idle Hours] (Shanghai: Liangyou tushu chuban gongsi, 1936);

Dafu shici ji [Dafu's Poetry] (Guangzhou: Yuzhoufeng she, 1948; enlarged edition, Hong Kong: Xiandai chubanshe, 1954);

Yu Dafu wenji [Yu Dafu's Collected Works], 12 volumes (Guangzhou: Huacheng chubanshe, 1982–1984)—includes in volume 4, "Xueye (zizhuan zhi yi zhang)" [Snowy Night (A Chapter of My Autobiography)], translated by Theodore Huters as "Early Autobiographical Fragments: A Young Sojourner in a Foreign Land," in *Modern Chinese Writers: Self-Portrayals*, edited by Helmut Martin and Jeffrey Kinkley (Armonk, N.Y.: Sharpe, 1992), pp. 308–312.

Collections: *Yu Dafu wenji* [A Collection of Yu Dafu's Work] (Shanghai: Chunming shudian, 1948);

Yu Dafu xuanji [Selected Works by Yu Dafu] (Beijing: Kaiming shudian, 1951);

Yu Dafu xuanji [Selected Works by Yu Dafu] (Hong Kong: Gangqing chubanshe, 1977);

Cover for Yu's first book, the story collection Chenlun (Sinking), published in 1921 (Wason Collection on East Asia–China, Kroch Asia Library, Cornell University)

Dafu wenyi lunwen ji [Dafu's Essays on Literature and Art], 3 volumes (Hong Kong: Gangqing chubanshe, 1978);

Yu Dafu quan ji [The Complete Works of Yu Dafu], 12 volumes (Hangzhou: Zhejiang wenyi chubanshe, 1992).

Editions in English: "Chunfeng chenzui de wanshang," translated as "One Intoxicating Evening of Spring Breeze," in *A Treasury of Chinese Literature: A New Prose Anthology, Including Fiction and Drama*, edited and translated by Ch'u Chai and Winberg Chai (New York: Appleton-Century-Crofts, 1965), pp. 276–288;

"Chunfeng chenzui de wanshang," translated by George A. Kennedy as "Intoxicating Spring Nights," in *Straw Sandals: Chinese Short Stories, 1918–1933*, edited by Harold R. Isaacs (Cambridge, Mass.: MIT Press, 1974), pp. 68–83;

Cover for Yu's short-story collection Yingluo ji (Convolvulus), published in 1923 (from Yu Runqi, ed., Tang Tao cang shu, 2004; Bruccoli Clark Layman Archives)

"Chenlun," translated by Joseph S. M. Lau and C. T. Hsia as "Sinking," in *Modern Chinese Stories and Novellas, 1919–1949,* edited by Lau, Hsia, and Leo Ou-fan Lee (New York: Columbia University Press, 1981), pp. 125–141;

Nights of Spring Fever and Other Writings (Beijing: Chinese Literature, 1984);

"Chenlun," translated by Lau and Hsia as "Sinking," in *The Columbia Anthology of Modern Chinese Literature,* edited by Lau and Howard Goldblatt (New York: Columbia University Press, 1995), pp. 44–69;

"The Winter Scene in Jiangnan" ("Jiangnan de dongjing") and "Village School and Academy" ("Shudian yu xuetang"), in *The Chinese Essay,* translated and edited by David E. Pollard (New York: Columbia University Press, 2000; London: Hurst, 2000), pp. 207–215.

TRANSLATIONS: *Xiao jia zhi wu* [Five Minor Authors] (Shanghai: Bexin shuju, 1930);

Jige weida de zuojia [A Few Great Authors] (Shanghai: Zhonghua shuju, 1934);

Dafu suo yi duanpian ji [Short Stories Translated by Dafu] (Shanghai: Shenghuo shudian, 1935).

Yu Dafu was one of China's most important twentieth-century writers. His exploration of the self, desolation, sexual desire, and decadence changed the face of the modern Chinese literary tradition. While he is perhaps best known for his short story "Chenlun" (1921; translated as "Sinking," 1971), Yu was also a poet, translator, essayist, and one of the founders of Chuangzao she (the Creation Society), a group of authors who championed individualism, free expression, democracy, and science in the early 1920s. During the final years of his life in Singapore, much of his writing focused on economic analysis and military issues. Although great lore has grown around Yu's romantic life and mysterious death, he is best remembered for writing the first modern historical story, "Cai shi ji" (1923, Colored Cliff); as the first author to bring the phrase "class struggle" into debates on literature; and for "Chunfeng chenzui de wanshang" (1924, Evenings of Intoxicating Spring Breeze; translated as "One Spring Night," 1932), one of the first modern stories to focus on the plight of workers. A romantic writer who wrote poignantly of sexual longing and the humiliations to which Chinese students in Japan were subjected during the early 1900s, Yu angered the older generation of writers with his candor while striking a strong chord with Chinese youth of the post–May Fourth 1919 generation. He was criticized for narcissism and for airing his dirty laundry in public. In Yu readers find the complexities of the early-twentieth-century Chinese writer-intellectual in all his splendor and with all his shortcomings.

Yu kept a diary until 1936 and wrote many essays on his life and writing. Much of his fiction is obviously autobiographical, and he acknowledged that he modeled characters such as the protagonist of "Chenlun" and Yu in "Mangmang ye" (1922, One Boundless Evening) on himself. In the latter story, which is collected in *Hanhui ji: Dafu quanji, di yi juan* (1927, Cold Ashes: Dafu's Complete Works, Volume One), he says of the character Yu: "If one looked closely between his eyebrows, one could see the anxiety hidden behind that feigned happiness.... His face was not common, but there was nothing special about it either. His flat face was graced with two tiny eyes and a rather large nose.... One could tell that he was an interesting person." As Lu Xun is known for the phrase that concludes "Kuangren riji" (1918; translated as "A Madman's Diary," 1981), "Save the children ...," Yu is remembered for the protagonist's last words in "Chenlun": "Oh China, my China, you are the cause of my death. Prosper! Grow strong! So many of your sons and daughters are still suffering in misery." Both phrases were calls to arms by authors who became close friends and who exposed the crumbling facade of Republican-era Chinese culture.

Yu was born Yu Wen on 7 December 1896 in Fuyang, Zhejiang province. He was the youngest son in a family of three boys and a girl. Like many other scholarly families, the Yus had fallen into poverty over the generations. Yu was two years old when his father, Yu Qizeng, died, leaving his mother, whose surname was Lu, to rely on a small piece of property and a tiny shop for her income. Because of the family's financial situation, the daughter, Yu Fengzhen, who was two years older than Yu Wen, was given to a family named Ye as a child bride at the age of seven; she died at twenty-six. The mother did manage to educate her three sons on her limited income. The oldest, Yu Qingyun, who later adopted the *zi* (style name) Mantuo, graduated from Tokyo Law School and returned to China to practice law. The second son, Yu Hao, studied medicine in Beijing and became a doctor in Fuyang. Yu Wen began school at seven and soon began writing poetry. He claimed the seventeenth-century writer Wu Meicun as his favorite classical poet. He traveled to Hangzhou to attend high school, only to find the tuition too high; he moved on to a school in Jiaxing, then back to Hangzhou, where he became a classmate of the future poet and founder of the Xin yue (New Moon) Society, Xu Zhimo. All schools closed when the Republican Revolution took place in 1911, and Yu returned home.

In September 1912 Yu entered the college preparatory class at Zhijiang University, an institution sponsored by an American-Chinese Benevolent Society, but was soon expelled for participating in a revolt against the oppressive practices of the university's president. In the spring of 1913 he enrolled in a Baptist school in Hangzhou to study English but left three months later, disappointed with what he deemed the enslaving practices of missionary schools. He wrote poetry at home throughout the summer. In September he followed his brother Mantuo to Tokyo, where, at Mantuo's suggestion, he began the study of medicine at the Tokyo Institute of Higher Learning. Soon after his arrival in Tokyo he met the future writers Guo Moruo, who was also studying medicine, and Zhang Ziping, who was then an engineering student. In the brief "Lun Yu Dafu" (On Yu Dafu), dated 6 March 1946 and included in *Yu Dafu yanjiu ziliao* (1986, A Catalogue of Reference Materials on Yu Dafu), edited by Chen Zishan and Wang Zili, Guo recalls that Yu was fluent in English and German, that his knowledge of Chinese literature was immense, and that he was already an accomplished poet when he arrived in Tokyo. Guo notes that Yu was deeply interested in European, American, and Japanese literature

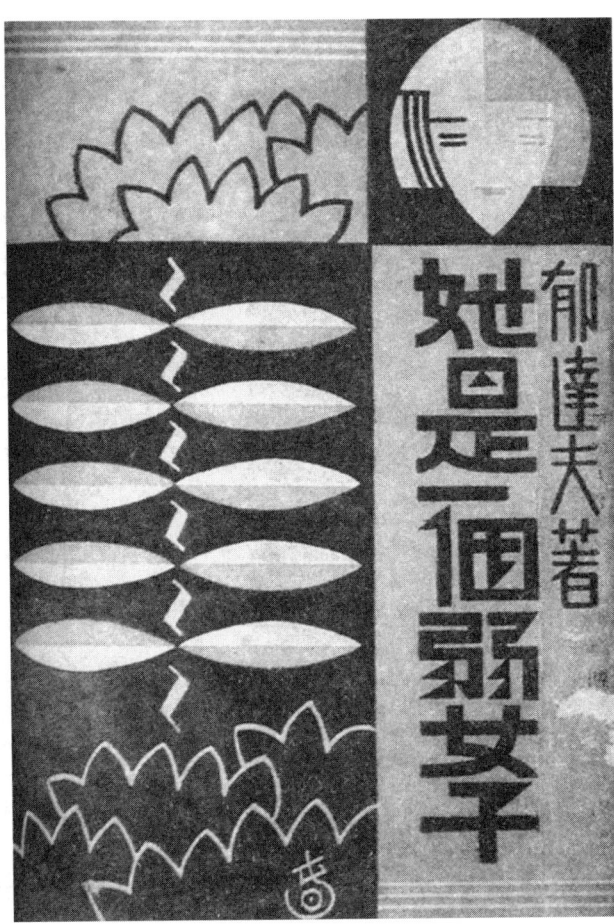

Cover for Yu's novel Ta shi yige ruo nüzi *(She Is a Weak Woman), published in April 1932. It was banned by the Nationalist regime in June (from Yu Runqi, ed.,* Tang Tao cang shu, *2004; Bruccoli Clark Layman Archives).*

and claimed to have read more than one thousand works during his four years at the university. In 1915 Yu published his first poems in Shanghai's *Shenzhou ribao* (Shenzhou Daily) and the *Zhijiang ribao* (Zhijiang Daily) under his style name, Yu Dafu. He continued to use that name throughout his life. The poems are collected in volume ten of *Yu Dafu wenji* (1982–1984, Yu Dafu's Collected Works).

In 1916 the high tuition at the medical school led Yu to switch to political science. At this time he was exposed to the political and economic theories of Karl Marx and Friedrich Engels and read Vladimir Ilich Lenin's *Gosudarstvo i revolyutsiya* (1917; translated as *The State and Revolution,* 1919). On 10 October 1916 he wrote to Mantuo: "In order to right a crumbling regime, we must revolutionize society."

During the next few years Yu continued to write classical-style poetry. According to his diary, in 1917 he began writing short stories in the vernacular; none of

Cover for Raole ta (Forgive Her), Yu's revision of his banned novel Ta shi yige ruo nüzi. It was published in December 1933 (from Yu Runqi, ed., Tang Tao cang shu, 2004; Bruccoli Clark Layman Archives).

those early stories survives. Also in 1917 he was engaged to Sun Quan, who had been chosen for him by his mother. They were married on 14 July 1920 and had two daughters and two sons; one of the sons died in infancy.

For Yu and other Chinese in Japan, the May Fourth Movement of 1919 was a monumental turning point. Enraged at what he termed the "carving up" of Chinese land, Yu vowed to take revenge if China's territory was not returned in twenty years. Similar sentiments were echoed by Chinese students and writers throughout the world.

The Creation Society was founded at a meeting at Yu's home in Tokyo on 8 June 1921; in addition to Yu, the founders included Guo, Zhang, and Cheng Fangwu. In September, Yu moved to Shanghai to manage the society's journal, *Chuangzao* (Creation). An announcement in the 29 September edition of the Shanghai newspaper *Shishi xinbao* (New Current Affairs Times) proclaimed the arrival of a literary quarterly dedicated to "pure literature" and promised that the Creation Society would "delve into society's darkest corners, advocate the independence of art, and work with countless unknown writers to create a future for Chinese literature." Earlier in 1921 a group of writers, including Mao Dun, Zheng Zhenduo, Zhu Ziqing, and Ye Shengtao, had founded the Wenxue yanjiu hui (Literary Research Association). Their publication, *Xiaoshuo yuebao* (Short Story Monthly), and *Chuangzao* represented opposite ends of the contemporary literary spectrum, with realist literature championed by the former and Romantic literature by the latter.

Also in 1921 Yu's first short-story collection, *Chenlun*, was published. In addition to the infamous title work, it comprises an introduction by Yu and the stories "Nan qian" (A Move South) and "Yinhuise de si" (A Silver-grey Death). "Chenlun" had a tremendous impact: young readers found a new voice, while moralists thought that "Chenlun" heralded the decadent demise of a generation. In "Chenlun" an unnamed Chinese youth studying in Japan whiles away his days reading the works of William Wordsworth, Ralph Waldo Emerson, and Henry David Thoreau as he wanders through the countryside, but his reading cannot allay the guilt he feels about his constant need for sexual gratification. He keeps his distance from other Chinese students, masturbates frequently, and one day finds himself peeking in on his innkeeper's daughter as she bathes. He flees back to his room and then, in search of peace, moves up the mountain to a house in a mei grove managed by a peasant. Soon his self-control is tested again by the "noise of undressing . . . the smacking of lips" and the woman's pleas when he comes upon a pair of lovers while taking a walk. That afternoon, he takes a trolley into the city and goes to a brothel. Japanese prostitutes, however, have little use for Chinese men. After an angry, drunken poetic recitation, he collapses. Later that evening, he awakes, pays his bill, and walks to the beach. His body is crawling with shame, a shame for which China is responsible: China is weak; he is ashamed of that weakness and embodies it. Uttering his famous cry, he walks slowly into the sea and drowns.

While "Chenlun" may not have seemed new in a world literary context, it was new to China. The protagonist realizes the shame of his nation via his own personal shame, sexual depravity, and depression. Yu's autobiographical protagonist's deep sense of failure mirrored the feelings of a generation of patriotic Chinese youth, whose cries for freedom were met with harsh reprimands from their elders.

In the second issue of *Chuangzao,* published in August 1922, Yu published an article that led to a literary war between members of the Creation Society and followers of the reformer Hu Shi. In "Xiyang lou riji" (Xiyang Tower Diary), which is collected in volume five of *Yu Dafu wenji*, Yu criticized the quality of a translation by one of Hu's students. Hu responded with a scathing critique of the Creation Society, calling its members base and boring. The conflict reached its pinnacle in 1923 with the publication in *Chuangzao* of Yu's story "Cai shi ji," which is acknowledged as the first modern historical story written in China. (It is collected in *Hanhui ji*.)

The protagonist of "Cai shi ji" is the proud, lonely eighteenth-century poet Huang Zhongze, who suffered from long and frequent bouts of depression. Though based on an actual person, the character is clearly autobiographical. Huang spends much of his time walking through the countryside composing poetry, and Yu quotes several poems by the real Huang. Huang travels to the grave of the Tang dynasty poet Li Bai, whom the historical Huang admired, and composes a poem in his memory. When Huang's archenemy, the scholar Dai Dongyuan—a favorite of Hu Shi—comes to town, Huang labels him a "little Confucius" and goes into a tirade on the weaknesses of classical scholars. The parallel between the relationship of the poet Huang and the scholar Dai, on the one hand, and the present-day relationship of Yu and Hu Shi, on the other hand, was obvious to knowledgeable readers. The personal motivation underlying the writing of "Cai shi ji" does not, however, diminish the literary quality of the work. The reader is lured into the world of a brilliant poet; like the protagonist of "Chenlun," Huang rises painfully from the page to represent the complexities of human existence.

In February 1923 Yu met Lu Xun, with whom he formed a friendship that flourished until Lu Xun's death in 1936. A few months after their meeting, Yu's article "Wenxue shang de jieji douzheng" (1923; translated as "Class Struggle in Literature," 1996) was published in the Creation Society's *Chuangzao zhoubao* (Creation Weekly); it is collected in Yu's *Wenyi lunji* (1926, On Literature and Art). Yu writes, "Class struggle in twentieth-century literature must adopt the same tactics as that of real class struggle in society." The article marks the first time that the phrase "class struggle" had been used in China in the context of literary production.

Later that same year, Yu wrote one of the first modern-day short stories to focus on the plight of the worker in China. Published in the 28 February 1924 issue of *Chuangzuo zhoubao* and collected in *Hanhui ji*, "Chunfeng chenzui de wanshang" concerns a young, impoverished writer who lives in a tiny attic room and his new neighbor, a young woman who works at a cigarette factory and must pass through his room on the

Advertisement for Raole ta *on the inside front cover of the magazine* Xiandai/Les Contemporains *(The Moderns), February 1934. The novel was banned by the Nationalist government in April (Collection of Thomas Moran).*

way to and from her own. The writer frequently goes out in the middle of the night to take a walk; believing that he must be a gang member or a thief, the woman keeps her distance from him for the first few weeks. She eventually becomes curious about him, however, and one evening they have their first conversation and share the food she has brought home. When the writer receives $5.00 for a translation, he spends the money on a shower, a new shirt, and some snacks. That night he shares his banana cake with his neighbor. She warns him not to smoke, especially the cigarettes made at her factory; touched by her kindness, he agrees to quit smoking. The story of a destitute writer and a penniless worker attests to the power of the human spirit and outlines the predicament of China's lower classes in the early twentieth century.

In 1923 Yu began teaching politics, economics, and history at Beijing University; in 1926 he moved to Zhongshan (Sun Yat-sen) University in Guangzhou to teach law. Soon afterward, Creation Society publications came to a halt under pressure from the Nationalist

Yu Dafu with his second wife, the leftist author Wang Yingxia, circa 1937 (from Jon Eugene von Kowallis, The Lyrical Lu Xun: A Study of His Classical-Style Verse, *1996; Thomas Cooper Library, University of South Carolina)*

Party. In January 1927 Yu fell in love with a woman named Wang Yingxia and left his wife for her. They were engaged in June and married in January 1928. In 1928 he published *Dafu daibiao zuo* (Representative Works by Dafu), but it was banned by the Nationalist regime. Yu left Guangzhou for Shanghai in 1929. In 1930 he and Lu Xun founded the Zhongguo ziyou yundong da tongmeng (Chinese Alliance for Freedom), and Yu traveled around the country condemning the Nationalist regime's oppression of the arts. The Zhongguo zuoyi zuojia lianmeng (Chinese League of Left-Wing Writers) was formed that same year, with Yu as a founding member. The other members soon began to criticize Yu for claiming to be a "*zuojia*" (writer) and not a "*zhanshi*" (warrior); they took the comment to mean that he did not support the revolution. In failing health and under constant attack, he moved to Hangzhou and built a home he called his "shelter from wind and rain." The short novel *Ta shi yige ruo nüzi* (1932, She Is a Weak Woman) was his second book to be banned by the Nationalist government. He was expelled from the Chinese League of Left-Wing Writers in 1933. He published a "revised" version of *Ta shi yige ruo nüzi* in December as *Raole ta* (Forgive Her); it was banned the following year.

War with Japan broke out in 1937. At the end of 1938 Yu assumed the editorship of the *Xingzhou ribao* (Singapore Daily). In Singapore he became involved in the Overseas Chinese Anti-Japanese Movement and edited the *Huaqiao zhoubao* (Overseas Chinese Weekly), which was published by British Intelligence. In 1939 Yu published in the 5 March issue of the Hong Kong journal *Dafeng* (Great Wind) a series of poems collectively titled "Huijia shiji" (Poems on a Crumbled Family) chronicling the demise of his relationship with Wang, with whom he had had three children; the poems are collected in volume ten of *Yu Dafu wenji*. Yu's brother Mantuo, who had joined the Nan she (Southern Society), an organization of poets with strong nationalist tendencies, was accused of being a spy and was killed by the Japanese on 23 November 1939 in Shanghai.

On the eve of the fall of Singapore to the Japanese in February 1942, Yu Dafu fled to Sumatra under an alias. Sumatra fell a few days later, and Yu was forced to become a translator for the Japanese. After six months he requested and was granted sick leave and established a series of businesses that served as fronts for anti-Japanese resistance. In February 1944 an informant revealed his identity to the Japanese. He was detained on 29 August 1945, fourteen days after Japan surrendered to the Allied forces, and a Japanese military-police squad leader identified in sources only as "D" ordered him hanged. He was executed shortly thereafter; the exact date is unknown.

Letters:

Dafu shujian: Zhi Wang Yingxia [Dafu's Letters: Letters to Wang Yingxia] (Tianjin: Tianjin renmin chubanshe, 1982).

Bibliographies:

Chen Zishan and Wang Zili, "Yu Dafu jian pu," in their *Yu Dafu yanjiu ziliao* (Hong Kong: Joint Publishing Company, 1986), pp. 759–866;

Guo Wenyou, ed., *Qianqiu yinhen: Yu Dafu nianpu changbian* (Chengdu: Sichuan renmin chubanshe, 1996).

Biographies:

Guo Wenyou, ed., *Qianqiu yinhen: Yu Dafu nianpu changbian* (Chengdu: Sichuan renmin chubanshe, 1996);

Chen Zishan, *Taobi chenlun: Mingren bixia de Yu Dafu* (Shanghai: Dongfang chuban zhongxin, 1998);

Wang Guanquan, *Tuifei zhong yinxian huihuan–Yu Dafu* (Shanghai: Shanghai shudian chubanshe, 2001);

Yuan Qiongqiong and Pan Ningdong, *Duoqing lei meiren: Yu Dafu–Wang Yingxia de shidai kulian* (Beijing: Zhongguo youyi chuban gongsi, 2001).

References:

Randall Oliver Chang, "Yu Ta-fu (1896–1945): The Alienated Artist in Modern Chinese Literature," dissertation, Claremont Graduate School and University Center, 1974;

Chen Zishan and Wang Zili, eds., *Yu Dafu yanjiu ziliao* (Hong Kong: Joint Publishing Company, 1986);

Kirk A. Denton, "The Distant Shore: The Nationalist Theme in Yu Dafu's *Sinking*," *Chinese Literature: Essays, Articles, and Reviews*, 14 (1992): 107–123;

Anna Dolezalová, *Yü Ta-fu: Specific Traits of His Literary Creation* (Bratislava: Slovak Academy of Sciences Publishing House, 1971?);

Michael Egan, "The Short Stories of Yu Dafu–Life Becomes Literature," dissertation, University of Toronto, 1980;

Egan, "Yu Dafu and the Transition to Modern Chinese Literature," in *Modern Chinese Literature in the May Fourth Era*, edited by Merle Goldman (Cambridge, Mass.: Harvard University Press, 1977), pp. 309–324;

Yi-tsi Mei Feuerwerker, "Text, Intertext, and the Representation of the Writing Self in Lu Xun, Yu Dafu, and Wang Meng," in *From May Fourth to June Fourth: Fiction and Film in Twentieth-Century China*, edited by Ellen Widmer and David Wang (Cambridge, Mass.: Harvard University Press, 1993), pp. 167–193;

Marián Gálik, "Yu Dafu and His Panaesthetic Criticism," in his *The Genesis of Modern Chinese Literary Criticism (1917–1930)* (London: Curzon Press / Bratislava: VEDA, 1980), pp. 104–128;

Kumagaya Hideo, "Quest for Truth: An Introductory Study of Yu Dafu's Fiction," *Journal of the Oriental Society of Australia*, 24 (1992): 49–63;

C. T. Hsia, "Yu Dafu," in his *A History of Modern Chinese Fiction*, second edition (New Haven: Yale University Press, 1971), pp. 102–111;

Jon Eugene von Kowallis, *The Lyrical Lu Xun: A Study of His Classical-Style Verse* (Honolulu: University of Hawai'i Press, 1996), pp. 300–301;

Leo Ou-fan Lee, "Yu Ta-fu," in his *The Romantic Generation of Modern Chinese Writers* (Cambridge, Mass.: Harvard University Press, 1973), pp. 81–123;

Sylvia Lin, "Unwelcome Heroines: Mao Dun and Yu Dafu's Creations of a New Chinese Woman," *Journal of Modern Chinese Literature in Chinese*, 1 (January 1998): 71–94;

Ng Mau-sang, "Yu Dafu's Superfluous Hero," in his *The Russian Hero in Modern Chinese Fiction* (Hong Kong: Chinese University Press, 1988), pp. 83–128;

Jaroslav Prusek, "On Mao Dun and Yu Dafu," in his *The Lyrical and the Epic: Studies of Modern Chinese Literature*, edited by Lee (Bloomington: Indiana University Press, 1980), pp. 121–177;

Shu-mei Shih, "The Libidinal and the National: The Morality of Decadence in Yu Dafu, Teng Gu, and Others," in her *The Lure of the Modern: Writing Modernism In Semicolonial China, 1917–1937* (Berkeley: University of California Press, 2001), pp. 110–127;

Suzuki Masao, *Yu Dafu* (Tokyo: Kenbun Shuppan, 1994);

Suzuki, *Yu Dafu in Sumatra* (Tokyo: Toho Shoten, 1995);

Jing Tsu, "Perversions of Masculinity: The Masochistic Male Subject in Yu Dafu, Guo Moruo, and Freud," *positions: east asia cultures critique*, 8 (Fall 2000): 269–316;

Wong Yoon Wah, "Yu Dafu in Exile: His Last Days in Sumatra," *Renditions*, no. 23 (1985): 71–83;

Yu Runqi, ed., *Tang Tao cang shu* (Beijing: Beijing chubanshe, 2004), pp. 43, 139.

Zeng Pu

(1 March 1872 – 23 June 1935)

Hu Ying
University of California, Irvine

BOOKS: *Weili ji* [A Collection of Unrefined Writings] (N.p.: Privately printed, 1889);

Tuishi heyi shi wencun [Essays from the "Pushing Ten into One" Studio], 2 volumes (N.p.: Privately printed, 1889);

Zhidan suoyu [Insignificant Words in Utter Sincerity], 2 volumes (N.p.: Privately printed, 1889);

Qiangwu ji [A Substanceless Collection] (N.p.: Privately printed, 1891);

Xuetanmeng yuanben [Dream of the White Tan Flower: An Opera] (N.p.: Privately printed, 1891);

Bu Houhanshu yiwenzhi [A Supplemental Historical Bibliography of the Later Han Dynasty with Critical Notes] (N.p.: Privately printed, 1895);

Niehai hua [A Flower in a Sinful Sea], 2 volumes (Shanghai: Xiaoshuo lin shushe, 1905; enlarged edition, Shanghai: Zhenmeishan shudian, 1928); chapters 1–5 translated by Rafe de Crespigny and Ts'un-yan Liu as "A Flower in a Sinful Sea," in *Chinese Middlebrow Fiction from the Ch'ing and Early Republican Eras*, edited by Liu and John Minford (Hong Kong: Chinese University Press, 1984), pp. 137–192;

Lu Nanzi: Lian [Lu Nanzi: Love] (Shanghai: Zhenmeishan shudian, 1928);

Niehai hua, erji [A Flower in a Sinful Sea, the Second Book] (Shanghai: Zhenmeishan shudian, 1929);

Niehai hua, sanji [A Flower in a Sinful Sea, the Third Book] (Shanghai: Zhenmeishan shudian, 1931); revised and enlarged as *Niehai hua, sanji heding ben* [A Flower in a Sinful Sea, the Complete Three Books] (Shanghai: Zhenmeishan shudian, 1931);

Yijia yan [Writings of One Family] (Shanghai: Zhenmeishan shudian, n.d.).

Editions and Collections: *Xuetanmeng yuanben* [Dream of the White Tan Flower: An Opera] (Shanghai: Zhenmeishan shudian, 1931);

Bu Houhanshu yiwenzhi [A Supplemental Historical Bibliography of the Later Han Dynasty with Critical Notes] (N.p.: Kaiming shudian, 1936);

Niehai hua; Lu Nanzi [A Flower in a Sinful Sea; Lu Nanzi] (Taibei: Guiguan tushu gufen youxian gongsi, 1983);

Lu Nanzi (Beijing: Renmin wenxue chubanshe, 1989).

TRANSLATIONS: Alexandre Dumas *père*, "Mage wanghou yishi" [Queen Margot *(La Reine Margot)*] *Xiaoshuo lin,* nos. 11–12 (1908);

Victor Hugo, *Jiushisan nian* [Ninety-Three *(Quatrevingt-treize)*] (Shanghai: Youzheng shuju, 1913);

Hugo, "Xiangri le" [Angelo, Tyrant of Padua *(Angelo, Tyran de Padoue)*], *Xiaoshuo yuebao* (1914);

Hugo, *Lükelanshi Baoxia* [Lucretia Borgia *(Lucrèce Borgia)*](Shanghai: Youzheng shuju, 1916);

Molière, *Furen xuetang* [The School for Wives *(L'Escole des femmes)*] (Shanghai: Zhenmeishan shudian, 1927);

Hugo, *Lübolan* [Ruy Blas *(Ruy Blas)*] (Shanghai: Zhenmeishan shudian, 1927);

Hugo, *O'nani* [Hernani *(Hernani)*] (Shanghai: Zhenmeishan shudian, 1927);

Pierre Louÿs, "Xila biliti ge" [The Songs of Bilitis *(Les Chansons de Bilitis)*] *Zhenmeishan*, nos. 1–3 (1927); nos. 6 and 8 (1928);

Jean Richepin, *Qi'er ge* [The Beggar's Song *(La Chanson des gueux)*] (Shanghai: Zhenmeishan shudian, 1928);

Hugo, *Zhonglou guairen* [La Esmeralda *(La Esmeralda)*] (Shanghai: Zhenmeishan shudian, 1928);

Emile Zola, *Nandan yu Nainong furen* [Nantos; Madame Neigeon *(Nantos; Madame Neigeon)*] (Shanghai: Zhenmeishan shudian, 1928);

Louÿs, *Rou yu si* [Flesh and Death *(Aphrodite)*], translated by Zeng Pu and Zeng Xubai (Shanghai: Zhenmeishan shudian, 1929).

SELECTED PERIODICAL PUBLICATIONS–UNCOLLECTED: "Lun Falanxi beiju yuanliu: Xila beiju yuanshi" [On the Origin of French Tragedy: The Source Material in Greek Tragedy], *Zhenmeishan,* 1, nos. 1–3, 6 (1928);

"Bingfu riji" [The Diary of a Sick Man], *Yuzhoufeng,* no. 2 (1928);

"Shijuan bei mo wu toubi kairan ti er lü" [Two Poems in Seven-Syllable Regulated Verse Written with Emotion after Throwing Down the Brush upon the Examination Paper becoming Stained with Ink], *Dawanbao*, 3 [or 30?] June 1935;

"Lanbang" [Disqualification], *Dawanbao*, 29–30 June 1935.

Zeng Pu is one of the most important of the authors who were active in the last decade of the Qing dynasty (1644 to 1911) and the early decades of the Republican era (1912 to 1949). His major work, *Niehai hua* (1905–1931, A Flower in a Sinful Sea), vividly captures a period of rapid change in China as it satirically depicts traditionally trained literati in the waning days of the Qing dynasty and engages new ideas such as anarchism and republican revolution. In addition to being a novelist, Zeng Pu was an important publisher of *xin xiaoshuo* (new fiction), an accomplished translator of works by French authors such as Victor Hugo and Emile Zola, and a public servant under the early Republican government.

Zeng Pu was born on 1 March 1872 into an old scholar-gentry family in Changshu, Jiangsu province. He was his parents' only son and grew up in an extended family that included sisters, a doting grandmother, and many cousins. His father, Zheng Zhizhuan, a *juren* (holder of the second-level degree in the civil examination system) and a *langzhong* (director) in the *xingbu* (Bureau of Punishments), was in Peter Li's words, "a typical traditional man of letters"; his mother's surname was You. His earliest education came from the romantic and historical tales that his maternal grandmother, surnamed Ding, recited to him in popular ballad form. Although not enthusiastic about memorizing the Confucian classics, Zeng Pu was given a solid traditional education by his father and tutors. He also read widely in vernacular fiction and drama but did so covertly, as was the rule with young people growing up in traditional households.

In September 1890 Zeng Pu married Wang Yuanshan. She died two weeks after giving birth to a daughter in November 1891; the baby died two months later. Zeng Pu wrote *Xuetanmeng yuanben* (Dream of the White Tan Flower), a *xiju* (operatic drama) in memory of his wife; it was privately published in 1891 and republished commercially in 1931.

Zeng Pu sat for the civil service examination between 1890 and 1892. He passed the local and provincial rounds with distinction, but at the metropolitan examination he disqualified himself by spilling ink on the papers. He quickly wrote two poems lamenting his fate and proclaiming that other paths were open to him in life, left the examination hall, and never sat for the examinations again. His failure ended the possibility of a career as a literati-official. His father purchased an official post, secretary of the Grand Secretariat, for him—buying offices was a common practice and was not considered a bribe—and for the next few years he had the opportunity to consort with eminent scholars in Beijing. He read widely in ancient and medieval Chinese literature and compiled the voluminous *Bu Houhanshu yiwenzhi* (1895, A Supplemental Historical Bibliography of the Later Han Dynasty with Critical Notes). In this formative period Zeng Pu laid down for himself a solid foundation in classical scholarship and formed personal associations with scholars and statesmen, some of whom make appearances in *Niehai hua*.

In 1893 Zeng Pu married Shen Xiangsheng. They had a son, Zeng Xubai, in 1895. That year Zeng Pu began studying French in the government-run special class for adults at the Tongwen guan (College of Foreign Languages). Unlike his classmates, who treated the class merely as a convenient ladder to officialdom, Zeng Pu continued his studies for several years with a tutor, read widely in European belles lettres, and made a systematic study of French literature. He and his wife had another son, Zeng Yuezhong, in 1896, and a daughter, Zeng De, in 1897. In a 1928 letter to Hu Shi, a leading May Fourth–era scholar, that was published as an appendix to *Niehai hua; Lu Nanzi* (1983, A Flower in a Sinful Sea; Lu Nanzi) Zeng Pu recalled his intellectual journey:

> I have never stepped through the gate of a modern school, not to mention never going abroad to study. The story of my learning French and the rudiments of world literature may be somewhat interesting, although by now it probably sounds like some trivial yarn from "a white-haired palace lady." I began studying French in the fall of 1895, soon after the Sino-Japanese War. . . . Later I contacted several bookshops in Paris, and within three or four years' time read quite a few literary and philosophical works in French. As a result of this, I found myself gripped by a literary fever, so much so that for days on end I would not go to sleep. Finally I became quite ill, which lasted a good five years.

In the decade following the Sino-Japanese War of 1894–1895 a political and cultural reform movement was underway that included the promotion of "new fiction." Reformers such as Liang Qichao believed that the novel, because of its power to affect ordinary people, was the best means of influencing public opinion. Zeng Pu shared this view of literature and this attitude toward social engagement, and around 1904 he and three friends from his hometown—Ding Zuyin, Xu Nianci, Zhu Yuansheng—established the Xiaoshuo lin shushe (Forest of Fiction Publishing Company) in Shanghai. All three were well trained in traditional literature, and each had studied a foreign language. Before going out of business in 1908, the company published seventeen original works and ninety-nine translations.

In 1903 Zeng Pu's friend Jin Tianyu (also known as Jin Songcen and Jin Tianhe) wrote six chapters of a novel titled *Niehai hua* and published the first two, which are largely allegorical, in *Jiangsu*, a magazine produced by Chinese students in Japan. Zeng Pu took over at Jin's request, heavily revised the first six chapters, and continued *Niehai hua* as an historical novel, intending to encompass the decades of rapid change beginning in the 1880s. In 1905 Xiaoshuolin shushe published Zeng Pu's version of *Niehai hua* in two volumes of ten chapters each. Layered with classical allusions, while at the same time striving to render the foreign in its authenticity, the novel depicts the journey of a Chinese diplomat and his concubine through Europe, recording the exotic events and personages they encounter and juxtaposing the narrative perspectives of "home" and "abroad." The novel went through fifty thousand copies in fifteen printings in the next few years.

In 1906 Zeng Pu became involved in the Yubei lixian gonghui (Association to Prepare for the Establishment of a Constitutional Government). Around 1907 he approached Lin Shu, the most popular translator of the day, and suggested using *baihua* (vernacular Chinese) in translation, rather than the Classical Chinese that was the prevailing practice at the time and of which Lin Shu was the undisputed master. Lin Shu did not follow Zeng Pu's advice, but Zeng Pu used the vernacular in his own translations. His choice of the modern vernacular makes him a forerunner of the New Culture Movement that swept China in the 1920s and 1930s and promoted the vernacular as the preferred literary medium. He was also one of the few among his contemporaries to translate literary works directly from the original language: many Chinese translators of the late Qing period did not read foreign languages and had to rely on assistants who did.

In addition to serving as the general manager of the publishing house, Zeng Pu was a principal contributor to its literary journal, *Xiaoshuo lin* (Forest of Fiction), which appeared in 1907–1908. He published a biographical sketch of Alexandre Dumas *père* and a translation of excerpts from Dumas's *La Reine Margot* (1845; translated as *Marguerite de Valois*, 1846), "Mage wanghou yishi," in the journal in 1908.

In 1910 Zeng Pu took a concubine, Zhang Cailuan. Before the revolution of 1911 he served as *houbu zhifu* (expectant prefect) in Zhejiang province, but he gave up the position after the revolution began. After the establishment of the Republic of China on 1 January 1912, he served in the Jiangsu provincial assembly. In the same year he took a second concubine, Yu Yizhu. In 1914 he became chairman of the provincial Guanchan chu (Bureau of Official Enterprises). Also in 1914 Zhang Cailuan gave birth to a son, Shumao. While serving in the government in Jiangsu, Zeng Pu continued to publish translations of French literature. His second son, who was studying in Germany, sent back many French works at his request; among the novels he rendered into vernacular Chinese were Hugo's *Quatrevingt-treize* (1874; translated as *Ninety-Three*, 1874) as *Jiushisan nian* (1913), *Angelo, Tyran de Padoue* (1835, Angelo, Tyrant of Padua; translated as *Angelo*, 1851) as "Xiangri le" (1914), and *Lucrèce Borgia* (1833; translated as *Lucretia Borgia: A Dramatic Tale*, 1842) as *Lükelanshi Baoxia* (1916). In 1918 Yu Yizhu gave birth to a son, Jiyang. De, Zeng Pu and Shen Xiangsheng's daughter, died that same year. Also in 1918 Zeng Pu resigned his position at the Guanchan chu. In 1924 he became the *Caizheng tingzhang* (Secretary of the Treasury) for Jiangsu province, then left the position to serve as *Zhengwu tingzhang* (Secretary of Administrative Affairs) for Sun Chuanfang, a warlord who controlled five southern provinces, including Jiangsu, in the mid 1920s. Zeng Pu retired from this position and from politics in 1926 and resumed his literary career full-time. In 1927 he established a publishing company, Zhenmeishan (Truth, Beauty, and Goodness) in partnership with his eldest son. Over the next six years he translated French plays and novels by Hugo, Zola, and Molière and published a series of essays introducing French literature to Chinese readers. He also published part of his diary and his largely confessional fictional autobiography *Lu Nanzi*. *Lu Nanzi: Lian* (Lu Nanzi: Love) began serial publication in the first issue of *Zhenmeishan* in November 1927; the eight chapters were published as a book in November 1928. Part 2, "Lu Nanzi: Hun" (Lu Nanzi: Marriage), was published in *Zhenmeishan* in 1929; it comprises one chapter. Parts 3 to 5 were never published. The first two installments of part 6, "Lu Nanzi: Zhan" (Lu Nanzi: War), were published in 1931 in a Zhenmeishan bookstore periodical; but the magazine was stopped, and the rest was not published.

The eponymous hero of *Lu Nanzi* is a youthful romantic ("Lu Nanzi" literally means "the Man of Lu," and the title is rendered as *The Real Man* in some English-language sources). Zeng Pu proclaimed the novel "true to the feelings I experienced, although the exact plot and timing may be at variance with reality." *La Nanzi: Lian* details the teenage protagonist's romance with a cousin. Prevented from marrying her by conservative social norms, Lu suffers a nervous breakdown and repeatedly considers suicide but eventually agrees to marry someone else. Meanwhile, two of his friends openly rebel against familial authority and conventional society in their pursuit of sexual love; their romance leads to their ostracism and ends in their double suicide. In its confessional style and high sentimentality, *Lu Nanzi* shows the influence of European Romantic literature, with which Zeng Pu was familiar and of which the most popular work in China at the time was Johann Wolfgang von Goethe's *Die Leiden des jungen Werthers* (1774; translated as *The Sorrows of Werther*, 1779). The novel also echoes main themes in the writing of the May Fourth generation: the conflict of individual love and familial obligation and the exploration of desire and sexuality.

Zeng Pu's fame rests primarily on *Niehai hua*. After the publication of the first twenty chapters in 1905, the next fifteen chapters took twenty-six years to appear—and then only intermittently and with significant changes of narrative direction. An enlarged 1928 edition comprises twenty-four chapters; chapters 11 through 20 were republished in 1929 as *Niehai hua, erji* (A Flower in a Sinful Sea, the Second Book); and chapters 21 through 30 appeared in 1931 as *Niehai hua, sanji* (A Flower in a Sinful Sea, the Third Book). Finally, *Niehai hua, sanji heding ben* (A Flower in a Sinful Sea, the Complete Three Books), comprising the first thirty chapters, was also published in 1931. This version is heavily revised, in part reflecting a more conservative political point of view on the part of the nearly sixty-year-old author. (The complicated publishing history of *Niehai hua* is detailed in *Niehai hua ziliao* [1982, Materials on Flower in a Sea of Retribution], edited by Wei Shaochang.) The novel was never finished; Zeng Pu's increasingly poor health and the burden of giving artistic structure to a vast social landscape and a tumultuous time—the last three decades of the Qing dynasty—prevented him from completing more than one of the five planned volumes of the work.

The name given to the narrator of the novel, Dongya Bingfu, signals an unflattering view of China: *dongya bingfu* (The Sick Man of East Asia) was popularly used at the time to describe the Qing empire and was coined after the cognomen for the dying Ottoman Empire, "the Sick Man of Europe." The novel opens with a discussion of the civil-service examination system, which had long been both the symbol of traditional high learning and the path to careers in officialdom; it was abolished in the year the first part of the novel was published. Speaking in the voice of a conventional storyteller—and mocking it somewhat—the narrator addresses his audience as though they were citizens of a foreign country and know nothing about the system:

> I don't suppose my dear citizens of the country have ever read "The Story of the Glorious Scholar," so you might fail to appreciate the honor and value of the first-degree holder. Of all the countries in the world, China alone possesses such an examination system, and then only once in three years is this highest degree awarded.

Thus the narrator reverses the roles of the familiar and the foreign, satirically emphasizing the "exoticness" of Chinese cultural practice. Four unique features of those who excel in the examinations are listed: "good deeds accumulated through several generations; capacity to withstand sexual temptation throughout one's lifetime; ripening of cultivated connections all over the capital city; and essays with appropriate praises and exaltations" of the empire and the

Cover for Rou yu si *(1929, Flesh and Death), a translation of Pierre Louÿs's 1895 novel* Aphrodite: Mours antiques *(translated as* Aphrodite: A Novel of Ancient Manners, *1900) by Zeng Pu and Zeng Xubai (from Yu Runqi, ed.,* Tang Tao cang shu, *2004; Bruccoli Clark Layman Archives)*

emperor. The narrator then says: "In wealth and honor, in wisdom and intelligence, even Su Shi and Li Po would keep respectful distance" from those who excel in the examinations, "not to mention Bacon of England and Rousseau of France." The narrator's claim that China's celebrated poets of antiquity, such as Su Shi and Li Po, would bow to late–Qing dynasty degree holders is conventional satire that ridicules the examination system. But by comparing Chinese scholars to foreign thinkers such as Francis Bacon and Jean-Jacques Rousseau, the narrator is rejecting the idea of "cultural uniqueness" and the national myth built around the examination system. The narrator's seemingly innocuous, joking remark thus serves to remove absolute authority from Chinese tradition.

The critique of the civil-service examination system extends to the portrayal of one of the central characters, Jin Wenqing, a member of the traditional literati who becomes an ambassador. Jin is based on the scholar Hong Jun, the Qing government's ambassador to Germany, Russia, Holland, and Austria from 1888 to 1891, whose acquaintance Zeng Pu had made during his years in Beijing. A "brilliant" product of the examination system, Jin purchases a set of thirty-five maps depicting the Sino-Russian border from a Russian of suspect character whom he meets on a journey abroad, and he presents the maps to the Qing court on his return. The maps turn out to have been drawn to justify Russia's territorial ambitions in the Pamirs. Because of Jin's mistake in presenting them to the court as authentic, the Qing empire nearly loses a territorial dispute with Russia. Jin's blunder is presented as inevitable, because he has been thrust into a role for which he is ill prepared and sent out into a world that he does not understand—and apparently does not care to understand. Jin's status as *zhuangyuan* (number one scholar), the man who placed first in the highest imperial examination, is repeatedly mentioned by the narrator and by other characters, marking him not just as a particularly inadequate individual but as a typical representative of the traditionally trained literati. His shortcomings, therefore, indicate the deficiency of the traditional scholar and, by extension, of the traditional system.

The other central character in *Niehai hua* is Jin's concubine, Fu Caiyun. She is based on the famous courtesan Sai Jinhua, who married Hong Jun in 1887. In the postscript to the 1928 edition of the novel Zeng Pu writes that he wanted the character to serve as the "thread" with which he would "attempt to link together the history of the past thirty years. . . . I wanted to avoid writing the 'front' side of history. Instead, I picked only interesting and minor anecdotes so that the context of the great events would be made clear." After Hong Jun's death, Sai returned to prostitution. She played a legendary role in the summer of 1900, when, in response to the Boxer Rebellion—the name given by foreigners to an anti-imperialist, antiforeign uprising led by the Yihetuan (Society United in Righteousness)—the allied forces of eight Western powers burned and looted Beijing and drove the Qing court into exile. Able to speak several European languages, Sai became the mistress of Count Alfred Waldersee, the commander in chief of the allied troops. According to legend, in the "dragon bed" of the Empress Dowager Cixi in the Imperial Palace, which Sai and Waldersee shared, Sai persuaded Waldersee to curb the brutality of his troops. Sai's role in the events of 1900 took on heavy symbolic value, and depictions of her by her contemporaries tended to opposite extremes: early in the twentieth century she was frequently represented as a femme fatale who brought down the empire, while in the 1930s she was more often portrayed as a nationalist heroine who single-handedly saved the country in a time of crisis. Most such positive renditions of her story came out in the late 1930s (she died in 1936); with all-out war with Japan impending, the use of a lower-class figure as an exemplar of patriotism appealed to popular taste. For authors who wrote under the banner of Guofang wenxue (Literature for National Defense), Sai seemed to provide just the right symbol: the lowly courtesan who upholds a high moral standard of loyalty—a long-established topos in Chinese literature.

In contrast to these black or white makeovers of Sai, her presence in *Niehai hua* is resolutely ambiguous. The narrative does not provide any interpretive frame to paint her as a heroine, nor does it condemn her as a villain. Zeng Pu is more intent on exploring the source of her power than on passing judgment on her exercise of it; he planned to deal with the Boxer Rebellion and the role of Sai/Fu in it, but the novel breaks off well before these events. Fu's power, the novel indicates, lies primarily in her ability to transform herself, which she first does when she "borrows" the official clothing—and, therefore, the status—of Jin's principal wife. Never forgetting that such power is not hers by right, Fu has no loyalty to the conventional principles underlying any position of power. Instead, she is dedicated to dealing with the needs of the present moment and acquiring the means to change her identity to meet each new challenge. Her lack of loyalty—to the Qing, to Jin, or to any ideology—makes it possible for her to act in moments of crisis, when rules and conventions are suspended and traditional hierarchies are overturned. Her chameleon-like nature enables her to play a pivotal role at a crucial moment in Chinese history, even though Zeng Pu did not bring her story through the year 1900 as he had originally planned to do.

In Zeng Pu's portrayal of Fu all the major issues of women's liberation are implicitly present: economic independence, education, participation in the public sphere, and sexual autonomy. In the 1920s and 1930s these issues were incorporated into the construction of the *xin nüxing* (new woman), a term common in reformist discourse. What is lacking in Zeng Pu's characterization of Fu, especially from the point of view of the May Fourth Movement, is any sense of dedication to an ideological agenda or political program that could legitimize her pursuit of freedom. In the final analysis, her own pleasure is Fu's only aim. The last chapter of the 1928 edition, in which Fu leaves the Jin household after Jin's death, is titled "The Jolly Bird Flies out of the Cage."

In addition to the main narrative strand of Jin and Fu, the novel includes several side plots. The most significant such plot involves Fu's German-language tutor, Sarah Aizenson, whom Fu and Jin meet en route to Europe and who turns out to be a Russian anarchist; the character is based on Sophia Perovskaia, who was hanged for her role in the assassination of Tsar Alexander II in 1881. Aizenson swindles Jin for the benefit of the Anarchist Party, and the narrative then digresses for three chapters to relate her story of political commitment and romance. In these chapters the philosophies of anarchism, democracy, and nationalism are explored at length. Aizenson sacrifices her love, and eventually her life, in the plot to assassinate the tsar. Another digression deals with the Franco-Vietnamese war of 1873 to 1885 and is initiated by a story that Jin hears at a party. The entertainers at the party include a young female tightrope walker who joined a troupe of performers after returning from fighting in Vietnam. As she walks the tightrope, she tells a story in song that mimics the structure of the novel and narrates history from the point of view of Huage, the possible legendary warrior concubine of Liu Yongfu, the Chinese warlord who led the *Hei qi* (Black Flag Army) against the French in Vietnam. Like the main narrative, it is a story filled with romantic passion and personal betrayal set against the backdrop of national crisis.

In the summer of 1931 Zeng Pu moved back to his hometown, Changshu, where he spent much of his time gardening. He died at his home on 23 June 1935. The name of the narrator of *Niehai hua*, Dongya Bingfu, had become Zeng Pu's nom de plume and adorns his tombstone in Changshu. During his lifetime his best-known novel had continued to develop as other writers produced sequels to it—mostly without his permission; this process continued well after his death. But the sequels fall short of Zeng Pu's ambitious historical scope. The original novel was never out of print throughout the first half of the twentieth century.

Zeng Pu's claim to an important position in modern Chinese literary history ultimately rests on his skillful portrayal of the rapidly changing Chinese society in *Niehai hua*. Some critics argue that in its structure *Niehai hua* largely follows the prototype of Wu Jingzi's novel *Rulin waishi* (circa 1750, Unofficial History of the Literati; translated as *The Scholars*, 1957) in loosely linking many episodic stories; others contend that Zeng Pu's work departs significantly from the traditional model by threading together a handful of stories in such as a way that the novel resembles a "pearl flower"—a blossom of loose pearls strung tightly together by a florist's wire. All agree that the structure is highly effective for covering a large canvas depicting many aspects of contemporary history.

Bibliographies:

Peter Li, "Selected Bibliography: Primary Sources," in his *Tseng P'u* (Boston: Twayne, 1980), pp. 140–142;

Shi Meng, "Zeng Pu zhu yi kao," in his *Zeng Pu yanjiu* (Shanghai: Guji chubanshe, 1982), pp. 61–76;

Zhang Ziwen, "Zeng Mengpu xiansheng zhuzuo ji yiwen mulu," in *Niehai hua; Lu Nanzi,* by Zeng Pu (Taibei: Guiguan tushu gufen youxian gongsi, 1983), pp. 423–428.

Biographies:

Shi Meng, "Zeng Pu shengping xinian," in his *Zeng Pu yanjiu* (Shanghai: Guji chubanshe, 1982), pp. 1–60;

Zeng Xubai, "Zeng Mengpu nianpu," in *"Niehai hua" ziliao,* edited by Wei Shaochang (Shanghai: Guji chubanshe, 1982), pp. 152–197.

References:

A Ying (Qian Xingcun), *Wanqing xiaoshuo shi* (Beijing: Renmin wenxue chubanshe, 1980), pp. 23–29;

Chen Pingyuan, *Zhongguo xiaoshuo xushi moshi de zhuanbian* (Shanghai: Shanghai renmin chubanshe, 1988), pp. 175–177;

Milena Dolezelová-Velingerová, ed., *The Chinese Novel at the Turn of the Century* (Toronto: University of Toronto Press, 1980), pp. 150–164;

Peter Li, *Tseng P'u* (Boston: Twayne, 1980);

Lin Mingde, ed., *Wanqing xiaoshuo yanjiu* (Taibei: Lianjing chuban gongsi, 1988), pp. 361–404;

Lu Xun, *Zhongguo xiaoshuo shilue* (Beijing: Renmin wenxue chubanshe, 1963), pp. 244–246;

Jaroslav Prusék, "The Changing Role of the Narrator in Chinese Novels at the Beginning of the Twentieth Century," *Archiv Orientální,* 38, no. 2 (1970): 169–178;

Shi Meng, *Zeng Pu yanjiu* (Shanghai: Guji chubanshe, 1982);

Dewei Wang, "Pan Jinlian, Sai Jinhua, Ying Xueyan: Zhongguo xiaoshuo shijiezhong 'huoshui' zaoxing de yanbian," in his *Cong Liu Er dao Wang Zhenhe: Zhongguo xiandai xieshi xiaoshuo sanlun* (Taibei: Shibao, 1986), pp. 77–94;

Wei Shaochang, ed., *Niehai hua ziliao* (Shanghai: Guji chubanshe, 1982);

Catherine Yeh, "Zeng Pu's *Niehai hua* as a Political Novella: A World Genre in a Chinese Form," dissertation, Harvard University, 1990;

Yu Runqi, ed., *Tang Tao cang shu* (Beijing: Beijing chubanshe, 2004), p. 18;

Paola Zamperini, "The Harlot's Progress: Fu Caiyun's Journey in the Sea of Retribution," M.A. thesis, University of California, Berkeley, 1994.

Papers:

Zeng Pu's manuscripts and other important materials are in the Gest Oriental Library, Princeton University.

Zhang Ailing
(Eileen Chang)
(30 September 1920 – September 1995)

Zhang Jingyuan
Georgetown University

BOOKS: *Chuanqi* [Romances] (Shanghai: Zazhishe, 1944; enlarged edition, Shanghai: Shanhe tushu gongci, 1946)–includes "Fengsuo," translated by Karen Kingsbury as "Sealed Off," in *The Columbia Anthology of Modern Chinese Literature,* edited by Lau and Howard Goldblatt (New York: Columbia University Press, 1995), pp. 188–197; "Guihuazheng: A'xiao bei qiu," translated by Zhang as "Shame, Amah!" in *Eight Stories by Chinese Women,* edited by Hua-ling Nieh (Taibei: Heritage Press, 1962), pp. 92–114; "Hong luan xi," translated by Janet Ng and Janice Wickeri as "Great Felicity," *Renditions,* no. 45 (1996): 101–111; "Hong meigui yu bai meigui," translated by Carolyn Thompson Brown as "Red Rose and White Rose," in her "Eileen Chang's 'Red Rose and White Rose': A Translation and Afterword," dissertation, American University, 1978, pp. 1–77; "Jinsuo ji," translated by Zhang as "The Golden Cangue," in *Twentieth-Century Chinese Stories,* edited by C. T. Hsia (New York: Columbia University Press, 1971), pp. 138–191; "Liu qing," translated by Eva Hung as "Traces of Love," *Renditions,* no. 45 (1996): 112–127; "Qing cheng zhi lian," translated by Karen Kingsbury as "Love in a Fallen City," *Renditions,* no. 45 (1996): 61–92; "Xin jing," translated by Roslyn Tom as "The Heart Sutra," in her "The Parent-Child Relationship in the Three Stories by Eileen Chang, with a Translation of 'The Heart Sutra,'" B.A. thesis, Harvard University, 1985, pp. 45–98;

Liu yan [Gossip] (Shanghai: Zhongguo kexue gongsi, 1944)–includes "Gengyi ji" [On Changing Clothes], translated by Zhang from her "Chinese Life and Fashions," *XXth Century,* 4 (January 1943): 54–61; "Yangren kan Jingxi ji qita" [On Foreigners Watching Peking Opera and Other Subjects], translated by Zhang from her "Still Alive," *XXth Century,* 4 (June 1943): 432–438;

Zhang Ailing (from the back cover for Ren Ruwen and Wang Yan, Zhang Ailing huazhuan: Meili yu cangjing, *2004; Collection of Thomas Moran)*

"Jin yu lu," translated by Oliver Stunt as "From the Ashes," *Renditions,* no. 45 (1996): 47–57; "Da ren," translated by David E. Pollard as "A Beating," *Renditions,* no. 45 (1996): 58–59; "Bi ye zheng ming hu," translated by Karen Kingsbury as "What Is Essential Is That the Names Be Right," *Renditions,* no. 45 (1996): 28–32; "Si yu," translated by Ng as "Intimate Words," *Renditions,* no. 45 (1996): 33-46; "Ziji de wenzhang," translated by Wendy Larson as "My Writing," in *Modern Chinese Literary Thought: Writings on Literature, 1893-1945,* edited by Kirk A. Denton (Stanford, Cal.: Stanford University Press, 1996), pp. 436-442;

Shiba chun [Eighteen Springs], as Liang Jing (Shanghai: Yibaoshe, 1951);

Chi di zhi lian [Love in Redland] (Hong Kong: Tianfeng chubanshe, 1954); translated by Zhang as *Naked Earth* (Hong Kong: Union Press, 1956);

Yang ge, translated into Chinese by Zhang (Hong Kong: Jinri shijie she, 1954); original English version published as *The Rice-Sprout Song* (New York: Scribners, 1955); republished as *The Rice Sprout Song: A Novel of Modern China* (Hong Kong: Dragonfly, 1955);

The Rouge of the North, as Chang (London: Cassell, 1967); translated into Chinese by Zhang as *Yuan nü* [The Embittered Woman] (Taibei: Huangguan chubanshe, 1968); English version republished, with foreword by David Der-wei Wang (Berkeley: University of California Press, 1998);

Ban sheng yuan [Destined for Half a Lifetime] (Taibei: Huangguan chubanshe, 1968);

Zhang kan [Zhang's Outlook] (Taibei: Huangguan chubanshe, 1976)–includes "Tiancai meng," translated by Karen Kingsbury as "Dream of Genius," *Renditions,* no. 45 (1996): 25-27;

Honglou meng yan [An Obsession with *Dream of the Red Chamber*] (Taibei: Huangguan chubanshe, 1977);

Wangran ji [Bewilderment] (Taibei: Huangguan chubanshe, 1983);

Yu yun [Lingering Melody] (Taibei: Huangguan chubanshe, 1987)–includes "Zhongguoren de zongjiao," translated into Chinese by Zhang from her "Demons and Fairies," *XXth Century,* 5 (December 1943): 421-429; "Shuansheng" (Alliteration), translated by Edward Gunn as "International Shanghai, 1941: Coffee House Chat about Sexual Intimacy and the Childlike Charm of the Japanese," in *Modern Chinese Writers: Self-Portrayals,* edited by Helmut Martin and Jeffrey Kinkley (Armonk, N.Y.: Sharpe, 1992), pp. 296-301;

Xu ji [A Sequel] (Taibei: Huangguan chubanshe, 1988)–includes "Wu si yi shi," translated by Zhang, originally written in English as "Stale Mates," *Reporter,* 15 (20 September 1956): 34-38;

Di yi lu xiang [Aloeswood Ashes: The First Burning] (Taibei: Huangguan chubanshe, 1991);

Qing cheng zhi lian [Love in a Fallen City] (Taibei: Huangguan chubanshe, 1991);

Zhang Ailing wenji [Zhang Ailing's Collected Works], 4 volumes, edited by Jin Hongta and Yu Qing (Hefei: Anhui wenyi chubanshe, 1992);

Duizhao ji: Kan lao zhaoxiangbu [Reflections: On Looking at an Old Photo Album] (Taibei: Huangguan chubanshe, 1994); excerpts translated by Janice Wickeri as "Reflections: Words and Pictures: Excerpts," *Renditions,* 45 (1996): 13-23;

Tongxue shaonian dou bu jian [The Kids Are All Right] (Taibei: Huangguan chubanshe, 2004);

Chenxiang [Aloeswood] (Taibei: Huangguan chubanshe, 2005).

Editions and Collections: *Zhang Ailing duanpian xiaoshuoji* [A Collection of Zhang Ailing's Short Stories] (Taibei: Huangguan chubanshe, 1954);

Zhang Ailing xiaoshuoji [A Collection of Stories by Zhang Ailing] (Taibei: Huangguan chubanshe, 1968);

Zhang Ailing sanwen quan bian [The Complete Essays of Zhang Ailing], edited by Lai Fengyi (Hangzhou: Zhejiang wenyi chubanshe, 1992);

Zhang Ailing ji: Daodi shi Shanghairen [Works of Zhang Ailing: At Bottom a Shanghainese], edited by Xu Daoming and Feng Jinniu (Shanghai: Hanyu da cidian chubanshe, 1995);

The Rice-Sprout Song, foreword by David Der-wei Wang (Berkeley: University of California Press, 1998).

Editions in English: "Jinsuo ji," translated by Zhang as "The Golden Cangue," in *Modern Chinese Stories and Novellas 1919-1949,* edited by Joseph S. M. Lau, C. T. Hsia, and Leo Ou-fan Lee (New York: Columbia University Press, 1981), pp. 530-559;

"Guihuazheng: A'xiao bei qiu," translated by Zhang Ailing as "Shame, Amah!" in *Bamboo Shoots after the Rain: Contemporary Stories by Women Writers of Taiwan,* edited by Ann C. Carver and Sung-sheng Yvonne Chang (New York: Feminist Press, 1990), pp. 3-16;

"Fengsuo," translated by Janet Ng and Janice Wickeri as "Shutdown," *Renditions,* no. 45 (1996): 93-100;

"The Religion of the Chinese" ("Zhongguoren de zongjiao"), in *The Chinese Essay,* translated and edited by David E. Pollard (New York: Columbia University Press, 2000; London: Hurst, 2000), pp. 283-292;

Traces of Love and Other Stories, edited by Eva Hung (Hong Kong: Research Center for Translation, Chinese University of Hong Kong, 2000)–comprises "Shutdown" ("Fengsuo"), translated by Ng and Wickeri; "Great Felicity" ("Hong luan xi"), translated by Ng and Wickeri; "Steamed Osmanthus Flower: Ah Xiao's Unhappy Autumn" ("Guihuazheng: A'xiao bei qiu"), translated by Simon Patton; "Traces of Love" ("Liu qing"), translated by Hung; and "Stale Mates," written in English by Zhang;

"Love in the Fallen City" ("Qing cheng zhi lian"), translated by Shu-ning Sciban, in *Dragonflies: Fiction by Chinese Women in the Twentieth Century,* edited by Shu-ning Sciban and Fred Edwards (Ithaca, N.Y.: East Asian Program, Cornell University, 2003), pp. 32–70;

Written on Water (Liu yan), translated by Andrew F. Jones (New York: Columbia University Press, 2005).

PRODUCED SCRIPTS: *Taitai wansui* [Long Live the Wife!], motion picture, Shanghai wenhua yingye gongsi, 1947;

Bu liao qing [Lingering Passion], motion picture, Shanghai wenhua yingye gongsi, 1947;

Qingchang ru zhanchang [The Battle of Love], motion picture, Guoji dianying maoye youxian gongsi, 1956;

Ren cai liang de [A Tale of Two Wives], motion picture, Guoji dianying maoye youxian gongsi, 1958;

Taohua yun [The Wayward Husband], motion picture, Guoji dianying maoye youxian gongsi, 1959;

Liu yue xin niang [June Bride], motion picture, Guoji dianying maoye youxian gongsi, 1960;

Nan bei yi jia qin [The Greatest Wedding on Earth], motion picture, Guoji dianying maoye youxian gongsi, 1962;

Xiao er'nü [Father Takes a Bride], motion picture, Guoji dianying maoye youxian gongsi, 1962;

Yi qu nan wang [Please Remember Me], motion picture, Guoji dianying maoye youxian gongsi, 1964.

TRANSLATIONS: Chen Jiying, *Fool in the Reeds,* translated by Zhang, as Chang (Hong Kong: Rainbow Press, 1959);

Mark Van Doren, ed., *Aimosen xuan ji* [The Portable Emerson] (Hong Kong: Jinri shijie she, 1963);

Ernest Hemingway, *Laoren yu hai* [The Old Man and the Sea] (Hong Kong: Jinri shijie she, 1976);

Han Bangqing, *Hai shang hua liezhuan* [Flowers of Shanghai], translated by Zhang from the Suzhou dialect to Mandarin (Taibei: Huangguan chubanshe, 1981); translated by Zhang, as Chang, as *The Sing-Song Girls of Shanghai,* revised and edited by Eva Hung (New York: Columbia University Press, 2005).

SELECTED PERIODICAL PUBLICATIONS– UNCOLLECTED: "Chinese Life and Fashions," *XXth Century,* 4 (January 1943): 54–61;

"On the Screen: Wife, Vamp, Child," *XXth Century,* 4 (May 1943): 392;

"Still Alive," *XXth Century,* 4 (June 1943): 432–438.

"On the Screen: *The Opium War,*" *XXth Century,* 4 (June 1943): 464;

"On the Screen: *Song of Autumn* and *Cloud Over Moon,*" *XXth Century,* 5 (July 1943): 75–76;

"On the Screen: *Mothers and Daughters-in-Law,*" *XXth Century,* 5 (August/September 1943): 202;

"On the Screen: *On with the Show* and *The Call of Spring,*" *XXth Century,* 5 (October 1943): 278;

"On the Screen: *China: Educating the Family* and *The Fisher Girl,*" *XXth Century,* 5 (November 1943): 358;

"Demons and Fairies," *XXth Century,* 5 (December 1943): 421–429.

Best known as a fiction writer and essayist, Zhang Ailing (Eileen Chang) rose to literary fame in Shanghai during the Japanese occupation in the early 1940s but fell into relative obscurity until Columbia University professor C. T. Hsia praised her in his pioneering *A History of Modern Chinese Fiction* (1961) as one of the best Chinese writers of the twentieth century and her story "Jinsuo ji" (1943; translated as "The Golden Cangue," 1971) as "the greatest novelette in the history of Chinese literature." After this rediscovery, Zhang's works became popular in Taiwan, in Hong Kong, in mainland China after the death of Mao Zedong in 1976, and among readers of Chinese the world over. Since the 1980s Zhang's position as one of the literary giants of modern China has been firmly established.

More than any other major literary figure of twentieth-century China, Zhang has drawn media attention and been treated almost voyeuristically as an item for public consumption. One of her fans even traveled from Taibei to Los Angeles to rummage through her garbage for personal information and souvenirs. The fascination with her is partly accounted for by the paradox that Zhang often wrote about her personal life in her fiction and essays while living in utter seclusion during the last twenty-five years of her life– the period when she was at the height of her literary fame. A year before her death she published a photograph album of herself and her ancestors to reshape her public persona and create yet another myth about herself, provoking even further frantic public curiosity about her and her works. The media branded her a *qinü* (unusual woman) and called her "the last member of the Chinese aristocracy."

Zhang was born into an aristocratic family in Shanghai on 30 September 1920 and named Zhang Ying. On her father's side her grandmother's father was Li Hongzhang, a nineteenth-century Qing dynasty statesman responsible for signing many peace treaties with the Western powers; her grandfather was Zhang Peilun, a high-ranking scholar-official who was

Drawings by Zhang for her story "Jinsuo ji" (1943), which she translated in 1971 as "The Golden Cangue" (from Ren Ruwen and Wang Yan, Zhang Ailing huazhuan: Meili yu cangjing, 2004; Collection of Thomas Moran)

demoted by the Qing court after the Sino-French War of 1884. Zhang's father, Zhang Zhiyi, lived mainly on the family's declining fortune during the Republican era. He smoked opium, was addicted to gambling, frequented brothels, kept a concubine, and mistreated his wife and children. Zhang's mother, Huang Yifan, was a "Modern Girl" who unbound her feet and read translated Western novels of romance and liberty.

During her childhood Zhang witnessed a dissipated style of life among remnants of the Qing who were nostalgic for the imperial days and could find no place in the new Republic. She had an excellent classical education; like the clichéd child of good breeding, she was able to recite poems of the Tang dynasty (618 to 907) at age three. She was shy and took great pleasure in solitary writing and drawing.

When Zhang was four, Huang went to Europe with her sister-in-law to study art and oil painting, leaving Zhang and Zhang's three-year-old brother, Zhang Zijing, in the care of their tyrannical father and his concubine. Four years later, Huang returned from Europe. Zhang Zhiyi tried to make amends with his wife: he got rid of the concubine and tried to give up his opium addiction. After living together for less than two years, the couple were formally divorced. Zhang Zhiyi later married Sun Yongfan, an opium addict from an old official-scholar family.

Zhang wrote her first story, a family drama, at age seven, and went on to try her hand at historical fiction and romances. She even wrote a modern version of Cao Xuequin's classical novel *Honglou meng* (1791, Dream of the Red Chamber; translated as *The Story of the Stone*, 1973–1986) in the "Mandarin Ducks and Butterflies" mode, giving the characters modern experiences and comic adventures. None of these childhood works have been published. Her first publication was a cartoon in the English-language newspaper *Evening Post* when she was nine; she earned five yuan, which she immediately spent on a tube of lipstick. In 1930 her mother changed Zhang's name to Eileen Chang to register her in St. Mary's Hall Girls' School, an Episcopalian missionary school in Shanghai; Zhang Ailing is the Chinese transliteration of Eileen Chang. Zhang entered St. Mary's Hall in the fall of 1931. Her mother went to

Europe again in 1932; she returned to China in 1936 but left for Europe again soon afterward. From that time on she largely remained out of Zhang's life.

Zhang published essays and short stories in *Guo guang* (The Light of the Nation), the St. Mary's Hall school journal. Among them was "Niu" (Ox), which appeared in the first issue of the journal on 20 October 1936. It describes the miserable lot of a poor peasant family; Zhang particularly touches on the devastating prospect that faces the wife on the loss of her husband and of her chickens, her only source of livelihood. This piece is Zhang's only story in the new literary style characteristic of the May Fourth Movement of the early 1920s, when young urban writers favored rural themes and evinced a sentimental benevolence toward poor peasants bound to the earth and constrained by a harsh environment. "Bawang bie ji" (Farewell My Concubine) was published in the ninth and final issue of *Guo guang* on 10 May 1937; it is a rewriting of a tragic historical story. During a military siege Yu, the king of Chu's concubine, commits suicide. Zhang focuses on Yu's thoughts instead of those of the king—a reversal of the traditional narrative, in which Yu's act would have been depicted as an expression of her loyalty to the king and a way to highlight the bravery of the king besieged by enemy troops and abandoned by his own soldiers. In Zhang's version, Yu commits suicide not out of blind devotion to the king but because she is afraid that if the king overcomes the siege and conquers the country, she will face a gloomy future as a kept woman. Her farewell is a decisive step of self-assertion in opposition to the king. "Bawang bie ji" is the beginning of Zhang's exploration of the dilemma of modern women unable to free themselves from their dependence on men. The two stories were discovered in 1987 by Chen Zishan, a Shanghai scholar, and are included in volume one of *Zhang Ailing wenji* (1992, Zhang Ailing's Collected Works). Even in her first stories Zhang shows stylistic and psychological maturity by paying attention to the interior worlds of her protagonists, particularly female ones.

After graduating from high school in 1937, Zhang submitted "Tiancai meng" (translated as "Dream of Genius," 1996) to an essay competition held by the Shanghai literary journal *Xifeng* (West Wind); it came in thirteenth, received an honorary award, and was published in the journal in 1941; it is collected in her *Zhang kan* (1976, Zhang's Outlook). In the essay she describes herself as a child: she was full of dreams, clumsy at daily chores, and awkward on social occasions but loved literature and her own imaginative writing; she felt strongly the appeal of music, paintings, and colored fabrics; and, in general, she appreciated the aesthetic pleasures of a solitary life. But, Zhang writes, her dreams were plagued by the petty annoyances of daily reality. The essay ends with a typically fin de siècle maxim: "Life is a gorgeous gown swarming with lice."

Zhang was accepted by the University of London but was unable to travel to Europe because of the outbreak of war in the Pacific in 1937. She entered the University of Hong Kong as an English major in 1939. She resolved to write only in English during her time at the university. She later used her observations of the colony's hybridized culture in her writing. During her third year at the university the Japanese besieged and then attacked the colony. Zhang worked as a nurse, attending to wounded civilians at the school's hospital.

The war forced the university to close in 1942, a year before Zhang was scheduled to graduate. She returned to Shanghai, which was called Gudao (Orphan Island) because it was cut off from the rest of China by blockades and fighting. She briefly attended a college-preparatory class at St. John's College before becoming a freelance writer. In 1943 she began contributing articles on Chinese culture and reviews of movies in the Shanghai-based English-language journal *The XXth Century*. Published from 1941 to 1946, *The XXth Century* advocated the victory of the Axis powers in World War II; but Zhang's articles and reviews have no apparent political content, nor was she otherwise involved in the politics of the journal. The articles on Chinese culture were well received; the editor of *The XXth Century* commented that they offered "an amusing psychoanalysis of modern China . . . conveying to us a great deal of information on the mentality of the Chinese masses" and that "it is her deep curiosity about her own people which enables her to interpret the Chinese to the foreigners." Zhang's *XXth Century* articles have never been collected, but Chinese versions of some of them are included in her essay collections *Liu yan* (1944, Gossip; translated as *Written on Water*, 2005) and *Yu yun* (1987, Lingering Melody). Zhang also published essays and stories in popular Chinese-language literary magazines, including *Ziluolan* (Violet), *Tiandi* (Heaven and Earth), *Zazhi yuekan* (Miscellaneous Records Monthly), *Wanxiang* (Panorama), *Dajia* (Everyone), and *Gu jin* (Then and Now), illustrating many of them with her own drawings. Her Chinese stories met with instant success, making her one of the most popular writers in Shanghai during the Japanese occupation.

Zhang's fiction is not easy to place among the main schools and trends of early- and mid-twentieth-century Chinese writing. Though she wrote of relationships between women and men, she objected to the association of her writing with that of the "Romantic Generation"—the lyrically sentimentalist side of the May Fourth Movement represented by women writers such as Bing Xin and Bai Wei. And while the personal

Illustration by Zhang for her story "Xin jing" (translated as "The Heart Sutra," 1985) in the journal Wanxiang *(Panorama), August–September 1943 (Collection of Thomas Moran)*

affairs of her characters are placed against a backdrop of social transformation, she also differs from the other main group of May Fourth writers, who focused on making powerful arguments for social change. Nor does she belong among the equally political writers to whom that group gave way in the late 1930s and who emphasized patriotic or leftist antiwar rhetoric. Her writing perhaps most resembles that of the "Modernist" movement represented by the journal *Xiandai/Les Contemporains* (The Moderns), which was published from 1932 to 1935. The Modernists were chiefly concerned with literary technique, with catching the sophisticated urban ambience, and with speaking for the "third type" of people–those in the socioeconomic middle and the political center. But Zhang's literary achievement surpasses that of the Modernists and offers an alternative approach to literary modernism. Her writing combines the techniques of traditional Chinese vernacular fiction with modern narrative innovations, and her outlook is one of profound world-weariness–a view that is associated with her favorite post–World War I British writers W. Somerset Maugham, Aldous Huxley, and H. G. Wells. The older and newer styles combine to add texture and significance to her works. Her mastery of Chinese is, perhaps, the outstanding element in her fiction and essays: readers are mesmerized by her linguistic sophistication; rich clusters of brilliant colors, images, and symbols; and her ingeniously caustic tongue.

Although some critics insist that Zhang's writing is apolitical, she shows her political concerns indirectly in many ways. The war and its effects lurk in the background of most of her writing and in terms she uses frequently such as "desolation," "annihilation," and "destruction." Again and again she conveys a sense of the transience of all things. In the preface to her first book, the short-story collection *Chuanqi* (1944, Romances), she writes: "Our times are undergoing rapid transformation; order is already breaking down, and even greater demolition is ahead. One day our civilization will cease to exist, no matter whether we see this as China ascending or descending. If the word I use most often is 'desolation' *[huangliang]*, that is because at the back of my mind looms large the threat of such a great annihilation." In "Tiancai meng" Zhang described her preferred styles of writing as those of "splendor" and "melancholy." Beneath individual human dramas, she believed, a broader tragedy always lies. Her stories unfold in the context of the destruction of societies and civilizations.

Zhang's stories of the 1940s take place in cosmopolitan settings, either in the treaty port of Shanghai or the colony of Hong Kong. She grew up in Shanghai and felt most at home there, and her Shanghai stories outnumber her Hong Kong stories; sometimes she views Hong Kong from the standpoint of characters from Shanghai, using an outsider's cultural shock to give her observations of urban life greater force.

Zhang published ten of her Shanghai and Hong Kong stories in the collection *Chuanqi* in 1944; an enlarged edition with five more stories appeared in 1946. The term *chuanqi* originally referred to a genre of Tang dynasty fiction: tales of marvels and strange adventures. Later it was applied to translations of Western medieval literature of romance and thus gained the modern meaning of "love stories." Most of Zhang's stories—all of those that are considered her best—are about love relationships between men and women, but they are not "romantic." Edward Gunn, in fact, calls her fiction "antiromantic," for she writes about love not with May Fourth romanticism but with skepticism, irony, and disillusionment. The romantic relationships in Zhang's stories are based on calculated maneuvers, circumstances, and acts of fate. Both in her stories and in her essays Zhang takes a critical stance toward fantasies of romance and visions of transcendent union between men and women. In her fiction women's need for material provision and social recognition underlies their quest for love and marriage.

Zhang examines Chinese culture and customs from a Western perspective and looks at traditional ways of life from a modern one. The cover for the enlarged edition of *Chuanqi,* designed by her friend Yan Ying at her direction, features a common after-dinner household scene of the late Qing period: a woman in traditional costume, apparently the mistress of the household, sits at a table playing solitaire; next to her a nanny holds a baby. But in the upper-right quarter of the picture a faceless figure, apparently of Western origin and clearly representing the modern, leans into the room through a window like a ghost. This juxtaposition of the old and the new creates an odd and unsettling atmosphere.

Chuanqi includes the first two stories by Zhang that immediately caught readers' attention. Set against the background of colonial Hong Kong, "Chenxiang xie: Diyi lu xiang" (Aloeswood Ashes: The First Burning) and "Chenxiang xie: Di'er lu xiang" (Aloeswood Ashes: The Second Burning) were originally published in the popular journal *Ziluolan* in 1943. The editor of *Ziluolan,* Zhou Shoujuan, himself a skilled writer of the commercially popular Mandarin Ducks and Butterflies style of romance with a melancholy touch, praised the stories highly and noted that they have the flavor both of Maugham, who is known for the stark cynicism of his unadorned portraits of human nature and the conflicts of Europeans in the colonial environment, and of *Honglou meng,* the prime example of the traditional Chinese "domestic" novel—what Hsia calls "intimate boudoir realism." The stories are stylistically conservative in that they are narrated by detached, omniscient observers, as in the older school of romance—a form that readers would find familiar and comfortable. At certain moments, however, Zhang changes the narrative viewpoint to that of one of the protagonists.

"Chenxiang xie: Diyi lu xiang" is about the fall of Weilong, a student from Shanghai who is lured by the materially rich world of Hong Kong and becomes entangled in games of seduction. The story is set in the mansion that an elderly concubine, whose professional stock in trade is flirtation and endless entertaining, inherited from her late husband. Zhang's story reworks the traditional tale of an older woman managing the seduction of a girl to show a decaying Chinese culture unable to resist the encroachment of the hybridized colonial culture and the seductive power of material self-interest. At times the mansion appears as a haunted imperial tomb, stubbornly persisting in spite of changing times and affecting everyone who enters it. The story provides an example of the way in which Zhang went farther than most Chinese fiction writers in using description of the characters' surroundings to represent their feelings and concerns when Weilong, feeling torn and frustrated by the hollow temptations of life in Hong Kong and thinking of returning to Shanghai, walks outside the mansion: "It is getting dark. The entire world is like a gray Christmas card, all vague and shadowy; the only things in existence are those huge red flowers, simple, primitive, as big as bowls, and as big as barrels." The material temptations of the city are as "simple" and "primitive" as they are alien.

"Chenxiang xie: Di'er lu xiang" touches on a favorite theme of Maugham's: the prudish British social codes and their influence on colonial Europeans—in Zhang's story, the British expatriate community in Hong Kong. The rigid Victorian moral outlook was the cause of hysteria and divorce for several women in the family of the protagonist, Susie, and led to the suicide of her new husband, Roger. As is common in Zhang's stories, contrasting viewpoints highlight the absurdity of situations and predicaments. Although the story proper is told by a conventional third-person narrator, it is introduced by a prelude related in the first person. The prelude is set in a library and takes the form of a conversation in which a gossipy Irish classmate of the narrator, Ailing, excitedly discloses the latest gossip circulating in the colonial community. Ailing remarks that a library is a refrigerator of emotions, storing centuries of books about human lives but without human warmth: the years have given the books a cold feel. To hear a living story in such a place is like watching a fistfight from the clouds. Ailing has been immersed in reading historical documents regarding Lord George McCartney's eighteenth-century mission to the emperor Qian Long. This major effort by the British Empire to engage China failed because McCartney stubbornly refused to follow Chinese court etiquette and express appropriately humble respect for the Son of Heaven and Emperor of the Middle Kingdom. The story that Ailing has heard, and is about to tell, is a modern version of the failed mission that involves several expatriates. The juxtaposition of McCartney's mission reported by cold books and the modern story of colonial experience is itself juxtaposed to a comparison of a jaded and demystified view of sex passed down among the Chinese in books with the confining morals and pathological phobias of the British expatriates.

The protagonist of "Moli xiangpian" (Jasmine Tea), first published in the journal *Zazhi yuekan* in July 1943, is Nie Chuanqing. Nie is a college student who grew up in Hong Kong in an old gentry family that was originally from Shanghai. His mother died young, and his father and stepmother smoked opium and neglected him. Lonely, shy, and filled with self-loathing, Nie finds his only consolation in daydreaming. He becomes friends with a classmate, Yan Danzhu, the daughter of the professor who teaches Nie's Chinese literature class. When he finds out that Professor Yan was his mother's first love, Nie's daydreams continually turn to the life he might have had if he had been the professor's son. Scolded and eventually rejected by his ideal father figure for his poor performance in class, Nie is overwhelmed by envy and jealousy of Yan Danzhu and brutally beats her. The tension in Nie's mind is so convincingly developed that his final act, though cruel, is perfectly understandable.

"Qing cheng zhi lian" (translated as "Love in a Fallen City," 1996) was originally published in *Zazhi yuekan* in September 1943. The title has a double meaning: on the one hand, it is an idiom for a woman so beautiful that an entire city could fall in love with her; on the other hand, it is a name for a love that distracts a ruler and leaves the city defenseless. In Zhang's story it refers to a wartime realization of the temporality and uncertainty of human life that leads two calculating and selfish people who are skeptical about romance to form the union that they both need. The marriage of Bai Liusu, a divorcée approaching thirty who is being pressed by her family to get married, and Fan Liuyuan,

Zhang in the early 1940s (from Joseph S. M. Lau, C. T. Hsia, and Leo Ou-fan Lee, eds., Modern Chinese Stories and Novellas 1919–1949, *1981; Middlebury College Library)*

a playboy who does not believe in the institution of marriage, becomes possible only when Hong Kong falls to Japan and the two suddenly realize their mutual dependency and vulnerability.

In "Fengsuo" (translated as "Sealed Off," 1995), originally published in the journal *Xiao tiandi* (Small World) in November 1943, war temporarily lifts customary limitations and offers people who lead conventional, unexciting lives a chance to venture outside the boundaries to toy with the "dangerous" and the "impossible." Two strangers on a Shanghai trolley that has stopped during a Japanese air raid begin a romance and make plans for the future. The man complains about his unhappy arranged marriage and proposes to the woman; she amuses herself with the idea of becoming his concubine. But when the air raid is over, the man quickly resumes the face of a stranger, moves away from the woman, and gets off the trolley without saying good-bye, and life goes on as before. "It was as though the whole of Shanghai suddenly dozed off and had an absurd dream," the narrator comments.

Zhang explores many psychological dimensions of the urbanites who people her stories. "Xin jing" (1943; translated as "The Heart Sutra," 1985), first published in the journal *Wanxiang* in August 1943, explores the Freudian theme of incestuous attraction between a father and daughter. Though the father takes his daughter's look-alike classmate as his mistress to divert him from his obsession with his daughter, life will never again have the same joy for either of them.

In the 1940s Shanghai was the "Jewel of the Orient." Zhang's "Jinsuo ji," originally published in *Zazhi yuekan* in November 1943 and also known in her own English version as "The Golden Cangue," is a tale of manners set in the old Shanghai of a few decades earlier—a time when money was not the sole determinant of social status, and the city was not so different from the rest of the country. A *cangue* is a traditional Chinese punishment device, intermediate between handcuffs and stocks, consisting of a board locked around the convict's head and hands; here it is a metaphor for the way in which money handicaps human souls. Cao Qiqiao becomes enslaved by the desire for money; while May Fourth literature usually portrays women as victims of the traditional society, Cao bears much of the responsibility for her own destruction. Sold by her brother to be the wife of a wealthy invalid, she is a willing participant in the "business transaction." But the marriage brings her only material comfort, not social respectability, and she is cut off from her family and friends. Her desire to hold onto her money makes her suspicious of everyone; she gradually goes mad, destroying herself and those around her, including her children. The symbolism and the use of cinematic montage in the novella have drawn the attention of many literary critics.

In 1940s Shanghai, with the institution of arranged marriage a thing of the past, the responsibility of matching girls to suitable men of equal, or preferably higher, social class had devolved from parents onto the shoulders of the young women themselves. Three stories in *Chuanqi*—"Liuli wa" (Glazed Tiles), "Hua diao" (Withering of Flowers), and "Hong luan xi" (translated as "Great Felicity," 1996)—are about urban girls whose social class places them above any gainful employment as, for example, store clerks or typists; their only profession is to get married—in "Hua diao" Zhang calls them "nü jiehun yuan" (female "weddingists")—and their success is measured by the social status and wealth of the husband. Zhang's stories of young women and their parents preoccupied with age-old games designed to ensure a good marriage demonstrate the vulnerability of women in the economic marketplace and the damage that expectations of "marrying up" inflict on them. "Liuli wa" was first published in *Wanxiang* in November 1943, and "Hua diao" was first published in *Zazhi yuekan* in March 1944. Both are in the first edition of *Chuanqi*. "Hong luan xi" appears in the enlarged edition.

Also added to the enlarged edition is "Hong meigui yu bai meigui" (1944; translated as "Red Rose and White Rose," 1978), which was first published in three installments in *Zazhi yuekan* in May, June, and July 1944. The title refers to a code developed by Tong Zhenbao, a senior manager in a foreign textile-dying company in Shanghai, who prides himself on being upright and responsible and wants his world to be in strict order. He divides the women in his life into two mutually exclusive categories: red roses and white roses. The red rose represents passion, taboo, illegitimacy, and hybridization; the white rose represents purity, chastity, asexuality, and legitimacy. He oscillates between the two, eventually choosing to stay with his wife, the white rose. The story, narrated in a sarcastic tone, reveals the hypocrisy of this "ideal modern Chinese" man, whose world of rationality and authority falls apart as he tries in vain to maintain surface order with his clear-cut formulas.

In 1944 Zhang published her collection of essays *Liu yan*, which includes some of her photographs and drawings; the cover features a self-portrait in pencil. Like many of Zhang's titles, *Liu yan* has a double meaning. It can mean "gossip"; by implication, Zhang wanted her essays to spread as fast as rumors. Literally, it means "flowing words"—or, in Zhang's paraphrase in "Houloumeng yan zixu" (1977, Preface to *An Obsession with* Dream of the Red Chamber), "written on water," suggesting transience. The implication here is that Zhang's words will float away with the passage of time; they are not designed for eternity. Written in a lively, witty, and often humorous style and featuring intimate topics, fresh ideas, and revealing observations on apparently trivial details of human life and its environment, Zhang's essays are an important part of her literary legacy.

The essays in *Liu yan* can be divided into two groups: cultural commentaries on Beijing opera, movies, music, dance, painting, and fashion, as well as Zhang's views on social topics such as the character of Shanghai people and the situation of women; and autobiographical essays. The first category includes Chinese-language versions of articles originally published in English in *The XXth Century*: among them are "Gengyi ji" (On Changing Clothes), originally published in Chinese in the journal *Gujin* (Then and Now) in December 1943 and in English as "Chinese Life and Fashions" in *The XXth Century* in January 1943; "Yangren kan Jingxi ji qita" (On Foreigners Watching Peking Opera and Other Subjects), first published in Chinese in *Gujin* in November 1943 and as "Still Alive" in *The XXth Century* in June 1943; and "Jie yindeng"

(Borrowing Silver Lanterns), originally published in *The XXth Century* as "On the Screen: Wife, Vamp, Child" in May 1943. The original articles were intended to introduce English-speaking readers to aspects of Chinese culture, and the Chinese versions are revised to appeal to a Chinese audience. In her essays, both in English and in Chinese, Zhang does not deal with large issues but observes telling details of cultural life. Even so, now and then she makes remarks that bring out the deeper significance of what is perceived as trivial. For example, discussing the early Republican period in "Gengyi ji," she writes that "In an age of political disorder, people were powerless to modify existing conditions closer to their ideal. All they could do was to create their own atmosphere, with clothes, which constitute for most men and all women their immediate environments. We live in our clothes."

What life might be like were one just to lose control is a theme in many of Zhang's stories and essays. In "Gengyi ji," for example, a boy riding his bicycle down a busy street takes his hands off the handlebars and rides on unsteadily; the pedestrians stop and watch in fascination. The narrator says, "Perhaps the loveliest time in one's life is in this moment of 'letting go'!" This episode does not appear in the English version of the essay, "Chinese Life and Fashions," in *The XXth Century*.

Also among the essays of social commentary in *Liu yan* is "Zou, zou dao loushang qu" (Let's Go, Go Upstairs), in which Zhang mentions that she once wrote a play and is particularly fond of comic episode in which a character responds to a family dispute by going upstairs. She notes that Henrik Ibsen's play *Et Dukkehjem* (1879; translated as *A Doll's House*, 1889), in which the protagonist, Nora, awakens from her doll-like domestic status, had an immense impact on the Chinese public. During the May Fourth period the ending of the play, in which Nora leaves home, provoked many public discussions on the future of women's liberation in China. The most powerful and influential voice on the topic was the writer Lu Xun. His speech "Nuola zuohou zenyang" (1924, What Happens after Nora Leaves Home?) posits three possible outcomes for any woman who refuses to be a puppet at home and walks out: she will become a prostitute, die of starvation, or return home. In an indirect reply to Lu Xun, Zhang proposes another path, less dramatic but more practical: go upstairs and come down whenever the dinner bell rings: "In fact, even if we just walk from the back building to the front building, inhale some fresh air, and open a window to see some new scenery, that is not bad." This suggestion is a cheerful cynicism. Ultimate solutions are important, but they may not come soon and may not come at all; in the meantime, one can

Self-portrait by Zhang (from Hu Lancheng, "Ping Zhang Ailing," Zazhi, 13 [10 May 1944]; Collection of Thomas Moran)

make small improvements and find diversions on a human scale.

In "Daodi shi Shanghairen" (At Bottom a Shanghainese), first published in *Zazhi yuekan* in July 1943, Zhang writes: "Shanghainese means traditional Chinese plus the temper of modern high-pressure life. The exchange among the aberrant of the new culture and the old culture may not be very healthy, but there is an astounding wisdom there."

In the autobiographical essays in *Liu yan* Zhang playfully describes herself as an ordinary, independent city dweller who loves money, clothes, and food and takes pleasure in trivial matters. The persona she creates in these essays is genial, intimate, trusting, and curious—the kind of popular writer that readers can be expected to like. Aware of the changes in the role of Chinese writers in the modern world, Zhang became a master at managing the writer-reader relationship. She told her readers that she preferred the modern role of the writer, which is to appeal to the public in the free market, over the traditional role of the intellectual as a didact at the mercy of the emperor. In "Tong yan wu ji" (The Words of a Child Have No Taboos) she writes that she is happy that her source of income is not the imperial family but the magazine-buying masses, for "the masses are an abstraction. If I have to serve a master, then of course I'd prefer an abstract one." She spoke to the reading public not as a preacher but as a fellow petty urbanite, and common readers could enjoy and empathize with the joy and pain of her daily life. She retained this "friend-of-the-readers" approach to the end of her life. In "Jin yu lu" (translated as "From the Ashes," 1996), first published in *Wanxiang* in 1944, Zhang describes her experiences as a student in Hong Kong during the war. She calls for attention to be paid to irrelevant matters, because "Man's *joie de vivre* is solely to be found in life's irrelevancies." Like a true modernist, she says: "This thing we call reality is without structure, a confusion of gramophones playing in chaotic cacophony, each singing its own song. But amid the unintelligible clamor is the unexpected lucid interval that sours the heart and moistens the eye, a discernible melody instantly reclaimed by the weighty gloom, the spark of understanding swamped."

Zhang believed that in an age of rapid change, people sense that something is wrong with their daily lives; her work portrays the terror of banal everyday life. Her works are about ordinary people's pitfalls and pathos and the lives of individuals and families that have spun out of control. Her fictional world is filled with callous, cowardly, and otherwise morally flawed petty urbanites. Zhang never considered herself an elite writer and, therefore, did not think that she had to carry the burden of being a spokesperson for moral uprightness and social justice; she saw herself as a popular writer whose aim was to entertain. Until the 1990s critics of Chinese literature paid little attention to popular writers, believing that their works were of low literary value. In spite of Zhang's vast popularity in Shanghai in the 1940s, only a few serious critics wrote about her stories at the time.

Zhang's career suffered after World War II as a result of her wartime association with some journals that had been financed by the Japanese and also because of her 1944 marriage to Hu Lansheng, deputy minister of the Propaganda Department of Shanghai in the Japanese puppet Nanjing government. After the war, Hu went into hiding and lived with two other women, and he and Zhang were divorced in 1947. Some literary magazines that formerly welcomed Zhang's works shunned her; others that had flourished during the war went out of business. Zhang turned to writing movie scripts. During high school she had subscribed to English-language movie magazines such as *Screen* and *Movie Star* for bedside reading. She was an avid moviegoer and saw practically all the movies, both foreign and Chinese, shown in Shanghai. She had begun publishing reviews of Chinese movies in *The XXth Century* in 1943, the same time as she began publishing short stories, and many of her stories employ cinematic devices such as close-ups, fade-outs, montage, and panorama. *Taitai wansui* (Long Live the Wife!), which was produced by a Shanghai film studio in 1947, is a characteristic work of domestic conflict and romance. The most notable difference between the script and her stories is the comic, lighthearted, storm-in-a-teacup quality of the former. Contrary to the left-wing trend dominant in the Shanghai movie industry after the end of the war with Japan, *Taitai wansui* does not deliver a political message but centers around family, marriage, and love. Mrs. Tang, a middle-class Shanghai housewife, has to help her husband get out of his involvement with another woman, Chen Mimi. Her solution is an amusing variant of the traditional method for dealing with such a situation: she invites Chen, who has been blackmailing Mr. Tang by claiming to be pregnant, to live with her and her husband in an old-fashioned husband, wife, and concubine arrangement but casually reveals to her rival that her husband has no money. After that, Chen leaves Mr. Tang alone, and Mrs. Tang reconciles with her husband at the divorce-signing table. Hers is not a revolutionary solution to a modern urban woman's problems but something a woman in such a situation might, in accord with the social code of the day, actually do.

After the founding of the People's Republic of China in 1949, Zhang tried to adapt to the new socialist mode of writing. She attended the First Congress of the

Shanghai Federation of Literary and Art Circles in 1950 and published two serial novellas under the pen name Liang Jing in the Shanghai newspaper *Yibao* (Yi Times): *Shiba chun* (Eighteen Springs) from 25 March 1950 to 11 February 1951 and "Xiao Ai" from 4 November 1951 to 24 January 1952. Although *Shiba chun,* which was republished in book form in 1951, maintains Zhang's focus on domestic scenes, family drama, and interpersonal relationships during the social upheavals of the first half of the twentieth century, it ends on a note of hope for a better life under the new regime. "Xiao Ai" depicts the life of a domestic servant whose life changes drastically for the better after the founding of the People's Republic. It was republished in the second volume of *Zhang Ailing wenji* (1992, Zhang Ailing's Collected Works).

Despite her efforts to conform to the new state ideology, however, Zhang sensed that her career was in jeopardy. In 1952 she moved to Hong Kong, where she went to work for the United States Information Agency. She translated some American works into Chinese, including Mark Van Doren's *The Portable Emerson* (1946) as *Aimosen xuan ji* (1963) and Ernest Hemingway's *The Old Man and the Sea* (1952) as *Laoren yu hai* (1976). She also translated into English Chen Jiying's novel *Di cun zhuang* (1954), which portrays a peasant's life in the first half of the twentieth century, as *Fool in the Reeds* (1959).

While in Hong Kong, Zhang wrote two political novels. *Chi di zhi lian* (1954, Love in Redland) was written and published in Chinese and then translated by Zhang into English as *Naked Earth* (1956). *The Rice-Sprout Song* was written in English but published first in Zhang's Chinese translation as *Yang ge* in 1954 and in the original English version in 1955. Both novels are products of the Cold War and anti-Communism—particularly the former, which was a disappointment to the reading public and to Zhang herself, who later said wryly that it was "commissioned." *The Rice-Sprout Song* deals with the disastrous effects of the land-reform movement on the rural population in China, examines the role of Chinese intellectuals in the movement, and culminates in a peasant riot. The motif of hunger appears here both as a devastating human problem stimulating class consciousness and as a sign of the heroic self-sacrifice valued by the Communists. *The Rice-Sprout Song* received warm reviews in the Western media, and Zhang sold the rights for twenty-three foreign translations and a television adaptation of the book.

Zhang moved to the United States in 1955. The following year she was awarded a two-year stay at the MacDowell Colony, an artists' colony in Peterborough, New Hampshire. There she met Ferdinand Reyher, a playwright; they were married in August 1956. For the

"Rose," illustration by Zhang for her story "Hong Meigui yu Bai Meigui" (Red Rose and White Rose) in the 10 May 1944 issue of Zazhi *(Collection of Thomas Moran)*

most part Zhang remained a freelance writer and independent scholar, publishing both in English and in Chinese. She wrote and adapted movie scripts for studios in Hong Kong and visited Taiwan briefly in 1963. She was writer in residence at Miami University in Oxford, Ohio, in 1966. Her husband died in 1967 after a long illness.

In 1967 Zhang published the novel *The Rouge of the North;* her own Chinese translation, *Yuan nü* (The Embittered Woman), appeared in 1968. It was characteristic of Zhang in her later years to publish revised versions of her earlier works: *The Rouge of the North* is a longer version of her 1943 story "The Golden Cangue." Yindi, the protagonist of *The Rouge of the North,* is a less demonic and more sympathetic,

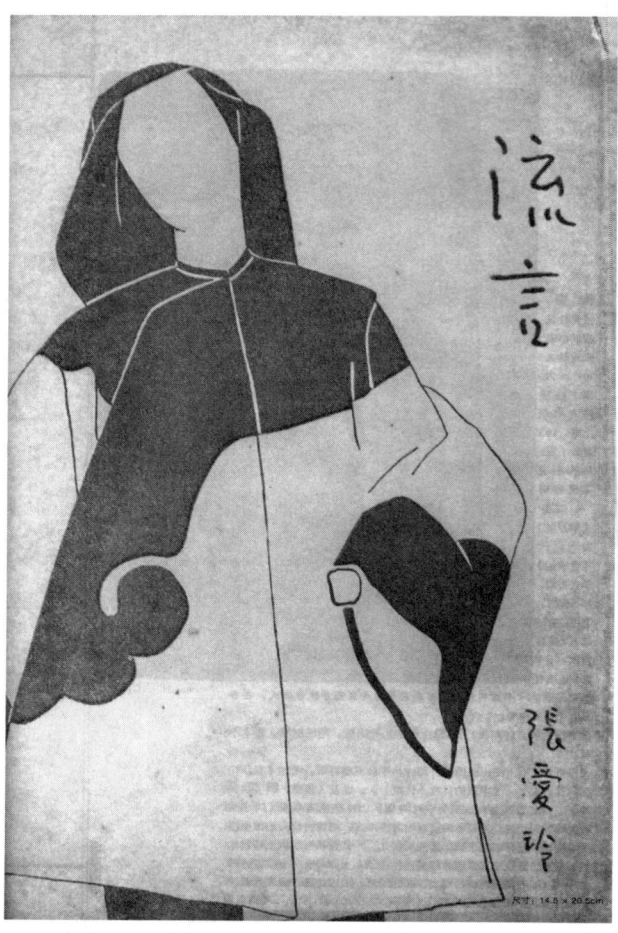

Cover for Zhang's second book, Liu yan *(1944, Gossip; translated as* Written on Water, *2005), a collection of essays (from Yu Runqi, ed.,* Tang Tao cang shu, *2004; Bruccoli Clark Layman Archives)*

rounded, and convincing character than Cao Qiqiao in "The Golden Cangue." Zhang also revised *Shiba chun* as *Ban sheng yuan* (1968, Destined for Half a Lifetime), removing an episode in which the Nationalist Party arrests one of the protagonists and tortures his wife to death and the optimistic ending about the future under the new socialist regime.

Zhang was a fellow of the Radcliffe Institute for Advanced Study in Cambridge, Massachusetts, from 1967 to 1969 and a researcher at the Center for Chinese Studies at the University of California, Berkeley, from 1969 to 1971. Although she continued to write–and rewrite–fiction, she began to give most of her attention to scholarly work. She spent nearly ten years on a close textual study of the various editions of *Honglou meng* and published the results under the title *Honglou meng yan* (An Obsession with *Dream of the Red Chamber*) in 1977. Zhang notes that she had been fasci-

nated with the novel since childhood, and she acknowledges her literary debt to it. She compares the task to going through a labyrinth, doing a word puzzle, or writing a detective novel. In 1981 she published an annotated Mandarin translation of the Shanghai Wu-dialect *Hai shang hua liezhuan* (1892, Flowers of Shanghai), by Han Bangqing; the book includes a translation of part of the novel into English (Zhang's complete translation was published posthumously in 2005 as *The Sing-Song Girls of Shanghai*). These works reflect Zhang's general literary interest in traditional-style novels, whether they be masterpieces of the traditional vernacular or middlebrow popular novels of the late-Qing and early Republican periods, a literary affinity from which her works draw inspiration in both substance and technique.

In 1994 Zhang's final work, *Duizhao ji: Kan lao zhaoxiangbu* (Reflections: On Looking at an Old Photo Album; excerpts translated as "Reflections: Words and Pictures: Excerpts," 1996) was published by the Huangguan chubanshe (Crown Press) in Taibei. It consists of fifty-four old family photos, each with a brief introduction. Photographs of Zhang in chronological order, from childhood to adulthood, are included, but much of the work comprises pictures of her maternal and paternal ancestors with especially detailed commentaries on those who were mostly absent from her life and yet remained important in the realm of her imagination: her great-grandparents, her grandparents, and her mother. The pictures of Zhang in adulthood mostly show her alone. Her two husbands are omitted from the book. With this photographic autobiography Zhang presents a carefully controlled set of images to satisfy the curiosity of her fans and her critics, long frustrated by her hermit-like reclusiveness, while at the same time leaving them unsure of the significance of what they were seeing. Zhang was found dead in her Los Angeles apartment on 8 September 1995.

Zhang Ailing is, perhaps, the only Chinese fiction writer of the twentieth century to have attained the status of a media celebrity, with a following among both the general reading public and academics. Her cultural and literary standing can be indicated by the currency of two special phrases constructed from her quite common surname: "Zhang mi" (Zhang's Fans) and "Zhang xue" (Studies on Zhang Ailing). Her works have influenced a generation of writers in Taiwan and on the mainland. Several of her works have been turned into popular movies, including *Qing cheng zhi lian* (1984), directed by Ann Hui; *Yuan nü* (1990), directed by Dan Hanzhang; *Hong meigui yu bai meigui* (1994), directed by Stanley Kwan; *Ban sheng yuan/ Eighteen Springs* (1997), directed by Hui; and *Hai shang hua* (1998), directed by Hou Hsiao-hsien. In 1998, as Zhang's fame soared in the Chinese-speaking world, the University of California Press republished *The Rice-Sprout Song* and *The Rouge of the North* to ensure the continuation of her literary legacy in English.

Bibliography:

Li Yingping, "Zhang Ailing shengping, zuopin nianbiao," in *Wode jiejie Zhang Ailing,* by Zhang Zijing and Ji Ji (Shanghai: Xuelin chubanshe, 1997), pp. 188–197.

Biographies:

Hu Lancheng, "Ping Zhang Ailing," *Zazhi,* 13 (10 May 1944): 76–81;

Hu Lancheng, *Jin shi jin sheng* (Nagoya: Janarusha, 1958); excerpts translated by David E. Pollard as "This Life, These Times," *Renditions,* no. 45 (1996): 129–135;

Yu Qing, *Tiancai qi nü Zhang Ailing* (Shijiazhuang: Huashan wenyi chubanshe, 1992);

Hu Xin, *Zhang Ailing zhuan* (Beijing: Zuojia chubanshe, 1996);

Ji Ji and Guan Hong, eds., *Yongyuande Zhang Ailing: didi, zhangfu, qinyou bixia de chuanqi* (Shanghai: Xuelin chubanshe, 1996);

Sima Xin, *Zhang Ailing yu Laiya* (Taibei: Dadi chubanshe, 1996);

Tam Pak Shan, "Eileen Chang: A Chronology," *Renditions,* no. 45 (1996): 6–12;

Zhang Zijing and Ji Ji, *Wo de jiejie Zhang Ailing* (Shanghai: Xuelin chubanshe, 1997);

Ren Ruwen, *Chenxiangxie li de jiushi: Zhang Ailing zhuan* (Beijing: Tuanjie chubanshe, 2001);

Yu Bin, *Zhang Ailing zhuan* (Guilin: Guangxi shifan daxue chubanshe, 2001);

Zhang Jun, *Yueguang xia de beiliang: Zhang Ailing zhuan* (Guangzhou: Huacheng chubanshe, 2001);

Ren and Wang Yan, *Zhang Ailing huazhuan: Meili yu cangjing* (Beijing: Tuanjie chubanshe, 2004).

References:

Jeanine Bohlmeyer, "Eileen Chang's Bridges to China," *Tamkang Review,* 5, no. 1 (1974): 111–128;

Carolyn Thompson Brown, "Eileen Chang's 'Red Rose and White Rose': A Translation and Afterword," dissertation, American University, 1978;

Sung-sheng Yvonne Chang, "Yuan Qiongqiong and the Rage for Eileen Zhang," *Modern Chinese Literature,* 4, nos. 1–2 (1988): 201–223;

Chen Bingliang, *Zhang Ailing duanpian xiaoshuo lun ji* (Taibei: Yuanjing chuban shiye gongsi, 1983);

Stephen Chen, "Themes and Techniques in Eileen Chang's Stories," *Tamkang Review,* 8, no. 2 (1977): 169–200;

Ya-Shu Chen, "Love Demythologized: The Significance and Impact of Zhang Ailing's (1921–1995)

Cover designed at Zhang's direction for the enlarged edition (1946) of her short-story collection Chuanqi *(Romances). The original edition, published in 1944, was her first book (Collection of Zhang Jingyuan).*

Works," dissertation, University of Wisconsin, 1998;

Chen Zishan, ed., *Si yu Zhang Ailing* (Hangzhou: Zhejiang wenyi chubanshe, 1995);

Rey Chow, "Modernity and Narration–in Feminine Detail," in her *Women and Chinese Modernity: The Politics of Reading Between West and East* (Minneapolis: University of Minnesota Press, 1991), pp. 84–120;

Chow, "Seminal Dispersal, Fecal Retention, and Related Narrative Matters: Eileen Chang's Tale of Roses in the Problematic of Modern Writing," *Differences: A Journal of Feminist Cultural Studies,* 11, no. 2 (1999): 153–176;

Poshek Fu, "Eileen Chang, Women's Film, and the Domestic Culture of Modern Shanghai," *Tamkang Review,* 29, no. 4 (1999), pp. 9–28;

Edward Gunn, "Chang Ai-ling," in his *Unwelcome Muse: Chinese Literature in Shanghai and Peking 1937–1945* (New York: Columbia University Press, 1980), pp. 200–231;

C. T. Hsia, "Eileen Chang," in his *A History of Modern Chinese Fiction* (New Haven: Yale University Press, 1961), pp. 389–431;

Hu Lancheng, "Ping Zhang Ailing," *Zazhi*, 13 (10 May 1944): 76–81;

Hu Xin, *Zuihou de guizu: Zhang Ailing* (Taibei: Guoji cunwenku shudian, 1995);

Nicole Huang, "Eileen Chang and the Modern Essay," in *The Modern Chinese Literary Essay: Defining the Chinese Self in the 20th Century*, edited by Martin Woesler (Bochum, Germany: Bochum University Press, 2000), pp. 67–96;

Hsin-sheng C. Kao, "The Shaping of a Life: Structure and Narrative Process in Eileen Chang's *The Rouge of the North*," in *Women Writers of Twentieth Century China*, edited by A. Palandri (Eugene: Asian Studies Publications, University of Oregon, 1982), pp. 111–137;

Leo Ou-fan Lee, "Eileen Chang and Cinema," *Journal of Modern Literature in Chinese*, 2 (January 1999), pp. 37–60;

Lee, "Eileen Chang: Romances of a Fallen City," in his *Shanghai Modern: The Flowering of a New Urban Culture in China, 1930–1945* (Cambridge, Mass.: Harvard University Press, 1999), pp. 267–303;

Ping-kwan Leung, "Two Discourses on Colonialism: Huang Guliu and Eileen Chang on Hong Kong in the Forties," *Boundary 2*, 25 (Fall 1998), pp. 77–96; also in *Modern Chinese Literary and Cultural Studies in the Age of Theory: Reimagining a Field*, edited by Rey Chow (Durham, N.C. & London: Duke University Press, 2000), pp. 78–98;

Chin-chown Lim, "Reading 'The Golden Cangue': Iron Boudoirs and Symbols of Oppressed Confucian Women," translated by Louise Edwards and Kam Louie, *Renditions*, no. 45 (1996): 141–149;

Lin Xingqian, *Lishi, nüxing yu xingbie zhengzhi: Chongdu Zhang Ailing* (Taibei: Maitian chubanshe, 2000);

Helmut Martin, "'Like a Film Abruptly Torn Off': Tension and Despair in Zhang Ailing's Writing Experience," in *Symbols of Anguish: In Search of Melancholy in China*, edited by Wolfgang Kubin (Bern: Peter Lang, 2001), pp. 353–383;

Meng Yue and Dai Jinhua, "Zhang Ailing: Cangliang de wan'er yi xiao," in their *Fuchu lishi dibiao* (Henan: Henan renmin chubanshe, 1989), pp. 245–262;

Lucien Miller and Hui-chuan Chang, "Fiction and Autobiography: Spatial Form in 'The Golden Cangue' and *The Woman Warrior*," in *Modern Chinese Women Writers: Critical Appraisals*, edited by Michael S. Duke (New York: Sharpe, 1989), pp. 24–43;

Sherry Mou, "Between History and Literature: Chang Ai-ling's Lao Tai-tai Characters," *Jindai Zhongguo funü shi yanjiu* (Taiwan), no. 2 (June 1994): 203–227;

Laikwan Pang, "Photography and Autobiography: Zhang Ailing's *Looking at Each Other*," *Modern Chinese Literature and Culture*, 13 (Spring 2001), pp. 73–106;

Shirley J. Paolini and Yen Chen-shen, "Moon, Madness and Mutilation in Eileen Chang's English Translation of 'The Golden Cangue'," *Tamkang Review*, 19, nos. 1–4 (1988–1989): 547–557;

Shui Jing, *Pao zhuan ji* (Taibei: Sanmin shuju, 1986);

Shui, *Zhang Ailing de xiaoshuo yishu* (Taibei: Dadi chubanshe, 1973);

Shui, *Zhang Ailing weiwan: Jiedu Zhang Ailing de zuopin* (Taibei: Dadi chubanshe, 1996);

Elizabeth Cheng Stewart, "Awareness of the Woman Question in the Novels of George Elliot and Eileen Chang," dissertation, University of Illinois at Urbana-Champaign, 1988;

Tang Wenbiao, ed., *Zhang Ailing ziliao daquan ji* (Taibei: Shibao wenhua chuban shiye youxian gongsi, 1984);

Roslyn Tom, "The Parent-Child Relationship in the Three Stories by Eileen Chang, with a Translation of 'The Heart Sutra,'" B.A. thesis, Harvard University, 1985;

Xiaoming Wang, "The 'Good Fortune' of Eileen Chang," translated by Cecile Chu-chin Sun, *Renditions*, no. 45 (1996): 136–140;

Philip F. C. Williams, "Back from Extremity: Eileen Chang's Literary Return," *Tamkang Review*, 29, no. 3 (1999): 127–138;

Xiaoling Yin, "Shadow of *The Dream of the Red Chamber*: An Intertextual Critique of 'The Golden Cangue,'" *Tamkang Review*, 21, no. 1 (1990): 1–28;

Yang Ze, ed., *Yuedu Zhang Ailing: Zhang Ailing guoji yantaohui lunwen ji* (Taibei: Maitian chubanshe, 1999);

Yu Qing, ed., *Xun zhao Zhang Ailing* (Beijing: Zhongguo youyi chuban gongsi, 1995);

Yu Qing and Jin Hongda, eds., *Zhang Ailing yanjiu ziliao* (Fuzhou: Haixia wenyi chubanshe, 1994);

Yu Runqi, ed., *Tang Tao cang shu* (Beijing: Beijing chubanshe, 2004), pp. 193–194;

Zhang Jian, *Zhang Ailing xinlun* (Taibei: Shuquan chubanshe, 1996);

Zhang Jian, ed., *Zhang Ailing de xiaoshuo shijie* (Taibei: Xuesheng shuju, 1984);

Zheng Shusen, ed., *Zhang Ailing de shijie* (Taibei: Yuncheng wenhua shiye gufen youxian gongsi, 1989).

Zhang Henshui

(18 May 1895 – 15 February 1967)

T. M. McClellan
University of Edinburgh

SELECTED BOOKS: *Chunming waishi* [An Unofficial History of Beijing], 3 volumes (Shanghai: Shijie shuju, 1930);

Tixiao yinyuan [Fate in Tears and Laughter], 3 volumes (Shanghai: Sanyou shushe, 1930); excerpts translated by Sally Borthwick in *Chinese Middlebrow Fiction from the Ch'ing and Early Republican Eras,* edited by Liu Ts'un-yan (Hong Kong: Renditions Books, Chinese University Press, 1984), pp. 254–287;

Jian dan qin xin [Swords and Dulcimers] (Beiping: Xin chenbao, 1930);

Man jiang hong [Sunset on the Yangtze] (Shanghai: Shijie shuju, 1931);

Luo xia gu wu [Rose-Colored Clouds], 4 volumes (Shanghai: Shijie shuju, 1931);

Wan gong ji [Bent Bow Collection] (Shanghai: Yuanheng shushe, 1932);

Jinfen shijia [Gold-Dust Dynasty], 12 volumes (Shanghai: Shijie shuju, 1933);

Taiping hua [The Flowers of Peace] (Shanghai: Sanyou shushe, 1933);

Re xue zhi hua [Flower of Ardent Blood] (Guangzhou & Hong Kong: Wu gui tang, 1933);

Meiren en [A Beauty's Favor] (Shanghai: Shijie shuju, 1934);

Man cheng fengyu [Cities in Uproar], 3 volumes (Hankou: Dazhong shuju, 1934);

Xiandai qingnian [Modern Youth], 3 volumes (Shanghai: Sheying she, 1934);

Qinhuai shijia [Singsong Girls of Nanjing] (Shanghai: Baixin shuju, 1940);

Ye shenchen [Heavy Is the Night] (Shanghai: Sanyou shushe, 1941);

Mimi gu [The Secret Valley] (Shanghai: Baixin shuju, 1941);

Ping Hu tongche [The Beiping-Shanghai Express] (Shanghai: Baixin shuju, 1941); translated by William A. Lyell as *Shanghai Express* (Honolulu: University of Hawai'i Press, 1997);

Zhang Henshui (from Tang Wenyi, Mu Dingsheng, and Ji Lei, eds., 20 shiji Zhongguo wenxue tudian, *2001; Collection of Thomas Moran)*

Yan guilai [Return of the Swallow] (Tianjin: Weiyi shudian, 1942);

Xiangzhan zhi ye [Nights of Street Fighting] (Chongqing: Xinmin baoshe, 1942);

Bashiyi meng [Eighty-One Dreams] (Chongqing: Xinmin baoshe, 1942)—includes "Xiezi: Shu chi xia de shengyu," translated by T. M. McClellan as "Prologue: Remnants from Rats' Teeth," *Renditions,* 57 (Spring 2002): 38–41; "Di qishi'er meng: Wo shi Sun Wukong," translated by McClellan as "Dream the Seventy-Second: 'I Am the Monkey King,'" *Renditions,* 57 (Spring

2002): 42–67; "Di shiwu meng: Tuihuiqu le ershi nian," translated by McClellan as "Dream the Fifteenth: 'Twenty Years Ago,'" *Renditions,* 60 (Spring 2004): 27–49; and "Di sanshiliu meng: Tiantang zhi you," translated by McClellan as "Dream the Thirty-Sixth: 'A Tour of Heaven,'" *Renditions,* 61 (Autumn 2004): 41–69;
Da jiang dong qu [The Great River Flows East] (Chongqing: Xinmin baoshe, 1943);
Shuihu xin zhuan [New *Outlaws of the Marsh*], 4 volumes (Chongqing: Jianzhong, 1943);
Shuihu renwu lunzan [Discussions and Appraisals of Characters from *Outlaws of the Marsh*] (Chongqing: Wanxiang shuwu, 1944);
Si ren ji [This Man's Tale], 2 volumes (Shanghai: Baixin shuju, 1944);
Danfeng jie [Crimson Phoenix Street] (third edition [earliest extant edition], Shanghai: Jiaoyu shudian, 1944);
Shanchuang xiaopin [Informal Essays from a Mountain Window] (Shanghai: Shanghai zazhi gongsi, 1945);
Bei yan nan fei [The Wild Goose Flies South], 2 volumes (Chongqing: Shancheng, 1946);
Huben wan sui! [Tigers Forever!] (Shanghai: Baixin shuju, 1946);
Ao shuang hua [A Hardy Perennial] (Shanghai: Baixin shuju, 1947);
Zhi zui jin mi [Cash Drunk, Money Mad] (Shanghai: Baixin shuju, 1949);
Liang Shanbo yu Zhu Yingtai [Liang Shanbo and Zhu Yingtai] (Beijing: Baowentang shudian, 1954);
Bai she zhuan [The Story of White Snake] (Beijing: Tongsu wenyi chubanshe, 1955);
Meng Jiangnü (Beijing: Beijing chubanshe, 1957);
Wangliang shijie [Goblin Market] (Shanghai: Wenhua chubanshe, 1957);
Wu zi dengke [Five Sons Pass the Examinations; or, The Carpetbaggers] (Shanghai: Wenhua chubanshe, 1957);
Wo de xiezuo shengya [My Career as a Writer] (Chengdu: Sichuan renmin chubanshe, 1981);
Zhang Henshui quanji [The Complete Works of Zhang Henshui], 62 volumes (Taiyuan: Beiyue wenyi chubanshe, 1993).

OTHER: "Zong da xie: Bing ziwo jiantao" [An Open Letter of Thanks–and a Self-Criticism], in *Zhang Henshui yanjiu ziliao,* edited by Zhang Zhanguo and Wei Shouzhong (Tianjin: Tianjin renmin chubanshe, 1986), pp. 277–282.

SELECTED PERIODICAL PUBLICATION–UNCOLLECTED: "Wo de shenghuo he chuangzuo" [My Life and Work], *Ming bao yuekan,* 132 (December 1976: 74–78); 133 (January 1977: 29–34).

In his time Zhang Henshui was regarded as the chief exponent of China's "Saturday School" or "Mandarin Ducks and Butterflies School" of popular fiction during its decline, which coincided with the rise of May Fourth literature in the late 1910s. As such, Zhang was attacked by "progressive" May Fourth writers and was thereafter mostly ignored by critics until a revival of interest in his work began in mainland China around 1980. More than twenty of his novels were republished there in the 1980s and aroused significant interest among general readers.

Zhang's career as a novelist began in 1930, around the same time as those of such leading lights of twentieth-century Chinese fiction as Mao Dun and Lao She. He took a different road from theirs, however; in the essay "Zong da xie: Bing ziwo jiantao" (An Open Letter of Thanks–and a Self-Criticism), first published in the Chongqing newspaper *Xinmin bao* (New People's Post) on 20 May 1944, he justifies this divergence as an attempt to "improve the old linked-chapter Chinese novel" instead of abolishing it, which he saw as the aim of his more radical literary contemporaries. *Zhanghui* (linked-chapter) is the predominant form of the traditional Chinese novel; its main features include the verse-couplet title and conventional leads-in and leads-out to each chapter. It remains unclear to what extent Zhang succeeded in his "improvements" or reforms, but his fiction did "ganshang shidai" (catch up with the times), another retrospectively avowed intention–he uses the expression "ganshang shidai" in the title of a section of "Wo de shenghuo he chuangzuo" (My Life and Work), a short autobiography published posthumously in *Ming bao yuekan* (Ming Pao Monthly) in 1976–1977. Even his last novels retain some of the central features of traditional Chinese fiction, while doing away with some of its more obviously archaic linguistic and stylistic features. From his youth Zhang was interested in Classical Chinese poetry, as well as in fiction; his poetry is not highly regarded, but his essays, particularly his classical essays written in Chongqing during the war with Japan, have received high praise from scholars such as King-fai Tam.

The first of six children, Zhang was born on 18 May 1895 in eastern Jiangxi province; his original name was Zhang Xinyuan. The Zhangs, who were from

Qianshan in central Anhui, were "scholar gentry" with a military pedigree, having raised and served in local militias since the Taiping Rebellion of 1851 to 1864. Zhang's father, Zhang Yu, left an early career as a soldier to enter the civil service; his mother's name is not recorded in the standard sources. Zhang Yu was assigned to a rural customs and excise post near Jingdezhen in 1895 or 1896. Zhang Xinyuan's brother Xiaokong was born in 1898. In 1901 Zhang Xinyuan entered a traditional private elementary school, where he studied the usual primers and Confucian classics for three years.

In 1904 Zhang Yu was promoted to a posting in Nanchang, the capital of Jiangxi. There Zhang Xinyuan entered a *jiaguan* (family school) run by the family of a friend. After six months, he transferred to a larger private school. Also in 1904 his sister Zhang Qiwei was born. Twin brothers Buye and Muye followed in 1907.

In 1909, after several years of traditional schooling, sometimes with tutors at home as the family moved several times in Anhui and Jiangxi provinces, Zhang entered a modern-style school in Nanchang. From the fall of 1909 until 1912 he followed the new Westernized curriculum in two schools in Nanchang, studying subjects such as English, physics, and mathematics; in his free time he read traditional fiction and classical poetry. In 1910, in a demonstration of anti-Qing patriotism, he cut off the Manchu-style *bianzi* (queue) in which Chinese men were required to wear their hair. That same year his sister Zhang Qifan was born.

In the autumn of 1912 Zhang Yu died of an illness. His father's death left Zhang Xinyuan with no money for tuition. He withdrew from school, abandoned his plans to study abroad, and returned to Qianshan.

In 1913 Zhang was admitted to the Meng Zang kenzhi xuexiao (College for the Development of Mongolia and Tibet), founded by Sun Yat-sen, in Suzhou. Hoping to earn money to help with tuition, he wrote two stories in three days in response to an advertisement in one of the most important journals of the Saturday School of popular Chinese literature, *Xiaoshuo yuebao* (Short Story Monthly). "Jiu xinniang" (Secondhand Bride) is in Classical Chinese and is a humorous tale about the marriage of two young people; "Meihua jie" (Plunder of Plum Blossom) is in vernacular Chinese and is about a widow's suicide. Neither was accepted for publication, but Zhang received an encouraging letter from the editor, Yun Tieqiao.

In July 1913, in what is known as the "Second Revolution," several southern provinces declared themselves independent of the Republic of China and its autocratic president, Yuan Shikai, and organized their own military forces. The Meng Zang kenzhi xuexiao

Cover for a 1960 edition of Zhang's best-selling novel Tixiao yinyuan *(1930, Fate in Tears and Laughter), about a young man attracted to two women who look exactly alike but are opposites in character (Wason Collection on East Asia–China, Kroch Asia Library, Cornell University)*

was disbanded that month for its involvement in the Second Revolution. Zhang went home to Qianshan and was married by family arrangement to Xu Wenshu; they had no children. In early September the Second Revolution ended in defeat, with Yuan still in power.

According to T. M. McClellan's *Zhang Henshui and Chinese Popular Fiction, 1919–1949* (2005), "during the next six years Zhang led a somewhat bohemian existence, punctuated by attempts to resume formal studies." His state of mind during these years is reflected in the pen name he began to use. His stories of 1913 were submitted under the name "Chouhua Henshui sheng" (He-Who-Pines-for-Flowers-and-Bemoans-[the-Flowing-of-] Water). The phrase refers to a tenth-century poem in the *ci* (lyric) form by Li Yu, the last emperor of the

Southern Tang dynasty. By 1914 Zhang was using the shortened form "Henshui," which expresses regret for the passage of time or, more positively, the resolve not to waste it.

In 1916 Zhang began to apply himself to the study of Chinese traditional literature and translations of Western fiction. Having previously done unpaid journalistic work for an uncle in Hankou, in January 1918 he took an editorial job on *Wan jiang ribao* (The Anhui River Daily) in Wuhu. McClellan writes that in the spring of 1919 Zhang, with the encouragement of friends, "made his début as a published novelist in *Anhui River Daily* and elsewhere with five works," of which "only one short story and one novella have survived due to their inclusion in the same year in an anthology," *Xiaoshuo bawang* (Storylords), "edited by the prominent Saturday School writer Yao Min'ai." According to McClellan, "both are written in a lively vernacular Chinese and in the traditional popular style of flippant scandalmongery" that characterized the Saturday School.

On 4 May 1919 patriotic riots in Beijing galvanized a wider campaign for changes in China's politics and culture that became known as the May Fourth Movement. In the fall, Zhang resigned from the *Wan jiang ribao* and took the train to Beijing, intending to apply to Beijing University. Instead, he went to work for the Beijing correspondent of the Shanghai newspaper *Shen bao* and then, in addition, for the Beijing newspaper *Yishibao* (Social Welfare News). His work schedule left him no time to pursue a formal education, but in 1920 he studied English through a correspondence course offered by the Shangwu yinshuguan (Commercial Press). He continued to take on positions until, by 1922, he had so many jobs that, as he puts it in "Wo de shenghuo he chuangzuo," he was "a coolie for the news business." That year he moved his family from Qianshan to Wuhu; he sent much of his income there for his brothers' and sisters' schooling.

In 1924 Zhang quit all of his jobs and went to work as news editor for *Shijie wanbao* (The World Evening News), founded by Cheng Shewo. One of Cheng's partners in the venture knew that Zhang wrote stories and asked him to compose something for the literary supplement of the paper. Zhang's first important novel, *Chunming waishi* (An Unofficial History of Beijing) ran in the *Shijie wanbao* literary supplement from April 1924 until January 1929; it was published in book form in 1930. In 1925 Cheng started *Shijie ribao* (The World News) and made Zhang editor of its literary supplement. In the fall of 1926 Zhang added a second wife, Hu Qiuxia; their only surviving child, son Zhang Xiaoshui, was born in 1928. Zhang's novel *Jinfen shijia* (Gold Dust Dynasty) was serialized in *Shijie ribao* from 14 February 1927 to 22 May 1932 and published in book form in twelve volumes in 1933.

Zhang's first significant works of fiction, *Chunming waishi* and *Jinfen shijia,* are the two longest, and among the most popular, of his career. Each is around one million Chinese characters in length, rivaling some of the great Chinese novels such as Cao Xueqin's *Honglou meng* (1791, Dream of the Red Chamber; translated as *The Story of the Stone,* 1973–1986). McClellan writes that, like many of the old Chinese novels, such as *Shuihu zhuan* (circa 1600, The Story of the Water Margin; translated as *All Men Are Brothers,* 1933), *Rulin waishi* (circa 1750, Unofficial History of the Literati; translated as *The Scholars,* 1957), and even more like the "novels of exposure" of the last decade of the Qing dynasty (1900 to 1911), *Chunming waishi* and *Jinfen shijia* "may appear lacking in structure to the Western reader" because, in comparison "to the May Fourth novel being born of Western realism at the same time, their central plots are relatively weak," and "subsidiary characters and storylines are profuse." The two novels attempt something different from Western fiction: a panoramic view of society and human relationships that is not constrained by coherence of plot.

The central character of *Chunming waishi,* Yang Xingyuan, is a journalist from Anhui working in Beijing; through him a wide range of contemporary social trends are observed, including scandals involving politicians in gambling dens, young women taking off their clothes in art schools, and college tutors bedding their students. Yang's own romantic story—the successive tragedies of liaisons with two highly dissimilar women, a prostitute and a scholar—runs through the book but is sometimes neglected for two or more chapters at a time. A provincial and an old-fashioned scholar, Yang represents a traditional Chinese culture that is under threat in the metropolis of Beijing, where modern Western urban values are growing stronger daily.

Jinfen shijia is the story of the decline—brought about to a great extent by the modernization process observed in *Chunming waishi*—of the Jin family. The plot is structured by the rise and fall of the relationship of Jin Yanxi, the youngest and most flamboyant of the four sons of Premier Jin, and his quieter and more pragmatic humbly born wife, Leng Qingqiu. In temperament Yanxi is reminiscent of Jia Baoyu, the flawed romantic hero of *Honglou meng*—an important influence on Zhang. Like Baoyu, Yanxi is spoiled by his family and allowed to neglect his academic and moral education. Qingqiu, unlike any female character in the old Chinese fiction, takes desperate action to escape from her loveless marriage. Under cover of the confusion caused when her rooms catch fire, she runs away with her baby boy and goes back to her own family. Thus, Qingqiu chooses a traditional Chinese way out that lies between the extremes of capitulation or prostitution that Lu Xun predicted as the only alternatives for divorcées in his 1923 speech "Nuola zou hou zenyang" (translated as "What Happens after Nora Leaves Home?" 1957), a locus classicus of May Fourth thinking on the woman question. By the end of the novel the former premier "Gold" (the literal meaning of his surname) has died, and, for all its grand modern ways, his once-great family is scattering like dust. Qingqiu, like her small but honest traditional family, represents the older Chinese values. The moral superiority of ordinary, respectable, old-fashioned families—often with prodigal members—is a persistent theme in Zhang's fiction.

When *Chunming waishi* was published as a book in 1930, demand for Zhang's work increased. He was already the most popular novelist in north China, but his nationwide preeminence in the popular-literature market began when the Shanghai paper *Xinwen bao* (The News) commissioned a novel from him. *Tixiao yinyuan* (Fate in Tears and Laughter) was serialized in *Kuaihuo lin* (Forest of Happiness), the literary supplement of *Xinwen bao*, from 17 March to 30 November 1930 and published in book form in three volumes that same year. One of the publishing sensations of the twentieth century in China, this huge best-seller was attacked by May Fourth critics partly because its success proved that the Saturday School remained more popular than the new literature. According to Zhang biographer Yuan Jin, however, *Tixiao yinyuan* "reached the artistic pinnacle of the linked-chapter novel of the time" and "is an extremely important work in the history of the development of the linked-chapter novel and of popular fiction."

The success of *Tixiao yinyuan* stems from an exuberant mix of traditional and modern styles, techniques, contents, and themes. Only a quarter as long as *Chunming waishi* or *Jinfen shijia*, *Tixiao yinyuan* begins with the young southerner Fan Jiashu arriving in Beijing in the 1920s to spend the summer preparing to enter the university there. He stays with his wealthy and fashionable aunt and uncle, in whose Westernized social circle he meets Helena He (He Lina). Ill at ease in such company, Jiashu prefers to wander alone in atmospheric districts of Old Beijing such as Tianqiao. Amid the heady sights, sounds, and smells of the markets, stalls, and shops he watches a performance by a strikingly pretty drum singer, Fengxi, and falls in love with her. Among the many coincidences and extraordinary misunderstandings that delighted the readers of the novel, the most preposterous is that the two beauties who are the main rivals for Jiashu's love are physically indistinguishable. Spiritually and socially, however, Helena and

Cover for volume four of Zhang's twelve-volume novel Jinfen shijia *(1933, Gold-Dust Dynasty), the story of the decline of the Jin family (from Tang Wenyi, Mu Dingsheng, and Ji Lei, eds.,* 20 shiji Zhongguo wenxue tudian, *2001; Collection of Thomas Moran)*

Fengxi are worlds apart. The wealthy, educated, and liberated Helena is much more his social equal, but Jiashu prefers the illiterate Fengxi. Although in some ways a modern man, he is drawn to Fengxi's Chinese ways—especially her more passive nature compared to the Westernized *xin nüxing* (new woman). In Tianqiao, Jiashu also meets a martial-arts performer, Guan Shoufeng, whom he admires as the embodiment of traditional Chinese rugged masculine virtues. Guan has a daughter, Xiugu, who is also an accomplished fighter as well as a girl of profound spirituality. While occasionally going to social events or on dates with Helena as his aunt and uncle wish, Jiashu spends most of his energy and funds on getting Fengxi and her mother decent housing and sending Fengxi to a modern school for girls. His mother falls ill, however, and Jiashu has to return south. While he is away, Fengxi is kidnapped and made the concubine of a warlord general. Guan sets out to save her but does not go through with the rescue because of what he misconstrues as evidence that Fengxi has betrayed Jiashu. After many more plot twists, Fengxi is driven insane by the general's beatings, Xiugu avenges her by murdering the general, and Jiashu seems set to find solace in Helena's arms.

In 1931 Zhang married a third wife, Zhou Shuqin; she took the name Zhou Nan, which was given to her by Zhang. In the summer of 1932 Zhang and Hu's daughters Wei'r and Kang'r died (their years of birth are unknown). That same year Zhang and Zhou Nan had a son, Zhang Ershui.

Established as the most popular novelist in China, Zhang devoted more of his efforts to fiction and less to journalism. A trip to the poverty-stricken provinces of Shaanxi and Gansu in 1934 was the basis for a series of travel essays. In his autobiography, *Wo de xiezuo shengya* (1981, My Career as a Writer), first published in *Xinmin bao* between 1 January and 15 February 1949, Zhang says that this journey of about six weeks began partly as a pilgrimage to the cradle of Chinese civilization and seat of early imperial glory, but that his glimpses of the warlord politics and the subhuman conditions of the poor "completely changed my thinking."

Zhang and Zhou Nan's son Zhang Quan was born in 1935. Zhang rented a *siheyuan* (house built around a courtyard) in Beiping (as Beijing was known from 28 June 1928 to 27 September 1949) for his family and taught courses in Chinese fiction and classics as principal of the Beihua meishu zhuanke xuexiao (North China School of Fine Art), which he founded in 1931 with some of his royalties. The college's low fees and distinguished faculty—including two of twentieth-century China's greatest painters, Qi Baishi and Xu Beihong—attracted up to two hundred students at its peak and remained in operation until 1937.

During the 1930s Zhang built on the modest "improvements" he had made in *Tixiao yinyuan* to provide more-positive roles for some of his female characters. Yang Yanqiu, the protagonist of *Yan guilai* (Return of the Swallow), which was serialized in *Kuaihuo lin* from 31 July 1934 to 26 June 1936 and published as a book in 1942, is the most positive of all:

> Nineteen years old. . . . Not only do her fair, rosy complexion and dark eyes call forth exclamations wherever she goes, but with her sturdy physique, there's no hint about her of the sickly aspect of the old-style beauty. Apart from being captain of her school's girls' basketball team, she is also the South China two hundred meters sprint champion.

Yanqiu is a refugee from famine in her native Gansu, and her heroic return there from the comfort of Nanjing forms the backbone of the novel. She is an extreme example: most of Zhang's female characters tend to conform to the Saturday School "magnolia and pear" dichotomy that E. Perry Link Jr. describes:

> the magnolia and pear represent two horns of a dilemma which pervaded modern urban life: whether [a woman should] be modern, foreign-influenced, stylish, and aggressive or old-style, purely Chinese, plain, and retiring. . . . This symbolic opposition of the foreign or "new" style represented by a brilliant, aggressive woman, and the Chinese or "old" style represented by a comely, retiring one was common to a good number of love stories in the 1910s and 1920s, many of which were triangular affairs involving a male protagonist and these two female types.

This typology is generally applicable to Zhang's fiction, but most of his female characters are more modern and assertive than Fengxi and less Westernized and aggressive than Helena.

While Zhang's novels of the 1930s differ from May Fourth fiction in treatment of gender, they are relevant to the times and so are comparable to the writings of the May Fourth school in theme. In *Yan guilai* this similarity of theme is seen in the gentle parody of the semi-autobiographical *yishao* (young fogey) Gao Yihong and his "romantic pessimism," as well as in the modernity of the central plot and the female protagonist. Elsewhere in Zhang's works of this period, however, it is difficult to find central characters and themes that are truly modern. Often the settings are contemporary, while the messages are traditional. In *Xiandai qingnian* (1934, Modern Youth), for example, a forward-looking father saves money to send his son to the capital to study in the modern fashion; yet, the novel is a conservative lament for the loss of traditional values—in particular, filial piety. The author's sympathy is with the long-suffering father, a poor maker and vendor of bean curd. He sacrifices for the education of his son, Zhou Jichun, but Jichun falls into rapid moral decline under the influence of urban Westernized "modern youths" who teach him to womanize and waste money. The ethics of the novel are reinforced linguistically and stylistically by the selective use of Classical Chinese and premodern *baihua* (vernacular Chinese) and stock phrases from traditional fiction, which continued, though decreasingly, to characterize Zhang's novels.

Chunming waishi, *Jinfen shijia*, *Tixiao yinyuan*, *Xiandai qingnian*, and *Yan guilai* all adhere to the basic form of the linked-chapter novel: the chapters are named *hui* (sessions) and are headed by verse couplets. *Bei yan nan fei* (1946, The Wild Goose Flies South) appears even more traditional: one of Zhang's few period novels, it is set principally in the last years of the Qing dynasty. In the preface Zhang claims that *Bei yan nan fei* is an antifeudal work: the heroes are teenage lovers who rebel against the arranged marriage system. But this theme is found in many traditional Chinese literary works at least since Dong Jieyuan's *Xixiang ji zhugongdiao* (circa late twelfth–early thirteenth century, The Story of the Western Chamber Suite), the original story of which dates to the Tang dynasty (618 to 907), and it is prominent in Saturday School writing. The theme did not, therefore, meet the definition of "modern" used by May Fourth writers and critics.

Bei yan nan fei is the story of the doomed love of sixteen-year-old Li Xiaoqiu and fourteen-year-old Yao Chunhua. Their innocent but intense affair includes many of the tropes of the traditional Chinese *caizi jiaren* (talent and beauty) tale as the lovers fall ill and contemplate or attempt suicide when their parents thwart their plans. Just as they are plotting to elope, Chunhua is tricked into marrying her childhood betrothed ahead of schedule. In the final chapter Xiaoqiu passes through Chunhua's village about twenty years later as commander of a Beifa (Northern Expeditionary) regiment. Circumstances limit the former sweethearts to a few poignant words shouted across the widening water between them as Xiaoqiu and his troops set sail on the river. This final episode is Zhang's attempt to "catch up with the times": Xiaoqiu is presented as a revolutionary hero of the Nationalist Party, which was in its heyday as the government of China at the time the novel was written in the mid 1930s. That both Xiaoqiu and Chunhua are shown to have moved on with their lives runs counter to the extreme romanticism of the "talent and beauty" and Mandarin Ducks and Butterflies traditions. Also, the young people's illnesses and attempts at suicide earlier in the novel sometimes appear parodic. The treatment of lower-class characters in *Bei yan nan fei* also gives the novel some claim to modernity. The story of the pretty young serving woman Feng Cuiying and her divorce from her dishonest and drunken husband, Mao Sanshu (Third Uncle Mao), is given prominence in the novel and is livelier in many ways than the central story of Xiaoqiu and Chunhua. The outcome, in which Mao Sanshu begins to examine his own faults, is compassionate and sensible. *Bei yan nan fei* is, thus, a good-humored rendering of the classic Chinese romance in a more modern era. As such, it is emblematic of Zhang's attempts at "improvement."

By the beginning of 1936 Zhang had made himself persona non grata in northern China with anti-Japanese writings such as the two poems, one play, and six short stories of *Wan gong ji* (1932, Bent Bow Collection). He went to Nanjing, which was then the national capital, and started a newspaper, the *Nanjingren bao* (Nanjing People's News).

Cover for Zhang's Bashiyi meng *(1942, Eighty-One Dreams), a series of fourteen independent stories presented as the dreams of a single narrator (from Tang Wenyi, Mu Dingsheng, and Ji Lei, eds.,* 20 shiji Zhongguo wenxue tudian, *2001; Collection of Thomas Moran)*

In several novels of the mid to late 1930s Zhang continued to accentuate the position of lower-class heroes and heroines. Among them is *Ye shenchen* (Heavy Is the Night), which was serialized in *Chahua* (Tea Talk), a literary supplement of *Xinwen bao*, from 27 June 1936 to 7 March 1939 and published as a book in 1941. It is almost entirely lacking in modern content. The action is apparently set in 1920s Beijing, but there is little evidence of the influence of the twentieth century on the hero, Ding Erhe: he is a paragon of traditional virtues, of which filial piety is the chief. Ding is the antithesis of Zhou Jichun, the prodigal son in *Xiandai qingnian;* all of the positive characters in *Ye shenchen* are similarly old-fashioned, while the "modern youth" are, once again, the villains: selfish, opportunistic, enthralled by fashion, and immoral. *Ye shenchen* uses melodrama to produce nostalgia for neglected superior morals and behavior, rather than providing a modern realistic description of the lower-class city life such as Lao She, a May Fourth writer, achieved in his acclaimed novel *Luotuo Xiangzi*

Zhang with his third wife, Zhou Nan, in 1946 (from E. Perry Link Jr., Mandarin Ducks and Butterflies: Popular Fiction in Early Twentieth-Century Chinese Cities, *1981; Collection of Thomas Moran)*

(1939, Camel Xiangzi; translated as *Rickshaw: The Novel Lo-t'o Hsiang Tzu*, 1979).

Zhang remained in Nanjing until shortly before the city fell to the Japanese in December 1937. Following the government in its retreat westward to Chongqing in Sichuan, Zhang was appointed chief editor of *Xinmin bao* and took charge of the literary section of the paper. He lived with Zhou Nan and their children in the Chongqing area for the rest of the war, while Xu Wenshu, Hu Qiuxia, and Hu and Zhang's only surviving child remained in his ancestral home in Qianshan.

Zhang wrote or attempted to write several fictional treatments of the war, including *Xiangzhan zhi ye* (Nights of Street Fighting), a tale of close-quarters warfare written in 1938 and published in 1942. His most significant works of 1937 to 1949, however, are centered on civilian life in Chongqing during the war. It is clear from these works that Zhang was a keen, patriotic observer of social and political events in China's wartime capital and that he was outraged by the moral and economic abuses that he witnessed.

Bashiyi meng (Eighty-One Dreams) is generally considered Zhang's most significant work of fiction from the Chongqing years. Serialized in *Zuihou guantou* (The Final Juncture), the literary supplement of *Xinmin bao*, from 1 December 1939 to 25 April 1941, it was published in book form in 1942. Beneath the anachronistic allegory and nonrealist content, *Bashiyi meng* is a modern social novel; it can also be categorized as a linked-short-story novel, as it comprises fourteen (not eighty-one) self-contained stories that are presented as the dreams of the narrator. The dreams are numbered at random intervals from "Dream the Fifth" to "Dream the Eightieth." Five deal extensively with the supernatural; three do so to a lesser extent; and six have no supernatural content. The six prosaic dreams of government and mercantile abuse and corruption read like journalism and express Zhang's indignation. In the supernatural dreams, however, he draws on traditional Chinese myth, legend, fiction, and drama. In "Di qishi'er meng: Wo shi Sun Wukong" (translated as "Dream the Seventy-Second: 'I Am the Monkey King,'" 2002) the narrator dreams that he is the Monkey King in the novel *Xiyou ji* (circa 1592; translated as *Journey to the West*, 1977–1983), ascribed to Wu Cheng'en. He battles man-eating demons but is unable to defeat the greatest evil of all, a huge monster that is identified with material greed.

In 1940 Zhang and Zhou Nan had a daughter, Zhang Mingming; in 1943 they had another daughter, Zhang Rongrong. In early 1946 Zhang returned to Beiping to found an edition of *Xinmin bao* there. His resignation in autumn 1948 brought his journalistic career to an end. That same year he and Zhou Nan had a third daughter, Zhang Zheng. His first two wives and eldest son joined the rest of the family in Beiping, where Zhou Nan gave birth to their fourth daughter, Zhang Tong, in 1949.

Zhang's novel *Zhi zui jin mi* (1949, Cash Drunk, Money Mad) unites the panoramic approach of the traditional Chinese novel with the structured, plot-driven aesthetic of Western and May Fourth fiction to examine middle-class mores and economic realities in wartime Chongqing. Modern-style interior monologue reveals the character of the antiheroine, Tian Peizhi, but that character is simple and patriarchal. Like most of Zhang's novels at this stage in his career, *Zhi zui jin mi* employs few obtrusive stylistic features of the linked-chapter novel. The chapter headings are simple words or phrases, rather than the finely crafted classical couplets in which he took such pride (a pride he expresses in *Wo de xiezuo shengya*).

The People's Liberation Army took control of Beiping on 31 January. In early March, Zhang was accused in *Xinmin bao* of having collaborated with the Nationalist Party to turn the paper into a reactionary organ; there were no further repercussions, however. In June he suffered a stroke that left him paralyzed on one side and with impaired speech and memory, but he made a partial recovery. In 1949 and 1950 he was admitted to the major writers' organizations of the People's Republic of China and the Beijing Municipality. Although he wrote some novelizations of legends and old tales during the 1950s, his career as a major novelist was at an end. He lived in Beijing with his large family until another stroke killed him on 15 February 1967.

The first academic conference devoted to Zhang Henshui studies was held in Zhang's native district in 1988 by the Anhui Academy of Social Sciences, and papers from the conference were published in 1990. The "Zhang Henshui re" (Zhang Henshui craze) of the 1980s cooled in the early 1990s but led to commercially successful television dramatizations of his works such as *Jinfen shijia* (2002), directed by Li Dawei and starring Chen Kun, Dong Jie, and Liu Yifei. It is now generally accepted among Chinese and non-Chinese scholars of Chinese literature that Zhang is an important transitional and crossover author between the May Fourth and Saturday Schools, the new and the old, and the Chinese and the Westernized during the first half of the twentieth century.

Bibliographies:

Zhang Zhanguo and Wei Shouzhong, "Zhang Henshui zhuzuo xinian" and "Zhang Henshui zhuzuo (dan xing ben) mulu suoyin," in *Zhang Henshui yanjiu ziliao*, edited by Zhang and Wei (Tianjin: Tianjin renmin chubanshe, 1986), pp. 377–698.

Biographies:

Yuan Jin, *Zhang Henshui pingzhuan* (Changsha: Hunan wenyi chubanshe, 1988);

Shi Nan, *Zhang Henshui zhuan* (Nanjing: Jiangsu wenyi chubanshe, 2000).

References:

Sally Borthwick, "Mandarin Ducks and Butterflies," *Papers on Far Eastern History*, 10 (1974): 29–53;

Hilary Chung and Tommy McClellan, "Images of Women: Exploring Apparent Changes of Attitude towards Women in the May 4th Era through Literary Imagery," in *Notions et perceptions du changement en Chine,* edited by Viviane Alleton and Alexeï Volkov (Paris: College de France, 1994), pp. 187–198;

E Jirui and others, *Zhang Henshui yanjiu lunwen ji* (Hefei: Anhui wenyi, 1990);

Fan Boqun, *Minguo tongsu xiaoshuo: Yuanyang hudie pai* (Beijing: Renmin wenxue, 1989);

Fan, ed., *Zhongguo jin-xiandai tongsu wenxue shi*, 2 volumes (Nanjing: Jiangsu jiaoyu, 1999);

E. Perry Link Jr., *Mandarin Ducks and Butterflies: Popular Fiction in Early Twentieth-Century Chinese Cities* (Berkeley: University of California Press, 1981);

Liu Yangti, ed., *Yuanyang hudie pai xin lun* (Beijing: Zhongguo wenlian, 1997);

T. M. McClellan, "Change and Continuity in the Fiction of Zhang Henshui: From Oneiric Romanticism to Nightmare Realism," *Modern Chinese Literature*, 10 (May 1998): 113–134;

McClellan, *Zhang Henshui and Chinese Popular Fiction, 1919–1949* (Lewiston, N.Y.: Edwin Mellen Press, 2005);

Hsiao-wei Wang Rupprecht, *Departure and Return: Chang Hen-shui and the Chinese Narrative Tradition* (Hong Kong: Joint Publishing Company, 1987);

King-fai Tam, "The Significance of the Zhang Henshui Revival," *Gest Library Journal*, 3, nos. 1–2 (1989): 30–45;

Tang Wenyi, Mu Dingsheng, and Ji Lei, eds., *20 shiji Zhongguo wenxue tudian* (Chengdu: Sichuan renmin chubanshe, 2001), pp. 137–138;

Yan Shichao, *Zhang Henshui lun* (Hefei: Anhui Daxue, 1998);

Yang Yi, *Zhang Henshui mingzuo xinshang* (Beijing: Zhongguo heping, 1996);

Zhang Zhanguo and Wei Shouzhong, eds., *Zhang Henshui yanjiu ziliao* (Tianjin: Tianjin renmin chubanshe, 1986);

Zhao Xiaoxuan, *Zhang Henshui xiaoshuo xin lun: Shiqing xiaoshuo chuantong de chengji yu zhuanhua* (Taibei: Taiwan xuesheng shuju, 2002).

Zhang Tianyi

(26 September 1906 – 28 April 1985)

Thomas Moran
Middlebury College

BOOKS: *Cong kongxu dao chongshi* [From Emptiness to Fullness] (Shanghai: Lianhe shudian, 1931);

Guitu riji [Ghostland Diary] (Shanghai: Zhengwu shuju, 1931);

Xiao Bide [Little Peter] (Shanghai: Chunguang shudian, 1931; Shanghai: Hufeng shuju, 1931)—includes "Ershiyige," translated by Ming-ting Sze (George A. Kennedy) as "Twenty-One Men: A Story," *China Today*, 1, no. 4 (1935): 75–77;

Chilun [Cogwheel], as Tie Chihan (Shanghai: Hufeng shuju, 1932); as Zhang Tianyi (Shanghai: Changjiang shudian, 1936);

Yinian [One Year] (Shanghai: Liangyou tushu yinshua gongsi, 1933);

Mifeng [Honeybees] (Shanghai: Xiandai shuju, 1933)—includes "Lu," translated by Chi-chen Wang as "The Road," in *Contemporary Chinese Stories*, edited by Wang (New York: Columbia University Press, 1944), pp. 1–8; "Meng," translated by Shu-ying Tsau as "Dream," in his "Zhang Tianyi's Fiction: The Beginning of Proletarian Literature in China," dissertation, University of Toronto, 1976, pp. 217–232; and "Chouhen," translated by Tsau as "Hatred," *Bulletin of Concerned Asian Scholars*, 8 (1976): 63–71;

Jibei yu naizi [Back and Breasts] (Shanghai: Liangyou tushu yinshua gongsi, 1933); abridged and translated by Chia-hua Yuan and Robert Payne as "The Breasts of a Girl," in *Contemporary Chinese Short Stories*, edited and translated by Yuan and Payne (London: Noel Carrington, 1946), pp. 97–117;

Da Lin yu Xiao Lin (Shanghai: Xiandai shuju, 1933; revised edition, Beijing: Zhongguo shaonian ertong chubanshe, 1956); translated by Gladys Yang as *Big Lin and Little Lin* (Beijing: Foreign Languages Press, 1958);

Fangong [Counterattack] (Shanghai: Shenghuo shudian, 1934);

Yixing [Mutation] (Shanghai: Liangyou tushu yinshua gongsi, 1934)—includes "Wenruo zhizaozhe," translated by Stephen L. Smith as "Manufacturer of Tenderness," *Renditions*, no. 32 (Fall 1989): 46–58; title story translated by Edgar Snow as "Mutation," in *Living China: Modern Chinese Short Stories*, edited by Snow (London: Harrap, 1936; New York: Reynal & Hitchcock, 1937), pp. 267–288; and "Xiao," abridged and translated by Wang as "Smile!" in *Contemporary Chinese Stories*, pp. 108–118;

Tuanyuan (Shanghai: Wenhua shenghuo chubanshe, 1935); title story translated by Wang as "Reunion," in *Contemporary Chinese Stories*, pp. 119–126;

Yang jingbang qixia [The Strange Knight-Errant of Shanghai] (Shanghai: Xinzhong shuju, 1936);

Jiren ji [The Collected Works of an Unbalanced Man or A Collection of Stories about Unbalanced People] (Shanghai: Liangyou tushu yinshua gongsi, 1936);

Qingming shijie [Grave-Sweeping Season] (Shanghai: Wenxue chubanshe, 1936); title story revised as *Qingming shijie* (Beijing: Zuojia chubanshe, 1954);

Wanren yue [The Wanren Association] (Shanghai: Shangwu yinshuguan, 1936)—includes "Lao Ming de gushi," translated by Wang as "The Inside Story," in *Contemporary Chinese Stories*, pp. 9–17;

Chun feng (Shanghai: Wenhua shenghuo chubanshe, 1936)—title story translated by Hou Chien as "Spring Breeze," in *Twentieth-Century Chinese Stories*, edited by C. T. Hsia and Joseph S. M. Lau (New York: Columbia University Press, 1971), pp. 64–89;

Zhui [Pursuit] (Shanghai: Kaiming shudian, 1936)—includes "Dizhu," translated by Nathan K. Mao as "The Bulwark," in *Modern Chinese Stories and Novellas, 1919–1949*, edited by Lau, Hsia, and Leo Ou-fan Lee (New York: Columbia University Press, 1981), pp. 336–344; "Zhongqiu," translated by Ronald Miao as "Midautumn Festival," in *The Columbia Anthology of Modern Chinese Literature*, edited by Lau and Howard Goldblatt (New

Zhang Tianyi (from Joseph S. M. Lau, C. T. Hsia, and Leo Ou-fan Lee, eds., Modern Chinese Stories and Novellas, 1919–1949, 1981; Middlebury College Library)

York: Columbia University Press, 1995), pp. 136–142; "Duliang," translated by Yang and W. J. F. Jenner as "Generosity," in *Modern Chinese Stories,* edited and translated by Jenner and Yang (London & New York: Oxford University Press, 1970), pp. 101–106; and "Lütu zhong," translated by Stanley R. Munro as "The Journey," in *Genesis of a Revolution: An Anthology of Modern Chinese Short Stories,* edited and translated by Munro (Singapore: Heinemann Educational, 1979), pp. 179–198;

Tutu dawang ji hao xiongdi [King Baldy and the Good Brothers] (Shanghai: Duoyangshe chubanbu, 1936; revised edition, Tianjin: Xinjiu chubanshe, 1980);

Zai chengshi li [In the City] (Shanghai: Liangyou tushu yinshua gongsi, 1937);

Qiguai de difang [Strange Place] (Shanghai: Wenhua shenghuo chubanshe, 1937);

Xuexiao li de gushi [Stories from School] (Shanghai: Dushu shenghuo chubanshe, 1937);

Tongxiangmen [Townspeople] (Shanghai: Wenhua shenghuo chubanshe, 1939)—includes "Xiaye meng," translated by Sidney Shapiro as "A Summer Night's Dream," *Chinese Literature,* 1 (1962): 3–39;

Tan renwu miaoxie [On the Description of Character] (Chongqing: Zuojia shuwu, 1942);

Suxie sanpian [Three Sketches] (Chongqing: Wenhua shenghuo chubanshe, 1943; revised edition, Beijing: Renmin wenxue chubanshe, 1963)—includes "Hua Wei xiansheng," translated by Chun-chan Yeh as "Mr. Hua Wei," in *Three Seasons and Other Stories,* edited by Yeh (London: Staples, 1946), pp. 111–118; and "Xin sheng," abridged and translated by Wang as "A New Life," in *Stories of China at War,* edited by Wang (New York: Columbia University Press, 1947), pp. 133–144;

Luo Wenying de gushi [The Story of Luo Wenying] (Beijing: Zhongguo qingnian chubanshe, 1952); title story republished as *Luo Wenying de gushi* (Beijing: Zuojia chubanshe, 1960);

Rong Sheng zai jiali [Rong Sheng at Home] (Beijing: Qingnian chubanshe, 1953);

Da huilang (Beijing: Qingnian chubanshe, 1954); translated as *The Big Grey Wolf: A Play for Children* (Beijing: Foreign Languages Press, 1961);

Bu dong naojin de gushi [Stories for Dummies] (Beijing: Zhongguo shaonian ertong chubanshe, 1956);

Wenxue zaping [Random Comments on Literature] (Beijing: Zuojia chubanshe, 1958);

Bao hulu de mimi [The Secret of the Precious Gourd] (Beijing: Zhongguo shaonian ertong chubanshe, 1958); translated by Yang as *The Magic Gourd*

(Beijing: Foreign Languages Press, 1959); Chinese version revised (Beijing: Zhongguo shaonian ertong chubanshe, 1978);

Gei haizimen [For the Children] (Beijing: Renmin wenxue chubanshe, 1959; revised, 1977);

Jinya diguo [The Empire of the Golden Duck] (Changsha: Hunan renmin wenxue chubanshe, 1980);

Zhang Tianyi wenji [The Collected Works of Zhang Tianyi], 10 volumes (Shanghai: Wenyi chubanshe, 1985–1993).

Collections: *Zhang Tianyi lun chuangzuo* [Zhang Tianyi on Writing], edited by Zhang Liaomin (Shanghai: Wenyi chubanshe, 1982);

Zhang Tianyi wenxue pinglunji [The Collected Literary Criticism of Zhang Tianyi] (Beijing: Renmin wenxue chubanshe, 1984).

Editions in English: *Stories of Chinese Young Pioneers* (Beijing: Foreign Languages Press, 1954)—includes "Going to the Cinema," ("Qu kan dianying"), "How Lo [sic] Wen-ying Became a Young Pioneer" ("Luo Wenying de gushi"), "They and We" ("Tamen he women"), and "Yung-sheng at Home" ("Rong Sheng zai jiali");

"A New Life" ("Xinsheng"), translated by Carl B. Durley, *Renditions,* no. 2 (Spring 1974): 31–49.

In C. T. Hsia's estimation, Zhang Tianyi was the most brilliant short-story writer of the 1930s. He was certainly prolific, publishing eleven books of short stories, five novels, four works of children's literature, and two one-act plays betwen 1929 and 1938, the period of his greatest productivity. Zhang lived in Shanghai, Nanjing, and Hangzhou and moved in the circles of Communist and left-leaning intellectuals in those cities. He read English and named Charles Dickens, Guy de Maupassant, Emile Zola, Leo Tolstoy, Anton Chekhov, Maksim Gor'ky, and Lu Xun among the writers who influenced him. His best stories are tightly structured, closely observed satires that target universal human failings or the specific hypocrisy of bourgeois intellectuals. Zhang's satire is more funny than bitter. By the mid 1930s he was known for having helped Chinese critical realism break with the formula of "revolution plus romance" that had dominated the 1920s. He wrote about violence, squalor, and sex with a frankness that few of his peers matched, and his characters' speech can be marvelously obscene. Zhang's ear for dialogue and his entertaining ability to capture the flavor of regional and class idioms were major reasons for his popularity.

Zhang was born in Nanjing on 26 September 1906; his original name was Zhang Yuanding. His ancestors were from Xiangxiang, Hunan province. His grandfather served Zeng Guofan. Zhang's father, Zhang Tongmo, held a second-level civil service degree but quit his position in the Qing bureaucracy to work as an educator. He was an open-minded, sometimes shy man with a taste for poetry and wine. Zhang Tianyi's mother, Wei Maoxian, was also from a family of scholars. Zhang Yuanding was the youngest of five children. His two brothers and eldest sister died before he reached his teens. His surviving sister, Zhang Jiamei, liked literature, knew English, and took an interest in her younger brother's education. Zhang Yuanding ranked fifteenth in age among paternal cousins (not siblings, as some sources claim). The best known of his four paternal uncles was Zhang Tongdian (whom *The Biographical Dictionary of Republican China* [1967–1979] misidentifies as his father), a Hanlin scholar who was education commissioner in Nanjing during the last years of the Qing dynasty. Zhang Tongdian's wife was a poet, and his daughter, Zhang Mojun (who was, thus, Zhang Tianyi's cousin—not his sister, as *The Biographical Dictionary of Republican China* maintains), was a prominent feminist and educator who served the Nationalist government through the 1950s. According to his friend Jiang Muliang, Zhang Tianyi was not close to, and did not have much in common with, his wealthier relatives.

Zhang Tongmo joined Sun Yat-sen's new administration in January 1912 but lost his job sometime between 12 February, when Sun was replaced by Yuan Shikai as provisional president of the Chinese Republic, and 1 April, when Sun's resignation became official. In search of work, he moved the family to Hangzhou. Zhang Yuanding attended the prestigious but conservative Zongwen High School; outside of school he read traditional Chinese fiction and translations of foreign fiction. Inspired by stories in the popular periodical *Libailiu* (Saturday), he began to write when he was fifteen. He started a literary journal with his classmates Dai Kechong and Dai Chaosheng and a student at a local college, Shi Depu. (Under their respective pen names—Du Heng and Su Wen; Dai Wangshu; and Shi Zhecun—his three collaborators have important places in the history of modern Chinese literature.) Zhang wrote farces, detective stories, and essays, and in 1922 his first published work, the short story "Xinshi" (New Poetry), appeared in *Libailiu;* no copy of the story is known to survive. By late 1923 he had published thirteen more stories under the pen names Zhang Wuzheng and Wu Zheng.

Zhang graduated from high school in 1924 and enrolled in an art school in Shanghai; dissatisfied and short of money, he withdrew before the end of the year. He was in Beijing from the fall of 1925 until the summer of 1927 preparing for the entrance examination for Beijing University; there he was introduced to Marxism and, according to most sources, joined the Communist Party. He first used the pen name Zhang Tianyi in

1926, taking *Tianyi* (skywings) from the Peng bird, mentioned in the ancient Daoist text *Zhuangzi*, which has wings like clouds across the sky.

Zhang cut his studies for the examination short and returned to Hangzhou. Throughout 1928 he moved around the area of Shanghai and Nanjing, both of which are just a few hours by train from Hangzhou, and worked at a variety of jobs. In November 1928 he wrote the autobiographical story "Santianban de meng" (Three and a Half Days' Dream). Early in the following year he exchanged letters with Lu Xun, who was editing *Benliu* (Torrent), and in March he sent "Santianban de meng" to Lu Xun for publication in the journal; it appeared in the 24 April 1929 issue. Lu Xun remained Zhang's patron and occasional correspondent. In "Santianban de meng" a young man writes letters to a friend recounting a visit home to Hangzhou. He loves his aging parents but pities them, laughs at them for being old and helpless, is impatient with their small talk and constrained lives, and is eager to escape their suffocating affection. The narrator's annoyance at his parents stems from his dissatisfaction with his own life—he has not realized his ambitions. The story is an example of Zhang's talent for looking squarely at contradictory and unflattering aspects of the human psyche. He settled on the Zhang Tianyi pseudonym permanently in 1929.

Zhang's first story collection, *Cong kongxu dao chongshi* (From Emptiness to Fullness), was published in early 1931. In the title story the vacillating intellectual Jing Ye lives a banal life in the capital, seeking stimulation from women, wine, and art. When a friend is arrested and executed as a revolutionary, Jing Ye resolves to move from the "emptiness" of dissipation to the "fullness" of political action. The story, which was retitled "Jing Ye xiansheng" (Mr. Jing Ye) in later collections, ends with contradictory gossip about what has happened to Jing Ye. In "Baofu" (Revenge) the vacillating intellectual becomes an irredeemable degenerate. The philanderer Huang sets out to ruin an impetuous college student, Bu, because she has spurned him. He arranges a last meeting with her and seduces her. The story ends with Huang's internal monologue as they have sex: he hopes that Bu will get pregnant so he can abandon her and complete his revenge. In "San Taiye yu Guisheng" (Third Great-Grandfather and Guisheng) revolutionary impulses subside in a village, allowing the old order to reestablish itself.

Zhang's first novel, *Guitu riji* (Ghostland Diary), was published in July 1931. It is an allegorical fantasy told in the form of the diary of Han Shiqian, who has traveled to the land of the ghosts. Ghostland stands for China, and Ghostland's ills are China's ills. The broad satire of *Guitu riji* targets politicians, capitalists, and

Cover for Zhang's first novel, Guitu riji *(1931, Ghostland Diary), an allegorical fantasy in which Ghostland stands for China (from Yu Runqi, ed.,* Tang Tao cang shu, *2004; Bruccoli Clark Layman Archives)*

intellectuals. In the premiere issue (20 September 1931) of *Beidou* (Big Dipper) the leading Marxist critic Qu Qiubai expressed disappointment with *Guitu riji*, saying that it simplifies real problems and drifts into frivolity.

Zhang Tianyi joined the League of Left-Wing Writers in the fall of 1931. His second story collection, *Xiao Bide* (Little Peter), appeared at the end of 1931. The title story is about workers who get back at their boss by killing his dog. "Pidai" (The Leather Belt), "Mianbao xian" (The Bread Line), and "Ershiyige" (Twenty-One; translated as "Twenty-One Men: A Story," 1935) are set during the fighting in the late 1920s between the National Revolutionary Army and the armies of various warlords and serve as the vehicles for Zhang's meditations on resistance to authority. The twenty-one men of "Ershiyige" are exhausted survivors of a skirmish; ordered to continue a suicidal march, they mutiny and kill or scare off their officers. They help a wounded enemy soldier and take him into their ranks, and the twenty-two men walk away from the fighting. The stories suggest that the enlisted men in

Cover for Zhang's second story collection, Xiao Bide (Little Peter), which appeared at the end of 1931 (from Yu Runqi, ed., Tang Tao cang shu, 2004; Bruccoli Clark Layman Archives)

opposing armies are actually class allies and that civilians' hatred of soldiers ought to be directed at officers and politicians. "Ershiyige" attracted positive attention from the Left and was one of three stories by Zhang that Lu Xun and the writer and critic Mao Dun recommended for translation and inclusion in Harold R. Isaacs's *Straw Sandals* (1974); the book as published, however, includes no stories by Zhang. The figure of the vacillating intellectual reappears in "Xisong de lian'ai gushi" (A Trivial Love Story), "Zhaoxun ciji de ren" (A Man in Search of Stimulation), and "Zhuchangzi de beiai" (The Sorrows of Pig Guts). In "Zhuchangzi de beiai," as in Lu Xun's "Zai jiulou shang" (1924, In the Wine Shop), the narrator meets a classmate who has abandoned his ideals. "Zhuchangzi" (Pig Guts) is the nickname of a famous writer who has surrendered to alcohol and other debilitating pleasures because he cannot, or does not wish to, adjust to revolutionary times.

Zhang's first story for children, "Da Lin yu Xiao Lin" (translated as *Big Lin and Little Lin*, 1958), ran serially in *Beidou* on 20 January and 20 July 1932 and was published as a book in 1933. Two poor orphaned brothers are chased by the "People-eating Ogre," the symbol of imperialists, capitalists, and other oppressors of the poor. Little Lin, the hero, heeds his late father's admonition to work hard and be honest, while Big Lin wants to become rich and powerful. Mary Ann Farquhar calls the story a classic of modern Chinese children's literature.

Zhang left Shanghai when resistance to the invading Japanese escalated into violence in January 1932. He moved in with his sister in Nanjing, took a job in a government military-affairs office, and helped to organize a branch of the League of Left-Wing Writers. His second novel, *Chilun* (Cogwheel), was published in September; it describes the lives of young men and women in Nanjing and Shanghai during the tumultuous period between the seizure of the northeastern city of Shenyang on 18 September 1931 and the Japanese bombing of Shanghai on 29 January 1932. In late 1932 *Chilun* was banned as "proletarian literature," and Zhang had to leave his job when his superiors realized that he was the author. Reviewing the work in *Wenxue* (Literature) for 1 August 1933, Mao Dun complained that the characters in *Chilun* are poorly differentiated and float free of connections to what is going on around them. Mao Dun also disliked the novel's loose structure and argued that its humor is out of keeping with its subject matter.

In February 1933 Lu Xun wrote to Zhang with friendly criticism, pointing out that his early stories were overly farcical and his more recent work tediously long. Zhang's third novel, *Yinian* (One Year), was published in April 1933. In *Yinian*, as in "Pidai" in *Xiao Bide*, a man travels from the countryside to the city in hopes of rising in the world with the help of his relatives. As Marston Anderson summarizes the plot in *The Limits of Realism: Chinese Fiction in the Revolutionary Period* (1990), Bai Muyi is "forced to take up one humiliating job after another, eventually becoming involved with a band of drug dealers." He learns that to advance, one must bully inferiors and flatter superiors. Anderson cites an article in the 26 August 1933 issue of *Wenxue zhoukan* (Literature Weekly), the supplement to the Tianjin newspaper *Yishi bao* (Social Welfare News), in which the critic Shen Wu complained that the episodic *Yinian* could easily end at any point or go on for several hundred pages more. The novel was banned in 1934.

Published in May 1933, *Mifeng* (Honeybees) is a collection of seven stories that had appeared in journals between May 1932 and January 1933. The title piece tells of poor farmers' resentment of the rich through a country boy's letters to his sister in the city. Three stories—"Zuihou lieche" (The Last Train), "Lu" (translated as "The Road," 1944), and "Chouhen" (translated as

"Hatred," 1976)—repeat themes and situations from *Xiao Bide,* dealing with soldiers who mutiny when their officers order them to retreat rather than fight the Japanese and encouraging solidarity between soldiers and the common people. "Meng" (translated as "Dream," 1976) borrows its protagonist and basic situation from the last twelve chapters (fifty-nine to seventy) of Jin Shengtan's seventeenth-century version of the traditional *Shuihu zhuan* (The Story of the Water Margin), in which Lu Junyi is exiled from his wealthy family and his position of power in the capital and becomes the "Jade Unicorn of Hebei," one of the bandits of the Mount Liang Marsh. In Zhang's story Lu awakens in the night, wanders to a hilltop, and wishes that his murder of his wife and rebellion against the authorities were only a dream. He falls back to sleep and dreams that he betrays his brother outlaws and precipitates their defeat by the imperial army. When Lu wakes up this time, he is reconciled to his new situation and accepts the ideology of his rebellion. Shu-ying Tsau points out that "The theme of the test—in which a non-proletarian character must define his relation to the revolution—is constant with Zhang Tianyi throughout his first ten years as a writer."

Published in installments in the journal *Xiandai/ Les Contemporains* (The Moderns) from May 1933 through March 1934 and as a book in 1936, *Yang jingbang qixia* (The Strange Knight-Errant of Shanghai) is generally considered Zhang's best novel. Like *Chilun,* it covers the months from the Mukden Incident to the Japanese bombing of Shanghai; unlike the earlier novel, it is tightly structured and consistent in its comedic tone. The title character is twenty-six-year-old Shi Zhaochang, whose family flees to Shanghai when the Japanese advance on Beiping (as Beijing was known from 1928 to 1949). A Don Quixote–like figure, Shi Zhaochang has lost sight of the fact that the martial-arts novels he loves are fiction; he thinks that he can actually acquire the powers of the kung fu masters, flying swordsmen, and Daoist adepts of his favorite books, and he plans to use these powers to defeat the Japanese and set the world to right. He is appalled by insolent peasants, striking workers, and modern mores. He also tells himself that he does not like loose women, but he is tantalized by the thought that proper form requires that he have the help of an attractive female knight-errant. He believes that he has found his partner in "Mary" He, an actress who plays a knight-errant on the stage but whom Shi takes to be a real martial heroine, which leads to confusion and comedy. Confidence men posing as Daoist immortals reinforce Shi's delusion that he is destined to rescue China; their prophecies allow him to feel superior to his obnoxious younger brother, of whom a fortune-teller has predicted great

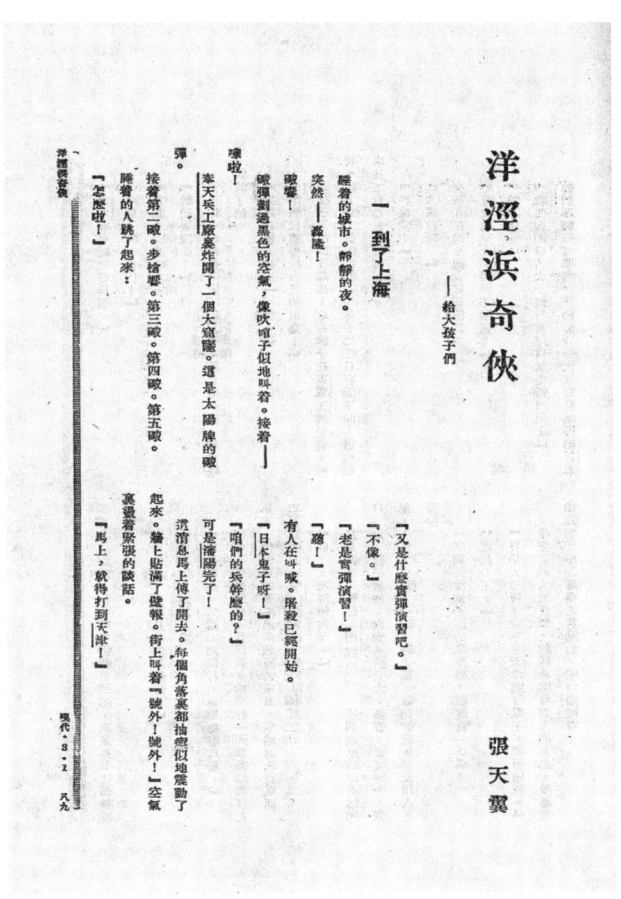

First page of the first installment of Zhang's novel Yang jingbang qixia *(The Strange Knight-Errant of Shanghai) in the magazine* Xiandai/Les Contemporains *(The Moderns), May 1933. It was published in book form in 1936 (Collection of Thomas Moran).*

things. In the final chapters Shi is joined by a Sancho Panza figure: when the rest of the family moves to safety in the French Concession, Shi forces their cook, Mr. Wang, to stay with him in the Zhabei district as the Japanese bombs fall. Wang is scared witless, but Shi trusts in the "flying sword" (actually a penknife) and "magic pills" (candy) given to him by the fake Daoist immortals, who have in the meantime swindled him out of his inheritance. Shi is injured in the bombing and hospitalized, and at the end of the book his despised stepmother chatters away at the mahjongg table at home.

The well-meaning Shi Zhaochang is merely ridiculous; the real targets of satire in *Yang jingbang qixia* are hypocrites who profit from China's crisis. As Hsia points out, the novel mocks the use of patriotism to sell everything from government projects to commercial goods. The third-person narrator is at times gratuitously silly, and there is much play with language. Mary He, who is from Shanghai, speaks what Hsia calls

Cover for a 1945 edition of Zhang's novel Yinian (One Year), first published in 1933 and banned in 1934, about a man who travels from the country to the city in hopes of rising in the world and learns that to do so, one must bully one's inferiors and flatter one's superiors (Collection of John Berninghausen)

"peculiar imitation-Mandarin," and Shi's horrible younger brother lets fly once or twice with incredible strings of invective. *Yang jingbang qixia* parodies clichés of plot and language in the martial-arts novels that were popular in the first decades of the twentieth century.

Zhang published *Tutu dawang ji hao xiongdi* (King Baldy and the Good Brothers), a work for children, in serial form in *Xiandai ertong* (Modern Child) from 1 March to 16 August 1933; it was banned before it finished its run but was published as a book in 1936. (A publishing law passed in 1930 and amended in 1931—and strengthened by the formation of a censorship board in Shanghai in 1934—banned the publication of material that undermined the Nationalist regime and its policies, required publishers to register with the government, and called for prepublication review of the entire contents of periodicals and of summaries of books. Bookstores that sold banned material were subject to raids and enforced closures. Nationalist control over publishing was never total, however. Shanghai was the center of the publishing industry, and parts of it were controlled by foreign powers; this situation gave writers and publishers some immunity from government censorship. That *Tutu dawang* was banned in 1933 but published as a book in 1936 might be explained by inconsistencies in enforcement, the difference between regulations for periodicals and books, or the daring of the publisher of the book. (Publishers sometimes did not know what was banned, and they could evade censorship when they wanted to.) The title character sits in a chair made of human bones and uses lanterns made of human skins. He hunts ants and eats them boiled in opium. He is so stupid that he sometimes forgets his own name. When he is angry, his teeth grow so long that he is lifted to the moon. He has tens of thousands of wives, on whom he occasionally snacks. When he takes a fancy to a village girl named Gan'gan and has her dragged back to his palace, her little brother, the girl next door, and a confident yellow cat come to the rescue. Before they can liberate Gan'gan, they have to deal with hungry kittens, a dishonest monk, and a shifty pug dog who works for the king. The tale is extravagantly silly and gross and so presumably appealed to young readers.

In *Jibei yu naizi* (1933, Back and Breasts; translated as "The Breasts of a Girl," 1946) Ren San's wife takes a lover in another village. At Ren San's bidding, the chief elder of the Ren clan punishes her; the elder, however, is plotting to get Ren San out of the way and Ren's wife into bed. Through courage and cunning, Ren's wife humiliates her husband and the elder and escapes with her lover. The elder's lewd internal monologue as he sizes up Ren's wife (he wants to bite her lips) and the story's memorable descriptive detail (sunflower-seed husks dance in the lap of the elder's gown as he sits and fidgets) are signs of Zhang's mature craft as a storyteller.

"Jibei yu naizi" was included in Zhang's 1934 collection *Fangong* (Counterattack). Most of the fourteen stories in that book and *Yixing* (Mutation), also published in 1934, stick to his established themes: they place miserable people in difficult situations, look at the empty lives of the rich, or take the side of Communists in their conflict with the Nationalists while sympathizing with those caught in the middle. Two of the more frequently remarked upon are "Bao shi fu zi" (Mr. Bao and Son) and "Xiao" (translated as "Smile!" 1944), both of which are included in *Yixing*. The title characters of "Bao shi fu zi" are based on the father and son who were doormen at Zhang's sister's apartment in Nanjing: a man invests his money and his dreams of higher social status in his son, who squanders them.

The story offers an incisive portrayal of an adolescent boy's desperation for acceptance by his peers and his callous treatment of his father, who embarrasses him. In "Xiao" a warlord gives a woman a choice: sleep with him, or he will have her husband killed. The warlord wants revenge on the husband, who has insulted him, but he is also simply sadistic. It is not enough that the woman give in to him; she must smile as she does so. He has sex with her, cheats her of a promised payment, publicly humiliates her, and—as the reader knows but she does not—will have her husband killed anyway. "Xiao" is noteworthy for its crisp economy in allowing dialogue and internal monologue to carry the plot and for its disturbing use of detail that both disgusts and fascinates—for example, the warlord licks the woman's cheek during their first interview. In many of his works Zhang narrates horrors with cool detachment and puts readers inside the minds of repulsive men. According to Yifeng Sun, Zhang learned the narrative device of revealing characters' objectionable secret thoughts from one of his favorite novels, the late-eighteenth-century *Rulin waishi* (The Unofficial History of the Literati).

In 1934–1935 Zhang moved between Nanjing, Hangzhou, and Shanghai. He taught Chinese literature at two schools and did what he could to help friends on the Left, such as the writer and translator Luo Shiyi, who were imprisoned for their political activities. Zhang and Lu Xun first met face to face at a coffee shop in Shanghai on 10 April 1934. Zhang's first novel, *Guitu riji*, was banned in 1935. In June of that year he signed an open letter criticizing the authoritarian Xin shenghuo yundong (New Life Movement), an initiative that Chiang Kai-shek and the Nationalist Party had begun in February 1934 to promote nationalism and Confucianism as the ideological counterpart of the effort to defeat the Communists militarily. His collection *Tuanyuan* (1935, Reunion) comprises, in David E. Pollard's words, six stories "of the poor and desperate, mostly set in filth and squalor."

In January 1936 Zhang brought out *Jiren ji*; the title can be translated as "The Collected Works of an Unbalanced Man" or as "A Collection of Stories about Unbalanced People." It comprises seventeen stories that had appeared in earlier collections, two play scripts, and five previously uncollected stories about corrupt clergy, timid bureaucrats, and self-deceiving intellectuals. "Yijiuersi–sansi" (1924–1934) and "Jiren shouji" (Notes from an Unbalanced Man) are about men who belong to the last category. In "Yijiuersi–sansi" a member of the Xin wenhua yundong (New Culture Movement) generation is revealed as a hypocrite who talks about revolution but always finds a reason to postpone participating in it. As a young man, the narrator of "Jiren shouji" was a May Fourth devotee of Mr. Democracy

Cover for a 1951 edition of Zhang's short-story volume Jiren ji *(The Collected Works of an Unbalanced Man or A Collection of Stories about Unbalanced People), first published in 1936 (Collection of John Berninghausen)*

and Mr. Science, rebelled against his father, ended his arranged marriage, wrote vernacular poems, and demonstrated at Tiananmen (The Gate of Heavenly Peace); now middle-aged and a failure, he regrets his wasted youth. Over his wife's objections he has brought her and their children to his ancestral village to live with his rich uncle. He hopes to regain his place in the family and secure an income from its property; but he has put himself in the impossible position of trying to ingratiate himself with his conservative uncle, impress his progressive young cousins, and maintain the fiction that he is morally superior to all of them. His uncle, who never believes that the prodigal nephew has truly reformed, swindles him out of a few dollars, and his cousins, who are deaf to his lectures, mock him. In the last paragraph the narrator, now a paranoid wreck who does not know what to do or where to turn, locks himself in his room.

Jiren ji was followed in February by *Qingming shijie* (Grave-Sweeping Season), a collection of three stories. In the long title piece the teacher Xie sells Mr. Luo, his social superior, some land but demands a high price for the part of the plot that holds the Xie ancestral graves.

Cover for an undated Shanghai edition of Zhang's novel Tutu dawang ji hao xiongdi (King Baldy and the Good Brothers), originally published in 1936 and revised in 1980 (Wason Collection on East Asia–China, Kroch Asia Library, Cornell University)

The imperious Luo builds a fence around the graves. On the day of the spring Qingming festival Xie arrives to sweep the graves and burn incense, and Luo's men assault him. Vowing revenge, Xie ingratiates himself with the soldiers who are billeted at his house. Goaded by Xie and motivated by righteousness, the soldiers ambush and beat Luo. Xie is initially pleased, but he is horrified to learn the soldiers said things to Luo during the attack that implicate him. He nervously awaits Luo's next move. Luo offers Xie a deal: in exchange for the names of the soldiers and a low price for the remaining parcel of land, Luo will absolve Xie of responsibility. The reader assumes that the honest, hapless soldiers will be arrested and shot. The main appeal of the story lies in its clever structure: it repeatedly returns to the tables at the teahouse, where the local gentry spend time in idle gossip about the spat between Luo and Xie. "Qiang'an" (A Case of Robbery), an almost cinematic vignette about villagers who defend their homes against a night raid by bandits, begins with a gunshot that startles a woman nursing her baby and ends ten pages later with a corpse lying in the street. Zhang takes just a few sentences to give the local history and bring his characters to life. The protagonist, Liu Gui, and his wife are used to violence; their fear is tempered by experience, and their six-year-old daughter is inured to the sound of gunfire. Readers are shown, rather than told, that the village security force is lazy, incompetent, cowardly, and allied with the bandits. In "Youyi" (Friendship) yet another social climber has his ladder to the top pulled out from under him.

Wanren yue (The Wanren Association) was published in March 1936. The stories in this collection deal with children who witness degradation and dishonesty, people caught in the crossfire of civil wars and revolutions, class conflict in the countryside, and the hypocrisy of the petit bourgeoisie. In "Shanju" (A Charitable Deed), which recalls Lu Xun's "Feizao" (1924, Soap), a mood of charity washes over Mr. Chai but then fades into irritation with the poor. Chai praises himself in his diary, carefully eliding his more uncharitable thoughts and deeds. "Lao Ming de gushi" (Old Ming's Story; translated as "The Inside Story," 1944) is darkly comic and ironic. After dinner Old Ming pushes his chair back from the table and tells his companions the story of how a warlord named Kuang came to power and wealth. A sycophant named Diao Jinsheng who made himself useful to Kuang was thanked with a bullet in the head when Kuang needed to sacrifice him. Old Ming's story, which teaches the lesson that everybody needs a patsy like Diao, is amusing; but it is disturbing because it is told entirely from an amoral point of view. In a discussion of humor, satire, and parody in Zhang's work, Yifeng Sun makes the case that Zhang preferred neutral, objective "youmo" (humor) to what he saw as subjective, obvious, and sometimes overly personal "fengci" (satire). Zhang left room for his readers to make up their own minds about what he showed them.

Zhang was a pallbearer at Lu Xun's funeral on 22 October 1936. The following month he published two collections of stories. The title piece in *Chun feng* (translated as "Spring Breeze," 1991) depicts the relentless chaos and bickering at a primary school. Moving from playground to classroom to teacher's lounge to cafeteria, the narrator pauses to focus on a day in the lives of the principal and three members of his faculty, all of whom are lazy, sadistic, apathetic, or pedantic. Moments of perfectly observed comedy form the background to the main action: a child idly picks at a hole in his shirt, making it bigger and bigger; smug Mr. Ding amuses himself mightily, but no one else notices his clowning; the male teachers ask their favorite students for just a little more detail about their mothers and

Zhang (left) and the poet Luo Binji in Hong Kong in 1949 (Museum of Modern Chinese Literature, Beijing)

older sisters. The narrator of "Yige ticai" (A Subject Matter) is a writer who travels to his ancestral home and is visited by a distant relative, Aunt Qing Er. She has a vague idea of what writers do and wants the narrator to write an essay she can sell. Aunt Qing Er is more than sixty years old and has been a widow since the age of sixteen. She appeals to the narrator's sympathy by telling him how difficult her life is. He knows, however, that Aunt Qing Er's tenants call her "The Locust" and that she once drove a woman to suicide over a debt. Telling her that he needs a subject that is fresh, preferably involving sex, he gets her to reveal that she had intercourse several times with a member of the local gentry. She claims that the man raped her, but the narrative has long since put the reader in a position to doubt her version of events. The narrator is hard-hearted, but there is no doubt that the reader is meant to believe that Aunt Qing Er gets what she deserves when he brings the tale to a conclusion by reporting that he is publishing the story despite Aunt Qing Er's request that he not do so. (Several details in "Yige ticai" suggest that the story is partly autobiographical.) "Miwei de ye" (Honey-Flavored Night) is an even more disturbing depiction of cruelty. Mimi has just come to Shanghai from the north and has no money or connections. She meets a rich young man named Jin Weili, who gives her $50 for reasons she does not understand. Jin brings Mimi home and introduces her to friends of his who are drinking in his apartment. Jin, too, is drunk; he bristles at a perceived slight from Mimi and drags her to a bedroom. Characteristically, Zhang does not take the reader inside the bedroom as Jin assaults Mimi; he focuses on the other men as they take turns watching the "montage" through the keyhole, sharing jealousy and prurient interest.

Much of Zhang's reputation in the English-speaking world is built on the stories in *Zhui* (Pursuit), the other collection he published in November 1936; they provide the material for about a fourth of Hsia's chapter on Zhang in his influential *A History of Modern Chinese Fiction* (1961). Hsia divides Zhang's work into three categories. The "agitational" stories are "standard proletarian exercises in the manner of Socialist Realism"; one of his examples is "She Taiye de shibai" (The Failure of Lord Snake), which is included in *Zhui*. Lord Snake prides himself on having earned the goodwill of his peasant tenants. He tells himself that he is not to blame when his private security force fires on hungry peasants who raid his granary. Lord Snake feels sorry for himself because he has tried to be a good man but has failed because of famine and impatient peasants. Hsia places Zhang's tales about vacillating bourgeois intellectuals into the category of "ideological" stories. Although he does not discuss the title story of *Zhui*, it is a rough fit for this category. A widower in late middle age tries to impress his son by keeping up with intellectual fashions.

Cover for a 1979 edition of Gladys Yang's 1959 translation of Zhang's Bao hulu de mimi (1958, The Secret of the Precious Gourd), one of the dozen stories he wrote for children (Collection of Thomas Moran)

He reads works by Gor'ky and a book on imperialism, but the concepts and the vernacular language confuse and tire him. For Hsia, Zhang's best stories are those in the third category: satires. His examples are three pieces in *Zhui*: "Dizhu" (translated as "The Bulwark," 1981), "Zhongqiu" (translated as "Midautumn Festival," 1995), and "Lütu zhong" (translated as "The Journey," 1979) mock hypocritical, selfish, and pompous members of the middle and upper classes. The stories in *Zhui* suggest that by late 1936 political exigency was overcoming, to some degree, Zhang's invention and craft. His ideological position was hardening in response to China's deepening crisis, and he may also have been reaching a point of creative exhaustion.

Zhang's last published novel, *Zai chengshi li* (In the City), was serialized from 6 July 1936 to 31 May 1937 in *Guowen zhoubao* (National News Weekly) and appeared in book form in June 1937. As in *Yinian*, a man comes to the city from the countryside and does his best to compete with swindlers and crooks. The complex plot involves a tangle of family relationships; at the center is a struggle between the sycophantic Ding Shousong, the new arrival to the city, and his overbearing in-law, Tang Er, who plans to sell the family land and pocket the profit. Anderson writes in "Mao Dun, Zhang Tianyi, and the Social Impediments to Realism" that in works such as *Zai chengshi li* it seems that "Zhang has taken the criticism of his earlier novels too much to heart and consciously suppressed his instincts for formal innovation in the interests of a conventionally realistic representation of Chinese society."

War with Japan began in July 1937, and by September the fighting had reached Shanghai. In the middle of the month Zhang left for Changsha in Hunan, where he remained through the end of 1938. From 1937 through 1942 the bulk of his published work consisted of essays and criticism related to the cultural side of the war effort, but in 1937–1938 he published two influential short stories. The rich, ridiculous protagonist of "Hua Wei xiansheng" (translated as "Mr. Hua Wei," 1946), published in *Wenyi zhendi* (The Literature and Art Grant) on 16 April 1938, is successful at self-promotion. Hua Wei complains of overwork as he rushes from meeting to meeting, always arriving late and leaving early after delivering, with great gravitas, the same short speech: everybody must work hard to contribute to the war effort, and this work must proceed under the proper leadership. The proper leadership, of course, is that of men like Hua Wei. In "Xin sheng" (translated as "New Life," 1947), published in *Wenyi zhendi* on 1 November 1938, Li Yimo takes a job teaching art at a high school after he is driven from his home by war. Li is a literatus with epicurean tastes. The war inconveniences him. He understands that propaganda is needed but is embarrassed by it, and he is uncomfortable around progressive students and colleagues. Desperate for companionship, he befriends Zhang, a teacher of the Chinese classics who advocates nonresistance to the Japanese and is, therefore, presented as a negative character. Li is not without conscience or patriotism, but he is weak and spoiled. His attempt to occupy the middle ground between commitment to the war effort and capitulation to the enemy is untenable. "Tan Jiu xiansheng de gongzuo," "Hua Wei xiansheng," and "Xin sheng" were collected in 1943 as *Suxie san pian* (Three Sketches).

"Hua Wei xiansheng" is a slight story that caused a big stir. Zhang wrote the story to satirize a type of self-important, incompetent official he observed in Changsha in 1938; in 1952 he claimed that he wrote it specifically to criticize Nationalist bureaucrats who interfered with the work of anti-Japanese cultural organizations. But when the story was first published, some readers took it as an attack on the Chinese people in general. According to Shen Chengkuan, Huang Hou-

Zhang and his wife, Shen Chengkuan, at their home in 1984 (Museum of Modern Chinese Literature, Beijing)

xing, and Wu Fuhui, debate intensified when an article by Lin Lin in the Guilin edition of the newspaper *Jiuwang ribao* (Salvation Daily) on 22 February 1939 pointed out that a translation of "Hua Wei xiansheng" had been published in Japan and suggested that the story aided the enemy. The debate over "Hua Wei xiansheng" widened into one over satire in general and continued throughout 1939; the consensus reached was that satire was useful and legitimate. In "Realism's Last Stand: Character and Ideology in Zhang Tianyi's *Three Sketches*" (1989), Anderson observes that although Zhang's supporters were victorious, they "conceded the legitimacy of ideological appraisals of literary merit and indirectly contributed to the further politicization of literature in progressive intellectual circles."

After leaving Changsha, Zhang lived in various cities in Hunan. *Tongxiangmen* (Townspeople), a collection of four stories that had appeared in periodicals in 1936 and 1937, was published in 1939. Before falling ill with tuberculosis in the fall of 1942, Zhang participated energetically in the war effort by serving on committees, editing, and teaching. "Hua Wei xiansheng," "Xin sheng," and the previously unpublished "Tan Jiu xiansheng de gongzuo" (Mr. Tan Jiu's Work), which Zhang had written in 1937, were collected in 1943 as *Suxie sanpian* (Three Sketches). "Tan Jiu xiansheng de gongzuo"

is told from the blinkered perspective of the title character, a fool who believes that his law degree makes him the natural leader of his town's anti-Japanese war effort. Tan Jiu is interested in profit and perks. When others undertake real work–such as organizing an air-raid drill, which Tan Jiu misunderstands as some sort of theater performance)–he attempts to sabotage it out of jealousy.

Reports of Zhang's illness appeared in newspapers in Chongqing and Yan'an, and a campaign began to solicit contributions to help him pay for treatment. In November 1944 a Japanese advance overran south central China; Zhang made the difficult trip from Hunan to Chongqing in Sichuan, where he was housed at the headquarters of the Zhongua quanguo wenyijie kangdi xiehui (All-China Association of Literary Resistance). In the summer of 1945 he accepted an invitation from Chen Baichen, a playwright and fiction writer he had met in 1935, to move to Chengdu. He was hospitalized there and then moved to the countryside near the city to recuperate. While in Chengdu, Zhang learned Esperanto, read early Chinese history, collected folktales, took notes on rural life, and did research for an essay on *Xiyou ji* (Journey to the West), a novel that dates to 1592 in its oldest extant edition and is traditionally ascribed to the sixteenth-century author Wu

Cheng'en. The essay was published as "*Xiyou ji zhaji*" (Notes on *Journey to the West*) in *Renmin wenxue* (People's Literature) on 7 February 1954. Zhang went to Shanghai in August 1948 and to Hong Kong in November. Through 1949 he published a series of parables in the Hong Kong press.

Zhang moved to Beiping in May 1949. The name of the city reverted to Beijing in September. Beginning in 1951 he held positions in several cultural organizations, including the Zhongyang wenxue yanjiusuo (Central Literary Research Institute) and the Zhongguo zuojia xiehui (Chinese Writers' Association). He was also a delegate to the National People's Congress. He joined the editorial staff of *Renmin wenxue* in 1953. In December 1953 he married Shen Chengkuan, a colleague at *Renmin wenxue*. Their daughter, Zhang Zhang, was born in August 1954.

Zhang does not seem to have participated in the Hundred Flowers Movement of May and June 1957. In July 1957, after the start of the Anti-Rightist Campaign, he wrote character sketches for a play that was to be called "Hua Wei xiansheng zai jintian" (Mr. Hua Wei Today). He never finished the work; in fact, he abandoned all of the stories and novels that he began after 1949. The only fiction he published after that time was children's literature, and he became China's best-known children's author. The dozen works for children he published include "Luo Wenying de gushi" (1952, The Story of Luo Wenying; translated as "How Lo Wen-ying Became a Young Pioneer," 1954), "Da huilang" (1954; translated as "The Big Grey Wolf," 1961), and "Bao hulu de mimi" (1958, The Secret of the Precious Gourd; translated as *The Magic Gourd*, 1959).

In December 1957 Zhang became editor in chief of *Renmin wenxue*. During the Cultural Revolution of 1966 to 1976 he was suspended from his position, his books were banned, and he was sent to the countryside for more than two and a half years. He was partially disabled by a stroke in 1975. He died in Beijing on 28 April 1985.

Many readers in China know Zhang Tianyi best as the author of high-quality children's literature and the artful propaganda of *Suxie sanpian*. His major contribution to literature comprises *Yang jingbang qixia* and the several short stories in which his imagination is still fresh and his craft still uncompromised by politics.

Bibliography:

"Zhang Tianyi zhuzuo xinian, shumu" and "Zhang Tianyi chuangzuo de yanjiu, pingjie ziliao mulu suoyin," in *Zhang Tianyi yanjiu ziliao*, edited by Shen Chengkuan, Huang Houxing, and Wu Fuhui (Beijing: Zhongguo shehui kexue chubanshe, 1982), pp. 501–551.

Biographies:

Shen Chengkuan, Huang Houxing, and Wu Fuhui, "Zhang Tianyi shengping yu wenxue huodong nianbiao," in *Zhang Tianyi yanjiu ziliao*, edited by Shen, Huang, and Wu (Beijing: Zhongguo shehui kexue chubanshe, 1982), pp. 8–45;

Liu Shaotang, ed., *Minguo renwu xiaozhuan*, volume 9 (Taibei: Zhuanji wenxue chubanshe, 1987), pp. 202–215.

References:

Marston Anderson, *The Limits of Realism: Chinese Fiction in the Revolutionary Period* (Berkeley: University of California Press, 1990), pp. 119–179;

Anderson, "Realism's Last Stand: Character and Ideology in Zhang Tianyi's *Three Sketches*," *Modern Chinese Literature*, 5 (Fall 1989): 179–196;

Mary Ann Farquhar, *Children's Literature in China: From Lu Xun to Mao Zedong* (Armonk, N.Y.: Sharpe, 1988), pp. 143–165, 251–282;

Michel Hockx, "In Defense of the Censor: Literary Autonomy and State Authority in Shanghai, 1930–1936," *Journal of Modern Literature in Chinese*, 2 (July 1998): 1–30;

C. T. Hsia, "Chang T'ien-i (1906–)," in his *A History of Modern Chinese Fiction* (New Haven: Yale University Press, 1961), pp. 212–236;

Jiang Muliang, "Ji Zhang Tianyi," *Wenyi shenghuo (haiwai ban)*, 15 October 1948;

Stephen R. MacKinnon, "Toward a History of the Chinese Press in the Republican Period," *Modern China*, 23 (January 1997): 3–32;

David E. Pollard, "Zhang Tianyi, *Tuanyuan* (Family Reunion), 1935," in *A Selective Guide to Chinese Literature 1900–1949*, volume 2: *The Short Story*, edited by Zbigniew Slupski (Leiden: Brill, 1988), pp. 278–281;

Shen Chengkuan, Huang Houxing, and Wu Fuhui, eds., *Zhang Tianyi yanjiu ziliao* (Beijing: Zhongguo shehui kexue chubanshe, 1982);

Yifeng Sun, "Humour, Satire, and Parody in Zhang Tianyi's Writings," *Chinese Culture*, 40 (June 1999): 1–44;

Shu-ying Tsau, "Zhang Tianyi's Fiction: The Beginning of Proletarian Literature in China," dissertation, University of Toronto, 1976;

Yu Runqi, ed., *Tang Tao cang shu* (Beijing: Beijing chubanshe, 2004), pp. 132, 136.

Zhao Shuli

(24 September 1906 – 23 September 1970)

T. M. McClellan
University of Edinburgh

BOOKS: *Xiao Erhei jiehun* [Young Blacky Gets Married] (Shanxi: Huabei xinhua shudian, 1943); translated as "Little Erhei's Marriage," *Chinese Literature,* 5 (1979): 28–54;

Li Youcai banhua [The Rhymes of Li Youcai] (Shanxi: Huabei xinhua shudian, 1943);

Meng Xiangying fanshen [Meng Xiangying's Emancipation] (Shanxi: Huabei xinhua shudian, 1945);

Zhandou yu shengchan jiehe–yi deng yingxiong Pang Rulin [Uniting Struggle and Production: First-Class Hero Pang Rulin (Shanxi: Suobao xinhua shudian, 1945);

Lijiazhuang de bianqian (Licheng: Huabei xinhua shudian, 1946); translated by Gladys Yang as *Changes in Li Village* (Beijing: Foreign Languages Press, 1953);

Fugui (N.p.: Huabei xinhua shudian, 1946)–translated by Cyril Birch as "Lucky," in *Modern Chinese Stories and Novellas, 1919–1949,* edited by Joseph S. M. Lau, C. T. Hsia, and Leo Ou-fan Lee (New York: Columbia University Press, 1981), pp. 324–333; enlarged (N.p.: Huabei xinhua shudian, 1948)–includes "Cuiliangchai," translated by Joseph Kalmer as "The Tax Collector," *Eastern World,* 4 (1950);

Xie bu ya zheng [Evil Won't Overcome Right] (N.p.: Ji'nan xinhua shudian, 1948);

Chuan jia bao [The Heirloom] (Beijing: Tianxia tushu gongsi, 1949)–includes "Tian guafu kan gua," translated by Jeffrey C. Kinkley as "The Widow Tian and Her Pumpkins," in, *Furrows: Peasants, Intellectuals, and the State. Stories and Histories From Modern China,* edited by Helen Siu (Stanford, Cal.: Stanford University Press, 1990), pp. 103–105;

Dengji (Beijing: Gongren chubanshe, 1950); translated as "Registration," in *Registration and Other Stories by Contemporary Chinese Writers* (Beijing: Foreign Languages Press, 1954), pp. 55–92;

Shi Bulan ganche [Shi Bulan Drives His Cart] (Beijing: Gongren chubanshe, 1950);

Wanxiang Lou [The Hall of Myriad Phenomena] (Beijing: Gongren chubanshe, 1950);

Zhao Shuli (from Zhao Shuli, *1994; Baker-Berry Library, East Asian, Dartmouth College)*

Zhao Shuli xuanji [Selected Works of Zhao Shuli] (Beijing: Kaiming shudian, 1951);

Sanliwan (Beijing: Tongsu duwu chubanshe, 1955); translated by Yang as *Sanliwan Village* (Beijing: Foreign Languages Press, 1957);

Liu Erhe yu Wang Jisheng [Liu Erhe and Wang Jisheng] (Beijing: Tongsu duwu chubanshe, 1956);

Biaoming taidu [Make Your Position Clear] (Beijing: Tongsu duwu chubanshe, 1957);

"*Duanlian duanlian*" ["Come on, Shape Up"] (Taiyuan: Shanxi renmin chubanshe, 1958);

Lingquan dong [Fairy Spring Cave] (Beijing: Zuojia chubanshe, 1959);

Sanfu ji [Thrice Over Collection] (Beijing: Zuojia chubanshe, 1960)—includes "Xin shitang li yi guren," translated by Yang Hsien-yi as "A New Canteen and Old Memories," *Chinese Literature,* 12 (1959): 107–111;

Taobuzhu de shou [The Unglovable Hands] (Taiyuan: Shanxi renmin chubanshe, 1962); translated by Nathan K. Mao and Winston L. Y. Yang as "The Unglovable Hands," in *Literature of the People's Republic of China,* edited by Kai-yu Hsu (Bloomington: Indiana University Press, 1980), pp. 494–502;

Xiaxiang ji [The Down to the Villages Collection] (Beijing: Zuojia chubanshe, 1963)—includes "Yang Laotaiye," translated by Sidney Shapiro as "Patriarch," *Chinese Literature,* 3 (1964): 19–30;

Zhao Shuli lun chuangzuo [Zhao Shuli on Literary Creation] (Shanghai: Shanghai wenyi chubanshe, 1985);

Zhao Shuli quanji [Complete Works of Zhao Shuli], 5 volumes (Taiyuan: Beiyue wenyi chubanshe, 2000).

Collections: *Zhao Shuli xiaoshuo xuanji* [Selected Fiction of Zhao Shuli] (N.p.: Lüliang wenhua jiaoyu chubanshe, 1947);

Zhao Shuli duanpian xiaoshuo xuanji [Selected Short Stories of Zhao Shuli] (N.p.: Huazhong xinhua shudian, 1949);

Zhao Shuli xiaoshuo xuan [A Selection of Zhao Shuli's Fiction] (Taiyuan: Shanxi renmin chubanshe, 1979);

Zhao Shuli xiju quyi xuan [A Selection of Zhao Shuli's Plays and Popular Performance Works] (Taiyuan: Shanxi renmin chubanshe, 1980);

Zhao Shuli wen ji [Zhao Shuli's Works], 4 volumes (Beijing: Gongren chubanshe, 1980);

Zhao Shuli wenji buyi [Supplement to *Zhao Shuli's Works*] (Taiyuan: Zhongguo zuojia xiehui Shanxi fenhui, 1982);

Zhao Shuli wenji xubian [Continuation of *Zhao Shuli's Works*] (Beijing: Gongren chubanshe, 1984);

Zhao Shuli daibiaozuo [Representative Works of Zhao Shuli] (Zhengzhou: Huanghe wenyi, 1986);

Zhao Shuli (Hong Kong & Beijing: Sanlian shudian, Renmin wenxue chubanshe, 1994).

Edition in English: *Rhymes of Li Yu-ts'ai and Other Stories,* translated by Sydney Shapiro (Beijing: Foreign Languages Press, 1950); republished as *Rhymes of Li Youcai and Other Stories* (Beijing: Foreign Languages Press, 1980)—includes "The Rhymes of Li Yu-ts'ai" (*Li Youcai banhua*) and "The Heirloom" ("Chuan jia bao").

PLAY PRODUCTION: *Shilidian,* Changzhi, 8 August 1964.

Zhao Shuli is one of the greatest names of Chinese communist literature. After the Yan'an Forum on Literature and Art of 1942, his stories became the leading examples of the new literature sanctioned by Mao Zedong's Communist government in the areas of wartime China that it controlled. He was, nevertheless, mercilessly attacked during the Cultural Revolution launched by Mao in 1966.

Zhao was born Zhao Deyi on 24 September 1906 in the village of Weichi, Qinshui county, in the Taihang Mountain region of southeast Shanxi province. He was the second child of Zhao Heqing, a farmer, and Wang Jinlian; his sister Zhao Xiaohao had been born in 1903. In the essay "Ye suan jingyan" (Experiences of a Sort), published in *Renmin ribao* (People's Daily) on 26 June 1949, Zhao writes that "my family went from middle peasant to poor peasant under the oppression of loan sharks." During the eighteenth century two Zhao brothers had achieved high office and built two mansions in Weichi. The family fortunes had waned by the time of Zhao Shuli's paternal grandfather, Zhao Zhongfang, who repeatedly failed the first level of civil service examinations, and they were devastated by a famine in the late 1870s. Zhao Zhongfang fled to Henan province, where he became a shop assistant and then a shopkeeper and restored some of the family's wealth. Zhao Zhongfang then returned to Qinshui county, hoping to restore the family socially as well as economically by resuming the scholar-gentry life and preparing the next generation for the civil service examinations. But the examination system was abolished in 1905, and land rents proved insufficient to keep the Zhao clan in its accustomed lifestyle. Thus, Zhao Heqing was the first in his family to be forced to take up the plow.

Zhao Heqing loved literature and was a musician and a devotee of the local opera form known as Shangdang *bangzi* (southeast Shanxi "clapper opera"). From him Zhao Shuli gained a lifelong love of the traditional performing arts of the region. In Zhao's fiction musicians and other performers are always worker-heroes and correct political activists, while Zhao Heqing serves as the model for one of his best-known negative characters, the superstitious and backward father of Erhai (Blacky) in *Xiao Erhei jiehun* (1943, Young Blacky Gets Married; translated as "Little Erhei's Marriage," 1979).

In 1911 Zhao Deyi's given name was changed to Shuli. His sister Shuiyi, whose childhood name was Yuhua, was born on 7 March of that year. Zhao Zhongfang was Zhao Shuli's first teacher and hoped that his grandson would be the family's scholarly success. Zhao Zhongfang's wife died in the summer of 1915, and Zhao Zhongfang died in February 1916. In the spring Zhao Shuli enrolled in a *sishu* (old-style private school) in Weichi. Medical care and funerals for Zhao Zhongfang and his wife exhausted the family savings, and Zhao Shuli was bullied by classmates and mistreated by teachers because he was poor. In 1917 he persuaded his parents to let him quit school, and he began to learn farming from his father. His sister Yuqin, whose childhood name was Cuihua, was born on 30 August 1917.

In the summer of 1919 Zhao studied in a *buxiban* (tutorial) at a provincial *gaoji xiaoxue* (higher primary school) in Keshan, about ten miles from his home. In the spring of 1920 he enrolled in the first-year level at the school. His sister Xiaowang was born on 31 January 1921. On 23 January 1922 Zhao married Ma Suying, who was four months older than he. At the end of 1922 he graduated from the higher primary school, and the next year he went to work as a teacher in a lower primary school in the village of Yelu in Qinshui county. In 1924 he transferred to a lower primary school in the village of Banzhang, also in Qinshui county.

On 13 February 1925 Zhao and Ma had a son, Taihu. In the same month Zhao went to the village of Xifeng in Yangcheng county to teach at a *sishu*. In the summer he was admitted to the Shanxi shengli di si shifan (Shanxi Number Four Normal School) in Changzhi. In the winter of 1926 he joined the Nationalist Party. In the spring of 1927 Chang Wenyu, one of those who had recommended Zhao for membership in the party, gave Zhao a book on communism; Chang told Zhao that he was a Communist but that the fact should be kept secret. Shortly thereafter, Zhao secretly joined the Chinese Communist Party. A crackdown on Communists in Shanxi began in 1928, and Zhao went into hiding in the late spring and lost contact with the party.

Zhao's wife died on 25 April 1929. On 28 April he was arrested on suspicion of being a Communist. Zhao did not believe that the evidence against him was convincing, and he never admitted that he was a Communist. He was sentenced to a *zixin yuan* (reformatory) in Taiyuan. His first two stories were published in *Zixin yuekan* (Reformatory Monthly) in the fall of 1929: "Hui" (Regret), about filial love overcoming a teenage delinquent's fear of his father, and "Bai ma de gushi" (The Story of a White Horse), about a runaway horse's reunion with his master. Both stories are in collected volume one of *Zhao Shuli quanqi* (2000, The Complete Works of Zhao Shuli). He was released in the early summer of 1930 and returned to Taiyuan in August after a visit to Weichi. In Taiyuan he worked in a variety of jobs, including teacher's assistant. At this time he replaced the second character in his given name, changing the meaning from "establish the rites" to "establish reason" to symbolize his desire to replace the rites of feudal society with Marxist reason. Twice in the latter half of 1930 the Communist Party sent emissaries to ask Zhao to return, but he declined. In April or May 1931 he took a teaching job at a higher primary school in

Cover for a 1947 edition of Zhao's first book, Xiao Erhei jiehun (Young Blacky Gets Married; translated as "Little Erhei's Marriage," 1979), originally published in 1943 (Wason Collection on East Asia–China, Kroch Asia Library, Cornell University)

Dong'an, Qinshui county. On 24 December 1931 he married nineteen-year-old Guan Lianzhong, the adopted daughter of a landlord in the village.

In August 1933 Zhao took a job teaching language arts at a higher primary school in the village of Beiguan in Taigu county. He was also publishing fiction and essays; two of his stories of 1933, "Youge ren" (There Was a Man) and "Jinzi" (Gold), are included in the first volume of his complete works. In January 1934 he quit his job; he traveled in southern Shanxi and visited Henan, but otherwise his whereabouts and activities during 1934 and the first half of 1935 cannot be confirmed. He continued to work on a novel about the struggle between farmers and the forces of feudalism, "Panlongyu" (Coiled Dragon Gulch), which he had begun in 1933. The first chapter was serialized in *Zhongguo wenhua jianshe xiehui Shanxi fenhui yuekan* (The Monthly Journal of the Shanxi Branch of the Association for Chinese Culture) from February to April 1935 under the pen name Yexiao. That chapter is all that survives of the novel, and it is collected in the first volume of his complete works. On 31 May 1935 Zhao and Guan's daughter Xiaofen was born; her name was later changed to Guangjian. From late July to mid October 1935 Zhao took an acting class at the Xibei yingye gongsi (Northwest Film Company) in Taiyuan.

In May or June 1936 Zhao returned to Weichi. On 18 June he went to Changzhi to teach at the Shangdang gongli jianyi xiangcun shifan xuexiao (Southeast Shanxi Countryside Public Elementary Teachers Training School), a progressive school founded by friends of his. In December he wrote *Dadao Hanjian* (Down with Traitors), a play in rhyme; it appeared in two parts on 14 and 21 January 1937 in *Kaizhan* (The Beginning), a publication of the *Taiyuan ribao* (Taiyuan Daily).

Zhao left the school in Changzhi in late April 1937. War with Japan began in July, and that winter Zhao rejoined the Communist Party. In 1938 he held various positions and did propaganda and other work to mobilize the populace to support the war effort. In August or September 1939 the party assigned him to work on *Huanghe ribao* (The Yellow River Daily) in Huguan. In March 1940 he participated in the launching of *Renmin bao* (The People's Press) and became editor in chief of its literary supplement, *Dajia gan* (Everybody Get to Work). In late May 1940 he moved to *Xinhua ribao* (New China Daily), which was also published in southeastern Shanxi province.

In 1940–1941 Zhao published *kuaiban* (clapper talks), *guci* (drum songs), editorials, essays, poems, and many stories. Most of these works appeared in *Zhongguo ren* (The Chinese), another publication of *Xinhua ribao* for which Zhao served as editor. Volume one of *Zhao Shuli quanji* includes thirty-two of Zhao's stories from 1941.

Mao's "Zai Yan'an wenyi zuotanhui shang de jianghua" (Talks at the Yan'an Forum on Literature and Art) in May 1942 set the agenda for mainland Chinese writing from 1942 until the end of the Cultural Revolution in 1976, and Zhao became the first champion of Mao's line on literature. Mao declared that "natural" forms that were "crude but also extremely lively" were "the sole source of literature and art in conceptualized form" but that it was necessary to "process" them to produce a more organized and concentrated typification and idealization of reality. Zhao was thirty-seven years old *(sanshiqi sui)* by Chinese reckoning at the time of the forum; in a 14 September 1957 letter to his daughter Guangjian, Zhao wrote, "I acquired my love for literature and art in my early twenties, and I made some efforts of my own, but I didn't start writing in earnest until I was thirty-eight *[sanshiba sui]*" in 1943.

Zhao wrote *Xiao Erhei jiehun* in May 1943, and it was published as a book in September. The work opposes arranged marriages and treason. Erhei and Xiaoqin get engaged with the help of the enlightened revolutionaries who have taken control of their district, overcoming the interference of their superstitious, vain, and ignorant parents and attacks by two local despots who collaborated with the Japanese and who are salacious and vindictive. Erhei and Xiaoqin are good-looking, even tempered, and confident; their enemies are easily defeated; and their parents see the error of their ways and reform. *Xiao Erhei jiehun* was republished by several firms across China. It was successful largely because of the language in which it is written, which incorporates local dialect and was accessible to peasants but not to the extent of alienating a wider readership, and also because it engages a commonplace yet important issue of the time: whereas May Fourth writers such as Ding Ling created female protagonists who struggled to adapt to new sexual roles, Zhao wrote for the village people he knew–both "backward" and "progressive" ones–about down-to-earth, practical matters set against the background of wider political and national developments, and he did so without sacrificing romanticism. Romanticism persisted as a characteristic of much of his fiction; romantic interest is, however, absent from his next work, which is his best-known and possibly his most important publication.

In October 1943 Zhao started work as an editor at the Huabei xinhua shudian (Northern China New China Bookstore) in Liao county, Shanxi province, which had published his first book. In October the Huabei xinhua shudian published his second book, the novella *Li Youcai banhua* (1943, The Rhymes of Li Youcai; translated as "The Rhymes of Li Yu-ts'ai," 1950). According to Cyril Birch, *Li Youcai banhua* was successful in Communist-controlled areas of China before 1949 and in the People's Republic of China after 1949, both with general readers and with the leadership, because it incorporates, in a "natural and organic" way, elements from traditional oral and literate popular culture. *Li Youcai banhua* is written in a free-flowing, natural, and demotic Chinese that echoes the narrative formulae of traditional Chinese vernacular fiction and is exemplary of the ideologically sound and strategically effective "processing" of "natural forms" of art and literature that Mao encouraged in his Yan'an talks. This exemplary status derives largely from the function of the rhymes in the story. The Chinese word designating these "rhymes," *banhua,* is more properly translated as "clapper ballads" or "clapper ditties"–rhymed folk poems recited to the rhythmic accompaniment of a bamboo or wooden clapper. Variations of the clapper-ballad form can be found in every region of China. In northern China the typical version takes the form of short-lined, staccato recitation at breakneck speed. Traditionally, the content of clapper ballads was witty, generally satirical, and often lewd.

Li Youcai banhua is set in Yanjiashan, a village in northern China, during the Japanese occupation of the late 1930s and early 1940s. Although Yanjiashan has been controlled by the Communists for some time, the Yan family has preserved the traditional power structure by bullying and bribing the locals and hoodwinking the inexperienced party worker, Comrade Zhang. At the beginning of the novella Yan Xifu's abuses of power are exposed, and he is removed as mayor and punished. But Yan Xifu's uncle Yan Hengyuan is able to keep his own reputation as "enlightened gentry" while ensuring that a protégé is installed as the new mayor in a rigged election. As the village's largest landowner, Yan Hengyuan proceeds to manipulate the process of land reform to his own advantage and to corrupt the villagers who rose to official positions after his nephew's disgrace. Meanwhile, the naive Comrade Zhang periodically recommends that the party's county headquarters–where he seems to spend most of his time–accord the village this model status or that commendation. The poorest villagers have only one outlet for their long-harbored resentment: the witty satirical rhymes of their bard, the irrepressible Li Youcai. When the streetwise County Peasant Association chairman, Comrade Yang, arrives in the so-called model village, it takes him only a few hours of conversation with the poor peasants, who regale him with Li Youcai's rhymes, to form the assessment: "your village is controlled by feudal racketeers." He rapidly reforms the moribund Peasant Association with the help of the younger peasants; heavyweight reinforcements arrive from county party headquarters; and a mass meeting puts everything to rights. Under the leadership of the Communist Party, the peasants are victorious over the enemy landlord class.

The rhymes already constitute Mao's "crude but also extremely lively" elements of "national form" at the beginning of the novella: they are a vibrant and organic part of the cultural and social life of the village, and in their satirical function they increasingly appear as an embodiment of the peasants' "mass outlook." Until correct guidance is made available to the poor peasants in the person of Comrade Yang, however, the rhymes can serve only as an impotent outlet for popular grievance. Under the leadership of the party the rhymes are transformed into a progressive force and begin to act as a principal means of raising consciousness among the people and as a weapon in the struggle against class enemies.

In the article "Zhao Shuli de chuangzuo" (translated as "The Creative Works of Chao Shu-li," 1950), published on 26 August 1946 in *Yan'an jiefang ribao* (Yan'an Liberation Daily), the Communist Party's chief literary commissar, Zhou Yang, noted that "Zhao Shuli deliberately calls his works 'popular stories'"; but "they are not, of course, popular stories in the ordinary sense of the word, but real works of art, in which artistry and popular appeal blend." Zhao's accomplishment in *Li Youcai banhua* exhibits both Mao's "processing" and "idealization" of "literature and

Cover for the 1950 book that includes the English translation of Zhao's Li Youcai banhua *(1943, The Rhymes of Li Youcai), about the overthrow of the corrupt power structure of a village by peasants and the local Communist Party leadership (Collection of Thomas Moran)*

art in their natural form" and Zhou Yang's "blend" of "artistry and popular appeal."

The fact that the closing eulogy in rhyme form does not mention the Communist Party was, perhaps, one reason why Zhao and *Li Youcai banhua* did not retain model status beyond the late 1950s. During the Cultural Revolution, writing that did not emphasize the centrality of the party was suspect, no matter how "correctly" it depicted class contradictions and the positive role of the poor peasantry. The early 1940s were Zhao's golden age as a writer of fiction.

In the fall of 1943 Zhao's father and thirty other villagers were bayoneted to death by Japanese troops. In the fall of 1946 Zhao and his family moved to Wu'an county in Hebei province, where the Huabei xinhua shudian had relocated.

Lijiazhuang de bianqian (1946; translated as *Changes in Li Village*, 1953), Zhao's longest work of fiction of the 1940s, attempts a more naturalistic and comprehensive treatment of the rural revolution than the tightly controlled politico-literary metaphor of *Li Youcai banhua*. *Lijiazhuang de bianqian* might be termed an historical novella in that it begins in the late 1920s, although by the end it brings events up to the time of writing–in rather a rush: here, as in many other places in his fiction, Zhao appears to have been writing to a schedule dictated by events, and *Lijiazhuang de bianqian* suffers artistically as a result. Exploitation of the poor in the village of Lijiazhuang is exemplified by the poor peasant Zhang Tiesuo's conviction by a landlord-controlled kangaroo court because his feisty wife cut down a mulberry tree unjustly adjudged to belong to the schoolteacher Li Chunxi, a nephew of the leading local landlord. The fine reduces Zhang and his wife and child to near destitution. Zhang finds work as a carpenter in Taiyuan, where he meets the Communist activist Xiao Chang. He regards Xiao Chang as the one truly good person he has ever known; on the other hand, he also encounters Li Chunxi's brother, Li Xiaoxi, an officer in forces loyal to the Shanxi warlord Yan Xishan. Li Xiaoxi is a vicious gangster, militarist, and upholder of all things advantageous to his landlord class. Nevertheless, Zhang serves for a time as Li Xiaoxi's orderly. Fearing for the safety of the money he has earned from his labor in the city, Zhang accepts Li Xiaoxi's protection for his journey home to Lijiazhuang.

At this point *Lijiazhuang de bianqian* becomes formulaic. Zhang's tales of the moral giant Xiao Chang soon dispel his peers' fear of the Communists, and they look forward to their "liberation" by the Eighth Route Army, the main Communist force that operated in northern China during the war with Japan. That liberation arrives after Xiao Chang comes to the village and exercises his leadership. Half of the villagers are killed by Nationalist or Japanese forces–Xiao Chang is buried alive by the former–but finally, the Japanese are defeated. With Zhang Tiesuo as a somewhat unlikely village head, the men of Lijiazhuang, including Zhang's thirteen-year-old son, set off to fight in the impending civil war between the Nationalists and the Communists.

The ambivalence of the central character, Zhang Tiesuo, is one of the most striking features of *Lijiazhuang de bianqian*. At the beginning of the novella Zhang, if not craven, is clearly downtrodden, weeping over his fate while his formidable wife, who typifies the strong female characters in Zhao's oeuvre, rants against adversity. In the middle of the story he becomes a lackey of the landlord, bully, and right-wing militarist Li Xiaoxi. Yet, toward the end Zhang is elevated to leadership status–largely, it seems, because he was the first to bring the Communist gospel to the village.

Zhang Tiesuo's characterization in *Lijiazhuang de bianqian* contrasts with that of the eponymous hero of *Fugui* (translated as "Lucky," 1981), a short story that was published as a book in 1946. Fugui is a wretched, downtrodden, and destitute peasant. Driven to steal and–almost worse–to hire himself out as a funeral musician, Fugui is suddenly catapulted into a heroic role when he is called on to denounce his oppressor, a kinsman, at the cathartic "struggle meeting" in the story.

Zhao and Guan's second son, Erhu, was born on 12 June 1947. On 15 December 1948 Zhao published "Dui gaige nongcun xiju ji dian jianyi" (A Few Suggestions on the Reform of Village Theater) in the premiere issue of *Huabei wenyi* (North China Literature and Art). In January 1949 he moved back to Weichi with his wife and their youngest son. In April he went to Beiping (as Beijing was known from 28 June 1928 to 27 September 1949), taking his daughter Guangjian with him. On 29 September 1949 Guan gave birth to their son Sanhu. In 1950 she, the rest of their children, and Zhao's mother joined him in Beijing. In 1951 Zhao returned to his native district to immerse himself in peasant life. The following year he took part in the establishment of rural collectives in a village near Pingshun.

Zhao's only completed novel, *Sanliwan* (translated as *Sanliwan Village*, 1957), is set in a large Shanxi village during the collectivization movement of the early to mid 1950s. It was serialized in the first four issues of *Renmin wenxue* (People's Literature) for 1955 and published as a book in May. The novel opens with a short prelude describing the allocation of the various wings of the Liu family mansion after "Liu Laowu . . . was executed by the government." The rest of the work is concerned with what Mao in a 1957 speech termed "renmin neibu maodun" (contradictions among the people). Arrayed against stubborn middle-level peasants intent on going their own way and old revolutionaries who have become set in their ways are honest though unsophisticated peasants and paragon families. Although it describes intricate details of land collectivization, *Sanliwan* retains interest not only through its well-crafted melodrama but also through the political choices involved in two central romances and a subsidiary one: Fan Lingzhi has to abandon her prejudice to find happiness with the sturdy but uneducated model worker Wang Yusheng; Wang Yumei has to wait for Ma Youyi to "revolutionize" himself–escape from his "feudal" family– before she can have the man she desired all along; the political significance of the mariage of Wang Manxi and Xiaojun is much less clear, but the timing, which allows for a triple wedding on the Moon Festival coinciding with National Day, affords a spectacular *datuanyuan* ("grand reunion" or "happily ever after") ending to the novel.

Zhao was celebrated as a leading writer during the 1950s. He published several essays during this time, including the 1957 letter to his daughter, Guangjian, who had failed to get into a university. He castigates her for "looking down on the working people" and refusing to listen to his advice either to get a job as a shop assistant or hairdresser in the city or to go home to their village and engage in production in the newly established commune. The letter was obtained by a journalist and published in the *Shanxi ribao* (Shanxi Daily) on 11 November 1957 under the title "Yuan ni zuo yi ge laodongzhe" (Hoping You'll Be a Laborer); it was republished in *Renmin ribao* and other papers and is included in Zhao's *Sanfu ji* (1960, Thrice Over Collection).

In October 1959 Zhao was subjected to party criticism; the charge was that rightist tendencies could be found in some of his comments on communes and agricultural development. The investigation concluded in January 1960, and Zhao was not disciplined. His mother died on 21 January 1962. One of the last official eulogies of Zhao as a model man of letters appeared in the English-language magazine *Chinese Literature* in 1964; otherwise, the issue was devoted to the 1964 Festival of Beijing Opera on Contemporary Themes, a "cultural" event that, above any other, foreshadowed the "Great Proletarian Cultural Revolution." At the time, Zhao was writing his major dramatic work, a Shangdang *bangzi* titled *Shilidian*. The plot centers on the efforts of Ma Hongying, a "model worker" in the village of the title, to unite her fellow commune members to struggle for justice and, above all, for increased production. The play was performed for the public in Changzhi on 8 August 1964; but after a September performance for a *neibu* (internal) audience of party officials, further performance was banned. The principal complaint seems to have been that it was too "hei'an" (dark) in that it highlighted problems instead of heroic successes.

In January 1964, in a talk that was published in 2000 as "Zai Zhongguo zuoxie zhaokai de zuojia, bianji zuotanhui shang de fayan" (Remarks at a Conference of Writers and Editors Convened by the Chinese Writers' Association) in volume five of his complete works, Zhao said, "I haven't the courage to write even a little more idealism into my works, I prefer to trust in my own eyes." In the fall of 1964 Zhao made minor revisions to *Shilidian*. In February 1965 Zhao and his family moved back to Taiyuan. *Shilidian* was again performed for a *neibu* audience in mid August 1965, and again the play was found to be unacceptable. Zhao continued to make revisions, but it was never again performed. *Shilidian* was published posthumously in *Renmin wenxue* in 1978 and is included in volume three of *Zhao Shuli quanji*.

While the 1942 Yan'an Conference began Mao's ultimately victorious battle against the May Fourth generation of bourgeois writers to establish socialist realism in literature, by 1962 the post–socialist realist mode of "the combination of revolutionary realism and revolutionary Romanticism" was being advanced by Jiang Qing under Mao's supervision. During the Great Leap Forward, from around 1958, and during the Cultural Revolution the new Romanticism, with its emphasis on the "three prominences" of idealized revolutionary heroes, was predominant. In August 1962, however, it was still possible for established Communist writers to gather in Dalian at a

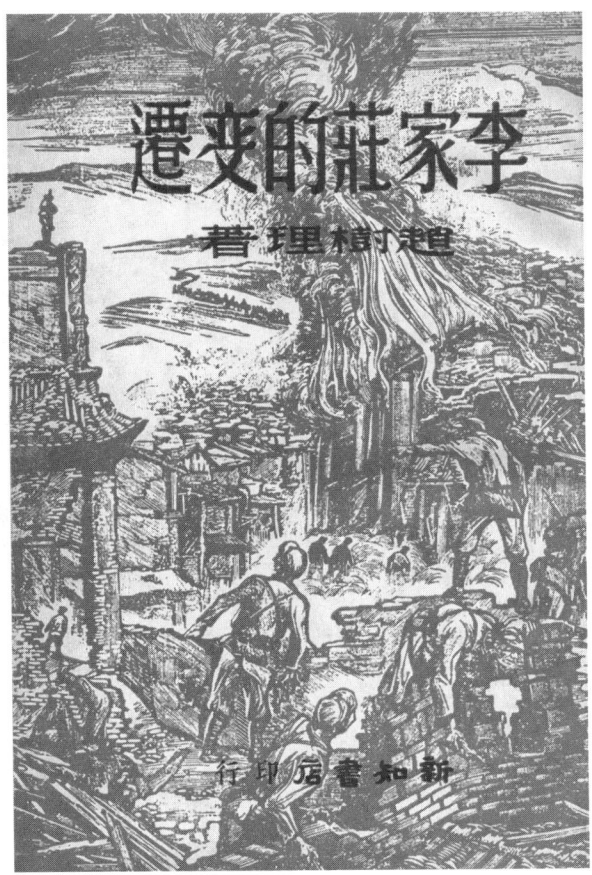

Cover for a 1947 edition of Zhao's novella Lijiazhuang de bianqian *(translated as* Changes in Li Village, *1953), first published in 1946 (Wason Collection on East Asia–China, Kroch Asia Library, Cornell University)*

conference on rural subject matter in short fiction, under the sponsorship of Zhao's old mentor Zhou Yang, a giant of Communist Party cultural affairs, to discuss the question of "middle characters"—that is, characters who are neither red nor white (Communist or anti-Communist). But in 1966 Zhou Yang, who was far too powerful a rival for Jiang's Cultural Revolution Group to ignore, became one of the first major targets for criticism and "struggle." As Zhou Yang's most famous literary protégé and a participant at the Dalian conference, Zhao soon came under attack, and in August he was put under the supervision of the Southeast Shanxi Revolutionary Rebels, a faction of Red Guards. During the next four years he was periodically paraded, humiliated, and "struggled" against. Frequently, he was forced to assume the "airplane" position: standing on a stool, bent double, with his arms behind his back and a placard around his neck announcing his "counterrevolutionary" crimes—that is, some of the more-humanistic depictions in his writing. In September 1970, at the height of hysterical denunciations of Zhao, the stool was kicked out from under him—a common ploy—breaking

*Zhao, the poet Wang Yaping, and the fiction writer Lao She in 1951 (from Zhongguo dabaike quanshu zongbianji weiyuanhui, ed.,
Zhongguo wenxue, volume 2, 1986; Collection of Thomas Moran)*

one of his ribs and puncturing one of his lungs. He did not receive medical treatment and died a few days later, on 23 September.

Zhao Shuli was a peasant writer who was not of such pure poor peasant stock as would have been more consistent with his canonization in the 1940s and 1950s as the prime example of literary fiction in the Yan'an mode of Chinese communist literature. His work shows his deep commitment to the party that he first joined at the age of twenty-one. Equally, it shows his subtle and humane understanding of the villages and communities in which he grew up.

Bibliographies:

"Zhao Shuli zuopin mulu suoyin," in *Zhongguo dangdai wenxue yanjiu ziliao: Zhao Shuli zhuanji*, volume 2, edited by Fudan Zhongwen xi (Shanghai: Fudan daxue, neibu faxing, 1979), pp. 494–522;

Wang Chaobing, "Zhao Shuli zhuzuo shumu," in *Zhongguo xiandai zuojia da cidian*, edited by Yang Li (Beijing: Xin shijie chubanshe, 1992), pp. 629–630.

Biographies:

Huang Xiuji, *Zhao Shuli yanjiu* (Taiyuan: Shanxi renmin chubanshe, 1985);

Dai Guangzhong, *Zhao Shuli zhuan* (Beijing: Beijing shiyue wenyi, 1987);

Dong Dazhong, *Zhao Shuli nianpu*, revised and enlarged edition (Taiyuan: Beiyue wenyi chubanshe, 1993);

Zhongguo zuojia zishu (Shanghai: Shanghai jiaoyu chubanshe, 1998).

References:

Cyril Birch, *Chinese Communist Literature* (New York: Praeger, 1963);

Hilary Chung, ed., *Critical Studies,* volume 6: *In the Party Spirit: Socialist Realism and Literary Practice in the Soviet Union, East Germany and China* (Amsterdam & Atlanta: Rodopi, 1996);

Fudan daxue Zhongwen xi, ed., *Zhongguo dangdai wenxue yanjiu ziliao: Zhao Shuli zhuanji*, 2 volumes (Shanghai: Fudan daxue, neibu faxing, 1979)—includes in volume 1, Zhou Yang, "Zhao Shuli de chuangzuo," pp. 158–171; translated as "The Creative Works of Chao Shu-li," in Zhao's *Rhymes of Li Yu-ts'ai and Other Stories,* translated by Sidney Shapiro (Beijing: Foreign Languages Press, 1950), pp. 7–30;

Bonnie S. McDougall and Kam Louie, *The Literature of China in the Twentieth Century* (London: Hurst, 1997), pp. 196, 208, 220–224, 226–227, 444;

Anne F. Thurston, *Enemies of the People: The Ordeal of the Intellectuals in China's Great Cultural Revolution* (Cambridge, Mass.: Harvard University Press, 1988);

Yang Lan, *Chinese Fiction of the Cultural Revolution* (Hong Kong: Hong Kong University Press, 1998);

Zhongguo dabaike quanshu zongbianji weiyuanhui, ed., *Zhongguo wenxue*, volume 2 (Beijing & Shanghai: Zhongguo dabaike quanshu chubanshe, 1986).

Books for Further Reading

Anderson, Marston. *The Limits of Realism: Chinese Fiction in the Revolutionary Period.* Berkeley, Los Angeles & Oxford: University of California Press, 1990.

Beijing tushuguan shumu bianjizu, ed. *Zhongguo xiandai zuojia zhuyi shumu* (A Catalogue of Modern Chinese Writers, Their Works and Translations), 2 volumes. Beijing: Shumu wenxian chubanshe, 1982.

Boorman, Howard L., and Richard C. Howard, eds. *Biographical Dictionary of Republican China,* 5 volumes. New York: Columbia University Press, 1967–1979.

Chen Mingshu, ed. *Ershi shiji Zhongguo wenxue dadian* (The Encyclopedia of Twentieth-Century Chinese Literature), 3 volumes. Shanghai: Shanghai jiaoyu chubanshe, 1994–1996.

Chen Pingyuan and Xia Xiaohong, eds. *Ershi shiji Zhongguo xiaoshuo lilun ziliao* (Materials on Twentieth-Century Chinese Literary Theory), 4 volumes. Beijing: Beijing daxue chubanshe, 1997.

Chow Tse-tsung. *The May Fourth Movement: Intellectual Revolution in Modern China.* Cambridge, Mass. & London: Harvard University Press, 1960.

Chu, Pao-liang. *Twentieth-Century Chinese Writers and Their Pen Names,* enlarged edition, 2 volumes. Taibei: Center for Chinese Studies, 1989.

Denton, Kirk A., ed. *Modern Chinese Literary Thought: Writings on Literature, 1893–1945.* Stanford, Cal.: Stanford University Press, 1996.

Doleželová-Velingerová, Milena, ed. *The Chinese Novel at the Turn of the Century.* Toronto, Buffalo, N.Y. & London: University of Toronto Press, 1980.

Doleželová-Velingerová, ed. *A Selective Guide to Chinese Literature 1900–1949,* volume 1: *The Novel.* Leiden, New York, Copenhagen & Cologne: Brill, 1988.

Dooling, Amy D., and Kristina M. Torgeson, eds. *Writing Women in Modern China: An Anthology of Women's Literature from the Early Twentieth Century.* New York: Columbia University Press, 1998.

Gibbs, Donald A., and Yun-chen Li. *A Bibliography of Studies and Translations of Modern Chinese Literature 1918–1942.* Cambridge, Mass. & London: East Asian Research Center, Harvard University, 1975.

Goldman, Merle, ed. *Modern Chinese Literature in the May Fourth Era.* Cambridge, Mass. & London: Harvard University Press, 1977.

Goldman and Leo Ou-fan Lee, eds. *An Intellectual History of Modern China.* Cambridge: Cambridge University Press, 2002.

Gunn, Edward. *Rewriting Chinese: Style and Innovation in Twentieth-Century Chinese Prose.* Stanford, Cal.: Stanford University Press, 1991.

Gunn. *Unwelcome Muse: Chinese Literature in Shanghai and Peking, 1937–1945.* New York: Columbia University Press, 1980.

Hsia, C. T. *C. T. Hsia on Chinese Literature.* New York: Columbia University Press, 2004.

Hsia. *A History of Modern Chinese Fiction,* third edition, introduction by David Der-wei Wang. Bloomington & Indianapolis: Indiana University Press, 1999.

Hsia, Tsi-an. *The Gate of Darkness: Studies on the Leftist Literary Movement in China.* Seattle & London: University of Washington Press, 1968.

Hu Shi. *Baihua wenxue shi, shang juan* (A History of Vernacular Literature, Volume One). Shanghai: Xinyue shudian, 1928.

Hummel, Arthur W. *Eminent Chinese of the Ch'ing Period.* 2 volumes, Washington, D.C.: U.S. Government Printing Office, 1943, 1944; 1 volume, Taipei: Ch'eng Wen, 1970.

Hung, Chang-tai. *War and Popular Culture: Resistance in Modern China, 1937–1945.* Berkeley: University of California Press, 1994.

Idema, Wilt, and Lloyd Haft. *A Guide to Chinese Literature.* Ann Arbor: Center for Chinese Studies, University of Michigan, 1997.

Johnson, David G., Andrew J. Nathan, Evelyn Sakakida Rawski, and Judith A. Berling, eds. *Popular Culture in Late Imperial China.* Berkeley: University of California Press, 1985.

Lee, Leo Ou-fan. *The Romantic Generation of Modern Chinese Writers.* Cambridge, Mass.: Harvard University Press, 1973.

Lee, Lily Xiao Hong, and A. D. Stefanowska, eds. in chief, assisted by Sue Wiles; Clara Wing-chung Ho, volume ed. *Biographical Dictionary of Chinese Women: The Qing Period 1644–1911.* Armonk, N.Y. & London: Sharpe, 1998.

Lee and Stefanowska, eds. in chief; Wiles, assistant ed. in chief; Lee, volume ed. *Biographical Dictionary of Chinese Women: The Twentieth Century 1912–2000.* Armonk, N.Y. & London: Sharpe, 2003.

Link, E. Perry, Jr., *Mandarin Ducks and Butterflies: Popular Fiction in Early Twentieth-Century Chinese Cities.* Berkeley, Los Angeles & London: University of California Press, 1981.

Liu Jianmei. *Revolution plus Love: Literary History, Women's Bodies, and Thematic Repetition in Twentieth-Century Chinese Fiction.* Honolulu: University of Hawai'i Press, 2003.

Liu, Ts'un-yan, ed., assisted by John Minford, *Chinese Middlebrow Fiction from the Ch'ing and Early Republican Eras.* Hong Kong: Chinese University Press, 1984.

Lu Xun. *A Brief History of Chinese Fiction,* translated by Yang Xianyi and Gladys Yang. Beijing: Foreign Languages Press, 1959.

Ma Liangchun and Li Futian, eds. *Zhongguo wenxue da cidian* (Encyclopedia of Chinese Literature), 8 volumes. Tianjin: Tianjin renmin chubanshe, 1991.

Mackerras, Colin, assisted by Robert Chan. *Modern China: A Chronology from 1842 to the Present.* San Francisco: W. H. Freeman, 1982.

Martin, Helmut, and Jeffrey Kinkley, eds. *Modern Chinese Writers: Self-Portrayals.* Armonk, N.Y. & London: Sharpe, 1992.

McDougall, Bonnie S., and Kam Louie. *The Literature of China in the Twentieth Century.* New York: Columbia University Press, 1997.

Mostow, Joshua S., Kirk A. Denton, Bruce Fulton, and Sharalyn Orbaugh, eds. *The Columbia Companion to Modern East Asian Literature.* New York: Columbia University Press, 2003.

Nienhauser, William H., Jr., Charles Hartman, Y. A. Ma, Stephen H. West, and Scott W. Galer, eds. *The Indiana Companion to Traditional Chinese Literature,* 2 volumes. Bloomington & Indianapolis: Indiana University Press, 1986, 1998.

Qian Xingcun, as A Ying. *Wan Qing xiaoshuo shi* (A History of Late-Qing Fiction). Beijing: Renmin wenxue chubanshe, 1980.

Ramsey, S. Robert. *The Languages of China.* Princeton: Princeton University Press, 1987.

Rubinstein, Murray A., ed. *Taiwan: A New History.* Armonk, N.Y. & London: Sharpe, 1999.

Schoppa, R. Keith. *The Columbia Guide to Modern Chinese History.* New York: Columbia University Press, 2000.

Shih, Shu-mei. *The Lure of the Modern: Writing Modernism in Semicolonial China, 1917–1937.* Berkeley, Los Angeles & London: University of California Press, 2001.

Sima Changfeng. *Zhongguo xin wenxue shi* (A History of the New Chinese Literature), 3 volumes. Hong Kong: Zhaoming chubanshe, 1975–1978.

Slupski, Zbigniew, ed. *A Selective Guide to Chinese Literature 1900–1949,* volume 2: *The Short Story.* Leiden, New York, Copenhagen & Cologne: Brill, 1988.

Spence, Jonathan D. *The Search for Modern China.* New York: Norton, 1990.

Tang Tao and Yan Jiayan, eds. *Zhongguo xiandai wenxue shi* (A History of Modern Chinese Literature), 3 volumes. Beijing: Renmin wenxue chubanshe, 1988.

Wang, David Der-wei. *Fin-de-Siècle Splendor: Repressed Modernities of Late Qing Fiction, 1849–1911.* Stanford, Cal.: Stanford University Press, 1997.

Wang Yao. *Zhongguo xin wenxue shigao* (A Draft History of China's New Literature), 2 volumes. Shanghai: Shanghai wenyi chubanshe, 1982.

Wilkinson, Endymion. *Chinese History: A Manual,* revised and enlarged edition. Cambridge, Mass. & London: Harvard University Asia Center, 2000.

Wong, Timothy C., ed. *Stories for Saturday: Twentieth-Century Chinese Popular Fiction.* Honolulu: University of Hawai'i Press, 2003.

Wong, Wang-chi. *Politics and Literature in Shanghai: The Chinese League of Left-Wing Writers, 1930-1936.* Manchester, U.K. & New York: Manchester University Press, 1991.

Xu Naixiang and Qin Hong, eds. *Zhongguo xiandai wenxue zuozhe biming lu* (A List of Pen Names of Modern Chinese Authors). Changsha: Hunan wenyi chubanshe, 1988.

Yan Jiayan. *Zhongguo xiandai xiaoshuo liupai shi* (A History of the Schools of Modern Chinese Fiction). Beijing: Renmin wenxue chubanshe, 1989.

Yang Li, Hu Zhihui, and Wu Fuhui, eds. *Zhongguo xiandai zuojia da cidian* (A Biographical Dictionary of Modern Chinese Writers). Beijing: Xin shijie chubanshe, 1992. Revised and translated by Hu Zhihui, Yue Cheng, He Fei, and Hu Shaowei as *A Biographical Dictionary of Modern Chinese Writers.* Beijing: New World Press, 1994.

Yang, Winston L. Y., and Nathan K. Mao, eds. *Modern Chinese Fiction: A Guide to Its Study and Appreciation, Essays and Bibliographies.* Boston: G. K. Hall, 1981.

Zhong Jingwen, Qian Zhonglian, Wang Yao, Ji Zhenhuai, Wang Yuanhua, Xu Juemin, and Deng Shaoji, eds. *Zhongguo daibake quanshu: Zhongguo wenxue* (The Encyclopedia of China: Chinese Literature), 2 volumes. Beijing: Zhongguo dabaike quanshu chubanshe, 1986.

Contributors

Roland Altenburger . . . . *Universität Zürich*
Jianhua Chen . . . . *Hong Kong University of Science and Technology*
John A. Crespi . . . . *Colgate University*
Steven P. Day . . . . *Swarthmore College*
Kirk A. Denton . . . . *Ohio State University*
Amy D. Dooling . . . . *Connecticut College*
Rosemary M. Haddon . . . . *Massey University*
Nicole Huang . . . . *University of Wisconsin–Madison*
Ann Huss . . . . *Wellesley College*
Theodore Huters . . . . *University of California, Los Angeles*
Nicholas A. Kaldis . . . . *Binghamton University*
Jeffrey C. Kinkley . . . . *St. John's University, New York*
Jon Eugene von Kowallis . . . . *University of New South Wales, Sydney*
Charles A. Laughlin . . . . *Yale University*
Xinmin Liu . . . . *University of Pittsburgh*
Christopher Lupke . . . . *Washington State University*
William A. Lyell . . . . *Stanford University*
T. M. McClellan . . . . *University of Edinburgh*
Feng-ying Ming . . . . *California State University, Long Beach*
Thomas Moran . . . . *Middlebury College*
Steven Riep . . . . *Brigham Young University*
Carlos Rojas . . . . *University of Florida*
Kristina M. Torgeson . . . .
Alexandra R. Wagner . . . .
Lingzhen Wang . . . . *Brown University*
Philip F. Williams . . . . *Massey University*
Timothy C. Wong . . . . *Arizona State University*
Xiaobin Yang . . . . *Academia Sinica*
Angelina C. Yee . . . . *Hong Kong University of Science and Technology*
Hu Ying . . . . *University of California, Irvine*
Zhang Jingyuan . . . . *Georgetown University*
Yingjin Zhang . . . . *University of California, San Diego*

Cumulative Index

Dictionary of Literary Biography, Volumes 1-328
Dictionary of Literary Biography Yearbook, 1980-2002
Dictionary of Literary Biography Documentary Series, Volumes 1-19
Concise Dictionary of American Literary Biography, Volumes 1-7
Concise Dictionary of British Literary Biography, Volumes 1-8
Concise Dictionary of World Literary Biography, Volumes 1-4

Cumulative Index

DLB before number: *Dictionary of Literary Biography,* Volumes 1-328
Y before number: *Dictionary of Literary Biography Yearbook,* 1980-2002
DS before number: *Dictionary of Literary Biography Documentary Series,* Volumes 1-19
CDALB before number: *Concise Dictionary of American Literary Biography,* Volumes 1-7
CDBLB before number: *Concise Dictionary of British Literary Biography,* Volumes 1-8
CDWLB before number: *Concise Dictionary of World Literary Biography,* Volumes 1-4

A

Aakjær, Jeppe 1866-1930 .... DLB-214

Aarestrup, Emil 1800-1856 .... DLB-300

Abbey, Edward 1927-1989 .... DLB-256, 275

Abbey, Edwin Austin 1852-1911 .... DLB-188

Abbey, Maj. J. R. 1894-1969 .... DLB-201

Abbey Press DLB-49

The Abbey Theatre and Irish Drama, 1900-1945 .... DLB-10

Abbot, Willis J. 1863-1934 .... DLB-29

Abbott, Edwin A. 1838-1926 .... DLB-178

Abbott, Jacob 1803-1879 .... DLB-1, 42, 243

Abbott, Lee K. 1947- DLB-130

Abbott, Lyman 1835-1922 .... DLB-79

Abbott, Robert S. 1868-1940 .... DLB-29, 91

'Abd al-Hamid al-Katib circa 689-750 .... DLB-311

Abe Kōbō 1924-1993 .... DLB-182

Abelaira, Augusto 1926- DLB-287

Abelard, Peter circa 1079-1142? DLB-115, 208

Abelard-Schuman DLB-46

Abell, Arunah S. 1806-1888 .... DLB-43

Abell, Kjeld 1901-1961 .... DLB-214

Abercrombie, Lascelles 1881-1938 .... DLB-19

The Friends of the Dymock Poets Y-00

Aberdeen University Press Limited DLB-106

Abish, Walter 1931- DLB-130, 227

Ablesimov, Aleksandr Onisimovich 1742-1783 .... DLB-150

Abraham à Sancta Clara 1644-1709 ...... DLB-168

Abrahams, Peter 1919- DLB-117, 225; CDWLB-3

Abramov, Fedor Aleksandrovich 1920-1983 .... DLB-302

Abrams, M. H. 1912- DLB-67

Abramson, Jesse 1904-1979 .... DLB-241

Abrogans circa 790-800 .... DLB-148

Abschatz, Hans Aßmann von 1646-1699 .... DLB-168

Abse, Dannie 1923- DLB-27, 245

Abu al-'Atahiyah 748-825? DLB-311

Abu Nuwas circa 757-814 or 815 .... DLB-311

Abu Tammam circa 805-845 .... DLB-311

Abutsu-ni 1221-1283 .... DLB-203

Academy Chicago Publishers DLB-46

Accius circa 170 B.C.-circa 80 B.C. DLB-211

"An account of the death of the Chevalier de La Barre," Voltaire DLB-314

Accrocca, Elio Filippo 1923-1996 .... DLB-128

Ace Books DLB-46

Achebe, Chinua 1930- DLB-117; CDWLB-3

Achtenberg, Herbert 1938- DLB-124

Ackerman, Diane 1948- DLB-120

Ackroyd, Peter 1949- DLB-155, 231

Acorn, Milton 1923-1986 .... DLB-53

Acosta, José de 1540-1600 .... DLB-318

Acosta, Oscar Zeta 1935?-1974? DLB-82

Acosta Torres, José 1925- DLB-209

Actors Theatre of Louisville DLB-7

Adair, Gilbert 1944- DLB-194

Adair, James 1709?-1783? DLB-30

Aðalsteinn Kristmundsson (see Steinn Steinarr)

Adam, Graeme Mercer 1839-1912 .... DLB-99

Adam, Robert Borthwick, II 1863-1940 .... DLB-187

Adame, Leonard 1947- DLB-82

Adameșteanu, Gabriel 1942- DLB-232

Adamic, Louis 1898-1951 .... DLB-9

Adamov, Arthur Surenovitch 1908-1970 .... DLB-321

Adamovich, Georgii 1894-1972 .... DLB-317

Adams, Abigail 1744-1818 .... DLB-183, 200

Adams, Alice 1926-1999 .... DLB-234; Y-86

Adams, Bertha Leith (Mrs. Leith Adams, Mrs. R. S. de Courcy Laffan) 1837?-1912 .... DLB-240

Adams, Brooks 1848-1927 .... DLB-47

Adams, Charles Francis, Jr. 1835-1915 .... DLB-47

Adams, Douglas 1952-2001 .... DLB-261; Y-83

Adams, Franklin P. 1881-1960 .... DLB-29

Adams, Glenda 1939- DLB-325

Adams, Hannah 1755-1832 .... DLB-200

Adams, Henry 1838-1918 ...... DLB-12, 47, 189

Adams, Herbert Baxter 1850-1901 .... DLB-47

Adams, James Truslow 1878-1949 .... DLB-17; DS-17

Adams, John 1735-1826 .... DLB-31, 183

Adams, John Quincy 1767-1848 .... DLB-37

Adams, Léonie 1899-1988 .... DLB-48

Adams, Levi 1802-1832 .... DLB-99

Adams, Richard 1920- DLB-261

Adams, Samuel 1722-1803 .... DLB-31, 43

Adams, Sarah Fuller Flower 1805-1848 .... DLB-199

Adams, Thomas 1582/1583-1652 .... DLB-151

Adams, William Taylor 1822-1897 .... DLB-42

J. S. and C. Adams [publishing house] DLB-49

Adamson, Harold 1906-1980 .... DLB-265

Adamson, Sir John 1867-1950 .... DLB-98

Adamson, Robert 1943- DLB-289

Adcock, Arthur St. John 1864-1930 .... DLB-135

Adcock, Betty 1938- DLB-105

"Certain Gifts" DLB-105

Tribute to James Dickey Y-97

Adcock, Fleur 1934- DLB-40

Addams, Jane 1860-1935 .... DLB-303

Addison, Joseph 1672-1719 .... DLB-101; CDBLB-2

Ade, George 1866-1944 .... DLB-11, 25

Adeler, Max (see Clark, Charles Heber)

Adlard, Mark 1932- DLB-261

Adler, Richard 1921- DLB-265

Adonias Filho (Adonias Aguiar Filho) 1915-1990 .... DLB-145, 307

Adorno, Theodor W. 1903-1969 .... DLB-242

Adoum, Jorge Enrique 1926- DLB-283

349

Cumulative Index

Advance Publishing Company DLB-49

Ady, Endre 1877-1919. . . . . . DLB-215; CDWLB-4

AE 1867-1935 . . . . DLB-19; CDBLB-5

Ælfric circa 955-circa 1010 . . . . DLB-146

Aeschines circa 390 B.C.-circa 320 B.C. DLB-176

Aeschylus 525-524 B.C.-456-455 B.C.
. . . . .DLB-176; CDWLB-1

Aesthetic Papers DLB-1

Aesthetics
   Eighteenth-Century Aesthetic
     Theories DLB-31

African Literature
   Letter from Khartoum Y-90

African American
   Afro-American Literary Critics:
     An Introduction DLB-33

   The Black Aesthetic: Background DS-8

   The Black Arts Movement,
     by Larry Neal DLB-38

   Black Theaters and Theater Organizations
     in America, 1961-1982:
     A Research List DLB-38

   Black Theatre: A Forum [excerpts] . . . DLB-38

   Callaloo [journal] Y-87

   Community and Commentators:
     Black Theatre and Its Critics DLB-38

   The Emergence of Black
     Women Writers DS-8

   The Hatch-Billops Collection. DLB-76

   A Look at the Contemporary Black
     Theatre Movement DLB-38

   The Moorland-Spingarn Research
     Center DLB-76

   "The Negro as a Writer," by
     G. M. McClellan DLB-50

   "Negro Poets and Their Poetry," by
     Wallace Thurman DLB-50

   Olaudah Equiano and Unfinished Journeys:
     The Slave-Narrative Tradition and
     Twentieth-Century Continuities, by
     Paul Edwards and Pauline T.
     Wangman DLB-117

   PHYLON (Fourth Quarter, 1950),
     The Negro in Literature:
     The Current Scene DLB-76

   The Schomburg Center for Research
     in Black Culture DLB-76

   Three Documents [poets], by John
     Edward Bruce DLB-50

After Dinner Opera Company Y-92

Agassiz, Elizabeth Cary 1822-1907 . . . . . . DLB-189

Agassiz, Louis 1807-1873 . . . . DLB-1, 235

Agee, James
   1909-1955 . . . . DLB-2, 26, 152; CDALB-1

   The Agee Legacy: A Conference at
     the University of Tennessee
     at Knoxville Y-89

Aguilera Malta, Demetrio 1909-1981 . . . . DLB-145

Aguirre, Isidora 1919- DLB-305

Agustini, Delmira 1886-1914 . . . . DLB-290

Ahlin, Lars 1915-1997 . . . . DLB-257

Ai 1947- DLB-120

Ai Wu 1904-1992 . . . . DLB-328

Aichinger, Ilse 1921- DLB-85, 299

Aickman, Robert 1914-1981 . . . . DLB-261

Aidoo, Ama Ata 1942- DLB-117; CDWLB-3

Aiken, Conrad
   1889-1973 . . . . DLB-9, 45, 102; CDALB-5

Aiken, Joan 1924-2004 . . . . DLB-161

Aikin, Lucy 1781-1864 . . . . DLB-144, 163

Ainsworth, William Harrison
   1805-1882 . . . . DLB-21

Aïssé, Charlotte-Elizabeth 1694?-1733 . . . DLB-313

Aistis, Jonas 1904-1973 . . . . . DLB-220; CDWLB-4

Aitken, Adam 1960- DLB-325

Aitken, George A. 1860-1917 . . . . DLB-149

Robert Aitken [publishing house] DLB-49

Aitmatov, Chingiz 1928- DLB-302

Akenside, Mark 1721-1770 . . . . DLB-109

Akhmatova, Anna Andreevna
   1889-1966 . . . . DLB-295

Akins, Zoë 1886-1958 . . . . DLB-26

Aksakov, Ivan Sergeevich 1823-1826 . . . . .DLB-277

Aksakov, Sergei Timofeevich
   1791-1859 . . . . DLB-198

Aksyonov, Vassily 1932- DLB-302

Akunin, Boris (Grigorii Shalvovich
   Chkhartishvili) 1956- DLB-285

Akutagawa Ryūnosuke 1892-1927 . . . . . . DLB-180

Alabaster, William 1568-1640 . . . . DLB-132

Alain de Lille circa 1116-1202/1203 . . . . . DLB-208

Alain-Fournier 1886-1914 . . . . DLB-65

Alanus de Insulis (see Alain de Lille)

Alarcón, Francisco X. 1954- DLB-122

Alarcón, Justo S. 1930- DLB-209

Alba, Nanina 1915-1968 . . . . DLB-41

Albee, Edward 1928- . . . DLB-7, 266; CDALB-1

Albert, Octavia 1853-ca. 1889 . . . . DLB-221

Albert the Great circa 1200-1280 . . . . DLB-115

Alberti, Rafael 1902-1999 . . . . DLB-108

Albertinus, Aegidius circa 1560-1620 . . . . DLB-164

Alcaeus born circa 620 B.C. DLB-176

Alcoforado, Mariana, the Portuguese Nun
   1640-1723 . . . . DLB-287

Alcott, Amos Bronson
   1799-1888 . . . . DLB-1, 223; DS-5

Alcott, Louisa May 1832-1888
   . . . DLB-1, 42, 79, 223, 239; DS-14; CDALB-3

Alcott, William Andrus 1798-1859 . . . . DLB-1, 243

Alcuin circa 732-804 . . . . DLB-148

Aldana, Francisco de 1537-1578 . . . . DLB-318

Aldanov, Mark (Mark Landau)
   1886-1957 . . . . DLB-317

Alden, Henry Mills 1836-1919 . . . . DLB-79

Alden, Isabella 1841-1930 . . . . DLB-42

John B. Alden [publishing house] DLB-49

Alden, Beardsley, and Company DLB-49

Aldington, Richard
   1892-1962 . . . . .DLB-20, 36, 100, 149

Aldis, Dorothy 1896-1966 . . . . DLB-22

Aldis, H. G. 1863-1919 . . . . DLB-184

Aldiss, Brian W. 1925- DLB-14, 261, 271

Aldrich, Thomas Bailey
   1836-1907 . . . . .DLB-42, 71, 74, 79

Alegría, Ciro 1909-1967 . . . . DLB-113

Alegría, Claribel 1924- DLB-145, 283

Aleixandre, Vicente 1898-1984 . . . . DLB-108

Aleksandravičius, Jonas (see Aistis, Jonas)

Aleksandrov, Aleksandr Andreevich
   (see Durova, Nadezhda Andreevna)

Alekseeva, Marina Anatol'evna
   (see Marinina, Aleksandra)

d'Alembert, Jean Le Rond 1717-1783 . . . . DLB-313

Alencar, José de 1829-1877 . . . . DLB-307

Aleramo, Sibilla (Rena Pierangeli Faccio)
   1876-1960 . . . . DLB-114, 264

Aleshkovsky, Petr Markovich 1957- . . . DLB-285

Aleshkovsky, Yuz 1929- DLB-317

Alexander, Cecil Frances 1818-1895 . . . . . DLB-199

Alexander, Charles 1868-1923 . . . . DLB-91

Charles Wesley Alexander
   [publishing house] DLB-49

Alexander, James 1691-1756 . . . . DLB-24

Alexander, Lloyd 1924- DLB-52

Alexander, Meena 1951- DLB-323

Alexander, Sir William, Earl of Stirling
   1577?-1640 . . . . DLB-121

Alexie, Sherman 1966- DLB-175, 206, 278

Alexis, Willibald 1798-1871 . . . . DLB-133

Alf laylah wa laylah
   ninth century onward DLB-311

Alfred, King 849-899 . . . . DLB-146

Alger, Horatio, Jr. 1832-1899 . . . . DLB-42

Algonquin Books of Chapel Hill DLB-46

Algren, Nelson
   1909-1981 . . . . . . .DLB-9; Y-81, 82; CDALB-1

   Nelson Algren: An International
     Symposium Y-00

Ali, Agha Shahid 1949-2001 . . . . DLB-323

Ali, Ahmed 1908-1994 . . . . DLB-323

Ali, Monica 1967- DLB-323

'Ali ibn Abi Talib circa 600-661 . . . . DLB-311

Aljamiado Literature DLB-286

Allan, Andrew 1907-1974 . . . . DLB-88

Allan, Ted 1916-1995 . . . . DLB-68

Allbeury, Ted 1917- DLB-87

Alldritt, Keith 1935- DLB-14

Allen, Dick 1939- DLB-282

Allen, Ethan 1738-1789 . . . . .DLB-31

Allen, Frederick Lewis 1890-1954 . . . . . . .DLB-137

Allen, Gay Wilson 1903-1995 . . . . . DLB-103; Y-95

Allen, George 1808-1876 . . . . .DLB-59

Allen, Grant 1848-1899 . . . . DLB-70, 92, 178

Allen, Henry W. 1912-1991. . . . . .Y-85

Allen, Hervey 1889-1949. . . . . . . .DLB-9, 45, 316

Allen, James 1739-1808 . . . . .DLB-31

Allen, James Lane 1849-1925. . . . . .DLB-71

Allen, Jay Presson 1922- DLB-26

John Allen and Company DLB-49

Allen, Paula Gunn 1939- DLB-175

Allen, Samuel W. 1917- DLB-41

Allen, Woody 1935- DLB-44

George Allen [publishing house] DLB-106

George Allen and Unwin Limited DLB-112

Allende, Isabel 1942- DLB-145; CDWLB-3

Alline, Henry 1748-1784 . . . . .DLB-99

Allingham, Margery 1904-1966. . . . . .DLB-77

The Margery Allingham Society. Y-98

Allingham, William 1824-1889 . . . . .DLB-35

W. L. Allison [publishing house] DLB-49

The *Alliterative Morte Arthure and the Stanzaic Morte Arthur* circa 1350-1400 . . . . .DLB-146

Allott, Kenneth 1912-1973 . . . . .DLB-20

Allston, Washington 1779-1843 . . . . . . .DLB-1, 235

Almeida, Manuel Antônio de 1831-1861 . . . . .DLB-307

John Almon [publishing house] DLB-154

Alonzo, Dámaso 1898-1990. . . . . .DLB-108

Alsop, George 1636-post 1673 . . . . .DLB-24

Alsop, Richard 1761-1815 . . . . .DLB-37

Henry Altemus and Company. DLB-49

Altenberg, Peter 1885-1919 . . . . .DLB-81

Althusser, Louis 1918-1990 . . . . .DLB-242

Altolaguirre, Manuel 1905-1959 . . . . .DLB-108

Aluko, T. M. 1918- DLB-117

Alurista 1947- DLB-82

Alvarez, A. 1929- DLB-14, 40

Alvarez, Julia 1950- DLB-282

Alvaro, Corrado 1895-1956. . . . . .DLB-264

Alver, Betti 1906-1989 . . . . . .DLB-220; CDWLB-4

Amadi, Elechi 1934- DLB-117

Amado, Jorge 1912-2001 . . . . .DLB-113

Amalrik, Andrei 1938-1980 . . . . .DLB-302

Ambler, Eric 1909-1998 . . . . .DLB-77

The Library of America. DLB-46

The Library of America: An Assessment After Two Decades Y-02

America: or, A Poem on the Settlement of the British Colonies, by Timothy Dwight DLB-37

American Bible Society Department of Library, Archives, and Institutional Research Y-97

American Conservatory Theatre DLB-7

American Culture American Proletarian Culture: The Twenties and Thirties DS-11

Studies in American Jewish Literature Y-02

The American Library in Paris Y-93

American Literature The Literary Scene and Situation and . . . (Who Besides Oprah) Really Runs American Literature? Y-99

Who Owns American Literature, by Henry Taylor Y-94

Who Runs American Literature? Y-94

American News Company. DLB-49

A Century of Poetry, a Lifetime of Collecting: J. M. Edelstein's Collection of Twentieth-Century American Poetry Y-02

The American Poets' Corner: The First Three Years (1983-1986) Y-86

American Publishing Company. DLB-49

American Spectator [Editorial] Rationale From the Initial Issue of the American Spectator (November 1932). DLB-137

American Stationers' Company. DLB-49

The American Studies Association of Norway. Y-00

American Sunday-School Union DLB-49

American Temperance Union DLB-49

American Tract Society. DLB-49

The American Trust for the British Library . . .Y-96

American Writers' Congress 25-27 April 1935 . . . . .DLB-303

American Writers Congress The American Writers Congress (9-12 October 1981) Y-81

The American Writers Congress: A Report on Continuing Business Y-81

Ames, Fisher 1758-1808. . . . . .DLB-37

Ames, Mary Clemmer 1831-1884 . . . . .DLB-23

Ames, William 1576-1633 . . . . .DLB-281

Amfiteatrov, Aleksandr 1862-1938 . . . . . . .DLB-317

Amiel, Henri-Frédéric 1821-1881. . . . . . . .DLB-217

Amini, Johari M. 1935- DLB-41

Amis, Kingsley 1922-1995 . . .DLB-15, 27, 100, 139, 326; Y-96; CDBLB-7

Amis, Martin 1949- DLB-14, 194

Ammianus Marcellinus circa A.D. 330-A.D. 395 . . . . .DLB-211

Ammons, A. R. 1926-2001 . . . . .DLB-5, 165

Amory, Thomas 1691?-1788 . . . . .DLB-39

Amsterdam, 1998 Booker Prize winner, Ian McEwan DLB-326

Amyot, Jacques 1513-1593. . . . . .DLB-327

Anand, Mulk Raj 1905-2004 . . . . .DLB-323

Anania, Michael 1939- DLB-193

Anaya, Rudolfo A. 1937- DLB-82, 206, 278

Ancrene Riwle circa 1200-1225 . . . . .DLB-146

Andersch, Alfred 1914-1980 . . . . .DLB-69

Andersen, Benny 1929- DLB-214

Andersen, Hans Christian 1805-1875 . . . .DLB-300

Anderson, Alexander 1775-1870 . . . . .DLB-188

Anderson, David 1929- DLB-241

Anderson, Frederick Irving 1877-1947. . . .DLB-202

Anderson, Jessica 1916- DLB-325

Anderson, Margaret 1886-1973 . . . . .DLB-4, 91

Anderson, Maxwell 1888-1959 . . . . DLB-7, 228

Anderson, Patrick 1915-1979 . . . . .DLB-68

Anderson, Paul Y. 1893-1938 . . . . .DLB-29

Anderson, Poul 1926-2001 . . . . .DLB-8

Tribute to Isaac Asimov Y-92

Anderson, Robert 1750-1830. . . . . .DLB-142

Anderson, Robert 1917- DLB-7

Anderson, Sherwood 1876-1941 . . . . .DLB-4, 9, 86; DS-1; CDALB-4

Andrade, Jorge (Aluísio Jorge Andrade Franco) 1922-1984 . . . . .DLB-307

Andrade, Mario de 1893-1945. . . . . .DLB-307

Andrade, Oswald de (José Oswald de Sousa Andrade) 1890-1954 . . . . .DLB-307

Andreae, Johann Valentin 1586-1654 . . . .DLB-164

Andreas Capellanus fl. circa 1185 .DLB-208

Andreas-Salomé, Lou 1861-1937 . . . . .DLB-66

Andreev, Leonid Nikolaevich 1871-1919 . . . . .DLB-295

Andres, Stefan 1906-1970 . . . . .DLB-69

Andresen, Sophia de Mello Breyner 1919- DLB-287

Andreu, Blanca 1959- DLB-134

Andrewes, Lancelot 1555-1626 . . . . .DLB-151, 172

Andrews, Charles M. 1863-1943 . . . . .DLB-17

Andrews, Miles Peter ?-1814 . . . . .DLB-89

Andrews, Stephen Pearl 1812-1886 . . . . . .DLB-250

Andrian, Leopold von 1875-1951 . . . . .DLB-81

Andrić, Ivo 1892-1975 . . . . . .DLB-147; CDWLB-4

Andrieux, Louis (see Aragon, Louis)

Andrus, Silas, and Son. DLB-49

Andrzejewski, Jerzy 1909-1983 . . . . .DLB-215

Angell, James Burrill 1829-1916 . . . . .DLB-64

Angell, Roger 1920- DLB-171, 185

Angelou, Maya 1928- DLB-38; CDALB-7

Tribute to Julian Mayfield Y-84

Anger, Jane fl. 1589 . . . . .DLB-136

Angers, Félicité (see Conan, Laure)

The Anglo-Saxon Chronicle
circa 890-1154 . . . . DLB-146

Angus and Robertson (UK) Limited DLB-112

Anhalt, Edward 1914-2000. . . . . DLB-26

Anissimov, Myriam 1943- DLB-299

Anker, Nini Roll 1873-1942 . . . . DLB-297

Annenkov, Pavel Vasil'evich
1813?-1887. . . . . DLB-277

Annensky, Innokentii Fedorovich
1855-1909 . . . . DLB-295

Henry F. Anners [publishing house]. DLB-49

Annolied between 1077 and 1081 . . . . DLB-148

Anouilh, Jean 1910-1987. . . . . DLB-321

Anscombe, G. E. M. 1919-2001 . . . . DLB-262

Anselm of Canterbury 1033-1109. . . . . . . DLB-115

Anstey, F. 1856-1934 . . . . DLB-141, 178

'Antarah ('Antar ibn Shaddad al-'Absi)
?-early seventh century?. DLB-311

Anthologizing New Formalism DLB-282

Anthony, Michael 1932- DLB-125

Anthony, Piers 1934- DLB-8

Anthony, Susanna 1726-1791 . . . . DLB-200

Antin, David 1932- DLB-169

Antin, Mary 1881-1949 . . . . DLB-221; Y-84

Anton Ulrich, Duke of Brunswick-Lüneburg
1633-1714. . . . . DLB-168

Antschel, Paul (see Celan, Paul)

Antunes, António Lobo 1942- DLB-287

Anyidoho, Kofi 1947- DLB-157

Anzaldúa, Gloria 1942- DLB-122

Anzengruber, Ludwig 1839-1889 . . . . DLB-129

Apess, William 1798-1839. . . . . DLB-175, 243

Apodaca, Rudy S. 1939- DLB-82

Apollinaire, Guillaume 1880-1918 . . DLB-258, 321

Apollonius Rhodius third century B.C.. . . . DLB-176

Apple, Max 1941- DLB-130

Appelfeld, Aharon 1932- DLB-299

D. Appleton and Company DLB-49

Appleton-Century-Crofts DLB-46

Applewhite, James 1935- DLB-105

Tribute to James Dickey. Y-97

Apple-wood Books DLB-46

April, Jean-Pierre 1948- DLB-251

Apukhtin, Aleksei Nikolaevich
1840-1893 . . . . DLB-277

Apuleius circa A.D. 125-post A.D. 164
. . . . DLB-211; CDWLB-1

Aquin, Hubert 1929-1977 . . . . DLB-53

Aquinas, Thomas 1224/1225-1274 . . . . . . DLB-115

Aragon, Louis 1897-1982 . . . . DLB-72, 258

Aragon, Vernacular Translations in the
Crowns of Castile and 1352-1515 . . . DLB-286

Aralica, Ivan 1930- DLB-181

Aratus of Soli
circa 315 B.C.-circa 239 B.C. DLB-176

Arbasino, Alberto 1930- DLB-196

Arbor House Publishing Company DLB-46

Arbuthnot, John 1667-1735. . . . . DLB-101

Arcadia House DLB-46

Arce, Julio G. (see Ulica, Jorge)

Archer, William 1856-1924. . . . . DLB-10

Archilochhus
mid seventh century B.C.E.. . . . . DLB-176

The Archpoet circa 1130?-? DLB-148

Archpriest Avvakum (Petrovich)
1620?-1682. DLB-150

Arden, John 1930- DLB-13, 245

Arden of Faversham DLB-62

Ardis Publishers Y-89

Ardizzone, Edward 1900-1979 . . . . DLB-160

Arellano, Juan Estevan 1947- DLB-122

The Arena Publishing Company DLB-49

Arena Stage. DLB-7

Arenas, Reinaldo 1943-1990. . . . . DLB-145

Arendt, Hannah 1906-1975 . . . . DLB-242

Arensberg, Ann 1937- Y-82

Arghezi, Tudor 1880-1967 . . . DLB-220; CDWLB-4

Arguedas, José María 1911-1969 . . . . DLB-113

Argüelles, Hugo 1932-2003 . . . . DLB-305

Argueta, Manlio 1936- DLB-145

'Arib al-Ma'muniyah 797-890 . . . . DLB-311

Arias, Ron 1941- DLB-82

Arishima Takeo 1878-1923. . . . . DLB-180

Aristophanes circa 446 B.C.-circa 386 B.C.
. . . . DLB-176; CDWLB-1

Aristotle 384 B.C.-322 B.C.
. . . . DLB-176; CDWLB-1

Ariyoshi Sawako 1931-1984 . . . . DLB-182

Arland, Marcel 1899-1986 . . . . DLB-72

Arlen, Michael 1895-1956 . . . . DLB-36, 77, 162

Arlt, Roberto 1900-1942. . . . . DLB-305

Armah, Ayi Kwei 1939- . . . DLB-117; CDWLB-3

Armantrout, Rae 1947- DLB-193

Der arme Hartmann ?-after 1150 . . . . DLB-148

Armed Services Editions. DLB-46

Armitage, G. E. (Robert Edric) 1956- . . DLB-267

Armstrong, Martin Donisthorpe
1882-1974. . . . . DLB-197

Armstrong, Richard 1903-1986 . . . . DLB-160

Armstrong, Terence Ian Fytton (see Gawsworth, John)

Arnauld, Antoine 1612-1694 . . . . DLB-268

Arndt, Ernst Moritz 1769-1860 . . . . DLB-90

Arnim, Achim von 1781-1831 . . . . DLB-90

Arnim, Bettina von 1785-1859 . . . . DLB-90

Arnim, Elizabeth von (Countess Mary Annette
Beauchamp Russell) 1866-1941 . . . . DLB-197

Arno Press DLB-46

Arnold, Edwin 1832-1904 . . . . DLB-35

Arnold, Edwin L. 1857-1935 . . . . DLB-178

Arnold, Matthew
1822-1888 . . . . DLB-32, 57; CDBLB-4

Preface to *Poems* (1853) DLB-32

Arnold, Thomas 1795-1842 . . . . DLB-55

Edward Arnold [publishing house]. DLB-112

Arnott, Peter 1962- DLB-233

Arnow, Harriette Simpson 1908-1986 . . . . . DLB-6

Arp, Bill (see Smith, Charles Henry)

Arpino, Giovanni 1927-1987. . . . . DLB-177

Arrabal, Fernando 1932- DLB-321

Arrebo, Anders 1587-1637 . . . . DLB-300

Arreola, Juan José 1918-2001 . . . . DLB-113

Arrian circa 89-circa 155. . . . . DLB-176

J. W. Arrowsmith [publishing house] DLB-106

Arrufat, Antón 1935- DLB-305

Art
John Dos Passos: Artist Y-99
The First Post-Impressionist
Exhibition. DS-5
The Omega Workshops. DS-10
The Second Post-Impressionist
Exhibition DS-5

Artaud, Antonin 1896-1948 . . . . DLB-258, 321

Artel, Jorge 1909-1994 . . . . DLB-283

Arthur, Timothy Shay
1809-1885 . . . . DLB-3, 42, 79, 250; DS-13

Artmann, H. C. 1921-2000. . . . . DLB-85

Artsybashev, Mikhail Petrovich
1878-1927. . . . . DLB-295

Arvin, Newton 1900-1963 . . . . DLB-103

Asch, Nathan 1902-1964 . . . . DLB-4, 28

Nathan Asch Remembers Ford Madox
Ford, Sam Roth, and Hart Crane Y-02

Ascham, Roger 1515/1516-1568. . . . . DLB-236

Aseev, Nikolai Nikolaevich
1889-1963 . . . . DLB-295

Ash, John 1948- DLB-40

Ashbery, John 1927- DLB-5, 165; Y-81

Ashbridge, Elizabeth 1713-1755 . . . . DLB-200

Ashburnham, Bertram Lord
1797-1878 . . . . DLB-184

Ashendene Press. DLB-112

Asher, Sandy 1942- Y-83

Ashton, Winifred (see Dane, Clemence)

Asimov, Isaac 1920-1992 . . . . DLB-8; Y-92

Tribute to John Ciardi Y-86

Askew, Anne circa 1521-1546. . . . . DLB-136

Aspazija 1865-1943. . . . . DLB-220; CDWLB-4

Asselin, Olivar 1874-1937 . . . . DLB-92

The Association of American Publishers Y-99

The Association for Documentary Editing. . . . Y-00

The Association for the Study of
    Literature and Environment (ASLE)......Y-99
Astell, Mary 1666-1731 ....DLB-252
Astley, Thea 1925- DLB-289
Astley, William (see Warung, Price)
Asturias, Miguel Ángel
    1899-1974 ....DLB-113, 290; CDWLB-3
Atava, S. (see Terpigorev, Sergei Nikolaevich)
Atheneum Publishers..................DLB-46
Atherton, Gertrude 1857-1948.....DLB-9, 78, 186
Athlone Press......................DLB-112
Atkins, Josiah circa 1755-1781 ....DLB-31
Atkins, Russell 1926- DLB-41
Atkinson, Kate 1951- DLB-267
Atkinson, Louisa 1834-1872............DLB-230
The Atlantic Monthly Press.............DLB-46
Attaway, William 1911-1986............DLB-76
Atwood, Margaret 1939- DLB-53, 251, 326
Aubert, Alvin 1930- DLB-41
Aub, Max 1903-1972..................DLB-322
Aubert de Gaspé, Phillipe-Ignace-François
    1814-1841.......................DLB-99
Aubert de Gaspé, Phillipe-Joseph
    1786-1871.......................DLB-99
Aubigné, Théodore Agrippa d'
    1552-1630......................DLB-327
Aubin, Napoléon 1812-1890 ....DLB-99
Aubin, Penelope
    1685-circa 1731 ....DLB-39
    Preface to *The Life of Charlotta
    du Pont* (1723) DLB-39
Aubrey-Fletcher, Henry Lancelot (see Wade, Henry)
Auchincloss, Louis 1917- DLB-2, 244; Y-80
Auden, W. H.
    1907-1973..........DLB-10, 20; CDBLB-6
Audiberti, Jacques 1899-1965 ....DLB-321
Audio Art in America: A Personal Memoir....Y-85
Audubon, John James 1785-1851........DLB-248
Audubon, John Woodhouse
    1812-1862......................DLB-183
Auerbach, Berthold 1812-1882 ....DLB-133
Auernheimer, Raoul 1876-1948..........DLB-81
Augier, Emile 1820-1889 ....DLB-192
Augustine 354-430...................DLB-115
Aulnoy, Marie-Catherine Le Jumel
    de Barneville, comtesse d'
    1650/1651-1705 ....DLB-268
Aulus Gellius
    circa A.D. 125-circa A.D. 180? DLB-211
Austen, Jane 1775-1817 .....DLB-116; CDBLB-3
Auster, Paul 1947- DLB-227
Austin, Alfred 1835-1913...............DLB-35
Austin, J. L. 1911-1960 ....DLB-262
Austin, Jane Goodwin 1831-1894.........DLB-202
Austin, John 1790-1859 ....DLB-262

Austin, Mary Hunter
    1868-1934 ....DLB-9, 78, 206, 221, 275
Austin, William 1778-1841..............DLB-74
Australie (Emily Manning)
    1845-1890.....................DLB-230
Authors and Newspapers Association DLB-46
Authors' Publishing Company...........DLB-49
Avallone, Michael 1924-1999 .....DLB-306; Y-99
    Tribute to John D. MacDonald........Y-86
    Tribute to Kenneth Millar............Y-83
    Tribute to Raymond Chandler.........Y-88
Avalon Books DLB-46
Avancini, Nicolaus 1611-1686..........DLB-164
Avendaño, Fausto 1941- DLB-82
Averroës 1126-1198..................DLB-115
Avery, Gillian 1926- DLB-161
Avicenna 980-1037..................DLB-115
Ávila Jiménez, Antonio 1898-1965 ......DLB-283
Avison, Margaret 1918-1987............DLB-53
Avon Books........................DLB-46
Avyžius, Jonas 1922-1999 ....DLB-220
Awdry, Wilbert Vere 1911-1997 ....DLB-160
Awoonor, Kofi 1935- DLB-117
Ayala, Francisco 1906- DLB-322
Ayckbourn, Alan 1939- DLB-13, 245
Ayer, A. J. 1910-1989.................DLB-262
Aymé, Marcel 1902-1967...............DLB-72
Aytoun, Sir Robert 1570-1638..........DLB-121
Aytoun, William Edmondstoune
    1813-1865.................DLB-32, 159
Azevedo, Aluísio 1857-1913............DLB-307
Azevedo, Manuel Antônio Álvares de
    1831-1852......................DLB-307
Azorín (José Martínez Ruiz)
    1873-1967......................DLB-322

B

B.V. (see Thomson, James)
Ba Jin 1904-2005 ....DLB-328
Babbitt, Irving 1865-1933 ....DLB-63
Babbitt, Natalie 1932- DLB-52
John Babcock [publishing house]........DLB-49
Babel, Isaak Emmanuilovich
    1894-1940.....................DLB-272
Babits, Mihály 1883-1941 ...DLB-215; CDWLB-4
Babrius circa 150-200.................DLB-176
Babson, Marian 1929- DLB-276
Baca, Jimmy Santiago 1952- DLB-122
Bacchelli, Riccardo 1891-1985..........DLB-264
Bache, Benjamin Franklin 1769-1798......DLB-43
Bachelard, Gaston 1884-1962 ....DLB-296
Bacheller, Irving 1859-1950 ....DLB-202
Bachmann, Ingeborg 1926-1973 ....DLB-85

Bačinskaitė-Bučienė, Salomėja (see Nėris, Salomėja)
Bacon, Delia 1811-1859.............DLB-1, 243
Bacon, Francis
    1561-1626......DLB-151, 236, 252; CDBLB-1
Bacon, Sir Nicholas circa 1510-1579 .....DLB-132
Bacon, Roger circa 1214/1220-1292 .....DLB-115
Bacon, Thomas circa 1700-1768.........DLB-31
Bacovia, George
    1881-1957 ....DLB-220; CDWLB-4
Richard G. Badger and Company........DLB-49
Bagaduce Music Lending Library Y-00
Bage, Robert 1728-1801................DLB-39
Bagehot, Walter 1826-1877 ....DLB-55
Baggesen, Jens 1764-1826 ....DLB-300
Bagley, Desmond 1923-1983 ....DLB-87
Bagley, Sarah G. 1806-1848?..........DLB-239
Bagnold, Enid
    1889-1981 ....DLB-13, 160, 191, 245
Bagryana, Elisaveta
    1893-1991 ....DLB-147; CDWLB-4
Bahr, Hermann 1863-1934 ....DLB-81, 118
Baïf, Jean-Antoine de 1532-1589 ....DLB-327
Bail, Murray 1941- DLB-325
Bailey, Abigail Abbot
    1746-1815......................DLB-200
Bailey, Alfred Goldsworthy 1905-1997 ....DLB-68
Bailey, H. C. 1878-1961................DLB-77
Bailey, Jacob 1731-1808 ....DLB-99
Bailey, Paul 1937- DLB-14, 271
Bailey, Philip James 1816-1902 ....DLB-32
Francis Bailey [publishing house].........DLB-49
Baillargeon, Pierre 1916-1967 ....DLB-88
Baillie, Hugh 1890-1966 ....DLB-29
Baillie, Joanna 1762-1851...............DLB-93
Bailyn, Bernard 1922- DLB-17
Bain, Alexander
    English Composition and Rhetoric (1866)
    [excerpt] DLB-57
Bainbridge, Beryl 1933- DLB-14, 231
Baird, Irene 1901-1981 ....DLB-68
Baker, Augustine 1575-1641.............DLB-151
Baker, Carlos 1909-1987 ....DLB-103
Baker, David 1954-..................DLB-120
Baker, George Pierce 1866-1935 ....DLB-266
Baker, Herschel C. 1914-1990..........DLB-111
Baker, Houston A., Jr. 1943- DLB-67
Baker, Howard
    Tribute to Caroline Gordon Y-81
    Tribute to Katherine Anne Porter Y-80
Baker, Nicholson 1957- DLB-227; Y-00
    Review of Nicholson Baker's *Double Fold:
    Libraries and the Assault on Paper* Y-00
Baker, Samuel White 1821-1893 ....DLB-166
Baker, Thomas 1656-1740 ....DLB-213

Cumulative Index

Walter H. Baker Company
  ("Baker's Plays") DLB-49
The Baker and Taylor Company DLB-49
Bakhtin, Mikhail Mikhailovich
  1895-1975...................... DLB-242
Bakunin, Mikhail Aleksandrovich
  1814-1876...................... DLB-277
Balaban, John 1943- DLB-120
Bald, Wambly 1902-1990............... DLB-4
Balde, Jacob 1604-1668............... DLB-164
Balderston, John 1889-1954 .... DLB-26
Baldwin, James 1924-1987
  ...... DLB-2, 7, 33, 249, 278; Y-87; CDALB-1
Baldwin, Joseph Glover
  1815-1864................. DLB-3, 11, 248
Baldwin, Louisa (Mrs. Alfred Baldwin)
  1845-1925..................... DLB-240
Baldwin, William circa 1515-1563 ...... DLB-132
Richard and Anne Baldwin
  [publishing house] DLB-170
Bale, John 1495-1563 .... DLB-132
Balestrini, Nanni 1935- DLB-128, 196
Balfour, Sir Andrew 1630-1694 .... DLB-213
Balfour, Arthur James 1848-1930....... DLB-190
Balfour, Sir James 1600-1657 .... DLB-213
Ballantine Books................... DLB-46
Ballantyne, R. M. 1825-1894 .... DLB-163
Ballard, J. G. 1930- DLB-14, 207, 261, 319
Ballard, Martha Moore 1735-1812 ...... DLB-200
Ballerini, Luigi 1940- DLB-128
Ballou, Maturin Murray (Lieutenant Murray)
  1820-1895 .... DLB-79, 189
Robert O. Ballou [publishing house] DLB-46
Bal'mont, Konstantin Dmitrievich
  1867-1942 .... DLB-295
Balzac, Guez de 1597?-1654 .... DLB-268
Balzac, Honoré de 1799-1855 .... DLB-119
Bambara, Toni Cade
  1939-1995 .... DLB-38, 218; CDALB-7
Bamford, Samuel 1788-1872 .... DLB-190
A. L. Bancroft and Company DLB-49
Bancroft, George 1800-1891... DLB-1, 30, 59, 243
Bancroft, Hubert Howe 1832-1918....DLB-47, 140
Bandeira, Manuel 1886-1968 .... DLB-307
Bandelier, Adolph F. 1840-1914 .... DLB-186
Bang, Herman 1857-1912 .... DLB-300
Bangs, John Kendrick 1862-1922 ..... DLB-11, 79
Banim, John 1798-1842........DLB-116, 158, 159
Banim, Michael 1796-1874 .... DLB-158, 159
Banks, Iain (M.) 1954- DLB-194, 261
Banks, John circa 1653-1706........... DLB-80
Banks, Russell 1940- DLB-130, 278
Bannerman, Helen 1862-1946 .... DLB-141
Bantam Books..................... DLB-46

Banti, Anna 1895-1985................DLB-177
Banville, John 1945- DLB-14, 271, 326
Banville, Théodore de 1823-1891....... DLB-217
Bao Tianxiao 1876-1973 .... DLB-328
Baraka, Amiri
  1934- DLB-5, 7, 16, 38; DS-8; CDALB-1
Barańczak, Stanisław 1946- DLB-232
Baranskaia, Natal'ia Vladimirovna
  1908- DLB-302
Baratynsky, Evgenii Abramovich
  1800-1844 .... DLB-205
Barba-Jacob, Porfirio 1883-1942........ DLB-283
Barbauld, Anna Laetitia
  1743-1825........... DLB-107, 109, 142, 158
Barbeau, Marius 1883-1969 .... DLB-92
Barber, John Warner 1798-1885 .... DLB-30
Bàrberi Squarotti, Giorgio 1929- DLB-128
Barbey d'Aurevilly, Jules-Amédée
  1808-1889 .... DLB-119
Barbier, Auguste 1805-1882 .... DLB-217
Barbilian, Dan (see Barbu, Ion)
Barbour, John circa 1316-1395 .... DLB-146
Barbour, Ralph Henry 1870-1944........ DLB-22
Barbu, Ion 1895-1961...... DLB-220; CDWLB-4
Barbusse, Henri 1873-1935............ DLB-65
Barclay, Alexander circa 1475-1552 ..... DLB-132
E. E. Barclay and Company DLB-49
C. W. Bardeen [publishing house] DLB-49
Barham, Richard Harris 1788-1845 ..... DLB-159
Barich, Bill 1943- DLB-185
Baring, Maurice 1874-1945........... DLB-34
Baring-Gould, Sabine 1834-1924 ... DLB-156, 190
Barker, A. L. 1918-2002 .... DLB-14, 139
Barker, Clive 1952- DLB-261
Barker, Dudley (see Black, Lionel)
Barker, George 1913-1991 .... DLB-20
Barker, Harley Granville 1877-1946 ...... DLB-10
Barker, Howard 1946- DLB-13, 233
Barker, James Nelson 1784-1858......... DLB-37
Barker, Jane 1652-1727 .... DLB-39, 131
Barker, Lady Mary Anne 1831-1911 .... DLB-166
Barker, Pat 1943- DLB-271, 326
Barker, William circa 1520-after 1576.... DLB-132
Arthur Barker Limited DLB-112
Barkov, Ivan Semenovich 1732-1768..... DLB-150
Barks, Coleman 1937- DLB-5
Barlach, Ernst 1870-1938 .... DLB-56, 118
Barlow, Joel 1754-1812 .... DLB-37
  The Prospect of Peace (1778) DLB-37
Barnard, John 1681-1770 .... DLB-24
Barnard, Marjorie (M. Barnard Eldershaw)
  1897-1987..................... DLB-260

Barnard, Robert 1936- DLB-276
Barne, Kitty (Mary Catherine Barne)
  1883-1957 .... DLB-160
Barnes, Barnabe 1571-1609 .... DLB-132
Barnes, Djuna 1892-1982.... DLB-4, 9, 45; DS-15
Barnes, Jim 1933- DLB-175
Barnes, Julian 1946- DLB-194; Y-93
  Notes for a Checklist of Publications Y-01
Barnes, Margaret Ayer 1886-1967 .... DLB-9
Barnes, Peter 1931- DLB-13, 233
Barnes, William 1801-1886 .... DLB-32
A. S. Barnes and Company DLB-49
Barnes and Noble Books DLB-46
Barnet, Miguel 1940- DLB-145
Barney, Natalie 1876-1972 .... DLB-4; DS-15
Barnfield, Richard 1574-1627 ....DLB-172
Baroja, Pío 1872-1956................ DLB-322
Richard W. Baron [publishing house]..... DLB-46
Barr, Amelia Edith Huddleston
  1831-1919 .... DLB-202, 221
Barr, Robert 1850-1912 ....DLB-70, 92
Barral, Carlos 1928-1989 .... DLB-134
Barrax, Gerald William 1933- DLB-41, 120
Barrès, Maurice 1862-1923............ DLB-123
Barreno, Maria Isabel (see The Three Marias:
  A Landmark Case in Portuguese
  Literary History)
Barrett, Eaton Stannard 1786-1820...... DLB-116
Barrie, J. M.
  1860-1937 ..... DLB-10, 141, 156; CDBLB-5
Barrie and Jenkins DLB-112
Barrio, Raymond 1921- DLB-82
Barrios, Gregg 1945- DLB-122
Barry, Philip 1896-1949 ....DLB-7, 228
Barry, Robertine (see Françoise)
Barry, Sebastian 1955- DLB-245
Barse and Hopkins................... DLB-46
Barstow, Stan 1928- DLB-14, 139, 207
  Tribute to John Braine Y-86
Barth, John 1930- DLB-2, 227
Barthelme, Donald
  1931-1989 ....DLB-2, 234; Y-80, 89
Barthelme, Frederick 1943- DLB-244; Y-85
Barthes, Roland 1915-1980 .... DLB-296
Bartholomew, Frank 1898-1985 ....DLB-127
Bartlett, John 1820-1905............. DLB-1, 235
Bartol, Cyrus Augustus 1813-1900.... DLB-1, 235
Barton, Bernard 1784-1849............. DLB-96
Barton, John ca. 1610-1675 .... DLB-236
Barton, Thomas Pennant 1803-1869 .... DLB-140
Bartram, John 1699-1777 .... DLB-31
Bartram, William 1739-1823........... DLB-37

Barykova, Anna Pavlovna 1839-1893 .... DLB-277

Bashshar ibn Burd circa 714-circa 784 ....DLB-311

Basic Books DLB-46

Basille, Theodore (see Becon, Thomas)

Bass, Rick 1958- DLB-212, 275

Bass, T. J. 1932- Y-81

Bassani, Giorgio 1916-2000 .... DLB-128, 177, 299

Basse, William circa 1583-1653 ....DLB-121

Bassett, John Spencer 1867-1928 ....DLB-17

Bassler, Thomas Joseph (see Bass, T. J.)

Bate, Walter Jackson 1918-1999...... DLB-67, 103

Bateman, Stephen circa 1510-1584.......DLB-136

Christopher Bateman
   [publishing house] DLB-170

Bates, H. E. 1905-1974............DLB-162, 191

Bates, Katharine Lee 1859-1929 ....DLB-71

Batiushkov, Konstantin Nikolaevich
   1787-1855......................DLB-205

B. T. Batsford [publishing house]........DLB-106

Batteux, Charles 1713-1780 ....DLB-313

Battiscombe, Georgina 1905- DLB-155

The Battle of Maldon circa 1000 ....DLB-146

Baudelaire, Charles 1821-1867 ....DLB-217

Baudrillard, Jean 1929- DLB-296

Bauer, Bruno 1809-1882 ....DLB-133

Bauer, Wolfgang 1941- DLB-124

Baum, L. Frank 1856-1919 ....DLB-22

Baum, Vicki 1888-1960 ....DLB-85

Baumbach, Jonathan 1933- Y-80

   Tribute to James Dickey Y-97

   Tribute to Peter Taylor Y-94

Bausch, Robert 1945- DLB-218

Bawden, Nina 1925- DLB-14, 161, 207

Bax, Clifford 1886-1962............ DLB-10, 100

Baxter, Charles 1947- DLB-130

Bayer, Eleanor (see Perry, Eleanor)

Bayer, Konrad 1932-1964 ....DLB-85

Bayle, Pierre 1647-1706.............DLB-268, 313

Bayley, Barrington J. 1937- DLB-261

Baynes, Pauline 1922- DLB-160

Baynton, Barbara 1857-1929 ....DLB-230

Bazin, Hervé (Jean Pierre Marie Hervé-Bazin)
   1911-1996 ....DLB-83

The BBC Four Samuel Johnson Prize
   for Non-fiction......................Y-02

Beach, Sylvia 1887-1962..........DLB-4; DS-15

Beacon Press DLB-49

Beadle and Adams...................DLB-49

Beagle, Peter S. 1939- Y-80

Beal, M. F. 1937- Y-81

Beale, Howard K. 1899-1959 ....DLB-17

Beard, Charles A. 1874-1948 ....DLB-17

Beat Generation (Beats)
   As I See It, by Carolyn Cassady DLB-16

   A Beat Chronology: The First Twenty-five
     Years, 1944-1969................DLB-16

   The Commercialization of the Image
     of Revolt, by Kenneth Rexroth....DLB-16

   Four Essays on the Beat Generation ...DLB-16

   in New York City DLB-237

   in the West DLB-237

   Outlaw Days.....................DLB-16

   Periodicals of....................DLB-16

Beattie, Ann 1947- DLB-218, 278; Y-82

Beattie, James 1735-1803 ....DLB-109

Beatty, Chester 1875-1968 ....DLB-201

Beauchemin, Nérée 1850-1931 ....DLB-92

Beauchemin, Yves 1941- DLB-60

Beaugrand, Honoré 1848-1906 ....DLB-99

Beaulieu, Victor-Lévy 1945- DLB-53

Beaumarchais, Pierre-Augustin Caron de
   1732-1799 ....DLB-313

Beaumer, Mme de ?-1766..............DLB-313

Beaumont, Francis circa 1584-1616
   and Fletcher, John
   1579-1625 .... DLB-58; CDBLB-1

Beaumont, Sir John 1583?-1627........DLB-121

Beaumont, Joseph 1616-1699..........DLB-126

Beauvoir, Simone de 1908-1986..... DLB-72; Y-86

   Personal Tribute to Simone de Beauvoir Y-86

Beaver, Bruce 1928- DLB-289

Becher, Ulrich 1910-1990...............DLB-69

Becker, Carl 1873-1945 ....DLB-17

Becker, Jurek 1937-1997 ....DLB-75, 299

Becker, Jurgen 1932- DLB-75

Beckett, Mary 1926- DLB-319

Beckett, Samuel 1906-1989
  .. DLB-13, 15, 233, 319, 321; Y-90; CDBLB-7

Beckford, William 1760-1844........DLB-39, 213

Beckham, Barry 1944- DLB-33

Bećković, Matija 1939- DLB-181

Becon, Thomas circa 1512-1567 ......DLB-136

Becque, Henry 1837-1899 ....DLB-192

Beddoes, Thomas 1760-1808..........DLB-158

Beddoes, Thomas Lovell 1803-1849 .....DLB-96

Bede circa 673-735 ....DLB-146

Bedford-Jones, H. 1887-1949 ....DLB-251

Bedregal, Yolanda 1913-1999..........DLB-283

Beebe, William 1877-1962 ....DLB-275

Beecher, Catharine Esther
   1800-1878 ....DLB-1, 243

Beecher, Henry Ward
   1813-1887 ....DLB-3, 43, 250

Beer, George L. 1872-1920 ....DLB-47

Beer, Johann 1655-1700 ....DLB-168

Beer, Patricia 1919-1999 ....DLB-40

Beerbohm, Max 1872-1956 .... DLB-34, 100

Beer-Hofmann, Richard 1866-1945.......DLB-81

Beers, Henry A. 1847-1926 ....DLB-71

S. O. Beeton [publishing house].........DLB-106

Begley, Louis 1933- DLB-299

Bégon, Elisabeth 1696-1755..............DLB-99

Behan, Brendan
   1923-1964 ....DLB-13, 233; CDBLB-7

Behn, Aphra 1640?-1689........ DLB-39, 80, 131

Behn, Harry 1898-1973 ....DLB-61

Behrman, S. N. 1893-1973 .... DLB-7, 44

Beklemishev, Iurii Solomonvich
   (see Krymov, Iurii Solomonovich)

Belaney, Archibald Stansfeld (see Grey Owl)

Belasco, David 1853-1931 ....DLB-7

Clarke Belford and Company DLB-49

Belgian Luxembourg American Studies
   Association Y-01

Belinsky, Vissarion Grigor'evich
   1811-1848 ....DLB-198

Belitt, Ben 1911-2003....................DLB-5

Belknap, Jeremy 1744-1798 .... DLB-30, 37

Bell, Adrian 1901-1980 ....DLB-191

Bell, Clive 1881-1964. .... DS-10

Bell, Daniel 1919- DLB-246

Bell, Gertrude Margaret Lowthian
   1868-1926 ....DLB-174

Bell, James Madison 1826-1902.........DLB-50

Bell, Madison Smartt 1957- DLB-218, 278

   Tribute to Andrew Nelson Lytle Y-95

   Tribute to Peter Taylor Y-94

Bell, Marvin 1937- DLB-5

Bell, Millicent 1919- DLB-111

Bell, Quentin 1910-1996 ....DLB-155

Bell, Vanessa 1879-1961................ DS-10

George Bell and Sons.................DLB-106

Robert Bell [publishing house]..........DLB-49

Bellamy, Edward 1850-1898 ....DLB-12

Bellamy, Joseph 1719-1790..............DLB-31

John Bellamy [publishing house] DLB-170

La Belle Assemblée 1806-1837 ....DLB-110

Bellezza, Dario 1944-1996 ....DLB-128

Belli, Carlos Germán 1927- DLB-290

Belli, Gioconda 1948- DLB-290

Belloc, Hilaire 1870-1953 .... DLB-19, 100, 141, 174

Belloc, Madame (see Parkes, Bessie Rayner)

Bellonci, Maria 1902-1986.............DLB-196

Bellow, Saul 1915-2005
   ....DLB-2, 28, 299; Y-82;
                  DS-3; CDALB-1

   Tribute to Isaac Bashevis Singer Y-91

Belmont Productions DLB-46

Belov, Vasilii Ivanovich 1932- DLB-302
Bels, Alberts 1938- DLB-232
Belševica, Vizma 1931- ... DLB-232; CDWLB-4
Bely, Andrei 1880-1934 .... DLB-295
Bemelmans, Ludwig 1898-1962 .... DLB-22
Bemis, Samuel Flagg 1891-1973 .... DLB-17
William Bemrose [publishing house] DLB-106
Ben no Naishi 1228?-1271?. DLB-203
Benchley, Robert 1889-1945. .... DLB-11
Bencúr, Matej (see Kukučin, Martin)
Benedetti, Mario 1920- DLB-113
Benedict, Pinckney 1964- DLB-244
Benedict, Ruth 1887-1948............. DLB-246
Benedictus, David 1938- DLB-14
Benedikt Gröndal 1826-1907 .... DLB-293
Benedikt, Michael 1935- DLB-5
Benediktov, Vladimir Grigor'evich
  1807-1873..................... DLB-205
Benét, Stephen Vincent
  1898-1943 .... DLB-4, 48, 102, 249
  Stephen Vincent Benét Centenary Y-97
Benét, William Rose 1886-1950 .... DLB-45
Benford, Gregory 1941- Y-82
Benítez, Sandra 1941- DLB-292
Benjamin, Park 1809-1864 .... DLB-3, 59, 73, 250
Benjamin, Peter (see Cunningham, Peter)
Benjamin, S. G. W. 1837-1914 .... DLB-189
Benjamin, Walter 1892-1940 .... DLB-242
Benlowes, Edward 1602-1676.......... DLB-126
Benn, Gottfried 1886-1956............. DLB-56
Benn Brothers Limited DLB-106
Bennett, Alan 1934- DLB-310
Bennett, Arnold
  1867-1931.... DLB-10, 34, 98, 135; CDBLB-5
  The Arnold Bennett Society............ Y-98
Bennett, Charles 1899-1995 .... DLB-44
Bennett, Emerson 1822-1905 .... DLB-202
Bennett, Gwendolyn 1902-1981 .... DLB-51
Bennett, Hal 1930- DLB-33
Bennett, James Gordon 1795-1872 ...... DLB-43
Bennett, James Gordon, Jr. 1841-1918 .... DLB-23
Bennett, John 1865-1956 .... DLB-42
Bennett, Louise 1919- DLB-117; CDWLB-3
Benni, Stefano 1947- DLB-196
Benoist, Françoise-Albine Puzin de
  La Martinière 1731-1809 .... DLB-313
Benoit, Jacques 1941- DLB-60
Benson, A. C. 1862-1925 .... DLB-98
Benson, E. F. 1867-1940 .... DLB-135, 153
  The E. F. Benson Society............. Y-98
  The Tilling Society.................. Y-98
Benson, Jackson J. 1930- DLB-111

Benson, Robert Hugh 1871-1914 .... DLB-153
Benson, Stella 1892-1933 .... DLB-36, 162
Bent, James Theodore 1852-1897........DLB-174
Bent, Mabel Virginia Anna ?-?..........DLB-174
Bentham, Jeremy 1748-1832.... DLB-107, 158, 252
Bentley, E. C. 1875-1956............... DLB-70
Bentley, Phyllis 1894-1977 .... DLB-191
Bentley, Richard 1662-1742 .... DLB-252
Richard Bentley [publishing house] DLB-106
Benton, Robert 1932- DLB-44
Benziger Brothers DLB-49
Beowulf circa 900-1000 or 790-825
  .... DLB-146; CDBLB-1
Berberova, Nina 1901-1993 .... DLB-317
Berent, Wacław 1873-1940............ DLB-215
Beresford, Anne 1929- DLB-40
Beresford, John Davys
  1873-1947............... DLB-162, 178, 197
  "Experiment in the Novel" (1929)
  [excerpt].................... DLB-36
Beresford-Howe, Constance 1922- DLB-88
R. G. Berford Company............... DLB-49
Berg, Elizabeth 1948- DLB-292
Berg, Stephen 1934- DLB-5
Bergengruen, Werner 1892-1964 .... DLB-56
Berger, John 1926- DLB-14, 207, 319, 326
Berger, Meyer 1898-1959 .... DLB-29
Berger, Thomas 1924- DLB-2; Y-80
  A Statement by Thomas Berger......... Y-80
Bergman, Hjalmar 1883-1931.......... DLB-259
Bergman, Ingmar 1918- DLB-257
Berkeley, Anthony 1893-1971.......... DLB-77
Berkeley, George 1685-1753 .... DLB-31, 101, 252
The Berkley Publishing Corporation DLB-46
Berkman, Alexander 1870-1936 .... DLB-303
Berlin, Irving 1888-1989.............. DLB-265
Berlin, Lucia 1936- DLB-130
Berman, Marshall 1940- DLB-246
Berman, Sabina 1955- DLB-305
Bernal, Vicente J. 1888-1915........... DLB-82
Bernanos, Georges 1888-1948 .... DLB-72
Bernard, Catherine 1663?-1712........DLB-268
Bernard, Harry 1898-1979 .... DLB-92
Bernard, John 1756-1828 .... DLB-37
Bernard of Chartres circa 1060-1124? ... DLB-115
Bernard of Clairvaux 1090-1153 .... DLB-208
Bernard, Richard 1568-1641/1642 ..... DLB-281
Bernard Silvestris
  fl. circa 1130-1160 .... DLB-208
Bernardin de Saint-Pierre 1737-1814 ..... DLB-313
Bernari, Carlo 1909-1992 ....DLB-177

Bernhard, Thomas
  1931-1989 ....DLB-85, 124; CDWLB-2
Berniéres, Louis de 1954- DLB-271
Bernstein, Charles 1950- DLB-169
Béroalde de Verville, François
  1556-1626 .... DLB-327
Berriault, Gina 1926-1999 .... DLB-130
Berrigan, Daniel 1921- DLB-5
Berrigan, Ted 1934-1983 .... DLB-5, 169
Berry, Wendell 1934- DLB-5, 6, 234, 275
Berryman, John 1914-1972.... DLB-48; CDALB-1
Bersianik, Louky 1930- DLB-60
Berssenbrugge, Mei-mei 1947- DLB-312
Thomas Berthelet [publishing house].....DLB-170
Berto, Giuseppe 1914-1978.............DLB-177
Bertocci, Peter Anthony 1910-1989 ......DLB-279
Bertolucci, Attilio 1911-2000 .... DLB-128
Berton, Pierre 1920-2004 .... DLB-68
Bertrand, Louis "Aloysius" 1807-1841 ....DLB-217
Besant, Sir Walter 1836-1901 ...... DLB-135, 190
Bessa-Luís, Agustina 1922- DLB-287
Bessette, Gerard 1920- DLB-53
Bessie, Alvah 1904-1985.............. DLB-26
Bester, Alfred 1913-1987.............. DLB-8
Besterman, Theodore 1904-1976 .... DLB-201
Beston, Henry (Henry Beston Sheahan)
  1888-1968 ....DLB-275
Best-Seller Lists
  An Assessment.................... Y-84
  What's Really Wrong With
  Bestseller Lists.................. Y-84
Bestuzhev, Aleksandr Aleksandrovich
  (Marlinsky) 1797-1837 .... DLB-198
Bestuzhev, Nikolai Aleksandrovich
  1791-1855..................... DLB-198
Betham-Edwards, Matilda Barbara
  (see Edwards, Matilda Barbara Betham-)
Betjeman, John
  1906-1984 ....DLB-20; Y-84; CDBLB-7
Betocchi, Carlo 1899-1986 .... DLB-128
Bettarini, Mariella 1942- DLB-128
Betts, Doris 1932- DLB-218; Y-82
Beveridge, Albert J. 1862-1927...........DLB-17
Beveridge, Judith 1956- DLB-325
Beverley, Robert circa 1673-1722 ..... DLB-24, 30
Bevilacqua, Alberto 1934- DLB-196
Bevington, Louisa Sarah 1845-1895..... DLB-199
Beyle, Marie-Henri (see Stendhal)
Bèze, Théodore de (Theodore Beza)
  1519-1605 .... DLB-327
Bhatt, Sujata 1956- DLB-323
Białoszewski, Miron 1922-1983 .... DLB-232
Bianco, Margery Williams 1881-1944 ... DLB-160
Bibaud, Adèle 1854-1941 .... DLB-92

Bibaud, Michel 1782-1857 .... DLB-99

Bibliography
  Bibliographical and Textual Scholarship
    Since World War II. Y-89
  Center for Bibliographical Studies and
    Research at the University of
    California, Riverside. Y-91
  The Great Bibliographers Series Y-93
  Primary Bibliography: A Retrospective. ... Y-95

Bichsel, Peter 1935- DLB-75

Bickerstaff, Isaac John 1733-circa 1808 .... DLB-89

Drexel Biddle [publishing house] DLB-49

Bidermann, Jacob
  1577 or 1578-1639 .... DLB-164

Bidwell, Walter Hilliard 1798-1881 .... DLB-79

Biehl, Charlotta Dorothea 1731-1788 ..... DLB-300

Bienek, Horst 1930-1990 .... DLB-75

Bierbaum, Otto Julius 1865-1910 .... DLB-66

Bierce, Ambrose 1842-1914?
    . . . . . . DLB-11, 12, 23, 71, 74, 186; CDALB-3

Bigelow, William F. 1879-1966 .... DLB-91

Biggers, Earl Derr 1884-1933 .... DLB-306

Biggle, Lloyd, Jr. 1923-2002 .... DLB-8

Bigiaretti, Libero 1905-1993 .... DLB-177

Bigland, Eileen 1898-1970 .... DLB-195

Biglow, Hosea (see Lowell, James Russell)

Bigongiari, Piero 1914-1997 .... DLB-128

Bilac, Olavo 1865-1918 .... DLB-307

Bilenchi, Romano 1909-1989 .... DLB-264

Billinger, Richard 1890-1965 .... DLB-124

Billings, Hammatt 1818-1874 .... DLB-188

Billings, John Shaw 1898-1975 .... DLB-137

Billings, Josh (see Shaw, Henry Wheeler)

Binchy, Maeve 1940- DLB-319

Binding, Rudolf G. 1867-1938 .... DLB-66

Bing Xin 1900-1999 .... DLB-328

Bingay, Malcolm 1884-1953 .... DLB-241

Bingham, Caleb 1757-1817 .... DLB-42

Bingham, George Barry 1906-1988 ..... DLB-127

Bingham, Sallie 1937- DLB-234

William Bingley [publishing house] DLB-154

Binyon, Laurence 1869-1943 .... DLB-19

Biographia Brittanica DLB-142

Biography
  Biographical Documents Y-84, 85
  A Celebration of Literary Biography Y-98
  Conference on Modern Biography Y-85
  The Cult of Biography
    Excerpts from the Second Folio Debate:
    "Biographies are generally a disease of
    English Literature" Y-86
  New Approaches to Biography: Challenges
    from Critical Theory, USC Conference
    on Literary Studies, 1990 .... Y-90

"The New Biography," by Virginia Woolf,
  New York Herald Tribune,
  30 October 1927 .... DLB-149

"The Practice of Biography," in *The English
  Sense of Humour and Other Essays*, by
  Harold Nicolson DLB-149

"Principles of Biography," in *Elizabethan
  and Other Essays*, by Sidney Lee ... DLB-149

Remarks at the Opening of "The Biographical
  Part of Literature" Exhibition, by
  William R. Cagle Y-98

Survey of Literary Biographies Y-00

A Transit of Poets and Others: American
  Biography in 1982 .... Y-82

The Year in Literary
  Biography Y-83–01

Biography, The Practice of:
  An Interview with B. L. Reid Y-83
  An Interview with David Herbert Donald ... Y-87
  An Interview with Humphrey Carpenter Y-84
  An Interview with Joan Mellen Y-94
  An Interview with John Caldwell Guilds Y-92
  An Interview with William Manchester ... Y-85

John Bioren [publishing house] DLB-49

Bioy Casares, Adolfo 1914-1999 .... DLB-113

Bird, Isabella Lucy 1831-1904 .... DLB-166

Bird, Robert Montgomery 1806-1854 .... DLB-202

Bird, William 1888-1963 .... DLB-4; DS-15

The Cost of the *Cantos*: William Bird
  to Ezra Pound Y-01

Birken, Sigmund von 1626-1681 .... DLB-164

Birney, Earle 1904-1995 .... DLB-88

Birrell, Augustine 1850-1933 .... DLB-98

Bisher, Furman 1918- DLB-171

Bishop, Elizabeth
  1911-1979 .... DLB-5, 169; CDALB-6
  The Elizabeth Bishop Society Y-01

Bishop, John Peale 1892-1944 .... DLB-4, 9, 45

Bismarck, Otto von 1815-1898 .... DLB-129

Bisset, Robert 1759-1805 .... DLB-142

Bissett, Bill 1939- DLB-53

Bitov, Andrei Georgievich 1937- DLB-302

Bitzius, Albert (see Gotthelf, Jeremias)

Bjørnboe, Jens 1920-1976 .... DLB-297

Bjørnvig, Thorkild 1918- DLB-214

Black, David (D. M.) 1941- DLB-40

Black, Gavin (Oswald Morris Wynd)
  1913-1998 .... DLB-276

Black, Lionel (Dudley Barker)
  1910-1980 .... DLB-276

Black, Winifred 1863-1936 .... DLB-25

Walter J. Black [publishing house] DLB-46

Blackamore, Arthur 1679-? DLB-24, 39

Blackburn, Alexander L. 1929- Y-85

Blackburn, John 1923-1993 .... DLB-261

Blackburn, Paul 1926-1971 .... DLB-16; Y-81

Blackburn, Thomas 1916-1977 .... DLB-27

Blacker, Terence 1948- DLB-271

Blackmore, R. D. 1825-1900 .... DLB-18

Blackmore, Sir Richard 1654-1729 ...... DLB-131

Blackmur, R. P. 1904-1965 .... DLB-63

Blackwell, Alice Stone 1857-1950 .... DLB-303

Basil Blackwell, Publisher DLB-106

Blackwood, Algernon Henry
  1869-1951 .... DLB-153, 156, 178

Blackwood, Caroline 1931-1996 ..... DLB-14, 207

William Blackwood and Sons, Ltd. DLB-154

Blackwood's Edinburgh Magazine
  1817-1980 .... DLB-110

Blades, William 1824-1890 .... DLB-184

Blaga, Lucian 1895-1961 .... DLB-220

Blagden, Isabella 1817?-1873 .... DLB-199

Blair, Eric Arthur (see Orwell, George)

Blair, Francis Preston 1791-1876 .... DLB-43

Blair, Hugh
  Lectures on Rhetoric and Belles Lettres (1783),
    [excerpts] DLB-31

Blair, James circa 1655-1743 .... DLB-24

Blair, John Durburrow 1759-1823 .... DLB-37

Blais, Marie-Claire 1939- DLB-53

Blaise, Clark 1940- DLB-53

Blake, George 1893-1961 .... DLB-191

Blake, Lillie Devereux 1833-1913 .... DLB-202, 221

Blake, Nicholas (C. Day Lewis)
  1904-1972 .... DLB-77

Blake, William
  1757-1827 .... DLB-93, 154, 163; CDBLB-3

The Blakiston Company DLB-49

Blanchard, Stephen 1950- DLB-267

Blanchot, Maurice 1907-2003 .... DLB-72, 296

Blanckenburg, Christian Friedrich von
  1744-1796 .... DLB-94

Blandiana, Ana 1942- DLB-232; CDWLB-4

Blanshard, Brand 1892-1987 .... DLB-279

Blasco Ibáñez, Vicente 1867-1928 ...... DLB-322

Blaser, Robin 1925- DLB-165

Blaumanis, Rudolfs 1863-1908 .... DLB-220

Bleasdale, Alan 1946- DLB-245

Bledsoe, Albert Taylor
  1809-1877 .... DLB-3, 79, 248

Bleecker, Ann Eliza 1752-1783 .... DLB-200

Blelock and Company DLB-49

Blennerhassett, Margaret Agnew
  1773-1842 .... DLB-99

Geoffrey Bles [publishing house] DLB-112

Blessington, Marguerite, Countess of
  1789-1849 .... DLB-166

Blew, Mary Clearman 1939- DLB-256

Blicher, Steen Steensen 1782-1848 ...... DLB-300

The Blickling Homilies circa 971 .... DLB-146

Blind, Mathilde 1841-1896 . . . . DLB-199

The Blind Assassin, 2000 Booker Prize winner,
Margaret Atwood DLB-326

Blish, James 1921-1975 . . . . DLB-8

E. Bliss and E. White
[publishing house] DLB-49

Bliven, Bruce 1889-1977 . . . . DLB-137

Blixen, Karen 1885-1962 . . . . DLB-214

Bloch, Ernst 1885-1977 . . . . DLB-296

Bloch, Robert 1917-1994 . . . . DLB-44

 Tribute to John D. MacDonald Y-86

Block, Lawrence 1938- DLB-226

Block, Rudolph (see Lessing, Bruno)

Blok, Aleksandr Aleksandrovich
1880-1921 . . . . DLB-295

Blondal, Patricia 1926-1959 . . . . DLB-88

Bloom, Harold 1930- DLB-67

Bloomer, Amelia 1818-1894 . . . . DLB-79

Bloomfield, Robert 1766-1823 . . . . DLB-93

Bloomsbury Group DS-10

 The *Dreannought* Hoax DS-10

Bloor, Ella Reeve 1862-1951 . . . . DLB-303

Blotner, Joseph 1923- DLB-111

Blount, Thomas 1618?-1679 . . . . DLB-236

Bloy, Léon 1846-1917 . . . . DLB-123

Blume, Judy 1938- DLB-52

 Tribute to Theodor Seuss Geisel Y-91

Blunck, Hans Friedrich 1888-1961 . . . . . . DLB-66

Blunden, Edmund 1896-1974 . . . .DLB-20, 100, 155

Blundeville, Thomas 1522?-1606 . . . . DLB-236

Blunt, Lady Anne Isabella Noel
1837-1917 . . . . .DLB-174

Blunt, Wilfrid Scawen 1840-1922 . . . . .DLB-19, 174

Bly, Nellie (see Cochrane, Elizabeth)

Bly, Robert 1926- DLB-5

Blyton, Enid 1897-1968 . . . . DLB-160

Boaden, James 1762-1839 . . . . DLB-89

Boal, Augusto 1931- DLB-307

Boas, Frederick S. 1862-1957 . . . . DLB-149

The Bobbs-Merrill Company DLB-46, 291

 The Bobbs-Merrill Archive at the
 Lilly Library, Indiana University Y-90

Boborykin, Petr Dmitrievich
1836-1921 . . . . DLB-238

Bobrov, Semen Sergeevich
1763?-1810 . . . . DLB-150

Bobrowski, Johannes 1917-1965 . . . . DLB-75

Bocage, Manuel Maria Barbosa du
1765-1805 . . . . DLB-287

Bodenheim, Maxwell 1892-1954 . . . . . . DLB-9, 45

Bodenstedt, Friedrich von 1819-1892 . . . . DLB-129

Bodini, Vittorio 1914-1970 . . . . DLB-128

Bodkin, M. McDonnell 1850-1933 . . . . DLB-70

Bodley, Sir Thomas 1545-1613 . . . . DLB-213

Bodley Head DLB-112

Bodmer, Johann Jakob 1698-1783 . . . . . . DLB-97

Bodmershof, Imma von 1895-1982 . . . . . DLB-85

Bodsworth, Fred 1918- DLB-68

Böðvar Guðmundsson 1939- DLB-293

Boehm, Sydney 1908-1990 . . . . DLB-44

Boer, Charles 1939- DLB-5

Boethius circa 480-circa 524 . . . . DLB-115

Boethius of Dacia circa 1240-? DLB-115

Bogan, Louise 1897-1970 . . . . DLB-45, 169

Bogarde, Dirk 1921-1999 . . . . DLB-14

Bogdanov, Aleksandr Aleksandrovich
1873-1928 . . . . DLB-295

Bogdanovich, Ippolit Fedorovich
circa 1743-1803 . . . . DLB-150

David Bogue [publishing house] DLB-106

Bohjalian, Chris 1960- DLB-292

Böhme, Jakob 1575-1624 . . . . DLB-164

H. G. Bohn [publishing house] DLB-106

Bohse, August 1661-1742 . . . . DLB-168

Boie, Heinrich Christian 1744-1806 . . . . . DLB-94

Boileau-Despréaux, Nicolas 1636-1711 . . . DLB-268

Bojunga, Lygia 1932- DLB-307

Bok, Edward W. 1863-1930 . . . . . . DLB-91; DS-16

Boland, Eavan 1944- DLB-40

Boldrewood, Rolf (Thomas Alexander Browne)
1826?-1915 . . . . DLB-230

Bolingbroke, Henry St. John, Viscount
1678-1751 . . . . DLB-101

Böll, Heinrich
1917-1985 . . . . DLB-69; Y-85; CDWLB-2

Bolling, Robert 1738-1775 . . . . DLB-31

Bolotov, Andrei Timofeevich
1738-1833 . . . . DLB-150

Bolt, Carol 1941- DLB-60

Bolt, Robert 1924-1995 . . . . DLB-13, 233

Bolton, Herbert E. 1870-1953 . . . . DLB-17

Bonaventura DLB-90

Bonaventure circa 1217-1274 . . . . DLB-115

Bonaviri, Giuseppe 1924- DLB-177

Bond, Edward 1934- DLB-13, 310

Bond, Michael 1926- DLB-161

Bondarev, Iurii Vasil'evich 1924- DLB-302

The Bone People, 1985 Booker Prize winner,
Keri Hulme DLB-326

Albert and Charles Boni
[publishing house] DLB-46

Boni and Liveright DLB-46

Bonnefoy, Yves 1923- DLB-258

Bonner, Marita 1899-1971 . . . . DLB-228

Bonner, Paul Hyde 1893-1968 . . . . DS-17

Bonner, Sherwood (see McDowell, Katharine
Sherwood Bonner)

Robert Bonner's Sons DLB-49

Bonnin, Gertrude Simmons (see Zitkala-Ša)

Bonsanti, Alessandro 1904-1984 . . . . .DLB-177

Bontempelli, Massimo 1878-1960 . . . . DLB-264

Bontemps, Arna 1902-1973 . . . . DLB-48, 51

The Book Buyer (1867-1880, 1884-1918,
1935-1938 . . . . .DS-13

The Book League of America DLB-46

Book Reviewing

 The American Book Review: A Sketch . . . Y-92

 Book Reviewing and the
  Literary Scene Y-96, 97

 Book Reviewing in America Y-87–94

 Book Reviewing in America and the
  Literary Scene Y-95

 Book Reviewing in Texas Y-94

 Book Reviews in Glossy Magazines Y-95

 Do They or Don't They?
  Writers Reading Book Reviews Y-01

 The Most Powerful Book Review
  in America [*New York Times
  Book Review*] Y-82

 Some Surprises and Universal Truths Y-92

 The Year in Book Reviewing and the
  Literary Situation Y-98

Book Supply Company DLB-49

The Book Trade History Group Y-93

The Booker Prize Y-96–98

 Address by Anthony Thwaite,
 Chairman of the Booker Prize Judges
 Comments from Former Booker
 Prize Winners Y-86

Boorde, Andrew circa 1490-1549 . . . . DLB-136

Boorstin, Daniel J. 1914- DLB-17

 Tribute to Archibald MacLeish Y-82

 Tribute to Charles Scribner Jr. Y-95

Booth, Franklin 1874-1948 . . . . DLB-188

Booth, Mary L. 1831-1889 . . . . DLB-79

Booth, Philip 1925- Y-82

Booth, Wayne C. 1921- DLB-67

Booth, William 1829-1912 . . . . DLB-190

Bor, Josef 1906-1979 . . . . DLB-299

Borchardt, Rudolf 1877-1945 . . . . DLB-66

Borchert, Wolfgang 1921-1947 . . . . . . DLB-69, 124

Bording, Anders 1619-1677 . . . . DLB-300

Borel, Pétrus 1809-1859 . . . . DLB-119

Borgen, Johan 1902-1979 . . . . DLB-297

Borges, Jorge Luis
1899-1986 . . . DLB-113, 283; Y-86; CDWLB-3

 The Poetry of Jorge Luis Borges Y-86

 A Personal Tribute Y-86

Borgese, Giuseppe Antonio 1882-1952 . . . DLB-264

Börne, Ludwig 1786-1837 . . . . DLB-90

Bornstein, Miriam 1950- DLB-209

Borowski, Tadeusz 1922-1951 . . . . DLB-215; CDWLB-4

Borrow, George 1803-1881 . . . . . . DLB-21, 55, 166

Bosanquet, Bernard 1848-1923 . . . . DLB-262

Boscán, Juan circa 1490-1542 . . . . DLB-318

Bosch, Juan 1909-2001. . . . . DLB-145

Bosco, Henri 1888-1976. . . . . DLB-72

Bosco, Monique 1927- DLB-53

Bosman, Herman Charles 1905-1951 . . . . DLB-225

Bossuet, Jacques-Bénigne 1627-1704 . . . . . . DLB-268

Bostic, Joe 1908-1988. . . . . DLB-241

Boston, Lucy M. 1892-1990 . . . . DLB-161

Boston Quarterly Review DLB-1

Boston University
  Editorial Institute at Boston University Y-00
  Special Collections at Boston University . . . Y-99

Boswell, James 1740-1795. . . . . DLB-104, 142; CDBLB-2

Boswell, Robert 1953- DLB-234

Bosworth, David Y-82
  Excerpt from "Excerpts from a Report of the Commission," in *The Death of Descartes* Y-82

Bote, Hermann circa 1460-circa 1520. . . . DLB-179

Botev, Khristo 1847-1876 . . . . DLB-147

Botkin, Vasilii Petrovich 1811-1869 . . . . . . DLB-277

Botta, Anne C. Lynch 1815-1891 . . . . . DLB-3, 250

Botto, Ján (see Krasko, Ivan)

Bottome, Phyllis 1882-1963 . . . . DLB-197

Bottomley, Gordon 1874-1948 . . . . DLB-10

Bottoms, David 1949- DLB-120; Y-83
  Tribute to James Dickey Y-97

Bottrall, Ronald 1906-1959 . . . . DLB-20

Bouchardy, Joseph 1810-1870 . . . . DLB-192

Boucher, Anthony 1911-1968 . . . . DLB-8

Boucher, Jonathan 1738-1804. . . . . DLB-31

Boucher de Boucherville, Georges 1814-1894 . . . . DLB-99

Boudreau, Daniel (see Coste, Donat)

Bouhours, Dominique 1628-1702 . . . . DLB-268

Bourassa, Napoléon 1827-1916 . . . . DLB-99

Bourget, Paul 1852-1935 . . . . DLB-123

Bourinot, John George 1837-1902 . . . . DLB-99

Bourjaily, Vance 1922- DLB-2, 143

Bourne, Edward Gaylord 1860-1908. . . . . . DLB-47

Bourne, Randolph 1886-1918 . . . . DLB-63

Bousoño, Carlos 1923- DLB-108

Bousquet, Joë 1897-1950 . . . . DLB-72

Bova, Ben 1932- Y-81

Bovard, Oliver K. 1872-1945 . . . . DLB-25

Bove, Emmanuel 1898-1945 . . . . DLB-72

Bowen, Elizabeth 1899-1973 . . . . DLB-15, 162; CDBLB-7

Bowen, Francis 1811-1890 . . . . DLB-1, 59, 235

Bowen, John 1924- DLB-13

Bowen, Marjorie 1886-1952. . . . . DLB-153

Bowen-Merrill Company DLB-49

Bowering, George 1935- DLB-53

Bowers, Bathsheba 1671-1718 . . . . DLB-200

Bowers, Claude G. 1878-1958 . . . . DLB-17

Bowers, Edgar 1924-2000 . . . . DLB-5

Bowers, Fredson Thayer 1905-1991 . . . . DLB-140; Y-91
  The Editorial Style of Fredson Bowers Y-91
  Fredson Bowers and Studies in Bibliography Y-91
  Fredson Bowers and the Cambridge Beaumont and Fletcher Y-91
  Fredson Bowers as Critic of Renaissance Dramatic Literature Y-91
  Fredson Bowers as Music Critic Y-91
  Fredson Bowers, Master Teacher Y-91
  An Interview [on Nabokov] Y-80
  Working with Fredson Bowers Y-91

Bowles, Paul 1910-1999 . . . . . . DLB-5, 6, 218; Y-99

Bowles, Samuel, III 1826-1878. . . . . DLB-43

Bowles, William Lisle 1762-1850 . . . . DLB-93

Bowman, Louise Morey 1882-1944 . . . . . . DLB-68

Bowne, Borden Parker 1847-1919 . . . . DLB-270

Boyd, James 1888-1944 . . . . DLB-9; DS-16

Boyd, John 1912-2002 . . . . DLB-310

Boyd, John 1919- DLB-8

Boyd, Martin 1893-1972 . . . . DLB-260

Boyd, Thomas 1898-1935 . . . . . DLB-9, 316; DS-16

Boyd, William 1952- DLB-231

Boye, Karin 1900-1941 . . . . DLB-259

Boyesen, Hjalmar Hjorth 1848-1895 . . . . DLB-12, 71; DS-13

Boylan, Clare 1948- DLB-267

Boyle, Kay 1902-1992 . . . . DLB-4, 9, 48, 86; DS-15; Y-93

Boyle, Roger, Earl of Orrery 1621-1679 . . . DLB-80

Boyle, T. Coraghessan 1948- DLB-218, 278; Y-86

Božić, Mirko 1919- DLB-181

Brackenbury, Alison 1953- DLB-40

Brackenridge, Hugh Henry 1748-1816 . . . . DLB-11, 37
  The Rising Glory of America DLB-37

Brackett, Charles 1892-1969 . . . . DLB-26

Brackett, Leigh 1915-1978 . . . . DLB-8, 26

John Bradburn [publishing house] DLB-49

Bradbury, Malcolm 1932-2000 . . . . . DLB-14, 207

Bradbury, Ray 1920- DLB-2, 8; CDALB-6

Bradbury and Evans DLB-106

Braddon, Mary Elizabeth 1835-1915 . . . . DLB-18, 70, 156

Bradford, Andrew 1686-1742. . . . . DLB-43, 73

Bradford, Gamaliel 1863-1932. . . . . DLB-17

Bradford, John 1749-1830 . . . . DLB-43

Bradford, Roark 1896-1948. . . . . DLB-86

Bradford, William 1590-1657 . . . . . . DLB-24, 30

Bradford, William, III 1719-1791. . . . . DLB-43, 73

Bradlaugh, Charles 1833-1891 . . . . DLB-57

Bradley, David 1950- DLB-33

Bradley, F. H. 1846-1924. . . . . DLB-262

Bradley, Katherine Harris (see Field, Michael)

Bradley, Marion Zimmer 1930-1999 . . . . . . DLB-8

Bradley, William Aspenwall 1878-1939 . . . . . DLB-4

Ira Bradley and Company DLB-49

J. W. Bradley and Company DLB-49

Bradshaw, Henry 1831-1886 . . . . DLB-184

Bradstreet, Anne 1612 or 1613-1672. . . . . DLB-24; CDALB-2

Bradūnas, Kazys 1917- DLB-220

Bradwardine, Thomas circa 1295-1349 . . . DLB-115

Brady, Frank 1924-1986 . . . . DLB-111

Frederic A. Brady [publishing house] DLB-49

Braga, Rubem 1913-1990 . . . . DLB-307

Bragg, Melvyn 1939- DLB-14, 271

Brahe, Tycho 1546-1601 . . . . DLB-300

Charles H. Brainard [publishing house] DLB-49

Braine, John 1922-1986 . . . . DLB-15; Y-86; CDBLB-7

Braithwait, Richard 1588-1673 . . . . DLB-151

Braithwaite, William Stanley 1878-1962 . . . . DLB-50, 54

Bräker, Ulrich 1735-1798 . . . . DLB-94

Bramah, Ernest 1868-1942 . . . . DLB-70

Branagan, Thomas 1774-1843 . . . . DLB-37

Brancati, Vitaliano 1907-1954 . . . . DLB-264

Branch, William Blackwell 1927- DLB-76

Brand, Christianna 1907-1988 . . . . DLB-276

Brand, Max (see Faust, Frederick Schiller)

Brandão, Raul 1867-1930 . . . . DLB-287

Branden Press DLB-46

Brandes, Georg 1842-1927 . . . . DLB-300

Branner, H.C. 1903-1966 . . . . DLB-214

Brant, Sebastian 1457-1521 . . . . DLB-179

Brantôme (Pierre de Bourdeille) 1540?-1614 . . . . DLB-327

Brassey, Lady Annie (Allnutt) 1839-1887 . . . . DLB-166

Brathwaite, Edward Kamau 1930- DLB-125; CDWLB-3

Brault, Jacques 1933- DLB-53

Braun, Matt 1932- DLB-212

Braun, Volker 1939- DLB-75, 124

Brautigan, Richard 1935-1984 . . . . DLB-2, 5, 206; Y-80, 84

Cumulative Index

Braxton, Joanne M. 1950- DLB-41
Bray, Anne Eliza 1790-1883 .... DLB-116
Bray, Thomas 1656-1730 .... DLB-24
Brazdžionis, Bernardas 1907-2002 ...... DLB-220
George Braziller [publishing house] DLB-46
The Bread Loaf Writers' Conference 1983.... Y-84
Breasted, James Henry 1865-1935 .... DLB-47
Brecht, Bertolt
   1898-1956 .... DLB-56, 124; CDWLB-2
Bredel, Willi 1901-1964 .... DLB-56
Bregendahl, Marie 1867-1940 .... DLB-214
Breitinger, Johann Jakob 1701-1776....... DLB-97
Brekke, Paal 1923-1993 .... DLB-297
Bremser, Bonnie 1939- DLB-16
Bremser, Ray 1934-1998............... DLB-16
Brennan, Christopher 1870-1932 .... DLB-230
Brentano, Bernard von 1901-1964 ...... DLB-56
Brentano, Clemens 1778-1842 .... DLB-90
Brentano, Franz 1838-1917............ DLB-296
Brentano's....................... DLB-49
Brenton, Howard 1942- DLB-13
Breslin, Jimmy 1929-1996............ DLB-185
Breton, André 1896-1966 .... DLB-65, 258
Breton, Nicholas circa 1555-circa 1626... DLB-136
The Breton Lays
   1300-early fifteenth century DLB-146
Brett, Lily 1946- DLB-325
Brett, Simon 1945- DLB-276
Brewer, Gil 1922-1983 .... DLB-306
Brewer, Luther A. 1858-1933 .... DLB-187
Brewer, Warren and Putnam DLB-46
Brewster, Elizabeth 1922- DLB-60
Breytenbach, Breyten 1939- DLB-225
Bridge, Ann (Lady Mary Dolling Sanders
   O'Malley) 1889-1974 .... DLB-191
Bridge, Horatio 1806-1893 .... DLB-183
Bridgers, Sue Ellen 1942- DLB-52
Bridges, Robert
   1844-1930 .... DLB-19, 98; CDBLB-5
The Bridgewater Library DLB-213
Bridie, James 1888-1951............... DLB-10
Brieux, Eugene 1858-1932 .... DLB-192
Brigadere, Anna
   1861-1933 .... DLB-220; CDWLB-4
Briggs, Charles Frederick
   1804-1877................... DLB-3, 250
Brighouse, Harold 1882-1958......... DLB-10
Bright, Mary Chavelita Dunne
   (see Egerton, George)
Brightman, Edgar Sheffield 1884-1953.....DLB-270
B. J. Brimmer Company................ DLB-46
Brines, Francisco 1932- DLB-134
Brink, André 1935- DLB-225

Brinley, George, Jr. 1817-1875......... DLB-140
Brinnin, John Malcolm 1916-1998 .... DLB-48
Brisbane, Albert 1809-1890 .... DLB-3, 250
Brisbane, Arthur 1864-1936........... DLB-25
British Academy................... DLB-112
The British Critic 1793-1843 .... DLB-110
British Library
   The American Trust for the
     British Library................... Y-96
   The British Library and the Regular
     Readers' Group................. Y-91
   Building the New British Library
     at St Pancras Y-94
British Literary Prizes........... DLB-207; Y-98
British Literature
   The "Angry Young Men".......... DLB-15
   Author-Printers, 1476-1599 .... DLB-167
   The Comic Tradition Continued..... DLB-15
   Documents on Sixteenth-Century
     Literature................ DLB-167, 172
   Eikon Basilike 1649 .... DLB-151
   Letter from London Y-96
   A Mirror for Magistrates............. DLB-167
   "Modern English Prose" (1876),
     by George Saintsbury DLB-57
   Sex, Class, Politics, and Religion [in the
     British Novel, 1930-1959] DLB-15
   Victorians on Rhetoric and Prose
     Style....................... DLB-57
   The Year in British Fiction Y-99-01
   "You've Never Had It So Good," Gusted
     by "Winds of Change": British
     Fiction in the 1950s, 1960s,
     and After.................... DLB-14
British Literature, Old and Middle English
   Anglo-Norman Literature in the
     Development of Middle English
     Literature................... DLB-146
   The Alliterative Morte Arthure and the
     Stanzaic Morte Arthur
     circa 1350-1400 .... DLB-146
   Ancrene Riwle circa 1200-1225 .... DLB-146
   The Anglo-Saxon Chronicle circa
     890-1154 .... DLB-146
   The Battle of Maldon circa 1000 ...... DLB-146
   Beowulf circa 900-1000 or
     790-825 .... DLB-146; CDBLB-1
   The Blickling Homilies circa 971 .... DLB-146
   The Breton Lays
     1300-early fifteenth century..... DLB-146
   The Castle of Perserverance
     circa 1400-1425 .... DLB-146
   The Celtic Background to Medieval
     English Literature DLB-146
   The Chester Plays circa 1505-1532;
     revisions until 1575 .... DLB-146
   Cursor Mundi circa 1300 .... DLB-146
   The English Language: 410
     to 1500 .... DLB-146
   The Germanic Epic and Old English
     Heroic Poetry: Widsith, Waldere,
     and The Fight at Finnsburg...... DLB-146

   Judith circa 930 .... DLB-146
   The Matter of England 1240-1400... DLB-146
   The Matter of Rome early twelfth to
     late fifteenth centuries DLB-146
   Middle English Literature:
     An Introduction.............. DLB-146
   The Middle English Lyric DLB-146
   Morality Plays: Mankind circa 1450-1500
     and Everyman circa 1500......... DLB-146
   N-Town Plays circa 1468 to early
     sixteenth century............. DLB-146
   Old English Literature:
     An Introduction.............. DLB-146
   Old English Riddles
     eighth to tenth centuries DLB-146
   The Owl and the Nightingale
     circa 1189-1199 .... DLB-146
   The Paston Letters 1422-1509 .... DLB-146
   The Seafarer circa 970 .... DLB-146
   The South English Legendary circa
     thirteenth to fifteenth centuries ... DLB-146
The British Review and London Critical
   Journal 1811-1825................ DLB-110
Brito, Aristeo 1942- DLB-122
Brittain, Vera 1893-1970 .... DLB-191
Briusov, Valerii Iakovlevich
   1873-1924................... DLB-295
Brizeux, Auguste 1803-1858............DLB-217
Broadway Publishing Company......... DLB-46
Broch, Hermann
   1886-1951 ....DLB-85, 124; CDWLB-2
Brochu, André 1942- DLB-53
Brock, Edwin 1927-1997.............. DLB-40
Brockes, Barthold Heinrich 1680-1747... DLB-168
Brod, Max 1884-1968................. DLB-81
Brodber, Erna 1940- DLB-157
Brodhead, John R. 1814-1873......... DLB-30
Brodkey, Harold 1930-1996 .... DLB-130
Brodsky, Joseph (Iosif Aleksandrovich
   Brodsky) 1940-1996......... DLB-285; Y-87
   Nobel Lecture 1987 .... Y-87
Brodsky, Michael 1948- DLB-244
Broeg, Bob 1918- DLB-171
Brøgger, Suzanne 1944- DLB-214
Brome, Richard circa 1590-1652 .... DLB-58
Brome, Vincent 1910-2004 .... DLB-155
Bromfield, Louis 1896-1956......... DLB-4, 9, 86
Bromige, David 1933- DLB-193
Broner, E. M. 1930- DLB-28
   Tribute to Bernard Malamud.......... Y-86
Bronk, William 1918-1999 .... DLB-165
Bronnen, Arnolt 1895-1959 .... DLB-124
Brontë, Anne 1820-1849............ DLB-21, 199
Brontë, Charlotte
   1816-1855 ..... DLB-21, 159, 199; CDBLB-4

Brontë, Emily
   1818-1848 ..... DLB-21, 32, 199; CDBLB-4

The Brontë Society Y-98

Brook, Stephen 1947- DLB-204

Brook Farm 1841-1847 .... DLB-1; 223; DS-5

Brooke, Frances 1724-1789.......... DLB-39, 99

Brooke, Henry 1703?-1783.............. DLB-39

Brooke, L. Leslie 1862-1940 .... DLB-141

Brooke, Margaret, Ranee of Sarawak
   1849-1936 .... DLB-174

Brooke, Rupert
   1887-1915 .... DLB-19, 216; CDBLB-6

   The Friends of the Dymock Poets........ Y-00

Brooker, Bertram 1888-1955 .... DLB-88

Brooke-Rose, Christine 1923- DLB-14, 231

Brookner, Anita 1928- DLB-194, 326; Y-87

Brooks, Charles Timothy 1813-1883... DLB-1, 243

Brooks, Cleanth 1906-1994 .... DLB-63; Y-94

   Tribute to Katherine Anne Porter Y-80

   Tribute to Walker Percy Y-90

Brooks, Gwendolyn
   1917-2000 .... DLB-5, 76, 165; CDALB-1

   Tribute to Julian Mayfield Y-84

Brooks, Jeremy 1926-1994.............. DLB-14

Brooks, Mel 1926- DLB-26

Brooks, Noah 1830-1903......... DLB-42; DS-13

Brooks, Richard 1912-1992 .... DLB-44

Brooks, Van Wyck 1886-1963 .... DLB-45, 63, 103

Brophy, Brigid 1929-1995 .... DLB-14, 70, 271

Brophy, John 1899-1965 .... DLB-191

Brorson, Hans Adolph 1694-1764 .... DLB-300

Brossard, Chandler 1922-1993 .... DLB-16

Brossard, Nicole 1943- DLB-53

Broster, Dorothy Kathleen 1877-1950 .... DLB-160

Brother Antoninus (see Everson, William)

Brotherton, Lord 1856-1930 .... DLB-184

Brougham, John 1810-1880.............. DLB-11

Brougham and Vaux, Henry Peter
   Brougham, Baron 1778-1868.... DLB-110, 158

Broughton, James 1913-1999............. DLB-5

Broughton, Rhoda 1840-1920 .... DLB-18

Broun, Heywood 1888-1939 .... DLB-29, 171

Browder, Earl 1891-1973 .... DLB-303

Brown, Alice 1856-1948................. DLB-78

Brown, Bob 1886-1959 .... DLB-4, 45; DS-15

Brown, Cecil 1943- DLB-33

Brown, Charles Brockden
   1771-1810 .... DLB-37, 59, 73; CDALB-2

Brown, Christy 1932-1981.............. DLB-14

Brown, Dee 1908-2002 .... Y-80

Brown, Frank London 1927-1962 .... DLB-76

Brown, Fredric 1906-1972 .... DLB-8

Brown, George Mackay
   1921-1996 .... DLB-14, 27, 139, 271

Brown, Harry 1917-1986 .... DLB-26

Brown, Ian 1945- DLB-310

Brown, Larry 1951- DLB-234, 292

Brown, Lew 1893-1958 .... DLB-265

Brown, Marcia 1918- DLB-61

Brown, Margaret Wise 1910-1952........ DLB-22

Brown, Morna Doris (see Ferrars, Elizabeth)

Brown, Oliver Madox 1855-1874......... DLB-21

Brown, Sterling 1901-1989........ DLB-48, 51, 63

Brown, T. E. 1830-1897................ DLB-35

Brown, Thomas Alexander (see Boldrewood, Rolf)

Brown, Warren 1894-1978............. DLB-241

Brown, William Hill 1765-1793 .... DLB-37

Brown, William Wells
   1815-1884 .... DLB-3, 50, 183, 248

Brown University
   The Festival of Vanguard Narrative...... Y-93

Browne, Charles Farrar 1834-1867 .... DLB-11

Browne, Frances 1816-1879 .... DLB-199

Browne, Francis Fisher 1843-1913........ DLB-79

Browne, Howard 1908-1999 .... DLB-226

Browne, J. Ross 1821-1875.............. DLB-202

Browne, Michael Dennis 1940- DLB-40

Browne, Sir Thomas 1605-1682 .... DLB-151

Browne, William, of Tavistock
   1590-1645 .... DLB-121

Browne, Wynyard 1911-1964 .... DLB-13, 233

Browne and Nolan.................... DLB-106

Brownell, W. C. 1851-1928 .... DLB-71

Browning, Elizabeth Barrett
   1806-1861 .... DLB-32, 199; CDBLB-4

Browning, Robert
   1812-1889 .... DLB-32, 163; CDBLB-4

   Essay on Chatterton DLB-32

   Introductory Essay: *Letters of Percy
   Bysshe Shelley* (1852)............. DLB-32

   "The Novel in [Robert Browning's]
   'The Ring and the Book'" (1912),
   by Henry James DLB-32

Brownjohn, Allan 1931- DLB-40

   Tribute to John Betjeman Y-84

Brownson, Orestes Augustus
   1803-1876 .... DLB-1, 59, 73, 243; DS-5

Bruccoli, Matthew J. 1931- DLB-103

   Joseph [Heller] and George [V. Higgins] Y-99

   Response [to Busch on Fitzgerald]........ Y-96

   Tribute to Albert Erskine Y-93

   Tribute to Charles E. Feinberg Y-88

   Working with Fredson Bowers Y-91

Bruce, Charles 1906-1971 .... DLB-68

Bruce, John Edward 1856-1924

   Three Documents [African American
   poets] DLB-50

Bruce, Leo 1903-1979 .... DLB-77

Bruce, Mary Grant 1878-1958.......... DLB-230

Bruce, Philip Alexander 1856-1933....... DLB-47

Bruce-Novoa, Juan 1944- DLB-82

Bruckman, Clyde 1894-1955............ DLB-26

Bruckner, Ferdinand 1891-1958......... DLB-118

Brundage, John Herbert (see Herbert, John)

Brunner, John 1934-1995.............. DLB-261

   Tribute to Theodore Sturgeon Y-85

Brutus, Dennis
   1924- DLB-117, 225; CDWLB-3

Bryan, C. D. B. 1936- DLB-185

Bryan, William Jennings 1860-1925 ..... DLB-303

Bryant, Arthur 1899-1985 .... DLB-149

Bryant, William Cullen 1794-1878
   .... DLB-3, 43, 59, 189, 250; CDALB-2

Bryce, James 1838-1922............ DLB-166, 190

Bryce Echenique, Alfredo
   1939- DLB-145; CDWLB-3

Bryden, Bill 1942- DLB-233

Brydges, Sir Samuel Egerton
   1762-1837 .... DLB-107, 142

Bryskett, Lodowick 1546?-1612 .... DLB-167

Buchan, John 1875-1940 .... DLB-34, 70, 156

Buchanan, George 1506-1582 .... DLB-132

Buchanan, Robert 1841-1901 .... DLB-18, 35

   "The Fleshly School of Poetry and
   Other Phenomena of the Day"
   (1872) DLB-35

   "The Fleshly School of Poetry:
   Mr. D. G. Rossetti" (1871),
   by Thomas Maitland DLB-35

Buchler, Justus 1914-1991 .... DLB-279

Buchman, Sidney 1902-1975 .... DLB-26

Buchner, Augustus 1591-1661.......... DLB-164

Büchner, Georg
   1813-1837 .... DLB-133; CDWLB-2

Bucholtz, Andreas Heinrich 1607-1671..... DLB-168

Buck, Pearl S. 1892-1973 ... DLB-9, 102; CDALB-7

Bucke, Charles 1781-1846 .... DLB-110

Bucke, Richard Maurice 1837-1902....... DLB-99

Buckingham, Edwin 1810-1833.......... DLB-73

Buckingham, Joseph Tinker 1779-1861 .... DLB-73

Buckler, Ernest 1908-1984 .... DLB-68

Buckley, Vincent 1925-1988 .... DLB-289

Buckley, William F., Jr. 1925- ... DLB-137; Y-80

   Publisher's Statement From the
   Initial Issue of *National Review*
   (19 November 1955)............ DLB-137

Buckminster, Joseph Stevens
   1784-1812 .... DLB-37

Buckner, Robert 1906-1989............. DLB-26

Budd, Thomas ?-1698 .... DLB-24

Budé, Guillaume 1468-1540 .... DLB-327

Budrys, A. J. 1931- DLB-8

Cumulative Index   DLB 328

Buechner, Frederick 1926- Y-80

Buell, John 1927- DLB-53

Buenaventura, Enrique 1925-2003 ...... DLB-305

Bufalino, Gesualdo 1920-1996 .... DLB-196

Buffon, Georges-Louis Leclerc de
  1707-1788 .... DLB-313

  "Le Discours sur le style" DLB-314

Job Buffum [publishing house] DLB-49

Bugnet, Georges 1879-1981 .... DLB-92

al-Buhturi 821-897 .... DLB-311

Buies, Arthur 1840-1901 .... DLB-99

Bukiet, Melvin Jules 1953- DLB-299

Bukowski, Charles 1920-1994 ... DLB-5, 130, 169

Bulatović, Miodrag
  1930-1991 .... DLB-181; CDWLB-4

Bulgakov, Mikhail Afanas'evich
  1891-1940 .... DLB-272

Bulgarin, Faddei Venediktovich
  1789-1859 .... DLB-198

Bulger, Bozeman 1877-1932 .... DLB-171

Bull, Olaf 1883-1933 .... DLB-297

Bullein, William
  between 1520 and 1530-1576 .... DLB-167

Bullins, Ed 1935- DLB-7, 38, 249

Bulosan, Carlos 1911-1956 .... DLB-312

Bulwer, John 1606-1656 .... DLB-236

Bulwer-Lytton, Edward (also Edward
  Bulwer) 1803-1873 .... DLB-21

  "On Art in Fiction" (1838) DLB-21

Bumpus, Jerry 1937- Y-81

Bunce and Brother DLB-49

Bunin, Ivan 1870-1953 .... DLB-317

Bunner, H. C. 1855-1896 .... DLB-78, 79

Bunting, Basil 1900-1985 .... DLB-20

Buntline, Ned (Edward Zane Carroll
  Judson) 1821-1886 .... DLB-186

Bunyan, John 1628-1688 ..... DLB-39; CDBLB-2

  The Author's Apology for
    His Book DLB-39

Burch, Robert 1925- DLB-52

Burciaga, José Antonio 1940- DLB-82

Burdekin, Katharine (Murray Constantine)
  1896-1963 .... DLB-255

Bürger, Gottfried August 1747-1794 ...... DLB-94

Burgess, Anthony (John Anthony Burgess Wilson)
  1917-1993 ...... DLB-14, 194, 261; CDBLB-8

  The Anthony Burgess Archive at
    the Harry Ransom Humanities
    Research Center Y-98

  Anthony Burgess's 99 Novels:
    An Opinion Poll Y-84

Burgess, Gelett 1866-1951 .... DLB-11

Burgess, John W. 1844-1931 .... DLB-47

Burgess, Thornton W. 1874-1965 .... DLB-22

Burgess, Stringer and Company DLB-49

Burgos, Julia de 1914-1953 .... DLB-290

Burick, Si 1909-1986 .... DLB-171

Burk, John Daly circa 1772-1808 .... DLB-37

Burk, Ronnie 1955- DLB-209

Burke, Edmund 1729?-1797 .... DLB-104, 252

Burke, James Lee 1936- DLB-226

Burke, Johnny 1908-1964 .... DLB-265

Burke, Kenneth 1897-1993 .... DLB-45, 63

Burke, Thomas 1886-1945 .... DLB-197

Burley, Dan 1907-1962 .... DLB-241

Burley, W. J. 1914- DLB-276

Burlingame, Edward Livermore
  1848-1922 .... DLB-79

Burliuk, David 1882-1967 .... DLB-317

Burman, Carina 1960- DLB-257

Burnet, Gilbert 1643-1715 .... DLB-101

Burnett, Frances Hodgson
  1849-1924 .... DLB-42, 141; DS-13, 14

Burnett, W. R. 1899-1982 .... DLB-9, 226

Burnett, Whit 1899-1973 .... DLB-137

Burney, Fanny 1752-1840 .... DLB-39

  Dedication, The Wanderer (1814) DLB-39

  Preface to Evelina (1778) DLB-39

Burns, Alan 1929- DLB-14, 194

Burns, Joanne 1945- DLB-289

Burns, John Horne 1916-1953 .... Y-85

Burns, Robert 1759-1796 .... DLB-109; CDBLB-3

Burns and Oates DLB-106

Burnshaw, Stanley 1906- DLB-48; Y-97

  James Dickey and Stanley Burnshaw
    Correspondence Y-02

  Review of Stanley Burnshaw: The
    Collected Poems and Selected
    Prose Y-02

  Tribute to Robert Penn Warren Y-89

Burr, C. Chauncey 1815?-1883 .... DLB-79

Burr, Esther Edwards 1732-1758 .... DLB-200

Burroughs, Edgar Rice 1875-1950 .... DLB-8

  The Burroughs Bibliophiles Y-98

Burroughs, John 1837-1921 .... DLB-64, 275

Burroughs, Margaret T. G. 1917- DLB-41

Burroughs, William S., Jr. 1947-1981 ..... DLB-16

Burroughs, William Seward 1914-1997
  .... DLB-2, 8, 16, 152, 237; Y-81, 97

Burroway, Janet 1936- DLB-6

Burt, Maxwell Struthers
  1882-1954 .... DLB-86; DS-16

A. L. Burt and Company DLB-49

Burton, Hester 1913-2000 .... DLB-161

Burton, Isabel Arundell 1831-1896 ..... DLB-166

Burton, Miles (see Rhode, John)

Burton, Richard Francis
  1821-1890 .... DLB-55, 166, 184

Burton, Robert 1577-1640 .... DLB-151

Burton, Virginia Lee 1909-1968 .... DLB-22

Burton, William Evans 1804-1860 .... DLB-73

Burwell, Adam Hood 1790-1849 .... DLB-99

Bury, Lady Charlotte 1775-1861 .... DLB-116

Busch, Frederick 1941-2006 .... DLB-6, 218

  Excerpts from Frederick Busch's USC
    Remarks [on F. Scott Fitzgerald] Y-96

  Tribute to James Laughlin Y-97

  Tribute to Raymond Carver Y-88

Busch, Niven 1903-1991 .... DLB-44

Bushnell, Horace 1802-1876 .... DS-13

Business & Literature
  The Claims of Business and Literature:
    An Undergraduate Essay by
    Maxwell Perkins Y-01

Bussières, Arthur de 1877-1913 .... DLB-92

Butler, Charles circa 1560-1647 .... DLB-236

Butler, Guy 1918- DLB-225

Butler, Joseph 1692-1752 .... DLB-252

Butler, Josephine Elizabeth 1828-1906 ... DLB-190

Butler, Juan 1942-1981 .... DLB-53

Butler, Judith 1956- DLB-246

Butler, Octavia E. 1947-2006 .... DLB-33

Butler, Pierce 1884-1953 .... DLB-187

Butler, Robert Olen 1945- DLB-173

Butler, Samuel 1613-1680 .... DLB-101, 126

Butler, Samuel
  1835-1902 .... DLB-18, 57, 174; CDBLB-5

Butler, William Francis 1838-1910 ...... DLB-166

E. H. Butler and Company DLB-49

Butor, Michel 1926- DLB-83

Nathaniel Butter
  [publishing house] DLB-170

Butterworth, Hezekiah 1839-1905 .... DLB-42

Buttitta, Ignazio 1899-1997 .... DLB-114

Butts, Mary 1890-1937 .... DLB-240

Buzo, Alex 1944- DLB-289

Buzzati, Dino 1906-1972 .... DLB-177

Byars, Betsy 1928- DLB-52

Byatt, A. S. 1936- DLB-14, 194, 319, 326

Byles, Mather 1707-1788 .... DLB-24

Henry Bynneman
  [publishing house] DLB-170

Bynner, Witter 1881-1968 .... DLB-54

Byrd, William circa 1543-1623 .... DLB-172

Byrd, William, II 1674-1744 .... DLB-24, 140

Byrne, John Keyes (see Leonard, Hugh)

Byron, George Gordon, Lord
  1788-1824 .... DLB-96, 110; CDBLB-3

  The Byron Society of America Y-00

Byron, Robert 1905-1941 .... DLB-195

Byzantine Novel, The Spanish DLB-318

C

Caballero Bonald, José Manuel
1926- DLB-108

Cabañero, Eladio 1930- DLB-134

Cabell, James Branch 1879-1958 .... DLB-9, 78

Cabeza de Baca, Manuel 1853-1915 ..... DLB-122

Cabeza de Baca Gilbert, Fabiola
1898-1993 .... DLB-122

Cable, George Washington
1844-1925 .... DLB-12, 74; DS-13

Cable, Mildred 1878-1952 .... DLB-195

Cabral, Manuel del 1907-1999 .... DLB-283

Cabral de Melo Neto, João
1920-1999 .... DLB-307

Cabrera, Lydia 1900-1991 .... DLB-145

Cabrera Infante, Guillermo
1929- DLB-113; CDWLB-3

Cabrujas, José Ignacio 1937-1995 .... DLB-305

Cadell [publishing house] DLB-154

Cady, Edwin H. 1917- DLB-103

Caedmon fl. 658-680 .... DLB-146

Caedmon School circa 660-899 .... DLB-146

Caesar, Irving 1895-1996 .... DLB-265

Cafés, Brasseries, and Bistros DS-15

Cage, John 1912-1992 .... DLB-193

Cahan, Abraham 1860-1951 .... DLB-9, 25, 28

Cahn, Sammy 1913-1993 .... DLB-265

Cain, George 1943- DLB-33

Cain, James M. 1892-1977 .... DLB-226

Cain, Paul (Peter Ruric, George Sims)
1902-1966 .... DLB-306

Caird, Edward 1835-1908 .... DLB-262

Caird, Mona 1854-1932 .... DLB-197

Čaks, Aleksandrs
1901-1950 .... DLB-220; CDWLB-4

Caldecott, Randolph 1846-1886 .... DLB-163

John Calder Limited
[Publishing house] DLB-112

Calderón de la Barca, Fanny
1804-1882 .... DLB-183

Caldwell, Ben 1937- DLB-38

Caldwell, Erskine 1903-1987 .... DLB-9, 86

H. M. Caldwell Company DLB-49

Caldwell, Taylor 1900-1985 .... DS-17

Calhoun, John C. 1782-1850 .... DLB-3, 248

Călinescu, George 1899-1965 .... DLB-220

Calisher, Hortense 1911- DLB-2, 218

Calkins, Mary Whiton 1863-1930 .... DLB-270

Callaghan, Mary Rose 1944- DLB-207

Callaghan, Morley 1903-1990 ..... DLB-68; DS-15

Callahan, S. Alice 1868-1894 .... DLB-175, 221

Callaloo [journal] Y-87

Callimachus circa 305 B.C.-240 B.C. DLB-176

Calmer, Edgar 1907-1986 .... DLB-4

Calverley, C. S. 1831-1884 .... DLB-35

Calvert, George Henry
1803-1889 .... DLB-1, 64, 248

Calverton, V. F. (George Goetz)
1900-1940 .... DLB-303

Calvin, Jean 1509-1564 .... DLB-327

Calvino, Italo 1923-1985 .... DLB-196

Cambridge, Ada 1844-1926 .... DLB-230

Cambridge Press DLB-49

Cambridge Songs (Carmina Cantabrigensia)
circa 1050 .... DLB-148

Cambridge University
Cambridge and the Apostles DS-5

Cambridge University Press DLB-170

Camden, William 1551-1623 .... DLB-172

Camden House: An Interview with
James Hardin...................... Y-92

Cameron, Eleanor 1912-2000 .... DLB-52

Cameron, George Frederick
1854-1885 .... DLB-99

Cameron, Lucy Lyttelton 1781-1858..... DLB-163

Cameron, Peter 1959- DLB-234

Cameron, William Bleasdell 1862-1951.... DLB-99

Camm, John 1718-1778 .... DLB-31

Camões, Luís de 1524-1580............ DLB-287

Camon, Ferdinando 1935- DLB-196

Camp, Walter 1859-1925 .... DLB-241

Campana, Dino 1885-1932 .... DLB-114

Campbell, Bebe Moore 1950- DLB-227

Campbell, David 1915-1979 .... DLB-260

Campbell, Gabrielle Margaret Vere
(see Shearing, Joseph, and Bowen, Marjorie)

Campbell, James Dykes 1838-1895 ...... DLB-144

Campbell, James Edwin 1867-1896 .... DLB-50

Campbell, John 1653-1728 .... DLB-43

Campbell, John W., Jr. 1910-1971 .... DLB-8

Campbell, Ramsey 1946- DLB-261

Campbell, Robert 1927-2000 .... DLB-306

Campbell, Roy 1901-1957 .... DLB-20, 225

Campbell, Thomas 1777-1844 .... DLB-93, 144

Campbell, William Edward (see March, William)

Campbell, William Wilfred 1858-1918 .... DLB-92

Campion, Edmund 1539-1581 .... DLB-167

Campion, Thomas
1567-1620 .... DLB-58, 172; CDBLB-1

Campo, Rafael 1964- DLB-282

Campton, David 1924- DLB-245

Camus, Albert 1913-1960 .... DLB-72, 321

Camus, Jean-Pierre 1584-1652 .... DLB-268

The Canadian Publishers' Records Database ...Y-96

Canby, Henry Seidel 1878-1961 .... DLB-91

Cancioneros DLB-286

Candelaria, Cordelia 1943- DLB-82

Candelaria, Nash 1928- DLB-82

Candide, Voltaire DLB-314

Canetti, Elias
1905-1994 .... DLB-85, 124; CDWLB-2

Canham, Erwin Dain 1904-1982........ DLB-127

Canitz, Friedrich Rudolph Ludwig von
1654-1699 .... DLB-168

Cankar, Ivan 1876-1918..... DLB-147; CDWLB-4

Cannan, Gilbert 1884-1955 .... DLB-10, 197

Cannan, Joanna 1896-1961 .... DLB-191

Cannell, Kathleen 1891-1974 .... DLB-4

Cannell, Skipwith 1887-1957 .... DLB-45

Canning, George 1770-1827 .... DLB-158

Cannon, Jimmy 1910-1973 .... DLB-171

Cano, Daniel 1947- DLB-209

Old Dogs / New Tricks? New
Technologies, the Canon, and the
Structure of the Profession Y-02

Cantú, Norma Elia 1947- DLB-209

Cantwell, Robert 1908-1978 .... DLB-9

Jonathan Cape and Harrison Smith
[publishing house] DLB-46

Jonathan Cape Limited DLB-112

Čapek, Karel 1890-1938 .... DLB-215; CDWLB-4

Capen, Joseph 1658-1725............... DLB-24

Capes, Bernard 1854-1918............. DLB-156

Capote, Truman 1924-1984
.... DLB-2, 185, 227; Y-80, 84; CDALB-1

Capps, Benjamin 1922- DLB-256

Caproni, Giorgio 1912-1990 .... DLB-128

Caragiale, Mateiu Ioan 1885-1936....... DLB-220

Carballido, Emilio 1925- DLB-305

Cardarelli, Vincenzo 1887-1959 .... DLB-114

Cardenal, Ernesto 1925- DLB-290

Cárdenas, Reyes 1948- DLB-122

Cardinal, Marie 1929-2001 .... DLB-83

Cardoza y Aragón, Luis 1901-1992...... DLB-290

Carew, Jan 1920- DLB-157

Carew, Thomas 1594 or 1595-1640..... DLB-126

Carey, Henry circa 1687-1689-1743....... DLB-84

Carey, Mathew 1760-1839 .... DLB-37, 73

M. Carey and Company DLB-49

Carey, Peter 1943- DLB-289, 326

Carey and Hart DLB-49

Carlell, Lodowick 1602-1675........... DLB-58

Carleton, William 1794-1869........... DLB-159

G. W. Carleton [publishing house] DLB-49

Carlile, Richard 1790-1843 .... DLB-110, 158

Carlson, Ron 1947- DLB-244

Carlyle, Jane Welsh 1801-1866 .... DLB-55

Carlyle, Thomas
1795-1881 .... DLB-55, 144; CDBLB-3

"The Hero as Man of Letters:
  Johnson, Rousseau, Burns"
  (1841) [excerpt] DLB-57

The Hero as Poet. Dante; Shakspeare
  (1841) DLB-32

Carman, Bliss 1861-1929 .... DLB-92

Carmina Burana circa 1230 .... DLB-138

Carnap, Rudolf 1891-1970 .... DLB-270

Carnero, Guillermo 1947- DLB-108

Carossa, Hans 1878-1956 .... DLB-66

Carpenter, Humphrey
  1946-2005 .... DLB-155; Y-84, 99

Carpenter, Stephen Cullen ?-1820? DLB-73

Carpentier, Alejo
  1904-1980 .... DLB-113; CDWLB-3

Carr, Emily 1871-1945 .... DLB-68

Carr, John Dickson 1906-1977 .... DLB-306

Carr, Marina 1964- DLB-245

Carr, Virginia Spencer 1929- DLB-111; Y-00

Carrera Andrade, Jorge 1903-1978 ...... DLB-283

Carrier, Roch 1937- DLB-53

Carrillo, Adolfo 1855-1926 .... DLB-122

Carroll, Gladys Hasty 1904-1999 .... DLB-9

Carroll, John 1735-1815 .... DLB-37

Carroll, John 1809-1884 .... DLB-99

Carroll, Lewis
  1832-1898 ..... DLB-18, 163, 178; CDBLB-4

  The Lewis Carroll Centenary Y-98

  The Lewis Carroll Society
    of North America Y-00

Carroll, Paul 1927-1996 .... DLB-16

Carroll, Paul Vincent 1900-1968 .... DLB-10

Carroll and Graf Publishers DLB-46

Carruth, Hayden 1921- DLB-5, 165

  Tribute to James Dickey............... Y-97

  Tribute to Raymond Carver............ Y-88

Carryl, Charles E. 1841-1920 .... DLB-42

Carson, Anne 1950- DLB-193

Carson, Rachel 1907-1964 .... DLB-275

Carswell, Catherine 1879-1946.......... DLB-36

Cartagena, Alfonso de circa 1384-1456 .. DLB-286

Cartagena, Teresa de 1425?-? DLB-286

Cărtărescu, Mirea 1956- DLB-232

Carter, Angela
  1940-1992 .... DLB-14, 207, 261, 319

Carter, Elizabeth 1717-1806............ DLB-109

Carter, Henry (see Leslie, Frank)

Carter, Hodding, Jr. 1907-1972 .... DLB-127

Carter, Jared 1939- DLB-282

Carter, John 1905-1975................ DLB-201

Carter, Landon 1710-1778.............. DLB-31

Carter, Lin 1930-1988.................. Y-81

Carter, Martin 1927-1997 ....DLB-117; CDWLB-3

Carter, Robert, and Brothers DLB-49

Carter and Hendee.................... DLB-49

Cartwright, Jim 1958- DLB-245

Cartwright, John 1740-1824 .... DLB-158

Cartwright, William circa 1611-1643 .... DLB-126

Caruthers, William Alexander
  1802-1846 .... DLB-3, 248

Carver, Jonathan 1710-1780 .... DLB-31

Carver, Raymond 1938-1988 ... DLB-130; Y-83,88

  First Strauss "Livings" Awarded to Cynthia
    Ozick and Raymond Carver
    An Interview with Raymond Carver.... Y-83

Carvic, Heron 1917?-1980 ....DLB-276

Cary, Alice 1820-1871................. DLB-202

Cary, Joyce 1888-1957 ... DLB-15, 100; CDBLB-6

Cary, Patrick 1623?-1657 .... DLB-131

Casal, Julián del 1863-1893 .... DLB-283

Case, John 1540-1600.................. DLB-281

Casey, Gavin 1907-1964................ DLB-260

Casey, Juanita 1925- DLB-14

Casey, Michael 1947- DLB-5

Cassady, Carolyn 1923- DLB-16

  "As I See It" DLB-16

Cassady, Neal 1926-1968 ....DLB-16, 237

Cassell and Company.................. DLB-106

Cassell Publishing Company DLB-49

Cassill, R. V. 1919-2002 ....DLB-6, 218; Y-02

  Tribute to James Dickey............... Y-97

Cassity, Turner 1929- DLB-105; Y-02

Cassius Dio circa 155/164-post 229 .....DLB-176

Cassola, Carlo 1917-1987 ....DLB-177

Castellano, Olivia 1944- DLB-122

Castellanos, Rosario
  1925-1974..........DLB-113, 290; CDWLB-3

Castelo Branco, Camilo 1825-1890 ..... DLB-287

Castile, Protest Poetry in.............. DLB-286

Castile and Aragon, Vernacular Translations
  in Crowns of 1352-1515............ DLB-286

Castillejo, Cristóbal de 1490?-1550 ..... DLB-318

Castillo, Ana 1953- DLB-122, 227

Castillo, Rafael C. 1950- DLB-209

The Castle of Perseverance
  circa 1400-1425 .... DLB-146

Castlemon, Harry (see Fosdick, Charles Austin)

Castro, Brian 1950- DLB-325

Castro, Consuelo de 1946- DLB-307

Castro Alves, Antônio de 1847-1871..... DLB-307

Čašule, Kole 1921- DLB-181

Caswall, Edward 1814-1878 .... DLB-32

Catacalos, Rosemary 1944- DLB-122

Cather, Willa 1873-1947
  .... DLB-9, 54, 78, 256; DS-1; CDALB-3

The Willa Cather Pioneer Memorial
  and Education Foundation Y-00

Catherine II (Ekaterina Alekseevna), "The Great,"
  Empress of Russia 1729-1796....... DLB-150

Catherwood, Mary Hartwell 1847-1902... DLB-78

Catledge, Turner 1901-1983............DLB-127

Catlin, George 1796-1872 .... DLB-186, 189

Cato the Elder 234 B.C.-149 B.C. DLB-211

Cattafi, Bartolo 1922-1979 .... DLB-128

Catton, Bruce 1899-1978 ....DLB-17

Catullus circa 84 B.C.-54 B.C.
  ....DLB-211; CDWLB-1

Causley, Charles 1917-2003 .... DLB-27

Caute, David 1936- DLB-14, 231

Cavendish, Duchess of Newcastle,
  Margaret Lucas
  1623?-1673.......... DLB-131, 252, 281

Cawein, Madison 1865-1914 .... DLB-54

William Caxton [publishing house] DLB-170

The Caxton Printers, Limited DLB-46

Caylor, O. P. 1849-1897 .... DLB-241

Caylus, Marthe-Marguerite de
  1671-1729..................... DLB-313

Cayrol, Jean 1911-2005 .... DLB-83

Cecil, Lord David 1902-1986.......... DLB-155

Cela, Camilo José 1916-2002 ......DLB-322; Y-89

  Nobel Lecture 1989 .... Y-89

Celan, Paul 1920-1970 ...... DLB-69; CDWLB-2

Celati, Gianni 1937- DLB-196

Celaya, Gabriel 1911-1991 .... DLB-108

Céline, Louis-Ferdinand 1894-1961 ...... DLB-72

Celtis, Conrad 1459-1508..............DLB-179

Cendrars, Blaise 1887-1961 .... DLB-258

The Steinbeck Centennial Y-02

Censorship
  The Island Trees Case: A Symposium on
    School Library Censorship Y-82

Center for Bibliographical Studies and
  Research at the University of
  California, Riverside Y-91

Center for Book Research Y-84

The Center for the Book in the Library
  of Congress Y-93

  A New Voice: The Center for the
    Book's First Five Years............ Y-83

Centlivre, Susanna 1669?-1723.......... DLB-84

The Centre for Writing, Publishing and
  Printing History at the University
  of Reading....................... Y-00

The Century Company DLB-49

A Century of Poetry, a Lifetime of Collecting:
  J. M. Edelstein's Collection of
  Twentieth-Century American Poetry..... Y-02

Cernuda, Luis 1902-1963............. DLB-134

Cerruto, Oscar 1912-1981 .... DLB-283

Cervantes, Lorna Dee 1954- DLB-82

Césaire, Aimé 1913- DLB-321

de Céspedes, Alba 1911-1997 ....DLB-264

Cetina, Gutierre de 1514-17?-1556 ......DLB-318

Ch., T. (see Marchenko, Anastasiia Iakovlevna)

Cha, Theresa Hak Kyung 1951-1982 ....DLB-312

Chaadaev, Petr Iakovlevich
1794-1856 ....DLB-198

Chabon, Michael 1963- DLB-278

Chacel, Rosa 1898-1994 ....DLB-134, 322

Chacón, Eusebio 1869-1948 ....DLB-82

Chacón, Felipe Maximiliano 1873-? DLB-82

Chadwick, Henry 1824-1908...........DLB-241

Chadwyck-Healey's Full-Text Literary Databases:
Editing Commercial Databases of
Primary Literary Texts Y-95

Challans, Eileen Mary (see Renault, Mary)

Chalmers, George 1742-1825............DLB-30

Chaloner, Sir Thomas 1520-1565 ....DLB-167

Chamberlain, Samuel S. 1851-1916.......DLB-25

Chamberland, Paul 1939- DLB-60

Chamberlin, William Henry 1897-1969....DLB-29

Chambers, Charles Haddon 1860-1921 ...DLB-10

Chambers, María Cristina (see Mena, María Cristina)

Chambers, Robert W. 1865-1933 ....DLB-202

W. and R. Chambers
[publishing house] DLB-106

Chambers, Whittaker 1901-1961 ....DLB-303

Chamfort, Sébastien-Roch Nicolas de
1740?-1794.....................DLB-313

Chamisso, Adelbert von 1781-1838.......DLB-90

Champfleury 1821-1889 ....DLB-119

Champier, Symphorien 1472?-1539? DLB-327

Chan, Jeffery Paul 1942- DLB-312

Chandler, Harry 1864-1944.............DLB-29

Chandler, Norman 1899-1973 ....DLB-127

Chandler, Otis 1927-2006.............DLB-127

Chandler, Raymond
1888-1959 ....DLB-226, 253; DS-6; CDALB-5

Raymond Chandler Centenary..........Y-88

Chang, Diana 1934- DLB-312

Channing, Edward 1856-1931 ....DLB-17

Channing, Edward Tyrrell
1790-1856 ....DLB-1, 59, 235

Channing, William Ellery
1780-1842 ....DLB-1, 59, 235

Channing, William Ellery, II
1817-1901 ....DLB-1, 223

Channing, William Henry
1810-1884 ....DLB-1, 59, 243

Chapelain, Jean 1595-1674............DLB-268

Chaplin, Charlie 1889-1977 ....DLB-44

Chapman, George
1559 or 1560-1634 ....DLB-62, 121

Chapman, Olive Murray 1892-1977 .....DLB-195

Chapman, R. W. 1881-1960 ....DLB-201

Chapman, William 1850-1917..........DLB-99

John Chapman [publishing house].......DLB-106

Chapman and Hall [publishing house] ...DLB-106

Chappell, Fred 1936- DLB-6, 105

    "A Detail in a Poem" DLB-105

    Tribute to Peter Taylor Y-94

Chappell, William 1582-1649 ....DLB-236

Char, René 1907-1988 ....DLB-258

Charbonneau, Jean 1875-1960..........DLB-92

Charbonneau, Robert 1911-1967 ....DLB-68

Charles, Gerda 1914-1996..............DLB-14

William Charles [publishing house].......DLB-49

Charles d'Orléans 1394-1465 ....DLB-208

Charley (see Mann, Charles)

Charrière, Isabelle de 1740-1805 ....DLB-313

Charskaia, Lidiia 1875-1937............DLB-295

Charteris, Leslie 1907-1993 ....DLB-77

Chartier, Alain circa 1385-1430 ....DLB-208

Charyn, Jerome 1937- Y-83

Chase, Borden 1900-1971 ....DLB-26

Chase, Edna Woolman 1877-1957 ....DLB-91

Chase, James Hadley (René Raymond)
1906-1985 ....DLB-276

Chase, Mary Coyle 1907-1981..........DLB-228

Chase-Riboud, Barbara 1936- DLB-33

Chateaubriand, François-René de
1768-1848 ....DLB-119

Châtelet, Gabrielle-Emilie Du
1706-1749 ....DLB-313

Chatterjee, Upamanyu 1959- DLB-323

Chatterton, Thomas 1752-1770 ....DLB-109

    Essay on Chatterton (1842), by
    Robert Browning DLB-32

Chatto and Windus DLB-106

Chatwin, Bruce 1940-1989 ....DLB-194, 204

Chaucer, Geoffrey
1340?-1400 ....DLB-146; CDBLB-1

    New Chaucer Society Y-00

Chaudhuri, Amit 1962- DLB-267, 323

Chaudhuri, Nirad C. 1897-1999 ....DLB-323

Chauncy, Charles 1705-1787 ....DLB-24

Chauveau, Pierre-Joseph-Olivier
1820-1890 ....DLB-99

Chávez, Denise 1948- DLB-122

Chávez, Fray Angélico 1910-1996 ....DLB-82

Chayefsky, Paddy 1923-1981..... DLB-7, 44; Y-81

Cheesman, Evelyn 1881-1969 ....DLB-195

Cheever, Ezekiel 1615-1708 ....DLB-24

Cheever, George Barrell 1807-1890 ......DLB-59

Cheever, John 1912-1982
.... DLB-2, 102, 227; Y-80, 82; CDALB-1

Cheever, Susan 1943- Y-82

Cheke, Sir John 1514-1557 ....DLB-132

Chekhov, Anton Pavlovich 1860-1904 ...DLB-277

Chelsea House DLB-46

Chênedollé, Charles de 1769-1833 ......DLB-217

Cheney, Brainard
    Tribute to Caroline Gordon Y-81

Cheney, Ednah Dow 1824-1904 ......DLB-1, 223

Cheney, Harriet Vaughan 1796-1889......DLB-99

Chénier, Marie-Joseph 1764-1811 ....DLB-192

Cheng Xiaoqing 1893-1976............DLB-328

Cherny, Sasha 1880-1932 ....DLB-317

Chernyshevsky, Nikolai Gavrilovich
1828-1889 ....DLB-238

Cherry, Kelly 1940 ....Y-83

Cherryh, C. J. 1942- Y-80

Chesebro', Caroline 1825-1873 ....DLB-202

Chesney, Sir George Tomkyns
1830-1895 ....DLB-190

Chesnut, Mary Boykin 1823-1886.......DLB-239

Chesnutt, Charles Waddell
1858-1932 .... DLB-12, 50, 78

Chesson, Mrs. Nora (see Hopper, Nora)

Chester, Alfred 1928-1971 ....DLB-130

Chester, George Randolph 1869-1924 ....DLB-78

The Chester Plays circa 1505-1532;
revisions until 1575 ....DLB-146

Chesterfield, Philip Dormer Stanhope,
Fourth Earl of 1694-1773...........DLB-104

Chesterton, G. K. 1874-1936
.. DLB-10, 19, 34, 70, 98, 149, 178; CDBLB-6

    "The Ethics of Elfland" (1908) DLB-178

Chettle, Henry
circa 1560-circa 1607.............DLB-136

Cheuse, Alan 1940- DLB-244

Chew, Ada Nield 1870-1945 ....DLB-135

Cheyney, Edward P. 1861-1947..........DLB-47

Chiang Yee 1903-1977 ....DLB-312

Chiara, Piero 1913-1986 ....DLB-177

Chicanos
    Chicano History DLB-82
    Chicano Language DLB-82
    Chicano Literature: A Bibliography .. DLB-209
    A Contemporary Flourescence of Chicano
    Literature Y-84
    Literatura Chicanesca: The View From
    Without DLB-82

Child, Francis James 1825-1896.... DLB-1, 64, 235

Child, Lydia Maria 1802-1880 .... DLB-1, 74, 243

Child, Philip 1898-1978 ....DLB-68

Childers, Erskine 1870-1922 ....DLB-70

Children's Literature
    Afterword: Propaganda, Namby-Pamby,
    and Some Books of Distinction ...DLB-52
    Children's Book Awards and Prizes ...DLB-61
    Children's Book Illustration in the
    Twentieth Century DLB-61

Children's Illustrators, 1800-1880 . . . DLB-163
    The Harry Potter Phenomenon Y-99
    Pony Stories, Omnibus
      Essay on DLB-160
    The Reality of One Woman's Dream:
      The de Grummond Children's
      Literature Collection Y-99
    School Stories, 1914-1960 . . . . DLB-160
    The Year in Children's
      Books Y-92–96, 98–01
    The Year in Children's Literature Y-97
Childress, Alice 1916-1994 . . . . DLB-7, 38, 249
Childress, Mark 1957- DLB-292
Childs, George W. 1829-1894 . . . . DLB-23
Chilton Book Company DLB-46
Chin, Frank 1940- DLB-206, 312
Chin, Justin 1969- DLB-312
Chin, Marilyn 1955- DLB-312
Chinweizu 1943- DLB-157
Chinnov, Igor' 1909-1996 . . . . DLB-317
Chitham, Edward 1932- DLB-155
Chittenden, Hiram Martin 1858-1917 . . . . DLB-47
Chivers, Thomas Holley 1809-1858 . . . DLB-3, 248
Chkhartishvili, Grigorii Shalvovich
    (see Akunin, Boris)
Chocano, José Santos 1875-1934 . . . . DLB-290
Cholmondeley, Mary 1859-1925 . . . . DLB-197
Chomsky, Noam 1928- DLB-246
Chopin, Kate 1850-1904 . . . DLB-12, 78; CDALB-3
Chopin, René 1885-1953 . . . . DLB-92
Choquette, Adrienne 1915-1973 . . . . DLB-68
Choquette, Robert 1905-1991 . . . . DLB-68
Choyce, Lesley 1951- DLB-251
Chrétien de Troyes
    circa 1140-circa 1190 . . . . DLB-208
Christensen, Inger 1935- DLB-214
Christensen, Lars Saabye 1953- DLB-297
The Christian Examiner DLB-1
The Christian Publishing Company DLB-49
Christie, Agatha
    1890-1976 . . . . DLB-13, 77, 245; CDBLB-6
Christine de Pizan
    circa 1365-circa 1431 . . . . DLB-208
Christopher, John (Sam Youd) 1922- . . DLB-255
Christus und die Samariterin circa 950 . . . . . DLB-148
Christy, Howard Chandler 1873-1952 . . . DLB-188
Chu, Louis 1915-1970 . . . . DLB-312
Chukovskaia, Lidiia 1907-1996 . . . . DLB-302
Chulkov, Mikhail Dmitrievich
    1743?-1792 . . . . DLB-150
Church, Benjamin 1734-1778 . . . . DLB-31
Church, Francis Pharcellus 1839-1906 . . . . DLB-79
Church, Peggy Pond 1903-1986 . . . . DLB-212
Church, Richard 1893-1972 . . . . DLB-191

Church, William Conant 1836-1917 . . . . . DLB-79
Churchill, Caryl 1938- DLB-13, 310
Churchill, Charles 1731-1764 . . . . DLB-109
Churchill, Winston 1871-1947 . . . . DLB-202
Churchill, Sir Winston
    1874-1965 . . . . DLB-100; DS-16; CDBLB-5
Churchyard, Thomas 1520?-1604 . . . . . . DLB-132
E. Churton and Company DLB-106
Chute, Marchette 1909-1994 . . . . DLB-103
Ciardi, John 1916-1986 . . . . DLB-5; Y-86
Cibber, Colley 1671-1757 . . . . DLB-84
Cicero 106 B.C.-43 B.C. DLB-211, CDWLB-1
Cima, Annalisa 1941- DLB-128
Čingo, Živko 1935-1987 . . . . DLB-181
Cioran, E. M. 1911-1995 . . . . DLB-220
Čipkus, Alfonsas (see Nyka-Niliūnas, Alfonsas)
Cirese, Eugenio 1884-1955 . . . . DLB-114
Cīrulis, Jānis (see Bels, Alberts)
Cisneros, Antonio 1942- DLB-290
Cisneros, Sandra 1954- DLB-122, 152
City Lights Books DLB-46
Civil War (1861–1865)
    Battles and Leaders of the Civil War DLB-47
    Official Records of the Rebellion DLB-47
    Recording the Civil War DLB-47
Cixous, Hélène 1937- DLB-83, 242
Claire d'Albe, Sophie Cottin DLB-314
Clampitt, Amy 1920-1994 . . . . DLB-105
    Tribute to Alfred A. Knopf Y-84
Clancy, Tom 1947- DLB-227
Clapper, Raymond 1892-1944 . . . . DLB-29
Clare, John 1793-1864 . . . . DLB-55, 96
Clarendon, Edward Hyde, Earl of
    1609-1674 . . . . DLB-101
Clark, Alfred Alexander Gordon
    (see Hare, Cyril)
Clark, Ann Nolan 1896-1995 . . . . DLB-52
Clark, C. E. Frazer, Jr. 1925-2001 . . . DLB-187; Y-01
    C. E. Frazer Clark Jr. and
      Hawthorne Bibliography DLB-269
    The Publications of C. E. Frazer
      Clark Jr. DLB-269
Clark, Catherine Anthony 1892-1977 . . . . DLB-68
Clark, Charles Heber 1841-1915 . . . . DLB-11
Clark, Davis Wasgatt 1812-1871 . . . . DLB-79
Clark, Douglas 1919-1993 . . . . DLB-276
Clark, Eleanor 1913-1996 . . . . DLB-6
Clark, J. P. 1935- DLB-117; CDWLB-3
Clark, Lewis Gaylord
    1808-1873 . . . . DLB-3, 64, 73, 250
Clark, Mary Higgins 1929- DLB-306
Clark, Walter Van Tilburg
    1909-1971 . . . . DLB-9, 206

Clark, William 1770-1838 . . . . DLB-183, 186
Clark, William Andrews, Jr.
    1877-1934 . . . . DLB-187
C. M. Clark Publishing Company DLB-46
Clarke, Sir Arthur C. 1917- DLB-261
    Tribute to Theodore Sturgeon Y-85
Clarke, Austin 1896-1974 . . . . DLB-10, 20
Clarke, Austin C. 1934- DLB-53, 125
Clarke, Gillian 1937- DLB-40
Clarke, James Freeman
    1810-1888 . . . . DLB-1, 59, 235; DS-5
Clarke, John circa 1596-1658 . . . . DLB-281
Clarke, Lindsay 1939- DLB-231
Clarke, Marcus 1846-1881 . . . . DLB-230
Clarke, Pauline 1921- DLB-161
Clarke, Rebecca Sophia 1833-1906 . . . . . . DLB-42
Clarke, Samuel 1675-1729 . . . . DLB-252
Robert Clarke and Company DLB-49
Clarkson, Thomas 1760-1846 . . . . DLB-158
Claudel, Paul 1868-1955 . . . . . DLB-192, 258, 321
Claudius, Matthias 1740-1815 . . . . DLB-97
Clausen, Andy 1943- DLB-16
Claussen, Sophus 1865-1931 . . . . DLB-300
Clawson, John L. 1865-1933 . . . . DLB-187
Claxton, Remsen and Haffelfinger DLB-49
Clay, Cassius Marcellus 1810-1903 . . . . . . DLB-43
Clayton, Richard (see Haggard, William)
Cleage, Pearl 1948- DLB-228
Cleary, Beverly 1916- DLB-52
Cleary, Kate McPhelim 1863-1905 . . . . . . DLB-221
Cleaver, Vera 1919-1992 and
    Cleaver, Bill 1920-1981 . . . . DLB-52
Cleeve, Brian 1921-2003 . . . . DLB-276
Cleland, John 1710-1789 . . . . DLB-39
Clemens, Samuel Langhorne (Mark Twain)
    1835-1910 . . . . DLB-11, 12, 23, 64, 74,
                                186, 189; CDALB-3
    Comments From Authors and Scholars on
      their First Reading of *Huck Finn* Y-85
    Huck at 100: How Old Is
      Huckleberry Finn? Y-85
    Mark Twain on Perpetual Copyright Y-92
    A New Edition of *Huck Finn* Y-85
Clement, Hal 1922-2003 . . . . DLB-8
Clemo, Jack 1916-1994 . . . . DLB-27
Clephane, Elizabeth Cecilia 1830-1869 . . DLB-199
Cleveland, John 1613-1658 . . . . DLB-126
Cliff, Michelle 1946- DLB-157; CDWLB-3
Clifford, Lady Anne 1590-1676 . . . . DLB-151
Clifford, James L. 1901-1978 . . . . DLB-103
Clifford, Lucy 1853?-1929 . . . . . DLB-135, 141, 197
Clift, Charmian 1923-1969 . . . . DLB-260
Clifton, Lucille 1936- DLB-5, 41

Clines, Francis X. 1938- DLB-185

Clive, Caroline (V) 1801-1873..........DLB-199

Edward J. Clode [publishing house].......DLB-46

Clough, Arthur Hugh 1819-1861 ....DLB-32

Cloutier, Cécile 1930- DLB-60

Clouts, Sidney 1926-1982 ....DLB-225

Clutton-Brock, Arthur 1868-1924 ....DLB-98

Coates, Robert M.
1897-1973.............DLB-4, 9, 102; DS-15

Coatsworth, Elizabeth 1893-1986 ....DLB-22

Cobb, Charles E., Jr. 1943- DLB-41

Cobb, Frank I. 1869-1923 ....DLB-25

Cobb, Irvin S. 1876-1944.........DLB-11, 25, 86

Cobbe, Frances Power 1822-1904 ....DLB-190

Cobbett, William 1763-1835 .... DLB-43, 107, 158

Cobbledick, Gordon 1898-1969.........DLB-171

Cochran, Thomas C. 1902-1999 ....DLB-17

Cochrane, Elizabeth 1867-1922 ......DLB-25, 189

Cockerell, Sir Sydney 1867-1962 ....DLB-201

Cockerill, John A. 1845-1896..........DLB-23

Cocteau, Jean 1889-1963 ....DLB-65, 258, 321

Coderre, Emile (see Jean Narrache)

Cody, Liza 1944- DLB-276

Coe, Jonathan 1961- DLB-231

Coetzee, J. M. 1940- DLB-225, 326

Coffee, Lenore J. 1900?-1984...........DLB-44

Coffin, Robert P. Tristram 1892-1955.....DLB-45

Coghill, Mrs. Harry (see Walker, Anna Louisa)

Cogswell, Fred 1917- DLB-60

Cogswell, Mason Fitch 1761-1830 ....DLB-37

Cohan, George M. 1878-1942 ....DLB-249

Cohen, Arthur A. 1928-1986............DLB-28

Cohen, Leonard 1934- DLB-53

Cohen, Matt 1942- DLB-53

Cohen, Morris Raphael 1880-1947 ......DLB-270

Colasanti, Marina 1937- DLB-307

Colbeck, Norman 1903-1987..........DLB-201

Colden, Cadwallader
1688-1776 ....DLB-24, 30, 270

Colden, Jane 1724-1766 ....DLB-200

Cole, Barry 1936- DLB-14

Cole, George Watson 1850-1939........DLB-140

Colegate, Isabel 1931- DLB-14, 231

Coleman, Emily Holmes 1899-1974 ....DLB-4

Coleman, Wanda 1946- DLB-130

Coleridge, Hartley 1796-1849 ....DLB-96

Coleridge, Mary 1861-1907.........DLB-19, 98

Coleridge, Samuel Taylor
1772-1834 ....DLB-93, 107; CDBLB-3

Coleridge, Sara 1802-1852............DLB-199

Colet, John 1467-1519 ....DLB-132

Colette 1873-1954 ....DLB-65

Colette, Sidonie Gabrielle (see Colette)

Colinas, Antonio 1946- DLB-134

Coll, Joseph Clement 1881-1921 ....DLB-188

A Century of Poetry, a Lifetime of Collecting:
J. M. Edelstein's Collection of
Twentieth-Century American Poetry Y-02

Collier, John 1901-1980........... DLB-77, 255

Collier, John Payne 1789-1883..........DLB-184

Collier, Mary 1690-1762 ....DLB-95

Collier, Robert J. 1876-1918...........DLB-91

P. F. Collier [publishing house] DLB-49

Collin and Small DLB-49

Collingwood, R. G. 1889-1943 ....DLB-262

Collingwood, W. G. 1854-1932.........DLB-149

Collins, An floruit circa 1653...........DLB-131

Collins, Anthony 1676-1729............DLB-252

Collins, Merle 1950- DLB-157

Collins, Michael 1964- DLB-267

Collins, Michael (see Lynds, Dennis)

Collins, Mortimer 1827-1876 ....DLB-21, 35

Collins, Tom (see Furphy, Joseph)

Collins, Wilkie
1824-1889 ....DLB-18, 70, 159; CDBLB-4

"The Unknown Public" (1858)
[excerpt] DLB-57

The Wilkie Collins Society Y-98

Collins, William 1721-1759 ....DLB-109

Isaac Collins [publishing house]..........DLB-49

William Collins, Sons and Company.....DLB-154

Collis, Maurice 1889-1973 ....DLB-195

Collyer, Mary 1716?-1763? DLB-39

Colman, Benjamin 1673-1747 ....DLB-24

Colman, George, the Elder 1732-1794.....DLB-89

Colman, George, the Younger
1762-1836 ....DLB-89

S. Colman [publishing house] DLB-49

Colombo, John Robert 1936- DLB-53

Colonial Literature...................DLB-307

Colquhoun, Patrick 1745-1820 ....DLB-158

Colter, Cyrus 1910-2002 ....DLB-33

Colum, Padraic 1881-1972..............DLB-19

The Columbia History of the American Novel
A Symposium on....................Y-92

Columbus, Christopher 1451-1506......DLB-318

Columella fl. first century A.D..........DLB-211

Colvin, Sir Sidney 1845-1927 ....DLB-149

Colwin, Laurie 1944-1992........ DLB-218; Y-80

Comden, Betty 1915- and
Green, Adolph 1918-2002......DLB-44, 265

Comi, Girolamo 1890-1968 ....DLB-114

Comisso, Giovanni 1895-1969..........DLB-264

Commager, Henry Steele 1902-1998 ......DLB-17

Commynes, Philippe de
circa 1447-1511 ....DLB-208

Compton, D. G. 1930- DLB-261

Compton-Burnett, Ivy 1884?-1969 ....DLB-36

Conan, Laure (Félicité Angers)
1845-1924 ....DLB-99

Concord, Massachusetts
Concord History and Life.........DLB-223

Concord: Literary History
of a Town DLB-223

The Old Manse, by Hawthorne DLB-223

The Thoreauvian Pilgrimage: The
Structure of an American Cult ...DLB-223

Concrete Poetry....................DLB-307

Conde, Carmen 1901-1996 ....DLB-108

Condillac, Etienne Bonnot de
1714-1780 ....DLB-313

Condorcet, Marie-Jean-Antoine-Nicolas Caritat,
marquis de 1743-1794 ....DLB-313

"The Tenth Stage"................DLB-314

Congreve, William
1670-1729 ....DLB-39, 84; CDBLB-2

Preface to *Incognita* (1692) DLB-39

W. B. Conkey Company DLB-49

Conlon, Evelyn 1952- DLB-319

Conn, Stewart 1936- DLB-233

Connell, Evan S., Jr. 1924- DLB-2; Y-81

Connelly, Marc 1890-1980 .... DLB-7; Y-80

Connolly, Cyril 1903-1974..............DLB-98

Connolly, James B. 1868-1957...........DLB-78

Connor, Ralph (Charles William Gordon)
1860-1937 ....DLB-92

Connor, Tony 1930- DLB-40

Conquest, Robert 1917- DLB-27

Conrad, Joseph
1857-1924 ....DLB-10, 34, 98, 156; CDBLB-5

John Conrad and Company DLB-49

Conroy, Jack 1899-1990...................Y-81

A Tribute [to Nelson Algren]............Y-81

Conroy, Pat 1945- DLB-6

The Conservationist, 1974 Booker Prize winner,
Nadine Gordimer DLB-326

Considine, Bob 1906-1975.............DLB-241

Consolo, Vincenzo 1933- DLB-196

Constable, Henry 1562-1613............DLB-136

Archibald Constable and Company DLB-154

Constable and Company Limited DLB-112

Constant, Benjamin 1767-1830..........DLB-119

Constant de Rebecque, Henri-Benjamin de
(see Constant, Benjamin)

Constantine, David 1944- DLB-40

Constantine, Murray (see Burdekin, Katharine)

Constantin-Weyer, Maurice 1881-1964 ....DLB-92

Contempo (magazine)
Contempo Caravan:
Kites in a Windstorm Y-85

Cumulative Index

The Continental Publishing Company.... DLB-49

A Conversation between William Riggan
and Janette Turner Hospital............ Y-02

Conversations with Editors Y-95

Conway, Anne 1631-1679............. DLB-252

Conway, Moncure Daniel
1832-1907.................... DLB-1, 223

Cook, Ebenezer circa 1667-circa 1732..... DLB-24

Cook, Edward Tyas 1857-1919......... DLB-149

Cook, Eliza 1818-1889................ DLB-199

Cook, George Cram 1873-1924........ DLB-266

Cook, Michael 1933-1994 .... DLB-53

David C. Cook Publishing Company..... DLB-49

Cooke, George Willis 1848-1923......... DLB-71

Cooke, John Esten 1830-1886 .... DLB-3, 248

Cooke, Philip Pendleton
1816-1850.................. DLB-3, 59, 248

Cooke, Rose Terry 1827-1892 .... DLB-12, 74

Increase Cooke and Company DLB-49

Cook-Lynn, Elizabeth 1930- DLB-175

Coolbrith, Ina 1841-1928........... DLB-54, 186

Cooley, Peter 1940- DLB-105

"Into the Mirror" DLB-105

Coolidge, Clark 1939- DLB-193

Coolidge, Susan
(see Woolsey, Sarah Chauncy)

George Coolidge [publishing house]...... DLB-49

Coomaraswamy, Ananda 1877-1947..... DLB-323

Cooper, Anna Julia 1858-1964 .... DLB-221

Cooper, Edith Emma 1862-1913 .... DLB-240

Cooper, Giles 1918-1966 .... DLB-13

Cooper, J. California 19??- DLB-212

Cooper, James Fenimore
1789-1851....... DLB-3, 183, 250; CDALB-2

The Bicentennial of James Fenimore Cooper:
An International Celebration........ Y-89

The James Fenimore Cooper Society..... Y-01

Cooper, Kent 1880-1965................ DLB-29

Cooper, Susan 1935- DLB-161, 261

Cooper, Susan Fenimore 1813-1894..... DLB-239

William Cooper [publishing house] DLB-170

J. Coote [publishing house]............ DLB-154

Coover, Robert 1932- DLB-2, 227; Y-81

Tribute to Donald Barthelme........ Y-89

Tribute to Theodor Seuss Geisel Y-91

Copeland and Day DLB-49

Ćopić, Branko 1915-1984............. DLB-181

Copland, Robert 1470?-1548 .... DLB-136

Coppard, A. E. 1878-1957............. DLB-162

Coppée, François 1842-1908 .... DLB-217

Coppel, Alfred 1921-2004................. Y-83

Tribute to Jessamyn West.......... Y-84

Coppola, Francis Ford 1939- DLB-44

Copway, George (Kah-ge-ga-gah-bowh)
1818-1869 ....DLB-175, 183

Copyright
The Development of the Author's
Copyright in Britain DLB-154

The Digital Millennium Copyright Act:
Expanding Copyright Protection in
Cyberspace and Beyond Y-98

Editorial: The Extension of Copyright ... Y-02

Mark Twain on Perpetual Copyright..... Y-92

Public Domain and the Violation
of Texts Y-97

The Question of American Copyright
in the Nineteenth Century
Preface, by George Haven Putnam
The Evolution of Copyright, by
Brander Matthews
Summary of Copyright Legislation in
the United States, by R. R. Bowker
Analysis of the Provisions of the
Copyright Law of 1891, by
George Haven Putnam
The Contest for International Copyright,
by George Haven Putnam
Cheap Books and Good Books,
by Brander Matthews DLB-49

Writers and Their Copyright Holders:
the WATCH Project Y-94

Corazzini, Sergio 1886-1907........... DLB-114

Corbett, Richard 1582-1635........... DLB-121

Corbière, Tristan 1845-1875........... DLB-217

Corcoran, Barbara 1911- DLB-52

Cordelli, Franco 1943- DLB-196

Corelli, Marie 1855-1924 .... DLB-34, 156

Corle, Edwin 1906-1956................ Y-85

Corman, Cid 1924-2004............ DLB-5, 193

Cormier, Robert 1925-2000 ... DLB-52; CDALB-6

Tribute to Theodor Seuss Geisel Y-91

Corn, Alfred 1943- DLB-120, 282; Y-80

Corneille, Pierre 1606-1684............DLB-268

Cornford, Frances 1886-1960......... DLB-240

Cornish, Sam 1935- DLB-41

Cornish, William
circa 1465-circa 1524 .... DLB-132

Cornwall, Barry (see Procter, Bryan Waller)

Cornwallis, Sir William, the Younger
circa 1579-1614.................. DLB-151

Cornwell, David John Moore (see le Carré, John)

Cornwell, Patricia 1956- DLB-306

Coronel Urtecho, José 1906-1994........ DLB-290

Corpi, Lucha 1945- DLB-82

Corrington, John William
1932-1988 .... DLB-6, 244

Corriveau, Monique 1927-1976 .... DLB-251

Corrothers, James D. 1869-1917......... DLB-50

Corso, Gregory 1930-2001........DLB-5, 16, 237

Cortázar, Julio 1914-1984....DLB-113; CDWLB-3

Cortéz, Carlos 1923-2005............ DLB-209

Cortez, Jayne 1936- DLB-41

Corvinus, Gottlieb Siegmund
1677-1746.................... DLB-168

Corvo, Baron (see Rolfe, Frederick William)

Cory, Annie Sophie (see Cross, Victoria)

Cory, Desmond (Shaun Lloyd McCarthy)
1928- DLB-276

Cory, William Johnson 1823-1892....... DLB-35

Coryate, Thomas 1577?-1617.......DLB-151, 172

Ćosić, Dobrica 1921- DLB-181; CDWLB-4

Cosin, John 1595-1672 .... DLB-151, 213

Cosmopolitan Book Corporation........ DLB-46

Cossa, Roberto 1934- DLB-305

Costa, Maria Velho da (see The Three Marias:
A Landmark Case in Portuguese
Literary History)

Costain, Thomas B. 1885-1965 .... DLB-9

Coste, Donat (Daniel Boudreau)
1912-1957.................... DLB-88

Costello, Louisa Stuart 1799-1870....... DLB-166

Cota-Cárdenas, Margarita 1941- DLB-122

Côté, Denis 1954- DLB-251

Cotten, Bruce 1873-1954 ....DLB-187

Cotter, Joseph Seamon, Jr. 1895-1919..... DLB-50

Cotter, Joseph Seamon, Sr. 1861-1949 .... DLB-50

Cottin, Sophie 1770-1807 .... DLB-313

Claire d'Albe..................... DLB-314

Joseph Cottle [publishing house] DLB-154

Cotton, Charles 1630-1687............ DLB-131

Cotton, John 1584-1652 .... DLB-24

Cotton, Sir Robert Bruce 1571-1631 .... DLB-213

Couani, Anna 1948- DLB-325

Coulter, John 1888-1980............... DLB-68

Cournos, John 1881-1966 .... DLB-54

Courteline, Georges 1858-1929 .... DLB-192

Cousins, Margaret 1905-1996 ....DLB-137

Cousins, Norman 1915-1990 ....DLB-137

Couvreur, Jessie (see Tasma)

Coventry, Francis 1725-1754............ DLB-39

Dedication, *The History of Pompey
the Little* (1751)................ DLB-39

Coverdale, Miles 1487 or 1488-1569 .... DLB-167

N. Coverly [publishing house] DLB-49

Covici-Friede DLB-46

Cowan, Peter 1914-2002............. DLB-260

Coward, Noel
1899-1973......... DLB-10, 245; CDBLB-6

Coward, McCann and Geoghegan....... DLB-46

Cowles, Gardner 1861-1946........... DLB-29

Cowles, Gardner "Mike", Jr.
1903-1985 .... DLB-127, 137

Cowley, Abraham 1618-1667...... DLB-131, 151

Cowley, Hannah 1743-1809 .... DLB-89

Cowley, Malcolm
1898-1989 .... DLB-4, 48; DS-15; Y-81, 89

Cowper, Richard (John Middleton Murry Jr.)
1926-2002 .... DLB-261

Cowper, William 1731-1800........ DLB-104, 109

Cox, A. B. (see Berkeley, Anthony)

Cox, James McMahon 1903-1974 .... DLB-127

Cox, James Middleton 1870-1957 .... DLB-127

Cox, Leonard circa 1495-circa 1550 ..... DLB-281

Cox, Palmer 1840-1924 .... DLB-42

Coxe, Louis 1918-1993 .... DLB-5

Coxe, Tench 1755-1824 .... DLB-37

Cozzens, Frederick S. 1818-1869 .... DLB-202

Cozzens, James Gould 1903-1978 ....
.... DLB-9, 294; Y-84; DS-2; CDALB-1

   Cozzens's *Michael Scarlett* Y-97

   Ernest Hemingway's Reaction to
   James Gould Cozzens Y-98

   James Gould Cozzens–A View
   from Afar Y-97

   James Gould Cozzens: How to
   Read Him Y-97

   James Gould Cozzens Symposium and
   Exhibition at the University of
   South Carolina, Columbia Y-00

   Mens Rea (or Something) Y-97

   Novels for Grown-Ups Y-97

Crabbe, George 1754-1832 .... DLB-93

Crace, Jim 1946- DLB-231

Crackanthorpe, Hubert 1870-1896 ...... DLB-135

Craddock, Charles Egbert (see Murfree, Mary N.)

Cradock, Thomas 1718-1770 .... DLB-31

Craig, Daniel H. 1811-1895........... DLB-43

Craik, Dinah Maria 1826-1887 ...... DLB-35, 163

Cramer, Richard Ben 1950- DLB-185

Cranch, Christopher Pearse
1813-1892 .... DLB-1, 42, 243; DS-5

Crane, Hart 1899-1932 ..... DLB-4, 48; CDALB-4

   Nathan Asch Remembers Ford Madox
   Ford, Sam Roth, and Hart Crane Y-02

Crane, R. S. 1886-1967 .... DLB-63

Crane, Stephen
1871-1900 .... DLB-12, 54, 78; CDALB-3

   Stephen Crane: A Revaluation, Virginia
   Tech Conference, 1989............. Y-89

   The Stephen Crane Society......... Y-98, 01

Crane, Walter 1845-1915................ DLB-163

Cranmer, Thomas 1489-1556 .... DLB-132, 213

Crapsey, Adelaide 1878-1914 .... DLB-54

Crashaw, Richard 1612/1613-1649 ...... DLB-126

Craven, Avery 1885-1980 .... DLB-17

Crawford, Charles 1752-circa 1815 ..... DLB-31

Crawford, F. Marion 1854-1909 .... DLB-71

Crawford, Isabel Valancy 1850-1887...... DLB-92

Crawley, Alan 1887-1975 .... DLB-68

Crayon, Geoffrey (see Irving, Washington)

Crayon, Porte (see Strother, David Hunter)

Creamer, Robert W. 1922- DLB-171

Creasey, John 1908-1973 .... DLB-77

Creative Age Press.................... DLB-46

Creative Nonfiction Y-02

Crébillon, Claude-Prosper Jolyot de *fils*
1707-1777 .... DLB-313

Crébillon, Claude-Prosper Jolyot de *père*
1674-1762 .... DLB-313

William Creech [publishing house] DLB-154

Thomas Creede [publishing house] DLB-170

Creel, George 1876-1953 .... DLB-25

Creeley, Robert 1926-2005
.... DLB-5, 16, 169; DS-17

Creelman, James
1859-1915 .... DLB-23

Cregan, David 1931- DLB-13

Creighton, Donald 1902-1979 .... DLB-88

Crémazie, Octave 1827-1879 .... DLB-99

Crémer, Victoriano 1909?- DLB-108

Crenne, Helisenne de (Marguerite de Briet)
1510?-1560? DLB-327

Crescas, Hasdai circa 1340-1412? DLB-115

Crespo, Angel 1926-1995 .... DLB-134

Cresset Press DLB-112

Cresswell, Helen 1934- DLB-161

Crèvecoeur, Michel Guillaume Jean de
1735-1813 .... DLB-37

Crewe, Candida 1964- DLB-207

Crews, Harry 1935- DLB-6, 143, 185

Crichton, Michael (John Lange, Jeffrey Hudson,
Michael Douglas) 1942- DLB-292; Y-81

Crispin, Edmund (Robert Bruce Montgomery)
1921-1978 .... DLB-87

Cristofer, Michael 1946- DLB-7

Criticism
   Afro-American Literary Critics:
   An Introduction DLB-33

   The Consolidation of Opinion: Critical
   Responses to the Modernists DLB-36

   "Criticism in Relation to Novels"
   (1863), by G. H. Lewes DLB-21

   The Limits of Pluralism DLB-67

   Modern Critical Terms, Schools, and
   Movements................... DLB-67

   "Panic Among the Philistines":
   A Postscript, An Interview
   with Bryan Griffin Y-81

   The Recovery of Literature: Criticism
   in the 1990s: A Symposium Y-91

   The Stealthy School of Criticism (1871),
   by Dante Gabriel Rossetti........ DLB-35

Crnjanski, Miloš
1893-1977 .... DLB-147; CDWLB-4

Crocker, Hannah Mather 1752-1829 ..... DLB-200

Crockett, David (Davy)
1786-1836 .... DLB-3, 11, 183, 248

Croft-Cooke, Rupert (see Bruce, Leo)

Crofts, Freeman Wills 1879-1957......... DLB-77

Croker, John Wilson 1780-1857......... DLB-110

Croly, George 1780-1860............... DLB-159

Croly, Herbert 1869-1930 .... DLB-91

Croly, Jane Cunningham 1829-1901 ..... DLB-23

Crompton, Richmal 1890-1969......... DLB-160

Cronin, A. J. 1896-1981................ DLB-191

Cros, Charles 1842-1888................ DLB-217

Crosby, Caresse 1892-1970 and
   Crosby, Harry 1898-1929 and .. DLB-4; DS-15

Crosby, Harry 1898-1929 .... DLB-48

Crosland, Camilla Toulmin (Mrs. Newton
Crosland) 1812-1895................ DLB-240

Cross, Amanda (Carolyn G. Heilbrun)
1926-2003 .... DLB-306

Cross, Gillian 1945- DLB-161

Cross, Victoria 1868-1952 .... DLB-135, 197

Crossley-Holland, Kevin 1941- DLB-40, 161

Crothers, Rachel 1870-1958.......... DLB-7, 266

Thomas Y. Crowell Company.......... DLB-49

Crowley, John 1942- Y-82

Crowley, Mart 1935- DLB-7, 266

Crown Publishers DLB-46

Crowne, John 1641-1712 .... DLB-80

Crowninshield, Edward Augustus
1817-1859 .... DLB-140

Crowninshield, Frank 1872-1947......... DLB-91

Croy, Homer 1883-1965 .... DLB-4

Crumley, James 1939- DLB-226; Y-84

Cruse, Mary Anne 1825?-1910 .... DLB-239

Cruz, Migdalia 1958- DLB-249

Cruz, Sor Juana Inés de la 1651-1695 .... DLB-305

Cruz, Victor Hernández 1949- DLB-41

Cruz e Sousa, João 1861-1898.......... DLB-307

Csokor, Franz Theodor 1885-1969 .... DLB-81

Csoóri, Sándor 1930- DLB-232; CDWLB-4

Cuadra, Pablo Antonio 1912-2002 ...... DLB-290

Cuala Press DLB-112

Cudworth, Ralph 1617-1688 .... DLB-252

Cueva, Juan de la 1543-1612 .... DLB-318

Cugoano, Quobna Ottabah 1797-?.......... Y-02

Cullen, Countee
1903-1946 .... DLB-4, 48, 51; CDALB-4

Culler, Jonathan D. 1944- DLB-67, 246

Cullinan, Elizabeth 1933- DLB-234

Culverwel, Nathaniel 1619?-1651? DLB-252

Cumberland, Richard 1732-1811 .... DLB-89

Cummings, Constance Gordon
1837-1924 .... DLB-174

Cummings, E. E.
1894-1962 .... DLB-4, 48; CDALB-5

   The E. E. Cummings Society Y-01

Cumulative Index

Cummings, Ray 1887-1957 .... DLB-8
Cummings and Hilliard DLB-49
Cummins, Maria Susanna 1827-1866 ..... DLB-42
Cumpián, Carlos 1953- DLB-209
Cunard, Nancy 1896-1965 .... DLB-240
Joseph Cundall [publishing house] DLB-106
Cuney, Waring 1906-1976 .... DLB-51
Cuney-Hare, Maude 1874-1936 .... DLB-52
Cunha, Euclides da 1866-1909 .... DLB-307
Cunningham, Allan 1784-1842 .... DLB-116, 144
Cunningham, J. V. 1911-1985 .... DLB-5
Cunningham, Michael 1952- DLB-292
Cunningham, Peter (Peter Lauder, Peter Benjamin) 1947- DLB-267
Peter F. Cunningham [publishing house] DLB-49
Cunqueiro, Alvaro 1911-1981 .... DLB-134
Cuomo, George 1929- Y-80
Cupples, Upham and Company DLB-49
Cupples and Leon DLB-46
Cuppy, Will 1884-1949 .... DLB-11
Curiel, Barbara Brinson 1956- DLB-209
Edmund Curll [publishing house] DLB-154
Currie, James 1756-1805 .... DLB-142
Currie, Mary Montgomerie Lamb Singleton, Lady Currie (see Fane, Violet)
Cursor Mundi circa 1300 .... DLB-146
Curti, Merle E. 1897-1996 .... DLB-17
Curtis, Anthony 1926- DLB-155
Curtis, Cyrus H. K. 1850-1933 .... DLB-91
Curtis, George William 1824-1892 .... DLB-1, 43, 223
Curzon, Robert 1810-1873 .... DLB-166
Curzon, Sarah Anne 1833-1898 .... DLB-99
Cusack, Dymphna 1902-1981 .... DLB-260
Cushing, Eliza Lanesford 1794-1886 .... DLB-99
Cushing, Harvey 1869-1939 .... DLB-187
Custance, Olive (Lady Alfred Douglas) 1874-1944 .... DLB-240
Cynewulf circa 770-840 .... DLB-146
Cyrano de Bergerac, Savinien de 1619-1655 .... DLB-268
Czepko, Daniel 1605-1660 .... DLB-164
Czerniawski, Adam 1934- DLB-232

D

Dabit, Eugène 1898-1936 .... DLB-65
Daborne, Robert circa 1580-1628 .... DLB-58
Dąbrowska, Maria 1889-1965 .... DLB-215; CDWLB-4
Dacey, Philip 1939- DLB-105

"Eyes Across Centuries: Contemporary Poetry and 'That Vision Thing,'" DLB-105
Dach, Simon 1605-1659 .... DLB-164
Dacier, Anne Le Fèvre 1647-1720 ...... DLB-313
Dagerman, Stig 1923-1954 .... DLB-259
Daggett, Rollin M. 1831-1901 .... DLB-79
D'Aguiar, Fred 1960- DLB-157
Dahl, Roald 1916-1990 .... DLB-139, 255
Tribute to Alfred A. Knopf Y-84
Dahlberg, Edward 1900-1977 .... DLB-48
Dahn, Felix 1834-1912 .... DLB-129
The Daily Worker DLB-303
Dal', Vladimir Ivanovich (Kazak Vladimir Lugansky) 1801-1872 .... DLB-198
Dale, Peter 1938- DLB-40
Daley, Arthur 1904-1974 .... DLB-171
Dall, Caroline Healey 1822-1912 ..... DLB-1, 235
Dallas, E. S. 1828-1879 .... DLB-55
The Gay Science [excerpt](1866) DLB-21
The Dallas Theater Center DLB-7
D'Alton, Louis 1900-1951 .... DLB-10
Dalton, Roque 1935-1975 .... DLB-283
Daly, Carroll John 1889-1958 .... DLB-226
Daly, T. A. 1871-1948 .... DLB-11
Damon, S. Foster 1893-1971 .... DLB-45
William S. Damrell [publishing house] DLB-49
Dana, Charles A. 1819-1897 .... DLB-3, 23, 250
Dana, Richard Henry, Jr. 1815-1882 .... DLB-1, 183, 235
Dandridge, Ray Garfield 1882-1930 ..... DLB-51
Dane, Clemence 1887-1965 ....DLB-10, 197
Danforth, John 1660-1730 .... DLB-24
Danforth, Samuel, I 1626-1674 .... DLB-24
Danforth, Samuel, II 1666-1727 .... DLB-24
Dangerous Acquaintances, Pierre-Ambroise-François Choderlos de Laclos DLB-314
Daniel, John M. 1825-1865 .... DLB-43
Daniel, Samuel 1562 or 1563-1619 ...... DLB-62
Daniel Press DLB-106
Daniel', Iulii 1925-1988 .... DLB-302
Daniells, Roy 1902-1979 .... DLB-68
Daniels, Jim 1956- DLB-120
Daniels, Jonathan 1902-1981 .... DLB-127
Daniels, Josephus 1862-1948 .... DLB-29
Daniels, Sarah 1957- DLB-245
Danilevsky, Grigorii Petrovich 1829-1890 .... DLB-238
Dannay, Frederic 1905-1982 .... DLB-137
Danner, Margaret Esse 1915- DLB-41
John Danter [publishing house] DLB-170
Dantin, Louis (Eugene Seers) 1865-1945 .... DLB-92

Danto, Arthur C. 1924- DLB-279
Danzig, Allison 1898-1987 ....DLB-171
D'Arcy, Ella circa 1857-1937 .... DLB-135
Darío, Rubén 1867-1916 .... DLB-290
Dark, Eleanor 1901-1985 .... DLB-260
Darke, Nick 1948- DLB-233
Darley, Felix Octavious Carr 1822-1888 .... DLB-188
Darley, George 1795-1846 .... DLB-96
Darmesteter, Madame James (see Robinson, A. Mary F.)
Darrow, Clarence 1857-1938 .... DLB-303
Darwin, Charles 1809-1882 ....DLB-57, 166
Darwin, Erasmus 1731-1802 .... DLB-93
Daryush, Elizabeth 1887-1977 .... DLB-20
Das, Kamala 1934- DLB-323
Dashkova, Ekaterina Romanovna (née Vorontsova) 1743-1810 .... DLB-150
Dashwood, Edmée Elizabeth Monica de la Pasture (see Delafield, E. M.)
Dattani, Mahesh 1958- DLB-323
Daudet, Alphonse 1840-1897 .... DLB-123
d'Aulaire, Edgar Parin 1898-1986 and d'Aulaire, Ingri 1904-1980 .... DLB-22
Davenant, Sir William 1606-1668 .... DLB-58, 126
Davenport, Guy 1927-2005 .... DLB-130
Tribute to John Gardner Y-82
Davenport, Marcia 1903-1996 .... DS-17
Davenport, Robert circa 17th century DLB-58
Daves, Delmer 1904-1977 .... DLB-26
Davey, Frank 1940- DLB-53
Davidson, Avram 1923-1993 .... DLB-8
Davidson, Donald 1893-1968 .... DLB-45
Davidson, Donald 1917-2003 ....DLB-279
Davidson, John 1857-1909 .... DLB-19
Davidson, Lionel 1922- DLB-14, 276
Davidson, Robyn 1950- DLB-204
Davidson, Sara 1943- DLB-185
Davið Stefánsson frá Fagraskógi 1895-1964 .... DLB-293
Davie, Donald 1922-1995 .... DLB-27
Davie, Elspeth 1919-1995 .... DLB-139
Davies, Sir John 1569-1626 ....DLB-172
Davies, John, of Hereford 1565?-1618 ... DLB-121
Davies, Rhys 1901-1978 .... DLB-139, 191
Davies, Robertson 1913-1995 .... DLB-68
Davies, Samuel 1723-1761 .... DLB-31
Davies, Thomas 1712?-1785 .... DLB-142, 154
Davies, W. H. 1871-1940 ....DLB-19, 174
Peter Davies Limited DLB-112
Davin, Nicholas Flood 1840?-1901 .... DLB-99

Daviot, Gordon 1896?-1952 ....DLB-10
(see also Tey, Josephine)

Davis, Arthur Hoey (see Rudd, Steele)

Davis, Benjamin J. 1903-1964 ....DLB-303

Davis, Charles A. (Major J. Downing)
1795-1867 ....DLB-11

Davis, Clyde Brion 1894-1962...........DLB-9

Davis, Dick 1945- DLB-40, 282

Davis, Frank Marshall 1905-1987 ....DLB-51

Davis, H. L. 1894-1960 ....DLB-9, 206

Davis, Jack 1917-2000 ....DLB-325

Davis, John 1774-1854 ....DLB-37

Davis, Lydia 1947- DLB-130

Davis, Margaret Thomson 1926- DLB-14

Davis, Ossie 1917-2005 .... DLB-7, 38, 249

Davis, Owen 1874-1956................DLB-249

Davis, Paxton 1925-1994..................Y-89

Davis, Rebecca Harding
1831-1910 ....DLB-74, 239

Davis, Richard Harding 1864-1916
.... DLB-12, 23, 78, 79, 189; DS-13

Davis, Samuel Cole 1764-1809............DLB-37

Davis, Samuel Post 1850-1918...........DLB-202

Davison, Frank Dalby 1893-1970........DLB-260

Davison, Peter 1928- DLB-5

Davydov, Denis Vasil'evich
1784-1839 ....DLB-205

Davys, Mary 1674-1732..................DLB-39

Preface to *The Works of Mrs. Davys*
(1725) DLB-39

DAW Books DLB-46

Dawe, Bruce 1930- DLB-289

Dawson, Ernest 1882-1947 .... DLB-140; Y-02

Dawson, Fielding 1930- DLB-130

Dawson, Sarah Morgan 1842-1909 ......DLB-239

Dawson, William 1704-1752.............DLB-31

Day, Angel fl. 1583-1599 .... DLB-167, 236

Day, Benjamin Henry 1810-1889.........DLB-43

Day, Clarence 1874-1935 ....DLB-11

Day, Dorothy 1897-1980 ....DLB-29

Day, Frank Parker 1881-1950 ....DLB-92

Day, John circa 1574-circa 1640 ....DLB-62

Day, Marele 1947- DLB-325

Day, Thomas 1748-1789..................DLB-39

John Day [publishing house] DLB-170

The John Day Company DLB-46

Mahlon Day [publishing house]..........DLB-49

Day Lewis, C. (see Blake, Nicholas)

Dazai Osamu 1909-1948 ....DLB-182

Deacon, William Arthur 1890-1977........DLB-68

Deal, Borden 1922-1985 ....DLB-6

de Angeli, Marguerite 1889-1987........DLB-22

De Angelis, Milo 1951- DLB-128

Debord, Guy 1931-1994 ....DLB-296

De Bow, J. D. B. 1820-1867 .... DLB-3, 79, 248

Debs, Eugene V. 1855-1926...........DLB-303

de Bruyn, Günter 1926- DLB-75

de Camp, L. Sprague 1907-2000 ....DLB-8

De Carlo, Andrea 1952- DLB-196

De Casas, Celso A. 1944- DLB-209

Dechert, Robert 1895-1975 ....DLB-187

Declaration of the Rights of Man and of
the Citizen....................DLB-314

Declaration of the Rights of Woman, Olympe
de Gouges DLB-314

Dedications, Inscriptions, and
Annotations....................Y-01–02

Dee, John 1527-1608 or 1609....... DLB-136, 213

Deeping, George Warwick 1877-1950 ....DLB-153

Deffand, Marie de Vichy-Chamrond,
marquise Du 1696-1780 ....DLB-313

Defoe, Daniel
1660-1731 .... DLB-39, 95, 101; CDBLB-2

Preface to *Colonel Jack* (1722).........DLB-39

Preface to *The Farther Adventures of
Robinson Crusoe* (1719) DLB-39

Preface to *Moll Flanders* (1722) DLB-39

Preface to *Robinson Crusoe* (1719) DLB-39

Preface to *Roxana* (1724) DLB-39

de Fontaine, Felix Gregory 1834-1896.....DLB-43

De Forest, John William
1826-1906 ....DLB-12, 189

DeFrees, Madeline 1919- DLB-105

"The Poet's Kaleidoscope: The
Element of Surprise in the
Making of the Poem" DLB-105

DeGolyer, Everette Lee 1886-1956 ......DLB-187

de Graff, Robert 1895-1981................Y-81

de Graft, Joe 1924-1978 ....DLB-117

De Groen, Alma 1941- DLB-325

De Heinrico circa 980?..................DLB-148

Deighton, Len 1929- DLB-87; CDBLB-8

DeJong, Meindert 1906-1991............DLB-52

Dekker, Thomas
circa 1572-1632 .... DLB-62, 172; CDBLB-1

Delacorte, George T., Jr. 1894-1991........DLB-91

Delafield, E. M. 1890-1943 ....DLB-34

Delahaye, Guy (Guillaume Lahaise)
1888-1969 ....DLB-92

de la Mare, Walter 1873-1956
.... DLB-19, 153, 162, 255; CDBLB-6

Deland, Margaret 1857-1945 ....DLB-78

Delaney, Shelagh 1939- DLB-13; CDBLB-8

Delano, Amasa 1763-1823 ....DLB-183

Delany, Martin Robinson 1812-1885......DLB-50

Delany, Samuel R. 1942- DLB-8, 33

de la Roche, Mazo 1879-1961 ....DLB-68

Delavigne, Jean François Casimir
1793-1843 ....DLB-192

Delbanco, Nicholas 1942- DLB-6, 234

Delblanc, Sven 1931-1992 ....DLB-257

Del Castillo, Ramón 1949- DLB-209

Deledda, Grazia 1871-1936 ....DLB-264

De León, Nephtalí 1945- DLB-82

Deleuze, Gilles 1925-1995 ....DLB-296

Delfini, Antonio 1907-1963 ....DLB-264

Delgado, Abelardo Barrientos 1931- DLB-82

Del Giudice, Daniele 1949- DLB-196

De Libero, Libero 1906-1981 ....DLB-114

Delibes, Miguel 1920- DLB-322

Delicado, Francisco
circa 1475-circa 1540? DLB-318

DeLillo, Don 1936- DLB-6, 173

de Lint, Charles 1951- DLB-251

de Lisser H. G. 1878-1944............DLB-117

Dell, Floyd 1887-1969 ....DLB-9

Dell Publishing Company DLB-46

delle Grazie, Marie Eugene 1864-1931 ....DLB-81

Deloney, Thomas died 1600 ....DLB-167

Deloria, Ella C. 1889-1971..............DLB-175

Deloria, Vine, Jr. 1933- DLB-175

del Rey, Lester 1915-1993 ....DLB-8

Del Vecchio, John M. 1947- DS-9

Del'vig, Anton Antonovich 1798-1831....DLB-205

de Man, Paul 1919-1983 ....DLB-67

DeMarinis, Rick 1934- DLB-218

Demby, William 1922- DLB-33

De Mille, James 1833-1880 ....DLB-99, 251

de Mille, William 1878-1955 ....DLB-266

Deming, Philander 1829-1915..........DLB-74

Deml, Jakub 1878-1961 ....DLB-215

Demorest, William Jennings 1822-1895....DLB-79

De Morgan, William 1839-1917 ....DLB-153

Demosthenes 384 B.C.-322 B.C. DLB-176

Henry Denham [publishing house] DLB-170

Denham, Sir John 1615-1669........DLB-58, 126

Denison, Merrill 1893-1975 ....DLB-92

T. S. Denison and Company DLB-49

Dennery, Adolphe Philippe 1811-1899 ...DLB-192

Dennie, Joseph 1768-1812 ..... DLB-37, 43, 59, 73

Dennis, C. J. 1876-1938 ....DLB-260

Dennis, John 1658-1734 ....DLB-101

Dennis, Nigel 1912-1989 .... DLB-13, 15, 233

Denslow, W. W. 1856-1915..............DLB-188

Dent, J. M., and Sons..................DLB-112

Dent, Lester 1904-1959 ....DLB-306

Dent, Tom 1932-1998 ....DLB-38

Denton, Daniel circa 1626-1703..........DLB-24

DePaola, Tomie 1934- DLB-61	Deveaux, Alexis 1948- DLB-38	Tribute to Truman Capote............ Y-84
De Quille, Dan 1829-1898 .... DLB-186	De Vere, Aubrey 1814-1902........... DLB-35	Tributes [to Dickey]................. Y-97
De Quincey, Thomas 1785-1859........ DLB-110, 144; CDBLB-3	Devereux, second Earl of Essex, Robert 1565-1601 .... DLB-136	Dickey, William 1928-1994 .... DLB-5
"Rhetoric" (1828; revised, 1859) [excerpt]................... DLB-57	The Devin-Adair Company DLB-46	Dickinson, Emily 1830-1886......... DLB-1, 243; CDALB-3
"Style" (1840; revised, 1859) [excerpt]................... DLB-57	De Vinne, Theodore Low 1828-1914 .... DLB-187	Dickinson, John 1732-1808............ DLB-31
Derby, George Horatio 1823-1861 .... DLB-11	Devlin, Anne 1951- DLB-245	Dickinson, Jonathan 1688-1747 .... DLB-24
J. C. Derby and Company DLB-49	DeVoto, Bernard 1897-1955 .... DLB-9, 256	Dickinson, Patric 1914-1994............ DLB-27
Derby and Miller DLB-49	De Vries, Peter 1910-1993 ....DLB-6; Y-82	Dickinson, Peter 1927- DLB-87, 161, 276
De Ricci, Seymour 1881-1942 .... DLB-201	Tribute to Albert Erskine.............. Y-93	John Dicks [publishing house] DLB-106
Derleth, August 1909-1971 .... DLB-9; DS-17	Dewart, Edward Hartley 1828-1903...... DLB-99	Dickson, Gordon R. 1923-2001 .... DLB-8
Derrida, Jacques 1930-2004 .... DLB-242	Dewdney, Christopher 1951- DLB-60	*Dictionary of Literary Biography* Annual Awards for Dictionary of Literary Biography Editors and Contributors Y-98–02
The Derrydale Press................. DLB-46	Dewdney, Selwyn 1909-1979 .... DLB-68	
Derzhavin, Gavriil Romanovich 1743-1816.................... DLB-150	Dewey, John 1859-1952 ....DLB-246, 270	
Desai, Anita 1937- DLB-271, 323	Dewey, Orville 1794-1882............ DLB-243	*Dictionary of Literary Biography Yearbook* Awards..........Y-92–93, 97–02
Desani, G. V. 1909-2000............. DLB-323	Dewey, Thomas B. 1915-1981 .... DLB-226	*The Dictionary of National Biography* DLB-144
Desaulniers, Gonzalve 1863-1934........ DLB-92	DeWitt, Robert M., Publisher DLB-49	Diderot, Denis 1713-1784 .... DLB-313
Desbordes-Valmore, Marceline 1786-1859..................... DLB-217	DeWolfe, Fiske and Company DLB-49	"The Encyclopedia"............... DLB-314
	Dexter, Colin 1930- DLB-87	Didion, Joan 1934- DLB-2, 173, 185; Y-81, 86; CDALB-6
Descartes, René 1596-1650 .... DLB-268	de Young, M. H. 1849-1925 .... DLB-25	
Deschamps, Emile 1791-1871 .... DLB-217	Dhlomo, H. I. E. 1903-1956........DLB-157, 225	Di Donato, Pietro 1911-1992 .... DLB-9
Deschamps, Eustache 1340?-1404 .... DLB-208	Dhu al-Rummah (Abu al-Harith Ghaylan ibn 'Uqbah) circa 696-circa 735 .... DLB-311	Die Fürstliche Bibliothek Corvey........... Y-96
Desbiens, Jean-Paul 1927- DLB-53		Diego, Gerardo 1896-1987 .... DLB-134
des Forêts, Louis-Rene 1918-2001 .... DLB-83	Dhuoda circa 803-after 843 .... DLB-148	Dietz, Howard 1896-1983............. DLB-265
Deshpande, Shashi 1938- DLB-323	*The Dial* 1840-1844.................. DLB-223	Díez, Luis Mateo 1942- DLB-322
Desiato, Luca 1941- DLB-196	The Dial Press DLB-46	Digby, Everard 1550?-1605 .... DLB-281
Desjardins, Marie-Catherine (see Villedieu, Madame de)	"Dialogue entre un prêtre et un moribond," Marquis de Sade................. DLB-314	Digges, Thomas circa 1546-1595 .... DLB-136
Desnica, Vladan 1905-1967 .... DLB-181	Diamond, I. A. L. 1920-1988 .... DLB-26	The Digital Millennium Copyright Act: Expanding Copyright Protection in Cyberspace and Beyond Y-98
Desnos, Robert 1900-1945 .... DLB-258	Dias Gomes, Alfredo 1922-1999. .... DLB-307	
Des Périers, Bonaventure 1510?-1543?.................... DLB-327	Díaz del Castillo, Bernal circa 1496-1584 .... DLB-318	Diktonius, Elmer 1896-1961........... DLB-259
		Dillard, Annie 1945- DLB-275, 278; Y-80
Desportes, Philippe 1546-1606 .... DLB-327	Dibble, L. Grace 1902-1998 .... DLB-204	Dillard, R. H. W. 1937- DLB-5, 244
DesRochers, Alfred 1901-1978 .... DLB-68	Dibdin, Thomas Frognall 1776-1847..................... DLB-184	Charles T. Dillingham Company DLB-49
Des Roches, Madeleine 1520?-1587? and Catherine des Roches 1542-1587?.....DLB-327	Di Cicco, Pier Giorgio 1949- DLB-60	G. W. Dillingham Company DLB-49
Des Roches, Madeleine 1520?-1587?................... DLB-327	Dick, Philip K. 1928-1982 .... DLB-8	Edward and Charles Dilly [publishing house] DLB-154
	Dick and Fitzgerald.................. DLB-49	
Desrosiers, Léo-Paul 1896-1967 .... DLB-68	Dickens, Charles 1812-1870 .... DLB-21, 55, 70, 159, 166; DS-5; CDBLB-4	Dilthey, Wilhelm 1833-1911 .... DLB-129
Dessaulles, Louis-Antoine 1819-1895 ..... DLB-99		Dimitrova, Blaga 1922- DLB-181; CDWLB-4
Dessì, Giuseppe 1909-1977 ....DLB-177		Dimov, Dimitr 1909-1966............. DLB-181
Destouches, Louis-Ferdinand (see Céline, Louis-Ferdinand)	Dickey, Eric Jerome 1961- DLB-292	Dimsdale, Thomas J. 1831?-1866....... DLB-186
	Dickey, James 1923-1997 ....DLB-5, 193; Y-82, 93, 96, 97; DS-7, 19; CDALB-6	Dinescu, Mircea 1950- DLB-232
Desvignes, Lucette 1926- DLB-321		Dinesen, Isak (see Blixen, Karen)
DeSylva, Buddy 1895-1950 .... DLB-265	James Dickey and Stanley Burnshaw Correspondence Y-02	Ding Ling 1904-1986 .... DLB-328
De Tabley, Lord 1835-1895 .... DLB-35	James Dickey at Seventy–A Tribute Y-93	Dingelstedt, Franz von 1814-1881 ...... DLB-133
Deutsch, Babette 1895-1982........... DLB-45	James Dickey, American Poet........... Y-96	Dinis, Júlio (Joaquim Guilherme Gomes Coelho) 1839-1871......... DLB-287
Deutsch, Niklaus Manuel (see Manuel, Niklaus)	The James Dickey Society Y-99	Dintenfass, Mark 1941- Y-84
	The Life of James Dickey: A Lecture to the Friends of the Emory Libraries, by Henry Hart................ Y-98	Diogenes, Jr. (see Brougham, John)
André Deutsch Limited DLB-112		Diogenes Laertius circa 200 ....DLB-176
Devanny, Jean 1894-1962............ DLB-260	Tribute to Archibald MacLeish Y-82	DiPrima, Diane 1934- DLB-5, 16
	Tribute to Malcolm Cowley Y-89	Disch, Thomas M. 1940- DLB-8, 282

"Le Discours sur le style," Georges-Louis Leclerc de Buffon.....................DLB-314

Disgrace, 1999 Booker Prize winner, J. M. Coetzee................DLB-326

Diski, Jenny 1947-.................DLB-271

Disney, Walt 1901-1966.............DLB-22

Disraeli, Benjamin 1804-1881........DLB-21, 55

D'Israeli, Isaac 1766-1848...........DLB-107

DLB Award for Distinguished Literary Criticism..................Y-02

Ditlevsen, Tove 1917-1976...........DLB-214

Ditzen, Rudolf (see Fallada, Hans)

Divakaruni, Chitra Banerjee 1956-....DLB-323

Dix, Dorothea Lynde 1802-1887......DLB-1, 235

Dix, Dorothy (see Gilmer, Elizabeth Meriwether)

Dix, Edwards and Company...........DLB-49

Dix, Gertrude circa 1874-?..........DLB-197

Dixie, Florence Douglas 1857-1905.....DLB-174

Dixon, Ella Hepworth 1855 or 1857-1932...............DLB-197

Dixon, Paige (see Corcoran, Barbara)

Dixon, Richard Watson 1833-1900.......DLB-19

Dixon, Stephen 1936-...............DLB-130

DLB Award for Distinguished Literary Criticism..................Y-02

Dmitriev, Andrei Viktorovich 1956-....DLB-285

Dmitriev, Ivan Ivanovich 1760-1837......DLB-150

Dobell, Bertram 1842-1914...........DLB-184

Dobell, Sydney 1824-1874............DLB-32

Dobie, J. Frank 1888-1964...........DLB-212

Dobles Yzaguirre, Julieta 1943-......DLB-283

Döblin, Alfred 1878-1957.....DLB-66; CDWLB-2

Dobroliubov, Nikolai Aleksandrovich 1836-1861...................DLB-277

Dobson, Austin 1840-1921.........DLB-35, 144

Dobson, Rosemary 1920-.............DLB-260

Doctorow, E. L. 1931-.....DLB-2, 28, 173; Y-80; CDALB-6

Dodd, Susan M. 1946-...............DLB-244

Dodd, William E. 1869-1940..........DLB-17

Anne Dodd [publishing house].........DLB-154

Dodd, Mead and Company............DLB-49

Doderer, Heimito von 1896-1966......DLB-85

B. W. Dodge and Company............DLB-46

Dodge, Mary Abigail 1833-1896........DLB-221

Dodge, Mary Mapes 1831?-1905..........DLB-42, 79; DS-13

Dodge Publishing Company...........DLB-49

Dodgson, Charles Lutwidge (see Carroll, Lewis)

Dodsley, Robert 1703-1764...........DLB-95

R. Dodsley [publishing house].........DLB-154

Dodson, Owen 1914-1983.............DLB-76

Dodwell, Christina 1951-............DLB-204

Doesticks, Q. K. Philander, P. B. (see Thomson, Mortimer)

Doheny, Carrie Estelle 1875-1958.......DLB-140

Doherty, John 1798?-1854............DLB-190

Doig, Ivan 1939-...................DLB-206

Doinaș, Ștefan Augustin 1922-.......DLB-232

Dolet, Etienne 1509-1546............DLB-327

Domínguez, Sylvia Maida 1935-......DLB-122

Donaghy, Michael 1954-.............DLB-282

Patrick Donahoe [publishing house]......DLB-49

Donald, David H. 1920-........DLB-17; Y-87

Donaldson, Scott 1928-..............DLB-111

Doni, Rodolfo 1919-................DLB-177

Donleavy, J. P. 1926-............DLB-6, 173

Donnadieu, Marguerite (see Duras, Marguerite)

Donne, John 1572-1631.........DLB-121, 151; CDBLB-1

Donnelly, Ignatius 1831-1901..........DLB-12

R. R. Donnelley and Sons Company......DLB-49

Donoghue, Emma 1969-..............DLB-267

Donohue and Henneberry.............DLB-49

Donoso, José 1924-1996....DLB-113; CDWLB-3

M. Doolady [publishing house]........DLB-49

Dooley, Ebon (see Ebon)

Doolittle, Hilda 1886-1961......DLB-4, 45; DS-15

Doplicher, Fabio 1938-..............DLB-128

Dor, Milo 1923-...................DLB-85

George H. Doran Company...........DLB-46

Dorat, Jean 1508-1588...............DLB-327

Dorcey, Mary 1950-.................DLB-319

Dorgelès, Roland 1886-1973..........DLB-65

Dorn, Edward 1929-1999.............DLB-5

Dorr, Rheta Childe 1866-1948.........DLB-25

Dorris, Michael 1945-1997............DLB-175

Dorset and Middlesex, Charles Sackville, Lord Buckhurst, Earl of 1643-1706....DLB-131

Dorsey, Candas Jane 1952-...........DLB-251

Dorst, Tankred 1925-............DLB-75, 124

Dos Passos, John 1896-1970 ....DLB-4, 9, 316; DS-1, 15; CDALB-5

John Dos Passos: A Centennial Commemoration..................Y-96

John Dos Passos: Artist...............Y-99

John Dos Passos Newsletter............Y-00

U.S.A. (Documentary).............DLB-274

Dostoevsky, Fyodor 1821-1881.........DLB-238

Doubleday and Company.............DLB-49

Doubrovsky, Serge 1928-............DLB-299

Dougall, Lily 1858-1923..............DLB-92

Doughty, Charles M. 1843-1926..................DLB-19, 57, 174

Douglas, Lady Alfred (see Custance, Olive)

Douglas, Ellen (Josephine Ayres Haxton) 1921-........................DLB-292

Douglas, Gavin 1476-1522............DLB-132

Douglas, Keith 1920-1944............DLB-27

Douglas, Norman 1868-1952........DLB-34, 195

Douglass, Frederick 1817-1895 ....DLB-1, 43, 50, 79, 243; CDALB-2

Frederick Douglass Creative Arts Center   Y-01

Douglass, William circa 1691-1752......DLB-24

Dourado, Autran 1926-.........DLB-145, 307

Dove, Arthur G. 1880-1946...........DLB-188

Dove, Rita 1952-.........DLB-120; CDALB-7

Dover Publications...................DLB-46

Doves Press......................DLB-112

Dovlatov, Sergei Donatovich 1941-1990....................DLB-285

Dowden, Edward 1843-1913........DLB-35, 149

Dowell, Coleman 1925-1985..........DLB-130

Dowland, John 1563-1626............DLB-172

Downes, Gwladys 1915-..............DLB-88

Downing, J., Major (see Davis, Charles A.)

Downing, Major Jack (see Smith, Seba)

Dowriche, Anne before 1560-after 1613..........DLB-172

Dowson, Ernest 1867-1900........DLB-19, 135

William Doxey [publishing house].......DLB-49

Doyle, Sir Arthur Conan 1859-1930...DLB-18, 70, 156, 178; CDBLB-5

The Priory Scholars of New York........Y-99

Doyle, Kirby 1932-..................DLB-16

Doyle, Roddy 1958-.............DLB-194, 326

Drabble, Margaret 1939-........DLB-14, 155, 231; CDBLB-8

Tribute to Graham Greene.............Y-91

Drach, Albert 1902-1995..............DLB-85

Drachmann, Holger 1846-1908.........DLB-300

Dracula (Documentary).............DLB-304

Dragojević, Danijel 1934-............DLB-181

Dragún, Osvaldo 1929-1999..........DLB-305

Drake, Samuel Gardner 1798-1875.....DLB-187

Drama (*See* Theater)

The Dramatic Publishing Company......DLB-49

Dramatists Play Service..............DLB-46

Drant, Thomas early 1540s?-1578...............DLB-167

Draper, John W. 1811-1882...........DLB-30

Draper, Lyman C. 1815-1891..........DLB-30

Drayton, Michael 1563-1631..........DLB-121

Dreiser, Theodore 1871-1945 ....DLB-9, 12, 102, 137; DS-1; CDALB-3

The International Theodore Dreiser Society........................Y-01

Notes from the Underground of *Sister Carrie*..................Y-01

Dresser, Davis 1904-1977 . . . . DLB-226

Drew, Elizabeth A.
"A Note on Technique" [excerpt] (1926) DLB-36

Drewe, Robert 1943- DLB-325

Drewitz, Ingeborg 1923-1986 . . . . DLB-75

Drieu La Rochelle, Pierre 1893-1945 . . . . . DLB-72

Drinker, Elizabeth 1735-1807 . . . . DLB-200

Drinkwater, John 1882-1937 . . . . . . DLB-10, 19, 149

    The Friends of the Dymock Poets Y-00

Droste-Hülshoff, Annette von 1797-1848 . . . . DLB-133; CDWLB-2

The Drue Heinz Literature Prize
Excerpt from "Excerpts from a Report of the Commission," in David Bosworth's *The Death of Descartes* An Interview with David Bosworth Y-82

Drummond, William, of Hawthornden 1585-1649 . . . . DLB-121, 213

Drummond, William Henry 1854-1907 . . . DLB-92

Drummond de Andrade, Carlos 1902-1987 . . . . DLB-307

Druzhinin, Aleksandr Vasil'evich 1824-1864 . . . . DLB-238

Druzhnikov, Yuri 1933- DLB-317

Dryden, Charles 1860?-1931 . . . . DLB-171

Dryden, John 1631-1700 . . . . . . DLB-80, 101, 131; CDBLB-2

Držić, Marin circa 1508-1567 . . . . DLB-147; CDWLB-4

Duane, William 1760-1835 . . . . DLB-43

Du Bartas, Guillaume 1544-1590 . . . . DLB-327

Dubé, Marcel 1930- DLB-53

Dubé, Rodolphe (see Hertel, François)

Du Bellay, Joachim 1522?-1560 . . . . DLB-327

Dubie, Norman 1945- DLB-120

Dubin, Al 1891-1945 . . . . DLB-265

Du Boccage, Anne-Marie 1710-1802 . . . . . DLB-313

Dubois, Silvia 1788 or 1789?-1889 . . . . DLB-239

Du Bois, W. E. B. 1868-1963 . . . . DLB-47, 50, 91, 246; CDALB-3

Du Bois, William Pène 1916-1993 . . . . DLB-61

Dubrovina, Ekaterina Oskarovna 1846-1913 . . . . DLB-238

Dubus, Andre 1936-1999 . . . . DLB-130

    Tribute to Michael M. Rea Y-97

Dubus, Andre, III 1959- DLB-292

Ducange, Victor 1783-1833 . . . . DLB-192

Du Chaillu, Paul Belloni 1831?-1903 . . . . DLB-189

Ducharme, Réjean 1941- DLB-60

Dučić, Jovan 1871-1943 . . . . . DLB-147; CDWLB-4

Duck, Stephen 1705?-1756 . . . . DLB-95

Gerald Duckworth and Company Limited DLB-112

Duclaux, Madame Mary (see Robinson, A. Mary F.)

Dudek, Louis 1918-2001 . . . . DLB-88

Dudintsev, Vladimir Dmitrievich 1918-1998 . . . . DLB-302

Dudley-Smith, Trevor (see Hall, Adam)

Duell, Sloan and Pearce DLB-46

Duerer, Albrecht 1471-1528 . . . . DLB-179

Duff Gordon, Lucie 1821-1869 . . . . DLB-166

Dufferin, Helen Lady, Countess of Gifford 1807-1867 . . . . DLB-199

Duffield and Green DLB-46

Duffy, Maureen 1933- DLB-14, 310

Dufief, Nicholas Gouin 1776-1834 . . . . . . DLB-187

Dufresne, John 1948- DLB-292

Dugan, Alan 1923-2003 . . . . DLB-5

Dugard, William 1606-1662 . . . . DLB-170, 281

William Dugard [publishing house] DLB-170

Dugas, Marcel 1883-1947 . . . . DLB-92

William Dugdale [publishing house] DLB-106

Du Guillet, Pernette 1520?-1545 . . . . DLB-327

Duhamel, Georges 1884-1966 . . . . DLB-65

Dujardin, Edouard 1861-1949 . . . . DLB-123

Dukes, Ashley 1885-1959 . . . . DLB-10

Dumas, Alexandre *fils* 1824-1895 . . . . DLB-192

Dumas, Alexandre *père* 1802-1870 . . . . DLB-119, 192

Dumas, Henry 1934-1968 . . . . DLB-41

du Maurier, Daphne 1907-1989 . . . . DLB-191

Du Maurier, George 1834-1896 . . . . . DLB-153, 178

Dummett, Michael 1925- DLB-262

Dunbar, Paul Laurence 1872-1906 . . . . DLB-50, 54, 78; CDALB-3

    Introduction to *Lyrics of Lowly Life* (1896), by William Dean Howells DLB-50

Dunbar, William circa 1460-circa 1522 . . . . DLB-132, 146

Duncan, Dave 1933- DLB-251

Duncan, David James 1952- DLB-256

Duncan, Norman 1871-1916 . . . . DLB-92

Duncan, Quince 1940- DLB-145

Duncan, Robert 1919-1988 . . . . . . DLB-5, 16, 193

Duncan, Ronald 1914-1982 . . . . DLB-13

Duncan, Sara Jeannette 1861-1922 . . . . . . DLB-92

Dunigan, Edward, and Brother DLB-49

Dunlap, John 1747-1812 . . . . DLB-43

Dunlap, William 1766-1839 . . . . DLB-30, 37, 59

Dunlop, William "Tiger" 1792-1848 . . . . . DLB-99

Dunmore, Helen 1952- DLB-267

Dunn, Douglas 1942- DLB-40

Dunn, Harvey Thomas 1884-1952 . . . . . . DLB-188

Dunn, Stephen 1939- DLB-105

    "The Good, The Not So Good" DLB-105

Dunne, Dominick 1925- DLB-306

Dunne, Finley Peter 1867-1936 . . . . . . DLB-11, 23

Dunne, John Gregory 1932- Y-80

Dunne, Philip 1908-1992 . . . . DLB-26

Dunning, Ralph Cheever 1878-1930 . . . . . . DLB-4

Dunning, William A. 1857-1922 . . . . DLB-17

Duns Scotus, John circa 1266-1308 . . . . . DLB-115

Dunsany, Lord (Edward John Moreton Drax Plunkett, Baron Dunsany) 1878-1957 . . . . DLB-10, 77, 153, 156, 255

Dunton, W. Herbert 1878-1936 . . . . DLB-188

John Dunton [publishing house] DLB-170

Dupin, Amantine-Aurore-Lucile (see Sand, George)

Du Pont de Nemours, Pierre Samuel 1739-1817 . . . . DLB-313

Dupuy, Eliza Ann 1814-1880 . . . . DLB-248

Durack, Mary 1913-1994 . . . . DLB-260

Durand, Lucile (see Bersianik, Louky)

Duranti, Francesca 1935- DLB-196

Duranty, Walter 1884-1957 . . . . DLB-29

Duras, Marguerite (Marguerite Donnadieu) 1914-1996 . . . . DLB-83, 321

Durfey, Thomas 1653-1723 . . . . DLB-80

Durova, Nadezhda Andreevna (Aleksandr Andreevich Aleksandrov) 1783-1866 . . . . DLB-198

Durrell, Lawrence 1912-1990 . . . . DLB-15, 27, 204; Y-90; CDBLB-7

William Durrell [publishing house] DLB-49

Dürrenmatt, Friedrich 1921-1990 . . . . DLB-69, 124; CDWLB-2

Duston, Hannah 1657-1737 . . . . DLB-200

Dutt, Toru 1856-1877 . . . . DLB-240

E. P. Dutton and Company DLB-49

Duun, Olav 1876-1939 . . . . DLB-297

Duvoisin, Roger 1904-1980 . . . . DLB-61

Duyckinck, Evert Augustus 1816-1878 . . . . DLB-3, 64, 250

Duyckinck, George L. 1823-1863 . . . . DLB-3, 250

Duyckinck and Company DLB-49

Dwight, John Sullivan 1813-1893 . . . . . DLB-1, 235

Dwight, Timothy 1752-1817 . . . . DLB-37

    America: or, A Poem on the Settlement of the British Colonies, by Timothy Dwight DLB-37

Dybek, Stuart 1942- DLB-130

    Tribute to Michael M. Rea Y-97

Dyer, Charles 1928- DLB-13

Dyer, Sir Edward 1543-1607 . . . . DLB-136

Dyer, George 1755-1841 . . . . DLB-93

Dyer, John 1699-1757 . . . . DLB-95

Dyk, Viktor 1877-1931 . . . . DLB-215

Dylan, Bob 1941- DLB-16

E

Eager, Edward 1911-1964 . . . . DLB-22

Eagleton, Terry 1943- DLB-242

Eames, Wilberforce 1855-1937 ..... DLB-140

Earle, Alice Morse 1853-1911 ..... DLB-221

Earle, John 1600 or 1601-1665 ..... DLB-151

James H. Earle and Company DLB-49

East Europe
Independence and Destruction, 1918-1941 ..... DLB-220

Social Theory and Ethnography: Language and Ethnicity in Western versus Eastern Man DLB-220

Eastlake, William 1917-1997 ..... DLB-6, 206

Eastman, Carol ?- DLB-44

Eastman, Charles A. (Ohiyesa) 1858-1939 ..... DLB-175

Eastman, Max 1883-1969 ..... DLB-91

Eaton, Daniel Isaac 1753-1814 ..... DLB-158

Eaton, Edith Maude 1865-1914 ..... DLB-221, 312

Eaton, Winnifred 1875-1954 ..... DLB-221, 312

Eberhart, Richard 1904-2005 ... DLB-48; CDALB-1

Tribute to Robert Penn Warren Y-89

Ebner, Jeannie 1918-2004 ..... DLB-85

Ebner-Eschenbach, Marie von 1830-1916 ..... DLB-81

Ebon 1942- DLB-41

E-Books' Second Act in Libraries Y-02

Ecbasis Captivi circa 1045 ..... DLB-148

Ecco Press DLB-46

Eckhart, Meister circa 1260-circa 1328 ... DLB-115

The Eclectic Review 1805-1868 ..... DLB-110

Eco, Umberto 1932- DLB-196, 242

Eddison, E. R. 1882-1945 ..... DLB-255

Edel, Leon 1907-1997 ..... DLB-103

Edelfeldt, Inger 1956- DLB-257

J. M. Edelstein's Collection of Twentieth-Century American Poetry (A Century of Poetry, a Lifetime of Collecting) Y-02

Edes, Benjamin 1732-1803 ..... DLB-43

Edgar, David 1948- DLB-13, 233

Viewpoint: Politics and Performance DLB-13

Edgerton, Clyde 1944- DLB-278

Edgeworth, Maria 1768-1849 ..... DLB-116, 159, 163

The Edinburgh Review 1802-1929 ..... DLB-110

Edinburgh University Press DLB-112

Editing
Conversations with Editors Y-95

Editorial Statements DLB-137

The Editorial Style of Fredson Bowers Y-91

Editorial: The Extension of Copyright Y-02

We See the Editor at Work Y-97

Whose *Ulysses*? The Function of Editing ... Y-97

The Editor Publishing Company DLB-49

Editorial Institute at Boston University Y-00

Edmonds, Helen Woods Ferguson (see Kavan, Anna)

Edmonds, Randolph 1900-1983 ..... DLB-51

Edmonds, Walter D. 1903-1998 ..... DLB-9

Edric, Robert (see Armitage, G. E.)

Edschmid, Kasimir 1890-1966 ..... DLB-56

Edson, Margaret 1961- DLB-266

Edson, Russell 1935- DLB-244

Edwards, Amelia Anne Blandford 1831-1892 ..... DLB-174

Edwards, Dic 1953- DLB-245

Edwards, Edward 1812-1886 ..... DLB-184

Edwards, Jonathan 1703-1758 ..... DLB-24, 270

Edwards, Jonathan, Jr. 1745-1801 ..... DLB-37

Edwards, Junius 1929- DLB-33

Edwards. Matilda Barbara Betham 1836-1919 ..... DLB-174

Edwards, Richard 1524-1566 ..... DLB-62

Edwards, Sarah Pierpont 1710-1758 ..... DLB-200

James Edwards [publishing house] DLB-154

Effinger, George Alec 1947- DLB-8

Egerton, George 1859-1945 ..... DLB-135

Eggleston, Edward 1837-1902 ..... DLB-12

Eggleston, Wilfred 1901-1986 ..... DLB-92

Eglītis, Anšlavs 1906-1993 ..... DLB-220

Eguren, José María 1874-1942 ..... DLB-290

Ehrenreich, Barbara 1941- DLB-246

Ehrenstein, Albert 1886-1950 ..... DLB-81

Ehrhart, W. D. 1948- DS-9

Ehrlich, Gretel 1946- DLB-212, 275

Eich, Günter 1907-1972 ..... DLB-69, 124

Eichendorff, Joseph Freiherr von 1788-1857 ..... DLB-90

Eifukumon'in 1271-1342 ..... DLB-203

Eigner, Larry 1926-1996 ..... DLB-5, 193

Eikon Basilike 1649 ..... DLB-151

Eilhart von Oberge circa 1140-circa 1195 ..... DLB-148

Einar Benediktsson 1864-1940 ..... DLB-293

Einar Kárason 1955- DLB-293

Einar Már Guðmundsson 1954- DLB-293

Einhard circa 770-840 ..... DLB-148

Eiseley, Loren 1907-1977 ..... DLB-275, DS-17

Eisenberg, Deborah 1945- DLB-244

Eisenreich, Herbert 1925-1986 ..... DLB-85

Eisner, Kurt 1867-1919 ..... DLB-66

Ekelöf, Gunnar 1907-1968 ..... DLB-259

Eklund, Gordon 1945- Y-83

Ekman, Kerstin 1933- DLB-257

Ekwensi, Cyprian 1921- ... DLB-117; CDWLB-3

Elaw, Zilpha circa 1790-? DLB-239

George Eld [publishing house] DLB-170

Elder, Lonne, III 1931- DLB-7, 38, 44

Paul Elder and Company DLB-49

Eldershaw, Flora (M. Barnard Eldershaw) 1897-1956 ..... DLB-260

Eldershaw, M. Barnard (see Barnard, Marjorie and Eldershaw, Flora)

The Elected Member, 1970 Booker Prize winner, Bernice Rubens DLB-326

The Electronic Text Center and the Electronic Archive of Early American Fiction at the University of Virginia Library Y-98

Eliade, Mircea 1907-1986 .... DLB-220; CDWLB-4

Elie, Robert 1915-1973 ..... DLB-88

Elin Pelin 1877-1949 ..... DLB-147; CDWLB-4

Eliot, George 1819-1880 ..... DLB-21, 35, 55; CDBLB-4

The George Eliot Fellowship Y-99

Eliot, John 1604-1690 ..... DLB-24

Eliot, T. S. 1888-1965 ..... DLB-7, 10, 45, 63, 245; CDALB-5

T. S. Eliot Centennial: The Return of the Old Possum Y-88

The T. S. Eliot Society: Celebration and Scholarship, 1980-1999 ..... Y-99

Eliot's Court Press DLB-170

Elizabeth I 1533-1603 ..... DLB-136

Elizabeth von Nassau-Saarbrücken after 1393-1456 ..... DLB-179

Elizondo, Salvador 1932- DLB-145

Elizondo, Sergio 1930- DLB-82

Elkin, Stanley 1930-1995 ..... DLB-2, 28, 218, 278; Y-80

Elles, Dora Amy (see Wentworth, Patricia)

Ellet, Elizabeth F. 1818?-1877 ..... DLB-30

Elliot, Ebenezer 1781-1849 ..... DLB-96, 190

Elliot, Frances Minto (Dickinson) 1820-1898 ..... DLB-166

Elliott, Charlotte 1789-1871 ..... DLB-199

Elliott, George 1923- DLB-68

Elliott, George P. 1918-1980 ..... DLB-244

Elliott, Janice 1931-1995 ..... DLB-14

Elliott, Sarah Barnwell 1848-1928 ..... DLB-221

Elliott, Sumner Locke 1917-1991 ..... DLB-289

Elliott, Thomes and Talbot DLB-49

Elliott, William, III 1788-1863 ..... DLB-3, 248

Ellin, Stanley 1916-1986 ..... DLB-306

Ellis, Alice Thomas (Anna Margaret Haycraft) 1932- DLB-194

Ellis, Bret Easton 1964- DLB-292

Ellis, Edward S. 1840-1916 ..... DLB-42

Frederick Staridge Ellis [publishing house] DLB-106

Ellis, George E.
"The New Controversy Concerning Miracles DS-5

The George H. Ellis Company DLB-49

Cumulative Index   DLB 328

Ellis, Havelock 1859-1939 . . . . DLB-190
Ellison, Harlan 1934- DLB-8
    Tribute to Isaac Asimov Y-92
Ellison, Ralph
    1914-1994. . . . DLB-2, 76, 227; Y-94; CDALB-1
Ellmann, Richard 1918-1987 . . . . . . DLB-103; Y-87
Ellroy, James 1948- DLB-226; Y-91
    Tribute to John D. MacDonald Y-86
    Tribute to Raymond Chandler Y-88
Eluard, Paul 1895-1952 . . . . DLB-258
Elyot, Thomas 1490?-1546 . . . . DLB-136
Emanuel, James Andrew 1921- DLB-41
Emecheta, Buchi 1944- DLB-117; CDWLB-3
Emerson, Ralph Waldo
    1803-1882 . . . . . DLB-1, 59, 73, 183, 223, 270;
                                  DS-5; CDALB-2
    Ralph Waldo Emerson in 1982 . . . . Y-82
    The Ralph Waldo Emerson Society Y-99
Emerson, William 1769-1811 . . . . DLB-37
Emerson, William R. 1923-1997 . . . . Y-97
Emin, Fedor Aleksandrovich
    circa 1735-1770 . . . . DLB-150
Emmanuel, Pierre 1916-1984 . . . . DLB-258
Empedocles fifth century B.C. DLB-176
Empson, William 1906-1984 . . . . DLB-20
Enchi Fumiko 1905-1986 . . . . DLB-182
"The Encyclopedia," Denis Diderot DLB-314
Ende, Michael 1929-1995 . . . . DLB-75
Endō Shūsaku 1923-1996 . . . . DLB-182
Engel, Marian 1933-1985 . . . . DLB-53
Engel'gardt, Sof'ia Vladimirovna
    1828-1894 . . . . DLB-277
Engels, Friedrich 1820-1895 . . . . DLB-129
Engle, Paul 1908-1991 . . . . DLB-48
    Tribute to Robert Penn Warren Y-89
English, Thomas Dunn 1819-1902 . . . . . . DLB-202
The English Patient, 1992 Booker Prize winner,
    Michael Ondaatje DLB-326
Ennius 239 B.C.-169 B.C. DLB-211
Enquist, Per Olov 1934- DLB-257
Enright, Anne 1962- DLB-267
Enright, D. J. 1920-2002 . . . . DLB-27
Enright, Elizabeth 1909-1968 . . . . DLB-22
Enright, Nick 1950-2003 . . . . DLB-325
Epic, The Sixteenth-Century Spanish DLB-318
Epictetus circa 55-circa 125-130 . . . . DLB-176
Epicurus 342/341 B.C.-271/270 B.C. DLB-176
d'Epinay, Louise (Louise-Florence-Pétronille Tardieu
    d'Esclavelles, marquise d'Epinay)
    1726-1783 . . . . DLB-313
Epps, Bernard 1936- DLB-53
Epshtein, Mikhail Naumovich 1950- . . DLB-285
Epstein, Julius 1909-2000 and
    Epstein, Philip 1909-1952 . . . . DLB-26

Epstein, Leslie 1938- DLB-299
Editors, Conversations with Y-95
Equiano, Olaudah
    circa 1745-1797 . . . . . . DLB-37, 50; CDWLB-3
    Olaudah Equiano and Unfinished
        Journeys: The Slave-Narrative
        Tradition and Twentieth-Century
        Continuities DLB-117
Eragny Press DLB-112
Erasmus, Desiderius 1467-1536 . . . . DLB-136
Erba, Luciano 1922- DLB-128
Erdman, Nikolai Robertovich
    1900-1970 . . . . DLB-272
Erdrich, Louise
    1954- DLB-152, 175, 206; CDALB-7
Erenburg, Il'ia Grigor'evich 1891-1967 . . . DLB-272
Erichsen-Brown, Gwethalyn Graham
    (see Graham, Gwethalyn)
Eriugena, John Scottus circa 810-877 . . . . DLB-115
Ernst, Paul 1866-1933 . . . . DLB-66, 118
Erofeev, Venedikt Vasil'evich
    1938-1990 . . . . DLB-285
Erofeev, Viktor Vladimirovich 1947- . . . DLB-285
Ershov, Petr Pavlovich 1815-1869 . . . . . . DLB-205
Erskine, Albert 1911-1993 . . . . Y-93
    At Home with Albert Erskine Y-00
Erskine, John 1879-1951 . . . . DLB-9, 102
Erskine, Mrs. Steuart ?-1948 . . . . DLB-195
Ertel', Aleksandr Ivanovich
    1855-1908 . . . . DLB-238
Ervine, St. John Greer 1883-1971 . . . . DLB-10
Eschenburg, Johann Joachim
    1743-1820 . . . . DLB-97
Escofet, Cristina 1945- DLB-305
Escoto, Julio 1944- DLB-145
Esdaile, Arundell 1880-1956 . . . . DLB-201
Esenin, Sergei Aleksandrovich
    1895-1925 . . . . DLB-295
Eshleman, Clayton 1935- DLB-5
Espaillat, Rhina P. 1932- DLB-282
Espanca, Florbela 1894-1930 . . . . DLB-287
Espriu, Salvador 1913-1985 . . . . DLB-134
Ess Ess Publishing Company DLB-49
Essex House Press DLB-112
Esson, Louis 1878-1943 . . . . DLB-260
Essop, Ahmed 1931- DLB-225
Esterházy, Péter 1950- DLB-232; CDWLB-4
Estes, Eleanor 1906-1988 . . . . DLB-22
Estes and Lauriat DLB-49
Estienne, Henri II (Henricus Stephanus)
    1531-1597 . . . . DLB-327
Estleman, Loren D. 1952- DLB-226
Eszterhas, Joe 1944- DLB-185
Etherege, George 1636-circa 1692 . . . . DLB-80
Ethridge, Mark, Sr. 1896-1981 . . . . DLB-127

Ets, Marie Hall 1893-1984 . . . . DLB-22
Etter, David 1928- DLB-105
Ettner, Johann Christoph 1654-1724 . . . . DLB-168
Eudora Welty Remembered in
    Two Exhibits Y-02
Eugene Gant's Projected Works Y-01
Eupolemius fl. circa 1095 . . . . DLB-148
Euripides circa 484 B.C.-407/406 B.C.
    . . . . DLB-176; CDWLB-1
Evans, Augusta Jane 1835-1909 . . . . DLB-239
Evans, Caradoc 1878-1945 . . . . DLB-162
Evans, Charles 1850-1935 . . . . DLB-187
Evans, Donald 1884-1921 . . . . DLB-54
Evans, George Henry 1805-1856 . . . . DLB-43
Evans, Hubert 1892-1986 . . . . DLB-92
Evans, Mari 1923- DLB-41
Evans, Mary Ann (see Eliot, George)
Evans, Nathaniel 1742-1767 . . . . DLB-31
Evans, Sebastian 1830-1909 . . . . DLB-35
Evans, Ray 1915- DLB-265
M. Evans and Company DLB-46
Evaristi, Marcella 1953- DLB-233
Everett, Alexander Hill 1790-1847 . . . . . . DLB-59
Everett, Edward 1794-1865 . . . . . . DLB-1, 59, 235
Everson, R. G. 1903- DLB-88
Everson, William 1912-1994 . . . . . DLB-5, 16, 212
Evreinov, Nikolai 1879-1953 . . . . DLB-317
Ewald, Johannes 1743-1781 . . . . DLB-300
Ewart, Gavin 1916-1995 . . . . DLB-40
Ewing, Juliana Horatia 1841-1885 . . . DLB-21, 163
The Examiner 1808-1881 . . . . DLB-110
Exley, Frederick 1929-1992 . . . . DLB-143; Y-81
Editorial: The Extension of Copyright Y-02
von Eyb, Albrecht 1420-1475 . . . . DLB-179
Eyre and Spottiswoode DLB-106
Ezekiel, Nissim 1924-2004 . . . . DLB-323
Ezera, Regīna 1930- DLB-232
Ezzo ?-after 1065 . . . . DLB-148

F

Faber, Frederick William 1814-1863 . . . . . DLB-32
Faber and Faber Limited DLB-112
Faccio, Rena (see Aleramo, Sibilla)
Facsimiles
    The Uses of Facsimile: A Symposium Y-90
Fadeev, Aleksandr Aleksandrovich
    1901-1956 . . . . DLB-272
Fagundo, Ana María 1938- DLB-134
Fainzil'berg, Il'ia Arnol'dovich
    (see Il'f, Il'ia and Petrov, Evgenii)
Fair, Ronald L. 1932- DLB-33
Fairfax, Beatrice (see Manning, Marie)

Fairlie, Gerard 1899-1983 . . . . .DLB-77	George Faulkner [publishing house] DLB-154	Ferber, Edna 1885-1968. . . . . . .DLB-9, 28, 86. 266
Faldbakken, Knut 1941- DLB-297	Faulks, Sebastian 1953- DLB-207	Ferdinand, Vallery, III (see Salaam, Kalamu ya)
Falkberget, Johan (Johan Petter Lillebakken) 1879-1967 . . . . .DLB-297	Fauset, Jessie Redmon 1882-1961 . . . . .DLB-51	Ferguson, Sir Samuel 1810-1886 . . . . .DLB-32
Fallada, Hans 1893-1947 . . . . .DLB-56	Faust, Frederick Schiller (Max Brand) 1892-1944 . . . . .DLB-256	Ferguson, William Scott 1875-1954 . . . . . . .DLB-47
The Famished Road, 1991 Booker Prize winner, Ben Okri DLB-326	Faust, Irvin 1924- DLB-2, 28, 218, 278; Y-80, 00	Fergusson, Robert 1750-1774 . . . . .DLB-109
Fancher, Betsy 1928- Y-83	I Wake Up Screaming [Response to Ken Auletta] .Y-97	Ferland, Albert 1872-1943 . . . . .DLB-92
Fane, Violet 1843-1905 . . . . .DLB-35	Tribute to Bernard Malamud Y-86	Ferlinghetti, Lawrence 1919- DLB-5, 16; CDALB-1
Fanfrolico Press .DLB-112	Tribute to Isaac Bashevis Singer Y-91	Tribute to Kenneth Rexroth Y-82
Fanning, Katherine 1927- DLB-127	Tribute to Meyer Levin. Y-81	Fermor, Patrick Leigh 1915- DLB-204
Fanon, Frantz 1925-1961 . . . . .DLB-296	Fawcett, Edgar 1847-1904 . . . . .DLB-202	Fern, Fanny (see Parton, Sara Payson Willis)
Fanshawe, Sir Richard 1608-1666 . . . . . . .DLB-126	Fawcett, Millicent Garrett 1847-1929 . . . . .DLB-190	Ferrars, Elizabeth (Morna Doris Brown) 1907-1995 . . . . .DLB-87
Fantasy Press Publishers DLB-46	Fawcett Books DLB-46	Ferré, Rosario 1942- DLB-145
Fante, John 1909-1983 . . . . .DLB-130; Y-83	Fay, Theodore Sedgwick 1807-1898. . . . . .DLB-202	Ferreira, Vergílio 1916-1996. . . . . .DLB-287
Al-Farabi circa 870-950. . . . . .DLB-115	Fearing, Kenneth 1902-1961 . . . . .DLB-9	E. Ferret and Company DLB-49
Farabough, Laura 1949- DLB-228	Federal Writers' Project DLB-46	Ferrier, Susan 1782-1854 . . . . .DLB-116
Farah, Nuruddin 1945- . . .DLB-125; CDWLB-3	Federman, Raymond 1928- Y-80	Ferril, Thomas Hornsby 1896-1988. . . . . .DLB-206
Farber, Norma 1909-1984 . . . . .DLB-61	Fedin, Konstantin Aleksandrovich 1892-1977 . . . . .DLB-272	Ferrini, Vincent 1913- DLB-48
A Farewell to Arms (Documentary) DLB-308	Fedorov, Innokentii Vasil'evich (see Omulevsky, Innokentii Vasil'evich)	Ferron, Jacques 1921-1985. . . . . .DLB-60
Fargue, Léon-Paul 1876-1947 . . . . .DLB-258	Feiffer, Jules 1929- DLB-7, 44	Ferron, Madeleine 1922- DLB-53
Farigoule, Louis (see Romains, Jules)	Feinberg, Charles E. 1899-1988. . . . DLB-187; Y-88	Ferrucci, Franco 1936- DLB-196
Farjeon, Eleanor 1881-1965 . . . . .DLB-160	Feind, Barthold 1678-1721 . . . . .DLB-168	Fet, Afanasii Afanas'evich 1820?-1892 . . . . .DLB-277
Farley, Harriet 1812-1907. . . . . .DLB-239	Feinstein, Elaine 1930- DLB-14, 40	Fetridge and Company DLB-49
Farley, Walter 1920-1989. . . . . .DLB-22	Feirstein, Frederick 1940- DLB-282	Feuchtersleben, Ernst Freiherr von 1806-1849 . . . . .DLB-133
Farmborough, Florence 1887-1978 . . . . . .DLB-204	Feiss, Paul Louis 1875-1952 . . . . .DLB-187	Feuchtwanger, Lion 1884-1958 . . . . .DLB-66
Farmer, Beverley 1941- DLB-325	Feldman, Irving 1928- DLB-169	Feuerbach, Ludwig 1804-1872 . . . . .DLB-133
Farmer, Penelope 1939- DLB-161	Felipe, Carlos 1911-1975 . . . . .DLB-305	Feuillet, Octave 1821-1890. . . . . .DLB-192
Farmer, Philip José 1918- DLB-8	Felipe, Léon 1884-1968 . . . . .DLB-108	Feydeau, Georges 1862-1921 . . . . .DLB-192
Farnaby, Thomas 1575?-1647. . . . . .DLB-236	Fell, Frederick, Publishers DLB-46	Fibiger, Mathilde 1830-1872 . . . . .DLB-300
Farningham, Marianne (see Hearn, Mary Anne)	Fellowship of Southern Writers Y-98	Fichte, Johann Gottlieb 1762-1814 . . . . . . .DLB-90
Farquhar, George circa 1677-1707. . . . . . . .DLB-84	Felltham, Owen 1602?-1668 . . . . DLB-126, 151	Ficke, Arthur Davison 1883-1945 . . . . .DLB-54
Farquharson, Martha (see Finley, Martha)	Felman, Shoshana 1942- DLB-246	Fiction
Farrar, Frederic William 1831-1903 . . . . . .DLB-163	Fels, Ludwig 1946- DLB-75	American Fiction and the 1930s DLB-9
Farrar, Straus and Giroux DLB-46	Felton, Cornelius Conway 1807-1862 .DLB-1, 235	Fiction Best-Sellers, 1910-1945 . . . . .DLB-9
Farrar and Rinehart DLB-46	Fel'zen, Iurii (Nikolai Berngardovich Freidenshtein) 1894?-1943 . . . . .DLB-317	Postmodern Holocaust Fiction DLB-299
Farrell, J. G. 1935-1979 . . . . DLB-14, 271, 326	Mothe-Fénelon, François de Salignac de la 1651-1715 . . . . .DLB-268	The Year in Fiction Y-84, 86, 89, 94–99
Farrell, James T. 1904-1979 . . . .DLB-4, 9, 86; DS-2	Fenn, Harry 1837-1911 . . . . .DLB-188	The Year in Fiction: A Biased View Y-83
Fast, Howard 1914-2003 . . . . .DLB-9	Fennario, David 1947- DLB-60	The Year in U.S. Fiction Y-00, 01
Faulkner, William 1897-1962 . . . . DLB-9, 11, 44, 102, 316; DS-2; Y-86; CDALB-5	Fenner, Dudley 1558?-1587? DLB-236	The Year's Work in Fiction: A Survey Y-82
Faulkner and Yoknapatawpha Conference, Oxford, Mississippi. Y-97	Fenno, Jenny 1765?-1803 . . . . .DLB-200	Fiedler, Leslie A. 1917-2003 . . . . .DLB-28, 67
Faulkner Centennial Addresses Y-97	Fenno, John 1751-1798. . . . . .DLB-43	Tribute to Bernard Malamud Y-86
"Faulkner 100–Celebrating the Work," University of South Carolina, Columbia Y-97	R. F. Fenno and Company. DLB-49	Tribute to James Dickey Y-97
Impressions of William Faulkner. Y-97	Fenoglio, Beppe 1922-1963 . . . . .DLB-177	Field, Barron 1789-1846. . . . . .DLB-230
William Faulkner and the People-to-People Program Y-86	Fenton, Geoffrey 1539?-1608 . . . . .DLB-136	Field, Edward 1924- DLB-105
William Faulkner Centenary Celebrations .Y-97	Fenton, James 1949- DLB-40	Field, Eugene 1850-1895 . . DLB-23, 42, 140; DS-13
	The Hemingway/Fenton Correspondence Y-02	Field, John 1545?-1588 . . . . .DLB-167
The William Faulkner Society. Y-99		Field, Joseph M. 1810-1856 . . . . .DLB-248
		Field, Marshall, III 1893-1956 . . . . .DLB-127
		Field, Marshall, IV 1916-1965 . . . . .DLB-127
		Field, Marshall, V 1941- DLB-127

Cumulative Index

Field, Michael (Katherine Harris Bradley)
  1846-1914. . . . . DLB-240
  "The Poetry File" DLB-105
Field, Nathan 1587-1619 or 1620 . . . . DLB-58
Field, Rachel 1894-1942 . . . . DLB-9, 22
Fielding, Helen 1958- DLB-231
Fielding, Henry
  1707-1754 . . . . DLB-39, 84, 101; CDBLB-2
  "Defense of *Amelia*" (1752) DLB-39
  The History of the Adventures of Joseph Andrews
    [excerpt] (1742) DLB-39
  Letter to [Samuel] Richardson on *Clarissa*
    (1748). DLB-39
  Preface to *Joseph Andrews* (1742) DLB-39
  Preface to Sarah Fielding's *Familiar
    Letters* (1747) [excerpt] DLB-39
  Preface to Sarah Fielding's *The
    Adventures of David Simple* (1744) . . . DLB-39
  Review of *Clarissa* (1748) DLB-39
  Tom Jones (1749) [excerpt] DLB-39
Fielding, Sarah 1710-1768 . . . . DLB-39
  Preface to *The Cry* (1754) DLB-39
Fields, Annie Adams 1834-1915 . . . . DLB-221
Fields, Dorothy 1905-1974 . . . . DLB-265
Fields, James T. 1817-1881 . . . . DLB-1, 235
Fields, Julia 1938- DLB-41
Fields, Osgood and Company DLB-49
Fields, W. C. 1880-1946 . . . . DLB-44
Fierstein, Harvey 1954- DLB-266
Figes, Eva 1932- DLB-14, 271
Figuera, Angela 1902-1984 . . . . DLB-108
Filmer, Sir Robert 1586-1653 . . . . DLB-151
Filson, John circa 1753-1788 . . . . DLB-37
Finch, Anne, Countess of Winchilsea
  1661-1720. DLB-95
Finch, Annie 1956- DLB-282
Finch, Robert 1900- DLB-88
Findley, Timothy 1930-2002. . . . . DLB-53
Finlay, Ian Hamilton 1925- DLB-40
Finley, Martha 1828-1909. . . . . DLB-42
Finn, Elizabeth Anne (McCaul)
  1825-1921 . . . . DLB-166
Finnegan, Seamus 1949- DLB-245
Finney, Jack 1911-1995. . . . . DLB-8
Finney, Walter Braden (see Finney, Jack)
Firbank, Ronald 1886-1926 . . . . DLB-36
Firmin, Giles 1615-1697 . . . . DLB-24
First Edition Library/Collectors'
  Reprints, Inc. Y-91
Fischart, Johann
  1546 or 1547-1590 or 1591 . . . . DLB-179
Fischer, Karoline Auguste Fernandine
  1764-1842. DLB-94
Fischer, Tibor 1959- DLB-231
Fish, Stanley 1938- DLB-67
Fishacre, Richard 1205-1248. . . . . DLB-115
Fisher, Clay (see Allen, Henry W.)
Fisher, Dorothy Canfield 1879-1958 . . . DLB-9, 102

Fisher, Leonard Everett 1924- DLB-61
Fisher, Roy 1930- DLB-40
Fisher, Rudolph 1897-1934 . . . . DLB-51, 102
Fisher, Steve 1913-1980 . . . . DLB-226
Fisher, Sydney George 1856-1927. . . . . . . DLB-47
Fisher, Vardis 1895-1968. . . . . DLB-9, 206
Fiske, John 1608-1677. . . . . DLB-24
Fiske, John 1842-1901 . . . . DLB-47, 64
Fitch, Thomas circa 1700-1774 . . . . DLB-31
Fitch, William Clyde 1865-1909. . . . . DLB-7
FitzGerald, Edward 1809-1883. . . . . DLB-32
Fitzgerald, F. Scott 1896-1940
  . . . . DLB-4, 9, 86; Y-81, 92;
                              DS-1, 15, 16; CDALB-4
  F. Scott Fitzgerald: A Descriptive
    Bibliography, Supplement (2001) Y-01
  F. Scott Fitzgerald Centenary
    Celebrations Y-96
  F. Scott Fitzgerald Inducted into the
    American Poets' Corner at St. John
    the Divine; Ezra Pound Banned Y-99
  "F. Scott Fitzgerald: St. Paul's Native Son
    and Distinguished American Writer":
    University of Minnesota Conference,
    29-31 October 1982. . . . . Y-82
  First International F. Scott Fitzgerald
    Conference Y-92
  The Great Gatsby (Documentary). DLB-219
  Tender Is the Night (Documentary) DLB-273
Fitzgerald, Penelope
  1916-2000. . . . . DLB-14, 194, 326
Fitzgerald, Robert 1910-1985 . . . . Y-80
FitzGerald, Robert D. 1902-1987 . . . . DLB-260
Fitzgerald, Thomas 1819-1891 . . . . DLB-23
Fitzgerald, Zelda Sayre 1900-1948 . . . . . . Y-84
Fitzhugh, Louise 1928-1974 . . . . DLB-52
Fitzhugh, William circa 1651-1701 . . . . . . DLB-24
Flagg, James Montgomery 1877-1960. . . . DLB-188
Flanagan, Thomas 1923-2002 . . . . Y-80
Flanner, Hildegarde 1899-1987. . . . . DLB-48
Flanner, Janet 1892-1978. . . . . DLB-4; DS-15
Flannery, Peter 1951- DLB-233
Flaubert, Gustave 1821-1880 . . . . . . DLB-119, 301
Flavin, Martin 1883-1967 . . . . DLB-9
Fleck, Konrad (fl. circa 1220) DLB-138
Flecker, James Elroy 1884-1915 . . . . . . DLB-10, 19
Fleeson, Doris 1901-1970 . . . . DLB-29
Fleißer, Marieluise 1901-1974 . . . . DLB-56, 124
Fleischer, Nat 1887-1972 . . . . DLB-241
Fleming, Abraham 1552?-1607 . . . . DLB-236
Fleming, Ian 1908-1964 . . .DLB-87, 201; CDBLB-7
Fleming, Joan 1908-1980 . . . . .DLB-276
Fleming, May Agnes 1840-1880 . . . . DLB-99
Fleming, Paul 1609-1640 . . . . DLB-164
Fleming, Peter 1907-1971 . . . . DLB-195
Fletcher, Giles, the Elder 1546-1611 . . . . . DLB-136

Fletcher, Giles, the Younger
  1585 or 1586-1623. . . . . DLB-121
Fletcher, J. S. 1863-1935 . . . . DLB-70
Fletcher, John 1579-1625. . . . . DLB-58
Fletcher, John Gould 1886-1950. . . . . . DLB-4, 45
Fletcher, Phineas 1582-1650 . . . . DLB-121
Flieg, Helmut (see Heym, Stefan)
Flint, F. S. 1885-1960 . . . . DLB-19
Flint, Timothy 1780-1840 . . . . .DLB-73, 186
Fløgstad, Kjartan 1944- DLB-297
Florensky, Pavel Aleksandrovich
  1882-1937 . . . . DLB-295
Flores, Juan de fl. 1470-1500. . . . . DLB-286
Flores-Williams, Jason 1969- DLB-209
Florio, John 1553?-1625. . . . . .DLB-172
Fludd, Robert 1574-1637 . . . . DLB-281
Flynn, Elizabeth Gurley 1890-1964 . . . . . DLB-303
Fo, Dario 1926- Y-97
  Nobel Lecture 1997: Contra Jogulatores
    Obloquentes Y-97
Foden, Giles 1967- DLB-267
Fofanov, Konstantin Mikhailovich
  1862-1911 .DLB-277
Foix, J. V. 1893-1987. . . . . DLB-134
Foley, Martha 1897-1977 . . . . .DLB-137
Folger, Henry Clay 1857-1930 . . . . DLB-140
Folio Society DLB-112
Follain, Jean 1903-1971 . . . . DLB-258
Follen, Charles 1796-1840. . . . . DLB-235
Follen, Eliza Lee (Cabot) 1787-1860 . . . DLB-1, 235
Follett, Ken 1949- DLB-87; Y-81
Follett Publishing Company DLB-46
John West Folsom [publishing house]. DLB-49
Folz, Hans
  between 1435 and 1440-1513 . . . . . . .DLB-179
Fonseca, Manuel da 1911-1993 . . . . DLB-287
Fonseca, Rubem 1925- DLB-307
Fontane, Theodor
  1819-1898 . . . . .DLB-129; CDWLB-2
Fontenelle, Bernard Le Bovier de
  1657-1757 . . . . .DLB-268, 313
Fontes, Montserrat 1940- DLB-209
Fonvisin, Denis Ivanovich
  1744 or 1745-1792 . . . . DLB-150
Foote, Horton 1916- DLB-26, 266
Foote, Mary Hallock
  1847-1938. . . . . . . .DLB-186, 188, 202, 221
Foote, Samuel 1721-1777 . . . . DLB-89
Foote, Shelby 1916-2005. . . . . .DLB-2, 17
Forbes, Calvin 1945- DLB-41
Forbes, Ester 1891-1967 . . . . DLB-22
Forbes, John 1950-1998 . . . . .DLB=325
Forbes, Rosita 1893?-1967 . . . . DLB-195

Forbes and Company..................DLB-49	Foster, John 1648-1681.................DLB-24	Franzos, Karl Emil 1848-1904..........DLB-129
Force, Peter 1790-1868................DLB-30	Foster, Michael 1904-1956..............DLB-9	Fraser, Antonia 1932- DLB-276
Forché, Carolyn 1950- DLB-5, 193	Foster, Myles Birket 1825-1899.........DLB-184	Fraser, G. S. 1915-1980................DLB-27
Ford, Charles Henri 1913-2002.......DLB-4, 48	Foster, William Z. 1881-1961...........DLB-303	Fraser, Kathleen 1935- DLB-169
Ford, Corey 1902-1969................DLB-11	Foucault, Michel 1926-1984.............DLB-242	Frattini, Alberto 1922- DLB-128

Ford, Ford Madox
  1873-1939 ....DLB-34, 98, 162; CDBLB-6
	Robert and Andrew Foulis
	  [publishing house]..............DLB-154
		Frau Ava ?-1127......................DLB-148

Nathan Asch Remembers Ford Madox Ford, Sam Roth, and Hart Crane.....Y-02	Fouqué, Caroline de la Motte 1774-1831....DLB-90	Fraunce, Abraham 1558?-1592 or 1593 ..DLB-236
J. B. Ford and Company DLB-49	Fouqué, Friedrich de la Motte 1777-1843......................DLB-90	Frayn, Michael 1933- DLB-13, 14, 194, 245
Ford, Jesse Hill 1928-1996..............DLB-6	Four Seas Company...................DLB-46	Frazier, Charles 1950- DLB-292
Ford, John 1586-?...........DLB-58; CDBLB-1	Four Winds Press....................DLB-46	Fréchette, Louis-Honoré 1839-1908......DLB-99
Ford, R. A. D. 1915-1998...............DLB-88	Fournier, Henri Alban (see Alain-Fournier)	Frederic, Harold 1856-1898....DLB-12, 23; DS-13
Ford, Richard 1944- DLB-227	Fowler, Christopher 1953- DLB-267	Freed, Arthur 1894-1973..............DLB-265
Ford, Worthington C. 1858-1941.........DLB-47	Fowler, Connie May 1958- DLB-292	Freeling, Nicolas 1927-2003.............DLB-87
Fords, Howard, and Hulbert DLB-49	Fowler and Wells Company............DLB-49	Tribute to Georges Simenon............Y-89

Foreman, Carl 1914-1984 ....DLB-26	Fowles, John
	  1926- DLB-14, 139, 207; CDBLB-8
		Freeman, Douglas Southall
		  1886-1953................ DLB-17; DS-17

Forester, C. S. 1899-1966..............DLB-191	Fox, John 1939- DLB-245	Freeman, Joseph 1897-1965............DLB-303
The C. S. Forester Society.............Y-00	Fox, John, Jr. 1862 or 1863-1919....DLB-9; DS-13	Freeman, Judith 1946- DLB-256
Forester, Frank (see Herbert, Henry William)	Fox, Paula 1923- DLB-52	Freeman, Legh Richmond 1842-1915.....DLB-23
Formalism, New	Fox, Richard Kyle 1846-1922............DLB-79	Freeman, Mary E. Wilkins 1852-1930................DLB-12, 78, 221
Anthologizing New Formalism DLB-282	Fox, William Price 1926- DLB-2; Y-81	Freeman, R. Austin 1862-1943 ....DLB-70
The Little Magazines of the New Formalism.................DLB-282	Remembering Joe Heller.............Y-99	Freidank circa 1170-circa 1233..........DLB-138
The New Narrative Poetry DLB-282	Richard K. Fox [publishing house]........DLB-49	Freiligrath, Ferdinand 1810-1876........DLB-133
Presses of the New Formalism and the New Narrative DLB-282	Foxe, John 1517-1587.................DLB-132	Fremlin, Celia 1914- DLB-276
The Prosody of the New Formalism ..DLB-282	Fraenkel, Michael 1896-1957.............DLB-4	Frémont, Jessie Benton 1834-1902.......DLB-183

Younger Women Poets of the
  New Formalism.................DLB-282
	Frame, Ronald 1953- DLB-319	Frémont, John Charles
		  1813-1890..................DLB-183, 186

Forman, Harry Buxton 1842-1917.......DLB-184	France, Anatole 1844-1924.............DLB-123	French, Alice 1850-1934 ....DLB-74; DS-13
Fornés, María Irene 1930- DLB-7	France, Richard 1938- DLB-7	French, David 1939- DLB-53
Forrest, Leon 1937-1997................DLB-33	Francis, Convers 1795-1863..........DLB-1, 235	French, Evangeline 1869-1960..........DLB-195
Forsh, Ol'ga Dmitrievna 1873-1961......DLB-272	Francis, Dick 1920- DLB-87; CDBLB-8	French, Francesca 1871-1960...........DLB-195
Forster, E. M. 1879-1970 . DLB-34, 98, 162, 178, 195; DS-10; CDBLB-6	Francis, Sir Frank 1901-1988............DLB-201	James French [publishing house] DLB-49
"Fantasy," from *Aspects of the Novel* (1927) DLB-178	Francis, Jeffrey, Lord 1773-1850.........DLB-107	Samuel French [publishing house]........DLB-49
Forster, Georg 1754-1794 ....DLB-94	C. S. Francis [publishing house].........DLB-49	Samuel French, Limited..............DLB-106
Forster, John 1812-1876 ....DLB-144	Franck, Sebastian 1499-1542 ....DLB-179	French Literature
Forster, Margaret 1938- DLB-155, 271	Francke, Kuno 1855-1930...............DLB-71	Georges-Louis Leclerc de Buffon, "Le Discours sur le style"..................DLB-314
Forsyth, Frederick 1938- DLB-87	Françoise (Robertine Barry) 1863-1910....DLB-92	Marie-Jean-Antoine-Nicolas Caritat, marquis de Condorcet, "The Tenth Stage"...DLB-314
Forsyth, William "Literary Style" (1857) [excerpt] DLB-57	François, Louise von 1817-1893.........DLB-129	Sophie Cottin, *Claire d'Albe* DLB-314
Forten, Charlotte L. 1837-1914 ......DLB-50, 239	Frank, Bruno 1887-1945 ....DLB-118	Declaration of the Rights of Man and of the Citizen DLB-314
Pages from Her Diary DLB-50	Frank, Leonhard 1882-1961 ....DLB-56, 118	Denis Diderot, "The Encyclopedia" ..DLB-314
Fortini, Franco 1917-1994..............DLB-128	Frank, Melvin 1913-1988................DLB-26	Epic and Beast Epic..............DLB-208
Fortune, Mary ca. 1833-ca. 1910 ....DLB-230	Frank, Waldo 1889-1967..............DLB-9, 63	French Arthurian Literature DLB-208
Fortune, T. Thomas 1856-1928..........DLB-23	Franken, Rose 1895?-1988 ...... DLB-228, Y-84	Olympe de Gouges, *Declaration of the Rights of Woman*....................DLB-314

Fosdick, Charles Austin 1842-1915.......DLB-42	Franklin, Benjamin
	  1706-1790 ....DLB-24, 43, 73, 183; CDALB-2
		Françoise d'Issembourg de Graffigny, *Letters from
		  a Peruvian Woman*..............DLB-314

Fosse, Jon 1959- DLB-297	Franklin, James 1697-1735 ....DLB-43	Claude-Adrien Helvétius, *The Spirit of Laws* DLB-314

Foster, David 1944- DLB-289	Franklin, John 1786-1847...............DLB-99	Paul Henri Thiry, baron d'Holbach (writing as
		  Jean-Baptiste de Mirabaud), *The System
		  of Nature*....................DLB-314

Foster, Genevieve 1893-1979 ....DLB-61	Franklin, Miles 1879-1954 ....DLB-230	
Foster, Hannah Webster 1758-1840 .... DLB-37, 200	Franklin Library DLB-46	
	Frantz, Ralph Jules 1902-1979 ....DLB-4	

Pierre-Ambroise-François Choderlos de Laclos, *Dangerous Acquaintances* DLB-314

Lyric Poetry DLB-268

Louis-Sébastien Mercier, *Le Tableau de Paris* DLB-314

Charles-Louis de Secondat, baron de Montesquieu, *The Spirit of Laws* .. DLB-314

Other Poets DLB-217

Poetry in Nineteenth-Century France: Cultural Background and Critical Commentary DLB-217

Roman de la Rose: Guillaume de Lorris 1200 to 1205-circa 1230, Jean de Meun 1235/1240-circa 1305 .... DLB-208

Jean-Jacques Rousseau, *The Social Contract* DLB-314

Marquis de Sade, "Dialogue entre un prêtre et un moribond" DLB-314

Saints' Lives DLB-208

Troubadours, *Trobairitz,* and Trouvères DLB-208

Anne-Robert-Jacques Turgot, baron de l'Aulne, "Memorandum on Local Government" DLB-314

Voltaire, "An account of the death of the chevalier de La Barre" DLB-314

Voltaire, *Candide* DLB-314

Voltaire, *Philosophical Dictionary* DLB-314

French Theater
Medieval French Drama DLB-208

Parisian Theater, Fall 1984: Toward a New Baroque Y-85

Freneau, Philip 1752-1832 .... DLB-37, 43

The Rising Glory of America DLB-37

Freni, Melo 1934- DLB-128

Fréron, Elie Catherine 1718-1776 ...... DLB-313

Freshfield, Douglas W. 1845-1934 .... DLB-174

Freud, Sigmund 1856-1939 .... DLB-296

Freytag, Gustav 1816-1895 .... DLB-129

Fríða Á. Sigurðardóttir 1940- DLB-293

Fridegård, Jan 1897-1968 .... DLB-259

Fried, Erich 1921-1988 .... DLB-85

Friedan, Betty 1921-2006 .... DLB-246

Friedman, Bruce Jay 1930- DLB-2, 28, 244

Friedman, Carl 1952- DLB-299

Friedman, Kinky 1944- DLB-292

Friedrich von Hausen circa 1171-1190 ... DLB-138

Friel, Brian 1929- DLB-13, 319

Friend, Krebs 1895?-1967? DLB-4

Fries, Fritz Rudolf 1935- DLB-75

Frisch, Max 1911-1991 .... DLB-69, 124; CDWLB-2

Frischlin, Nicodemus 1547-1590 .... DLB-179

Frischmuth, Barbara 1941- DLB-85

Fritz, Jean 1915- DLB-52

Froissart, Jean circa 1337-circa 1404 ..... DLB-208

Fromm, Erich 1900-1980 .... DLB-296

Fromentin, Eugene 1820-1876 .... DLB-123

Frontinus circa A.D. 35-A.D. 103/104 .... DLB-211

Frost, A. B. 1851-1928 .... DLB-188; DS-13

Frost, Robert 1874-1963 .... DLB-54; DS-7; CDALB-4

The Friends of the Dymock Poets Y-00

Frostenson, Katarina 1953- DLB-257

Frothingham, Octavius Brooks 1822-1895 .... DLB-1, 243

Froude, James Anthony 1818-1894 .... DLB-18, 57, 144

Fruitlands 1843-1844 .... DLB-1, 223; DS-5

Fry, Christopher 1907-2005 .... DLB-13

Tribute to John Betjeman Y-84

Fry, Roger 1866-1934 .... DS-10

Fry, Stephen 1957- DLB-207

Frye, Northrop 1912-1991 ...... DLB-67, 68, 246

Fuchs, Daniel 1909-1993 ..... DLB-9, 26, 28; Y-93

Tribute to Isaac Bashevis Singer Y-91

Fuentes, Carlos 1928- DLB-113; CDWLB-3

Fuertes, Gloria 1918-1998 .... DLB-108

Fugard, Athol 1932- DLB-225

The Fugitives and the Agrarians: The First Exhibition Y-85

Fujiwara no Shunzei 1114-1204 .... DLB-203

Fujiwara no Tameaki 1230s?-1290s? DLB-203

Fujiwara no Tameie 1198-1275 .... DLB-203

Fujiwara no Teika 1162-1241 .... DLB-203

Fuks, Ladislav 1923-1994 .... DLB-299

Fulbecke, William 1560-1603? DLB-172

Fuller, Charles 1939- DLB-38, 266

Fuller, Henry Blake 1857-1929 .... DLB-12

Fuller, John 1937- DLB-40

Fuller, Margaret (see Fuller, Sarah)

Fuller, Roy 1912-1991 .... DLB-15, 20

Tribute to Christopher Isherwood Y-86

Fuller, Samuel 1912-1997 .... DLB-26

Fuller, Sarah 1810-1850 ...... DLB-1, 59, 73, 183, 223, 239; DS-5; CDALB-2

Fuller, Thomas 1608-1661 .... DLB-151

Fullerton, Hugh 1873-1945 .... DLB-171

Fullwood, William fl. 1568 .... DLB-236

Fulton, Alice 1952- DLB-193

Fulton, Len 1934- Y-86

Fulton, Robin 1937- DLB-40

Furbank, P. N. 1920- DLB-155

Furetière, Antoine 1619-1688 .... DLB-268

Furman, Laura 1945- Y-86

Furmanov, Dmitrii Andreevich 1891-1926 .... DLB-272

Furness, Horace Howard 1833-1912 ... DLB-64

Furness, William Henry 1802-1896 .... DLB-1, 235

Furnivall, Frederick James 1825-1910 .... DLB-184

Furphy, Joseph (Tom Collins) 1843-1912 .... DLB-230

Furthman, Jules 1888-1966 .... DLB-26

Shakespeare and Montaigne: A Symposium by Jules Furthman Y-02

Furui Yoshikichi 1937- DLB-182

Fushimi, Emperor 1265-1317 .... DLB-203

Futabatei Shimei (Hasegawa Tatsunosuke) 1864-1909 .... DLB-180

Fyleman, Rose 1877-1957 .... DLB-160

G

G., 1972 Booker Prize winner, John Berger DLB-326

Gaarder, Jostein 1952- DLB-297

Gadallah, Leslie 1939- DLB-251

Gadamer, Hans-Georg 1900-2002 ..... DLB-296

Gadda, Carlo Emilio 1893-1973 .... DLB-177

Gaddis, William 1922-1998 .... DLB-2, 278

William Gaddis: A Tribute Y-99

Gág, Wanda 1893-1946 .... DLB-22

Gagarin, Ivan Sergeevich 1814-1882 .... DLB-198

Gagnon, Madeleine 1938- DLB-60

Gaiman, Neil 1960- DLB-261

Gaine, Hugh 1726-1807 .... DLB-43

Hugh Gaine [publishing house] DLB-49

Gaines, Ernest J. 1933- DLB-2, 33, 152; Y-80; CDALB-6

Gaiser, Gerd 1908-1976 .... DLB-69

Gaitskill, Mary 1954- DLB-244

Galarza, Ernesto 1905-1984 .... DLB-122

Galaxy Science Fiction Novels DLB-46

Galbraith, Robert (or Caubraith) circa 1483-1544 .... DLB-281

Gale, Zona 1874-1938 .... DLB-9, 228, 78

Galen of Pergamon 129-after 210 ...... DLB-176

Gales, Winifred Marshall 1761-1839 .... DLB-200

Galich, Aleksandr 1918-1977 .... DLB-317

Medieval Galician-Portuguese Poetry ... DLB-287

Gall, Louise von 1815-1855 .... DLB-133

Gallagher, Tess 1943- DLB-120, 212, 244

Gallagher, Wes 1911-1997 .... DLB-127

Gallagher, William Davis 1808-1894 .... DLB-73

Gallant, Mavis 1922- DLB-53

Gallegos, María Magdalena 1935- DLB-209

Gallico, Paul 1897-1976 .... DLB-9, 171

Gallop, Jane 1952- DLB-246

Galloway, Grace Growden 1727-1782 ... DLB-200

Galloway, Janice 1956- DLB-319

Gallup, Donald 1913-2000 .... DLB-187

Galsworthy, John 1867-1933
...... DLB-10, 34, 98, 162; DS-16; CDBLB-5

Galt, John 1779-1839 . . . . DLB-99, 116, 159
Galton, Sir Francis 1822-1911 . . . . DLB-166
Galvin, Brendan 1938- DLB-5
Gambaro, Griselda 1928- DLB-305
Gambit DLB-46
Gamboa, Reymundo 1948- DLB-122
Gammer Gurton's Needle DLB-62
Gan, Elena Andreevna (Zeneida R-va)
   1814-1842 . . . . DLB-198
Gandhi, Mohandas Karamchand
   1869-1948 . . . . DLB-323
Gandlevsky, Sergei Markovich
   1952- DLB-285
Gannett, Frank E. 1876-1957 . . . . DLB-29
Gant, Eugene: Projected Works Y-01
Gao Xingjian 1940- Y-00
   Nobel Lecture 2000: "The Case for
      Literature" Y-00
Gaos, Vicente 1919-1980 . . . . DLB-134
García, Andrew 1854?-1943 . . . . DLB-209
García, Cristina 1958- DLB-292
García, Lionel G. 1935- DLB-82
García, Richard 1941- DLB-209
García, Santiago 1928- DLB-305
García Márquez, Gabriel
   1928- DLB-113; Y-82; CDWLB-3
   The Magical World of Macondo Y-82
   Nobel Lecture 1982: The Solitude of
      Latin America Y-82
   A Tribute to Gabriel García Márquez Y-82
García Marruz, Fina 1923- DLB-283
García-Camarillo, Cecilio 1943- DLB-209
Garcilaso de la Vega circa 1503-1536 . . . . . DLB-318
Garcilaso de la Vega, Inca 1539-1616 . . . . DLB-318
Gardam, Jane 1928- DLB-14, 161, 231
Gardell, Jonas 1963- DLB-257
Garden, Alexander circa 1685-1756 . . . . DLB-31
Gardiner, John Rolfe 1936- DLB-244
Gardiner, Margaret Power Farmer
   (see Blessington, Marguerite, Countess of)
Gardner, John
   1933-1982 . . . . DLB-2; Y-82; CDALB-7
Garfield, Leon 1921-1996 . . . . DLB-161
Garis, Howard R. 1873-1962 . . . . DLB-22
Garland, Hamlin 1860-1940 . . DLB-12, 71, 78, 186
   The Hamlin Garland Society Y-01
Garneau, François-Xavier 1809-1866 . . . . . DLB-99
Garneau, Hector de Saint-Denys
   1912-1943 . . . . DLB-88
Garneau, Michel 1939- DLB-53
Garner, Alan 1934- DLB-161, 261
Garner, Helen 1942- DLB-325
Garner, Hugh 1913-1979 . . . . DLB-68
Garnett, David 1892-1981 . . . . DLB-34

Garnett, Eve 1900-1991 . . . . DLB-160
Garnett, Richard 1835-1906 . . . . DLB-184
Garnier, Robert 1545?-1590 . . . . DLB-327
Garrard, Lewis H. 1829-1887 . . . . DLB-186
Garraty, John A. 1920- DLB-17
Garrett, Almeida (João Baptista da Silva
   Leitão de Almeida Garrett)
   1799-1854 . . . . DLB-287
Garrett, George
   1929- DLB-2, 5, 130, 152; Y-83
   Literary Prizes Y-00
   My Summer Reading Orgy: Reading
      for Fun and Games: One Reader's
      Report on the Summer of 2001 . . . . . . Y-01
   A Summing Up at Century's End Y-99
   Tribute to James Dickey Y-97
   Tribute to Michael M. Rea Y-97
   Tribute to Paxton Davis Y-94
   Tribute to Peter Taylor Y-94
   Tribute to William Goyen Y-83
   A Writer Talking: A Collage Y-00
Garrett, John Work 1872-1942 . . . . DLB-187
Garrick, David 1717-1779 . . . . DLB-84, 213
Garrison, William Lloyd
   1805-1879 . . . . DLB-1, 43, 235; CDALB-2
Garro, Elena 1920-1998 . . . . DLB-145
Garshin, Vsevolod Mikhailovich
   1855-1888 . . . . DLB-277
Garth, Samuel 1661-1719 . . . . DLB-95
Garve, Andrew 1908-2001 . . . . DLB-87
Gary, Romain 1914-1980 . . . . DLB-83, 299
Gascoigne, George 1539?-1577 . . . . DLB-136
Gascoyne, David 1916-2001 . . . . DLB-20
Gash, Jonathan (John Grant) 1933- DLB-276
Gaskell, Elizabeth Cleghorn
   1810-1865 . . . . . . DLB-21, 144, 159; CDBLB-4
   The Gaskell Society Y-98
Gaskell, Jane 1941- DLB-261
Gaspey, Thomas 1788-1871 . . . . DLB-116
Gass, William H. 1924- DLB-2, 227
Gates, Doris 1901-1987 . . . . DLB-22
Gates, Henry Louis, Jr. 1950- DLB-67
Gates, Lewis E. 1860-1924 . . . . DLB-71
Gatto, Alfonso 1909-1976 . . . . DLB-114
Gault, William Campbell 1910-1995 . . . . DLB-226
   Tribute to Kenneth Millar Y-83
Gaunt, Mary 1861-1942 . . . . DLB-174, 230
Gautier, Théophile 1811-1872 . . . . DLB-119
Gautreaux, Tim 1947- DLB-292
Gauvreau, Claude 1925-1971 . . . . DLB-88
The *Gawain*-Poet
   fl. circa 1350-1400 . . . . DLB-146
Gawsworth, John (Terence Ian Fytton
   Armstrong) 1912-1970 . . . . DLB-255

Gay, Ebenezer 1696-1787 . . . . DLB-24
Gay, John 1685-1732 . . . . DLB-84, 95
Gayarré, Charles E. A. 1805-1895 . . . . DLB-30
Charles Gaylord [publishing house] DLB-49
Gaylord, Edward King 1873-1974 . . . . . . DLB-127
Gaylord, Edward Lewis 1919-2003 . . . . . . DLB-127
Gazdanov, Gaito 1903-1971 . . . . DLB-317
Gébler, Carlo 1954- DLB-271
Geda, Sigitas 1943- DLB-232
Geddes, Gary 1940- DLB-60
Geddes, Virgil 1897-1989 . . . . DLB-4
Gedeon (Georgii Andreevich Krinovsky)
   circa 1730-1763 . . . . DLB-150
Gee, Maggie 1948- DLB-207
Gee, Shirley 1932- DLB-245
Geibel, Emanuel 1815-1884 . . . . DLB-129
Geiogamah, Hanay 1945- DLB-175
Geis, Bernard, Associates DLB-46
Geisel, Theodor Seuss 1904-1991 . . . DLB-61; Y-91
Gelb, Arthur 1924- DLB-103
Gelb, Barbara 1926- DLB-103
Gelber, Jack 1932- DLB-7, 228
Gélinas, Gratien 1909-1999 . . . . DLB-88
Gellert, Christian Fuerchtegott
   1715-1769 . . . . DLB-97
Gellhorn, Martha 1908-1998 . . . . Y-82, 98
Gems, Pam 1925- DLB-13
Genet, Jean 1910-1986 . . . . DLB-72, 321; Y-86
Genette, Gérard 1930- DLB-242
Genevoix, Maurice 1890-1980 . . . . DLB-65
Genis, Aleksandr Aleksandrovich
   1953- DLB-285
Genlis, Stéphanie-Félicité Ducrest, comtesse de
   1746-1830 . . . . DLB-313
Genovese, Eugene D. 1930- DLB-17
Gent, Peter 1942- Y-82
Geoffrey of Monmouth
   circa 1100-1155 . . . . DLB-146
George, Elizabeth 1949- DLB-306
George, Henry 1839-1897 . . . . DLB-23
George, Jean Craighead 1919- DLB-52
George, W. L. 1882-1926 . . . . DLB-197
George III, King of Great Britain
   and Ireland 1738-1820 . . . . DLB-213
Georgslied 896? DLB-148
Gerber, Merrill Joan 1938- DLB-218
Gerhardie, William 1895-1977 . . . . DLB-36
Gerhardt, Paul 1607-1676 . . . . DLB-164
Gérin, Winifred 1901-1981 . . . . DLB-155
Gérin-Lajoie, Antoine 1824-1882 . . . . DLB-99
German Literature
   A Call to Letters and an Invitation
      to the Electric Chair DLB-75

The Conversion of an Unpolitical
    Man...................... DLB-66
The German Radio Play DLB-124
The German Transformation from the
    Baroque to the Enlightenment.... DLB-97
Germanophilism.................. DLB-66
A Letter from a New Germany Y-90
The Making of a People............ DLB-66
The Novel of Impressionism DLB-66
Pattern and Paradigm: History as
    Design..................... DLB-75
Premisses DLB-66
The 'Twenties and Berlin........... DLB-66
Wolfram von Eschenbach's *Parzival*:
    Prologue and Book 3......... DLB-138
Writers and Politics: 1871-1918 ...... DLB-66

German Literature, Middle Ages
    Abrogans circa 790-800 .... DLB-148
    Annolied between 1077 and 1081..... DLB-148
    The Arthurian Tradition and
        Its European Context DLB-138
    Cambridge Songs (Carmina Cantabrigensia)
        circa 1050 .... DLB-148
    Christus und die Samariterin circa 950... DLB-148
    De Heinrico circa 980?............ DLB-148
    Ecbasis Captivi circa 1045........... DLB-148
    Georgslied 896?................. DLB-148
    German Literature and Culture from
        Charlemagne to the Early Courtly
        Period DLB-148; CDWLB-2
    The Germanic Epic and Old English
        Heroic Poetry: *Widsith, Waldere*,
        and *The Fight at Finnsburg*....... DLB-146
    Graf Rudolf between circa
        1170 and circa 1185.......... DLB-148
    Heliand circa 850................ DLB-148
    Das Hildesbrandslied
        circa 820 .... DLB-148; CDWLB-2
    Kaiserchronik circa 1147 .... DLB-148
    The Legends of the Saints and a
        Medieval Christian
        Worldview................ DLB-148
    Ludus de Antichristo circa 1160 .... DLB-148
    Ludwigslied 881 or 882 .... DLB-148
    Muspilli circa 790-circa 850 .... DLB-148
    Old German Genesis and *Old German
        Exodus* circa 1050-circa 1130 .... DLB-148
    Old High German Charms
        and Blessings...... DLB-148; CDWLB-2
    The *Old High German Isidor*
        circa 790-800 .... DLB-148
    Petruslied circa 854?.............. DLB-148
    Physiologus circa 1070-circa 1150 ..... DLB-148
    Ruodlieb circa 1050-1075 .... DLB-148
    "Spielmannsepen" (circa 1152
        circa 1500)................. DLB-148
    The Strasbourg Oaths 842.......... DLB-148
    Tatian circa 830................. DLB-148
    Waltharius circa 825............... DLB-148
    Wessobrunner Gebet circa 787-815..... DLB-148

German Theater
    German Drama 800-1280 .... DLB-138
    German Drama from Naturalism
        to Fascism: 1889-1933......... DLB-118
Gernsback, Hugo 1884-1967 .... DLB-8, 137
Gerould, Katharine Fullerton
    1879-1944.................... DLB-78
Samuel Gerrish [publishing house]....... DLB-49
Gerrold, David 1944- DLB-8
Gersão, Teolinda 1940- DLB-287
Gershon, Karen 1923-1993........... DLB-299
Gershwin, Ira 1896-1983 .... DLB-265
    The Ira Gershwin Centenary.......... Y-96
Gerson, Jean 1363-1429 .... DLB-208
Gersonides 1288-1344 .... DLB-115
Gerstäcker, Friedrich 1816-1872........ DLB-129
Gertsen, Aleksandr Ivanovich
    (see Herzen, Alexander)
Gerstenberg, Heinrich Wilhelm von
    1737-1823..................... DLB-97
Gervinus, Georg Gottfried
    1805-1871.................... DLB-133
Gery, John 1953- DLB-282
Geßner, Solomon 1730-1788 .... DLB-97
Geston, Mark S. 1946- DLB-8
Al-Ghazali 1058-1111 .... DLB-115
Ghelderode, Michel de (Adolphe-Adhémar Martens)
    1898-1962 .... DLB-321
Ghose, Zulfikar 1935- DLB-323
Ghosh, Amitav 1956- DLB-323
The Ghost Road, 1995 Booker Prize winner,
    Pat Barker DLB-326
Gibbings, Robert 1889-1958........... DLB-195
Gibbon, Edward 1737-1794............ DLB-104
Gibbon, John Murray 1875-1952 .... DLB-92
Gibbon, Lewis Grassic (see Mitchell, James Leslie)
Gibbons, Floyd 1887-1939 .... DLB-25
Gibbons, Kaye 1960- DLB-292
Gibbons, Reginald 1947- DLB-120
Gibbons, William eighteenth century..... DLB-73
Gibson, Charles Dana
    1867-1944................ DLB-188; DS-13
Gibson, Graeme 1934- DLB-53
Gibson, Margaret 1944- DLB-120
Gibson, Margaret Dunlop 1843-1920.....DLB-174
Gibson, Wilfrid 1878-1962 .... DLB-19
    The Friends of the Dymock Poets Y-00
Gibson, William 1914- DLB-7
Gibson, William 1948- DLB-251
Gide, André 1869-1951 .... DLB-65, 321
Giguère, Diane 1937- DLB-53
Giguère, Roland 1929- DLB-60
Gil de Biedma, Jaime 1929-1990 .... DLB-108
Gil-Albert, Juan 1906-1994........... DLB-134

Gilbert, Anthony 1899-1973............ DLB-77
Gilbert, Elizabeth 1969- DLB-292
Gilbert, Sir Humphrey 1537-1583 ...... DLB-136
Gilbert, Michael 1912- DLB-87
Gilbert, Sandra M. 1936- DLB-120, 246
Gilchrist, Alexander 1828-1861 .... DLB-144
Gilchrist, Ellen 1935- DLB-130
Gilder, Jeannette L. 1849-1916......... DLB-79
Gilder, Richard Watson 1844-1909 ....DLB-64, 79
Gildersleeve, Basil 1831-1924.......... DLB-71
Giles, Henry 1809-1882 .... DLB-64
Giles of Rome circa 1243-1316......... DLB-115
Gilfillan, George 1813-1878 .... DLB-144
Gill, Eric 1882-1940 .... DLB-98
Gill, Sarah Prince 1728-1771 .... DLB-200
William F. Gill Company DLB-49
Gillespie, A. Lincoln, Jr. 1895-1950 .... DLB-4
Gillespie, Haven 1883-1975 .... DLB-265
Gilliam, Florence fl. twentieth century DLB-4
Gilliatt, Penelope 1932-1993 .... DLB-14
Gillott, Jacky 1939-1980 .... DLB-14
Gilman, Caroline H. 1794-1888 ...... DLB-3, 73
Gilman, Charlotte Perkins 1860-1935 ... DLB-221
    The Charlotte Perkins Gilman Society ... Y-99
W. and J. Gilman [publishing house] DLB-49
Gilmer, Elizabeth Meriwether
    1861-1951 .... DLB-29
Gilmer, Francis Walker 1790-1826 .... DLB-37
Gilmore, Mary 1865-1962 .... DLB-260
Gilroy, Frank D. 1925- DLB-7
Gimferrer, Pere (Pedro) 1945- DLB-134
Ginger, Aleksandr S. 1897-1965 ....DLB-317
Gingrich, Arnold 1903-1976............DLB-137
    Prospectus From the Initial Issue of
        Esquire (Autumn 1933)..........DLB-137
    "With the Editorial Ken," Prospectus
        From the Initial Issue of *Ken*
        (7 April 1938) DLB-137
Ginibi, Ruby Langford 1934- DLB-325
Ginsberg, Allen
    1926-1997 ....DLB-5, 16, 169, 237; CDALB-1
Ginzburg, Evgeniia
    1904-1977 .... DLB-302
Ginzburg, Lidiia Iakovlevna
    1902-1990 .... DLB-302
Ginzburg, Natalia 1916-1991 ....DLB-177
Ginzkey, Franz Karl 1871-1963......... DLB-81
Gioia, Dana 1950- DLB-120, 282
Giono, Jean 1895-1970 .... DLB-72, 321
Giotti, Virgilio 1885-1957 .... DLB-114
Giovanni, Nikki 1943- DLB-5, 41; CDALB-7
Giovannitti, Arturo 1884-1959......... DLB-303
Gipson, Lawrence Henry 1880-1971 .....DLB-17

Girard, Rodolphe 1879-1956 .... DLB-92
Giraudoux, Jean 1882-1944 .... DLB-65, 321
Girondo, Oliverio 1891-1967 .... DLB-283
Gissing, George 1857-1903 ...... DLB-18, 135, 184
    The Place of Realism in Fiction (1895) ... DLB-18
Giudici, Giovanni 1924- DLB-128
Giuliani, Alfredo 1924- DLB-128
Gjellerup, Karl 1857-1919 .... DLB-300
Glackens, William J. 1870-1938 .... DLB-188
Gladilin, Anatolii Tikhonovich
    1935- DLB-302
Gladkov, Fedor Vasil'evich 1883-1958 .... DLB-272
Gladstone, William Ewart
    1809-1898 .... DLB-57, 184
Glaeser, Ernst 1902-1963 .... DLB-69
Glancy, Diane 1941- DLB-175
Glanvill, Joseph 1636-1680 .... DLB-252
Glanville, Brian 1931- DLB-15, 139
Glapthorne, Henry 1610-1643? DLB-58
Glasgow, Ellen 1873-1945 .... DLB-9, 12
    The Ellen Glasgow Society Y-01
Glasier, Katharine Bruce 1867-1950 ...... DLB-190
Glaspell, Susan 1876-1948 ...... DLB-7, 9, 78, 228
Glass, Montague 1877-1934 .... DLB-11
Glassco, John 1909-1981 .... DLB-68
Glauser, Friedrich 1896-1938 .... DLB-56
Glavin, Anthony 1946- DLB-319
F. Gleason's Publishing Hall DLB-49
Gleim, Johann Wilhelm Ludwig
    1719-1803 .... DLB-97
Glendinning, Robin 1938- DLB-310
Glendinning, Victoria 1937- DLB-155
Glidden, Frederick Dilley (Luke Short)
    1908-1975 .... DLB-256
Glinka, Fedor Nikolaevich 1786-1880 .... DLB-205
Glover, Keith 1966- DLB-249
Glover, Richard 1712-1785 .... DLB-95
Glover, Sue 1943- DLB-310
Glück, Louise 1943- DLB-5
Glyn, Elinor 1864-1943 .... DLB-153
Gnedich, Nikolai Ivanovich 1784-1833 ... DLB-205
Gobineau, Joseph-Arthur de
    1816-1882 .... DLB-123
The God of Small Things, 1997 Booker Prize winner,
    Arundhati Roy DLB-326
Godber, John 1956- DLB-233
Godbout, Jacques 1933- DLB-53
Goddard, Morrill 1865-1937 .... DLB-25
Goddard, William 1740-1817 .... DLB-43
Godden, Rumer 1907-1998 .... DLB-161
Godey, Louis A. 1804-1878 .... DLB-73
Godey and McMichael DLB-49

Godfrey, Dave 1938- DLB-60
Godfrey, Thomas 1736-1763 .... DLB-31
Godine, David R., Publisher DLB-46
Godkin, E. L. 1831-1902 .... DLB-79
Godolphin, Sidney 1610-1643 .... DLB-126
Godwin, Gail 1937- DLB-6, 234
M. J. Godwin and Company DLB-154
Godwin, Mary Jane Clairmont
    1766-1841 .... DLB-163
Godwin, Parke 1816-1904 .... DLB-3, 64, 250
Godwin, William 1756-1836 .... DLB-39, 104,
    142, 158, 163, 262; CDBLB-3
    Preface to *St. Leon* (1799) DLB-39
Goering, Reinhard 1887-1936 .... DLB-118
Goes, Albrecht 1908- DLB-69
Goethe, Johann Wolfgang von
    1749-1832 .... DLB-94; CDWLB-2
Goetz, Curt 1888-1960 .... DLB-124
Goffe, Thomas circa 1592-1629 .... DLB-58
Goffstein, M. B. 1940- DLB-61
Gogarty, Oliver St. John 1878-1957 .... DLB-15, 19
Gogol, Nikolai Vasil'evich 1809-1852 .... DLB-198
Goines, Donald 1937-1974 .... DLB-33
Gold, Herbert 1924- DLB-2; Y-81
    Tribute to William Saroyan Y-81
Gold, Michael 1893-1967 .... DLB-9, 28
Goldbarth, Albert 1948- DLB-120
Goldberg, Dick 1947- DLB-7
Golden Cockerel Press DLB-112
Golding, Arthur 1536-1606 .... DLB-136
Golding, Louis 1895-1958 .... DLB-195
Golding, William 1911-1993
    .... DLB-15, 100, 255, 326; Y-83; CDBLB-7
    Nobel Lecture 1993 .... Y-83
    The Stature of William Golding Y-83
Goldman, Emma 1869-1940 .... DLB-221
Goldman, William 1931- DLB-44
Goldring, Douglas 1887-1960 .... DLB-197
Goldschmidt, Meir Aron 1819-1887 ..... DLB-300
Goldsmith, Oliver 1730?-1774
    ...... DLB-39, 89, 104, 109, 142; CDBLB-2
Goldsmith, Oliver 1794-1861 .... DLB-99
Goldsmith Publishing Company DLB-46
Goldstein, Richard 1944- DLB-185
Goldsworthy, Peter 1951- DLB-325
Gollancz, Sir Israel 1864-1930 .... DLB-201
Victor Gollancz Limited DLB-112
Gomberville, Marin Le Roy, sieur de
    1600?-1674 .... DLB-268
Gombrowicz, Witold
    1904-1969 .... DLB-215; CDWLB-4
Gomez, Madeleine-Angélique Poisson de
    1684-1770 .... DLB-313

Gómez de Ciudad Real, Alvar (Alvar Gómez
    de Guadalajara) 1488-1538 .... DLB-318
Gómez-Quiñones, Juan 1942- DLB-122
Laurence James Gomme
    [publishing house] DLB-46
Gompers, Samuel 1850-1924 .... DLB-303
Gonçalves Dias, Antônio 1823-1864 ..... DLB-307
Goncharov, Ivan Aleksandrovich
    1812-1891 .... DLB-238
Goncourt, Edmond de 1822-1896 .... DLB-123
Goncourt, Jules de 1830-1870 .... DLB-123
Gonzales, Rodolfo "Corky" 1928- DLB-122
Gonzales-Berry, Erlinda 1942- DLB-209
    "Chicano Language" DLB-82
González, Angel 1925- DLB-108
Gonzalez, Genaro 1949- DLB-122
Gonzalez, N. V. M. 1915-1999 .... DLB-312
González, Otto-Raúl 1921- DLB-290
Gonzalez, Ray 1952- DLB-122
González de Mireles, Jovita
    1899-1983 .... DLB-122
González Martínez, Enrique 1871-1952 ... DLB-290
González-T., César A. 1931- DLB-82
Goodis, David 1917-1967 .... DLB-226
Goodison, Lorna 1947- DLB-157
Goodman, Allegra 1967- DLB-244
Goodman, Nelson 1906-1998 .... DLB-279
Goodman, Paul 1911-1972 .... DLB-130, 246
The Goodman Theatre DLB-7
Goodrich, Frances 1891-1984 and
    Hackett, Albert 1900-1995 .... DLB-26
Goodrich, Samuel Griswold
    1793-1860 .... DLB-1, 42, 73, 243
S. G. Goodrich [publishing house] DLB-49
C. E. Goodspeed and Company DLB-49
Goodwin, Stephen 1943- Y-82
Googe, Barnabe 1540-1594 .... DLB-132
Gookin, Daniel 1612-1687 .... DLB-24
Gopegui, Belén 1963- DLB-322
Goran, Lester 1928- DLB-244
Gordimer, Nadine 1923- DLB-225, 326; Y-91
    Nobel Lecture 1991 .... Y-91
Gordon, Adam Lindsay 1833-1870 ...... DLB-230
Gordon, Caroline
    1895-1981 .... DLB-4, 9, 102; DS-17; Y-81
Gordon, Charles F. (see OyamO)
Gordon, Charles William (see Connor, Ralph)
Gordon, Giles 1940- DLB-14, 139, 207
Gordon, Helen Cameron, Lady Russell
    1867-1949 .... DLB-195
Gordon, Lyndall 1941- DLB-155
Gordon, Mack 1904-1959 .... DLB-265
Gordon, Mary 1949- DLB-6; Y-81

Cumulative Index

Gordone, Charles 1925-1995 .... DLB-7
Gore, Catherine 1800-1861 .... DLB-116
Gore-Booth, Eva 1870-1926 .... DLB-240
Gores, Joe 1931- DLB-226; Y-02
    Tribute to Kenneth Millar Y-83
    Tribute to Raymond Chandler Y-88
Gorey, Edward 1925-2000 .... DLB-61
Gorgias of Leontini
    circa 485 B.C.-376 B.C. DLB-176
Gor'ky, Maksim 1868-1936 .... DLB-295
Gorodetsky, Sergei Mitrofanovich
    1884-1967 .... DLB-295
Gorostiza, José 1901-1979 .... DLB-290
Görres, Joseph 1776-1848 .... DLB-90
Gosse, Edmund 1849-1928 ...... DLB-57, 144, 184
Gosson, Stephen 1554-1624 .... DLB-172
    The Schoole of Abuse (1579) DLB-172
Gotanda, Philip Kan 1951- DLB-266
Gotlieb, Phyllis 1926- DLB-88, 251
Go-Toba 1180-1239 .... DLB-203
Gottfried von Straßburg
    died before 1230 ...... DLB-138; CDWLB-2
Gotthelf, Jeremias 1797-1854 .... DLB-133
Gottschalk circa 804/808-869 .... DLB-148
Gottsched, Johann Christoph
    1700-1766 .... DLB-97
Götz, Johann Nikolaus 1721-1781 .... DLB-97
Goudge, Elizabeth 1900-1984 .... DLB-191
Gouges, Olympe de 1748-1793 .... DLB-313
    Declaration of the Rights of Woman DLB-314
Gough, John B. 1817-1886 .... DLB-243
Gould, Wallace 1882-1940 .... DLB-54
Gournay, Marie de 1565-1645 .... DLB-327
Govoni, Corrado 1884-1965 .... DLB-114
Govrin, Michal 1950- DLB-299
Gower, John circa 1330-1408 .... DLB-146
Goyen, William 1915-1983 ...... DLB-2, 218; Y-83
Goytisolo, José Augustín 1928- DLB-134
Goytisolo, Juan 1931- DLB-322
Goytisolo, Luis 1935- DLB-322
Gozzano, Guido 1883-1916 .... DLB-114
Grabbe, Christian Dietrich 1801-1836 ... DLB-133
Gracq, Julien (Louis Poirier) 1910- DLB-83
Grady, Henry W. 1850-1889 .... DLB-23
Graf, Oskar Maria 1894-1967 .... DLB-56
Graf Rudolf between circa 1170 and
    circa 1185 .... DLB-148
Graff, Gerald 1937- DLB-246
Graffigny, Françoise d'Issembourg de
    1695-1758 .... DLB-313
    Letters from a Peruvian Woman DLB-314
Richard Grafton [publishing house] DLB-170
Grafton, Sue 1940- DLB-226

Graham, Frank 1893-1965 .... DLB-241
Graham, George Rex 1813-1894 .... DLB-73
Graham, Gwethalyn (Gwethalyn Graham
    Erichsen-Brown) 1913-1965 .... DLB-88
Graham, Jorie 1951- DLB-120
Graham, Katharine 1917-2001 .... DLB-127
Graham, Lorenz 1902-1989 .... DLB-76
Graham, Philip 1915-1963 .... DLB-127
Graham, R. B. Cunninghame
    1852-1936 .... DLB-98, 135, 174
Graham, Shirley 1896-1977 .... DLB-76
Graham, Stephen 1884-1975 .... DLB-195
Graham, W. S. 1918-1986 .... DLB-20
William H. Graham [publishing house] ... DLB-49
Graham, Winston 1910-2003 .... DLB-77
Grahame, Kenneth 1859-1932 ...DLB-34, 141, 178
Grainger, Martin Allerdale 1874-1941 .... DLB-92
Gramatky, Hardie 1907-1979 .... DLB-22
Gramcko, Ida 1924-1994 .... DLB-290
Gramsci, Antonio 1891-1937 .... DLB-296
Granada, Fray Luis de 1504-1588 ..... DLB-318
Grand, Sarah 1854-1943 .... DLB-135, 197
Grandbois, Alain 1900-1975 .... DLB-92
Grandson, Oton de circa 1345-1397 .... DLB-208
Grange, John circa 1556-? DLB-136
Granger, Thomas 1578-1627 .... DLB-281
Granich, Irwin (see Gold, Michael)
Granin, Daniil 1918- DLB-302
Granovsky, Timofei Nikolaevich
    1813-1855 .... DLB-198
Grant, Anne MacVicar 1755-1838 ..... DLB-200
Grant, Duncan 1885-1978 .... DS-10
Grant, George 1918-1988 .... DLB-88
Grant, George Monro 1835-1902 ...... DLB-99
Grant, Harry J. 1881-1963 .... DLB-29
Grant, James Edward 1905-1966 ...... DLB-26
Grant, John (see Gash, Jonathan)
War of the Words (and Pictures): The Creation
    of a Graphic Novel Y-02
Grass, Günter 1927- ...DLB-75, 124; CDWLB-2
    Nobel Lecture 1999:
    "To Be Continued..." Y-99
    Tribute to Helen Wolff Y-94
Grasty, Charles H. 1863-1924 .... DLB-25
Grau, Shirley Ann 1929- DLB-2, 218
Graves, John 1920- Y-83
Graves, Richard 1715-1804 .... DLB-39
Graves, Robert 1895-1985
    ....DLB-20, 100, 191; DS-18; Y-85; CDBLB-6
    The St. John's College
    Robert Graves Trust Y-96
Gray, Alasdair 1934- DLB-194, 261, 319
Gray, Asa 1810-1888 .... DLB-1, 235

Gray, David 1838-1861 .... DLB-32
Gray, Simon 1936- DLB-13
Gray, Robert 1945- DLB-325
Gray, Thomas 1716-1771 .... DLB-109; CDBLB-2
Grayson, Richard 1951- DLB-234
Grayson, William J. 1788-1863.... DLB-3, 64, 248
The Great Bibliographers Series Y-93
The Great Gatsby (Documentary) DLB-219
"The Greatness of Southern Literature":
    League of the South Institute for the
    Study of Southern Culture and History
    .... Y-02
Grech, Nikolai Ivanovich 1787-1867 ..... DLB-198
Greeley, Horace 1811-1872....DLB-3, 43, 189, 250
Green, Adolph 1915-2002 .... DLB-44, 265
Green, Anna Katharine
    1846-1935 .... DLB-202, 221
Green, Duff 1791-1875 .... DLB-43
Green, Elizabeth Shippen 1871-1954 .... DLB-188
Green, Gerald 1922- DLB-28
Green, Henry 1905-1973 .... DLB-15
Green, Jonas 1712-1767 .... DLB-31
Green, Joseph 1706-1780 .... DLB-31
Green, Julien 1900-1998 .... DLB-4, 72
Green, Paul 1894-1981 .... DLB-7, 9, 249; Y-81
Green, T. H. 1836-1882 .... DLB-190, 262
Green, Terence M. 1947- DLB-251
T. and S. Green [publishing house] DLB-49
Green Tiger Press DLB-46
Timothy Green [publishing house] DLB-49
Greenaway, Kate 1846-1901 .... DLB-141
Greenberg: Publisher DLB-46
Greene, Asa 1789-1838 .... DLB-11
Greene, Belle da Costa 1883-1950 .....DLB-187
Greene, Graham 1904-1991
    .... DLB-13, 15, 77, 100, 162, 201, 204;
    Y-85, 91; CDBLB-7
    Tribute to Christopher Isherwood Y-86
Greene, Robert 1558-1592 ....DLB-62, 167
Greene, Robert Bernard (Bob), Jr.
    1947- DLB-185
Benjamin H Greene [publishing house] ... DLB-49
Greenfield, George 1917-2000 .... Y-91, 00
    Derek Robinson's Review of George
    Greenfield's *Rich Dust* Y-02
Greenhow, Robert 1800-1854 .... DLB-30
Greenlee, William B. 1872-1953 ....DLB-187
Greenough, Horatio 1805-1852 ..... DLB-1, 235
Greenwell, Dora 1821-1882 .... DLB-35, 199
Greenwillow Books DLB-46
Greenwood, Grace (see Lippincott, Sara Jane Clarke)
Greenwood, Walter 1903-1974 .....DLB-10, 191
Greer, Ben 1948- DLB-6

Greflinger, Georg 1620?-1677 ....DLB-164	Grigson, Geoffrey 1905-1985 ....DLB-27	Guðbergur Bergsson 1932- DLB-293
Greg, W. R. 1809-1881 ....DLB-55	Grillparzer, Franz 1791-1872 ....DLB-133; CDWLB-2	Guðmundur Bödvarsson 1904-1974 .....DLB-293
Greg, W. W. 1875-1959 ....DLB-201	Grimald, Nicholas circa 1519-circa 1562..............DLB-136	Guðmundur Gíslason Hagalín 1898-1985 ....DLB-293
Gregg, Josiah 1806-1850 ....DLB-183, 186	Grimké, Angelina Weld 1880-1958 ....DLB-50, 54	Guðmundur Magnússon (see Jón Trausti)
Gregg Press DLB-46	Grimké, Sarah Moore 1792-1873 ....DLB-239	Guerra, Tonino 1920- DLB-128
Gregory, Horace 1898-1982...........DLB-48	Grimm, Frédéric Melchior 1723-1807 ....DLB-313	Guest, Barbara 1920- DLB-5, 193
Gregory, Isabella Augusta Persse, Lady 1852-1932 ....DLB-10	Grimm, Hans 1875-1959 ....DLB-66	Guevara, Fray Antonio de 1480?-1545 ...DLB-318
Gregory of Rimini circa 1300-1358 ......DLB-115	Grimm, Jacob 1785-1863 ....DLB-90	Guèvremont, Germaine 1893-1968.......DLB-68
Gregynog Press DLB-112	Grimm, Wilhelm 1786-1859 ....DLB-90; CDWLB-2	Guglielminetti, Amalia 1881-1941.......DLB-264
Greiff, León de 1895-1976 ....DLB-283	Grimmelshausen, Johann Jacob Christoffel von 1621 or 1622-1676.......DLB-168; CDWLB-2	Guidacci, Margherita 1921-1992........DLB-128
Greiffenberg, Catharina Regina von 1633-1694 ....DLB-168	Grimshaw, Beatrice Ethel 1871-1953 .....DLB-174	Guillén, Jorge 1893-1984..............DLB-108
Greig, Noël 1944- DLB-245	Grímur Thomsen 1820-1896...........DLB-293	Guillén, Nicolás 1902-1989 ....DLB-283
Grekova, Irina (Elena Sergeevna Venttsel') 1907-2002 ....DLB-302	Grin, Aleksandr Stepanovich 1880-1932 ....DLB-272	Guilloux, Louis 1899-1980 ....DLB-72
Grenfell, Wilfred Thomason 1865-1940.....................DLB-92	Grindal, Edmund 1519 or 1520-1583 ....DLB-132	Guilpin, Everard circa 1572-after 1608? DLB-136
Grenville, Kate 1950- DLB-325	Gripe, Maria (Kristina) 1923- DLB-257	Guiney, Louise Imogen 1861-1920 ....DLB-54
Gress, Elsa 1919-1988 ....DLB-214	Griswold, Rufus Wilmot 1815-1857 ....DLB-3, 59, 250	Guiterman, Arthur 1871-1943 ....DLB-11
Greve, Felix Paul (see Grove, Frederick Philip)	Gronlund, Laurence 1846-1899.........DLB-303	Gul', Roman 1896-1986...............DLB-317
Greville, Fulke, First Lord Brooke 1554-1628 ....DLB-62, 172	Grosart, Alexander Balloch 1827-1899 ...DLB-184	Gumilev, Nikolai Stepanovich 1886-1921 ....DLB-295
Grey, Sir George, K.C.B. 1812-1898 .....DLB-184	Grosholz, Emily 1950- DLB-282	Günderrode, Caroline von 1780-1806 ....DLB-90
Grey, Lady Jane 1537-1554 ....DLB-132	Gross, Milt 1895-1953 ....DLB-11	Gundulić, Ivan 1589-1638... DLB-147; CDWLB-4
Grey, Zane 1872-1939 ....DLB-9, 212	Grosset and Dunlap..................DLB-49	Gunesekera, Romesh 1954- DLB-267, 323
Zane Grey's West Society Y-00	Grosseteste, Robert circa 1160-1253 .....DLB-115	Gunn, Bill 1934-1989.................DLB-38
Grey Owl (Archibald Stansfeld Belaney) 1888-1938 ....DLB-92; DS-17	Grossman, Allen 1932- DLB-193	Gunn, James E. 1923- DLB-8
Grey Walls Press DLB-112	Grossman, David 1954- DLB-299	Gunn, Neil M. 1891-1973 ....DLB-15
Griboedov, Aleksandr Sergeevich 1795?-1829 ....DLB-205	Grossman, Vasilii Semenovich 1905?-1964 ....DLB-272	Gunn, Thom 1929- DLB-27; CDBLB-8
Grice, Paul 1913-1988 ....DLB-279	Grossman Publishers..................DLB-46	Gunnar Gunnarsson 1889-1975.........DLB-293
Grier, Eldon 1917- DLB-88	Grosvenor, Gilbert H. 1875-1966.........DLB-91	Gunnars, Kristjana 1948- DLB-60
Grieve, C. M. (see MacDiarmid, Hugh)	Groth, Klaus 1819-1899...............DLB-129	Günther, Johann Christian 1695-1723 ....DLB-168
Griffin, Bartholomew fl. 1596 ....DLB-172	Groulx, Lionel 1878-1967 ....DLB-68	Gupta, Sunetra 1965- DLB-323
Griffin, Bryan	Grove, Frederick Philip (Felix Paul Greve) 1879-1948 ....DLB-92	Gurik, Robert 1932- DLB-60
"Panic Among the Philistines": A Postscript, An Interview with Bryan Griffin Y-81		Gurney, A. R. 1930- DLB-266
	Grove Press DLB-46	Gurney, Ivor 1890-1937..................Y-02
Griffin, Gerald 1803-1840 ....DLB-159	Groys, Boris Efimovich 1947- DLB-285	The Ivor Gurney Society Y-98
The Griffin Poetry Prize................Y-00	Grubb, Davis 1919-1980 ....DLB-6	Guro, Elena Genrikhovna 1877-1913.....DLB-295
Griffith, Elizabeth 1727?-1793 ....DLB-39, 89	Gruelle, Johnny 1880-1938 ....DLB-22	Gustafson, Ralph 1909-1995 ....DLB-88
Preface to The Delicate Distress (1769) ...DLB-39	von Grumbach, Argula 1492-after 1563? DLB-179	Gustafsson, Lars 1936- DLB-257
Griffith, George 1857-1906 ....DLB-178	Grundtvig, N. F. S. 1783-1872 ....DLB-300	Gütersloh, Albert Paris 1887-1973 ....DLB-81
Ralph Griffiths [publishing house] DLB-154	Grymeston, Elizabeth before 1563-before 1604 ....DLB-136	Guterson, David 1956- DLB-292
Griffiths, Trevor 1935- DLB-13, 245	Grynberg, Henryk 1936- DLB-299	Guthrie, A. B., Jr. 1901-1991 ....DLB-6, 212
S. C. Griggs and Company DLB-49	Gryphius, Andreas 1616-1664 ....DLB-164; CDWLB-2	Guthrie, Ramon 1896-1973 ....DLB-4
Griggs, Sutton Elbert 1872-1930 ....DLB-50		Guthrie, Thomas Anstey (see Anstey, FC)
Grignon, Claude-Henri 1894-1976........DLB-68	Gryphius, Christian 1649-1706 ....DLB-168	Guthrie, Woody 1912-1967 ....DLB-303
Grigor'ev, Apollon Aleksandrovich 1822-1864 ....DLB-277	Guare, John 1938- DLB-7, 249	The Guthrie Theater DLB-7
Grigorovich, Dmitrii Vasil'evich 1822-1899 ....DLB-238	Guarnieri, Gianfrancesco 1934- DLB-307	Gutiérrez Nájera, Manuel 1859-1895.....DLB-290
	Guberman, Igor Mironovich 1936- DLB-285	Guttormur J. Guttormsson 1878-1966 ...DLB-293
		Gutzkow, Karl 1811-1878..............DLB-133
		Guy, Ray 1939- DLB-60

Cumulative Index

Guy, Rosa 1925- DLB-33

Guyot, Arnold 1807-1884................DS-13

Gwynn, R. S. 1948- DLB-282

Gwynne, Erskine 1898-1948............ DLB-4

Gyles, John 1680-1755 .... DLB-99

Gyllembourg, Thomasine 1773-1856 .... DLB-300

Gyllensten, Lars 1921- DLB-257

Gyrðir Elíasson 1961- DLB-293

Gysin, Brion 1916-1986 .... DLB-16

H

H.D. (see Doolittle, Hilda)

Habermas, Jürgen 1929- DLB-242

Habington, William 1605-1654 .... DLB-126

Hacker, Marilyn 1942- DLB-120, 282

Hackett, Albert 1900-1995 .... DLB-26

Hacks, Peter 1928- DLB-124

Hadas, Rachel 1948- DLB-120, 282

Hadden, Briton 1898-1929............. DLB-91

Hagedorn, Friedrich von 1708-1754 ..... DLB-168

Hagedorn, Jessica Tarahata 1949- DLB-312

Hagelstange, Rudolf 1912-1984 .... DLB-69

Hagerup, Inger 1905-1985 .... DLB-297

Haggard, H. Rider
  1856-1925 .... DLB-70, 156, 174, 178

Haggard, William (Richard Clayton)
  1907-1993................DLB-276; Y-93

Hagy, Alyson 1960- DLB-244

Hahn-Hahn, Ida Gräfin von 1805-1880 .. DLB-133

Haig-Brown, Roderick 1908-1976........ DLB-88

Haight, Gordon S. 1901-1985.......... DLB-103

Hailey, Arthur 1920-2004..........DLB-88; Y-82

Haines, John 1924- DLB-5, 212

Hake, Edward fl. 1566-1604........... DLB-136

Hake, Thomas Gordon 1809-1895....... DLB-32

Hakluyt, Richard 1552?-1616.......... DLB-136

Halas, František 1901-1949........... DLB-215

Halbe, Max 1865-1944................. DLB-118

Halberstam, David 1934- DLB-241

Haldane, Charlotte 1894-1969 .... DLB-191

Haldane, J. B. S. 1892-1964 .... DLB-160

Haldeman, Joe 1943- DLB-8

Haldeman-Julius Company.............. DLB-46

Hale, E. J., and Son.................. DLB-49

Hale, Edward Everett
  1822-1909 ....DLB-1, 42, 74, 235

Hale, Janet Campbell 1946- DLB-175

Hale, Kathleen 1898-2000 .... DLB-160

Hale, Leo Thomas (see Ebon)

Hale, Lucretia Peabody 1820-1900....... DLB-42

Hale, Nancy
  1908-1988 ....DLB-86; DS-17; Y-80, 88

Hale, Sarah Josepha (Buell)
  1788-1879...............DLB-1, 42, 73, 243

Hale, Susan 1833-1910............... DLB-221

Hales, John 1584-1656 .... DLB-151

Halévy, Ludovic 1834-1908 .... DLB-192

Haley, Alex 1921-1992 .... DLB-38; CDALB-7

Haliburton, Thomas Chandler
  1796-1865................... DLB-11, 99

Hall, Adam (Trevor Dudley-Smith)
  1920-1995 ....DLB-276

Hall, Anna Maria 1800-1881 .... DLB-159

Hall, Donald 1928- DLB-5

Hall, Edward 1497-1547 .... DLB-132

Hall, Halsey 1898-1977............... DLB-241

Hall, James 1793-1868 ....DLB-73, 74

Hall, Joseph 1574-1656............ DLB-121, 151

Hall, Radclyffe 1880-1943 .... DLB-191

Hall, Rodney 1935- DLB-289

Hall, Sarah Ewing 1761-1830 .... DLB-200

Hall, Stuart 1932- DLB-242

Samuel Hall [publishing house] DLB-49

al-Hallaj 857-922.................... DLB-311

Hallam, Arthur Henry 1811-1833 .... DLB-32

On Some of the Characteristics of
  Modern Poetry and On the
  Lyrical Poems of Alfred
  Tennyson (1831) DLB-32

Halldór Laxness (Halldór Guðjónsson)
  1902-1998 .... DLB-293

Halleck, Fitz-Greene 1790-1867 ...... DLB-3, 250

Haller, Albrecht von 1708-1777......... DLB-168

Halliday, Brett (see Dresser, Davis)

Halligan, Marion 1940- DLB-325

Halliwell-Phillipps, James Orchard
  1820-1889 .... DLB-184

Hallmann, Johann Christian
  1640-1704 or 1716? DLB-168

Hallmark Editions DLB-46

Halper, Albert 1904-1984.............. DLB-9

Halperin, John William 1941- DLB-111

Halstead, Murat 1829-1908 .... DLB-23

Hamann, Johann Georg 1730-1788....... DLB-97

Hamburger, Michael 1924- DLB-27

Hamilton, Alexander 1712-1756 .... DLB-31

Hamilton, Alexander 1755?-1804....... DLB-37

Hamilton, Cicely 1872-1952..........DLB-10, 197

Hamilton, Edmond 1904-1977 .... DLB-8

Hamilton, Elizabeth 1758-1816..... DLB-116, 158

Hamilton, Gail (see Corcoran, Barbara)

Hamilton, Gail (see Dodge, Mary Abigail)

Hamish Hamilton Limited DLB-112

Hamilton, Hugo 1953- DLB-267

Hamilton, Ian 1938-2001 .... DLB-40, 155

Hamilton, Janet 1795-1873 .... DLB-199

Hamilton, Mary Agnes 1884-1962........DLB-197

Hamilton, Patrick 1904-1962 ....DLB-10, 191

Hamilton, Virginia 1936-2002 ...DLB-33, 52; Y-01

Hamilton, Sir William 1788-1856..... DLB-262

Hamilton-Paterson, James 1941- DLB-267

Hammerstein, Oscar, 2nd 1895-1960.... DLB-265

Hammett, Dashiell
  1894-1961 .... DLB-226; DS-6; CDALB-5

  An Appeal in *TAC* Y-91

  The Glass Key and Other Dashiell
    Hammett Mysteries............... Y-96

  Knopf to Hammett: The Editoral
    Correspondence Y-00

  The Maltese Falcon (Documentary).... DLB-280

Hammon, Jupiter 1711-died between
  1790 and 1806 .... DLB-31, 50

Hammond, John ?-1663 .... DLB-24

Hamner, Earl 1923- DLB-6

Hampson, John 1901-1955 .... DLB-191

Hampton, Christopher 1946- DLB-13

Hamsun, Knut 1859-1952 .... DLB-297

Handel-Mazzetti, Enrica von 1871-1955... DLB-81

Handke, Peter 1942- DLB-85, 124

Handlin, Oscar 1915- DLB-17

Hankin, St. John 1869-1909 .... DLB-10

Hanley, Clifford 1922- DLB-14

Hanley, James 1901-1985 .... DLB-191

Hannah, Barry 1942- DLB-6, 234

Hannay, James 1827-1873 .... DLB-21

Hannes Hafstein 1861-1922 .... DLB-293

Hano, Arnold 1922- DLB-241

Hanrahan, Barbara 1939-1991 .... DLB-289

Hansberry, Lorraine
  1930-1965 ....DLB-7, 38; CDALB-1

Hansen, Joseph 1923-2004 .... DLB-226

Hansen, Martin A. 1909-1955 .... DLB-214

Hansen, Thorkild 1927-1989 .... DLB-214

Hanson, Elizabeth 1684-1737 .... DLB-200

Hapgood, Norman 1868-1937 .... DLB-91

Happel, Eberhard Werner 1647-1690.... DLB-168

Haq, Kaiser 1950- DLB-323

Harbach, Otto 1873-1963.............. DLB-265

The Harbinger 1845-1849 .... DLB-1, 223

Harburg, E. Y. "Yip" 1896-1981........ DLB-265

Harcourt Brace Jovanovich............ DLB-46

Hardenberg, Friedrich von (see Novalis)

Harding, Walter 1917-1996 .... DLB-111

Hardwick, Elizabeth 1916- DLB-6

Hardy, Alexandre 1572?-1632 ....DLB-268

Hardy, Frank 1917-1994 .... DLB-260

Hardy, Thomas
   1840-1928 . . . . . . .DLB-18, 19, 135; CDBLB-5

   "Candour in English Fiction" (1890) . . .DLB-18

Hare, Cyril 1900-1958. . . . . .DLB-77

Hare, David 1947- DLB-13, 310

Hare, R. M. 1919-2002 . . . . .DLB-262

Hargrove, Marion 1919-2003 . . . . .DLB-11

Häring, Georg Wilhelm Heinrich
   (see Alexis, Willibald)

Harington, Donald 1935- DLB-152

Harington, Sir John 1560-1612 . . . . . . .DLB-136

Harjo, Joy 1951- DLB-120, 175

Harkness, Margaret (John Law)
   1854-1923 .DLB-197

Harley, Edward, second Earl of Oxford
   1689-1741 .DLB-213

Harley, Robert, first Earl of Oxford
   1661-1724 .DLB-213

Harlow, Robert 1923- DLB-60

Harman, Thomas fl. 1566-1573. . . . . . . .DLB-136

Harness, Charles L. 1915- DLB-8

Harnett, Cynthia 1893-1981 . . . . .DLB-161

Harnick, Sheldon 1924- DLB-265

   Tribute to Ira Gershwin. Y-96

   Tribute to Lorenz Hart Y-95

Harper, Edith Alice Mary (see Wickham, Anna)

Harper, Fletcher 1806-1877 . . . . .DLB-79

Harper, Frances Ellen Watkins
   1825-1911 . . . . .DLB-50, 221

Harper, Michael S. 1938- DLB-41

Harper and Brothers DLB-49

Harpur, Charles 1813-1868 . . . . .DLB-230

Harraden, Beatrice 1864-1943 . . . . .DLB-153

George G. Harrap and Company
   Limited DLB-112

Harriot, Thomas 1560-1621 . . . . .DLB-136

Harris, Alexander 1805-1874 . . . . .DLB-230

Harris, Benjamin ?-circa 1720 . . . . . . .DLB-42, 43

Harris, Christie 1907-2002 . . . . .DLB-88

Harris, Errol E. 1908- DLB-279

Harris, Frank 1856-1931 . . . . .DLB-156, 197

Harris, George Washington
   1814-1869 . . . . .DLB-3, 11, 248

Harris, Joanne 1964- DLB-271

Harris, Joel Chandler
   1848-1908 . . . . .DLB-11, 23, 42, 78, 91

   The Joel Chandler Harris Association. Y-99

Harris, Mark 1922- DLB-2; Y-80

   Tribute to Frederick A. Pottle Y-87

Harris, William Torrey 1835-1909. . . . . . .DLB-270

Harris, Wilson 1921- DLB-117; CDWLB-3

Harrison, Mrs. Burton
   (see Harrison, Constance Cary)

Harrison, Charles Yale 1898-1954 . . . . . . .DLB-68

Harrison, Constance Cary 1843-1920. . . .DLB-221

Harrison, Frederic 1831-1923 . . . . . . .DLB-57, 190

   "On Style in English Prose" (1898). . . .DLB-57

Harrison, Harry 1925- DLB-8

James P. Harrison Company DLB-49

Harrison, Jim 1937- Y-82

Harrison, M. John 1945- DLB-261

Harrison, Mary St. Leger Kingsley
   (see Malet, Lucas)

Harrison, Paul Carter 1936- DLB-38

Harrison, Susan Frances 1859-1935. . . . . . .DLB-99

Harrison, Tony 1937- DLB-40, 245

Harrison, William 1535-1593 . . . . .DLB-136

Harrison, William 1933- DLB-234

Harrisse, Henry 1829-1910 . . . . .DLB-47

Harry, J. S. 1939- DLB-325

The Harry Ransom Humanities Research Center
   at the University of Texas at Austin. Y-00

Harryman, Carla 1952- DLB-193

Harsdörffer, Georg Philipp 1607-1658 . . . .DLB-164

Harsent, David 1942- DLB-40

Hart, Albert Bushnell 1854-1943. . . . . . . .DLB-17

Hart, Anne 1768-1834 . . . . .DLB-200

Hart, Elizabeth 1771-1833 . . . . .DLB-200

Hart, Julia Catherine 1796-1867 . . . . .DLB-99

Hart, Kevin 1954- DLB-325

Hart, Lorenz 1895-1943. . . . . .DLB-265

   Larry Hart: Still an Influence Y-95

   Lorenz Hart: An American Lyricist Y-95

   The Lorenz Hart Centenary Y-95

Hart, Moss 1904-1961 . . . . .DLB-7, 266

Hart, Oliver 1723-1795 . . . . .DLB-31

Rupert Hart-Davis Limited DLB-112

Harte, Bret 1836-1902
   . . . . .DLB-12, 64, 74, 79, 186; CDALB-3

Harte, Edward Holmead 1922- DLB-127

Harte, Houston Harriman 1927- DLB-127

Harte, Jack 1944- DLB-319

Hartlaub, Felix 1913-1945 . . . . .DLB-56

Hartlebon, Otto Erich 1864-1905 . . . . . . .DLB-118

Hartley, David 1705-1757 . . . . .DLB-252

Hartley, L. P. 1895-1972 . . . . .DLB-15, 139

Hartley, Marsden 1877-1943 . . . . .DLB-54

Hartling, Peter 1933- DLB-75

Hartman, Geoffrey H. 1929- DLB-67

Hartmann, Sadakichi 1867-1944 . . . . .DLB-54

Hartmann von Aue
   circa 1160-circa 1205. . . . .DLB-138; CDWLB-2

Hartshorne, Charles 1897-2000 . . . . .DLB-270

Haruf, Kent 1943- DLB-292

Harvey, Gabriel 1550?-1631 . . .DLB-167, 213, 281

Harvey, Jack (see Rankin, Ian)

Harvey, Jean-Charles 1891-1967 . . . . .DLB-88

Harvill Press Limited. DLB-112

Harwood, Gwen 1920-1995. . . . . .DLB-289

Harwood, Lee 1939- DLB-40

Harwood, Ronald 1934- DLB-13

al-Hasan al-Basri 642-728 . . . . .DLB-311

Hašek, Jaroslav 1883-1923. . . DLB-215; CDWLB-4

Haskins, Charles Homer 1870-1937 . . . . . .DLB-47

Haslam, Gerald 1937- DLB-212

Hass, Robert 1941- DLB-105, 206

Hasselstrom, Linda M. 1943- DLB-256

Hastings, Michael 1938- DLB-233

Hatar, Győző 1914- DLB-215

The Hatch-Billops Collection DLB-76

Hathaway, William 1944- DLB-120

Hatherly, Ana 1929- DLB-287

Hauch, Carsten 1790-1872. . . . . .DLB-300

Hauff, Wilhelm 1802-1827 . . . . .DLB-90

Hauge, Olav H. 1908-1994 . . . . .DLB-297

Haugen, Paal-Helge 1945- DLB-297

Haugwitz, August Adolph von
   1647-1706. .DLB-168

Hauptmann, Carl 1858-1921. . . . . . .DLB-66, 118

Hauptmann, Gerhart
   1862-1946 . . . . .DLB-66, 118; CDWLB-2

Hauser, Marianne 1910- Y-83

Havel, Václav 1936- DLB-232; CDWLB-4

Haven, Alice B. Neal 1827-1863 . . . . . . .DLB-250

Havergal, Frances Ridley 1836-1879 . . . . .DLB-199

Hawes, Stephen 1475?-before 1529 . . . . .DLB-132

Hawker, Robert Stephen 1803-1875 . . . . . .DLB-32

Hawkes, John
   1925-1998 . . . . DLB-2, 7, 227; Y-80, Y-98

   John Hawkes: A Tribute Y-98

   Tribute to Donald Barthelme Y-89

Hawkesworth, John 1720-1773. . . . . .DLB-142

Hawkins, Sir Anthony Hope (see Hope, Anthony)

Hawkins, Sir John 1719-1789 . . . . . .DLB-104, 142

Hawkins, Walter Everette 1883-? DLB-50

Hawthorne, Nathaniel 1804-1864
   . . .DLB-1, 74, 183, 223, 269; DS-5; CDALB-2

   The Nathaniel Hawthorne Society Y-00

   The Old Manse. DLB-223

Hawthorne, Sophia Peabody
   1809-1871 . . . . .DLB-183, 239

Hay, John 1835-1905 . . . . .DLB-12, 47, 189

Hay, John 1915- DLB-275

Hayashi Fumiko 1903-1951 . . . . .DLB-180

Haycox, Ernest 1899-1950. . . . . .DLB-206

Haycraft, Anna Margaret (see Ellis, Alice Thomas)

Hayden, Robert
   1913-1980 . . . . .DLB-5, 76; CDALB-1

Cumulative Index

Haydon, Benjamin Robert 1786-1846 ... DLB-110

Hayes, John Michael 1919- DLB-26

Hayley, William 1745-1820......... DLB-93, 142

Haym, Rudolf 1821-1901............. DLB-129

Hayman, Robert 1575-1629 .... DLB-99

Hayman, Ronald 1932- DLB-155

Hayne, Paul Hamilton
1830-1886 .... DLB-3, 64, 79, 248

Hays, Mary 1760-1843 .... DLB-142, 158

Hayslip, Le Ly 1949- DLB-312

Hayward, John 1905-1965 .... DLB-201

Haywood, Eliza 1693?-1756 .... DLB-39

   Dedication of *Lasselia* [excerpt]
   (1723)..................... DLB-39

   Preface to *The Disguis'd Prince*
   [excerpt] (1723) DLB-39

   The Tea-Table [excerpt]............. DLB-39

Haywood, William D. 1869-1928....... DLB-303

Willis P. Hazard [publishing house] DLB-49

Hazlitt, William 1778-1830 .... DLB-110, 158

Hazzard, Shirley 1931- DLB-289; Y-82

Head, Bessie
1937-1986......... DLB-117, 225; CDWLB-3

Headley, Joel T. 1813-1897... DLB-30, 183; DS-13

Heaney, Seamus 1939- .. DLB-40; Y-95; CDBLB-8

   Nobel Lecture 1994: Crediting Poetry.... Y-95

Heard, Nathan C. 1936- DLB-33

Hearn, Lafcadio 1850-1904 ......DLB-12, 78, 189

Hearn, Mary Anne (Marianne Farningham,
Eva Hope) 1834-1909 .... DLB-240

Hearne, John 1926- DLB-117

Hearne, Samuel 1745-1792 .... DLB-99

Hearne, Thomas 1678?-1735 .... DLB-213

Hearst, William Randolph 1863-1951 .... DLB-25

Hearst, William Randolph, Jr.
1908-1993 .... DLB-127

Heartman, Charles Frederick
1883-1953 .... DLB-187

Heat and Dust, 1975 Booker Prize winner,
Ruth Prawer Jhabvala............. DLB-326

Heath, Catherine 1924- DLB-14

Heath, James Ewell 1792-1862 .... DLB-248

Heath, Roy A. K. 1926- DLB-117

Heath-Stubbs, John 1918- DLB-27

Heavysege, Charles 1816-1876........ DLB-99

Hebbel, Friedrich
1813-1863........... DLB-129; CDWLB-2

Hebel, Johann Peter 1760-1826......... DLB-90

Heber, Richard 1774-1833 .... DLB-184

Hébert, Anne 1916-2000 .... DLB-68

Hébert, Jacques 1923- DLB-53

Hebreo, León circa 1460-1520 .... DLB-318

Hecht, Anthony 1923- DLB-5, 169

Hecht, Ben 1894-1964 ....DLB-7, 9, 25, 26, 28, 86

Hecker, Isaac Thomas 1819-1888..... DLB-1, 243

Hedge, Frederic Henry
1805-1890 .... DLB-1, 59, 243; DS-5

Hefner, Hugh M. 1926- DLB-137

Hegel, Georg Wilhelm Friedrich
1770-1831..................... DLB-90

Heiberg, Johan Ludvig 1791-1860 ...... DLB-300

Heiberg, Johanne Luise 1812-1890...... DLB-300

Heide, Robert 1939- DLB-249

Heidegger, Martin 1889-1976 .... DLB-296

Heidish, Marcy 1947- Y-82

Heißenbüttel, Helmut 1921-1996 .... DLB-75

Heike monogatari................. DLB-203

Hein, Christoph 1944- ... DLB-124; CDWLB-2

Hein, Piet 1905-1996 .... DLB-214

Heine, Heinrich 1797-1856 ... DLB-90; CDWLB-2

Heinemann, Larry 1944- DS-9

William Heinemann Limited DLB-112

Heinesen, William 1900-1991........... DLB-214

Heinlein, Robert A. 1907-1988 .... DLB-8

Heinrich, Willi 1920- DLB-75

Heinrich Julius of Brunswick
1564-1613 .... DLB-164

Heinrich von dem Türlîn
fl. circa 1230................. DLB-138

Heinrich von Melk
fl. after 1160................. DLB-148

Heinrich von Veldeke
circa 1145-circa 1190 .... DLB-138

Heinse, Wilhelm 1746-1803 .... DLB-94

Heinz, W. C. 1915- DLB-171

Heiskell, John 1872-1972.............. DLB-127

Hejinian, Lyn 1941- DLB-165

Helder, Herberto 1930- DLB-287

Heliand circa 850................... DLB-148

Heller, Joseph
1923-1999 ...... DLB-2, 28, 227; Y-80, 99, 02

   Excerpts from Joseph Heller's
   USC Address, "The Literature
   of Despair" Y-96

   Remembering Joe Heller, by William
   Price Fox Y-99

   A Tribute to Joseph Heller............ Y-99

Heller, Michael 1937- DLB-165

Hellman, Lillian 1906-1984 ..... DLB-7, 228; Y-84

Hellwig, Johann 1609-1674............ DLB-164

Helprin, Mark 1947- Y-85; CDALB-7

Helvétius, Claude-Adrien 1715-1771..... DLB-313

   The Spirit of Laws................ DLB-314

Helwig, David 1938- DLB-60

Hemans, Felicia 1793-1835 .... DLB-96

Hemenway, Abby Maria 1828-1890..... DLB-243

Hemingway, Ernest 1899-1961 ... DLB-4, 9, 102, 210, 316; Y-81, 87, 99; DS-1, 15, 16; CDALB-4

   A Centennial Celebration Y-99

   Come to Papa Y-99

   The Ernest Hemingway Collection at
   the John F. Kennedy Library........ Y-99

   Ernest Hemingway Declines to
   Introduce *War and Peace* Y-01

   Ernest Hemingway's Reaction to
   James Gould Cozzens Y-98

   Ernest Hemingway's Toronto Journalism
   Revisited: With Three Previously
   Unrecorded Stories Y-92

   Falsifying Hemingway Y-96

   A Farewell to Arms (Documentary).... DLB-308

   Hemingway Centenary Celebration
   at the JFK Library............... Y-99

   The Hemingway/Fenton
   Correspondence Y-02

   Hemingway in the JFK Y-99

   The Hemingway Letters Project
   Finds an Editor Y-02

   Hemingway Salesmen's Dummies....... Y-00

   Hemingway: Twenty-Five Years Later.... Y-85

   A Literary Archaeologist Digs On:
   A Brief Interview with Michael
   Reynolds..................... Y-99

   Not Immediately Discernible ... but
   Eventually Quite Clear: The *First
   Light* and *Final Years* of
   Hemingway's Centenary Y-99

   Packaging Papa: *The Garden of Eden* Y-86

   Second International Hemingway
   Colloquium: Cuba Y-98

Hémon, Louis 1880-1913............. DLB-92

Hempel, Amy 1951- DLB-218

Hempel, Carl G. 1905-1997 ....DLB-279

Hemphill, Paul 1936- Y-87

Hénault, Gilles 1920-1996 .... DLB-88

Henchman, Daniel 1689-1761 .... DLB-24

Henderson, Alice Corbin 1881-1949 ..... DLB-54

Henderson, Archibald 1877-1963 .... DLB-103

Henderson, David 1942- DLB-41

Henderson, George Wylie 1904-1965 .... DLB-51

Henderson, Zenna 1917-1983 .... DLB-8

Henighan, Tom 1934- DLB-251

Henisch, Peter 1943- DLB-85

Henley, Beth 1952- Y-86

Henley, William Ernest 1849-1903....... DLB-19

Henniker, Florence 1855-1923 .... DLB-135

Henning, Rachel 1826-1914 .... DLB-230

Henningsen, Agnes 1868-1962 .... DLB-214

Henry, Alexander 1739-1824 .... DLB-99

Henry, Buck 1930- DLB-26

Henry, Marguerite 1902-1997 .... DLB-22

Henry, O. (see Porter, William Sydney)

Henry, Robert Selph 1889-1970 ....DLB-17

Henry, Will (see Allen, Henry W.)

Henry VIII of England 1491-1547 ...... DLB-132

Henry of Ghent
circa 1217-1229 - 1293............DLB-115

Henryson, Robert
1420s or 1430s-circa 1505.........DLB-146

Henschke, Alfred (see Klabund)

Hensher, Philip 1965- DLB-267

Hensley, Sophie Almon 1866-1946.......DLB-99

Henson, Lance 1944- DLB-175

Henty, G. A. 1832-1902............DLB-18, 141

The Henty Society Y-98

Hentz, Caroline Lee 1800-1856.......DLB-3, 248

Heraclitus
fl. circa 500 B.C..................DLB-176

Herbert, Agnes circa 1880-1960........DLB-174

Herbert, Alan Patrick 1890-1971.....DLB-10, 191

Herbert, Edward, Lord, of Cherbury
1582-1648 ....DLB-121, 151, 252

Herbert, Frank 1920-1986......DLB-8; CDALB-7

Herbert, George 1593-1633.. DLB-126; CDBLB-1

Herbert, Henry William 1807-1858.....DLB-3, 73

Herbert, John 1926-2001...............DLB-53

Herbert, Mary Sidney, Countess of Pembroke
(see Sidney, Mary)

Herbert, Xavier 1901-1984 ....DLB-260

Herbert, Zbigniew
1924-1998.............DLB-232; CDWLB-4

Herbst, Josephine 1892-1969.............DLB-9

Herburger, Gunter 1932- DLB-75, 124

Herculano, Alexandre 1810-1877........DLB-287

Hercules, Frank E. M. 1917-1996.........DLB-33

Herder, Johann Gottfried 1744-1803......DLB-97

B. Herder Book Company.............DLB-49

Heredia, José-María de 1842-1905.......DLB-217

Herford, Charles Harold 1853-1931.....DLB-149

Hergesheimer, Joseph 1880-1954......DLB-9, 102

Heritage Press DLB-46

Hermann the Lame 1013-1054 ....DLB-148

Hermes, Johann Timotheu 1738-1821.....DLB-97

Hermlin, Stephan 1915-1997 ....DLB-69

Hernández, Alfonso C. 1938-..........DLB-122

Hernández, Inés 1947- DLB-122

Hernández, Miguel 1910-1942..........DLB-134

Hernton, Calvin C. 1932- DLB-38

Herodotus circa 484 B.C.-circa 420 B.C.
.... DLB-176; CDWLB-1

Héroët, Antoine 1490?-1567?..........DLB-327

Heron, Robert 1764-1807..............DLB-142

Herr, Michael 1940- DLB-185

Herrera, Darío 1870-1914 ....DLB-290

Herrera, Fernando de 1534?-1597........DLB-318

Herrera, Juan Felipe 1948- DLB-122

E. R. Herrick and Company DLB-49

Herrick, Robert 1591-1674..............DLB-126

Herrick, Robert 1868-1938 ....DLB-9, 12, 78

Herrick, William 1915-2004 ....Y-83

Herrmann, John 1900-1959...............DLB-4

Hersey, John
1914-1993 ... DLB-6, 185, 278, 299; CDALB-7

Hertel, François 1905-1985 ....DLB-68

Hervé-Bazin, Jean Pierre Marie (see Bazin, Hervé)

Hervey, John, Lord 1696-1743..........DLB-101

Herwig, Georg 1817-1875..............DLB-133

Herzen, Alexander (Aleksandr Ivanovich
Gersten) 1812-1870 ....DLB-277

Herzog, Emile Salomon Wilhelm
(see Maurois, André)

Hesiod eighth century B.C. DLB-176

Hesse, Hermann
1877-1962 ....DLB-66; CDWLB-2

Hessus, Eobanus 1488-1540 ....DLB-179

Heureka! (see Kertész, Imre and Nobel Prize
in Literature: 2002)..................Y-02

Hewat, Alexander circa 1743-circa 1824 ...DLB-30

Hewett, Dorothy 1923-2002 ....DLB-289

Hewitt, John 1907-1987 ....DLB-27

Hewlett, Maurice 1861-1923 ....DLB-34, 156

Heyen, William 1940- DLB-5

Heyer, Georgette 1902-1974. ....DLB-77, 191

Heym, Stefan 1913-2001...............DLB-69

Heyse, Paul 1830-1914 ....DLB-129

Heytesbury, William
circa 1310-1372 or 1373...........DLB-115

Heyward, Dorothy 1890-1961........DLB-7, 249

Heyward, DuBose 1885-1940 ... DLB-7, 9, 45, 249

Heywood, John 1497?-1580?...........DLB-136

Heywood, Thomas 1573 or 1574-1641 ....DLB-62

Hiaasen, Carl 1953- DLB-292

Hibberd, Jack 1940- DLB-289

Hibbs, Ben 1901-1975 ....DLB-137

"The Saturday Evening Post reaffirms
a policy," Ben Hibb's Statement
in *The Saturday Evening Post*
(16 May 1942) DLB-137

Hichens, Robert S. 1864-1950..........DLB-153

Hickey, Emily 1845-1924...............DLB-199

Hickman, William Albert 1877-1957......DLB-92

Hicks, Granville 1901-1982............DLB-246

Hidalgo, José Luis 1919-1947 ....DLB-108

Hiebert, Paul 1892-1987................DLB-68

Hieng, Andrej 1925- DLB-181

Hierro, José 1922-2002 ....DLB-108

Higgins, Aidan 1927- DLB-14

Higgins, Colin 1941-1988 ....DLB-26

Higgins, George V.
1939-1999 .... DLB-2; Y-81, 98–99

Afterword [in response to Cozzen's
Mens Rea (or Something)] Y-97

At End of Day: The Last George V.
Higgins Novel...................Y-99

The Books of George V. Higgins:
A Checklist of Editions
and Printings Y-00

George V. Higgins in Class...........Y-02

Tribute to Alfred A. Knopf Y-84

Tributes to George V. Higgins Y-99

"What You Lose on the Swings You Make
Up on the Merry-Go-Round"....Y-99

Higginson, Thomas Wentworth
1823-1911 ....DLB-1, 64, 243

Highsmith, Patricia 1921-1995.........DLB-306

Highwater, Jamake 1942?- DLB-52; Y-85

Hijuelos, Oscar 1951- DLB-145

Hildegard von Bingen 1098-1179........DLB-148

Das Hildesbrandslied
circa 820 ....DLB-148; CDWLB-2

Hildesheimer, Wolfgang 1916-1991...DLB-69, 124

Hildreth, Richard 1807-1865 ... DLB-1, 30, 59, 235

Hill, Aaron 1685-1750 ....DLB-84

Hill, Geoffrey 1932- DLB-40; CDBLB-8

George M. Hill Company DLB-49

Hill, "Sir" John 1714?-1775.............DLB-39

Lawrence Hill and Company,
Publishers DLB-46

Hill, Joe 1879-1915..................DLB-303

Hill, Leslie 1880-1960 ....DLB-51

Hill, Reginald 1936- DLB-276

Hill, Susan 1942- DLB-14, 139

Hill, Walter 1942- DLB-44

Hill and Wang.......................DLB-46

Hillberry, Conrad 1928- DLB-120

Hillerman, Tony 1925- DLB-206, 306

Hilliard, Gray and Company...........DLB-49

Hills, Lee 1906-2000 ....DLB-127

Hillyer, Robert 1895-1961.............DLB-54

Hilsenrath, Edgar 1926- DLB-299

Hilton, James 1900-1954 ....DLB-34, 77

Hilton, Walter died 1396..............DLB-146

Hilton and Company..................DLB-49

Himes, Chester 1909-1984 ... DLB-2, 76, 143, 226

Joseph Hindmarsh [publishing house] DLB-170

Hine, Daryl 1936- DLB-60

Hingley, Ronald 1920- DLB-155

Hinojosa-Smith, Rolando 1929- DLB-82

Hinton, S. E. 1948- CDALB-7

Hippel, Theodor Gottlieb von
1741-1796 ....DLB-97

Hippius, Zinaida Nikolaevna
1869-1945 ....DLB-295

Hippocrates of Cos fl. circa
425 B.C. DLB-176; CDWLB-1

Hirabayashi Taiko 1905-1972 ....DLB-180

Cumulative Index

Hirsch, E. D., Jr. 1928- DLB-67
Hirsch, Edward 1950- DLB-120
"Historical Novel," The Holocaust...... DLB-299
Hoagland, Edward 1932- DLB-6
Hoagland, Everett H., III 1942- DLB-41
Hoban, Russell 1925- DLB-52; Y-90
Hobbes, Thomas 1588-1679... DLB-151, 252, 281
Hobby, Oveta 1905-1995 .... DLB-127
Hobby, William 1878-1964............ DLB-127
Hobsbaum, Philip 1932- DLB-40
Hobsbawm, Eric (Francis Newton) 1917- DLB-296
Hobson, Laura Z. 1900-1986 .... DLB-28
Hobson, Sarah 1947- DLB-204
Hoby, Thomas 1530-1566 .... DLB-132
Hoccleve, Thomas circa 1368-circa 1437 .... DLB-146
Hoch, Edward D. 1930- DLB-306
Hochhuth, Rolf 1931- DLB-124
Hochman, Sandra 1936- DLB-5
Hocken, Thomas Morland 1836-1910 ... DLB-184
Hocking, William Ernest 1873-1966......DLB-270
Hodder and Stoughton, Limited........ DLB-106
Hodgins, Jack 1938- DLB-60
Hodgman, Helen 1945- DLB-14
Hodgskin, Thomas 1787-1869 .... DLB-158
Hodgson, Ralph 1871-1962 .... DLB-19
Hodgson, William Hope 1877-1918...........DLB-70, 153, 156, 178
Hoe, Robert, III 1839-1909 .... DLB-187
Hoeg, Peter 1957- DLB-214
Hoel, Sigurd 1890-1960 .... DLB-297
Hoem, Edvard 1949- DLB-297
Hoffenstein, Samuel 1890-1947 .... DLB-11
Hoffman, Alice 1952- DLB-292
Hoffman, Charles Fenno 1806-1884... DLB-3, 250
Hoffman, Daniel 1923- DLB-5
    Tribute to Robert Graves............. Y-85
Hoffmann, E. T. A. 1776-1822............. DLB-90; CDWLB-2
Hoffman, Frank B. 1888-1958 .... DLB-188
Hoffman, William 1925- DLB-234
    Tribute to Paxton Davis............... Y-94
Hoffmanswaldau, Christian Hoffman von 1616-1679...................... DLB-168
Hofmann, Michael 1957- DLB-40
Hofmannsthal, Hugo von 1874-1929..........DLB-81, 118; CDWLB-2
Hofmo, Gunvor 1921-1995 .... DLB-297
Hofstadter, Richard 1916-1970 ....DLB-17, 246
Hogan, Desmond 1950- DLB-14, 319
Hogan, Linda 1947- DLB-175

Hogan and Thompson................ DLB-49
Hogarth Press................ DLB-112; DS-10
Hogg, James 1770-1835.........DLB-93, 116, 159
Hohberg, Wolfgang Helmhard Freiherr von 1612-1688 .... DLB-168
von Hohenheim, Philippus Aureolus Theophrastus Bombastus (see Paracelsus)
Hohl, Ludwig 1904-1980 .... DLB-56
Højholt, Per 1928- DLB-214
Holan, Vladimir 1905-1980 .... DLB-215
d'Holbach, Paul Henri Thiry, baron 1723-1789..................... DLB-313
    The System of Nature (as Jean-Baptiste de Mirabaud) DLB-314
Holberg, Ludvig 1684-1754 .... DLB-300
Holbrook, David 1923- DLB-14, 40
Holcroft, Thomas 1745-1809 .... DLB-39, 89, 158
    Preface to *Alwyn* (1780).............. DLB-39
Holden, Jonathan 1941- DLB-105
    "Contemporary Verse Story-telling"... DLB-105
Holden, Molly 1927-1981 .... DLB-40
Hölderlin, Friedrich 1770-1843.............. DLB-90; CDWLB-2
Holdstock, Robert 1948- DLB-261
Holiday, 1974 Booker Prize winner, Stanley Middleton DLB-326
Holiday House DLB-46
Holinshed, Raphael died 1580 .... DLB-167
Holland, J. G. 1819-1881 ....DS-13
Holland, Norman N. 1927- DLB-67
Hollander, John 1929- DLB-5
Holley, Marietta 1836-1926 .... DLB-11
Hollinghurst, Alan 1954- DLB-207, 326
Hollingsworth, Margaret 1940- DLB-60
Hollo, Anselm 1934- DLB-40
Holloway, Emory 1885-1977 .... DLB-103
Holloway, John 1920- DLB-27
Holloway House Publishing Company ... DLB-46
Holme, Constance 1880-1955 .... DLB-34
Holmes, Abraham S. 1821?-1908 .... DLB-99
Holmes, John Clellon 1926-1988 .....DLB-16, 237
    "Four Essays on the Beat Generation"................... DLB-16
Holmes, Mary Jane 1825-1907..... DLB-202, 221
Holmes, Oliver Wendell 1809-1894 ...... DLB-1, 189, 235; CDALB-2
Holmes, Richard 1945- DLB-155
Holmes, Thomas James 1874-1959...... DLB-187
The Holocaust "Historical Novel" DLB-299
Holocaust Fiction, Postmodern......... DLB-299
Holocaust Novel, The "Second-Generation" DLB-299
Holroyd, Michael 1935- DLB-155; Y-99
Holst, Hermann E. von 1841-1904....... DLB-47

Holt, John 1721-1784 .... DLB-43
Henry Holt and Company DLB-49, 284
Holt, Rinehart and Winston........... DLB-46
Holtby, Winifred 1898-1935........... DLB-191
Holthusen, Hans Egon 1913-1997 .... DLB-69
Hölty, Ludwig Christoph Heinrich 1748-1776 .... DLB-94
Holub, Miroslav 1923-1998 .... DLB-232; CDWLB-4
Holz, Arno 1863-1929 .... DLB-118
Home, Henry, Lord Kames (see Kames, Henry Home, Lord)
Home, John 1722-1808................ DLB-84
Home, William Douglas 1912-1992...... DLB-13
Home Publishing Company DLB-49
Homer circa eighth-seventh centuries B.C. DLB-176; CDWLB-1
Homer, Winslow 1836-1910........... DLB-188
Homes, Geoffrey (see Mainwaring, Daniel)
Honan, Park 1928- DLB-111
Hone, William 1780-1842..........DLB-110, 158
Hongo, Garrett Kaoru 1951- DLB-120, 312
Honig, Edwin 1919- DLB-5
Hood, Hugh 1928-2000 .... DLB-53
Hood, Mary 1946- DLB-234
Hood, Thomas 1799-1845 .... DLB-96
Hook, Sidney 1902-1989 ....DLB-279
Hook, Theodore 1788-1841 .... DLB-116
Hooker, Jeremy 1941- DLB-40
Hooker, Richard 1554-1600 .... DLB-132
Hooker, Thomas 1586-1647 .... DLB-24
hooks, bell 1952- DLB-246
Hooper, Johnson Jones 1815-1862 .... DLB-3, 11, 248
Hope, A. D. 1907-2000................ DLB-289
Hope, Anthony 1863-1933 .... DLB-153, 156
Hope, Christopher 1944- DLB-225
Hope, Eva (see Hearn, Mary Anne)
Hope, Laurence (Adela Florence Cory Nicolson) 1865-1904.......... DLB-240
Hopkins, Ellice 1836-1904 .... DLB-190
Hopkins, Gerard Manley 1844-1889 .... DLB-35, 57; CDBLB-5
Hopkins, John ?-1570 .... DLB-132
Hopkins, John H., and Son DLB-46
Hopkins, Lemuel 1750-1801............ DLB-37
Hopkins, Pauline Elizabeth 1859-1930.... DLB-50
Hopkins, Samuel 1721-1803 .... DLB-31
Hopkinson, Francis 1737-1791 .... DLB-31
Hopkinson, Nalo 1960- DLB-251
Hopper, Nora (Mrs. Nora Chesson) 1871-1906.................... DLB-240
Hoppin, Augustus 1828-1896.......... DLB-188

Hora, Josef 1891-1945 . . . . . . DLB-215; CDWLB-4

Horace 65 B.C.-8 B.C. DLB-211; CDWLB-1

Horgan, Paul 1903-1995 . . . . . DLB-102, 212; Y-85

    Tribute to Alfred A. Knopf Y-84

Horizon Press DLB-46

Horkheimer, Max 1895-1973 . . . . DLB-296

Hornby, C. H. St. John 1867-1946 . . . . . . DLB-201

Hornby, Nick 1957- DLB-207

Horne, Frank 1899-1974 . . . . DLB-51

Horne, Richard Henry (Hengist)
    1802 or 1803-1884 . . . . DLB-32

Horne, Thomas 1608-1654 . . . . DLB-281

Horney, Karen 1885-1952 . . . . DLB-246

Hornung, E. W. 1866-1921 . . . . DLB-70

Horovitz, Israel 1939- DLB-7

Horta, Maria Teresa (see The Three Marias:
    A Landmark Case in Portuguese
    Literary History)

Horton, George Moses 1797?-1883? DLB-50

    George Moses Horton Society Y-99

Horváth, Ödön von 1901-1938 . . . . . . DLB-85, 124

Horwood, Harold 1923- DLB-60

E. and E. Hosford [publishing house] DLB-49

Hoskens, Jane Fenn 1693-1770? DLB-200

Hoskyns, John circa 1566-1638 . . . . . DLB-121, 281

Hosokawa Yūsai 1535-1610 . . . . DLB-203

Hospers, John 1918- DLB-279

Hospital, Janette Turner 1942- DLB-325

Hostovský, Egon 1908-1973 . . . . DLB-215

Hotchkiss and Company DLB-49

Hotel du Lac, 1984 Booker Prize winner,
    Anita Brookner DLB-326

Hough, Emerson 1857-1923 . . . . DLB-9, 212

Houghton, Stanley 1881-1913 . . . . DLB-10

Houghton Mifflin Company DLB-49

Hours at Home DS-13

Household, Geoffrey 1900-1988 . . . . DLB-87

Housman, A. E. 1859-1936 . . . DLB-19; CDBLB-5

Housman, Laurence 1865-1959 . . . . DLB-10

Houston, Pam 1962- DLB-244

Houwald, Ernst von 1778-1845 . . . . DLB-90

Hovey, Richard 1864-1900 . . . . DLB-54

How Late It Was, How Late, 1994 Booker Prize winner,
    James Kelman DLB-326

Howard, Donald R. 1927-1987 . . . . DLB-111

Howard, Maureen 1930- Y-83

Howard, Richard 1929- DLB-5

Howard, Roy W. 1883-1964 . . . . DLB-29

Howard, Sidney 1891-1939 . . . . . . DLB-7, 26, 249

Howard, Thomas, second Earl of Arundel
    1585-1646 . . . . DLB-213

Howe, E. W. 1853-1937 . . . . DLB-12, 25

Howe, Henry 1816-1893 . . . . DLB-30

Howe, Irving 1920-1993 . . . . DLB-67

Howe, Joseph 1804-1873 . . . . DLB-99

Howe, Julia Ward 1819-1910 . . . . . DLB-1, 189, 235

Howe, Percival Presland 1886-1944 . . . . . . DLB-149

Howe, Susan 1937- DLB-120

Howell, Clark, Sr. 1863-1936 . . . . DLB-25

Howell, Evan P. 1839-1905 . . . . DLB-23

Howell, James 1594?-1666 . . . . DLB-151

Howell, Soskin and Company DLB-46

Howell, Warren Richardson
    1912-1984 . . . . DLB-140

Howells, William Dean 1837-1920
    . . . . DLB-12, 64, 74, 79, 189; CDALB-3

    Introduction to Paul Laurence
    Dunbar's *Lyrics of Lowly Life*
    (1896) DLB-50

    The William Dean Howells Society Y-01

Howitt, Mary 1799-1888 . . . . DLB-110, 199

Howitt, William 1792-1879 . . . . DLB-110

Hoyem, Andrew 1935- DLB-5

Hoyers, Anna Ovena 1584-1655 . . . . DLB-164

Hoyle, Fred 1915-2001 . . . . DLB-261

Hoyos, Angela de 1940- DLB-82

Henry Hoyt [publishing house] DLB-49

Hoyt, Palmer 1897-1979 . . . . DLB-127

Hrabal, Bohumil 1914-1997 . . . . DLB-232

Hrabanus Maurus 776?-856 . . . . DLB-148

Hronský, Josef Cíger 1896-1960 . . . . DLB-215

Hrotsvit of Gandersheim
    circa 935-circa 1000 . . . . DLB-148

Hubbard, Elbert 1856-1915 . . . . DLB-91

Hubbard, Kin 1868-1930 . . . . DLB-11

Hubbard, William circa 1621-1704 . . . . DLB-24

Huber, Therese 1764-1829 . . . . DLB-90

Huch, Friedrich 1873-1913 . . . . DLB-66

Huch, Ricarda 1864-1947 . . . . DLB-66

Huddle, David 1942- DLB-130

Hudgins, Andrew 1951- DLB-120, 282

Hudson, Henry Norman 1814-1886 . . . . . . DLB-64

Hudson, Stephen 1868?-1944 . . . . DLB-197

Hudson, W. H. 1841-1922 . . . . . DLB-98, 153, 174

Hudson and Goodwin DLB-49

Huebsch, B. W., oral history Y-99

B. W. Huebsch [publishing house] DLB-46

Hueffer, Oliver Madox 1876-1931 . . . . DLB-197

Huet, Pierre Daniel
    Preface to *The History of Romances*
    (1715) DLB-39

Hugh of St. Victor circa 1096-1141 . . . . . . DLB-208

Hughes, David 1930- DLB-14

Hughes, Dusty 1947- DLB-233

Hughes, Hatcher 1881-1945 . . . . DLB-249

Hughes, John 1677-1720 . . . . DLB-84

Hughes, Langston 1902-1967 . . . . . . DLB-4, 7, 48,
    51, 86, 228, 315; DS-15; CDALB-5

Hughes, Richard 1900-1976 . . . . DLB-15, 161

Hughes, Ted 1930-1998 . . . . DLB-40, 161

Hughes, Thomas 1822-1896 . . . . DLB-18, 163

Hugo, Richard 1923-1982 . . . . DLB-5, 206

Hugo, Victor 1802-1885 . . . . . . DLB-119, 192, 217

Hugo Awards and Nebula Awards DLB-8

Huidobro, Vicente 1893-1948 . . . . DLB-283

Hull, Richard 1896-1973 . . . . DLB-77

Hulda (Unnur Benediktsdóttir Bjarklind)
    1881-1946 . . . . DLB-293

Hulme, Keri 1947- DLB-326

Hulme, T. E. 1883-1917 . . . . DLB-19

Hulton, Anne ?-1779? DLB-200

Humanism, Sixteenth-Century
    Spanish DLB-318

Humboldt, Alexander von 1769-1859 . . . . . DLB-90

Humboldt, Wilhelm von 1767-1835 . . . . . . DLB-90

Hume, David 1711-1776 . . . . DLB-104, 252

Hume, Fergus 1859-1932 . . . . DLB-70

Hume, Sophia 1702-1774 . . . . DLB-200

Hume-Rothery, Mary Catherine
    1824-1885 . . . . DLB-240

Humishuma
    (see Mourning Dove)

Hummer, T. R. 1950- DLB-120

Humor
    American Humor: A Historical
    Survey DLB-11

    American Humor Studies Association Y-99

    The Comic Tradition Continued
    [in the British Novel] DLB-15

    Humorous Book Illustration DLB-11

    International Society for Humor Studies . . . Y-99

    Newspaper Syndication of American
    Humor DLB-11

    Selected Humorous Magazines
    (1820-1950) DLB-11

Bruce Humphries [publishing house] DLB-46

Humphrey, Duke of Gloucester
    1391-1447 . . . . DLB-213

Humphrey, William
    1924-1997 . . . . DLB-6, 212, 234, 278

Humphreys, David 1752-1818 . . . . DLB-37

Humphreys, Emyr 1919- DLB-15

Humphreys, Josephine 1945- DLB-292

Hunayn ibn Ishaq 809-873 or 877 . . . . DLB-311

Huncke, Herbert 1915-1996 . . . . DLB-16

Huneker, James Gibbons
    1857-1921 . . . . DLB-71

Hunold, Christian Friedrich
    1681-1721 . . . . DLB-168

Hunt, Irene 1907- DLB-52

Hunt, Leigh 1784-1859 . . . . DLB-96, 110, 144

Cumulative Index

Hunt, Violet 1862-1942 . . . . DLB-162, 197

Hunt, William Gibbes 1791-1833 . . . . DLB-73

Hunter, Evan (Ed McBain)
1926-2005 . . . . DLB-306; Y-82

    Tribute to John D. MacDonald Y-86

Hunter, Jim 1939- DLB-14

Hunter, Kristin 1931- DLB-33

    Tribute to Julian Mayfield Y-84

Hunter, Mollie 1922- DLB-161

Hunter, N. C. 1908-1971 . . . . DLB-10

Hunter-Duvar, John 1821-1899 . . . . DLB-99

Huntington, Henry E. 1850-1927 . . . . DLB-140

    The Henry E. Huntington Library Y-92

Huntington, Susan Mansfield
1791-1823 . . . . DLB-200

Hurd and Houghton DLB-49

Hurst, Fannie 1889-1968 . . . . DLB-86

Hurst and Blackett DLB-106

Hurst and Company DLB-49

Hurston, Zora Neale
1901?-1960 . . . . DLB-51, 86; CDALB-7

Husserl, Edmund 1859-1938 . . . . DLB-296

Husson, Jules-François-Félix (see Champfleury)

Huston, John 1906-1987 . . . . DLB-26

Hutcheson, Francis 1694-1746 . . . . . DLB-31, 252

Hutchinson, Ron 1947- DLB-245

Hutchinson, R. C. 1907-1975 . . . . DLB-191

Hutchinson, Thomas 1711-1780 . . . . . DLB-30, 31

Hutchinson and Company
(Publishers) Limited DLB-112

Huth, Angela 1938- DLB-271

Hutton, Richard Holt
1826-1897 . . . . DLB-57

von Hutten, Ulrich 1488-1523 . . . . DLB-179

Huxley, Aldous 1894-1963
. . . . . . DLB-36, 100, 162, 195, 255; CDBLB-6

Huxley, Elspeth Josceline
1907-1997 . . . . DLB-77, 204

Huxley, T. H. 1825-1895 . . . . DLB-57

Huyghue, Douglas Smith 1816-1891 . . . . . DLB-99

Huysmans, Joris-Karl 1848-1907 . . . . DLB-123

Hwang, David Henry
1957- DLB-212, 228, 312

Hyde, Donald 1909-1966 . . . . DLB-187

Hyde, Mary 1912-2003 . . . . DLB-187

Hyman, Trina Schart 1939- DLB-61

I

Iavorsky, Stefan 1658-1722 . . . . DLB-150

Iazykov, Nikolai Mikhailovich
1803-1846 . . . . DLB-205

Ibáñez, Armando P. 1949- DLB-209

Ibáñez, Sara de 1909-1971 . . . . DLB-290

Ibarbourou, Juana de 1892-1979 . . . . DLB-290

Ibn Abi Tahir Tayfur 820-893 . . . . DLB-311

Ibn Qutaybah 828-889 . . . . DLB-311

Ibn al-Rumi 836-896 . . . . DLB-311

Ibn Sa'd 784-845 . . . . DLB-311

Ibrahim al-Mawsili 742 or 743-803 or 804 DLB-311

Ibn Bajja circa 1077-1138 . . . . DLB-115

Ibn Gabirol, Solomon
circa 1021-circa 1058 . . . . DLB-115

Ibn al-Muqaffa' circa 723-759 . . . . DLB-311

Ibn al-Mu'tazz 861-908 . . . . DLB-311

Ibuse Masuji 1898-1993 . . . . DLB-180

Ichijō Kanera
(see Ichijō Kaneyoshi)

Ichijō Kaneyoshi (Ichijō Kanera)
1402-1481 . . . . DLB-203

Iffland, August Wilhelm
1759-1814 . . . . DLB-94

Iggulden, John 1917- DLB-289

Ignatieff, Michael 1947- DLB-267

Ignatow, David 1914-1997 . . . . DLB-5

Ike, Chukwuemeka 1931- DLB-157

Ikkyū Sōjun 1394-1481 . . . . DLB-203

Iles, Francis
(see Berkeley, Anthony)

Il'f, Il'ia (Il'ia Arnol'dovich Fainzil'berg)
1897-1937 . . . . DLB-272

Illich, Ivan 1926-2002 . . . . DLB-242

Illustration
    Children's Book Illustration in the
        Twentieth Century DLB-61

    Children's Illustrators, 1800-1880 . . . DLB-163

    Early American Book Illustration DLB-49

    The Iconography of Science-Fiction
        Art DLB-8

    The Illustration of Early German
        Literary Manuscripts, circa
        1150-circa 1300 . . . . DLB-148

    Minor Illustrators, 1880-1914 . . . . . . DLB-141

Illyés, Gyula 1902-1983 . . . . DLB-215; CDWLB-4

Imbs, Bravig 1904-1946 . . . . DLB-4; DS-15

Imbuga, Francis D. 1947- DLB-157

Immermann, Karl 1796-1840 . . . . DLB-133

Imru' al-Qays circa 526-circa 565 . . . . . . DLB-311

In a Free State, 1971 Booker Prize winner,
V. S. Naipaul DLB-326

Inchbald, Elizabeth 1753-1821 . . . . DLB-39, 89

Inchon, Elizabeth (see Inchbald)

Indiana University Press Y-02

Ingamells, Rex 1913-1955 . . . . DLB-260

Inge, William 1913-1973 . . . DLB-7, 249; CDALB-1

Ingelow, Jean 1820-1897 . . . . DLB-35, 163

Ingemann, B. S. 1789-1862 . . . . DLB-300

Ingersoll, Ralph 1900-1985 . . . . DLB-127

The Ingersoll Prizes Y-84

Ingoldsby, Thomas (see Barham, Richard Harris)

Ingraham, Joseph Holt 1809-1860 . . . . DLB-3, 248

Inman, John 1805-1850 . . . . DLB-73

Innerhofer, Franz 1944- DLB-85

Innes, Michael (J. I. M. Stewart)
1906-1994 . . . . DLB-276

Innis, Harold Adams 1894-1952 . . . . DLB-88

Innis, Mary Quayle 1899-1972 . . . . DLB-88

Inō Sōgi 1421-1502 . . . . DLB-203

Inoue Yasushi 1907-1991 . . . . DLB-182

"The Greatness of Southern Literature":
League of the South Institute for the
Study of Southern Culture and History
. . . . Y-02

International Publishers Company DLB-46

Internet (publishing and commerce)
    Author Websites Y-97

    The Book Trade and the Internet Y-00

    E-Books Turn the Corner Y-98

    The E-Researcher: Possibilities
        and Pitfalls Y-00

    Interviews on E-publishing Y-00

    John Updike on the Internet Y-97

    LitCheck Website Y-01

    Virtual Books and Enemies of Books . . . Y-00

Interviews
    Adoff, Arnold Y-01

    Aldridge, John W. Y-91

    Anastas, Benjamin Y-98

    Baker, Nicholson Y-00

    Bank, Melissa Y-98

    Bass, T. J. Y-80

    Bernstein, Harriet Y-82

    Betts, Doris Y-82

    Bosworth, David Y-82

    Bottoms, David Y-83

    Bowers, Fredson Y-80

    Burnshaw, Stanley Y-97

    Carpenter, Humphrey Y-84, 99

    Carr, Virginia Spencer Y-00

    Carver, Raymond Y-83

    Cherry, Kelly Y-83

    Conroy, Jack Y-81

    Coppel, Alfred Y-83

    Cowley, Malcolm Y-81

    Davis, Paxton Y-89

    Devito, Carlo Y-94

    De Vries, Peter Y-82

    Dickey, James Y-82

    Donald, David Herbert Y-87

    Editors, Conversations with Y-95

    Ellroy, James Y-91

    Fancher, Betsy Y-83

    Faust, Irvin Y-00

    Fulton, Len Y-86

    Furst, Alan Y-01

    Garrett, George Y-83

    Gelfman, Jane Y-93

Goldwater, Walter Y-93	Schlafly, Phyllis Y-82	M. J. Ivers and Company. DLB-49
Gores, Joe Y-02	Schroeder, Patricia. Y-99	Iwaniuk, Wacław 1915-2001 . . . . DLB-215
Greenfield, George Y-91	Schulberg, Budd Y-81, 01	Iwano Hōmei 1873-1920 . . . . DLB-180
Griffin, Bryan Y-81	Scribner, Charles, III. Y-94	Iwaszkiewicz, Jarosláv 1894-1980 . . . . DLB-215
Groom, Winston Y-01	Sipper, Ralph. Y-94	Iyayi, Festus 1947- DLB-157
Guilds, John Caldwell Y-92	Smith, Cork. Y-95	Izumi Kyōka 1873-1939 . . . . DLB-180
Hamilton, Virginia Y-01	Staley, Thomas F. Y-00	
Hardin, James Y-92	Styron, William. Y-80	# J
Harris, Mark Y-80	Talese, Nan Y-94	
Harrison, Jim. Y-82	Thornton, John Y-94	Jackmon, Marvin E. (see Marvin X)
Hazzard, Shirley Y-82	Toth, Susan Allen Y-86	Jacks, L. P. 1860-1955 . . . . DLB-135
Herrick, William Y-01	Tyler, Anne Y-82	Jackson, Angela 1951- DLB-41
Higgins, George V. Y-98	Vaughan, Samuel. Y-97	Jackson, Charles 1903-1968. . . . . DLB-234
Hoban, Russell Y-90	Von Ogtrop, Kristin Y-92	Jackson, Helen Hunt
Holroyd, Michael Y-99	Wallenstein, Barry. Y-92	1830-1885 . . . . DLB-42, 47, 186, 189
Horowitz, Glen Y-90	Weintraub, Stanley Y-82	Jackson, Holbrook 1874-1948 . . . . DLB-98
Iggulden, John. Y-01	Williams, J. Chamberlain Y-84	Jackson, Laura Riding 1901-1991 . . . . DLB-48
Jakes, John. Y-83	Into the Past: William Jovanovich's	Jackson, Shirley
Jenkinson, Edward B. Y-82	Reflections in Publishing Y-02	1916-1965 . . . . DLB-6, 234; CDALB-1
Jenks, Tom. Y-86	Ionesco, Eugène 1909-1994 . . . . DLB-321	Jacob, Max 1876-1944 . . . . DLB-258
Kaplan, Justin Y-86	Ireland, David 1927- DLB-289	Jacob, Naomi 1884?-1964 . . . . DLB-191
King, Florence. Y-85	The National Library of Ireland's	Jacob, Piers Anthony Dillingham
Klopfer, Donald S. Y-97	New James Joyce Manuscripts. Y-02	(see Anthony, Piers)
Krug, Judith. Y-82	Irigaray, Luce 1930- DLB-296	Jacob, Violet 1863-1946. . . . . DLB-240
Lamm, Donald Y-95	Irving, John 1942- DLB-6, 278; Y-82	Jacobi, Friedrich Heinrich 1743-1819 . . . . . DLB-94
Laughlin, James Y-96	Irving, Washington 1783-1859	Jacobi, Johann Georg 1740-1841 . . . . DLB-97
Lawrence, Starling. Y-95	. . . . DLB-3, 11, 30, 59, 73, 74,	George W. Jacobs and Company. DLB-49
Lindsay, Jack Y-84	183, 186, 250; CDALB-2	Jacobs, Harriet 1813-1897 . . . . DLB-239
Mailer, Norman. Y-97	Irwin, Grace 1907- DLB-68	Jacobs, Joseph 1854-1916. . . . . DLB-141
Manchester, William Y-85	Irwin, Will 1873-1948 . . . . DLB-25	Jacobs, W. W. 1863-1943 . . . . DLB-135
Max, D. T. Y-94	Isaksson, Ulla 1916-2000 . . . . DLB-257	The W. W. Jacobs Appreciation Society . . . Y-98
McCormack, Thomas Y-98	Iser, Wolfgang 1926- DLB-242	Jacobsen, J. P. 1847-1885 . . . . DLB-300
McNamara, Katherine. Y-97	Isherwood, Christopher	Jacobsen, Jørgen-Frantz 1900-1938 . . . . . . DLB-214
Mellen, Joan Y-94	1904-1986 . . . . DLB-15, 195; Y-86	Jacobsen, Josephine 1908- DLB-244
Menaker, Daniel Y-97	The Christopher Isherwood Archive,	Jacobsen, Rolf 1907-1994 . . . . DLB-297
Mooneyham, Lamarr Y-82	The Huntington Library Y-99	Jacobson, Dan 1929- DLB-14, 207, 225, 319
Murray, Les. Y-01	Ishiguro, Kazuo 1954- DLB-194, 326	Jacobson, Howard 1942- DLB-207
Nosworth, David. Y-82	Ishikawa Jun 1899-1987 . . . . DLB-182	Jacques de Vitry circa 1160/1170-1240. . . . DLB-208
O'Connor, Patrick Y-84, 99	Iskander, Fazil' Abdulevich 1929- DLB-302	Jæger, Frank 1926-1977 . . . . DLB-214
Ozick, Cynthia Y-83	The Island Trees Case: A Symposium on	Ja'far al-Sadiq circa 702-765 . . . . DLB-311
Penner, Jonathan Y-83	School Library Censorship	William Jaggard [publishing house] DLB-170
Pennington, Lee. Y-82	An Interview with Judith Krug	Jahier, Piero 1884-1966 . . . . DLB-114, 264
Penzler, Otto Y-96	An Interview with Phyllis Schlafly	al-Jahiz circa 776-868 or 869 . . . . DLB-311
Plimpton, George Y-99	An Interview with Edward B. Jenkinson	Jahnn, Hans Henny 1894-1959 . . . . . . DLB-56, 124
Potok, Chaim Y-84	An Interview with Lamarr Mooneyham	Jaimes, Freyre, Ricardo 1866?-1933. . . . . . DLB-283
Powell, Padgett Y-01	An Interview with Harriet Bernstein. Y-82	Jakes, John 1932- DLB-278; Y-83
Prescott, Peter S. Y-86	Islas, Arturo	Tribute to John Gardner Y-82
Rabe, David Y-91	1938-1991 . . . . DLB-122	Tribute to John D. MacDonald. Y-86
Rechy, John Y-82	Issit, Debbie 1966- DLB-233	Jakobína Johnson (Jakobína Sigurbjarnardóttir)
Reid, B. L. Y-83	Ivanišević, Drago 1907-1981 . . . . DLB-181	1883-1977 . . . . DLB-293
Reynolds, Michael. Y-95, 99	Ivanov, Georgii 1894-1954. . . . . DLB-317	Jakobson, Roman 1896-1982. . . . . DLB-242
Robinson, Derek Y-02	Ivanov, Viacheslav Ivanovich	James, Alice 1848-1892 . . . . DLB-221
Rollyson, Carl Y-97	1866-1949 . . . . DLB-295	James, C. L. R. 1901-1989. . . . . DLB-125
Rosset, Barney Y-02	Ivanov, Vsevolod Viacheslavovich	
	1895-1963 . . . . DLB-272	
	Ivask, Yuri 1907-1986 . . . . DLB-317	
	Ivaska, Astrīde 1926- DLB-232	

Cumulative Index

James, Clive 1939- DLB-325

James, George P. R. 1801-1860 .... DLB-116

James, Henry 1843-1916
.... DLB-12, 71, 74, 189; DS-13; CDALB-3

"The Future of the Novel" (1899) DLB-18

"The Novel in [Robert Browning's]
'The Ring and the Book'"
(1912) DLB-32

James, John circa 1633-1729 .... DLB-24

James, M. R. 1862-1936 .... DLB-156, 201

James, Naomi 1949- DLB-204

James, P. D. (Phyllis Dorothy James White)
1920- DLB-87, 276; DS-17; CDBLB-8

Tribute to Charles Scribner Jr. Y-95

James, Thomas 1572?-1629 .... DLB-213

U. P. James [publishing house] DLB-49

James, Will 1892-1942 .... DS-16

James, William 1842-1910 .... DLB-270

James VI of Scotland, I of England
1566-1625 .... DLB-151, 172

*Ane Schort Treatise Conteining Some Revlis
and Cautelis to Be Obseruit and
Eschewit in Scottis Poesi* (1584)...... DLB-172

Jameson, Anna 1794-1860 .... DLB-99, 166

Jameson, Fredric 1934- DLB-67

Jameson, J. Franklin 1859-1937 .... DLB-17

Jameson, Storm 1891-1986 .... DLB-36

Jančar, Drago 1948- DLB-181

Janés, Clara 1940- DLB-134

Janevski, Slavko 1920-2000 . DLB-181; CDWLB-4

Janowitz, Tama 1957- DLB-292

Jansson, Tove 1914-2001 .... DLB-257

Janvier, Thomas 1849-1913 .... DLB-202

Japan
"The Development of Meiji Japan" .. DLB-180

"Encounter with the West"......... DLB-180

Japanese Literature
Letter from Japan Y-94, 98

Medieval Travel Diaries DLB-203

Surveys: 1987-1995 .... DLB-182

Jaramillo, Cleofas M. 1878-1956 .... DLB-122

Jaramillo Levi, Enrique 1944- DLB-290

Jarir after 650-circa 730 .... DLB-311

Jarman, Mark 1952- DLB-120, 282

Jarrell, Randall
1914-1965 .... DLB-48, 52; CDALB-1

Jarrold and Sons DLB-106

Jarry, Alfred 1873-1907 .... DLB-192, 258

Jarves, James Jackson 1818-1888 .... DLB-189

Jasmin, Claude 1930- DLB-60

Jaunsudrabiņš, Jānis 1877-1962 .... DLB-220

Jay, John 1745-1829 .... DLB-31

Jean de Garlande (see John of Garland)

Jefferies, Richard 1848-1887 .... DLB-98, 141

The Richard Jefferies Society Y-98

Jeffers, Lance 1919-1985 .... DLB-41

Jeffers, Robinson
1887-1962 .... DLB-45, 212; CDALB-4

Jefferson, Thomas
1743-1826 .... DLB-31, 183; CDALB-2

Jégé 1866-1940 .... DLB-215

Jelinek, Elfriede 1946- DLB-85

Jellicoe, Ann 1927- DLB-13, 233

Jemison, Mary circa 1742-1833 .... DLB-239

Jen, Gish 1955- DLB-312

Jenkins, Dan 1929- DLB-241

Jenkins, Elizabeth 1905- DLB-155

Jenkins, Robin 1912-2005 .... DLB-14, 271

Jenkins, William Fitzgerald (see Leinster, Murray)

Herbert Jenkins Limited DLB-112

Jennings, Elizabeth 1926- DLB-27

Jens, Walter 1923- DLB-69

Jensen, Axel 1932-2003 .... DLB-297

Jensen, Johannes V. 1873-1950 .... DLB-214

Jensen, Merrill 1905-1980 .... DLB-17

Jensen, Thit 1876-1957 .... DLB-214

Jephson, Robert 1736-1803 .... DLB-89

Jerome, Jerome K. 1859-1927 ..... DLB-10, 34, 135

The Jerome K. Jerome Society Y-98

Jerome, Judson 1927-1991 .... DLB-105

"Reflections: After a Tornado" DLB-105

Jerrold, Douglas 1803-1857 .... DLB-158, 159

Jersild, Per Christian 1935- DLB-257

Jesse, F. Tennyson 1888-1958 .... DLB-77

Jewel, John 1522-1571 .... DLB-236

John P. Jewett and Company DLB-49

Jewett, Sarah Orne 1849-1909 ....DLB-12, 74, 221

The Jewish Publication Society DLB-49

Studies in American Jewish Literature Y-02

Jewitt, John Rodgers 1783-1821 .... DLB-99

Jewsbury, Geraldine 1812-1880 .... DLB-21

Jewsbury, Maria Jane 1800-1833 .... DLB-199

Jhabvala, Ruth Prawer
1927- DLB-139, 194, 323, 326

Jiang Guangci 1901-1931 .... DLB-328

Jiménez, Juan Ramón 1881-1958 .... DLB-134

Jin, Ha 1956- DLB-244, 292

Joans, Ted 1928-2003 .... DLB-16, 41

Jodelle, Estienne 1532?-1573 .... DLB-327

Jōha 1525-1602 .... DLB-203

Jóhann Sigurjónsson 1880-1919 .... DLB-293

Jóhannes úr Kötlum 1899-1972 .... DLB-293

Johannis de Garlandia (see John of Garland)

John, Errol 1924-1988 .... DLB-233

John, Eugenie (see Marlitt, E.)

John of Dumbleton
circa 1310-circa 1349 .... DLB-115

John of Garland (Jean de Garlande,
Johannis de Garlandia)
circa 1195-circa 1272 .... DLB-208

The John Reed Clubs DLB-303

Johns, Captain W. E. 1893-1968 .... DLB-160

Johnson, Mrs. A. E. ca. 1858-1922 ..... DLB-221

Johnson, Amelia (see Johnson, Mrs. A. E.)

Johnson, B. S. 1933-1973 .... DLB-14, 40

Johnson, Charles 1679-1748 .... DLB-84

Johnson, Charles 1948- DLB-33, 278

Johnson, Charles S. 1893-1956 ...... DLB-51, 91

Johnson, Colin (Mudrooroo) 1938- ... DLB-289

Johnson, Denis 1949- DLB-120

Johnson, Diane 1934- Y-80

Johnson, Dorothy M. 1905-1984 ...... DLB-206

Johnson, E. Pauline (Tekahionwake)
1861-1913 .... DLB-175

Johnson, Edgar 1901-1995 .... DLB-103

Johnson, Edward 1598-1672 .... DLB-24

Johnson, Eyvind 1900-1976 .... DLB-259

Johnson, Fenton 1888-1958 .... DLB-45, 50

Johnson, Georgia Douglas
1877?-1966 .... DLB-51, 249

Johnson, Gerald W. 1890-1980 .... DLB-29

Johnson, Greg 1953- DLB-234

Johnson, Helene 1907-1995 .... DLB-51

Jacob Johnson and Company DLB-49

Johnson, James Weldon
1871-1938 .... DLB-51; CDALB-4

Johnson, John H. 1918-2005 .... DLB-137

"Backstage," Statement From the
Initial Issue of *Ebony*
(November 1945 .... DLB-137

Johnson, Joseph [publishing house] DLB-154

Johnson, Linton Kwesi 1952- DLB-157

Johnson, Lionel 1867-1902 .... DLB-19

Johnson, Nunnally 1897-1977 .... DLB-26

Johnson, Owen 1878-1952 .... Y-87

Johnson, Pamela Hansford 1912-1981 .... DLB-15

Johnson, Pauline 1861-1913 .... DLB-92

Johnson, Ronald 1935-1998 .... DLB-169

Johnson, Samuel 1696-1772 ... DLB-24; CDBLB-2

Johnson, Samuel
1709-1784 .... DLB-39, 95, 104, 142, 213

Rambler, no. 4 (1750) [excerpt] DLB-39

The BBC Four Samuel Johnson Prize
for Non-fiction Y-02

Johnson, Samuel 1822-1882 .... DLB-1, 243

Johnson, Susanna 1730-1810 .... DLB-200

Johnson, Terry 1955- DLB-233

Johnson, Uwe 1934-1984 ..... DLB-75; CDWLB-2

Benjamin Johnson [publishing house]..... DLB-49

Benjamin, Jacob, and Robert Johnson
 [publishing house]..................DLB-49
Johnston, Annie Fellows 1863-1931.......DLB-42
Johnston, Basil H. 1929- DLB-60
Johnston, David Claypole 1798?-1865....DLB-188
Johnston, Denis 1901-1984 ....DLB-10
Johnston, Ellen 1835-1873 ....DLB-199
Johnston, George 1912-1970 ....DLB-260
Johnston, George 1913-1970 ....DLB-88
Johnston, Sir Harry 1858-1927 ....DLB-174
Johnston, Jennifer 1930- DLB-14
Johnston, Mary 1870-1936..............DLB-9
Johnston, Richard Malcolm 1822-1898....DLB-74
Johnstone, Charles 1719?-1800?.........DLB-39
Johst, Hanns 1890-1978................DLB-124
Jökull Jakobsson 1933-1978 ....DLB-293
Jolas, Eugene 1894-1952 ....DLB-4, 45
Jolley, Elizabeth 1923- DLB-325
Jón Stefán Sveinsson or Svensson (see Nonni)
Jón Trausti (Guðmundur Magnússon)
 1873-1918 ....DLB-293
Jón úr Vör (Jón Jónsson) 1917-2000 .....DLB-293
Jónas Hallgrímsson 1807-1845..........DLB-293
Jones, Alice C. 1853-1933 ....DLB-92
Jones, Charles C., Jr. 1831-1893 ....DLB-30
Jones, D. G. 1929- DLB-53
Jones, David 1895-1974 ...DLB-20, 100; CDBLB-7
Jones, Diana Wynne 1934- DLB-161
Jones, Ebenezer 1820-1860 ....DLB-32
Jones, Ernest 1819-1868................DLB-32
Jones, Gayl 1949- DLB-33, 278
Jones, George 1800-1870 ....DLB-183
Jones, Glyn 1905-1995.................DLB-15
Jones, Gwyn 1907- DLB-15, 139
Jones, Henry Arthur 1851-1929..........DLB-10
Jones, Hugh circa 1692-1760 ....DLB-24
Jones, James 1921-1977 ....DLB-2, 143; DS-17
 James Jones Papers in the Handy
 Writers' Colony Collection at
 the University of Illinois at
 Springfield......................Y-98
 The James Jones Society Y-92
Jones, Jenkin Lloyd 1911-2004.........DLB-127
Jones, John Beauchamp 1810-1866 ......DLB-202
Jones, Joseph, Major
 (see Thompson, William Tappan)
Jones, LeRoi (see Baraka, Amiri)
Jones, Lewis 1897-1939 ....DLB-15
Jones, Madison 1925- DLB-152
Jones, Marie 1951- DLB-233
Jones, Preston 1936-1979 ....DLB-7
Jones, Rodney 1950- DLB-120

Jones, Thom 1945- DLB-244
Jones, Sir William 1746-1794 ....DLB-109
Jones, William Alfred 1817-1900 ....DLB-59
Jones's Publishing House................DLB-49
Jong, Erica 1942- DLB-2, 5, 28, 152
Jonke, Gert F. 1946-..................DLB-85
Jonson, Ben
 1572?-1637 ....DLB-62, 121; CDBLB-1
Jonsson, Tor 1916-1951 ....DLB-297
Jordan, June 1936- DLB-38
Jorgensen, Johannes 1866-1956.........DLB-300
Jose, Nicholas 1952- DLB-325
Joseph, Jenny 1932- DLB-40
Joseph and George.....................Y-99
Michael Joseph Limited DLB-112
Josephson, Matthew 1899-1978 ....DLB-4
Josephus, Flavius 37-100................DLB-176
Josephy, Alvin M., Jr.
 Tribute to Alfred A. Knopf Y-84
Josiah Allen's Wife (see Holley, Marietta)
Josipovici, Gabriel 1940- DLB-14, 319
Josselyn, John ?-1675 ....DLB-24
Joudry, Patricia 1921-2000..............DLB-88
Jouve, Pierre Jean 1887-1976 ....DLB-258
Jovanovich, William 1920-2001 ....Y-01
 Into the Past: William Jovanovich's
 Reflections on Publishing Y-02
 [Response to Ken Auletta].............Y-97
 The Temper of the West: William
 Jovanovich Y-02
 Tribute to Charles Scribner Jr...........Y-95
Jovine, Francesco 1902-1950 ....DLB-264
Jovine, Giuseppe 1922- DLB-128
Joyaux, Philippe (see Sollers, Philippe)
Joyce, Adrien (see Eastman, Carol)
Joyce, James 1882-1941
 ....DLB-10, 19, 36, 162, 247; CDBLB-6
 Danis Rose and the Rendering of Ulysses....Y-97
 James Joyce Centenary: Dublin, 1982......Y-82
 James Joyce Conference Y-85
 A Joyce (Con)Text: Danis Rose and the
 Remaking of Ulysses.................Y-97
 The National Library of Ireland's
 New James Joyce Manuscripts Y-02
 The New Ulysses......................Y-84
 Public Domain and the Violation of
 Texts..........................Y-97
 The Quinn Draft of James Joyce's
 Circe Manuscript Y-00
 Stephen Joyce's Letter to the Editor of
 The Irish Times Y-97
 Ulysses, Reader's Edition: First Reactions...Y-97
 We See the Editor at Work Y-97
 Whose Ulysses? The Function of Editing...Y-97
Jozsef, Attila 1905-1937 .....DLB-215; CDWLB-4

San Juan de la Cruz 1542-1591 ....DLB-318
Juarroz, Roberto 1925-1995............DLB-283
Orange Judd Publishing Company DLB-49
Judd, Sylvester 1813-1853 ....DLB-1, 243
Judith circa 930 ....DLB-146
Juel-Hansen, Erna 1845-1922 ....DLB-300
Julian of Norwich 1342-circa 1420......DLB-1146
Julius Caesar
 100 B.C.-44 B.C.........DLB-211; CDWLB-1
June, Jennie
 (see Croly, Jane Cunningham)
Jung, Carl Gustav 1875-1961...........DLB-296
Jung, Franz 1888-1963................DLB-118
Jünger, Ernst 1895-1998......DLB-56; CDWLB-2
Der jüngere Titurel circa 1275 ....DLB-138
Jung-Stilling, Johann Heinrich
 1740-1817......................DLB-94
Junqueiro, Abílio Manuel Guerra
 1850-1923 ....DLB-287
Justice, Donald 1925- Y-83
Juvenal circa A.D. 60-circa A.D. 130
 ....DLB-211; CDWLB-1
The Juvenile Library
 (see M. J. Godwin and Company)

K

Kacew, Romain (see Gary, Romain)
Kafka, Franz 1883-1924......DLB-81; CDWLB-2
Kahn, Gus 1886-1941 ....DLB-265
Kahn, Roger 1927- DLB-171
Kaikō Takeshi 1939-1989 ....DLB-182
Káinn (Kristján Níels Jónsson/Kristjan
 Niels Julius) 1860-1936 ....DLB-293
Kaiser, Georg 1878-1945 ....DLB-124; CDWLB-2
Kaiserchronik circa 1147 ....DLB-148
Kaleb, Vjekoslav 1905- DLB-181
Kalechofsky, Roberta 1931- DLB-28
Kaler, James Otis 1848-1912 ....DLB-12, 42
Kalmar, Bert 1884-1947 ....DLB-265
Kamensky, Vasilii Vasil'evich
 1884-1961 ....DLB-295
Kames, Henry Home, Lord
 1696-1782 ....DLB-31, 104
Kamo no Chōmei (Kamo no Nagaakira)
 1153 or 1155-1216 ....DLB-203
Kamo no Nagaakira (see Kamo no Chōmei)
Kampmann, Christian 1939-1988 ....DLB-214
Kandel, Lenore 1932- DLB-16
Kane, Sarah 1971-1999 ....DLB-310
Kaneko, Lonny 1939- DLB-312
Kang, Younghill 1903-1972 ....DLB-312
Kanin, Garson 1912-1999 ....DLB-7
 A Tribute (to Marc Connelly)...........Y-80
Kaniuk, Yoram 1930- DLB-299

Kant, Hermann 1926- DLB-75	Keary, Annie 1825-1879 .... DLB-163	Kennedy, A. L. 1965- DLB-271
Kant, Immanuel 1724-1804. .... DLB-94	Keary, Eliza 1827-1918 .... DLB-240	Kennedy, Adrienne 1931- DLB-38
Kantemir, Antiokh Dmitrievich 1708-1744 .... DLB-150	Keating, H. R. F. 1926- DLB-87	Kennedy, John Pendleton 1795-1870. . . DLB-3, 248
Kantor, MacKinlay 1904-1977 .... DLB-9, 102	Keatley, Charlotte 1960- DLB-245	Kennedy, Leo 1907-2000. .... DLB-88
Kanze Kōjirō Nobumitsu 1435-1516 .... DLB-203	Keats, Ezra Jack 1916-1983. .... DLB-61	Kennedy, Margaret 1896-1967 .... DLB-36
Kanze Motokiyo (see Zeimi)	Keats, John 1795-1821 . . . DLB-96, 110; CDBLB-3	Kennedy, Patrick 1801-1873 .... DLB-159
Kaplan, Fred 1937- DLB-111	Keble, John 1792-1866 .... DLB-32, 55	Kennedy, Richard S. 1920- DLB-111; Y-02
Kaplan, Johanna 1942- DLB-28	Keckley, Elizabeth 1818?-1907 .... DLB-239	Kennedy, William 1928- DLB-143; Y-85
Kaplan, Justin 1925- DLB-111; Y-86	Keeble, John 1944- Y-83	Kennedy, X. J. 1929- DLB-5
Kaplinski, Jaan 1941- DLB-232	Keeffe, Barrie 1945- DLB-13, 245	Tribute to John Ciardi Y-86
Kapnist, Vasilii Vasilevich 1758?-1823 . . . DLB-150	Keeley, James 1867-1934. .... DLB-25	Kennelly, Brendan 1936- DLB-40
Karadžić, Vuk Stefanović 1787-1864 .... DLB-147; CDWLB-4	W. B. Keen, Cooke and Company DLB-49	Kenner, Hugh 1923-2003 .... DLB-67
Karamzin, Nikolai Mikhailovich 1766-1826. .... DLB-150	The Mystery of Carolyn Keene Y-02	Tribute to Cleanth Brooks Y-80
	Kefala, Antigone 1935- DLB-289	Mitchell Kennerley [publishing house] DLB-46
	Keillor, Garrison 1942- Y-87	Kenny, Maurice 1929- DLB-175
Karinthy, Frigyes 1887-1938 .... DLB-215	Keith, Marian (Mary Esther MacGregor) 1874?-1961 .... DLB-92	Kent, Frank R. 1877-1958 .... DLB-29
Karmel, Ilona 1925-2000 .... DLB-299		Kenyon, Jane 1947-1995 .... DLB-120
Karnad, Girish 1938- DLB-323	Keller, Gary D. 1943- DLB-82	Kenzheev, Bakhyt Shkurullaevich 1950- DLB-285
Karsch, Anna Louisa 1722-1791 .... DLB-97	Keller, Gottfried 1819-1890 .... DLB-129; CDWLB-2	
Kasack, Hermann 1896-1966 .... DLB-69	Keller, Helen 1880-1968 .... DLB-303	Keough, Hugh Edmund 1864-1912 ......DLB-171
Kasai Zenzō 1887-1927 .... DLB-180	Kelley, Edith Summers 1884-1956 .... DLB-9	Keppler and Schwartzmann DLB-49
Kaschnitz, Marie Luise 1901-1974 .... DLB-69	Kelley, Emma Dunham ?-? DLB-221	Ker, John, third Duke of Roxburghe 1740-1804. .... DLB-213
Kassák, Lajos 1887-1967 .... DLB-215	Kelley, Florence 1859-1932. .... DLB-303	Ker, N. R. 1908-1982 .... DLB-201
Kaštelan, Jure 1919-1990 .... DLB-147	Kelley, William Melvin 1937- DLB-33	Keralio-Robert, Louise-Félicité de 1758-1822. .... DLB-313
Kästner, Erich 1899-1974 .... DLB-56	Kellogg, Ansel Nash 1832-1886 .... DLB-23	
Kataev, Evgenii Petrovich (see Il'f, Il'ia and Petrov, Evgenii)	Kellogg, Steven 1941- DLB-61	Kerlan, Irvin 1912-1963 ....DLB-187
	Kelly, George E. 1887-1974 ....DLB-7, 249	Kermode, Frank 1919- DLB-242
Kataev, Valentin Petrovich 1897-1986. . . . DLB-272	Kelly, Hugh 1739-1777 .... DLB-89	Kern, Jerome 1885-1945 ....DLB-187
Katenin, Pavel Aleksandrovich 1792-1853. .... DLB-205	Kelly, Piet and Company DLB-49	Kernaghan, Eileen 1939- DLB-251
Kattan, Naim 1928- DLB-53	Kelly, Robert 1935- DLB-5, 130, 165	Kerner, Justinus 1786-1862 .... DLB-90
Katz, Steve 1935- Y-83	Kelman, James 1946- DLB-194, 319, 326	Kerouac, Jack 1922-1969 . . DLB-2, 16, 237; DS-3; CDALB-1
Ka-Tzetnik 135633 (Yehiel Dinur) 1909-2001 .... DLB-299	Kelmscott Press. DLB-112	
	Kelton, Elmer 1926- DLB-256	Auction of Jack Kerouac's On the Road Scroll. Y-01
Kauffman, Janet 1945- DLB-218; Y-86	Kemble, E. W. 1861-1933. .... DLB-188	
Kauffmann, Samuel 1898-1971 .... DLB-127	Kemble, Fanny 1809-1893 .... DLB-32	The Jack Kerouac Revival Y-95
Kaufman, Bob 1925-1986. .... DLB-16, 41	Kemelman, Harry 1908-1996 .... DLB-28	"Re-meeting of Old Friends": The Jack Kerouac Conference. Y-82
Kaufman, George S. 1889-1961 .... DLB-7	Kempe, Margery circa 1373-1438 .... DLB-146	
Kaufmann, Walter 1921-1980. ....DLB-279	Kempinski, Tom 1938- DLB-310	Statement of Correction to "The Jack Kerouac Revival" Y-96
Kavan, Anna (Helen Woods Ferguson Edmonds) 1901-1968. .... DLB-255	Kempner, Friederike 1836-1904 .... DLB-129	Kerouac, Jan 1952-1996 .... DLB-16
	Kempowski, Walter 1929- DLB-75	Charles H. Kerr and Company DLB-49
Kavanagh, P. J. 1931- DLB-40	Kenan, Randall 1963- DLB-292	Kerr, Orpheus C. (see Newell, Robert Henry)
Kavanagh, Patrick 1904-1967 .... DLB-15, 20	Claude Kendall [publishing company] DLB-46	Kersh, Gerald 1911-1968 .... DLB-255
Kaverin, Veniamin Aleksandrovich (Veniamin Aleksandrovich Zil'ber) 1902-1989 .... DLB-272	Kendall, Henry 1839-1882 .... DLB-230	Kertész, Imre. DLB-299; Y-02
	Kendall, May 1861-1943. .... DLB-240	Kesey, Ken 1935-2001 .... DLB-2, 16, 206; CDALB-6
Kawabata Yasunari 1899-1972 .... DLB-180	Kendell, George 1809-1867 .... DLB-43	
Kay, Guy Gavriel 1954- DLB-251	Keneally, Thomas 1935- DLB-289, 299, 326	Kessel, Joseph 1898-1979 .... DLB-72
Kaye-Smith, Sheila 1887-1956 .... DLB-36	Kenedy, P. J., and Sons. DLB-49	Kessel, Martin 1901-1990 .... DLB-56
Kazakov, Iurii Pavlovich 1927-1982 ..... DLB-302	Kenkō circa 1283-circa 1352. .... DLB-203	Kesten, Hermann 1900-1996 .... DLB-56
Kazin, Alfred 1915-1998 .... DLB-67	Kenna, Peter 1930-1987 .... DLB-289	Keun, Irmgard 1905-1982 .... DLB-69
Keane, John B. 1928-2002 .... DLB-13	Kennan, George 1845-1924 .... DLB-189	Key, Ellen 1849-1926 .... DLB-259
		Key and Biddle. DLB-49

Keynes, Sir Geoffrey 1887-1982 . . . . DLB-201	King, Clarence 1842-1901 . . . . DLB-12	Kitchin, C. H. B. 1895-1967 . . . . DLB-77
Keynes, John Maynard 1883-1946 . . . . DS-10	King, Florence 1936- Y-85	Kittredge, William 1932- DLB-212, 244
Keyserling, Eduard von 1855-1918 . . . . DLB-66	King, Francis 1923- DLB-15, 139	Kiukhel'beker, Vil'gel'm Karlovich 1797-1846 . . . . DLB-205
al-Khalil ibn Ahmad circa 718-791 . . . . DLB-311	King, Grace 1852-1932 . . . . DLB-12, 78	Kizer, Carolyn 1925- DLB-5, 169
Khan, Adib 1949- DLB-323	King, Harriet Hamilton 1840-1920 . . . . . . DLB-199	Kjaerstad, Jan 1953- DLB-297
Khan, Ismith 1925-2002 . . . . DLB-125	King, Henry 1592-1669 . . . . DLB-126	Klabund 1890-1928 . . . . DLB-66
al-Khansa' fl. late sixth-mid seventh centuries DLB-311	Solomon King [publishing house] DLB-49	Klaj, Johann 1616-1656 . . . . DLB-164
Kharitonov, Evgenii Vladimirovich 1941-1981 . . . . DLB-285	King, Stephen 1947- DLB-143; Y-80	Klappert, Peter 1942- DLB-5
Kharitonov, Mark Sergeevich 1937- DLB-285	King, Susan Petigru 1824-1875 . . . . DLB-239	Klass, Philip (see Tenn, William)
Khaytov, Nikolay 1919- DLB-181	King, Thomas 1943- DLB-175	Klein, A. M. 1909-1972 . . . . DLB-68
Khemnitser, Ivan Ivanovich 1745-1784 . . . . DLB-150	King, Woodie, Jr. 1937- DLB-38	Kleist, Ewald von 1715-1759 . . . . DLB-97
Kheraskov, Mikhail Matveevich 1733-1807 . . . . DLB-150	Kinglake, Alexander William 1809-1891 . . . . DLB-55, 166	Kleist, Heinrich von 1777-1811 . . . . DLB-90; CDWLB-2
Khlebnikov, Velimir 1885-1922 . . . . DLB-295	Kingo, Thomas 1634-1703 . . . . DLB-300	Klíma, Ivan 1931- DLB-232; CDWLB-4
Khodasevich, Vladislav 1886-1939 . . . . . . DLB-317	Kingsbury, Donald 1929- DLB-251	Klimentev, Andrei Platonovic (see Platonov, Andrei Platonovich)
Khomiakov, Aleksei Stepanovich 1804-1860 . . . . DLB-205	Kingsley, Charles 1819-1875 . . . . DLB-21, 32, 163, 178, 190	Klinger, Friedrich Maximilian 1752-1831 . . . . DLB-94
Khristov, Boris 1945- DLB-181	Kingsley, Henry 1830-1876 . . . . DLB-21, 230	Kliuev, Nikolai Alekseevich 1884-1937 . . . DLB-295
Khvoshchinskaia, Nadezhda Dmitrievna 1824-1889 . . . . DLB-238	Kingsley, Mary Henrietta 1862-1900 . . . . . DLB-174	Kliushnikov, Viktor Petrovich 1841-1892 . . . . DLB-238
Khvostov, Dmitrii Ivanovich 1757-1835 . . . . DLB-150	Kingsley, Sidney 1906-1995 . . . . DLB-7	Klopfer, Donald S. Impressions of William Faulkner Y-97
Kibirov, Timur Iur'evich (Timur Iur'evich Zapoev) 1955- DLB-285	Kingsmill, Hugh 1889-1949 . . . . DLB-149	Oral History Interview with Donald S. Klopfer Y-97
Kidd, Adam 1802?-1831 . . . . DLB-99	Kingsolver, Barbara 1955- DLB-206; CDALB-7	Tribute to Alfred A. Knopf Y-84
William Kidd [publishing house] DLB-106	Kingston, Maxine Hong 1940- . . DLB-173, 212, 312; Y-80; CDALB-7	Klopstock, Friedrich Gottlieb 1724-1803 . . . . DLB-97
Kidde, Harald 1878-1918 . . . . DLB-300	Kingston, William Henry Giles 1814-1880 . . . . DLB-163	Klopstock, Meta 1728-1758 . . . . DLB-97
Kidder, Tracy 1945- DLB-185	Kinnan, Mary Lewis 1763-1848 . . . . DLB-200	Kluge, Alexander 1932- DLB-75
Kiely, Benedict 1919- DLB-15, 319	Kinnell, Galway 1927- DLB-5; Y-87	Kluge, P. F. 1942- Y-02
Kieran, John 1892-1981 . . . . DLB-171	Kinsella, John 1963- DLB-325	Knapp, Joseph Palmer 1864-1951 . . . . DLB-91
Kierkegaard, Søren 1813-1855 . . . . DLB-300	Kinsella, Thomas 1928- DLB-27	Knapp, Samuel Lorenzo 1783-1838 . . . . DLB-59
Kies, Marietta 1853-1899 . . . . DLB-270	Kipling, Rudyard 1865-1936 . . . . DLB-19, 34, 141, 156; CDBLB-5	J. J. and P. Knapton [publishing house] . . . DLB-154
Kiggins and Kellogg DLB-49	Kipphardt, Heinar 1922-1982 . . . . DLB-124	Kniazhnin, Iakov Borisovich 1740-1791 . . . . DLB-150
Kiley, Jed 1889-1962 . . . . DLB-4	Kirby, William 1817-1906 . . . . DLB-99	Knickerbocker, Diedrich (see Irving, Washington)
Kilgore, Bernard 1908-1967 . . . . DLB-127	Kircher, Athanasius 1602-1680 . . . . DLB-164	Knigge, Adolph Franz Friedrich Ludwig, Freiherr von 1752-1796 . . . . DLB-94
Kilian, Crawford 1941- DLB-251	Kireevsky, Ivan Vasil'evich 1806-1856 . . . . DLB-198	Charles Knight and Company DLB-106
Killens, John Oliver 1916-1987 . . . . DLB-33	Kireevsky, Petr Vasil'evich 1808-1856 . . . . DLB-205	Knight, Damon 1922-2002 . . . . DLB-8
Tribute to Julian Mayfield Y-84	Kirk, Hans 1898-1962 . . . . DLB-214	Knight, Etheridge 1931-1992 . . . . DLB-41
Killigrew, Anne 1660-1685 . . . . DLB-131	Kirk, John Foster 1824-1904 . . . . DLB-79	Knight, John S. 1894-1981 . . . . DLB-29
Killigrew, Thomas 1612-1683 . . . . DLB-58	Kirkconnell, Watson 1895-1977 . . . . DLB-68	Knight, Sarah Kemble 1666-1727 . . . . . DLB-24, 200
Kilmer, Joyce 1886-1918 . . . . DLB-45	Kirkland, Caroline M. 1801-1864 . . . . DLB-3, 73, 74, 250; DS-13	Knight-Bruce, G. W. H. 1852-1896 . . . . . . DLB-174
Kilroy, Thomas 1934- DLB-233	Kirkland, Joseph 1830-1893 . . . . DLB-12	Knister, Raymond 1899-1932 . . . . DLB-68
Kilwardby, Robert circa 1215-1279 . . . . . . DLB-115	Francis Kirkman [publishing house] DLB-170	Knoblock, Edward 1874-1945 . . . . DLB-10
Kilworth, Garry 1941- DLB-261	Kirkpatrick, Clayton 1915-2004 . . . . DLB-127	Knopf, Alfred A. 1892-1984 . . . . Y-84
Kim, Anatolii Andreevich 1939- DLB-285	Kirkup, James 1918- DLB-27	Knopf to Hammett: The Editoral Correspondence Y-00
Kimball, Richard Burleigh 1816-1892 . . . . DLB-202	Kirouac, Conrad (see Marie-Victorin, Frère)	Alfred A. Knopf [publishing house] DLB-46
Kincaid, Jamaica 1949- DLB-157, 227; CDALB-7; CDWLB-3	Kirsch, Sarah 1935- DLB-75	Knorr von Rosenroth, Christian 1636-1689 . . . . DLB-168
Kinck, Hans Ernst 1865-1926 . . . . DLB-297	Kirst, Hans Hellmut 1914-1989 . . . . DLB-69	
King, Charles 1844-1933 . . . . DLB-186	Kiš, Danilo 1935-1989 . . . . . . DLB-181; CDWLB-4	
	Kita Morio 1927- DLB-182	
	Kitcat, Mabel Greenhow 1859-1922 . . . . . DLB-135	Knowles, John 1926-2001 . . . . . . DLB-6; CDALB-6

Cumulative Index

Knox, Frank 1874-1944 .... DLB-29
Knox, John circa 1514-1572 .... DLB-132
Knox, John Armoy 1850-1906 .... DLB-23
Knox, Lucy 1845-1884 .... DLB-240
Knox, Ronald Arbuthnott 1888-1957 .... DLB-77
Knox, Thomas Wallace 1835-1896...... DLB-189
Knudsen, Jakob 1858-1917 .... DLB-300
Knut, Dovid 1900-1955 .... DLB-317
Kobayashi Takiji 1903-1933 .... DLB-180
Kober, Arthur 1900-1975 .... DLB-11
Kobiakova, Aleksandra Petrovna
   1823-1892 .... DLB-238
Kocbek, Edvard 1904-1981 ...DLB-147; CDWLB-4
Koch, C. J. 1932- DLB-289
Koch, Howard 1902-1995.............. DLB-26
Koch, Kenneth 1925-2002 .... DLB-5
Kōda Rohan 1867-1947 .... DLB-180
Koehler, Ted 1894-1973 .... DLB-265
Koenigsberg, Moses 1879-1945.......... DLB-25
Koeppen, Wolfgang 1906-1996......... DLB-69
Koertge, Ronald 1940- DLB-105
Koestler, Arthur 1905-1983 ...... Y-83; CDBLB-7
Kohn, John S. Van E. 1906-1976........ DLB-187
Kokhanovskaia
   (see Sokhanskaia, Nadezhda Stepanova)
Kokoschka, Oskar 1886-1980.......... DLB-124
Kolatkar, Arun 1932-2004 .... DLB-323
Kolb, Annette 1870-1967............. DLB-66
Kolbenheyer, Erwin Guido
   1878-1962................... DLB-66, 124
Kolleritsch, Alfred 1931- DLB-85
Kolodny, Annette 1941- DLB-67
Koltès, Bernard-Marie 1948-1989....... DLB-321
Kol'tsov, Aleksei Vasil'evich
   1809-1842 .... DLB-205
Komarov, Matvei circa 1730-1812....... DLB-150
Komroff, Manuel 1890-1974............ DLB-4
Komunyakaa, Yusef 1947- DLB-120
Kondoleon, Harry 1955-1994.......... DLB-266
Koneski, Blaže 1921-1993... DLB-181; CDWLB-4
Konigsburg, E. L. 1930- DLB-52
Konparu Zenchiku 1405-1468? DLB-203
Konrád, György 1933- DLB-232; CDWLB-4
Konrad von Würzburg
   circa 1230-1287 .... DLB-138
Konstantinov, Aleko 1863-1897 .... DLB-147
Konwicki, Tadeusz 1926- DLB-232
Koontz, Dean 1945- DLB-292
Kooser, Ted 1939- DLB-105
Kopit, Arthur 1937- DLB-7
Kops, Bernard 1926?- DLB-13
Kornbluth, C. M. 1923-1958 .... DLB-8

Körner, Theodor 1791-1813........... DLB-90
Kornfeld, Paul 1889-1942............ DLB-118
Korolenko, Vladimir Galaktionovich
   1853-1921 .... DLB-277
Kosinski, Jerzy 1933-1991........ DLB-2, 299; Y-82
Kosmač, Ciril 1910-1980 .... DLB-181
Kosovel, Srečko 1904-1926........... DLB-147
Kostrov, Ermil Ivanovich 1755-1796 ..... DLB-150
Kotzebue, August von 1761-1819 .... DLB-94
Kotzwinkle, William 1938- DLB-173
Kovačić, Ante 1854-1889 .... DLB-147
Kovalevskaia, Sof'ia Vasil'evna
   1850-1891 .... DLB-277
Kovič, Kajetan 1931- DLB-181
Kozlov, Ivan Ivanovich 1779-1840....... DLB-205
Kracauer, Siegfried 1889-1966 .... DLB-296
Kraf, Elaine 1946- Y-81
Kramer, Jane 1938- DLB-185
Kramer, Larry 1935- DLB-249
Kramer, Mark 1944- DLB-185
Kranjčević, Silvije Strahimir 1865-1908 .. DLB-147
Krasko, Ivan 1876-1958 .... DLB-215
Krasna, Norman 1909-1984 .... DLB-26
Kraus, Hans Peter 1907-1988 .... DLB-187
Kraus, Karl 1874-1936 .... DLB-118
Krause, Herbert 1905-1976............ DLB-256
Krauss, Ruth 1911-1993.............. DLB-52
Krauth, Nigel 1949- DLB-325
Kreisel, Henry 1922-1991............. DLB-88
Krestovsky V.
   (see Khvoshchinskaia, Nadezhda Dmitrievna)
Krestovsky, Vsevolod Vladimirovich
   1839-1895 .... DLB-238
Kreuder, Ernst 1903-1972............. DLB-69
Krėvė-Mickevičius, Vincas 1882-1954 ... DLB-220
Kreymborg, Alfred 1883-1966 .... DLB-4, 54
Krieger, Murray 1923-2000 .... DLB-67
Krim, Seymour 1922-1989............. DLB-16
Kripke, Saul 1940- DLB-279
Kristensen, Tom 1893-1974 .... DLB-214
Kristeva, Julia 1941- DLB-242
Kristján Níels Jónsson/Kristjan Niels Julius
   (see Káinn)
Kritzer, Hyman W. 1918-2002 .... Y-02
Krivulin, Viktor Borisovich 1944-2001... DLB-285
Krleža, Miroslav
   1893-1981 .... DLB-147; CDWLB-4
Krock, Arthur 1886-1974 .... DLB-29
Kroetsch, Robert 1927- DLB-53
Kropotkin, Petr Alekseevich 1842-1921 ..DLB-277
Kross, Jaan 1920- DLB-232
Kruchenykh, Aleksei Eliseevich
   1886-1968 .... DLB-295

Krúdy, Gyula 1878-1933.............. DLB-215
Krutch, Joseph Wood
   1893-1970................DLB-63, 206, 275
Krylov, Ivan Andreevich 1769-1844 ..... DLB-150
Krymov, Iurii Solomonovich
   (Iurii Solomonovich Beklemishev)
   1908-1941 ....DLB-272
Kubin, Alfred 1877-1959.............. DLB-81
Kubrick, Stanley 1928-1999 .... DLB-26
Kudrun circa 1230-1240.............. DLB-138
Kuffstein, Hans Ludwig von 1582-1656.. DLB-164
Kuhlmann, Quirinus 1651-1689........ DLB-168
Kuhn, Thomas S. 1922-1996 ....DLB-279
Kuhnau, Johann 1660-1722 .... DLB-168
Kukol'nik, Nestor Vasil'evich
   1809-1868 .... DLB-205
Kukučín, Martin
   1860-1928 ....DLB-215; CDWLB-4
Kumin, Maxine 1925- DLB-5
Kuncewicz, Maria 1895-1989 .... DLB-215
Kundera, Milan 1929- DLB-232; CDWLB-4
Kunene, Mazisi 1930- DLB-117
Kunikida Doppo 1869-1908 .... DLB-180
Kunitz, Stanley 1905-2006 .... DLB-48
Kunjufu, Johari M. (see Amini, Johari M.)
Kunnert, Gunter 1929- DLB-75
Kunze, Reiner 1933- DLB-75
Kuo, Helena 1911-1999 .... DLB-312
Kupferberg, Tuli 1923- DLB-16
Kuprin, Aleksandr Ivanovich
   1870-1938 .... DLB-295
Kuraev, Mikhail Nikolaevich 1939- ... DLB-285
Kurahashi Yumiko 1935- DLB-182
Kureishi, Hanif 1954- DLB-194, 245
Kürnberger, Ferdinand 1821-1879 ..... DLB-129
Kurz, Isolde 1853-1944.............. DLB-66
Kusenberg, Kurt 1904-1983 .... DLB-69
Kushchevsky, Ivan Afanas'evich
   1847-1876 .... DLB-238
Kushner, Tony 1956- DLB-228
Kuttner, Henry 1915-1958 .... DLB-8
Kuzmin, Mikhail Alekseevich
   1872-1936..................... DLB-295
Kuznetsov, Anatoli
   1929-1979................. DLB-299, 302
Kyd, Thomas 1558-1594 .... DLB-62
Kyffin, Maurice circa 1560?-1598........ DLB-136
Kyger, Joanne 1934- DLB-16
Kyne, Peter B. 1880-1957 .... DLB-78
Kyōgoku Tamekane 1254-1332 .... DLB-203
Kyrklund, Willy 1921- DLB-257

L

L. E. L. (see Landon, Letitia Elizabeth)

Labé, Louise 1520?-1566...............DLB-327	Lamb, Charles 1775-1834......DLB-93, 107, 163; CDBLB-3	Larcom, Lucy 1824-1893.........DLB-221, 243
Laberge, Albert 1871-1960..............DLB-68	Lamb, Mary 1764-1874...............DLB-163	Lardner, John 1912-1960...............DLB-171
Laberge, Marie 1950- DLB-60	Lambert, Angela 1940- DLB-271	Lardner, Ring 1885-1933 ......DLB-11, 25, 86, 171; DS-16; CDALB-4
Labiche, Eugène 1815-1888...........DLB-192	Lambert, Anne-Thérèse de (Anne-Thérèse de Marguenat de Courcelles, marquise de Lambert) 1647-1733....................DLB-313	Lardner 100: Ring Lardner Centennial Symposium.............Y-85
Labrunie, Gerard (see Nerval, Gerard de)	Lambert, Betty 1933-1983.............DLB-60	Lardner, Ring, Jr. 1915-2000.......DLB-26, Y-00
La Bruyère, Jean de 1645-1696.........DLB-268	La Mettrie, Julien Offroy de 1709-1751....................DLB-313	Larivey, Pierre de 1541-1619...........DLB-327
La Calprenède 1609?-1663............DLB-268	Lamm, Donald Goodbye, Gutenberg? A Lecture at the New York Public Library, 18 April 1995...................Y-95	Larkin, Philip 1922-1985......DLB-27; CDBLB-8
Lacan, Jacques 1901-1981.............DLB-296		The Philip Larkin Society..............Y-99
La Capria, Raffaele 1922- DLB-196		La Roche, Sophie von 1730-1807.........DLB-94
La Ceppède, Jean de 1550?-1623........DLB-327	Lamming, George 1927- DLB-125; CDWLB-3	La Rochefoucauld, François duc de 1613-1680......................DLB-268
La Chaussée, Pierre-Claude Nivelle de 1692-1754......................DLB-313	La Mothe Le Vayer, François de 1588-1672......................DLB-268	La Rocque, Gilbert 1943-1984.........DLB-60
Laclos, Pierre-Ambroise-François Choderlos de 1741-1803......................DLB-313	L'Amour, Louis 1908-1988........DLB-206; Y-80	Laroque de Roquebrune, Robert (see Roquebrune, Robert de)
Dangerous Acquaintances.............DLB-314	Lampman, Archibald 1861-1899.........DLB-92	Larrick, Nancy 1910-2004..............DLB-61
Lacombe, Patrice (see Trullier-Lacombe, Joseph Patrice)	Lamson, Wolffe and Company..........DLB-49	Lars, Claudia 1899-1974..............DLB-283
	Lancer Books.......................DLB-46	Larsen, Nella 1893-1964..............DLB-51
Lacretelle, Jacques de 1888-1985.........DLB-65	Lanchester, John 1962-................DLB-267	Larsen, Thøger 1875-1928.............DLB-300
Lacy, Ed 1911-1968..................DLB-226	Lander, Peter (see Cunningham, Peter)	Larson, Clinton F. 1919-1994..........DLB-256
Lacy, Sam 1903- DLB-171	Landesman, Jay 1919- and Landesman, Fran 1927-.............DLB-16	La Sale, Antoine de circa 1386-1460/1467..............DLB-208
Ladd, Joseph Brown 1764-1786..........DLB-37		
La Farge, Oliver 1901-1963..............DLB-9	Landolfi, Tommaso 1908-1979..........DLB-177	Las Casas, Fray Bartolomé de 1474-1566......................DLB-318
Lafayette, Marie-Madeleine, comtesse de 1634-1693......................DLB-268	Landon, Letitia Elizabeth 1802-1838......DLB-96	Lasch, Christopher 1932-1994..........DLB-246
	Landor, Walter Savage 1775-1864....DLB-93, 107	Lasdun, James 1958- DLB-319
Laffan, Mrs. R. S. de Courcy (see Adams, Bertha Leith)	Landry, Napoléon-P. 1884-1956..........DLB-92	Lasker-Schüler, Else 1869-1945......DLB-66, 124
Lafferty, R. A. 1914-2002................DLB-8	Landvik, Lorna 1954- DLB-292	Lasnier, Rina 1915-1997...............DLB-88
La Flesche, Francis 1857-1932..........DLB-175	Lane, Charles 1800-1870.......DLB-1, 223; DS-5	Lassalle, Ferdinand 1825-1864..........DLB-129
La Fontaine, Jean de 1621-1695.........DLB-268	Lane, F. C. 1885-1984................DLB-241	*Last Orders*, 1996 Booker Prize winner, Graham Swift...................DLB-326
Laforet, Carmen 1921-2004............DLB-322	Lane, Laurence W. 1890-1967...........DLB-91	
Laforge, Jules 1860-1887..............DLB-217	Lane, M. Travis 1934- DLB-60	La Taille, Jean de 1534?-1611?..........DLB-327
Lagerkvist, Pär 1891-1974.............DLB-259	Lane, Patrick 1939- DLB-53	Late-Medieval Castilian Theater........DLB-286
Lagerlöf, Selma 1858-1940......................DLB-259	Lane, Pinkie Gordon 1923- DLB-41	Latham, Robert 1912-1995............DLB-201
	John Lane Company.................DLB-49	Lathan, Emma (Mary Jane Latsis [1927-1997] and Martha Henissart [1929-]).......DLB-306
Lagorio, Gina 1922- DLB-196	Laney, Al 1896-1988................DLB-4, 171	
La Guma, Alex 1925-1985.......DLB-117, 225; CDWLB-3	Lang, Andrew 1844-1912......DLB-98, 141, 184	Lathrop, Dorothy P. 1891-1980.........DLB-22
	Langer, Susanne K. 1895-1985..........DLB-270	Lathrop, George Parsons 1851-1898......DLB-71
Lahaise, Guillaume (see Delahaye, Guy)	Langevin, André 1927- DLB-60	Lathrop, John, Jr. 1772-1820............DLB-37
La Harpe, Jean-François de 1739-1803....DLB-313	Langford, David 1953- DLB-261	Latimer, Hugh 1492?-1555............DLB-136
Lahiri, Jhumpa 1967- DLB-323	Langgässer, Elisabeth 1899-1950........DLB-69	Latimore, Jewel Christine McLawler (see Amini, Johari M.)
Lahontan, Louis-Armand de Lom d'Arce, Baron de 1666-1715?..............DLB-99	Langhorne, John 1735-1779............DLB-109	
	Langland, William circa 1330-circa 1400..DLB-146	Latin Literature, The Uniqueness of....DLB-211
Lai He 1894-1943....................DLB-328	Langton, Anna 1804-1893..............DLB-99	La Tour du Pin, Patrice de 1911-1975....DLB-258
Laing, Kojo 1946- DLB-157	Lanham, Edwin 1904-1979.............DLB-4	Latymer, William 1498-1583...........DLB-132
Laird, Caroreth 1895-1983...............Y-82	Lanier, Sidney 1842-1881.........DLB-64; DS-13	Laube, Heinrich 1806-1884............DLB-133
Laird and Lee......................DLB-49	Lanyer, Aemilia 1569-1645.............DLB-121	Laud, William 1573-1645.............DLB-213
Lake, Paul 1951- DLB-282	Lao She 1899-1966...................DLB-328	Laughlin, James 1914-1997.....DLB-48; Y-96, 97
Lalić, Ivan V. 1931-1996..............DLB-181	Lapointe, Gatien 1931-1983.............DLB-88	A Tribute [to Henry Miller].........Y-80
Lalić, Mihailo 1914-1992..............DLB-181	Lapointe, Paul-Marie 1929- DLB-88	Tribute to Albert Erskine............Y-93
Lalonde, Michèle 1937- DLB-60	La Ramée, Pierre de (Petrus Ramus, Peter Ramus) 1515-1572....................DLB-327	Tribute to Kenneth Rexroth..........Y-82
Lamantia, Philip 1927- DLB-16		Tribute to Malcolm Cowley..........Y-89
Lamartine, Alphonse de 1790-1869......................DLB-217		Laumer, Keith 1925-1993...............DLB-8
Lamb, Lady Caroline 1785-1828......................DLB-116		

Lauremberg, Johann 1590-1658 . . . . DLB-164

Laurence, Margaret 1926-1987 . . . . DLB-53

Laurentius von Schnüffis 1633-1702 . . . . . DLB-168

Laurents, Arthur 1918- DLB-26

Laurie, Annie (see Black, Winifred)

Laut, Agnes Christiana 1871-1936 . . . . DLB-92

Lauterbach, Ann 1942- DLB-193

Lautréamont, Isidore Lucien Ducasse,
Comte de 1846-1870 . . . . DLB-217

Lavater, Johann Kaspar 1741-1801 . . . . DLB-97

Lavin, Mary 1912-1996 . . . . DLB-15, 319

Law, John (see Harkness, Margaret)

Lawes, Henry 1596-1662 . . . . DLB-126

Lawler, Ray 1922- DLB-289

Lawless, Anthony (see MacDonald, Philip)

Lawless, Emily (The Hon. Emily Lawless)
1845-1913 . . . . DLB-240

Lawrence, D. H. 1885-1930
. . . . . DLB-10, 19, 36, 98, 162, 195; CDBLB-6

The D. H. Lawrence Society of
North America Y-00

Lawrence, David 1888-1973 . . . . DLB-29

Lawrence, Jerome 1915-2004 . . . . DLB-228

Lawrence, Seymour 1926-1994 . . . . Y-94

Tribute to Richard Yates Y-92

Lawrence, T. E. 1888-1935 . . . . DLB-195

The T. E. Lawrence Society Y-98

Lawson, George 1598-1678 . . . . DLB-213

Lawson, Henry 1867-1922 . . . . DLB-230

Lawson, John ?-1711 . . . . DLB-24

Lawson, John Howard 1894-1977 . . . . DLB-228

Lawson, Louisa Albury 1848-1920 . . . . . . DLB-230

Lawson, Robert 1892-1957 . . . . DLB-22

Lawson, Victor F. 1850-1925 . . . . DLB-25

Layard, Austen Henry 1817-1894 . . . . DLB-166

Layton, Irving 1912- DLB-88

LaZamon fl. circa 1200 . . . . DLB-146

Lazarević, Laza K. 1851-1890 . . . . DLB-147

Lazarus, George 1904-1997 . . . . DLB-201

Lazhechnikov, Ivan Ivanovich
1792-1869 . . . . DLB-198

Lea, Henry Charles 1825-1909 . . . . DLB-47

Lea, Sydney 1942- DLB-120, 282

Lea, Tom 1907-2001 . . . . DLB-6

Leacock, John 1729-1802 . . . . DLB-31

Leacock, Stephen 1869-1944 . . . . DLB-92

Lead, Jane Ward 1623-1704 . . . . DLB-131

Leadenhall Press DLB-106

"The Greatness of Southern Literature":
League of the South Institute for the
Study of Southern Culture and History
. . . . Y-02

Leakey, Caroline Woolmer 1827-1881 . . . . . DLB-230

Leapor, Mary 1722-1746 . . . . DLB-109

Lear, Edward 1812-1888 . . . . . . DLB-32, 163, 166

Leary, Timothy 1920-1996 . . . . DLB-16

W. A. Leary and Company DLB-49

Léautaud, Paul 1872-1956 . . . . DLB-65

Leavis, F. R. 1895-1978 . . . . DLB-242

Leavitt, David 1961- DLB-130

Leavitt and Allen DLB-49

Le Blond, Mrs. Aubrey 1861-1934 . . . . DLB-174

le Carré, John (David John Moore Cornwell)
1931- DLB-87; CDBLB-8

Tribute to Graham Greene Y-91

Tribute to George Greenfield Y-00

Lécavelé, Roland (see Dorgeles, Roland)

Lechlitner, Ruth 1901- DLB-48

Leclerc, Félix 1914-1988 . . . . DLB-60

Le Clézio, J. M. G. 1940- DLB-83

Leder, Rudolf (see Hermlin, Stephan)

Lederer, Charles 1910-1976 . . . . DLB-26

Ledwidge, Francis 1887-1917 . . . . DLB-20

Lee, Chang-rae 1965- DLB-312

Lee, Cherylene 1953- DLB-312

Lee, Dennis 1939- DLB-53

Lee, Don L. (see Madhubuti, Haki R.)

Lee, George W. 1894-1976 . . . . DLB-51

Lee, Gus 1946- DLB-312

Lee, Harper 1926- DLB-6; CDALB-1

Lee, Harriet 1757-1851 and
Lee, Sophia 1750-1824 . . . . DLB-39

Lee, Laurie 1914-1997 . . . . DLB-27

Lee, Leslie 1935- DLB-266

Lee, Li-Young 1957- DLB-165, 312

Lee, Manfred B. 1905-1971 . . . . DLB-137

Lee, Nathaniel circa 1645-1692 . . . . DLB-80

Lee, Robert E. 1918-1994 . . . . DLB-228

Lee, Sir Sidney 1859-1926 . . . . DLB-149, 184

"Principles of Biography," in
Elizabethan and Other Essays DLB-149

Lee, Tanith 1947- DLB-261

Lee, Vernon
1856-1935 . . . . DLB-57, 153, 156, 174, 178

Lee and Shepard DLB-49

Le Fanu, Joseph Sheridan
1814-1873 . . . . DLB-21, 70, 159, 178

Lefèvre d'Etaples, Jacques
1460?-1536 . . . . DLB-327

Leffland, Ella 1931- Y-84

le Fort, Gertrud von 1876-1971 . . . . DLB-66

Le Gallienne, Richard 1866-1947 . . . . DLB-4

Legaré, Hugh Swinton
1797-1843 . . . . DLB-3, 59, 73, 248

Legaré, James Mathewes 1823-1859 . . . DLB-3, 248

Léger, Antoine-J. 1880-1950 . . . . DLB-88

Leggett, William 1801-1839 . . . . DLB-250

Le Guin, Ursula K.
1929- DLB-8, 52, 256, 275; CDALB-6

Lehman, Ernest 1920- DLB-44

Lehmann, John 1907-1989 . . . . DLB-27, 100

John Lehmann Limited DLB-112

Lehmann, Rosamond 1901-1990 . . . . DLB-15

Lehmann, Wilhelm 1882-1968 . . . . DLB-56

Leiber, Fritz 1910-1992 . . . . DLB-8

Leibniz, Gottfried Wilhelm 1646-1716 . . . DLB-168

Leicester University Press DLB-112

Leigh, Carolyn 1926-1983 . . . . DLB-265

Leigh, W. R. 1866-1955 . . . . DLB-188

Leinster, Murray 1896-1975 . . . . DLB-8

Leiser, Bill 1898-1965 . . . . DLB-241

Leisewitz, Johann Anton 1752-1806 . . . . . . DLB-94

Leitch, Maurice 1933- DLB-14

Leithauser, Brad 1943- DLB-120, 282

Leland, Charles G. 1824-1903 . . . . DLB-11

Leland, John 1503?-1552 . . . . DLB-136

Lemaire de Belges, Jean 1473-? DLB-327

Lemay, Pamphile 1837-1918 . . . . DLB-99

Lemelin, Roger 1919-1992 . . . . DLB-88

Lemercier, Louis-Jean-Népomucène
1771-1840 . . . . DLB-192

Le Moine, James MacPherson 1825-1912 . DLB-99

Lemon, Mark 1809-1870 . . . . DLB-163

Le Moyne, Jean 1913-1996 . . . . DLB-88

Lemperly, Paul 1858-1939 . . . . DLB-187

Leñero, Vicente 1933- DLB-305

L'Engle, Madeleine 1918- DLB-52

Lennart, Isobel 1915-1971 . . . . DLB-44

Lennox, Charlotte 1729 or 1730-1804 . . . . DLB-39

Lenox, James 1800-1880 . . . . DLB-140

Lenski, Lois 1893-1974 . . . . DLB-22

Lentricchia, Frank 1940- DLB-246

Lenz, Hermann 1913-1998 . . . . DLB-69

Lenz, J. M. R. 1751-1792 . . . . DLB-94

Lenz, Siegfried 1926- DLB-75

León, Fray Luis de 1527-1591 . . . . DLB-318

Leonard, Elmore 1925- DLB-173, 226

Leonard, Hugh 1926- DLB-13

Leonard, William Ellery 1876-1944 . . . . . . DLB-54

Leong, Russell C. 1950- DLB-312

Leonov, Leonid Maksimovich
1899-1994 . . . . DLB-272

Leonowens, Anna 1834-1914 . . . . DLB-99, 166

Leont'ev, Konstantin Nikolaevich
1831-1891 . . . . DLB-277

Leopold, Aldo 1887-1948 . . . . DLB-275

LePan, Douglas 1914-1998 . . . . DLB-88

Lepik, Kalju 1920-1999 . . . . .DLB-232

Leprohon, Rosanna Eleanor 1829-1879. . . .DLB-99

Le Queux, William 1864-1927. . . . . .DLB-70

Lermontov, Mikhail Iur'evich
 1814-1841 . . . . .DLB-205

Lerner, Alan Jay 1918-1986 . . . . .DLB-265

Lerner, Max 1902-1992 . . . . .DLB-29

Lernet-Holenia, Alexander 1897-1976 . . . . .DLB-85

Le Rossignol, James 1866-1969 . . . . .DLB-92

Lesage, Alain-René 1668-1747 . . . . .DLB-313

Lescarbot, Marc circa 1570-1642 . . . . .DLB-99

LeSeur, William Dawson 1840-1917 . . . . . .DLB-92

LeSieg, Theo. (see Geisel, Theodor Seuss)

Leskov, Nikolai Semenovich
 1831-1895 . . . . .DLB-238

Leslie, Doris before 1902-1982 . . . . .DLB-191

Leslie, Eliza 1787-1858 . . . . .DLB-202

Leslie, Frank (Henry Carter)
 1821-1880 . . . . .DLB-43, 79

Frank Leslie [publishing house] DLB-49

Leśmian, Bolesław 1878-1937 . . . . .DLB-215

Lesperance, John 1835?-1891 . . . . .DLB-99

Lespinasse, Julie de 1732-1776 . . . . .DLB-313

Lessing, Bruno 1870-1940 . . . . .DLB-28

Lessing, Doris
 1919- DLB-15, 139; Y-85; CDBLB-8

Lessing, Gotthold Ephraim
 1729-1781 . . . . .DLB-97; CDWLB-2

The Lessing Society Y-00

L'Estoile, Pierre de 1546-1611 . . . . .DLB-327

Le Sueur, Meridel 1900-1996. . . . . .DLB-303

Lettau, Reinhard 1929-1996 . . . . .DLB-75

Letters from a Peruvian Woman, Françoise d'Issembourg
 de Graffigny DLB-314

The Hemingway Letters Project Finds
 an Editor Y-02

Lever, Charles 1806-1872. . . . . .DLB-21

Lever, Ralph ca. 1527-1585 . . . . .DLB-236

Leverson, Ada 1862-1933 . . . . .DLB-153

Levertov, Denise
 1923-1997 . . . . .DLB-5, 165; CDALB-7

Levi, Peter 1931-2000 . . . . .DLB-40

Levi, Primo 1919-1987. . . . . DLB-177, 299

Levien, Sonya 1888-1960. . . . . .DLB-44

Levin, Meyer 1905-1981 . . . . DLB-9, 28; Y-81

Levin, Phillis 1954- DLB-282

Lévinas, Emmanuel 1906-1995 . . . . .DLB-296

Levine, Norman 1923- DLB-88

Levine, Philip 1928- DLB-5

Levis, Larry 1946- DLB-120

Lévi-Strauss, Claude 1908- DLB-242

Levitov, Aleksandr Ivanovich
 1835?-1877 .DLB-277

Levy, Amy 1861-1889 . . . . .DLB-156, 240

Levy, Benn Wolfe 1900-1973 . . . . . . .DLB-13; Y-81

Levy, Deborah 1959- DLB-310

Lewald, Fanny 1811-1889 . . . . .DLB-129

Lewes, George Henry 1817-1878 . . . . .DLB-55, 144

 "Criticism in Relation to Novels"
  (1863) DLB-21

 The Principles of Success in Literature
  (1865) [excerpt]. DLB-57

Lewis, Agnes Smith 1843-1926 . . . . .DLB-174

Lewis, Alfred H. 1857-1914 . . . . .DLB-25, 186

Lewis, Alun 1915-1944 . . . . .DLB-20, 162

Lewis, C. Day (see Day Lewis, C.)

Lewis, C. I. 1883-1964. . . . . .DLB-270

Lewis, C. S. 1898-1963
 . . . . DLB-15, 100, 160, 255; CDBLB-7

 The New York C. S. Lewis Society Y-99

Lewis, Charles B. 1842-1924 . . . . .DLB-11

Lewis, David 1941-2001 . . . . .DLB-279

Lewis, Henry Clay 1825-1850. . . . . . . .DLB-3, 248

Lewis, Janet 1899-1999 . . . . .Y-87

 Tribute to Katherine Anne Porter Y-80

Lewis, Matthew Gregory
 1775-1818 . . . . DLB-39, 158, 178

Lewis, Meriwether 1774-1809 . . . . . .DLB-183, 186

Lewis, Norman 1908-2003 . . . . .DLB-204

Lewis, R. W. B. 1917-2002. . . . . .DLB-111

Lewis, Richard circa 1700-1734 . . . . .DLB-24

Lewis, Saunders 1893-1985 . . . . .DLB-310

Lewis, Sinclair
 1885-1951 . . . . . . .DLB-9, 102; DS-1; CDALB-4

 Sinclair Lewis Centennial Conference. Y-85

 The Sinclair Lewis Society Y-99

Lewis, Wilmarth Sheldon 1895-1979 . . . . .DLB-140

Lewis, Wyndham 1882-1957 . . . . .DLB-15

 Time and Western Man
  [excerpt] (1927). DLB-36

Lewisohn, Ludwig 1882-1955 . . .DLB-4, 9, 28, 102

Leyendecker, J. C. 1874-1951. . . . . .DLB-188

Leyner, Mark 1956- DLB-292

Lezama Lima, José 1910-1976 . . . . . .DLB-113, 283

Lézardière, Marie-Charlotte-Pauline Robert de
 1754-1835 . . . . .DLB-313

L'Heureux, John 1934- DLB-244

Libbey, Laura Jean 1862-1924 . . . . .DLB-221

Libedinsky, Iurii Nikolaevich
 1898-1959 . . . . .DLB-272

The Liberator .DLB-303

Library History Group Y-01

E-Books' Second Act in Libraries. Y-02

The Library of America. DLB-46

The Library of America: An Assessment
 After Two Decades Y-02

Licensing Act of 1737. . . . . .DLB-84

Leonard Lichfield I [publishing house] . . .DLB-170

Lichtenberg, Georg Christoph
 1742-1799 . . . . .DLB-94

The Liddle Collection Y-97

Lidman, Sara 1923-2004 . . . . .DLB-257

Lieb, Fred 1888-1980. . . . . .DLB-171

Liebling, A. J. 1904-1963 . . . . .DLB-4, 171

Lieutenant Murray (see Ballou, Maturin Murray)

Life and Times of Michael K, 1983 Booker Prize winner,
 J. M. Coetzee. DLB-326

Life of Pi, 2002 Booker Prize winner,
 Yann Martel DLB-326

Lighthall, William Douw 1857-1954 . . . . . .DLB-92

Lihn, Enrique 1929-1988. . . . . .DLB-283

Lilar, Françoise (see Mallet-Joris, Françoise)

Lili'uokalani, Queen 1838-1917. . . . . .DLB-221

Lillo, George 1691-1739. . . . . .DLB-84

Lilly, J. K., Jr. 1893-1966 . . . . .DLB-140

Lilly, Wait and Company DLB-49

Lily, William circa 1468-1522 . . . . .DLB-132

Lim, Shirley Geok-lin 1944- DLB-312

Lima, Jorge de 1893-1953 . . . . .DLB-307

Lima Barreto, Afonso Henriques de
 1881-1922 . . . . .DLB-307

Limited Editions Club DLB-46

Limón, Graciela 1938- DLB-209

Limonov, Eduard 1943- DLB-317

Lincoln and Edmands DLB-49

Lind, Jakov 1927- DLB-299

Linda Vilhjálmsdóttir 1958- DLB-293

Lindesay, Ethel Forence
 (see Richardson, Henry Handel)

Lindgren, Astrid 1907-2002 . . . . .DLB-257

Lindgren, Torgny 1938- DLB-257

Lindsay, Alexander William, Twenty-fifth
 Earl of Crawford 1812-1880 . . . . .DLB-184

Lindsay, Sir David circa 1485-1555 . . . . . .DLB-132

Lindsay, David 1878-1945 . . . . .DLB-255

Lindsay, Jack 1900-1990 . . . . .Y-84

Lindsay, Lady (Caroline Blanche
 Elizabeth Fitzroy Lindsay)
 1844-1912 . . . . .DLB-199

Lindsay, Norman 1879-1969 . . . . .DLB-260

Lindsay, Vachel
 1879-1931 . . . . .DLB-54; CDALB-3

The Line of Beauty, 2004 Booker Prize winner,
 Alan Hollinghurst DLB-326

Linebarger, Paul Myron Anthony
 (see Smith, Cordwainer)

Ling Shuhua 1900-1990. . . . . .DLB-328

Link, Arthur S. 1920-1998. . . . . .DLB-17

Linn, Ed 1922-2000 . . . . .DLB-241

Linn, John Blair 1777-1804. . . . . .DLB-37

Lins, Osman 1924-1978 . . . . .DLB-145, 307

Cumulative Index

Linton, Eliza Lynn 1822-1898 .... DLB-18
Linton, William James 1812-1897 .... DLB-32
Barnaby Bernard Lintot
   [publishing house] DLB-170
Lion Books DLB-46
Lionni, Leo 1910-1999 .... DLB-61
Lippard, George 1822-1854 .... DLB-202
Lippincott, Sara Jane Clarke
   1823-1904 .... DLB-43
J. B. Lippincott Company DLB-49
Lippmann, Walter 1889-1974 .... DLB-29
Lipton, Lawrence 1898-1975 .... DLB-16
Lisboa, Irene 1892-1958 .... DLB-287
Liscow, Christian Ludwig
   1701-1760 .... DLB-97
Lish, Gordon 1934- DLB-130
   Tribute to Donald Barthelme Y-89
   Tribute to James Dickey Y-97
Lisle, Charles-Marie-René Leconte de
   1818-1894 .... DLB-217
Lispector, Clarice
   1925?-1977 .... DLB-113, 307; CDWLB-3
LitCheck Website Y-01
Literary Awards and Honors Y-81-02
   Booker Prize Y-86, 96-98
   The Drue Heinz Literature Prize Y-82
   The Elmer Holmes Bobst Awards
     in Arts and Letters Y-87
   The Griffin Poetry Prize Y-00
   Literary Prizes [British] DLB-15, 207
   National Book Critics Circle
     Awards Y-00-01
   The National Jewish
     Book Awards Y-85
   Nobel Prize Y-80-02
   Winning an Edgar Y-98
The Literary Chronicle and Weekly Review
   1819-1828 .... DLB-110
Literary Periodicals:
   Callaloo Y-87
   Expatriates in Paris DS-15
   New Literary Periodicals:
     A Report for 1987 .... Y-87
   A Report for 1988 .... Y-88
   A Report for 1989 .... Y-89
   A Report for 1990 .... Y-90
   A Report for 1991 .... Y-91
   A Report for 1992 .... Y-92
   A Report for 1993 .... Y-93
Literary Research Archives
   The Anthony Burgess Archive at
     the Harry Ransom Humanities
     Research Center Y-98
   Archives of Charles Scribner's Sons DS-17
   Berg Collection of English and
     American Literature of the
     New York Public Library Y-83

The Bobbs-Merrill Archive at the
   Lilly Library, Indiana University Y-90
Die Fürstliche Bibliothek Corvey Y-96
Guide to the Archives of Publishers,
   Journals, and Literary Agents in
   North American Libraries Y-93
The Henry E. Huntington Library Y-92
The Humanities Research Center,
   University of Texas Y-82
The John Carter Brown Library Y-85
Kent State Special Collections Y-86
The Lilly Library Y-84
The Modern Literary Manuscripts
   Collection in the Special
   Collections of the Washington
   University Libraries Y-87
A Publisher's Archives: G. P. Putnam Y-92
Special Collections at Boston
   University Y-99
The University of Virginia Libraries Y-91
The William Charvat American Fiction
   Collection at the Ohio State
   University Libraries Y-92
Literary Societies Y-98–02
   The Margery Allingham Society Y-98
   The American Studies Association
     of Norway Y-00
   The Arnold Bennett Society Y-98
   The Association for the Study of
     Literature and Environment
     (ASLE) Y-99
   Belgian Luxembourg American Studies
     Association Y-01
   The E. F. Benson Society Y-98
   The Elizabeth Bishop Society Y-01
   The [Edgar Rice] Burroughs
     Bibliophiles Y-98
   The Byron Society of America Y-00
   The Lewis Carroll Society
     of North America Y-00
   The Willa Cather Pioneer Memorial
     and Education Foundation Y-00
   New Chaucer Society Y-00
   The Wilkie Collins Society Y-98
   The James Fenimore Cooper Society Y-01
   The Stephen Crane Society Y-98, 01
   The E. E. Cummings Society Y-01
   The James Dickey Society Y-99
   John Dos Passos Newsletter Y-00
   The Priory Scholars [Sir Arthur Conan
     Doyle] of New York Y-99
   The International Theodore Dreiser
     Society Y-01
   The Friends of the Dymock Poets Y-00
   The George Eliot Fellowship Y-99
   The T. S. Eliot Society: Celebration and
     Scholarship, 1980-1999 .... Y-99
   The Ralph Waldo Emerson Society Y-99
   The William Faulkner Society Y-99
   The C. S. Forester Society Y-00
   The Hamlin Garland Society Y-01

The [Elizabeth] Gaskell Society Y-98
The Charlotte Perkins Gilman Society ... Y-99
The Ellen Glasgow Society Y-01
Zane Grey's West Society Y-00
The Ivor Gurney Society Y-98
The Joel Chandler Harris Association Y-99
The Nathaniel Hawthorne Society Y-00
The [George Alfred] Henty Society Y-98
George Moses Horton Society Y-99
The William Dean Howells Society Y-01
WW2 HMSO Paperbacks Society Y-98
American Humor Studies Association Y-99
International Society for Humor Studies ... Y-99
The W. W. Jacobs Appreciation Society .. Y-98
The Richard Jefferies Society Y-98
The Jerome K. Jerome Society Y-98
The D. H. Lawrence Society of
   North America Y-00
The T. E. Lawrence Society Y-98
The [Gotthold] Lessing Society Y-00
The New York C. S. Lewis Society Y-99
The Sinclair Lewis Society Y-99
The Jack London Research Center Y-00
The Jack London Society Y-99
The Cormac McCarthy Society Y-99
The Melville Society Y-01
The Arthur Miller Society Y-01
The Milton Society of America Y-00
International Marianne Moore Society ... Y-98
International Nabokov Society Y-99
The Vladimir Nabokov Society Y-01
The Flannery O'Connor Society Y-99
The Wilfred Owen Association Y-98
Penguin Collectors' Society Y-98
The [E. A.] Poe Studies Association Y-99
The Katherine Anne Porter Society Y-01
The Beatrix Potter Society Y-98
The Ezra Pound Society Y-01
The Powys Society Y-98
Proust Society of America Y-00
The Dorothy L. Sayers Society Y-98
The Bernard Shaw Society Y-99
The Society for the Study of
   Southern Literature Y-00
The Wallace Stevens Society Y-99
The Harriet Beecher Stowe Center Y-00
The R. S. Surtees Society Y-98
The Thoreau Society Y-99
The Tilling [E. F. Benson] Society Y-98
The Trollope Societies Y-00
H. G. Wells Society Y-98
The Western Literature Association Y-99
The William Carlos Williams Society Y-99
The Henry Williamson Society Y-98
The [Nero] Wolfe Pack Y-99

The Thomas Wolfe Society............Y-99

Worldwide Wodehouse Societies........Y-98

The W. B. Yeats Society of N.Y. Y-99

The Charlotte M. Yonge Fellowship Y-98

Literary Theory
   The Year in Literary Theory.......Y-92–Y-93

Literature at Nurse, or Circulating Morals (1885),
   by George Moore DLB-18

Litt, Toby 1968- DLB-267, 319

Littell, Eliakim 1797-1870 ....DLB-79

Littell, Robert S. 1831-1896...............DLB-79

Little, Brown and Company DLB-49

Little Magazines and Newspapers DS-15

   Selected English-Language Little
   Magazines and Newspapers
   [France, 1920-1939] DLB-4

The Little Magazines of the
   New Formalism.................DLB-282

The Little Review 1914-1929 .... DS-15

Littlewood, Joan 1914-2002.............DLB-13

Liu, Aimee E. 1953- DLB-312

Liu E 1857-1909...................DLB-328

Lively, Penelope 1933- ... DLB-14, 161, 207, 326

Liverpool University Press...............DLB-112

The Lives of the Poets (1753) DLB-142

Livesay, Dorothy 1909-1996 ....DLB-68

Livesay, Florence Randal 1874-1953 ......DLB-92

Livings, Henry 1929-1998...............DLB-13

Livingston, Anne Howe 1763-1841 ... DLB-37, 200

Livingston, Jay 1915-2001 ....DLB-265

Livingston, Myra Cohn 1926-1996 ....DLB-61

Livingston, William 1723-1790..........DLB-31

Livingstone, David 1813-1873 ....DLB-166

Livingstone, Douglas 1932-1996 ....DLB-225

Livshits, Benedikt Konstantinovich
   1886-1938 or 1939 ....DLB-295

Livy 59 B.C.-A.D. 17 ....DLB-211; CDWLB-1

Liyong, Taban lo (see Taban lo Liyong)

Lizárraga, Sylvia S. 1925- DLB-82

Llamazares, Julio 1955- DLB-322

Llewellyn, Kate 1936- DLB-325

Llewellyn, Richard 1906-1983...........DLB-15

Lloréns Torres, Luis 1876-1944 ....DLB-290

Edward Lloyd [publishing house]........DLB-106

Lobato, José Bento Monteiro
   1882-1948 ....DLB-307

Lobel, Arnold 1933- DLB-61

Lochhead, Liz 1947- DLB-310

Lochridge, Betsy Hopkins (see Fancher, Betsy)

Locke, Alain 1886-1954................DLB-51

Locke, David Ross 1833-1888........DLB-11, 23

Locke, John 1632-1704.....DLB-31, 101, 213, 252

Locke, Richard Adams 1800-1871 ....DLB-43

Locker-Lampson, Frederick
   1821-1895 ....DLB-35, 184

Lockhart, John Gibson
   1794-1854 ....DLB-110, 116 144

Lockridge, Francis 1896-1963 ....DLB-306

Lockridge, Richard 1898-1982..........DLB-306

Lockridge, Ross, Jr. 1914-1948 .... DLB-143; Y-80

Locrine and Selimus...................DLB-62

Lodge, David 1935- DLB-14, 194

Lodge, George Cabot 1873-1909.........DLB-54

Lodge, Henry Cabot 1850-1924 ....DLB-47

Lodge, Thomas 1558-1625 .... DLB-172

   Defence of Poetry (1579) [excerpt] DLB-172

Loeb, Harold 1891-1974 ....DLB-4; DS-15

Loeb, William 1905-1981 ....DLB-127

Loesser, Frank 1910-1969 ....DLB-265

Lofting, Hugh 1886-1947...............DLB-160

Logan, Deborah Norris 1761-1839 ......DLB-200

Logan, James 1674-1751.........DLB-24, 140

Logan, John 1923-1987 ....DLB-5

Logan, Martha Daniell 1704?-1779 ......DLB-200

Logan, William 1950- DLB-120

Logau, Friedrich von 1605-1655 ....DLB-164

Logue, Christopher 1926- DLB-27

Lohenstein, Daniel Casper von
   1635-1683 ....DLB-168

Lohrey, Amanda 1947- DLB-325

Lo-Johansson, Ivar 1901-1990 ....DLB-259

Lokert, George (or Lockhart)
   circa 1485-1547 ....DLB-281

Lomonosov, Mikhail Vasil'evich
   1711-1765......................DLB-150

London, Jack
   1876-1916 .....DLB-8, 12, 78, 212; CDALB-3

   The Jack London Research Center.......Y-00

   The Jack London Society Y-99

The London Magazine 1820-1829 ....DLB-110

Long, David 1948- DLB-244

Long, H., and Brother................DLB-49

Long, Haniel 1888-1956 ....DLB-45

Long, Ray 1878-1935................DLB-137

Longfellow, Henry Wadsworth
   1807-1882 ....DLB-1, 59, 235; CDALB-2

Longfellow, Samuel 1819-1892 ....DLB-1

Longford, Elizabeth 1906-2002 ....DLB-155

   Tribute to Alfred A. Knopf Y-84

Longinus circa first century DLB-176

Longley, Michael 1939- DLB-40

T. Longman [publishing house]..........DLB-154

Longmans, Green and Company..........DLB-49

Longmore, George 1793?-1867 ....DLB-99

Longstreet, Augustus Baldwin
   1790-1870 .... DLB-3, 11, 74, 248

D. Longworth [publishing house] DLB-49

Lønn, Øystein 1936- DLB-297

Lonsdale, Frederick 1881-1954 ....DLB-10

Loos, Anita 1893-1981..... DLB-11, 26, 228; Y-81

Lopate, Phillip 1943- Y-80

Lope de Rueda 1510?-1565? DLB-318

Lopes, Fernão 1380/1390?-1460? DLB-287

Lopez, Barry 1945- DLB-256, 275

López, Diana (see Isabella, Ríos)

López, Josefina 1969- DLB-209

López de Mendoza, Íñigo
   (see Santillana, Marqués de)

López Velarde, Ramón 1888-1921.......DLB-290

Loranger, Jean-Aubert 1896-1942 ....DLB-92

Lorca, Federico García 1898-1936.......DLB-108

Lord, John Keast 1818-1872..............DLB-99

Lorde, Audre 1934-1992 ....DLB-41

Lorimer, George Horace 1867-1937.......DLB-91

A. K. Loring [publishing house]..........DLB-49

Loring and Mussey DLB-46

Lorris, Guillaume de (see *Roman de la Rose*)

Lossing, Benson J. 1813-1891 ....DLB-30

Lothar, Ernst 1890-1974.................DLB-81

D. Lothrop and Company...............DLB-49

Lothrop, Harriet M. 1844-1924..........DLB-42

Loti, Pierre 1850-1923 ....DLB-123

Lotichius Secundus, Petrus 1528-1560.... DLB-179

Lott, Emmeline fl. nineteenth century DLB-166

Louisiana State University Press Y-97

Lounsbury, Thomas R. 1838-1915 ....DLB-71

Louÿs, Pierre 1870-1925 ....DLB-123

Løveid, Cecile 1951- DLB-297

Lovejoy, Arthur O. 1873-1962...........DLB-270

Lovelace, Earl 1935- DLB-125; CDWLB-3

Lovelace, Richard 1618-1657 ....DLB-131

John W. Lovell Company DLB-49

Lovell, Coryell and Company DLB-49

Lover, Samuel 1797-1868 ....DLB-159, 190

Lovesey, Peter 1936- DLB-87

   Tribute to Georges Simenon Y-89

Lovinescu, Eugen
   1881-1943............DLB-220; CDWLB-4

Lovingood, Sut
   (see Harris, George Washington)

Low, Samuel 1765-? DLB-37

Lowell, Amy 1874-1925............DLB-54, 140

Lowell, James Russell 1819-1891
   ...... DLB-1, 11, 64, 79, 189, 235; CDALB-2

Lowell, Robert
   1917-1977............DLB-5, 169; CDALB-7

Lowenfels, Walter 1897-1976 ....DLB-4

Lowndes, Marie Belloc 1868-1947........DLB-70

Lowndes, William Thomas 1798-1843 ... DLB-184

Humphrey Lownes [publishing house] DLB-170

Lowry, Lois 1937- DLB-52

Lowry, Malcolm 1909-1957 ... DLB-15; CDBLB-7

Lowther, Pat 1935-1975 .... DLB-53

Loy, Mina 1882-1966 .... DLB-4, 54

Loynaz, Dulce María 1902-1997 .... DLB-283

Lozeau, Albert 1878-1924 .... DLB-92

Lu Ling 1923-1994 .... DLB-328

Lu Xun 1881-1936 .... DLB-328

Lu Yin 1898?-1934 .... DLB-328

Lubbock, Percy 1879-1965 .... DLB-149

Lucan A.D. 39-A.D. 65 .... DLB-211

Lucas, E. V. 1868-1938 .... DLB-98, 149, 153

Fielding Lucas Jr. [publishing house] DLB-49

Luce, Clare Booth 1903-1987 .... DLB-228

Luce, Henry R. 1898-1967 .... DLB-91

John W. Luce and Company DLB-46

Lucena, Juan de ca. 1430-1501 .... DLB-286

Lucian circa 120-180 .... DLB-176

Lucie-Smith, Edward 1933- DLB-40

Lucilius circa 180 B.C.-102/101 B.C. DLB-211

Lucini, Gian Pietro 1867-1914 .... DLB-114

Luco Cruchaga, Germán 1894-1936 .... DLB-305

Lucretius circa 94 B.C.-circa 49 B.C.
.... DLB-211; CDWLB-1

Luder, Peter circa 1415-1472 .... DLB-179

Ludlam, Charles 1943-1987 .... DLB-266

Ludlum, Robert 1927-2001 .... Y-82

Ludus de Antichristo circa 1160 .... DLB-148

Ludvigson, Susan 1942- DLB-120

Ludwig, Jack 1922- DLB-60

Ludwig, Otto 1813-1865 .... DLB-129

Ludwigslied 881 or 882 .... DLB-148

Luera, Yolanda 1953- DLB-122

Luft, Lya 1938- DLB-145

Lugansky, Kazak Vladimir
(see Dal', Vladimir Ivanovich)

Lugn, Kristina 1948- DLB-257

Lugones, Leopoldo 1874-1938 .... DLB-283

Luhan, Mabel Dodge 1879-1962 .... DLB-303

Lukács, Georg (see Lukács, György)

Lukács, György
1885-1971 .... DLB-215, 242; CDWLB-4

Luke, Peter 1919-1995 .... DLB-13

Lummis, Charles F. 1859-1928 .... DLB-186

Lundkvist, Artur 1906-1991 .... DLB-259

Lunts, Lev Natanovich
1901-1924 .... DLB-272

F. M. Lupton Company DLB-49

Lupus of Ferrières
circa 805-circa 862 .... DLB-148

Lurie, Alison 1926- DLB-2

Lussu, Emilio 1890-1975 .... DLB-264

Lustig, Arnošt 1926- DLB-232, 299

Luther, Martin
1483-1546 .... DLB-179; CDWLB-2

Luzi, Mario 1914-2005 .... DLB-128

L'vov, Nikolai Aleksandrovich
1751-1803 .... DLB-150

Lyall, Gavin 1932-2003 .... DLB-87

Lydgate, John circa 1370-1450 .... DLB-146

Lyly, John circa 1554-1606 .... DLB-62, 167

Lynch, Martin 1950- DLB-310

Lynch, Patricia 1898-1972 .... DLB-160

Lynch, Richard fl. 1596-1601 .... DLB-172

Lynd, Robert 1879-1949 .... DLB-98

Lynds, Dennis (Michael Collins)
1924- DLB-306

Tribute to John D. MacDonald Y-86

Tribute to Kenneth Millar Y-83

Why I Write Mysteries: Night and Day... Y-85

Lyon, Matthew 1749-1822 .... DLB-43

Lyotard, Jean-François 1924-1998 ...... DLB-242

Lyricists
Additional Lyricists: 1920-1960 ..... DLB-265

Lysias circa 459 B.C.-circa 380 B.C. DLB-176

Lytle, Andrew 1902-1995 .... DLB-6; Y-95

Tribute to Caroline Gordon Y-81

Tribute to Katherine Anne Porter Y-80

Lytton, Edward
(see Bulwer-Lytton, Edward)

Lytton, Edward Robert Bulwer
1831-1891 .... DLB-32

M

Maass, Joachim 1901-1972 .... DLB-69

Mabie, Hamilton Wright 1845-1916 ...... DLB-71

Mac A'Ghobhainn, Iain (see Smith, Iain Crichton)

MacArthur, Charles 1895-1956 ..... DLB-7, 25, 44

Macaulay, Catherine 1731-1791 .... DLB-104

Macaulay, David 1945- DLB-61

Macaulay, Rose 1881-1958 .... DLB-36

Macaulay, Thomas Babington
1800-1859 .... DLB-32, 55; CDBLB-4

Macaulay Company DLB-46

MacBeth, George 1932-1992 .... DLB-40

Macbeth, Madge 1880-1965 .... DLB-92

MacCaig, Norman 1910-1996 .... DLB-27

MacDiarmid, Hugh
1892-1978 .... DLB-20; CDBLB-7

MacDonald, Cynthia 1928- DLB-105

MacDonald, George 1824-1905 .... DLB-18, 163, 178

MacDonald, John D.
1916-1986 .... DLB-8, 306; Y-86

MacDonald, Philip 1899?-1980 .... DLB-77

Macdonald, Ross (see Millar, Kenneth)

Macdonald, Sharman 1951- DLB-245

MacDonald, Wilson 1880-1967 .... DLB-92

Macdonald and Company (Publishers) .. DLB-112

MacEwen, Gwendolyn 1941-1987 ... DLB-53, 251

Macfadden, Bernarr 1868-1955 ...... DLB-25, 91

MacGregor, John 1825-1892 .... DLB-166

MacGregor, Mary Esther (see Keith, Marian)

Macherey, Pierre 1938- DLB-296

Machado, Antonio 1875-1939 .... DLB-108

Machado, Manuel 1874-1947 .... DLB-108

Machado de Assis, Joaquim Maria
1839-1908 .... DLB-307

Machar, Agnes Maule 1837-1927 .... DLB-92

Machaut, Guillaume de
circa 1300-1377 .... DLB-208

Machen, Arthur Llewelyn Jones
1863-1947 .... DLB-36, 156, 178

MacIlmaine, Roland fl. 1574 .... DLB-281

MacInnes, Colin 1914-1976 .... DLB-14

MacInnes, Helen 1907-1985 .... DLB-87

Mac Intyre, Tom 1931- DLB-245

Mačiulis, Jonas (see Maironis, Jonas)

Mack, Maynard 1909-2001 .... DLB-111

Mackall, Leonard L. 1879-1937 .... DLB-140

MacKay, Isabel Ecclestone 1875-1928 ..... DLB-92

Mackay, Shena 1944- DLB-231, 319

MacKaye, Percy 1875-1956 .... DLB-54

Macken, Walter 1915-1967 .... DLB-13

MacKenna, John 1952- DLB-319

Mackenzie, Alexander 1763-1820 .... DLB-99

Mackenzie, Alexander Slidell
1803-1848 .... DLB-183

Mackenzie, Compton 1883-1972 ..... DLB-34, 100

Mackenzie, Henry 1745-1831 .... DLB-39

The Lounger, no. 20 (1785) DLB-39

Mackenzie, Kenneth (Seaforth Mackenzie)
1913-1955 .... DLB-260

Mackenzie, William 1758-1828 .... DLB-187

Mackey, Nathaniel 1947- DLB-169

Mackey, William Wellington 1937- DLB-38

Mackintosh, Elizabeth (see Tey, Josephine)

Mackintosh, Sir James 1765-1832 .... DLB-158

Macklin, Charles 1699-1797 .... DLB-89

Maclaren, Ian (see Watson, John)

Maclaren-Ross, Julian 1912-1964 .... DLB-319

MacLaverty, Bernard 1942- DLB-267

MacLean, Alistair 1922-1987 .... DLB-276

MacLean, Katherine Anne 1925- DLB-8

Maclean, Norman 1902-1990 .... DLB-206

MacLeish, Archibald 1892-1982
.... DLB-4, 7, 45; Y-82; DS-15; CDALB-7

MacLennan, Hugh 1907-1990 . . . . DLB-68

MacLeod, Alistair 1936- DLB-60

Macleod, Fiona (see Sharp, William)

Macleod, Norman 1906-1985 . . . . DLB-4

Mac Low, Jackson 1922-2004 . . . . DLB-193

MacMahon, Bryan 1909-1998 . . . . DLB-319

Macmillan and Company DLB-106

The Macmillan Company DLB-49

Macmillan's English Men of Letters, First Series (1878-1892) DLB-144

MacNamara, Brinsley 1890-1963 . . . . DLB-10

MacNeice, Louis 1907-1963 . . . . DLB-10, 20

Macphail, Andrew 1864-1938 . . . . DLB-92

Macpherson, James 1736-1796 . . . . DLB-109

Macpherson, Jay 1931- DLB-53

Macpherson, Jeanie 1884-1946 . . . . DLB-44

Macrae Smith Company DLB-46

MacRaye, Lucy Betty (see Webling, Lucy)

John Macrone [publishing house] DLB-106

MacShane, Frank 1927-1999 . . . . DLB-111

Macy-Masius DLB-46

Madden, David 1933- DLB-6

Madden, Sir Frederic 1801-1873 . . . . DLB-184

Maddow, Ben 1909-1992 . . . . DLB-44

Maddux, Rachel 1912-1983 . . . . DLB-234; Y-93

Madgett, Naomi Long 1923- DLB-76

Madhubuti, Haki R. 1942- DLB-5, 41; DS-8

Madison, James 1751-1836 . . . . DLB-37

Madsen, Svend Åge 1939- DLB-214

Madrigal, Alfonso Fernández de (El Tostado) ca. 1405-1455 . . . . DLB-286

Maeterlinck, Maurice 1862-1949 . . . . DLB-192

Mafūz, Najīb 1911- Y-88

Nobel Lecture 1988 . . . . Y-88

The Little Magazines of the New Formalism DLB-282

Magee, David 1905-1977 . . . . DLB-187

Maginn, William 1794-1842 . . . . DLB-110, 159

Magoffin, Susan Shelby 1827-1855 . . . . DLB-239

Mahan, Alfred Thayer 1840-1914 . . . . DLB-47

Mahapatra, Jayanta 1928- DLB-323

Maheux-Forcier, Louise 1929- DLB-60

Mahin, John Lee 1902-1984 . . . . DLB-44

Mahon, Derek 1941- DLB-40

Maiakovsky, Vladimir Vladimirovich 1893-1930 . . . . DLB-295

Maikov, Apollon Nikolaevich 1821-1897 . . . . DLB-277

Maikov, Vasilii Ivanovich 1728-1778 . . . . . DLB-150

Mailer, Norman 1923-
. . . . . . DLB-2, 16, 28, 185, 278; Y-80, 83, 97; DS-3; CDALB-6

Tribute to Isaac Bashevis Singer Y-91

Tribute to Meyer Levin Y-81

Maillart, Ella 1903-1997 . . . . DLB-195

Maillet, Adrienne 1885-1963 . . . . DLB-68

Maillet, Antonine 1929- DLB-60

Maillu, David G. 1939- DLB-157

Maimonides, Moses 1138-1204 . . . . DLB-115

Main Selections of the Book-of-the-Month Club, 1926-1945 . . . . DLB-9

Mainwaring, Daniel 1902-1977 . . . . DLB-44

Mair, Charles 1838-1927 . . . . DLB-99

Mair, John circa 1467-1550 . . . . DLB-281

Maironis, Jonas 1862-1932 . . DLB-220; CDWLB-4

Mais, Roger 1905-1955 . . . . . DLB-125; CDWLB-3

Maitland, Sara 1950- DLB-271

Major, Andre 1942- DLB-60

Major, Charles 1856-1913 . . . . DLB-202

Major, Clarence 1936- DLB-33

Major, Kevin 1949- DLB-60

Major Books DLB-46

Makanin, Vladimir Semenovich 1937- DLB-285

Makarenko, Anton Semenovich 1888-1939 . . . . DLB-272

Makemie, Francis circa 1658-1708 . . . . DLB-24

The Making of Americans Contract Y-98

Makovsky, Sergei 1877-1962 . . . . DLB-317

Maksimov, Vladimir Emel'ianovich 1930-1995 . . . . DLB-302

Maksimović, Desanka 1898-1993 . . . . DLB-147; CDWLB-4

Malamud, Bernard 1914-1986 . . . . DLB-2, 28, 152; Y-80, 86; CDALB-1

Bernard Malamud Archive at the Harry Ransom Humanities Research Center Y-00

Mălăncioiu, Ileana 1940- DLB-232

Malaparte, Curzio (Kurt Erich Suckert) 1898-1957 . . . . . . DLB-264

Malerba, Luigi 1927- DLB-196

Malet, Lucas 1852-1931 . . . . DLB-153

Malherbe, François de 1555-1628 . . . . DLB-327

Mallarmé, Stéphane 1842-1898 . . . . DLB-217

Malleson, Lucy Beatrice (see Gilbert, Anthony)

Mallet-Joris, Françoise (Françoise Lilar) 1930- DLB-83

Mallock, W. H. 1849-1923 . . . . DLB-18, 57

"Every Man His Own Poet; or, The Inspired Singer's Recipe Book" (1877) DLB-35

"Le Style c'est l'homme" (1892) DLB-57

Memoirs of Life and Literature (1920), [excerpt] DLB-57

Malone, Dumas 1892-1986 . . . . DLB-17

Malone, Edmond 1741-1812 . . . . DLB-142

Malory, Sir Thomas circa 1400-1410 - 1471 . . . DLB-146; CDBLB-1

Malouf, David 1934- DLB-289

Malpede, Karen 1945- DLB-249

Malraux, André 1901-1976 . . . . DLB-72

The Maltese Falcon (Documentary) DLB-280

Malthus, Thomas Robert 1766-1834 . . . . DLB-107, 158

Maltz, Albert 1908-1985 . . . . DLB-102

Malzberg, Barry N. 1939- DLB-8

Mamet, David 1947- DLB-7

Mamin, Dmitrii Narkisovich 1852-1912 . . . . DLB-238

Manaka, Matsemela 1956- DLB-157

Mañas, José Ángel 1971- DLB-322

Manchester University Press DLB-112

Mandel, Eli 1922-1992 . . . . DLB-53

Mandel'shtam, Nadezhda Iakovlevna 1899-1980 . . . . DLB-302

Mandel'shtam, Osip Emil'evich 1891-1938 . . . . DLB-295

Mandeville, Bernard 1670-1733 . . . . DLB-101

Mandeville, Sir John mid fourteenth century DLB-146

Mandiargues, André Pieyre de 1909-1991 . . . . DLB-83

Manea, Norman 1936- DLB-232

Manfred, Frederick 1912-1994 . . . . DLB-6, 212, 227

Manfredi, Gianfranco 1948- DLB-196

Mangan, Sherry 1904-1961 . . . . DLB-4

Manganelli, Giorgio 1922-1990 . . . . DLB-196

Manilius fl. first century A.D. DLB-211

Mankiewicz, Herman 1897-1953 . . . . DLB-26

Mankiewicz, Joseph L. 1909-1993 . . . . DLB-44

Mankowitz, Wolf 1924-1998 . . . . DLB-15

Manley, Delarivière 1672?-1724 . . . . DLB-39, 80

Preface to The Secret History, of Queen Zarah, and the Zarazians (1705) DLB-39

Mann, Abby 1927- DLB-44

Mann, Charles 1929-1998 . . . . Y-98

Mann, Emily 1952- DLB-266

Mann, Heinrich 1871-1950 . . . . DLB-66, 118

Mann, Horace 1796-1859 . . . . DLB-1, 235

Mann, Klaus 1906-1949 . . . . DLB-56

Mann, Mary Peabody 1806-1887 . . . . DLB-239

Mann, Thomas 1875-1955 . . . . DLB-66; CDWLB-2

Mann, William D'Alton 1839-1920 . . . . . . DLB-137

Mannin, Ethel 1900-1984 . . . . DLB-191, 195

Manning, Emily (see Australie)

Manning, Frederic 1882-1935 . . . . DLB-260

Manning, Laurence 1899-1972 . . . . DLB-251

Manning, Marie 1873?-1945 . . . . DLB-29

Manning and Loring DLB-49

Mannyng, Robert fl. 1303-1338 . . . . DLB-146

Cumulative Index

Mano, D. Keith 1942- DLB-6	Markfield, Wallace 1926-2002 .... DLB-2, 28	Martin, Charles 1942- DLB-120, 282
Manor Books DLB-46	Markham, E. A. 1939- DLB-319	Martin, Claire 1914- DLB-60
Manrique, Gómez 1412?-1490 .... DLB-286	Markham, Edwin 1852-1940 .... DLB-54, 186	Martin, David 1915-1997 .... DLB-260
Manrique, Jorge ca. 1440-1479 .... DLB-286	Markish, David 1938- DLB-317	Martin, Jay 1935- DLB-111
Mansfield, Katherine 1888-1923 .... DLB-162	Markle, Fletcher 1921-1991 .... DLB-68; Y-91	Martin, Johann (see Laurentius von Schnüffis)
Mantel, Hilary 1952- DLB-271	Marlatt, Daphne 1942- DLB-60	Martin, Thomas 1696-1771 .... DLB-213
Manuel, Niklaus circa 1484-1530 .... DLB-179	Marlitt, E. 1825-1887 .... DLB-129	Martin, Violet Florence (see Ross, Martin)
Manzini, Gianna 1896-1974 .... DLB-177	Marlowe, Christopher 1564-1593 .... DLB-62; CDBLB-1	Martin du Gard, Roger 1881-1958 .... DLB-65
Mao Dun 1896-1981 .... DLB-328	Marlyn, John 1912-1985............... DLB-88	Martineau, Harriet 1802-1876..... DLB-21, 55, 159, 163, 166, 190
Mapanje, Jack 1944- DLB-157	Marmion, Shakerley 1603-1639 .... DLB-58	Martínez, Demetria 1960- DLB-209
Maraini, Dacia 1936- DLB-196	Marmontel, Jean-François 1723-1799 .... DLB-314	Martínez de Toledo, Alfonso 1398?-1468.................... DLB-286
Maraise, Marie-Catherine-Renée Darcel de 1737-1822 .... DLB-314	Der Marner before 1230-circa 1287 ..... DLB-138	Martínez, Eliud 1935- DLB-122
Maramzin, Vladimir Rafailovich 1934- DLB-302	Marnham, Patrick 1943- DLB-204	Martínez, Max 1943- DLB-82
March, William (William Edward Campbell) 1893-1954 .... DLB-9, 86, 316	Marot, Clément 1496-1544............ DLB-327	Martínez, Rubén 1962- DLB-209
	The *Marprelate Tracts* 1588-1589 .... DLB-132	Martín Gaite, Carmen 1925-2000 ...... DLB-322
Marchand, Leslie A. 1900-1999 .... DLB-103	Marquand, John P. 1893-1960 .... DLB-9, 102	Martín-Santos, Luis 1924-1964......... DLB-322
Marchant, Bessie 1862-1941 .... DLB-160	Marques, Helena 1935- DLB-287	Martinson, Harry 1904-1978 .... DLB-259
Marchant, Tony 1959- DLB-245	Marqués, René 1919-1979 .... DLB-113, 305	Martinson, Moa 1890-1964 .... DLB-259
Marchenko, Anastasiia Iakovlevna 1830-1880 .... DLB-238	Marquis, Don 1878-1937 .... DLB-11, 25	Martone, Michael 1955- DLB-218
Marchessault, Jovette 1938- DLB-60	Marriott, Anne 1913-1997 .... DLB-68	Martyn, Edward 1859-1923 .... DLB-10
Marcinkevičius, Justinas 1930- DLB-232	Marryat, Frederick 1792-1848 ...... DLB-21, 163	Marvell, Andrew 1621-1678............. DLB-131; CDBLB-2
Marcos, Plínio (Plínio Marcos de Barros) 1935-1999 .... DLB-307	Marsé, Juan 1933- DLB-322	Marvin X 1944- DLB-38
Marcus, Frank 1928- DLB-13	Marsh, Capen, Lyon and Webb DLB-49	Marx, Karl 1818-1883 .... DLB-129
Marcuse, Herbert 1898-1979 .... DLB-242	Marsh, George Perkins 1801-1882 .... DLB-1, 64, 243	Marzials, Theo 1850-1920 .... DLB-35
Marden, Orison Swett 1850-1924....... DLB-137	Marsh, James 1794-1842............... DLB-1, 59	Masefield, John 1878-1967 .... DLB-10, 19, 153, 160; CDBLB-5
Marechera, Dambudzo 1952-1987 ..... DLB-157	Marsh, Narcissus 1638-1713........... DLB-213	Masham, Damaris Cudworth, Lady 1659-1708..................... DLB-252
Marek, Richard, Books DLB-46	Marsh, Ngaio 1899-1982 .... DLB-77	Masino, Paola 1908-1989 .... DLB-264
Mares, E. A. 1938- DLB-122	Marshall, Alan 1902-1984 .... DLB-260	Mason, A. E. W. 1865-1948 .... DLB-70
Marguerite de Navarre 1492-1549 ...... DLB-327	Marshall, Edison 1894-1967........... DLB-102	Mason, Bobbie Ann 1940- DLB-173; Y-87; CDALB-7
Margulies, Donald 1954- DLB-228	Marshall, Edward 1932- DLB-16	Mason, F. van Wyck (Geoffrey Coffin, Frank W. Mason, Ward Weaver) 1901-1978 .... DLB-306
Mariana, Juan de 1535 or 1536-1624 .... DLB-318	Marshall, Emma 1828-1899 .... DLB-163	Mason, William 1725-1797 .... DLB-142
Mariani, Paul 1940- DLB-111	Marshall, James 1942-1992............. DLB-61	Mason Brothers DLB-49
Marías, Javier 1951- DLB-322	Marshall, Joyce 1913- DLB-88	*The Massachusetts Quarterly Review* 1847-1850...................... DLB-1
Marie de France fl. 1160-1178.......... DLB-208	Marshall, Paule 1929- DLB-33, 157, 227	*The Masses*....................... DLB-303
Marie-Victorin, Frère (Conrad Kirouac) 1885-1944 .... DLB-92	Marshall, Tom 1938-1993............... DLB-60	Massey, Gerald 1828-1907 .... DLB-32
Marin, Biagio 1891-1985 .... DLB-128	Marsilius of Padua circa 1275-circa 1342 .... DLB-115	Massey, Linton R. 1900-1974 ....DLB-187
Marinetti, Filippo Tommaso 1876-1944................... DLB-114, 264	Mars-Jones, Adam 1954- DLB-207, 319	Massie, Allan 1938- DLB-271
Marinina, Aleksandra (Marina Anatol'evna Alekseeva) 1957- DLB-285	Marson, Una 1905-1965............... DLB-157	Massinger, Philip 1583-1640............ DLB-58
	Marston, John 1576-1634 ....DLB-58, 172	Masson, David 1822-1907 .... DLB-144
Marinković, Ranko 1913-2001.............DLB-147; CDWLB-4	Marston, Philip Bourke 1850-1887........ DLB-35	Masters, Edgar Lee 1868-1950 .... DLB-54; CDALB-3
Marion, Frances 1886-1973............. DLB-44	Martel, Yann 1963- DLB-326	Masters, Hilary 1928- DLB-244
Marius, Richard C. 1933-1999............. Y-85	Martens, Kurt 1870-1945 .... DLB-66	Masters, Olga 1919-1986 .... DLB-325
Marivaux, Pierre Carlet de Chamblain de 1688-1763..................... DLB-314	Martí, José 1853-1895.............. DLB-290	Mastronardi, Lucio 1930-1979 ....DLB-177
Markandaya, Kamala 1924-2004 .... DLB-323	Martial circa A.D. 40-circa A.D. 103 .... DLB-211; CDWLB-1	Mat' Maria (Elizaveta Kuz'mina-Karavdeva Skobtsova, née Pilenko) 1891-1945.....DLB-317
Markevich, Boleslav Mikhailovich 1822-1884 .... DLB-238	William S. Martien [publishing house] DLB-49	
	Martin, Abe (see Hubbard, Kin)	
	Martin, Catherine ca. 1847-1937........ DLB-230	

Matevski, Mateja 1929- ...DLB-181; CDWLB-4

Mather, Cotton
1663-1728 ....DLB-24, 30, 140; CDALB-2

Mather, Increase 1639-1723 ....DLB-24

Mather, Richard 1596-1669 ....DLB-24

Matheson, Annie 1853-1924 ....DLB-240

Matheson, Richard 1926- DLB-8, 44

Matheus, John F. 1887-1986.............DLB-51

Mathews, Aidan 1956- DLB-319

Mathews, Cornelius 1817?-1889 ...DLB-3, 64, 250

Elkin Mathews [publishing house].......DLB-112

Mathews, John Joseph 1894-1979 ....DLB-175

Mathias, Roland 1915- DLB-27

Mathis, June 1892-1927 ....DLB-44

Mathis, Sharon Bell 1937- DLB-33

Matković, Marijan 1915-1985 ....DLB-181

Matoš, Antun Gustav 1873-1914 ....DLB-147

Matos Paoli, Francisco 1915-2000 ....DLB-290

Matsumoto Seichō 1909-1992 ....DLB-182

The Matter of England 1240-1400.......DLB-146

The Matter of Rome early twelfth to late
fifteenth century DLB-146

Matthew of Vendôme
circa 1130-circa 1200 ....DLB-208

Matthews, Brander 1852-1929.. DLB-71, 78; DS-13

Matthews, Brian 1936- DLB-325

Matthews, Jack 1925- DLB-6

Matthews, Victoria Earle 1861-1907 .....DLB-221

Matthews, William 1942-1997...........DLB-5

Matthías Jochumsson 1835-1920........DLB-293

Matthías Johannessen 1930- DLB-293

Matthiessen, F. O. 1902-1950 ....DLB-63

Matthiessen, Peter 1927- DLB-6, 173, 275

Maturin, Charles Robert 1780-1824 .....DLB-178

Matute, Ana María 1926- DLB-322

Maugham, W. Somerset 1874-1965
.... DLB-10, 36, 77, 100, 162, 195; CDBLB-6

Maupassant, Guy de 1850-1893 ....DLB-123

Maupertuis, Pierre-Louis Moreau de
1698-1759 ....DLB-314

Maupin, Armistead 1944- DLB-278

Mauriac, Claude 1914-1996.............DLB-83

Mauriac, François 1885-1970.............DLB-65

Maurice, Frederick Denison 1805-1872....DLB-55

Maurois, André 1885-1967.............DLB-65

Maury, James 1718-1769 ....DLB-31

Mavor, Elizabeth 1927- DLB-14

Mavor, Osborne Henry (see Bridie, James)

Maxwell, Gavin 1914-1969 ....DLB-204

Maxwell, William
1908-2000 .... DLB-218, 278; Y-80

Tribute to Nancy Hale Y-88

H. Maxwell [publishing house] DLB-49

John Maxwell [publishing house]........DLB-106

May, Elaine 1932- DLB-44

May, Karl 1842-1912 ....DLB-129

May, Thomas 1595/1596-1650 ....DLB-58

Mayer, Bernadette 1945- DLB-165

Mayer, Mercer 1943- DLB-61

Mayer, O. B. 1818-1891.............DLB-3, 248

Mayes, Herbert R. 1900-1987 ....DLB-137

Mayes, Wendell 1919-1992 ....DLB-26

Mayfield, Julian 1928-1984 .... DLB-33; Y-84

Mayhew, Henry 1812-1887 ...... DLB-18, 55, 190

Mayhew, Jonathan 1720-1766 ....DLB-31

Mayne, Ethel Colburn 1865-1941 ....DLB-197

Mayne, Jasper 1604-1672...............DLB-126

Mayne, Seymour 1944- DLB-60

Mayor, Flora Macdonald 1872-1932 .....DLB-36

Mayröcker, Friederike 1924- DLB-85

Mazrui, Ali A. 1933- DLB-125

Mažuranić, Ivan 1814-1890 ....DLB-147

Mazursky, Paul 1930- DLB-44

McAlmon, Robert 1896-1956 ... DLB-4, 45; DS-15

"A Night at Bricktop's" Y-01

McArthur, Peter 1866-1924 ....DLB-92

McAuley, James 1917-1976..............DLB-260

Robert M. McBride and Company DLB-46

McCabe, Patrick 1955- DLB-194

McCafferty, Owen 1961- DLB-310

McCaffrey, Anne 1926- DLB-8

McCann, Colum 1965- DLB-267

McCarthy, Cormac 1933- DLB-6, 143, 256

The Cormac McCarthy Society Y-99

McCarthy, Mary 1912-1989 .... DLB-2; Y-81

McCarthy, Shaun Lloyd (see Cory, Desmond)

McCay, Winsor 1871-1934 ....DLB-22

McClane, Albert Jules 1922-1991 ....DLB-171

McClatchy, C. K. 1858-1936.............DLB-25

McClellan, George Marion 1860-1934 ....DLB-50

"The Negro as a Writer"..............DLB-50

McCloskey, Robert 1914-2003 ....DLB-22

McCloy, Helen 1904-1992.............DLB-306

McClung, Nellie Letitia 1873-1951 ....DLB-92

McClure, James 1939- DLB-276

McClure, Joanna 1930- DLB-16

McClure, Michael 1932- DLB-16

McClure, Phillips and Company DLB-46

McClure, S. S. 1857-1949................DLB-91

A. C. McClurg and Company DLB-49

McCluskey, John A., Jr. 1944- DLB-33

McCollum, Michael A. 1946- Y-87

McConnell, William C. 1917- DLB-88

McCord, David 1897-1997..............DLB-61

McCord, Louisa S. 1810-1879 ....DLB-248

McCorkle, Jill 1958- DLB-234; Y-87

McCorkle, Samuel Eusebius 1746-1811....DLB-37

McCormick, Anne O'Hare 1880-1954 ....DLB-29

McCormick, Kenneth Dale 1906-1997 ....Y-97

McCormick, Robert R. 1880-1955 ....DLB-29

McCourt, Edward 1907-1972............DLB-88

McCoy, Horace 1897-1955 ....DLB-9

McCrae, Hugh 1876-1958 ....DLB-260

McCrae, John 1872-1918................DLB-92

McCrumb, Sharyn 1948- DLB-306

McCullagh, Joseph B. 1842-1896 ....DLB-23

McCullers, Carson
1917-1967 ..... DLB-2, 7, 173, 228; CDALB-1

McCulloch, Thomas 1776-1843..........DLB-99

McCunn, Ruthanne Lum 1946- DLB-312

McDermott, Alice 1953- DLB-292

McDonald, Forrest 1927- DLB-17

McDonald, Walter 1934- DLB-105, DS-9

"Getting Started: Accepting the
Regions You Own–or Which
Own You"...................DLB-105

Tribute to James Dickey Y-97

McDougall, Colin 1917-1984............DLB-68

McDowell, Katharine Sherwood Bonner
1849-1883 .... DLB-202, 239

Obolensky McDowell
[publishing house].................DLB-46

McEwan, Ian 1948- DLB-14, 194, 319, 326

McFadden, David 1940- DLB-60

McFall, Frances Elizabeth Clarke
(see Grand, Sarah)

McFarland, Ron 1942- DLB-256

McFarlane, Leslie 1902-1977 ....DLB-88

McFee, William 1881-1966 ....DLB-153

McGahan, Andrew 1966- DLB-325

McGahern, John 1934- DLB-14, 231, 319

McGee, Thomas D'Arcy 1825-1868 ......DLB-99

McGeehan, W. O. 1879-1933 .... DLB-25, 171

McGill, Ralph 1898-1969 ....DLB-29

McGinley, Phyllis 1905-1978 .... DLB-11, 48

McGinniss, Joe 1942- DLB-185

McGirt, James E. 1874-1930 ....DLB-50

McGlashan and Gill...................DLB-106

McGough, Roger 1937- DLB-40

McGrath, John 1935- DLB-233

McGrath, Patrick 1950- DLB-231

McGraw-Hill......................DLB-46

McGuane, Thomas 1939- DLB-2, 212; Y-80

Tribute to Seymour Lawrence..........Y-94

McGuckian, Medbh 1950- DLB-40

McGuffey, William Holmes 1800-1873.... DLB-42

McGuinness, Frank 1953- DLB-245

McHenry, James 1785-1845 .... DLB-202

McIlvanney, William 1936- DLB-14, 207

McIlwraith, Jean Newton 1859-1938 ..... DLB-92

McInerney, Jay 1955- DLB-292

McInerny, Ralph 1929- DLB-306

McIntosh, Maria Jane 1803-1878 ... DLB-239, 248

McIntyre, James 1827-1906............ DLB-99

McIntyre, O. O. 1884-1938 .... DLB-25

McKay, Claude 1889-1948 ..... DLB-4, 45, 51, 117

The David McKay Company DLB-49

McKean, William V. 1820-1903 .... DLB-23

McKenna, Stephen 1888-1967 .... DLB-197

The McKenzie Trust.................... Y-96

McKerrow, R. B. 1872-1940 .... DLB-201

McKinley, Robin 1952- DLB-52

McKnight, Reginald 1956- DLB-234

McLachlan, Alexander 1818-1896 ...... DLB-99

McLaren, Floris Clark 1904-1978 .... DLB-68

McLaverty, Michael 1907-1992 .... DLB-15

McLean, Duncan 1964- DLB-267

McLean, John R. 1848-1916. .... DLB-23

McLean, William L. 1852-1931 .... DLB-25

McLennan, William 1856-1904 .... DLB-92

McLoughlin Brothers DLB-49

McLuhan, Marshall 1911-1980 .... DLB-88

McMaster, John Bach 1852-1932 .... DLB-47

McMillan, Terri 1951- DLB-292

McMurtry, Larry 1936-
........DLB-2, 143, 256; Y-80, 87; CDALB-6

McNally, Terrence 1939- DLB-7, 249

McNeil, Florence 1937- DLB-60

McNeile, Herman Cyril 1888-1937 ...... DLB-77

McNickle, D'Arcy 1904-1977 ....DLB-175, 212

McPhee, John 1931- DLB-185, 275

McPherson, James Alan 1943- DLB-38, 244

McPherson, Sandra 1943- Y-86

McTaggart, J. M. E. 1866-1925 .... DLB-262

McWhirter, George 1939- DLB-60

McWilliam, Candia 1955- DLB-267

McWilliams, Carey 1905-1980......... DLB-137

"*The Nation's* Future," Carey
McWilliams's Editorial Policy
in *Nation*.................... DLB-137

Mda, Zakes 1948- DLB-225

Mead, George Herbert 1863-1931 ....DLB-270

Mead, L. T. 1844-1914................ DLB-141

Mead, Matthew 1924- DLB-40

Mead, Taylor circa 1931- DLB-16

Meany, Tom 1903-1964 ....DLB-171

Mears, Gillian 1964- DLB-325

Mechthild von Magdeburg
circa 1207-circa 1282 .... DLB-138

Medieval Galician-Portuguese Poetry.... DLB-287

Medill, Joseph 1823-1899.............. DLB-43

Medoff, Mark 1940- DLB-7

Meek, Alexander Beaufort
1814-1865 .... DLB-3, 248

Meeke, Mary ?-1816................. DLB-116

Mehta, Ved 1934- DLB-323

Mei, Lev Aleksandrovich 1822-1862 .....DLB-277

Meinke, Peter 1932- DLB-5

Meireles, Cecília 1901-1964 .... DLB-307

Mejía, Pedro 1497-1551............... DLB-318

Mejia Vallejo, Manuel 1923- DLB-113

Melanchthon, Philipp 1497-1560 ....DLB-179

Melançon, Robert 1947- DLB-60

Mell, Max 1882-1971 .... DLB-81, 124

Mellow, James R. 1926-1997.......... DLB-111

Mel'nikov, Pavel Ivanovich 1818-1883 ... DLB-238

Meltzer, David 1937- DLB-16

Meltzer, Milton 1915- DLB-61

Melville, Elizabeth, Lady Culross
circa 1585-1640 ....DLB-172

Melville, Herman
1819-1891 .... DLB-3, 74, 250; CDALB-2

The Melville Society Y-01

Melville, James
(Roy Peter Martin) 1931- DLB-276

"Memorandum on Local Government," Anne-Robert-Jacques Turgot, bacon de
l'Aulne DLB-314

Mena, Juan de 1411-1456............. DLB-286

Mena, María Cristina 1893-1965 ... DLB-209, 221

Menander 342-341 B.C.-circa 292-291 B.C.
.... DLB-176; CDWLB-1

Menantes (see Hunold, Christian Friedrich)

Mencke, Johann Burckhard 1674-1732 ... DLB-168

Mencken, H. L. 1880-1956
.... DLB-11, 29, 63, 137, 222; CDALB-4

"Berlin, February, 1917"............... Y-00

From the Initial Issue of *American Mercury*
(January 1924) DLB-137

Mencken and Nietzsche: An
Unpublished Excerpt from H. L.
Mencken's *My Life as Author and
Editor* Y-93

Mendelssohn, Moses 1729-1786 .... DLB-97

Mendes, Catulle 1841-1909 .... DLB-217

Méndez M., Miguel 1930- DLB-82

Mendoza, Diego Hurtado de
1504-1575..................... DLB-318

Mendoza, Eduardo 1943- DLB-322

The Mercantile Library of New York........ Y-96

Mercer, Cecil William (see Yates, Dornford)

Mercer, David 1928-1980..........DLB-13, 310

Mercer, John 1704-1768 .... DLB-31

Mercer, Johnny 1909-1976 .... DLB-265

Mercier, Louis-Sébastien 1740-1814 ..... DLB-314

Le Tableau de Paris DLB-314

Meredith, George
1828-1909 ....DLB-18, 35, 57, 159; CDBLB-4

Meredith, Louisa Anne 1812-1895 .. DLB-166, 230

Meredith, Owen
(see Lytton, Edward Robert Bulwer)

Meredith, William 1919- DLB-5

Meres, Francis
Palladis Tamia, Wits Treasurie (1598)
[excerpt]................DLB-172

Merezhkovsky, Dmitrii Sergeevich
1865-1941 .... DLB-295

Mergerle, Johann Ulrich
(see Abraham ä Sancta Clara)

Mérimée, Prosper 1803-1870 ....DLB-119, 192

Merino, José María 1941- DLB-322

Merivale, John Herman 1779-1844....... DLB-96

Meriwether, Louise 1923- DLB-33

Merleau-Ponty, Maurice 1908-1961 ..... DLB-296

Merlin Press DLB-112

Merriam, Eve 1916-1992 .... DLB-61

The Merriam Company............ DLB-49

Merril, Judith 1923-1997 .... DLB-251

Tribute to Theodore Sturgeon Y-85

Merrill, James 1926-1995 ....DLB-5, 165; Y-85

Merrill and Baker.................... DLB-49

The Mershon Company.............. DLB-49

Merton, Thomas 1915-1968........DLB-48; Y-81

Merwin, W. S. 1927- DLB-5, 169

Julian Messner [publishing house] DLB-46

Mészöly, Miklós 1921- DLB-232

J. Metcalf [publishing house]........... DLB-49

Metcalf, John 1938- DLB-60

The Methodist Book Concern DLB-49

Methuen and Company.............. DLB-112

Meun, Jean de (see *Roman de la Rose*)

Mew, Charlotte 1869-1928 .... DLB-19, 135

Mewshaw, Michael 1943- Y-80

Tribute to Albert Erskine.............. Y-93

Meyer, Conrad Ferdinand 1825-1898.... DLB-129

Meyer, E. Y. 1946- DLB-75

Meyer, Eugene 1875-1959............. DLB-29

Meyer, Michael 1921-2000 .... DLB-155

Meyers, Jeffrey 1939- DLB-111

Meynell, Alice 1847-1922 .... DLB-19, 98

Meynell, Viola 1885-1956 .... DLB-153

Meyrink, Gustav 1868-1932........... DLB-81

Mézières, Philipe de circa 1327-1405..... DLB-208

Michael, Ib 1945- DLB-214

Michael, Livi 1960- DLB-267

Michaëlis, Karen 1872-1950...........DLB-214

Michaels, Anne 1958- DLB-299

Michaels, Leonard 1933-2003 ....DLB-130

Michaux, Henri 1899-1984 ....DLB-258

Micheaux, Oscar 1884-1951 ....DLB-50

Michel of Northgate, Dan
  circa 1265-circa 1340..............DLB-146

Micheline, Jack 1929-1998.............DLB-16

Michener, James A. 1907?-1997 ....DLB-6

Micklejohn, George circa 1717-1818.......DLB-31

Middle Hill Press....................DLB-106

Middleton, Christopher 1926- DLB-40

Middleton, Richard 1882-1911 ....DLB-156

Middleton, Stanley 1919- DLB-14, 326

Middleton, Thomas 1580-1627 ....DLB-58

Midnight's Children, 1981 Booker Prize winner,
  Salman Rushdie...................DLB-326

Miegel, Agnes 1879-1964..............DLB-56

Miežėlaitis, Eduardas 1919-1997 ....DLB-220

Miguéis, José Rodrigues 1901-1980......DLB-287

Mihailović, Dragoslav 1930- DLB-181

Mihalić, Slavko 1928- DLB-181

Mikhailov, A.
  (see Sheller, Aleksandr Konstantinovich)

Mikhailov, Mikhail Larionovich
  1829-1865 ....DLB-238

Mikhailovsky, Nikolai Konstantinovich
  1842-1904 ....DLB-277

Miles, Josephine 1911-1985 ....DLB-48

Miles, Susan (Ursula Wyllie Roberts)
  1888-1975 ....DLB-240

Miliković, Branko 1934-1961...........DLB-181

Milius, John 1944- DLB-44

Mill, James 1773-1836 ....DLB-107, 158, 262

Mill, John Stuart
  1806-1873 .....DLB-55, 190, 262; CDBLB-4

  Thoughts on Poetry and Its Varieties
    (1833) DLB-32

Andrew Millar [publishing house] DLB-154

Millar, Kenneth
  1915-1983 ....DLB-2, 226; Y-83; DS-6

Millás, Juan José 1946- DLB-322

Millay, Edna St. Vincent
  1892-1950 ....DLB-45, 249; CDALB-4

Millen, Sarah Gertrude 1888-1968 ......DLB-225

Miller, Andrew 1960- DLB-267

Miller, Arthur 1915-2005 ...DLB-7, 266; CDALB-1

  The Arthur Miller Society............Y-01

Miller, Caroline 1903-1992 ....DLB-9

Miller, Eugene Ethelbert 1950- DLB-41

  Tribute to Julian Mayfield Y-84

Miller, Heather Ross 1939- DLB-120

Miller, Henry
  1891-1980 ....DLB-4, 9; Y-80; CDALB-5

Miller, Hugh 1802-1856...............DLB-190

Miller, J. Hillis 1928- DLB-67

Miller, Jason 1939- DLB-7

Miller, Joaquin 1839-1913 ....DLB-186

Miller, May 1899-1995................DLB-41

Miller, Paul 1906-1991................DLB-127

Miller, Perry 1905-1963 ....DLB-17, 63

Miller, Sue 1943- DLB-143

Miller, Vassar 1924-1998 ....DLB-105

Miller, Walter M., Jr. 1923-1996 ....DLB-8

Miller, Webb 1892-1940................DLB-29

James Miller [publishing house]..........DLB-49

Millett, Kate 1934- DLB-246

Millhauser, Steven 1943- DLB-2

Millican, Arthenia J. Bates 1920- DLB-38

Milligan, Alice 1866-1953 ....DLB-240

Mills, Magnus 1954- DLB-267

Mills and Boon DLB-112

Milman, Henry Hart 1796-1868 ....DLB-96

Milne, A. A. 1882-1956 .....DLB-10, 77, 100, 160

Milner, Ron 1938- DLB-38

William Milner [publishing house].......DLB-106

Milnes, Richard Monckton (Lord Houghton)
  1809-1885 ....DLB-32, 184

Milton, John
  1608-1674 .....DLB-131, 151, 281; CDBLB-2

  The Milton Society of America..........Y-00

Miłosz, Czesław
  1911-2004 ....DLB-215; CDWLB-4

Minakami Tsutomu 1919- DLB-182

Minamoto no Sanetomo 1192-1219......DLB-203

Minco, Marga 1920- DLB-299

The Minerva Press...................DLB-154

Minns, Susan 1839-1938 ....DLB-140

Minsky, Nikolai 1855-1937 ....DLB-317

Minton, Balch and Company DLB-46

Minyana, Philippe 1946- DLB-321

Mirbeau, Octave 1848-1917........DLB-123, 192

Mirikitani, Janice 1941- DLB-312

Mirk, John died after 1414?............DLB-146

Miró, Gabriel 1879-1930 ....DLB-322

Miró, Ricardo 1883-1940...............DLB-290

Miron, Gaston 1928-1996 ....DLB-60

A Mirror for Magistrates DLB-167

Mirsky, D. S. 1890-1939 ....DLB-317

Mishima Yukio 1925-1970 ....DLB-182

Mistral, Gabriela 1889-1957............DLB-283

Mitchel, Jonathan 1624-1668...........DLB-24

Mitchell, Adrian 1932- DLB-40

Mitchell, Donald Grant
  1822-1908 ....DLB-1, 243; DS-13

Mitchell, Gladys 1901-1983.............DLB-77

Mitchell, James Leslie 1901-1935.........DLB-15

Mitchell, John (see Slater, Patrick)

Mitchell, John Ames 1845-1918..........DLB-79

Mitchell, Joseph 1908-1996 ....DLB-185; Y-96

Mitchell, Julian 1935- DLB-14

Mitchell, Ken 1940- DLB-60

Mitchell, Langdon 1862-1935 ....DLB-7

Mitchell, Loften 1919-2001 ....DLB-38

Mitchell, Margaret 1900-1949 ...DLB-9; CDALB-7

Mitchell, S. Weir 1829-1914............DLB-202

Mitchell, W. J. T. 1942- DLB-246

Mitchell, W. O. 1914-1998 ....DLB-88

Mitchison, Naomi Margaret (Haldane)
  1897-1999 ....DLB-160, 191, 255, 319

Mitford, Mary Russell 1787-1855....DLB-110, 116

Mitford, Nancy 1904-1973.............DLB-191

Mittelholzer, Edgar
  1909-1965 ....DLB-117; CDWLB-3

Mitterer, Erika 1906-2001 ....DLB-85

Mitterer, Felix 1948- DLB-124

Mitternacht, Johann Sebastian
  1613-1679 ....DLB-168

Miyamoto Yuriko 1899-1951............DLB-180

Mizener, Arthur 1907-1988 ....DLB-103

Mo, Timothy 1950- DLB-194

Moberg, Vilhelm 1898-1973 ....DLB-259

Modern Age Books....................DLB-46

Modern Language Association of America
  The Modern Language Association of
    America Celebrates Its Centennial ...Y-84

The Modern Library...................DLB-46

Modiano, Patrick 1945- DLB-83, 299

Modjeska, Drusilla 1946- DLB-325

Moffat, Yard and Company.............DLB-46

Moffet, Thomas 1553-1604 ....DLB-136

Mofolo, Thomas 1876-1948.............DLB-225

Mohr, Nicholasa 1938- DLB-145

Moix, Ana María 1947- DLB-134

Molesworth, Louisa 1839-1921 ....DLB-135

Molière (Jean-Baptiste Poquelin)
  1622-1673 ....DLB-268

Møller, Poul Martin 1794-1838 ....DLB-300

Möllhausen, Balduin 1825-1905 ....DLB-129

Molnár, Ferenc 1878-1952 ...DLB-215; CDWLB-4

Molnár, Miklós (see Mészöly, Miklós)

Momaday, N. Scott
  1934- DLB-143, 175, 256; CDALB-7

Monkhouse, Allan 1858-1936 ....DLB-10

Cumulative Index

Monro, Harold 1879-1932 .... DLB-19
Monroe, Harriet 1860-1936 .... DLB-54, 91
Monsarrat, Nicholas 1910-1979 .... DLB-15
Montagu, Lady Mary Wortley
    1689-1762 .... DLB-95, 101
Montague, C. E. 1867-1928 .... DLB-197
Montague, John 1929- DLB-40
Montaigne, Michel de 1533-1592 .... DLB-327
Montale, Eugenio 1896-1981 .... DLB-114
Montalvo, Garci Rodríguez de
    ca. 1450?-before 1505 .... DLB-286
Montalvo, José 1946-1994 .... DLB-209
Montemayor, Jorge de 1521?-1561? DLB-318
Montero, Rosa 1951- DLB-322
Monterroso, Augusto 1921-2003 .... DLB-145
Montesquieu, Charles-Louis de Secondat, baron de
    1689-1755 .... DLB-314
The Spirit of Laws DLB-314
Montesquiou, Robert de 1855-1921 ..... DLB-217
Montgomerie, Alexander
    circa 1550?-1598 .... DLB-167
Montgomery, James 1771-1854 ...... DLB-93, 158
Montgomery, John 1919- DLB-16
Montgomery, Lucy Maud
    1874-1942 .... DLB-92; DS-14
Montgomery, Marion 1925- DLB-6
Montgomery, Robert Bruce (see Crispin, Edmund)
Montherlant, Henry de 1896-1972 ... DLB-72, 321
The Monthly Review 1749-1844 .... DLB-110
Monti, Ricardo 1944- DLB-305
Montigny, Louvigny de 1876-1955 .... DLB-92
Montoya, José 1932- DLB-122
Moodie, John Wedderburn Dunbar
    1797-1869 .... DLB-99
Moodie, Susanna 1803-1885 .... DLB-99
Moody, Joshua circa 1633-1697 .... DLB-24
Moody, William Vaughn 1869-1910 .... DLB-7, 54
Moon Tiger, 1987 Booker Prize winner,
    Penelope Lively DLB-326
Moorcock, Michael 1939- DLB-14, 231, 261, 319
Moore, Alan 1953- DLB-261
Moore, Brian 1921-1999 .... DLB-251
Moore, Catherine L. 1911-1987 .... DLB-8
Moore, Clement Clarke 1779-1863 .... DLB-42
Moore, Dora Mavor 1888-1979 .... DLB-92
Moore, G. E. 1873-1958 .... DLB-262
Moore, George 1852-1933 .... DLB-10, 18, 57, 135
    Literature at Nurse, or Circulating Morals
    (1885) DLB-18
Moore, Lorrie 1957- DLB-234
Moore, Marianne
    1887-1972 .... DLB-45; DS-7; CDALB-5
    International Marianne Moore Society ... Y-98
Moore, Mavor 1919- DLB-88

Moore, Richard 1927- DLB-105
    "The No Self, the Little Self, and
    the Poets" DLB-105
Moore, T. Sturge 1870-1944 .... DLB-19
Moore, Thomas 1779-1852 .... DLB-96, 144
Moore, Ward 1903-1978 .... DLB-8
Moore, Wilstach, Keys and Company DLB-49
Moorehead, Alan 1901-1983 .... DLB-204
Moorhouse, Frank 1938- DLB-289
Moorhouse, Geoffrey 1931- DLB-204
Moorish Novel of the Sixteenth
    Century, The DLB-318
The Moorland-Spingarn Research
    Center DLB-76
Moorman, Mary C. 1905-1994 .... DLB-155
Mora, Pat 1942- DLB-209
Moraes, Dom 1938-2004 .... DLB-323
Moraes, Vinicius de 1913-1980 .... DLB-307
Moraga, Cherríe 1952- DLB-82, 249
Morales, Alejandro 1944- DLB-82
Morales, Mario Roberto 1947- DLB-145
Morales, Rafael 1919- DLB-108
Morality Plays: *Mankind* circa 1450-1500
    and *Everyman* circa 1500 .... DLB-146
Morand, Paul (1888-1976) DLB-65
Morante, Elsa 1912-1985 .... DLB-177
Morata, Olympia Fulvia 1526-1555 ...... DLB-179
Moravia, Alberto 1907-1990 .... DLB-177
Mordaunt, Elinor 1872-1942 .... DLB-174
Mordovtsev, Daniil Lukich 1830-1905 ... DLB-238
More, Hannah
    1745-1833 .... DLB-107, 109, 116, 158
More, Henry 1614-1687 .... DLB-126, 252
More, Sir Thomas
    1477/1478-1535 .... DLB-136, 281
Morejón, Nancy 1944- DLB-283
Morellet, André 1727-1819 .... DLB-314
Morency, Pierre 1942- DLB-60
Moreno, Dorinda 1939- DLB-122
Moretti, Marino 1885-1979 .... DLB-114, 264
Morgan, Berry 1919-2002 .... DLB-6
Morgan, Charles 1894-1958 .... DLB-34, 100
Morgan, Edmund S. 1916- DLB-17
Morgan, Edwin 1920- DLB-27
Morgan, John Pierpont 1837-1913 ..... DLB-140
Morgan, John Pierpont, Jr. 1867-1943 ... DLB-140
Morgan, Robert 1944- DLB-120, 292
Morgan, Sally 1951- DLB-325
Morgan, Sydney Owenson, Lady
    1776?-1859 .... DLB-116, 158
Morgner, Irmtraud 1933-1990 .... DLB-75
Morhof, Daniel Georg 1639-1691 ...... DLB-164
Mori, Kyoko 1957- DLB-312

Mori Ōgai 1862-1922 .... DLB-180
Mori, Toshio 1910-1980 .... DLB-312
Móricz, Zsigmond 1879-1942 .... DLB-215
Morier, James Justinian
    1782 or 1783?-1849 .... DLB-116
Mörike, Eduard 1804-1875 .... DLB-133
Morin, Paul 1889-1963 .... DLB-92
Morison, Richard 1514?-1556 .... DLB-136
Morison, Samuel Eliot 1887-1976 .... DLB-17
Morison, Stanley 1889-1967 .... DLB-201
Moritz, Karl Philipp 1756-1793 .... DLB-94
Moriz von Craûn circa 1220-1230 .... DLB-138
Morley, Christopher 1890-1957 .... DLB-9
Morley, John 1838-1923 .... DLB-57, 144, 190
Moro, César 1903-1956 .... DLB-290
Morris, George Pope 1802-1864 .... DLB-73
Morris, James Humphrey (see Morris, Jan)
Morris, Jan 1926- DLB-204
Morris, Lewis 1833-1907 .... DLB-35
Morris, Margaret 1737-1816 .... DLB-200
Morris, Mary McGarry 1943- DLB-292
Morris, Richard B. 1904-1989 .... DLB-17
Morris, William 1834-1896
    ..... DLB-18, 35, 57, 156, 178, 184; CDBLB-4
Morris, Willie 1934-1999 .... Y-80
    Tribute to Irwin Shaw Y-84
    Tribute to James Dickey Y-97
Morris, Wright
    1910-1998 .... DLB-2, 206, 218; Y-81
Morrison, Arthur 1863-1945 .... DLB-70, 135, 197
Morrison, Charles Clayton 1874-1966 .... DLB-91
Morrison, John 1904-1998 .... DLB-260
Morrison, Toni 1931-
    .... DLB-6, 33, 143; Y-81, 93; CDALB-6
    Nobel Lecture 1993 .... Y-93
Morrissy, Mary 1957- DLB-267
William Morrow and Company DLB-46
Morse, James Herbert 1841-1923 .... DLB-71
Morse, Jedidiah 1761-1826 .... DLB-37
Morse, John T., Jr. 1840-1937 .... DLB-47
Morselli, Guido 1912-1973 .... DLB-177
Morte Arthure, the *Alliterative* and the
    Stanzaic circa 1350-1400 .... DLB-146
Mortimer, Favell Lee 1802-1878 .... DLB-163
Mortimer, John
    1923- DLB-13, 245, 271; CDBLB-8
Morton, Carlos 1942- DLB-122
Morton, H. V. 1892-1979 .... DLB-195
John P. Morton and Company DLB-49
Morton, Nathaniel 1613-1685 .... DLB-24
Morton, Sarah Wentworth 1759-1846 .... DLB-37
Morton, Thomas circa 1579-circa 1647 ... DLB-24

Moscherosch, Johann Michael 1601-1669 ....DLB-164

Humphrey Moseley [publishing house] DLB-170

Möser, Justus 1720-1794................DLB-97

Mosley, Nicholas 1923- DLB-14, 207

Mosley, Walter 1952- DLB-306

Moss, Arthur 1889-1969 ....DLB-4

Moss, Howard 1922-1987 ....DLB-5

Moss, Thylias 1954- DLB-120

Motion, Andrew 1952- DLB-40

Motley, John Lothrop 1814-1877 ....DLB-1, 30, 59, 235

Motley, Willard 1909-1965 ....DLB-76, 143

Mott, Lucretia 1793-1880..............DLB-239

Benjamin Motte Jr. [publishing house] DLB-154

Motteux, Peter Anthony 1663-1718.......DLB-80

Mottram, R. H. 1883-1971...............DLB-36

Mount, Ferdinand 1939- DLB-231

Mouré, Erin 1955- DLB-60

Mourning Dove (Humishuma) between 1882 and 1888?-1936 ....DLB-175, 221

Movies
Fiction into Film, 1928-1975: A List of Movies Based on the Works of Authors in British Novelists, 1930-1959...................DLB-15

Movies from Books, 1920-1974.......DLB-9

Mowat, Farley 1921- DLB-68

A. R. Mowbray and Company, Limited DLB-106

Mowrer, Edgar Ansel 1892-1977 ....DLB-29

Mowrer, Paul Scott 1887-1971 ....DLB-29

Edward Moxon [publishing house] DLB-106

Joseph Moxon [publishing house] DLB-170

Moyes, Patricia 1923-2000.............DLB-276

Mphahlele, Es'kia (Ezekiel) 1919- DLB-125, 225; CDWLB-3

Mrożek, Sławomir 1930- ...DLB-232; CDWLB-4

Mtshali, Oswald Mbuyiseni 1940- DLB-125, 225

Mu Shiying 1912-1940.................DLB-328

al-Mubarrad 826-898 or 899 ....DLB-311

Mucedorus........................DLB-62

Mudford, William 1782-1848............DLB-159

Mudrooroo (see Johnson, Colin)

Mueller, Lisel 1924- DLB-105

Muhajir, El (see Marvin X)

Muhajir, Nazzam Al Fitnah (see Marvin X)

Muhammad the Prophet circa 570-632 ...DLB-311

Mühlbach, Luise 1814-1873...........DLB-133

Muir, Edwin 1887-1959 ....DLB-20, 100, 191

Muir, Helen 1937- DLB-14

Muir, John 1838-1914 ....DLB-186, 275

Muir, Percy 1894-1979................DLB-201

Mujū Ichien 1226-1312 ....DLB-203

Mukherjee, Bharati 1940- DLB-60, 218, 323

Mulcaster, Richard 1531 or 1532-1611 ...DLB-167

Muldoon, Paul 1951- DLB-40

Mulisch, Harry 1927- DLB-299

Mulkerns, Val 1925- DLB-319

Müller, Friedrich (see Müller, Maler)

Müller, Heiner 1929-1995 ....DLB-124

Müller, Maler 1749-1825 ....DLB-94

Muller, Marcia 1944- DLB-226

Müller, Wilhelm 1794-1827 ....DLB-90

Mumford, Lewis 1895-1990 ....DLB-63

Munby, A. N. L. 1913-1974 ....DLB-201

Munby, Arthur Joseph 1828-1910 ....DLB-35

Munday, Anthony 1560-1633 ....DLB-62, 172

Mundt, Clara (see Mühlbach, Luise)

Mundt, Theodore 1808-1861 ....DLB-133

Munford, Robert circa 1737-1783.........DLB-31

Mungoshi, Charles 1947- DLB-157

Munk, Kaj 1898-1944 ....DLB-214

Munonye, John 1929- DLB-117

Muñoz Molina, Antonio 1956- DLB-322

Munro, Alice 1931- DLB-53

George Munro [publishing house] DLB-49

Munro, H. H. 1870-1916 ....DLB-34, 162; CDBLB-5

Munro, Neil 1864-1930 ....DLB-156

Norman L. Munro [publishing house] DLB-49

Munroe, Kirk 1850-1930...............DLB-42

Munroe and Francis.................DLB-49

James Munroe and Company DLB-49

Joel Munsell [publishing house] DLB-49

Munsey, Frank A. 1854-1925..........DLB-25, 91

Frank A. Munsey and Company........DLB-49

Mura, David 1952- DLB-312

Murakami Haruki 1949- DLB-182

Muratov, Pavel 1881-1950..............DLB-317

Murayama, Milton 1923- DLB-312

Murav'ev, Mikhail Nikitich 1757-1807 ....DLB-150

Murdoch, Iris 1919-1999 ....DLB-14, 194, 233, 326; CDBLB-8

Murdock, James From *Sketches of Modern Philosophy*........DS-5

Murdoch, Rupert 1931- DLB-127

Murfree, Mary N. 1850-1922 ....DLB-12, 74

Murger, Henry 1822-1861 ....DLB-119

Murger, Louis-Henri (see Murger, Henry)

Murnane, Gerald 1939- DLB-289

Murner, Thomas 1475-1537............DLB-179

Muro, Amado 1915-1971...............DLB-82

Murphy, Arthur 1727-1805 ....DLB-89, 142

Murphy, Beatrice M. 1908-1992 ....DLB-76

Murphy, Dervla 1931- DLB-204

Murphy, Emily 1868-1933..............DLB-99

Murphy, Jack 1923-1980 ....DLB-241

John Murphy and Company DLB-49

Murphy, John H., III 1916- DLB-127

Murphy, Richard 1927-1993 ....DLB-40

Murphy, Tom 1935- DLB-310

Murray, Albert L. 1916- DLB-38

Murray, Gilbert 1866-1957 ....DLB-10

Murray, Jim 1919-1998 ....DLB-241

John Murray [publishing house] DLB-154

Murray, Judith Sargent 1751-1820 ....DLB-37, 200

Murray, Les 1938- DLB-289

Murray, Pauli 1910-1985 ....DLB-41

Murry, John Middleton 1889-1957 ......DLB-149

"The Break-Up of the Novel" (1922).....................DLB-36

Murry, John Middleton, Jr. (see Cowper, Richard)

Musäus, Johann Karl August 1735-1787......................DLB-97

Muschg, Adolf 1934- DLB-75

Musil, Robert 1880-1942 ....DLB-81, 124; CDWLB-2

Muspilli circa 790-circa 850.............DLB-148

Musset, Alfred de 1810-1857 ....DLB-192, 217

Benjamin B. Mussey and Company.................DLB-49

Muste, A. J. 1885-1967 ....DLB-303

Mutafchieva, Vera 1929- DLB-181

Mutis, Alvaro 1923- DLB-283

Mwangi, Meja 1948- DLB-125

Myers, Frederic W. H. 1843-1901.....................DLB-190

Myers, Gustavus 1872-1942.............DLB-47

Myers, L. H. 1881-1944................DLB-15

Myers, Walter Dean 1937- DLB-33

Myerson, Julie 1960- DLB-267

Mykle, Agnar 1915-1994 ....DLB-297

Mykolaitis-Putinas, Vincas 1893-1967 ....DLB-220

Myles, Eileen 1949- DLB-193

Myrdal, Jan 1927- DLB-257

Mystery
1985: The Year of the Mystery: A Symposium....................Y-85

Comments from Other Writers.........Y-85

The Second Annual New York Festival of Mystery Y-00

Why I Read Mysteries Y-85

Why I Write Mysteries: Night and Day, by Michael Collins Y-85

Cumulative Index

N

Na Prous Boneta circa 1296-1328....... DLB-208
Nabl, Franz 1883-1974 .... DLB-81
Nabokov, Véra 1902-1991 .... Y-91
Nabokov, Vladimir 1899-1977 .... DLB-2, 244, 278, 317; Y-80, 91; DS-3; CDALB-1
   International Nabokov Society.......... Y-99
   An Interview [On Nabokov], by Fredson Bowers................. Y-80
   Nabokov Festival at Cornell........... Y-83
   The Vladimir Nabokov Archive in the Berg Collection of the New York Public Library: An Overview Y-91
   The Vladimir Nabokov Society......... Y-01
Nádaši, Ladislav (see Jégé)
Naden, Constance 1858-1889......... DLB-199
Nadezhdin, Nikolai Ivanovich 1804-1856 .... DLB-198
Nadson, Semen Iakovlevich 1862-1887 ...DLB-277
Naevius circa 265 B.C.-201 B.C. DLB-211
Nafis and Cornish................... DLB-49
Nagai Kafū 1879-1959 .... DLB-180
Nagel, Ernest 1901-1985............ .DLB-279
Nagibin, Iurii Markovich 1920-1994 .... DLB-302
Nagrodskaia, Evdokiia Apollonovna 1866-1930 .... DLB-295
Naipaul, Shiva 1945-1985........DLB-157; Y-85
Naipaul, V. S. 1932- ... DLB-125, 204, 207, 326; Y-85, Y-01; CDBLB-8; CDWLB-3
   Nobel Lecture 2001: "Two Worlds"...... Y-01
Nakagami Kenji 1946-1992 .... DLB-182
Nakano-in Masatada no Musume (see Nijō, Lady)
Nałkowska, Zofia 1884-1954 .... DLB-215
Namora, Fernando 1919-1989 .... DLB-287
Joseph Nancrede [publishing house]...... DLB-49
Naranjo, Carmen 1930- DLB-145
Narayan, R. K. 1906-2001 .... DLB-323
Narbikova, Valeriia Spartakovna 1958- DLB-285
Narezhny, Vasilii Trofimovich 1780-1825.................... DLB-198
Narrache, Jean (Emile Coderre) 1893-1970..................... DLB-92
Nasby, Petroleum Vesuvius (see Locke, David Ross)
Eveleigh Nash [publishing house]....... DLB-112
Nash, Ogden 1902-1971 .... DLB-11
Nashe, Thomas 1567-1601?........... DLB-167
Nason, Jerry 1910-1986 .... DLB-241
Nasr, Seyyed Hossein 1933- DLB-279
Nast, Condé 1873-1942 .... DLB-91
Nast, Thomas 1840-1902 .... DLB-188
Nastasijević, Momčilo 1894-1938....... DLB-147
Nathan, George Jean 1882-1958 .... DLB-137
Nathan, Robert 1894-1985 .... DLB-9

Nation, Carry A. 1846-1911.......... DLB-303
National Book Critics Circle Awards Y-00–01
The National Jewish Book Awards.......... Y-85
Natsume Sōseki 1867-1916 .... DLB-180
Naughton, Bill 1910-1992............ DLB-13
Nava, Michael 1954- DLB-306
Navarro, Joe 1953- DLB-209
Naylor, Gloria 1950- DLB-173
Nazor, Vladimir 1876-1949........... DLB-147
Ndebele, Njabulo 1948-........DLB-157, 225
Neagoe, Peter 1881-1960 .... DLB-4
Neal, John 1793-1876 .... DLB-1, 59, 243
Neal, Joseph C. 1807-1847 .... DLB-11
Neal, Larry 1937-1981 .... DLB-38
The Neale Publishing Company......... DLB-49
Nearing, Scott 1883-1983............. DLB-303
Nebel, Frederick 1903-1967 .... DLB-226
Nebrija, Antonio de 1442 or 1444-1522.. DLB-286
Nedreaas, Torborg 1906-1987 .... DLB-297
F. Tennyson Neely [publishing house] DLB-49
Negoiţescu, Ion 1921-1993............ DLB-220
Negri, Ada 1870-1945................ DLB-114
Nehru, Pandit Jawaharlal 1889-1964 .... DLB-323
Neihardt, John G. 1881-1973 ..... DLB-9, 54, 256
Neidhart von Reuental circa 1185-circa 1240 .... DLB-138
Neilson, John Shaw 1872-1942 .... DLB-230
Nekrasov, Nikolai Alekseevich 1821-1877.....................DLB-277
Nekrasov, Viktor Platonovich 1911-1987..................... DLB-302
Neledinsky-Meletsky, Iurii Aleksandrovich 1752-1828..................... DLB-150
Nelligan, Emile 1879-1941 .... DLB-92
Nelson, Alice Moore Dunbar 1875-1935 .. DLB-50
Nelson, Antonya 1961- DLB-244
Nelson, Kent 1943- DLB-234
Nelson, Richard K. 1941- DLB-275
Nelson, Thomas, and Sons [U.K.] DLB-106
Nelson, Thomas, and Sons [U.S.] DLB-49
Nelson, William 1908-1978............ DLB-103
Nelson, William Rockhill 1841-1915 ..... DLB-23
Nemerov, Howard 1920-1991......DLB-5, 6; Y-83
Németh, László 1901-1975 .... DLB-215
Nepos circa 100 B.C.-post 27 B.C. DLB-211
Nėris, Salomėja 1904-1945 .. DLB-220; CDWLB-4
Neruda, Pablo 1904-1973 .... DLB-283
Nerval, Gérard de 1808-1855.......... DLB-217
Nervo, Amado 1870-1919............ DLB-290
Nesbit, E. 1858-1924 ....DLB-141, 153, 178
Ness, Evaline 1911-1986............... DLB-61

Nestroy, Johann 1801-1862........... DLB-133
Nettleship, R. L. 1846-1892 .... DLB-262
Neugeboren, Jay 1938- DLB-28
Neukirch, Benjamin 1655-1729......... DLB-168
Neumann, Alfred 1895-1952 .... DLB-56
Neumann, Ferenc (see Molnár, Ferenc)
Neumark, Georg 1621-1681........... DLB-164
Neumeister, Erdmann 1671-1756 .... DLB-168
Nevins, Allan 1890-1971..........DLB-17; DS-17
Nevinson, Henry Woodd 1856-1941 .... DLB-135
The New American Library............ DLB-46
New Directions Publishing Corporation... DLB-46
The New Monthly Magazine 1814-1884 .... DLB-110
New York Times Book Review Y-82
John Newbery [publishing house]....... DLB-154
Newbolt, Henry 1862-1938 .... DLB-19
Newbound, Bernard Slade (see Slade, Bernard)
Newby, Eric 1919- DLB-204
Newby, P. H. 1918-1997............ DLB-15, 326
Thomas Cautley Newby [publishing house] DLB-106
Newcomb, Charles King 1820-1894... DLB-1, 223
Newell, Peter 1862-1924............... DLB-42
Newell, Robert Henry 1836-1901 .... DLB-11
Newhouse, Samuel I. 1895-1979.........DLB-127
Newman, Cecil Earl 1903-1976 ....DLB-127
Newman, David 1937- DLB-44
Newman, Frances 1883-1928 .... Y-80
Newman, Francis William 1805-1897.... DLB-190
Newman, G. F. 1946- DLB-310
Newman, John Henry 1801-1890 .... DLB-18, 32, 55
Mark Newman [publishing house]....... DLB-49
Newmarch, Rosa Harriet 1857-1940..... DLB-240
George Newnes Limited.............. DLB-112
Newsome, Effie Lee 1885-1979.......... DLB-76
Newton, A. Edward 1864-1940 .... DLB-140
Newton, Sir Isaac 1642-1727 .... DLB-252
Nexø, Martin Andersen 1869-1954 ..... DLB-214
Nezval, Vítěslav 1900-1958 ....DLB-215; CDWLB-4
Ngugi wa Thiong'o 1938- DLB-125; CDWLB-3
Niatum, Duane 1938- DLB-175
The *Nibelungenlied* and the *Klage* circa 1200..................... DLB-138
Nichol, B. P. 1944-1988 .... DLB-53
Nicholas of Cusa 1401-1464........... DLB-115
Nichols, Ann 1891?-1966 .... DLB-249
Nichols, Beverly 1898-1983 .... DLB-191
Nichols, Dudley 1895-1960 .... DLB-26
Nichols, Grace 1950- DLB-157

412

Nichols, John 1940- Y-82

Nichols, Mary Sargeant (Neal) Gove
　1810-1884 ....DLB-1, 243

Nichols, Peter 1927- DLB-13, 245

Nichols, Roy F. 1896-1973..............DLB-17

Nichols, Ruth 1948- DLB-60

Nicholson, Edward Williams Byron
　1849-1912 ....DLB-184

Nicholson, Geoff 1953- DLB-271

Nicholson, Norman 1914-1987...........DLB-27

Nicholson, William 1872-1949..........DLB-141

Ní Chuilleanáin, Eiléan 1942- DLB-40

Nicol, Eric 1919- DLB-68

Nicolai, Friedrich 1733-1811 ....DLB-97

Nicolas de Clamanges circa 1363-1437 ...DLB-208

Nicolay, John G. 1832-1901 and
　Hay, John 1838-1905...............DLB-47

Nicole, Pierre 1625-1695 ....DLB-268

Nicolson, Adela Florence Cory (see Hope, Laurence)

Nicolson, Harold 1886-1968 ....DLB-100, 149

　"The Practice of Biography," in
　　*The English Sense of Humour and
　　Other Essays* DLB-149

Nicolson, Nigel 1917-2004 ....DLB-155

Ní Dhuibhne, Éilís 1954- DLB-319

Niebuhr, Reinhold 1892-1971 .....DLB-17; DS-17

Niedecker, Lorine 1903-1970............DLB-48

Nieman, Lucius W. 1857-1935...........DLB-25

Nietzsche, Friedrich
　1844-1900 ....DLB-129; CDWLB-2

　Mencken and Nietzsche: An Unpublished
　　Excerpt from H. L. Mencken's *My Life
　　as Author and Editor* Y-93

Nievo, Stanislao 1928- DLB-196

Niggli, Josefina 1910-1983 ....Y-80

Nightingale, Florence 1820-1910 ....DLB-166

Nijō, Lady (Nakano-in Masatada no Musume)
　1258-after 1306 ....DLB-203

Nijō Yoshimoto 1320-1388..............DLB-203

Nikitin, Ivan Savvich 1824-1861 ....DLB-277

Nikitin, Nikolai Nikolaevich 1895-1963...DLB-272

Nikolev, Nikolai Petrovich 1758-1815 ....DLB-150

Niles, Hezekiah 1777-1839 ....DLB-43

Nims, John Frederick 1913-1999 ....DLB-5

　Tribute to Nancy Hale Y-88

Nin, Anaïs 1903-1977...........DLB-2, 4, 152

Nína Björk Árnadóttir 1941-2000 ......DLB-293

Niño, Raúl 1961- DLB-209

Nissenson, Hugh 1933- DLB-28

Niven, Frederick John 1878-1944........DLB-92

Niven, Larry 1938- DLB-8

Nixon, Howard M. 1909-1983..........DLB-201

Nizan, Paul 1905-1940..................DLB-72

Njegoš, Petar II Petrović
　1813-1851 ....DLB-147; CDWLB-4

Nkosi, Lewis 1936- DLB-157, 225

Noah, Mordecai M. 1785-1851 ....DLB-250

Noailles, Anna de 1876-1933 ....DLB-258

Nobel Peace Prize
　The Nobel Prize and Literary Politics.....Y-88
　Elie Wiesel Y-86

Nobel Prize in Literature
　Joseph Brodsky.....................Y-87
　Camilo José Cela...................Y-89
　Dario Fo Y-97
　Gabriel García Márquez Y-82
　William Golding Y-83
　Nadine Gordimer Y-91
　Günter Grass.......................Y-99
　Seamus Heaney......................Y-95
　Imre Kertész Y-02
　Najīb Mahfūz Y-88
　Toni Morrison......................Y-93
　V. S. Naipaul......................Y-01
　Kenzaburō Oe......................Y-94
　Octavio Paz........................Y-90
　José Saramago Y-98
　Jaroslav Seifert...................Y-84
　Claude Simon Y-85
　Wole Soyinka Y-86
　Wisława Szymborska Y-96
　Derek Walcott......................Y-92
　Gao Xingjian.......................Y-00

Nobre, António 1867-1900.............DLB-287

Nodier, Charles 1780-1844.............DLB-119

Noël, Marie (Marie Mélanie Rouget)
　1883-1967 ....DLB-258

Noel, Roden 1834-1894.................DLB-35

Nogami Yaeko 1885-1985 ....DLB-180

Nogo, Rajko Petrov 1945- DLB-181

Nolan, William F. 1928- DLB-8

　Tribute to Raymond Chandler Y-88

Noland, C. F. M. 1810?-1858 ....DLB-11

Noma Hiroshi 1915-1991 ....DLB-182

Nonesuch Press DLB-112

Creative Nonfiction Y-02

Nonni (Jón Stefán Sveinsson or Svensson)
　1857-1944 ....DLB-293

Noon, Jeff 1957- DLB-267

Noonan, Robert Phillipe (see Tressell, Robert)

Noonday Press........................DLB-46

Noone, John 1936- DLB-14

Nora, Eugenio de 1923- DLB-134

Nordan, Lewis 1939- DLB-234

Nordbrandt, Henrik 1945- DLB-214

Nordhoff, Charles 1887-1947............DLB-9

Norén, Lars 1944- DLB-257

Norfolk, Lawrence 1963- DLB-267

Norman, Charles 1904-1996...........DLB-111

Norman, Marsha 1947- DLB-266; Y-84

Norris, Charles G. 1881-1945............DLB-9

Norris, Frank
　1870-1902 ....DLB-12, 71, 186; CDALB-3

Norris, Helen 1916- DLB-292

Norris, John 1657-1712................DLB-252

Norris, Leslie 1921- DLB-27, 256

Norse, Harold 1916- DLB-16

Norte, Marisela 1955- DLB-209

North, Marianne 1830-1890 ....DLB-174

North Point Press.....................DLB-46

Nortje, Arthur 1942-1970.........DLB-125, 225

Norton, Alice Mary (see Norton, Andre)

Norton, Andre 1912-2005 ....DLB-8, 52

Norton, Andrews 1786-1853 ....DLB-1, 235; DS-5

Norton, Caroline 1808-1877....DLB-21, 159, 199

Norton, Charles Eliot 1827-1908...DLB-1, 64, 235

Norton, John 1606-1663 ....DLB-24

Norton, Mary 1903-1992...............DLB-160

Norton, Thomas 1532-1584 ....DLB-62

W. W. Norton and Company DLB-46

Norwood, Robert 1874-1932...........DLB-92

Nosaka Akiyuki 1930- DLB-182

Nossack, Hans Erich 1901-1977 ....DLB-69

Notker Balbulus circa 840-912..........DLB-148

Notker III of Saint Gall
　circa 950-1022...................DLB-148

Notker von Zweifalten ?-1095 ....DLB-148

Nourse, Alan E. 1928-1992 ....DLB-8

Novak, Slobodan 1924- DLB-181

Novak, Vjenceslav 1859-1905 ....DLB-147

Novakovich, Josip 1956- DLB-244

Novalis 1772-1801 ....DLB-90; CDWLB-2

Novaro, Mario 1868-1944.............DLB-114

Novás Calvo, Lino 1903-1983..........DLB-145

Novelists
　Library Journal Statements and
　　Questionnaires from First Novelists Y-87

Novels
　The Columbia History of the American Novel
　　A Symposium on Y-92
　The Great Modern Library Scam........Y-98
　Novels for Grown-Ups Y-97
　The Proletarian Novel................DLB-9
　Novel, The "Second-Generation" Holocaust
　　.........................DLB-299
　The Year in the Novel...... Y-87–88, Y-90–93

Novels, British
　"The Break-Up of the Novel" (1922),
　　by John Middleton Murry DLB-36
　The Consolidation of Opinion: Critical
　　Responses to the Modernists DLB-36

"Criticism in Relation to Novels" (1863), by G. H. Lewes DLB-21
"Experiment in the Novel" (1929) [excerpt], by John D. Beresford ... DLB-36
"The Future of the Novel" (1899), by Henry James DLB-18
The Gay Science (1866), by E. S. Dallas [excerpt].................... DLB-21
A Haughty and Proud Generation (1922), by Ford Madox Hueffer .. DLB-36
Literary Effects of World War II DLB-15
"Modern Novelists – Great and Small" (1855), by Margaret Oliphant DLB-21
The Modernists (1932), by Joseph Warren Beach DLB-36
A Note on Technique (1926), by Elizabeth A. Drew [excerpts] DLB-36
Novel-Reading: *The Works of Charles Dickens; The Works of W. Makepeace Thackeray* (1879), by Anthony Trollope DLB-21
Novels with a Purpose (1864), by Justin M'Carthy................ DLB-21
"On Art in Fiction" (1838), by Edward Bulwer.............. DLB-21
The Present State of the English Novel (1892), by George Saintsbury DLB-18
Representative Men and Women: A Historical Perspective on the British Novel, 1930-1960..... DLB-15
"The Revolt" (1937), by Mary Colum [excerpts].................... DLB-36
"Sensation Novels" (1863), by H. L. Manse DLB-21
Sex, Class, Politics, and Religion [in the British Novel, 1930-1959] ... DLB-15
Time and Western Man (1927), by Wyndham Lewis [excerpts] ... DLB-36
Noventa, Giacomo 1898-1960 .... DLB-114
Novikov, Nikolai Ivanovich 1744-1818..................... DLB-150
Novomeský, Laco 1904-1976 .... DLB-215
Nowlan, Alden 1933-1983 .... DLB-53
Nowra, Louis 1950- DLB-325
Noyes, Alfred 1880-1958 .... DLB-20
Noyes, Crosby S. 1825-1908............ DLB-23
Noyes, Nicholas 1647-1717 .... DLB-24
Noyes, Theodore W. 1858-1946......... DLB-29
Nozick, Robert 1938-2002 ....DLB-279
N-Town Plays circa 1468 to early sixteenth century................ DLB-146
Nugent, Frank 1908-1965.............. DLB-44
Nunez, Sigrid 1951- DLB-312
Nušić, Branislav 1864-1938 ....DLB-147; CDWLB-4
David Nutt [publishing house] DLB-106
Nwapa, Flora 1931-1993 .... DLB-125; CDWLB-3
Nye, Edgar Wilson (Bill) 1850-1896 .... DLB-11, 23, 186
Nye, Naomi Shihab 1952- DLB-120

Nye, Robert 1939- DLB-14, 271
Nyka-Niliūnas, Alfonsas 1919- DLB-220

O

Oakes, Urian circa 1631-1681 .... DLB-24
Oakes Smith, Elizabeth 1806-1893 .... DLB-1, 239, 243
Oakley, Violet 1874-1961 .... DLB-188
Oates, Joyce Carol 1938- DLB-2, 5, 130; Y-81; CDALB-6
Tribute to Michael M. Rea............. Y-97
Ōba Minako 1930- DLB-182
Ober, Frederick Albion 1849-1913 ...... DLB-189
Ober, William 1920-1993................. Y-93
Oberholtzer, Ellis Paxson 1868-1936 ..... DLB-47
The Obituary as Literary Form Y-02
Obradović, Dositej 1740?-1811......... DLB-147
O'Brien, Charlotte Grace 1845-1909 .... DLB-240
O'Brien, Edna 1932- DLB-14, 231, 319; CDBLB-8
O'Brien, Fitz-James 1828-1862 .... DLB-74
O'Brien, Flann (see O'Nolan, Brian)
O'Brien, Kate 1897-1974 .... DLB-15
O'Brien, Tim 1946- DLB-152; Y-80; DS-9; CDALB-7
Ó Cadhain, Máirtín 1905-1970......... DLB-319
O'Casey, Sean 1880-1964..... DLB-10; CDBLB-6
Occom, Samson 1723-1792............DLB-175
Occomy, Marita Bonner 1899-1971 ...... DLB-51
Ochs, Adolph S. 1858-1935 .... DLB-25
Ochs-Oakes, George Washington 1861-1931 .... DLB-137
O'Connor, Flannery 1925-1964 ....DLB-2, 152; Y-80; DS-12; CDALB-1
The Flannery O'Connor Society Y-99
O'Connor, Frank 1903-1966 .... DLB-162
O'Connor, Joseph 1963- DLB-267
Octopus Publishing Group............ DLB-112
Oda Sakunosuke 1913-1947........... DLB-182
Odell, Jonathan 1737-1818 .... DLB-31, 99
O'Dell, Scott 1903-1989 .... DLB-52
Odets, Clifford 1906-1963 ....DLB-7, 26
Odhams Press Limited DLB-112
Odio, Eunice 1922-1974 .... DLB-283
Odoevsky, Aleksandr Ivanovich 1802-1839 .... DLB-205
Odoevsky, Vladimir Fedorovich 1804 or 1803-1869............ DLB-198
Odoevtseva, Irina 1895-1990 .... DLB-317
O'Donnell, Peter 1920- DLB-87
O'Donovan, Michael (see O'Connor, Frank)
O'Dowd, Bernard 1866-1953 .... DLB-230
Ōe, Kenzaburō 1935- DLB-182; Y-94

Nobel Lecture 1994: Japan, the Ambiguous, and Myself Y-94
Oehlenschläger, Adam 1779-1850....... DLB-300
O'Faolain, Julia 1932- DLB-14, 231, 319
O'Faolain, Sean 1900-1991 .... DLB-15, 162
Off-Loop Theatres DLB-7
Offord, Carl Ruthven 1910-1990 .... DLB-76
Offshore, 1979 Booker Prize winner, Penelope Fitzgerald DLB-326
O'Flaherty, Liam 1896-1984.... DLB-36, 162; Y-84
Ogarev, Nikolai Platonovich 1813-1877 ...DLB-277
J. S. Ogilvie and Company............ DLB-49
Ogilvy, Eliza 1822-1912 .... DLB-199
Ogot, Grace 1930- DLB-125
O'Grady, Desmond 1935- DLB-40
Ogunyemi, Wale 1939- DLB-157
O'Hagan, Howard 1902-1982 .... DLB-68
O'Hara, Frank 1926-1966 ....DLB-5, 16, 193
O'Hara, John 1905-1970... DLB-9, 86, 324; DS-2; CDALB-5
John O'Hara's Pottsville Journalism...... Y-88
O'Hare, Kate Richards 1876-1948 ...... DLB-303
O'Hegarty, P. S. 1879-1955............ DLB-201
Ohio State University
The William Charvat American Fiction Collection at the Ohio State University Libraries Y-92
Okada, John 1923-1971 .... DLB-312
Okara, Gabriel 1921- DLB-125; CDWLB-3
O'Keeffe, John 1747-1833 .... DLB-89
Nicholas Okes [publishing house]........DLB-170
Okigbo, Christopher 1930-1967 ....DLB-125; CDWLB-3
Okot p'Bitek 1931-1982 .....DLB-125; CDWLB-3
Okpewho, Isidore 1941- DLB-157
Okri, Ben 1959- DLB-157, 231, 319, 326
Ólafur Jóhann Sigurðsson 1918-1988.... DLB-293
The Old Devils, 1986 Booker Prize winner, Kingsley Amis DLB-326
Old Dogs / New Tricks? New Technologies, the Canon, and the Structure of the Profession..................... Y-02
Old Franklin Publishing House DLB-49
Old German Genesis and *Old German Exodus* circa 1050-circa 1130 .... DLB-148
The *Old High German Isidor* circa 790-800 .... DLB-148
Older, Fremont 1856-1935............. DLB-25
Oldham, John 1653-1683 .... DLB-131
Oldman, C. B. 1894-1969 .... DLB-201
Olds, Sharon 1942- DLB-120
Olearius, Adam 1599-1671............. DLB-164
O'Leary, Ellen 1831-1889............. DLB-240
O'Leary, Juan E. 1879-1969 .... DLB-290
Olesha, Iurii Karlovich 1899-1960 ....DLB-272

Oliphant, Laurence 1829?-1888......DLB-18, 166

Oliphant, Margaret 1828-1897...DLB-18, 159, 190

   "Modern Novelists—Great and Small"
      (1855).......................DLB-21

Oliveira, Carlos de 1921-1981..........DLB-287

Oliver, Chad 1928-1993.................DLB-8

Oliver, Mary 1935- DLB-5, 193

Ollier, Claude 1922- DLB-83

Olsen, Tillie 1912/1913-
      ....DLB-28, 206; Y-80; CDALB-7

Olson, Charles 1910-1970 ....DLB-5, 16, 193

Olson, Elder 1909-1992............DLB-48, 63

Olson, Sigurd F. 1899-1982 ....DLB-275

The Omega Workshops..................DS-10

Omotoso, Kole 1943- DLB-125

Omulevsky, Innokentii Vasil'evich
   1836 [or 1837]-1883 ....DLB-238

Ondaatje, Michael 1943- DLB-60, 323, 326

O'Neill, Eugene 1888-1953 .....DLB-7; CDALB-5

   Eugene O'Neill Memorial Theater
     Center......................DLB-7

   Eugene O'Neill's Letters: A Review Y-88

Onetti, Juan Carlos
   1909-1994 ....DLB-113; CDWLB-3

Onions, George Oliver 1872-1961.......DLB-153

Onofri, Arturo 1885-1928 ....DLB-114

O'Nolan, Brian 1911-1966............DLB-231

Oodgeroo of the Tribe Noonuccal
   (Kath Walker) 1920-1993 ....DLB-289

Opie, Amelia 1769-1853..........DLB-116, 159

Opitz, Martin 1597-1639 ....DLB-164

Oppen, George 1908-1984..........DLB-5, 165

Oppenheim, E. Phillips 1866-1946........DLB-70

Oppenheim, James 1882-1932 ....DLB-28

Oppenheimer, Joel 1930-1988 ....DLB-5, 193

Optic, Oliver (see Adams, William Taylor)

Orczy, Emma, Baroness 1865-1947 ....DLB-70

Oregon Shakespeare Festival Y-00

Origo, Iris 1902-1988..................DLB-155

O'Riordan, Kate 1960- DLB-267

Orlovitz, Gil 1918-1973 ....DLB-2, 5

Orlovsky, Peter 1933- DLB-16

Ormond, John 1923- DLB-27

Ornitz, Samuel 1890-1957 ....DLB-28, 44

O'Rourke, P. J. 1947- DLB-185

Orozco, Olga 1920-1999 ....DLB-283

Orten, Jiří 1919-1941................DLB-215

Ortese, Anna Maria 1914- DLB-177

Ortiz, Lourdes 1943- DLB-322

Ortiz, Simon J. 1941- DLB-120, 175, 256

Ortnit and *Wolfdietrich* circa 1225-1250.....DLB-138

Orton, Joe 1933-1967.....DLB-13, 310; CDBLB-8

Orwell, George (Eric Arthur Blair)
   1903-1950 ...DLB-15, 98, 195, 255; CDBLB-7

   The Orwell Year Y-84

   (Re-)Publishing Orwell Y-86

Ory, Carlos Edmundo de 1923- DLB-134

Osbey, Brenda Marie 1957- DLB-120

Osbon, B. S. 1827-1912 ....DLB-43

Osborn, Sarah 1714-1796.............DLB-200

Osborne, John 1929-1994 .....DLB-13; CDBLB-7

Oscar and Lucinda, 1988 Booker Prize winner,
   Peter Carey DLB-326

Osgood, Frances Sargent 1811-1850 .....DLB-250

Osgood, Herbert L. 1855-1918 ....DLB-47

James R. Osgood and Company DLB-49

Osgood, McIlvaine and Company.......DLB-112

O'Shaughnessy, Arthur 1844-1881 ....DLB-35

Patrick O'Shea [publishing house] DLB-49

Osipov, Nikolai Petrovich 1751-1799 ....DLB-150

Oskison, John Milton 1879-1947 ....DLB-175

Osler, Sir William 1849-1919...........DLB-184

Osofisan, Femi 1946- DLB-125; CDWLB-3

Ostenso, Martha 1900-1963.............DLB-92

Ostrauskas, Kostas 1926- DLB-232

Ostriker, Alicia 1937- DLB-120

Ostrovsky, Aleksandr Nikolaevich
   1823-1886 ....DLB-277

Ostrovsky, Nikolai Alekseevich
   1904-1936 ....DLB-272

Osundare, Niyi 1947- DLB-157; CDWLB-3

Oswald, Eleazer 1755-1795 ....DLB-43

Oswald von Wolkenstein
   1376 or 1377-1445 ....DLB-179

Otero, Blas de 1916-1979..............DLB-134

Otero, Miguel Antonio 1859-1944........DLB-82

Otero, Nina 1881-1965 ....DLB-209

Otero Silva, Miguel 1908-1985 ....DLB-145

Otfried von Weißenburg
   circa 800-circa 875? DLB-148

Otis, Broaders and Company DLB-49

Otis, James (see Kaler, James Otis)

Otis, James, Jr. 1725-1783................DLB-31

Otsup, Nikolai 1894-1958 ....DLB-317

Ottaway, James 1911-2000.............DLB-127

Ottendorfer, Oswald 1826-1900 ....DLB-23

Ottieri, Ottiero 1924-2002 ....DLB-177

Otto-Peters, Louise 1819-1895.........DLB-129

Otway, Thomas 1652-1685 ....DLB-80

Ouellette, Fernand 1930- DLB-60

Ouida 1839-1908..................DLB-18, 156

Outing Publishing Company DLB-46

Overbury, Sir Thomas
   circa 1581-1613 ....DLB-151

The Overlook Press...................DLB-46

Ovid 43 B.C.-A.D. 17 ....DLB-211; CDWLB-1

Oviedo, Gonzalo Fernández de
   1478-1557 ....DLB-318

Owen, Guy 1925-1981 ....DLB-5

Owen, John 1564-1622 ....DLB-121

John Owen [publishing house]..........DLB-49

Peter Owen Limited...................DLB-112

Owen, Robert 1771-1858......... DLB-107, 158

Owen, Wilfred
   1893-1918........DLB-20; DS-18; CDBLB-6

   A Centenary Celebration Y-93

   The Wilfred Owen Association..........Y-98

The Owl and the Nightingale
   circa 1189-1199..................DLB-146

Owsley, Frank L. 1890-1956 ....DLB-17

Oxford, Seventeenth Earl of, Edward
   de Vere 1550-1604 ....DLB-172

OyamO (Charles F. Gordon)
   1943- DLB-266

Ozerov, Vladislav Aleksandrovich
   1769-1816 ....DLB-150

Ozick, Cynthia 1928- ...DLB-28, 152, 299; Y-82

   First Strauss "Livings" Awarded
     to Cynthia Ozick and
     Raymond Carver
     An Interview with Cynthia Ozick.....Y-83

   Tribute to Michael M. Rea Y-97

P

Pace, Richard 1482?-1536 ....DLB-167

Pacey, Desmond 1917-1975 ....DLB-88

Pacheco, José Emilio 1939- DLB-290

Pack, Robert 1929- DLB-5

Paddy Clarke Ha Ha Ha, 1993 Booker Prize winner,
   Roddy Doyle....................DLB-326

Padell Publishing Company.............DLB-46

Padgett, Ron 1942- DLB-5

Padilla, Ernesto Chávez 1944- DLB-122

L. C. Page and Company DLB-49

Page, Louise 1955- DLB-233

Page, P. K. 1916- DLB-68

Page, Thomas Nelson
   1853-1922 ....DLB-12, 78; DS-13

Page, Walter Hines 1855-1918........DLB-71, 91

Paget, Francis Edward 1806-1882 ....DLB-163

Paget, Violet (see Lee, Vernon)

Pagliarani, Elio 1927- DLB-128

Pagnol, Marcel 1895-1974 ....DLB-321

Pain, Barry 1864-1928............DLB-135, 197

Pain, Philip ?-circa 1666................DLB-24

Paine, Robert Treat, Jr. 1773-1811 ....DLB-37

Paine, Thomas
   1737-1809 ....DLB-31, 43, 73, 158; CDALB-2

Painter, George D. 1914- DLB-155

Painter, William 1540?-1594 ....DLB-136

Palazzeschi, Aldo 1885-1974 . . . . DLB-114, 264

Palei, Marina Anatol'evna 1955- DLB-285

Palencia, Alfonso de 1424-1492 . . . . DLB-286

Palés Matos, Luis 1898-1959 . . . . DLB-290

Paley, Grace 1922- DLB-28, 218

Paley, William 1743-1805 . . . . DLB-252

Palfrey, John Gorham 1796-1881 . . . . DLB-1, 30, 235

Palgrave, Francis Turner 1824-1897 . . . . . . DLB-35

Palissy, Bernard 1510?-1590? DLB-327

Palmer, Joe H. 1904-1952 . . . . DLB-171

Palmer, Michael 1943- DLB-169

Palmer, Nettie 1885-1964 . . . . DLB-260

Palmer, Vance 1885-1959 . . . . DLB-260

Paltock, Robert 1697-1767 . . . . DLB-39

Paludan, Jacob 1896-1975 . . . . DLB-214

Paludin-Müller, Frederik 1809-1876 . . . . . DLB-300

Pan Books Limited DLB-112

Panaev, Ivan Ivanovich 1812-1862 . . . . . . DLB-198

Panaeva, Avdot'ia Iakovlevna 1820-1893 . . . . DLB-238

Panama, Norman 1914-2003 and Frank, Melvin 1913-1988 . . . . DLB-26

Pancake, Breece D'J 1952-1979 . . . . DLB-130

Panduro, Leif 1923-1977 . . . . DLB-214

Panero, Leopoldo 1909-1962 . . . . DLB-108

Pangborn, Edgar 1909-1976 . . . . DLB-8

Panizzi, Sir Anthony 1797-1879 . . . . DLB-184

Panneton, Philippe (see Ringuet)

Panova, Vera Fedorovna 1905-1973 . . . . . DLB-302

Panshin, Alexei 1940- DLB-8

Pansy (see Alden, Isabella)

Pantheon Books DLB-46

Papadat-Bengescu, Hortensia 1876-1955 . . . . DLB-220

Papantonio, Michael 1907-1976 . . . . DLB-187

Paperback Library DLB-46

Paperback Science Fiction DLB-8

Papini, Giovanni 1881-1956 . . . . DLB-264

Paquet, Alfons 1881-1944 . . . . DLB-66

Paracelsus 1493-1541 . . . . DLB-179

Paradis, Suzanne 1936- DLB-53

Páral, Vladimír, 1932- DLB-232

Pardoe, Julia 1804-1862 . . . . DLB-166

Paré, Ambroise 1510 or 1517?-1590 . . . . . DLB-327

Paredes, Américo 1915-1999 . . . . DLB-209

Pareja Diezcanseco, Alfredo 1908-1993 . . DLB-145

Parents' Magazine Press DLB-46

Paretsky, Sara 1947- DLB-306

Parfit, Derek 1942- DLB-262

Parise, Goffredo 1929-1986 . . . . DLB-177

Parish, Mitchell 1900-1993 . . . . DLB-265

Parizeau, Alice 1930-1990 . . . . DLB-60

Park, Ruth 1923?- DLB-260

Parke, John 1754-1789 . . . . DLB-31

Parker, Dan 1893-1967 . . . . DLB-241

Parker, Dorothy 1893-1967 . . . . . . DLB-11, 45, 86

Parker, Gilbert 1860-1932 . . . . DLB-99

Parker, James 1714-1770 . . . . DLB-43

Parker, John [publishing house] DLB-106

Parker, Matthew 1504-1575 . . . . DLB-213

Parker, Robert B. 1932- DLB-306

Parker, Stewart 1941-1988 . . . . DLB-245

Parker, Theodore 1810-1860 . . . DLB-1, 235; DS-5

Parker, William Riley 1906-1968 . . . . DLB-103

J. H. Parker [publishing house] DLB-106

Parkes, Bessie Rayner (Madame Belloc) 1829-1925 . . . . DLB-240

Parkman, Francis 1823-1893 . . . . DLB-1, 30, 183, 186, 235

Parks, Gordon 1912- DLB-33

Parks, Tim 1954- DLB-231

Parks, William 1698-1750 . . . . DLB-43

William Parks [publishing house] DLB-49

Parley, Peter (see Goodrich, Samuel Griswold)

Parmenides late sixth-fifth century B.C. . . . DLB-176

Parnell, Thomas 1679-1718 . . . . DLB-95

Parnicki, Teodor 1908-1988 . . . . DLB-215

Parnok, Sofiia Iakovlevna (Parnokh) 1885-1933 . . . . DLB-295

Parr, Catherine 1513?-1548 . . . . DLB-136

Parra, Nicanor 1914- DLB-283

Parrington, Vernon L. 1871-1929 . . . . . DLB-17, 63

Parrish, Maxfield 1870-1966 . . . . DLB-188

Parronchi, Alessandro 1914- DLB-128

Parshchikov, Aleksei Maksimovich (Raiderman) 1954- DLB-285

Partisan Review DLB-303

Parton, James 1822-1891 . . . . DLB-30

Parton, Sara Payson Willis 1811-1872 . . . . DLB-43, 74, 239

S. W. Partridge and Company DLB-106

Parun, Vesna 1922- DLB-181; CDWLB-4

Pascal, Blaise 1623-1662 . . . . DLB-268

Pasinetti, Pier Maria 1913- DLB-177

Tribute to Albert Erskine Y-93

Pasolini, Pier Paolo 1922-1975 . . . . . DLB-128, 177

Pastan, Linda 1932- DLB-5

Pasternak, Boris 1890-1960 . . . . DLB-302

Paston, George (Emily Morse Symonds) 1860-1936 . . . . DLB-149, 197

The Paston Letters 1422-1509 . . . . DLB-146

Pastoral Novel of the Sixteenth Century, The DLB-318

Pastorius, Francis Daniel 1651-circa 1720 . . . . DLB-24

Patchen, Kenneth 1911-1972 . . . . DLB-16, 48

Pater, Walter 1839-1894 . . . DLB-57, 156; CDBLB-4

Aesthetic Poetry (1873) DLB-35

"Style" (1888) [excerpt] DLB-57

Paterson, A. B. "Banjo" 1864-1941 . . . . . . DLB-230

Paterson, Katherine 1932- DLB-52

Patmore, Coventry 1823-1896 . . . . DLB-35, 98

Paton, Alan 1903-1988 . . . . DLB-225; DS-17

Paton, Joseph Noel 1821-1901 . . . . DLB-35

Paton Walsh, Jill 1937- DLB-161

Patrick, Edwin Hill ("Ted") 1901-1964 . . . DLB-137

Patrick, John 1906-1995 . . . . DLB-7

Pattee, Fred Lewis 1863-1950 . . . . DLB-71

Patterson, Alicia 1906-1963 . . . . DLB-127

Patterson, Eleanor Medill 1881-1948 . . . . . DLB-29

Patterson, Eugene 1923- DLB-127

Patterson, Joseph Medill 1879-1946 . . . . . DLB-29

Pattillo, Henry 1726-1801 . . . . DLB-37

Paul, Elliot 1891-1958 . . . . DLB-4; DS-15

Paul, Jean (see Richter, Johann Paul Friedrich)

Paul, Kegan, Trench, Trubner and Company Limited DLB-106

Peter Paul Book Company DLB-49

Stanley Paul and Company Limited DLB-112

Paulding, James Kirke 1778-1860 . . . . DLB-3, 59, 74, 250

Paulin, Tom 1949- DLB-40

Pauper, Peter, Press DLB-46

Paustovsky, Konstantin Georgievich 1892-1968 . . . . DLB-272

Pavese, Cesare 1908-1950 . . . . DLB-128, 177

Pavić, Milorad 1929- DLB-181; CDWLB-4

Pavlov, Konstantin 1933- DLB-181

Pavlov, Nikolai Filippovich 1803-1864 . . . . DLB-198

Pavlova, Karolina Karlovna 1807-1893 . . . . DLB-205

Pavlović, Miodrag 1928- DLB-181; CDWLB-4

Pavlovsky, Eduardo 1933- DLB-305

Paxton, John 1911-1985 . . . . DLB-44

Payn, James 1830-1898 . . . . DLB-18

Payne, John 1842-1916 . . . . DLB-35

Payne, John Howard 1791-1852 . . . . DLB-37

Payson and Clarke DLB-46

Paz, Octavio 1914-1998 . . . . DLB-290; Y-90, 98

Nobel Lecture 1990 . . . . Y-90

Pazzi, Roberto 1946- DLB-196

Pea, Enrico 1881-1958 . . . . DLB-264

Peabody, Elizabeth Palmer 1804-1894 . . . . DLB-1, 223

Preface to *Record of a School: Exemplifying the General Principles of Spiritual Culture* DS-5	Pennell, Joseph 1857-1926 .... DLB-188	Peters, Robert 1924- DLB-105
Elizabeth Palmer Peabody [publishing house] DLB-49	Penner, Jonathan 1940- Y-83	"Foreword to *Ludwig of Baviria*"...... DLB-105
Peabody, Josephine Preston 1874-1922 ... DLB-249	Pennington, Lee 1939- Y-82	Petersham, Maud 1889-1971 and Petersham, Miska 1888-1960 .... DLB-22
Peabody, Oliver William Bourn 1799-1848 .... DLB-59	Penton, Brian 1904-1951 .... DLB-260	Peterson, Charles Jacobs 1819-1887....... DLB-79
Peace, Roger 1899-1968 .... DLB-127	Pepper, Stephen C. 1891-1972 .... DLB-270	Peterson, Len 1917- DLB-88
Peacham, Henry 1578-1644? DLB-151	Pepys, Samuel 1633-1703 .... DLB-101, 213; CDBLB-2	Peterson, Levi S. 1933- DLB-206
Peacham, Henry, the Elder 1547-1634 .... DLB-172, 236	Percy, Thomas 1729-1811 .... DLB-104	Peterson, Louis 1922-1998 .... DLB-76
Peachtree Publishers, Limited DLB-46	Percy, Walker 1916-1990 .... DLB-2; Y-80, 90	Peterson, T. B., and Brothers DLB-49
Peacock, Molly 1947- DLB-120	Tribute to Caroline Gordon Y-81	Petitclair, Pierre 1813-1860 .... DLB-99
Peacock, Thomas Love 1785-1866 .... DLB-96, 116	Percy, William 1575-1648 .... DLB-172	Petrescu, Camil 1894-1957 .... DLB-220
Pead, Deuel ?-1727 .... DLB-24	Perec, Georges 1936-1982 .... DLB-83, 299	Petronius circa A.D. 20-A.D. 66 .... DLB-211; CDWLB-1
Peake, Mervyn 1911-1968 ...... DLB-15, 160, 255	Perelman, Bob 1947- DLB-193	Petrov, Aleksandar 1938- DLB-181
Peale, Rembrandt 1778-1860 .... DLB-183	Perelman, S. J. 1904-1979 .... DLB-11, 44	Petrov, Evgenii (Evgenii Petrovich Kataev) 1903-1942 .... DLB-272
Pear Tree Press DLB-112	Perez, Raymundo "Tigre" 1946- DLB-122	Petrov, Gavriil 1730-1801 .... DLB-150
Pearce, Philippa 1920- DLB-161	Pérez de Ayala, Ramón 1880-1962 ...... DLB-322	Petrov, Valeri 1920- DLB-181
H. B. Pearson [publishing house] DLB-49	Pérez de Guzmán, Fernán ca. 1377-ca. 1460 .... DLB-286	Petrov, Vasilii Petrovich 1736-1799 .... DLB-150
Pearson, Hesketh 1887-1964 .... DLB-149	Pérez-Reverte, Arturo 1951- DLB-322	Petrović, Rastko 1898-1949 .... DLB-147; CDWLB-4
Peattie, Donald Culross 1898-1964 ...... DLB-275	Peri Rossi, Cristina 1941- DLB-145, 290	Petrushevskaia, Liudmila Stefanovna 1938- DLB-285
Pechersky, Andrei (see Mel'nikov, Pavel Ivanovich)	Perkins, Eugene 1932- DLB-41	*Petruslied* circa 854?.................. DLB-148
Peck, George W. 1840-1916 .... DLB-23, 42	Perkins, Maxwell The Claims of Business and Literature: An Undergraduate Essay Y-01	Petry, Ann 1908-1997 .... DLB-76
H. C. Peck and Theo. Bliss [publishing house] DLB-49	Perkins, William 1558-1602 .... DLB-281	Pettie, George circa 1548-1589 .... DLB-136
Peck, Harry Thurston 1856-1914 ..... DLB-71, 91	Perkoff, Stuart Z. 1930-1974 .... DLB-16	Pétur Gunnarsson 1947- DLB-293
Peden, William 1913-1999 .... DLB-234	Perley, Moses Henry 1804-1862 .... DLB-99	Peyton, K. M. 1929- DLB-161
Tribute to William Goyen Y-83	Permabooks DLB-46	Pfaffe Konrad fl. circa 1172 .... DLB-148
Peele, George 1556-1596 .... DLB-62, 167	Perovsky, Aleksei Alekseevich (Antonii Pogorel'sky) 1787-1836 ..... DLB-198	Pfaffe Lamprecht fl. circa 1150 .... DLB-148
Pegler, Westbrook 1894-1969 .... DLB-171	Perrault, Charles 1628-1703 .... DLB-268	Pfeiffer, Emily 1827-1890 .... DLB-199
Péguy, Charles 1873-1914 .... DLB-258	Perri, Henry 1561-1617 .... DLB-236	Pforzheimer, Carl H. 1879-1957 .... DLB-140
Peirce, Charles Sanders 1839-1914 ...... DLB-270	Perrin, Alice 1867-1934 .... DLB-156	Phaedrus circa 18 B.C.-circa A.D. 50 ...... DLB-211
Pekić, Borislav 1930-1992 ... DLB-181; CDWLB-4	Perry, Anne 1938- DLB-276	Phaer, Thomas 1510?-1560 .... DLB-167
Pelecanos, George P. 1957- DLB-306	Perry, Bliss 1860-1954 .... DLB-71	Phaidon Press Limited DLB-112
Peletier du Mans, Jacques 1517-1582 ..... DLB-327	Perry, Eleanor 1915-1981 .... DLB-44	Pharr, Robert Deane 1916-1992 .... DLB-33
Pelevin, Viktor Olegovich 1962- DLB-285	Perry, Henry (see Perri, Henry)	Phelps, Elizabeth Stuart 1815-1852 ...... DLB-202
Pellegrini and Cudahy DLB-46	Perry, Matthew 1794-1858 .... DLB-183	Phelps, Elizabeth Stuart 1844-1911 ... DLB-74, 221
Pelletier, Aimé (see Vac, Bertrand)	Perry, Sampson 1747-1823 .... DLB-158	Philander von der Linde (see Mencke, Johann Burckhard)
Pelletier, Francine 1959- DLB-251	Perse, Saint-John 1887-1975 .... DLB-258	Philby, H. St. John B. 1885-1960 .... DLB-195
Pellicer, Carlos 1897?-1977 .... DLB-290	Persius A.D. 34-A.D. 62 .... DLB-211	Philip, Marlene Nourbese 1947- DLB-157
Pemberton, Sir Max 1863-1950 .... DLB-70	Perutz, Leo 1882-1957 .... DLB-81	Philippe, Charles-Louis 1874-1909........ DLB-65
de la Peña, Terri 1947- DLB-209	Pesetsky, Bette 1932- DLB-130	Philips, John 1676-1708 .... DLB-95
Penfield, Edward 1866-1925 .... DLB-188	Pessanha, Camilo 1867-1926 .... DLB-287	Philips, Katherine 1632-1664 .... DLB-131
Penguin Books [U.K.] DLB-112	Pessoa, Fernando 1888-1935 .... DLB-287	Phillipps, Sir Thomas 1792-1872 .... DLB-184
Fifty Penguin Years Y-85	Pestalozzi, Johann Heinrich 1746-1827..... DLB-94	Phillips, Caryl 1958- DLB-157
Penguin Collectors' Society Y-98	Peter, Laurence J. 1919-1990 .... DLB-53	Phillips, David Graham 1867-1911 .... DLB-9, 12, 303
Penguin Books [U.S.] DLB-46	Peter of Spain circa 1205-1277 .... DLB-115	Phillips, Jayne Anne 1952- DLB-292; Y-80
Penn, William 1644-1718 .... DLB-24	Peterkin, Julia 1880-1961 .... DLB-9	Tribute to Seymour Lawrence........... Y-94
Penn Publishing Company DLB-49	Peters, Ellis (Edith Pargeter) 1913-1995 .... DLB-276	Phillips, Robert 1938- DLB-105
Penna, Sandro 1906-1977 .... DLB-114	Peters, Lenrie 1932- DLB-117	

Cumulative Index

"Finding, Losing, Reclaiming: A Note
 on My Poems" DLB-105
 Tribute to William Goyen Y-83
Phillips, Stephen 1864-1915 . . . . DLB-10
Phillips, Ulrich B. 1877-1934. . . . . DLB-17
Phillips, Wendell 1811-1884 . . . . DLB-235
Phillips, Willard 1784-1873 . . . . DLB-59
Phillips, William 1907-2002 . . . . DLB-137
Phillips, Sampson and Company DLB-49
Phillpotts, Adelaide Eden (Adelaide Ross)
 1896-1993 . . . . DLB-191
Phillpotts, Eden 1862-1960. . . DLB-10, 70, 135, 153
Philo circa 20-15 B.C.-circa A.D. 50 . . . . . . .DLB-176
Philosophical Dictionary, Voltaire DLB-314
Philosophical Library DLB-46
Philosophy
 Eighteenth-Century Philosophical
  Background DLB-31
 Philosophic Thought in Boston DLB-235
 Translators of the Twelfth Century:
  Literary Issues Raised and
  Impact Created DLB-115
Elihu Phinney [publishing house] DLB-49
Phoenix, John (see Derby, George Horatio)
PHYLON (Fourth Quarter, 1950),
 The Negro in Literature:
 The Current Scene DLB-76
Physiologus circa 1070-circa 1150 . . . . DLB-148
П.О. (Pi O, Peter Oustabasides)
 1951- DLB-325
Piccolo, Lucio 1903-1969 . . . . DLB-114
Pichette, Henri 1924-2000 . . . . DLB-321
Pickard, Tom 1946- DLB-40
William Pickering [publishing house] DLB-106
Pickthall, Marjorie 1883-1922 . . . . DLB-92
Picoult, Jodi 1966- DLB-292
Pictorial Printing Company DLB-49
Piel, Gerard 1915-2004 . . . . DLB-137
"An Announcement to Our Readers,"
 Gerard Piel's Statement in *Scientific
 American* (April 1948) DLB-137
Pielmeier, John 1949- DLB-266
Piercy, Marge 1936- DLB-120, 227
Pierre, DBC 1961- DLB-326
Pierro, Albino 1916-1995 . . . . DLB-128
Pignotti, Lamberto 1926- DLB-128
Pike, Albert 1809-1891 . . . . DLB-74
Pike, Zebulon Montgomery 1779-1813 . . . DLB-183
Pillat, Ion 1891-1945 . . . . DLB-220
Pil'niak, Boris Andreevich (Boris Andreevich
 Vogau) 1894-1938 . . . . DLB-272
Pilon, Jean-Guy 1930- DLB-60
Pinar, Florencia fl. ca. late
 fifteenth century DLB-286
Pinckney, Eliza Lucas 1722-1793 . . . . DLB-200

Pinckney, Josephine 1895-1957 . . . . DLB-6
Pindar circa 518 B.C.-circa 438 B.C.
 . . . . DLB-176; CDWLB-1
Pindar, Peter (see Wolcot, John)
Pineda, Cecile 1942- DLB-209
Pinero, Arthur Wing 1855-1934 . . . . DLB-10
Piñero, Miguel 1946-1988 . . . . DLB-266
Pinget, Robert 1919-1997 . . . . DLB-83
Pinkney, Edward Coote
 1802-1828 . . . . DLB-248
Pinnacle Books DLB-46
Piñon, Nélida 1935- DLB-145, 307
Pinsky, Robert 1940- Y-82
 Reappointed Poet Laureate Y-98
Pinter, Harold 1930- . . . DLB-13, 310; CDBLB-8
 Writing for the Theatre DLB-13
Pinto, Fernão Mendes 1509/1511?-1583. . DLB-287
Piontek, Heinz 1925- DLB-75
Piozzi, Hester Lynch [Thrale]
 1741-1821 . . . . DLB-104, 142
Piper, H. Beam 1904-1964 . . . . DLB-8
Piper, Watty DLB-22
Pirandello, Luigi 1867-1936 . . . . DLB-264
Pirckheimer, Caritas 1467-1532 . . . . .DLB-179
Pirckheimer, Willibald 1470-1530 . . . . DLB-179
Pires, José Cardoso 1925-1998 . . . . DLB-287
Pisar, Samuel 1929- Y-83
Pisarev, Dmitrii Ivanovich 1840-1868 . . . . . DLB-277
Pisemsky, Aleksei Feofilaktovich
 1821-1881 . . . . DLB-238
Pitkin, Timothy 1766-1847 . . . . DLB-30
Pitter, Ruth 1897-1992 . . . . DLB-20
Pix, Mary 1666-1709 . . . . DLB-80
Pixerécourt, René Charles Guilbert de
 1773-1844 . . . . DLB-192
Pizarnik, Alejandra 1936-1972 . . . . DLB-283
Plá, Josefina 1909-1999 . . . . DLB-290
Plaatje, Sol T. 1876-1932 . . . . DLB-125, 225
Planchon, Roger 1931- DLB-321
Plante, David 1940- Y-83
Plantinga, Alvin 1932- DLB-279
Platen, August von 1796-1835 . . . . DLB-90
Plath, Sylvia
 1932-1963 . . . . DLB-5, 6, 152; CDALB-1
Plato circa 428 B.C.-348-347 B.C.
 . . . . DLB-176; CDWLB-1
Plato, Ann 1824-? DLB-239
Platon 1737-1812 . . . . DLB-150
Platonov, Andrei Platonovich (Andrei
 Platonovich Klimentev)
 1899-1951 . . . . DLB-272
Platt, Charles 1945- DLB-261
Platt and Munk Company DLB-46

Plautus circa 254 B.C.-184 B.C.
 . . . . DLB-211; CDWLB-1
Playboy Press DLB-46
John Playford [publishing house] DLB-170
Der Pleier fl. circa 1250 . . . . DLB-138
Pleijel, Agneta 1940- DLB-257
Plenzdorf, Ulrich 1934- DLB-75
Pleshcheev, Aleksei Nikolaevich
 1825?-1893 . . . . DLB-277
Plessen, Elizabeth 1944- DLB-75
Pletnev, Petr Aleksandrovich
 1792-1865 . . . . DLB-205
Pliekšāne, Elza Rozenberga (see Aspazija)
Pliekšāns, Jānis (see Rainis, Jānis)
Plievier, Theodor 1892-1955 . . . . DLB-69
Plimpton, George 1927-2003 . . DLB-185, 241; Y-99
Pliny the Elder A.D. 23/24-A.D. 79 . . . . . . DLB-211
Pliny the Younger
 circa A.D. 61-A.D. 112 . . . . DLB-211
Plomer, William
 1903-1973 . . . . DLB-20, 162, 191, 225
Plotinus 204-270 . . . . DLB-176; CDWLB-1
Plowright, Teresa 1952- DLB-251
Plume, Thomas 1630-1704 . . . . DLB-213
Plumly, Stanley 1939- DLB-5, 193
Plumpp, Sterling D. 1940- DLB-41
Plunkett, James 1920-2003 . . . . DLB-14
Plutarch
 circa 46-circa 120 . . . . DLB-176; CDWLB-1
Plymell, Charles 1935- DLB-16
Pocket Books DLB-46
Podestá, José J. 1858-1937 . . . . DLB-305
Poe, Edgar Allan 1809-1849
 . . . . DLB-3, 59, 73, 74, 248; CDALB-2
 The Poe Studies Association Y-99
Poe, James 1921-1980 . . . . DLB-44
The Poet Laureate of the United States Y-86
 Statements from Former Consultants
  in Poetry Y-86
Poetry
 Aesthetic Poetry (1873) DLB-35
 A Century of Poetry, a Lifetime of
  Collecting: J. M. Edelstein's
  Collection of Twentieth-
  Century American Poetry Y-02
 "Certain Gifts," by Betty Adcock DLB-105
 Concrete Poetry DLB-307
 Contempo Caravan: Kites in a
  Windstorm Y-85
 "Contemporary Verse Story-telling,"
  by Jonathan Holden DLB-105
 "A Detail in a Poem," by Fred
  Chappell DLB-105
 "The English Renaissance of Art"
  (1908), by Oscar Wilde DLB-35
 "Every Man His Own Poet; or,
  The Inspired Singer's Recipe

Book" (1877), by
H. W. Mallock DLB-35

"Eyes Across Centuries: Contemporary
Poetry and 'That Vision Thing,'"
by Philip Dacey. DLB-105

A Field Guide to Recent Schools
of American Poetry. Y-86

"Finding, Losing, Reclaiming:
A Note on My Poems,
by Robert Phillips" DLB-105

"The Fleshly School of Poetry and Other
Phenomena of the Day" (1872). . . . DLB-35

"The Fleshly School of Poetry:
Mr. D. G. Rossetti" (1871) DLB-35

The G. Ross Roy Scottish Poetry Collection
at the University of South Carolina . . . Y-89

"Getting Started: Accepting the Regions
You Own–or Which Own You,"
by Walter McDonald DLB-105

"The Good, The Not So Good," by
Stephen Dunn. DLB-105

The Griffin Poetry Prize Y-00

The Hero as Poet. Dante; Shakspeare
(1841), by Thomas Carlyle. DLB-32

"Images and 'Images,'" by Charles
Simic. DLB-105

"Into the Mirror," by Peter Cooley . . . DLB-105

"Knots into Webs: Some Autobiographical
Sources," by Dabney Stuart DLB-105

"L'Envoi" (1882), by Oscar Wilde. DLB-35

"Living in Ruin," by Gerald Stern. . . . DLB-105

Looking for the Golden Mountain:
Poetry Reviewing Y-89

Lyric Poetry (French) DLB-268

Medieval Galician-Portuguese
Poetry. DLB-287

"The No Self, the Little Self, and the
Poets," by Richard Moore. DLB-105

On Some of the Characteristics of Modern
Poetry and On the Lyrical Poems of
Alfred Tennyson (1831) DLB-32

The Pitt Poetry Series: Poetry Publishing
Today Y-85

"The Poetry File," by Edward
Field DLB-105

Poetry in Nineteenth-Century France:
Cultural Background and Critical
Commentary DLB-217

The Poetry of Jorge Luis Borges Y-86

"The Poet's Kaleidoscope: The Element
of Surprise in the Making of the
Poem" by Madeline DeFrees. DLB-105

The Pre-Raphaelite Controversy. DLB-35

Protest Poetry in Castile DLB-286

"Reflections: After a Tornado,"
by Judson Jerome DLB-105

Statements from Former Consultants
in Poetry Y-86

Statements on the Art of Poetry DLB-54

The Study of Poetry (1880), by
Matthew Arnold. DLB-35

A Survey of Poetry Anthologies,
1879-1960 . . . . DLB-54

Thoughts on Poetry and Its Varieties
(1833), by John Stuart Mill. DLB-32

Under the Microscope (1872), by
A. C. Swinburne. DLB-35

The Unterberg Poetry Center of the
92nd Street Y Y-98

Victorian Poetry: Five Critical
Views DLBV-35

Year in Poetry Y-83–92, 94–01

Year's Work in American Poetry Y-82

Poets
  The Lives of the Poets (1753) DLB-142
  Minor Poets of the Earlier
    Seventeenth Century DLB-121
  Other British Poets Who Fell
    in the Great War. DLB-216
  Other Poets [French] DLB-217
  Second-Generation Minor Poets of
    the Seventeenth Century DLB-126
  Third-Generation Minor Poets of
    the Seventeenth Century DLB-131

Pogodin, Mikhail Petrovich 1800-1875. . . . DLB-198

Pogorel'sky, Antonii
  (see Perovsky, Aleksei Alekseevich)

Pohl, Frederik 1919- DLB-8
  Tribute to Isaac Asimov Y-92
  Tribute to Theodore Sturgeon Y-85

Poirier, Louis (see Gracq, Julien)

Poláček, Karel 1892-1945 . . . DLB-215; CDWLB-4

Polanyi, Michael 1891-1976. . . . . DLB-100

Pole, Reginald 1500-1558 . . . . DLB-132

Polevoi, Nikolai Alekseevich 1796-1846. . . DLB-198

Polezhaev, Aleksandr Ivanovich
  1804-1838. . . . . DLB-205

Poliakoff, Stephen 1952- DLB-13

Polidori, John William 1795-1821 . . . . . . DLB-116

Polite, Carlene Hatcher 1932- DLB-33

Pollard, Alfred W. 1859-1944 . . . . DLB-201

Pollard, Edward A. 1832-1872. . . . . DLB-30

Pollard, Graham 1903-1976 . . . . DLB-201

Pollard, Percival 1869-1911 . . . . DLB-71

Pollard and Moss. DLB-49

Pollock, Sharon 1936- DLB-60

Polonsky, Abraham 1910-1999 . . . . DLB-26

Polonsky, Iakov Petrovich 1819-1898 . . . . DLB-277

Polotsky, Simeon 1629-1680 . . . . DLB-150

Polybius circa 200 B.C.-118 B.C.. . . . . DLB-176

Pomialovsky, Nikolai Gerasimovich
  1835-1863. . . . . DLB-238

Pomilio, Mario 1921-1990 . . . . DLB-177

Pompéia, Raul (Raul d'Avila Pompéia)
  1863-1895. . . . . DLB-307

Ponce, Mary Helen 1938- DLB-122

Ponce-Montoya, Juanita 1949- DLB-122

Ponet, John 1516?-1556 . . . . DLB-132

Ponge, Francis 1899-1988 . . . . DLB-258; Y-02

Poniatowska, Elena
  1933- DLB-113; CDWLB-3

Ponsard, François 1814-1867 . . . . DLB-192

William Ponsonby [publishing house] DLB-170

Pontiggia, Giuseppe 1934- DLB-196

Pontoppidan, Henrik 1857-1943 . . . . DLB-300

Pony Stories, Omnibus Essay on DLB-160

Poole, Ernest 1880-1950 . . . . DLB-9

Poole, Sophia 1804-1891 . . . . DLB-166

Poore, Benjamin Perley 1820-1887 . . . . . . DLB-23

Popa, Vasko 1922-1991 . . . . . DLB-181; CDWLB-4

Pope, Abbie Hanscom 1858-1894 . . . . . . DLB-140

Pope, Alexander
  1688-1744 . . . . . . DLB-95, 101, 213; CDBLB-2

Poplavsky, Boris 1903-1935. . . . . DLB-317

Popov, Aleksandr Serafimovich
  (see Serafimovich, Aleksandr Serafimovich)

Popov, Evgenii Anatol'evich 1946- DLB-285

Popov, Mikhail Ivanovich
  1742-circa 1790 . . . . DLB-150

Popović, Aleksandar 1929-1996. . . . . DLB-181

Popper, Karl 1902-1994 . . . . DLB-262

Popular Culture Association/
  American Culture Association. Y-99

Popular Library DLB-46

Poquelin, Jean-Baptiste (see Molière)

Porete, Marguerite ?-1310 . . . . DLB-208

Porlock, Martin (see MacDonald, Philip)

Porpoise Press DLB-112

Porta, Antonio 1935-1989 . . . . DLB-128

Porter, Anna Maria 1780-1832. . . . . . DLB-116, 159

Porter, Cole 1891-1964 . . . . DLB-265

Porter, David 1780-1843 . . . . DLB-183

Porter, Dorothy 1954- DLB-325

Porter, Eleanor H. 1868-1920 . . . . DLB-9

Porter, Gene Stratton (see Stratton-Porter, Gene)

Porter, Hal 1911-1984 . . . . DLB-260

Porter, Henry circa sixteenth century DLB-62

Porter, Jane 1776-1850 . . . . DLB-116, 159

Porter, Katherine Anne 1890-1980
  . . . . . . DLB-4, 9, 102; Y-80; DS-12; CDALB-7
  The Katherine Anne Porter Society Y-01

Porter, Peter 1929- DLB-40, 289

Porter, William Sydney (O. Henry)
  1862-1910 . . . . DLB-12, 78, 79; CDALB-3

Porter, William T. 1809-1858. . . . . . DLB-3, 43, 250

Porter and Coates DLB-49

Portillo Trambley, Estela 1927-1998. . . . . DLB-209

Portis, Charles 1933- DLB-6

Medieval Galician-Portuguese Poetry DLB-287

Posey, Alexander 1873-1908 . . . . DLB-175

Possession, 1990 Booker Prize winner,
  A. S. Byatt. DLB-326

Postans, Marianne circa 1810-1865...... DLB-166

Postgate, Raymond 1896-1971 .... DLB-276

Postl, Carl (see Sealsfield, Carl)

Postmodern Holocaust Fiction DLB-299

Poston, Ted 1906-1974 .... DLB-51

Potekhin, Aleksei Antipovich
1829-1908 .... DLB-238

Potok, Chaim 1929-2002 .... DLB-28, 152

    A Conversation with Chaim Potok Y-84

    Tribute to Bernard Malamud.......... Y-86

Potter, Beatrix 1866-1943 .... DLB-141

    The Beatrix Potter Society Y-98

Potter, David M. 1910-1971 .... DLB-17

Potter, Dennis 1935-1994 .... DLB-233

John E. Potter and Company DLB-49

Pottle, Frederick A. 1897-1987 .....DLB-103; Y-87

Poulin, Jacques 1937- DLB-60

Pound, Ezra 1885-1972
.... DLB-4, 45, 63; DS-15; CDALB-4

    The Cost of the *Cantos:* William Bird
    to Ezra Pound Y-01

    The Ezra Pound Society.............. Y-01

Poverman, C. E. 1944- DLB-234

Povey, Meic 1950- DLB-310

Povich, Shirley 1905-1998 ....DLB-171

Powell, Anthony 1905-2000 ... DLB-15; CDBLB-7

    The Anthony Powell Society: Powell and
    the First Biennial Conference Y-01

Powell, Dawn 1897-1965
    Dawn Powell, Where Have You Been
    All Our Lives?................... Y-97

Powell, John Wesley 1834-1902 .... DLB-186

Powell, Padgett 1952- DLB-234

Powers, J. F. 1917-1999 .... DLB-130

Powers, Jimmy 1903-1995 .... DLB-241

Pownall, David 1938- DLB-14

Powys, John Cowper 1872-1963..... DLB-15, 255

Powys, Llewelyn 1884-1939 .... DLB-98

Powys, T. F. 1875-1953........... DLB-36, 162

    The Powys Society................... Y-98

Poynter, Nelson 1903-1978 .... DLB-127

Prada, Juan Manuel de 1970- DLB-322

Prado, Adélia 1935- DLB-307

Prado, Pedro 1886-1952............. DLB-283

Prados, Emilio 1899-1962........... DLB-134

Praed, Mrs. Caroline (see Praed, Rosa)

Praed, Rosa (Mrs. Caroline Praed)
1851-1935 .... DLB-230

Praed, Winthrop Mackworth 1802-1839 .. DLB-96

Praeger Publishers DLB-46

Praetorius, Johannes 1630-1680 .... DLB-168

Pratolini, Vasco 1913-1991 ....DLB-177

Pratt, E. J. 1882-1964 .... DLB-92

Pratt, Samuel Jackson 1749-1814 .... DLB-39

Preciado Martin, Patricia 1939- DLB-209

Préfontaine, Yves 1937- DLB-53

Prelutsky, Jack 1940- DLB-61

Prentice, George D. 1802-1870 .... DLB-43

Prentice-Hall..................... DLB-46

Prescott, Orville 1906-1996 .... Y-96

Prescott, William Hickling
1796-1859 .... DLB-1, 30, 59, 235

Prešeren, Francè
1800-1849 ....DLB-147; CDWLB-4

Presses (*See also* Publishing)
    Small Presses in Great Britain and
    Ireland, 1960-1985............. DLB-40

    Small Presses I: Jargon Society......... Y-84

    Small Presses II: The Spirit That Moves
    Us Press..................... Y-85

    Small Presses III: Pushcart Press Y-87

Preston, Margaret Junkin
1820-1897................. DLB-239, 248

Preston, May Wilson 1873-1949....... DLB-188

Preston, Thomas 1537-1598 .... DLB-62

Prévert, Jacques 1900-1977 .... DLB-258

Prévost d'Exiles, Antoine François
1697-1763.................... DLB-314

Price, Anthony 1928- DLB-276

Price, Reynolds 1933- DLB-2, 218, 278

Price, Richard 1723-1791 .... DLB-158

Price, Richard 1949- Y-81

Prichard, Katharine Susannah
1883-1969 .... DLB-260

Prideaux, John 1578-1650............. DLB-236

Priest, Christopher 1943- DLB-14, 207, 261

Priestley, J. B. 1894-1984
.... DLB-10, 34, 77, 100, 139; Y-84; CDBLB-6

Priestley, Joseph 1733-1804........... DLB-252

Prigov, Dmitrii Aleksandrovich 1940- .. DLB-285

Prime, Benjamin Young 1733-1791 .... DLB-31

Primrose, Diana floruit circa 1630 ...... DLB-126

Prince, F. T. 1912-2003................ DLB-20

Prince, Nancy Gardner
1799-circa 1856 .... DLB-239

Prince, Thomas 1687-1758 .... DLB-24, 140

Pringle, Thomas 1789-1834 .... DLB-225

Printz, Wolfgang Casper 1641-1717 ..... DLB-168

Prior, Matthew 1664-1721 .... DLB-95

Prisco, Michele 1920-2003 ....DLB-177

Prishvin, Mikhail Mikhailovich
1873-1954.....................DLB-272

Pritchard, William H. 1932- DLB-111

Pritchett, V. S. 1900-1997 .... DLB-15, 139

Probyn, May 1856 or 1857-1909....... DLB-199

Procter, Adelaide Anne 1825-1864 ... DLB-32, 199

Procter, Bryan Waller 1787-1874..... DLB-96, 144

Proctor, Robert 1868-1903 .... DLB-184

Prokopovich, Feofan 1681?-1736 .... DLB-150

Prokosch, Frederic 1906-1989 .... DLB-48

Pronzini, Bill 1943- DLB-226

Propertius circa 50 B.C.-post 16 B.C.
.....................DLB-211; CDWLB-1

Propper, Dan 1937- DLB-16

Prose, Francine 1947- DLB-234

Protagoras circa 490 B.C.-420 B.C. DLB-176

Protest Poetry in Castile
ca. 1445-ca. 1506 .... DLB-286

Proud, Robert 1728-1813 .... DLB-30

Proust, Marcel 1871-1922............... DLB-65

    Marcel Proust at 129 and the Proust
    Society of America................ Y-00

    Marcel Proust's *Remembrance of Things Past:*
    The Rediscovered Galley Proofs Y-00

Prutkov, Koz'ma Petrovich
1803-1863 ....DLB-277

Prynne, J. H. 1936- DLB-40

Przybyszewski, Stanislaw 1868-1927...... DLB-66

Pseudo-Dionysius the Areopagite floruit
circa 500..................... DLB-115

Public Lending Right in America
    PLR and the Meaning of Literary
    Property...................... Y-83

    Statement by Sen. Charles
    McC. Mathias, Jr. PLR Y-83

    Statements on PLR by American Writers.... Y-83

Public Lending Right in the United Kingdom
    The First Year in the United Kingdom.... Y-83

Publishers [listed by individual names]
    Publishers, Conversations with:
    An Interview with Charles Scribner III... Y-94

    An Interview with Donald Lamm Y-95

    An Interview with James Laughlin....... Y-96

    An Interview with Patrick O'Connor Y-84

Publishing
    The Art and Mystery of Publishing:
    Interviews Y-97

    Book Publishing Accounting: Some Basic
    Concepts Y-98

    1873 Publishers' Catalogues......... DLB-49

    The Literary Scene 2002: Publishing, Book
    Reviewing, and Literary Journalism .. Y-02

    Main Trends in Twentieth-Century
    Book Clubs DLB-46

    Overview of U.S. Book Publishing,
    1910-1945 .... DLB-9

    The Pitt Poetry Series: Poetry Publishing
    Today Y-85

    Publishing Fiction at LSU Press......... Y-87

    The Publishing Industry in 1998:
    Sturm-und-drang.com................ Y-98

    The Publishing Industry in 1999 .... Y-99

    Publishers and Agents: The Columbia
    Connection Y-87

    Responses to Ken Auletta Y-97

    Southern Writers Between the Wars ... DLB-9

The State of Publishing Y-97
Trends in Twentieth-Century
    Mass Market Publishing DLB-46
The Year in Book Publishing Y-86
Pückler-Muskau, Hermann von
    1785-1871 . . . . .DLB-133
Puértolas, Soledad 1947- DLB-322
Pufendorf, Samuel von 1632-1694 . . . . . . .DLB-168
Pugh, Edwin William 1874-1930 . . . . .DLB-135
Pugin, A. Welby 1812-1852 . . . . .DLB-55
Puig, Manuel 1932-1990 . . . . DLB-113; CDWLB-3
Puisieux, Madeleine d'Arsant de
    1720-1798 . . . . .DLB-314
Pulgar, Hernando del (Fernando del Pulgar)
    ca. 1436-ca. 1492 . . . . .DLB-286
Pulitzer, Joseph 1847-1911 . . . . .DLB-23
Pulitzer, Joseph, Jr. 1885-1955 . . . . .DLB-29
Pulitzer Prizes for the Novel, 1917-1945 . . . . .DLB-9
Pulliam, Eugene 1889-1975 . . . . .DLB-127
Purcell, Deirdre 1945- DLB-267
Purchas, Samuel 1577?-1626 . . . . .DLB-151
Purdy, Al 1918-2000 . . . . .DLB-88
Purdy, James 1923- DLB-2, 218
Purdy, Ken W. 1913-1972 . . . . .DLB-137
Pusey, Edward Bouverie 1800-1882 . . . . . . .DLB-55
Pushkin, Aleksandr Sergeevich
    1799-1837 . . . . .DLB-205
Pushkin, Vasilii L'vovich
    1766-1830 . . . . .DLB-205
Putnam, George Palmer
    1814-1872 . . . . .DLB-3, 79, 250, 254
G. P. Putnam [publishing house] DLB-254
G. P. Putnam's Sons [U.K.] DLB-106
G. P. Putnam's Sons [U.S.] DLB-49
    A Publisher's Archives: G. P. Putnam Y-92
Putnam, Hilary 1926- DLB-279
Putnam, Samuel 1892-1950 . . . . . . .DLB-4; DS-15
Puttenham, George 1529?-1590 . . . . .DLB-281
Puzo, Mario 1920-1999 . . . . .DLB-6
Pyle, Ernie 1900-1945 . . . . .DLB-29
Pyle, Howard
    1853-1911 . . . . .DLB-42, 188; DS-13
Pyle, Robert Michael 1947- DLB-275
Pym, Barbara 1913-1980 . . . . . . DLB-14, 207; Y-87
Pynchon, Thomas 1937- DLB-2, 173
Pyramid Books DLB-46
Pyrnelle, Louise-Clarke 1850-1907 . . . . . . .DLB-42
Pythagoras circa 570 B.C.-? DLB-176

Q

Qays ibn al-Mulawwah circa 680-710 . . . .DLB-311
Qian Zhongshu 1910-1998 . . . . .DLB-328
Quad, M. (see Lewis, Charles B.)
Quaritch, Bernard 1819-1899 . . . . .DLB-184

Quarles, Francis 1592-1644 . . . . .DLB-126
The Quarterly Review 1809-1967 . . . . .DLB-110
Quasimodo, Salvatore 1901-1968 . . . . .DLB-114
Queen, Ellery (see Dannay, Frederic, and
    Manfred B. Lee)
Queen, Frank 1822-1882 . . . . .DLB-241
The Queen City Publishing House DLB-49
Queirós, Eça de 1845-1900 . . . . .DLB-287
Queneau, Raymond 1903-1976 . . . . . .DLB-72, 258
Quennell, Peter 1905-1993 . . . . .DLB-155, 195
Quental, Antero de
    1842-1891 . . . . .DLB-287
Quesada, José Luis 1948- DLB-290
Quesnel, Joseph 1746-1809 . . . . .DLB-99
Quiller-Couch, Sir Arthur Thomas
    1863-1944 . . . . .DLB-135, 153, 190
Quin, Ann 1936-1973 . . . . .DLB-14, 231
Quinault, Philippe 1635-1688 . . . . .DLB-268
Quincy, Samuel, of Georgia
    fl. eighteenth century DLB-31
Quincy, Samuel, of Massachusetts
    1734-1789 . . . . .DLB-31
Quindlen, Anna 1952- DLB-292
Quine, W. V. 1908-2000 . . . . .DLB-279
Quinn, Anthony 1915-2001 . . . . .DLB-122
Quinn, John 1870-1924 . . . . .DLB-187
Quiñónez, Naomi 1951- DLB-209
Quintana, Leroy V. 1944- DLB-82
Quintana, Miguel de 1671-1748
    A Forerunner of Chicano
        Literature .DLB-122
Quintilian circa A.D. 40-circa A.D. 96 . . . . .DLB-211
Quintus Curtius Rufus
    fl. A.D. 35 . . . . .DLB-211
Harlin Quist Books DLB-46
Quoirez, Françoise (see Sagan, Françoise)

R

Raabe, Wilhelm 1831-1910 . . . . .DLB-129
Raban, Jonathan 1942- DLB-204
Rabe, David 1940- DLB-7, 228; Y-91
Rabelais, François 1494?-1593 . . . . .DLB-327
Rabi'ah al-'Adawiyyah circa 720-801 . . . . .DLB-311
Raboni, Giovanni 1932- DLB-128
Rachilde 1860-1953 . . . . .DLB-123, 192
Racin, Koço 1908-1943 . . . . .DLB-147
Racine, Jean 1639-1699 . . . . .DLB-268
Rackham, Arthur 1867-1939 . . . . .DLB-141
Raczymow, Henri 1948- DLB-299
Radauskas, Henrikas
    1910-1970 . . . . .DLB-220; CDWLB-4
Radcliffe, Ann 1764-1823 . . . . .DLB-39, 178
Raddall, Thomas 1903-1994 . . . . .DLB-68

Radford, Dollie 1858-1920 . . . . .DLB-240
Radichkov, Yordan 1929-2004 . . . . .DLB-181
Radiguet, Raymond 1903-1923 . . . . .DLB-65
Radishchev, Aleksandr Nikolaevich
    1749-1802 . . . . .DLB-150
Radnóti, Miklós
    1909-1944 . . . . DLB-215; CDWLB-4
Radrigán, Juan 1937- DLB-305
Radványi, Netty Reiling (see Seghers, Anna)
Rafat, Taufiq 1927-1998 . . . . .DLB-323
Rahv, Philip 1908-1973 . . . . .DLB-137
Raich, Semen Egorovich 1792-1855 . . . . . .DLB-205
Raičković, Stevan 1928- DLB-181
Raiderman (see Parshchikov, Aleksei Maksimovich)
Raimund, Ferdinand Jakob 1790-1836 . . . . .DLB-90
Raine, Craig 1944- DLB-40
Raine, Kathleen 1908-2003 . . . . .DLB-20
Rainis, Jānis 1865-1929 . . . . . DLB-220; CDWLB-4
Rainolde, Richard
    circa 1530-1606 . . . . .DLB-136, 236
Rainolds, John 1549-1607 . . . . .DLB-281
Rakić, Milan 1876-1938 . . . . . . DLB-147; CDWLB-4
Rakosi, Carl 1903-2004 . . . . .DLB-193
Ralegh, Sir Walter
    1554?-1618 . . . . DLB-172; CDBLB-1
Raleigh, Walter
    Style (1897) [excerpt] DLB-57
Ralin, Radoy 1923-2004 . . . . .DLB-181
Ralph, Julian 1853-1903 . . . . .DLB-23
Ramanujan, A. K. 1929-1993 . . . . .DLB-323
Ramat, Silvio 1939- DLB-128
Ramée, Marie Louise de la (see Ouida)
Ramírez, Sergío 1942- DLB-145
Ramke, Bin 1947- DLB-120
Ramler, Karl Wilhelm 1725-1798 . . . . .DLB-97
Ramon Ribeyro, Julio 1929-1994 . . . . .DLB-145
Ramos, Graciliano 1892-1953 . . . . .DLB-307
Ramos, Manuel 1948- DLB-209
Ramos Sucre, José Antonio 1890-1930 . . .DLB-290
Ramous, Mario 1924- DLB-128
Rampersad, Arnold 1941- DLB-111
Ramsay, Allan 1684 or 1685-1758 . . . . .DLB-95
Ramsay, David 1749-1815 . . . . .DLB-30
Ramsay, Martha Laurens 1759-1811 . . . . .DLB-200
Ramsey, Frank P. 1903-1930 . . . . .DLB-262
Ranch, Hieronimus Justesen
    1539-1607 . . . . .DLB-300
Ranck, Katherine Quintana 1942- DLB-122
Rand, Avery and Company DLB-49
Rand, Ayn 1905-1982 . . . DLB-227, 279; CDALB-7
Rand McNally and Company DLB-49
Randall, David Anton 1905-1975 . . . . .DLB-140

Randall, Dudley 1914-2000 .... DLB-41
Randall, Henry S. 1811-1876 .... DLB-30
Randall, James G. 1881-1953 .... DLB-17
    The Randall Jarrell Symposium: A Small
        Collection of Randall Jarrells Y-86
    Excerpts From Papers Delivered at the
        Randall Jarrel Symposium Y-86
Randall, John Herman, Jr. 1899-1980 ..... DLB-279
Randolph, A. Philip 1889-1979 .... DLB-91
Anson D. F. Randolph
    [publishing house] DLB-49
Randolph, Thomas 1605-1635 ...... DLB-58, 126
Random House DLB-46
Rankin, Ian (Jack Harvey) 1960- DLB-267
Henry Ranlet [publishing house] DLB-49
Ransom, Harry 1908-1976 .... DLB-187
Ransom, John Crowe
    1888-1974 .... DLB-45, 63; CDALB-7
Ransome, Arthur 1884-1967 .... DLB-160
Rao, Raja 1908- DLB-323
Raphael, Frederic 1931- DLB-14, 319
Raphaelson, Samson 1896-1983 .... DLB-44
Rare Book Dealers
    Bertram Rota and His Bookshop Y-91
    An Interview with Glenn Horowitz Y-90
    An Interview with Otto Penzler Y-96
    An Interview with Ralph Sipper Y-94
    New York City Bookshops in the
        1930s and 1940s: The Recollections
        of Walter Goldwater Y-93
Rare Books
    Research in the American Antiquarian
        Book Trade Y-97
    Two Hundred Years of Rare Books and
        Literary Collections at the
        University of South Carolina Y-00
Rascón Banda, Víctor Hugo 1948- DLB-305
Rashi circa 1040-1105 .... DLB-208
Raskin, Ellen 1928-1984 .... DLB-52
Rasputin, Valentin Grigor'evich
    1937- DLB-302
Rastell, John 1475?-1536 .... DLB-136, 170
Rattigan, Terence
    1911-1977 .... DLB-13; CDBLB-7
Raven, Simon 1927-2001 .... DLB-271
Ravenhill, Mark 1966- DLB-310
Ravnkilde, Adda 1862-1883 .... DLB-300
Rawicz, Piotr 1919-1982 .... DLB-299
Rawlings, Marjorie Kinnan 1896-1953
    .... DLB-9, 22, 102; DS-17; CDALB-7
Rawlinson, Richard 1690-1755 .... DLB-213
Rawlinson, Thomas 1681-1725 .... DLB-213
Rawls, John 1921-2002 .... DLB-279
Raworth, Tom 1938- DLB-40
Ray, David 1932- DLB-5
Ray, Gordon Norton 1915-1986 .... DLB-103, 140

Ray, Henrietta Cordelia 1849-1916 ...... DLB-50
Raymond, Ernest 1888-1974 .... DLB-191
Raymond, Henry J. 1820-1869 ...... DLB-43, 79
Raymond, René (see Chase, James Hadley)
Razaf, Andy 1895-1973 .... DLB-265
al-Razi 865?-925? DLB-311
Rea, Michael 1927-1996 .... Y-97
    Michael M. Rea and the Rea Award for
        the Short Story Y-97
Reach, Angus 1821-1856 .... DLB-70
Read, Herbert 1893-1968 .... DLB-20, 149
Read, Martha Meredith
    fl. nineteenth century DLB-200
Read, Opie 1852-1939 .... DLB-23
Read, Piers Paul 1941- DLB-14
Reade, Charles 1814-1884 .... DLB-21
Reader's Digest Condensed Books DLB-46
Readers Ulysses Symposium Y-97
Reading, Peter 1946- DLB-40
Reading Series in New York City Y-96
Reaney, James 1926- DLB-68
Rebhun, Paul 1500?-1546 .... DLB-179
Rèbora, Clemente 1885-1957 .... DLB-114
Rebreanu, Liviu 1885-1944 .... DLB-220
Rechy, John 1934- DLB-122, 278; Y-82
Redding, J. Saunders 1906-1988 ..... DLB-63, 76
J. S. Redfield [publishing house] DLB-49
Redgrove, Peter 1932-2003 .... DLB-40
Redmon, Anne 1943- Y-86
Redmond, Eugene B. 1937- DLB-41
Redol, Alves 1911-1969 .... DLB-287
James Redpath [publishing house] DLB-49
Reed, Henry 1808-1854 .... DLB-59
Reed, Henry 1914-1986 .... DLB-27
Reed, Ishmael
    1938- DLB-2, 5, 33, 169, 227; DS-8
Reed, Rex 1938- DLB-185
Reed, Sampson 1800-1880 .... DLB-1, 235
Reed, Talbot Baines 1852-1893 .... DLB-141
Reedy, William Marion 1862-1920 .... DLB-91
Reese, Lizette Woodworth 1856-1935 .... DLB-54
Reese, Thomas 1742-1796 .... DLB-37
Reeve, Clara 1729-1807 .... DLB-39
    Preface to *The Old English Baron*
        (1778) DLB-39
    The Progress of Romance (1785)
        [excerpt] DLB-39
Reeves, James 1909-1978 .... DLB-161
Reeves, John 1926- DLB-88
Reeves-Stevens, Garfield 1953- DLB-251
Régio, José (José Maria dos Reis Pereira)
    1901-1969 .... DLB-287

Henry Regnery Company DLB-46
Rêgo, José Lins do 1901-1957 .... DLB-307
Rehberg, Hans 1901-1963 .... DLB-124
Rehfisch, Hans José 1891-1960 .... DLB-124
Reich, Ebbe Kløvedal 1940- DLB-214
Reid, Alastair 1926- DLB-27
Reid, B. L. 1918-1990 .... DLB-111
Reid, Christopher 1949- DLB-40
Reid, Forrest 1875-1947 .... DLB-153
Reid, Helen Rogers 1882-1970 .... DLB-29
Reid, James fl. eighteenth century DLB-31
Reid, Mayne 1818-1883 .... DLB-21, 163
Reid, Thomas 1710-1796 .... DLB-31, 252
Reid, V. S. (Vic) 1913-1987 .... DLB-125
Reid, Whitelaw 1837-1912 .... DLB-23
Reilly and Lee Publishing Company DLB-46
Reimann, Brigitte 1933-1973 .... DLB-75
Reinmar der Alte circa 1165-circa 1205 .. DLB-138
Reinmar von Zweter
    circa 1200-circa 1250 .... DLB-138
Reisch, Walter 1903-1983 .... DLB-44
Reizei Family DLB-203
Religion
    A Crisis of Culture: The Changing
        Role of Religion in the
        New Republic DLB-37
The Remains of the Day, 1989 Booker Prize winner,
    Kazuo Ishiguro DLB-326
Remarque, Erich Maria
    1898-1970 .... DLB-56; CDWLB-2
Remington, Frederic
    1861-1909 .... DLB-12, 186, 188
Remizov, Aleksei Mikhailovich
    1877-1957 .... DLB-295
Renaud, Jacques 1943- DLB-60
Renault, Mary 1905-1983 .... Y-83
Rendell, Ruth (Barbara Vine)
    1930- DLB-87, 276
Rensselaer, Maria van Cortlandt van
    1645-1689 .... DLB-200
Repplier, Agnes 1855-1950 .... DLB-221
Reshetnikov, Fedor Mikhailovich
    1841-1871 .... DLB-238
Restif (Rétif) de La Bretonne, Nicolas-Edme
    1734-1806 .... DLB-314
Rettenbacher, Simon 1634-1706 .... DLB-168
Retz, Jean-François-Paul de Gondi,
    cardinal de 1613-1679 .... DLB-268
Reuchlin, Johannes 1455-1522 .... DLB-179
Reuter, Christian 1665-after 1712 ...... DLB-168
Fleming H. Revell Company DLB-49
Reverdy, Pierre 1889-1960 .... DLB-258
Reuter, Fritz 1810-1874 .... DLB-129
Reuter, Gabriele 1859-1941 .... DLB-66

Reventlow, Franziska Gräfin zu
1871-1918 .... DLB-66

Review of Reviews Office DLB-112

Rexroth, Kenneth 1905-1982
..... DLB-16, 48, 165, 212; Y-82; CDALB-1

    The Commercialization of the Image
    of Revolt..................... DLB-16

Rey, H. A. 1898-1977................. DLB-22

Reyes, Carlos José 1941- DLB-305

Reynal and Hitchcock DLB-46

Reynolds, G. W. M. 1814-1879 .... DLB-21

Reynolds, John Hamilton
1794-1852 .... DLB-96

Reynolds, Sir Joshua 1723-1792 .... DLB-104

Reynolds, Mack 1917-1983 .... DLB-8

Reza, Yazmina 1959- DLB-321

Reznikoff, Charles 1894-1976 .... DLB-28, 45

Rhetoric
    Continental European Rhetoricians,
    1400-1600, and Their Influence
    in Reaissance England DLB-236

    A Finding Guide to Key Works on
    Microfilm DLB-236

    Glossary of Terms and Definitions of
    Rhetoic and Logic DLB-236

Rhett, Robert Barnwell 1800-1876....... DLB-43

Rhode, John 1884-1964................ DLB-77

Rhodes, Eugene Manlove 1869-1934..... DLB-256

Rhodes, James Ford 1848-1927 .... DLB-47

Rhodes, Richard 1937- DLB-185

Rhys, Jean 1890-1979
.... DLB-36, 117, 162; CDBLB-7; CDWLB-3

Ribeiro, Bernadim
fl. ca. 1475/1482-1526/1544.......... DLB-287

Ricardo, David 1772-1823 .... DLB-107, 158

Ricardou, Jean 1932- DLB-83

Ricciboni, Marie-Jeanne (Marie-Jeanne de
Heurles Laboras de Mézières Riccoboni)
1713-1792....................... DLB-314

Rice, Anne (A. N. Roquelare, Anne Rampling)
1941- DLB-292

Rice, Christopher 1978- DLB-292

Rice, Elmer 1892-1967................. DLB-4, 7

Rice, Grantland 1880-1954 .... DLB-29, 171

Rich, Adrienne 1929- DLB-5, 67; CDALB-7

Richard, Mark 1955- DLB-234

Richard de Fournival
1201-1259 or 1260 .... DLB-208

Richards, David Adams 1950- DLB-53

Richards, George circa 1760-1814 .... DLB-37

Richards, I. A. 1893-1979................ DLB-27

Richards, Laura E. 1850-1943 .... DLB-42

Richards, William Carey 1818-1892 ...... DLB-73

Grant Richards [publishing house]....... DLB-112

Richardson, Charles F. 1851-1913........ DLB-71

Richardson, Dorothy M. 1873-1957....... DLB-36

The Novels of Dorothy Richardson
(1918), by May Sinclair.......... DLB-36

Richardson, Henry Handel
(Ethel Florence Lindesay Robertson)
1870-1946 .... DLB-197, 230

Richardson, Jack 1935- DLB-7

Richardson, John 1796-1852 .... DLB-99

Richardson, Samuel
1689-1761 .... DLB-39, 154; CDBLB-2

    Introductory Letters from the Second
    Edition of *Pamela* (1741) DLB-39

    Postscript to [the Third Edition of]
    Clarissa (1751) DLB-39

    Preface to the First Edition of
    Pamela (1740) DLB-39

    Preface to the Third Edition of
    Clarissa (1751) [excerpt]......... DLB-39

    Preface to Volume 1 of *Clarissa*
    (1747) DLB-39

    Preface to Volume 3 of *Clarissa*
    (1748) DLB-39

Richardson, Willis 1889-1977 .... DLB-51

Riche, Barnabe 1542-1617............. DLB-136

Richepin, Jean 1849-1926 .... DLB-192

Richler, Mordecai 1931-2001............ DLB-53

Richter, Conrad 1890-1968 .... DLB-9, 212

Richter, Hans Werner 1908-1993......... DLB-69

Richter, Johann Paul Friedrich
1763-1825 .... DLB-94; CDWLB-2

Joseph Rickerby [publishing house]...... DLB-106

Rickword, Edgell 1898-1982 .... DLB-20

Riddell, Charlotte 1832-1906........... DLB-156

Riddell, John (see Ford, Corey)

Ridge, John Rollin 1827-1867........... DLB-175

Ridge, Lola 1873-1941................. DLB-54

Ridge, William Pett 1859-1930 .... DLB-135

Riding, Laura (see Jackson, Laura Riding)

Ridler, Anne 1912-2001................ DLB-27

Ridruego, Dionisio 1912-1975 .... DLB-108

Riel, Louis 1844-1885 .... DLB-99

Riemer, Johannes 1648-1714 .... DLB-168

Riera, Carme 1948- DLB-322

Rifbjerg, Klaus 1931- DLB-214

Riffaterre, Michael 1924- DLB-67

A Conversation between William Riggan
and Janette Turner Hospital Y-02

Riggs, Lynn 1899-1954 .... DLB-175

Riis, Jacob 1849-1914.................. DLB-23

John C. Riker [publishing house]......... DLB-49

Riley, James 1777-1840................ DLB-183

Riley, John 1938-1978 .... DLB-40

Rilke, Rainer Maria
1875-1926 .... DLB-81; CDWLB-2

Rimanelli, Giose 1926- DLB-177

Rimbaud, Jean-Nicolas-Arthur
1854-1891 .... DLB-217

Rinehart and Company................ DLB-46

Ringuet 1895-1960.................... DLB-68

Ringwood, Gwen Pharis 1910-1984....... DLB-88

Rinser, Luise 1911-2002................ DLB-69

Ríos, Alberto 1952- DLB-122

Ríos, Isabella 1948- DLB-82

Ripley, Arthur 1895-1961 .... DLB-44

Ripley, George 1802-1880 ..... DLB-1, 64, 73, 235

The Rising Glory of America:
Three Poems..................... DLB-37

The Rising Glory of America: Written in 1771
(1786), by Hugh Henry Brackenridge
and Philip Freneau DLB-37

Riskin, Robert 1897-1955 .... DLB-26

Risse, Heinz 1898-1989 .... DLB-69

Rist, Johann 1607-1667 .... DLB-164

Ristikivi, Karl 1912-1977 .... DLB-220

Ritchie, Anna Mowatt 1819-1870 ..... DLB-3, 250

Ritchie, Anne Thackeray 1837-1919 ...... DLB-18

Ritchie, Thomas 1778-1854 .... DLB-43

Rites of Passage, 1980 Booker Prize winner,
William Golding DLB-326

The Ritz Paris Hemingway Award Y-85

    Mario Varga Llosa's Acceptance Speech... Y-85

Rivard, Adjutor 1868-1945 .... DLB-92

Rive, Richard 1931-1989.......... DLB-125, 225

Rivera, José 1955- DLB-249

Rivera, Marina 1942- DLB-122

Rivera, Tomás 1935-1984 .... DLB-82

Rivers, Conrad Kent 1933-1968 .... DLB-41

Riverside Press...................... DLB-49

Rivington, James circa 1724-1802 .... DLB-43

Charles Rivington [publishing house] DLB-154

Rivkin, Allen 1903-1990 .... DLB-26

Roa Bastos, Augusto 1917-2005......... DLB-113

Robbe-Grillet, Alain 1922- DLB-83

Robbins, Tom 1936- Y-80

Roberts, Charles G. D. 1860-1943 .... DLB-92

Roberts, Dorothy 1906-1993........... DLB-88

Roberts, Elizabeth Madox
1881-1941 .... DLB-9, 54, 102

Roberts, John (see Swynnerton, Thomas)

Roberts, Kate 1891-1985 .... DLB-319

Roberts, Keith 1935-2000 .... DLB-261

Roberts, Kenneth 1885-1957 ....DLB-9

Roberts, Michèle 1949- DLB-231

Roberts, Theodore Goodridge
1877-1953 .... DLB-92

Roberts, Ursula Wyllie (see Miles, Susan)

Roberts, William 1767-1849............ DLB-142

James Roberts [publishing house] DLB-154

Roberts Brothers DLB-49

A. M. Robertson and Company........ DLB-49

Robertson, Ethel Florence Lindesay
(see Richardson, Henry Handel)

Robertson, William 1721-1793......... DLB-104

Robin, Leo 1895-1984............... DLB-265

Robins, Elizabeth 1862-1952.......... DLB-197

Robinson, A. Mary F. (Madame James
Darmesteter, Madame Mary
Duclaux) 1857-1944............. DLB-240

Robinson, Casey 1903-1979........... DLB-44

Robinson, Derek 1932-............... Y-02

Robinson, Edwin Arlington
1869-1935............. DLB-54; CDALB-3

Review by Derek Robinson of George
Greenfield's Rich Dust.............. Y-02

Robinson, Henry Crabb 1775-1867..... DLB-107

Robinson, James Harvey 1863-1936...... DLB-47

Robinson, Lennox 1886-1958........... DLB-10

Robinson, Mabel Louise 1874-1962...... DLB-22

Robinson, Marilynne 1943-.......... DLB-206

Robinson, Mary 1758-1800........... DLB-158

Robinson, Richard circa 1545-1607..... DLB-167

Robinson, Therese 1797-1870....... DLB-59, 133

Robison, Mary 1949-............... DLB-130

Roblès, Emmanuel 1914-1995.......... DLB-83

Roccatagliata Ceccardi, Ceccardo
1871-1919..................... DLB-114

Rocha, Adolfo Correira da (see Torga, Miguel)

Roche, Billy 1949-................. DLB-233

Rochester, John Wilmot, Earl of
1647-1680..................... DLB-131

Rochon, Esther 1948-............... DLB-251

Rock, Howard 1911-1976............. DLB-127

Rockwell, Norman Perceval 1894-1978.. DLB-188

Rodgers, Carolyn M. 1945-......... DLB-41

Rodgers, W. R. 1909-1969............ DLB-20

Rodney, Lester 1911-............... DLB-241

Rodoreda, Mercé 1908-1983........... DLB-322

Rodrigues, Nelson 1912-1980.......... DLB-307

Rodríguez, Claudio 1934-1999........ DLB-134

Rodríguez, Joe D. 1943-............ DLB-209

Rodriguez, Judith 1936-............ DLB-325

Rodríguez, Luis J. 1954-........... DLB-209

Rodriguez, Richard 1944-........ DLB-82, 256

Rodríguez Julia, Edgardo 1946-..... DLB-145

Roe, E. P. 1838-1888................ DLB-202

Roethke, Theodore
1908-1963......... DLB-5, 206; CDALB-1

Rogers, Jane 1952-................. DLB-194

Rogers, Pattiann 1940-............. DLB-105

Rogers, Samuel 1763-1855........... DLB-93

Rogers, Will 1879-1935.............. DLB-11

Rohmer, Sax 1883-1959.............. DLB-70

Roig, Montserrat 1946-1991........... DLB-322

Roiphe, Anne 1935-.................. Y-80

Rojas, Arnold R. 1896-1988.......... DLB-82

Rojas, Fernando de ca. 1475-1541..... DLB-286

Roland de la Platière, Marie-Jeanne
(Madame Roland) 1754-1793....... DLB-314

Rolfe, Edwin (Solomon Fishman)
1909-1954.................... DLB-303

Rolfe, Frederick William
1860-1913................. DLB-34, 156

Rolland, Romain 1866-1944........... DLB-65

Rolle, Richard circa 1290-1300 - 1349... DLB-146

Rölvaag, O. E. 1876-1931.......... DLB-9, 212

Romains, Jules 1885-1972........ DLB-65, 321

A. Roman and Company............. DLB-49

Roman de la Rose: Guillaume de Lorris
1200/1205-circa 1230, Jean de
Meun 1235-1240-circa 1305........ DLB-208

Romano, Lalla 1906-2001............ DLB-177

Romano, Octavio 1923-............ DLB-122

Rome, Harold 1908-1993............ DLB-265

Romero, Leo 1950-................. DLB-122

Romero, Lin 1947-................. DLB-122

Romero, Orlando 1945-............. DLB-82

Ronsard, Pierre de 1524-1585........ DLB-327

Rook, Clarence 1863-1915........... DLB-135

Roosevelt, Theodore
1858-1919.............. DLB-47, 186, 275

Root, Waverley 1903-1982............ DLB-4

Root, William Pitt 1941-........... DLB-120

Roquebrune, Robert de 1889-1978..... DLB-68

Rorty, Richard 1931-............ DLB-246, 279

Rosa, João Guimarães 1908-1967... DLB-113, 307

Rosales, Luis 1910-1992............ DLB-134

Roscoe, William 1753-1831.......... DLB-163

Rose, Dilys 1954-................. DLB-319

Rose, Reginald 1920-2002............ DLB-26

Rose, Wendy 1948-................ DLB-175

Rosegger, Peter 1843-1918.......... DLB-129

Rosei, Peter 1946-................. DLB-85

Rosen, Norma 1925-................ DLB-28

Rosenbach, A. S. W. 1876-1952........ DLB-140

Rosenbaum, Ron 1946-.............. DLB-185

Rosenbaum, Thane 1960-............ DLB-299

Rosenberg, Isaac 1890-1918........ DLB-20, 216

Rosenfeld, Isaac 1918-1956......... DLB-28

Rosenthal, Harold 1914-1999......... DLB-241

Jimmy, Red, and Others: Harold
Rosenthal Remembers the Stars of
the Press Box................... Y-01

Rosenthal, M. L. 1917-1996........... DLB-5

Rosenwald, Lessing J. 1891-1979..... DLB-187

Ross, Alexander 1591-1654.......... DLB-151

Ross, Harold 1892-1951..............DLB-137

Ross, Jerry 1926-1955.............. DLB-265

Ross, Leonard Q. (see Rosten, Leo)

Ross, Lillian 1927-................ DLB-185

Ross, Martin 1862-1915............. DLB-135

Ross, Sinclair 1908-1996............ DLB-88

Ross, W. W. E. 1894-1966........... DLB-88

Rosselli, Amelia 1930-1996.......... DLB-128

Rossen, Robert 1908-1966........... DLB-26

Rosset, Barney 1922-................ Y-02

Rossetti, Christina 1830-1894... DLB-35, 163, 240

Rossetti, Dante Gabriel
1828-1882............. DLB-35; CDBLB-4

The Stealthy School of
Criticism (1871)................ DLB-35

Rossner, Judith 1935-............... DLB-6

Rostand, Edmond 1868-1918.......... DLB-192

Rosten, Leo 1908-1997.............. DLB-11

Rostenberg, Leona 1908-2005........ DLB-140

Rostopchina, Evdokiia Petrovna
1811-1858.................... DLB-205

Rostovsky, Dimitrii 1651-1709........ DLB-150

Rota, Bertram 1903-1966............ DLB-201

Bertram Rota and His Bookshop........ Y-91

Roth, Gerhard 1942-............ DLB-85, 124

Roth, Henry 1906?-1995............. DLB-28

Roth, Joseph 1894-1939............. DLB-85

Roth, Philip
1933-..... DLB-2, 28, 173; Y-82; CDALB-6

Rothenberg, Jerome 1931-......... DLB-5, 193

Rothschild Family.................. DLB-184

Rotimi, Ola 1938-................. DLB-125

Rotrou, Jean 1609-1650.............DLB-268

Rousseau, Jean-Jacques 1712-1778...... DLB-314

The Social Contract............... DLB-314

Routhier, Adolphe-Basile 1839-1920..... DLB-99

Routier, Simone 1901-1987........... DLB-88

George Routledge and Sons.......... DLB-106

Roversi, Roberto 1923-............. DLB-128

Rowe, Elizabeth Singer 1674-1737.... DLB-39, 95

Rowe, Nicholas 1674-1718........... DLB-84

Rowlands, Ian 1964-............... DLB-310

Rowlands, Samuel circa 1570-1630...... DLB-121

Rowlandson, Mary
circa 1637-circa 1711.......... DLB-24, 200

Rowley, William circa 1585-1626...... DLB-58

Rowling, J. K.
The Harry Potter Phenomenon......... Y-99

Rowse, A. L. 1903-1997............ DLB-155

Rowson, Susanna Haswell
circa 1762-1824.................DLB-37, 200

Roy, Arundhati 1961-.......... DLB-323, 326

Roy, Camille 1870-1943............. DLB-92

DLB 328   Cumulative Index

The G. Ross Roy Scottish Poetry Collection
   at the University of South Carolina Y-89

Roy, Gabrielle 1909-1983................DLB-68

Roy, Jules 1907-2000 ....DLB-83

The Royal Court Theatre and the English
   Stage Company...................DLB-13

The Royal Court Theatre and the New
   Drama.......................DLB-10

The Royal Shakespeare Company
   at the Swan Y-88

Royall, Anne Newport 1769-1854 ....DLB-43, 248

Royce, Josiah 1855-1916 ....DLB-270

The Roycroft Printing Shop............DLB-49

Royde-Smith, Naomi 1875-1964 ....DLB-191

Royster, Vermont 1914-1996 ....DLB-127

Richard Royston [publishing house] DLB-170

Rozanov, Vasilii Vasil'evich
   1856-1919 ....DLB-295

Różewicz, Tadeusz 1921- DLB-232

Ruark, Gibbons 1941- DLB-120

Ruban, Vasilii Grigorevich 1742-1795 ....DLB-150

Rubens, Bernice 1928-2004 ..... DLB-14, 207, 326

Rubião, Murilo 1916-1991............DLB-307

Rubina, Dina Il'inichna 1953- DLB-285

Rubinshtein, Lev Semenovich 1947- DLB-285

Rudd and Carleton DLB-49

Rudd, Steele (Arthur Hoey Davis).......DLB-230

Rudkin, David 1936- DLB-13

Rudnick, Paul 1957- DLB-266

Rudnicki, Adolf 1909-1990 ....DLB-299

Rudolf von Ems circa 1200-circa 1254....DLB-138

Ruffin, Josephine St. Pierre 1842-1924.....DLB-79

Rufo, Juan Gutiérrez 1547?-1620?.......DLB-318

Ruganda, John 1941- DLB-157

Ruggles, Henry Joseph 1813-1906.......DLB-64

Ruiz de Burton, María Amparo
   1832-1895 ....DLB-209, 221

Rukeyser, Muriel 1913-1980 ....DLB-48

Rule, Jane 1931- DLB-60

Rulfo, Juan 1918-1986......DLB-113; CDWLB-3

Rumaker, Michael 1932- DLB-16

Rumens, Carol 1944- DLB-40

Rummo, Paul-Eerik 1942- DLB-232

Runyon, Damon
   1880-1946 ....DLB-11, 86, 171

Ruodlieb circa 1050-1075 ....DLB-148

Rush, Benjamin 1746-1813 ....DLB-37

Rush, Rebecca 1779-?..................DLB-200

Rushdie, Salman 1947- DLB-194, 323, 326

Rusk, Ralph L. 1888-1962 ....DLB-103

Ruskin, John
   1819-1900 ......DLB-55, 163, 190; CDBLB-4

Russ, Joanna 1937- DLB-8

Russell, Benjamin 1761-1845 ....DLB-43

Russell, Bertrand 1872-1970........DLB-100, 262

Russell, Charles Edward 1860-1941 ......DLB-25

Russell, Charles M. 1864-1926 ....DLB-188

Russell, Eric Frank 1905-1978 ....DLB-255

Russell, Fred 1906-2003...............DLB-241

Russell, George William (see AE)

Russell, Countess Mary Annette Beauchamp
   (see Arnim, Elizabeth von)

Russell, Willy 1947- DLB-233

B. B. Russell and Company...........DLB-49

R. H. Russell and Son DLB-49

Rutebeuf fl.1249-1277 ....DLB-208

Rutherford, Mark 1831-1913...........DLB-18

Ruxton, George Frederick
   1821-1848 ....DLB-186

R-va, Zeneida (see Gan, Elena Andreevna)

Ryan, Gig 1956- DLB-325

Ryan, James 1952- DLB-267

Ryan, Michael 1946- Y-82

Ryan, Oscar 1904- DLB-68

Rybakov, Anatolii Naumovich
   1911-1994 ....DLB-302

Ryder, Jack 1871-1936 ....DLB-241

Ryga, George 1932-1987 ....DLB-60

Rylands, Enriqueta Augustina Tennant
   1843-1908 ....DLB-184

Rylands, John 1801-1888 ....DLB-184

Ryle, Gilbert 1900-1976...............DLB-262

Ryleev, Kondratii Fedorovich
   1795-1826 ....DLB-205

Rymer, Thomas 1643?-1713 ....DLB-101

Ryskind, Morrie 1895-1985............DLB-26

Rzhevsky, Aleksei Andreevich
   1737-1804....................DLB-150

S

The Saalfield Publishing Company DLB-46

Saba, Umberto 1883-1957 ....DLB-114

Sábato, Ernesto 1911- DLB-145; CDWLB-3

Saberhagen, Fred 1930- DLB-8

Sabin, Joseph 1821-1881 ....DLB-187

Sabino, Fernando (Fernando Tavares Sabino)
   1923-2004 ....DLB-307

Sacer, Gottfried Wilhelm 1635-1699 .....DLB-168

Sachs, Hans 1494-1576 ..... DLB-179; CDWLB-2

Sá-Carneiro, Mário de 1890-1916 ....DLB-287

Sack, John 1930-2004 ....DLB-185

Sackler, Howard 1929-1982..............DLB-7

Sackville, Lady Margaret 1881-1963 .....DLB-240

Sackville, Thomas 1536-1608 and
   Norton, Thomas 1532-1584 ....DLB-62

Sackville, Thomas 1536-1608 ....DLB-132

Sackville-West, Edward 1901-1965 .....DLB-191

Sackville-West, Vita 1892-1962 ......DLB-34, 195

Sacred Hunger, 1992 Booker Prize winner,
   Barry Unsworth DLB-326

Sá de Miranda, Francisco de
   1481-1588? DLB-287

Sade, Marquis de (Donatien-Alphonse-François,
   comte de Sade) 1740-1814...........DLB-314

   "Dialogue entre un prêtre et un
      moribond" DLB-314

Sadlier, Mary Anne 1820-1903 ....DLB-99

D. and J. Sadlier and Company..........DLB-49

Sadoff, Ira 1945- DLB-120

Sadoveanu, Mihail 1880-1961 ....DLB-220

Sadur, Nina Nikolaevna 1950- DLB-285

Sáenz, Benjamin Alire 1954- DLB-209

Saenz, Jaime 1921-1986 ....DLB-145, 283

Saffin, John circa 1626-1710............DLB-24

Sagan, Françoise 1935- DLB-83

Sage, Robert 1899-1962.................DLB-4

Sagel, Jim 1947- DLB-82

Sagendorph, Robb Hansell 1900-1970....DLB-137

Sahagún, Carlos 1938- DLB-108

Sahgal, Nayantara 1927- DLB-323

Sahkomaapii, Piitai (see Highwater, Jamake)

Sahl, Hans 1902-1993 ....DLB-69

Said, Edward W. 1935- DLB-67

Saigyō 1118-1190.....................DLB-203

Saijo, Albert 1926- DLB-312

Saiko, George 1892-1962..............DLB-85

Sainte-Beuve, Charles-Augustin
   1804-1869 ....DLB-217

Saint-Exupéry, Antoine de 1900-1944 .....DLB-72

Saint-Gelais, Mellin de 1490?-1558 ......DLB-327

St. John, J. Allen 1872-1957 ....DLB-188

St John, Madeleine 1942- DLB-267

St. Johns, Adela Rogers 1894-1988 ....DLB-29

St. Omer, Garth 1931- DLB-117

Saint Pierre, Michel de 1916-1987 ....DLB-83

Saintsbury, George 1845-1933........ DLB-57, 149

   "Modern English Prose" (1876) DLB-57

   The Present State of the English
      Novel (1892),.................DLB-18

Saint-Simon, Louis de Rouvroy, duc de
   1675-1755 ....DLB-314

St. Dominic's Press DLB-112

The St. John's College Robert Graves Trust ...Y-96

St. Martin's Press DLB-46

St. Nicholas 1873-1881...................DS-13

Saiokuken Sōchō 1448-1532 ....DLB-203

Saki (see Munro, H. H.)

Salaam, Kalamu ya 1947- DLB-38

Salacrou, Armand 1899-1989 ....DLB-321

Šalamun, Tomaž 1941- ... DLB-181; CDWLB-4
Salas, Floyd 1931- ... DLB-82
Sálaz-Marquez, Rubén 1935- ... DLB-122
Salcedo, Hugo 1964- ... DLB-305
Salemson, Harold J. 1910-1988 ... DLB-4
Salesbury, William 1520?-1584? ... DLB-281
Salinas, Luis Omar 1937- ... DLB-82
Salinas, Pedro 1891-1951 ... DLB-134
Salinger, J. D. 1919- ... DLB-2, 102, 173; CDALB-1
Salkey, Andrew 1928-1995 ... DLB-125
Sallust circa 86 B.C.-35 B.C. ... DLB-211; CDWLB-1
Salt, Waldo 1914-1987 ... DLB-44
Salter, James 1925- ... DLB-130
Salter, Mary Jo 1954- ... DLB-120
Saltus, Edgar 1855-1921 ... DLB-202
Saltykov, Mikhail Evgrafovich 1826-1889 ... DLB-238
Salustri, Carlo Alberto (see Trilussa)
Salverson, Laura Goodman 1890-1970 ... DLB-92
Samain, Albert 1858-1900 ... DLB-217
Sampson, Richard Henry (see Hull, Richard)
Samuels, Ernest 1903-1996 ... DLB-111
Sanborn, Franklin Benjamin 1831-1917 ... DLB-1, 223
Sánchez, Florencio 1875-1910 ... DLB-305
Sánchez, Luis Rafael 1936- ... DLB-145, 305
Sánchez, Philomeno "Phil" 1917- ... DLB-122
Sánchez, Ricardo 1941-1995 ... DLB-82
Sánchez, Saúl 1943- ... DLB-209
Sanchez, Sonia 1934- ... DLB-41; DS-8
Sánchez de Arévalo, Rodrigo 1404-1470 ... DLB-286
Sánchez de Badajoz, Diego ?-1552? ... DLB-318
Sánchez Ferlosio, Rafael 1927- ... DLB-322
Sand, George 1804-1876 ... DLB-119, 192
Sandburg, Carl 1878-1967 ... DLB-17, 54; CDALB-3
Sandel, Cora (Sara Fabricius) 1880-1974 ... DLB-297
Sandemose, Aksel 1899-1965 ... DLB-297
Sanders, Edward 1939- ... DLB-16, 244
Sanderson, Robert 1587-1663 ... DLB-281
Sandoz, Mari 1896-1966 ... DLB-9, 212
Sandwell, B. K. 1876-1954 ... DLB-92
Sandy, Stephen 1934- ... DLB-165
Sandys, George 1578-1644 ... DLB-24, 121
Sangster, Charles 1822-1893 ... DLB-99
Sanguineti, Edoardo 1930- ... DLB-128
Sanjōnishi Sanetaka 1455-1537 ... DLB-203
San Pedro, Diego de fl. ca. 1492 ... DLB-286
Sansay, Leonora ?-after 1823 ... DLB-200

Sansom, William 1912-1976 ... DLB-139
Sant'Anna, Affonso Romano de 1937- ... DLB-307
Santayana, George 1863-1952 ... DLB-54, 71, 246, 270; DS-13
Santiago, Danny 1911-1988 ... DLB-122
Santillana, Marqués de (Íñigo López de Mendoza) 1398-1458 ... DLB-286
Santmyer, Helen Hooven 1895-1986 ... Y-84
Santos, Bienvenido 1911-1996 ... DLB-312
Sanvitale, Francesca 1928- ... DLB-196
Sapidus, Joannes 1490-1561 ... DLB-179
Sapir, Edward 1884-1939 ... DLB-92
Sapper (see McNeile, Herman Cyril)
Sappho circa 620 B.C.-circa 550 B.C. ... DLB-176; CDWLB-1
Saramago, José 1922- ... DLB-287; Y-98
  Nobel Lecture 1998: How Characters Became the Masters and the Author Their Apprentice ... Y-98
Sarban (John W. Wall) 1910-1989 ... DLB-255
Sardou, Victorien 1831-1908 ... DLB-192
Sarduy, Severo 1937-1993 ... DLB-113
Sargent, Pamela 1948- ... DLB-8
Saro-Wiwa, Ken 1941- ... DLB-157
Saroyan, Aram
  Rites of Passage [on William Saroyan] ... Y-83
Saroyan, William 1908-1981 ... DLB-7, 9, 86; Y-81; CDALB-7
Sarraute, Nathalie 1900-1999 ... DLB-83, 321
Sarrazin, Albertine 1937-1967 ... DLB-83
Sarris, Greg 1952- ... DLB-175
Sarton, May 1912-1995 ... DLB-48; Y-81
Sartre, Jean-Paul 1905-1980 ... DLB-72, 296, 321
Sassoon, Siegfried 1886-1967 ... DLB-20, 191; DS-18
  A Centenary Essay ... Y-86
  Tributes from Vivien F. Clarke and Michael Thorpe ... Y-86
Sata Ineko 1904-1998 ... DLB-180
Saturday Review Press ... DLB-46
Saunders, James 1925-2004 ... DLB-13
Saunders, John Monk 1897-1940 ... DLB-26
Saunders, Margaret Marshall 1861-1947 ... DLB-92
Saunders and Otley ... DLB-106
Saussure, Ferdinand de 1857-1913 ... DLB-242
Savage, James 1784-1873 ... DLB-30
Savage, Marmion W. 1803?-1872 ... DLB-21
Savage, Richard 1697?-1743 ... DLB-95
Savard, Félix-Antoine 1896-1982 ... DLB-68
Savery, Henry 1791-1842 ... DLB-230
Saville, (Leonard) Malcolm 1901-1982 ... DLB-160
Saville, 1976 Booker Prize winner, David Storey ... DLB-326

Savinio, Alberto 1891-1952 ... DLB-264
Sawyer, Robert J. 1960- ... DLB-251
Sawyer, Ruth 1880-1970 ... DLB-22
Sayer, Mandy 1963- ... DLB-325
Sayers, Dorothy L. 1893-1957 ... DLB-10, 36, 77, 100; CDBLB-6
  The Dorothy L. Sayers Society ... Y-98
Sayle, Charles Edward 1864-1924 ... DLB-184
Sayles, John Thomas 1950- ... DLB-44
Sbarbaro, Camillo 1888-1967 ... DLB-114
Scalapino, Leslie 1947- ... DLB-193
Scannell, Vernon 1922- ... DLB-27
Scarry, Richard 1919-1994 ... DLB-61
Scève, Maurice circa 1502-circa 1564 ... DLB-327
Schack, Hans Egede 1820-1859 ... DLB-300
Schaefer, Jack 1907-1991 ... DLB-212
Schaeffer, Albrecht 1885-1950 ... DLB-66
Schaeffer, Susan Fromberg 1941- ... DLB-28, 299
Schaff, Philip 1819-1893 ... DS-13
Schaper, Edzard 1908-1984 ... DLB-69
Scharf, J. Thomas 1843-1898 ... DLB-47
Schede, Paul Melissus 1539-1602 ... DLB-179
Scheffel, Joseph Viktor von 1826-1886 ... DLB-129
Scheffler, Johann 1624-1677 ... DLB-164
Schéhadé, Georges 1905-1999 ... DLB-321
Schelling, Friedrich Wilhelm Joseph von 1775-1854 ... DLB-90
Scherer, Wilhelm 1841-1886 ... DLB-129
Scherfig, Hans 1905-1979 ... DLB-214
Schickele, René 1883-1940 ... DLB-66
Schiff, Dorothy 1903-1989 ... DLB-127
Schiller, Friedrich 1759-1805 ... DLB-94; CDWLB-2
Schindler's Ark, 1982 Booker Prize winner, Thomas Keneally ... DLB-326
Schirmer, David 1623-1687 ... DLB-164
Schlaf, Johannes 1862-1941 ... DLB-118
Schlegel, August Wilhelm 1767-1845 ... DLB-94
Schlegel, Dorothea 1763-1839 ... DLB-90
Schlegel, Friedrich 1772-1829 ... DLB-90
Schleiermacher, Friedrich 1768-1834 ... DLB-90
Schlesinger, Arthur M., Jr. 1917- ... DLB-17
Schlumberger, Jean 1877-1968 ... DLB-65
Schmid, Eduard Hermann Wilhelm (see Edschmid, Kasimir)
Schmidt, Arno 1914-1979 ... DLB-69
Schmidt, Johann Kaspar (see Stirner, Max)
Schmidt, Michael 1947- ... DLB-40
Schmidtbonn, Wilhelm August 1876-1952 ... DLB-118
Schmitz, Aron Hector (see Svevo, Italo)
Schmitz, James H. 1911-1981 ... DLB-8

Schnabel, Johann Gottfried 1692-1760....DLB-168

Schnackenberg, Gjertrud 1953- DLB-120

Schnitzler, Arthur
1862-1931 ....DLB-81, 118; CDWLB-2

Schnurre, Wolfdietrich 1920-1989........DLB-69

Schocken Books.......................DLB-46

Scholartis Press DLB-112

Scholderer, Victor 1880-1971..........DLB-201

The Schomburg Center for Research
in Black Culture DLB-76

Schönbeck, Virgilio (see Giotti, Virgilio)

Schönherr, Karl 1867-1943.............DLB-118

Schoolcraft, Jane Johnston 1800-1841 ....DLB-175

School Stories, 1914-1960 ....DLB-160

Schopenhauer, Arthur 1788-1860.........DLB-90

Schopenhauer, Johanna 1766-1838........DLB-90

Schorer, Mark 1908-1977...............DLB-103

Schottelius, Justus Georg 1612-1676 .....DLB-164

Schouler, James 1839-1920..............DLB-47

Schoultz, Solveig von 1907-1996 ....DLB-259

Schrader, Paul 1946- DLB-44

Schreiner, Olive
1855-1920 ....DLB-18, 156, 190, 225

Schroeder, Andreas 1946- DLB-53

Schubart, Christian Friedrich Daniel
1739-1791 ....DLB-97

Schubert, Gotthilf Heinrich 1780-1860 ....DLB-90

Schücking, Levin 1814-1883 ....DLB-133

Schulberg, Budd 1914- DLB-6, 26, 28; Y-81

Excerpts from USC Presentation
[on F. Scott Fitzgerald] Y-96

F. J. Schulte and Company..............DLB-49

Schulz, Bruno 1892-1942....DLB-215; CDWLB-4

Schulze, Hans (see Praetorius, Johannes)

Schupp, Johann Balthasar 1610-1661.....DLB-164

Schurz, Carl 1829-1906 ....DLB-23

Schuyler, George S. 1895-1977........DLB-29, 51

Schuyler, James 1923-1991..........DLB-5, 169

Schwartz, Delmore 1913-1966........DLB-28, 48

Schwartz, Jonathan 1938- Y-82

Schwartz, Lynne Sharon 1939- DLB-218

Schwarz, Sibylle 1621-1638 ....DLB-164

Schwarz-Bart, Andre 1928- DLB-299

Schwerner, Armand 1927-1999 ....DLB-165

Schwob, Marcel 1867-1905..............DLB-123

Sciascia, Leonardo 1921-1989 ....DLB-177

Science Fiction and Fantasy
Documents in British Fantasy and
Science Fiction DLB-178

Hugo Awards and Nebula Awards DLB-8

The Iconography of Science-Fiction
Art DLB-8

The New Wave....................DLB-8

Paperback Science Fiction DLB-8

Science Fantasy DLB-8

Science-Fiction Fandom and
Conventions DLB-8

Science-Fiction Fanzines: The Time
Binders DLB-8

Science-Fiction Films DLB-8

Science Fiction Writers of America
and the Nebula Award DLB-8

Selected Science-Fiction Magazines and
Anthologies....................DLB-8

A World Chronology of Important Science
Fiction Works (1818-1979) DLB-8

The Year in Science Fiction
and Fantasy....................Y-00, 01

Scot, Reginald circa 1538-1599 ....DLB-136

Scotellaro, Rocco 1923-1953 ....DLB-128

Scott, Alicia Anne (Lady John Scott)
1810-1900 ....DLB-240

Scott, Catharine Amy Dawson
1865-1934 ....DLB-240

Scott, Dennis 1939-1991 ....DLB-125

Scott, Dixon 1881-1915 ....DLB-98

Scott, Duncan Campbell 1862-1947.......DLB-92

Scott, Evelyn 1893-1963 ....DLB-9, 48

Scott, F. R. 1899-1985 ....DLB-88

Scott, Frederick George 1861-1944 ....DLB-92

Scott, Geoffrey 1884-1929 ....DLB-149

Scott, Harvey W. 1838-1910 ....DLB-23

Scott, John 1948- DLB-325

Scott, Lady Jane (see Scott, Alicia Anne)

Scott, Paul 1920-1978.......... DLB-14, 207, 326

Scott, Sarah 1723-1795 ....DLB-39

Scott, Tom 1918-1995 ....DLB-27

Scott, Sir Walter 1771-1832
...... DLB-93, 107, 116, 144, 159; CDBLB-3

Scott, William Bell 1811-1890 ....DLB-32

Walter Scott Publishing Company
Limited DLB-112

William R. Scott [publishing house].......DLB-46

Scott-Heron, Gil 1949- DLB-41

Scribe, Eugene 1791-1861 ....DLB-192

Scribner, Arthur Hawley 1859-1932 .... DS-13, 16

Scribner, Charles 1854-1930 .... DS-13, 16

Scribner, Charles, Jr. 1921-1995.............Y-95

Reminiscences....................DS-17

Charles Scribner's Sons DLB-49; DS-13, 16, 17

Archives of Charles Scribner's Sons DS-17

Scribner's Magazine.......................DS-13

Scribner's Monthly......................DS-13

Scripps, E. W. 1854-1926................DLB-25

Scudder, Horace Elisha 1838-1902 .... DLB-42, 71

Scudder, Vida Dutton 1861-1954.........DLB-71

Scudéry, Madeleine de 1607-1701 ....DLB-268

Scupham, Peter 1933- DLB-40

The Sea, 2005 Booker Prize winner,
John Banville...................DLB-326

The Sea, The Sea, 1978 Booker Prize winner,
Iris Murdoch....................DLB-326

Seabrook, William 1886-1945 ....DLB-4

Seabury, Samuel 1729-1796 ....DLB-31

Seacole, Mary Jane Grant 1805-1881 ....DLB-166

The Seafarer circa 970 ....DLB-146

Sealsfield, Charles (Carl Postl)
1793-1864 ....DLB-133, 186

Searle, John R. 1932- DLB-279

Sears, Edward I. 1819?-1876 ....DLB-79

Sears Publishing Company DLB-46

Seaton, George 1911-1979 ....DLB-44

Seaton, William Winston 1785-1866 ......DLB-43

Sebillet, Thomas 1512-1589..............DLB-327

Martin Secker [publishing house]........DLB-112

Martin Secker, and Warburg Limited DLB-112

The "Second Generation" Holocaust
Novel........................DLB-299

Sedgwick, Arthur George 1844-1915......DLB-64

Sedgwick, Catharine Maria
1789-1867 .... DLB-1, 74, 183, 239, 243

Sedgwick, Ellery 1872-1960.............DLB-91

Sedgwick, Eve Kosofsky 1950- DLB-246

Sedley, Sir Charles 1639-1701 ....DLB-131

Seeberg, Peter 1925-1999...............DLB-214

Seeger, Alan 1888-1916 ....DLB-45

Seers, Eugene (see Dantin, Louis)

Segal, Erich 1937- Y-86

Segal, Lore 1928- DLB-299

Šegedin, Petar 1909-1998...............DLB-181

Seghers, Anna 1900-1983 .... DLB-69; CDWLB-2

Seid, Ruth (see Sinclair, Jo)

Seidel, Frederick Lewis 1936- Y-84

Seidel, Ina 1885-1974..................DLB-56

Seifert, Jaroslav
1901-1986 .... DLB-215; Y-84; CDWLB-4

Jaroslav Seifert Through the Eyes of
the English-Speaking Reader Y-84

Three Poems by Jaroslav Seifert Y-84

Seifullina, Lidiia Nikolaevna 1889-1954 .. DLB-272

Seigenthaler, John 1927- DLB-127

Seizin Press DLB-112

Séjour, Victor 1817-1874................DLB-50

Séjour Marcou et Ferrand, Juan Victor
(see Séjour, Victor)

Sekowski, Józef-Julian, Baron Brambeus
(see Senkovsky, Osip Ivanovich)

Selby, Bettina 1934- DLB-204

Selby, Hubert Jr. 1928-2004..........DLB-2, 227

Selden, George 1929-1989 ....DLB-52

Selden, John 1584-1654 ....DLB-213

Cumulative Index

Selenić, Slobodan 1933-1995 . . . . DLB-181

Self, Edwin F. 1920- DLB-137

Self, Will 1961- DLB-207

Seligman, Edwin R. A. 1861-1939 . . . . DLB-47

Selimović, Meša
1910-1982. . . . . DLB-181; CDWLB-4

Sellars, Wilfrid 1912-1989 . . . . .DLB-279

Sellings, Arthur (Arthur Gordon Ley)
1911-1968. DLB-261

Selous, Frederick Courteney 1851-1917 . . .DLB-174

Seltzer, Chester E. (see Muro, Amado)

Thomas Seltzer [publishing house] DLB-46

Selvadurai, Shyam 1965- DLB-323

Selvon, Sam 1923-1994. . . . . DLB-125; CDWLB-3

Semel, Nava 1954- DLB-299

Semmes, Raphael 1809-1877. . . . . DLB-189

Senancour, Etienne de 1770-1846 . . . . DLB-119

Sena, Jorge de 1919-1978 . . . . DLB-287

Sendak, Maurice 1928- DLB-61

Sender, Ramón J. 1901-1982. . . . . DLB-322

Seneca the Elder
circa 54 B.C.-circa A.D. 40. . . . . DLB-211

Seneca the Younger
circa 1 B.C.-A.D. 65 . . . . . DLB-211; CDWLB-1

Senécal, Eva 1905-1988 . . . . DLB-92

Sengstacke, John 1912-1997 . . . . DLB-127

Senior, Olive 1941- DLB-157

Senkovsky, Osip Ivanovich
(Józef-Julian Sekowski, Baron Brambeus)
1800-1858. . . . . DLB-198

Šenoa, August 1838-1881 . . . . DLB-147; CDWLB-4

Sentimental Fiction of the Sixteenth
Century DLB-318

Sepamla, Sipho 1932- DLB-157, 225

Serafimovich, Aleksandr Serafimovich
(Aleksandr Serafimovich Popov)
1863-1949 . . . . DLB-272

Serao, Matilde 1856-1927 . . . . DLB-264

Seredy, Kate 1899-1975. . . . . DLB-22

Sereni, Vittorio 1913-1983 . . . . DLB-128

William Seres [publishing house] DLB-170

Sergeev-Tsensky, Sergei Nikolaevich (Sergei
Nikolaevich Sergeev) 1875-1958 . . . . DLB-272

Serling, Rod 1924-1975. . . . . DLB-26

Sernine, Daniel 1955- DLB-251

Serote, Mongane Wally 1944- DLB-125, 225

Serraillier, Ian 1912-1994 . . . . DLB-161

Serrano, Nina 1934- DLB-122

Service, Robert 1874-1958 . . . . DLB-92

Sessler, Charles 1854-1935 . . . . DLB-187

Seth, Vikram 1952- DLB-120, 271, 323

Seton, Elizabeth Ann 1774-1821 . . . . DLB-200

Seton, Ernest Thompson
1860-1942 . . . . DLB-92; DS-13

Seton, John circa 1509-1567 . . . . DLB-281

Setouchi Harumi 1922- DLB-182

Settle, Mary Lee 1918- DLB-6

Seume, Johann Gottfried 1763-1810 . . . . . . DLB-94

Seuse, Heinrich 1295?-1366 . . . . .DLB-179

Seuss, Dr. (see Geisel, Theodor Seuss)

Severianin, Igor' 1887-1941. . . . . DLB-295

Severin, Timothy 1940- DLB-204

Sévigné, Marie de Rabutin Chantal,
Madame de 1626-1696 . . . . DLB-268

Sewall, Joseph 1688-1769 . . . . DLB-24

Sewall, Richard B. 1908-2003. . . . . DLB-111

Sewall, Samuel 1652-1730. . . . . DLB-24

Sewell, Anna 1820-1878 . . . . DLB-163

Sewell, Stephen 1953- DLB-325

Sexton, Anne 1928-1974. . . DLB-5, 169; CDALB-1

Seymour-Smith, Martin 1928-1998. . . . . . DLB-155

Sgorlon, Carlo 1930- DLB-196

Shaara, Michael 1929-1988. . . . . Y-83

Shabel'skaia, Aleksandra Stanislavovna
1845-1921 . . . . DLB-238

Shadwell, Thomas 1641?-1692. . . . . DLB-80

Shaffer, Anthony 1926-2001 . . . . DLB-13

Shaffer, Peter 1926- DLB-13, 233; CDBLB-8

Muhammad ibn Idris al-Shafi'i 767-820 . . DLB-311

Shaftesbury, Anthony Ashley Cooper,
Third Earl of 1671-1713 . . . . DLB-101

Shaginian, Marietta Sergeevna
1888-1982 .DLB-272

Shairp, Mordaunt 1887-1939 . . . . DLB-10

Shakespeare, Nicholas 1957- DLB-231

Shakespeare, William
1564-1616 . . . . . DLB-62, 172, 263; CDBLB-1

The New Variorum Shakespeare Y-85

Shakespeare and Montaigne: A Symposium
by Jules Furthman Y-02

$6,166,000 for a *Book!* Observations on
*The Shakespeare First Folio: The History
of the Book*. Y-01

Taylor-Made Shakespeare? Or Is
"Shall I Die?" the Long-Lost Text
of Bottom's Dream? Y-85

The Shakespeare Globe Trust Y-93

Shakespeare Head Press DLB-112

Shakhova, Elisaveta Nikitichna
1822-1899 .DLB-277

Shakhovskoi, Aleksandr Aleksandrovich
1777-1846 . . . . DLB-150

Shalamov, Varlam Tikhonovich
1907-1982. DLB-302

al-Shanfara fl. sixth century DLB-311

Shange, Ntozake 1948- DLB-38, 249

Shapcott, Thomas W. 1935- DLB-289

Shapir, Ol'ga Andreevna 1850-1916. . . . . DLB-295

Shapiro, Karl 1913-2000 . . . . DLB-48

Sharon Publications DLB-46

Sharov, Vladimir Aleksandrovich
1952- DLB-285

Sharp, Margery 1905-1991. . . . . DLB-161

Sharp, William 1855-1905 . . . . DLB-156

Sharpe, Tom 1928- DLB-14, 231

Shaw, Albert 1857-1947. . . . . DLB-91

Shaw, George Bernard
1856-1950 . . . . DLB-10, 57, 190, CDBLB-6

The Bernard Shaw Society. Y-99

"Stage Censorship: The Rejected
Statement" (1911) [excerpts]. DLB-10

Shaw, Henry Wheeler 1818-1885. . . . . DLB-11

Shaw, Irwin
1913-1984 . . . . . .DLB-6, 102; Y-84; CDALB-1

Shaw, Joseph T. 1874-1952 . . . . .DLB-137

"As I Was Saying," Joseph T. Shaw's
Editorial Rationale in *Black Mask*
(January 1927) DLB-137

Shaw, Mary 1854-1929. . . . . DLB-228

Shaw, Robert 1927-1978 . . . . DLB-13, 14

Shaw, Robert B. 1947- DLB-120

Shawn, Wallace 1943- DLB-266

Shawn, William 1907-1992 . . . . .DLB-137

Frank Shay [publishing house] DLB-46

Shchedrin, N. (see Saltykov, Mikhail Evgrafovich)

Shcherbakova, Galina Nikolaevna
1932- DLB-285

Shcherbina, Nikolai Fedorovich
1821-1869 .DLB-277

Shea, John Gilmary 1824-1892. . . . . DLB-30

Sheaffer, Louis 1912-1993. . . . . DLB-103

Sheahan, Henry Beston (see Beston, Henry)

Shearing, Joseph 1886-1952 . . . . DLB-70

Shebbeare, John 1709-1788 . . . . DLB-39

Sheckley, Robert 1928- DLB-8

Shedd, William G. T. 1820-1894 . . . . DLB-64

Sheed, Wilfrid 1930- DLB-6

Sheed and Ward [U.S.]. DLB-46

Sheed and Ward Limited [U.K.] DLB-112

Sheldon, Alice B. (see Tiptree, James, Jr.)

Sheldon, Edward 1886-1946. . . . . DLB-7

Sheldon and Company. DLB-49

Sheller, Aleksandr Konstantinovich
1838-1900 . . . . DLB-238

Shelley, Mary Wollstonecraft 1797-1851
. . . . .DLB-110, 116, 159, 178; CDBLB-3

Preface to *Frankenstein; or, The
Modern Prometheus* (1818) DLB-178

Shelley, Percy Bysshe
1792-1822. . . . . DLB-96, 110, 158; CDBLB-3

Shelnutt, Eve 1941- DLB-130

Shen Congwen 1902-1988 . . . . DLB-328

Shenshin (see Fet, Afanasii Afanas'evich)

Shenstone, William 1714-1763 . . . . DLB-95

Shepard, Clark and Brown DLB-49	Short Stories Michael M. Rea and the Rea Award for the Short Story Y-97	Silverberg, Robert 1935- DLB-8
Shepard, Ernest Howard 1879-1976 . . . . . . DLB-160		Silverman, Kaja 1947- DLB-246
Shepard, Sam 1943- DLB-7, 212	The Year in Short Stories Y-87	Silverman, Kenneth 1936- DLB-111
Shepard, Thomas I, 1604 or 1605-1649 . . . DLB-24	The Year in the Short Story Y-88, 90–93	Simak, Clifford D. 1904-1988 . . . . DLB-8
Shepard, Thomas, II, 1635-1677 . . . . DLB-24	Shōtetsu 1381-1459 . . . . DLB-203	Simcoe, Elizabeth 1762-1850 . . . . DLB-99
Shepherd, Luke fl. 1547-1554. . . . . DLB-136	Showalter, Elaine 1941- DLB-67	Simcox, Edith Jemima 1844-1901 . . . . DLB-190
Sherburne, Edward 1616-1702. . . . . DLB-131	Shreve, Anita 1946- DLB-292	Simcox, George Augustus 1841-1905 . . . . . DLB-35
Sheridan, Frances 1724-1766 . . . . DLB-39, 84	Shteiger, Anatolii 1907-1944 . . . . DLB-317	Sime, Jessie Georgina 1868-1958 . . . . DLB-92
Sheridan, Richard Brinsley 1751-1816 . . . . DLB-89; CDBLB-2	Shukshin, Vasilii Makarovich 1929-1974 . . . . DLB-302	Simenon, Georges 1903-1989 . . . . . . DLB-72; Y-89
Sherman, Francis 1871-1926 . . . . DLB-92	Shulevitz, Uri 1935- DLB-61	Simic, Charles 1938- DLB-105
Sherman, Martin 1938- DLB-228	Shulman, Max 1919-1988 . . . . DLB-11	"Images and 'Images'" DLB-105
Sherriff, R. C. 1896-1975 . . . . DLB-10, 191, 233	Shute, Henry A. 1856-1943 . . . . DLB-9	Simionescu, Mircea Horia 1928- DLB-232
Sherrod, Blackie 1919- DLB-241	Shute, Nevil (Nevil Shute Norway)	Simmel, Georg 1858-1918 . . . . DLB-296
Sherry, Norman 1935- DLB-155	1899-1960 . . . . DLB-255	Simmel, Johannes Mario 1924- DLB-69
Tribute to Graham Greene Y-91	Shuttle, Penelope 1947- DLB-14, 40	Valentine Simmes [publishing house] DLB-170
Sherry, Richard 1506-1551 or 1555 . . . . . . DLB-236	Shvarts, Evgenii L'vovich 1896-1958 . . . . . DLB-272	Simmons, Ernest J. 1903-1972 . . . . DLB-103
Sherwood, Mary Martha 1775-1851 . . . . . DLB-163	Sibawayhi circa 750-circa 795 . . . . DLB-311	Simmons, Herbert Alfred 1930- DLB-33
Sherwood, Robert E. 1896-1955 . . . DLB-7, 26, 249	Sibbes, Richard 1577-1635 . . . . DLB-151	Simmons, James 1933- DLB-40
Shevyrev, Stepan Petrovich 1806-1864 . . . . DLB-205	Sibiriak, D. (see Mamin, Dmitrii Narkisovich)	Simms, William Gilmore 1806-1870 . . . . DLB-3, 30, 59, 73, 248
Shi Tuo (Lu Fen) 1910-1988 . . . . DLB-328	Siddal, Elizabeth Eleanor 1829-1862 . . . . . DLB-199	Simms and M'Intyre DLB-106
Shiel, M. P. 1865-1947 . . . . DLB-153	Sidgwick, Ethel 1877-1970 . . . . DLB-197	Simon, Claude 1913-2005 . . . . DLB-83; Y-85
Shiels, George 1886-1949 . . . . DLB-10	Sidgwick, Henry 1838-1900 . . . . DLB-262	Nobel Lecture Y-85
Shiga Naoya 1883-1971 . . . . DLB-180	Sidgwick and Jackson Limited DLB-112	Simon, Neil 1927- DLB-7, 266
Shiina Rinzō 1911-1973 . . . . DLB-182	Sidhwa, Bapsi 1939- DLB-323	Simon and Schuster DLB-46
Shikishi Naishinnō 1153?-1201 . . . . DLB-203	Sidney, Margaret (see Lothrop, Harriet M.)	Simonov, Konstantin Mikhailovich
Shillaber, Benjamin Penhallow 1814-1890 . . . . DLB-1, 11, 235	Sidney, Mary 1561-1621 . . . . DLB-167	1915-1979 . . . . DLB-302
Shimao Toshio 1917-1986 . . . . DLB-182	Sidney, Sir Philip 1554-1586 . . . . DLB-167; CDBLB-1	Simons, Katherine Drayton Mayrant 1890-1969 . . . . Y-83
Shimazaki Tōson 1872-1943 . . . . DLB-180	An Apologie for Poetrie (the Olney edition, 1595, of Defence of Poesie) DLB-167	Simović, Ljubomir 1935- DLB-181
Shimose, Pedro 1940- DLB-283	Sidney's Press DLB-49	Simpkin and Marshall [publishing house] DLB-154
Shine, Ted 1931- DLB-38	The Siege of Krishnapur, 1973 Booker Prize winner,	Simpson, Helen 1897-1940 . . . . DLB-77
Shinkei 1406-1475 . . . . DLB-203	J. G. Farrell DLB-326	Simpson, Louis 1923- DLB-5
Ship, Reuben 1915-1975 . . . . DLB-88	Sierra, Rubén 1946- DLB-122	Simpson, N. F. 1919- DLB-13
Shirer, William L. 1904-1993 . . . . DLB-4	Sierra Club Books DLB-49	Sims, George 1923-1999 . . . . DLB-87; Y-99
Shirinsky-Shikhmatov, Sergii Aleksandrovich 1783-1837 . . . . DLB-150	Siger of Brabant circa 1240-circa 1284 . . . . DLB-115	Sims, George Robert 1847-1922 . . . DLB-35, 70, 135
Shirley, James 1596-1666 . . . . DLB-58	Sigourney, Lydia Huntley 1791-1865 . . . . . . DLB-1, 42, 73, 183, 239, 243	Sinán, Rogelio 1902-1994 . . . . DLB-145, 290
Shishkov, Aleksandr Semenovich 1753-1841 . . . . DLB-150	Silkin, Jon 1930-1997 . . . . DLB-27	Sinclair, Andrew 1935- DLB-14
Shmelev, I. S. 1873-1950 . . . . DLB-317	Silko, Leslie Marmon 1948- DLB-143, 175, 256, 275	Sinclair, Bertrand William 1881-1972 . . . . . DLB-92
Shockley, Ann Allen 1927- DLB-33	Silliman, Benjamin 1779-1864 . . . . DLB-183	Sinclair, Catherine 1800-1864 . . . . DLB-163
Sholokhov, Mikhail Aleksandrovich 1905-1984 . . . . DLB-272	Silliman, Ron 1946- DLB-169	Sinclair, Clive 1948- DLB-319
Shōno Junzō 1921- DLB-182	Silliphant, Stirling 1918-1996 . . . . DLB-26	Sinclair, Jo 1913-1995 . . . . DLB-28
Shore, Arabella 1820?-1901 . . . . DLB-199	Sillitoe, Alan 1928- DLB-14, 139; CDBLB-8	Sinclair, Lister 1921- DLB-88
Shore, Louisa 1824-1895 . . . . DLB-199	Tribute to J. B. Priestly Y-84	Sinclair, May 1863-1946 . . . . DLB-36, 135
Short, Luke (see Glidden, Frederick Dilley)	Silman, Roberta 1934- DLB-28	The Novels of Dorothy Richardson (1918) DLB-36
Peter Short [publishing house] DLB-170	Silone, Ignazio (Secondino Tranquilli) 1900-1978 . . . . DLB-264	Sinclair, Upton 1878-1968 . . . . . . DLB-9; CDALB-5
Shorter, Dora Sigerson 1866-1918 . . . . DLB-240	Silva, Beverly 1930- DLB-122	Upton Sinclair [publishing house] DLB-46
Shorthouse, Joseph Henry 1834-1903 . . . . . DLB-18	Silva, Clara 1905-1976 . . . . DLB-290	Singer, Isaac Bashevis 1904-1991 . . . . DLB-6, 28, 52, 278; Y-91; CDALB-1
	Silva, José Asunció 1865-1896 . . . . DLB-283	Singer, Mark 1950- DLB-185

Singh, Khushwant 1915- DLB-323

Singmaster, Elsie 1879-1958 .... DLB-9

Siniavsky, Andrei (Abram Tertz)
1925-1997..................... DLB-302

Sinisgalli, Leonardo 1908-1981......... DLB-114

Siodmak, Curt 1902-2000............. DLB-44

Sîrbu, Ion D. 1919-1989 .... DLB-232

Siringo, Charles A. 1855-1928 .... DLB-186

Sissman, L. E. 1928-1976 .... DLB-5

Sisson, C. H. 1914-2003 .... DLB-27

Sitwell, Edith 1887-1964 ...... DLB-20; CDBLB-7

Sitwell, Osbert 1892-1969......... DLB-100, 195

Sivanandan, Ambalavaner 1923- DLB-323

Sixteenth-Century Spanish Epic, The.... DLB-318

Skácel, Jan 1922-1989................ DLB-232

Skalbe, Kārlis 1879-1945............. DLB-220

Skármeta, Antonio
1940- DLB-145; CDWLB-3

Skavronsky, A. (see Danilevsky, Grigorii Petrovich)

Skeat, Walter W. 1835-1912.......... DLB-184

William Skeffington [publishing house] .. DLB-106

Skelton, John 1463-1529.............. DLB-136

Skelton, Robin 1925-1997............DLB-27, 53

Škėma, Antanas 1910-1961............ DLB-220

Skinner, Constance Lindsay
1877-1939...................... DLB-92

Skinner, John Stuart 1788-1851.......... DLB-73

Skipsey, Joseph 1832-1903 .... DLB-35

Skou-Hansen, Tage 1925- DLB-214

Skrzynecki, Peter 1945- DLB-289

Škvorecký, Josef 1924- DLB-232; CDWLB-4

Slade, Bernard 1930- DLB-53

Slamnig, Ivan 1930- DLB-181

Slančeková, Božena (see Timrava)

Slataper, Scipio 1888-1915 .... DLB-264

Slater, Patrick 1880-1951 .... DLB-68

Slaveykov, Pencho 1866-1912.......... DLB-147

Slaviček, Milivoj 1929- DLB-181

Slavitt, David 1935- DLB-5, 6

Sleigh, Burrows Willcocks Arthur
1821-1869 .... DLB-99

Sleptsov, Vasilii Alekseevich 1836-1878 ...DLB-277

Slesinger, Tess 1905-1945 .... DLB-102

Slessor, Kenneth 1901-1971 .... DLB-260

Slick, Sam (see Haliburton, Thomas Chandler)

Sloan, John 1871-1951 .... DLB-188

Sloane, William, Associates DLB-46

Slonimsky, Mikhail Leonidovich
1897-1972..................... DLB-272

Sluchevsky, Konstantin Konstantinovich
1837-1904.....................DLB-277

Small, Maynard and Company.......... DLB-49

Smart, Christopher 1722-1771......... DLB-109

Smart, David A. 1892-1957 .... DLB-137

Smart, Elizabeth 1913-1986 .... DLB-88

Smart, J. J. C. 1920- DLB-262

Smedley, Menella Bute 1820?-1877...... DLB-199

William Smellie [publishing house]...... DLB-154

Smiles, Samuel 1812-1904 .... DLB-55

Smiley, Jane 1949- DLB-227, 234

Smith, A. J. M. 1902-1980 .... DLB-88

Smith, Adam 1723-1790 .... DLB-104, 252

Smith, Adam (George Jerome Waldo
Goodman) 1930- DLB-185

Smith, Alexander 1829-1867 .... DLB-32, 55

"On the Writing of Essays" (1862) ... DLB-57

Smith, Amanda 1837-1915 .... DLB-221

Smith, Betty 1896-1972.................... Y-82

Smith, Carol Sturm 1938- Y-81

Smith, Charles Henry 1826-1903........ DLB-11

Smith, Charlotte 1749-1806 .... DLB-39, 109

Smith, Chet 1899-1973 ....DLB-171

Smith, Cordwainer 1913-1966 .... DLB-8

Smith, Dave 1942- DLB-5

Tribute to James Dickey............... Y-97

Tribute to John Gardner Y-82

Smith, Dodie 1896-1990............... DLB-10

Smith, Doris Buchanan 1934-2002....... DLB-52

Smith, E. E. 1890-1965 .... DLB-8

Smith, Elihu Hubbard 1771-1798 .... DLB-37

Smith, Elizabeth Oakes (Prince)
(see Oakes Smith, Elizabeth)

Smith, Eunice 1757-1823.............. DLB-200

Smith, F. Hopkinson 1838-1915 ....DS-13

Smith, George D. 1870-1920........... DLB-140

Smith, George O. 1911-1981 .... DLB-8

Smith, Goldwin 1823-1910............. DLB-99

Smith, H. Allen 1907-1976 .... DLB-11, 29

Smith, Harry B. 1860-1936............ DLB-187

Smith, Hazel Brannon 1914-1994....... DLB-127

Smith, Henry circa 1560-circa 1591 ..... DLB-136

Smith, Horatio (Horace)
1779-1849................... DLB-96, 116

Smith, Iain Crichton (Iain Mac A'Ghobhainn)
1928-1998 .... DLB-40, 139, 319

Smith, J. Allen 1860-1924............. DLB-47

Smith, James 1775-1839 .... DLB-96

Smith, Jessie Willcox 1863-1935........ DLB-188

Smith, John 1580-1631 .... DLB-24, 30

Smith, John 1618-1652 .... DLB-252

Smith, Josiah 1704-1781 .... DLB-24

Smith, Ken 1938- DLB-40

Smith, Lee 1944- DLB-143; Y-83

Smith, Logan Pearsall 1865-1946 .... DLB-98

Smith, Margaret Bayard 1778-1844 ..... DLB-248

Smith, Mark 1935- Y-82

Smith, Michael 1698-circa 1771 .... DLB-31

Smith, Pauline 1882-1959............. DLB-225

Smith, Red 1905-1982 ....DLB-29, 171

Smith, Roswell 1829-1892 .... DLB-79

Smith, Samuel Harrison 1772-1845 ..... DLB-43

Smith, Samuel Stanhope 1751-1819 ...... DLB-37

Smith, Sarah (see Stretton, Hesba)

Smith, Sarah Pogson 1774-1870 .... DLB-200

Smith, Seba 1792-1868 .... DLB-1, 11, 243

Smith, Stevie 1902-1971 .... DLB-20

Smith, Sydney 1771-1845 ....DLB-107

Smith, Sydney Goodsir 1915-1975 .... DLB-27

Smith, Sir Thomas 1513-1577.......... DLB-132

Smith, Vivian 1933- DLB-325

Smith, W. Gordon 1928-1996.......... DLB-310

Smith, Wendell 1914-1972 ....DLB-171

Smith, William fl. 1595-1597 .... DLB-136

Smith, William 1727-1803.............. DLB-31

A General Idea of the College of Mirania
(1753) [excerpts] DLB-31

Smith, William 1728-1793.............. DLB-30

Smith, William Gardner 1927-1974....... DLB-76

Smith, William Henry 1808-1872....... DLB-159

Smith, William Jay 1918- DLB-5

Smith, Elder and Company DLB-154

Harrison Smith and Robert Haas
[publishing house] DLB-46

J. Stilman Smith and Company DLB-49

W. B. Smith and Company............. DLB-49

W. H. Smith and Son DLB-106

Leonard Smithers [publishing house] DLB-112

Smollett, Tobias
1721-1771 .... DLB-39, 104; CDBLB-2

Dedication to *Ferdinand Count Fathom*
(1753)....................... DLB-39

Preface to *Ferdinand Count Fathom*
(1753)....................... DLB-39

Preface to *Roderick Random* (1748)..... DLB-39

Smythe, Francis Sydney 1900-1949 ..... DLB-195

Snelling, William Joseph 1804-1848..... DLB-202

Snellings, Rolland (see Touré, Askia Muhammad)

Snodgrass, W. D. 1926- DLB-5

Snorri Hjartarson 1906-1986 .... DLB-293

Snow, C. P.
1905-1980 .... DLB-15, 77; DS-17; CDBLB-7

Snyder, Gary
1930- DLB-5, 16, 165, 212, 237, 275

Sobiloff, Hy 1912-1970 .... DLB-48

The Social Contract, Jean-Jacques
Rousseau DLB-314

The Society for Textual Scholarship and
TEXT....................... Y-87

The Society for the History of Authorship,
  Reading and Publishing................Y-92
Söderberg, Hjalmar 1869-1941.........DLB-259
Södergran, Edith 1892-1923............DLB-259
Soffici, Ardengo 1879-1964.........DLB-114, 264
Sofola, 'Zulu 1938-..................DLB-157
Sokhanskaia, Nadezhda Stepanovna
  (Kokhanovskaia) 1823?-1884........DLB-277
Sokolov, Sasha (Aleksandr Vsevolodovich
  Sokolov) 1943-....................DLB-285
Solano, Solita 1888-1975................DLB-4
Soldati, Mario 1906-1999..............DLB-177
Soledad (see Zamudio, Adela)
Šoljan, Antun 1932-1993...............DLB-181
Sollers, Philippe (Philippe Joyaux)
  1936-..............................DLB-83
Sollogub, Vladimir Aleksandrovich
  1813-1882..........................DLB-198
Sollors, Werner 1943-.................DBL-246
Solmi, Sergio 1899-1981...............DLB-114
Sologub, Fedor 1863-1927..............DLB-295
Solomon, Carl 1928-....................DLB-16
Solórzano, Carlos 1922-...............DLB-305
Soloukhin, Vladimir Alekseevich
  1924-1997..........................DLB-302
Solov'ev, Sergei Mikhailovich
  1885-1942..........................DLB-295
Solov'ev, Vladimir Sergeevich
  1853-1900..........................DLB-295
Solstad, Dag 1941-....................DLB-297
Solway, David 1941-....................DLB-53
Solzhenitsyn, Aleksandr
  1918-..............................DLB-302
  Solzhenitsyn and America..............Y-85
Some Basic Notes on Three Modern Genres:
  Interview, Blurb, and Obituary........Y-02
Somerville, Edith Œnone 1858-1949.....DLB-135
Something to Answer For, 1969 Booker Prize winner,
  P. H. Newby........................DLB-326
Somov, Orest Mikhailovich 1793-1833...DLB-198
Sønderby, Knud 1909-1966..............DLB-214
Sone, Monica 1919-....................DLB-312
Song, Cathy 1955-.................DLB-169, 312
Sonnevi, Göran 1939-..................DLB-257
Sono Ayako 1931-......................DLB-182
Sontag, Susan 1933-2004.............DLB-2, 67
Sophocles 497/496 B.C.-406/405 B.C.
  ....DLB-176; CDWLB-1
Šopov, Aco 1923-1982..................DLB-181
Sorel, Charles ca.1600-1674...........DLB-268
Sørensen, Villy 1929-.................DLB-214
Sorensen, Virginia 1912-1991..........DLB-206
Sorge, Reinhard Johannes 1892-1916...DLB-118
Sorokin, Vladimir Georgievich
  1955-..............................DLB-285

Sorrentino, Gilbert 1929-.......DLB-5, 173; Y-80
Sosa, Roberto 1930-...................DLB-290
Sotheby, James 1682-1742..............DLB-213
Sotheby, John 1740-1807...............DLB-213
Sotheby, Samuel 1771-1842.............DLB-213
Sotheby, Samuel Leigh 1805-1861.......DLB-213
Sotheby, William 1757-1833.........DLB-93, 213
Soto, Gary 1952-.......................DLB-82
Soueif, Ahdaf 1950-...................DLB-267
Souster, Raymond 1921-.................DLB-88
The *South English Legendary* circa
  thirteenth-fifteenth centuries.......DLB-146
Southerland, Ellease 1943-.............DLB-33
Southern, Terry 1924-1995...............DLB-2
Southern Illinois University Press.......Y-95
Southern Literature
  Fellowship of Southern Writers........Y-98
  The Fugitives and the Agrarians:
    The First Exhibition................Y-85
  "The Greatness of Southern Literature":
    League of the South Institute for the
    Study of Southern Culture and
    History.............................Y-02
  The Society for the Study of
    Southern Literature.................Y-00
  Southern Writers Between the Wars....DLB-9
Southerne, Thomas 1659-1746............DLB-80
Southey, Caroline Anne Bowles
  1786-1854..........................DLB-116
Southey, Robert 1774-1843......DLB-93, 107, 142
Southwell, Robert 1561?-1595..........DLB-167
Southworth, E. D. E. N. 1819-1899.....DLB-239
Sowande, Bode 1948-...................DLB-157
Tace Sowle [publishing house].........DLB-170
Soyfer, Jura 1912-1939................DLB-124
Soyinka, Wole
  1934-........DLB-125; Y-86, Y-87; CDWLB-3
  Nobel Lecture 1986: This Past Must
    Address Its Present.................Y-86
Spacks, Barry 1931-...................DLB-105
Spalding, Frances 1950-...............DLB-155
Spanish Byzantine Novel, The..........DLB-318
Spanish Travel Writers of the
  Late Middle Ages....................DLB-286
Spark, Muriel 1918-.......DLB-15, 139; CDBLB-7
Michael Sparke [publishing house].....DLB-170
Sparks, Jared 1789-1866............DLB-1, 30, 235
Sparshott, Francis 1926-...............DLB-60
Späth, Gerold 1939-....................DLB-75
Spatola, Adriano 1941-1988............DLB-128
Spaziani, Maria Luisa 1924-...........DLB-128
Specimens of Foreign Standard Literature
  1838-1842............................DLB-1
The *Spectator* 1828-.................DLB-110
Spedding, James 1808-1881.............DLB-144

Spee von Langenfeld, Friedrich
  1591-1635..........................DLB-164
Speght, Rachel 1597-after 1630........DLB-126
Speke, John Hanning 1827-1864.........DLB-166
Spellman, A. B. 1935-..................DLB-41
Spence, Catherine Helen 1825-1910.....DLB-230
Spence, Thomas 1750-1814..............DLB-158
Spencer, Anne 1882-1975.............DLB-51, 54
Spencer, Charles, third Earl of Sunderland
  1674-1722..........................DLB-213
Spencer, Elizabeth 1921-............DLB-6, 218
Spencer, George John, Second Earl Spencer
  1758-1834..........................DLB-184
Spencer, Herbert 1820-1903.........DLB-57, 262
  "The Philosophy of Style" (1852).....DLB-57
Spencer, Scott 1945-....................Y-86
Spender, J. A. 1862-1942..............DLB-98
Spender, Stephen 1909-1995...DLB-20; CDBLB-7
Spener, Philipp Jakob 1635-1705.......DLB-164
Spenser, Edmund
  circa 1552-1599.........DLB-167; CDBLB-1
  Envoy from *The Shepheardes Calender*....DLB-167
  "The Generall Argument of the
    Whole Booke," from
    The Shepheardes Calender.........DLB-167
  "A Letter of the Authors Expounding
    His Whole Intention in the Course
    of this Worke: Which for that It
    Giueth Great Light to the Reader,
    for the Better Vnderstanding
    Is Hereunto Annexed,"
    from *The Faerie Queene* (1590)....DLB-167
  "To His Booke," from
    The Shepheardes Calender (1579)..DLB-167
  "To the Most Excellent and Learned
    Both Orator and Poete, Mayster
    Gabriell Haruey, His Verie Special
    and Singular Good Frend E. K.
    Commendeth the Good Lyking of
    This His Labour, and the Patronage
    of the New Poete," from
    The Shepheardes Calender.........DLB-167
Sperr, Martin 1944-...................DLB-124
Spewack, Bella Cowen 1899-1990........DLB-266
Spewack, Samuel 1899-1971.............DLB-266
Spicer, Jack 1925-1965............DLB-5, 16, 193
Spiegelman, Art 1948-.................DLB-299
Spielberg, Peter 1929-..................Y-81
Spielhagen, Friedrich 1829-1911.......DLB-129
"Spielmannsepen" (circa 1152-circa 1500)...DLB-148
Spier, Peter 1927-.....................DLB-61
Spillane, Mickey 1918-2006............DLB-226
Spink, J. G. Taylor 1888-1962.........DLB-241
Spinrad, Norman 1940-...................DLB-8
  Tribute to Isaac Asimov...............Y-92
Spires, Elizabeth 1952-...............DLB-120
The Spirit of Laws, Claude-Adrien
  Helvétius..........................DLB-314

Cumulative Index

The Spirit of Laws, Charles-Louis de Secondat, baron de Montesquieu DLB-314

Spitteler, Carl 1845-1924 .... DLB-129

Spivak, Lawrence E. 1900-1994 .... DLB-137

Spofford, Harriet Prescott 1835-1921 .... DLB-74, 221

Sponde, Jean de 1557-1595 .... DLB-327

Sports
    Jimmy, Red, and Others: Harold Rosenthal Remembers the Stars of the Press Box Y-01
    The Literature of Boxing in England through Arthur Conan Doyle Y-01
    Notable Twentieth-Century Books about Sports DLB-241

Sprigge, Timothy L. S. 1932- DLB-262

Spring, Howard 1889-1965 .... DLB-191

Springs, Elliott White 1896-1959 .... DLB-316

Squibob (see Derby, George Horatio)

Squier, E. G. 1821-1888 .... DLB-189

Staal-Delaunay, Marguerite-Jeanne Cordier de 1684-1750 .... DLB-314

Stableford, Brian 1948- DLB-261

Stacpoole, H. de Vere 1863-1951 ..... DLB-153

Staël, Germaine de 1766-1817 ...... DLB-119, 192

Staël-Holstein, Anne-Louise Germaine de (see Staël, Germaine de)

Staffeldt, Schack 1769-1826 .... DLB-300

Stafford, Jean 1915-1979 .... DLB-2, 173

Stafford, William 1914-1993 .... DLB-5, 206

Stallings, Laurence 1894-1968 ..... DLB-7, 44, 316

Stallworthy, Jon 1935- DLB-40

Stampp, Kenneth M. 1912- DLB-17

Stănescu, Nichita 1933-1983 .... DLB-232

Stanev, Emiliyan 1907-1979 .... DLB-181

Stanford, Ann 1916-1987 .... DLB-5

Stangerup, Henrik 1937-1998 .... DLB-214

Stanihurst, Richard 1547-1618 .... DLB-281

Stanitsky, N. (see Panaeva, Avdot'ia Iakovlevna)

Stankevich, Nikolai Vladimirovich 1813-1840 .... DLB-198

Stanković, Borisav ("Bora") 1876-1927 .... DLB-147; CDWLB-4

Stanley, Henry M. 1841-1904 .... DLB-189; DS-13

Stanley, Thomas 1625-1678 .... DLB-131

Stannard, Martin 1947- DLB-155

William Stansby [publishing house] DLB-170

Stanton, Elizabeth Cady 1815-1902 ...... DLB-79

Stanton, Frank L. 1857-1927 .... DLB-25

Stanton, Maura 1946- DLB-120

Stapledon, Olaf 1886-1950 .... DLB-15, 255

Star Spangled Banner Office DLB-49

Stark, Freya 1893-1993 .... DLB-195

Starkey, Thomas circa 1499-1538 ...... DLB-132

Starkie, Walter 1894-1976 .... DLB-195

Starkweather, David 1935- DLB-7

Starrett, Vincent 1886-1974 .... DLB-187

Stationers' Company of London, The DLB-170

Statius circa A.D. 45-A.D. 96 .... DLB-211

Staying On, 1977 Booker Prize winner, Paul Scott DLB-326

Stead, Christina 1902-1983 .... DLB-260

Stead, Robert J. C. 1880-1959 .... DLB-92

Steadman, Mark 1930- DLB-6

Stearns, Harold E. 1891-1943 ...... DLB-4; DS-15

Stebnitsky, M. (see Leskov, Nikolai Semenovich)

Stedman, Edmund Clarence 1833-1908 ... DLB-64

Steegmuller, Francis 1906-1994 .... DLB-111

Steel, Flora Annie 1847-1929 ...... DLB-153, 156

Steele, Max 1922-2005 .... Y-80

Steele, Richard 1672-1729 .... DLB-84, 101; CDBLB-2

Steele, Timothy 1948- DLB-120

Steele, Wilbur Daniel 1886-1970 .... DLB-86

Wallace Markfield's "Steeplechase" Y-02

Steere, Richard circa 1643-1721 .... DLB-24

Stefán frá Hvítadal (Stefán Sigurðsson) 1887-1933 .... DLB-293

Stefán Guðmundsson (see Stephan G. Stephansson)

Stefán Hörður Grímsson 1919 or 1920-2002 .... DLB-293

Steffens, Lincoln 1866-1936 .... DLB-303

Stefanovski, Goran 1952- DLB-181

Stegner, Wallace 1909-1993 .... DLB-9, 206, 275; Y-93

Stehr, Hermann 1864-1940 .... DLB-66

Steig, William 1907-2003 .... DLB-61

Stein, Gertrude 1874-1946 .... DLB-4, 54, 86, 228; DS-15; CDALB-4

Stein, Leo 1872-1947 .... DLB-4

Stein and Day Publishers DLB-46

Steinbeck, John 1902-1968 .... DLB-7, 9, 212, 275, 309; DS-2; CDALB-5
    John Steinbeck Research Center, San Jose State University Y-85
    The Steinbeck Centennial Y-02

Steinem, Gloria 1934- DLB-246

Steiner, George 1929- DLB-67, 299

Steinhoewel, Heinrich 1411/1412-1479 .... DLB-179

Steinn Steinarr (Aðalsteinn Kristmundsson) 1908-1958 .... DLB-293

Steinunn Sigurðardóttir 1950- DLB-293

Steloff, Ida Frances 1887-1989 .... DLB-187

Stendhal 1783-1842 .... DLB-119

Stephan G. Stephansson (Stefán Guðmundsson) 1853-1927 .... DLB-293

Stephen, Leslie 1832-1904 ...... DLB-57, 144, 190

Stephen Family (Bloomsbury Group) DS-10

Stephens, A. G. 1865-1933 .... DLB-230

Stephens, Alexander H. 1812-1883 ...... DLB-47

Stephens, Alice Barber 1858-1932 ...... DLB-188

Stephens, Ann 1810-1886 .... DLB-3, 73, 250

Stephens, Charles Asbury 1844?-1931 .... DLB-42

Stephens, James 1882?-1950 ..... DLB-19, 153, 162

Stephens, John Lloyd 1805-1852 ... DLB-183, 250

Stephens, Michael 1946- DLB-234

Stephensen, P. R. 1901-1965 .... DLB-260

Sterling, George 1869-1926 .... DLB-54

Sterling, James 1701-1763 .... DLB-24

Sterling, John 1806-1844 .... DLB-116

Stern, Gerald 1925- DLB-105
    "Living in Ruin" DLB-105

Stern, Gladys B. 1890-1973 .... DLB-197

Stern, Madeleine B. 1912- DLB-111, 140

Stern, Richard 1928- DLB-218; Y-87

Stern, Stewart 1922- DLB-26

Sterne, Laurence 1713-1768 ... DLB-39; CDBLB-2

Sternheim, Carl 1878-1942 .... DLB-56, 118

Sternhold, Thomas ?-1549 .... DLB-132

Steuart, David 1747-1824 .... DLB-213

Stevens, Henry 1819-1886 .... DLB-140

Stevens, Wallace 1879-1955 ... DLB-54; CDALB-5
    The Wallace Stevens Society Y-99

Stevenson, Anne 1933- DLB-40

Stevenson, D. E. 1892-1973 .... DLB-191

Stevenson, Lionel 1902-1973 .... DLB-155

Stevenson, Robert Louis 1850-1894 .... DLB-18, 57, 141, 156, 174; DS-13; CDBLB-5
    "On Style in Literature: Its Technical Elements" (1885) ... DLB-57

Stewart, Donald Ogden 1894-1980 .... DLB-4, 11, 26; DS-15

Stewart, Douglas 1913-1985 .... DLB-260

Stewart, Dugald 1753-1828 .... DLB-31

Stewart, George, Jr. 1848-1906 .... DLB-99

Stewart, George R. 1895-1980 .... DLB-8

Stewart, Harold 1916-1995 .... DLB-260

Stewart, J. I. M. (see Innes, Michael)

Stewart, Maria W. 1803?-1879 .... DLB-239

Stewart, Randall 1896-1964 .... DLB-103

Stewart, Sean 1965- DLB-251

Stewart and Kidd Company DLB-46

Sthen, Hans Christensen 1544-1610 ..... DLB-300

Stickney, Trumbull 1874-1904 .... DLB-54

Stieler, Caspar 1632-1707 .... DLB-164

Stifter, Adalbert 1805-1868 .... DLB-133; CDWLB-2

Stiles, Ezra 1727-1795 .... DLB-31

Still, James 1906-2001 .... DLB-9; Y-01

Stirling, S. M. 1953- DLB-251

Stirner, Max 1806-1856 . . . . DLB-129
Stith, William 1707-1755 . . . . DLB-31
Stivens, Dal 1911-1997 . . . . DLB-260
Elliot Stock [publishing house] DLB-106
Stockton, Annis Boudinot 1736-1801 . . . . . DLB-200
Stockton, Frank R.
   1834-1902 . . . . DLB-42, 74; DS-13
Stockton, J. Roy 1892-1972 . . . . DLB-241
Ashbel Stoddard [publishing house] DLB-49
Stoddard, Charles Warren 1843-1909 . . . . DLB-186
Stoddard, Elizabeth 1823-1902 . . . . DLB-202
Stoddard, Richard Henry
   1825-1903 . . . . DLB-3, 64, 250; DS-13
Stoddard, Solomon 1643-1729 . . . . DLB-24
Stoker, Bram
   1847-1912 . . . . DLB-36, 70, 178; CDBLB-5
   On Writing *Dracula,* from the
      Introduction to *Dracula* (1897) DLB-178
   Dracula (Documentary) DLB-304
Frederick A. Stokes Company DLB-49
Stokes, Thomas L. 1898-1958 . . . . DLB-29
Stokesbury, Leon 1945- DLB-120
Stolberg, Christian Graf zu 1748-1821 . . . . . DLB-94
Stolberg, Friedrich Leopold Graf zu
   1750-1819 . . . . DLB-94
Stone, Lucy 1818-1893 . . . . DLB-79, 239
Stone, Melville 1848-1929 . . . . DLB-25
Stone, Robert 1937- DLB-152
Stone, Ruth 1915- DLB-105
Stone, Samuel 1602-1663 . . . . DLB-24
Stone, William Leete 1792-1844 . . . . DLB-202
Herbert S. Stone and Company DLB-49
Stone and Kimball DLB-49
Stoppard, Tom
   1937- DLB-13, 233; Y-85; CDBLB-8
   Playwrights and Professors DLB-13
Storey, Anthony 1928- DLB-14
Storey, David 1933- . . . DLB-13, 14, 207, 245, 326
Storm, Theodor
   1817-1888 . . . . DLB-129; CDWLB-2
Storni, Alfonsina 1892-1938 . . . . DLB-283
Story, Thomas circa 1670-1742 . . . . DLB-31
Story, William Wetmore 1819-1895 . . . . DLB-1, 235
Storytelling: A Contemporary Renaissance Y-84
Stoughton, William 1631-1701 . . . . DLB-24
Stout, Rex 1886-1975 . . . . DLB-306
Stow, John 1525-1605 . . . . DLB-132
Stow, Randolph 1935- DLB-260
Stowe, Harriet Beecher 1811-1896 . . . . . . DLB-1,12,
         42, 74, 189, 239, 243; CDALB-3
   The Harriet Beecher Stowe Center Y-00
Stowe, Leland 1899-1994 . . . . DLB-29
Stoyanov, Dimitr Ivanov (see Elin Pelin)

Strabo 64/63 B.C.-circa A.D. 25 . . . . DLB-176
Strachey, Lytton 1880-1932 . . . . . . DLB-149; DS-10
   Preface to *Eminent Victorians* DLB-149
William Strahan [publishing house] DLB-154
Strahan and Company DLB-106
Strand, Mark 1934- DLB-5
The Strasbourg Oaths 842 . . . . DLB-148
Stratemeyer, Edward 1862-1930 . . . . DLB-42
Strati, Saverio 1924- DLB-177
Stratton and Barnard DLB-49
Stratton-Porter, Gene
   1863-1924 . . . . DLB-221; DS-14
Straub, Peter 1943- Y-84
Strauß, Botho 1944- DLB-124
Strauß, David Friedrich 1808-1874 . . . . DLB-133
Strauss, Jennifer 1933- DLB-325
The Strawberry Hill Press DLB-154
Strawson, P. F. 1919- DLB-262
Streatfeild, Noel 1895-1986 . . . . DLB-160
Street, Cecil John Charles (see Rhode, John)
Street, G. S. 1867-1936 . . . . DLB-135
Street and Smith DLB-49
Streeter, Edward 1891-1976 . . . . DLB-11
Streeter, Thomas Winthrop 1883-1965 . . . DLB-140
Stretton, Hesba 1832-1911 . . . . DLB-163, 190
Stribling, T. S. 1881-1965 . . . . DLB-9
Der Stricker circa 1190-circa 1250 . . . . DLB-138
Strickland, Samuel 1804-1867 . . . . DLB-99
Strindberg, August 1849-1912 . . . . DLB-259
Stringer, Arthur 1874-1950 . . . . DLB-92
Stringer and Townsend DLB-49
Strittmatter, Erwin 1912-1994 . . . . DLB-69
Strniša, Gregor 1930-1987 . . . . DLB-181
Strode, William 1630-1645 . . . . DLB-126
Strong, L. A. G. 1896-1958 . . . . DLB-191
Strother, David Hunter (Porte Crayon)
   1816-1888 . . . . DLB-3, 248
Strouse, Jean 1945- DLB-111
Strugatsky, Arkadii Natanovich
   1925- DLB-302
Strugatsky, Boris Natanovich 1933- DLB-302
Stuart, Dabney 1937- DLB-105
   "Knots into Webs: Some
      Autobiographical Sources" DLB-105
Stuart, Jesse 1906-1984 . . . . . DLB-9, 48, 102; Y-84
Lyle Stuart [publishing house] DLB-46
Stuart, Ruth McEnery 1849?-1917 . . . . DLB-202
Stub, Ambrosius 1705-1758 . . . . DLB-300
Stubbs, Harry Clement (see Clement, Hal)
Stubenberg, Johann Wilhelm von
   1619-1663 . . . . DLB-164
Stuckenberg, Viggo 1763-1905 . . . . DLB-300

Studebaker, William V. 1947- DLB-256
Studies in American Jewish Literature Y-02
Studio DLB-112
Stump, Al 1916-1995 . . . . DLB-241
Sturgeon, Theodore
   1918-1985 . . . . DLB-8; Y-85
Sturges, Preston 1898-1959 . . . . DLB-26
Styron, William
   1925- DLB-2, 143, 299; Y-80; CDALB-6
   Tribute to James Dickey Y-97
Suard, Jean-Baptiste-Antoine
   1732-1817 . . . . DLB-314
Suárez, Clementina 1902-1991 . . . . DLB-290
Suárez, Mario 1925- DLB-82
Suassuna, Ariano 1927- DLB-307
Such, Peter 1939- DLB-60
Suckling, Sir John 1609-1641? DLB-58, 126
Suckow, Ruth 1892-1960 . . . . DLB-9, 102
Sudermann, Hermann 1857-1928 . . . . DLB-118
Sue, Eugène 1804-1857 . . . . DLB-119
Sue, Marie-Joseph (see Sue, Eugène)
Suetonius circa A.D. 69-post A.D. 122 . . . . . DLB-211
Suggs, Simon (see Hooper, Johnson Jones)
Sui Sin Far (see Eaton, Edith Maude)
Suits, Gustav 1883-1956 . . . . DLB-220; CDWLB-4
Sukenick, Ronald 1932-2004 . . . . . . DLB-173; Y-81
   An Author's Response Y-82
Sukhovo-Kobylin, Aleksandr Vasil'evich
   1817-1903 . . . . DLB-277
Suknaski, Andrew 1942- DLB-53
Sullivan, Alan 1868-1947 . . . . DLB-92
Sullivan, C. Gardner 1886-1965 . . . . DLB-26
Sullivan, Frank 1892-1976 . . . . DLB-11
Sulte, Benjamin 1841-1923 . . . . DLB-99
Sulzberger, Arthur Hays 1891-1968 . . . . . . DLB-127
Sulzberger, Arthur Ochs 1926- DLB-127
Sulzer, Johann Georg 1720-1779 . . . . DLB-97
Sumarokov, Aleksandr Petrovich
   1717-1777 . . . . DLB-150
Summers, Hollis 1916-1987 . . . . DLB-6
Sumner, Charles 1811-1874 . . . . DLB-235
Sumner, William Graham 1840-1910 . . . . DLB-270
Henry A. Sumner
   [publishing house] DLB-49
Sundman, Per Olof 1922-1992 . . . . DLB-257
Supervielle, Jules 1884-1960 . . . . DLB-258
Surtees, Robert Smith 1803-1864 . . . . DLB-21
   The R. S. Surtees Society Y-98
Sutcliffe, Matthew 1550?-1629 . . . . DLB-281
Sutcliffe, William 1971- DLB-271
Sutherland, Efua Theodora 1924-1996 . . . DLB-117
Sutherland, John 1919-1956 . . . . DLB-68

Sutro, Alfred 1863-1933 .... DLB-10

Svava Jakobsdóttir 1930- DLB-293

Svendsen, Hanne Marie 1933- DLB-214

Svevo, Italo (Ettore Schmitz)
1861-1928 .... DLB-264

Swados, Harvey 1920-1972. .... DLB-2

Swain, Charles 1801-1874. .... DLB-32

Swallow Press DLB-46

Swan Sonnenschein Limited DLB-106

Swanberg, W. A. 1907-1992 .... DLB-103

Swedish Literature
The Literature of the Modern
Breakthrough. DLB-259

Swenson, May 1919-1989 .... DLB-5

Swerling, Jo 1897-1964 .... DLB-44

Swift, Graham 1949- DLB-194, 326

Swift, Jonathan
1667-1745 .... DLB-39, 95, 101; CDBLB-2

Swinburne, A. C.
1837-1909 .... DLB-35, 57; CDBLB-4

Under the Microscope (1872)........ DLB-35

Swineshead, Richard floruit circa 1350... DLB-115

Swinnerton, Frank 1884-1982........... DLB-34

Swisshelm, Jane Grey 1815-1884 .... DLB-43

Swope, Herbert Bayard 1882-1958....... DLB-25

Swords, James ?-1844 .... DLB-73

Swords, Thomas 1763-1843 .... DLB-73

T. and J. Swords and Company DLB-49

Swynnerton, Thomas (John Roberts)
circa 1500-1554 .... DLB-281

Sykes, Ella C. ?-1939 ....DLB-174

Sylvester, Josuah 1562 or 1563-1618 .... DLB-121

Symonds, Emily Morse (see Paston, George)

Symonds, John Addington
1840-1893 ....DLB-57, 144

"Personal Style" (1890) DLB-57

Symons, A. J. A. 1900-1941 .... DLB-149

Symons, Arthur 1865-1945....... DLB-19, 57, 149

Symons, Julian 1912-1994...... DLB-87, 155; Y-92

Julian Symons at Eighty Y-92

Symons, Scott 1933- DLB-53

Synge, John Millington
1871-1909........... DLB-10, 19; CDBLB-5

Synge Summer School: J. M. Synge
and the Irish Theater, Rathdrum,
County Wiclow, Ireland Y-93

Syrett, Netta 1865-1943 ....DLB-135, 197

The System of Nature, Paul Henri Thiry,
baron d'Holbach (as Jean-Baptiste
de Mirabaud) DLB-314

Szabó, Lőrinc 1900-1957 .... DLB-215

Szabó, Magda 1917- DLB-215

Szymborska, Wisława
1923- DLB-232, Y-96; CDWLB-4

Nobel Lecture 1996:
The Poet and the World Y-96

T

Taban lo Liyong 1939?- DLB-125

al-Tabari 839-923 .... DLB-311

Tablada, José Juan 1871-1945 .... DLB-290

Le Tableau de Paris, Louis-Sébastien
Mercier...................... DLB-314

Tabori, George 1914- DLB-245

Tabucchi, Antonio 1943- DLB-196

Taché, Joseph-Charles 1820-1894....... DLB-99

Tachihara Masaaki 1926-1980 .... DLB-182

Tacitus circa A.D. 55-circa A.D. 117
.... DLB-211; CDWLB-1

Tadijanović, Dragutin 1905- DLB-181

Tafdrup, Pia 1952- DLB-214

Tafolla, Carmen 1951- DLB-82

Taggard, Genevieve 1894-1948 .... DLB-45

Taggart, John 1942- DLB-193

Tagger, Theodor (see Bruckner, Ferdinand)

Tagore, Rabindranath 1861-1941 .... DLB-323

Taiheiki late fourteenth century DLB-203

Tait, J. Selwin, and Sons DLB-49

Tait's Edinburgh Magazine 1832-1861...... DLB-110

The Takarazaka Revue Company Y-91

Talander (see Bohse, August)

Talese, Gay 1932- DLB-185

Tribute to Irwin Shaw Y-84

Talev, Dimitr 1898-1966.............. DLB-181

Taliaferro, H. E. 1811-1875........... DLB-202

Tallent, Elizabeth 1954- DLB-130

TallMountain, Mary 1918-1994 .... DLB-193

Talvj 1797-1870 .... DLB-59, 133

Tamási, Áron 1897-1966............. DLB-215

Tammsaare, A. H.
1878-1940............ DLB-220; CDWLB-4

Tan, Amy 1952- DLB-173, 312; CDALB-7

Tandori, Dezső 1938- DLB-232

Tanner, Thomas 1673/1674-1735 ..... DLB-213

Tanizaki Jun'ichirō 1886-1965 .... DLB-180

Tapahonso, Luci 1953- DLB-175

The Mark Taper Forum DLB-7

Taradash, Daniel 1913-2003........... DLB-44

Tarasov-Rodionov, Aleksandr Ignat'evich
1885-1938 ....DLB-272

Tarbell, Ida M. 1857-1944............. DLB-47

Tardieu, Jean 1903-1995 .... DLB-321

Tardivel, Jules-Paul 1851-1905 .... DLB-99

Targan, Barry 1932- DLB-130

Tribute to John Gardner Y-82

Tarkington, Booth 1869-1946......... DLB-9, 102

Tashlin, Frank 1913-1972 .... DLB-44

Tasma (Jessie Couvreur) 1848-1897 ... DLB-230

Tate, Allen 1899-1979.......DLB-4, 45, 63; DS-17

Tate, James 1943- DLB-5, 169

Tate, Nahum circa 1652-1715........... DLB-80

Tatian circa 830 .... DLB-148

Taufer, Veno 1933- DLB-181

Tauler, Johannes circa 1300-1361........DLB-179

Tavares, Salette 1922-1994 .... DLB-287

Tavčar, Ivan 1851-1923 ....DLB-147

Taverner, Richard ca. 1505-1575 .... DLB-236

Taylor, Ann 1782-1866................ DLB-163

Taylor, Bayard 1825-1878....... DLB-3, 189, 250

Taylor, Bert Leston 1866-1921 .... DLB-25

Taylor, Charles H. 1846-1921 .... DLB-25

Taylor, Edward circa 1642-1729 .... DLB-24

Taylor, Elizabeth 1912-1975 .... DLB-139

Taylor, Sir Henry 1800-1886 .... DLB-32

Taylor, Henry 1942- DLB-5

Who Owns American Literature Y-94

Taylor, Jane 1783-1824 .... DLB-163

Taylor, Jeremy circa 1613-1667......... DLB-151

Taylor, John 1577 or 1578 - 1653 .... DLB-121

Taylor, Mildred D. 1943- DLB-52

Taylor, Peter 1917-1994.... DLB-218, 278; Y-81, 94

Taylor, Susie King 1848-1912.......... DLB-221

Taylor, William Howland 1901-1966 .... DLB-241

William Taylor and Company DLB-49

Teale, Edwin Way 1899-1980...........DLB-275

Teasdale, Sara 1884-1933 .... DLB-45

Teffi, Nadezhda 1872-1952.............DLB-317

Teillier, Jorge 1935-1996............... DLB-283

Telles, Lygia Fagundes 1924- DLB-113, 307

The Temper of the West: William Jovanovich Y-02

Temple, Sir William 1555?-1627........ DLB-281

Temple, Sir William 1628-1699 .... DLB-101

Temple, William F. 1914-1989 .... DLB-255

Temrizov, A. (see Marchenko, Anastasia Iakovlevna)

Tench, Watkin ca. 1758-1833 .... DLB-230

Tencin, Alexandrine-Claude Guérin de
1682-1749..................... DLB-314

Tender Is the Night (Documentary)........DLB-273

Tendriakov, Vladimir Fedorovich
1923-1984 .... DLB-302

Tenn, William 1919- DLB-8

Tennant, Emma 1937- DLB-14

Tenney, Tabitha Gilman 1762-1837 ...DLB-37, 200

Tennyson, Alfred 1809-1892 .. DLB-32; CDBLB-4

On Some of the Characteristics of
Modern Poetry and On the Lyrical
Poems of Alfred Tennyson
(1831) DLB-32

Tennyson, Frederick 1807-1898 .... DLB-32

Tenorio, Arthur 1924- DLB-209

"The Tenth Stage," Marie-Jean-Antoine-Nicolas
Caritat, marquis de Condorcet......DLB-314

Tepl, Johannes von
circa 1350-1414/1415..............DLB-179

Tepliakov, Viktor Grigor'evich
1804-1842.....................DLB-205

Terence circa 184 B.C.-159 B.C. or after
...................DLB-211; CDWLB-1

St. Teresa of Ávila 1515-1582..........DLB-318

Terhune, Albert Payson 1872-1942........DLB-9

Terhune, Mary Virginia 1830-1922........DS-13

Terpigorev, Sergei Nikolaevich (S. Atava)
1841-1895.....................DLB-277

Terry, Megan 1932-............DLB-7, 249

Terson, Peter 1932-...................DLB-13

Tesich, Steve 1943-1996...................Y-83

Tessa, Delio 1886-1939..............DLB-114

Testori, Giovanni 1923-1993
.........................DLB-128, 177

Texas
The Year in Texas Literature............Y-98

Tey, Josephine 1896?-1952..............DLB-77

Thacher, James 1754-1844..............DLB-37

Thacher, John Boyd 1847-1909.........DLB-187

Thackeray, William Makepeace
1811-1863...DLB-21, 55, 159, 163; CDBLB-4

Thames and Hudson Limited.........DLB-112

Thanet, Octave (see French, Alice)

Thaxter, Celia Laighton
1835-1894.....................DLB-239

Thayer, Caroline Matilda Warren
1785-1844.....................DLB-200

Thayer, Douglas H. 1929-..........DLB-256

Theater
Black Theatre: A Forum [excerpts]....DLB-38

Community and Commentators:
Black Theatre and Its Critics.....DLB-38

German Drama from Naturalism
to Fascism: 1889-1933.........DLB-118

A Look at the Contemporary Black
Theatre Movement..............DLB-38

The Lord Chamberlain's Office and
Stage Censorship in England.....DLB-10

New Forces at Work in the American
Theatre: 1915-1925.............DLB-7

Off Broadway and Off-Off Broadway...DLB-7

Oregon Shakespeare Festival............Y-00

Plays, Playwrights, and Playgoers.....DLB-84

Playwrights on the Theater.........DLB-80

Playwrights and Professors.........DLB-13

Producing *Dear Bunny, Dear Volodya*:
The Friendship and the Feud...........Y-97

Viewpoint: Politics and Performance,
by David Edgar..................DLB-13

Writing for the Theatre,
by Harold Pinter.................DLB-13

The Year in Drama.........Y-82–85, 87–98

The Year in U.S. Drama...............Y-00

Theater, English and Irish
Anti-Theatrical Tracts.............DLB-263

The Chester Plays circa 1505-1532;
revisions until 1575............DLB-146

Dangerous Years: London Theater,
1939-1945....................DLB-10

A Defense of Actors.............DLB-263

The Development of Lighting in the
Staging of Drama, 1900-1945....DLB-10

Education....................DLB-263

The End of English Stage Censorship,
1945-1968....................DLB-13

Epigrams and Satires..............DLB-263

Eyewitnesses and Historians.......DLB-263

Fringe and Alternative Theater in
Great Britain..................DLB-13

The Great War and the Theater,
1914-1918 [Great Britain]........DLB-10

Licensing Act of 1737..............DLB-84

Morality Plays: *Mankind* circa 1450-1500
and *Everyman* circa 1500........DLB-146

The New Variorum Shakespeare........Y-85

N-Town Plays circa 1468 to early
sixteenth century.............DLB-146

Politics and the Theater...........DLB-263

Practical Matters..................DLB-263

Prologues, Epilogues, Epistles to
Readers, and Excerpts from
Plays.....................DLB-263

The Publication of English
Renaissance Plays..............DLB-62

Regulations for the Theater........DLB-263

Sources for the Study of Tudor and
Stuart Drama..................DLB-62

Stage Censorship: "The Rejected
Statement" (1911), by Bernard
Shaw [excerpts]................DLB-10

Synge Summer School: J. M. Synge and
the Irish Theater, Rathdrum,
County Wiclow, Ireland...........Y-93

The Theater in Shakespeare's Time...DLB-62

The Theatre Guild..................DLB-7

The Townely Plays fifteenth and
sixteenth centuries...........DLB-146

The Year in British Drama.........Y-99–01

The Year in Drama: London............Y-90

The Year in London Theatre..........Y-92

A Yorkshire Tragedy..............DLB-58

Theaters
The Abbey Theatre and Irish Drama,
1900-1945....................DLB-10

Actors Theatre of Louisville..........DLB-7

American Conservatory Theatre......DLB-7

Arena Stage......................DLB-7

Black Theaters and Theater
Organizations in America,
1961-1982: A Research List......DLB-38

The Dallas Theater Center...........DLB-7

Eugene O'Neill Memorial Theater
Center.......................DLB-7

The Goodman Theatre..............DLB-7

The Guthrie Theater...............DLB-7

The Mark Taper Forum.............DLB-7

The National Theatre and the Royal
Shakespeare Company: The
National Companies...........DLB-13

Off-Loop Theatres.................DLB-7

The Royal Court Theatre and the
English Stage Company.........DLB-13

The Royal Court Theatre and the
New Drama..................DLB-10

The Takarazaka Revue Company.......Y-91

Thegan and the Astronomer
fl. circa 850.....................DLB-148

Thelwall, John 1764-1834.........DLB-93, 158

Theocritus circa 300 B.C.-260 B.C.......DLB-176

Theodorescu, Ion N. (see Arghezi, Tudor)

Theodulf circa 760-circa 821..........DLB-148

Theophrastus circa 371 B.C.-287 B.C......DLB-176

Thériault, Yves 1915-1983..............DLB-88

Thério, Adrien 1925-...................DLB-53

Theroux, Paul 1941-....DLB-2, 218; CDALB-7

Thesiger, Wilfred 1910-2003..........DLB-204

They All Came to Paris..................DS-15

Thibaudeau, Colleen 1925-..........DLB-88

Thiele, Colin 1920-.................DLB-289

Thielen, Benedict 1903-1965..........DLB-102

Thiong'o Ngugi wa (see Ngugi wa Thiong'o)

Thiroux d'Arconville, Marie-Geneviève
1720-1805.....................DLB-314

This Quarter 1925-1927, 1929-1932.........DS-15

Thoma, Ludwig 1867-1921.............DLB-66

Thoma, Richard 1902-1974..............DLB-4

Thomas, Audrey 1935-................DLB-60

Thomas, D. M.
1935-....DLB-40, 207, 299; Y-82; CDBLB-8

The Plagiarism Controversy..........Y-82

Thomas, Dylan
1914-1953.......DLB-13, 20, 139; CDBLB-7

The Dylan Thomas Celebration.........Y-99

Thomas, Ed 1961-..................DLB-310

Thomas, Edward
1878-1917............DLB-19, 98, 156, 216

The Friends of the Dymock Poets........Y-00

Thomas, Frederick William 1806-1866...DLB-202

Thomas, Gwyn 1913-1981.........DLB-15, 245

Thomas, Isaiah 1750-1831.......DLB-43, 73, 187

Thomas, Johann 1624-1679...........DLB-168

Thomas, John 1900-1932.................DLB-4

Thomas, Joyce Carol 1938-............DLB-33

Thomas, Lewis 1913-1993..............DLB-275

Thomas, Lorenzo 1944-..............DLB-41

Thomas, Norman 1884-1968..........DLB-303

Thomas, R. S. 1915-2000.....DLB-27; CDBLB-8

Isaiah Thomas [publishing house]........DLB-49

Cumulative Index

Thomasîn von Zerclære circa 1186-circa 1259 . . . . DLB-138

Thomason, George 1602?-1666 . . . . DLB-213

Thomasius, Christian 1655-1728 . . . . DLB-168

Thompson, Daniel Pierce 1795-1868 . . . . DLB-202

Thompson, David 1770-1857 . . . . DLB-99

Thompson, Dorothy 1893-1961 . . . . DLB-29

Thompson, E. P. 1924-1993 . . . . DLB-242

Thompson, Flora 1876-1947 . . . . DLB-240

Thompson, Francis 1859-1907 . . . . DLB-19; CDBLB-5

Thompson, George Selden (see Selden, George)

Thompson, Henry Yates 1838-1928 . . . . . DLB-184

Thompson, Hunter S. 1939-2005 . . . . DLB-185

Thompson, Jim 1906-1977 . . . . DLB-226

Thompson, John 1938-1976 . . . . DLB-60

Thompson, John R. 1823-1873 . . . . DLB-3, 73, 248

Thompson, Lawrance 1906-1973 . . . . DLB-103

Thompson, Maurice 1844-1901 . . . . DLB-71, 74

Thompson, Ruth Plumly 1891-1976 . . . . . . DLB-22

Thompson, Thomas Phillips 1843-1933 . . . DLB-99

Thompson, William 1775-1833 . . . . DLB-158

Thompson, William Tappan 1812-1882 . . . . DLB-3, 11, 248

Thomson, Cockburn "Modern Style" (1857) [excerpt] DLB-57

Thomson, Edward William 1849-1924 . . . DLB-92

Thomson, James 1700-1748 . . . . DLB-95

Thomson, James 1834-1882 . . . . DLB-35

Thomson, Joseph 1858-1895 . . . . DLB-174

Thomson, Mortimer 1831-1875 . . . . DLB-11

Thomson, Rupert 1955- DLB-267

Thon, Melanie Rae 1957- DLB-244

Thor Vilhjálmsson 1925- DLB-293

Þórarinn Eldjárn 1949- DLB-293

Þórbergur Þórðarson 1888-1974 . . . . DLB-293

Thoreau, Henry David 1817-1862 . . . . DLB-1, 183, 223, 270, 298; DS-5; CDALB-2

The Thoreau Society Y-99

The Thoreauvian Pilgrimage: The Structure of an American Cult . . . DLB-223

Thorne, William 1568?-1630 . . . . DLB-281

Thornton, John F. [Repsonse to Ken Auletta] Y-97

Thorpe, Adam 1956- DLB-231

Thorpe, Thomas Bangs 1815-1878 . . . . DLB-3, 11, 248

Thorup, Kirsten 1942- DLB-214

Thotl, Birgitte 1610-1662 . . . . DLB-300

Thrale, Hester Lynch (see Piozzi, Hester Lynch [Thrale])

The Three Marias: A Landmark Case in Portuguese Literary History (Maria Isabel Barreno, 1939- ;

Maria Teresa Horta, 1937- ; Maria Velho da Costa, 1938-) DLB-287

Thubron, Colin 1939- DLB-204, 231

Thucydides circa 455 B.C.-circa 395 B.C. DLB-176

Thulstrup, Thure de 1848-1930 . . . . DLB-188

Thümmel, Moritz August von 1738-1817 . . . . DLB-97

Thurber, James 1894-1961 . . . . DLB-4, 11, 22, 102; CDALB-5

Thurman, Wallace 1902-1934 . . . . DLB-51

"Negro Poets and Their Poetry" DLB-50

Thwaite, Anthony 1930- DLB-40

The Booker Prize, Address Y-86

Thwaites, Reuben Gold 1853-1913 . . . . . . DLB-47

Tibullus circa 54 B.C.-circa 19 B.C. DLB-211

Ticknor, George 1791-1871 . . . . . DLB-1, 59, 140, 235

Ticknor and Fields DLB-49

Ticknor and Fields (revived) DLB-46

Tieck, Ludwig 1773-1853 . . . . DLB-90; CDWLB-2

Tietjens, Eunice 1884-1944 . . . . DLB-54

Tikkanen, Märta 1935- DLB-257

Tilghman, Christopher circa 1948 . . . . . . DLB-244

Tilney, Edmund circa 1536-1610 . . . . DLB-136

Charles Tilt [publishing house] DLB-106

J. E. Tilton and Company DLB-49

Time-Life Books DLB-46

Times Books DLB-46

Timothy, Peter circa 1725-1782 . . . . DLB-43

Timrava 1867-1951 . . . . DLB-215

Timrod, Henry 1828-1867 . . . . DLB-3, 248

Tindal, Henrietta 1818?-1879 . . . . DLB-199

Tinker, Chauncey Brewster 1876-1963 . . . DLB-140

Tinsley Brothers DLB-106

Tiptree, James, Jr. 1915-1987 . . . . DLB-8

Tišma, Aleksandar 1924-2003 . . . . DLB-181

Titus, Edward William 1870-1952 . . . . DLB-4; DS-15

Tiutchev, Fedor Ivanovich 1803-1873 . . . . DLB-205

Tlali, Miriam 1933- DLB-157, 225

Todd, Barbara Euphan 1890-1976 . . . . . . DLB-160

Todorov, Tzvetan 1939- DLB-242

Tofte, Robert 1561 or 1562-1619 or 1620 . . . . DLB-172

Tóibín, Colm 1955- DLB-271

Toklas, Alice B. 1877-1967 . . . . DLB-4; DS-15

Tokuda Shūsei 1872-1943 . . . . DLB-180

Toland, John 1670-1722 . . . . DLB-252

Tolkien, J. R. R. 1892-1973 . . . . . . DLB-15, 160, 255; CDBLB-6

Toller, Ernst 1893-1939 . . . . DLB-124

Tollet, Elizabeth 1694-1754 . . . . DLB-95

Tolson, Melvin B. 1898-1966 . . . . DLB-48, 76

Tolstaya, Tatyana 1951- DLB-285

Tolstoy, Aleksei Konstantinovich 1817-1875 . . . . DLB-238

Tolstoy, Aleksei Nikolaevich 1883-1945 . . . DLB-272

Tolstoy, Leo 1828-1910 . . . . DLB-238

Tomalin, Claire 1933- DLB-155

Tómas Guðmundsson 1901-1983 . . . . . . DLB-293

Tomasi di Lampedusa, Giuseppe 1896-1957 . . . . DLB-177

Tomlinson, Charles 1927- DLB-40

Tomlinson, H. M. 1873-1958 . . . . DLB-36, 100, 195

Abel Tompkins [publishing house] DLB-49

Tompson, Benjamin 1642-1714 . . . . DLB-24

Tomson, Graham R. (see Watson, Rosamund Marriott)

Ton'a 1289-1372 . . . . DLB-203

Tondelli, Pier Vittorio 1955-1991 . . . . DLB-196

Tonks, Rosemary 1932- DLB-14, 207

Tonna, Charlotte Elizabeth 1790-1846 . . . DLB-163

Jacob Tonson the Elder [publishing house] DLB-170

Toole, John Kennedy 1937-1969 . . . . Y-81

Toomer, Jean 1894-1967 . . . . DLB-45, 51; CDALB-4

Topsoe, Vilhelm 1840-1881 . . . . DLB-300

Tor Books DLB-46

Torberg, Friedrich 1908-1979 . . . . DLB-85

Torga, Miguel (Adolfo Correira da Rocha) 1907-1995 . . . . DLB-287

Torre, Francisco de la ?-? DLB-318

Torrence, Ridgely 1874-1950 . . . . DLB-54, 249

Torrente Ballester, Gonzalo 1910-1999 . . . . DLB-322

Torres-Metzger, Joseph V. 1933- DLB-122

Torres Naharro, Bartolomé de 1485?-1523? DLB-318

El Tostado (see Madrigal, Alfonso Fernández de)

Toth, Susan Allen 1940- Y-86

Richard Tottell [publishing house] DLB-170

"The Printer to the Reader," (1557) DLB-167

Tough-Guy Literature DLB-9

Touré, Askia Muhammad 1938- DLB-41

Tourgée, Albion W. 1838-1905 . . . . DLB-79

Tournemir, Elizaveta Sailhas de (see Tur, Evgeniia)

Tourneur, Cyril circa 1580-1626 . . . . DLB-58

Tournier, Michel 1924- DLB-83

Frank Tousey [publishing house] DLB-49

Tower Publications DLB-46

Towne, Benjamin circa 1740-1793 . . . . . . DLB-43

Towne, Robert 1936- DLB-44

The Towneley Plays fifteenth and sixteenth centuries DLB-146

Townsend, Sue 1946- DLB-271

Townshend, Aurelian
 by 1583-circa 1651 ....DLB-121
Toy, Barbara 1908-2001..............DLB-204
Tozzi, Federigo 1883-1920 ....DLB-264
Tracy, Honor 1913-1989 ....DLB-15
Traherne, Thomas 1637?-1674 ....DLB-131
Traill, Catharine Parr 1802-1899.........DLB-99
Train, Arthur 1875-1945 ....DLB-86; DS-16
Tranquilli, Secondino (see Silone, Ignazio)
The Transatlantic Publishing Company ...DLB-49
The Transatlantic Review 1924-1925 .... DS-15
The Transcendental Club
 1836-1840 .... DLB-1; DLB-223
Transcendentalism....... DLB-1; DLB-223; DS-5
   "A Response from America," by
    John A. Heraud DS-5
   Publications and Social Movements DLB-1
   The Rise of Transcendentalism,
    1815-1860..................... DS-5
   Transcendentalists, American DS-5
   "What Is Transcendentalism? By a
    Thinking Man," by James
    Kinnard Jr.................... DS-5
transition 1927-1938 .... DS-15
Translations (Vernacular) in the Crowns of
 Castile and Aragon 1352-1515 ......DLB-286
Tranströmer, Tomas 1931- DLB-257
Tranter, John 1943- DLB-289
Travel Writing
   American Travel Writing, 1776-1864
    (checklist) DLB-183
   British Travel Writing, 1940-1997
    (checklist) DLB-204
   Travel Writers of the Late
    Middle Ages DLB-286
   (1876-1909.....................DLB-174
   (1837-1875.....................DLB-166
   (1910-1939.....................DLB-195
Traven, B. 1882?/1890?-1969?.........DLB-9, 56
Travers, Ben 1886-1980............DLB-10, 233
Travers, P. L. (Pamela Lyndon)
 1899-1996....................DLB-160
Trediakovsky, Vasilii Kirillovich
 1703-1769.....................DLB-150
Treece, Henry 1911-1966..............DLB-160
Treitel, Jonathan 1959- DLB-267
Trejo, Ernesto 1950-1991...............DLB-122
Trelawny, Edward John
 1792-1881 .... DLB-110, 116, 144
Tremain, Rose 1943- DLB-14, 271
Tremblay, Michel 1942- DLB-60
Trent, William P. 1862-1939 .... DLB-47, 71
Trescot, William Henry 1822-1898 ....DLB-30
Tressell, Robert (Robert Phillipe Noonan)
 1870-1911 ....DLB-197
Trevelyan, Sir George Otto
 1838-1928 ....DLB-144

Trevisa, John circa 1342-circa 1402 ......DLB-146
Trevisan, Dalton 1925- DLB-307
Trevor, William 1928- DLB-14, 139
Triana, José 1931- DLB-305
Trierer Floyris circa 1170-1180 ....DLB-138
Trifonov, Iurii Valentinovich
 1925-1981.....................DLB-302
Trillin, Calvin 1935- DLB-185
Trilling, Lionel 1905-1975 ....DLB-28, 63
Trilussa 1871-1950..................DLB-114
Trimmer, Sarah 1741-1810 ....DLB-158
Triolet, Elsa 1896-1970.................DLB-72
Tripp, John 1927- DLB-40
Trocchi, Alexander 1925-1984...........DLB-15
Troisi, Dante 1920-1989 ....DLB-196
Trollope, Anthony
 1815-1882 .... DLB-21, 57, 159; CDBLB-4
   Novel-Reading: *The Works of Charles
   Dickens; The Works of W. Makepeace
   Thackeray* (1879) DLB-21
   The Trollope Societies................Y-00
Trollope, Frances 1779-1863.........DLB-21, 166
Trollope, Joanna 1943- DLB-207
Troop, Elizabeth 1931- DLB-14
Tropicália........................DLB-307
Trotter, Catharine 1679-1749 ....DLB-84, 252
Trotti, Lamar 1898-1952 ....DLB-44
Trottier, Pierre 1925- DLB-60
Trotzig, Birgitta 1929- DLB-257
Troupe, Quincy Thomas, Jr. 1943- DLB-41
John F. Trow and Company DLB-49
Trowbridge, John Townsend 1827-1916...DLB-202
Trudel, Jean-Louis 1967- DLB-251
True History of the Kelly Gang, 2001 Booker Prize winner,
 Peter Carey DLB-326
Truillier-Lacombe, Joseph-Patrice
 1807-1863 ....DLB-99
Trumbo, Dalton 1905-1976 ....DLB-26
Trumbull, Benjamin 1735-1820 ....DLB-30
Trumbull, John 1750-1831 ....DLB-31
Trumbull, John 1756-1843 ....DLB-183
Truth, Sojourner 1797?-1883 ....DLB-239
Tscherning, Andreas 1611-1659........DLB-164
Tsubouchi Shōyō 1859-1935 ....DLB-180
Tsvetaeva, Marina Ivanovna
 1892-1941 ....DLB-295
Tuchman, Barbara W.
   Tribute to Alfred A. Knopf..............Y-84
Tucholsky, Kurt 1890-1935 ....DLB-56
Tucker, Charlotte Maria
 1821-1893 ....DLB-163, 190
Tucker, George 1775-1861 ....DLB-3, 30, 248
Tucker, James 1808?-1866? DLB-230

Tucker, Nathaniel Beverley
 1784-1851 ....DLB-3, 248
Tucker, St. George 1752-1827 ....DLB-37
Tuckerman, Frederick Goddard
 1821-1873 ....DLB-243
Tuckerman, Henry Theodore 1813-1871.....DLB-64
Tumas, Juozas (see Vaizgantas)
Tunis, John R. 1889-1975.......... DLB-22, 171
Tunstall, Cuthbert 1474-1559 ....DLB-132
Tunström, Göran 1937-2000 ....DLB-257
Tuohy, Frank 1925- DLB-14, 139
Tupper, Martin F. 1810-1889...........DLB-32
Tur, Evgeniia 1815-1892 ....DLB-238
Turbyfill, Mark 1896-1991..............DLB-45
Turco, Lewis 1934- Y-84
   Tribute to John Ciardi.................Y-86
Turgenev, Aleksandr Ivanovich
 1784-1845 ....DLB-198
Turgenev, Ivan Sergeevich
 1818-1883 ....DLB-238
Turgot, baron de l'Aulne, Anne-Robert-Jacques
 1727-1781 ....DLB-314
   "Memorandum on Local
   Government" DLB-314
Turnbull, Alexander H. 1868-1918 ......DLB-184
Turnbull, Andrew 1921-1970..........DLB-103
Turnbull, Gael 1928- DLB-40
Turnèbe, Odet de 1552-1581.........DLB-327
Turner, Arlin 1909-1980 ....DLB-103
Turner, Charles (Tennyson)
 1808-1879 ....DLB-32
Turner, Ethel 1872-1958 ....DLB-230
Turner, Frederick 1943- DLB-40
Turner, Frederick Jackson
 1861-1932 ....DLB-17, 186
   A Conversation between William Riggan
   and Janette Turner Hospital Y-02
Turner, Joseph Addison 1826-1868 ....DLB-79
Turpin, Waters Edward 1910-1968 ....DLB-51
Turrini, Peter 1944- DLB-124
Tusquets, Esther 1936- DLB-322
Tutuola, Amos 1920-1997 ... DLB-125; CDWLB-3
Twain, Mark (see Clemens, Samuel Langhorne)
Tweedie, Ethel Brilliana
 circa 1860-1940 ....DLB-174
A Century of Poetry, a Lifetime of
 Collecting: J. M. Edelstein's
 Collection of Twentieth-
 Century American Poetry............ YB-02
Twombly, Wells 1935-1977 ....DLB-241
Twysden, Sir Roger 1597-1672..........DLB-213
Tyard, Pontus de 1521?-1605 ....DLB-327
Ty-Casper, Linda 1931- DLB-312
Tyler, Anne 1941- ... DLB-6, 143; Y-82; CDALB-7
Tyler, Mary Palmer 1775-1866..........DLB-200

Tyler, Moses Coit 1835-1900 . . . . .DLB-47, 64
Tyler, Royall 1757-1826. . . . . DLB-37
Tylor, Edward Burnett 1832-1917. . . . . . . DLB-57
Tynan, Katharine 1861-1931 . . . . . . DLB-153, 240
Tyndale, William circa 1494-1536 . . . . . . DLB-132
Tyree, Omar 1969- DLB-292

U

Uchida, Yoshiko 1921-1992 . . DLB-312; CDALB-7
Udall, Nicholas 1504-1556. . . . . DLB-62
Ugrêsić, Dubravka 1949- DLB-181
Uhland, Ludwig 1787-1862. . . . . DLB-90
Uhse, Bodo 1904-1963. . . . . DLB-69
Ujević, Augustin "Tin"
  1891-1955 . . . . DLB-147
Ulenhart, Niclas fl. circa 1600. . . . . DLB-164
Ulfeldt, Leonora Christina 1621-1698 . . . DLB-300
Ulibarrí, Sabine R. 1919-2003 . . . . DLB-82
Ulica, Jorge 1870-1926 . . . . DLB-82
Ulitskaya, Liudmila Evgen'evna
  1943- DLB-285
Ulivi, Ferruccio 1912- DLB-196
Ulizio, B. George 1889-1969 . . . . DLB-140
Ulrich von Liechtenstein
  circa 1200-circa 1275 . . . . DLB-138
Ulrich von Zatzikhoven
  before 1194-after 1214 . . . . DLB-138
'Umar ibn Abi Rabi'ah 644-712 or 721 . . DLB-311
Unaipon, David 1872-1967. . . . . DLB-230
Unamuno, Miguel de 1864-1936 . . . DLB-108, 322
Under, Marie 1883-1980 . . . DLB-220; CDWLB-4
Underhill, Evelyn 1875-1941 . . . . DLB-240
Undset, Sigrid 1882-1949. . . . . DLB-297
Ungaretti, Giuseppe 1888-1970. . . . . DLB-114
Unger, Friederike Helene
  1741-1813. DLB-94
United States Book Company DLB-49
Universal Publishing and Distributing
  Corporation. DLB-46
University of Colorado
  Special Collections at the University of
  Colorado at Boulder Y-98
Indiana University Press. Y-02
The University of Iowa
  Writers' Workshop Golden Jubilee Y-86
University of Missouri Press. Y-01
University of South Carolina
  The G. Ross Roy Scottish
  Poetry Collection Y-89
  Two Hundred Years of Rare Books and
  Literary Collections at the
  University of South Carolina. Y-00
The University of South Carolina Press. Y-94
University of Virginia
  The Book Arts Press at the University
  of Virginia. Y-96

The Electronic Text Center and the
  Electronic Archive of Early American
  Fiction at the University of Virginia
  Library Y-98
University of Virginia Libraries Y-91
University of Wales Press. DLB-112
University Press of Florida. Y-00
University Press of Kansas Y-98
University Press of Mississippi Y-99
Unnur Benediktsdóttir Bjarklind (see Hulda)
Uno Chiyo 1897-1996 . . . . DLB-180
Unruh, Fritz von 1885-1970 . . . . DLB-56, 118
Unsworth, Barry 1930- DLB-194, 326
Unt, Mati 1944- DLB-232
The Unterberg Poetry Center of the
  92nd Street Y Y-98
Untermeyer, Louis 1885-1977. . . . . DLB-303
T. Fisher Unwin [publishing house] DLB-106
Upchurch, Boyd B. (see Boyd, John)
Updike, John 1932- DLB-2, 5, 143, 218, 227;
  Y-80, 82; DS-3; CDALB-6
  John Updike on the Internet Y-97
  Tribute to Alfred A. Knopf. Y-84
  Tribute to John Ciardi Y-86
Upīts, Andrejs 1877-1970 . . . . DLB-220
Uppdal, Kristofer 1878-1961. . . . . DLB-297
Upton, Bertha 1849-1912. . . . . DLB-141
Upton, Charles 1948- DLB-16
Upton, Florence K. 1873-1922 . . . . DLB-141
Upward, Allen 1863-1926 . . . . DLB-36
Urban, Milo 1904-1982 . . . . DLB-215
Ureña de Henríquez, Salomé 1850-1897 . DLB-283
Urfé, Honoré d' 1567-1625 . . . . DLB-268
Urista, Alberto Baltazar (see Alurista)
Urquhart, Fred 1912-1995 . . . . DLB-139
Urrea, Luis Alberto 1955- DLB-209
Urzidil, Johannes 1896-1970 . . . . DLB-85
U.S.A. (Documentary) DLB-274
Usigli, Rodolfo 1905-1979 . . . . DLB-305
Usk, Thomas died 1388. . . . . DLB-146
Uslar Pietri, Arturo 1906-2001 . . . . DLB-113
Uspensky, Gleb Ivanovich
  1843-1902 .DLB-277
Ussher, James 1581-1656 . . . . DLB-213
Ustinov, Peter 1921-2004 . . . . DLB-13
Uttley, Alison 1884-1976. . . . . DLB-160
Uz, Johann Peter 1720-1796 . . . . DLB-97

V

Vadianus, Joachim 1484-1551. . . . . .DLB-179
Vac, Bertrand (Aimé Pelletier) 1914- . . . DLB-88
Vācietis, Ojārs 1933-1983 . . . . DLB-232
Vaculík, Ludvík 1926- DLB-232

Vaičiulaitis, Antanas 1906-1992 . . . . DLB-220
Vaičiūnaite, Judita 1937- DLB-232
Vail, Laurence 1891-1968. . . . . DLB-4
Vail, Petr L'vovich 1949- DLB-285
Vailland, Roger 1907-1965 . . . . DLB-83
Vaižgantas 1869-1933. . . . . DLB-220
Vajda, Ernest 1887-1954. . . . . DLB-44
Valdés, Alfonso de circa 1490?-1532 . . . . DLB-318
Valdés, Gina 1943- DLB-122
Valdes, Juan de 1508-1541 . . . . DLB-318
Valdez, Luis Miguel 1940- DLB-122
Valduga, Patrizia 1953- DLB-128
Vale Press DLB-112
Valente, José Angel 1929-2000 . . . . DLB-108
Valenzuela, Luisa 1938- . . .DLB-113; CDWLB-3
Valera, Diego de 1412-1488 . . . . DLB-286
Valeri, Diego 1887-1976 . . . . DLB-128
Valerius Flaccus fl. circa A.D. 92 . . . . . . DLB-211
Valerius Maximus fl. circa A.D. 31 . . . . . DLB-211
Valéry, Paul 1871-1945 . . . . DLB-258
Valesio, Paolo 1939- DLB-196
Valgardson, W. D. 1939- DLB-60
Valle, Luz 1899-1971 . . . . DLB-290
Valle, Víctor Manuel 1950- DLB-122
Valle-Inclán, Ramón del
  1866-1936 . . . . DLB-134, 322
Vallejo, Armando 1949- DLB-122
Vallejo, César Abraham 1892-1938 . . . . . DLB-290
Vallès, Jules 1832-1885 . . . . DLB-123
Vallette, Marguerite Eymery (see Rachilde)
Valverde, José María 1926-1996. . . . . DLB-108
Vampilov, Aleksandr Valentinovich (A. Sanin)
  1937-1972 . . . . DLB-302
Van Allsburg, Chris 1949- DLB-61
Van Anda, Carr 1864-1945 . . . . DLB-25
Vanbrugh, Sir John 1664-1726 . . . . DLB-80
Vance, Jack 1916?- DLB-8
Vančura, Vladislav
  1891-1942 . . . . .DLB-215; CDWLB-4
van der Post, Laurens 1906-1996 . . . . DLB-204
Van Dine, S. S. (see Wright, Willard Huntington)
Van Doren, Mark 1894-1972 . . . . DLB-45
van Druten, John 1901-1957 . . . . DLB-10
Van Duyn, Mona 1921-2004 . . . . DLB-5
  Tribute to James Dickey. Y-97
Van Dyke, Henry 1852-1933 . . . . . .DLB-71; DS-13
Van Dyke, Henry 1928- DLB-33
Van Dyke, John C. 1856-1932 . . . . DLB-186
Vane, Sutton 1888-1963 . . . . DLB-10
Van Gieson, Judith 1941- DLB-306
Vanguard Press. DLB-46

van Gulik, Robert Hans 1910-1967 . . . . DS-17
van Itallie, Jean-Claude 1936- DLB-7
Van Loan, Charles E. 1876-1919 . . . . .DLB-171
Vann, Robert L. 1879-1940 . . . . .DLB-29
Van Rensselaer, Mariana Griswold
  1851-1934 . . . . .DLB-47
Van Rensselaer, Mrs. Schuyler
  (see Van Rensselaer, Mariana Griswold)
Van Vechten, Carl 1880-1964 . . . . . . .DLB-4, 9, 51
van Vogt, A. E. 1912-2000 . . . . .DLB-8, 251
Varela, Blanca 1926- DLB-290
Vargas Llosa, Mario
  1936- DLB-145; CDWLB-3
  Acceptance Speech for the Ritz Paris
    Hemingway Award. Y-85
Varley, John 1947- .Y-81
Varnhagen von Ense, Karl August
  1785-1858 . . . . .DLB-90
Varnhagen von Ense, Rahel
  1771-1833 . . . . .DLB-90
Varro 116 B.C.-27 B.C. DLB-211
Vasilenko, Svetlana Vladimirovna
  1956- DLB-285
Vasiliu, George (see Bacovia, George)
Vásquez, Richard 1928- DLB-209
Vassa, Gustavus (see Equiano, Olaudah)
Vassalli, Sebastiano 1941- DLB-128, 196
Vaugelas, Claude Favre de 1585-1650 . . . . DLB-268
Vaughan, Henry 1621-1695. . . . . .DLB-131
Vaughan, Thomas 1621-1666 . . . . .DLB-131
Vaughn, Robert 1592?-1667 . . . . .DLB-213
Vaux, Thomas, Lord 1509-1556 . . . . .DLB-132
Vazov, Ivan 1850-1921. . . . . . DLB-147; CDWLB-4
Vázquez Montalbán, Manuel
  1939- DLB-134, 322
Véa, Alfredo, Jr. 1950- DLB-209
Veblen, Thorstein 1857-1929 . . . . .DLB-246
Vedel, Anders Sørensen 1542-1616 . . . . . .DLB-300
Vega, Janine Pommy 1942- DLB-16
Veiller, Anthony 1903-1965 . . . . .DLB-44
Velásquez-Trevino, Gloria 1949- DLB-122
Veley, Margaret 1843-1887 . . . . .DLB-199
Velleius Paterculus
  circa 20 B.C.-circa A.D. 30 . . . . .DLB-211
Veloz Maggiolo, Marcio 1936- DLB-145
Vel'tman, Aleksandr Fomich
  1800-1870 . . . . .DLB-198
Venegas, Daniel ?-? DLB-82
Venevitinov, Dmitrii Vladimirovich
  1805-1827 . . . . .DLB-205
Verbitskaia, Anastasiia Alekseevna
  1861-1928 . . . . .DLB-295
Verde, Cesário 1855-1886 . . . . .DLB-287
Vergil, Polydore circa 1470-1555 . . . . .DLB-132
Veríssimo, Erico 1905-1975 . . . . .DLB-145, 307

Verlaine, Paul 1844-1896 . . . . .DLB-217
Vernacular Translations in the Crowns of
  Castile and Aragon 1352-1515 . . . . . .DLB-286
Verne, Jules 1828-1905 . . . . .DLB-123
Vernon God Little, 2003 Booker Prize winner,
  DBC Pierre DLB-326
Verplanck, Gulian C. 1786-1870 . . . . .DLB-59
Vertinsky, Aleksandr 1889-1957 . . . . .DLB-317
Very, Jones 1813-1880 . . . . .DLB-1, 243; DS-5
Vesaas, Halldis Moren 1907-1995 . . . . . . .DLB-297
Vesaas, Tarjei 1897-1970. . . . . .DLB-297
Vian, Boris 1920-1959 . . . . .DLB-72, 321
Viazemsky, Petr Andreevich
  1792-1878 . . . . .DLB-205
Vicars, Thomas 1591-1638 . . . . .DLB-236
Vicente, Gil 1465-1536/1540? DLB-287, 318
Vickers, Roy 1888?-1965. . . . . .DLB-77
Vickery, Sukey 1779-1821 . . . . .DLB-200
Victoria 1819-1901. . . . . .DLB-55
Victoria Press DLB-106
La vida de Lazarillo de Tormes DLB-318
Vidal, Gore 1925- DLB-6, 152; CDALB-7
Vidal, Mary Theresa 1815-1873 . . . . .DLB-230
Vidmer, Richards 1898-1978 . . . . .DLB-241
Viebig, Clara 1860-1952 . . . . .DLB-66
Vieira, António, S. J. (Antonio Vieyra)
  1608-1697 . . . . .DLB-307
Viereck, George Sylvester 1884-1962 . . . . .DLB-54
Viereck, Peter 1916- DLB-5
Vietnam War (ended 1975)
  Resources for the Study of Vietnam War
    Literature DLB-9
Viets, Roger 1738-1811 . . . . .DLB-99
Vigil-Piñon, Evangelina 1949- DLB-122
Vigneault, Gilles 1928- DLB-60
Vigny, Alfred de 1797-1863 . . . . DLB-119, 192, 217
Vigolo, Giorgio 1894-1983 . . . . .DLB-114
Vik, Bjørg 1935- .DLB-297
The Viking Press .DLB-46
Vila-Matas, Enrique 1948- DLB-322
Vilde, Eduard 1865-1933. . . . . .DLB-220
Vilinskaia, Mariia Aleksandrovna
  (see Vovchok, Marko)
Villa, José García 1908-1997 . . . . .DLB-312
Villanueva, Alma Luz 1944- DLB-122
Villanueva, Tino 1941- DLB-82
Villard, Henry 1835-1900 . . . . .DLB-23
Villard, Oswald Garrison 1872-1949 . . .DLB-25, 91
Villarreal, Edit 1944- DLB-209
Villarreal, José Antonio 1924- DLB-82
Villaseñor, Victor 1940- DLB-209
Villedieu, Madame de (Marie-Catherine
  Desjardins) 1640?-1683 . . . . .DLB-268

Villegas, Antonio de ?-? DLB-318
Villegas de Magnón, Leonor
  1876-1955 . . . . .DLB-122
Villehardouin, Geoffroi de
  circa 1150-1215 . . . . .DLB-208
Villemaire, Yolande 1949- DLB-60
Villena, Enrique de
  ca. 1382/84-1432 . . . . .DLB-286
Villena, Luis Antonio de 1951- DLB-134
Villiers, George, Second Duke
  of Buckingham 1628-1687 . . . . .DLB-80
Villiers de l'Isle-Adam, Jean-Marie
  Mathias Philippe-Auguste,
  Comte de 1838-1889 . . . . .DLB-123, 192
Villon, François 1431-circa 1463? DLB-208
Vinaver, Michel (Michel Grinberg)
  1927- DLB-321
Vine Press DLB-112
Viorst, Judith 1931- DLB-52
Vipont, Elfrida (Elfrida Vipont Foulds,
  Charles Vipont) 1902-1992 . . . . .DLB-160
Viramontes, Helena María 1954- DLB-122
Virgil 70 B.C.-19 B.C. DLB-211; CDWLB-1
Vischer, Friedrich Theodor 1807-1887. . . .DLB-133
Vitier, Cintio 1921- DLB-283
Vitrac, Roger 1899-1952 . . . . .DLB-321
Vitruvius circa 85 B.C.-circa 15 B.C. DLB-211
Vitry, Philippe de 1291-1361 . . . . .DLB-208
Vittorini, Elio 1908-1966 . . . . .DLB-264
Vivanco, Luis Felipe 1907-1975 . . . . .DLB-108
Vives, Juan Luis 1493-1540 . . . . .DLB-318
Vivian, E. Charles (Charles Henry Cannell,
  Charles Henry Vivian, Jack Mann,
  Barry Lynd) 1882-1947 . . . . .DLB-255
Viviani, Cesare 1947- DLB-128
Vivien, Renée 1877-1909 . . . . .DLB-217
Vizenor, Gerald 1934- DLB-175, 227
Vizetelly and Company DLB-106
Vladimov, Georgii
  1931-2003 . . . . .DLB-302
Voaden, Herman 1903-1991 . . . . .DLB-88
Voß, Johann Heinrich 1751-1826 . . . . .DLB-90
Vogau, Boris Andreevich
  (see Pil'niak, Boris Andreevich)
Voigt, Ellen Bryant 1943- DLB-120
Voinovich, Vladimir Nikolaevich
  1932- DLB-302
Vojnović, Ivo 1857-1929 . . . . . DLB-147; CDWLB-4
Vold, Jan Erik 1939- DLB-297
Volkoff, Vladimir 1932- DLB-83
P. F. Volland Company DLB-46
Vollbehr, Otto H. F.
  1872?-1945 or 1946. . . . . .DLB-187
Vologdin (see Zasodimsky, Pavel Vladimirovich)
Voloshin, Maksimilian Aleksandrovich
  1877-1932 . . . . .DLB-295

439

Volponi, Paolo 1924-1994............DLB-177

Voltaire (François-Marie Arouet)
   1694-1778..................... DLB-314

   "An account of the death of the chevalier de
     La Barre".................. DLB-314

   Candide..................... DLB-314

   Philosophical Dictionary............. DLB-314

Vonarburg, Élisabeth 1947-......... DLB-251

von der Grün, Max 1926-........ DLB-75

Vonnegut, Kurt 1922-.........DLB-2, 8, 152;
          Y-80; DS-3; CDALB-6

   Tribute to Isaac Asimov............... Y-92

   Tribute to Richard Brautigan.......... Y-84

Voranc, Prežihov 1893-1950......... DLB-147

Voronsky, Aleksandr Konstantinovich
   1884-1937.................... DLB-272

Vorse, Mary Heaton 1874-1966....... DLB-303

Vovchok, Marko 1833-1907.......... DLB-238

Voynich, E. L. 1864-1960............. DLB-197

Vroman, Mary Elizabeth
   circa 1924-1967 .... DLB-33

W

Wace, Robert ("Maistre")
   circa 1100-circa 1175.............. DLB-146

Wackenroder, Wilhelm Heinrich
   1773-1798...................... DLB-90

Wackernagel, Wilhelm 1806-1869...... DLB-133

Waddell, Helen 1889-1965........... DLB-240

Waddington, Miriam 1917-2004........ DLB-68

Wade, Henry 1887-1969............. DLB-77

Wagenknecht, Edward 1900-2004...... DLB-103

Wägner, Elin 1882-1949............. DLB-259

Wagner, Heinrich Leopold 1747-1779..... DLB-94

Wagner, Henry R. 1862-1957......... DLB-140

Wagner, Richard 1813-1883........... DLB-129

Wagoner, David 1926-........... DLB-5, 256

Wah, Fred 1939-.................. DLB-60

Waiblinger, Wilhelm 1804-1830........ DLB-90

Wain, John
   1925-1994 ...DLB-15, 27, 139, 155; CDBLB-8
   Tribute to J. B. Priestly................. Y-84

Wainwright, Jeffrey 1944-........... DLB-40

Waite, Peirce and Company........... DLB-49

Wakeman, Stephen H. 1859-1924...... DLB-187

Wakoski, Diane 1937-............... DLB-5

Walahfrid Strabo circa 808-849....... DLB-148

Henry Z. Walck [publishing house]..... DLB-46

Walcott, Derek
   1930- DLB-117; Y-81, 92; CDWLB-3

   Nobel Lecture 1992: The Antilles:
     Fragments of Epic Memory......... Y-92

Robert Waldegrave [publishing house]....DLB-170

Waldis, Burkhard circa 1490-1556?......DLB-178

Waldman, Anne 1945-.............. DLB-16

Waldrop, Rosmarie 1935-........... DLB-169

Walker, Alice 1900-1982............. DLB-201

Walker, Alice
   1944- DLB-6, 33, 143; CDALB-6

Walker, Annie Louisa (Mrs. Harry Coghill)
   circa 1836-1907 .... DLB-240

Walker, George F. 1947-............ DLB-60

Walker, John Brisben 1847-1931........ DLB-79

Walker, Joseph A. 1935-............ DLB-38

Walker, Kath (see Oodgeroo of the Tribe Noonuccal)

Walker, Margaret 1915-1998 ....DLB-76, 152

Walker, Obadiah 1616-1699........... DLB-281

Walker, Ted 1934-................. DLB-40

Walker, Evans and Cogswell Company... DLB-49

Wall, John F. (see Sarban)

Wallace, Alfred Russel 1823-1913....... DLB-190

Wallace, Dewitt 1889-1981........... DLB-137

Wallace, Edgar 1875-1932............. DLB-70

Wallace, Lew 1827-1905.............. DLB-202

Wallace, Lila Acheson 1889-1984....... DLB-137

   "A Word of Thanks," From the Initial
     Issue of *Reader's Digest*
     (February 1922)............... DLB-137

Wallace, Naomi 1960-.............. DLB-249

Wallace Markfield's "Steeplechase"......... Y-02

Wallace-Crabbe, Chris 1934-........ DLB-289

Wallant, Edward Lewis
   1926-1962 .... DLB-2, 28, 143, 299

Waller, Edmund 1606-1687........... DLB-126

Walpole, Horace 1717-1797......DLB-39, 104, 213

   Preface to the First Edition of
     The Castle of Otranto (1764)....DLB-39, 178

   Preface to the Second Edition of
     The Castle of Otranto (1765) DLB-39, 178

Walpole, Hugh 1884-1941............ DLB-34

Walrond, Eric 1898-1966............. DLB-51

Walser, Martin 1927-.............DLB-75, 124

Walser, Robert 1878-1956............ DLB-66

Walsh, Ernest 1895-1926............ DLB-4, 45

Walsh, Robert 1784-1859............. DLB-59

Walters, Henry 1848-1931........... DLB-140

Waltharius circa 825 .... DLB-148

Walther von der Vogelweide
   circa 1170-circa 1230 .... DLB-138

Walton, Izaak
   1593-1683 .... DLB-151, 213; CDBLB-1

Walwicz, Ania 1951-............... DLB-325

Wambaugh, Joseph 1937-...........DLB-6; Y-83

Wand, Alfred Rudolph 1828-1891...... DLB-188

Wandor, Michelene 1940-........... DLB-310

Waniek, Marilyn Nelson 1946-....... DLB-120

Wanley, Humphrey 1672-1726......... DLB-213

War of the Words (and Pictures):
   The Creation of a Graphic Novel Y-02

Warburton, William 1698-1779........ DLB-104

Ward, Aileen 1919-................ DLB-111

Ward, Artemus (see Browne, Charles Farrar)

Ward, Arthur Henry Sarsfield (see Rohmer, Sax)

Ward, Douglas Turner 1930-........DLB-7, 38

Ward, Mrs. Humphry 1851-1920........ DLB-18

Ward, James 1843-1925............. DLB-262

Ward, Lynd 1905-1985.............. DLB-22

Ward, Lock and Company............ DLB-106

Ward, Nathaniel circa 1578-1652 .... DLB-24

Ward, Theodore 1902-1983........... DLB-76

Wardle, Ralph 1909-1988............. DLB-103

Ware, Henry, Jr. 1794-1843........... DLB-235

Ware, William 1797-1852 .... DLB-1, 235

Warfield, Catherine Ann 1816-1877........DLB-248

Waring, Anna Letitia 1823-1910 ....DLB-240

Frederick Warne and Company [U.K.].... DLB-106

Frederick Warne and Company [U.S.] DLB-49

Warner, Anne 1869-1913............. DLB-202

Warner, Charles Dudley 1829-1900...... DLB-64

Warner, Marina 1946-.............. DLB-194

Warner, Rex 1905-1986............. DLB-15

Warner, Susan 1819-1885....DLB-3, 42, 239, 250

Warner, Sylvia Townsend
   1893-1978.................. DLB-34, 139

Warner, William 1558-1609............DLB-172

Warner Books..................... DLB-46

Warr, Bertram 1917-1943............ DLB-88

Warren, John Byrne Leicester
   (see De Tabley, Lord)

Warren, Lella 1899-1982................. Y-83

Warren, Mercy Otis 1728-1814 ...... DLB-31, 200

Warren, Robert Penn 1905-1989 ......DLB-2, 48,
          152, 320; Y-80, 89; CDALB-6

   Tribute to Katherine Anne Porter Y-80

Warren, Samuel 1807-1877............ DLB-190

Die Wartburgkrieg circa 1230-circa 1280 ... DLB-138

Warton, Joseph 1722-1800 ....DLB-104, 109

Warton, Thomas 1728-1790........DLB-104, 109

Warung, Price (William Astley)
   1855-1911 .... DLB-230

Washington, George 1732-1799......... DLB-31

Washington, Ned 1901-1976.......... DLB-265

Wassermann, Jakob 1873-1934........ DLB-66

Wasserstein, Wendy 1950-2006........ DLB-228

Wassmo, Herbjorg 1942-............ DLB-297

Wasson, David Atwood 1823-1887 ... DLB-1, 223

Watanna, Onoto (see Eaton, Winnifred)

Waten, Judah 1911?-1985........... DLB-289

Waterhouse, Keith 1929-...........DLB-13, 15

Waterman, Andrew 1940-........... DLB-40

Waters, Frank 1902-1995 . . . . DLB-212; Y-86
Waters, Michael 1949- DLB-120
Watkins, Tobias 1780-1855 . . . . DLB-73
Watkins, Vernon 1906-1967 . . . . DLB-20
Watmough, David 1926- DLB-53
Watson, Colin 1920-1983 . . . . DLB-276
Watson, Ian 1943- DLB-261
Watson, James Wreford (see Wreford, James)
Watson, John 1850-1907 . . . . DLB-156
Watson, Rosamund Marriott
 (Graham R. Tomson) 1860-1911 . . . . . DLB-240
Watson, Sheila 1909-1998 . . . . DLB-60
Watson, Thomas 1545?-1592 . . . . DLB-132
Watson, Wilfred 1911-1998 . . . . DLB-60
W. J. Watt and Company DLB-46
Watten, Barrett 1948- DLB-193
Watterson, Henry 1840-1921 . . . . DLB-25
Watts, Alan 1915-1973 . . . . DLB-16
Watts, Isaac 1674-1748 . . . . DLB-95
Franklin Watts [publishing house] DLB-46
Waugh, Alec 1898-1981 . . . . DLB-191
Waugh, Auberon 1939-2000 . . . DLB-14, 194; Y-00
Waugh, Evelyn 1903-1966
 . . . . DLB-15, 162, 195; CDBLB-6
Way and Williams DLB-49
Wayman, Tom 1945- DLB-53
Wearne, Alan 1948- DLB-325
Weatherly, Tom 1942- DLB-41
Weaver, Gordon 1937- DLB-130
Weaver, Robert 1921- DLB-88
Webb, Beatrice 1858-1943 . . . . DLB-190
Webb, Francis 1925-1973 . . . . DLB-260
Webb, Frank J. fl. 1857 . . . . DLB-50
Webb, James Watson 1802-1884 . . . . DLB-43
Webb, Mary 1881-1927 . . . . DLB-34
Webb, Phyllis 1927- DLB-53
Webb, Sidney 1859-1947 . . . . DLB-190
Webb, Walter Prescott 1888-1963 . . . . DLB-17
Webbe, William ?-1591 . . . . DLB-132
Webber, Charles Wilkins
 1819-1856? DLB-202
Weber, Max 1864-1920 . . . . DLB-296
Webling, Lucy (Lucy Betty MacRaye)
 1877-1952 . . . . DLB-240
Webling, Peggy (Arthur Weston)
 1871-1949 . . . . DLB-240
Webster, Augusta 1837-1894 . . . . DLB-35, 240
Webster, John
 1579 or 1580-1634? DLB-58; CDBLB-1
 The Melbourne Manuscript Y-86
Webster, Noah
 1758-1843 . . . . DLB-1, 37, 42, 43, 73, 243
Webster, Paul Francis 1907-1984 . . . . DLB-265

Charles L. Webster and Company DLB-49
Weckherlin, Georg Rodolf 1584-1653 . . . . DLB-164
Wedekind, Frank
 1864-1918 . . . . DLB-118; CDWLB-2
Weeks, Edward Augustus, Jr.
 1898-1989 . . . . DLB-137
Weeks, Stephen B. 1865-1918 . . . . DLB-187
Weems, Mason Locke 1759-1825 . . . DLB-30, 37, 42
Weerth, Georg 1822-1856 . . . . DLB-129
Weidenfeld and Nicolson DLB-112
Weidman, Jerome 1913-1998 . . . . DLB-28
Weigl, Bruce 1949- DLB-120
Weil, Jiří 1900-1959 . . . . DLB-299
Weinbaum, Stanley Grauman
 1902-1935 . . . . DLB-8
Weiner, Andrew 1949- DLB-251
Weintraub, Stanley 1929- DLB-111; Y82
Weise, Christian 1642-1708 . . . . DLB-168
Weisenborn, Gunther 1902-1969 . . . . DLB-69, 124
Weiss, John 1818-1879 . . . . DLB-1, 243
Weiss, Paul 1901-2002 . . . . DLB-279
Weiss, Peter 1916-1982 . . . . DLB-69, 124
Weiss, Theodore 1916-2003 . . . . DLB-5
Weiß, Ernst 1882-1940 . . . . DLB-81
Weiße, Christian Felix 1726-1804 . . . . DLB-97
Weitling, Wilhelm 1808-1871 . . . . DLB-129
Welch, Denton 1915-1948 . . . . DLB-319
Welch, James 1940- DLB-175, 256
Welch, Lew 1926-1971? DLB-16
Weldon, Fay 1931- . . DLB-14, 194, 319; CDBLB-8
Wellek, René 1903-1995 . . . . DLB-63
Weller, Archie 1957- DLB-325
Wells, Carolyn 1862-1942 . . . . DLB-11
Wells, Charles Jeremiah
 circa 1800-1879 . . . . DLB-32
Wells, Gabriel 1862-1946 . . . . DLB-140
Wells, H. G. 1866-1946
 . . . . DLB-34, 70, 156, 178; CDBLB-6
 H. G. Wells Society Y-98
 Preface to The Scientific Romances of
  H. G. Wells (1933) DLB-178
Wells, Helena 1758?-1824 . . . . DLB-200
Wells, Rebecca 1952- DLB-292
Wells, Robert 1947- DLB-40
Wells-Barnett, Ida B. 1862-1931 . . . . . DLB-23, 221
Welsh, Irvine 1958- DLB-271
Welty, Eudora 1909-2001 . . . . . . DLB-2, 102, 143;
  Y-87, 01; DS-12; CDALB-1
 Eudora Welty: Eye of the Storyteller Y-87
 Eudora Welty Newsletter Y-99
 Eudora Welty's Funeral Y-01
 Eudora Welty's Ninetieth Birthday Y-99
 Eudora Welty Remembered in
  Two Exhibits Y-02

Wendell, Barrett 1855-1921 . . . . DLB-71
Wentworth, Patricia 1878-1961 . . . . DLB-77
Wentworth, William Charles
 1790-1872 . . . . DLB-230
Wenzel, Jean-Paul 1947- DLB-321
Werder, Diederich von dem 1584-1657 . . . DLB-164
Werfel, Franz 1890-1945 . . . . DLB-81, 124
Werner, Zacharias 1768-1823 . . . . DLB-94
The Werner Company DLB-49
Wersba, Barbara 1932- DLB-52
Wescott, Glenway
 1901-1987 . . . . DLB-4, 9, 102; DS-15
Wesker, Arnold
 1932- DLB-13, 310, 319; CDBLB-8
Wesley, Charles 1707-1788 . . . . DLB-95
Wesley, John 1703-1791 . . . . DLB-104
Wesley, Mary 1912-2002 . . . . DLB-231
Wesley, Richard 1945- DLB-38
Wessel, Johan Herman 1742-1785 . . . . . . DLB-300
A. Wessels and Company DLB-46
Wessobrunner Gebet circa 787-815 . . . . DLB-148
West, Anthony 1914-1988 . . . . DLB-15
 Tribute to Liam O'Flaherty Y-84
West, Cheryl L. 1957- DLB-266
West, Cornel 1953- DLB-246
West, Dorothy 1907-1998 . . . . DLB-76
West, Jessamyn 1902-1984 . . . . DLB-6; Y-84
West, Mae 1892-1980 . . . . DLB-44
West, Michael Lee 1953- DLB-292
West, Michelle Sagara 1963- DLB-251
West, Morris 1916-1999 . . . . DLB-289
West, Nathanael
 1903-1940 . . . . DLB-4, 9, 28; CDALB-5
West, Paul 1930- DLB-14
West, Rebecca 1892-1983 . . . . DLB-36; Y-83
West, Richard 1941- DLB-185
West and Johnson DLB-49
Westcott, Edward Noyes 1846-1898 . . . . . DLB-202
The Western Literature Association Y-99
The Western Messenger
 1835-1841 . . . . DLB-1; DLB-223
Western Publishing Company DLB-46
Western Writers of America Y-99
The Westminster Review 1824-1914 . . . . . . DLB-110
Weston, Arthur (see Webling, Peggy)
Weston, Elizabeth Jane circa 1582-1612 . . . DLB-172
Wetherald, Agnes Ethelwyn 1857-1940 . . . . DLB-99
Wetherell, Elizabeth (see Warner, Susan)
Wetherell, W. D. 1948- DLB-234
Wetzel, Friedrich Gottlob 1779-1819 . . . . . . DLB-90
Weyman, Stanley J. 1855-1928 . . . . . . DLB-141, 156
Wezel, Johann Karl 1747-1819 . . . . DLB-94

Cumulative Index

Whalen, Philip 1923-2002 .... DLB-16

Whalley, George 1915-1983 .... DLB-88

Wharton, Edith 1862-1937 .... DLB-4, 9, 12, 78, 189; DS-13; CDALB-3

Wharton, William 1925- Y-80

Whately, Mary Louisa 1824-1889 ...... DLB-166

Whately, Richard 1787-1863 .... DLB-190

   Elements of Rhetoric (1828; revised, 1846) [excerpt] DLB-57

Wheatley, Dennis 1897-1977 .... DLB-77, 255

Wheatley, Phillis circa 1754-1784 .... DLB-31, 50; CDALB-2

Wheeler, Anna Doyle 1785-1848? DLB-158

Wheeler, Charles Stearns 1816-1843 .. DLB-1, 223

Wheeler, Monroe 1900-1988 .... DLB-4

Wheelock, John Hall 1886-1978 .... DLB-45

   From John Hall Wheelock's Oral Memoir Y-01

Wheelwright, J. B. 1897-1940 .... DLB-45

Wheelwright, John circa 1592-1679 ..... DLB-24

Whetstone, George 1550-1587 .... DLB-136

Whetstone, Colonel Pete (see Noland, C. F. M.)

Whewell, William 1794-1866 .... DLB-262

Whichcote, Benjamin 1609?-1683 ...... DLB-252

Whicher, Stephen E. 1915-1961 .... DLB-111

Whipple, Edwin Percy 1819-1886 ...... DLB-1, 64

Whitaker, Alexander 1585-1617 .... DLB-24

Whitaker, Daniel K. 1801-1881 .... DLB-73

Whitcher, Frances Miriam 1812-1852 .... DLB-11, 202

White, Andrew 1579-1656 .... DLB-24

White, Andrew Dickson 1832-1918 ...... DLB-47

White, E. B. 1899-1985 ... DLB-11, 22; CDALB-7

White, Edgar B. 1947- DLB-38

White, Edmund 1940- DLB-227

White, Ethel Lina 1887-1944 .... DLB-77

White, Hayden V. 1928- DLB-246

White, Henry Kirke 1785-1806 .... DLB-96

White, Horace 1834-1916 .... DLB-23

White, James 1928-1999 .... DLB-261

White, Patrick 1912-1990 .... DLB-260

White, Phyllis Dorothy James (see James, P. D.)

White, Richard Grant 1821-1885 .... DLB-64

White, T. H. 1906-1964 .... DLB-160, 255

White, Walter 1893-1955 .... DLB-51

Wilcox, James 1949- DLB-292

William White and Company DLB-49

White, William Allen 1868-1944 ...... DLB-9, 25

White, William Anthony Parker (see Boucher, Anthony)

White, William Hale (see Rutherford, Mark)

Whitchurch, Victor L. 1868-1933 .... DLB-70

Whitehead, Alfred North 1861-1947 .... DLB-100, 262

Whitehead, E. A. (Ted Whitehead) 1933- DLB-310

Whitehead, James 1936- Y-81

Whitehead, William 1715-1785 ...... DLB-84, 109

Whitfield, James Monroe 1822-1871 ..... DLB-50

Whitfield, Raoul 1898-1945 .... DLB-226

Whitgift, John circa 1533-1604 .... DLB-132

Whiting, John 1917-1963 .... DLB-13

Whiting, Samuel 1597-1679 .... DLB-24

Whitlock, Brand 1869-1934 .... DLB-12

Whitman, Albery Allson 1851-1901 ...... DLB-50

Whitman, Alden 1913-1990 .... Y-91

Whitman, Sarah Helen (Power) 1803-1878 .... DLB-1, 243

Whitman, Walt 1819-1892 ... DLB-3, 64, 224, 250; CDALB-2

Albert Whitman and Company DLB-46

Whitman Publishing Company DLB-46

Whitney, Geoffrey 1548 or 1552?-1601 .... DLB-136

Whitney, Isabella fl. 1566-1573 .... DLB-136

Whitney, John Hay 1904-1982 .... DLB-127

Whittemore, Reed 1919-1995 .... DLB-5

Whittier, John Greenleaf 1807-1892 .... DLB-1, 243; CDALB-2

Whittlesey House DLB-46

Wickham, Anna (Edith Alice Mary Harper) 1884-1947 .... DLB-240

Wickram, Georg circa 1505-circa 1561 ... DLB-179

Wicomb, Zoë 1948- DLB-225

Wideman, John Edgar 1941- DLB-33, 143

Widener, Harry Elkins 1885-1912 .... DLB-140

Wiebe, Rudy 1934- DLB-60

Wiechert, Ernst 1887-1950 .... DLB-56

Wied, Gustav 1858-1914 .... DLB-300

Wied, Martina 1882-1957 .... DLB-85

Wiehe, Evelyn May Clowes (see Mordaunt, Elinor)

Wieland, Christoph Martin 1733-1813 .... DLB-97

Wienbarg, Ludolf 1802-1872 .... DLB-133

Wieners, John 1934- DLB-16

Wier, Ester 1910-2000 .... DLB-52

Wiesel, Elie 1928- DLB-83, 299; Y-86, 87; CDALB-7

   Nobel Lecture 1986: Hope, Despair and Memory Y-86

Wiggin, Kate Douglas 1856-1923 .... DLB-42

Wigglesworth, Michael 1631-1705 .... DLB-24

Wilberforce, William 1759-1833 .... DLB-158

Wilbrandt, Adolf 1837-1911 .... DLB-129

Wilbur, Richard 1921- .. DLB-5, 169; CDALB-7

   Tribute to Robert Penn Warren Y-89

Wilcox, James 1949- DLB-292

Wild, Peter 1940- DLB-5

Wilde, Lady Jane Francesca Elgee 1821?-1896 .... DLB-199

Wilde, Oscar 1854-1900 .. DLB-10, 19, 34, 57, 141, 156, 190; CDBLB-5

   "The Critic as Artist" (1891) DLB-57

   "The Decay of Lying" (1889) DLB-18

   "The English Renaissance of Art" (1908) DLB-35

   "L'Envoi" (1882) DLB-35

   Oscar Wilde Conference at Hofstra University Y-00

Wilde, Richard Henry 1789-1847 ...... DLB-3, 59

W. A. Wilde Company DLB-49

Wilder, Billy 1906-2002 .... DLB-26

Wilder, Laura Ingalls 1867-1957 ..... DLB-22, 256

Wilder, Thornton 1897-1975 .... DLB-4, 7, 9, 228; CDALB-7

   Thornton Wilder Centenary at Yale Y-97

Wildgans, Anton 1881-1932 .... DLB-118

Wilding, Michael 1942- DLB-325

Wiley, Bell Irvin 1906-1980 .... DLB-17

John Wiley and Sons DLB-49

Wilhelm, Kate 1928- DLB-8

Wilkes, Charles 1798-1877 .... DLB-183

Wilkes, George 1817-1885 .... DLB-79

Wilkins, John 1614-1672 .... DLB-236

Wilkinson, Anne 1910-1961 .... DLB-88

Wilkinson, Christopher 1941- DLB-310

Wilkinson, Eliza Yonge 1757-circa 1813 .... DLB-200

Wilkinson, Sylvia 1940- Y-86

Wilkinson, William Cleaver 1833-1920 ... DLB-71

Willard, Barbara 1909-1994 .... DLB-161

Willard, Emma 1787-1870 .... DLB-239

Willard, Frances E. 1839-1898 .... DLB-221

Willard, Nancy 1936- DLB-5, 52

Willard, Samuel 1640-1707 .... DLB-24

L. Willard [publishing house] DLB-49

Willeford, Charles 1919-1988 .... DLB-226

William of Auvergne 1190-1249 .... DLB-115

William of Conches circa 1090-circa 1154 .... DLB-115

William of Ockham circa 1285-1347 .... DLB-115

William of Sherwood 1200/1205-1266/1271 .... DLB-115

The William Charvat American Fiction Collection at the Ohio State University Libraries Y-92

Williams, Ben Ames 1889-1953 .... DLB-102

Williams, C. K. 1936- DLB-5

Williams, Chancellor 1905-1992 .... DLB-76

Williams, Charles 1886-1945 ... DLB-100, 153, 255

Williams, Denis 1923-1998 .... DLB-117

Williams, Emlyn 1905-1987 .... DLB-10, 77

Williams, Garth 1912-1996 .... DLB-22

Williams, George Washington 1849-1891 .... DLB-47

ISBN-13: 978-0-7876-8146-3
ISBN-10: 0-7876-8146-6

PL
2652
.C4175

2007